D1831271

THE SCHEDULED CASTES IN INDIA

VOL. I

THE SCHEDULED CASTES IN INDIA

VOL. I

S.K. Chatterjee

GYAN

GYAN PUBLISHING HOUSE

NEW DELHI-110 002

THE SCHEDULED CASTES IN INDIA (VOL. I)
(Anthropology, Tribal Studies, Sociology)

ISBN : 81-212-0511-5 (Set)

ISBN : 81-212-0535-2 (Vol. I)

Published in 2008 in India by
Gyan Publishing House
5 Ansari Road
New Delhi-110 002

All rights reserved. No part of this book may be reproduced in any manner without written permission

Printed at Vishal Kaushik Printers Delhi - 110093

CONTENTS

PREFACE VOL. I

While doing the research work for my books "Communalism and Constitution" and "Disintegration and Constitution", I stumbled upon the fact that as the process of constitution-making advanced, the Constituent Assembly decided to do away with the original scheme of providing safeguards to the minority communities because that would have perpetuated the communal divide. It, however, provided safeguards for the Scheduled Castes because their representatives had not only specifically asked for the same but also persistently demanded for their categorisation as a separate political economic and social minority. The debates in the Constituent Assembly and the compulsions of the Framers to provide safeguards for 'a section of Hindu community known as Scheduled Castes' prompted me to undertake an indepth study of the Scheduled Castes in all its facets. I knew it was a vast and complex subject and would require a lot of painstaking research. When I took up this project in 1992 my plan was to write a single book on this subject. As the study progressed I found that the subject was so enormous and engrossing that it would be difficult to do justice to it within the confine of a single book. So I planned to spread it to four volumes—all self-contained, yet continuum of the same subject.

To understand the emergence of the 'Scheduled Castes'

in its proper perspective, it is imperative to have a first-hand knowledge about the caste system that developed in India through the ages and its relevance in the Indian context as also the role of the Britishers in caste matters. The first volume is, therefore, devoted to the study of the origin and growth of the caste system upto the British period, because the Scheduled Castes emerged as a separate entity in our body politic only towards the fag end of the British rule.

The second volume discusses the framing of the constitutional provisions relating to the Scheduled Castes.

The third volume deals with the genesis, growth and demographic pattern of the Scheduled Castes.

The fourth volume deals with the tables related to the scheduled castes of India.

I am highly thankful to those who assisted me in completing this project, though it is not possible here to mention all of them.

In the first place, I am extremely greatful to Dr. A.K. Das and Sri S.K. Das Sharma. Frankly speaking, I would not able to repay their debt throughout my life. The way they helped me is beyond description. Despite his multifarious activities, as it is usual with a renowned Anthropologist and presently a Member of the West Bengal Backward Classes Commission, Dr. Das went out of his way in discussing all the chapters with me in great details and guiding me in every conceivable way. Sri S.K. Das Sharma, in spite of his old age and busy schedule, scrutinised the manuscript very minutely and offered his valuable suggestions for improvement.

I should also acknowledge with gratitude the assistance and sincere cooperation received from Sri A.M. Patra, Sri S.N. Bhaduri and Dr. S.K. Mishra, Assistant Librarians and other staff of the National Library, Dr. M.K. Chowdhuri, Director, Dr. Swapan De, Assistant Planner, Sri Ramen Saha, Cultural Research Officer and Shrimati Kabita Chatterjee, Librarian of the Cultural Research Institute, Calcutta, Dr. M. Raha, Joint Director and

Dr. Palash Chandra Coomar, Assistant Director Census Operations, West Bengal and Sri Durga Prasad Bhattacharjee, Secretary, Socio-Economic Research Institute, Calcutta.

My thanks are also due to the staff of the West Bengal State Archives, West Bengal Secretariat Library and West Bengal Assembly Library, for the assistance extended to me.

I would be failing in my duty if I do not place on record the assistance extended to me by Sri M.K. Jain, Deputy Registrar General (Social Studies Division), Dr. B.P. Mahapatra, Deputy Registrar General (Language), Sri A.K. Dutta, Deputy Director, Census Operations, West Bengal, Dr. S. Naskar, Assistant Director, National Commission for Scheduled Castes and Scheduled Tribes, Dr. S.K. Sengupta, Reader, Department of Anthropology, University of Calcutta, Sri Kumarananda Chattopadhaya of the Indian Statistical Institute, Calcutta, Director, Tribal Research & Training Institute, Maharashtra and Director, Bihar Tribal Welfare Research Institute, Ranchi.

In the end, I express my deepest gratitude to the eminent authorities whose works I had the privilege to quote.

I should also acknowledge the assistance and help received from my wife. But for her encouragement, inspiration and cooperation, this project would not have been complete. I am indebted to Sri B.P. Garg of the Gyan Publishing House for bringing out all the four volumes within a very short time.

This is rather an ambitious project which took about three years to complete. The labour, energy and time spent on it will be worth spending if this study generates interest of the researchers, academicians and the general public for whom it is meant.

S.K. Chatterjee

Salt Lake,
Calcutta

1

Origin and Growth of Caste in India

It is perhaps true that the most frequently mentioned peculiarity of the traditional Hindu society is the institution of caste, or as it is more frequently called, the caste system. Social institutions that resemble caste in one respect or the other are not difficult to find elsewhere, but it is only in India that it is known as 'caste'. The caste system has survived in a far perfect form in India than elsewhere, but Hocart shows that the Indian caste system is not an isolated phenomenon as it is often thought to be, but a specis of a very widespread genus. Comparable forms still exist in Polynesia and Melanesia, and that clear traces of them can be seen in ancient Greece and Rome, and in modern Egypt.[1] Hutton finds analogus institutions which resemble caste in one or other of its aspect in various parts of the world like Ceylon, Fiji, Egypt, Somali, Ruanda and Urundi in modern Africa and Burma.[2] Ghurye traces elements of caste outside India like Egypt, Western Asia, China, Japan, America, Rome and tribal Europe.[3] It is true that social and racial differences in some form or the other do prevail in other parts of the world, but the kind of system found in India is characterised more by its specific unique features like the complexity, elaboration and rigidity than by such features which it shares with caste structures elsewhere. The caste system that has developed in India is the natural result of the interaction of a number of geographical, social, religious, and economic factors not elsewhere found in conjuction.[4] It is the peculiarity of India that it recognised the social differences inherent in human nature and gave them an institutional and mystic form with a religious and spiritual background.[5]

Racial Composition

The population of India is composed of all sorts of different elements of great diversity, of different creeds, different customs, and even different colours. All these varied peoples have been enabled to live together in conditions of comparative stability and forming what may be described as a multiple society, by the caste system, which most probably be regarded as having developed as a sort of organic response to the requirements of the particular case. Geographical circumstances have imposed a certain unity on the inhabitants of the peninsula, whereas the diverse origins of the people have dictated variety.[6]

Although it is difficult to come to a conclusive opinion on the manner of fission and fusion of the different races in India, from the latest books on caste it will be seen that the Anthropologists have divided the racial elements in India as (1) Negritos, (2) Proto-Australoids or Pre-Dravidians, (3) Dravidians (Mediterranean), (4) Round-heads (Brachycephals-Alpenoid), (5) Indo-Aryans (Nordic-Caucasoid), and (6) Mongoloids. These divisions are based on inferences drawn from language, culture and anthropometry, i.e. a science which seeks, by measuring certain leading physical characters, such as the stature and the proportions of the head, features, and limbs, to ascertain and classify the chief types of mankind and the probable origin of the various race-stocks.[7]

The Negritos are pygmies ranging from four to five feet in height, very dark in colour and distinguished by their "pepper-corn" hair. They are generally found in Malaya, the Philippines and in the Andaman islands. Strictly speaking, they are not found in India but certain Negrito characteristics have been observed in the eastern and south-eastern parts of India among the Kadar tribe of the Cochin forest and occasionally among the tribes of the Rajmahal Hills, Bihar, and among the Naga tribes on the frontier of Assam and Burma.

They are followed by the Proto-Australoids whose earliest ancestors could be traced to Palestine. The Proto-Australoids or Pre-Dravidians, as they are sometimes called, are characterised by very wavy and even curly hair, a broad nose, coarse feature and a dark-brown skin. They are allied to the aborigines of Australia and are widely spread all over India, particularly among the lower castes and humbler classes of society. It is admitted that they formed the bulk of the population of the Indian peninsula at some very early date. As there are two distinct families of Austric languages in India, they are supposed to have entered India by two different routes, one round the west end of the Himalayas, and the other through the eastern section. The language spoken by the former is said to be Kolarian and by the latter Mon-Khmer. The Mon-Khmer-speaking people are confined to one area in Assam; while those speaking Kolarian are few in number but widespread. They include Mundas, Kols and Santhals. The Australoids who later came to be known as Kolarians, must have come before 3000 B.C. According to Sir John Campbell, Kolara was the name by which India was known to the ancient world.[8]

They are followed by the Dravidians who are also supposed to have come from outside India. Though their language affinity has not been established outside India, their cultural parallels have been traced to the old civilization of Mesopotamia, Syria and Crete. According to Elliot Smith, they are a branch of the Mediterranean race, who from somewhere in East Africa wandered into India via Arabia and South Persia many centuries before the coming of the stone-culture.[9] The relation of the Mediterranean race with some section of the people in South India is established by means of certain common peculiarities, such as the structure of the hair, softness of the skin and scarcity of hair on the body. Whether they came from outside or not, the Dravidians were in the Indus Valley about 3000 B.C.

The Roundheads are supposed to have come to India about the third milleneum B.C. from the southern steppes of Russia through Iran, due to some disturbances in their native land. They came through the north-western passes and passed down the west coast as far as Coorg, then avoiding Malabar, trickled through Mysore into Tamil and Telegu-speaking areas, until they met in Bengal another batch of theirs that came down from the frontier through the southern banks of the Jamuna and the Ganges. From the east there was a widespread movement of the southern Mongoloids southwards to the Bay of Bengal, and into Indonesia which had some reflex influence on India from the east. Finally, the Indo-Aryan race entered India about 2000-1500 B.C. These people occupied and settled in the Punjab; later sending colonies further east and filtering through central India into the south. These people definitely used an Indo-European language and had fair skin and blue eyes.

These Indo-Europeans were followed in subsequent centuries by many invasions on a smaller scale. Between 500 B.C. and the beginning of the Christian era northern India was invaded by the Persians and Greeks, and after them by the Sakas or Seythians and by the Kusans, who were a nomad tribe from Central Asia. Again in the fifth century A.D. another horde of nomads from Central Asia, the Huns, invaded northern India. The Shans from the headwaters of the Irwaddy began to conquer Assam at the end of the eighth century A.D. and Mongolians occupied the higher mountains all along the northern fringe of India. In the eighth century the Muslim invasions began with an Arab invasion in Sind, and Muslim invasions of one sort or another continued until the establishment of the Mughal Empire in the sixteenth century, by which time the Portuguese had already founded their settlement at Goa.[10] Thus Negritos, Pre-Dravidians, Dravidians, Roundheads, Indo-Aryans and Mongolians constitute the racial elements in the population of India, though Risley mentioned Aryan, Dravidian and Mongoloid as the three broad types of races contributing to the formation of the Indian population.[11]

It was when these diverse racial elements, indigenous as well as immigrant, got mixed in different degrees under different climatic and geographical conditions at short and long intervals through a process of ethnic combination that the peoples of India were derived. It is an admitted fact that a man's skin gets darker in tropical climate and geographical environment affects his physical features. The racial changes that are seen in India are mainly the result of environment and climate. It is imperative to keep this racial composition in view for a proper evaluation of the caste structure in India in its proper perspective.

Definition of Caste

It is difficult to define what a caste precisely connotes. The word 'caste' comes from the Portuguese word 'casta', signifying 'breed, race or kind', *homem de boa casta* is a "man of good family". The Portuguese of the sixteenth century applied the term indiscriminately to the various social and occupational groups found in the subcontinent, and this confusion has continued to the present time. On the one hand, the term is used to describe in the broadest sense the total system of social stratification peculiar to India; on the other hand, it is used to denote three, perhaps four, more or less distinct aspects of this total system, i.e. *varna, jati* and *gotra. Varna* is not the same thing as *jati*, the former representing the four-fold division of society which the authors of the Dharamsutras sought to derive from one or other of the four *varnas*. By contrast, the gotra, or clan, described by Hutton as "an exogamous unit of individuals theoretically descended from a single ancestor,"[12] cuts freely across *jati* lines and possibly across *varna* lines. To this confusion of interlocking hierarchies may be added a fourth division when dealing with South India, where by the time of the Chola period (A.D. 850-1267) there had occurred a great and still unexplained bisection of the *sudra varna* into the "jatis of the left hand" and the "jatis of the right hand", a division that still exists today and is reflected in the continuing rivalry between jatis of opposing hands.[13] Careless use of the English word "caste" has been the source of considerable confusion. Manu distinctly says that there are only four *varnas*, Brahman, Kshtriya, Vaisya and Sudra and there is no fifth *varna*,[14] while he admits of over fifty *jatis*. *Varna*, according to Manu, are four divisions into which the castes are grouped.[15] But, Dutt points out that, even Manu, not to speak of later writers, has confused *jati* with *varna*. The confusion is due to the fact that Brahman can be called both a *varna* and a *jati*, and so Sudra is also called a *jati*; though there are many *jatis* which are comprehended under the name Sudra, and a group cannot be found today which is known simply by the name of Sudra.[16] Ketkar also thinks that this confusion existed at a period still more remote.[17] As K. de B. Codringten has very rightly pointed out, the abstract, semi-literary and wholly arbitrary definitions of the Portuguese word 'caste' should be avoided and we should revert to the Sanskrit words which were used by the ancients to describe the social grouping. That will give the clue to the origin of the unique system.[18]

Foreign writers have attempted to define the term, but it will be readily seen that these so-called definitions are often descriptions of only those characteristics of the caste system which the particular writer wishes to emphasise. Nesfield defines caste as "a class of the community which disowns connection with any other class and can neither intermarry, nor eat and drink with any but persons of their own communitys." Bains defines it as "the perpetuation of status or function by heredity and endogamy."[19]

According to Risley, "a caste may be defined as a collection of families or groups of families bearing a common name;

claiming common descent from a mythical ancestor; human or divine; professing to follow the same hereditary calling; and regarded by those who are competent to give opinion as forming a single homogeneous community. The name generally denotes or is associated with a specific occupation. A caste is almost invariably endogamous in the sense that a member of the large circle denoted by the common name may not marry outside that circle, but within the circle there are usually a number of smaller circles each of which is also endogamous."[20]

Ketkar defines a caste as "a social group having two characteristics: (1) membership is confined to those who are born of members and includes all persons so born; (2) the members are forbidden by an inexorable social law to marry outside the group. Each one of such groups has a special name by which it is called. Several of such small aggregates are grouped together under a common name, while these larger groups are but subdivisions of groups still larger which have independent names."[21] Hutton considers this definition, generally speaking, valid.[22]

Gait says that caste is "an endogamous group or a collection of such groups bearing a common name who by reason of traditional occupation and reputed origin, are generally regarded, by those of their countrymen who are competent to give an opinion, as forming a single homogeneous community, the constituent parts of which are nearly related to each other than they are to any other section of the society."[23]

Beteille has attempted to define caste "as a small and named group of persons characterised by endogamy, hereditary membership, and a specific style of life which sometimes includes the pursuit by tradition of a particular occupation and is usually associated with a more or less distinct ritual status in a hierarchical system."[24]

In the terminology of Weber, castes constitute status groups. "In contrast to classes", Weber writes, "status groups are normally communities. They are, however, often of an amorphous kind."[25]

Majumdar and Madan define caste thus: "If a number of people constitute a group, not because of physical "togetherness" but because they have some common interests and common ways of doing things, as a consequence of which stratification of society into higher and lower groups emerges, then these groups may be called *status groups*. If a status group is open to entry, that is, if anybody can become its member by fulfilling certain prerequisite conditions, like obtaining a degree, or paying an admission fee, or earning a particular income, then the status group may be called a class. The restrictions of the term class to mean an income group has no sociological sanction; such a group is properly called an economic class. If the recruitment is not free, that is, if a status group is not open to anybody, but only those are its members who have certain *ascribed* attributes, which cannot be acquired by others, then it is called a caste."[26] Bougle, the French writer, concludes that the caste system divides the whole society into a large number of hereditary groups, distinguished from one another and connected together by three characteristics: separation in matters of marriage and contact, whether direct or indirect (food); division of labour, each group having, in theory or by tradition, a profession from which their members can depart only with certain limits; and finally *hierarchy*, which ranks the groups as relatively superior or inferior to one another.[27] This definition indicates the main apparent characteristics of the system. Dutt refrains from defining caste, but describes its features: members of the different castes cannot have matrimonial connections with any but persons of their own castes; there are restrictions, though not so rigid as in the matter of marriage, about a member of one caste eating and drinking with that of a different castes; in many cases there are fixed occupations for different castes; there is some hierarchical gradation among the castes, the most recognised position being that of the Brahmanas at the top; birth alone decides a man's connection with his caste for life, unless expelled for violation of his caste rules, and transition from one caste to another, high or low, is not possible. The prestige of the Brahman caste is the corner-stone of the whole organisation.[28] This description generally fits in with the caste system evolved in India.

Origin of Caste System

Caste in India is a social institution, deriving sanction from and intimately interwoven with the Hindu religion. Membership of a caste is compulsory and not a matter of choice. A person is born into it. It is practically impossible for individuals to change their caste. Each caste boasts of a peculiar tradition of culture and tries to preserve it tenaciously. The customs by which it lives are generally different in some respects from those of any other castes and are sometimes in marked contrast to those of any other caste. The caste system provides the individual member of caste with rules which must be observed by him in the matters of food, marriage, divorce, birth, initiation and death. Wilson sums up in his own inimitable way as follows:

"Caste gives its directions for recognition, acceptance, consecration, and sacramental dedication and vice versa, of a human being on his appearance in this world. It has for infancy, pupilage and manhood, its ordained methods of sucking, sipping, drinking, eating, and voiding, of washing, rinsing, anointing, and smearing; of clothing, dressing, and ornamenting; of sitting, rising, and reclining; of moving, visiting, and travelling; of speaking, reading, listening, and reciting; and of meditating, singing, working, playing and fighting. It has its laws for social and religious rights, privileges, and occupations; for instructing, training, and educating; for obligation, duty, and practice; for divine recognition, duty, and ceremony; for errors, sins, and transgressions; for intercommunion, avoidance; and excommunications; for defilement, ablution, and purification; for fines, chastisements, imprisonments, mutilations, banishments, and capital executions. It unfolds the ways of committing what it calls sin, accumulating merit, and losing merit. It treats of inheritance, conveyance, possession, and dispossession; of bargains, gain, loss and ruin. It deals with death, burial, burning; and with commemoration, assistance, and injury after death. It interferes, in short, with all the relations and events of life, and with what precedes and follows...life."[29]

Caste sanctions and strictures still govern all social, religious and economic activities of an average Indian in the villages and, to a decreasing extent, in the towns and the cities. The cost of breaking down the caste sanctions is pollution, i.e., temporary fall from ritual purity through association with a ritually less pure or impure person, food or occupation. This fall becomes permanent if no attempt is made to regain the lost purity by ritualistic expiation. If a man is excommunicated by his caste-fellows, nobody in the caste will marry with him or will accept water from his hands, or will invite him to dinner. Sometimes, if the offence is very bad, as the killing of a cow, the whole village will outcaste him. The priests will not attend any ceremonial in his house. The barbers will not shave him, and the washerman will not wash his clothes. These are the methods of bringing pressures on the man.

It is obvious that such a system of social stratification divides the society into thousands of small, hereditary and endogamous groups, each cluster of groups having its own distinctive set of customs and practices, which together form a hierarchy. Each such group of caste (or *jati*) is associated with one or more traditional occupations and related to the others by means of an elaborate division of labour. Each caste pursues, within limits, its own style of life, having distinctive customs in the matter of dress, diet, rituals, etc.[30] and is characterised by a degree of social and cultural identity. Within the country every region has its distinctive culture as well as its distinctive pattern of castes and sub-castes. As Louis Dumont puts it, "the caste, unified from the outside, is divided within. More generally, a particular caste is a complex group, a successive inclusion of groups of diverse orders or levels, in which different functions (profession, endogamy, etc.) are attached to different levels. Finally, far more than a 'group' in the ordinary sense, the caste is a *state of mind*, a state of mind which is expressed by the emergence, in various situations, of groups of various orders generally called 'castes'.... The caste system is above all a system of ideas and values, a formal, comprehensible, rational system, a system in the intellectual sense of the term."[31] According to Ketkar, in India there are over three thousand castes, most of them having sub-castes.[32]

The caste system on which the traditional order of the Hindu society is based is believed to have been of immemorial antiquity. The complex nature of the caste structure is evident from the fact that, even after a century and a half of painstaking and meticulous research in the history and function of the social system, we do not possess any conclusive explanation of the circumstances that might have contributed to the formation and development of this unique system in India. As very rightly commented by D.N. Majumdar, there are today as many theories regarding the origin of the caste system as there are writers on the subject.[32a]

The earliest speculation regarding the origin of caste system can be traced to the mythological story of creation of the four *varnas* embodied in the *Purusasukta* (hymn of man) of the *Rg Veda*. The hymn appear in the *Rg Veda* as well as in the *Atharva Veda*; in the *Rg Veda* it is RV.X.90.12 and in the *Atharva Veda* AV.XIX.6.6. Both stand in the name of one Rishi Narayan. It is reproduced with slight changes in the later vedic literature[33] and in the traditions of the epic,[34] Puranas,[35] and Dharmasastras.[36] It states that the Brahmans emanated from the mouth of the primeval man, the Kshatriya from his arms, the Vaisya from his thighs and the Sudra from his feet.[37] In point of time, the *Purusasukta* version may be ascribed to the end of the period of the *Atharva Veda*, in which it occurs in the latest portion. It seems to provide a theoretical justification for the disintegration of tribal society into classes. Already in the *Rg Vedic* period, division of labour had gone a long way. But although members of the same family worked as poet, physician and grinder, this did not involve any social differentiation. Towards the end of the period of the *Atharva Veda*, however, differentiations of functions tended to develop into differentiation of rank, and tribes and clans gradually disintegrated into social classes. Obviously, the old tradition of the common origin of the varnas could not explain the accession of the non-Aryan tribes to the Brahmanical fold, but it could serve as a useful fiction. It could help to assimilate and keep the heterogenous elements together, and, in so far as the Sudras were supposed to have been born from the feet of the first man, it could justify their servile position in Brahmanical society.[38]

European writers on the subject of caste origins knew about the racial difference between castes, high and low, and consciously or unconsciously, linked their findings to race, Weale who wrote that the whole history of India, from the earliest times, had been one long story of colour prejudice and that more cruelty had probably been displayed there than in the rest of the world, believed that the Aryan races, who were 'white', simply devised the iron system of castes to prevent the undue mixing of a dominant race with a 'black' inferior race. W.J. Thomas finds marked physical contrasts in the population, correlated with superior and inferior cultures, and this, according to him, is the basis of caste distinctions. Dudley Buxton thinks that caste is still of assistance in dividing up the complex races of the Indian peninsula. Gillin thinks that it is possible that caste in India originated in the racial differentiations between various populations. Maclver also leans towards the theory of the racial origin of caste structures. He says that caste perhaps arose out of the superimposition of one endogamous community on another. Religion came in to rationalise the power, prestige and pride of race which such a superimposition must have engendered. Kroebar finds a race element in caste but he regards religious, cultural and occupational elements also as significant. He further believes that any factor which sets off a group may lead to the emergence of a caste in India. Tozzar thinks that in North India caste came to be based on occupations with no contact allowed among different castes, but in South India, where there were many aboriginal peoples, the racial question was the main basis on the division into castes.[39] The racial significance of the caste system was recognised by Sir Herbert Risley, who traced the origin of castes from Indo-Aryan immigration into India. The prehistoric migration of the Indo-Aryans from Persia, where a four-fold division of society was known, laid down the structure of social grouping; and the clash and fusion of cultures between the invading people, on the one hand, and the indigenes, on the other, who belonged to separate racial stock inferior to the immigrants, brought about the super-structure which was the caste system. The motive principle of Indian caste is to be sought in the antipathy of the higher race for the lower, of the fair-skinned Aryan for the black Dravidian. The invading Aryan displayed a marked antipathy to marriage with persons of alien black race and devised an elaborate system of taboo for the prevention of such unions. But intermarriage could not altogether be prevented. The continual contact between the Aryan and Dravidian elements created a series of endogamous groups, which may be roughly classified as *Ethnic, Provincial or Linguistic, Territorial or Local, Functional or Occupational, Sectarian, and Social.* In the first of these classes the race basis is palpable and acknowledged whereas in the remaining other classes a fiction has been generated that they must be of a fundamentally different race. Risley, therefore, concluded that "caste was an institution evolved by the Aryans in the attempt to preserve the purity of their own stock, and afterwards expanded and adapted, by the influence of a series of fictions, to fit an endless variety of social, religious, and industrial conditions."[40]

Among the Indian writers Hayavadana Rao,[41] S.C. Roy,[42] N.K.Dutt,[43], G.S. Ghurye[44] and D.N. Majumdar[45] have linked caste with the racial factor. The initiation of the Indian caste structure has been credited to the Indo-Aryans, and the *varna* is regarded as a concept of racial origin, diluted in course of time through race mixture and hybridization which have resulted from intermarriage on the principles of hypergamy and of Anuloma (meaning 'with the hair', i.e. natural) and Pratiloma (meaning 'against the hair', i.e. unnatural) unions, as they are found even in present times. Dr. Ghurye emphasizes in particular the factor of priestly manipulation by Brahmanas attempting to maintain the purity of Aryan invaders. According to him, "caste in India is a Brahminic child of the Indo-Aryan culture, cradled in the land of the Ganges and the Jamuna and thence transferred to other parts of India."[46] He also thinks that endogamy, the outstanding feature of the system, was first developed by the Brahmins in the plains of northern India and thence conveyed as a cultural trait to the other areas.[47] Dutt thinks that some of the seeds of caste were a common stock of the Aryan peoples in all countries. But while they failed to grow elsewhere, they found a more fertile soil in India because of the absencc in Vedic and Epic times of any strong political power wielding supremacy over a large area and crushing tribal differences and enforcing uniform laws and customs.[48]

The colour question in the formation of caste has also been considered. There was little colour distinction between the Aryans and the non-Aryans in Europe. But the extreme divergence of colour between the Aryans and the non-Aryans in India made the invading Aryans conscious of colour or complexion. That the colour question was at the root of the *varna* system is apparent from the meaning of the word *varna* which means colour as well as class and from the great emphasis with which the Vedic Indians distinguished themselves from the non-Aryans in respect of colour. The three higher *varnas* were originally distinguished one from the other by the various shades of colour that were found in earlier days, resulting from the intermixture between the immigrants of Indo-Aryan racial stock and the indigenes, either of Dravidian or pre-Dravidian or Roundhead racial affiliation. Various factors contributed to such race mixture-scarcity of women among the invading group; the settled life with a house and all that it connoted among the indigenous population which naturally attracted the nomadic elements of the immigrant population; highly developed Dravidian culture with its matriarchial system; temple-worship of the mother goddess, rites, rituals and temple architecture, priesthood and learning, all have contributed to a racial miscegenation.[49] That class which retained utmost purity of colour by avoiding intermixture normally gained precedence in the social scale. The status also depended on the extent of isolation maintained by the social groups.[50] The Brahmans were white, the Kshatriyas red, the Vaisayas because of large absorption of black blood were yellowish like the Mullattoes of America and the Sudras black, as described in the Mahabharat.[51] The three higher varnas have tried to maintain their claims to superior status by keeping to themselves the important professions and avocations and jealously restricting the liberties of others with respect to their means of livelihood. Moreover, in course of time, the Brahman ritualism became so complicated and the Brahmanic literature became so developed at a time when writing was not known to them and everything had to be preserved by memory alone that a special class of men were required for the purpose who could carry on the profession from father to son and who could improve their skill and mnemonical power by the adoption of strictly hereditary principle. The same system developed in Persia where the Atharva or priests in particular formed something like a caste. "They had their secrets which they were prohibited from divulging; they were spiritual guides of their nation, and none but the son of a priest could become a priest, a rule which the Persis still maintain."[52] When two such parallel institutions are noticed in the two neighbouring countries in a high state of development, it is not difficult to assign the beginning of caste system in the shape of varna division to the Indo-Iranian period of history as the four-fold division of society is found both in the Avestan Persia and the Rg Vedic India. In ancient Persia there were the Atharvas (priests), Rathaesthas (warriors), Vastriya Fshuyants (cultivators) and Huitis (artisans), the only important difference lay with regard to fourth class, which was the artisan class in Persia, and the servile or Sudra class in India. But the difference is more apparent than real if we consider that the pursuit of handicrafts was mostly assigned to the slaves or Sudras in India.[53]

Karve, however, does not accept the view that the original meaning of varna was 'colour'. She argues that in the early sacred literature and in grammatical works varna meant 'class'. Karve continues that "at a later time the word...came to mean 'colour' and the fourfold division of the ancients was then taken to be based on a physical feature, namely, colour."[54]

The racial factor in the formation of the caste structure is, in a sense, admitted by most of the scholars and yet the development of the caste system cannot be explained wholly on the basis of race.

Occupational basis of the origin of caste has also been propounded. Common occupation or division of labour is the chief, if not the sole, cause of the foundation of the caste system. This theory was advocated by Nesfield who regarded occupation as the exclusive basis of caste distinction. In his opinion caste originated in India long after the Aryan invaders had been absorbed in the mass of the native people and all racial distinction between the two sets of people, Aryan and aboriginal, had disappeared. Different occupations grouped together men from different tribes into guild castes, which then borrowed the principles of endogamy and prohibition of commensality from the customs of the old tribes and thereby solidified themselves into isolated units. The ranking of any caste as high or low depended upon whether the industry represented by the caste belonged to an advanced or backward stage of culture and thus the natural history of human industries afforded the chief clue to the gradation as well as the formation of the Indian castes. Thus the castes following the most primitive occupations like hunting, fishing, basket-making, etc., were regarded as the lowest, the metal-workers, agriculturists, and traders were higher in rank, while the highest caste was of those who were priests and teachers. He went on to add that "function, and function only was the foundation upon which the whole caste system of India was built up."[55] This view is supported by Dahlmann.[56]

A theory of the origin of caste which combines both functional and racial origins has been put forward by Slater in his *Dravidian Elements in Indian Culture*. He emphasizes the fact that caste is actually stronger in southern than in northern India, and suggests that caste arose in India before the Aryan invasion as a result of occupations becoming hereditary and marriages being arranged by parents within the society of the common craft because sexual maturity developed early and trade secrets were thus preserved. As a result of magic and religious ceremonies also, exclusive occupational groups were built up, marriage outside which became prejudicial and contrary to practice. The Aryan invasion had the effect of strengthening a tendency to associate difference of caste with a difference of colour and of strengthening also a tendency for castes to be placed in a scale of social precedence. He also maintains the existence in the pre-Aryan society of India of an order of priest magicians.[57]

The existence of tribes in various stages of cultural progress and transition of tribes to one of interdependence, provided the starting point of the evolutionary hypothesis of Denzil Ibbetson. He explains caste as arising from a combination of tribal origins, functional guilds and a 'levitical religion' and lays great stress on the tribe. The turning-point in the career of a tribe comes when it abandons its wild and nomadic life and adopts a particular occupation as its principal method of economic subsistence. This is the guild stage in caste history, and is common at some period or other of economic progress to all peoples in the world. The formation of guilds of occupational groups naturally led to the recognition of skills and importance of the various guilds. In an industrial society, the technicians have assumed a dominant and even dictatorial status. In medieval times, the guilds vied with one another for predominance in accordance with their economic status exercising various degrees of pressure on the social life of the country. The exaltation of the priestly guild was soon followed by the priests insisting on the hereditary nature of their occupational status, and this led to the formation of endogamous units, as more and more of the guilds wanted to conserve the social status and privileges they enjoyed and to secure these permanently for the members of the guild. The Brahmins set the ball rolling and the various other guilds followed suit and a hierarchical organisation established itself.[58]

Chappel and Coon trace the origin of castes to the absorption of aboriginal types, and they also explain the formation of new castes with reference to the emergence of new occupations.[59]

Quite a different origin for caste is argued by Hocart, who apprently regards the whole system as originating in ritual. According to him, the basis of the caste system is two-fold—descent and sacrifice. Of the two, sacrifice is the essential one; descent is merely a qualification which at times may be dispensed with, for even a boy of non-sacrificial lineage can be admitted to royal, priestly or farmer rank by going through the initiation ceremony appropriate to that rank as a result of which he is reborn as a member of the particular rank. Every son of a Brahmin is born of his father, but he is also born of the sacrifice, and so is every Kshatriya and Farmer. Hence, such expressions as 'the twice-born, first born of ritual'. Castes are merely families to whom various offices of the ritual are assigned by heredity. Since rank depends upon certain qualifications, a family can lose its rank by losing its qualifications, i.e. observance of rules which go with certain offices. Since the offices are ritual, the rules are ritual. He regards the caste system as a system for distributing throughout the community the various duties connected with the royal ritual and the king's service, which are largely the same, and for ensuring that these duties are performed only by those properly qualified to perform them—qualified, that is to say, both by heredity and knowledge of the rites. Hocart shows that it was not only kings, priests and nobles who took part in the rites, but all members of the community. All human communities were originally bodies of persons organised for ritual purposes. At the head of the rites, from very early times, stood the divine king. His principal duty was to be just—that is to say, to see that all, whether gods or men, received their due. If this were done, the rites would be performed correctly and without disturbance, and the rain would fall in due season. Since the king was both divine and human, the whole of his service was a ritual service, and his cook, barber, drummer, etc., were sacred persons, and the families which furnished them (the 'castes') received, as a reward for their services to the king, and through him to the community as a whole, lands and other privileges. This does not mean that all members of the cook were always cooks. The king's cook, in fact, need not actually cook at all, but was merely to supervise the preparation of the king's food. Hocart's theory, in essence, laid emphasis on the 'religious man', who, though he tilled and built and reared a family, believed that he could do these things successfully only so long as he played his allotted part in the ritual activities of his community.[60]

Hutton lays emphasis on the importance of the primitive conceptions of taboo, *mana*, magic and soul-staff in contributing to the formation of the caste system. He thinks that the primitive attitude to taboo, belief in *mana* and the resulting taboo on food of, or other contacts with, strangers, which may be infected with the dangerous soul-matter of strangers, the occupational division of society as is found among the Naga tribes in Assam, and superstitious regard for everything strange and unfamiliar, might have shaped the structure of Indian society. In other words, the fundamental elements of the caste system have been functioning in the primitive society from very early times and the *Rg Vedic* invaders had only to superimpose their definitely graded social classes on a society already divided into groups isolated by taboos.[61] Roy also stresses the importance of the primitive ideas of taboo, *mana* and 'soul-staff' in the formation of the caste system.[62] Max Weber's view becomes significant in this context. Caste, according to him, signifies the enhancement and transformation of social distance into a religious or more strictly a magical principle.[63]

It is not difficult to trace endogamy, occupational division and untouchability from the dread of uncanny *mana*. The untouchability that developed in this country has been found to be mutual. It is practised not only by the Brahmins but by all other castes. Thus, "when a Brahman has been in a Kurcchan's house, the moment he leaves it, the place where he was seated is besmeared with cowdung to remove the pollution."[64] Or, when a Brahmin enters the *paracherry* of the Holiyas, men and women from the settlement come to the outskirt of the village to greet him with cowdung solution, broomstick and a garland of torn shoes; these, the Holiyas say, disarm the Brahmin of his evil *mana* and the Holiyas have little to fear from consequent social intercourse with the Brahmin.[65] In many areas of South India, the sight of a Brahmin was considered ill omen. Several communities even observe pollution from the visit of a Brahmin to their village, and *Parpane Nambakoodatu* (Trust Not The Brahmin) has become a saying widespread among the villagers of Tamilnad.[66] The concept of *mana* or *bonga* does explain the social distance and personality fixation. It has given rise to innumerable taboos and avoidances. It regulates individual behaviour and group responses, and its importance to tribal life and conduct must be conceded. The fear of pollution has also been stressed by Ketkar, who points out that "the chief principle on which the entire (caste) system depends is that of purity and pollution."[67]

The social distance theory was also supported by W.H.R. Rivers who found that the various castes of the South recognised social distance among them and a quantitative estimate of avoidance could be had from the social incompetence traditionally prescribed.[68]

Rice ascribes the origin of caste to totemism and the taboos which accompany it. He emphasises in this connection the holiness of Kitchen and the principle that food is a ready conveyor of injurious qualities in totemistic and primitive belief.[69] Hutton says that B. Bonnerjee's article in the *Indian Antiquary*, published in 1932, and the theory advanced by Dr. B.S. Guha are somewhat similar to that of Rice.[70] Pillai argues that caste is neither based on political grounds as advanced by the Europeans, nor it is based on divine dispensation as is believed by the orthodox Hindus. The political basis of caste is the presumed invasion of India by the Aryans, and consequent enslavement of the original inhabitants. As there is no historical or traditional or archaeological evidence to establish an Aryan invasion, the development of caste on a political basis should be discredited as it is much more based on mistaken interpretation of certain terms used in a single hymn in the Vedas. Hence, Pillai thinks that in the absence of any other evidence, it can safely be stated that *Jati* or caste originated with the totem and maintained by prohibitions on interdining and intermarriage.[71]

Then there is the theory of *Karma* and trans-migration of soul, which seeks to justify the caste system.[72] The various conditions of men, the highest, the middling, and the lowest are caused by *Karma*. One's status in life is determined by one's action (*Karma*) in past incarnations. Whatever a man enjoys or suffers is a result of his own actions. His bad actions would bear bitter fruit, whether they were done overtly or covertly. In consequence of many sinful acts committed by one's body, voice or mind, that individual in the next birth will become a bird, or a beast, or a low caste person, respectively. Those who commit sins go into inferior existence or wombs; those who do good *Karma* pass into superior wombs; and those who lead an ideal life obtain *nirbana* from birth and death. Such being the idea of retribution and justice, not only one is dissuaded from bad life but he is also persuaded into a meritorious life by promises of birth in a family of a Brahmana or a King, promises of absolution, of heaven, of expiation of sins of himself and also of his ancestors. Thus even the most wretched man with his most degrading occupation remains satisfied with the belief that the miseries of his present life are the result of his sins in his previous life, and if he submissively performs his caste duties in this life he will be born in a higher caste in the next life.

Roy also stresses the importance of the Indo-Aryan concept of *Karma* in caste formation.[73]

Though the caste system as it exists is peculiarly an Indian product, it must be admitted that the elements of the system existed or still exist in other countries also. One may refer to the colour problem in the United States of America as essentially a caste problem, though the commensal taboo does not operate there with any rigour, or to comparable forms as existed in Medieval Ceylon, Ancient Iran, Ancient Rome and Greece, Ancient Egypt, or as exists in Polynesia, Melanesia or even in modern Egypt. One may also refer to the occupational hereditary groups in the Western Roman Empire as created by the Theodesian Code. Such groups could not have been created overnight unless elements of social segregation were there.[74] In many societies there is a tendency of division of occupation on racial lines—so much so that a particular occupation becomes associated with a particular tribe. Ketkar finds numerous cases of this kind in America. The fact that the Chinese are a caste of laundrymen is something every American knows. There are also occupational castes of Negro porters and of Japanese butlers. In many cities Italians and Greeks are found in the occupation of shoe blacking. In two or three cities buying and selling of second-hand clothes and shoes is a trade which is monopolized or relegated to Russian Jews. Buying watches and jewellery or loaning money on them is also a trade of this tribe. In fashionable circles it has become customary to employ

French nurses, and in some cities domestic service is the occupation of Irish girls. It is also considered a fashion to have a Negro waiter, so much so that the Negroes have begun to feel that to wait on tables is their peculiar occupation and privilege. Strangely enough in the eastern part of America the native of India has become associated with palmistry, astrology, fortune telling and jugglery, so much so that it pays a man to pass for a Hindu when he is not. Spaniards in this profession advertise themselves as Hindu astrologers and palmists. There are various causes which bring about such a condition. Ability to do no other work but some peculiar work, and willingness to work for less, on the part of certain tribes, contribute to this phenomena. It may somewhat be a result of fashion. Preponderance of fellow countrymen, in a particular trade becomes of great help to the new-comer. All these circumstances have their effect in dividing occupations on racial lines.[75]

The different theories, mentioned above, only go to show that only one or two factors cannot be indicated as probably contributing to the emergence and development of the caste system in India. On the other hand, it can be stated that caste in India is unique and peculiar because it is a composite institution, having a complex origin in the combination of geographical, historical, ethnic, social, economic, religious and political factors which have been operative only in India. These various factors have been summarised by Hutton thus:

(1) The geographical isolation and climate of India as a whole and of individual areas within it.

(2) Primitive beliefs (i) about power of food to transmit qualities; (ii) suspicion of strangers; (iii) totems, taboos, mana and soul-staff or life-matter; (iv) magic associated with crafts and trade-secrets.

(3) Clash of antagonistic cultures, particularly between cultures with patrilineal and matrilineal modes of descent.

(4) Clash of races and colour prejudice.

(5) Ideas of the exclusive family and ancestor worships and the sacramental meal.

(6) Idea of pollution, ablution, purification, and ceremonial purity with associations of ritual sacrifice.

(7) Development of classes with exclusive religious and social privileges and exploitation of the mass of the people by these classes. Evolution of a religious philosophy by these classes involving beliefs in reincarnation and the doctrine of Karma.

(8) Hereditary occupations, and hereditary guilds and associations for preservation of trade and craft secrets.

(9) Deliberate economic and administrative policies. Inclusion of isolated tribes and polities without absorption in larger administrative units.[76]

Tribe-Caste Continuum

Although tribe, caste, sept, clan, racial group and class are the various types of social groups found in India, it is the tribe and caste which dominate, the former among primitive communities and the latter in the traditional Hindu society. A tribe is a collection of families or groups of families bearing a common name, members of which occupy the same territory, speak the same language and observe certain taboos regarding marriage, profession or occupation and have developed a well-assured system of reciprocity and mutuality of obligations. A tribe is ordinarily an endogamous unit, the members of which confine their marriages within the tribe. Several clans constitute a tribe, each of which claims kinship between the members belonging to it, based on totemistic division, territorial contiguity or common residence. A tribe is a political unit in the sense that the tribal society owns a political organisation, either recognises hereditary tribal chiefs or the several sections of it are welded into a territorial group ruled over by clan chiefs or hereditary kings. Each section of a tribe, a clan or sept has a council of elders who assist the hereditary headman in tribal affairs, and perfect solidarity and group affiliation characterise the attitude of the members towards the tribal authority. Majumdar has defined the tribe as a social group with territorial affiliation, endogamous, with no specialization of functions, ruled by tribal officers, hereditary or otherwise, united in language or dialect, recognising social distance with other tribes or castes, without any social obloquy attaching to them, as it does in the caste structure, following tribal traditions, beliefs and customs, illiberal of naturalization of ideas from alien sources, above all, conscious of a homogeneity of ethnic and territorial integration.[77]

From very early times, there has been a gradual and silent change from tribe to caste. This change has taken place in a number of ways, and it is believed that most of the lower or exterior castes of today were formerly tribes. Actually the earliest references to the Hindu caste system mention four castes (*varnas*) and a fifth caste of *patit* (fallen or *antayaj* or *chandala*). The process of incorporation of tribes into castes has, therefore, proceeded ever since the coming of the Aryan people into India.

Risley has mentioned four processes by which the transformation of tribes into castes is effected. The processes are: (1) the leading men of an aboriginal tribe, having somehow got on in the world and become independent landed proprietors, manage to enrol themselves in one of the more distinguished castes. They usually set up as Rajputs, their first step being to 'rope in' a Brahmin priest who invents for them a pedigree hitherto unknown. In their earlier stage of the advancement they generally find great difficulties in getting their daughters married but after a generation or two their persistency obtains a reward and they intermarry, if not with pure Rajputs, at least with a superior order of manufactured Rajputs. Thus a real change of blood may take place and they have been absorbed in the fullest sense of the word, henceforth pose, and are locally accepted, as high-caste Hindus; (2) a number of aborigines embrace the tenets of a Hindu religious sect, and becoming Vaishnabs, Ramayats and the like, thereby losing their tribal name; (3) a whole tribe of aborigines, or a section of a tribe, enrol themselves in the ranks of Hinduism, under the style of a new caste which, though claiming an origin of remote antiquity is really distinguishable by its name from any of the standard and recognised castes. Risley says that the great majority of the Koch inhabitants of Rungpore of North Bengal now invariably describe themselves as Rajbansis or Bhanga Kshatriyas—a designation which enables them to represent themselves as an outlying brand of the Kshyatriyas who fled to North-Eastern Bengal in order to escape from the wrath of Parasuram. They claim descent from Raja Dasarath, father of Rama; they keep Brahmanas, immitate the Brahmanical ritual in their marriage ceremony, and have begun to adopt the Brahmanical system of gotras. There would be nothing in their custom to distinguish them from Aryan Hindus, although there has been no mixture of blood, and they remain thoroughly Koch under the new name of Rajbanshi; (4) a whole tribe of aborigines, or a section thereof, become gradually converted to Hinduism without abandoning their tribal designation. Risley mentions the case of the Bhumij of Western Bengal, a pure Dravidian race, who lost their original language and now speak only Bengali; they worship Hindu gods in addition to their own (the tendency being to relegate the tribal gods to the women), and the more advanced among them employ Brahmans as family priests. They still retain a set of totemistic exogamous subdivisions closely resembling those of the Mundas and the Santhals, but they are beginning to forget the totems and the names themselves will probably soon be abandoned in favour of more aristocratic designations. The tribe will then have become a caste and will go on striping itself of all customs likely to betray its true descent.[78] To these four processes Majumdar has added a fifth in which an individual member of an aboriginal or semi-aboriginal tribe adopts the surname and *gotra* of a particular caste, manages to enrol himself as a member of that particular caste and gradually intermarries with the members of that caste. His wealth and influence attract members of the caste he aspires to belong and thus in the long run he may establish himself as a permanent member of that caste.[79] Cultural contact with Hindu castes leads to the adoption by the tribes of Hindu beliefs, rituals, customs and to participation in Hindu festivals and attendance at Hindu temples.

The process of gradual evolution from the aborigines to a higher class Hindu is a main feature of social evolution in India. Often government officers have noticed and commented upon it. Buchanan stated in 1810-11 that "some men of the families of Thakurs, Thakoits and Baboos, whom in Captain Brown's time (1772-8) every one called Bhuiyas, and were then commonly called as such by other tribes said that nobody called them so; and that they were Suraji Bangs and knew nothing of Bhuiyas."[80] Here is an example of the members of a tribe not only discharging their ancestry, but also claiming a high descent from the Sun, like the kings of the Ikshavku dynasty. Instances like these are many. Many a petty chief or members of the landowning class, though they may not have any land now, claim descent from the Sun, like Ikshavku, or from the Moon, like the Purus. Change from Bhuiya to Suraj Bangs, or Surya Vanshi, was immediately attended by two things. One, the appointment of a Brahman priest, and the other, certain restrictions in diet. If one was not rich enough to appoint a Brahman purohit or priest, he had to be content often with ministration in Brahman style by one of his own caste. The Suryavanshi Bhuiyas did not give up meat-eating and wine-drinking all at once. Though their successors have done so in later years, they abstained only from eating beef, but they like Hindus eat meat of 'goats', fowls and pig, and drink spirituous liquors'. One hundred years later Sir High Mcpherson, in his settlement report of the Santhal Parganas, says that "their chiefs make the usual Kshatriya pretensions and calling themselves Suryabansis disclaim connection with their Bhuiya kinsmen."[81]

Bhuiyas present an excellent example of how from the original aboriginal state, the caste or group differences and distinctions arose gradually as men disclaimed association with their brethren in toil, and claimed new importance to themselves, both divine and social. The formation of the four varnas may also be found among the Bhuiyas. Roy classified them into five divisions: (1) the Des or primitive Bhuiyas represented by the Pauri Bhuiyas of the hills of Keonjhar, (2) the Khandait or Paik Bhuiya of the Orissa plains and southern part of Chotonagpur, (3) the mixed Rajkoli or Rajkuli Bhuiyas of Orissa States, (4) the Praja or Rautali Bhuiyas of Orissa and southern Chotonagpur, and (5) the land-holding Ghatwar, Tikait, or Rae Bhuiyas of the Santhal Parganas, Hazaribagh, Gaya, Monghyr and Bhagalpur districts. The latter usually wear the sacred thread, indicating that they have become 'dwijas', or twice born; the next step for them is to become Brahmanas; but among them Brahmanhood do not hold out much in comparison to Kshtriyahood, with its pelf and power. The Paiks or Khandaits have a semi-military organisation, and they carry a sword or axe as the emblem of their nobility. They are evidently Kshatriyas in the making, without the sacred thread of the dwijas. The Praja Bhuiya, the agriculturists, represent the vis of the Vedic days, or the Vaisyas of the post-Vedic days. In the Rajkoli Bhuiya, one may trace the making of the Sudras, as they are attached to the ruling chiefs as personal servants, attendants and the like. The last but not the least is the Pauri, or the oldest Bhuiya, the aborigine who are least affected by Brahmanism or caste organisation, and as such they have retreated to the tangled hill tracts of Keonjhar and Benea states, between the rivers Baitarni in the North and the Brahmani in the South, over the hills with an elevation of 2,000 to 3,000 feet above the sea level. There they live undisturbed by the Hindus and uninfluenced by Brahmanism.[82]

Similarly, there is a great parallel between the Munda social organisations and the Hindu organisations of 'gotra' and 'varna'. The Mundas are now found in certain parts of Bengal, Bihar and Orissa, where they are known under three different names, the Mundas, Santhals and Hos. The Santhals are divided into 12 Nija or main septs of which the trace of one sept only could not be found. Most probably the lost sept has become completely Brahmanised or Kshatriyaised and their descendents are not likely to give out their secrets. The eleven septs are divided into 203 sub-septs.

On comparing the sub-septs, it will be found that

(1) Every sept has a sub-sept called its own, indicating an original division into tribes.

(2) Every sept has a Naeke or priestly sub-sept, the fore-runner of the Brahman priest.

(3) Every sept, except Hasdak, has a Manjhi or ruling sub-section representing the royal families equivalent of the Kshatriyas.

(4) Every sept has a Bitol, or outcaste sub-sept, probably the fore-runners of the Chamars. These may have consisted of members who offend against the social laws of the tribe.

(5) In the main Nij sept there is a sub-sept called Kasa, meaning farmer, though such a sub-sept is not found in other septs. This may indicate their taking up agriculture for the first time.

The formation of sub-sept under different profession or calling shows the initial stage of caste formation in the casteless society of the Santhals.

Another element in the increase in the number of caste can also be traced back to the Santhals, namely, the formation of new sub-septs by new-comers from other tribes or from other septs. Among the Baske sept, there is one sub-sept called Munda-Baske and among the Murmu sept there is a Munda-Murmu sub-sept; these could not have happened without the Mundas mixing with the Santhals. Similarly, sub-sept like Baske-Besra, and Gua-Hembran-Kora, will indicate blending of the old septs resulting in the creation of new ones. Many a caste among the Hindus is formed on a similar basis. (The higher the number of caste taboos, the greater the chance for formation of new castes and sub-castes. The Santhal sept and the Brahman varna are based on the same principle of division of labour, though the Brahmanas made their division more water-tight.) The Santhals are as fanatic against marriage within the same gotra as the Brahmanas are.[83]

Essential Features of Caste System

The caste system, on which the traditional order of Hindu society is based, attached particular importance to purity of blood which was maintained—though not as inviolably as was earlier believed—by the all-pervasive rules of endogamy, and commensality. In the *Rg Veda* restrictions on marriage seem to have been of the simplest kind. Only two kinds of marriage were directly forbidden, of brothers and sisters, and of parents and children.[84] There were no definite restrictions on intermarriage between the different classes of the Aryan race; actual examples of mixed marriage are not found in the body of the *Rg Veda* because caste in its present sense did not exist at that time. The question of purity of blood was first raised during the post-Vedic period (1400-800 B.C.) and the Brahmanas took the lead in the matter of exclusiveness from the Sudras. Partly because of the fear of pollution of their Aryan blood, and partly because of their claim of class superiority and sacredness, the Brahmans in course of time became practically endogamous, allowing some freedom with the Kshatriyas, and less with the Vaisayas, who by the nature of things could not keep their blood very much untainted. But such self-denying regulations took a long time in the making, and more in the attainment of logical perfection, and so during this period the marriage restrictions had not assumed the rigidity of later times. Thus there was no legal bar to the Brahman marrying girls from any or all of the four varnas, and the offspring of a lawful marriage obtained the status of the father. Though the marrying of a Sudra girl was not legally prohibited, it was generally disliked. Separate castes for the children of the mixed marriage, as to be found in the next period, were not recognised during the *Brahmana* period.[85] Marriage between a twice-born male, not excepting a Brahman, and a Sudra female was not forbidden, though great disapproval was expressed by the Sutra-writers (800-300 B.C.) towards such a union and greater handicaps and disabilities were put on the recalcitrant party and the offspring. The wedding lost its sanctity as the Vedic mantras were not to be recited on the occasion. While the children of a Brahman by wives of the higher castes were full-fledged members of the sacrificing community and generally took the rank of the father, those by a Sudra wife were treated as more akin to the mother's caste. It is almost certain that very little disqualification attached to the offspring of a Vaisya-Sudra marriage, and that little vigilance was exercised to keep up the distinction between the children of Vaisya and Sudra mothers by a Vaisya father, especially when many groups of the Vaisya community had descended to the level of the Sudra. The Kshatriyas, on the other hand, unwilling to be excelled by the Brahmans in the pride of birth were probably more strict than the Vaisyas towards the children of their Sudra wives.[86] But, by what may be called the new testaments of the Hindus, i.e. the Puranas and Tantras, intermarriage between the different castes is prohibited altogether.[87] In fact, as Risley rightly observes, "caste is mainly a matter of marriage."[88] Jagjivan Ram, a Harijan leader, however, thinks that endogamy was, to a certain extent, a tribal characteristic. Primitive nations in embryo used to be divided into an infinite number of tribes, which usually bore an intense hatred towards each other and did not inter-marry even though they might have lived in contiguous areas and spoken the same language.[89]

Ketkar says that the conditions in the United States supply us with a parallel. There are laws in the Southern and Western States preventing marriages between whites and other races. The laws define that a person who has one-eighth or more coloured blood in him is a coloured person and may not marry with a white person. This is a positive statute and not moral law (dharma). But facts are entirely different from those stated in the law; the mulattoes try to smuggle themselves into white society as soon as they can, and in many cases they do so successfully before they have more than seven-eighths of white blood in them. There are several cases of young beautiful mulatto women marrying white men without revealing to them real composition. The sentiment in the white community is extremely strong against marrying with persons who have one drop of Negro blood in them. Though law would permit a white man to marry a Negro woman who has less than one-eighth of Negro blood a white man of respectability would not marry a woman who has any at all. The important fact is that the prevention of mixed marriage depends not on the degree of previous intermixture, but on the knowledge or ignorance of the blemish.[90] In the South Sea Islands it was the common belief among the members of the Mariami group that only the nobles were endowed with an immortal soul and a nobleman who married a girl of the people was punished with death. In the Polynesia the commoners were looked upon by the nobility as a different species of being. Hence in the higher ranks the marriage was concluded only with persons of corresponding positions; and in Tahiti, if a woman of condition chose an inferior person as a husband the children he had by her were killed.[91] In Sweden in the seventeenth century marriages outside the class were punished. According to the German civil law the marriage of a man belonging to the high nobility with a woman of inferior birth is still regarded as disparaging and the woman is not entitled to the rank of her husband nor is the full right of inheritance possessed by her and her children.[92] People of different religions also show a sectarian attitude regarding inter-marriage. Mohammedans and Christians do not inter-marry. Even the adherents of different churches have been prohibited from intermarrying. In the Roman Catholic Church the prohibition of marriage with heathens and Jews was soon followed by the prohibition of marriage with Protestants. Protestants also originally forbade such unions.[93] The 'upper caste' Muslims, namely, the Sheikhs, Saiyads, Maghals and the Pathans, are intensely cautious of their lineage and scrupulously avoid marital status with the 'low caste' Muslims like Ansaris and Julahas.

The other most important feature of the caste system is its commensal taboo. In primitive people, it is either based on a belief that anything connected with a stranger is dangerous, or on a belief in the magical effects of food. This belief may be at the origin of the practice still obtaining in many castes in India which insists that food which is touched or even seen by persons belonging to a different caste must be thrown away. In some cases, a person cannot take the food even if it is cooked by his own daughter after she has been given in marriage. In the next place, it is also a very widespread belief among primitive tribes in Asia that not only animate but most inanimate objects, like the house, the boat and the implements of craftsmen are all endowed with life-matter. What is more important is the belief that this life-matter may be attracted away or harmed by magic. Accordingly such life-matter must be protected by magic and taboo. The importance of this primitive beliefs in explaining the origin of commensal taboos and caste differentiations has to be admitted. Jagjivan Ram, however, gives a different interpretation to this practice of commensality. He says that inter-dining, or the practice of distributing food only to one's own kith and kin, did not start from any idea of pollution; it was because of the need to preserve scarce food which had been collected with great endeavour.[94] It is no doubt a good conjecture but the sociologists give a different version of this practice.

It may be noted that upto the Pre-Maurayan period (4th century B.C.) there was not much of prohibition on taking food from the people of lower castes. Food cooked by the Sudras was not objectionable. Sudras might prepare the food under the superintendence of men of the first three varnas.[95] There was little objection to taking food cooked by a Sudra servant provided he kept himself sufficiently clean. But even an independent Sudra could offer not only cooked food as alms to Brahman beggars but prepared food at certain sacrificial offerings.[96] The later-day Shastras, however, enjoin that a Brahman must avoid, if possible, the eating of any kind of food in the house of a Sudra, and that under no circumstances is he to eat any food cooked with water and salt by a Sudra, or touched by a Sudra after being cooked. The prejudice against eating cooked food that has been touched by a man of inferior caste is so strong that, although the Shastras do not prohibit the eating of food cooked by a Kshatriya or Vaisya, yet the Brahmana, in most parts of the country, would not eat such food. For these reasons, every Hindu household—whether Brahman, Kshatriya or Sudra—that can afford to keep a paid cook generally entertain the services of a Brahman for the performance of its *cuisine*—the result being that, in the larger towns, the very name of Brahman has suffered a strange degeneration so as to mean only a cook. Such Brahman cooks are also employed in sweetmeat shops or eating houses or even during social functions so as to ensure easy acceptability of the cooked articles by all sections of people. In towns and cities, the rigours of commensality has died down considerably, though it is still in vogue in villages.

Though the Hindu legislators made the castes exclusive by prohibiting intermarriage and interchange of hospitality, they also laid down specific occupations for each caste. The lawful occupations of a Brahman in all the law-books were (1) studying, (2) teaching, (3) sacrificing for himself, (4) officiating as priest for others, (5) giving alms and (6) receiving alms. Those of a Kshatriya were (1) studying, but not teaching, (2) sacrificing for himself, but not officiating as priest for others, (3) giving, but not receiving alms, (4) governing and (5) fighting. Those of a Vaisya were (1) studying, (2) sacrificing for himself, (3) giving alms, (4) cultivating, (5) cattle-breeding, (6) trading, and (7) lending money at interest. The Sudra was to obtain his livelihood (1) by serving the higher castes, and if necessary, (2) by practising mechanical arts. By the close of the Vedic period the distinction between the Vaisyas and the Sudras so far as their occupations were concerned, had become very slight, because in the time of Kautilya (4th century B.C.) among the lawful occupations of a Sudra were agriculture and cattle-breeding not only in times of distress but in normal circumstances. In course of time agriculture and cattle-breeding came to be regarded as degrading even for a Vaisya. The degradation of agriculture, like handicrafts, was due more to the growing dislike of the Indo-Aryans, like the Romans of later times, for manual labour of any kind and to the overwhelming association of non-Aryan Sudras in that profession than to the idea of Ahimsa, or non-injury to living creatures.[97]

Now the question arises as to what a man should do in case he failed to find employment within the limits of his prescribed occupations, or if he had not the necessary qualifications for them. So some latitude had to be allowed in order to let him live and not die of starvation. But he must not choose any and every profession for his livelihood. The Shastras lay down that a person unable to earn his livelihood otherwise may take to a profession which is ordinarily prohibited to his class. Manu says:

80. Among the several occupations for gaining a *livelihood* the most commendable respectively for the sacerdotal, military, and mercantile classes are teaching the Vedas, defending, and commerce or keeping herds and flocks.

81. Yet a Brahman unable to subsist by his duties just mentioned may live by the duty of a soldier, for that is the next in rank.

82. If it be asked, how he must live, should he be unable to get a subsistence by either of these employments, the *answer is,* he may subsist as a mercantile man, applying himself in person to tillage and attendance on cattle.

95. A military man in distress may subsist by all these means, but at no time must he have recourse to the highest, or a *sacerdotal* function.

98. A mercantile man, unable to subsist by his own duties, may descend even to the servile acts of a Sudra, taking care never to do what ought to be done; but, when he has gained a competence, let him depart from service.

99. A man of the fourth class, not finding employment by waiting on the twice-born, while his wife and son are tormented with hunger, may subsist by handicraft.[98]

Such being the precepts of the Shastras, it is often found that a Hindu of one caste is engaged in a profession which is the speciality of another and even Brahmans might be found in many non-Brahmanical professions and with non-Brahmanical habits. To-day a man can take to any occupation without changing his caste. The specific association between caste and traditional occupation is breaking down, although a broad relationship continues to exist.

Occupations are, according to traditional value, graded in an elaborate hierarchy in which ideas of purity and pollution play a significant part. Caste status is not the function of an occupation; instead of the occupation it is the ritual purity or impurity of a caste occupation which determines the status which a caste is to enjoy. The Aryan conquerors kept for themselves the profession of the priest, the ruler and the trader while assigning to the conquered aborigines all manual occupations, particularly those which were "regarded as low and contemptible".[99] A profane occupation like scavenging, burning the dead, or skinning, the dead animals, being ritually impure, entails a low or negative status.

Caste Status

The Hindu society has an irrevocable group and status system in the institution of caste, and the deadly efficiency of social control in Hindu society derives mainly from this.[100] Since the time of Manu, Hindu law-givers have attributed particular qualities to particular lines and the intermixture of lines has been circumscribed by strict rules of law and custom. The stratification of society into high castes and low castes, which are hereditary and often inelastic, accounts for considerable social disabilities of the latter. In traditional Hindu society there were legal and ritual sanctions which prevented lower castes from imitating the styles of life of the uppper castes. "There was no equality before law. The inequality resulting from caste was supposed to be ordained by God, and the law-givers, therefore, prescribed without any compunction different kinds of punishments and taxes for men belonging to different *varnas*."[101] The Sudras, who were at the lowest rung of the caste hierarchy, consisted of the servile and servicing castes. Though the word Sudras was often loosely used by ancient writers to denote all those who did not belong to the three higher *varnas*, there was always a distinction between those who had come or were coming under the Aryan influence, the Sudras proper, and those, sometimes called the fifth *varna*, who were too savage and unclean to be amenable to the Aryan culture and practices. Among the Sudras, too, there soon developed a distinction between those who followed the ideals and imitated the practice of the higher *varnas*, the 'clean' Sudras and those whose touch made impure the water of a Brahman, and to whom a good Brahman would not act as a priest. Those 'unclean' Sudras uptill recent times were variously called as 'Chandalas', 'Patita', 'Antajya', 'Depressed Classes', 'Untouchables', 'Harijans' and the like and were the worst affected by caste incompetence, mere contact with whom was believed to result in pollution. Terms exist for pollution and purity in every Indian language, and each of these terms has a certain amount of semantic stretch enabling it to move from one meaning to another as the context requires. Thus, Srinivas points out, pollution may refer to uncleanliness, defilement, impurity short of defilement, and indirectly even to sinfulness, while purity refers to cleanliness, spiritual merit, and indirectly to holiness.[102]

The superstition attaching to so-called pollution results in innumerable social and political disabilities, many of which are traditionally prescribed and socially enforced by the higher castes. Food and drink touched or in some cases even seen by them had to be thrown away. They could not draw water from a common well anywhere, or buy necessaries of life from a common shop, or, even talk to higher caste people from a distance nearer the prescribed limit. They were often denied the use of public conveyance, roads and schools. They were not to be given education, lest it would inspire them with a desire for their upliftment and a higher standard of living. Physicians would not go to their houses for treatment of their deseases, and even barbers would not shave them, though a barber had no objection to shave Muslims, Christians, even the newly converts to those religions. In some places, they could cremate their dead or bury them only in special areas. What was worse still, even the light of spiritualism and religion was denied to them. Vedic prayers and forms of worship and the religious practices of the Brahmanas were not to be theirs. Those among the Brahmanas who served the higher castes could not serve the depressed classes, for that would make them liable to excommunication or degradation. Some recruited their priests from their own castes and some employed barbers as priests. They were not allowed entry into temples, because their presence would impart impurity to the deities. In a word, they were not encouraged to feel that they were members of the same religious community as the higher-caste people. In South India, where casteism is predominant even in urban political life, there were also castes of 'unseeables', seeing whom would pollute a twice-born. Their shadow carried pollution and they should not approach public thoroughfares without warning, or walk on them in such a manner as to allow their shadow to fall on, or even be trodden over by, a Brahman. In one part of Madras Presidency the untouchables and pariahs could only use the roads at midday, when the sun is vertically overhead and the shadow is cast over a negligible distance. Consequently, in South India there was a definite check on the traditional mobility of lower castes. They could not go out of their localities and could venture outside only after nightfall. In *Annihilation of Caste* Ambedkar mentions that under the rule of Peswa in Maharastra, the Untouchables could not use the public street lest they should pollute a caste Hindu by their shadow. The Untouchables were to put a black thread either on their wrist or neck as a sign to demarcate them from the caste Hindus. In Poona, the capital of the Peswas, the Untouchables had to carry a broom to sweep away from behind the dust they treaded on for preventing a Hindu from polluting himself by walking on the same dust.[103]

Though these innumerable social and civic disabilities have disappeared over the years, the position was not very encouraging even in the late 20s. A leader of the Depressed Classes gave a graphic description of the pitiable conditions of the Depressed Classes in different parts of the country in his note prepared in 1929. He mentioned that the children of the Depressed Classes could not go to the same schools. The Untouchable children attending common schools in Bombay were victimised. The members of the Depressed Classes could not engage in occupations which would bring them into close contact with other Hindus, thus preventing all possibilities of social intercourse or economic betterment. The system of forced labour or *begar* was prevalent in the Punjab, and the Depressed Classes were harassed by officers throughout that province. In the lower courts of Bombay Depressed Classes witnesses must stand aloof when they gave evidence. No Untouchable could come into any public office for the transaction of business in the villages and minor towns of Bengal nor could he enter a post office to buy a stamp or post a letter. Hospitals maintained out of public funds had no accommodation for him. The right of using public rest houses was denied to him in Bombay. The Madras Council considered the question of throwing open all highways to the Depressed Classes. In the United Provinces Untouchables used to leave their pots near the public wells in the hope that some charitable samaritan would fill them. Resolutions were moved in the Madras Council, Bombay Council, Central Provinces Council and the Punjab Council to allow the members of the Depressed Classes to draw water from the public wells maintained by the Local Bodies. In the Punjab there were restrictive laws and customary rules that stood in the way of advancement of the Depressed Classes. They were forced to hold the lowest place in society, because of certain customary rules, which were enforceable in courts of law, debarring them from purchasing lands in village communities. The Land Alienation Act of Punjab prevented the Depressed Classes from purchasing lands from the privileged castes notified under the Act as agriculturists, though the Depressed Classes were themselves agriculturists. They, though Hindus, could not participate in common worship, not could they come into the Temples. They were not even admitted into a public conveyance in Bombay, not to speak of the barber's saloon and Indian Restaurants and Refreshment Rooms under the management of so-called caste Hindus.[104]

The Depressed Classes occupied a curiously ambiguous position in the traditional society. On the one hand, they were excluded from the *chaturvarna* scheme or the ideal model of Hindu society as this was developed by Brahminical jurists and literary scholars. On the other hand, they were an indispensable element in local society, rural and urban, everywhere. Thus, doctrinally they were not part of Hindu society while existentially they were an integral part of local communities.[105]

Social disabilities of a kind exist in all countries; they must be numerous and rigid in those where two or more distinct racial groups with graded cultural status have settled down and are in constant contacts. Among the higher castes in India, in view of the pre-eminent position of the Brahmanas in the Hindu society, other castes scarcely have any opinion of their own in regard to caste matters independent of the views of their priests. The Brahmanas have had for millenniums a fair monopoly of religious as well as secular learning and the fact that all learning used to be coded in Sanskrit, a language unknown to the masses, gave the Brahmanas a peculiar power to dominate the will of non-Brahmanas. The Brahmanas have so long secured to themselves rights, which are jealously guarded against being encroached upon, and the non-Brahmanas though recognised as "twice-born" suffer from disabilities not less irksome than those that have fallen to the lot of the Depressed Classes and were reduced to a position no better than intellectual serfs of the Brahmanas. The distinctions between Brahmanas and non-Brahmanas exist in all provinces. In the South such distinctions account for considerable social disabilities of the latter. In other parts, the disabilities are on the decline and are tending to disappear. Such distinctions have their origin in the ceremonial purity of the Brahmans, and do not have any racial significance. The disabilities of the so-called "depressed" castes are not ceremonial but founded on racial or cultural differences and therefore slow to disappear.

Social Disabilities in Vedic Period

According to Sharma, who has traced the social history of the Sudras upto A.D. 500 in his book *Sudras in Ancient India*, the different stratum in the caste society and the rigidity of the caste system are not found in the Vedic society. *Rg Vedic* society was basically tribal in character. According to Keith[106] the vedic Indians were primarily pastoral, at least this holds good of the Aryans known from the early parts of the *Rg Veda*. The Aryans encountered the urban population of Harappa society and ultimately conquered them in war. Social adjustment between the Aryans and survivors of Harappa society and other peoples naturally led to the rehabilitation of some of the surviving priests and chiefs into corresponding positions, possibly of inferior nature, in the new Aryan society. Early literature throws hardly any light on the process of assimilation between the Aryan commoners and those of the survivors of earlier societies. It is likely that most of them were reduced to what came to be known as the fourth *varna* in the Aryan society. In essence, the *Rg Vedic* Aryan society, and perhaps the society described in the

Atharva Veda, was characterised by the absence of sharp class divisions amongst its members, a feature which is usually found in early societies.[107] The Sudras appear as a social class only towards the end of the period of the *Atharva Veda*, when the *Purusasukta* version of their origin might have been inserted into the tenth book of the *Rg-Veda*.[108] In the opinion of Max Mullar, the hymn in *Purusasukta* is a later addition to Vedic text.[109]

This version indicates that Sudras were supposed to belong to the same stock as those of the other *varnas*. In addition to the slowly emerging military leaders and priests, there were husbandmen and artisans who practised a number of crafts and no social stigma was attached to them. Weavers, tanners, carpenters, printers and others, whose occupations were quite dignified in the *Rg Veda* and apparently practised by respected members of the Aryan community, later came to be reckoned as Sudra in the Pali texts,[110] and in this sense the tradition of the common origin of the four *varnas* may have an element of truth, but, as pointed out by Oldenberg, from the Vedic period onwards large numbers of aborigines of varying stocks were successively incorporated in the Sudra *varna*.[111] The Aryans, white-skinned, good-featured, making sacrifices and worshipping gods like Agni, Indra, Varun etc., were distinguishable ethnically and culturally from the Dasas or Dasyus, who were black-skinned (krishnathvach), noseless or flat-nosed (anas), of unintelligible speech (mridhravach), not sacrificing (ayajnan), worshipping no god (adevayu), and following strange customs (anyavrata). At first little quarter was given to the resisting natives of the soil. But gradually a milder policy was adopted, and large numbers of the Dasas were taken as slaves instead of being exterminated. In the *Rg Veda* mention is often made of slaves, sometimes in large numbers, and wealth was already to some extent made up of ownership of slaves. As the word Dasa became in the later literature synonymous with slave, it is supposed that the slaves were taken almost entirely from among the conquered non-Aryans.[112] The large number of natives reduced to serfdom in the Gangetic valley in the later Vedic period (1400-600 B.C.) resulted in the gradual withdrawal of the ruling race from all professions requiring manual labour and the generation of a spirit of contempt for industrial arts, which fell more and more into the hands of the Sudras. The greater association of slave or Sudra labour with certain branches of industry, together with the growing contempt for manual labour, brought the industries themselves low in the estimation of the higher classes, and made those engaged therein, even of pure Aryan birth, approximate more to their Sudra associates and fellow workmen.[113] Moreover, there were frequent conflicts amongst the members of the invading Aryan race over possession of cattle and laterly of land. Large sections of Aryan race who were thus dispossessed and impoverished came to be reckoned as the fourth varna in the society.[114] Hence, partly on account of the inter-mixture of blood and partly on account of their employment along with Sudras in the industrial professions and also partly through external and partly through internal conflicts, a large number of the Aryan race were assigned the degraded rank of Sudra in society. It is more likely that Dasas (slaves) and Sudras were originally the names of some prominent tribes conquered and reduced to slavery by the Aryans, as Karian became synonymous with slave at Athens,[115] but in course of time they came to include large groups of pre-Aryan and degraded Aryan populations. By the time the *Purusasukta* was composed the Dasa slaves of the Aryan conquerers had begun to be called Sudras, and hence the occurrence of the word therein instead of Dasa. In the later Vedic literature the Sudra is often contrasted with the Arya, instead of the Dasa or Dasyu of the *Rigveda*.[116] In the early Vedic period the Sudras, however, did not suffer from these disabilities which gradually fell on them from the late Vedic period onwards.[117]

The idea of ceremonial impurity of the Sudra involving prohibition of physical and visual contact with him appeared towards the close of the Vedic period (1000-600 B.C.). The first notice of such a marked degradation is found in the

Satapatha Brahmana (I 1.3.12) where a carpenter's touch is said to impart ceremonial impurity.[118] It is, however, inaccurate to think that Sudras were saddled with social restrictions regarding food and marriage, though there is some evidence of contempt for birth in a Chandala family and of the ascription of certain bad qualities to the Sudra. Religiously, the Sudra was permitted to take part in certain rites, and yet excluded from several specific rituals as well as from the Vedic sacrifice in general. In other words, in the Samhitas and Brahmanas (800 B.C.-600 B.C.), the position of the Sudras is ambiguous.[119]

Social Disabilities in Post-Vedic Period

In the pre-Maurayan period (600 B.C.-300 B.C.) the difference between the Vaisayas and the Sudras was getting narrower day by day. The occupations of the two castes were practically interchangeable. The gradual effacement of the distinction between the Vaisyas, at least a large part of them, and the Sudras was caused also by the increasing contempt with which the Brahmanas had begun to look upon the professions of the Vaisyas.[120] As the ruling class became more numerous and, therefore, more self-constituted, and as with the rapid expansion of Aryan domain in the Gangetic plains the Vedic society advanced more from tribalism towards feudalism, the difference between the Kshatriyas and the Vaisyas became much wider. Again, with the more abundant supply of Sudra slaves who were employed in all toilsome work, in ploughing, in pasturing and in industrial arts, the Aryan masters came to have a growing contempt for manual labour, and those Aryans who worked as labourers went down in the estimation of the higher classes. Thus a division arose between those Vaisyas whose professions were regarded as honourable and those whose occupations were regarded as being fit for Sudra slaves. To make matters worse, owing to their large number and diversity, to their lack of proper understanding and, above all, to their close association with the Sudras in various fields of work, the Vaisyas could not but receive a large admixture of non-Aryan blood. The proud higher castes, Brahmana and Kshatriya, began to adopt a more exclusive policy towards the proletarians of the community.[121] The social position of the Sudra underwent a change for the worse. With the complete substitution of society based on varna for tribal society during post-Vedic times, the members of the Sudra varna ceased to have any place in the work of administration. The law-givers emphasised the old fiction that the Sudra was born from the feet of the God, and apparently on this basis imposed on him numerous social disabilities in matters of company, food, marriage and education, amounting in several cases to his social boycott by the members of the higher varnas in general and the Brahmanas in particular.[122] The idea that food touched by the Sudra is defiled and cannot be taken by a Brahman is first expressed in the Dharamsutras (500 B.C.-300 B.C.) of this period.[123]

Although marriage with women of lower castes was permissible, the Dharamsutras show great aversion for connections of the reverse type. A son begotten by a Sudra on a woman of unequal caste was regarded as a *patita*. It is mostly to such marriages and connections that the early law-books trace the origin of about a dozen mixed (varnasamkara) castes, many of whom were relegated to the position of untouchables. But most of these mixed castes were nothing more than backward tribes, who were annexed to the four original and recognised varnas by giving them a wholly arbitrary genesis.[124] It seems that most of the so-called mixed castes owe their exclusiveness to either Brahmanical policy, or to the impossibility of including them within any of the four primary groups.[125]

While there was no bar to the imparting of Vedic education to the Sudras in earlier periods, it was denied to them during the pre-Maurayan period. Similarly, it was the view of this age that the Sudra cannot take part in Vedic sacrifices and sacraments. He came to be excluded from the Vedic sacrifices to such an extent that in the performance of certain rites even his presence and sight were avoided.[126] This period also saw the emergence of Buddhism and Jainism, as alternatives to the prevalent religious beliefs and practices. Gautama Buddha is very often complimented for fighting against the caste system and his creed is very often called a revolt against caste system. Rhys Davids has shown the fallacy of complimenting Buddha for breaking caste barriers in his various introductions to the Dialogues of Buddha. Robert Chalmors also exposed the attitude of Buddhism toward caste in his article "Madhura Sutta on Caste" (J.R.A.S., April, 1894, pp. 360-366).[127] Ghurey asserts that a close student of the early literature of these religious movements will feel convinced that the chief social aim of the writers was the assertion of the pre-eminence of the Kshatriyas. It is a well-known fact that no Jain Tirthamkara was ever born in any but a Kshatriya family. In Buddhist literature there are several examples where the enumeration of the four castes is headed by the Kshatriya, the Brahmin coming next. Many a time the Kshatriyas aggressively put forward claims for prior recognition over the Brahmins.[128] To Buddha himself is ascribed the saying that along with the Kshatriyas the Brahmins take precedence over the other castes in the matter of marks of respect to be shown to one's social superiors.[129] The early Buddhist writings also practically confirm the description of the Brahmana caste as given in the Sutras and concede to the Brahmanas the three exclusive privileges of teaching, performing sacrifices for others and receiving gifts.[130]

Untouchability probably appeared towards the end of the pre-Maurayan period.[131] Various explanations of the origin of untouchability have been offered. The Dharamsutras attribute it to the intermixture of castes. It has been suggested that in the majority instances the origin of untouchables took place as a result of complete isolation and loss of tradition of the Buddhist communities.[132] It has been contended that those who continued beef-eating were condemned as untouchables.[133] It is also argued that the spirit of contempt leading to untouchability was a thing borrowed from the Dravidians.[134] It has been said that the origin of untouchability may be traced back to pollution. Untouchability has its origin in hygiene first and then in religion.[135] Finally, the idea of untouchability has been traced to the theoretical impurity of certain occupations.[136]

Sharma thinks that one of the reasons for the origin of untouchability was the cultural lag of the aboriginal tribes, who were mainly hunters and fowlers, in contrast to the members of the Brahmanical society, who possessed the knowledge of metals and agriculture, and were developing urban life. The low material culture and the consequent wretched condition of these tribes suggest that they had a very precarious living and did not enjoy any security of livelihood. This contrast in material life was accentuated by the spirit of contempt for manual work and occupations growing in Brahmanical society itself. Gradually, as the upper varnas, especially of the Brahmans and Kshatriyas, withdrew more and more from the work of primary production and tended to be hereditary in their positions and functions, they not only developed a contempt for manual work but also extended it to the hands that practised it. He, therefore, concluded that against the background of a very low material culture of the aborigines, the increasing contempt for manual work, combined with primitive ideas of taboo and impurity associated with certain materials, produced the unique social phenomenon of untouchability.[137]

The Nishadas, Chandalas and Paulkasas, the earliest mention of whom is to be found in the Yajurveda, were aboriginal tribes, who had been on a very low cultural-level, lived in a repulsively dirty fashion and followed the primitive professions of hunting and fishing, when they were first met by the conquering Aryans. So little amenable to the Aryan culture were they, and such abhorrence did they generate in the minds of the Aryans, and also probably of the more cultured sections of the non-Aryans, that a wall of separation was raised between the men of society and these wild peoples, and they came to form the so-called "casteless castes" whose occupations were those which would not be followed by the higher classes. The humanitarian idea of elevating by slow and laborious work the culture-level and the standard of life of these unfortunate peoples was either under the circumstances impracticable or did not occur to the missionaries of the time. The great contempt with which these peoples were treated becomes somewhat explicable if we remember that, besides being of extremely dirty habits and low culture, they belonged to a Pre-Dravidian stock, probably Munda-Monkhmer race, who had remained unabsorbed by the Dravidians, and had been treated as pariahs even by the latter. The Nishadas, Chandalas, etc., originally denoted only unclean savage tribes living in hills and forests outside settled habitations. When a son was born of the most hated union between a Brahman woman and a Sudra male, he was expelled from the village and was compelled to live with the nomadic savage people outside, with whom he became one. Hence the statement of Dharamsastras that the issues of such detestable unions became Chandalas.[138]

The early Pali texts often mention the five despised castes of the Chandala, the Nishada, the Vena, the Rathakara and the Pukkasa. They are described as having low families (nicha kula) or inferior births (hina jati). But all of them were not treated as untouchables by the Dharamsutras. Only Chandalas and Nishadas were considered as untouchables in later Vedic society. Collectively, the untouchables were known as the *antyas* or the *bahyas*, i.e., people living outside villages and towns. Generally the untouchables lived at the end of villages or towns or in their own settlements. Their segregation was not the result of any deliberate policy of expulsion from old Aryan settlements. It seems rather that the whole population of tribal villages are condemned to the position of untouchables by the Brahmans.[139]

The Chandalas when absorbed in Brahmanical society were assigned the task of removing dead bodies of animals and human beings. They always appeared to be associated with the removal and cremation of corpses. They were also sometimes engaged for street sweeping. Gradually, the Chandalas came to be looked upon as untouchables. The Dharamsutras held that to touch and see a Chandala was sinful. In the Pali texts the Chandalas were clearly depicted as untouchables. A later Jataka described the Chandalas as the meanest men on earth. Contact with the air that touched a Chandala's body was regarded as pollution. The very sight of a Chandala forboded evil. Food and drink, if seen by him, were not to be taken. Partaking of his food, even without knowledge, led to social ostracism. In the Matanga Jataka it is related how sixteen thousand Brahmins lost their caste because they, though unknowingly, took food which had been polluted by contact with the leavings of a Chandala's meal. In the Satadhamma Jataka a Brahmin committed suicide because he had eaten the leavings from a Chandala's dish. In several Jatakas we find Brahmins running away to escape pollution by contact with Chandalas. This fear of pollution was not confined to the Brahmans alone. A merchant's daughter washed her eyes with scented water and went away from the place on seeing two Chandalas (Chitta-sambhuta Jataka). Matanga Jataka relates the story of another Sethi girl who did the same thing on seeing a Chandala at Benaras. The Chandalas led a life of misery and squalor. The Chandalas were not only despised and kept isolated from society but were distinguished from the rest of the population by their dress. We learn from Matanga Jataka that the Chandala possessed a pair of coloured garments, a girdle, a ragged robe and an earthen bowl.[140]

Almost equally despised with the Chandalas were the Pukkasas and Nishadas, who, however, were not so much noticed as their more unfortunate brethren, the Chandalas. As in the earlier writings which referred to the five-fold division of society, Brahman, Kshatriya, Vaisya, Sudra, Nishada, in the Buddhist Jataka literature also the social divisions were on similar lines, viz., Khattiya, Brahman, Vessa, Sudda, Chandalas, Pukkasa, the last two probably forming a pair. But soon confusion arose as the number of unclean castes increased. At the same time the authors of the Dharmasastras seeking their authority in the Vedic texts wanted to keep to the original four-fold division of society. So the fifth caste was altogether rejected, the Nishadas, Chandalas, Pukkasas, etc., being classified under mixed or casteless castes.[141]

Social Disabilities During Manu's Time and Thereafter

The law book of Manu is generally ascribed to the period 200 B.C.—A.D. 200. During this time the varna divided Brahmanical society was undermined by the activities of heretical sects and the incursions of foreign elements such as the Bactrian Greeks, Sakas, Parthians and Kusanas. Partly as a reaction to the Pro-Buddhist policy of Emperor Asoke (272-232 B.C.), and partly because of the advent of those new peoples, Manu desperately tries to preserve Brahmanical society, not only by ordaining rigorous measures against the Sudras, but also by inventing suitable geneologies for the incorporation of foreign elements into varna society. It should also be noted that some of these foreigners were Buddhists, some Brahmanists, while some were observing outlandish beliefs and practices. Again for a considerable period, the foreigners were dominant, and then stayed back in India permanently. Their relation with the Hindu social system must have been in the process of adjustment during this period. In order to assimilate numerous aboriginal tribes and foreign elements Manu made a far greater use of the fiction of *varnasamkara* (intermixture of varnas) than was done by his predecessors. In the majority instances the mixed castes were lumped with the Sudras in respect of their hereditary duties. Manu gives a list of *Jatis*, many of whom have changed in name and some of them have ceased to exist. He distinguishes the following categories:—

1. Four original Varnas.

2. Castes which were supposed to be produced by mixture with pure and mixed castes.

3. Castes which have lost their status on account of neglect of sacred rites.

4. Castes due to the exclusion of persons from the community.
5. Slaves and their descendants.
6. People excluded from the community of four Varnas as well as their descendants.[142]

Manu mentions the old mixed castes, who are said to have originated from the intermixture of the varnas and ascribes a similar origin to a long list of mixed castes, which are about thirty in number. These mixed castes resolve themselves into three types:

1. Caste produced from different pure castes;

2. Those produced by the mixture of pure castes on one side and mixed on the other;

3. And those produced from parents of mixed origin on both sides.[143]

Thus arose 1. Murdhavasikta (Brahmana and Kshatriya), 2. Mahisya (Kshatriya and Vaisya), 3. Karana (Vaisya and Sudra), 4. Ambastha (Brahmana and Vaisya), 5. Nishada or Parasava (Brahmana and Sudra), 6. Ugra (Kshatriya and Sudra), 7. Suta (Kshatriya and Brahmana), 8. Maghada (Vaisya and Kshatriya), 9. Vaidoha (Vaisya and Brahmana), 10. Ayogava (Sudra and Vaisya), 11. Kshattri (Sudra and Kshatriya), 12. Chandala (Sudra and Brahmana), 13. Avrita (Brahmana and Ugra), 14. Abhira (Brahmana and Ambastha), 15. Dhigvana (Brahmana and Ayogava), 16. Pukkasa (Nishada and Sudra), 17. Kukkutaka (Sudra and Nishada), 18. Svapaka (Kshattri and Ugra), 19. Vena (Vaideha and Ambastha), 20. Sairindhra (Dasyu and Ayogava), 21. Maitreyaka (Vaideha and Ayogava), 22. Margava or Kaivarta or Dasa (Nishada and Ayogava), 23. Karavara (Nishada and Vaideha), 24. Meda (Vaideha and Nishada), 25. Andhra (Vaideha and Karavara),

26. Pandusopaka (Chandala and Vaideha), 27. Ahindika (Nishada and Vaideha), 28. Sepaka (Chandala and Pukkasa), 29. Antyavasayin (Chandala and Nishada).[144]

Apart from Manu, other law-givers also give different lists of untouchables, and as it should be, there is divergence of opinion not only on their origin but also about their number. Though originally only Chandalas were the outcastes, later other castes also came to be considered outcastes. A researcher has compiled a fairly exhaustive list of such untouchables, which may be seen in Appendix A.[145]

These castes were to be distinguished by their occupations. Different tests ascribe different occupations to them. Manu says:

"To the Sutas (belong) the management of horses and chariots; to the Ambashthas, the art of healing; to the Vaidehaks, the service of women; to the Magadhas, trade.

"Killing fish to the Nishadas, carpentars' work to the Ayogava, to the Medas, the Andhras, the Chunchus and the Madgus the slaughter of wild animals.

"To Kshattris, Ugras, Pukkasas, catching and killing of (animals) living in holes; to Dhigvanas working in leather, to Venas, beating the drum."[146]

The other texts ascribe many more occupations to them. A consolidated chart of the occupations ascribed to these untouchables by the Hindu law-givers, compiled by the same researcher, may be seen in Appendix B.[147]

After stating the functions of the mixed castes, Manu ordains that they should live near well-known trees and burial grounds, on mountains and in groves. But the Chandalas and the Svapakas should live outside the village. Food vessels used by them were discarded for ever. Their sole property consisted of dogs and donkeys; they took their food in broken dishes, used ornaments of iron and clothes of dead people, and wandered from place to place.[148] They were not permitted to appear in towns and villages at night, where they could work only during the day. Manu provides that the Chandalas and Svapakas should be distinguished by marks at the king's command. Possibly the Chandalas and Svapakas were required to put on some kind of uniforms to distinguish them from the rest of the people. They could not enter into any transactions with others regarding marriage, debt, loan, etc., which could take place only with the members of their own castes. Manu ordains that members of the higher varnas should not give them even grain with their own hands. In particular, Manu wants to avoid all contact between the Brahmanas and untouchables. Manu further declares that, if a Brahman either has intercourse with Chandala or Antya women or takes their food, he shall fall from his Brahmanahood. But if he does these things intentionally, he shall be reduced to their status.[149]

Marriage between men of lower castes and women of higher castes was positively forbidden. The marriage regarded as the greatest horror was the marriage of a Brahmana woman to a man of Sudra varna. Such marriages are condemned severely by calling their progeny equal to the Chandalas. Such marriages must have been really rare and the object of the fiction is to prevent them. Neither Manu nor any other law-writer found it necessary to make the children by "marriages against grains" (marriages of women of higher castes with men of lower castes) a topic in the discussion of inheritence. But it seems probable that men of higher castes might have married women of lower castes, especially Sudras, but such practices were strongly condemned.[150]

Though it is not clear whether the untouchables and the mixed castes were regarded as Sudras by Manu, it seems that the mixed castes and the untouchables were being absorbed as inferior Sudras, who were distinguished from the ordinary Sudras by their separate habitations, backward culture and primitive religious beliefs.

There is a conflict of opinion regarding the status of the mixed castes. According to Sukraniti, all mixed castes except Murdhavasiktas were looked upon as Sudras. Kautilaya enjoins all mixed castes to take up the occupation of Sudras. In later times Brahmana writers hinted that in the Kali Age there are only two castes—Brahmanas and Sudras. According to Visnu, a mixed caste has the status of the mother's caste if that is inferior. According to Manu, the status of an offspring of a member of any caste by the wife of the immediately inferior caste would be "like" that of the father's caste but degraded due to the mother's inferior origin. In Mahabharata two views are recorded. According to one, the offspring of a Brahmana by a Kshatriya or a Vaisya woman would be a Brahmana. According to the other, the offspring of a Brahmana man and a Vaisya woman would be a Vaisya. The Markendya Purana gives an interesting rule. One must first marry a woman of one's own caste. He would be degraded to the caste of his wife if she were of an inferior caste unless his first wife was of his own caste. Sons of saints even by slave girls or women of untouchable castes were accepted as Brahmanas by society without any demur.[151]

Although the main distinction between the Sudras and the three upper varnas is retained by Manu as a matter of form, his work shows a far stronger tendency towards the approximation of the Vaisayas and Sudras in matters of legal provisions, food and marriage. The development was probably due to the fact that large numbers of Vaisyas were being thrown into the ranks of the Sudras.[152]

Many new castes were also formed by degradation from the original *varnas* on account of non-observance of Vedic rites and disobedience to Brahmanas. These are called Vratyas. Thus Vratyas are those people who are born of twice-born castes marrying girls of equal status, but have fallen in status as a consequence of neglecting sacraments. Vratya Brahmanas were known as 1. Bhrijjakantaka, 2. Avantya, 3. Vatadhana, 4. Pushpadha, and 5. Saikha. Vratya or degraded Kshatriyas became 1. Jhalla, 2. Malla, 3. Nata,

4. Lichchivi, 5. Karana, 6. Khasa, 7. Dravida (the people of South India), 8. Paundraka (the Pods), 9. Udra (the people of Orissa), 10. Kamboja (Kabulis), 11. Yavana (Bactrian Greeks), 12. Saka (Scythians), 13. Parada, 14. Pahlava (Persians), 15. China (Chinese), 16. Kirata (Kirantis), and 17. Darada (Darda, a frontier tribe). Degraded Vaisyas became 1. Sudhanvan, 2. Acharjya, 3. Karusha, 4. Vijanman, 5. Maitra and 6. Satvata. The observance of, and respect for, the Vedic rites determined the social status of the various tribes and nations. Manú and other sacred writers were not averse to giving the invading foreign peoples a place in the society and calling them Arya, irrespective of the fact whether they spoke Sanskrit, or Mlechcha or Barbarian languages, provided they followed the teachings of the Shastras, practised Vedic rites and consented to respect the Brahmanas. So it was not at all difficult to bring within the fold of Hinduism the various foreign elements who invaded India during this period. Thus the martial and ruling races like the Yavanas, Sakas, etc., were assigned the status of Kshatriya, but as they did not properly follow the usages of the Sanatan Dharma, or the Eternal Religion, they were called Vartya or degraded Kshatriyas. If any of them chose to fully adopt the Hindu ceremonial, the stigma would have been removed, and the party given an equal status with the existing Kshatriya groups.[153] Stein emphasizes this aspect of the Hindu civilization and feels that "the capacity of both ancient and medieval Indian society to ascribe to its actual rulers, frequently men of low social origins, a "clean" or "Kshatriya" rank may afford one of the explanations for the durability and longevity of the unique civilization of India".[154] Had the Moghuls or the Englishmen been without organized priesthood, and had they accepted the Brahmanas as their spiritual guides and taken pains to adopt the elevating sacraments, they also could have formed one of the Kshatriya castes.[155]

This gives us a clue to the success of Hinduism in keeping a firm hold upon the heterogeneous elements of the Indian population and its wonderful power of absorbing alien races and cultures, though apparently it is not a proselytising religion. In its earlier stages, points out Sovani, the Hindu social organization proved a powerful instrument of absorbing diverse kinds of peoples and tribes into the Hindu fold without disturbing their individual rituals and practices.[156] The Hindus of the period never attempted to derive the entirety of mankind from the Indian population. They believed that the world is made of various jatis and every one of these jatis belonged to one or the other of the four varnas. They never thought that the system of four varnas was peculiar to their land. They would not regard any foreign religion as antagonistic to their own. They would say to the foreigners that their religions were only varieties of the one eternal religion, the Sanatan Dharma, and that they belonged to one or the other of the four varnas into which the whole mankind was supposed to be divided. Those who would not care anything for Brahmanical usages were called Mlechchas or Dasyus and were let alone. But those who accepted the religious ideas of the Hindus were told that their status in society, that is, the estimation in which they would be regarded by the Brahmanas, would depend entirely upon the greater or less strictness with which they followed the teachings of the Sastras. When the foreigners accepted the social and religious usages of the Hindus, they probably found no difficulty in entering Hindu society. Their jati received the status which it could exact, as it always does. Formal conversion to Hinduism was unnecessary. No force was applied or even necessary. Unconsciously and imperceptibly the alien elements would be tempted by the unfailing bait of higher social status to give up their old practices and conform more and more to the Brahmanical usages. It is only when the catholic and tolerant Hinduism met the iconoclastic and anti-hierarchical creed of Islam that its progress was checked. Islam knew no compromise. "It was out to convert, not to be converted to any non-Quranic religious attitude or position, however, rational it might be. For the first time in its history, Hinduism faced a rival which it could not conquer and with which there could not be even easy peace. Under the circumstances, Hinduism like Roman

Catholicism in the sixteenth century was forced to redefine its dogma and institutions, and the caste system as the most obvious of these received in the succeeding centuries an exactitude, rigidity and definition that it probably had never possessed before. Tribes which had already become Hinduised and almost forgotten that their ancestors had once been non-Hindus began now to connect themselves with the Sun, the Moon, or even the Fire and the Sea in their search of pedigrees to prove that only the bluest of Kshatriya blood coursed through their veins".[157]

The advent of foreign peoples served to loosen the shackles of the varna system. Some improvement in the Sudra's legal and political status as also in their social and religious position might have been affected on account of the liberal religious outlook of the Kusana rulers (A.D. 78-226). Being mainly Saivites and Buddhists rather than supporters of the orthodox Brahmanism, they were probably better disposed towards the lower classes. This process was carried out further in the Gupta period (A.D. 300-500). The law books of the Gupta period retain the distinction between the Sudras and Untouchables. During this period there seems to have been an increase in the number of untouchable castes. Ten names are given for the Chandalas, some of which are rarely mentioned in the earlier texts. The Dombs, who came to form a numerous section of the untouchables in the Northern India in subsequent times, seem to have appeared as a caste in the Gupta period. The Jain sources describe them as a despised class. They were probably one of the aboriginal tribes, such as the Kiratas, Sabaras and Pulindas, who were absorbed in the Sudra community and assimilated to the lower orders of the Brahmanical society. During this period there seems to have been not only an increase in the number of the untouchables but also some intensification in the practice of untouchability. Fa-hsien (A.D. 399-414) informs as that, when the Chandalas enter the gate of a city or a market place, they strike a piece of wood to give prior notice of their arrival so that men may know and avoid them. But the practice of untouchability was observed mainly in respect of the Chandalas. Dombs or Charmakaras who came to be looked upon as untouchables in later times were probably not regarded as such during this period. The untouchables, and the Chandalas, in particular, are protrayed in very disparaging terms. It is stated that the *antyavasayins* are characterised by impurity, untruth, theft, heterodoxy, useless quarrels, passions, wrath and greed. Ferocity appears as a special trait of the Chandala's character.[158]

During the Gupta period the religious rights of the Sudras were considerably enlarged and in respect of several ceremonies they were placed on a level with the three higher *varnas*. While the champions of Buddhism continued to argue against birth as the basis of *varna*, the growth or certain reforming ideologies, especially the creed of Vaisnavism, secured a large measure of religious equality for the Sudras, Vaisnavism reached its high water-mark in the Gupta period. The doctrine of this sect, as propounded in the didactic sections of the Mahabharat and Puranas, show that, unlike the old orthodox form of Brahmanism, Vaisnavism did not keep the Sudras and untouchables at a distance, but extended to them the privileges of knowing God and attaining liberation.[159] Saivism also kept its door equally open to the Sudras. Tantricism, which was connected with both Vaisnavism and Saivism, also did not recognise *varna* distinctions in matters of religion.[160] Social degradation in the case of untouchables, who were regarded as Sudras only theoretically, but for all practical purposes were marked out as a separate community, continued in this period also.

Social Disabilities During Muslim Period

After the death of Harsha (A.D. 647), the dark days of Indian history began. Sind came under the occupation of the Arab in A.D. 712 and since then Muslims continued to come to India as travellers, traders and mercenaries. Mahmud's frequent raids, altogether fourteen in number (A.D. 1001-1026), must have given them more knowledge of the country. It also made them masters of Punjab and by the beginning of the 13th century A.D., the conquest of Northern India was completed by the Muslims. Their armies had over-run the entire country from Punjab to Assam and from Kashmir to the Vindhyas and the Muslims had now settled firmly in India. From the 11th century onwards, Moslem invasions, with cold-blooded murders, forcible conversions, looting, devastation of the countryside, breaking up of Hindu idols and desecration of Hindu temples began in India on a large scale and the Indians experienced perpetual insecurity. For fear of their culture being submerged under the impact of new forces, the Hindus framed rigid rules against intermarriage and inter-dining. The principle of heredity had come into prominence by c. 1000 A.D. *Pratiloma* marriages were discouraged by most of the higher castes and even *anuloma* marriages were frowned upon. This tendency towards rigidity was evidently an old legacy. In the *Mahabharata* period, Arjuna is said to have bewailed the possibility of annihilation in war of the Kuru warriors, the perishing of eternal family virtues, the prevalence of unrighteousness leading to a confusion of *varnas*. This fear grew whenever chaotic conditions prevailed because of foreign incursions. The epigraphs and literature of the period c. 600-1000 A.D. have references of a ruler's duty in keeping his people busy with the performance of the Varnasrama Dharma,[161] and this became more imperative when Ghazni's men occupied Punjab and their armies almost every year penetrated far into the interior. Evidently, Alberuni (A.D. 973-1048) was familiar with this idea when he wrote: "The kings of antiquity, who were industriously devoted to the duties of their office, spent most of their care on the division of their subjects into different classes and orders, which they tried to preserve from intermixture and disorder. Therefore they forbade people of different classes to have intercourse with each other, and laid upon each class a particular kind of work or art and handicraft. They did not allow anybody to transgress the limits of his class, and even punished those who would not be content with their class".[162]

During the 11th and 12th centuries, the number of castes, sub-castes and mixed castes increased greatly with the influence of Jainism on the Vaisyas, which made them confine themselves mainly to trade, commerce and lending. The position of the Sudra had improved a great deal. As the Vaisyas came under the doctrine of ahimsa, giving up agricultural activities, the Sudras were nearer true Vaisyas. They tilled soil and also acted as caravan-leader.[163] The Sudras gradually improved their economic condition. Their lot further improved when the reformist movement like Jainism and Saivism welcomed them in their fold, in no way treating them as inferior to the Brahmanas. But, intellectually they remained rather backward, because higher education was largely restricted to the elite—the Brahmanas and the Kshatriyas.

Generally speaking, woman's position seems to have deteriorated a bit during this period. She was not usually permitted to choose her own husband. The age of marriage went down to 12 years or lower still in the case of Brahmana maidens. The sphere of choice too became restricted because inter-caste marriages were discouraged and the offsprings of such a union were relegated either to the caste of the woman, if the marriage was of the *anuloma* type or considered as members of a mixed caste. The higher castes did not permit divorce and widow marriages were not approved. Among the Sudras, widow marriage was permissible, divorce could take place and the standard of morality expected was a little lower than that of the higher castes.[164]

Repeated Muslim attacks on the Hindu strongholds popularised the customs of *sati* and *jauhar*. The *sati* system was gaining popularity in Northern India after c. 1000 A.D., particularly in Rajasthan. The widows of not only the Kshatriyas, but also of the other three castes, adopted it. How far this custom was followed by the Brahmana widows is difficult to determine, as most of the inscriptional and literary evidences refer only to the case of the Kshatriya women.[165] But Altekar feels that the custom began to be followed by a few Brahmana families soon after 1000 A.D.[166]

When the Muslims invaded India once again towards the end of the twelfth century, the position became worse, because people of one part of the country got separated from those of the others and developed living and food habits which laid a premium on differences and led to the formation of further sub-castes and communities. This had a considerable effect on the Hindu social system. The migration of the Brahmanas, which was such a marked feature of the eleventh century and was meant perhaps to correct the imbalance of cultural development, almost came to an end in the 13th century A.D. As a result, the cultural exchange of ideas almost stopped and this may be regarded as one of the causes of the intellectual sterility of the 13th century.[167]

The advent of the Afgans and the Moghuls in the sixteenth century had a considerable effect on the Hindu social system. The immediate reaction, however, of the Afghan and Moghul conquest was the exodus of some people to the South. Those who remained behind became more exclusive and tried to protect themselves by early marriage and hardening of caste system. The Portuguese occupation of some parts of India in the early sixteenth century gave rise to fresh conversions of Hindus into Roman Catholics. When Hindu kings conquered the countries occupied by Moslems or Portuguese rulers, Muslim and Christian converts freely got themselves reconverted into Hinduism. All these further increased the number of castes.[168]

The medieval India also saw the resurgence of Hinduism. Adi-Jagatguru Sankaracharjya (788-820 A.D.) resurrected and reestablished the Hindu religion, purged it of heretical and fissiparous tendencies and opened its door to all sections of Hindu including the Chandalas and the down-trodden. Further, Vaisnavaite and Saivite devotees who did not give any place to the caste system, held the torch of Hinduism high in the hearts of the masses during this critical period when Hinduism was facing its greatest challenge from the proselytising religions, Islam and Christianity. The Bhakti movement led by Acharjya Ramanuj (1017-1200),

Madhavacharya (b.1238), Vallavacharya (1479-1531), Kabir (1440-1518), Nanak (1469-1539), Chaitanya (1486-1533), Tulsi Das (1532-1623), and many others did help check Islamisation of India. Under its influence, many who had converted to Islam, like Harihar and Bukka, came back to the Hindu fold. But it mainly served the Hindu society in another way—by giving it pride in its spiritual heritage and by bringing the truth of the Upanishads and the Gita to the doors of even the lowest classes of Hindu social order in their own language. When the Hindus failed militarily and politically, they learnt to assert themselves in the spiritual-bhakti place. It kept them going until better days returned.

The Bhakti saints were the leaders of the Hindu "protestant" movement which gave to the backward class Hindus a respectable position in the society. Even many Muslims were converted to Bhakti Hinduism. Namdeva, Ramdas, Eknath, Ramanand, Kabir, Nanak and Chaitanya and several other saints had Muslim disciples, many of whom converted themselves to the Hindu Bhakti cult. Chaitanya openly converted Muslims to Bhakti Hinduism.[169] The Bhakti movement also ignored the distinction between the sexes; and there were women saints such as Andal, Akkamahadevi, and Meera. It is indisputable that the net effect of the movement was to strike a blow for equality and prepare the higher castes for the more massive assault that came during the British rule.[170]

In the medieval India, the two mid-varnas, Kshatriya and Vaisya, approximated more towards the fourth *varna*, i.e. the Sudra. This process was more pronounced in Bengal than in other parts of the country. Modern expounders of Hindu Sastras in Bengal when referring to *varnas* and castes and their rights and duties, often cite a text to the effect that according to Yama there are in the Kali Age only two varnas, Brahmana and Sudra. Raghunandana,[171] in the sixteenth century, and Nagesabhatta,[172] in the eighteenth century, traced the extinction of Kshatriyas and Vaisyas from the prophecies in the Puranas regarding the Kali Age and that the Brahmanas had become Sudra-like by the non-observance of their rites. Ketkar, however, thinks that Kshatriyas and Vaisyas came to be regarded as extinct around third century A.D., i.e. the period attributed to Manu, the Hindu law-giver.[173] K.M. Panikkar maintains that there has been no such caste as the Kshatriya during the last two thousand years of history. The Nandas were the last "true" Kshatriyas, and they disappeared in the fifth century B.C. Since then every known royal family has come from a non-Kshatriya caste, including the famous Rajput dynasties of medieval India.[174] Panikkar also points out that "the Sudras seem to have produced an unusually large number of royal families even in more recent times. The Palas of Bengal belonged undoubtedly to that caste. The great Maratha Royal House, whatever their function today, could hardly sustain their genealogical pretensions connecting them with Rajput descent."[175]

The causes of degradation of the Kshatriya and Vaisya *varnas* had their deep roots in the past. As in medieval Europe so in ancient India there had been jealousy between the spiritual and temporal lords, and the Brahmanas had been seeking to widen the gulf between the two orders and to prove the inferiority of the Kshatriyas. The rise of Buddhism and Jainism no doubt represented a religious movement against the excessive ritualism practised by the Brahmanas and the extreme importance attached to the outer forms of observance. Both Jainism and Buddhism were Reform Movements started by Kshatriyas preaching against rituals and sacrifices and emphasising the performance of duty and the observance of right conduct. Buddhism spread over the whole of Northern India and a part of Southern India. The old ritualism of sacrifices was discarded and popular forms of worship were introduced. But the popular character of the movement was lost when it gradually developed degrading practices. While the Brahmanas later on with a surprising spirit of adaptability and accommodation adopted good many points from Buddhism in matters of theology and philosophy and even declared Gautam Buddha as one of the incarnations of Lord Vishnu, and thereby cut the ground from under the feet of their opponents, they not only yielded but rather strengthened their position in the matter of caste rules, with the result that with the decline of Buddhism the pretensions and prerogatives of the priestly caste became more strongly established than before. Yet so long as the Kshatriyas possessed temporal powers, the Brahmanas could not suppress them appreciably by means of their writings. It was not till after the Muslim conquest of the country when the function of ruling had passed away from the hands of Hindu royal families that any question could arise about the extinction of the Kshatriya *varna.* It was reserved for the Muslim conquerors to do this work for the Brahmanas, who could now say complacently that there was no longer any Kshatriya in the world.[176] When the Kshatriyas passed out of existence the Vaisyas, who had already come very close to the Sudras in social status, had no chance of survival.

We have seen earlier that in the pre-Mauryan period, the difference between the Vaisyas and the Sudras was getting narrower day by day. The occupations of the two *varnas* were practically interchangeable. The general rule was that "in times of distress each *varna* may follow the occupations of that next below it in rank". So the Vaisyas who were rigidly shut out from the occupations of the higher *varnas*, freely took to those of the Sudras, while the latter in distress were permitted to follow the professions of the Vaisya *varna.*[177] Later on, Sudras could be found in the professions of cattle-breeding and agriculture not only in exceptional circumstances but at all times.[178] Handicrafts passed entirely into the hands of the Sudra *varna.*[179]

Thus in the medieval India the artisan classes, such as carpenters, weavers, potters, smiths, etc., who had in the Rg Vedic society belonged to the Vaisya *varna* were ranked as Sudras. The recognised professions of a Vaisya were four in number, viz., agriculture, cattle-rearing, trade and money-lending.[180] Of these, agriculture and cattle-rearing were regarded as not quite honourable, and eventually, like industrial arts, fell to the share of the Sudras. Manu justified the aversion of the higher class Aryans towards agriculture by stating that it was not a noble profession as it involved the killing of insects and worms in the soil.[181] After this, trade and money-lending remained the only honourable occupations for a Vaisya. But such was the contempt with which even these were looked upon by the Brahmanas that some of the law-givers would not allow a Brahmana to follow them even in times of distress.[182] So it is not surprising to learn from Alberuni's accounts that in the eleventh century in some parts of India at least, the Vaisyas, like the Sudras, were "not allowed to hear it (i.e., the Vedas), much less to pronounce and recite it",[183] though this statement of Alberuni stands contradicted by Bhatta Laksmidhara, who had permitted the Vaisyas the study of the Vedas, but prohibited to trade in certain commodities like salt, hides, flesh, etc.[184] The next step of forbidding the use of sacred thread was practised in some areas of Bengal and thus the Vaisyas were reduced to the rank of the Sudras. This, however, did not happen in Northern and Western India, where the Vaisya is still a *dwija* or twice-born,[185] and some Vaisyas even followed the profession of the Kshatriyas. A few epigraphs from Chhattisgarh in Madhya Pradesh speak of the victories of a Vaisya, Vallabharaja, who was a feudatory of the Kalachuris of Ratnapur. Besides possessing martial prowess, he was religious-minded and built many temples, excavated tanks and reared mango groves. For his numerous good qualities Lachhalladevi, the queen of Ratnadeva II, treated him as her own son. There were many other members of this caste, who due to their great ability, served as high state ministers and commanders-in-chief.[186]

In Bengal, especially, two facts told adversely against the Vaisyas as compared with their brethren in Mid-India. First, most of them were heretics in faith, being Buddhist or Jaina, which together with their connections with the Pala rulers, who kept Buddhism in full vigour during their four long centuries of rule, drew upon them the displeasure of the Sena kings, who came from the Deccan and made the first serious attempt to regulate the loose social system of Bengal on the basis of the four-fold order, and their Brahmana supporters. Secondly, sea-voyage was freely indulged in by the traders of Bengal even when it was definitely prohibited in the Sastras.[187] It required, therefore, little effort on the part of the Brahmana legislators to reduce the Bengali Vaisyas to the status of Sudras.

Attempts were made to enforce in the Deccan also this convenient dictum that in the Kali Age there are only two *varnas*, Brahmana and Sudra. The revival of the Maratha military power, however, in the seventeenth century arrested the process of disappearance of the Kshatriya *varna* there, and the stubborn resistance offered by the Prabhu-Kayasthas in the eighteenth century foiled the Brahmanical efforts, though backed by the support of some of the Peshwas like Narayan Rao, to deprive them forcibly of the use of the sacred thread and to reduce them to the status of Sudras. Brahmanas were forbidden to officiate as priests for them, and they were ordered not to perform the rites of the twice-born. They were to call themselves Parbhus instead of Prabhus, and to say *Dandavat* instead of *Pranama* as a mark of degradation. Fortunately for the Prabhus, Narayan Rao met with a premature end, which was followed by troublous times when concessions had to be made to them. Besides, they were too much established in power in the country to be easily overcome, and they received in addition the valuable support of the Sankaracharyas of Sringeri Math.Thus the Deccan was saved from sharing the fate of Bengal.[188]

Social Disabilities During British Period

By the time the Britishers had consolidated their position in India, the Hindu social system had accumulated many undesirable features. Foreign invasions also rendered it more conservative.

The various policies of the British Rulers were designed mainly for the maintenance of law and order, for the collection of taxes, and for keeping an unrestricted market for British goods. Their centralised administration completely disrupted the old economy of the country. The old village economy which remained unaffected by the fortunes of political conflicts so long and which had given so much strength to the caste system, became disrupted under British Rule. The land policy created a new class of landlords and drove millions into the ranks of tenants and agricultural labourers. Unrestricted competition of imported goods caused the decay of rural industries and village handicrafts, and the artisan and occupational classes were rendered idle and swelled the ranks of agricultural labourers.[189] The caste-divided Hindu society which ensured employment and protection to its various caste-groups, could not effectively challenge the British policy. For the first time caste system faced a serious challenge from its foreign rulers. The western education also brought about a change in the outlook of the educated youth who under the leadership of social reformers like Raja Rammohan Roy (1772-1833), Iswar Chandra Vidyasagar (1820-1891), Swami Vivekananda (1863-1902), Swami Dayananda Swarasati (1824-1883), Justice Ranade (1842-1901), Lala Lajpat Rai (1865-1928), Mahatma Gandhi (1869-1948) and others introduced many social reforms including abolition of untouchability, elevating the status of women in society, abolition of *satidaha*, early marriage of girls, and widow remarriage. These movements no doubt had a salutary effect of cleansing the Hindu social order of some of its undesirable features, narrowing down the class and caste distinctions and changing the attitude of the high caste people towards the untouchables, who not only mixed with the lower castes but worked for their uplift.

The growth of towns, the establishment of industries in urban areas, the introduction of railways, the establishment of hotels and eating houses contributed to the relaxation of caste prejudices. New economic activities taken by the state gave birth to numerous non-caste occupations. A process was set into motion which began to attack the importance of caste as ritual-cum-occupational division of society. New bases of economic power appeared. The establishment of civil and criminal courts robbed the caste system and the caste panchayats of what authority they once had over the members of particular castes. The prestige of caste leaders and the pernicious effects of caste system gradually diminished.

As the impact of the British on the subcontinent became felt the process of change was accelerated. It was the West that introduced influences that were ultimately to disrupt craft-exclusiveness and shake the very foundations of the existing economic order. When the Indian economy became linked to the expanding world economy, new occupations were introduced and old trades attracted new workers by promises of greater financial rewards. Thus, Buchanan observed in 1934 that the *chamars* (leather workers), a caste extremely low in the Hindu hierarchy, had gained considerable prestige because the sale of hides to European countries had produced a new source of wealth out of all proportion to their traditional income. Similarly, the *teli* (oil pressers) of Bengal had profited greatly from the new markets, and many of their members had become wealthy bankers and merchants.[190]

In a more recent study (1947) of twenty eight jati in a rural Bengal village, it was found that only twelve were still performing their traditional occupations exclusively; five were in a state of transition between traditional occupations and new functions; and eleven no longer performed any part of their traditional roles.[191]

Davis, in his study of the Indian census reports of 1921 and 1941, furnishes the following table showing the percentages of Indians still engaged in their traditional occupations:[192]

	Per cent
Dealers in food and drink	37
Agricultural	21
Labourers and village menials	14
Pastoral	20
Learned professions	20
Boating and fishing	9
Trade and industry	
Unspecified	70
Specified	51

Similarly, Sharma, basing his conclusions on the study of a village about ten miles from Kanpur, shows statistically that a large percentage of the membership of each caste has forsaken its traditional occupation.[193] Clearly craft-exclusiveness has yielded to the pressures of changing times. As Davis concludes, mobility can be seen up and down the hierarchy, and with the mobility there is emerging a new middle class that draws from all castes, "some more than others to be sure, but certainly from no particular caste."[194]

But the British policy was not for fostering unity and cohesion of the various sections of people of India. Its policy was directed at dividing and subdividing the people at whatever level possible with a view to perpetuating its rule. They deliberately fostered distrust among the various sections of people, be it on the issue of religion, region, language or caste. In pursuance of their "divide and rule" policy, the British cultivated and nurtured the forces of disintegration, destabilization and discord. They never failed to exploit the antagonisms, cleavages and divisions in our body politic in order to justify the prolongation of their rule, and they failed to actively promote unity. The attitude of the British to such disruptive and disintegrating forces is quite plain and simple. Exploit and utilise them not only to perpetuate the rule but also to disintegrate the country. The policy of 'divide and rule', the introduction of separate electorates, and special recognition accorded to non-Brahmin castes in the South not only contributed to the disruption of whatever solidarity India once possessed and fostered jealousies between province and province and between creed and creed but also hardened the caste distinctions. A striking feature of the caste system in the pre-British period was its local character. There was no all-India horizontal organisation of castes. Formerly, the caste provided what Karve has called the 'cultural gestalt'. It practically coincided with linguistic and territorial boundaries. But British rule destroyed the local character of the caste system. It broke up the homogeneity of small groups over small areas and encouraged horizontal organisation of castes over vast stretches of land.

The British anthropologist, Miller, has demonstrated in a detailed case study of the Malayalam-speaking region that caste was traditionally 'a "system of territorial segmentation" in which the bedrock unit was either the village (desam) or at most the chiefdom (nad). With modern social change, the old boundaries dependent on political cleavages, now became porous, ceasing to mark the limits of social relations with individual castes. This has enabled castes to establish internal bonds of solidarity over wide areas. The last 50 years have seen the growth of a formal regional organisation for practically every caste, with the avowed aim of....raising the status and prestige of a caste as a whole and free its members from exploitation and victimization by the other castes.'[195] This increasing solidarity in caste over large geographical distance led to the strengthening of the caste spirit. It became the basis of economic and political enfranchisement and power politics, as well as increasing economic competition. Thus the associational functions of caste assumed a greater significance while the institutional functions receded into the background.[196] This became a major cause of the caste tensions and rivalries India has witnessed in recent years.

In their search for a uniform law code the British applied a unified, supposedly Brahminical legal system, for the first time, on an all-India scale. Laws in India had so far remained uncodified and the very process of codification destroyed the flexibility and the capacity to adapt to local customs and situations they had earlier displayed. The *Manusmriti* may have existed in the past but it had never sought to be uniformly applied to society.[197] The Britishers made the elastic Hindu law inelastic and non-progressive through their law courts.[198] One common characteristic of the upper caste is their abhorrence for physical labour. The system of education introduced by the British which was mainly designed for the training of a few people for the subordinate ranks of the administration[199] ultimately started churning out people for 'white colour jobs'. This system of education suited the upper castes well and also attracted other aspirants for these jobs.

It is not generally known that the India of rigid social stratification and hierarchial ranking was largely a British creation and that in their attempt to comprehend and control the Indian social order, the British set in motion forces that transformed the older system in a fundamental way. As late as the 18th century, the hierarchical ordering of Hindu society was not an established fact over large parts of the subcontinent. As some eminent historians have pointed out, till that time alternative ideologies and styles of life were strong, indeed dominant, in much of India.[200] It was only in the 19th century with the "pacification" of large parts of countryside that the Brahminical principles of social organisation could be said to have become operational on an all-India scale.[201]

Under the British many things happened to weaken as well as to strengthen the caste but on balance the latter outweighed the former. "The British, in contradistinction to their predecessors, progressively refused to perform certain social functions, perhaps the most important of which were those connected with the regulation of a caste society involving the functioning and relative status of castes. The Pre-British rulers, including the Muslims, by performing these functions helped maintain, even in a caste society, a degree of social integration. Thereby the process of continuous adjustment and wider integration was always at work. This process of over-all social regulation and integration could no longer be maintained when the British refused to perform these functions; as a result the social structure lost its adaptability and integration. In the pre-British days caste loyalty was tempered by the sense of loyalty to the Hindu society as a whole which was maintained by the secular authority. The loyalty to one's own caste increased under the British as occasions and opportunities for emphasizing or exhibiting the over-all sense of Hindu loyalties decreased. It is in this manner that the institution of caste became more rigid than before in the period of British rule.[202]

Srinivas also came to a conclusion that the *varna* model became more popular during the British period as a result of a variety of forces: the institution, which prevailed till 1864, of attaching Brahmin Pundits to British-established law courts, the presence in every town of a body of Western-educated lawyers who tried to apply Brahminical law to all Hindus, the translation of a vast mass of sacred literature from Sanskrit into English, the rise everywhere of caste *sabhas* who tried to introduce reforms by Sanskritizing the way of life of their respective castes, and the growth of a vigorous anti-Brahmin movement which attempted to displace Brahmins from the positions of power and influence which they occupied in some parts of the country.[203] Under the British economic and social dividing lines in society became parallel, which were not before.

J.S. Furnivall has observed that the impact of the West on India has been less violent than, for instance, on Burma, because of the caste system in India which afforded considerable protection to the social system.[204] Sovani, however, rightly points out that it is true that it prevented social disintegration, so characteristic of other societies, but it also left the Indian society loose and weak and hampered its transformation into a modern social and industrial community.[205]

While the liberal attitude of the Indians and the efforts of the social reformers were gradually obliterating caste-barriers and caste-prejudices, the endeavour of the British rulers to politicise the caste-issues in furtherence of its 'divide and rule' policy made a permanent inroad in the caste-ridden society and made the "casteless" castes a permanent feature in the Hindu social hierarchy. Their gullibility can easily be comprehended by the fact that their "divide and rule" policy ensured formation of a new caste, "Scheduled Castes", to mean any one of those castes, mainly untouchables, incorporated in the Schedule by the British Government. Not only they left enough loopholes in the entire scheme and ensured that the "Scheduled Castes" swelled in rank in future, thus reversing the efforts of all the social reformers during the last one thousand years, who were fighting for social uplift of these "casteless" castes in the Hindu social system, but also made it rather impossible for any of these castes included in the Schedule to come out of it in future, thus making them a permanent feature in the Hindu social system. That the British rulers succeeded in their endeavours is discernible by the fact that in spite of the avowed proclamation of the Constitution-makers to make India a casteless society, they also followed in the footstep of their past masters and perpetuated casteism, albiet in the name of obliterating it, so much so that the society is embroiled in caste-conflicts and caste-tensions even after forty-eight years of independence with no sign of abatement. Rather it is increasing with the passage of each day.

Notes and References

1. Hocart, A.M., *Caste—A Comparative Study*, Methuen & Co., London, 1950, pp. VI-VII.
2. Hutton, J.H., *Caste in India*, Oxford University Press, 1946, Chapter IX.
3. Ghurye, G.S., *Caste and Race in India*, Popular Prakashan, Bombay, Fifth edition, 1990, Chapter 6.
4. Hutton, *op. cit.*, p. 188.
5. Report of the Backward Classes Commission (K. Kalekar, Chairman), 1955, p. 14.
6. Hutton, *op. cit.*, p. 1.
7. Risley, H.H., *The Tribes and Castes of Bengal*, Calcutta, 1891, p. xxviii.
8. Pillai, G.K., *Origin and Development of Caste*, Kitab Mahal, Allahabad, 1959, p. 129.
9. *Ibid.*, p. 125.
10. Hutton, *op. cit.*, pp. 2-6; Pillai, *op. cit.*, pp. 121-136.
11. Risley, *op. cit.*, p. xxxi.
12. Hutton, *op. cit.*, p. 55.
13. Basham, A.L., *The Wonder That Was India*, London, 1954, p. 150.
14. *Manu* X. 4.
15. Ketkar, S.V., *History of Caste in India*, Rawat Publications, Jaipur, 1979, p. 76.

16. Dutt, N.K., *Origin and Growth of Caste in India*, Vol. I, Firma K.L. Mukhopadhyaya, Calcutta, 1968, p. 3.
17. Ketkar, *op. cit.*, p. 77.
18. Majumdar, D.N., and Madan, T.N., *An Introduction to Social Anthropology*, Asia Publishing House, 1956, p. 235.
19. *Census 1951 West Bengal*, The Tribes and Castes of West Bengal, Land and Land Revenue Department, Government of West Bengal, p. 16.
20. Risley, H.H., *The People of India*, W. Thacker Co., London, Second Edition, 1915, p. 67.
21. Ketkar, *op. cit.*, p. 15.
22. Hutton, *op. cit.*, p. 49.
23. *Census Report, Bengal*, 1901, p. 354.
24. Beteille, Andre, *Caste, Class and Power, Changing Patterns of Stratification on a Tanjore Village*, Berkeley : University of California Press, 1965, p. 46.
25. Weber, Max, *From Max Weber Essays on Sociology*, ed. by H.H. Gerth and C.W. Mills, London, 1948, p. 186.
26. Majumdar and Madan, *op. cit.*, p. 221.
27. Bouglé, Célestin : *Essais sur le régime des castes*, Paris, Alcan, (1st ed., 1908), 1927, p. 4; English translation of the introduction in *Contributions to Indian Sociology*, II, 1958, quoted by Louis Dumont, *Homo Hierarchicus*, Weidenfeld and Nicolson, London, 1970, p. 21.
28. Dutt, *op. cit.*, pp. 2-3.
29. Wilson, *Indian Castes*, I. 12, quoted in *Census 1951 West Bengal*, p. 19.
30. Bateille, Andre, *Castes: Old and New*, Asia Publishing House, 1969, p. 90.
31. Dumont, *op. cit.*, pp. 34-35.
32. Ketkar, *op. cit.*, p. 5.

32a. Majumdar, D.N., *Races and Cultures of India*, Asia Publishing House, Delhi, 1958, p. 279.

33. *Pancavimśa*, p. 113; *Brāhmanya*, Vol. I, 6-10; *Vajasanevi Samhita*, XXXI, 11; *Taittiriya Aranayaka*, III, 12.5 & 6, quoted by R.S. Sharma in *Sudras in Ancient India*, Motilal Banarasidass, 1958, p. 28.
34. *Mahabharat*, XII, 73, 4-8, quoted by Sharma, *Ibid.*
35. *Vāyu Purāna*, 1. VIII, 155-9; *Mārkandeya Purāna*, Ch. 49; *Visnu Purana*, I. Ch. VI, quoted by Sharma, *Ibid.*
36. *Vasistha Dharmasūtra*, IV. 2; *Baudhayāna Dharmasutra*, 1.10.19. 5-6; *Āpastamba Dharmasūtra*, I. 1.1.7; *Manu Smriti*, I. 31; *Yājñavalkya Smriti*, III, 126, quoted by Sharma, *Ibid.*
37. Buhler, G., *Laws of Manu* (1,31,87), pp. 14, 24, *Sacred Laws*, Pt. II, p. 25, (*Vasistha* IV, 2), etc. and vide Wilson, *Indian Caste*, I, p. 17, quoted by Hutton, *op. cit.*, p. 148.
38. Sharma, *op. cit.*, pp. 28-29.
39. Majumdar and Madan, *op. cit.*, pp. 226-28.

40. Risley, *The Tribes and Castes of Bengal*, *op. cit.*, pp. XXXVIII-XXXIX.
41. Rao Hayavadana, *Indian Caste System*, Bangalore, 1931, p. 66.
42. Roy, S.C., Caste, Race and Religion, in *Man in India*, XIV, No. 2.
43. Dutt, *op. cit.*, Chapter I.
44. Ghurye, *op. cit.*, Chapter VII.
45. Majumdar, *op. cit.*, Chapter III.
46. Ghurye, *op. cit.*, p. 176.
47. *Ibid.*, Chapter VII.
48. Dutt, *op. cit.*, p. 29.
49. Majumdar, *op. cit.*, p. 291.
50. Majumdar and Madan, *op. cit.*, pp. 235-36.
51. Dutt, *op. cit.*, pp. 18-19.
52. *Ibid.*, p. 33.
53. *Ibid.*, p. 15.
54. Karve, Iravati, *The Hindu Society--A New Interpretation*, Part I, Berkeley, (memographed), pp. 22-24, quoted by Robert O. Tilman, *The Influence of Caste on Indian Economic Development*, In : *Administration and Economic Development in India*, ed. by Ralph Braibanti and Joseph J. Spengler, Cambridge University Press, 1963, pp. 204-205.
55. Nesfield, J.C., *Brief view of the Caste System of the North-West Provinces and Oudh*, Allahabad, 1885, quoted by Dutt, *Ibid.*, pp. 20-21.
56. *Census 1951 West Bengal*, p. 17.
57. Quoted by Hutton, *op. cit.*, p. 176.
58. Ibbetson, Denzil., *Punjab Castes*, Pt. I, Lahore, 1916.
59. Majumdar and Madan, *op. cit.*, pp. 266-67.
60. Hocart, *op. cit.*, Chapter I, pp. VI-VIII.
61. Hutton, *op. cit.*, pp. 176-88.
62. Roy, S.C., Caste, Race and Religion in India, In : *Man in India*, Vol. XVII, No. 4.
63. Majumdar and Madan, *op. cit.*, p. 228.
64. Roy, Sarat Chandra, *Man in India*, Vol. XVII, No. 4, p. 242.
65. Majumdar, *op. cit.*, pp. 288-89.
66. Hardgrave, Robert L. Jr., *The Dravidian Movement*, Popular Prakashan, Bombay, 1965, p. 11
67. Ketkar, *op. cit.*, p. 121.
68. Majumdar, *op. cit.*, p. 283.
69. Rice, S., *The Origin of Caste*, Asiatic Review, Vol. XXV, 1929, quoted by Hutton, *op. cit.*, p. 176.
70. Hutton, *Ibid.*, p. 176.
71. Pillai, *op. cit.*, pp. 119 and 248.
72. Dutt, *op. cit.*, pp. 26-28.
73. Roy, Sarat Chandra, *Man in India*, Vol. XVII, No. 4.
74. *Census 1951, West Bengal*, p. 18.

75. Ketkar, *op. cit.*, p. 102.
76. Hutton, *op. cit.*, pp. 189-90.
77. Majumdar, D.N., *The Eastern Anthropologist*, September-November, 1958.
78. Risley, *The Tribes and Castes of Bengal*, *op. cit.*, pp. XVI-XVIII.
79. Majumdar, *op. cit.*, p. 358.
80. Quoted by Pillai, *op. cit.*, p. 146.
81. Quoted by Pillai, *Ibid.*, p. 147.
82. Roy, Sarat Chandra, *The Hill Bhuiyas of Orissa*, Ranchi, 1935, pp. 28-36.
83. Pillai, *op. cit.*, pp. 138-49.
84. Dutt, *op. cit.*, pp. 56-57.
85. *Ibid.*, pp. 92-93.
86. *Ibid.*, pp. 192-94.
87. Bhattacharjee, Jogendra Nath, *Hindu Caste and Sects*, Calcutta, 1896, p. 9.
88. Risley, *op. cit.*, p. XIII.
89. Ram Jagjivan, *Caste Challenge in India*, Vision Books, New Delhi, 1980, p. 9.
90. Ketkar, *op. cit.*, p. 108.
91. *Ibid.*, p. 29.
92. *Ibid.*
93. *Ibid.*, p. 31.
94. Ram Jagjivan, *op. cit.*, p. 9.
95. *Baudhayana Dharamasutra*, 1.5.10.20 quoted by Dutt, *op. cit.*, p. 152.
96. Dutt, *Ibid.*, pp. 152-53.
97. *Ibid.*, pp. 119-20.
98. *Manusmriti*, Chapter X, quoted by Bhattacharjee, *op. cit.*, p. 8.
99. Ram Jagjivan, *op. cit.*, p. 10.
100. Sovani, N.V., *Non-economic Aspects of India's Economic Development*, In : Administration and Economic Development in India, ed., *op. cit.*, p. 275.
101. Ram Jagjivan, *op. cit.*, p. 12.
102. Srinivas, M.N., *Social Change in Modern India*, Allied Publishers, 1966, p. 120.
103. Ambedkar, B.R., *Annihilation of Caste*, Dr. Babasaheb Ambedkar: Writings and Speeches, Govt. of Maharashtra, p. 39.
104. M.C. Rajah in his note on Depressed Classes given to the Indian Council Committee in 1929, vide *Report of the Indian Council Committee*, pp. 373-74.
105. Beteille, *Castes: Old and New*, *op. cit.*, p. 92.
106. Keith, A.B., *Cambridge History of India*, p. 99.
107. Sharma, *op. cit.*, pp. 18-26.
108. *Ibid.*, p. 30.

109. Quoted by Pillai, *op. cit.*, p. 12.
110. *Vedic Index*, II 265-66, quoted by Sharma, *op. cit.*, p. 28.
111. *Zeitschrift Der Deutschen Mergenlaondischen Geseuschaft*, Berlin, quoted by Sharma, *Ibid.*, p. 29.
112. Dutt, *op. cit.*, pp. 50-51.
113. *Ibid.*, p. 82.
114. Ambedkar, B.R., *Who were the Sudras*, Bombay, 1946, p. 239, Dutt, Bhupendra Nath, *Sudras in Indian Social Polity*, Calcutta, 1944, pp. 28-30.
115. Dutt, N.K., *op. cit.*, p. 51.
116. *Ibid.*, p. 85.
117. Sharma, *op. cit.*, p. 41.
118. *Ibid.*, p. 79.
119. Keith, A.B., *op. cit.*, p. 129.
120. Dutt, *op. cit.*, pp. 145-46.
121. Dutt, *Ibid.*, Vol. II, pp. 87-88.
122. Sharma, *op. cit.*, p. 111.
123. *Apastamba Dharamasutra*, I, 5.16.21 and 5.17.1, quoted by Sharma, *Ibid.*, p. 113.
124. Fick, Richard, *The Social Organization in North-East India in Buddha's Time*, Calcutta, 1920, p. 9.
125. Bhattacharjee, *op. cit.*, p. 11.
126. *Paraskara Gryasutra*, II, 8.3, quoted by Sharma, *op. cit.*, p. 122.
127. Ketkar, *op. cit.*, p. 122.
128. Ghure, *op. cit.*, p. 69.
129. Fick, *op. cit.*, p. 209.
130. Dutt, Vol. I, *op. cit.*, p. 225.
131. Sharma, *op. cit.*, p. 126.
132. This view has been further developed by Ambedkar, *The Untouchables*, Chapter IX.
133. *Ibid.*, Chapter X.
134. Dutt, Vol. I, *op. cit.*, p. 90.
135. Pillai, *op. cit.*, pp. 176-84.
136. Ghurye, *op. cit.*, p. 159.
137. Sharma, *op. cit.*, p. 132.
138. Dutt, Vol. II, *op. cit.*, pp. 89-91.
139. Sharma, *op. cit.*, pp. 130-32.
140. *Ibid.*, pp. 126-27.
141. Dutt, Vol. I, *op. cit.*, pp. 230-31.
142. Ketkar, *op. cit.*, p. 83.
143. *Ibid.*, p. 84.
144. Dutt, Vol. I, *op. cit.*, pp. 5-6.
145. *Census 1951, West Bengal*, pp. 47-48.
146. *Manu X 47-49.*, quoted by Ketkar, *op. cit.*, p. 104.

147. *Census 1951, West Bengal*, pp. 48-49.
148. *Manu* X 50-52, quoted by Ketkar, *op. cit.*, p. 104.
149. Sharma, *op. cit.*, pp. 204-8.
150. Ketkar, *op. cit.*, p. 144.
151. *Census 1951, West Bengal*, p. 28.
152. Sharma, *op. cit.*, p. 216.
153. Dutt, Vol. I., *op. cit.*, pp. 7-13.
154. Stein, B., *Social Mobility and Medieval South Indian Hindu Sects* in J. Silverberg (ed.), *Social Mobility in Caste in India*, special issue of Comparative Studies in Society and History, quoted by Srinivas, *Social Change in Modern India*, p. 32.
155. Ketkar, *op. cit.*, p. 94.
156. Sovani, *op. cit.*, p. 271.
157. Sharma, Dasarath, *The Early Chauhan Dynasties*, Delhi, 1959, pp. 244-45.
158. Sharma, R.S. *op. cit.*, pp. 257-64.
159. Roychaudhuri, H.C., *The Early History of the Vaisnava Sect*, Calcutta, 1920, p. 117.
160. Sharma, R.S., *op. cit.*, p. 275.
161. Sharma, Dr. Brijendra Nath, *Social and Cultural History of Northern India*, c. 1000-1200 A.D., Abhinav Publications, New Delhi, 1972, p. 9.
162. Sachau, E.C., *Alberuni's India*, two volumes in one, London, 1914, Vol. I, pp. 99-100.
163. Sharma, Dr. B.N., *op. cit.*, p. 28.
164. *Ibid.*, p. 77.
165. *Ibid.*, p. 67.
166. Altekar, Dr. A.S., *Position of Women in Hindu Civilization*, 3rd edition, Banaras, 1962, p. 129.
167. Sharma, Dr. B.N., *op. cit.*, p. 176.
168. Ramarao Adik, *Brahmanism without Casteism*, Bombay, 1961, pp. 44-45.
169. Lal, K.S., *Indian Muslims : Who Are They*, Voice of India, New Delhi, 1990, pp. 111-13.
170. Srinivas, *op. cit.*, pp. 25-26.
171. *Sudhitattam.*
172. *Vratyata-prayascitta-nirmaya.*
173. Ketkar, *op. cit.*, p. 164.
174. Panikkar, K.M., *Hindu Society at Cross Roads*, Bombay, 1955, p. 8.
175. *Ibid.*, p. 9.
176. Dutt, Vol. II, *op. cit.*, pp. 85-86, 93.
177. *Yajnavalkya Smriti*, I. 120.
178. *Kautilya Arthasastra*, I. 3.
179. *Gautama Dharmasutra*, X : *Vishnu Purana* II.
180. *Yajnavalkya Smriti*, I. 119.

181. *Manu* X. 83-84.
182. *Apastamba Dharmasutra* 1.7.20.10; *Baudhayana Dharmasutra* I. 5.10.24.
183. Sacahu, *op. cit.*, Vol. II, p. 136.
184. *Krtyakalpataru Grhasthakanda*, ed. with an introduction by K.V. Rangaswami Aiyangar, Gaekwad Oriental Series, Baroda, 1944, p. 258, quoted by Sharma, Dr. B.N., *op. cit.*, p. 24.
185. Dutt, *op. cit.*, Vol. II, p. 135.
186. Sharma, Dr. B.N., *op. cit.*, p. 25.
187. *Vrihannaradiya Purana*, XXII, 13-16.
188. Dutt, *op. cit.*, Vol. II, pp. 91-95, p. 105.
189. *Report of the First Backward Classes Commission*, 1955, p. 23, paras 44-45.
190. Buchanan, Daniel H., *The Development of Capitalist Enterprises in India*, New York, 1934, p. 24.
191. Bose, N.K., Some Aspects of Caste in Bengal, *Journal of American Folklore*, LXXI, July-Sept., 1958, pp. 398-99.
192. Davis, Kingsley, *The Population of India and Pakistan*, Princeton, 1951, p. 170.
193. *Southwestern Journal of Anthropology*, XVII (Summer, 1961), pp. 148-49.
194. Davis, *op. cit.*, p. 176.
195. Miller, Eric J., Caste and Territory in Malabar, *American Anthropologist*, Vol. 56, No. 3, June, 1954, pp. 418-19.
196. Saksena, R.N., Factor in social tensions, *Seminar*, No. 70, p. 23.
197. Jain, Meenakshi, The myth of caste tyranny, *Indian Express*, September, 26, 1991.
198. *Report of the First Backward Classes Commission*, 1955, p. 23, para 43.
199. *Ibid.*, p. 24, para 46.
200. Bayly, C.A., *The New Cambridge History of India*, Vol. II, Cambridge University Press, 1988.
201. Jain, Meenakshi, *op. cit.*
202. Sovani, N.V., *Journal of World History*, II, 1954, p. 101.
203. Srinivas, *op. cit.*, p. 6.
204. Furnivall, J.S., *Colonial Policy and Practice*, London, 1948, p. 9.
205. Sovani, N.V., *Non-Economic Aspects of Economic Development*, In Administration and Economic Development, ed., op. cit., p. 268.

2

Reformatory Movements

An important feature of traditional Hindu society was its segmentation into a large number of castes, sub-castes and sub-sub-castes, each of which was characterised by a degree of social and cultural identity. Within the country every region had its distinctive culture as well as its distinctive pattern of castes and sub-castes. This mode of organisation continues to play an important part in contemporary India, although it has now to compete with new principles of organisation. "If the Hindu social order could be summed up in a single phrase it would be this: It is the most thorough attempt known in Indian history to introduce inherited inequality as a guiding principle in social relationship."[1] The Hindu society has an irrevocable group and status system in the institution of caste, and the deadly efficiency of social control in Hindu society derives mainly from this.[2] It is perhaps true that social inequalities were legitimised to a greater extent in traditional India than elsewhere, although other countries are known to have their own forms of institutionalised inequality. Gradation of status arises out of the process of evaluation and the acceptance of framework of evaluation on which system of stratification rests is perhaps a universal feature of human societies.[3]

After reviewing the elements of caste as existed in countries like Egypt, Western Asia, China, Japan, South-East Asia, America, and the tribal peoples on the one hand and Rome and tribal Europe on the other, Ghurye concludes that distinction by birth has been usually recognised by many primitive peoples and almost all the major civilizations of ancient times. The primitive peoples, in so far as their arts and crafts are neither many, nor highly specialised, have few classes whose status is fixed. But wherever status is recognised, privileges and restrictions in the matter of the choice of avocation are very common. Restriction on the choice of one's mate based on birth is comparatively infrequent among them. In tribal England, in Rome, and in Asian civilizations, occupations not only tended to become hereditary but were actually prescribed to be followed by specific classes and graded in certain order as high and low. Specialized occupations had come to form themselves into units of community life. Society was divided into two, three, four, or five well-marked status-groups, intermarriage between which was often prohibited. The Chinese civilization, before it was influenced by Indian ideas, seemed to have been the most free in its social grouping. Well-marked status-groups within a society, distinguished from one another by rights and disabilities, separated from one another by the absence of freedom of intermarriage, may, therefore, be considered to be a common characteristic of the mental background and social picture of the Indo-European cultures. Specialization of occupations, accompanied by solidarity within specified occupations and great unfreedom about their choice, was a feature common to the ancient and medieval times. The circumstances that led to the abolition of distinctions, based on birth and occupation, in Rome and England are peculiar to each and cannot be gone into here. Suffice it for us to remember that in each case it was the special conditions, making for political unity and commercial aggrandisement, that slowly killed the ideas of status by birth and removed the unfreedom of occupation.[4]

It has been customary to condemn caste for all the ills and maladies afflicting the Hindu society in India. There has been unanimity in the condemnation of the institution characterised as inhuman and unjust in its application which has stagnated the Hindu religion, having outlived its utility. It has been held that castes, the building bricks of Hindu social structure, fragmented the social consciousness of Hindu society by dividing it into numerous groups arranged in a hierarchical order on the basis of birth. Secondly, the real triumph of the caste system lies not in upholding the supremacy of the Brahmin, but in conditioning the consciousness of lower castes in accepting their inferior status in the ritual hierarchy as a part of the natural order of things. Thirdly, it was through an elaborate, complex and subtle scheme of scripture, mythology and ritual that Brahminism succeeded in giving to the caste system, and to its inequality and discrimination towards majority of the people, a moral and divine authority that has seldom been challenged effectively, even by the most ardent social reformers. Fourthly, as exclusive custodians of higher knowledge, the Brahmins developed into a highly cultivated community with special flair for intellectual pursuits: the Sudras, continually subjected to all kinds of deprivation acquired all the unattractive traits of the unlettered rustic. Fifthly, if religion was ever used as the opium of the masses, it was done in India, where a small priest-class hypnotised the vast majority of the people into accepting with humility their role of servility. As labourers, cultivators, craftsmen, the Sudras were the life-blood of India's great civilization; yet they were treated as outcastes with no hope.[5] That the caste system creates dissensions in the Hindu society and promotes perpetuation of the low status of many castes must be universally admitted. Yet there are others who have not condemned the system outright but found some utility of it and the system has had admirers even amongst foreign scholars. They insisted that the caste system had also held Hindu society together, preserved some of its central values and had been a source of moral, social and emotional support. What was more, an institution that had lasted so long and struck much deep roots in the Hindu way of life and in which the Hindus had invested so much of their moral and emotional energy simply could not be 'abolished'. In view of this it is essential to draw attention to some important and significant socio-economic functions which the system has been performing for the individual, the caste-group and finally, for the society and the caste.

Looking at the system from the individual's point of view, it provides a security which no degree of unworthiness and incapability on his part will deprive him of unless, of course, he breaks the caste norms. He is assured of employment, shelter, protection and marriage. In the event of a disability he is not faced with disaster. In sum, caste is one's main line of defence in so far as it provides socio-economic security within a permanent milieu which is not based on changing individual caprice. It provides free training and education to its members in the skills in which it is traditionally proficient. Caste norms provide guidance to the individual in the ordering of his daily personal routine and social behaviour. By providing a common forum for collective effort and agitation one's caste increases the chances of mobility for an individual.[6]

Caste determines to a large extent the social status of each caste in regard to other castes. The caste system enables the caste to act corporately and to control behaviour of its component members. It is able in this way to raise its position in society.[7] Craft secrets are well safeguarded and perpetuated by occupational castes, and the caste generally functions as a guild or a trade union. The caste acting as an occupational guild can effectively influence the action of individuals or of corporate bodies outside its own membership.[8] In the religious sphere the caste system so operates that the caste can change or modify its social and religious observances in accordance with the changing ethical standards or the trend of public opinion.[9] Even the Kalelkar Commission conceded that "whatever may be the defects of caste it had nothing to do with wealth or power. The status of a person depended not on his wealth but on the traditional importance of his caste. There was thus social equality among all the members of caste in spite of extreme disparity in the status of individuals."[10]

The next important function is, or has been, to integrate Indian society, to weld into one community the various competing if not incompatible groups composing it, which includes not only occupational or religious groups but also the national, political and tribal societies and even the conquered peoples.[11] The caste system has afforded a place in the society for any kind of group or community, be it social, occupational, racial or religious, while retaining its own distinctive character and its separate individual life.[12] It has proved capable of absorbing many extraneous elements.[13] Caste has made Hindu society a liberal federation. Nehru saw in it an unique design for the solution of the minority problem; each caste, an autonomous unit, being tied to each other as he saw it, with an autocratic chain.[14] Sherring admits that 'caste promotes cleanliness and order, and is, in a certain sense, a bond of union among all classes of the Hindu community.'[15] Integration in so varied a country as India could have been achieved only through such an ingenious system. It is the caste system which has provided a way for assimilating outside influences. Religious and social revolts which have been punished with death by burning and stoning by other religions elsewhere have resulted in India only in the addition of new castes to the main system. In fact, the caste system has provided an outlet for very strong individual capacities and a scheme for social adjustment which some writers have compared favourably with the "European system of warring territorial nationalities."[16]

The second very important function of caste has been to act as a political and social stabilizer.[17] The caste system produced comparative stability and gave this multiple society its present form.[18] Caste kept the Hindu traditions and culture intact for thousands of years. Even the foreign domination for the best part of a thousand years has done little to obliterate them. The Peruvian culture disappeared at the first onslaught of the European invasion. India maintained hers all through the proselytising periods of the Mohammadan and Christian rule.[19] Basham, the renowned Indologist, holds the view that after the conquest of India by the Muslim invaders and, even throughout the period of British rule, the caste system fulfilled a definite social function, for whatever might have been its inherent disadvantages, "the organisation of the castes, independent of the government, and with social ostracism as its most severe sanction, was a powerful factor in the survival of Hinduism. The Hindu, living under an alien political order...retained his cultural individuality largely through his caste, which received most of the loyalty elsewhere felt toward king, nation and city."[20] Abbe Dubois regarded the caste system as being responsible for the preservation of India from complete barbarism, and as the sure basis of orderly government, as a defence against despotism, and a means for preserving the Hindu pattern of culture under the regime of alien conquerers.[21] S.C. Hill who has taken a similar view calls the caste system "the only Social System ever proposed upon a basis stronger than Force."[22] Caste has bestowed interrupted internal peace on, and engendered stability within, the very heterogeneous Hindu society. Provided with such internal integration and strength, Hindu society has faced calmly and adequately disasters and catastrophes of immense magnitude, like external invasions, the proselytizing activities of Christians, coerced conversion to Islam, internal upheavals like the egalitarian movements dating back to Buddhism, and also natural calamities like famines and earthquakes. It has put its stamp not only upon tribal social organization, but also on the daily life of Indian Christians and Muslims.[23]

Again, the caste system does provide for the various functions necessary to social life, functions ranging from education to scavenging, from government to domestic service of the most menial kind; and it makes this provision under the sanction of a religious dogma, the belief in *karma*,[24] i.e. the belief that one's status in life is determined by one's actions in past incarnations. Basing itself on the *karma* theory, the caste system has provided not only justification for the present disabilities of the inferior castes, but what is socially more significant, also an excellent motive for the peaceful acceptance of the present conditions along with the incentive for efforts to perform what are socially regarded as good actions, in order to ensure a better future. By so providing for strict adherence to custom as also the possibility of a cure for frustration social solidarity has been maintained uninterrupted by any conflicts.[25]

There is yet another function which the caste system probably performs, and that is a genetic one.[26] In Hindu society there is no peace of mind for a couple until they get a son, because without him there is no heaven nor peace hereafter. It has been found that inbreeding leads to a preponderance of males; and by prescribing endogamy the caste system has soothed the minds of generations of Hindus. Sodgwick, in his Report on the Census of Bombay, 1921 pointed out that the Indian caste system with its endogamous caste and its exogamous *gotras* "is a perfect method of preserving what is called in Genetics the "pure line". The endogamy prevents external hybridization, while the (internal) exogamy prevents the possibility of a fresh pure line arising within the old one by the isolation of any character not common to the whole line. With the preservation of the pure line the perpetuation of all characters common to it necessarily follows."[27]

In view of the functions which the caste system has so excellently performed, scientific investigators like Hutton have pleaded that there is no "necessity for destroying a social order which performs a number of useful functions both for the individual and the society" and that it should be reformed for improving "the position of the (inferior and exterior) castes within the system as it exists today."[28] Untouchability, exploitation of the inferior and exterior castes by the higher castes, degrading and inferior position of women in society and such other harmful concomitants of the system should be done away with, and not the whole system.

The history of the caste system in India is a record of a perpetual social tension and of protests and revolts against the prevailing social code. While the rigidity and elaborateness of the caste system, the two most striking characteristics of the status gradation in Indian society, have grown through centuries of practice and precepts, there have been at the same time concerted endeavours to remove the rigidity and orthodoxy in the caste system, cleanse the Hindu society of its rituals, extirpate the practice of social ostracisation of people on the basis of birth and heredity, dismantle the caste barrier, improve the social status of the socially disadvantaged sections of population by removing their disabilities and discriminations and induct the spirit of rationalism and secularism into the traditional caste stratification system, based on social, economic and religious status. There have been religious and social reform movements to fight against the ascriptive system of Indian society with all its ramifications like emphasis on ritual status, attribution, caste-ranking, pollution and purity, dominance of Brahminic culture, hierarchical ordering of occupations into high and low, the pernicious system of widow-burning and child-marriage, degrading and low position of women in society, exclusivism in imparting education and the like. This clash between two conflicting and divergent forces is going on in the Indian society for a very long time. "In every living society, there is always some movements from within, and some movements from without, and, therefore, there is always some change"[29] and Indian society is no exception. On the other hand, the glory of Indian civilization or Indian society is its remarkable capacity for absorbing factors making for change whether internal or external. The effect of the liberating forces and factors of change on the Indian society, particularly on its caste system may be categorised, for the purpose of our study, as under:

(a) The reformatory religious movements,

(b) The effect of Islam and Christianity,

(c) The efforts of social reformers,

(d) The urge to move up the caste ladder, and

(e) The impact of British contact.

Reformatory Religious Movements

During the period 600 B.C. to A.D. 300, which R.C. Majumdar mentions as the "Age of Revolt",[30] saw the birth of Jainism, Buddhism and Bhagavatism, developed and preached by Vardhamana Mahavira (539 B.C.—467 B.C.), Gautama Buddha (532 B.C.—487 B.C.) and Krsna-Vasudeva (before 6th century B.C.), who belonged to the independent republican clans of the Licchavis, the Sakyas and the Satvatas, respectively. All these three constitute a revolt against, or at least a decided break from, vedic cult of sacrifice, which involved mechanical, and sometimes cruel, ceremonials, the accepted creeds of the day.

Buddhism, which became a world religion in course of time, denied the vedic literature as divine revelation and refused to accept the social order of the day, particularly the system of caste. Neither Bhakti nor metaphysical and abstract knowledge of God had any place in it, and a highly developed ethical life was offered as the sole means of attaining salvation. The express ideas in the Buddhistic literature voice the feeling that caste has nothing to do either with material success in life or with reward after death. High caste is not protected from the effect of wrong doing, and to an ascetic caste ought to be a matter of utter indifference. One of the *Jataka* stories ends with the declaration from Bodhisattva that the virtuous do not ask one about his birth if his piety is well known. A person's worth in life is determined by right conduct and knowledge.[31] Nevertheless, in the various anecdotes about Buddha's former lives an individual's status is regarded as fixed by his conduct and even sometimes by his birth.[32] In a dispute between two youths as to whether a person is a Brahmin by birth or by his action, Buddha is said to have given his decision in favour of the latter alternative.[33] Thus Buddha is represented as being inclined to accept the divisions, basing them only on the individual's actions and not on his birth. That he meant these divisions to be status groups and not mere names is evident from another saying attributed to him, where the highest marks of social respect are claimed for the Kshatriyas and the Brahmins.[34]

In the matter of caste-restrictions the preachings and actions of Buddha had only a general liberalizing effect. He does not seem to have started with the idea of abolishing caste-distinctions, nor do his actions, as described in the *Jataka* stories, demonstrate an utter indifference towards the accident of birth; much less do they evince any conscious effort to annihilate caste.[35] Fick has rightly observed that it is wrong to look upon Buddhism as a revolt against caste.[36] And Sir Charles Eliot has summed up his judgement in the words, "though he (Buddha) denied that Brahmans were superior by birth to others he did not preach against caste."[37]

The probable genesis of Buddhism may be traced to the complete discomfiture of the Kshatriyas within the Brahminical fold and their effort to establish Kshatriya preeminence among the four castes. In their appeal to the masses to recognize them as the real leaders of society, they must have availed themselves of the general opinion of the non-Brahmans, specially the well-to-do sections who were dissatisfied with their low position within the Brahmanic fold. That is the reason why the largest bulk of its early followers were Kshatriyas and other well-to-do non-Brahmanas,[38] and the *Parivvajakas* (itinerant religious teachers) often belonged to non-Brahmanic castes in Buddha's time.[39]

By the twelfth century A.D. Buddhism which came to be unpopular due to the development of the Tantric beliefs and rituals and other debased forms, had well nigh vanished from India as an independent sect by which time Buddha was regarded as another *avatar* of Vishnu. This well-conceived and bold stroke of policy cut the ground under the feet of Buddhism. Moreover, the destruction of the Buddhist monastaries by the Islamic invaders dealt the final death-blow to Buddhism.[40]

Jainism, alone of all religions, was free from the Tantric development. The rigid conservatism, to which it owed this fortune, however, paved the way for its decline, as it failed to keep abreast with the changing spirit of the times. It still maintains its hold among a very influential section of the community in western India. This may partly be due to the fact that it preserved some essential Hindu practices like caste and winked at the worship of some popular deities like Ganesha.[41]

The evolution of different religious cults and sects in the post-vedic period was a noticeable phenomenon in the religious and cultural history of India. Thus, in course of time the five Brahminical Hindu cults of the Vaisnava (Bhagavata, Pancaratra, Satvata, Ekantika, etc., to mention some of its earlier designations), Saiva, Sakta, Saura and Ganapatya, apart from the non-Brahmanical cults of Buddha and Jaina, were developed.[42] This evolution was gradual and the element that played a great part in it was that of bhakti. The Bhakti-cult opened its door to all irrespective of caste, creed or sex. The Bhakti saints "preached the fundamental equality of all religions and the unity of Godhead, held that the dignity of man depended on his actions and not on his birth, protested against excessive ritualism and formalities of religion and domination of the priests, and emphasized simple devotion and faith as the means of salvation for one and all."[43] Even a Chandala is purged of the impurity of his caste by firm devotion to God.[44] Even a person of low birth is liberated from bondage, if he utters the name of God only once.[45] Nammahatya or the importance of muttering the name of God as a method of spiritual betterment gradually became an integral part of the developing creeds of Vaisnavism and Saivism.

Vaisnavism, which owed its origin to the original Bhagawata doctrine of Kṛṣṇa-Vasudeva of pre-sixth century B.C. became a part of Hindu religion and Kṛṣṇa was regarded as an *avatar* of Vishnu. It went through several phases of growth under different Acharyyas, Alvars and spiritual leaders, like Natha Muni (A.D. 824-924), Ramanuj (b. 1017), Nimbark

(12th century A.D.), Madhavacharya (13th century A.D.), Vallabha (1479-1531), Chaitnya (1485-1533), Sankara Deva (1486-1536). Many new sects depending on the tutelary deity or deities, also grew up. Mention may be made of the cult of Vithala or the Dasa Kutha sect. Though of Karnataka origin, it was made popular by Jnanadeva in Maharastra as it was done by Purandara, Kanaka, Vijayariththala and Jagannath in Karnataka. In Maharastra, this cult later developed and assumed different forms at the hands of Namdeva (1270-1338), Tukaram. (1608-1649), Ekanath and Ramadasa (b. 1608). In North India another sect was founded by Ramanand (14th century A.D.). The chief among his disciples were Ravidasa (b. 1377), Kabir (1440-1518), Dadu (1544-1603), Maludasa (1574-1682) and Tulsidasa (1532-1623). It is interesting to note that Kabir was a Mohammadan weaver, Dadu was a cotton-cleaner and Ravidasa, a leather-worker.

In addition to the purification of the Bhakti-cult and its elevation to a high spiritual level based on secure foundations of morality, these Vaisanava teachers made other notable contributions to the culture of the medieval age, one of which was admittance of people of even the lowest castes to its fold ignoring the caste distinctions. People of all classes and castes, including the Mohammadans, were taken into these sects and thus began a levelling process in the society. In the sphere of religion the lot of the so-called untouchables was sought to be improved for the first time in the history of Hinduism.

It is perhaps no coincidence that a number of 'Shudra saints of outstanding personality flourished in Maharastra, Bengal and other parts of India. They explored and perfected the easy method of salvation through Nammahatya for the Shudras. These saints produced a revolution without the uproar of rebellion. The Shudra, who was accustomed to look upon it as a great privilege to be allowed to practise the Brahminical rites, though only with the accompaniment of the Puranic mantras, now produced individuals who struck out a new path and established themselves as teachers. And the Brahmin, who was doubtful whether a Shudra was even capable of profiting by his religious teachings, had to accept some of the Shudras as his religious masters. This was more or less an all-India phenomenon. Mention may be made of Namdeva, a tailor by birth; of Ravidasa, the cobbler; Sena, the barber and Kabir, the Mohammedan weaver, who were all famous disciples of Ramanand; of Nabha, an 'untouchable' by birth but his name has become immortal as the author of the *Bhaktimala* or life stories of devotees;[46] of Kanakadas, a prominent member of the Dasa Kutha sect of Karnataka, a person of humble origin and is believed to have been a Kuruba (shepherd) or more probably a hunter chieftain (bede);[47] of Nandanar, a famous saiva saint of South India who belonged to the so-called untouchable caste; of Tirunilakanda Yalpanar, another saiva saint of low birth; of Arunagiri, a famous saiva saint of 15th century who had an infamous birth.[48]

The Alakhnami and Kumbhipatra sects also do not acknowledge the superiority of the higher castes. They are not sorry that they are debarred from entering the temples, for they regard these as low places, where one is diverted from truth.[49] Sivanarayan sect, which was founded by Sivanarayan, a Rajput of Ballia district born about A.D. 1710, who was inspired by the ideas of Dara Shikoh, is open to all creeds and castes, and the union of all forms of faith in one universal religion was the dream of Sivanarayan's life.[50]

The Swami Narayani sect founded by Sahajananda, who was born in A.D. 1780 in Gonda district, admits Mohammedans as well as Hindus from lower castes.[51] The Nanga (naked) sect founded by Dedraja, a Brahmin born in A.D. 1771, does not believe in image-worship, caste-distinctions and seclusion of women and believes in the fraternity of all faiths and in the kinship of all men and women.[52]

Dadu admitted both Hindus and Mohammedans to his discipleship and there have been many gurus in his sect who came of Mohammedan families. Even today, in Rajib's branch of Dadu's sect any one who attains to the height of spiritual realization is accepted as the head of the order, whether he be a Hindu or a Mohammedan.[53]

The followers of Dariya Saheb, who was deeply influenced in his religious life by the teachings of Kabir, pray like the Mohammedans in a standing posture called *kornis*, while their prayers in the sitting posture are known as *sizda*. They do not believe in scriptures, rites and observances, pilgrimages, vows, vestments, or the partaking of meat or wine, and all forms of violence are all strictly forbidden in this sect.[54]

Sankara Deva, the founder of Vaisnava sect in Assam, did not believe in distinctions between man and man on the basis of birth. He never refused admission to any one because he belonged to a low or impure caste. He even admitted members of the aboriginal tribes into his community such as Nagas, Miris, Garos and untouchable castes like Haris and Doms, and the Bhutias and even the Mohammedans who found equal position with others in his prayer house; and some of them were appointed leaders (atoi) of small groups of his followers.[55] Thus Damador, a Bhutia, became Atoi of the Bhutias, Gobinda Garo among the Garos, Narottam Naga among the Nagas, Narayan Miri among the Miris, and Jayhari, among the Muslim converts of the Deva.[56]

In the South, an influential and very powerful Saiva sect, known as the *Virasaivas* or *Lingayats* rose in Karnataka and Maharastra. It was founded in the twelfth century by Basava, the Brahmin Prime Minister of Bijjala. This new sect flourished at the cost of Jainism and Buddhism and was the main cause of their decay in the Deccan.[57] Virasaivism or Lingayat movement initially originated as a protest movement against Brahminical caste rigidity and ritualism, and hence was characterised as heterodox. It is essentially reformist with occasional revolutionary overtone. It is an offshoot of early Saivaism shorn of its Brahmanical or Vedic content in regard to certain ideas and practices. But Virasaivism did not repudiate the Vedas in toto.[58] When the founder of the sect started his movement, he was able to attract converts from a wide range of occupations. Consequently, the Lingayats of the princely state of Mysore included washermen, potters and others.[59] They shared a distinct body of religious and ethical teachings which entailed the abandonment of the principal Hindu rites of ceremonial purification and found tangible expression in adherence to vegetarianism and the wearing of the linga—symbolic of Siva—on the person of each believer.[60] Virasaivas no doubt preached the brotherhood of man but practice did not accord with precept. As the sect became established over the centuries, and monasteries were founded, they gave rise to fission and group formation and eventually reproduced within itself all the characteristics of Hindu caste society. In practice, today, Virasaivas recognise caste distinctions among themselves as well as with reference to non-Virasaivas. Indeed,Virasaivism includes within itself a number of castes and sub-castes which form a hierarchy based on differential ritual status.[61] The more important of these were the Jangama section of priests (over 6 per cent of the sect), the merchant Bansjigas (14 per cent), and the three main sections of agriculturists: Nonabas (14 per cent), Sadars (16 per cent) and Gowdas (about 25 per cent)[62]. One of the five codes of conduct for the individual member of the Lingayat community lays down that the members are required to make no difference between one Lingayat and another, as they are all devotees of Siva and therefore, demands that a Lingayat should dine and marry freely with other members of the same community, even if they follow different vocations. But in practice, intermarriage is a thing of the past and many sections refuse even to interdine and there are recorded instances of such refusals from very recent times.[63]

Another cult, which does not believe in caste, is the *Nath cult* or the cult of Goraksha (Gorakh Pantha of Hindi-Rajasthani). It is an esoteric cult professed by the yogi mendicants throughout northern, central and western India. It was essentially a Saiva yogic school, though Vaisnava association in western India, Buddhist affiliation in Nepal and eastern India, even Jaina and Islamic touches in isolated places make up the complicated texture of the widely spread Natha cult.[64] Mina Nath belonged to the fisherman's caste and in non-Bengali tradition Goraksha Nath, the most important figure of all the Siddhas, too is called a fisherman (Keotiya, i.e., Kaivarta). The derivative meaning of the name Jalandhari, another Siddha, is the net-holder.[65] The lay followers of the cult in Bengal were formed into a distinct 'Jugi' caste (weaver). It has subcastes with different secular and religious practices; greater divisions are found, however, elsewhere in India, each constituting a separate *Pantha*. In other parts of India, there are different subcastes attached to different monasteries ruled by elected *Mahantas*.[66] The distinctive surname of the caste is 'Natha'.[67]

The numerous religious schools of Bengal such as Khusi Visvasi, Saheb Dhani, Ramaballabhi, Jagamohini, Balarami, Neda (the shaven), Aul-Baul-Darbes-Sain, Samyogi, and Kartabhaja were all greatly influenced by the Niranjani and Natha cults, which were prevalent in Bengal and Orissa before Kabir preached his philosophy, and the Sahajia cult, and to a certain extent by Islam. These schools do not believe in castes or sects, temples or images, and do not also differentiate between the Hindus and the Mohammedans.[68]

Guru Nanak (1469-1538) founded the Sikh religion basing on the pure monotheistic doctrine of the Upanishads. He preached *nam* (the Name of God) as a potent means of religious realization. In his time, the impact of Islam on the people of North India was very powerful. He sought to harmonize the tenets of both Hinduism and Islam. He also established the organised fellowship (sangat). He tried to do away with caste-distinctions and to liberize other social practices.[69]

The impact of western thought led to a number of reform movements in Hinduism in the nineteenth century. It brought back the rationalism of the fifth century B.C.[70] and Raja Rammohan Roy was its great exponent. The new spirit led to the foundation of the Brahmo Samaj (including Parthana Samaj), the Arya Samaj and the Theosophical Society on the one hand and all-round reform in the orthodox Hindu religion and society on the other.

The fundamental truth of human fellowship and unity based on the bed-rock of Upanisadic idealism was the basic principle of *Brahmoism*, preached by the Brahmo Samaj, founded by Raja Rammohan Roy in 1828, which in course of time drew a large number of celebrities from all walks of life in furtherence of the cause of social, educational and political advancement of India. This primarily religious movement brought in its wake a wave of social reforms, the campaign for which was initiated by Raja Rammohan Roy with the anti-Suttee agitation. Instead of remaining as a mere intellectual pastime, it began attacking some of the fundamental iniquities and abuses of society. The Brahmo Samaj went solidly for the emancipation of women from all sorts of social iniquities. Intemperence, polygamy, etc. were denounced; widow remarriage and female education were strongly advocated by the Brahmo Samaj.[71] Later on, it launched a crusade against the caste system and succeeded in banishing it altogether from the Brahmo fold.[72] Courting persecution and social ostracism, these young reformers defied caste, promoted inter-caste marriages in this caste-ridden country and tried in many ways to remove the barrier between man and man and man and woman.[73] On the lines of the Brahmo Samaj, the Parthana Samaj of Bombay was organised in 1867 under the inspiration of eminent reformers of western India like Ranade and Bhandarkar.[74] At the time of its second schism in 1878 when the Sadharan Brahmo Samaj was formally organised, there were 124 Brahmo Samajas: 80 in Bengal, 8 in Assam, 6 in Bihar, 11 in North-Western Provinces, 5 in South India, 5 in Oudh, 7 in Bombay Presidency and 2 in Sind.[75] Thus it assumed the character of an all-India movement.

The Brahmo Samaj carried on its Mission work for the improvement of Backward Classes in Bengal, Assam and Bihar also. The people whose lot was improved by their attempt included the Khasi Hill people of Assam, Namasudras of East Bengal and Mehtars of Hazaribagh. Mission work was also carried on by Jayamangal Rath among the Oriya-speaking Hadis and Kaivartas of Ganjam. The noble-minded Maharaj of Pithapuram, a disciple of Raja Rammohan Roy, tried in various ways for the improvement of the Telegu-speaking depressed classes.[76]

Another powerful religious movement, namely the *Arya Samaj*, founded by Swami Dayanand on April 10, 1875 at Bombay, spread to different areas in course of time, mainly in North India. It takes its stand on the bed-rock of the Vedas, which, it believes, hold the key to all our socio-religious problems. To Swami Dayanand, truth, wherever it is found, is of the Vedas. Like every reform movement, the Arya Samaj set itself first to purge the society of its rampant evils. Swami Dayanand emphasised that the removal of inter-caste barriers, Harijan uplift, the raising of the age of marriage of Hindu girls, the remarriage of widows and the education of women would not degrade Hindu religion. The propaganda of the Arya Samaj extirpated social abuses, specially in the provinces in which it has had the opportunity of working. The caste system as a religious institution was abolished; the monopoly of the Brahmins over the Vedas was denied; women were liberated from a number of social disabilities. Untouchability being considered as un-Vedic, it invested lakhs of so-called 'untouchables' with the sacred thread and thus made them honourable members of the Hindu society, enjoying the same social rights as the so-called caste Hindus. The portals of the Vedic Church were thrown open even to non-Hindus. The practice of allowing the non-Hindus to join the ranks of their orthodox following as members of the same social organisation was revived by the Arya Samaj. The last two reforms, namely, the reclamation of the depressed classes and proselytization of non-Hindus, have cost the Arya Samaj a number of martyrs.[77]

Though both the Brahmo Samaj and the Arya Samaj were imbibed with the best of motives to put the entire house of the Hindus in order, the orthodox masses, rightly or wrongly, chose to stand or fall with the entirety of Hindu traditions and refused to accept any type of sectional Hinduism from the reformers. Ultimately, both the Brahmo Samaj and the Arya Samaj found themselves thrown out of the orthodox Hindu society, and were compelled to shift for themselves by creating independent folds.

Mention may be made here of another religious movement that put in a timely appearance in India from abroad and went to check, to a certain extent, the influx of the Christian as well as materialistic thoughts of the period. This was the *Theosophical Movement.* Theosophy, though ostensibly a new and electic creed, founded in 1875 in New York, initiated in this country a movement that resembled, to a considerable extent, the reform movements of Hinduism, so far as its salutary effect upon the Hindu society was concerned.[78] The Theosophist is characterised, first by a profound belief in the existence of a divine wisdom which explains all the intricate processes of nature; and secondly, by a determination to be an agent in God's plan for men. The Theosophist, therefore, is essentially a reformer engaged in the most strenuous forms of social service and believes in the universal brotherhood of humanity without distinction of race, creed, sex, caste, or social position.[79]

Towards the close of the nineteenth century flourished *Sri Ramakrishna* who sought to reconcile not only the rationalist doctrine with the emotionalism and ritualistic orthodoxy of the earlier ages, but also the different seemingly conflicting religions on the basis of experience gained through spiritual culture. His disciple Swami Vivekananda gave a definite shape to his catholic views and broadbased the doctrine of the Vedanta creed and founded the great Ramakrishna Mission which is now a potent force not only in India, but far beyond its boundaries. It is powerfully moulding the Hinduism of the present day and giving it a wide catholic character. But its sphere of activity far transcends the narrow circle of Hinduism. By carrying to its logical conclusion the Vedantic doctrine of the identity of man with God, it has established the fundamental equality of man on a secure basis. The rituals of the *Pauranic* religion are performed with meticulous care, but it knows no distinction of caste and creed and equally honours not only Buddha and Chaitanya, but Christ, Mohammad, Zoroaster, and other founders of great religious system of the world.[80]

The evolution of different religious sects and faiths showed that it was orthodoxy, and not reformation, that was mostly on the defensive all through the centuries. Conciliation, concession and compromise were the weapons with which orthodoxy fought daring innovations in thought, right from Jainism and Buddhism, Vaisnavism and Śaivism, down to the various Bhakti cults of medieval India, immortalised by Ramanand and Kabir, Nanak and Chaitanya and lastly, to the various reformist movements for revitalization of religion in modern India. The movements progressively helped obliterate caste-distinctions and purge the caste system of its pernicious traits. But its most important effect on the traditional Hindu society was that it created an environ which not only gave the lowest class Hindus including the 'untouchables' equal status with the highest but even threw up many persons of 'humble origin', who were regarded as saints. But for these movements, improvement in the position, status and rights of the lowest castes within the system would have been a far cry.

Effect of Islam and Christianity

The liberalizing influence of the Buddhist revolt and of Vaisnava compassion led the Brahmins to devise ways and means of assuring spiritual betterment to the Shudras in the Brahmanic way of rites and sacraments.[81] This process further gained momentum with the advent of two proselytizing religions-Islam and Christianity.

The advent of *Islam* in India resulted in an initial clash between two conflicting, and often incompatible, religions and cultures, which was followed by fusion and synthesis. India had so long assimilated almost all foreign races and cultures that entered the land at different times by broadening her faith and her social structure. Hinduism, for the first time, came face to face with a religion and culture that not only refused to be absorbed into the mainstream but also tried to convert people into its faith. For the invading Muslims, who came in successive waves, India represented a phenomenon which has few parallels elsewhere. "In most other countries Muslims have also assimilated the land into the mainstream of Islamic culture. India is the one exception where neither has Islam been overpowered by India, nor has India been absorbed into the Islamic world."[82]

The attempt at forcible conversion of Hindus to Islam was effectively checked by the Indian caste system. When the political and military power was passed on to an alien race, it was the Indian caste system that effectively stood the ground and kept the flocks under its arms. It is the general belief that the real cause of large scale conversion, especially of those belonging to the "casteless caste", was not political or economic, but social and religious. The caste-rules, particularly the invidious distinction between man and man, between the higher castes and the lower castes, and the failure to give due dignity and status to the so-called untouchables in the caste-bound Hindu society contributed to this conversion to Islam.[83] It is said that a large number of people belonging to lower castes, and in particular from the untouchables, became converted to Islam and Christianity to escape the rigour and humilation of the Hindu caste system.[84] Lal has very ably exploded this myth in his book *Indian Muslims: Who are They?* According to him, the caste system checked the process of Islamization at a most crucial moment. When Hindus lost their political-central authority, they fell back on their second line of defence, namely their castes which welded a lot of social authority. To the majority caste was synonymous with religion, and so there was a general reluctance and often resistance to conversion to Islam both by the high and the low caste Hindus. In fact, the lower castes were more particular about 'caste preservation' than even the higher caste ones.[85] Manucci tells us that even the castes called low were proud of their caste and were reluctant to convert. Their caste gave them freedom, dignity and security of the kind which the alien system and ideology failed to do.[86] In fact, Islam held no attraction for the Hindu low castes. By converting, they saw no improvement in their lot but suffered a double indignity. These converts were known as *Arzal* or *Ajlaf*, base-born, mean and despicable and treated as such by the Muslim immigrants. The common contemptuous name for these local converts is *Julaha*.[87] In reality, indigenous converts often failed to attain the social status of those who had foreign blood in their veins and, in a plutocratic regime, the poor tended to form a separate class.[88] They remained distinct from the descendants of the immigrants, classified as Saiyid, Shaikh, Mughal and Pathan. These latter social groups retained their distinct identity and considered themselves superior to the Indian Muslims who were considered inferior because they were thought to be lower in the Hindu caste hierarchy. They however quite often claimed equality with the Hindu upper castes.[89]

The interaction between these two forces at many levels had a profound influence on the way of life of the peoples inhabiting this land. The initial clash between the two religions and cultures was followed by fusion and synthesis, which, however, was not a one-sided affair. It is an admitted fact that Islam broke down the barriers of colour and birth absolutely in the formal act of worship and with negligible restrictions in daily social intercourse. Caste, which is a division of human beings into different grades, is repugnant to the non-Hindu mind, especially the Muslims. But the Indian Muslims, most of whom were converts, could not shake off the Indian tradition of rigid stratification according to caste. Converts tended to carry over their caste prejudices to their new faith. Difference in social esteem among converts from different castes could not thus be altogether avoided. "They thus acquired some of the habits and prejudices which characterized the later rigid form of the caste system, but, because of the Islamic insistence on equality of man, retained something of its original flexibility. This is clearly seen in the manner in which caste expressed itself in Indian Muslim society. Early Islam insisted on equality of man and repudiated even family names, as these tended to perpetuate distinctions. The Indian Muslims could not therefore accept a system of caste based on the fact of birth alone. In its place, Muslim society in India evolved a type of caste based on wealth and station."[90]

The synthesis in the field of religion had often been noticed and both from the Muslim and from the Hindu point of view there was an attempt at rapproachment. There were reasons for suspecting Muslim influence in some of the citadels of Hindu orthodoxy. It was not perhaps a mere accident that from the fourteenth century A.D., the two characteristic features of Islam, viz. the absence of social distinction among its followers and the total rejection of the worship of images, began to influence the Vaisnava reformers and mediaeval saints. A more direct and thorough influence of Islam may be traced in the severe monotheistic doctrine of Nanak,[91] Fawcett suggests that the growth of the Bhakti-cult in the South was due mainly to the influence of Islam.[92]

The advent of Muslim power created a new situation in which Sanskrit was gradually dethroned from its position of privilege and in its place, there was the remarkable phenomenon of the growth of literature in the different Indian languages. Religious reformers made their appeal in local dialects. The result was the achievement of a common outlook, which softened the sharp formalism of Islam and simplified the rituals of Hinduism.[93]

The interaction between *Christianity* and Hinduism was going on for a long time and the influence of the one on the other was more in evidence where Christianity had been established the longest. Notwithstanding the fact that though it suffered from the handicap of being considered the religion of the conqueror and an agent in the cultural conquest of India by the West,[94] it may be said that Christianity created a healthy ferment in Indian society, particularly in the nineteenth century. Dr. J.N. Farquhar claims that Christianity has exerted both a direct and an indirect influence on the development of the movements amongst Hindus, Muslims, and Parsis. He further says that the Christian doctrine of the love of God, which is a necessary element in the Fatherhood, passed into the teaching of the Brahmo Samaj and the Parthana Samaj, and has deeply influenced most of the other movements.[95]

Many parallels have been traced between the language of the *Bhagavad-Gita* and that of the *Gospel of St. John*, and some scholars explain this phenomenon as due to the influence of Christian ideas. The Bhakti movement in Hinduism, which reached its height about the twelfth and the thirteenth centuries, may also owe something to the Christian conception of love (*agape*) and faith (*pistis*) in a personal saviour from sin and death. On this last point, Dr. Grierson comments as follows: 'But it was in southern India that Christianity, as a doctrine, exercised the greatest influence on Hinduism generally. Although the conceptions of the fatherhood of God and of *bhakti* were indigenous to India, they received an immense impetus owing to the beliefs of Christian communities reacting upon the mediaeval Bhagavata reformers of the South.'[96]

Professor Garbe, R.G. Bhandarkar, and Dr. N. Macnicol are in substantial agreement with Dr. Grierson's contention.[97] Dr. Macnicol says: 'That the influence of Christian teaching on the ideas of later Vaisnavite and Saivite theism was considerable and increasing from about the thirteenth century onwards seems highly probable.'[98]

Christian service in the social, economic, educational and medical fields has got to be appreciated by all. The Christian missionary agencies carried on a relentless war against illiteracy, disease and poverty, the crying evils in society. Special emphasis was laid on the formation of schools and colleges for the spread of education. In course of time, these educational institutions played a notable part in imparting English education, which effected revolutionary changes in the social and political outlook of Indians of all classes. According to Jawaharlal Nehru, 'English education brought a widening of Indian horizons, an admiration for English literature and institutions, a revolt against some customs and aspects of Indian life, and a growing demand for political life.' [99] Referring to another aspect of the work of missions, Nehru observes: "The desire of the Christian missionaries to translate the Bible into every possible language thus resulted in the development of many Indian languages."[100]

In the matter of humanitarian services, social reform, and the creation of a society based on the worth and dignity of the individuals, Christian ideals have exerted a stimulating and beneficient influence on the thoughts and aspirations of the intelligentsia in Indian society for the last one and a half century. Hinduism has similarly influenced Christianity, which is best manifested in the South. In some of the social customs of the Syrian Christians of Malabar, we find a tendency to approximate to the code of behaviour obtaining among the Nairs of Malabar. The caste system was at one time nearly as widely prevalent in sections of the Church in South India as among Hindus; and the Church had to wage a war against it, before some of its worst features could be suppressed. Even today the shadow of caste hangs over certain groups of the Christian community in the South.[101] In Maharastra there are Konkanastha Brahman Christians, Saraswat Christians, Mahar Christians and these rigidly follow the taboos about intercaste marriages and inter-dining.[102]

Formation of caste-like structure even in the two religions, which denounce caste as an institution, goes to indicate the all-pervasive character of the Indian caste system. In the traditional system it was impossible for any alien community to function as a part of Indian society without acquiring some of the structural properties of castes which were the basic units of that society and these two religions are no exception. It would not be an exaggeration to say that it is possible in India to change one's religion but not one's caste. The influence of Hindu society has been so powerful that in some form or the other, the evils of the Hindu caste system have also crept into the Muslim and the Christian societies of India. Even more surprisingly the Sikh religion, which was founded on the basis of equality, has not been able to eliminate castes. Thus the strange and amazing phenomenon of untouchable Sikhs, untouchable Christians and Dalit Muslims is unique and peculiar to India—a reminder of the grip which caste has on the public mind.

The Efforts of Social Reformers

Since the time of Buddha attempts have been made by the social reformers to purge the Hindu society of the evils of the caste system and uplift the social position of the lowest rung in the society. Though Fick has reservation to look upon Buddha as a social reformer,[103] *Buddha* may be considered as the first social reformer, because, after all, it was his preaching which slackened many restrictions prevalent in Hinduism regarding the caste system, though caste in its present sense had not grown up then. After Buddha successive social reformers worked for cleansing the Hindu society of the ill-effects of the caste system. Since the rigidity of the caste system owed its origin in the Hindu legislation, it was in the fitness of things that these reformers were largely drawn from the religious teachers. It was *Ramanuj*, the great Vaisanava Acharya of the eleventh century, and a Brahmin, who took bold steps for the religious betterment of the outcaste section of the society. He secured for them the privilege of visiting the temple one day in the year and devised something which they might put on corresponding to the sacred thread of the Brahmans.[104] He was known as a friend of the lower classes, trying to uplift them in social and religious life. He gave them a place in Vaisanavism by allowing them to wear sect-marks, to dress themselves like Vaisanavas, to imitate their customs and habits and to study the *Prabandham*, venerated as the Tamil Veda by the Sri-Vaisanavas. *Basava*, another Brahmin of the twelfth century, opened the door of Virasaivism to all castes and was responsible for undertaking activities of social amelioration, such as the elevation of the social status of women, the abolition of caste distinctions and the removal of untouchability.[105] Even in the eleventh and twelfth centuries, the Brahmans, the Jains and other puritans opposed the regrettable institution of *devadasis* or the dedication of dancing girls to the temple gods, though deeply rooted in the Hindu society. In Northern India, the great reformers like Haribhadra Suri, Jinesvara Suri, Jinavallabha and their Kharataragachchha campaigned against the employment of *devadasis* in the temples, comparing a *vesya* to the washingstone of a washerman and the potsherd in which a dog had its meal. But they achieved only a partial success, because they not only provided entertainment to the people, but were also a source of revenue to the state.[106] Alberuni also mentions such an opposition in the North-Western parts of India, but aptly remarks that this reformatory campaign could not make any headway as the custom was supported by the kings and nobles.[107]

With the passage of time, especially in the mediaeval period, opposition to assign a place in the society, and to keep a large section of people outside the pale of orthodox Hinduism, on the basis of birth and occupation, was growing up from within, thanks to the efforts of the socio-religious leaders of this age. Their stand on caste, especially its rigidity and orthodoxy, succeeded on many an occasion to improve the status and position of these people in the social hierarchy and similarly failed on many instances when their protests landed them outside the pale of Brahmanic fold, even if for a temporary period, till they came to be recognised as distinct and separate religious sects like the Arya Samajists and the Brahmo Samajists of the later years.

The contribution of the *mediaeval mystics of India*, who inveighed against caste and religious custom alike, towards a better social organisation, cannot be over-estimated. A living faith was brought to the door of the meanest by preachers who often came from the submerged classes of Hindu society. We have seen that many sects like the Nathapanthis, Kabirpanthis, Satnami, Alakhnamis, Kumbhipatias, Sahajias, Dadupanthis, Khusi Visvasi, Saheb

Dhani, Ramavallabhi, Jagomohini, Balarami, Neda, Aul-Baul-Darbes-Sain, Samyogi, Karthabhaja, Niranjanis, Sivanarayana, Dhami, and many others grew up during this mediaeval period and their followers declared themselves against caste system and declined to accept the superior position of the Brahmanas.

As a matter of fact the attitude of the Vaisnavas and the Śaivas was not far different. Srinivas, a Brahmin, Ramchandra, a Vaisya, and Norottam, a Kshatriya, were all Vaisnavas, and as such, were not afraid to take their meals from the same plate.[108]

The saints or reformers in the middle ages tried to abolish the distinction between the high-caste Hindus and the so-called untouchables, by laying emphasis on the equality of members of all castes in the eyes of God and pointed out that through devotion or *Bhakti* all could achieve salvation. They took into their fold such men as barbers, weavers, shoemakers, etc., the so-called untouchables. But the privilege of equality was not extended to men as men, but to those individuals only who had washed off their untouchability with the love of God. The idea of equality propagated by these mediaeval saints therefore did not produce that much effect on the secular organization of society, as it should have been and untouchability could not altogether be removed from the stratified society. Caste barriers continued as of old. *Kabir*, the Mohammedan weaver, and *Rabidasa*, a shoemaker, were honoured by kings and high-caste men, but the same privilege was not extended to other weavers and shoemakers, who were still held as untouchables, Ravidasa took pride in the fact that even "the superior sort of Brahmanas came to bow before him;"[109] but the other members of his caste were not so honoured.

Moreover the caste system was so pervasive that even the religious groups formed in defiance of and in protest against the caste system, found themselves relegated, whether they wished it or not, precisely into the position of castes in that system which they had aspired to reform. This led Hutton to comment that unless these reformist groups were to succeed in destroying the caste system, as the followers of the Buddha nearly did, it is difficult to see what other outcome such a movement could have unless it broke away from Hinduism altogether, like the Sikhism. He cited the instances of Lingayats and Kabirpanthis as the two typical instances of religious sects turning into castes.[110] The lay followers of the Natha cult in Bengal were formed into a distinct 'Jugi' caste.[111]

New conceptions of social justice and political rights were brought about in the nineteenth century by the *Indian Renaissance*, which represented the dawn between the passing of the mediaeval age and the advent of the modern. The Renaissance in Bengal produced two men, *Rammohan Roy* and *Pandit Iswar Chandra Vidyasagar*, who symbolised all the historical characteristics of the Indian Renaissance. Rammohan Roy (1772-1833), father of modern India, is the awakener of us all. Many-sided is his achievement. He is a reformer who recognised that reforming could not be done piecemeal. If India is to be reformed, her education, religion, economic and political moves should be changed. One can say he is the initiator of the regionalization of the medium of instruction. The letter addressed to Lord Amherst in 1823 on English education is a veritable landmark in the educational history of modern India; for he urged therein for the promotion of a more liberal and enlightened system of education in India, embracing 'Mathematics, Natural Philosophy, Chemistry, Anatomy and other useful sciences, which the Nations of Europe have carried to a degree of perfection that has raised them above the inhabitants of other parts of the world.'[112] He led this movement till his departure for England in 1830. A new generation of young men, educated in the Hindu College sprang up in the meantime and strengthened his cause.[113] In those days, specially after the establishment of the Supreme Court in 1774 in Calcutta,' a knowledge of the English language appeared to be desirable and necessary'.[114] Moreover, the substitution of Persian by English in educational institutions and government business also necessitated the imparting of English education.

The Indian Renaissance of the nineteenth century was the result of English education and Western ideas which flowed along with it. Fifty years of English education brought greater changes in the minds of educated Hindus than the previous three thousand years.[115] The rationalizing effect of English education gave rise to a number of reform movements, one after another, for eradicating the society of the evil practices that had crept in and for uplifting the social position of the so-called 'untouchables', amongst others. The early reformers were highly influenced by the ideals of nationalism and rationalism. They owed these ideals to the influence of English education which brought them into contact with the thought-current of the Western world. The English-educated in India found that Indian society was organised on the basis of hierarchy, which was quite inconsistent with the high ideals of Liberty, Equality and Fraternity, thrown up by the French Revolution, and it was this inconsistency that made them realise the need for giving equality to women with men and for removing caste barriers and untouchability. They also realised that nationalism, so necessary to achieve political freedom, could not be a reality until the hierachical basis of society was replaced by the ideal of equality of all castes and communities, and the evils which made the life of women miserable—evils like *sati*, child marriage, forced widowhood, polygamy and kulinism in Bengal, and the denial of education to them,—were removed. Thus began a long era of reforms of Hindu Society and religion, and of reinterpretation of the latter. Rammohan Roy got the *Sati* Act passed in 1829, after eighteen years' of relentless crusade against the obnoxious custom of *sati*.

Pandit Iswar Chandra Vidyasagar (1820-1891) launched a movement for legislation for permitting widow remarriage and prohibiting polygamy: Though he could not achieve in his life time the prohibition of polygamy, the enactment of the Widow Remarriage Act in 1856 against all opposition was the culmination of his crusade against social iniquities. Vidyasagar's widow remarriage movement was not confined in Bengal only. In Maharastra, Vishnu Sastri Pandit translated into Marathi Vidyasagar's widow marriage tracts. He was one of the founders of the Widow Marriage Association in 1861 in Maharastra and the first widow marriage took place in Maharastra in 1861 itself. He himself also married a widow.[116] Dr. Dhando Keshav Karve (1858-1962), not only led this movement but himself married a widow in 1893.[117] In fact, many social reformers of the nineteenth and twentieth centuries, like Kandukari Veeresalingam Pantulu (1848-1919)[118] and Raghupati Venkataratnam Naidu (1862-1939)[119] of the Madras Presidency, Dr. M.Visvesvaraya (1860-1962)[120] of Mysore, Justice Mahadeo Govind Ranade (1842-1901)[121] of Maharastra, to mention only a few of them, faught against all the evils which were the bane of Hindu women.

Some writers[122] have pointed out that most of the social reformers of the nineteenth century, like Rammohan Roy, Iswar Chandra Vidyasagar, Keshab Chandra Sen, Shivnath Shastri, Atman Pandarang, M.G. Ranade and Gopal Krishna Gokhale, came from the highest castes—Brahmin and Kayastha, and the problems they attempted to solve, *sati*, infanticide, infant-marriage, unrestricted polygamy, shaving of widows, widow-marriage were really problems which affected their mothers and sisters. This was indeed the psychology behind their emphasis on the emancipation of women. By implication they wanted to say that these social reformers who belonged to higher castes did not take up the cause of removal of untouchability and other manifestations of social inequalities, which concerned the lower rung of the society most, with that characteristic vigour and energy of theirs and hence, these were left to leaders drawn from their own castes.[123] It was only in the twentieth century consequent on the growth of political consciousness among the non-Brahmins that equal stress came to be laid on the removal of caste barriers and untouchability.[124]

These great thinkers and social reformers of the nineteenth and early twentieth centuries perhaps do not deserve this sort of aspersions on their reformative activities, in the conduct of which they were inspired, least of all, by any casteist consideration. These pioneers of the Indian Renaissance did not distinguish between man and man on the basis of caste, rather they worked for the eradication of casteism and untouchability. We have already mentioned the activities of the Brahmo Samaj, the Parthana Samaj and the Arya Samaj in the matter of abolition of caste distinctions and caste barriers. Almost all the social reformers of this age were in the vanguard of these Samaj movements, either directly or indirectly, and worked actively for bringing about an all-round change in the condition and social position of the helpless victims of a dreadful system of social iniquity.

Rammohan Roy advocated abolition of caste and untouchability,[125] and Iswar Chandra Vidyasagar opened the door of Sanskrit College, so long restricted to pupils belonging to high castes only, to all sections of pupils irrespective of caste[126] and worked for the spread of female education till the last day of his life. Dr. M. Visvesvaraya, the architect of modern Karnataka, worked untiringly for raising the status of the so-called untouchables and socially backward classes, and for the amelioration of the backward classes and the untouchables for the first time through official auspices. This he did even before the advent of Mahatma Gandhi. He earmarked one lakh rupees, in those days a large sum, to grant scholarships to students of the backward communities annually and opened special schools for the Harijan Children. He campaigned vigorously for the spread of education among Harijans and girls.[127] Kandukuri Veereasalingam Pantulu[128] and Raghupati Venkataratnam Naidu[129] worked in the Madras Presidency for the welfare of the backward and unfortunate lot and uplift of the untouchables. In the western part of India, Bal Shastri Jambheker, Dadoba and Atmaram Pandurang, and Vishnu Parasuram Pandit were prominent among those who denounced the caste system.[130] Gopal Hari Deshmukh (1823-1892), Ramkrishna Gopal Bhandarkar (1837-1925) and Justice Ranade (1842-1901) worked relentlessly for the removal of untouchability and caste rigidity. G.K. Gokhale (1866-1915) founded in 1905 the Servants of India Society, the first secular organisation for the welfare of the underprivileged, rural and tribal people. And Jyotirao Govindrao Phule (1827-1890) of Poona was the pioneer in modern times of the movement calculated to improve the condition of and to secure social equality to the erstwhile untouchable and unapproachable classes.[131] V.R. Shinde, the twentieth century torch bearer of Phuley spirit, has stated[132] that the Bengali Brahmin Shashipada Bandyopadhyay started his uplift work among the labourers of Baranagar, among whom untouchables seem to have figured, in 1865. But definite mention of Bandyopadhya's relations with the Chandalas occurs in Shinde's account of the progressive Brahmin's work in 1870. He, we are informed, used to attend the religious discourses current among one sect of the Chandalas. In later years he used to dine with them and nurse their children.

As a matter of fact, it would be a travesty of truth if we do not admit that almost all the social and religious reformers of the nineteenth century, thrown up by the Indian Renaissance, being imbibed with the spirit of equality and social reform, worked for the alleviation of the sufferings of their fellow beings, especially those which were repugnant to enlightened opinion. And this spirit was not confined to any particular region or sect or community. Thus we find Sri Narayan Guru (1856-1928), a religious reformer of Kerala, propogating for the removal of caste system. It was mainly due to his untiring efforts that the Maharaja of Travancore ultimately made the 'Temple Entry Proclamation'.

Mention may be made of the efforts made by *Swami Vivekananda* (1863-1902) in redeeming the status and position of the untouchables and the downtrodden in the Hindu Society. He had valuable lessons from his first-hand readings regarding the social, economic and cultural life of the people during his extensive tour (*Paribrayya*) throughout the length and breadth of the country. His direct experience of the appalling misery of the unlettered and downtrodden masses, the helpless victims of the reprehensible excesses of caste prejudices encouraged in the name of religion made himrealise the fact that the Vedic religion, the epitome of catholicism, was so degraded that it came to be almost synonymous with a hot-bed of untouchability, sectarian hatred and social tyranny during the mediaeval period. He wanted that the sunken vitality of the helpless victims of social tyranny was to be restored by providing them with life-giving food, physical, intellectual as well as spiritual. He, however, encouraged neither drastic reform from above, nor fight from below; for both were ruinous. In the field of social reform, he preferred the process of evolution to that of revolution. The society was to be led gently to realise its own errors and made strong enough to eliminate by a healthy, natural, and evolutionary process all that would appear to it to be prejudicial to its progress.[133] He wanted that the privileges of caste system should go and not the caste system. There should be equal chances for all; every one be taught that the divine is within, and every one will work out his own salvation.[134] Swamiji used to invest the assembled devotees with the holy thread on the occasion of Sri Ramakrishna's *Tithipuja* (Nativity). In 1898 about forty to fifty *Bhaktas* were invested with the holy thread by the Swami.[135] He said that Europe began to advance from the date learning and power began to flow in among the poor lower classes. Lots of suffering poor people of other countries, cast off like refuse as it were, found a house and shelter in America, and these were the very backbone of America.[136] He also visualised the birth of New India arising from the awakening of the common men-the peasants, the fishermen, the cobblers, the sweepers, the labourers and such other lower classes of India who suffered oppression for thousand of years.[137] He castigated the so-called higher castes for regarding them as low-class people and vaunting their own culture without realising that the well-being of the higher classes now lay in helping the lower classes to get their legitimate rights.[138] He tried to bring home to the Hindu Society the injustice of treating a large section of the community as untouchables. Referring to the absence of the custom of inter-caste dining, he sarcastically remarked, 'caste has now entered our cooking pots'. On another occasion he said, "O, my countrymen O Indians, do not forget that those illiterate and ignorant cobblers and sweepers are your blood relations, your brothers."[139] A great champion for the well-being of the lower classes, this 'patriot saint of India' laid before his countrymen practical formulae of social service deduced from the fundamental teachings of the Vedanta. 'God is here before you in various forms', said the Swami, 'he who loves His creatures serves God.' He exhorted his countrymen to serve the underprivileged in the spirit of 'who serves Jiva, serves God indeed'. He was for rousing these lower classes from slumber by imparting learning and culture to them.[140] He said that if the Brahmin had more aptitude for learning on the ground of heredity than the Pariah, no more money should be spent on the Brahmin's education, but should be spent all on the Pariah. If the Brahmin is born clever, he can educate himself without help. If the others are not born clever, let them have all the teaching and the teachers they want. This is justice as he understood it.[141]

This endeavour to ameliorate the condition of the downtrodden gained further momentum in the twentieth century. Gandhiji started the Harijan movement in 1929 and defined Harijan as 'Children of God'. He founded All India Harijan Sevak Sangh for social reform and education of the depressed class in 1932. B.R. Ambedkar, and a number of other leaders took up the cause of social uplift of the socially degraded and ostracized people. This has been discussed in details in the next chapter.

Urge to Move up the Caste Ladder

In the past, various groups of Hindus of low castes had broken out of the traditional caste hierarchy in an attempt to improve their social status and either became converted to non-Hindu faiths or set up new groups within the Hindu fold that owed no allegiance to the Brahmanical caste and denied its claims to represent a superior or an ideal social status. We have already seen that a number of distinctive sects were formed, especially in the mediaeval period, which provided mobility to traditionally lower castes. The religious rivalries between Islam, Christianity and the Arya Samaj, apart from

The Dhobas or washerman are regarded as unclean Sudras, and Brahmanas do not take water touched by them. A section of them have given up their traditional profession, which is despised, and taken to agriculture. They call themselves Chasa-Dhobas, and are regarded as of superior status to the ordinary Dhobas.[148]

The original professions of the Kaivartas were those of a fisherman and a boatman. In later times a section of them gave up their traditional occupations and took to agriculture and adopted more closely the Brahmanical rules of life. They discarded the name of Kaivartas and assumed the name of Mahisya.[149]

Prof. M.S.A. Rao mentions the case of Yadavas who over the last several decades have succeeded in incorporating several allied castes like Ahirs (in Punjab, Haryana, Himachal Pradesh, Delhi, Uttar Pradesh, Bihar, Gujarat and Rajasthan); Goalas and Sadgopas (in Bengal and Orissa); Gavlis and Gopalas (in Maharastra); Gollas (in Andhra Pradesh and Karnataka) and Idayans and Konars (in Tamil Nadu) into the all-India Yadava category that today includes one-tenth of the total population of India. Though all groups included in the Yadava category belonged to the 'clean castes', the actual status varied from area to area. To improve their status, Yadavas at the turn of the century not only began to claim Kashatriya status but also to adopt Arya Samaj practices in a big way. Uttar Pradesh and Bihar witnessed widespread *jenevo* movements in the first two decades of the 20th century as Yadavas began to don the sacred thread in accordance with Arya Samaj practices. These years also saw the sprouting of Arya mandirs, pracharaks, priests and schools in many parts of India. This was accompanied by major changes in the life-style of the Yadavas. They began to follow Vedic life cycle ceremonies conducted by Arya priests. There was renewed emphasis on their Kashatriya identity and their links with Lord Krishna. Yadavas emerged as major protectors of cattle and the celebration of *Janmashtami* (Lord Krishna's birthday) became a major event in their social and religious life. Yadavas all over the country were quick to respond to the forces of change unleashed by the British rule. At the opening of the century itself, their regional associations concerned themselves with establishing educational institutions and seeking modern employment opportunities for their castemen. In Punjab, Western Uttar Pradesh and Madhya Pradesh, Yadavas turned mainly to the army for employment. In Punjab they even petitioned the government in the 1880s for recruitment of Ahirs into the army. The Punjab wing established English-language schools as well as a school for girls as early as 1920. Similar movements for educational advancement and modern employment were witnessed in Uttar Pradesh, Bombay, Bengal and Andhra Pradesh. The emergence of an English-educated elite among the Yadavas led to the formation of the All-India Yadava Mahasabha in 1923. The AIYM immediately engaged itself on two issues. It appealed to its castemen in all regions to add 'Yadava' to their names and at the same time launched on a major programme of social reform. In fact, as early as 1911, regional caste groups had been petitioning the Census Commissioners to change their caste name from Golla, Ahir etc., to Yadav. The regional organisation of the Gollas of Hyderabad, the Hyderabad Rashtra Yadava Mahajana Samajam, for example, appealed to the Census Commissioner that their caste names of Golla, Gowli, Gollawar and Ahir be changed to Yadava.[150]

Though the *Rajvanshis* and *Kochas* today are regarded as two distinct castes, there is little doubt that originally they belonged to the same ethnic stock. They came and settled in North Bengal as invaders from the North-East, like the Ahoms in the Brahmaputra valley. There they remained as rulers for a fairly long time, and hence the name Rajvanshi, meaning 'of the family of rulers', has been adopted by the caste. The Kochas are rather backward in the adoption of Hindu rites and usages, and are now-a-days found in humble professions. Hence they are not accepted as their castemen by the Rajvanshis, who are more Hinduised and more advanced in culture, and are mostly engaged in agriculture. They now claim to be regarded as Kshatriyas. Of late they have begun to adopt the practice of wearing sacred thread and also the

Hindu *gotra* names. At first they adopted only one *gotra*, namely Kashyap. Then they realised that it was un-Kshatriya like to have one gotra and to marry within the *same Gotra*. Now they have added twelve other *gotras* to the original one. The more backward and illiterate members of the Rajvanshi caste, however, have not been able to master the use of gotra nomenclature, nor have they ceased to maintain practices inconsistent with orthodox Hindu belief.[151] The Census Report of 1931 has commented on their customs and practices as follows: "Divorce is still practised amongst them as well as the system of 'companionate marriage' known as *gagoch* in Rangpur or *pani-sarpan* in the Terai of Darjeeling... The remarriage of widows is customary and attachments not amounting to formal marriage are also entered into by widows or divorced women. These are mainly of two kinds. In the *ghar-dhoka* type the woman betakes herself to the man to whom she has taken a fancy and is accepted by him; in the *dangua* or *pashua* relationship a widow, particularly if she has property, will secure to herself a protector...Practices like this and others at variance with the tenets of Hindu orthodoxy such as the indulgence in prohibited foods and liquors are discarded by the progressive members of the society".[152] All these indicate that even in traditional Hindu society the door was not entirely closed for admission from the lower to the higher direction.

Fuchs in his study of the Messianic movements in India has found traits of similar social changes among the tribal and the so-called untouchables and other low castes of the Hindu society by the process of social emulation and imitation of the Higher castes. He mentions, amongst others, the Messianic movements amongst the Mundas and Oroans of Bihar, the Virsaivism movement by Basava in the South, the Sankara Dev movement in Assam and the Satnami movement of the Chamars in Madhya Pradesh. His study reveals the great importance the backward peoples attach to social prestige. They are prepared to make great sacrifices in order to rise in social status. [153] Members of the Messianic movements feel very deeply that they belong to a community. This sense of solidarity certainly provides one of the greatest attractions to the masses. Persons of low social status are thrilled because they find themselves treated with a respect in these new communities such as they have never before experienced.[154]

Birsa Munda or Bhagwan Birsa, who later led a revolt against the British rule for establishing an independent Munda *Raj* in the last decade of the nineteenth century, propagated the Hindu ideals of ritual purity and asceticism. He forbade the worship of idols and spirits which used to play such a prominent role in Munda religion. Birsa's followers had to wear the sacred thread of the high-caste Hindus. This appealed strongly to the secret ambitions of the Mundas who aspired to the social status of the second Hindu caste, the Kshatriyas. He preached that theft, deception, murder, drunkenness and polygamy were sinful. He ordanied that pigs and fowls of a white colour were unclean and should be destroyed. The followers of Birsa form an endogamous group and abstain from flesh and liquor. They worship no other gods besides the High-God and do not propitiate the evil spirits. But their ranks are dwindling recently.[155]

The *Tana Bhagat Movement* amongst the Oraons began about the latter part of the year 1915. It spread practically over the whole of Chota Nagpur wherever Oraon villages were found. The bhagats (prophets), who were obviously under the influence of Hindu reformers demanded from their Oraon disciples abstinence from meat and liquor. In addition, objects of a red colour—the colour of blood—were forbidden to them; consequently the Oraons were forbidden to eat red pepper, as well as tomatoes and reddish rice. They were asked even to give up dancing. The members of the new sect gained great self-confidence; and in their desire for deliverance from economic exploitation and want they became a serious danger to their oppressors—the landlords and usurers, traders and officials. During the freedom movement the Tana Bhagats fought along with the revolutionary Hindu workers, and cheerfully went to jail or paid large fines in the interest of the national freedom movement. They even raided liquor shops, destroyed roads and telegraph lines, attacked police stations and government offices, held back flag demonstrations and offered satyagraha.[156]

The *Bachi-dan Bhagats* have to an even greater extent than the Tana Bhagats adopted Hindu ideology. This movement employs Gosains, or degraded Brahmins as priests and religious preceptors (gurus), and in a number of cases also Vaishnava Bairagis who usually belong to the lower Hindu castes. All bhagats are understood to maintain the rules of ritual purity in food and drink, and in other habits that high-caste Hindus observe. But at the same time they also observe most of the social customs and habits of the Oraon tribe which do not militate against Hindu ideas of ceremonial purity. They have succeeded in infusing a large amount of Hindu ideals into their tribal culture in a rather harmonious manner and without cutting themselves loose from their own tribal society. They follow a kind of Bhakti worship which is modified by tribal tradition and custom. This infusion of Hindu elements into the traditional Oraon culture and religion has immensely increased their self-respect, intensified their conservatism and stiffened their faithful adherence to ancient customs and beliefs. It has also rendered them immune to non-Hindu alien influences, such as Muslim and Christian influences.[157]

The *Satnami* sect of the Chamars of North India was founded by a Rajput named Jagjiwan Das (1682-1761) of Bara Banki district in U.P., who preached the worship of God under the name "Sat Nam" (True Name) and thought that the Deity was both creator and substance of all things. He conceived of God in popular Vedantic terms, that is, as an infinite and impersonal being void of sensible qualities and without a beginning or end. Jagjiwan Das urged that his followers should practise absolute indifference to the world, that they should depend on no one, and that they should practise implicit obedience to the *guru*. His followers enjoined tolerence, charity, consideration for others, prayer, study, and kindness to animals. He prohibited the use of meat, red lentils (on account of their red colour suggesting blood), of the brinjal or egg-plant which was believed, probably on account of its shape, to resemble flesh, and of intoxicating liquors.[158] He taught that spiritual realization was possible only through the grace of God, and he insisted on purity as the essence of a religious life. His aspiration was to unite the two streams of Hindu and Muslim religious life through love.[159] Between A.D. 1820 and 1830, one Ghasi Das (1780-1850), a cobbler by caste and a native of Bilaspur district, further reformed the movement. The seven precepts of Ghasi Das included abstinence from liquor, meat, and certain red vegetables such as lentils, chillies and tomatoes, because they had the colour of blood; the abolition of idol worship; the prohibition of the employment of cow for cultivation, and of ploughing after midday or taking food to the fields; and the worship of one solitary and supreme God. The use of *taroi* is said to have been forbidden on account of its fancied resemblance to the horn of the buffalo, and of brinjal from its likeness to the scrotum of the same animal. The prohibition against ploughing after midday meal was probably promulgated out of compassion for the plough animals and was already in force among Gonds of Bastar State. This precept is still observed by some Satnamis, and in case of necessity they will continue ploughing from early morning until the late afternoon without taking food in order not to violate it. The injunction against the use of the cow for ploughing was probably a sop to the Brahmins. The Satnamis were bidden to cast all idols from their homes, to dispense with temples and fixed prayers, but they were permitted to reverence the Sun. Caste was abolished and all men were to be socially equal except the family of Ghasi Das, in which the priesthood of the cult was to remain hereditary.[160] The Satnami movement is essentially a social revolt on the part of the despised Chamars or Tanners. A large proportion of the Satnami Chamars were owners or tenants of land, and this fact might have intensified their feeling of revolt against the degraded position to which they were relegated by the caste Hindus. The fundamental tenet of the Gospel of Ghasi Das, as in the case of so many dissenting sects, appeared to have been the abolition of caste and with it the authority of the Brahmins.[161] Ghurye thinks this is a "sort of a self-respect and social upgrading movement".[162]

This process of social mobility has been termed as *Brahminising* by Risley,[163] borrowing it from Sir Alfred Lyall's discription of the religious and social movement,[164] and Srinivas has termed it as Sanskritization, in the absence of a better term. "The only alternative word that suggests itself to me is Brahmanization and it is not any the less awkward".[165] By the term Sanskritization is meant the process by which a 'low' Hindu caste gives up its own rites, customs, and beliefs, and takes up, instead, the custom, rites, and beliefs of a higher caste. It is a much wider term than, and somewhat different from, the term Brahminization.[166] Generally such changes are followed by a claim to a higher position in the caste hierarchy than that traditionally conceded to the claimant caste by the local community. The claim is usually made over a period of time, in fact, a generation or two, before the "arrival" is conceded.[167] The lower castes accept one of the economically and politically dominant castes-normally a 'twice-born' caste, and not necessarily the Brahmin caste only—, which also enjoys a high ritual status, as the reference group and emulate its life style. They give up widow remarriage, go in for child marriage, abjure from non-vegetarian food, discourage out-door activities by their females. This imitative process of upward status mobility among lower castes begins by segments of caste or sub-caste breaking off from a larger whole of which they are a part, Sanskritize their customs and ritual, and eventually achieve a higher status than their parent body in the course of one or two generations.[168] This process is not confined to Hindu castes but also occurs among tribal and semi-tribal groups as well.[169] This usually takes place when there is either an improvement in the economic or political position of the group concerned or a higher group consciousness resulting from its contact with a source of the "Great Tradition" of Hinduism such as a pilgrimage-centre or monastery or proselytising sect.[170] Functionally such a process helps to break the barriers of parochialisation and brings about cultural uniformity among the various strata in a village, though analytically, it has been argued, it remains primarily cultural and not structural.[171] The mobility associated with Sanskritization results only in positional changes in the system and does not lead to any structural change.[172] The Sanskritization concept rests ultimately on the notion that the caste system, like all status hierarchies, causes the low to invidiously compare themselves with the high and to try in every way they can to soften, modify, reduce, and even eliminate altogether the basis for these status differences.[173] As a cultural phenomenon Sanskritization is peculiar to India and countries which have derived their civilization from India. But there is nothing peculiarly Indian about its social significance; it represents a means of claiming higher social status: it is a mechanism for social climbing by conforming to an all-India standard of respectable behaviour. In the caste system it can function as a safety-valve, enabling those who are economically and politically qualified for power to achieve recognition. Sanskritization does not represent necessarily a change in structure: positions in the structure change but the type of relationship which characterizes the structure does not change.[174] Rao thinks that Sanskritization is not only a description of a process of change but also an explanation, in so far as the *ideal* position was identified with the high caste, and any change either in consciousness for social emulation or both lead to imitation of the way of life associated with the higher caste.[175]

Sanskritization is said to have been going on for hundreds of years without impairing the structure of caste.[176] A low caste was able in a generation or two to rise to a higher position in the hierarchy by Sanskritizing its ritual and pantheon.[177] It is significant that it is mostly those who have improved their economic position through cultivation, trade or education, and have, in addition, contacts outside local society, tend to Sanskritize their life-style. This results in bringing about some consonance between their improved economic position and their social and ritual ranking.[178]

Bailey observes that there are in Sanskritization certain elements, which from the point of view of an ordered and stable caste political system, may be distrubing. Firstly and most obviously Sanskritization is an attack on the hierarchy. Such an attack is not necessarily revolutionary, but may merely be a rebellion which changes positions in society but does not change its form. Secondly, Sanskritization is sometimes a corporate activity with political implications by what was formerly a dependent caste with no corporate political existence. The most striking examples of this, are, of course, the assiduous attempts of the untouchables to Sanskritize their behaviour. The third element in which Sanskritization appears to be inimical to a caste system is in general levelling of culture. It is true, of course, that the protagonists do not see the process only in this light: an essential motive is to assert their superiority over others, and not merely to claim equality with the highest. But, whatever the protagonists think, in the long run the process tends to eliminate the diacritical differences between castes, which reflected and helped to maintain the hierarchy.[179]

The Impact of British Contact

The process of social mobility, however, started in a new form after the establishment of the British rule in India.The

Census operations which the British launched, contributed a new awareness to the caste identities and stimulated the aspiration for a kind of status mobility among the lower castes. From this aspiration sprang an urge to improve their status in the social hierarchy by assuming names other than those by which they were commonly known and getting such claims accepted by the government as well as the society at large. Caste associations sprang up to make these claims good as well as to give an organisational sustenance to these claims. In most cases, adoption of new names was coupled with adoption of new behaviour patterns usually practised by the upper caste. This process assumed a nation-wide spread in various forms during the early twentieth century.

As an example of this group mobility, in Bengal, the Yogi (a weaver *jati*) succeeded in moving into the *Brahman varna* in the space of just twenty years (1911-31) thanks to the concerted efforts of the caste panchayats, which undertook to rewrite the caste history—thereby discovering the true noble origins of the *jati*—and then to enlighten members on the duties and privileges of the newly acquired status.[180] Srinivas has listed eleven such castes which changed their claim to higher status from census to census and ultimately landed themselves in one of the three higher varnas by the 1931 census.[181]

The Census Report of 1911 for Bengal mentions how such a status mobility led to recognition of low castes as Vaisyas or Kshatriyas. "There is a general desire among the low castes of Bengal to merge the modern caste in the ancient class by calling themselves Kshatriyas and Vaisyas, two of these varnas... The castes that aspire to be recognised as Kshatriyas or Vaisyas obtain however a certain amount of support from the Pundits. Instead of recognising that a caste which used to be of poor repute has risen in the social scale the Pundits overcome the difficulty by the pleasing fiction that they never were that humble caste. They overlook questions of origin and descent, as well as the views of their predecessors and of the main body of Hindus, and consider avocation only. They compare, for instance, the present occupation of the caste and that of the old *varna*, and if it is the same, identify the caste with the *varna*. Thus, according to Manu, the Chandalas were a degraded race, whose principal occupation was that of burning the dead and hanging criminals; they were vagrants who kept dogs and asses, and were clothed in rags stripped from the dead. No Namasudra (a new name for the Chandal) at the present day does any of these things, and therefore, some Pundits rule that they are not Chandalas. Other castes, who have given up their traditional occupations and are engaged in trade, claim to be Vaisyas. The Pundit's argument in such cases is briefly—"These men are traders. The Vaisyas were traders. Therefore these men are Vaisyas". The following extracts from a resolution passed in June, 1912 by the Executive Committee of the Vanga Dharma Mandal (the Bengal Branch of the Bharat Dharma Mahamandal) illustrates the standpoint adopted:— "In view of the options expressed by the Pundits and leading members of the Bengali Hindu society and by the special officer deputed by the Vanga Dharma Mandal in this behalf to make local enquiries, the Vanga Dharma Mandal is of opinion that the Rarhi and Varendra Sahas of Eastern Bengal, as represented by the Eastern Bengal and Sylhet Vaisya Samity, whose manners and customs substantially resemble those of the upper classes of Hindu society and whose callings and professions do not differ from those of Vaisyas, are a distinct caste from the Sunri Sahas, and that their claim to be classed as Vaisyas may be conceded as being not inconsistent with the principles and practices enjoined by the Sastras."[182]

Mention may be made of the formation of Ramgharia caste. Since the beginning of the present century, the Sikhs of Tarkhan and Lohar descent, who were denied high status within the caste system, have increasingly applied to themselves the name Ramgharia, appropriating the name of an important *misl* (more or less a private army) of the Sikhs during the 18th century, whose leader had been a man of Tarkhan caste. By the 1930s, the term was coming into general use. The use of the name Ramgharia, for organisations and presumably for individuals, grew steadily, culminating in the emergence of Ramgharia caste, as an entity during the Censuses of 1921 and 1931.[183] We may take the case of the Okkaligas of erstwhile Mysore, now Karnataka. Okkaliga means cultivator and excludes those who tend animals. For the early census-takers of Mysore between 1799 and 1804, the Okkaligas were not a single community but a number of quite distinct castes of cultivators listed separately from one another under an occupational heading. By 1881, the Okkaligas had become a catch-all census grouping which included salt-makers, cowherds, dyers, extractors of iron, Tamil Vellalas and a Telegu group, which followed a vagrant and wandering life. Though 38 sections of Okkaligas were listed fully, 78 more were lumped together under a general heading for lack of space. The situation was further complicated in the Censuses of 1901 and subsequently, when for convenience the authors listed Okkaligas as a single category without sub-divisions. Inevitably, the extreme complexities of section definition were brushed aside and the Okkaligas were seen being discussed in Census literature of 1921 and in Mysore public life as a single "caste".[184]

In the traditional system the only way to become a Hindu was to belong to a caste, and the unit of mobility was usually a group, not an individual or a family.[185] It is quite likely that caste consciousness may be aroused as a result of such status mobility. This may lead to a streamlining of the community and hardening of the rules of separation from other communities. Dutt thinks that these attempts are no doubt good so far as the interests of the caste are concerned, but the tightening of caste barriers and the assumption of an air of caste superiority may excite corresponding jealousies among rival castes leading to a strengthening of casteism. He mentions the case of the Vaidyas of Bengal who have hardened their caste rules. Thus attempts were made to stop Vaidya-Kayastha marriage in all parts of the country, to universalise the use of the sacred thread among all sections of the community, to cut down the number of surnames, especially those which were regarded as not so respectable, to claim Brahmanhood by assuming the surname of Sharma, to wipe away the stigma attaching to some familiar sections, like the Hamvaid, and to break down the differences in social usages with a view to unify the four existing territorial divisions or samajas.[186] It may be mentioned that Vaidya-Kayastha marriage was never a regular phenomenon in Bengal except in three districts of Eastern Bengal-Assam, viz. Noakhali, Coomilla and Sylhet.

During the early period of its rule, the Britishers did not take any measure which might be construed as a confrontation with the caste-based Hindu society and wound the susceptability of the caste-conscious Hindus. But as the days rolled by, the administrative compulsions and conveniences, pressure of Hindu social reformers, need of following a "Divide and Rule" policy to keep at bay different segments of Indian population for prolongation of its rule at any cost had its manifestation in the different policies adopted by the Britishers in different fields like education, economic, occupation, communication and legislative. The fallout of these policies had been the opening-up of the closed Hindu society as well as the hardening of the caste rigidity in the stratified Hindu society. Opening of door of education to all sections of people irrespective of caste, creed and religion, introduction of Western system of education, collapse of village economy and village-based industry, urbanisation and industrialisation, establishment of a network of communication like Railways and Roadways, enactment of social legislation like prohibition of widow-burning, child-marriage, conferment of limited franchise, introduction of local-self government and the like hastened the process of social mobility and lessened caste rigidity and social distance between different caste groups. All these measures conjointly had the effect of disintegrating the caste-based Hindu society, at least in urban areas, and of initiating the process of transition from a caste-based society to a class-based society.

But the Britishers had something else in view. With the gradual rise in nationalism in India, the British had begun to be aware that, sooner or later, they would be obliged to concede political responsibility, even freedom to India. Their whole effort from 1906 onwards therefore was concentrated on delaying tactics; first by denying a parliamentary form of government in India, and secondly, as if to make this denial doubly sure, by falling back on the well-tried method of dividing the nationalist forces to stave off the day of Indian freedom as long as possible. By delaying a settlement, everytime the British Rulers saw to it that India remained firmly in their hands, while, with their support and encouragement, the disruptive forces within India grew in strength and numbers.[187]

As India became restive for attaining independence and people, irrespective of caste, creed or religion joined the freedom movement, Britishers ruthlessly pursued its policy of breaking the solidarity and integrity of the Indian people by whipping up the disintegrating tendencies inherent in our body politic. We have already seen how they succeeded in dividing the people on the basis of religion, region and language*. Similarly, they pursued the policy of dividing the Hindu society on the basis of caste. The efforts of India's

---

* Please see *Communalism and Constitution* and *Disintegration and Constitution* by the author.

colonial rulers and its pro-colonial elements were to use this unique feature of Indian society to divide the Indian people, to use caste against their growing political unity. "Not the colonial system but 'other' Indians, the upper castes, were regarded as holding back the progress of Indians belonging to the lower or intermediate castes. In western and south India, the Brahmins were said to be garnering, through careful manipulation, all the benefits of British rule. In Punjab, non-agricultural castes were held to be primarily responsible for the poverty of the peasants. As soon as the national movement entered the phase of mass struggle in 1905, the colonial administrators, ideologues and publicists began to portray it as a Brahmin and upper caste movement whose objective was to substitute the benevolent British rule by tyrannical upper caste rule. The fact that Ranade, Gokhale, Tilak, Aurobindo Ghosh, Lajpat Rai, Mahatma Gandhi, C.R. Das, Motilal and Jawaharlal Nehru, Sardar Patel, Dr. C. Rajagopalachari and Subhash Chandra Ghosh were upper caste by birth was held out as proof of the colonial theory of the upper caste character of the national movement. Similarly, the in-famous Rowlatt Committee Report emphasised the *bhadralok* character of the revolutionary terrorists of Bengal. Interestingly, the genesis of another popular idea of the Mandalist also came from colonial administrators and statesmen: Unite Muslims and other religious minorities, scheduled castes and backward castes against the upper castes. It was with this 'revolutionary' strategy that Churchill hoped to meet the challenge of the national movement."[188]

The Britishers thus not only suceeded in reversing the integrative processes set in motion by our religious saints, social reformers and by the so-called lower caste people themselves, as we have seen in the preceding paragraphs, but also reversed the effects of their own policies, mentioned earlier, which had a salutary effect on loosening caste barriers and caste distinctions. The policy of separate electorate, quota in service, educational institutions, scholarships, etc., purely on the basis of caste; enumeration of people on the basis of caste, sub-caste and occupation made the people conscious of their caste identity and hardened caste-barrier. So while the caste structure was being systematically disintegrated, consciously or unconsciously, the policy of differentiation on the basis of caste for extending various economic and political benefits in the name of abolition of caste-barrier and caste-rigidity, not only stratified the Hindu society beyond redemption but also gave rise to caste conflicts and caste tensions which have become a permanent feature in our social and political life. As the Britishers had ruthlessly pursued its policy of dividing the Indian people on the basis of religion, region, language and culture, so also they pursued the policy of dividing the Hindus on the basis of caste, so that the disintegrating tendencies set in motion by the Britishers would not allow the Indians to integrate themselves even when the Britishers had left India for good. That their policy had paid dividends need no further proof.

Notes and References

1. Davis, Kingsley, *Human Society*, p. 337, quoted by Mahesh H. Dave in *Dynamics of Reservation Policy*, ed. Haroobhai Mehta and Hasmukh Patel, Patriot Publishers, New Delhi, 1985, p. 62.
2. Sovani, *op. cit.*, p. 275.
3. Bateille, Castes : Old and New, *op. cit.*, p. 23.
4. Ghurye, *op. cit.*, pp. 159-60.
5. *Backward Classes Commission Report*, 1980, (Chairman, B.P. Mondal), pp. 14-16.
6. Majumdar and Madan, *op. cit.*, p. 237.
7. Hutton, *op. cit.*, p. 112.
8. *Ibid.*, p. 114.
9. *Ibid.*
10. *Report of the First Backward Classes Commission*, 1955, para 33, p. 20.
11. Hutton, *op. cit.*, p. 119.
12. *Ibid.*, p. 115.
13. *Report of the First Backward Classes Commission*, para 11, p. 15.

14. Nehru, Jawaharlal, *The Discovery of India*, Second Edition, Signet Press, Calcutta, 1946, p. 9.
15. Sherring, M.A., *Hindu Tribes and Castes*, III, Calcutta, 1881, p. 274, quoted by Hutton, *op. cit.*, p. 115.
16. Gilbert, W.H., *Peoples of India*, Washington, 1944, p. 82, quoted by Hutton, *Ibid.*, p. 120.
17. Hutton, *Ibid.*, pp. 120-21.
18. *Report of the First Backward Classes Commission*, para 11, p. 15.
19. Pillai, G.K., *op. cit.*, p. 212.
20. Basham, A.L., *The Wonder that was India*, London, 1954, p. 151.
21. Dubois, Abbe, *A Description of the People of India*, 1817, Pt. I, Ch. II, quoted by Hutton, *op. cit.*, p. 126.
22. Hill, S.C., *Origin of the Caste System in India*, XIII, I.A. March-October, 1931, quoted by Hutton, *Ibid.*, p. 120.
23. Majumdar and Madan, *op. cit.*, p. 238.
24. Hutton, *op. cit.*, p. 121.
25. Majumdar and Madan, *op. cit.*, p. 238.
26. Hutton, *op. cit.*, p. 131.
27. Sedgwick, L.J., *Report on the Census of Bombay Presidency* (Vol. VIII of Census of India, 1921), Bombay, 1922, p.103, quoted by Hutton, *Ibid.*, pp. 131-32.
28. Hutton, *Ibid.*, p. 130.
29. Rao, V.R.K.V., *Some Thoughts on Social Change in India*, In : Dimensions of Social Change in India, ed., by M.N. Srinivas, S. Seshaish and V.S. Parthasarathy, Allied Publishers, 1977, p. 21.
30. Majumdar, R.C., *Evolution of Religio-Philosophic Culture in India* In: *The Cultural Heritage of India*, Vol. IV, The Ramakrishna Mission Institute of Culture, Calcutta, 1956, p. 39.
31. Fick, R., *Social Organization in North-East India in Buddha's Time*, 1920, pp. 19-20, 28-30.
32. Ghurye, *op. cit.*, p. 70.
33. Fick, *op. cit.*, pp. 220-21.
34. *Ibid.*, p. 209.
35. Ghurye, *op. cit.*, p. 72.
36. Fick., *op. cit.*, p. 32.
37. Quoted by Ghurye, *op. cit.*, p. 72.
38. Ghurye, *Ibid.*, p. 72.
39. Das, Bhagwan, *Introduction to the Cultural Heritage of India*, Vol. IV, *op. cit.*, p. 11.
40. Majumdar, R.C., *op.*, *cit.*, p. 48.
41. *Ibid.*, pp. 48-49.
42. Banerjea, Jitendra Nath, *Cult-Syncretism*, In : *The Cultural Heritage of India*, *Ibid.*, p. 330.
43. Majumdar, R.C., Roy Chodhury, H.C. and Datta, K., *An Advanced History of India*, London, 1963, p. 8.

44. Bhagwata Gita, IX. 14.21.
45. *Ibid.*, V.I. 35.
46. Sen, Kshitimohan, *The Mediaeval Mystics of North India*, In : The Cultural Heritage of India, *op. cit.*, p. 383.
47. Sharma, B.N.K., *The Vaisanava Saints of Karnataka*, In : *Ibid.*, p. 352.
48. Pillai, S. Satchidanandam, *The Saiva Saints of South India*, In : *Ibid.*, pp. 345-47.
49. Sen, Kshitimohan, *op. cit.*, p. 390.
50. *Ibid.*, p. 391
51. *Ibid.*, p. 393.
52. *Ibid.*, p. 394.
53. *Ibid.*, p. 385.
54. *Ibid.*, p. 391.
55. Nath, Raj Mohan, *Sankara Deva and the Vaisanava Movement in Assam*, In : *Ibid.*, p. 203.
56. Fuchs, Stephen, *Rebellious Prophets*, Asia Publishing House, 1965, p. 131.
57. Majumdar, R.C., In : *The Cultural Heritage of India, op. cit.*, p. 51.
58. Parvathamma, C., *Religion and Social Change : A Study of Tradition and Change in Virasaivism.* In : Dimensions of Social Change in India, *op. cit.*, p. 245.
59. Manor, James, *The Evolution of Political Arenas and Units of Social Organization* : The Lingayats and Okkaligas of Princely Mysore, In: *Ibid.*, p. 175.
60. *Ibid.*
61. Parvathamma, C., *op. cit.*, p. 246.
62. Manor, *op. cit.*, p. 176.
63. Sadasivaiah, H.M., *A Comparative Study of Two Virasaiva Monastries: A Study in Sociology of Religion, Prasaranga*, Mysore, 1967, pp. 64-66.
64. Sen, Sukumar, *The Nath Cult*, In : The Cultural Heritage of India, *op. cit.*, p. 281.
65. *Ibid.*, p. 286.
66. *Ibid.*, p. 280.
67. *Ibid.*, p. 281.
68. Sen, Kshitimohan, In : *Ibid.*, p. 388.
69. Singh, Teja, *The Religion of the Sikh Gurus*, In : The Cultural Heritage of India, *Ibid.*, pp. 324-25.
70. Majumdar, R.C., *op. cit.*, p. 62.
71. Nag, Kalidas, The Brahmo Samaj, In : *Ibid.*, p. 627.
72. *Ibid.*, p. 654.
73. *Ibid.*, p. 628.
74. *Ibid.*
75. *Ibid.*, p. 631.

76. Coondo, R., *Dr. Ambedkar, the Iconoclast*, In : *Dr. Ambedkar, Pioneer of Human Rights*, Bodhisattva Publication, New Delhi, 1977, p. 46.
77. Pandit Champuti, *The Arya Samaj*, In : The Cultural Heritage of India, *op. cit.*, pp. 635-37.
78. Jinarajadas, C., *What Theosophists Believe*, In : *Ibid.*, p. 655.
79. *Ibid.*, pp. 648-649.
80. Majumdar, R.C., In : *Ibid.*, p. 62.
81. Ghurye, *op. cit.*, p. 92.
82. Kabir, Humayun, *Islam in India*, In : The Cultural Heritage of India, *op. cit.*, p. 579.
83. T.W. Arnold, Murray Titmus, Aziz Ahmad held this view.
84. Ketkar, *op. cit.*, p. 30.
85. Lal, K.S., *Indian Muslims, Who are They?* Voice of India, 1990, pp. 114-22.
86. Manucci, Niccolao, *Storia do Mogor*, English translation by W. Irvine, John Murray, London, 1906, Vol. III, p. 173, also II, p. 238.
87. Lal, *op. cit.*, pp. 90-102.
88. Kabir, *op. cit.*, p. 582.
89. Hasan, S. Nurul, *Caste System in Medieval Muslim Society*, *The Telegraph*, April 1, 1991.
90. Kabir, *op. cit.*, p. 582.
91. Majumdar, R.C., *Ibid.*, p. 61.
92. Kabir, *Ibid.*, p. 589.
93. *Ibid.*
94. Abraham, Rev. C.E., *The Rise and Growth of Christianity in India*, In : *Ibid.*, p. 569.
95. Farquhar, J.N., *Modern Religious Movements in India*, Lahore, 1943, pp. 433 and 436 quoted by Abraham, *Ibid.*, p. 569.
96. *Encyclopaedia of Religion and Ethics*, First Edition, Edinburgh, II, p. 550, quoted by Abraham, *Ibid.*, p. 558.
97. Abraham, *Ibid.*, p. 558.
98. Macnicol, Dr. N., *Indian Theism*, Oxford University Press, 1915, quoted by Abraham, *Ibid.*, p. 558.
99. Nehru, Jawaharlal, *op. cit.*, p. 337.
100. *Ibid.*, p. 376.
101. Abraham, *op. cit.*, p. 557.
102. Sirsikar V.M., Use in politics, *Seminar*, No. 70, p. 27.
103. Fick, *op. cit.*, p. 32.
104. Farquhar, J.N., *Outline of the Religous Literature of India*, (1920), pp. 244-45, quoted by Ghurye, *op. cit.*, p. 105.
105. Kumaraswamiji, Virasaivism, In : *Ibid.*, p. 99.
106. Sharma, B.N., *op. cit.*, p. 75.
107. Sachau, II, *op. cit.*, p. 157.
108. Ghurye, *op. cit.*, p. 105.

109. Singh, Teja, *The Religion of the Sikh Gurus*, In : The Cultural Heritage of India, *op. cit.*, p. 319.
110. Hutton, *op. cit.*, pp. 117-18.
111. Sen, Sukumar, *The Nath Cult*, In : The Cultural Heritage of India, *op. cit.*, pp. 280-81.
112. Ghose, Benoy, *Iswar Chandra Vidyasagar*, Builders of Modern India, Ministry of Information and Broadcasting, Government of India, 1971, p. 12.
113. *Ibid.*
114. Ramkamal Sen in his preface to the English-Bengali Dictionary, 1834, quoted by Ghose, *Ibid.*, p. 2.
115. Gopalaswamy, Prof. K.V., *Brahmarshi Raghupati Venkatratnam Naidu Guru, Moral and Social Reformer—Life and Times*, In : *Great Indian Social Reformers and Philanthropists*, ed. Prof. G.V.L.N. Sarma, Sri A.S. Chetti Sanmana Sangham, Narsapur, Andhra Pradesh, 1975, p. 65.
116. Mokkapati, Shivajee, *Justice Mahadeo Govind Ranade*, In : *Ibid.*, p. 85.
117. Ghose, *op. cit.*, p. 80.
118. Sriramamurti, Dr. P., *Sri Kandukuri Veeresalingam Pantulu*, In : Great Indian Social Reformers and Philanthropists, *op. cit.*, pp. 44-45.
119. Gopalaswamy, In : *Ibid.*, p. 71.
120. Tekur, S.M., *Bharat Ratna Sir Mokshagundam Visvesvarva*, In : *Ibid.*, p. 61.
121. Mokhapati, In : *Ibid.*, pp. 85-86.
122. Majumdar, R.C., *History and Culture of the Indian People*, Vol. X, Part II, Bharatiya Vidya Bhavan, pp. 260-61.
Prof. M. Venkatarangiya, *Foreward*, In : Great Indian Social Reformers and Philanthropists, *op. cit.*, p. III, Gopalaswami, *Ibid.*, p. 67.
Galantar, Marc, Competing Equalities, Oxford University Press, 1984, p. 22.
123. Gopalaswami, *op. cit.*, p. 67.
124. Prof. Venkatarangiya, *op. cit.*, p. III.
125. Mokkapati, *op. cit.*, p. 84.
126. Ghose, *op. cit.*, p. 31.
127. Tekur, Great Indian Social Reformers and Philanthropists, *op. cit.*, pp. 58-60
128. Sriramamurti, *Ibid.*, p. 47.
129. Gopalaswamy, *Ibid.*, p. 75.
130. Mokkapati, In : *Ibid.*, pp. 84-85.
131. Ghurye, *op. cit.*, p. 325.
132. Shinde, V.R., *The Problem of Untouchability*, (in Marathi), pp. 56-90, quoted by Ghurye, *Ibid.*, pp. 325-26.

133. Swami Nirvedananda, *Sri Ramakrishna and Spiritual Renaissance*, In : The Cultural Heritage of India, *op. cit.*, pp. 705, 717, 719.
134. *The Complete Works of Swami Vivekananda*, Advaita Ashram, Calcutta, 1990, Vol. III, pp. 245-46.
135. *Ibid.*, Vol. VII, p. 108.
136. *Ibid.*, p. 372.
137. *Ibid.*
138. *Ibid.*, pp. 148-49.
139. *Ibid.*, Vol. IV, p. 480.
140. *Ibid.*, Vol. VII, p. 150.
141. *Ibid.*, Vol. III, p. 193.
142. Risley : The Tribes and Castes of Bengal, op. cit., pp. XVI-XVIII.
143. Majumdar, D.N., *op. cit.*, p. 358.
144. Ketkar, *op. cit.*, p. 100.
145. Dutt, N.K., *op. cit.*, Vol. II, pp. 119-20.
146. *Ibid.*, pp. 122-23.
147. *Ibid.*, p. 124.
148. *Ibid.*
149. *Ibid.*, p. 135.
150. Rao, M.S.A., *Tradition, Rationality and Change*, (Essays in sociology of Economic Development and social change), Popular Prakashan, Bombay, 1972, pp. 75-87.

     Jain, Meenakshi, Establishing Yadav Raj, *Indian Express*, October, 30, 1990.
151. Dutt, N.K., *op. cit.*, Vol.II, pp. 136-38.
152. *Census Report, 1931, Bengal* I, p. 474, quoted by Dutt, *Ibid.*, p. 138.
153. Fuchs, *op. cit.*, p. 287.
154. *Ibid.*, p. 288.
155. *Ibid.*, pp. 28-29, 34.
156. *Ibid.*, pp. 40-42.
157. *Ibid.*, pp. 42-45.
158. *Ibid.*, p. 99.
159. Sen, Kshitimohan, *op. cit.*, p. 390.
160. Fuchs, *op. cit.*, p. 101.
161. *Ibid.*, pp. 104-5.
162. Ghurye, *op. cit.*, p. 322.
163. Risley : *The Tribes and Castes of Bengal, op. cit.*, p. XV.
164. *Asiatic Studies*, p. 102, quoted by Risley, *Ibid.*, p. XV.
165. Srinivas, M.N., *Sanskritization and Westernization*, In : *Society in India*, edited by Ayappan and Rathnam, SSA Publications, pp. 90-91.
166. *Ibid.*
167. Srinivas, *Social Change in Modern India*, *op. cit.*, p. 6.
168. Srinivas, M.N., *Religion and Society among the Coorgs of South India*, Clarendon, London, 1952, p. 30.

168. Srinivas, *Social Change in Modern India, op. cit.*, p. 7.
170. *Ibid.*, pp. 20-22.
171. Bandopadhaya, Suraj, *Caste Lost and Caste Regained : Some Aspects of Empirical Research on Village India*, In : Dimensions of Social Change in India, *op. cit.*, p. 119.
172. Srinivas, *Social Change in Modern India, op. cit.*, p. 7.
173. Gould, Harold A., *Sanskritization and Westernisation, A Dynamic View, The Economic Weekly*, June 24, 1961, p. 945.
174. Bailey, F.G., *Tribe, Caste and Nation*, Oxford University Press, 1960, p. 188.
175. Rao, V.K.R.V., *op. cit.*, p. 26.
176. Bailey, F.G., *Caste and the Economic Frontier, A Village in Highland Orissa*, Manchester Univ. Press 1957, Chapter IX.
177. Sachidananda, *The Harijan Elite*, Thomson Press (India) Limited, 1977, p. 141.
178. Bandopadhaya, Suraj, *op. cit.*, p. 128.
179. Bailey, *Tribe, Caste and Nation, op. cit.*, p. 189.
180. Bose, Nirmal Kumar, Some Aspects of Caste in Bengal, *Journal of American Folklore*, LXXI (July-Sept. 1958), pp. 405-6.
181. Srinivas, *Social Change in Modern India, op. cit.*, p. 97. For other examples, see Basham, *op. cit.*, pp. 145-46, 148; Adrian C. Mayer, *Caste and Kinship in Central India*, Berkeley, 1960, pp. 47-49; Eric, J.Miller, Caste and Territory in Malabar, *American Anthropologist LVI*, June, 1954, pp. 410-20.
182. *Census of Bengal*, 1911, pp. 442-43.
183. Saberwal, Satish, *States and Entrepreneurship : The Ramgharia Case*, In : *Dimensions of Social Change in India, op. cit.*, pp. 156-58.
184. Manor, *op. cit.*, pp. 172-73.
185. Srinivas, *Social Change in Modern India, op. cit.*, p. 7.
186. Dutt, N.K., *op. cit.*, Vol. II, pp. 76-77.
187. Sinha, Sasadhar, *Indian Independence in Perspective*, Asia Publishing House, Bombay, 1964, pp. 25 and 46.
188. Chandra, Bipan, *The struggle against caste and casteism, The Telegraph*, May 14, 1991.

3

Effects of British Rule on the Caste System—I

The British brought with them a casteless culture and a literature full of thoughts on individual liberty. As prudent foreigners wishing to consolidate their power over a strange land and people they decided to leave the peculiar institution of caste entirely alone except when it egregiously violated their cherished ideas of government. Uncertain of their position, the Britishers, like other invaders of India, adopted a policy of non-intervention in the religious observances and social institutions of the people. They recognised the integrity of caste organization and held that social privileges of the membership of a caste were to be wholly within the jurisdiction of the caste.[1] This was more or less their avowed policy till the first war of independence in 1857. The Rising opened the eyes of the administrators of the country as well as of the students of British Indian history to the potentialities of caste. It was almost the unanimous opinion of persons connected with the Government of India that the deep causes of the Rising were to be found in the fact that the Bengal Army was composed largely of the higher castes, viz. the Brahmins and the Rajputs. The lesson of the Rising, viz. that the safety of the British domination in India was very closely connected with keeping the Indian people divided on the lines of caste, was driven home to the British rulers. Some officials like Sir Lepel Griffin thought that caste was useful in preventing rebellion,[2] while James Kerr, the Principal of the Hindu College at Calcutta, commented in 1865 as follows: "It may be doubted if the existence of caste is on the whole unfavourable to the permanence of our rule. It may even be considered favourably to it, provided we act with prudence and forbearance. Its spirit is opposed to national union."[3] The maxim of 'divide and rule' began to be preached by historians and journalists alike.[4] Major-General H.T. Tucker, while giving evidence before the Special Commission presided over by Lord Peel, which was appointed to suggest a reorganisation of the Indian Army after the Rising of 1857, insisted on the necessity of keeping the country under British domination through the policy of dividing and separating into distinct bodies the nationalities and castes recruited to the Army.[5] Because the Rising was largely the work of soldiers of the high castes of Brahmins and Rajputs, there was a clamour in England that the high-caste sepoys should be removed. Suspicion on high castes, therefore, dates from the Rising. The valuable lesson so dearly acquired was not going to be lost. It being repeated in the form of the general principle of 'divide and rule' could not have failed to influence the policy and conduct of later officials.[6] It is perhaps no coincidence that in the post-Rising period a large number of British intellectuals, most of them being members of the Indian Civil Service, conducted studies of the various caste groups in different parts of the country. But for these studies, which provided a wealth of data on the life, customs, manners and religious beliefs of different castes, our knowledge about them would not have been complete. It is, however, a matter of debate whether these intellectuals were solely inspired by their intellectual curiosity or were guided by their administrative zeal to tighten the grip of the British rule in India, in particular to, find out about "the impact of Hinduism on the perpetuation of the ritual imbalances in the Indian caste system, the relation between clean castes and scheduled castes, and scheduled caste occupation, scheduled castes and Hindu religion, etc. The valuable ethnographical data available through the curiosity of British officials, the gazetteers, the reports on castes and tribes, the settlement reports, the learned journals, and the decennial censuses, etc., only provided to increase fissiparous tendencies in Indian society"[7] on the basis of caste.

Since then, the Briuishers pursued a dual policy—the policy of disintegration of the traditional Hindu caste system so that the institution of caste which has always been an important factor in the country's economic life and structure, trade, commerce and industry cannot be a centre of power in the changed governmental setup, and the policy of consolidation of caste system, that too, in the way they wished. This apparent contradictory approach was the outcome of a very well-conceived policy. Thus their policy of non-interference in caste matters changed in the second half of the nineteenth century, specially after the Rising, to a policy of active interference in caste matters so that the traditional hierarchical organization of caste became almost irrelevant. This policy was given a new orientation in the twentieth century, when the demand for independence gained momentum, to widening the existing cleavages and fostering separatism and new alignments in the hierarchy so that they could perpetuate their rule by dividing and sub-dividing the Hindus on the basis of caste as well. Thus, there was disintegration as well as crystallization of the caste system, displacement of caste as a unit of administration of justice as well as livening up of the caste spirit, loosening of caste bondage and hardening of caste solidarity, upward mobility of caste as well as downward mobility of caste and above all, groupings of certain castes at the dictation of government. Like the earlier Hindu kings, they assumed the 'power to raise and lower castes'[8] and also took upon themselves the responsibility of upholding the institution with the help of their civil power, and became the ardent champion of the very system which they deplored earlier, simply because it suited their very objective of prolongation of their rule by following the 'Divide and Rule' policy. Like any other predatory conquests where the ruling class was different from the people it ruled, the British rulers had to ensure that they were not outmaneuvered by any force inimical to their rule like the institution of caste which had always sprang into action in times of unstable political condition. They not only neutralised the caste as a potent weapon in power struggle but, on the other hand, nursed it as a powerful instrument of fission by creating new alignments and new loyalties and by opening new areas of conflict.

The impact of British rule on the traditional Indian caste system was broadly as follows:—

(1) The rigidity and orthodoxy of the caste hierarchy started breaking down, and at the same time, an all-round hardening of the system ensued.

(2) The process of upward social mobility not only suffered a severe jolt but actually a downward mobility ensued.

(3) Separatism and conflict became a permanent feature of the Hindu society.

(4) Caste became a tool in the political, religious and cultural battles that the Hindus fought amongst themselves.

Thus whatever measures they initiated in their 200-year rule, especially after the 1857 war of independence, in administrative, legislative, economic, educational and above all, in political fields, were aimed at achieving those objectives. The British Government assiduously 'nursed, rather than ignored, the spirit of caste'[9] in their actions and policies enunciated during this period.

Caste : Loosening of its Hold

Though the British Government recognised the integrity of caste for internal affairs, that did not protect the institution from inroads on some of its very vital powers. At first the British authorities wanted to sustain traditional Hindu and Muslim laws. After 1864 a new policy was adopted and the

British courts, administering a uniform criminal law, removed from the purview of caste many matters that used to be erstwhile adjudicated by it. Questions of assault, adultery, rape, and the like were taken before the British courts for decision, and the caste councils in proportion lost their former importance. Even in matters of civil law, such as marriage, divorce, etc., though the avowed intention of the British was to be guided by the caste-customs slowly but surely various decisions of the High Courts practically set aside the authority of caste.[10]

The hereditary and prescriptive right of the Brahmins to act as priests to all castes of the Hindus, with only a few exceptions, has been the one uniform and general principle inhering in caste-society through all its vicissitudes. But certain decisions of the High Courts have, however, emboldened the non-Brahmanic castes to dislodge the Brahmins from their monopoly of priesthood. In Bengal and in North India generally it is now settled that there is no office of priest recognised as such in law, and a householder may employ anyone he likes for the performance of any priestly service and pay the fees to him. A similar view has been taken in the Madras Presidency.[11] When in the Maratha country the non-Brahmin reformists started the practice of performing their religious rites without the aid of the Brahmin priests, the latter lodged a complaint asking for an injunction against the persons so violating their rights. The High Court of Bombay decreed that people could engage any priest they liked, and were not at all bound to call for the services of the hereditary priest; but unlike the High Court of Madras, they decreed that the hereditary priest must be paid some fees by way of compensation.[12] Ghurye, therefore, comments that this opens the way to the dissolution of the only bond holding together the diverse castes, viz. the employment of common priesthood.[13]

The Caste Disabilities Removal Act of 1850 dealt another blow at the integrity of caste. The Act does not, as may be expected from its title, remove civil disabilities existing between caste and caste but facilitates conversion to another religion or admission into another caste. Notwithstanding any custom of caste disinheriting a person for change of caste or religion, this Act provides that a person does not forfeit his ordinary rights of property by loss of caste or change of religion.[14]

Caste panchayats lost power. The Census Report of 1931 noted that, with the right to appeal to a court against them, "the power of the caste panchayats has thus greatly weakened in the last few decades and is now almost extinct. If a panchayat decreed a fine or penalty in the past, it could enforce its decision. In case the offender was recalcitrant it could prevent his intercourse with the community without fear of itself getting into trouble. Now such a recalcitrant member can file a suit in the civil court against the members of a panchayat or prosecute them for defaming him."[15]

Regarding the most important aspect, and almost the only surviving one, viz. that the prohibition against marriage outside the caste, the Special Marriage Act of 1872 made it possible for an Indian of whatever caste or creed to enter into a valid marriage with a person belonging to any caste or creed, provided the parties registered the contract of marriage, declaring, inter alia, that they did not belong to any religion. The clause requiring the solemn renunciation of caste and religion by the parties to a civil marriage was considered a great hardship and a moral dilemma by all progressive elements in the country. The Special Marriage Amendment Act of 1923 removed this hardship and persons marrying under the provisions of this Act, to whatever caste they may belong, are not required to renounce their religion in declaration but have to forfeit certain of their personal rights as Hindus. They cannot adopt. On their marriage they cease to be the members of the joint family to which they previously belonged. Whatever rights in the property of the family would have accrued to them by surviorship under the Hindu Law cease. As regards their own property they will be governed by the Indian Succession Act and not by the Hindu Law.[16]

Census : An Instrument of Hardening Caste Distinctions

Another aspect of British Administration which merit special attention is the census operations. When Lord Mayo organised the first population census in India in 1871, it was perhaps beyond his comprehension that the later British Administrators would make such a pernicious and malevolent use of caste in the census operations in pursuance of the 'Divide and Rule' policy. The largest single enquiry carried on regularly every ten years in our land covering every human life was too much of a temptation and opportunity to be brushed aside to unravel the niceties of a system so peculiar and strange to this country. What began primarily as a study to whet the 'intellectual curiosity among the more intelligent of the Britishers in India',[17] became, in course of time, a potent weapon in the hands of the British Administrators in dividing and subdividing the people on the basis of caste and in creating new alignments and new loyalties.

Plowden, as Census Commissioner of 1881 recommended that lists of castes and occupations should be prepared for each district. "A census now was tied to the apron-strings of castes and tribes and looking back on these censuses it is possible to argue that caste and tribe were indeed overdone."[18] From 1891 onwards Census Superintendents adopted the easier method of utilizing the decennial census for collecting and presenting the information and indulging in the theories of the origins of caste.[19] This procedure reached its culmination in the Census of 1901 under the guidance of Sir Herbert Risley. With a view to helping "us towards presenting an intelligible picture of the social grouping of that large proportion of the people of India which is organized, admittedly or tacitly, on the basis of caste" the Census Commissioner changed the classification of 1891 into one based on "social precedence as recognized by the native public opinion at the present day and manifesting itself in the facts that particular castes are supposed to be the modern representatives of one or other of the castes of the theoretical Hindu system." And this procedure Risley chose in spite of his clear admission that even in this caste-ridden society a person, when questioned about his caste, may offer a bewildering variety of replies: "He may give the name of a sect, of a sub-caste, of an exogamous sect or section, of a hypergamous group; he may mention some titular designation which sounds finer than the name of his caste; he may describe himself by his occupation or by the province or tract of country from which he comes."[20] Risley distinguished the castes into seven groups upon an elaborate classification. The first group contained Brahmans only as the acknowledged superiors of all other classes. In the second group were placed castes whose respectability was never in question and who are either twice-born or were held to be superior to all other Sudra castes. The third group consisted of the so-called Navasakh or nine branches all characterised to offer water the drinking of which would not pollute the higher classes. The fourth group contained clean castes with degraded Brahmans. The fifth contained castes lower than group four whose water is not usually accepted. The sixth comprised of low castes abstaining from beef, pork, and fowls, and the seventh embracing castes by whom forbidden foods were eaten and who pursued the most degraded occupations as scavengers, etc. Risley's attempt to draw up a list of castes according to their rank in society sowed the dragon's teeth of "depressed" and "scheduled" tribes and castes and left a most troublesome legacy and a vast field of political and social manoeuvring, and as Hutton remarks, "all the subsequent census officers in India have cursed the day when it occurred to Sir Herbert Risley to make the attempt."[21] Risley became, as Ashok Mitra, as Census Superintendent of West Bengal in 1951 puts it, "our modern Ballala Sen".[22]

Various ambitious castes quickly perceived the chance of raising their status. They invited conferences of their members, and formed councils to take steps to see that their status was recorded in the way they thought was honourable to them. Other castes that could not but resent this 'stealthy' procedure to advance, equally eagerly began to controvert their claims. Thus a campaign of mutual recrimination was set on foot.[23] "The leaders of all but the highest castes frankly looked upon the Census as an opportunity for pressing and perhaps obtaining some recognition of social claims which were denied by persons of castes higher than their own."[24] It provided an opportunity to castes to assert their claims for upward position in traditional hierarchy. This turned out to be "the equivalent of the traditional copper-plate grants of Indian Kings declaring the status, rank and privileges of a particular caste or castes."[25] In 1911 the Census-reporter for Madras wrote the following: "It has been pointed out to me by an Indian gentleman that the last few years, and especially the occasion of the present census, have witnessed an extraordinary revival of the caste spirit in certain aspects. For numerous caste "Shabhas" have sprung up, each keen to assert the dignity of the social group which it represents."[26]

The tendency on the part of castes to claim to be recorded in the census as a high caste increased as the years went by, and more and more people became aware of the existence of a new and government-sponsored channel of caste mobility. O 'Malley has recorded that at the time of the 1911 census operations, "there was a general idea in Bengal that the object of the census is not to show the number of persons belonging to each caste, but to fix the relative position of different castes and to deal with questions of social superiority. The feeling on the subject is largely the result of castes having been classified in the last census report in order of social precedence. This warrant of precedence gave rise to a considerable agitation when the census operations were instituted in 1911. Hundreds of petitions were received from different castes—their weight alone amounts to one and a half maunds—requesting that they might be known by a new name, be placed higher up in the order of precedence, be recognized as Kshatriya and Vaishya, etc. Many castes were aggrieved at the position assigned to them, and complained that it lowered them in public estimation."[27]

The method of making a claim was more or less stereotyped. The occupation, style of life, or name of the caste group would be mentioned in support of the claim. The similarity of caste name to the historical name of a respectable caste or tribe would be pointed out; the myth regarding the origin of the caste would be described, and its linkage with an epic hero, or divine or semidivine figure, would be stressed. Thus the Hunters (Bedas) of Mysore would claim kinship with Valmiki, the putative author of the epic Raṃayana about whom there is a legend that he was a hunter; and similarly the Shepherds (Kurubas) link their caste history with the name of the great Sanskrit poet and playwright, Kalidasa, who is believed to have been a shepherd by caste. Reference would also be made to the sacred literature of the Hindus and a few Sanskrit quotations thrown in to add strength to the claim. In Uttar Pradesh the ambitious claimants were able to find obliging Brahmin pandits who provided *vyasthas* or rulings to the effect that the caste in question was indeed a high one. The ruling was usually followed by citation of "evidence" of the kind mentioned above.[28]

Caste statistics became a nightmare to census officials more so because the return of caste, tribe or race, excited the only interest aroused by the census in the general public. The attempt to use the census to freeze the rank of castes had the opposite effect of stimulating mobility, and also increased intercaste rivalry. It is small wonder then, that nationalist Indians began to regard the recording of caste at the census as yet another manifestation of a sinister design on the part of the Imperialist British to keep alive if not to exacerbate the numerous divisions already present in Indian society. Their suspicions were further strengthened by the attempt to distinguish untouchables from other Hindus in the 1911 census operations. Moreover, while the earlier census reports recorded caste divisions not only among Hindus but also among Muslims and Christians, the later reports recorded only the former; this confirmed the nationalists in their worst suspicions.[29]

Two powerful movements now became atriculate—(a) Hindus were quick to detect the seeds of disintegration in these inquiries and, determined to keep themselves united, set afoot the movement that no Hindu henceforth should return his caste; and (b) while closing their ranks, realising that strength lay also in recruitment, they employed their energies in claiming all borderline and aboriginal peoples into the Hindu fold. While response to the first was lukewarm, the second movement caught on, owing to the age-old glamour that Brahminism held over the people.[30]

In 1911 the Census Superintendents were instructed to enumerate castes and tribes classed as Hindus who did not conform to certain standards, or were subject to certain disabilities. Those castes and tribes were generally described as untouchables who came within the following categories:—

(1) who are denied access into the interior of ordinary Hindu temples;

(2) who cause pollution by (a) touch or (b) within a certain distance;

(3) who bury their dead;

(4) who eat beef and do not reverence the cow.[31]

In 1921 the Census Commissioner prepared a list of 'depressed classes' but did not himself lay down any definition for the guidance of provincial superintendents. Nor does it appear from the reports that a classification was made during that census under the ten heads prescribed in 1911.

Risley was the first to count the *Depressed Classes* (the untouchables were known then as such) and the Census of 1911 found 24% of the Hindu population in that category. In 1916, and again in 1920, the Government of India called for a report as to the moral and material conditions of the *depressed classes* and for proposals for their amelioration from all local governments.[32] In response to that inquiry, the provincial governments (except Assam and Punjab), prepared a list of classes which they considered depressed.[33] The Census Superintendents prepared a list of *depressed classes* in 1921 and 1931.

There being no criterion by which one can objectively determine a particular caste to be *depressed*, these lists differed from one another. In the most elaborate attempt to specify criteria by which to identify untouchable groups, Hutton, the 1931 Census Commissioner, proposed a series of tests which revolved around the incidence of disabilities:

(1) Whether the caste or class in question can be served by Brahmins or not.

(2) Whether the caste or class in question can be served by the barbers, water-carriers, tailors, etc., who serve the caste Hindus.

(3) Whether the caste or class in question pollutes a high-caste Hindu by contact or proximity.

(4) Whether the caste or class in question is one from whose hands a caste Hindu can take water.

(5) Whether the caste or class in question is debarred from using public conveniences, such as roads, ferries, wells or schools.

(6) Whether the caste or class in question is debarred from use of Hindu temples.

(7) Whether in ordinary social intercourse a well-educated member of the caste or class in question will be treated as an equal by the high-caste men of the same educational qualifications.

(8) Whether the caste or class in question is merely depressed on account of its own ignorance, illiteracy or poverty and but for that, would be subject to no social disability.

(9) Whether it is depressed on account of the occupation followed, and whether but for that occupation it would be subject to no social disability.[34]

The existence of multiple criteria permitted regional variation by giving the Census Superintendents scope for discretion. Each provincial superintendent was instructed to draw up his own list, taking these tests into account, "and to reckon as depressed only those castes who definitely suffer from serious social and political handicap on account of their degraded position in the Hindu social scheme."[35] The final reckoning, then, did not apply Hutton's tests pure and simple. Excluded were some castes which were theoretically untouchable but who, by virtue of prosperity and vigorous organization, "have built up for themselves a strong position which obviates the need of any special measure for their social, political or religious protection."[36] Conversely, some groups were included even though theoretically they were not untouchables.[37] For instance, the Bengal list included several criminal tribes and aboriginals and consisted of thirty-one groups.[38]

Although the provincial governments compiled a list of Depressed Classes, the Government of India refrained from any official classification until 1936 on the ground that it would be unfair to stigmatize these groups by official acknowledgement of their low status. "The fluidity of social distinctions and the efforts of the classes lowest in the scale, aided by social reformers, to improve their status make it the more desirable that Government should abstain from doing which would tend to give rigidity to these distinctions."[39]

The groups in this category were finally listed (i.e. scheduled) in 1936 by the Government of India in the

Government of India (Scheduled Castes) Order, 1936 for purposes of giving effect to the provisions for special electoral representation in the Government of India Act, 1935. According to the Government of India (Scheduled Castes) Order of 1936, read with Article 26(i) of the First Schedule to the Government of India Act of 1935, scheduled castes means "such castes, races, or tribes, or parts of or groups within castes, races or tribes, being castes, races, or tribes, or parts or groups which appear to His Majesty in Council to correspond to the classes of persons formerly known as "the depressed classes", as His Majesty in Council may specify." The list issued under this Order did not correspond exactly with any of the earlier estimates: it hewed closely to the low figures for Assam, the high figures for the United Provinces and Bihar and Orissa, and took a middle course in Bengal. In the event, the list reflected definitions of untouchability with an admixture of economic and educational tests and considerations of local politics.[40] Lelah Dushkin observed that "the authorities who made up the final list made quite a departure from the original strict criterion of untouchability...many castes listed in the North would not have been included in the South. However, whatever the criteria were, all of the castes included in the final list were socially the lowest Hindu castes in their particular provinces and they were listed partly, at least, on that basis."[41]

Things being as they are, *Depressed Classes* or *Scheduled Castes* are a matter not of definition but of enumeration. For this reason the list of *Depressed Classes* or *Scheduled Castes* and *Tribes* has varied between wide limits. That any such list must contain the so-called 'untouchables' and a number of aboriginal groups is obvious. But the essential point stands out hard and clear: a caste is *depressed* or *scheduled* according as it is *so in the opinion of the Government* and no other's. The Government alone holds the key and decides whether its economic, social, or educational status is so backward as to deserve the special protection of the Government.[42] Though the British Government by their declared policy effectively discouraged any interference in caste matters, has, in effect, assumed to itself the role of the earlier Kings and Peshwas so far as it relates to inclusion of a caste in the schedule or not.

In 1941, tabulation was made of a large number of castes at the orders of the provincial governments. In Bengal, selection was made to include (a) all scheduled castes, including Hindu members of sixteen tribes; (b) all other castes which had at any time been considered for inclusion in the schedule; (c) such other castes, as according to the Census of 1931 were found to have a strength of not less than 4 per mile of the total population of Bengal; and (d) Bauris, Agarwallas (non-Jains), Baidyas and Rajputs.[43]

The utility of caste tabulations has been questioned. Sinister motives have been attributed and it has been criticised for promoting and perpetuating separatism and fission in the Hindu society.[44] Ghurye finds it difficult to see any valid public reason for this elaborate treatment of caste in the Census Report. The conclusion is unavoidable that the intellectual curiosity of some of the early officials is mostly responsible for the treatment of caste given to it in the Census, which has become progressively elaborate in each successive Census since 1872. The total result has been a livening up of the caste-spirit.[45]

The Census provided more than sufficient incentive for the consolidation of the caste-group. Mr. Middleton, one of the two Superintendents of Census Operations of 1921, makes eloquent remarks about the effects of the British Administration on caste in the Punjab. He observes: "I had intended pointing out that there is a very wide revolt against the classification of occupational castes; that these castes have been largely manufactured and almost entirely preserved as separate castes by the British Government. Our land records and official documents have added iron bonds to the old rigidity of caste. Caste in itself was rigid among higher castes, but malleable amongst the lower. We pigeonholed every one by caste, and if we could not find a true caste for them, labelled them with the name of an hereditary occupation. We deplore the caste-system and its effects on social and economic problems, but we are largely responsible for the system which we deplore. Left to themselves such castes as Sonar and Lohar would rapidly disappear and no one would suffer...Government's passion for labels and pigeon-holes has led to a crystallization of the caste system, which, except amongst the aristocratic castes, was really very fluid under indigenous rule... If the Government would ignore caste it would gradually be replaced by something very different amongst the lower castes."[46] The process of pigeon-holing and thus stereotyping of castes set in motion by caste tabulation has, in effect, kept caste-solidarity quite intact.[47] Though Hutton repudiates the suggestion that the recording of caste at the Censuses tends to stabilise the existence of the system, it cannot be denied that the mere recording of caste is an important factor in keeping the castes, especially those in the lower rungs of the ladder, more self-conscious. Hutton himself admits that "every census gives rise to a pestiferous deluge of representations accompanied by highly problematical histories, asking for recognition of some alleged fact or hypothesis of which the Census as a department is not legally competant to judge and of which its recognition if accorded would be socially valueless. As often as not, direct action is requested against the corresponding hypothesis of other castes. The caste that desires to improve its social position seems to regard the natural attempts of others as an infringement of its own prerogatives."[48]

The political uses to which caste tabulation has been put have been many and caste has always been, in the distant as well as recent past, a powerful weapon of political and social manoeuvring in the hands of a Government, which seeks to hold a country by force and guile, to rule by dividing the people. In the hands of such a government there can be few weapons as powerful and lethal as caste. Ashoke Mitra, the Census Superintendent of West Bengal in 1951 has very rightly observed that caste has certainly been put to many startling uses in the last forty years of the British rule.[49]

In view of the public outcry against tabulation of individual castes "which were required in India partly to satisfy the theory that it was a caste-ridden country and partly to meet the needs of administrative measures dependent on caste divisions,"[50] the All-India Census undertaken in independent India in 1951 had very little to do with the tabulation of individual castes, which ultimately disappeared in 1961, though tabulation of scheduled castes and scheduled tribes only continues to be a part of the census operations.

Disruption of Old Socio-economic Order

Under British rule the old village economy which had given so much strength to social order gradually became disrupted. Their centralised administration completely shattered the old economy of the country.[51] Muslim rule created and legitimised not only new structures of power but also new bases of status which were partly independent of caste. *Zamindars*, *jagirdars*, *manasabdars* and a whole host of other categories—mixed in their caste composition—found a permanent place in Indian society. They provided new bases of status which sometimes coincided with caste and sometimes cut across it. British rule eliminated some of these categories and added others.[52] The land policy created a new class of landlords who were recruited from a variety of different castes[53] and drove millions into the ranks of tenants and agricultural labourers. The growth of inequality in the ownership of land, land transfers to non-cultivators and migration to towns are evidence of the declining of the village community as a well-knit social organization. The old leadership in the village has been losing its position and influence without substantial signs of a new leadership stepping into its place. The institution of caste has less of social incidence, but it may well be that the economic incidence of caste accentuated. In this situation conflicts of interest within the village community have sharpened and the process continues.[54] Unrestricted competition of imported goods caused the collapse of the local cottage and rural industries.[55] "It is only in the course of the last eighty years (of the British rule), with rapid and preternatural destruction of traditional skills, designs, techniques, markets and patrons, with nothing in their place to offer to castes so long employed in them who suddenly found themselves cast off their moorings, obliged to take to vocations other than their own, that caste lost whatever significance it had in the organization of production. Stripped of its functional content, caste now seemed totally pointless... Simultaneously by the destruction of markets it was possible to drive a rail into the coffin of traditional caste occupations."[56]

In the past, the traditional order possessed its own sources of flexibility. Srinivas[57] in particular has drawn attention to two such factors operative in the past, viz. the fluidity of the political system and the availability of marginal land. Both these factors enables individual castes to move up and down with the system of castes. Both these sources of flexibility became greatly reduced in scope with the establishment of British rule. The imposition of the *pax Britannica* put a restraint on political fluidity and the rapid rise in population since the end of the nineteenth century made "marginal land" increasingly scarce.[58]

Effect of Sanskritization and Westernization Process

At the same time, establishment of new industries and development of trade and commerce ushered in the period of industrialisation. New urban centres grew up which became loci of power centre in the political and economic field. Construction of a network of communication system like Railways, Roadways, combined with the development of Road and Air transport, post and telegraph, telephone and science and technology started a chain of social change in India "that is more massive and national than anything that has been witnessed in the past."[59] Industrialisation, urbanisation, western education and technical advancement are producing social changes of widespread consequences, which has been termed by the Sociologists as Westernization, a term which 'subsumes changes occurring at different levels—technology, institutions, ideology, values'.[60] Both Sanskritization and Westernization reflect the contemporary as well as historical forces of changes in social stratification. Whereas Sanskritization involves a regional, sometimes even a village-level, mobilisation of the lower castes, Westernization is an urban and upper-middle class or caste phenomenon.[61] The process of mobility amongst the upper castes was through Westernization, that is acceptance of the cultural, scientific and technological values and roles innovated in India by the British regime.[62] It brings in its wake the new behaviour pattern and new symbols of prestige.[63] This mobility was in the direction of urban areas for availing of the opportunities of modern education and what is called "service", by which is meant a job in Government, either Provincial or Central, or in modern industry, which carry with them enormous power and prestige.

V.K.R.V. Rao puts forward the idea of de-Brahminisation which stands for a process of change in which the Brahmin, a term which includes all other high castes as well, denies his own high position in the traditional social systems and moves towards acquiring for himself higher education, and well paid and prestigious jobs in the bureaucracy. The Brahmin also leads in the modern professions, social reform and industrial entrepreneurship. In some ways, de-Brahminisation is the counterpart of Sanskritization. It is for reaching a state of Brahminisation that the process of Sanskritization is directed; and now the very custodians of Brahminisation have started de-Brahminising themselves. The de-Brahminised Brahmin may no longer be a caste; but his new ways, being in tune with the forces of change, are likely not only to ensure his survival but facilitate his retaining a position of high status and authority. When the lower castes are climbing up the social ladder by the process of Sanskritization, the Brahmin is responding to this challenge to his position by de-Brahminising himself or rather Westernising himself.[64] But this process of 'de-Brahminisation' is not restricted to the 'Brahminic' castes only. Some of the forces which impel the emerging elite to attach themselves to new models operate also among the Backward classes and low castes and tribes. As far as the lower castes were concerned, Westernization became doubly desirable—it subsumed not only things valuable in themselves but something which the high castes had and they did not. To catch up with the high castes, mere Sanskritization was not enough. Thus they became more determined to obtain Western education and the fruits that only it could yield. There is a decline in the temptation among low castes for Sanskritizing their way of living. Gould observes:

> "By the time they (the low castes) reach their destination (of Sanskritization), however, they will discover that Brahman has himself vacated the spot and moved on (to) the higher hill of Westernization where he still gazes contemptuously down upon them from an elevated porch...No doubt it will be at this point that the lower castes also commences abandoning their craze for Sanskritization and then the book will have to be closed on this chapter, as the resultant new Indian society comes to grip with the problem of hierarchy."[65]

Since the importance one gains in status, power and income is much more if one gets 'Westernized', the 'non-Brahminic' castes may simply repudiate the traditional urges like 'Sanskritization' in favour of modern urges like 'Westernization' and reestablish their original non-Brahminic identity to foster solidarities and legitimise their strivings in the modernistic sectors, as in the case of the various new industrial classes. This leads to inter-caste factional politics as an avenue of social mobility.[66]

In the past, social mobility under the traditional process like Sanskritization was no doubt 'slow and gradual'[67] but it did neither give rise to any widespread discord or social upheaval nor generate conflict of wider magnitude, because it was the culmination of a natural social phenomenon and therefore was not against the system. The social mobility of castes generated through Sanskritization reflected a process of change within the system. It did not lead to a structural change or change of the system as such.[68] According to Srinivas, it marked a positional change in the ranking of caste strata.[69] The unit of mobility was generally not the individual but a caste or a sub-caste. A caste had a more or less homogeneous culture and it was difficult for an individual to change his style of life effectively in the absence of corresponding changes in his caste or kin-group.[70] It was a caste-based achievement and none could normally move up the hierarchical ladder individually outside his caste or sub-caste. Sanskritization activated a series of latent structural processes within the system of stratification. Firstly, it contributed to the collective mobilisation of the aspirations of the lower castes for status ascendancy, and secondly, it implied a reference model for the aspired—for status, usually of the dominant castes in the villages or the regions concerned.[71] Sanskritization of the 'lower castes' and 'Backward classes', therefore, provided a stabilizing influence in Indian society. It can be seen not only as an idiom of mobility but also as an important source of continuity with the past.[72] Its symbols and values are essentially those of the traditional order.[73]

Sanskritization brings about a vertical mobility whereas horizontal mobility is the result of Westernization process. Westernization, which is more dependent on income, occupation and education than on caste, affords increasing scope for individual mobility. Western education, the expansion of caste-free occupations and the possibility of geographical mobility—all enable the individual to change his style of life on his own. He is no longer tied to the apron string of caste. Shorn of his caste moorings he can look beyond caste for his own individual mobility.

Through the impacts of western education, new economic opportunity, a slowly expanding franchise, industrialisation, urbanisation, technology, changing status symbols, new and more expanded networks of relationship came into being, new criteria of self-fulfilment were created, greater awareness of individual self-interest was generated, the craving for material benefits became all-pervasive and family and migration systems underwent drastic changes.[74] This essentially induces individual mobility, which is the *sine qua non* of the very process of Westernisation. Income, occupation, education and political power and not caste become the determinant factors of one's status and prestige in the society. In his study of stratification in the South Indian village, Sripuram, Beteille finds that many spheres of life have become relatively independent of caste.[75]

Westernization process not only refers 'to the adoption by a community of western elements in dress, habits, manners and customs,'[76] but also the inculcation of the spirit of rationalism and individualism, of proclaiming supremacy of reason over faith, of individual conscience over outside authority and above all, new conceptions of social justice and political rights. "Westernization results not only in the introduction of new institutions (for example, news papers, elections, Christian Missions) but also in fundamental changes in the old institutions. Implicit in Westernization are certain value preferences. A most important value is, what may be broadly characterised as humanitarianism, by which is meant an active concern for the welfare of all human beings irrespective of caste, economic position, religion, age, and sex. Equalitarianism and secularization are both included in humanitarianism. Humanitarianism underlay many of the reforms introduced by the British in the first half of the nineteenth century in the judicial system, as well as through administrative measures."[77] Rational thinking, secular outlook, equity of all, a new economic order, a new educational and political system, scientific thought—the resultant effect of the impact of Westernization—are expected to set in motion the process of modernisation which tends to loosen the rigidity of the traditional structure and to provide greater choice to the individual in entering into impersonal relations which cut across the boundaries of the old, established groups.

The dissociation between the traditional order of caste on the one hand and class, power and other elements of status on the other, is brought about or at least attended by the emergence of differentiated institutional structures of various kinds. Chief among these are (i) the growth of a money economy in which economic relations are governed by market conditions as opposed to inherited status; (ii) the emergence of a new "caste-free" occupational structure; (iii) the expansion of a new kind of educational system; and (iv) the development of differentiated political structures such as legislatures, parties and organs of local government.[78]

In normal course, all these factors and forces, either singly or conjointly, should have lessened the social differentiation and structural distance. But that could not be. When the people was eager to enjoy the benefits of the Westernisation process, and the Britishers realised that their very existence would be threatened by its impact, they manoeuvred it in such a manner that a distorted and malignant effect could ensue. The concomitant effect of Westernisation was channelised in such a manner that it subserved the very purpose of the British Administration. They superimposed their cherished policy of dividing and subdividing the people on the basis of caste, religion, region, etc., on the Westernisation process as well. They did not allow the tremendous potentialities of the Westernisation process to be fully explored and, instead, exploited the sentiments and feelings of the people so deftly that the caste-ridden society could not get itself rid of the bad effects of caste, which became another instrument in their hands for implementation of the "Divide and Rule" policy. The policy enunciated by the Britishers for perpetuation of their rule made such a permanent inroad in our body politic that even the free Indians could not deviate from it. On the other hand, they are following the same policy with a gusto. Westernisation acted as a counter-productive to the Sanskritization process, as the 'low castes' and tribes opted[79] for Westernisation, because it opened up more avenues for speedier and quicker social mobility which could be achieved in one generation even. But the effectiveness of the latter process was, in turn, scuttled and blunted by the Britishers when they made it caste-oriented and linked up the mobility with caste. The very system which was anathema to it became the most essential element for its sustenance. Thus in course of time the Westernisation process became a viable instrument for ensuring solidarity, rigidity and orthodoxy of the caste system.

Effect of Education Policy

In pre-British Indian Society, education was viewed as the special prerogative of the upper strata such as the Brahmin, Kshatriya and Vaisya castes. Thus, education contributed towards the maintenance of the caste structure. But with the establishment of British Rule in India, western system of education was introduced, which in theory at least, was based on the principle of equality and universalistic criteria of admittance. The doors of education were thrown open to all, irrespective of caste, class, sex or religion. It was indeed a far cry from the past where the traditional systems of education had contributed towards the traditional hierarchical order.

The British education policy was, however, primarily designed for the training of a few people for the subordinate ranks of the administration.[80] But by the first decade of the nineteenth century a small band of Indian intellectuals were already beginning to feel the need for radically changing the traditional system of education in India and introducing within it modern western concepts. In fact, the first attempts of encouraging education amongst Indians by the government during the Company days took the traditional models of *Madrasah* and *Vidyalaya*. A small but influential group of Indian intellectuals led by Raja Rammohan Roy protested against this policy, and suggested the wholesale introduction of western rational humanistic and scientific studies. Macaulay, in his famous Minute, written on

February 2, 1835 in favour of the "promotion of European literature and science among the natives of India", stated that "all the funds appropriated for the purpose of education would be best employed on English education alone."[81] Largely, as a result of the pressure of the liberal Indian intellectuals, three universities had been started in the Presidency cities of Calcutta, Bombay and Madras by the late fifties of the nineteenth century.

The western system of education in theory was open to all but in practice was restricted to the members of the upper castes such as Brahmin, Kshatriya and Vaisya among the Hindus. These castes with their long tradition of literacy and urban background were the first to sense the importance of the new opportunities. These opportunities were in line with their traditional involvement in administration and scholarship and offered high prestige. The new educational system and the opportunities it offered not only did not threaten their traditional position but proved to be the means of strengthening it. As the years rolled by increasing number of them took to English education without which a job could not be obtained in the government. Next to the higher castes were the rural rich and powerful peasant castes, whose awareness of the opportunities offered by education had sharpened considerably with the emergence of the backward classes movement around the first quarter of the 20th century. The numerous lower castes and untouchables with neither a tradition of literacy, nor economic and political power, lagged far behind the first two categories.[82]

Even when some lower caste children went to school the atmosphere was not conducive as discriminatory treatment was meted out by teachers as well. Briggs observed in 1920 that "both teachers and pupils make it most difficult for low caste boys to sit in the class rooms."[83] The Woods' Despatch of 1854 may be considered as the first official attempt to draw the attention of the Government to the neglected problem of transmitting useful but practical knowledge to the great mass of our people. One of their recommendations referred to the creation of separate departments of education in different provinces. The British officers who by their nature and nurture were averse to discrimination based on caste system, sympathized with and even encouraged the Harijan communities for seeking education and employment under their control. In the famous Dharwar case of 1856, when a Harijan boy was refused admission on the ground of alienating Hindus, the Court of Directors, quashing the order opined that 'all schools maintained at the sole cost of the Government shall be open to all classes of its subjects without distinction'.[84] Similar discriminations practised in educational institutions drew attention of a few free thinkers and consequently, certain

> "social reformers all over India started educational institutions which were open to all castes. In Maharashtra, for example, Phule started a school for untouchables in 1873. Education was soon recognised as a gateway to higher professions and a lever to enhance social status for lower castes, so that leaders of non-Brahmin Castes soon enthused their followers to become educated... Ambedkar and Bhaurao Patil started the Peoples' Education Society and Rayat Shikhan Sanstha which helped the spread of Education, especially among the non-Brahmins."[85]

It is not wrong to assume that social backwardness has largely contributed to the educational backwardness of a large number of social groups. But, as pointedout by the Kalelkar Commission, some who were not socially and economically low did not take to education, for instance, the Muslims, in the beginning of the British rule, were too proud to take to English education. There was at least one section among the Sikhs—Namdharis—which on patriotic grounds rejected British education.[86]

The initial control exercised by a few castes over higher education and the educational system in general nowhere lasted very long. Members of the other castes began to see the advantages of school and college education and made increasing demands for their share of the benefits. In Peninsular India these demands were put forward in an organized manner as a part of the non-Brahmin movement; elsewhere the upper caste domination was gradually eroded by the extension of schools and even colleges.

The Western education had achieved a measure of success in removing caste-barriers and caste-prejudices. If the spread of education was taken up in right earnest throughout the length and breadth of the country, in all probability, the distinction between man and man on the basis of birth would have been completely wiped out by this time. Unfortunately this immense potentiality of western education was not fully explored. On the other hand, the policy of restricting the scope of education, specially higher education, adversely affected this process. The educational institutions were only a few in number and consequently the scope of the facility of education was very limited. Further, whatever educational institutions were established, they were mainly in the cities and towns. 'No facilities were either created or thought of in the interest of the large body of the rural population'.[87] The light of education did not reach the majority of people who lived in villages. There was not even an effort to eradicate illiteracy, a legacy followed in independent India with equal equanimity as well. The percentage of literacy in 1911 was 5.9%, in 1931 8.0%, in 1951 16.6%, in 1971 29% and in 1991 52.11%. Consequently, the majority of the people remained illiterate, and ignorant, steeped in superstitions, orthodoxy and black magic. Secondly, educational facility was not within the easy reach of the poor. People coming from upper income group had greater access to higher education than those coming from middle and lower income groups. As a result, income, like caste, played a significant role in deciding a man's educational opportunities and chances of social mobility. In other words, a boy born in an upper income family had not only greater opportunities to receive higher education but his chances of social mobility were greater. And the converse was also true. Thus education as a channel of mobility had very limited significance for the lowest income groups.[88] Compared with the latter, people from middle and lower-middle income groups had better opportunities to receive higher education and could move up in society. This brought out the close relationship between income, education and social mobility.[89] Since those in the lower strata of society mostly belonged to the lowest income group, they suffered most. There was no policy to spread education amongst this section of people, which meant denial of the chances of receiving higher education, an important channel for securing higher level white collour jobs, which carried with them, besides good salary, more prestige and influence in the society.

And this is not all. When this section of people voiced demand for extending to them the benefit of English education, the Britishers pursued a mischievous policy, obviously in furtherence of its "divide and rule" policy. They sorted out this problem not by opening more educational institutions, especially in the rural areas and extending necessary financial support in the form of fee-concessions, scholarships, free hostel facilities, book grants, etc., to the indigent and needy students, but by earmarking certain percentage of scholarships, fee-concessions, and seats in various educational institutions on the basis of caste and religion. Thus in1885, the Education Department of the Government of Bombay, at the instance of a host of British Administrators like Sir Richard Temple, the Governor of Bombay, proposed to reserve 50 per cent of free scholarships for Muslims and 'backward' Hindu castes because the British felt that scholarships based on merit would 'perpetuate the Brahmin monopoly'.[90] While the policy of restricting the scope of education had the effect of denying this facility to the majority of the people and thus keeping them illiterate and ignorant, the policy of making caste a criterion for reservation of seats in educational institutions and extending other facilities like scholarships, book-grants, fee-studentships had the effect of dividing the students on the basis of caste. Instead of broad-basing the educational system to cater to the need of the people who were clamouring for higher education, the British policy was to divide the people on the basis of caste and further restricting the scope of the already-conscripted education. While western education acted as a tool for securing higher status in the caste-ridden society, thus loosening the grip of caste-consciousness and caste-rigidity, the policy of reservation of seats etc., in educational institutions on the basis of caste had the effect of further exciting caste-jealousies and dividing people on the basis of caste. The role of caste in our educational institutions, specially those of higher learning, therefore, cannot be viewed with equanimity. The obvious danger to educational standards and values comes from the surreptitious entry of caste. "Sometimes", points out Sirsikar, "it is naively argued in certain quarters that other things remaining equal, there is no harm in a selection being made on the basis of caste. It is conveniently forgotten that other things do not remain the same because of the weightage given to the factor of caste."[91]

Occupations : Old and New

Western education, industrialisation, urbanisation, economic and geographical mobility, expansion of internal market, easier communication and the like led to the emergence of a whole range of new occupations during the last fifty years of the British rule. Individuals were recruited to these not by birth but on the basis of educational and other abilities. Avenues of occupational mobility became wider and more diversified over the years. The different occupational strata were no longer as homogeneous in their caste composition as they used to be.

Earlier, occupation of an individual depended on his birth. These hereditary occupational castes were greatly interested in perpetuating a virtual monopoly over skill, technique, design, patrons, and markets, in making themselves indispensable to the life of the community, just as modern federations or combines are, and therefore all too eager to restrict intercourse to a select number of families and regions so that 'patents' might be strictly guarded and handed down from generation to generation in a virtually closed community. A great number of castes saw the possibility of their survival and prosperity, of perpetuating their monopoly in production in a greater rigidity of their caste custom, and in the success with which they could shut out interlopers. This is responsible for much rigidity, as competition grew in intensity and volume, as specialisation came into demand when variety threatened to overwhelm. Many castes thus threw a ring of cast-iron voluntarily around their community.[92]

The new occupations being no longer related to heredity, caste lost much of its hold and utility over the community. Individuals are no longer required to follow their traditional or hereditary occupations and could take up any occupation of their choice. The cast-iron ring of caste was thus broken. Whatever restrictions caste imposed on the choice of occupation largely ceased to guide individuals. The Kalelkar Commission concluded that "caste is bad because it bound a man to his hereditary profession; but when that binding is removed and full freedom is given caste distinction and the evil effects of caste will disappear."[93] Caste, as such, lost much of its rigidity. At the same time caste lost whatever significance it had in the matter of providing employment to its members. So long every member of a caste was assured of his traditional caste occupation. Now, caste could no longer provide employment to its members, who had to seek employment outside the hereditary or functional occupation. Unemployment and consequent competition for new jobs made caste dysfunctional.

There was much more freedom in the matter of choice of occupation during the British rule than under the old regime. New occupations, which require abilities similar to those displayed in older occupation, arose out of the new requirements. Many of those occupations, like those of draftsmanship and cabinet-making, came to be looked upon with greater esteem and with better remuneration than their older pro otypes. Draftsmanship is partially allied to clerkship and largely to the ancient designer's avocation. Recruits to this profession, therefore, hail both from the higher castes as well as from the lower castes. Secondly, dislocation of the economic order and provision of facilities for training in arts and crafts led to an extensive shifting of the old lines of division between occupations. The total result was that many members of the Brahmin caste were seen engaged in most of the occupations, excepting those of casual labourer, sweeper, and scavenger. Many members of the various artisan castes are teachers, shopkeepers, bank clerks, shop assistants, and architects.[94]

Most of the new occupations as opposed to the traditional ones are 'caste-free'. Jobs in the various branches of the Government, both civil and military, and in the non-Governmental and ancillary sectors like industries, business, private professions like Doctors, Engineers provided opportunities for achieving power and status outside the caste system. Recruitment to these new occupations was, at least theoretically, caste-free, though empirically there was a high correlation between certain castes and the new occupational system. This is so because the new occupations neither emerged *ex-nihilo* nor were they imposed on a social vacuum. In fact, as they were gradually introduced they tended at first to be absorbed or fitted into the existing system, which was based upon caste.[95]

Policy of Job Reservation

Along with the demand for higher education, the demand for representation in services, especially in the government, was articulated by the backward castes because government service, besides assuring a steady income, was regarded as a source of tremendous power and prestige for both the individual and the group. Government service, like education, became a new status symbol. Not only other caste groups but also the dominant linguistic groups began making claims for share in the 'divisive benefits'. The dominance of Bengalees over government services as well as the professions of law and teaching in Bihar was seen as a great obstacle for prospects by the educationally advanced castes of Bihar who spearheaded the movement for separation of Bihar from Bengal which ultimately materialised in 1911. Similarly, the dominance of Tamils in government services was successfully articulated in the movement for separation of Andhra from the Madras Presidency. Once competition for position of power and status became stiff, 'protection' and 'security' acquired a new dimension in the Backward class movements, like Non-Brahmin and Self-Respect Movements in the South.

The claim for representation of backward classes in the State services was voiced early in the South Indian States only. It gained great momentum by the Non-Brahmin Movement in Bombay, Madras (undivided), Mysore, and to some extent in Travancore-Cochin. There was at one time a recognition by the Bombay Government of the principle that the recruitment from amongst the advanced classes should be stopped till an adequate number of backward classes were recruited to the services. This, however, was not implemented. But the necessity and desirability of recruiting candidates belonging to backward classes was recognised and implemented. In Madras, a system of communal rotation was introduced to accord representation to all the recognised backward class groups in order to remove inequalities of representation in services. In Mysore the question of removing inequalities of representation in the State services of certain important communities was recognised as early as 1894. Strict instructions were issued in 1895 that certain reservation of posts should be earmarked for all communities except Brahmins who till then had a virtual monopoly of the entire services. The whole question was reviewed in 1918 by a Committee under the Chairmanship of Sir Leslie Miller, the then Chief Justice. Accepting the Committee's recomendations the Government directed that the proportion of members of backward communities in all Headquarters and District Offices of all Departments should be raised to fifty per cent of the total strength within seven years. To secure this end, standing instructions were issued to the appointing authorities to give preference to the candidates of the backward communities in making initial appointments, so long as those candidates possessed the prescribed qualifications. The age for entry into service was raised from 25 years to 28 in the case of these communities. The scheme of recruitment was altered in 1927 as progress was found to be slow, and the proportion of backward community candidates to be recruited was raised to 75 per cent of the total posts available, the remaining 25 per cent being filled up irrespective of communal considerations. Even these instructions were not fully implemented. Seven years later, in 1934, a revised set of rules of recruitment was issued, and the Central Recruitment Board was given greater powers to implement the rules of recruitment. Leading non-official members belonging to various communities were represented on this Board which reviewed the progress of representation of various communities in the State services. The rules of recruitment related only to non-gazetted service. But the same policy was followed by the Government in recruiting persons to the gazetted ranks of the State Services as well. It was realized in Mysore early enough that reservation of posts for backward communities did not by itself ensure equitable distribution over the whole range of communities included in this group. In actual practice it was found that the more backward among them did not receive sufficient representation. The Government, therefore, evolved a policy which would give representation to all communities by according representation to the unrepresented first, the under-represented next, and the represented last. The Governments of Travancore and Cochin States before merger had followed a policy of according representation to the several communities in the State approximately in proportion to their population.[96]

Though the non-Brahmin parties, which flourished in the South, erecting a system of preferences in educational admissions and recruitment to government, at first undertook to speak for the lowest strata as well, but as they prospered, their voices increasingly reflected their higher echelon constituents.[97] By the early thirties the non-Brahmin movements that had emerged so dramatically a generation earlier now bifurcated, as lower castes insisted on provisions separate from those for the upper non-Brahmin groups. Congress governments which took office in the provinces in 1937, continued and extended the regime of communal quotas in public services and college admissions, while non-Congress governments did the same thing elsewhere.[98] In the central services, the Government of India reserved quotas for Muslims and other religious minorities.[99]

As a matter of fact, the British initiated job reservations on communal basis in different parts of India from the end of the 19th century and followed it up with separate electorates along communal lines. For example, in U.P., in the late 1890s, the communal quota was fixed at three Muslims to five Hindus. In Punjab, reservation principle was applied both on communal and caste grounds.[100] This was more or less an all-India phenomenon. The reasons are not far to seek. As the literate class, the British were critically dependant on the high castes to man the administration and maintain order. But as their strength in the bureaucracy increased the British became increasingly fearful that they would use their hold over their people to manipulate unrest in other sections of society. Britishers of all pursuits, missionaries, administrators and orientalists, were quick to grasp the pivotal role of the high castes, specially of the Brahmins, in the Indian social arrangement. They were all agreed that religious ideas and practices underlay the entire social structure and that as custodians of the sacred tradition and head of the social order, Brahmins were the principal integrating force. This made them the natural target of those seeking to fragment, indeed atomise, Indian society. This was as true of the British conquerors as it was of the Muslim rulers in the preceding centuries. In fact, the British regarded the Brahmin 'a barrier to modernisation and an imperfect interpreter to his society of the aims and aspirations of British rule'. The British were not wrong in their distrust of educated Brahmins in whom they saw a potential threat to their supremacy in India. Most Britishers were convinced that the Brahmins secretly harboured 'treacherous' sentiments against their rule. Sir Richard Temple, Governor of Bombay, traced the Maharastrian Brahmin's hostility to British rule to the year 1818, that is from the time the British finally defeated the Peshwas in the third Anglo-Maratha war. He believed that the Chitpavan Brahmins were "inspired with a national sentiment and with an ambition bounded only with the bounds of India itself'".[101]

The tool of job reservation proved to be quite effective in the British pursuit of 'divide and rule'. It became a very emotive issue for the Muslim and Hindu middle class. The nationalist approach that instead of job reservation elimination of colonial rule was the answer to economic hardship fell on deaf ears as far as the Muslim middle class was concerned. The policy of job reservation, therefore, started the process of Hindu-Muslim divide which climaxed in 1947. On the consequences of reservation principle Bipan Chandra, the noted historian, comments that when after decades it became clear during the 1930s that reservations had in no way helped the Muslim masses, the result was not abandonment of the policy of reservations or even the development of a critique of the policy, but the propagation of the view that Hindu domination was so strong that even reservations had failed to affect it, and, therefore, a stronger medicine, that of the creation of a Muslim state, was needed. Similar were the consequences of reservations based on caste, the only result was the hardening of casteism.[102] The Kalelkar Commission observed in 1955 that reservation of a certain percentage of appointments in Government services in favour of minority communities and groups like the Muslims, Christians, Sikhs and the Scheduled Castes was accepted and given effect to by the British Government to weaken the Nationalistic forces.[103]

Reservations for Scheduled Castes in Central Government employment were provided since 1943. Instructions were issued in July, 1934, that duly qualified candidates belonging to the Depressed Classes should not be deprived of fair opportunities of appointments merely because they would not succeed in an open competition, but in view of the educational backwardness of these people, it was not considered necessary to reserve a definite percentage of vacancies for them. The position when reviewed in 1942, revealed that in spite of the various measures adopted to secure increased representation of Scheduled Castes in public services the results obtained were not substantial. While the Government of India recognised that this was mainly due to the difficulty in getting suitably qualified candidates, they considered that the reservation of a definite percentage of vacancies might provide the necessary stimulus to candidates of these castes to equip themselves with better qualifications and thus become eligible for various Government posts and services. It was also believed that the grant of age concession and the reduction in examination fees would also help secure qualified candidates from among members of the Scheduled Castes. It was, however, thought that sufficient number of candidates from the Scheduled Castes would not be forthcoming to fill the full number of vacancies to which they were entitled on a population basis, which was 12.75% then.The Government of India, therefore, issued orders in August, 1943 reserving $8^{1/3}$% of vacancies for them and proposed to consider the question of raising this percentage as soon as a sufficient number of qualified candidates from Scheduled Castes was available. The reservation was made applicable only in the case of direct recruitment and not in the case of recruitment by promotion. The orders applied to the Central Services (Class I and Class II) and the subordinate services under the administrative control of the government of India, with the exception of a few services and posts for which highly technical or specialised qualifications were required. It was decided that the maximum age limit prescribed for appointment to a service or a post should be increased by three years in the case of Scheduled Caste candidates. The fees prescribed for admission to an examination were also reduced to one fourth in their case. In June, 1946, however, the percentage of reserved vacancies was raised from $8^{1/3}$% to 12½ % to correspond to their percentage in the population.[104]

Thus, reservation in government services for a section of Hindu population, who have been put under the rubric of "Scheduled Castes" by the Government of the day, became a permanent feature in this country. While "caste-free" occupations have made caste redundant in the matter of providing employment to its members, the policy of giving employment in certain percentage of government posts solely on the basis of birth has underscored the importance of caste even in this new expanding occupational system. Moreover, there was increasing demand for new occupations from the people released from hereditary occupations. The disruption of old village economy, the disintegration of village handicrafts and the rapid rise in population since the end of the nineteenth century further accentuated the demand for "new occupations". But recruitment to public offices being a scarce commodity, it irrevocably generated rivalry among the claimants. Too many people vied for too few opportunities. Competition became stiff day by day. Under such circumstances, apart from educational qualifications, aptitude and ability, another parameter for selection was imported. And in a traditional hierarchical society what else could be that except caste? Actually caste is operating in a more disastrous but subtle way. "One now requires a 'correct' caste to join Government services and industrial employment, not to mention educational institutions."[105] Caste became the most important instrument for mobilising people under one platform—be it for higher education, representation in services or in the political structures, each of which could permit free mobility, in principle, within the caste system. Class and caste are not synonymous. Caste mobility should automatically lead to individual (class) mobility but the converse is not true. The process which could give mobility to an individual outside the caste system was subverted to make it applicable for upward movement within the caste as well. Individual mobility became subservient to caste mobility, which this process, in any case, is not designed to achieve. This policy of linking caste with this process made it not only caste-oriented but also caste-dependent, which got added momentum from the first decade of the twentieth century.

Western education, and employment in important managerial and administrative position, brought the high castes, specially the Brahmins, close to the new rulers of India, the British. They entered into the highly prestigious and powerful Indian Civil Service, and government Bureaucracies and other services and used the ties of kinship and affinity to recruit more high caste persons. They also dominated the professions of law, medicine and education. Since national awakenings first found expression among members of the professions and the urban middle classes in general, the leadership of the Congress as well as other such organisations which then existed, came to be dominated by them.

Politics of Castes and Creed

The other castes, however, did not for long remain reconciled to their inferior position. The changes under British power gave new scope to the impulse to self-government and advancement in many groups. In the late 19th century, people of many castes organized themselves, held conferences, brought out newspapers, and undertook internal reform efforts. At first they tended to seek advancement in traditional terms of ritual status, vying for prestigious entries on the census, putting forth claims to exalted *varna* position, and upgrading their practices in terms of perceived notions of respectability. The interest of caste organizations turned increasingly to secular betterment: they founded hospitals, schools, hostels, and loan funds; they sought representation, government jobs and scholarships.

New forms of organization were taken up by some castes at the lower end of the spectrum. Some embraced the opportunities afforded by missionaries; others were influenced by Hindu reform movements; still others developed their own organizations. The first militant action by low castes was the campaign of the Shanars (later known as Nadars) to enter the Hindu temple of Meenakshi Sundareswara in Madurai of Madras on 14th of May, 1897, a demand connected to their claim to be Kshatriyas.[106] The Ezhuvas (Iravas) of Kerala took a different tack; by the early years of the 20th century, they had developed their own system of temples and schools.[107]

The first decade of the twentieth century is marked as the trend-setter of the future course of events of Indian history. It legitimised the birth of two powerful forces—comunalism and casteism—, all in pursuance of the 'divide and rule' policy, which in course of time changed the entire complexion of Indian polity. As nationalism grew and the movement towards greater Indian participation in the governance gathered momentum in the late nineteenth century, the British Government was forced to revaluate its policy of giving more representation to the Indians in the Administration. Lord Minto, the new Viceroy, took a new approach to give representation to the Indian people in legislatures. He hit upon a novel idea which introduced communalism for the first time in the polity of the Indian state after the advent of the British rule and adopted a clever ploy of exacerbating the open rivalry between the two dominant religious communities—Hindus and Muslims. Colonel Dunlop Smith, private secretary to the Viceroy, wrote a letter to Archibald, the principal of the Aligarh Muslim College, that the Viceroy would be happy to receive a Muslim deputation. A deputation called the All-India Mohammedan Deputation, met the Viceroy on October 1, 1906 in Simla. Its leader was His Highness the Agha Khan of Bombay. This deputation made the demand for separate electorates for Muslims in any scheme of political reform and said that the representation of the Muslims should be more than what was warranted by their numerical strength in the country. They further demanded that only Muslims should be allowed to choose the Muslim members of the council, and also a "due share in the gazetted and the subordinate administerial services." Lord Minto went a step further than what was demanded or claimed. He said in his reply: "I am grateful to you for the opportunity you are affording me of expressing my appreciation of the just aims of the followers of Islam and their determination to share in the political history of our Empire. You justly claim that your position should be estimated not merely on your numerical strength but in respect of the political importance of your community and the service that it had rendered to the Empire." While the claim of the Deputationists was only related to the Imperial Legislative Council's election or nomination, the Viceroy went further to say: "The pith of your address is a demand that in any system of representation, whether it affects a municipality, a district board or a legislative council in which it is proposed to introduce or increase an electoral organisation, the Mahammedan community should be represented as a community." He further added that "his was a firm conviction that any electoral representation in India would be doomed to mischievous failure which aimed at granting a personal enfranchisement regardless of the beliefs and traditions of the communities composing the population of this continent."[108]

Lord Minto's assurance was reflected in the Minto-Morley Reforms of 1909 which introduced for the first time separate communal electorate with weightage to the Muslims, that became a permanent feature of Indian political system since then. At the suggestion of the British Rulers the first communal political setup in India, the Muslim League, was founded in December, 1906 to safeguard the interests of the Muslims who were smarting under the fear of being dominated by the Hindus, of falling behind the Hindus in modern callings and opportunities and of being reduced to a subordinate position.

Commenting on this provision for separate electorate Eleanor Zelliot observes:

> The granting of an electorate for Muslims in which they alone would vote brought the idea of communal electorate for minorities to the forefront in the minds of all communities which feared their submersion in a government run by the dominant caste Hindu community. The granting of special electorates to the Muslim community also made numbers important. Whether the vast number of Untouchables were truly Hindu and to be counted as such, or not, became an important question for the first time.[109]

At the same time the policy of enumerating Depressed Classes as a separate group from the Hindus in the Indian Census for 1911 accentuated concern about Hindu majority. The Muslim leaders quickly seized this opportunity and demanded that, properly speaking, the outcasts were beyond the pale of Hinduism, and therefore, their strength should not go to swell the numerical strength of the Hindus. Considering the fact that the estimates of Depressed Classes varied from one-fifth to one-sixth of the total population, the apprehensions about a continued Hindu majority were really genuine.

"Untouchability" was thus propelled into a prominent place on the Indian political stage, which it was to occupy until after Independence.[110] This new position was soon reflected by the reversal of the Indian National Congress's long-standing policy of excluding "social reform" from its program. At its Calcutta session in 1917, just one year after the Indian National Congress's historic decision in the Lucknow session of accepting the Muslim League's demand for the system of "Separate Electorate" for them, the Congress for the first time passed a mild and hesitant anti-disabilities resolution urging "upon the people of India the necessity, justice and righteousness of removing all disabilities imposed by custom upon the Depressed Classes, the disabilities being of a most vexatious and oppressive character, subjecting those classes to considerable hardship and inconvenience".[111] The Congress resolution, however, omitted a crucial passage of the original, as submitted by the Depressed Classes Mission Society, which specified "disabilities imposed by *religion and custom*".[112] As Congress had earlier avoided social reform because of its divisive potential, it now embraced it because of its unifying potential. From this point on, the social question was indissolubly linked to the political.[113]

During this time those among the lower castes who were able to acquire western education soon set about organising themselves politically and appealing to the British for a more equitable distribution of opportunities. Thus emerged the Non-Brahmin Movement and the Self-Respect Movement in the South and the Depressed Classes Movement in Bombay Presidency.

The Non-Brahmin Movement in Madras Presidency was formally launched with the issue of the Non-Brahmin Manifesto in December, 1916. The Manifesto presented detailed figures showing an extremely high concentration of Brahmins in the public services, in public bodies and in the educational system and contrasting this with the 3 per cent they formed of the total population of the Presidency.[114] The Movement gathered strength within a very short time. The Manifesto "was followed by the starting of three daily papers, in English, Telegu and Tamil, the English paper being called the *Justice* which became the mouthpiece of the movement, and supplied the name also to the party itself".[115] The Party held its first Conference at Coimbatore in August 1917. Thereafter a series of Conferences were held in Tamil and Telegu districts of the Presidency. The Conferences were evidently organized with expense and care and attended by a large number of notabilities.[116]

The leaders of the Non-Brahmin Movement expressed the fear that the transfer of power for which the Congress was agitating might lead to domination of the people by a small elite composed of Brahmins. They argued, therefore, for preferential treatment of Non-Brahmins to make up for the advantages which Brahmins had secured over them in the fields of education and employment.

The Justice Party sent a powerful delegation to England in 1919 to present the Non-Brahmin case before the Joint Parliamentary Committee set up in connection with the Government of India Bill. The Memorandum presented by K.V. Reddi Naidu on behalf of the Non-Brahmins was one of the longest and was once again armed with facts and figures showing the domination of the Brahmins in every field. It argued that the interests of Brahmins and non-Brahmins were incompatible, that they claimed different racial origins and that if power were transferred without communal representation,

> that power will be utilised for the aggrandisement of the Brahmins and to the detriment of the non-Brahmins; that a Brahmin oligarchy will be substituted for a British bureaucracy....and that the Brahmin oligarchy will never be responsible to the masses and the middle classes, the poor and the proletariat...[117]

Thanks to communal representation and to the Congress boycott of the elections, the Justice Party captured the polls in the elections of 1920, held under the Government of India Act, 1919. After their success in the 1920 elections the leaders of the Justice Party settled down to the task of improving the position of Non-Brahmins through legislative and executive action. One of the first moves was the appointment in every district of a Protector of Non-Brahmin Subordinates in Public Services (G.O. No. 114 dated 3.3.1921). Reservations for Non-Brahmins were introduced in increasing proportion in the services, in local bodies and in the institutions of higher learning. With the Justice Party acting as the watchdog of Non-Brahmin interests, changes began to come about in the distribution of power between castes.[118] For those aspiring to pass into the middle classes it became important at every stage whether they were Brahmins or Non-Brahmins.[119] A system of caste quotas was established; this often resulted in better qualified Brahmins being rejected in favour of less qualified Non-Brahmins. The principle of "protective discrimination" or "discrimination in reverse" became so firmly established that since 1920, in Madras Presidency, out of every twelve posts five had to go to non-Brahmin Hindus, two to Brahmins, two to Muslims, two to Anglo-Indians or Christians, and one to the Depressed Classes. (G.O. No. 1129 dated December 15, 1928). With regard to admission to medical and other colleges, out of every fourteen seats six were allotted to non-Brahmin Hindus, two to Backward Hindus, two to the Depressed Classes (Harijans), two to Brahmins, one to Anglo-Indian or Indian Christian, and one to a Muslim. Such a distribution of seats among the communities according to a fixed ratio continued for three decades till it was declared unconstitutional in 1951.[120]

The Non-Brahmin Movement appears to have achieved singular success within a remarkably short period of time. Although the full demands for communal representation were not met, 28 out of the 98 elected seats in the newly constituted Madras Council were reserved for Non-Brahmins.[121] The three Indian Ministers placed in charge of "transferred subjects" were all Non-Brahmins and Justicites. The same pattern was repeated in the succeeding Legislature constituted in 1923. In 1926 the Justice Party was defeated by the Swarajists, but the latter refused to form a Ministry and an Independent Ministry was formed under the Non-Brahmin leader, P. Subbaroyan. The Justice Party rode into power again in 1930 and, though defeated in the elections of 1934, was not finally dislodged till 1937 when the Congress formed a Ministry under the leadership of C. Rajagopalachari.[122]

The Non-Brahmins first organized their political interests around the Justice Party. The Manifesto of 1916 used the term Non-Brahmins in its most inclusive sense, to cover not only Muslims and Christians but also the Depressed Classes. For all practical purposes, the Justice Party, however, was a platform for only a small section of the Non-Brahmins—the urban, educated middle classes among them. Its impact on the rural masses was negligible, and it became virtually extinct after its rout in the 1937 elections.

Though the Non-Brahmin leaders of the Justice Party made occasional references to the Depressed Classes and the need for ameliorating their conditions of life, they had hardly any representation in the leadership of the Justice Party. In the Memorandum presented to the Joint Parliamentary Committee in 1919 by the Non-Brahmin delegation, the Depressed Classes were listed separately from the Non-Brahmins in the Table showing the population analysis of Madras Presidency. Further, the separateness of the Depressed Classes was given implicit recognition in the Constitution of 1919 in which 5 seats were reserved for them, to be filled through nomination by the Governor.[123]

For all this, the separateness of the Depressed Classes remained a persistent feature of social and political life in Madras. Isrchick states that the Justice Party did not seriously attempt to enlist the support of lower castes by including their demands in the party platform.[124]

The Justice Party was less strong in Andhra than in Tamilnad because, as a member testified to the Statutory Commission in London, "Brahmins and Non-Brahmins got along much better in Andhra than they did in Tamilnad".[125] It achieved its measure of success in Andhra by recruiting persons who held personal power as traditional notables in the locality. Thus a party which was founded to articulate caste interests was transformed in the Andhra setting to a party of landed elites.[126]

Perhaps the most important consequence of the Non-Brahmin Movement was the introduction of a "communal" or caste idiom into South Indian politics. The composition of political bodies was changed by it, sometimes artifically, through reserved seats, and everywhere communal loyalties became important in giving or withdrawing support. It is doubtful whether the Movement even attempted to organize politically the entire body on Non-Brahmins. But it certainly did succeed in creating a lasting impression that virtually in every political context it was important whether a person was a Brahmin or Non-Brahmin. It is this trend which gives the politics of South India (including Maharashtra but probably excluding Kerala) its distinctive character when compared with the politics of the North.[127]

In the twenties another movement known as Self-Respect Movement originated in Tamilnad. E.V. Ramaswami Naicker, popularly known as Periyar, had started an association called '*Suyamariyathai Sangham*' or 'Self-Respect Group' in 1923. Its main objective was to root out from 'Dravidians' all superstitious beliefs based on religion and caste and to debunk all Brahmanical or Sanskritic beliefs and practices.[128] Newspapers were started in English (The Liberator) and in Tamil (*Swayamariyadai*) in which Brahmins were denounced for their arrogance and the pursuit of their narrow group interests. Brahminism as a way of life came in for attack for its bigotry and duplicity, and for the exploitation which it practised and encouraged.[129]

From the late twenties onwards the Self-Respect Movement began to make concerted efforts to undermine the supremacy of the Brahmins in the ritual and social spheres. The Movement was welcomed by the Justice Party although its immediate objectives were not political. It sought rather to create for Non-Brahmins a climate of self-confidence and to liberate them from the ritual tyranny of the Brahmins. In the late twenties and early thirties it gained a measure of popular appeal under the leadership of Naicker. Through the columns of its own newspapers as well as through other newspapers it contributed a series of articles denouncing caste observances, child marriage, and enforced widowhood and decrying Hindu ceremonials and rituals. Attempts were made to do away with the service of Brahmin priests. The Purohit Maruppu Sangam (Association for the Elimination of Priests) was formed, and a general attitude of hostility towards Brahmins came to be built up on the social plane, and feelings ran high against them.

It advocated inter-caste marriage but also propounded what it called "self-respect marriage" or "reform marriage", in Tamil *Suyamariyathai* or *seerthirutha*. Its essence consisted in eschewing a priest and his rituals; someone from among the gathering for the wedding "irrespective of caste and creed was to discharge the function of the priest, the rituals consisting in exchange of garlands by the bride and bridegroom and tying of the 'tali' by bridegroom round the neck of the bride".[130] The first 'Self-Respect Marriage' took place in 1929. According to an estimate there were not less than 60,000 of such marriages current till 1968 [131]

The Self-Respect Movement had a tremendous impact on the life style of the Non-Brahmins and the Untouchables. Mention may be made of Nadars, who were somewhere between the Sudras and the outcaste Untouchables. During the latter part of the 19th century, the Nadar community began slowly to Sanskritize their manner of life. Among the men, many cropped their hair in the fashion of the Brahmin tuft. They adopted the sacred thread of the 'twice born' and vegetarianism came into vogue. Fathers named their children after the 'new' Sanskritic gods which had come into favour among the community, and Brahmin priests were found who were quite willing to provide their services to the wealthy Nadar temples and to officiate over the ceremonies of the caste. Behind these pretensions lay the newly-advanced Nadar claim to high Kshatriya status. Between 1860 and the early 1920s the Nadars assiduously advanced their claim through books, pamphlets, and periodicals.[132] Under the influence of the Self-Respect Movement, the first conference of which was held at Chinglepet in 1928 under the Presidentship of a Nadar, the Nadars began to de-Sanskritise their manner of life, in abandoning the pretensions to high caste adopted in the latter years of the 19th century. The sacred thread was thrown away and the use of Brahmin *purohits* was discouraged. The self-respect marriage became widespread as the people sought to release themselves from the priestly authority which had held them in at least psychological subservience to the high castes.[133]

Naicker, who spearheaded the Self-Respect Movement in the thirties and early forties, trained a band of educated young men with idealistic fervour as his disciples. In 1945, he reincarnated the Justice Party, liquidated in the elections of 1936-37, under the regional but locally supernational designation, Dravida Kazagham,[134] a militant organization devoted to anti-Brahmin and anti-North Indian activities. At the time of partition, Naicker tried to secure the help of Jinnah, so that Dravidasthan might be formed simultaneously with Pakistan. Jinnah refused assistance, and the British ignored the Dravidian agitations. Outraged at the British "betrayal"of the Dravidian peoples in turning the bureaucracy over to a Brahmin oligarchy, Naicker boycotted the Indpendence Day celebrations. He refused to honour the National Flag, just as he later refused to recognise the Indian Constitution, seeing it only as a tool of Brahmin tyranny.[135]

Resentment in the Dravida Kazagham soon surfaced mainly on the question of democratization of leadership within the party. On the issue of Naicker marrying a 28-year old girl at the age of 72, some of his ablest lieutenants seceded from the Dravida Kazagham in 1949 under the leadership of C.N. Annadurai and formed a separate party, the Dravida Munnetra Kazagham,[136] which emerged as the leading opposition party in the State. Though also rooted in anti-Brahminism, the D.M.K. is more moderate in its programme, even admitting Brahmins within its folds. It renounced its anti-Brahmin bias and canvassed actively for Brahmin support in the general elections held since 1962. It claims to be hostile not to Brahmins as such, but to the elements of obscurantism and exploitation in the Brahminical way of life.

In Maharashtra, Jyotirao Phooley (1827-90), who was born in a Mali (gardener) family, a subcaste of the Kunbi caste of Maharashtra, a cultivator caste above the untouchable groups, started organising the most deprived sections of the Non-Brahmin castes. He felt little enthusiasm for the rising tide of Hindu nationalism which was very largely the ideology of the western educated high caste Hindus; he feared that political independence without a social revolution would only mean combination of political power with cultural-social privileges in the hands of the entrenched caste elite groups. To Phooley the key to all that was basically wrong with the Hindu society was the monopoly of power and privilege traditionally enjoyed by the Brahmins and all his writings and public activities were directed towards subversion of this monopoly. However, instead of depending on the British, he took the initiative to instruct, inspire and organise the Non-Brahmin castes of Maharashtra. Besides writing extensively and running a journal Dinabandhu, started in 1871, he founded in 1873 the Satyashodhak Samaj (Society of the Seekers of Truth) with the aim of "saving the lower caste from the hypocritical Brahmins and their opportunistic scriptures". He also started the first schools in India for the children of untouchables in 1852 and a Home for the Prevention of Infanticide in 1863 where widowed mothers of illegitimate children were given protection and care. He advocated a socio-cultural revolution in India which would give to the poor and dispossessed dignity and self-respect, and a dynamic role in the shaping of their history. Phooley was doubly remarkable in that not only was he committed to a structural revolution of Indian society, but he was also the first intellectual of stature to emerge from a plebian caste in modern India.[137] Phooley attracted the support of the non-Brahmin heads of a few princely states, men like the Maharaja of Kolhapur, and in turn influenced their subsequent social reform programmes. More important, he propounded a philosophy of reform from below that would be taken up by low caste reformers of the succeeding generations, including Ambedkar.[138] It is no wonder that Dr. Ambedkar who brought the Depressed Classes in the centre stage of Indian politics and made them a viable political force within a span of three decades, considered Phooley as his spiritual mentor.

Notes and References

1. Ghurye, *op. cit.*, p. 271.
2. *Ibid.*, pp. 284-85.
3. Kerr, James, *The Domestic Life, Character and Customs of the Natives of India*, 1865, footnote, p. 361, quoted by Ghurye, *Ibid.*, p. 285.
4. *Ibid.*, p. 285.
5. *Report of the Peel Commission on the organization of the Indian Army*, 1859, quoted by Ghurye, *Ibid.*, p. 284.
6. *Ibid.*, p. 285.
7. Sinha, Dr. R.K., *Alienation Among Scheduled Castes*, Manas Publications, Delhi, 1986, p. 30.
8. *Census of 1931*, para 831, p 443.
9. Ghurye, *op. cit.*, p. 283.
10. *Ibid.*, p. 271.
11. Mulla, D.F., *Jurisdiction of Courts in Matters Relating to Rights and Powers of Castes*, 1901, pp. 49-63, quoted by Ghurye, *Ibid.*, p. 273.
12. Lathe, A.B., *Memoirs of His Highness Shri Sahu Chhattrapati, Maharaja of Kolhapur*, 1924, Vol. II, p. 373, quoted by Ghurye, *Ibid.*, p. 273.
13. *Ibid.*, p. 273.
14. *Ibid.*
15. Suri, Surinder, *Frontiers*, Seminar No. 70, p. 20.
16. Ghurye, *op. cit.*, pp. 274-75.
17. *Ibid.*, p. 278.
18. *Census 1951 West Bengal*, The Tribes and Castes of West Bengal, 1953, p. 1.
19. Ghurye, *op. cit.*, p. 278.
20. *Indian Census*, 1901, pp. 537-38.
21. *Census 1951 West Bengal*, *op. cit.*, p. 1.
22. *Ibid.*
23. Ghurye, *op. cit.*, p. 278.

24. *Bengal Census*, 1921, p. 346.
25. Srinivas, *Social Change in Modern India, op. cit.*, p. 95.
26. *Madras Census*, 1911, p. 178.
27. *Bengal, Bihar, Orissa and Sikkim Census Report, 1911*, p. 440.
28. Srinivas, *Social Change in Modern India, op. cit.*, p. 96.
29. Natarajan, S., *A Century of Social Reform in India*, Asia Publishing House, 1959, p. 118.
30. *Census 1951 West Bengal*, p. 2.
31. *Census 1911*, Part I, p. 232.
32. Hutton, *op. cit.*, p. 207.
33. *Indian Statutory Commission, 1930*, Vol. V, p. 1341.
34. Hutton, *op. cit.*, p. 194.
35. *Ibid.*, pp. 196-97.
36. *Ibid.*, p. 197.
37. Galantar, Marc., *Competing Equalities*, Oxford University Press, Delhi, 1984, p. 129.
38. *Census 1951 West Bengal*, pp. 4-5.
39. Indian Statutory Commission, 1930, Vol. V, p. 1341.
40. Galantar, *op. cit.*, p. 130.
41. Dushkin, Lelah, *The Policy of the Indian National Congress Toward the Depressed Classes : An Historical Study*, Master's thesis, University of Pennsylvania, p. 95, quoted by Galantar, *Ibid.*, p. 130.
42. *Census 1951 West Bengal*, p. 4.
43. *Ibid.*, p. 2.
44. *Ibid.*, p. 5.
45. Ghurye, *op. cit.*, p. 279.
46. *Punjab Census*, 1921, pp. 433-34.
47. Ghurye, *op. cit.*, p. 282.
48. *Census Report, 1931*, p. 433.
49. *Census 1951 West Bengal*, p. 5.
50. Sardar Vallabhbhai Patel, the Deputy Prime Minister and Home Minister, while opening the Conference of the Census Superintendents in New Delhi on 23rd February, 1950, quoted in the *Census 1951 West Bengal.*
51. *First Backward Classes Commission Report, 1955*, paras 44 and 45, p. 23.
52. Beteille, *Castes Old and New*, Asia Publishing House, 1969, p. 22.
53. *Ibid.*
54. Tarlok Singh, *The Village Panchayat and the Pattern of Village Development*, 1955, pp. 2-3, quoted by Hugh Tinker, *The Village in the Framework of Development*, In : *Administration and Economic Development in India*, (ed.) by Ralph Braibanti and Joseph J. Spengler, Cambridge University Press, 1963, p. 101.
55. *First Backward Classes Commission Report, 1955*, para 45, p. 23.
56. *Census 1951 West Bengal*, pp. 7-8.

57. Srinivas, *Social Change in Modern India, op. cit.*, p. 93.
58. Bateille, *Castes Old and New, op. cit.*, p. 58.
59. Rao, V.K.R.V., *Dimensions of Social Change in India*, (ed.), Allied Publishers, 1977, p. 22.
60. Srinivas, *op. cit.*, p. 47.
61. Singh, Yogendra, *The Changing Pattern of Social Stratification in India*, In : Dimensions of Social Change in India, *op. cit.*, p. 141.
62. *Ibid.*, p. 140.
63. Sachchidananda, *The Harijan Elite*, Thomson Press (India) Limited, 1977, p. 119.
64. Rao, V.K.R.V., *op. cit.*, pp. 30-31.
65. Gould, H.A. Sanskritization and Westernization : A Dynamic View, *Economic Weekly*, Vol. 25, 1961, p. 949.
66. Kothari, Rajani, *Caste in Indian Politics* (ed.), Orient Longman Ltd., 1970, p. 132.
67. Beteille, *op. cit.*, p. 132.
68. Singh, Yogendra, *op. cit.*, p. 140.
69. Srinivas, *op. cit.*, p. 93.
70. Bateille, *op. cit.*, p. 132.
71. Singh, Yogendra, *op. cit.*, p. 140.
72. Beteille, *op. cit.*, p. 127.
73. *Ibid.*, p. 119.
74. Kothari, Rajani, *op. cit.*, pp. 18-20.
75. Beteille, *Caste, Class and Power*, Oxford University Press, Bombay, 1966, p. 7.
76. Beteille, *Caste : Old and New, op. cit.*, p. 127.
77. Srinivas, *op. cit.*, pp. 48-49.
78. Beteille, *Caste : Old and New, op. cit.*, p. 60.
79. Orans, Martin, *The Santhal, A Tribe in Search of a Great Tradition*, Detroit, 1965, p. 101.
80. *First Backward Classes Commission Report*, p. 24, para 46.
81. *Minute by the Honourable T.B. Macaulay*, dated 2nd February, 1835, pp. 1-7.
82. Sivakumar, Chitra, *Higher Education, Social Stratification and Social Change in Mysore in the 1960s*, In : *Dimensions of Social Change in India, op. cit.*, pp. 190-91.
83. Sinha, R.K., *op. cit.*, p. 130.
84. *Selections from the records of Government of India*, Home Department, No. LXXVI, Calcutta, Government of India, Printing, 1870, quoted by Sinha, *Ibid.*, p. 42.
85. Paranjpe, A.C., *Caste, Prejudice and the Individual*, Lalwani Publishing House, Bombay, 1970, p. 17.
86. *First Backward Classes Commission Report*, para 11, p. 42.
87. *Ibid.*, para 284, p. 136.
88. Sivakumar, Chitra, *op. cit.*, p. 203.

89. *Ibid.*, p. 204.
90. Jain, Meenakshi, A myth the British created, *Indian Express*, October 5, 1990.
91. Sirsikar, V.M., Use in Politics, *Seminar No. 70.*
92. *Census 1951 West Bengal*, p. 7.
93. *First Backward Classes Commission Report*, para 207, p. 113.
94. Ghurye, *op. cit.*, pp. 295-96.
95. Beteille, *Caste : Old and New*, *op. cit.*, p. 69.
96. *First Backward Classes Commission Report*, paras 264-269, pp. 129-30.
97. Galantar, *op. cit.*, p. 27.
98. *Ibid.*, p. 36.
99. *Government of India Resolution No. F.14/17-B/33 dated July 4, 1934, Published in Gazette of India, Part I, July 7, 1934.*
100. Chandra, Bipan, The Struggle against Caste and Casteism, *The Telegraph*, May 14, 1991.
101. Jain, Meenakshi, The Plight of Brahamins, *Indian Expres*, September 18, 1990, and a myth the British created, *Indian Express*, October 5, 1990.
102. Chandra, Bipan, *op. cit.*
103. *First Backward Classes Commission Report*, para 256, p. 127.
104. *Report of the Commissioner for Scheduled Castes and Scheduled Tribes, 1951*, pp. 28-29.
105. Sirsikar, *op. cit.*
106. Hardgrave, Robert L. Jr., *Political Participation and Primordial Solidarity : The Nadars of Tamilnadu*, In : *Caste in Indian Politics*, (ed.), Orient Longman Ltd., 1970, pp. 110-13.
107. Galantar, *op. cit.*, p. 23.
108. Chaturvedi, J.P., The fragmentation of a nation, *The Telegraph*, March 19, 1991.
109. Zelliot, Eleanor, *Dr. Ambedkar and the Mahar Movement*, Ph.D. dissertation, University of Pennsylvania, 1969, p. 141, quoted by Galantar, *Ibid.*, p. 26.
110. *Ibid.*, p. 26.
111. Natarajan, Swaminath, *op. cit.*, p. 144.
112. Galantar, *op. cit.*, p. 27.
113. *Ibid.*, pp. 26-27.
114. Subba Rao, C.V., *Life and Times of Sir K.V. Reddi Naidu*, Rajahmundry 1957, pp. 17-23.
115. *Ibid.*, p. 30.
116. *Ibid.*, pp. 30-39.
117. *Ibid.*, p. 53.
118. Beteille, *Castes : Old and New*, *op. cit.*, pp. 174-75.
119. *Beteille, Caste, Class and Power*, op. cit., p. 210.
120. Srinivas, *op. cit.*, p. 109.

121. Hardgrave, Robert L. Jr., *The Dravidian Movement*, Bombay, 1968, p. 19.
122. Beteille, *Castes : Old and New*, *op. cit.*, p. 174.
123. *Ibid.*, p. 184.
124. Irschick, Eugene, *Politics and Social Change in South India : The Non-Brahmin Movement and Tamil Separatism, 1916-1929*, Ph.D. Thesis, Department of History, The University of Chicago, 1964, quoted by Elliot, Carolyn M., Caste and Faction among the *Dominant Caste : The Reddies and Kammas of Andhra*, In : *Caste in Politics*, p. 169.
125. *Great Britain, Parliamentary Papers, Vol. IV, House of Commons Paper No. 203, 1919, Joint Select Committee on Government of India Bill*, Vol. II, p. 218, quoted by Elliot, *Ibid.*, p. 151.
126. Elliot, *Ibid.*, p. 147.
127. Beteille, *Castes : Old and New*, *op. cit.*, pp. 163-64.
128. Jayaram, R., *The Times of India*, February 11, 1968.
129. Beteille, *Caste, Class and Power*, *op. cit.*, p. 211.
130. Jayaram, R., *op. cit.*
131. *Ibid.*
132. Hardgrave, In : *Caste in Indian Politics*, *op. cit.*, p. 110.
133. *Ibid.*, p. 123.
134. Ghurye, *op. cit.*, p. 455.
135. Hardgrave, *The Dravidian Movement*, *op. cit.*, pp. 32-33.
136. *Ibid.*, p. 33.
137. Ray, S., *From Phooley to Ambedkar : The Unaccomplished Revolution*, In : *Dr. Ambedkar, Pioneer of Human Rights*, ed., Boddhisttva Publication, New Delhi, 1977, pp. 103-7.
138. Joshi, Barbara R., *Democracy in Search of Equality : Untouchable Politics and Indian Social Change*, Hindustan Publishing Corporation (India), Delhi, 1982, p. 38.

4

Effects of British Rule on the Caste System—II

Ambedkar and Gandhi

The second decade of the twentieth century witnessed the emergence of two personalities in the Indian political field who worked for the amelioration of the conditions of the Untouchables. But there was a difference in their approach to the solution of the problems facing them. One of them was Mahatma Gandhi and the other was Dr. Bhimrao Ramji Ambedkar, both of whom hailed from the hinterlands of Bombay Presidency. Gandhi personified, what Galanter says, the 'evengelical' approach, while Ambedkar represented the 'secular' approach. The 'evengelical' approach stresses the uplift of untouchables to higher Hindu standards and the penance of caste Hindus for the injustices of untouchability, which is seen not as an integral part of Hinduism but as some external impurity. Uplifted untouchables and repentant Hindus will join together in a purified and redeemed Hinduism. At the other extreme, the secular approach stresses the denial of civil rights and economic opportunities and seeks to combat them by vigorous government intervention, and political action to obtain it. Untouchability is seen as an integral part of Hinduism. The secular approach does not seek to restore Hinduism to some original purity, but seeks instead to liberate all by dissolving the graded inequalities of caste into the common bond and common rights of citizenship in a secular state. In the 'evengelical' approach, the emphasis is on moral regeneration and philanthropic uplift; in the secular approach, it is on civic and economic improvement under government auspices.[1]

In 1916 Mohandas Karamchand Gandhi returned to India from Africa and assumed leadership of the Indian National Congress. In his autobiography, Gandhi tells as that from the age of twelve he was convinced that untouchability could not be sanctioned by Hinduism. From his first public statements on the subject, he describes untouchability as a sinful excrescence upon Hinduism. He calls upon caste Hindus to do penance, to purify themselves and Hinduism, while urging the untouchables to observe cleaner habits. The problem is one for voluntary private action, not for legal coercion. While rejecting caste in its modern manifestations, Gandhi accepted *varnashrama dharma* as a healthy division of labour by birth. Untouchability should be removed by abolishing the unwarranted fifth division and restoring the untouchables to their rightful estate as Sudras in a purified *varna* expressing not inequality but a horizontal and non-invidious division based on hereditary qualities. The notion that some are by birth polluting must be abolished, and those self-imposed restrictions on intercourse that are conducive to spiritual development should be retained.[2]

While Gandhi was a bania (merchant) by caste, Ambedkar was a Mahar, the dominant Depressed Class of Maharashtra and knew from his own experience what it meant to be born an untouchable in India. Ambedkar through his education, forensic ability, sagacity and political acumen made not only the Mahars but also the other 'untouchables' a political force to reckon with and equipped them for the use of political means toward a modern goal of social equality. While both were trained as lawyers, their attitude to law as an instrument of social redress was sharply divergent. Ambedkar reposed full faith in it and constantly sought to sharpen it; Gandhi had not much use for it. Instead he emphasised moral regeneration of individuals and societies undertaken on a voluntary basis. For Gandhi, unlike Ambedkar, legal intervention, or for that matter any other intervention by the state to re-order civil society along more humane lines, was an anathema. While Gandhi's appeals were directed principally to the caste Hindus, Ambedkar addressed the untouchables and directed their attention to the potentialities of action to be taken by government.

Ambedkar believed that only when the untouchables achieved political power could the social and economic conditions of theirs be improved. Through political action he wanted to force the hands of the caste Hindus to ameliorate the conditions in which the untouchables were living.[3] He shifted the political balance. Repeatedly he used the competitive manoeuvres of the major power blocs of the pre-independence era—the British, the Indian National Congress, and later the Muslim League—to get leverage for an untouchable population that had very few political resources of any sort.[4]

The antagonism between these two personalities was not of a purely personal nature. It echoed two very different temperaments and, more significantly, two radically opposed world views. Ambedkar's world view, nourished by his knowledge of the history of social reforms in Maharashtra and his economic and legal studies in the United States and Britain, was rooted in the enlightenment. To him fraternity and equality were the *sine qua non* of liberty. He trusted the instruments of the state to bring about social and economic change. He chose to be guided by reason rather than by faith. And he placed the individual at the very centre of the social order. Gandhi's world view, on the other hand, was rooted in morality. He was indifferent to economic mechanisms and political arrangements. He prized the qualities of self-abnegation and mercy. What is more, unlike Ambedkar, he seemed to regard the community rather than the individual as the prime social unit. For much the same reason he favoured the village against the city and, by extension, seemed to lay greater store by agriculture and agriculture-related activity rather than industrial endeavour. On the contrary Ambedkar urged his followers to desert the village, take to modern education (he himself founded several educational institutions) and seek to organise themselves politically.[5]

Mont-Ford Reforms

The First World War had generated a greater demand for self-government in India because it had created an awakening in India never witnessed before. Edwin S. Montague, the then Secretary of State for India, announced in the House of Commons on August 20, 1917, the new policy of the British Government towards India. This new policy was "that of the increasing association of Indians in every branch of the administration and gradual development of self-governing institutions with a view to the progressive realisation of responsible Government in India as an integral part of the British Empire."[6] Closely following upon this announcement, Montague along with Lord Chelmsford, the Viceroy, toured all over the country studying the Indian political problems. In anticipation of the declaration of a definite policy of the British Government, leading politicians got busy preparing schemes for changes in the constitutional structure of India. During this significant period two meetings of the Depressed Classes were held in the city of Bombay under two different Presidents. The first of these meetings was held under the banner of the Depressed Classes Mission Society on November 11, 1917 under the chairmanship of its president Sir Narayan Chandavarkar, an ex-President of the Indian National Congress. The meeting urged the British Government to protect the interests of the Depressed Classes by granting them the right to elect their own representatives to the Legislative Councils in proportion to their numbers. In another resolution the Indian National Congress was requested "to pass at its forthcoming session a distinct and independent resolution declaring to the people of India at large the necessity, justice, and righteousness of removing all the disabilities imposed by religion and custom upon the Depressed Classes, those disabilities being of a most vexatious and oppressive character, subjecting those classes to considerable hardship and inconvenience by prohibiting them from admission into public schools, hospitals, courts of justice and public offices, and the use of public wells, etc. These disabilities, social in origin, amount in law and practice to political disabilities and as such fall legitimately within the political mission and propaganda of the Indian National Congress."[7] The Indian National Congress, in pursuance of this resolution, passed for the first time the anti-untouchability resolution in its session held in Calcutta in 1917. The second meeting of the Depressed Classes was also held in November 1917, a week or so after the first meeting, under the chairmanship of Bapuji Namdeo Bagade, a leader of the Non-Brahmin Party. The chief concern of this meeting centred around a request to the British Government to "grant the Untouchables their own representatives in the various legislative bodies to ensure to them their civil and political rights."[8]

The Declaration of August 20, 1917 was followed by the publication on July 8, 1918, of the Report of Indian Constitutional Reforms, which was submitted by Montague and Chelmsford on April 22, 1918. This Report, known as 'Mont-Ford Report', laid down four formulae on which the reform proposals were based:—

1. "There should be, as far as possible, complete popular control in local bodies and the largest possible independence for them of outside control". 2. "The provinces are the domain in which the earlier steps towards the progressive realisation of responsible government should be taken. Some measure of responsibility should be given atonce, and our aim is to give complete responsibility as soon as conditions permit. This involves atonce giving the provinces the largest measure of independence, legislative, administrative, and financial, of the Government of India, which is compatible with the

due discharge by the latter of its own responsibilities". 3. "The Government of India must remain wholly responsible to Parliament, and, saving such responsibility, its authority in essential matters must remain indisputable, pending experience of the effect of the changes now to be introduced in the provinces. In the meantime the Indian Legislative Council should be enlarged and made more representative and its opportunities of influencing Government increased". 4. "In proportion as the foregoing changes take effect, the control of Parliament and the Secretary of State over the Government of India and Provincial Government must be relaxed."[9]

The Mont-Ford Report did not do more than enunciate principles on questions relating to functions of Central and Provincial Governments, franchise and the electoral system, and relations between the Secretary of State in Council, the Government of India, and the Provincial Governments. Three Committees were constituted to go into these questions. In October, 1918, the constitution and terms of reference of the Franchise and Functions Committees were publicly announced. Lord Southborough was appointed to preside over both the Committees, which were to meet in joint session when necessary. The other members of the Franchise Committee were Sir Frank G. Sly (Deputy Chairman), Sahibzada Aftab Ahmed Khan, W.M. Hailey, Surendra Nath Banerjee, Malcolm N. Hogg and Srinivasa Sastri. A third Committee presided over by Lord Crewe held its sittings in London at a later stage.

The work of the Franchise Committee lasted from November, 1918, till February, 1919. The report of the Committee was submitted to the Governor-General in Council on February 26, 1919. The Committee, after scrutinising the evidence received from the political parties and organisations, different associations representing various communities and interests like Anglo-Indians, Oriyas, Mahishyas, Depressed Classes, Ahoms, Zamindars and landholders, Agriculturists, Mining, Tea, Chamber of Commerce, Women and individuals, and the opinions of local Governments, recommended continuance of separate electorate for the

Muhammedans, extension of communal electorate to Sikhs in Punjab, separate electorates to Indian Christians in Madras, to Europeans in Madras, Bombay, Bengal, United Provinces, Bihar and Orissa and to Anglo-Indians in Madras and Bengal.[10] It also suggested representation of special interests like Zamindars and Landholders, University, Commerce and Industry.[11]

Claims for separate electorates were placed before the Committee by numerous other communities, such as the Mahishyas of Bengal and Assam, the Marwaris of Calcutta, the Bengali domiciled community of Bihar and Orissa, the Ahoms of Assam, the Mahars of the Central Provinces, the Uriyas of Madras and the Parsis of Bombay. In the southern parts of the Bombay Presidency and in Madras, claims were put forward by non-Brahmin Hindus for separate communal representation as a means of protection against the alleged ascendency of the Brahman. The Lingayats of the Bombay Presidency asked on this ground for the protection of their interests by reservation of seats in plural member constituencies. A similar claim on similar grounds was urged by the Marathas and allied castes in the Deccan and Southern divisions of the Bombay Presidency. In Madras a similar question was raised in a very acute form by the claim to communal representation of the Non-Brahmin Hindus of that Presidency. The Committee believed that these organised communities would find no difficulty in seeking representation through a general electorate in the districts where they were numerous and therefore, did not recommend any special provision for them.[12] The Committee, however, assigned a number of seats in each council to which non-official representatives of these who could not be expected to obtain representation by any particular system of election, might be appointed by nomination. In this category was included Indian Christians, Europeans, Depressed Classes, Labourers, Aborigines and others. The Committee was driven to the expedient of nomination for the representation of the Depressed Classes, because in no case did the Committee find it possible to provide an electorate on any satisfactory system of franchise.[13]

The Committee earmarked 47 seats to be filled by nomination in the provincial councils, of which 7 were allotted to the Depressed Classes as follows:- Madras 2, Bombay 1, Bengal 1, United Provinces 1, Bihar and Orissa 1 and Central Provinces 1.[14]

The views of the Government of India on the proposals made in the Mont-Ford Report and two Reports of the Southborough Committees were communicated to the India Office in certain despatches which aroused a good deal of criticism in this country. In their despatch of April 23, 1919, the Government of India suggested that there should be in each council enough representatives of the Depressed Classes to save them from being entirely submerged, and at the same time to stimulate some capacity for collective action. The Government of India suggested that Madras should be given six seats; in Bengal, the United Provinces and Bihar and Orissa four; in the Central Provinces and Bombay two and elsewhere one.[15] Accordingly in place of seven, they were given fourteen seats.[16]

To give effect to the proposed constitutional changes a Bill was introduced in the House of Commons on May 29, 1919. It was referred for consideration to a joint select committee of both Houses which suggested a number of modifications. The modifications proposed by the joint select committee were in many cases incorporated in the Bill which was passed into law in December 1919 and became the Government of India Act, 1919. Under the Act of 1919 communal representation has been provided not only "for the Muhammedan, Sikh, Indian Christian, European and Anglo-Indian communities (and in Burma, the Karen and Indian communities) but also the modified system of communal representation which has been provided for the non-Brahmin community in the Madras, and for the Maratha community, in the Bombay councils."[17] The 'Mont-Ford Report' said that with regard to the Depressed Classes "we intend to make the best arrangements that we can for their representation, in order that they too may ultimately learn the lesson of self-protection."[18] But when details of the constitution were framed, they were granted representation by nomination.

Again in 1924, the Secretary of State for India constituted the Reforms Enquiry Committee under the chairmanship of Home Member, Alexendar Muddiman with 8 others as members (1) to enquire into the difficulties arising from, or defects inherent in, the working of the Government of India Act and the Rules thereunder in regard to the Central Government and the Government of Governors' provinces; and (2) to investigate the feasibility and desirability of securing remedies for such difficulties or defects, consistent with the structure, policy and purpose of the Act, (a) by action taken under the Act and the Rules, or (b) by such amendments of the Act as appear necessary to rectify any administrative imperfections. The Committee in its report submitted on December 3, 1924 made certain recommendations and thought it desirable that the Depressed Classes and the factory labourers should receive further representation, as their representation was not considered adequate. "So far as the Depressed Classes are concerned we consider that unless in any particular case a local government is prepared to recommend a system of election, the further representation which we consider necessary can only be secured by nomination... If increased representation by nomination becomes necessary the provisions of the Act which place a minimum limit upon the proportion of elected members in each legislative body may in certain cases require amendment."[19] This recommendation was accepted by the Secretary of State who increased the number of seats to 20.[20]

The grant of representation to the Depressed Classes, even if by nomination, marked the beginning of a new era in Indian politics. It accorded legitimacy to the claim of the Depressed Classes for separate representation in the Legislatures, a claim which became a bone of contention in later years. The 1909 Act legitimised communal politics, which in course of time engulfed the country so much that it resulted in the vivisection of the country within a span of 40 years. The Muhammedans indeed pressed for and obtained from Lord Minto a promise that they should elect their own members in separate Muhammedan constituencies. Now it was the turn of the Depressed Classes. Once representation was offered to a section of population on the basis of their hierarchical position in the Hindu society, they could channelise their activities in building up enough pressure on the government to accede to their claim to representation on the basis of their number. As very aptly summed up by Dr. Ambedkar: "Thus the right of the Depressed Classes to special representation in the Legislature had become a principle which was not only accepted but adopted in the Constitution (of 1919). So well was this principle recognised that it had been extended even to District Local Boards, School Boards and Municipalities. A claim which had been given legal recognition in 1919 and which had thereby become a right and which had become perfected by the representatives of the Depressed Classes felt could not be disputed by any body."[21] The next step was consolidation of the gain and increasing the quota in future constitutions. The period from 1920 onwards till the enactment of the 1935 Act witnessed heightened activities on the part of the leaders of the Depressed Classes for more and more political power on the basis of their hierarchical position in the Hindu society. Commenting on the grant of communal electorate to the Muslims in the 1909 Act, the Mont-Ford Report observed that "it is probable that the far-reaching consequences of the decision and the difficulties which it would create at a later stage were not fully foreseen."[22] In the same vein it may be said that the authors of the 1919 Act did not foresee the cleavages and disunity that their decision on giving separate representation to a section of Hindu population on the basis of caste would create. Or was it a concerted move to divide the people on whatever pretext possible—be it religion or caste? Now the independence movement had to confront three forces—the ruling British Government, religion, and caste. Enough measures were taken, it seems, to delay the process of handing over power to Indians, though outwardly maintaining a facade of neutrality and urgency.

Caste Factor in Indian Politics

The first decade of the twentieth century saw a sharp increase in nationalism as well as caste-consciousness all over India. During the war years there was not only a striking growth of nationalist sentiment, but also an expectation that at the end of the war there would be a transfer of more power to Indian hands. The leaders of the non-Brahmin movement were afraid that this might be seized on by the Brahmins, and that they might be left high and dry. They wanted to make sure they would also benefit, and to this end they regarded communal representation as absolutely essential. Otherwise there would be a Brahmin oligarchy which would use its power to oppress everyone else. Some leaders of the movement in Madras openly gave expression to such a sentiment. The Maharajah of Kolhapur, the Maratha leader of the movement in Bombay, however, took a more nationalist stand, saying that he was for "home rule", but that communal (that is caste-based) representation was necessary for at least ten years in order to teach the non-Brahmin castes their rights. The Maharajah's position corresponded to that of the non-Brahmin leaders in the Madras Presidency. But the Justicites openly looked to the British to protect them from the more immediate if not more sinister foe, the Brahmin. It is indeed significant that an identical view was expressed in distant Bengal in the *Pataka*, a journal of the Namasudra caste: "The British government itself has now come to the aid of the uneducated; they have ever been the help of the poor, and the hope of the downtrodden castes."[23] Bose notes that the Namasudras had abstained from the anti-partition agitation of Bengal in 1905, and that at the height of the *Swadeshi* movement in 1907, "a deputation of representative Namasudra citizens waited upon the Lieutenant-Governor and prayed for the perpetuation of

British rule."[24] During the decade 1910-20 a section of the British in India made the Brahmin out to be their arch enemy. There was, first, the publication in 1910 of Valentine Chirol's *Indian Unrest*, the main thesis of which was that Brahminism and Western education constituted a serious threat to the continuance of British rule in India. The second was the publication, in 1918, of the Rowlatt Report (Report of the Committee Appointed to Investigate Revolutionary Conspiracies in India) which "showed conclusively that revolutionary conspiracy in Bombay was 'purely Brahmin and mostly Chitpavan' and that elsewhere in India the Brahmins had played a large part in fomenting and carrying out revolutionary crime."[25] The report gives details of the caste, age and occupation of "persons convicted in Bengal of revolutionary crimes or killed in commission of such crimes during the years 1907-1917." According to the report, almost 90 per cent of the revolutionaries belonged to the high castes of Bengal (Brahmin, Vaidya and Kayastha who comprise only about six per cent of the total population of Bengal) and were largely between 16 and 30 years in age.[26] Finally, there was the association of Brahmins, especially Madras Brahmins, with Mrs. Besant's Home Rule Movement (1916-17) and the playing up of this fact by the Justice Party in Madras to promote their interests.[27] It needed the inspiring leadership of Gandhiji and the Civil Disobedience Movements of the twenties and thirties to cut across caste and regional differences and bring the Indian masses into the nationalist stream.

The Indian National Congress, as we have seen, adopted for the first time an anti-untouchability resolution in the Calcutta session (December 26-29, 1917). Mrs. Annie Besant in her presidential address made a pointed reference to the anti-Brahmin movement in the Madras Presidency and the attempts of the official and non-official Europeans to stir the submerged classes into opposition to Home Rule and urged the delegates to work for a brighter future of the members of this class.[28] Since then eradication of untouchability became one of the aims of the Indian National Congress. Gandhiji wrote:

> Non-cooperation against the Government means cooperation among the governed, and if Hindus do not remove the sins of untouchability, there will be no Swaraj whether in one year or in hundred years...Swaraj is as unattainable without the removal of the sins of untouchability as it is without Hindu-Muslim Unity.[29]

In the Nagpur session (December 26-31, 1920) a resolution said: "The Hindu delegates of this Congress call upon the leading Hindus to settle all disputes between Brahmins and non-Brahmins, wherever they may be existing, and to make a special effort to rid Hinduism of the reproach of untouchability, and respectfully urges the religious heads to help the growing desires to reform Hinduism in the matter of its treatment of the suppressed classes."[30] In the very next session of the Congress at Ahmedabad (December 27-28, 1921), V.J. Patel, Chairman of the Reception Committee, informed the delegates that perhaps the greatest advance was made in the matter of untouchability. Untouchability was an attitude which had undergone a most noticeable change...The suppressed countrymen freely attended the Congress meetings.[31] In this very session Gandhiji made the issue of removal of untouchability as essential plank of Congress propaganda and at his suggestion it was resolved that a volunteer should be accepted only on signing a pledge which stipulated, amongst others, a declaration that "as a Hindu I believe in the justice and necessity of removing the evil of untouchability and shall, on all possible occasions, seek personal contact with an endeavour to render service to the submerged classes."[32] Incidentally, the Ahmedabad Congress gave sole executive authority to Gandhiji and invested him with full power of the All-India Congress Committee.[33]

The Working Committee of the Congress met at Bardoloi on February 11 and 12, 1922 and advised all Congress organisations "to organise the Depressed Classes for a better life, to improve their social, mental and moral condition, to induce them to send their children to national schools and to provide for them the ordinary facilities which the other citizens enjoy." The call continued with a note that "whilst, therefore, where the prejudice against the Untouchables is still strong in places, separate schools and separate wells must be maintained out of Congress funds, every effort should be made to draw such children to national schools and to persuade the people to allow the Untouchables to use the common wells."[34]

After this programme was confirmed by the All-India Congress Committee at its meeting at Delhi on February 24 and 25, 1922,[35] the All-India Congress Committee at its meeting at Lucknow on June 6, 7 and 10, 1922, appointed "a committee consisting of Swami Shraddhanandji, Mrs. Sarojini Naidu and Messers I.K. Yajnik and G.B. Deshpande to formulate a scheme embodying practical measures to be adopted for bettering the condition of the so-called Untouchables throughout the country and to place it for consideration before the next meeting of the Committee, the amount to be raised for the scheme to be Rs. 2 lacs for the present."[36] Swami Shradhanandji, a respected sanyasin of the Arya Samaj, however, resigned from this Committee on the question of release of fund and the Working Committee in its meeting at Bombay on July 18 and 19, 1922, appointed G.B. Deshpande the convenor of the Depressed Classes sub-committee.[37]

The Thirty-ninth session of the Indian National Congress was held at Belgaum on December 26 and 27, 1924 under the Presidentship of Gandhi. In his presidential address, Gandhiji exhorted that the removal of untouchability was just as essential for Swaraj as the attainment of Hindu-Muslim unity. This was an essentially Hindu question and Hindus could claim or take Swaraj till they had restored the liberty of the suppressed classes. To remove untouchability was a penance that caste Hindus owed to Hinduism and to themselves. He also warned against the tendency of exploiting the suppressed classes for political end.[38] At the end of the session a resolution on untouchability was adopted as follows:

> The Congress notes with satisfaction the progress in Hindu opinion regarding the removal of untouchability, but is of opinion that much yet remains to be done and therefore appeals to the Hindu members of all Congress organisations to make a greater effort in the cause. The Congress hereby urges the Hindu members of Provincial Congress Committees to devote greater attention to the amelioration of the lot of the Depressed Classes by ascertaining their wants, such as in regard to wells, places of worship, facilities for education, etc., and making provisions for meeting such wants. The Congress congratulates the Satyagrahis of Vaikom, who are engaged in asserting the right of way of untouchables through a thoroughfare which is open to caste Hindus, on their non-violence, patience, courage and endurance, and hopes that the State of Travancore which is regarded as enlightened will recognise the justice of the Satyagrahis' claim and grant speedy relief.[39]

The removal of untouchability was long confined to the platform of social or religious reform. By making it one of the items of constructive programme of the Congress, the attitude towards it of the educated classes and masses alike was changed perceptibly. In the subsequent Congress sessions held at Kanpur (December 26-28, 1925), Gauhati (December 26-28, 1926) and Calcutta (December 28-January 1, 1929), this programme of work was discussed and resolutions[40] were adopted including this task in its constructive programme of work. Immediately after the Congress session in Calcutta, a Sub-Committee for removal of untouchability under the charge of Jamnalal Bajaj was formed. As a result of the campaign of this Sub-Committee, many well known temples, which would not admit these classes, had been thrown open to them. Numerous wells and schools were opened to the people of these suppressed classes. Many municipalities also cooperated in this work. Further, it was claimed by the General Secretaries of the Indian National Congress in their report for the year 1929, that the effect of the propaganda for the removal of untouchability had been two-fold. The so-called higher castes had been induced in some measure to give up the exclusiveness which they had for long jealously kept, and the suppressed classes had become self-conscious and assertive of their rights.[41]

The All-India Hindu Maha Sabha, which was formed in 1915, because the Congress being a political party could not deal with questions which affected various communities in social and other non-political spheres,[42] also took programme for removal of untouchability from Hindu society. In the Gaya session of the Maha Sabha, held on December 30, 1922 a resolution was adopted requesting the Hindu religious leaders to impart religious training and improve social condition of low classes of Hindus including Untouchables and raise their status in every way.[43] This was a follow-up measure of the Nagpur Congress (1920) resolution calling upon the Hindus to make a special effort to rid Hinduism of the reproach of untouchability. In the seventh session of the Hindu Maha Sabha held in August, 1923, a resolution was adopted expressing its firm conviction that with a view to keep faith in Hinduism in the heart of Untouchables it was necessary to make arrangements for their education on sanitation and religion, also to allow them to read in schools, to draw water from wells, to have Darshan in temples and to sit in public meetings, which should be arranged in consultation with a sub-committee of Pandits.[44] The subsequent sessions of the Hindu Maha Sabha urged the Hindus to remove all restraints imposed on the Untouchables in the matter of use of public schools, public wells, roads and entry to temples.[45] A clear indication of the awakening of the Hindu social conscience can be had from the following resolutions passed by the Hindu Maha Sabha at its session in Surat on March 30-April 1, 1929:

> "This Hindu Maha Sabha declares that the so-called Untouchables have equal rights with other Hindus to study in public schools, to take water from public wells and other sources of drinking water, to sit with

> others in public meetings and to walk on public roads. The Maha Sabha calls upon all Hindus to remove such restrictions as may be existing anywhere at present in the way of the so-called Untouchable Hindus exercising these rights.
>
> "This Maha Sabha declares that the so-called Untouchables are fully entitled to have Dev Darshan, and the Maha Sabha calls upon all Hindus in general and all Hindu Sabhas in particular to provide the same facilities for Dev Darshan to them as are enjoyed at present by other Hindus.
>
> "This Maha Sabha calls upon Purohits (Priests), barbers and washermen to offer their services to the so-called Untouchables, especially the sweepers, and directs the local branches of the Hindu Maha Sabha to draw special attention of their Local Boards towards this matter.
>
> "This Maha Sabha looks upon the practice of nomination of the representatives of the Depressed Classes by the Government to the Local Bodies, Provincial Councils and the Assembly as most harmful and injurious to the true interests of the country and considers that this practice will become a source of creating a great gulf in the near future between other Hindus and the so-called Untouchable Classes. In the opinion of the Maha Sabha the right course to stop this practice is to put forward and back proper candidates belonging to the so-called Untouchable Classes to the elected bodies named above."[46]

Though the object of the Hindu Maha Sabha was to organise the Hindus, B.R. Jadhav, Minister of Education of Bombay and a leader of the Non-Brahmin movement in Bombay, as president of the ninth session of the Madras Non-Brahmin Confederation held at Madras on December 19, 1925, felt that organisation and unification of the Hindus would not be possible unless the Brahmin was ready to come down from his arrogant position. He might have been giving vent to the estranged feeling of a section of Non-Brahmins when he, in course of his presidential speech, said that "whatever Swarajism may stand for in other part of Northern India, Swarajism is synonymous with Brahminism in the Maratha-speaking districts of the Central Provinces and in Berar."[47] As if taking a cue from Jadav's speech, Dewan Bahadur Kumaraswami Raddiar, in his presidential address to the Non-Brahmin Confederation held at Coimbatore on July 2-4, 1927, declared: "Brahminism has acquired in the South Indian Brahmin vocabulary many synonyms—Swarajism, Nationalism and Patriotism."[48] Incidentally, this Conference accepted the scheme of entry into the Congress as an effective solution of the Non-Brahmin problems,[49] but the Bombay Non-Brahmin Conference meeting on August 27-28, 1927, rejected this move by a majority of 12-10 votes.[50]

The Indian Communists, however, had a different perception of the effect of Swaraj on the unfortunate lot of the Untouchables and their views were very succintly summed up by the President of the First Indian Communist's Conference held on December 26, 1925 thus:

> "From the standpoint of communism, this question of untouchability is purely an economic problem. Whether this class of people are admitted into temples or tanks or streets is not a question connected with our fight for Swaraj. With the advent of Swaraj, these social and religious disabilities will fall of themselves. Communists have neither caste nor creed nor religion. As Hindus, Mohammedans or Christians, they may have any private views about them. The question of untouchability is essentially associated with economic dependence of the vast mass of these Hindus. No sooner their economic dependence is solved, the social stigma of untouchability is bound to disappear. It is this inequality in the ownership of land which is mainly

responsible for the existence of helotry of the vast masses of the suppressed peoples. Not more entry into temples, tanks and roads will raise these unfortunates in the social scale in equal terms with their affluent brethren."[51]

The All-India Social Conference always stood for removal of untouchability and grant of equal social and religious rights and privileges to the neglected people.[52] It even took a resolution in 1924 that the depressed classes of Hindus must be represented by the elected members in the Councils to protect their interests.[53]

The National Liberal Federation also called upon the Hindu community to undo the grievous wrong done to the Untouchables and take all possible steps to ameliorate their condition socially, educationally and economically,[54] and give them preference for employment when fully qualified candidates were available.[55]

It may be noted that for five years from 1922 to 1927 the country passed through the horrible phase of Hindu-Muslim riots. The growing menace of Muslim intransgience which had no dearth of excuses for playing with the lives and property of the Hindus necessitated a strong Hindu organisation to protect the life and property of the Hindus. The Indian National Congress being a sort of an umbrella organisation for people of all creeds, castes and languages, was incapable of shielding the Hindus from the wrath of the Muslims. Pandit Madan Mohan Malaviya, Lala Lajpat Rai, Swami Shraddhanand, Dr. Moonje and others supported the cause of Hinduism, while continuing to be leaders of the Indian National Congress as well, as was the practice then. As a matter of fact almost all the leaders of the All-India Muslim League, All-India Hindu Maha Sabha, All-India Khialafat Committee and the like were not only important leaders of the Indian National Congress but also used to hold the sessions of these organisations at the same venue and in the same pandal where the Congress session was held. There was no bar in dual membership and becoming leaders of two or more organisations at the same time, even though such organisations more often than not championed sectarian or communal ideas. Under such circumstances the Hindu Maha Sabha came into existence. Swami Shraddhanand started *shuddhi* movement to counteract the *Tablig* movement launched by Mohammad Ali. It was a concerted campaign to take back the Hindus who had embraced Islam. Again it was he who sounded the clarion call of *Sangathan* with two-fold objectives— one of defending Hinduism against outside attacks and secondly, to promote harmony and goodwill between the different communities in India. Swamiji, however, fell a martyar to a shot fired by a young Muslim fanatic, Abdul Rashid, on December 23, 1926. In 1925, Dr. K.B. Hedgewar founded another organisation known as Rastriya Swayam Sevak Sangh to unite Hindus for the regeneration of Bharat. Inter-communal friction had always been evident in India but escalation of communal violence in all parts of the country in such an unprecedented scale as in the third decade of the twentieth century, that too after the introduction of constitutional reforms, made people to find out what had gone away in our body politic and whether the growing cleavages and dissensions among the two major communities of India had anything to do with the introduction of communal electorate in the 1909 Act and its perpetuation in the 1919 Act. One is inclined to agree with the findings of the Muddiman Committee that "it is more than probable that the view which has been indicated in some of the evidence produced before us that the introduction of the reforms scheme has contributed to the growth of such friction, is not without foundation. The desire of different communities each to strengthen its own position has been an underlying and deeper cause."[56]

In such an atmosphere an effort was made for drafting a constitution acceptable to all parties. An All Parties Conference was held on February 12-22, 1928. Twenty-nine parties including the Indian National Congress, the All-India Muslim League, the All-India Hindu Maha Sabha, the National Liberation Federation, Central Khilafat Committee, Central

Sikh League, Communist Party (Bombay), Bombay Non-Brahmin Party, Nationalist Non-Brahmin Party, other associations and organisations representing sectarian and communal interests participated in it.[57] After discussing the preliminaries, the Conference held its sitting in Bombay on May 19, 1928. It appointed a sub-committee, under the presidentship of Pandit Motilal Nehru, to draft a constitution. Other members of the committee were Subhas Bose, Sir Tej Bahadur Sapru, Shuaib Qureshi, Sir Ali Imam, Sardar Mangal Singh, M.S. Aney and C.R. Pradhan. It produced an unanimous report, which is popularly known as Nehru Report. For the first time in India's history all political parties laid their heads together to discuss constitutional problems and their mutually agreeable solutions. The salient points of the recommendations of the Nehru Report, amongst others, were, Dominion status and full responsible government, provincial autonomy with residuary powers to be exercised by the centre, joint electorate with reservation of seats instead of communal electorate, creation of new provinces etc. The Report did not make any special provision for the representation of the 'Non-Brahmins' and the 'Depressed Classes' in the legislatures. The Report felt strongly

> "that the Depressed Classes must be abolished or rather that they should be raised socially and economically so that they may take their proper place in the community. The only effective way to do this to give them educational and other facilities for this advance and to remove all obstacles in the way of this advance. Some of the articles in the Declaration of Rights, which we have recommended, will go a long way to remove the disabilities from which these classes suffer and will give them an opportunity to go ahead. The proposal that we should have adult suffrage will also automatically raise their level and increase their political power. Finally, we have strongly recommended that the education of the backward classes should be a special concern of the state. If all these recommendations are acted upon, we are convinced that the Depressed Classes will rapidly disappear and will be replaced by

a self-reliable and progressive group, cooperating with other groups in the welfare of the entire community".[58]

The Report was accepted unanimously by the All-Parties Conference at Lucknow (August 28-31, 1928)[59] but difficulties arose when it came up for scrutiny separately before all the parties which were represented at Lucknow Conference. They began to examine the report with a communal bias. Muslim League was divided on the issue. Maulana Azad, Hakim Ajmal Khan, Dr. Ansari and other nationalist leaders were in favour of accepting the report in its original form. Mohammad Shafi and others stood for rejecting it. The third section was led by Mohammad Ali Jinnah who was prepared to accept it but only after certain vital changes, proposed by him, were introduced in it. The report was placed before the All-Parties Convention which met under the presidentship of Dr. Ansari at Calcutta from December 22, 1928 to January 1, 1929. On January 1, 1929, on a motion moved by Mahatma Gandhi, the Convention adjourned sine die without coming to any agreement on any question, not even on the communal question, to meet when necessary for completing its work.[60]

Jinnah who did not agree to Nehru Report put forward his famous Fourteen Points as the minimum demands of the Muslims for any political settlement. They were in the following terms:—

1. The form of the future Constitution should be federal with residuary powers vested in the provinces.
2. A uniform measure of autonomy should be granted to all provinces.
3. All legislatures in the country and other elected bodies should be reconstituted on the definite principle of adequate and effective representation of minorities in every province without reducing the majority of any province to a minority or even equality.
4. In the Central Legislature, Muslim representation should not be less than one-third.

5. The representation of communal groups should continue to be by means of separate electorates as at present, provided that it should be open to any community, at any time, to abandon its separate electorate in favour of joint electorates.

6. Any territorial redistribution that might at any time be necessary should not in any way affect the Muslim majority in the Punjab, Bengal and North-West Frontier Province.

7. Full religious liberty, that is, liberty of belief, worship, observances, propaganda, association and education, should be guaranteed to all communities.

8. No bill or resolution, or any part thereof, should be passed in any legislature or any other elected body if three-fourths of the members of any community in that particular body oppose such a bill resolution or part thereof on the ground that it would be injurious to the interests of that community or, in the alternative, such other method as may be devised or as may be found feasible and practicable to deal with such cases.

9. Sind should be separated from the Bombay Presidency.

10. Reforms should be introduced in the North-West Frontier Province and Beluchistan on the same footing as in other provinces.

11. Provision should be made in the Constitution giving the Muslims an adequate share along with other Indians in all the Services of the State and in self-governing bodies, having due regard to the requirements of efficiency.

12. The Constitution should embody adequate safeguards for the protection of Muslim religion, culture and personal law, and the promotion of Muslim education,

language, religion, personal laws, Muslim charitable institutions, and for their due share in grants-in-aid given by the State and by self-governing bodies.

13. No Cabinet, either Central or Provincial, should be formed without there being a proportion of Muslim Ministers of at least one-third.

14. No change to be made in the Constitution by the Central Legislature except with the concurrence of the States constituting the Indian Federation.[61]

Jinnah by advancing his Fourteen Point formula offered no practicable solution of communal problem. He, however, succeeded in bringing the warring factions of the Muslim League together. Notwithstanding the opposition of the Hindus and the Sikhs and the rejection by the Simon Commission, the British Government when called upon to act as an arbiter, points out Dr. Ambedkar, granted the Muslims all their demands, old and new, as contained in the Fourteen Points of Jinnah.[62]

Simon Commission

The Government of India Act, 1919 had imposed an obligation on His Majesty's Government to appoint a Commission, at the expiration of 10 years from the passing of the Act, for the purpose of inquiring into the working of the system of government set up under the Act and certain kindred matters and reporting on the constitutional changes which might be considered desirable. Accordingly, on November 8, 1927 the formation of the Statutory Commission presided over by the celebrated constitutional lawyer Sir John Simon and assisted by six other members of the Parliament was announced.

The announcement in India—long advocated and anxiously awaited—of the appointment of the Statutory Commission aroused a storm of indignation and protest. The decision of His Majesty's Government to confine the personnel of the Commission to the members of the two Houses of Parliament was held as constituting an insult to Indians, and an arrogant repudiation of the claim which had been put forward that they should be given a predominant voice in the determination of the future constitution of their country. Almost all the major political parties like the Indian National Congress, All India Muslim League, All India Liberal Federation, All-India Hindu Maha Sabha, Indian Trade Union Congress passed resolution to boycott the Simon Commission.

The reaction of the Depressed Classes to the Simon Commission's tour of India was far different from that of these political parties and organisations. Eighteen Depressed Classes associations testified willingly to the Commission, sixteen of them asking for separate electorates for Untouchables.[63] While Ambedkar's students walked out of his class at Government Law College in protest, Ambedkar told the Commission that the Untouchables were relieved of anxiety because the Simon Commission did not include an Indian, since such a nominee could not be truly representative of all groups. He urged that the Depressed Classes should be treated as a distinct minority because they were outside the pale of Hindu society. As there was really no link between the Depressed Classes and the Hindu community, they must be regarded as a distinct and independent minority, entirely different from the Hindu community. He claimed for greater political protection than any other community in India because of educational backwardness, economic and social barriers. As a matter of demand for political protection, representation on the same basis as the Mohammedan community was asked for. Reserved seats if accompanied by adult franchise or separate electorate in the absence of adult franchise and certain safeguards either in the constitution or else in the way of advice in the instrument to the Governor regarding the education of Depressed Classes and the entry into public services were claimed by him. 22 seats reserved out of 140 seats, in case of adult suffrage, and the same number of seats through separate electorates in the Bombay Council if adult suffrage was not granted, he informed the Commission, would satisfy him and the organisation he spoke for, the Bahiskrit Hitakarini Sabha (Society for the uplift of the Depressed),[64] which he founded in 1924 to work for the social and economic betterment of the Depressed Classes. The Central Provinces Depressed Classes Association expressed a similar view of rights and privileges in even stronger and more distrustful language. This group requested (1) more governmental power of veto for protection of minority, (2) separate representation not only in legislatures but also in all public bodies including universities in proportion to numerical strength, (3) posts in government service for Depressed Class members, with minimum qualifications required, (4) representation in Cabinet dependent only upon Depressed Class votes, (5) no application of a bill affecting Depressed Classes if three-fourths of the community opposed it and (6) special grants for education.[65]

After two years of consistent work the Commission prepared and published its report in May, 1930. But even before the submission of the Simon Commission Report, the Labour Government of Great Britain, which came into office following the general election in May 1929, announced its intention of giving the Dominion Status to India and also of convening a Round Table Conference. The Viceroy of India made an announcement on October 31, 1929 of inviting representatives of different parties and interests in British India and representatives of the Indian States for the purpose of a conference and discussion in regard both to the British Indian and All-Indian problems after the submission of the reports of the Simon Commission and the Indian Central Committee.[66]

Round Table Conference

The report of the Simon Commission proved unacceptable to the major contenders. The British Government therefore convened a Round Table Conference in London to which it invited delegates from all parties and prominent interest groups "to discuss the future system of government for India and seek agreement for the guidance of British Parliament as to the foundation upon which it must stand."[67] The Indian National Congress leaders expressed their inability to attend the Conference unless previous assurance were given by His Majesty's Government that the purpose of the Conference was to draft a scheme for Dominion Status which His Majesty's Government would undertake to support.[68] Out of 88 delegates, who attended the Conference, 56 were from British India representing various interests like Hindus, Muslims, Sikhs, Anglo-Indians, Indian Christians, Depressed Classes, Landlords, Workers, Women, 16 from princely states and 16 represented British political parties.[69] Dr. Ambedkar and Dewan Bahadur R. Srinivasan of Madras represented the Depressed Classes. Their nomination, in the words of Ambedkar, meant "that the Untouchables were regarded not merely as a separate element from the Hindus but also of such importance as to have the right to be consulted in the framing of a constitution for India."[70] Subhas Chandra Bose voiced another interpretation of Ambedkar's political rise: "In 1930 and after, Dr. Ambedkar has had leadership thrust upon him by a benign British Government, because his services were necessary to embarrass the nationalist leaders."[71] Ambedkar, however, on his own terms identified himself with nationalism, if not with the nationalists. Before the first Round Table Conference, at a meeting of the All India Depressed Classes Conference held in August, 1930 at Nagpur, Ambedkar said:

> I agree with the Congressmen that no country is good enough to rule over another. But I must also take the liberty to tell them point-blank that the proposition does not end there and that it is equally true that no class is good enough to rule over another class.
>
> He added,
>
> It is only in a Swaraj constitution that you stand any chance of getting the political power into your own hands without which you cannot bring salvation to your people.[72]

But he found it necessary to continue to press for political safeguards for Depressed Classes while the British continued to rule India, distrusting that those who put independence above social reform would allow the Untouchables equality.

The First Round Table Conference began on November 12, 1930 in St. James Palace and was inaugurated by the King Emperor. The total work of the Conference was distributed among nine Sub-Committees, viz., Federal Structure Sub-Committee, Provincial Sub-Committee, Minorities Sub-Committee, Franchise Sub-Committee, Service Sub-Committee, Sind Sub-Committee, N.W.F.P. Sub-Committee, Burma Sub-Committee and Defence Sub-Committee. Reports of the Sub-Committees were then considered by the Committee of the Whole Conference.

The task of finding the solution to the communal question was assigned to the Minorities Sub-Committee of which Dr. Ambedkar was a member. Dr. Ambedkar and Rao Bahadur R. Srinivasan presented a joint memorandum, which may, without exaggeration, be described as a charter of the Untouchables' demands. These were set forth in the memorandum in legal language with penalties provided for their violation. It suggested that the Untouchables should elect their representatives on the basis of adult suffrage through separate electorates for the first ten years. Afterwards they might be elected by joint electorates with reserved seats. At the same time joint electorates should not be forced on the Untouchables against their will. It also made it clear that no community should be granted weightage at the cost of the untouchables and that the Depressed Classes would never agree to any community getting representation on better terms than themselves. The Charter of safeguards included the basic demand for equal citizenship and equal opportunity for the Untouchables. To ensure this there should be equality before the law for them. Provisions for the free enjoyment of equal rights were also suggested. Social boycott, which seriously affected the Depressed Classes, to be banned, condign punishment being provided for anybody who practised it. Along with adequate representation in the legislatures, the memorandum pressed for adequate representation of the Depressed Classes in the Services because it was necessary for their political and social development. It also asked for adequate provision for their education and for sanitation in the places where they lived. Creation of special department in charge of a Minister for the purpose of watching the interests of the Depressed Classes and promoting their welfare as well as representation of the Depressed Classes in the Cabinet were also demanded. The full text of the joint Memorandum can be seen in Appendix C.[73] When Ambedkar drafted this Memorandum for consideration of the Round Table Conference he had not even the faintest idea that it would devolve on him, as chairman of the Drafting Committee, to give constitutional recognition to his own demands in the Constitution of free India.

On December 22, speaking on the question of special representation Dr. Ambedkar said: "There is no reason why, for instance, all communities should have same franchise—in fact, there may even be cases which we find in the practical affairs of life, that in order to reach equality of status, we may have to adopt, so to speak, methods of inequality. In the matter of treating the richer class as against the poorer, for example, we do enact certain special measures for the benefit of the latter. We tax the richer class at a higher rate than the poorer, the object being that the principle of ability to pay the tax may be realised in practice. I think that the same consideration might be applied to the Depressed Classes."[74] On January 1, 1931 he further made it clear: "If you give us adult universal suffrage the Depressed Classes, barring a short transitional period which they want for their organization, will be prepared to accept joint electorates and reserved seats; but if you do not give us adult suffrage, then we must claim representation through separate electorates."[75] After discussion on the communal question, the Minorities Sub-Committee submitted its report to the Conference on January

16, 1931[76] and the Committee of the Whole Conference adopted it on January 19, the relevant extracts of which are as follows:

4. The possibility was expressed that under certain conditions the election of the Legislatures might be from a general register, but no agreement was come to regarding these conditions.

   Whilst it was generally admitted that a system of joint free electorates was in the abstract the most consistent with democratic principles as generally understood, and would be acceptable to the Depressed Classes after a short transitional period provided the franchise was based on adult suffrage, the opinion was expressed that, in view of the distribution of the communities in India and of their unequal economic, social and political effectiveness, there was a real danger that under such a system the representation secured by minorities would be totally inadequate, and that this system would therefore give no communal security.

5. Claims were therefore advanced by various communities that arrangements should be made for communal representation and for fixed proportions of seats. It was also urged that the number of seats reserved for a minority community should in no case be less than its proportion in the population. The methods by which this could be secured were mainly three: (1) nomination, (2) joint electorates with reservation of seats, and (3) separate electorates.

6. Nomination was unanimously deprecated.

7. Joint electorates were proposed, with the proviso that a proportion of seats should be reserved to the communities. Thus a more democratic form would be given to the elections, whilst the purpose of the separate electorate system would be secured. Doubts were expressed that, whilst such a system of election might secure the repre-

sentation of minorities, it provided no guarantee that the representation would be genuine, but that it might, in its working, mean the nomination or, in any event, the election of minority representatives by the majority communities.

It was pointed out that this was in fact only a form of community representation and had in practice all the objections to the more direct form of community electorates.

8. The discussion made it evident that the demand which remained as the only one which would be generally acceptable was separate electorates. The general objection to this scheme has been subject to much previous discussion in India. It involves what is a very difficult problem for solution, viz. what would be the amount of communal representation in the various Provinces and in the Centre; that, if the whole, or practically the whole, of the seats in a Legislature are to be assigned to communities, there will be no room for the growth of independent political opinion or of true political parties, and this problem received a serious complication by the demand of the representative of the Depressed Classes that they should be deducted from the Hindu population and be regarded, for electoral purposes, as a separate community.

9. It was suggested that, in order to meet the most obvious objection to the earmarking of seats to communities, only a proportion should be so assigned— say 80 per cent or 90 per cent—and that the rest should be filled by open election. This, however, was not regarded by some of the communities as giving them the guarantees they required.

10. The scheme proposed by Maulana Muhammad Ali, a member of the Sub-Committee, whose death we deplore, that, as far as possible, no communal candidate should be elected unless he secured at least 40 per cent of the votes of his own community and at least 5 or 10 per cent,

according to arrangement, of the votes of the other community, was also considered. It was, however, pointed out that such a scheme necessarily involved the maintenance of communal registers, and so was open to objections similar to those urged against separate electorates.

12. There was general agreement with the recommendation of Sub-Committee No. II (Provincial Constitution) that the representation on the Provincial Executives of important minority communities was a matter of the greatest practical importance for the successful working of the new constitution, and it was also agreed that, on the same grounds, Muhammedans should be represented on the Federal Executive. On behalf of the smaller minorities a claim was put forward for their representation, either individually or collectively, on the Provincial and Federal Executives, or that, if this should be found impossible, in each cabinet there should be a Minister specially charged with the duty of protecting minority interests.

(Dr. Ambedkar and Sardar Ujjal Singh would add the words "and other important minorities" after the word Muhammedans in line 6.)

The difficulties of working jointly responsible Executives under such a scheme as this were pointed out.

13. As regards the administration, it was agreed that recruitment to both Provincial and Central Services should be entrusted to Public Service Commissions, with instructions to reconcile the claims of the various communities to fair and adequate representation in the Public Services, whilst providing for the maintenance of a proper standard of efficiency.

16. It has also been made clear that the British Government cannot, with any chance of agreement, impose upon the communities an electoral principle which, in some feature or other, would be met by their opposition. It was, therefore, plain that, failing an agreement, separate electorates, with all their drawbacks and difficulties, would have to be retained as the basis of the

electoral arrangements under the new constitution. From this the question of proportions would arise. Under these circumstances, the claims of the Depressed Classes will have to be considered adequately.

17. The Sub-Committee, therefore, recommend that the Conference should register an opinion that it was desirable that an agreement upon the claims made to it should be reached, and that the negotiations should be continued between the representatives concerned, with a request that the result of their efforts should be reported to those engaged in the next stage of these negotiations.

18. The Minorities and Depressed Classes were definite in their assertion that they could not consent to any self-governing constitution for India unless their demands were met in a reasonable manner.[77]

The Federal Structure Sub-Committee had also to consider the question of the Depressed Classes in connection with the composition of the Federal Legislatures. In the report it made to the Conference it said:

> Opinion was unanimous in the Sub-Committee that, subject to any report of the Minorities Sub-Committee, provision should be made for the representation, possibly in both Chambers, and certainly in the Lower Chamber, of certain special interests, namely, the Depressed Classes, Indian Christians, Europeans, Anglo-Indians, Landlords, Commerce (European and Indian) and Labour.[78]

This report was considered and adopted by the Committee of the Whole Conference on January 15, 1931.[79]

Though the First Round Table Conference was adjourned without any decision, the representatives of the Depressed Classes did succeed in convincing the Conference that the Depressed Classes were entitled to recognition as a separate entity for political and constitutional purposes.

The Civil Disobedience Campaign, which had kept the Congress aloof from the First Round Table, ended with the signing of the Gandhi-Irwin Pact on March 5, 1931. It also paved the way for holding the Second Round Table Conference between September 7 and December 1, 1931, the only one Gandhi attended as the sole representative of the Congress. The names of the delegates were announced in the third week of July. This time the number of delegates was increased to 112. Of them, 69 were from British India representing various interests and parties like Hindus, Muslims, Sikhs, Parsis, Anglo-Indians, Indian Christians, Depressed Classes, Women and Labour, besides the Congress, 23 from the Indian States and 20 from the three British Parties. Dr. Ambedkar and Dewan Bahadur R. Srinivasan were nominated to represent the Depressed Classes.[80]

The work of second session of the Round Table Conference was to continue the process of finding solutions to the problems standing in the way of framing a constitution, initiated by the first session. The Indian National Congress not being a party to the decisions arrived at the meetings of the first session was now confronted with a curious situation. Either to reject the recommendations of the various Sub-Committees on which it had no representatives or to accept the recommendations, even if these were at variance with its principles and creeds. If the Congress had participated in full strength in the deliberations of the first session it could have ensured reflection of its views and principles on many crucial decisions like communal electorate, representation of special interests, provincial autonomy, federal structure and the like. Having boycotted the first session, it now fell on the frail shoulder of Mahatma Gandhi to fight an unequal battle and undo the decisions of the first session. "By going there in 1931, alone and unfriended, the Mahatma had the tactical disadvantage of having to meet a conference which had come into existence without the participation of the Congress and of having to build on sectarian foundations laid by communalist members."[81] But Mahatma Gandhi was ill-equipped to discharge this onerous duty. "From the point of view of knowledge Mr. Gandhi proved himself to be a very ill-equipped person. On the many constitutional and communal questions with which the Conference was confronted, Mr. Gandhi had no views or suggestions of a constructive character to offer."[82] This comment might be considered a little harsh considering that it came from the pen of Dr. Ambedkar, but even Subhas Chandra Bose contended that Mahatma Gandhi was not a proper choice of the Congress to represent at the Round Table Conference. "It was only in London that he realised what it meant to have a conference with members chosen by the Government, with the Congress as one of the several parties present there and with himself as the only representative of the Congress."[83] Moreover, "he was at a physical disadvantage, being a single frail individual in a group of 107. If he had accepted the offer made by the Government, of fifteen or sixteen seats for the Congress Delegation his position would have been stronger. His colleagues would have been of great help to him in meeting and crossing swords with a solid phalanx of reactionaries. Moreover, the Mahatma did not seem to be cut out for the role of a bargainer."[84] Gandhiji even highlighted the unrepresentative character of the delegates which stood in the way of arriving at an agreed solution of the problems. In the Minorities Committee meeting he blurted out: "We are almost all not elected representatives of the parties or groups whom we are presumed to represent; we are here by nomination of the Government. Nor are those whose presence was absolutely necessary for an agreed solution to be found here."[85] He might have been stating the truth but this plain-speaking, no doubt, made him unpopular amongst a section of the delegates. Opposed to separate electorates to any group, he grudgingly conceded that "the Congress has reconciled itself to special treatment of the Hindu-Muslim-Sikh tangle. There are sound historical reasons for it but the Congress will not extend that doctrine in any shape or form (to Untouchables)."[86] The efforts of Mahatma Gandhi of finding a mutually agreed solution to the questions of communal representation and safeguards having failed, the British Prime Minister suggested that the other smaller minorities might meet separately to consider if they could produce a settlement of the communal question.[87] Taking the hint of the British Government, the Muhammadans, the Depressed Classes, a section of the Indian Christians, the Anglo-Indians and the British Community met separately and produced a document which embodies an agreement that they had come to amongst themselves, which, according to them, covered something in the region of 46 per cent of the population of British India.[88] This document known as the Minorities Pact, which is reproduced as Appendix D, gave separate electorates and undue weightage to communities, the signatories sought to represent. Gandhiji objected to the inclusion of the Depressed Classes as a separate political entity. "I can understand the claims advanced by other minorities, but the claims advanced on behalf of the Untouchables, that to me is the unkindest cut of all. It means the perpetual bar-sinister. I would not sell the vital interests of the Untouchables even for the sake of winning the freedom of India. I claim myself in my own person to represent the vast mass of the Untouchables...We do not want on our register and on our census Untouchables classified as a separate class. Sikhs may remain as such in perpetuity, so may Muhammadans, so may Europeans. Will Untouchables remain Untouchables in perpetuity? I would far rather that Hinduism died than that Untouchability lived...It will create a division in Hinduism which I cannot possibly look forward to with any satisfaction whatsoever. I do not mind Untouchables, if they so desire, being converted to Islam and Christanity. I would tolerate that, but I cannot possibly tolerate what is in store for Hinduism if there are two divisions set forth in the villages...if I was the only person to resist this thing I would resist it with my life."[89] Dr. S.K. Dutta, a representative of the Indian Christians, wondered how the Depressed Classes being a section of the Hindus could be treated as a minority in relation to their co-religionists, and whether the five signatories could speak for 115 million people they claim to speak for. The question of separate electorates and undue weightage came in for sharp criticism not only from him[90] but also from the representatives of the Hindu Maha Sabha and the Sikhs.[91] Raja Narendra Nath also criticised it on the same line.[92] N.M. Joshi was critical for diluting the interest of the labours with communal interest.[93] Since the Minorities Pact was treated by the British Prime Minister as a part of the records of the Minorities Committee, representatives of the Hindu Maha Sabha, Sikhs, Anglo-Indians, Indian Christians, Women, Labour, Maratha and allied communities insisted and got their memoranda containing their point of view on solution of the communal problem and claims for protection of their interests, treated as part of the official documents, along with the Congress Scheme for a communal settlement.[94] B.R. Ambedkar and Dewan Bahadur R. Srinivasan submitted another supplementary memorandum on the claims of the Depressed Classes for separate representation,[95] which can be seen at Appendix E. Though the British Government did not take any decision on these documents furnished by the different claimants those became very handy, specially those reproduced as Appendices C to E while announcing the Communal Award on August 17, 1932.

In view of the stand taken by the delegates, the British Prime Minister adjourned the Minorities Committee *sine die* with a suggestion to the delegates to put in a signed requisition authorizing the Prime Minister to arbitrate and give his decision on the Communal issue.[96] Many delegates did it including Mahatma Gandhi.[97] Ambedkar, however, did not make any such requisition because he felt that "the demands of the Untouchables were so reasonable that no arbitration was necessary."[98] Or was he assured of separate electorates for the Depressed Classes beforehand?

Communal Award and Poona Pact

Ramsay Macdonald, the British Prime Minister, announced his decision known as Communal Award on August 4, 1932 (Appendix F). Along with it he also declared that he would be glad to accept any other solution of the communal problem provided it satisfied all communities. This Communal Award conceded separate electorates to the

Muslims, Sikhs, Indian Christians, Anglo-Indians, and Europeans. Labour, commerce, industry, mining and planting, land-holders and universities were also given separate constituencies and fixed seats. It also suggested the formation of general constituencies in which all persons other than Muslims, Sikhs, Christians, Anglo-Indians or Europeans were entitled to vote. Depressed Classes were recognised as a minority. Separate seats were allotted to them out of general seats. They were given right to exercise two votes each, one in the general constituency and the other in special constituency.

The Communal Award evoked a good deal of flutter and resentment in the country. The Award was a mischievous attempt to divide and weaken the Hindus by separating the Depressed Classes. For the first time the Depressed Classes were recognised as a separate community by awarding them separate electorates. The Simon Commission had rejected the claim of the Depressed Classes for separate electorates because of the difficulty of giving a definition of the Depressed Classes which should apply to all provinces,[99] and because it would mean "stigmatising each individual voter in the list, and militate against the process which is already beginning, and which needs to be in every way encouraged—that of helping those who are depressed to rise in the social and economic scale."[100] The Simon Commission Report was submitted in May, 1930 and the Communal Award was given in August, 1932. One wonders what happened in the interregnum of two years as to reject the recommendations of a Commission, set up by the Government and act contrary to its recommendations? One thing, however, had happened, i.e. formation of a National Government in Great Britain, which was virtually a Conservative Government, with its principle of perpetuating the British Rule at any cost by whipping up religious, parochial, casteist, and other disintegrating tendencies in our body politic.

The underlying motive of the Award was to split the Indian people into small and mutually hostile sections. The separatist system of representation on the basis of religion, sex, caste, race or sectional interest—instead of representation by the general mass of the people, usual in modern democracies—helped in the polarisation of sectional interests. Whereas the growth of a party or parties having commanding influences in all the Provinces should have checked the disintegrating tendencies, the set-up envisaged in the Communal Award, as it were, were against the growth of such parties having a fully national character. It was a direct attack on national solidarity. It provided for separate representation even in the case of Indian Christians and Women, although a majority of them did not make any demand for it.[101] The communal decision of the British Government accentuated communal dissension in the country, which ultimately paved the way for the partition of the country on the basis of religion.

The Award gave separate electorates for the Depressed Classes and allotted 78 seats to them. But the British Government did not give any definition of the Depressed Classes. As a result, there was now a reverse process for inclusion of castes in the list of depressed castes, which later came to be regarded as Scheduled Castes.

Even before the announcement of the Communal Award, Mahatma Gandhi informed the British Government that he would resort to 'fast unto death' if separate electorates for the Depressed Classes were accorded. After the announcement of the Communal Award Mahatma Gandhi commenced his 'fast unto death' on September 20, 1932. Leaders both from India and abroad became active to save Gandhiji's life. On the fifth day of the fast the leaders agreed on a formula. This settlement, called the Poona Pact, was signed on September 25, 1932, by Dr. Ambedkar on behalf of the Depressed Classes while Pt. Madan Mohan Malaviya did it on behalf of the caste Hindus. Ambedkar proved to be a hard bargainer and could extract a higher compensation for the Depressed Classes in place of the separate electorates given to them by the British Government. Poona Pact gave them 148 seats while the Award had given them only 78. The term of the

Poona Pact were given effect to by the British Government by embodying them in the Government of India Act, 1935 when the number of 148 seats was raised to 151 in making adjustments of seats for Bihar and Orissa.

The following is the text of the Poona Pact:

(1) There shall be seats reserved for the Depressed Classes out of the general electorate seats in the Provincial Legislatures as follows:

Madras 30; Bombay with Sind 15; Punjab 8; Bihar and Orissa 18; Central Provinces 20; Assam 7; Bengal 30: United Provinces 20; Total 148.

These figures are based on the total strength of the Provincial Councils, announced in the Prime Minister's decision.

(2) Election to these seats shall be by joint electorates subject, however, to the following procedure:

All the members of the Depressed Classes, registered in the general electoral roll in a constituency, will form an electoral college, which will elect a panel of four candidates belonging to the Depressed Classes for each of such reserved seats, by the method of the single vote; the four persons getting the highest number of votes in such primary election shall be candidates for election by the general electorate.

(3) Representation of the Depressed Classes in the Central Legislature shall likewise be on the principle of joint electorates and reserved seats by the method of primary election in the manner provided for in Clause 2 above, for their representation in the Provincial Legislatures.

(4) In the Central Legislature, eighteen percent of the seats allotted to the general electorate for British India in the said legislature shall be reserved for the Depressed Classes.

(5) The system of primary election to a panel of candidates for election to the Central and Provincial Legislatures, as herein before mentioned, shall come to an end after the first ten years, unless terminated sooner by mutual agreement under the provision of Clause 6 below.

(6) The system of representation of the Depressed Classes by reserved seats in the Provincial and Central Legislatures as provided for in Clauses 1 and 4 shall continue until determined by mutual agreement between the communities concerned in the settlement.

(7) Franchise for the Central and Provincial Legislatures for the Depressed Classes shall be as indicated in the Lothian Committee Report.

(8) There shall be no disabilities attaching to any one on the ground of his being a member of the Depressed Classes in regard to any elections to local bodies or appointment to the Public Services. Every endeavour shall be made to secure fair representation of the Depressed Classes in these respects, subject to such educational qualifications as may be laid down for appointment to the Public Services.

(9) In every province out of the educational grant, an adequate sum shall be earmarked for providing educational facilities to the Members of the Depressed Classes.[102]

Following the signing of the Poona Pact, an 'Untouchability Abolition Week' was observed throughout the country. Public meetings were addressed, inter-caste dinners were held, and temples were thrown open to the Untouchables. Attempts to fight against untouchability and caste superiority were so firm during 1931-32 that Gandhiji began calling them 'Harijans' (people of God) and established Harijan Sevak Sangh in September, 1932 for ameliorating their deplorable conditions by truthful and non-violent means. The Sangh with its branches all over the country, centred its activities around organisation of 'Melas' (fairs), camps, inter-caste dinners, publicity and propaganda through cinema vans, pamphlets and social workers. It tried and still tries to bring the entire Harijan-fold to a comparable and honourable position with that of the upper caste Hindus in toto. Also, it believed that actual emancipation could be realized by the spread of education, sanitary habits, medical care, gainful employment and enhanced economic condition. This uphill task, this philanthropic institution had taken voluntary with the government grants and other resources, however small or large, was really worth commendation by the welfare leaders. Besides Harijan Sevak Sangh, there were several voluntary organisations like the Arya Samaj, the Ram Krishna Mission, the Scheduled Caste Federation, the Servants of India Society, the Bharathiya Depressed Class League, and the Iswar Saran Ashram which came into existence and started working for the welfare of Scheduled Caste people.[103]

The substance of the Poona Pact was the reservation to the Depressed Classes of a number of seats out of the seats classified as general seats in the Award. which meant in effect out of Hindu seats, since Hindus formed the great bulk of the general electorates. These reserved seats would, however, be filled by an unusual form of double election. All members of the Depressed Classes who were registered on the general electoral roll of certain constituencies would elect a panel of four candidates belonging to their own body, and the four persons who received the highest number of votes in this primary election would be the only candidate for election to the reserved seat, but the candidate finally elected to the reserved seat would be elected by the general electorate, that is to say, by caste Hindus and by members of the Depressed Classes alike. The number of seats reserved for the Depressed Classes under the Poona Pact was practically double the number reserved under the Communal Award; but whereas under the latter there was to be a direct election to those seats by a separate Depressed Classes electorate, there would now be an election by the general electorate, although the candidates for election would have been previously selected by means of a primary election at which members of the Depressed Classes only would be entitled to vote. Since the Pact did not, and indeed could not, increase the total number of seats assigned by the Communal Award to the different Legislatures, it followed that any increase in the seats reserved for the Depressed Classes must involve a diminution in the seats which would be available for caste Hindus.[104]

Depressed Classes and Scheduling of Castes

Now that a substantial number of seats, about 19% of the general seats, were earmarked for representation of the Depressed Classes by election, the necessity of defining these Depressed Classes and also ascertaining their number arose. The Simon Commission recommended the appointment of a Franchise Committee which should undertake for each province the framing of a definition of Depressed Classes and the determination of their numbers so defined.[105] The Indian Franchise Committee, popularly known as Lothian Committee, so constituted, recommended that "the term 'depressed classes' should not include primitive or aboriginal tribes, nor should it include those Hindus who are only economically poor and in other ways backward but are not regarded as untouchables."[106] The Committee was of opinion that the term should be applied only to those who were 'untouchables', that is to say, those whose touch or approach caused pollution and who were denied access to the interior of Hindu temple.[107]

The Provincial Franchise Committees and provincial governments did furnish their recommendations to the Lothian Committee but the estimates of the number of depressed classes arrived at by them were not necessarily the total population of those who should form the depressed classes according to the Committee's definition. The Madras Government had already defined the term 'depressed classes' for the purpose of the Madras Local Boards Act, 1920 and their report conformed to that definion. Bombay's figures were estimated by a committee which had been appointed long before the Franchise Committee had defined the term 'depressed classes'.[108] In U.P. the position was little different. If the test of untouchability was strictly adhered to the number of depressed classes would be around 6 lakhs. But Blunt, a member of the Executive Committee estimated the untouchables at 9.2 millions. His interpretation of untouchability, however, went beyond the Committee's definition. The Census figures, which did not follow the Committee's definition, put the number at 12.6 millions.[109] And the most glaring case was that of Bengal which could not furnish the figure even because the list of castes to be included in the depressed classes was under revision.[110]

Now the definition and the number of depressed classes became a bone of contention. The representatives of caste Hindus from Bengal in their evidence before the Joint Committee on Indian Constitutional Reform suggested to Ambedkar that the Bengal Government should make an enquiry to determine who were the depressed classes on the twin criteria of untouchability and unapproachability but Ambedkar not only evaded the challenge but blamed the caste Hindu representatives for their failure to protect their interests at the time of signing the Poona Pact.[111] Ambedkar marshalled his argument for allotment of seats for the depressed classes on figures estimated by different committees at different point of time knowing it fully well that those committees' estimates could not be made applicable on this occasion, as none of them did follow the Lothian Committee's definition of depressed classes and even the census figures could not be sacroscant, because, as we have already seen, the censuses did not follow a uniform criteria everywhere. Even

Hutton's elaborate instructions on depressed classes were not adhered to at all places. Ambedkar himself conceded: "Before the time of the Lothian Committee the population of the Untouchables had no value. But after the Round Table Conference the Hindus had come to know that the Untouchables were demanding separate allotment of their share of representation, that such share must come out of the hump which the Hindus had been enjoying in the past and that the measure of the share must depend upon the population of the Untouchables."[112] For reasons obvious, Ambedkar could not allow any diminution in strength of the depressed classes, because the seats in the legislatures must have some bearing on population ratio as well. It must be commensurate to the seats allotted. Whereas the proper course should have been to define the depressed classes and then enumerate them and only after that allot a quota, if it has to be given, according to the population figure. This process was, however, reversed, in case of the Depressed Classes. First get a demand raised, then allot seats and after that enumerate them according to some definition. If the definition stands in the way, twist it in such a manner that it does not stand in the way of enumeration of such a class. This is precisely what the British Government did. The wording of Communal Award also supports this view. Para 9 of the Communal Award states: "The precise definition in each Province of those who will be entitled to vote in the special Depressed Class constituencies has not yet been finally determined. It will be based as a rule on the general principles advocated in the Franchise Committee's Report. Modification may, however, be found necessary in some Provinces in Northern India where the application of the general criteria of untouchability might result in a definition unsuitable in some respects to the special conditions of the Province".

Now that seats have been allotted, the question of 'Scheduling of castes' for the purpose of electoral arrangements brooked no delay. In view of the guideline in para 9 of the Communal Award, the lists prepared by the Provincial Governments did not necessarily conform to the definition settled I by the Lothian Committee. For instance, the Bengal Government found that the general criteria of untouchability would result in a definition (of depressed classes) unsuitable to the special conditions of the province. They, therefore, prepared a provisional list of "scheduled castes on the basis of the *social* and *political* backwardness of these castes and the necessity of securing for them special representation in order to protect their interests, and circulated the same to different caste organisations, individuals etc., with a view to obtaining their views regarding inclusion or non-inclusion of any caste in the provisional list. The list included not only Hindu castes but also some groups of aboriginal derivation now resident in Bengal which professed tribal or mixed religions."[113] It was also found that the list included Moslems and Christians as well as some castes which claimed to belong to the higher castes and had even in 1921, asked to be excluded from the category of Depressed Classes, e.g., Pod, Koch, Rajbanshi, Namsudras, etc.[114] But when the Bengal Government asked the District Officers and Commissioners of the Divisions to report whether the castes included in the list satisfied the above criteria, they were asked to examine "the *social, political, economic and educational position of the castes* in order to determine whether the castes were below the general level of development and so deserved special representation to protect their interests". Now it was not the untouchability but the level of social, political, economic and educational development of a caste which should determine whether it merited inclusion in the list. The District Officers and the Commissioners were asked to note that social precedence in itself was not a determining factor. The list was not a list of depressed classes in the sense in which that term was used in the Franchise Committee's Report and no caste was to be excluded from the list of 'Scheduled Castes' merely because it failed to satisfy the criteria adopted for depressed classes in that report. Its position in the list of Scheduled Castes must be considered on the basis of the more general criteria of social, educational, political and educational development,[115] because "Scheduled Castes" were a new political creation,[116] for the purpose of special electoral arrangements contemplated by the Communal Award.

Thus a special category of castes known as 'Scheduled Castes' was created by the British Government for the purpose of dividing the Hindu population in pursuance of its "Divide and Rule" policy. They were neither the 'untouchables' whose cause was so assiduously championed by Ambedkar, nor the depressed classes figuring in the census reports, and certainly not the depressed classes as defined by the Lothian Committee, specially constituted for the purpose of defining and enumerating the depressed classes, solely on the criteria of (a) denial of access to the interior of ordinary Hindu temples and (b) causing pollution by touch or within a certain distance, but "a group of castes, races or tribes which appear to correspond to the classes of persons formerly known as "the depressed classes"', as the Majesty in Council may specify."[117] Earlier the prevailing idea had been that inclusion in the list of Depressed Classes might affect the social prestige of the castes.[118] The scheduling of castes on the basis of social, political, economic and educational level of development removed that stigma so much so that even those castes which only a decade earlier had asked for exclusion from the list of Depressed Classes no longer pressed for it, because of the apparent political, economic and educational benefits. From now on, the process of upward mobility of castes either by the 'Sanskritization' process or by the 'Evengelical' process not only got stalled but actually a reverse process set in, that of inclusion of castes in the list of 'Scheduled Castes', which continues to remain the official designation for untouchables down to the present, though the term was primarily coined to denote those who would enjoy the special electoral arrangements for the 'Depressed Classes' under the 1935 Act. 'Scheduled Castes', according to Marc Galanter, "summons up the bureaucratic rigidification and torpor that overtook Ambedkar's measures for secular improvement."[119]

In a setting of Hindu-Muslim divergence, this sequence of events—the Communal Award, the fast and the Poona Pact—raised concern for untouchability to new heights, It was recognised as a problem that demanded a solution as part of the question of Indian nationhood. The salience of untouchability was not unconnected with concern about political alignments, especially after Ambedkar's efforts to obtain recognition for the depressed classes as a separate and distinct minority by siding with the Muslim League bloc during the Round Table Conferences. The exhortation of Dr. Ambedkar to his followers in the Yeola Conference on October 13, 1935 "to severe their connections with Hinduism and seek solace and self-respect in another religion"[120] was, therefore, a great shock to the Hindus and aroused a storm of opposition. On the other hand, it was a tantalizing source of hope for the non-Hindu leaders who saw in his announcement a possibility of bringing millions of untouchables into their fold. Whether Ambedkar was really in a position to get all the untouchables, now coming under the rubric of 'Scheduled Castes', converted into any other non-Hindu religion is a matter of conjecture, but as a writer has suggested, "the announcement about the decision for conversion could have been a calculated strategy to increase his bargaining power. Thus, so long as the threat to leave the pale of Hinduism persisted, the caste Hindu leaders might grant him greater concessions to avoid a loss of millions of their brothers. Had Dr. Ambedkar chosen to join the Muslim camp, the balance of power would have been decisively in their favour."[121] Gandhi charged that the religious feelings of the untouchables were being exploited in a political game.[122] Ambedkar's threat, however, did not materialise immediately, excepting an extended flirtation with Sikhism in 1936, and he waited for twenty long years before actual conversion to Buddhism.

Anxiety about the departure of the untouchables should be seen against a background of the much-discussed, long-term decline in the Hindu proportion of the total population of India roughly summarised in the following table :

Year	*Percentage*	*Source*
1881	74.3	1911 Census [123]
1891	72.3	-do-
1901	70.3	1941 Census[124]
1911	69.3	-do-
1921	68.4	-do-
1931	68.2	-do-
1941	65.9	-do-

Efforts to remove untouchability and help its victims proliferated in the wake of the Poona Pact. The new popular governments which took office in 1937 after the general elections held under the 1935 Act, avowed their opposition to untouchability. Madras passed the first legislation imposing criminal penalties for denying to untouchables the use of public facilities. Temple entry had been proclaimed earlier in a few progressive princely states. In 1938, for the first time in British India, government intervened to secure the opening of temples when Bombay and Madras passed temple-entry acts.[125] Encouragement of education for untouchables increased. Congress governments continued and extended the regime of communal quotas in public services and college admissions as did non-Congress governments elsewhere. In the Central services, the Government of India reserved quotas for Muslims and other religious minorities.[126]

Cripps Mission and Cabinet Mission

Over the questions of India's participation in the Second World War, started on September 3, 1939, and obtaining immediate independence, the Congress ministries resigned in October, 1939, and there was a constitutional dead-lock, when Governor's Rule was promulgated. The wavering fortune in the Second World War made the British Government feel the necessity of revising and softening of their attitude towards India. So, Sir Stafford Cripps, a member of the British War Cabinet, was sent to India on March 22, 1942 to negotiate with Indian political parties to find a just and final solution of the constitutional crisis and secure their cooperation in the war effort. His proposal, published on March 30, 1942, however, was rejected by all the political parties, though for different reasons.[127]

Dr. Ambedkar and M.C. Rajah, as representatives of the Depressed Classes, met Cripps on March 30, and asked whether they considered the Depressed Classes to be one of the racial and religious minorities, and Cripps replied that they did. They then asked what kind of provisions were likely to be made in the treaty for their protection. Cripps said that those would probably be along the lines of the League of Nations minority treaties, and that, if there were special provisions in the Constitution, these would probably be included in the Treaty, and that there would be some obligation to refer the matter to some outside authority in the event of a dispute, the Government of the Indian Union undertaking to abide by the decision given. If the Indian Government failed to do so this would constitute a breach of treaty, and the British Government could take such steps as it considered wise in the particular circumstances. Cripps further stated that though the form of protection might seem to them inadequate, it was the only possible one, once granted the principle of self-determination in India.

On April 1, 1942 Dr. Ambedkar and Rajah wrote to Cripps saying that the proposals were unacceptable to the

Depressed Classes, as they would place them under an unmitigated system of Hindu rule, and would be resisted by them by all the means at their disposal. They requested Cripps to convey their anxities to His Majesty's Government, and to impress upon them that the Depressed Classes would regard it as a breach of faith if a Constitution was forced upon them by His Majesty's Government which had not received their free and voluntary consent, and did not contain within itself the provisions necessary for safeguarding their interests.[128]

Later, in a press statement after the conclusion of the Nagpur session of the Depressed Class Conference, held on July 18-20, 1942, Dr. Ambedkar said that the Cripps proposals showed a sudden *volte face* on the part of His Majesty's Government. The proposal for a Constituent Assembly was intended to win over the Congress, while the proposal for Pakistan was designed to win over the Muslim League. Nothing was offered to the Depressed Classes. For the Constituent Assembly was nothing short of a betrayal of the Depressed Classes. In the Constituent Assembly there might be no representatives of the Depressed Classes at all because no communal quotas were fixed by these proposals. In the first place the representatives of the Depressed Classes would be in a hopeless minority. In the second place all decisions of the Constituent Assembly were not required to be by a unanimous vote. A majority vote was enough to decide any question no matter what its constitutional importance was. It was clear that under this system the voice of the Depressed Classes in the Constituent Assembly could not count. In the third place the present system of proportional representation by which the members to the Constituent Assembly were to bé elected under the terms contained in His Majesty's proposals could not but result in the caste Hindus having virtually the rights to nominate the representatives of the Depressed Classes to the Constitutent Assembly. Such representatives of the Depressed Classes would be the tools of the caste Hindus. In the fourth place the Constituent Assembly would be filled with the Congressites who would form the dominant majority party able to carry out its own programme. There was no doubt that Gandhi was totally opposed to giving political recognition to the Depressed Classes in the constitution as a separate and distinct element in the national life of India. That being the case the programme of the majority party in the Constituent Assembly would be to wipe out the political safeguards already granted to the Depressed Classes in the present constitution.[129]

This Conference also adopted resolutions declaring that no constitution would be acceptable to the Scheduled Castes unless :—

1. it has the consent of the Scheduled Castes,
2. it recognises the Scheduled Castes as a distinct and separate element,
3. it contains provisions for securing the following purposes—
   (a) earmarking a sum in the annual budget for promoting primary education and also advanced education among the children of the Scheduled Castes,
   (b) representation in proportion of their number, needs and importance,
   (i) in all Executive Governments—Central and Provincial,
   (ii) in the Public Services as also in the security services such as Judiciary, Police and Revenue,
   (iii) in all legislatures and local bodies which should be by the method of separate electorates,
   (c) representation in all Public Service Commissions, Central and Provincial,
   (d) separate settlements for the Scheduled Castes.[130]

The All-India Scheduled Castes Federation, founded by Ambedkar in 1943, gave further teeth to these demands and the Working Committee of the Federation meeting in Madras on September 23, 1944 adopted resolutions declaring that no Constitution shall be acceptable to the Scheduled Castes unless—

(a) it has the consent of the Scheduled Castes;

(b) it recognises the Scheduled Castes as distinct and separate element;

(c) it contains within itself provisions for securing the following purposes :

(1) for earmarking a definite sum in the Budgets of the Provincial and Central Governments for the Secondary, University and Advanced Education of the Scheduled Castes,

(2) for reservation of Government lands for separate settlements of the Scheduled Castes through a Settlement Commission,

(3) for Representation of the Scheduled Castes according to their needs, numbers and importance:—

(i) in the Legislature,

(ii) in the Executive,

(iii) in Municipalities and Local Boards,

(iv) in the Publice Services,

(v) on the Publice Service Commissions.

4. for the recognition of the above provisions as fundamental rights beyond the powers of the Legislature or the Executive to amend or alter or abrogate.

5. for the appointment of an Officer similar in status to that of the Auditor-General appointed under Section 166 of the Government of India Act of 1935 and removable from office in like manner and on the like grounds as a judge of the Federal Court to report on the working of the provisions relating to Fundamental rights.

It further demanded separate electorates for Scheduled Castes and representation of the minority communities on the Central and Provincial Executives, the representatives being chosen by the communities themselves.[131]

It is difficult to say how much the separate settlement resolution reflected the mind of the village Mahar, and how much it indicated an attempt by Ambedkar to establish the desperate seriousness of Scheduled Castes demands. It was made at a time when the Muslim League's demand for Pakistan was of great concern to both the Congress and the British. The demand for separate settlement was, however, ignored by the British as was the demand for separate electorates, although at least in the case of the latter, wide spread opinion had developed among the Scheduled Castes, thanks to the patronage extended by the Conservative British Government in the thirties that separate electorates were essential for them to be truely represented in the legislatures.

Earlier, Ambedkar, as a member of the Executive Council of the Governor-General of India, to which he was appointed on July 1, 1942, prepared and submitted on October 29, 1942, a Memorandum to the Governor-General containing the grievances of the Scheduled Castes and the remedies for removing them. It was a lengthy document, the bare outline of which were as follows:—

I. Political Grievances—

1. More representation in the Central Legislature.
2. More representation in the Central Executive.
3. Assurance of fair representation in the Public Services.

(i) By declaring the Scheduled Castes as minority and by reserving 13½ per cent of the annual vacancies for them.

(ii) Raising the age bar.

(iii) Reduction in Examination Fees.

(iv) Appointment of Scheduled Caste officer to protect Services rights of the Scheduled Castes.

4. Representation on the Federal Public Service Commission.

II. Educational Grievances—

1. An annual recurring grant of Rs. 2 lakhs for scholarships to Scheduled Castes students studying for Science, Engineering and Technology at the different Universities.

2. An annual grant of Rs. 1 lakh for education in Science, Technology and Engineering in foreign countries to students belonging to the Scheduled Castes.

3. Scholarships and free-ships for Scheduled Caste boys at the Indian School of Mines conducted by the Central Government.

4. Appointment of two representatives of the Scheduled Castes on the Central Board of Education established by the Government of India.

5. Facilities for technical training by reserving—

(a) apprenticeships in Government Printing Presses, and

(b) apprenticeships in Government Railway workshops.

III. Other Grievances—

1. Provision for adequate publicity of the social and political grievances of the Scheduled Castes.

2. Special provision for securing for members of the Scheduled Castes a footing in the Government Contracts system in the Public Works Department.[132]

In response to this Memorandum the Government of India announced on November 30, 1943, a number of concessions to Scheduled Castes, viz., a seat in the Council of State, an additional seat in the Central Assembly, reservation in the Indian Civil Services, reservations for technical training at railway workshops and the School of Mines and a provision of rupees three lakhs annually for scholarships for technical training in India and abroad.[133] The Government of India also modified its policy of communal representation in services announced in 1934 to extend the benefit to the Scheduled Castes and announced on August 11, 1943 that henceforth $8^1/^3$per cent of all vacancies in the Central and Subordinate Services including Railways be reserved for them, the age bar be raised by three years and examination fees be reduced to one-fourth.[134]

The imbroglio over finding a solution of Indian Constitutional problem, however, continued. On June 14, 1945, a new proposal, popularly known as Wavell Plan, was simultaneously announced by the Secretary of State for India and the Viceroy of India. Leaders of important political parties and groups including one representative each of the Sikhs and the Scheduled Castes attended the Conference in Simla from June 29, 1945. Rao Bahadur N. Siva Raj, M.L.A. and President of the All-India Scheduled Castes Federation represented the Scheduled Castes in the Conference. Though the Congress grudgingly agreed to equal representation of Hindus and Muslims in the cabinet, it was not willing to acquiesce in the League's demand that only the League was competent to send Muslim representatives in the Executive. Jinnah also could not agree to the appointment in the Executive Council of Muslims who did not belong to the League. The talk crashed on the rock of communalism. Lord Wavell announced the failure of the Conference on July 14, 1945.[135]

Following the general election that took place in Great Britain after the end of the World War on May 7, 1945, the Labour Party formed the Government on July 26, 1945, with Clement Attlee as Prime Minister. The coming of the anti-imperialist Labour Party to power marked a turning point in the history of the relation between Britain and India. With the installation of the Labour Ministry, the events moved in quick succession. The British Government announced on February 19, 1946 its plan of sending out to India a special mission of Cabinet Ministers consisting of the Secretary of State for India (Lord Pethick Lawrence), the President of the Board of Trade (Sir Stafford Cripps) and the First Lord of the Admirality (Mr. A.V. Alexander). The Cabinet Mission arrived in India on March 23, 1946, just 4 years after the visit of the Cripps Mission. The Cabinet Mission met the leaders of all politcal parties and groups and certain individuals. Ambedkar told the Cabinet Delegation on April 5, 1946 that "he did not want a Constituent Assembly at all. It would be dominated by the Caste Hindus, and the Scheduled Caste members would be more than a small minority which would always be outvoted even if a three-quarters or a two-thirds majority were required for the Assembly's decisions. All the assurances of protection which His Majesty's Government had given to the minorities would go by the board. Moreover there would be an immense amount of corruption in the Assembly-members would be bought over to vote against the interests of their communities". He, therefore, emphasised that for the Scheduled Castes "separate electorates were fundamental, since without them the Scheduled Castes would never have their own representatives."[136] Ambedkar again wrote to Lord Wavell on May 3, 1946 stating that the demands of the Scheduled Castes were such that they did not require the consent of other parties, at least in regard to three of their demands, namely (1) separate electorates, (2) proper representation in the Central Executive, and (3) undertaking from parties to accept certain general principles in regard to the safeguarding of the interest of the Scheduled Castes in the future constitution as a condition precedent for an interim Government.[137] He also requested A.V. Alexander, Member of the Cabinet Mission, who "came from the under-privileged classes of Great Britain" to do his best "to prevent a possible betrayal of the 60 millions of India's under-privileged" who had helped them (the British) to establish their rule and had defended it when it was menaced by a powerful combination of native forces in the Mutiny of 1857."[138] Since there was divergence of views among the principal parties, mainly the Congress and the Muslim League as to the setting-up of the Constituent Assembly for framing the future constitution of India, the Cabinet Mission and the Viceroy issued a statement on May 16 in which they gave their long-term scheme,[139] leaving the short-term arrangement for future negotiations. Exactly after a month i.e. on June 16, 1946, the short-term arrangement was disclosed.[140] Together, they give us the full picture of the Cabinet Mission Plan.

As regards the long term scheme, the Cabinet Mission rejected the Muslim League's demand for Pakistan. They recommended that the Constitution of India should take the following basic form—

(1) There should be a Union of India, embracing both British India and the States, which should deal with the following subjects: Foreign Affairs, Defence and Communications; and should have the powers necessary to raise the finances required for the above subjects.

(2) The Union should have an Executive and a Legislature constituted from British Indian and States representatives. Any question raising a major communal issue in the Legislature should require for its decision a majority of the representatives present and voting of each of the two major communities as well as a majority of all the members present and voting.

(3) All subjects other than the union subjects and all residuary powers should vest in the provinces.

(4) The States will retain all subjects and powers other than those ceded to the Union.

(5) Provinces should be free to form Groups with executives and legislatures, and each Group could determine the Provincial subjects to be taken in common.

(6) The constitutions of the Union and of the Groups should contain a provision whereby any Province could, by a majority vote of its Legislative Assembly, call for a reconsideration of the term of the constitution after an initial period of 10 years and at 10-yearly intervals thereafter.

(7) As soon as the new constitutional arrangements have come into operation, it shall be open to any Province to elect to come out of any Group in which it has been placed. Such a decision shall be taken by the new legislature of the Province after the first general election under the new constitution.

The method of selection of the representatives was spelt out in paras 18 & 19 (i) & (ii) of the Statement. The general procedure was specified in paragraph 19, sub-paragraphs iv to viii. Only 3 main communities in India were recognized. The General, Muslims & Sikhs, the 'General' community included all persons who were non-Muslims and non-Sikhs. Each Province was allotted a total of seats roughly in the ratio of one to a million, to be elected by the members of that community in its Legislative Assembly. As the smaller minorities would, upon the population basis, have little or no representation, since they would lose the weightage which assured them seats in the Provincial Legislature, arrangements were made to give them a full representation upon all matters of special interest to the minorities, for which an Advisory Committee on the rights of citizens, minorities, and tribal and excluded areas would be set up.

The short term plan as disclosed in the Statement of June 16, 1946, was regarding the formation of the Interim Government and the steps to be taken for the formation of Constitution making body.

The Muslim League Working Committee passed a resolution on June 25, agreeing to join the Interim Government, while the Congress Working Committee rejected on June 26 the Governor-General's proposals for the Interim Government. As the Congress refused to join the Interim Government the Governor-General adjourned negotiations relating to the formation of the Interim Government for the time being but elections to the Constituent Assembly were held and completed by the end of July, 1946. Congress won 206 seats, Muslim League 74 seats, Independent 8, Unionist Party 3, Akali Party 3, Communist 1 and Scheduled Castes Federation 1. Thus, in a house consisting of 296 members the Congress was in a commanding position, which Jinnah characterised as "brute majority". So the Council of the Muslim League withdrew its acceptance of the Cabinet Mission Plan by a resolution passed on July 29, 1946, being afraid that the Constituent Assembly, dominated by the Congress, might wreck the basic form of the grouping of the provinces and extend the scope, powers and subjects of the Union Centre, and resolved to resort to direct action to achieve Pakistan. 'Direct Action Day' was fixed on August 16, 1946.[141]

Reaction of Ambedkar to Cabinet Mission Plan

The Working Committee of the All-India Scheduled Castes Federation meeting on June 4, 1946, deplored the Statement issued by the Cabinet Mission for not mentioning the Scheduled Castes even once and also for non-fixation of any quota for the Scheduled Castes in the Constituent Assembly, and demanded that—

(1) The Scheduled Castes should have the right to be represented in the Legislatures through separate electorates.

(2) That the Constitution shall contain a provision making it obligatory on the Government to undertake the formation of separate settlements for the Scheduled Castes.

(3) Those members of the Scheduled Castes who topped the polls in the last primary elections be made members of the Advisory Committee and be allowed to elect five other representatives of the Scheduled Castes to the Advisory Committee.

The Working Committee even resolved to resort to direct action if the wrong done to them was not rectified.[142]

Ambedkar sent a lengthy letter to the British Prime Minister on July 1, 1946 making three specific requests— 1) to state openly that His Majesty's Government held that the Scheduled Castes were a minority within the meaning of paragraph 20 of the Cabinet Mission's Statement, 2) that His Majesty's Government would see that satisfactory safeguards which would enable them to live free from the fear of the Majority were provided for the Scheduled Castes before it agreed to sign the Treaty for cessation of sovereignty, and 3) that in the Interim Government the Scheduled Castes should have at least two representatives which should be the nominees of the Scheduled Castes Federation, because the Federation alone represented the Scheduled Castes and representations to Scheduled Castes Congressman was no representation to Scheduled Castes.[143]

In his reply on August 1, the British Prime Minister explained that "as regards the first, His Majesty's Government are anxious that the Constituent Assembly should have the fullest possible freedom of action consistent with the terms of the Cabinet Mission's Statements of May 16th, May 25th. We ourselves of course consider the Scheduled Castes to be an important minority which should be represented on the Minority Advisory Committee. But the declaration for which you ask could not be confined to the Scheduled Castes and would have to be a statement of all the elements who we consider should be included as Minorities in the Advisory Committee. Even though it would be only an expression of opinion on the part of His Majesty's Government, it would inevitably be interpreted as an attempt to interfere with the Assembly's freedom and as such would be likely to cause serious resentment. In these circumstances I cannot believe that such a declaration would be of value to the cause of the Scheduled Castes." Regarding the second request, the British Prime Minister informed that "they were very mindful of the rights of minorities and minorities should be able to live free from fear." That being the view, His Majesty's Government did not consider it wise to make any further pronouncement at that stage. As regards the nomination of two representatives who should be nominees of the Scheduled Castes Federation, the British Prime Minister regretted that he could not hold out any hope of that being possible.[144]

Not being satisfied with this attitude of the British Government, Ambedkar again wrote to the British Prime Minister on August 12 suggesting that the Scheduled Castes be declared as an important minority.[145] Lord Pethick-Lawrence's views on this suggestion were that neither the British Government could make a public declaration that the British Government regarded the Scheduled Castes as a minority who should be represented in the Minority Advisory Committee, nor could the British Government secure representation for Ambedkar's organization on the Minorities Advisory Committee.[146] Lord Pethick-Lawrence also counselled on September 9 that "we should not volunteer a pronouncement in response to Dr. Ambedkar's requests for a public declaration that the Scheduled Castes are a minority within the meaning of paragraph 20 of the Mission's Statement of May 16th. To do so would almost certainly arouse a controversy with Gandhi which might result in Congress opposing their inclusion as a demonstration. Even if we did not say that the Scheduled Castes are a minority but only that they should be included on the Committee, our statement would arouse requests for a similar statement in favour of the Anglo-Indians and others, and would be interpreted as interference with the Constitutent Assembly, which is what we are most anxious to avoid. There is no possibility that such a declaration would influence Congress to give the Scheduled Castes better treatment in the Advisory Committee than they would otherwise do, nor would it help Dr. Ambedkar, since it would refer simply to the Scheduled Castes, making no distinction between those who favour Congress and those who do not."[147] On this minute Attlee simply noted: "no further action."[148]

Like Jinnah, Ambedkar took the stand that the right to nominate Scheduled Caste member on the Interim Government rested with the Scheduled Castes Federation, the sole protector of Scheduled Caste interests. But what Jinnah could achieve, Ambedkar could not. This time he did not get any support from the British Government, who perhaps became wiser being confronted with the results of the elections held for the Provincial Legislatures in February, 1946, when Ambedkar's Scheduled Castes Federation was utterly defeated securing only two seats out of the 1585 seats of the Provincial Legislatures. Ambedkar produced official election figures for the Cabinet Mission which showed that in the primary elections held in December, 1945, in which Scheduled Castes alone voted, the Scheduled Castes Federation had received more votes than the Congress in Madras, Bombay and the Central Provinces.[149] He also offered proof that, in each province, the majority of Scheduled Caste votes had gone to non-Congress candidates.[150] There had been some violence in Nagpur and Bombay at the time of the elections, and Ambedkar also charged terrorism and intimidation as well as open hostility on the part of returning and polling officials as reasons for the election failure.[151] But Sir Stafford Cripps felt that "it had failed in the elections and we could not artificially restore its position."[152] This poor performance prompted A.V. Alexander, another member of the Cabinet Mission to make a statement in the House of Commons on July 18 that the majority of the Scheduled Castes were behind the Congress.[153]

The phenomenon of 'separatism' which marked the political movement under Ambedkar from 1930s until Independence was strong enough even before the formation of the Scheduled Castes Federation in 1942 for M.R. Jayakar, Bombay political figure and judge, to write to his fellow-moderate, Tej Bahadur Sapru, in April, 1941: "The depressed classes, under Ambedkar's guidance, are becoming more conscious of their separateness and not of their unity with Hinduism and perhaps in a short time a cry will go up for Mahar-stan."[154] Undoubtedly separatism was stimulated by the demands of the Muslims for Pakistan. It may also have been a macrocosm of what has been noticed on the village scale when Scheduled Castes' attempts to gain status are defeated. But both on the village and national level, separatism requires an outside force to relate to, if any gains are to be made.[155]

For the Muslims, it was the British, so also for the Scheduled Castes it was the British. Once the British changed its stance, the Scheduled Castes could not hold on to what they had gained earlier. But separatism as a political device did not altogether lose its value even in Independent India, mainly due to the inability of the founding fathers of the Constitution to effectively deal with the disintegrating tendencies let loose by the British in furtherence of its 'divide and rule' policy.

Policy that Blossomed

The Constituent Assembly was summoned to meet on December 9, 1946. Jinnah declined the invitation and said that no representative of the Muslim League should participate in the deliberations of the Constituent Assembly. Prime Minister Attlee made a last-minute attempt to save the situation. He invited two representatives each of the Congress and the League and, in addition, the Sikh member of the Interim Government, to go to London for further talks on the Constituent Assembly. At the conclusion of the coversations, the British Government issued a statement on 6th December, 1946. The Muslim League, however, persisted with its decision not to participate with the deliberations of the Constituent Assembly and demanded its dissolution forthwith.

The decisions of the British Government to leave India by June, 1948 was announced on February 20, 1947. This statement hinted at the possibility of a partition of the country in case the Muslim League continued its boycott of the Constituent Assembly. Lord Mountbatten, who succeeded Lord Wavell, assumed charge on March 29, 1947. He began a series of discussions with party leaders and other leading public men. Jinnah was adamant over his demand for Pakistan. The Congress had by now agreed to the principle of Pakistan but had insisted on a partition of the Provinces affected if Pakistan was unavoidable. The Mountbatten Plan for partition of the country into two Dominions—India and Pakistan—was announced on June 3, 1947.[156] The country was partitioned into two Dominions—India and Pakistan. Not only the country was partitioned, but the areas included in the then Provinces of the Punjab, Bengal and Assam were also partitioned.

The tendency towards disintegration adumbrated in the 1935 Act ultimately blossomed in the partition of the country formally legalised by the 1947 Act of Independence. Since the Cripps proposal the country had been torn asunder between the ideal of unity and the necessity of partition due to the failure to contain perpetuation of communal and sectarian politics. In the process, the forces of disintegration so very assiduously nurtured by the Britishers over the last several decades ultimately won.

Under such a social and political background, the Constituent Assembly, which had started functioning from December 9, 1946 was asked to frame a Constitution for India. The Independence Act of 1947, however, brought about a sea change in its functioning. The Constituent Assembly which was so long functioning under certain limitations under the Cabinet Mission Plan was not only free to come out of the stranglehold of communal, casteist and sectarian politics of the British Government but in a position to produce a document which would remove the virus of communalism, casteism, linguism and regionalism from our body politic for ever. It was a great opportunity for the Constituent Assembly to go beyond its class and socio-economic structure to translate the cherished objectives of the freedom movement. Was this opportunity seized for ushering in a really secular, casteless, creedless, exploitation-free society or the same old disintegrationist policy of the British Government got a new lease of life in our Constitution? Was the process of levelling of castes accelerated or the scope for perpetuating caste conflicts further widened?

Notes and References

1. Galantar, *op. cit.*, p. 28.
2. *Ibid.*, p. 29.
3. Sachchidananda, *op. cit.*, p. 6.
4. Joshi, *op. cit.*, p. 40.
5. Padgaonkar, Dileep, Ambedkar and Gandhi, *The Times of India*, April 14, 1990.
6. Agarwal, R.C., *Constitutional Development and National Movement of India*, S. Chand & Co., New Delhi, 1988, eighth edition, p. 172.
7. Ambedkar, *Dr. B.R., Writings and Speeches*, Vol. 9, *What Congress and Gandhi have done to the Untouchables*, Government of Maharashtra, 1970, p. 15.
8. *Ibid.*, p. 16.
9. *Report on Indian Constitutional Reforms*, 1918 (Mont-Ford Report) paras 188-91, pp. 123-25.
10. *Franchise Committee Report, 1919* (Southborough Committee Report), paras 15-17, p. 7.
11. *Ibid.*, paras 21-23, pp. 10-11.
12. *Ibid.*, paras 18-20, pp. 8-10.
13. *Ibid.*, para 24, p. 11.
14. *Ibid.*, pp. 13, 33, 41, 49, 64 and 72.
15. Quoted by Ambedkar, In : *Dr. Babasaheb Ambedkar : Writings and Speeches*, Vol. 9, *op. cit.*, p. 326.
16. Ambedkar, *Dr. B.R. : Writings and Speeches*, Vol. 5, *Under the Providence of Mr. Gandhi*, p. 312.

17. *Report of the Reforms Enquiry Committee* (Muddiman Committee), 1924, para 69, p. 60.
18. *Report on Indian Constitutional Reforms*, 1918, para 155.
19. *Report of the Reforms Enquiry Committee*, 1924, para 64, pp. 55-56.
20. *Report of the Indian Central Committee*, para 79, p. 45.
21. Ambedkar, *Dr. Babasaheb Ambedkar Writings and Speeches*, Vol. 5, *op. cit.*, p. 312.
22. *Report on Indian Constitutional Reforms, 1918*, para 75, p. 49
23. Srinivas, *op. cit.*, p. 107.
24. Bose, N.K., *Some Aspects of Caste in Bengal*, In : *The Social Organisation of Indian Civilization*, (ed.) Milton Singer, American Folklore Society, Philadelphia, 1959, p. 200.
25. Srinivas, *op. cit.*, pp. 107-8.
26. *Sedition Committee Report, 1918*, Annexure 2, p. 226.
27. Srinivas, *op. cit.*, p. 108.
28. Zaidi, A.M. & S.G., *The Encyclopaedia of the Indian National Congress*, Volume 7, 1916-20, pp. 202-03, 244.
29. *Young India*, December 20, 1920.
30. Zaidi, A.M. & S.G., *op. cit.*, Volume 7, p. 662.
31. *Ibid.*, Volume 8, p. 33.
32. *Indian Annual Register*, (henceforth *IAR*), *1922*, p. 386.
33. *Ibid.*, p. 387.
34. *Ibid.*, p. 309.
35. *Ibid.*, p. 317.
36. *IAR, 1923*, Volume II, p. 37.
37. Zaidi & Zaidi, *op. cit.*, Volume 8, p. 524.
38. *IAR, 1924*, Volume II, p. 408.
39. *Ibid.*, pp. 434-35.
40. Zaidi & Zaidi, *op. cit.*, Volume 9, pp. 71, 198 and 541.
41. *Ibid.*, p. 677.
42. Pt. Madan Mohan Malaviya in his presidential address in Belgaum in 1924, *IAR*, 1924, Volume II, p. 483.
43. *IAR, 1923*, p. 944.
44. *Indian Quarterly Register* (henceforth IQR), July-December, 1923, Vol. II, p. 139.
45. Resolution of the special session of the All-India Hindu Maha Sabha held at Belgaum on December 27 and 28, 1924, *IQR*, 1924, Vol. II, pp. 488-89; speech of the Indian National Congress President Mrs. Sarojini Naidu in the special session of the All-India Hindu Maha Sabha held at Kanpur on December 29, 1925, *IQR*, Vol. II, 1925, p. 349; resolution of the All-India Hindu Maha Sabha held at Delhi

on March 13, 1926, *IQR*, Vol. I, 1926, p. 401; resolution of the All-India Hindu Maha Sabha held at Patna on April 16-18, 1927, *IQR*, 1927, Vol. I, p. 422.

46. *IQR*, 1929, Vol. I, p. 359.
47. *IQR*, 1925, Vol. II, pp. 65-66.
48. *IQR*, 1927, Vol. II, p. 314.
49. *Ibid.*, p. 313.
50. *Ibid.*, p. 326.
51. Speech of Singaravelu, the president of the First Indian Communists' Conference held at Kanpur on December 26, 1925, *IQR*, 1925, Vol. II, pp. 370-71.
52. Resolutions taken in the Nagpur and Gaya sessions of the All-India Social Science Conference held on December 29 and 30, 1922, respectively, *IQR*, 1923, p. 984 (a) and 984 (g); resolution of the All-India Social Science Congress held at Calcutta on December 31, 1925, *IQR*, 1925, Vol. II, p. 400.
53. *IQR*, 1924, Vol. II, p. 519.
54. Resolution adopted at Lucknow session held on December 26-27, 1924, *IQR*, 1924, Vol. II, p. 467; resolution adopted at Calcutta session held on December 28-29, *IQR*, 1925, Vol. II, p. 389.
55. Resolution adopted in the annual conference held at Bombay on December 27-29, 1927, *IQR*, 1927, Vol. II, p. 437.
56. *Report of the Reforms Enquiry Committee* (Muddiman Committee), *1924*, para 59, p. 51.
57. *IQR*, 1928, Vol. I, p. 12.
58. *Ibid.*, p. 30.
59. *Ibid.*, p. 67.
60. *Ibid.*, pp. 141-42.
61. *IQR*, 1929, Vol. I, pp. 364-65.
62. Ambedkar, *Dr. B.R. : Writings and Speeches*, Vol. 8, *Pakistan or the Partition of India*, p. 259.
63. Zelliot Eleanor, *Learning the Use of Political Means : The Mahars of Maharashtra*, In : *Caste in Politics*, ed., *op. cit.*, p. 45.
64. *Indian Statutory Commission Report*, Vol. XVI, pp. 27-37.
65. *Petition to the Indian Statutory Commission from the Central Provinces Depressed Classes Association*, Nagpur, February 24, 1929, privately printed, quoted by Zelliot, *op. cit.*, p. 45.
66. *IQR*, 1929, Vol. II, pp. 47-48.
67. Inaugural speech of the Emperor in the First Round Table Conference, *Indian Round Table Conference—Report, 1930-31*, p. 11.
68. *IQR*, 1929, Vol. II, p. 52.
69. *Indian Round Table Conference—Report*, 1930-31, pp. 5-8.

70. Ambedkar, *Dr. B.R. : Writings and Speeches*, Vol. 9, *What Congress and Gandhi have done to the Untouchables*, pp. 40-41.
71. Bose, Subhas Chandra, *The Indian Struggle, Netaji's Life and Writings, 1920-34*, Part II, Calcutta, Thacker, Spink and Co., 1948, p. 40.
72. All-India Depressed Classes Conference, *IQR, 1930*, Vol. II, pp. 367-74.
73. *Proceedings of Sub-Committees*, Vol. III, *Sub-Committee No. III, Minorities, Indian Round Table Conference*, 12th November, 1930—19th January, 1931, pp. 168-74.
74. *Proceedings of Sub-Committees*, Vol. VI, *Sub-Committee No. VI, Franchise Sub-Committee, Indian Round Table Conference, 1930-31*, pp. 77-78.
75. *Proceedings of Sub-Committees*, Vol. III, *Minorities, op. cit.*, p. 78.
76. *Ibid.*, pp. 155-59.
77. Indian Round Table Conference, 12th November, 1930—19th January, 1931, (Proceedings), pp., 315-19.
78. *Proceedings of Sub-Committees*, Vol. I, *Sub-Committee No.I, Federal Structure Sub-Committee, Indian Round Table Conference, 1930-31*, p. 659.
79. *Indian Round Table Conference, 1930-31, Proceedings*, pp. 281-82.
80. *IQR*, 1931, Vol. II, pp. 429-32.
81. Bose, Subhas Chandra, *The Indian Struggle, 1920-42*, Asia Publishing House, 1964, p. 227.
82. Ambedkar, *What Congress and Gandhi have done to the Untouchables, op. cit.*, p. 55.
83. Bose, Subhas Chandra, *The Indian Struggle, 1920-42, op. cit.*, p. 226.
84. *Ibid.*, p. 228.
85. *Proceedings of Federal Structure and Minorities Committees, Indian Round Table Conference* (second session), 7th September, 1931—1st December, 1931, Vol. III, p. 1346.
86. *Ibid.*, Vol. I, p. 163.
87. *Ibid.*, Vol. III, p. 1364.
88. *Ibid.*, pp. 1394-99.
89. *Ibid.*, pp. 1384-85.
90. *Ibid.*, pp. 1438-39.
91. Sardar Ujjal Singh, *Ibid.*, p. 1368.
    Dr. B.S. Moonje, *Ibid.*, p. 1375.
92. *Ibid.*, pp. 1441-42.
93. *Ibid.*, p. 1369.
94. *Ibid.*, pp. 1391-94, 1399-1409 and 1411-42.

95. *Ibid.*, pp. 1409-11.
96. *Ibid.*, p. 1386.
97. Ambedkar, *What Congress and Gandhi have done to the Untouchables, op. cit.*, p. 74.
98. *Ibid.*
99. *Indian Statutory Commission Report, 1930*, Vol. I, para 58 and Vol. II, para 80, pp. 66-67.
100. *Ibid.*, Vol. II, para 79, p. 65.
101. Dr. S.K. Dutta, representing the Indian Christians, Smt. Sarojini Naidu and Begum Shah Nawaz, representing the Indian Women Organisations, did not ask for separate representation for the Indian Christians and Women, respectively. *Proceedings of Federal Structure and Minorities Committees, Indian Round Table Conference* (second session), pp. 1438-40, 1375-77.
102. Ambedkar, *What Congress and Gandhi have done to the Untouchables, op. cit.*, pp. 88-89.
103. Jha, M.L., *Untouchability and Education*, Namita Publications, Meerut, 1973, p. 7.
104. *Joint Committee on Indian Constitutional Reform* (session 1933-34) Vol. I, (Part II), *Proceedings*, para 120, p. 96.
105. *Indian Statutory Committee Report, 1930*, Vol. II, para 80.
106. *Indian Franchise Committee Report, 1932*, Vol. I, para 282.
107. *Ibid.*, paras 283-84.
108. *Ibid.*, p. 217.
109. *Ibid.*, pp. 114-16.
110. *Ibid.*, p. 117.
111. *Joint Committee on Indian Constitutional Reform* (session 1933-34) Minutes of Evidence, Vol. IIC, 31st July, 1933, pp. 1425-34.
112. Ambedkar, *What Congress and Gandhi have done to the Untouchables, op. cit.*, pp. 76-77.
113. *Resolution No. 122 A.R., dated 16th January, 1933 in File No. 1-R-2(4) of 1933 of the Government of Bengal, Appointment (Reforms) Department.*
114. *Memorandum of the Indian Association dated 15th February, 1933, in File No. 1-R-2-(10) of the Government of Bengal, Appointment (Reforms) Department.*
115. *Letter No. 1790-1820-A.R. dated 4th April, 1933 of the Government of Bengal, Appointment (Reforms) Department in File No. 1-R-2(14).*
116. *Note by W.D.R. Prentice, Member of Executive Council of Bengal in File No. 1-R-2 of 1933 dated 15th June, 1933.*
117. *Section 26(1) of Schedule I of the Government of India Act, 1935.*
118. *Letter No. 1790-1820-A.R. dated 4th April, 1933 of Appointment (Reforms) Department, Government of Bengal.*

119. Galantar, *op. cit.*, p. 34.
120. Keer, Dhananjoy, *Dr. Ambedkar : Life and Mission*, Popular Prakashan, Bombay, 1962, p. 252.
121. Paranjpe, A.C., *The Life History of Dr. B.R. Ambedkar*, In : *Dr. Ambedkar, Pioneer of Human Rights*, ed., *op. cit.*, p. 22.
122. Galantar, *op. cit.*, p. 34.
123. *Census of India, 1911.*
124. *Ibid., 1941*, Vol. I, p. 102.
125. *Mention may be made of the following enactments:*

    The Hyderabad Harijan (Removal of Social Disabilities) Regulation, 1358F (1938).

    The Hyderabad Harijan Temple Entry Regulation, 1358F (1938).

    The Travancore-Cochin Removal of Social Disabilities Act, 1925.

    The Madras Removal of Caste Disabilities Act, 1938.

    The Madras Village Court Act, 1889.

    The Madras District Municipalities Act, 1920.

    The Bombay Harijan (Removal of Social Disabilities) Act, 1946.

    The Removal of Civil Disabilities Act, 1943, (Mysore).

    The Orissa Removal of Civil Disabilities Act, 1946.
126. *Government of India Resolution No. F.14/17-B/33 dated July 4, 1934*, published in Gazette of India, Part I, July 7, 1934.
127. Kashyap, Anirban, *Communalism and Constitution*, Lancers Books, 1988, pp. 27-29.
128. *The Transfer of Power*, Nichlas Mansergh, Editor-in-Chief; published by His Majesty's Stationary Office, London, 1970, Vol. II, No. 227, pp. 336-37.
129. Ambedkar, *Dr. B.R. : Writings and Speeches*, Vol. 9, *op. cit.*, p. 336-43.
130. *Ibid.*, pp. 403-6.
131. Ambedkar, *What Congress and Gandhi have done to the Untouchables, op. cit.*, Appendix XI, pp. 346-58.
132. *The Transfer of Power, op. cit.*, Vol. III, No. 125, pp. 165-68.
133. Suman, R.D., In : *Dr. Ambedkar, Pioneer of Human Rights*, ed., *op. cit.*, pp. XLII-XLIII.
134. *Resolution No. 23/5/42-Ests(S)-dated August 11,1943 of the Government of India, Home Department*, published in the Gazette of India, Part I, August, 1943.
135. *IAR*, 1945, Part II, pp. 128-45.
136. *The Transfer of Power, op. cit.*, Vol. VII, No. 58, pp. 144-47.
137. Ambedkar, *Dr. B.R. : Writings and Speeches, op. cit.*, Vol. 10, pp. 487-90.

138. *Ibid.*, pp. 492-99.
139. Kashyap, *op. cit.*, Appendix I.
140. *IAR, 1946*, Vol. I, pp. 170-71.
141. Kashyap, *op. cit.*, pp. 29-33.
142. *The Transfer of Power, op. cit.*, Vol. VII, No. 454, pp. 808-12.
143. Ambedkar, *Dr. B.R. : Writings and Speeches, op. cit.*, Vol. 10, pp. 509-10.
144. *The Transfer of Power, op. cit.*, Vol. VIII, No. 105, pp. 170-72.
145. *Ibid.*, No. 142, pp. 221-23.
146. *Ibid.*, No. 250, pp. 411-12.
147. *Ibid.*, No. 288, pp. 466-68.
148. Ambedkar, *Dr. B.R. : Writings and Speeches, op. cit.*, Vol. 10, p. 519.
149. *Ibid.*, pp. 529-36.
150. Ambedkar, *What Congress and Gandhi have done to the Untouchables, op. cit.*, pp. 366-75.
151. Ambedkar, *Dr. B.R. : Writings and Speeches, op. cit.*, Vol. 10, p. 543.
152. Bannerjee, Anil Chandra and Bose, Dakhina Ranjan, *The Cabinet Mission in India*, 1946, A Mukherjee, Calcutta, p. 108.
153. *IAR, 1946*, Vol. II, p. 166.
154. Quoted by Zelliot Eleanor, *Learning the use of Political Means : The Mahars of Maharastra*, In : *Caste in Politics*, ed., *op. cit.*, p. 54.
155. *Ibid.*, p. 55.
156. Kashyap, *op. cit.*, pp. 36-37.

Appendix-A

List of Untouchables According to the Samhitas and Puranas

Abbreviations

[B = Baudhayana Dharma Sutra
BD = Brhaddharma purana
BV = Brahmavaivarta purana, Brahma Kanada, Ch. X, etc.
G = Gautama Dharma Sutra
K = Kane (History of Dharma Sastras, esp. Vol. II, Pt. I)
Kt = Kautilya, Artha Sastra, III. 7
M = Manu (Ch. X)
MB = Mahabharata. Anusasana Parvan, Chs. 48, 49
P = Parasara
S = Suta Samhita
U = Usanas Samhita
Vis = Visnu Dharma Sutra
Vas = Vasistha Dharma Sutra
Vaik= Vaikhanasa Samhita
Y = Yajnavalkya
=†Indicates birth out of clandestine or illicit union.]

Father	*Mother*	*Caste of offspring*	*Authority*
(1) Brahmana	Kshatriya	1. Murdhāvasikta	M, etc.
		2. Bhisak	U
(2) Do	Vaisya	1. Ambassta	M, P, B, Y, BD, etc.
		2. Ārdhika	

		3. Pāraśava	G
		4. Bhrjjakantaka	G also Medhatithi
		5. Nāpita†	U, Vaik
		6. Kumbhakara†	S
		7. Mlechha†	S
(3) Brahmana-Sudra		1. Ugra	U
		2. Nāpita	P
		3. Dāsa	P
		4. Nisāda	M, Y, Vas, B, etc.
		5. Parasava	G, MB, Narada
		6. Pāraśava†	U, Vaik
(4) Kshatriya Brahmana		1. Sūta	M, Y, S, Vas, G, B, Vis, MB, etc.
		2. Rathakāra†	U, Vaik
(5) Do	Vaisya	1. Ambastha	G, acc. to Haradatta
		2. Karana	MB (Adi 115.43)
		3. Bhoja	S
		4. Mādgu	Vaik
		5. Māhisya	G, V
		6. Avira†	S
		7. Āśvika†	Vaik
		8. Manikāra†	U
6) Ditto	Sudra	1. Ugra	B, M, Y, MB, etc.
		2. Nāpita	BD
		3. Pāraśava	MB, Narada
		4. Dausmanta	G.

		5. Mleccha	BV
		6. Gopāla	P
(7) Vaisya	Brahmana	1. Vaidehaka	M, B, MB Anu. 48.10, Vas
		2. Māgadha	G, U, Vaik, MB 49.9.10
		3. Krta	G
		4. Tāmbulin	BD
		5. Chakrin†	Vaik
		6. Kumbhakara†	U
		7. Rāmaka	Vas
(8) Do	Kshatriya	1. Māgadha	M, G, Y, MB Anu. 48.12, BD, etc.
		2. Āyogava	B, Vaik
		3, Pulkasa	Vas, Vis
		4. Dhivara	G
		5. Vandin	Harita (q. in Krtya-kalpataru) = Magadha, MB Anu 48.12
		6. Pulinda†	U, S, Vaik
		7. Bhupa	Yama (acc. Krtya-kalpataru)
		8. Ramaka (Vamaka)	MB Anu. 49.10
(9) Do	Sudra	1. Ugra	G
		2. Karana	G, Y, BD
		3. Rathakāra	B
		4. Katakāra	U, Vaik
		5. Sūchaka	U

		6. Āyogava	MB
		7. Taksan	MB
(10) Sudra	Brahmana	1. Chāndāla	M, Y, B, G, Vas, etc.
		2. Sūlika†	U
(11) Do	Ksatriya	1. Kṣatṛ	M, Y, B
		2. Charmakāra	U
		3. Māgadha	Vis
		4. Pulkasa	Vaik, U, S
		5. Yavana	G
		6. Vaina	Vas
		7. Vaidehaka	Vis
		8. Tantubāya	BD
		9. Ranjaka†	U
		10. Sūlika	Vaik, S
		11. Nisāda	Y, MB, Narada, S†
		12. Vrātya	MB Anu, 49.9.10
(12) Do	Vaisya	1. Antyāvasayin	Vas
		2. Āyogava	MB, G, M, Vis, Y, etc.
		3. Māgada	
		4. Pulkasa	Harita, Yama (in Krtyakal-pataru)
		5. Vaidehaka	G, U, Vaik
		6. Vaidya	MB
		7. Chakrin†	U
		8. Chākrika†	Vaik

male and a Brahmana female (G. 4.16, U. 17, Vaik. 10.13).
- (3) Born of a Sudra male and a Vaisya female (B. 1.9.7).
- (4) Born of a Sudra male and Ksatriya female (Vis. 16.5).

Occupation

- (1) Trade (M).
- (2) =Vandin : Praise of Kings (MB. Anu. 48.48).
- (3) "Clever in ornate prose, six languages and kalas... devotee of Kalika" (Skanda, Sahyadri 26.60.62).
- (4) Praise; singing; bearing messages (Vaik.). Untouchables (do.).
- (5) Praise; bearing messages; service of Vaisyas (U. 7.8).

13. Pulkasa, Pukkasa, Paulkasa
- (1) Born of Nisada father and Sudra mother (B. 1.9.14, M. 10.18).
- (2) Born of Nisada father and Ugra mother (Kt. 3.7).
- (3) Born of Sudra father and Ksatriya mother (Vaik. 10.14, U.7, S.).
- (4) Born of Vaisya father and Ksatriya mother (Vas. 18.5, Vis. 16.5).
- (5) Born of Sudra father and Vaiśya mother (Harita and Yama quoted in Krtyakal pataru).
- (6) Born of Chandala father and Ayogava mother (MB. Anu. 48.24).

Same as Mrtapa according to Ksirasvamin on Amarakosa.

Occupation

- (1) Hunting (Vis., Agni P.).
- (2) Catching and killing of animals living in holes. Same as of Ugra and Ksatr (M. 10.49).
- (3) Manufacture and sale of liquors and intoxicating drugs (Vaik. 10.14, S.).

14. Nisada
- (1) Born of Brahmana male and Sudra

female. Same as Parasava (B. 1.9.3, Vas. 18.8, M. 10.8, MB. Anu. 48.5, Y. 1.91, Kt. 3.7, U. 36-38, Vaik).

(2) Born of Brahmana father and Vaisya mother (G. 4.14).

(3) Born of Ksatriya male and Sudra female (Narada, MB. Anu. 48.12).

(4) Produced from left hand of king Vena (Vayu P. 2.1, 120-21, Bhagavata P. 4.14.42).

He is one of the Panchajanas (Nirukta 3.8) repository of all vices. He has reddish eyes and black hair (MB. Santi. 59. 96.97). He is short in stature, his hands and feet are short, hair brown, cheeks prominent and nose flat (Bhagavata). He lives killing wild animals (Vaik.)

15. Parasava

(1) Born of Brahmana father and Sudra mother (M. 10.8, G. 4.14, etc.). Origin same as Nisada according to many writers.

(2) Born of illicit union of a Brahmana male and a Sudra female (U. Vaik.). He is a devotee of Bhadrakali and lives by painting, beating drums, etc.

16. Yavana

(1) Born of Sudra father and Kshatriya mother (G.4.17).

(2) Ksatriyas reduced to sudra status (M. 10. 43-44).

(3) Sudras living outside Aryavarta (Mahabhasya on P. II. 4.10).

(4) Yenas. Yonas and Kambojas were tribes living outside Asoka's empire. Rock Edict V. XIII.

Also see Visnu P. 4.3.21. Yavanas are mlecchas shaving their heads as well as beards.

17. Rathakara

(1) Born of Vaisya father and Sudra mother (B. 1.9.6).

(2) Born of Mahisya

Appendix-B

Occupations of the Untouchables according to the Samhitas and Puranas

Abbreviations

[B = Baudhayana Dharma Sutra
BD = Brhaddharma purana
BV = Brahmavaivarta purana, Brahma Kanada, Ch. X, etc.
G = Gautama Dharma Sutra
K = Kane (History of Dharma Sastras, esp. Vol. II, Pt. I)
Kt = Kautilya, Artha Sastra, III. 7
M = Manu (Ch. X)
MB = Mahabharata. Anusasana Parvan, Chs. 48, 49
P = Parasara
S = Suta Samhita
U = Usanas Samhita
Vis = Visnu Dharma Sutra
Vas = Vasistha Dharma Sutra
Vaik = Vaikhanasa Samhita
Y = Yajnavalkya]

1. Antyavasayin
   (1) Offspring of Chandala male and Nisada female (M. 10.39).
   (2) Offspring of Sudra male and Vaisya female (Vas. 18.3).
   (3) Chandala (MB. Santi. 141.29-32).

2. Ambastha = Bhrjjakantaka
   (1) Offspring of Brahmana male and Vaisya female (P., B. 1.9.3, M. 10.8, Y. 1.91,U. 31, BD, etc.).
   (2) Offspring of Kshatriya male and Vaisya female (G. 4.14 according to Haradatta).

   Occupation

   Medicine (BD, M.10.47), Agriculture, firedancing, heraldry and singing (U. 31.32), see also Vaik. 10.12.

Skanda P. Sahyadri. 26.40-41.

(3) A tribe, see Raichaudhuri, Pol. Hist. Ind.

(4) A country of Mahabhasya on P. IV. 1.170.

3. Ayogava

(1) Offspring of Sudra male and Vaisya female. (M. 10.12, Kt. 3.7, G. 4.15, Vis. 16.4, MB. Anu. 48.13, Y.1.94).

(2) Offspring of Vaisya male and Kshatriya female (B. 1.9.7, U. 12, Vaik.10.14) = Pulkasa of Vas. 18.3.

Occupation

(1) Paring wood (M. 10.48).

(2) Weaving, making bronze vessels, cultivation, dealing in cloth (U. 13).

(3) Stage (acting) (Vis. 16.8. Agni P. 151.15).

(4) Working on stones and brick, white-washing, etc. (Skanda P. Sahyadri. 28.68-69).

We get Ayogu in Tait. Br. 3.4.1.

4. Ugra

(1) Offspring of Kshatriya male and Sudra female (B. 1.9.5, M. 10.9, Kt. 3.7, Y. 1.92, MB. Anu. 48.7).

(2) Offspring of Brahmana male and Sudra female (U.41).

(3) Offspring of Vaisya male and Sudra female (G. 4.14 = Rajputa (Skanda. Sahyadri and Kamalakara).

Occupation

(1) Catching and killing animals hiding in holes (M. 10.49).

(2) Bearing staff of the king and execution of punishments inflicted by the king (U.41).

5. Karana

(1) Vratya Ksatriya, also known variously as Jhalla Malla, Nicchivi, Nata, Khasa and Dravida (M.10.22).

(2) Offspring of a Kshatriya male and a Vaisya female (MB. Adi. 115-43 describ-

ing Yuyutsu, a son of Dhrtarastra).

(3) =Kayastha (Medini Kosa, Vaijayanti) meaning perhaps nothing more than a writer. Work of a Kayastha (Visva, Trikanda Sesa) Group of Kayasthas (Hema).

(4) =Charana or Vaitalika, a bard (Skanda-Sahyadri 26.1.49-51).

According to BD. a Karana is a Satsudra, his, occupation being writing or king's service. There can be little doubt that Karana is here identical with the Kayastha caste of Bengal.

6. Ksattr

(1) Offspring of Sudra male and Ksatriya female (B. 1.9.7, Kt. 3.7, M. 10.12, 13, 16, Y. 1.94, etc, = Vaina (Vas. 18.2).

Occupation

As of Ugra and Pulkasa (M. 104.9-50).

(2) Charioteer

(3) Doorkeeper (see Chhandogya, U. 4.1.5-8).

7. Chakrin

(1) Offspring of illicit union of Sudra male and Vaisya female (U. 22-23).

2) Offspring of Vaisya male and Brahmana female (Vaik. 10.13).

Occupation

(1) Selling of oil, oilcake and salt (U.), cf Telis of Bengal.

(2) Selling salt and oil (Vaik.)

(3) Pressing of sesame (Brahmanda P. quoted by Apararka on Y.).

8. Charmakara, Charmara, Charmavakrtta (M. 4.218). Karavara (M. 10.36).

(1) Offspring of Sudra male and Kshatriya female (U.4).

(2) Offspring of a Vaidehaka male and Brahmana female (U. 21, Vaik. 10.15).

(3) Offspring of an Ayogava male and Brahmana female (S).

(4) Offspring of a Vaidehaka male and Nisada female (MB. Anu. 48.26,

same origin as for Andhra).
(5) Offspring of a Tivara male and Chandala female (BV. Jatimala).
(6) Offspring of a Taksan male and Vaisya female (BD.).

9. Chakrika
(1) Offspring of an illicit union of a Sudra male and a Vaisya female (Vaik. 10.4).

Occupation

Selling of salt, oil and oilcakes (Vaik.), cf Chakrin=Tailaka (Hema).
(2) =Ghantika (bell-ringer) or Sravaka (Amara).

10. Chandal or Chandala
(1) Offspring of a Sudra male and Brahmana female (G. 4.15-16, Vas. 18.1, B. 1.9.7, M. 10.12, Y. 1.93, MB., etc.).
(2) Offspring of a union with sagotra girl (Yama, Vyasa, 1.9.10, Laghu Satatapa 59).
(3) =Matanga (MB. Anu. 29.17).

(4) =Antyavasayin, see above.

11. Napita
(1) Born of Brahmana father and Sudra mother (P. 11.21, same origin as Dasa).
(2) Born of Kshatriya male and Sudra female (BD.).
(3) Born of illicit union of a Brahmana male and Vaisya female (U. 32-34, Vaik. 10.12 = Urdhvanapita. Same origin as Kumbhakara (S.).
(4) Born of an Ambastha male and Kshatriya female (Vaik. 10.15).
(5) Born of Kshatriya male and Nisada female=Adho-Napita. (S).
(6) Born of Kuverin male and Pattikara female (Jatimala).

The Napita belongs to the Navasayaka group in Bengal.

12. Magadha
(1) Born of a Vaisya male and Kshatriya female (G. 4.5, Kt. 3.7, M. 10.11 & 17, Y. 1.93, BD., MB., Anu. 48.12).
(2) Born of a Vaisya

father and Karapa mother (Y. 1.95).
(3) Born of Kshatriya father and Brahmana mother (illicit union) (U. 5-6, Vaik. 10.13).

Occupation

(1) Taming horses, making chariots, building houses (Mitaksara quoting Samkha).
(2) Tending and driving horses and carts (U., Vaik).

They Formerly had upanayana ceremony but later became degraded to the status of Sudra (U. Vaik.). Originally their rank was just below Vaisya. Vide Kasika on P. 4.1.151.

18. Valdehaka
(1) Born of Vaisya father and Brahmana mother, Narada, Y. 1.93, MB. Anu. 48.10).
(2) Born of Sudra father and Kshatriya mother (G. 4.15).
(3) Born of Sudra father and Vaisya mother (G. 4.15, Vaik. 10.4, U.20).
(4) =Pulkasa (S.).
(5) =Merchant (Kt. 1.11 according to Pt. Shamasastrin. Also Medinikosa, etc.).

Occupation

(1) Guarding women (M. 10.47 Agni P. 151.14).
(2) Tending goats, cows, buffaloes; selling milk and milk products (U., Vaik.).

19. Suta
(1) Born of Ksatriya father and Brahmana mother (M. 10.11, G. 4.15, B. 1.9.9, Vas. 18.6., Kt. 3.7, Y. 1.9.3, S. Vis. 16.6, etc.).

Occupation

(1) Driving chariots (M., Vis).
(2) Reminding king about his duties and cooking for him (Vaik., U.).
(3) Attending on Brahmanas and Kshatriyas (MB. Karna 32.48).
(4) Preserving pedigrees

of kings and nobles; looking after chariots, elephants and horses; practice of medicine (Vayu P. 1.1, 33.35, etc.).	(5) All the work of a Kshatriya; charioteer; taming of elephants and riding horses (Skanda, Sahyadri 26.53-54).

Appendix-C

A Scheme of Political Safeguards for the Protection of the Depressed Classes in the Future Constitution of a Self-Governing India

†Appendix to Report of Sub-Committee No. III (Minorities)

(*Submitted by Dr. Bhimrao R. Ambedkar and Rao Bahadur R. Srinivasan*)

The following are the terms and conditions on which the Depressed Classes will consent to place themselves under a majority rule in a self-governing India:

Condition No. I
EQUAL CITIZENSHIP

The Depressed Classes cannot consent to subject themselves to majority rule in their present state of hereditary bondsmen. Before majority rule is established their emancipation from the system of untouchability must be an accomplished fact. It must not be left to the will of the majority. The Depressed Classes must be made free citizens entitled to all the rights of citizenship in common with other citizens of the State.

(A) To secure the abolition of untouchability and to create the equality of citizenship, it is proposed that the following fundamental right shall be made part of the constitution of India:

Fundamental Right

"All subjects of the State in India are equal before the law and possess equal civic rights. Any existing enactment,

---

†Proceedings of the sub-Committee No. III (Minorities), PP. 168-76,

U.S.A. Constitution Amendment XIV and Government of Ireland Act, 1920, 10 & 11, Geo V, Ch. 67, sec. 5 (2).

regulation, order, custom or interpretation of law by which any penalty, disadvantage, disability is imposed upon or any discrimination is made against any subject of the State on account of untouchability shall, as from the day on which this Constitution comes into operation, cease to have any effect in India."

This is so in all Constitutions, see Prof. Keith's remarks in Cmd. 207, p. 56

(B) To abolish the immunities and exemptions now enjoyed by executive officers by virtue of sections 110 and 111 of the Government of India Act, 1919 and their liability for executive action be made co-extensive with what it is in the case of a European British Subject.

Condition No. II

Free Enjoyment of Equal Rights

It is no use for the Depressed Classes to have a declaration of equal rights. There can be no doubt that the Depressed Classes will have to face the whole force of orthodox society, if they try to exercise the equal rights of citizenship. The Depressed Classes therefore feel that if these face the whole force of orthodox society if they try to exercise the equal rights of citizenship. The Depressed Classes therefore feel that if these declarations of rights are not to be mere pious pronouncements but are to be realities of everyday life then they should be protected by adequate pains and penalties from interference in the enjoyment of these declared rights.

(A) The Depressed Classes therefore propose that the following section should be added to part XI of the Government of India Act, 1919, dealing with Offences, Procedure and Penalties:

(i) *Offence of Infringement of Citizenship*

U.S. Statutes at arge. Civil Rights Protection Acts of April 9, 1866 and of March 1, 1875 passed in the interest of the Negroes after their emancipation.

"Whoever denies to any person except for reasons by law applicable to persons of all classes and regardless of any previous condition of untouchability the full enjoyment of any of the accommodations, advantages, facilities, privileges of inns, educational institutions, roads, paths, streets, tanks, wells and other watering places, public conveyances on land, air or water, theatres or other places of public amusement, resort or convenience whether they are dedicated to or maintained or licensed for the use of the public shall be punished with imprisonment of either description for a term which may extend to five years and shall also be liable to fine."

(B) Obstruction by orthodox individuals is not the only menace to the Depressed Classes in the way of peaceful enjoyment of their rights. The commonest form of obstruction is the social boycott. It is the most formidable weapon in the hands of the orthodox classes with which they beat down any attempt on the part of the Depressed Classes to undertake any activity if it happens to be unpalatable to them. The way it works and the occasions on which it is brought into operation are well described in the Report of the Committee appointed by the Government of Bombay in 1928 'to enquire into the educational, economic and social condition of the Depressed Classes (untouchables) and of the Aboriginal Tribes in the Presidency and to recommend measures for their uplift'. The following is an extract from the same:

Depressed Classes and Social Boycott

"102. Although we have recommended various remedies to secure to the Depressed Classes their rights to all public utilities we fear that there will be difficulties in the way of their exercising them for a long time to come. The first difficulty is the fear of open violence against them by the orthodox classes. It must be noted that the Depressed Classes form a small minority in every village, opposed to which is a great majority of the orthodox who are bent on protecting their interests and dignity from any supposed invasion by the Depressed Classes at any cost. The danger of prosecution by the Police has put a limitation upon the use of violence by the orthodox classes and consequently such cases are rare.

"The second difficulty arises from the economic position in which the Depressed Classes are found today. The Depressed Classes have no economic independence in most parts of the Presidency. Some cultivate the lands of the orthodox classes as their tenants at will. Others live on their earnings as farm labourers employed by the orthodox classes and the rest subsist on the food or grain given to them by the orthodox classes in lieu of service rendered to them as village servants. We have heard of numerous instances where the orthodox classes have used their economic power as a weapon against those Depressed Classes in their villages, when the latter have dared to exercise their rights, and have evicted them from their land, and stopped their employment and discontinued their remuneration as village servants. This boycott is often planned on such an extensive scale as to include the prevention of the Depressed Classes from using the commonly used paths and the stoppage of sale of the necessities of life by the village Bania. According to the evidence sometimes small cause suffice for the proclamation of a social boycott against the Depressed Classes. Frequently it follows on the exercise by the Depressed Classes of their right to the use of the common well, but cases have been by no means rare where a stringent boycott has been proclaimed simply because a Depressed Class man has put on the sacred thread, has bought a piece of land, has put on good clothes or ornaments, or has carried a marriage procession with the bridegroom on the horse through the public street.

"We do not know of any weapon more effective than this social boycott which would have been invented for the suppression of the Depressed Classes. The method of open violence pales away before it, for it has the most far-reaching and deadening effects. It is the most dangerous because it passes as a lawful method consistent with the theory of freedom of contact. We agree that this tyranny of the majority must be put down with a firm hand if we are to guarantee the Depressed Classes the freedom of speech and action necessary for their uplift."

In the opinion of the Depressed Classes the only way to overcome this kind of menace to their rights and liberties is to make social boycott an offence punishable by law. They are therefore bound to insist that the following sections should be added to those included in Part XI of the Government of India Act, 1919, dealing with Offences, Procedure and Penalties:

I. OFFENCE OF BOYCOTT DEFINED

(i) A person shall be deemed to boycott another who—

This and the following legal provisions are bodily taken from Burma Anti-Boycott Act, 1922, with a few changes to suit the necessities of the case.

(*a*) refuses to let or use or occupy any house or land, or to deal with, work for hire, or do business with another person, or to render to him or receive for him any service, or refuses to do any of the said things on the terms on which such things should commonly be done in the ordinary course of business, or

(*b*) abstains from such social, professional or business relations as he would, having regard to such existing customs in the Community which are not inconsistent with any fundamental right or other rights of citizenship declared in the Constitution, ordinarily maintain with such person, or

(*c*) in any way injures, annoys or interferes with such other person in the exercise of his lawful rights.

II. PUNISHMENT FOR BOYCOTTING

Whoever, in consequence of any person having done an

act which he was legally entitled to do or of his having omitted to do any act which he was legally entitled to omit to do or with intent to cause any person to do any act which he is not legally bound to do or to omit to do any act which he is legally entitled to do, or with intent to cause harm to such person in body, mind, reputation or property, or in his business or means of living, boycotts such person or any person in whom such person is interested, shall be punished with imprisonment of either description for a term which may extend to seven years or with fine or with both:

Provided that no offence shall be deemed to have been committed under this section if the Court is satisfied that the accused person has not acted at the instigation of or in collusion with any other person or in pursuance of or in collusion with any other person or in pursuance of any conspiracy or of any agreement or combination to boycott.

III. PUNISHMENT FOR INSTIGATING OR PROMOTING A BOYCOTT

Whoever—

(*a*) publicly makes or publishes or circulates a proposal for, or

(*b*) makes, publishes or circulates any statement, rumour or report with intent to, or which he has reason to believe to be likely to, cause, or

(*c*) in any other way instigates or promotes the boycotting of any person or class of persons, shall be punished with imprisonment which may extend to five years or with fine or with both.

Explanation.—An offence under this section shall be deemed to have been committed although the person affected or likely to be affected by any action of the nature referred to herein is not designated by name or class but only by his acting or abstaining from acting in some specified manner.

IV. PUNISHMENT FOR THREATENING A BOYCOTT

Whoever, in consequence of any person having done any act which he was legally entitled to do or of his having omitted to do an act which he was legally entitled to omit to do, or with intent to cause any person to do any act which he is not legally bound to do, or to omit to do any act which he is legally entitled to do, threatens to cause such person or any person in whom such person is interested, to be boycotted shall be punished with imprisonment of either description for a term which may extend to five years or with fine or with both.

Exception.—It is not boycott :—

(*i*) to do any act in furtherance of a *bona fide* labour dispute,

(*ii*) to do any act in the ordinary course of business competition.

N.B.—All these offences shall be deemed to be cognizable offences.

Condition No. III

PROTECTION AGAINST DISCRIMINATION

The Depressed Classes entertain grave fears of discrimination either by legislation or by executive order being made in the future. They cannot therefore consent to subject themselves to majority rule unless it is rendered impossible in law for the legislature or the executive to make any invidious discrimination against the Depressed Classes.

It is therefore proposed that the following statutory provision be made in the constitutional law of India:

"It shall not be competent for any Legislature or Executive in India to pass a law or issue an order, rule or regulation so as to violate the rights of the subjects of the State, regardless of any previous condition of untouchability, in all territories subject to the jurisdiction of the dominion of India:—

(1) to make and enforce contracts, to sue, be parties, and give evidence, to inherit, purchase, lease, sell, hold and convey real and personal property,

(2) to be eligible for entry into the civil and military employ and to all educational institutions except for such conditions and limitations as may be necessary to provide for the due and adequate representation of all classes of the subjects of the State,

(3) to be entitled to the full and equal enjoyment of the accommodations, advantages, facilities, educational institutions, privileges of inns, rivers, streams, wells, tanks, roads, paths, streets, public conveyances on land, air and water, theatres, and other places of public resort or amusement except for such conditions and limitations applicable alike to all subjects of every race, class, caste, colour or creed,

(4) to be deemed fit for and capable of sharing without distinction the benefits of any religious or charitable trust dedicated to or created, maintained or licensed for the general public or for persons of the same faith and religion,

(5) to claim full and equal benefit of all laws and proceedings for the security of person and property as is enjoyed by other subjects regardless of any previous condition of untouchability and be subject to like punishment, pains and penalties and to none other."

Condition No. IV

ADEQUATE REPRESENTATION IN THE LEGISLATURES

The Depressed Classes must be given sufficient political power to influence legislative and executive action for the purpose of securing their welfare. In view of this they demand that the following provisions shall be made in the electoral law so as to give them :—

(1) Right to adequate representation in the Legislatures of the Country, Provincial and Central.

(2) Right to elect their own men as their representatives, (a) by adult suffrage, and (b) by separate electorates for the first ten years and thereafter by joint electorates and reserved seats, it being understood that joint electorates shall not be forced upon the Depressed Classes against their will unless such joint electorates are accompanied by adult suffrage.

N.B.—Adequate Representation for the Depressed Classes cannot be defined in quantitative terms until the extent of representation allowed to other communities is known. But it must be understood that the Depressed Classes will not consent to the representation of any other community being settled on better terms than those allowed to them. They will not agree to being placed at a disadvantage in this matter. In any case the Depressed Classes of Bombay and Madras must have weightage over their population ratio of representation irrespective of the extent of representation allowed to other minorities in the Provinces.

Condition No. V

ADEQUATE REPRESENTATION IN THE SERVICES

The Depressed Classes have suffered enormously at the hands of the high caste officers who have monopolized the

Public Services by abusing the Law or by misusing the discretion vested in them in administering it to the prejudice of the Depressed Classes and to the advantage of the caste Hindus without any regard to justice, equity or good conscience. This mischief can only be avoided by destroying the monopoly of caste Hindus in the Public Services and by regulating the recruitment to them in such a manner that all communities including the Depressed Classes will have an adequate share in them. For this purpose the Depressed Classes have to make the following proposals for statutory enactment as part of the constitutional law :—

(1) There shall be established in India and in each Province in India a Public Service Commission to undertake the recruitment and control of the Public Services.

(2) No member of the Public Service Commission shall be removed except by a resolution passed by the Legislature nor shall he be appointed to any office under the Crown after his retirement.

(3) It shall be the duty of the Public Service Commission subject to the tests of efficiency as may be prescribed— (*a*) to recruit the Services in such a manner as will secure due and adequate representation of all communities, and (*b*) to regulate from time to time priority in employment in accordance with the existing extent of the representation of the various communities in any particular service concerned.

Condition No. VI

REDRESS AGAINST PREJUDICIAL ACTION OR NEGLECT OF INTERESTS

In view of the fact that the Majority Rule of the future will be the rule of the orthodox, the Depressed Classes fear that such a Majority Rule will not be sympathetic to them and that the probability of prejudice to their interests and neglect of their vital needs cannot be over-looked. It must be provided against, particularly because, however adequately represented, the Depressed Classes will be in a minority in all legislatures. The Depressed Classes think it very necessary that they should have the means of redress given to them in the constitution. It is therefore proposed that the following provision should be made in the constitution of India:—

British North America Act, 1867, sec. 93.

"In and for each Province and in and for India it shall be the duty and obligation of the Legislature and the Executive or any other Authority established by law to make adequate provision for the education, sanitation, recruitment in Public Services and other matters of social and political advancement of the Depressed Classes and to do nothing that will prejudicially affect them.

"(2) Where in any Province or in India the provisions of this section are violated an appeal shall lie to the Governor-General in Council from any act or decision of any Provincial Authority and to the Secretary of State from any act or decision of a Central Authority affecting the matter.

"(3) In every such case where it appears to the Governor-General in Council or to the Secretary of State the Provincial Authority or Central Authority does not take steps requisite for the due execution of the provisions of this section then and in every such case, and as far only as the circumstances of each case require, the Governor-General in Council or the Secretary of State acting as an appellate authority may prescribe, for such period as they may deem fit, remedial measures for the due execution of the provisions of this section and of any of its decisions under this section and which shall be binding upon the authority appealed against."

Condition No. VII
SPECIAL DEPARTMENTAL CARE

The helpless, hapless and sapless condition of the Depressed Classes must be entirely attributed to the dogged and determined opposition of the whole mass of the orthodox population which will not allow the Depressed Classes to have equality of status or equality of treatment. It is not enough to say of their economic condition that they are poverty-stricken or that they are a class of landless labourers, although both these statements are statements of fact. It has to be noted that the poverty of the Depressed Classes is due largely to the social prejudices in consequences of which many an occupation for earning a living is closed to them. This is a fact which differentiates the position of the Depressed Classes from that of the ordinary caste labourer and is often a source of trouble between the two. It has also to be borne in mind that the forms of tyranny and oppression practised against the Depressed Classes are very various and the capacity of the Depressed Classes to protect themselves is extremely limited. The facts which obtain in this connection and which are of common occurrence throughout India are well described in the Abstracts of Proceedings of the Board of Revenue of the Government of Madras dated 5th November 1882, No. 723, from which the following is an extract:

"134. There are forms of oppression only hitherto hinted at which must be at least cursorily mentioned. To punish disobedience of Pariahs, their masters :—

(*a*) Bring false cases in the village court or in the criminal courts.

(*b*) Obtain, on application, from Government, waste lands lying all round the paracheri, so as to impound the Pariahs' cattle or obstruct the way to their temple.

(*c*) Have mirasi names fraudulently entered in the

Government account against the paracheri.

(*d*) Pull down the huts and destroy the growth in the back-yards.

(*e*) Deny occupancy right in immemorial sub-tenancies.

(*f*) Forcibly cut the Pariahs' crops, and on being resisted charge them with theft and rioting.

(*g*) Under misrepresentations, get them to execute documents by which they are afterwards ruined.

(*h*) Cut off the flow of water from their fields.

(*i*) Without legal notice, have the property of sub-tenants attached for the landlords' arrears of revenue.

"135. It will be said there are civil and criminal courts for the redress of any of these injuries. There are the courts indeed; but India does not breed village Hampdens. One must have courage to go to the courts; money to employ legal knowledge, and meet legal expenses; and means to live during the case and the appeals. Further most cases depend upon the decision of the first court; and these courts are presided over by officials who are sometimes corrupt and who generally, for other reasons, sympathize with the wealthy and landed classes to which they belong.

"136. The influence of these classes with the official world can hardly be exaggerated. It is extreme with natives and great even with Europeans. Every office, from the highest to the lowest, is stocked with their representatives, and there is no proposal affecting their interests but they can bring a score of influence to bear upon it in its course from inception to execution."

There can be no doubt that in view of these circumstances the uplift of the Depressed Classes will remain a pious hope unless the task is placed in the forefront of all governmental activities and unless equalization of opportunities is realized in practice by a definite policy and determined effort on the part of the Government. To secure this end the proposal of the Depressed Classes is that the Constitutional Law should impose upon the Government of India a statutory obligation to maintain at all times a department to deal with their problems by the addition of a section in the Government of India Act to the following effect:—

"1. Simultaneously with the introduction of this Constitution and as part thereof there shall be created in the Government of India a Department to be in-charge of a Minister for the purpose of watching the interests of the Depressed Classes and promoting their welfare.

"2. The Minister shall hold office so long as he retains the confidence of the Central Legislature.

"3. It shall be the duty of the Minister in the exercise of any powers and duties conferred upon him or transferred to him by law, to take all such steps as may be desirable to secure the preparation, effectively carrying out and co-ordination of measures preventative of acts of social injustice, tyranny or oppression against the Depressed Classes and conducive to their welfare throughout India.

"4. It shall be lawful for the Governor-General :—

(*a*) to transfer to the Minister all or any powers or duties in respect of the welfare of the Depressed Classes arising from any enactment relating to education, sanitation, etc.,

(*b*) to appoint Depressed Classes welfare bureaux in each province to work under the authority of and in co-operation with the Minsiter."

Condition No. VIII

DEPRESSED CLASSES AND THE CABINET

Just as it is necessary that the Depressed Classes should have the power to influence governmental action by seats in the Legislature so also it is desirable that the Depressed Classes should have the opportunity to frame the general policy of the Government. This they can do only if they can find a seat in the Cabinet. The Depressed Classes therefore claim that in common with other minorities, their moral rights to be represented in the Cabinet should be recognized. With this purpose in view the Depressed Classes propose:

That in the Instrument of Instructions an obligation shall be placed upon the Governor and the Governor-General to endeavour to secure the representation of the Depressed Classes in his Cabinet.

Appendix-D

MINORITIES PACT

Provisions for a Settlement of the Communal Problem, put forward jointly by Muslims, Depressed Classes, Indian Christians, Anglo-Indians and Europeans.

CLAIMS OF MINORITY COMMUNITIES

1. No person shall by reason of his origin, religion, caste or creed, be prejudiced in any way in regard to public employment, office of power or honour, or with regard to enjoyment of his civic rights and the exercise of any trade or calling.

2. Statutory safeguards shall be incorporated in the constitution with a view to protect against enactments of the Legislature of discriminatory laws affecting any community.

3. Full religious liberty, that is, full liberty of belief, worship observances, propaganda, associations and education, shall be guaranteed to all communities subject to the maintenance of public order and morality.

   No person shall merely by change of faith lose any civic right or privilege, or be subject to any penalty.

4. The right to establish, manage and control, at their own expense, charitable, religious and social institutions, schools and other educational establishments with the right to exercise their religion therein.

5. The constitution shall embody adequate safeguards for the protection of religion, culture and personal law, and the promotion of education, language, charitable

institutions of the minority communities and for their due share in grants-in-aid given by the State and by the self-governing bodies.

6. Enjoyment of civic rights by all citizens shall be guaranteed by making any act or omission calculated to prevent full enjoyment an offence punishable by law.

7. In the formation of Cabinets in the Central Government and Provincial Governments, so far as possible, members belonging to the Mussalman community and other minorities of considerable number shall be included by convention.

8. There shall be Statutory Departments under the Central Provincial Governments to protect minority communities and to promote their welfare.

9. All communities at present enjoying representation in any Legislature through nomination or election shall have representation in all Legislatures through separate electorates and the minorities shall have not less than the proportion set forth in the Annexure but no majority shall be reduced to a minority or even an equality. Provided that after a lapse of ten years it will be open to Muslims in Punjab and Bengal and any minority communities in any other Provinces to accept joint electorates, or joint electorates with reservation of seats, by the consent of the community concerned. Similarly after the lapse of ten years, it will be open to any minority in the Central Legislature to accept joint electorates with or without reservation of seats with the consent of the community concerned.

   With regard to the Depressed Classes, no change to joint electorates and reserved seats shall be made until after 20 years' experience of separate electorates and until direct adult suffrage for the community has been established.

10. In every Province and in connection with the Central Government, a Public Services Commission shall be appointed, and the recruitment to the Public Services, except the proportion, if any, reserved to be filled by nomination by the Governor-General and the Governors, shall be made through such commission in such a way as to secure a fair representation to the various communities consistently with the considerations of efficiency and the possession of the necessary qualifications. Instructions to the Governor-General and the Governors in the Instrument of Instructions with regard to recruitment shall be embodied to give effect to this principle, and for that purpose to review periodically the composition of the Services.

11. If a Bill is passed which, in the opinion of two-thirds of the members of any Legislature representing a particular community, affects their religion or social practice based on religion, or in the case of fundamental rights of the subjects if one-third of the members object, it shall be open to such members to lodge their objection thereto, within a period of one month of the Bill being passed by the House, with the President of the House who shall forward the same to the Governor-General or the Governor, as the case may be, and he shall thereupon suspend the operation of that Bill for one year, upon the expiry of which period he shall remit the said Bill for further consideration by the Legislature. When such Bill has been further considered by the Legislature and the Legislature concerned has refused to revise or modify the Bill so as to meet the objection thereto, the Governor-General or the Governor, as the case may be, may give or withhold his assent to it in the exercise of his discretion, provided, further, that the validity of such Bill may be challenged in the Supreme Court by any two members of the denomination affected thereby on the ground that it contravenes one of their fundamental rights.

SPECIAL CLAIMS OF MUSSULMANS

(A)—The North-West Frontier Province shall be constituted a Governor's Province on the same footing as other Provinces with due regard to the necessary requirements for the security of the Frontier.

In the formation of the Provincial Legislature, the nominations shall not exceed more than 10 per cent of the whole.

(B)—Sind shall be separated from the Bombay Presidency and made a Governor's Province similar to and on the same footing as other Provinces in British India.

(C)—Mussulman representation in the Central Legislature shall be one-third of the total number of the House, and their representation in the Central Legislature shall not be less than the proportion set forth in the Annexure.

SPECIAL CLAIMS OF THE DEPRESSED CLASSES

(A)—The constitution shall declare invalid any custom or usage by which any penalty or disadvantage or disability is imposed upon or any discrimination is made against any subject of the State in regard to the enjoyment of the civic rights on account of Untouchability.

(B)—Generous treatment in the matter of recruitment to Public Services and the opening of enlistment in the Police and Military Service.

(C)—The Depressed Classes in the Punjab shall have the benefit of the Punjab Land Alienation Act extended to them.

(D)—Right of Appeal shall lie to the Governor or Governor-General for redress of prejudicial action or neglect of interest by any Executive Authority.

(E)—The Depressed Classes shall have representation not less than set forth in the Annexure.

SPECIAL CLAIMS OF THE ANGLO-INDIAN COMMUNITY

(A)—Generous interpretation of the claims admitted by Sub-Committee No. VIII (Services) to the effect that in recognition of the peculiar position of the community, special consideration should be given to the claim for public employment, having regard to the maintenance of an adequate standard of living.

(B)—The right to administer and contral its own educational institutions, i.e. European education, subject to the control of the Minister.

Provisions for generous and adequate grants-in-aid and scholarship on the basis of present grants.

(C)—Jury rights equal to those enjoyed by other communities in India unconditionally of proof of legitimacy and descent and the right of accused persons to claim trial by either a European or an Indian jury.

SPECIAL CLAIMS OF THE EUROPEAN COMMUNITY

(A)—Equal rights and privileges to those enjoyed by Indian-born subjects in all industrial and commercial activities.

(B)—The maintenance of existing rights in regard to procedure of criminal trials, and any measure or bill to amend, alter, or modify such a procedure cannot be introduced except with the previous consent of the Governor-General.

Agreed by:—

HIS HIGHESS THE AGA KHAN (Muslims)
DR. AMBEDKAR (Depressed Classes)
RAO BAHADUR PANNIR SELVAM (Indian Christians)
SIR HENRY GIDNEY (Anglo-Indians)
SIR HUBERT CARR (Europeans)

ANNEXURE—*Representation in Legislatures*

Figures in brackers=Population basis 1931 figures and depressed percentages as per Simon Report

---	Strength of Chamber	Hindu			Muslims	Christians	Sikhs	Anglo-Indians	Tribal, etc.	Euro-peans	Remarks
		Caste	Depressed	Total							
CENTRE All India (1931) Upper	200	(47.5) 101	(19)* 20	(66.5) 67	(21.5) 67	1	6	1	—	4	*Represents Percentage in Governor's Provinces of B.I.
Lower	300	123	45	168	100	7	10	3	—	12	
Assam	*100	(48.9) 38	(13.4) 13	(62.3) 51	(34.8) 35	3	—	1	—	10	*Pop. figures exclude Tribal Areas.
Bengal	200	(18.3) 38	(24.7) 35	(43) 73	(54.9) 102	(34.8) 2	—	3	—	20	
Bihar & Orissa	(67.8) 100	(14.5) 51	(82.3) 14	(11.3) 65	25	1	—	1	3	5	
Bombay	200	(68) 88	(8) 28	(76) 116	(20) 66	2	—	3	—	13	On Sind being separated weightage to Mussalmans in Bombay to be on the same footing as to the Hindus in the N.F.W.P.

—	Strength of Chamber	Hindu			Muslims	Christians	Sikhs	Anglo-Indians	Tribal, etc.	Euro-peans	Remarks
		Caste	Depressed	Total							
C.P.	100	(63.1) 58	(23.7) 20	(86.8) 78	(44) 15	1	—	2	2	2	
Madras	200	(71.3) 102	(15.4) 40	(86.7) 142	(7.1) 30	(3.7) 14	—	4	2	8	
Punjab	100	(15.1) 14	(13.5) 10	(28.6) 24	(56.5) 51	1.5	(13) 20	1.5	—	2	
U.P.	100	(58.1) 44	(26.4) 20	(84.5) 64	(14.8) 30	1	—	2	—	3	

Sind and N.W.F.P. Weightage similar to that enjoyed by the Mussalmans in the Provinces in which they constitute a minority of the population, shall be given to the Hindu minority in Sind and to the Hindu and Sikh minorities in the N.W.F.P.

Appendix-E

Political Safeguards for Depressed Classes

Supplementary Memorandum on the claims of the Depressed Classes for Special Representation, submitted to the R.T.C. by Dr. Bhimrao R. Ambedkar and Rao Bahadur R. Srinivasan.

In the memorandum that was submitted by us last year dealing with the question of political safeguards for the protection of the Depressed Classes in the constitution for a self-governing India, and which forms Appendix III to the printed volume of Proceedings of the Minorities Sub-Committee, we had demanded that special representation of the Depressed Classes must form one of such safeguards. But we did not then define the details of the special representation we claimed as being necessary for them. The reason was that the proceedings of the Minorities Sub-Committee came to an end before the question was reached. We now propose to make good the omission by this supplementary memorandum so that the Minorities Sub-Committee, if it comes to consider the question this year, should have the requisite details before it.

(1) EXTENT OF SPECIAL REPRESENTATION

(A)—Special Representation in Provincial Legislatures.

(i) In Bengal, Central Provinces, Assam, Bihar and Orissa, Punjab and the United Provinces, the Depressed Classes shall have representation in proportion to their population as estimated by the Simon Commission and the Indian Central Committee.

(ii) In Madras, the Depressed Classes shall have twenty-two per cent representation.

(iii) In Bombay :-

(a) in the event of Sind continuing to be a part of the Bombay Presidency, the Depressed Classes shall have sixteen per cent representation;

(b) in the event of Sind being separated from the Bombay Presidency the Depressed Classes shall enjoy the same degree of representation as the Presidency Muslims, both being equal in population.

(B)—Special Representation in the Federal Legislature.

In Both Houses of the Federal Legislature, the Depressed Classes shall have representation in proportion to their population in India.

RESERVATIONS

We have fixed this proportion of representation in the Legislatures on the following assumptions:—

(1) We have assumed that the figures for the population of the Depressed Classes given by the Simon Commission (Vol. I, p. 40) and the Indian Central Committee (Report p. 44) will be acceptable as sufficiently correct to form a basis for distributing seats.

(2) We have assumed that the Federal Legislature will comprise the whole of India, in which case the population of the Depressed Classes in Indian States, in Centrally Administered Areas, and in Excluded Territories, besides their population in Governor's Provinces, will form very properly an additional item in calculating the extent of representation of the Depressed Classes in the Federal Legislature.

(3) We have assumed that the administrative areas of the Provinces of British India will continue to be what they are at present.

But if the assumptions regarding figures of population are challenged, as some interested parties threaten to do, and if under a new census the Depressed Classes show a lower proportion, or if the administrative areas of the Provinces are altered, resulting in disturbing the existing balance of polulation, the Depressed Classes reserve their right to revise their proportion of representation and even to claim weightage. In the same way, if the All-India Federation does not come into being, they will be willing to submit to re-adjustment in their proportion of representation calculated on that basis in the Federal Legislature.

(2) METHOD OF REPRESENTATION

1. The Depressed Classes shall have the right to elect their representatives to the Provincial and Central Legislature through separate electorates of their voters.

For their representation in the Upper House of the Federal or Central Legislature, if it is decided to have indirect election by members of the Provincial Legislatures, the Depressed Classes will agree to abandon their right to separate electorates so far as their representation to the Upper House is concerned subject to this: that in any system of proportional representation arrangement shall be made to guarantee to them their quota of seats.

2. Separate electorates for the Depressed Classes shall not be liable to be replaced by a system of joint electorates and reserved seats, except when the following conditions are fulfilled:—

(a) A referendum of the voters held at the demand of a majority of their representatives in the Legislatures concerned and resulting in an absolute majority of the members of the Depressed Class having the franchise.

(b) No such referendum shall be resorted to until after twenty years and until universal adult suffrage has been established.

(3) NECESSITY OF DEFINING THE DEPRESSED CLASSES

The representation of the Depressed Classes has been grossly abused in the past inasmuch as persons other than the Depressed Classes were nominated to represent them in the Provincial Legislatures, and cases are not wanting in which persons not belonging to the Depressed Classes got themselves nominated as representatives of the Depressed Classes. This abuse was due to the fact that while the Governor was given the power to nominate persons to represent the Depressed Classes, he was not required to confine his nomination to persons belonging to the Depressed Classes. Since nomination is to be substituted by election under the new constitution, there will be no room for this abuse. But in order to leave no loophole for defeating the purpose of their special representation we claim:

(i) That the Depressed Classes shall not only have the right to their own separate electorates, but they shall also have the right to be represented by their own men.

(ii) That in each Province the Depressed Classes shall be strictly defined as meaning persons belonging to communities which are subjected to the system of Untouchability of the sort prevalent therein and which are enumerated by name in a shcedule prepared for electoral purposes.

(4) NOMENCLATURE

In dealing with this part of the question we would like to point out that the existing nomenclature of Depressed Classes is objected to by members of the Depressed Classes who have given thought to it and also by outsiders who take interest in them. It is degrading and contemptuous, and advantage may be taken of this occasion for drafting the new constitution to alter for official purposes the existing nomenclature. We think that they should be called "Non-Caste Hindus," "Protestant Hindus," or "Non-Conformist Hindus," or some such designation, instead of "Depressed Classes." We have no authority to press for any particular nomenclature. We can only suggest them, and we believe that if properly explained the Depressed Classes will not hesitate to accept the one most suitable for them.

We have received a large number of telegrams from the Depressed Classes all over India supporting the demands contained in this Memorandum.

Nov. 4th, 1931.

Appendix-F

Communal Award by his Majesty's Government—1932

In the statement made by the Prime Minister on 1st December last on behalf of His Majesty's Government at the close of the second session of the Round Table Conference, which was immediately afterwards endorsed by both Houses of Parliament, it was made plain that if the communities in India were unable to reach a settlement acceptable to all parties on the communal questions which the Conference had failed to solve His Majesty's Government were determined that India's constitutional advance should not on that account be frustrated, and that they would remove this obstacle by devising and applying themselves a provisional scheme.

2. On the 19th March last His Majesty's Government, having been informed that the continued failure of the communities to reach agreement was blocking the progress of the plans for the framing of a new Constitution, stated that they were engaged upon a careful re-examination of the difficult and controversial questions which arise. They are now satisfied that without a decision of at least some aspects of the problems connected with the position of minorities under the new Constitution, no further progress can be made with the framing of the Constitution.

3. His Majesty's Government have accordingly decided that they will include provisions to give effect to the scheme set out below in the proposals relating to the Indian Constitution to be laid in due course before Parliament. The scope of this scheme is purposely confined to the arrangements to be made for the representation of the British Indian communities in the Provincial

Legislatures, consideration of representation in the Legislature at the Centre being deferred for the reason given in paragraph 20 below. The decision to limit the scope of the scheme implies no failure to realise that the framing of the Constitution will necessitate the decision of a number of the problems of great importance to minorities, but has been taken in the hope that once a pronouncement has been made upon the basic questions of method and proportions of representation the communities themselves may find it possible to arrive at a *modus vivendi* on other communal problems, which have not as yet received the examination they require.

4. His Majesty's Government wish it to be most clearly understood that they themselves can be no parties to any negotiations which may be initiated with a view to the revision of their decision, and will not be prepared to give consideration to any representation aimed at securing the modification of it which is not supported by all the parties affected. But they are most desirous to close no door to an agreed settlement should such happily be forthcoming. If, therefore, before a new Government of India Act has passed into law, they are satisfied that the communities who are concerned are mutually agreed upon a practicable alternative scheme, either in respect of any one or more of the Governor's Provinces or in respect of the whole of the British India, they will be prepared to recommend to Parliament that alternative should be submitted for the provisions now outlined.

5. Seats in the Legislative Councils in the Governor's Provinces, or in the Lower House if there is an Upper Chamber, will be allocated as shown in the annexed table.*

6. Election to the seats allotted to Muhammadan, European and Sikh constituencies will be by voters voting in separate communal electorates covering between them the whole area of the Province (apart from any portions which may in special cases be excluded from the electoral area as 'backward").

Provision will be made in the Constitution itself to empower a revision of this electoral arrangement (and the other similar arrangements mentioned below) after 10 years with the assent of the communities affected, for the ascertainment of which suitable means will be devised.

7. All qualified electors, who are not voters either in a Muhammadan, Sikh, Indian Christian (see paragraph 10 below), Anglo-Indian (see paragraph 11 below) or European constituency, will be entitled to vote in a general constituency.

8. Seven seats will be reserved for Mahrattas in certain selected plural member general constituencies in Bombay.

9. Members of the "depressed classes" qualified to vote will vote in a general constituency. In view of the fact that for a considerable period these classes would be unlikely, by this means alone, to secure any adequate representation in the Legislature, a number of special seats will be assigned to them as shown in the table. These seats will be filled by election from special constituencies in which only members of the "depressed classes" electorally qualified will be entitled to vote. Any person voting in such a special constituency will, as stated above, be also entitled to vote in a general constituency. It is intended that these constituencies should be formed in selected areas where the Depressed Classes are most numerous, and that, except in Madras, they should not cover the whole area of the Province.

In Bengal it seems possible that in some general constituencies a majority of the voters will belong to the Depressed Classes. Accordingly, pending further investigation, no number has been fixed for the members to be returned from the special Depressed Classs constituencies in that Province. It is intended to secure that the Depressed Classes should obtain not less than 10 seats in the Bengal Legislature.

The precise definition in each province of those who (if electorally qualified) will be entitled to vote in the special Depressed Class constituencies has not yet been finally determined. It will be based as a rule on the general principles advocated in the Franchise Committee's Report. Modification may, however, be found necessary in some Provinces in Northern India where the application of the general criteria of untouchability might result in a definition unsuitable in some respects to the special conditions of the Province.

His Majesty's Government do not consider that these special Depressed Class constituencies will be required for more than a limited time. They intend that the Constitution shall provide that they shall come to an end after 20 years if they have not previously been abolished under the general powers of electoral revision referred to in paragraph 6.

10. Election to the seats allotted to Indian Christians will be by voters voting in separate communal electorates. It seems almost certain that practical difficulties will, except possibly in Madras, prevent the formation of Indian Christian constituencies covering the whole area of the Province, and that accordingly special Indian Christian constituencies will have to be formed only in one or two selected areas in the Province. Indian Christian voters in these areas will not vote in a general constituency. Indian Christian voters outside these areas will vote in a general constituency. Special arrangements may be needed in Bihar and Orissa, where a considerable proportion of the Indian Christian community belongs to the aboriginal tribes.

11. Election to the seats allotted to Anglo-Indians will be by voters voting in separate communal electorates. It is at present intended, subject to investigation of any practical difficulties that may arise, that the Anglo-Indian constituencies shall cover the whole area of each Province, a postal ballot being employed; but no final decision has yet been reached.

12. The method of filling the seats assigned for representatives from backward areas is still under investigation, and the number of seats so assigned should be regarded as provisional pending a final decision as to the constitutional arrangements to be made in relation to such areas.

13. His Majesty's Government attach great importance to securing that the new Legislatures should contain at least a small number of women members. They feel that at the outset this object could not be achieved without creating a certain number of seats specially allotted to women. They also feel that it is essential that women members should not be drawn disproportionately from one community. They have been unable to find any system which would avoid this risk, and would be consistent with the rest of the scheme for representation which they have found it necessary to adopt, except that of limiting the electorate for each special women's seat to voters from one community. The special women's seats have accordingly been specifically divided, as shown in the table, between the various communities. The precise electoral machinery to be employed in these special constituencies is still under consideration.

14. The seats allotted to "Labour" will be filled from non-communal constituencies. The electoral arrangements have still to be determined, but it is likely that in most Provinces the Labour constituencies will be partly trade union and partly special constituencies as recommended by the Franchise Committee.

15. The special seats allotted to Commerce and Industry, Mining and Planting will be filled by election through Chambers of Commerce and various Associations. The details of the electoral arrangements for these seats must await further investigation.

16. The special seats allotted to Land-holders will be filled

by election by special Land-holders' constituencies.

17. The method to be employed for election to the University seats is still under consideration.

18. His Majesty's Government have found it impossible in determining these questions of representation in the Provincial Legislatures to avoid entering into considerable detail. There remains, nevertheless, the determination of the constituencies. They intend that this task should be undertaken in India as early as possible.

    It is possible that in some instances delimitation of constituencies might be materially improved by slight variations from the numbers of seats now given. His Majesty's Government reserve the right to make such slight variations, for such purpose, provided that they would not materially affect the essential balance between communities. No such variations will, however, be made in the case of Bengal and Punjab.

19. The question of the composition of Second Chambers in the Provinces has so far received comparatively little attention in the constitutional discussions and requires further consideration before a decision is reached as to which Provinces shall have a Second Chamber or a scheme is drawn up for their composition.

    His Majesty's Government consider that the composition of the Upper House in a Province should be such as not to disturb in any essential the balance between the communities resulting from the composition of the Lower House.

20. His Majesty's Government do not propose at present to enter into the question of the size and composition of the Legislature at the Centre, since this involves among other questions that of representation of the Indian States which still needs further discussion. They will, of course, when considering the composition, pay full regard to the claims of all communities for adequate

representation therein.

21. His Majesty's Government have already accepted the principle that Sind should be constituted a separate Province, if satisfactory means of financing it can be found. As the financial problems involved still have to be reviewed in connection with other problems of federal finance, His Majesty's Government have thought preferable to include, at this stage, figures for a Legislature for the existing Province of Bombay, in addition to the schemes for separate Legislatures for Bombay Presidency proper and Sind.

22. The figures given for Bihar and Orissa relate to the existing Province. The question of constituting a separate Province of Orissa is still under investigation.

23. The inclusion in the table of figures relating to a Legislature for the Central Provinces including Berar does not imply that any decision has yet been reached regarding the future constitutional position of Berar.

London,
4th August, 1932.

ALLOCATION OF SEATS IN PROVINCIAL LEGISLATURES (LOWER HOUSE ONLY)

Province	General	Depressed Classes	Representatives from Backward Areas	Sikh	Muhammadan	Indian Christian	Anglo-Indian	European	Commerce and Industry, Mining and Planting, Special (*a*)	Landholders, Special	University Special	Labour, Special	Total
Madras	134 (including 6 women)	18	1	0	29 (including 1 woman)	9 (inc. 1 woman)	2	3	6	6	1	6	215
Bombay (including Sind)	97 (*b*) (including 5 women)	10	1	0	63 (including 1 woman)	3	2	4	8	3	1	8	200
Bengal	80 (*c*) (including 2 women)	(c)	0	0	119 (including 2 women)	2	4 (inc. 1 woman)	11	19	5	2	8	250
United Provinces	132 (including 4 women)	12	0	0	66 (including 2 women)	2	1	2	3	5	1	3	228
Punjab	43 (including 1 women)	0	0	32 (inc. 2 women)	86 (including 2 women)	2	1	1	1	5 (*d*)	1	3	175
Bihar and Orissa	99 (including 3 women)	7	8	0	42 (including 1 woman)	2	1	2	4	4	1	4	175
Central Provinces (including Berar)	77 (including 3 women)	10	1	0	14	0	1	1	2	3	1	2	112

Assam	44 (including 3 women) (*e*)	4		0	34	1	0	1	11		0	4	108
North-West Frontier Province	9	0	0	3	36	0	0	0	0	2	0	0	50
Bombay (without Sind)	109 (*b*) (including 5 women)	10	1	0	30 (including 1 woman)	3	2	3	7	2	1	7	175
Sind	19 (including 1 woman)	0	0	0	34 (including 1 woman)	0	0	2	2	2	0	1	60

(*a*) The Composition of the bodies through which election to these seats will be conducted, though in most cases neither predominantly European or predominantly Indian, will not be statutorily fixed. It is, accordingly, not possible in each Province to state with certainty how many Europeans and Indians respectively will be returned. It is, however, expected that, initially, the numbers will be approximately as follows :—Madras, 4 Europeans, 2 Indians; Bombay (including Sind), 5 Europeans, 3 Indians; Bengal, 14 Europeans, 5 Indians; United Provinces, 2 Europeans, 1 Indian; Punjab, 1 Indian; Bihar and Orissa, 2 Europeans, 2 Indians; Central Provinces including Berar, 1 European, 1 Indian; Assam, 8 Europeans, 3 Indians; Bombay without Sind, 4 Europeans, 3 Indians; Sind, 1 European, 1 Indian.

(*b*) Seven of these seats will be reserved for Mahrattas.

(*c*) As explained in paragraph 9 of the statement, the number of special Depressed Class seats in Bengal—which will not exceed 10—has not yet been fixed. The number of General seats will be 80, less the number of special Depressed Class seats.

(*d*) One of these seats is a Tumandar's seats. The four Land-holder's seats will be filled from special constituencies with joint electorates. It is probable, from the distribution of the electorate, that the members returned will be 1 Hindu, 1 Sikh, and 2 Mohammadans.

(*e*) This woman's seat will be filled from a non-communal constituency at Shillong.

Bibliography

Government Documents

Reports of the :—

Backward Classes Commission, 1955 (K. Kalelkar, Chairman).

Backward Classes Commission, 1980 (B.P. Mandal, Chairman).

Census of India, 1881.

Census of India, 1901, *India*.

Census of India, 1911, *India*.

Census of India, 1921, *India*.

Census of India, 1931, *India*.

Census of India, 1941, *India*.

Census of India, 1901, *Bengal*.

Census of India, 1911, *Bengal*.

Census of India, 1921, *Bengal*.

Census of India, 1931, *Bengal*.

Census of India, 1911, *Bengal, Bihar, Orissa, and Sikkim*.

Census of India, 1921, *Bombay Presidency*.

Census of India, 1911, *Madras*.

Census of India, 1921, *Punjab*.

Census of India, 1951, *West Bengal*.

Franchise Committee and the Committee on Division of Functions, 1919 (Lord Southborough, Chairman).

Indian Central Commitee, 1929 (Sankaran Nair, Chairman).

Indian Constitutional Reforms, 1918 (Mont-Ford Report).

Indian Franchise Committee, 1932 (Marquess of Lothian, Chairman)

Indian Round Table Conference (12th November, 1930-19th January, 1931).

Indian Round Table Conference (Second session, 7th September, 1931—1st December, 1931).

Indian Statutory Commission, 1930, Vol. I to V (Chairman, Lord Simon).

Joint Committee on Indian Constitutional Reforms (session 1933-34), Vol. I to III.

Peel Commission on the Organization of the Indian Army, 1859.

Proceedings of Sub-Committees, Vol. I to VIII, *Indian Round Table Conference*, 12th November, 1930 to 19th January, 1931.

Proceedings of Federal Structure and Minorities Committees, Indian Round Table Conference, (second session), 7th September, 1931 to 1st December, 1931, Vol. I to III.

Refroms Enquiry Committee, 1925 (Chairman, A.P. Muddiman).

Sedition Committee, 1918.

File Nos. 1-R-2(4) of 1933 of Government of Bengal.
1-R-2(10) of 1933 of Government of Bengal.
1-R-2(14) of 1933 of Government of Bengal.

The Transfer of Power, Nichlas Mansergh, Editor-in-Chief, His Majesty's Office, London, 1970.

Books and Articles

Abraham, Rev. C.E., *The Rise and Growth of Christianity in India, In The Cultural Heritage of India*, Vol. IV, The Ramakrishna Mission Institute of Culture, Calcutta, 1956.

Agarwal, R.C., *Constitutional Development and National Movement of India*, S. Chand & Co., New Delhi, eighth edition, 1988.

Altekar, Dr. A.S., *Position of women in Hindu Civilization*, 3rd edition, Banaras, 1962.

Ambedkar, Dr. B.R., *Annihilation of Castes*, Thacker & Co. 1946.

Ambedkar, Dr. B.R. *Who were the Sudras*, Bombay, 1946.

Ambedkar, Dr. B.R. *The Untouchables*, Amrit Book Co., New Delhi, 1948.

Ambedkar, Dr. B.R. *What Congress and Gandhi have done to the Untouchables*, Thacker & Co., 1948.

Ambedkar, Dr. B.R. *Dr. Babasaheb Ambedkar: Writings and Speeches*, Government of Maharashtra, Education Department, Vol. I to XI, 1991.

Aiyappan and Bala Ratnam, ed., *Society in India*, SSA Publications, 1956.

Apastamba Dharmasutra

Bandopadhaya, Suraj, *Caste Lost and Caste Regained: Some Aspects of Empirical Research on Village India*, In *Dimensions of Social Change in India*, edited by M.N. Srinivas, S. Seshaish and V.S. Parthasarathy, Allied Publishers, 1977.

Banerjee, Anil Chandra and Bose, Dakhina Ranjan, *The Cabinet Mission in India*, A. Mukherjee, Calcutta, 1946.

Banerjee, Jitendra Nath, *Cult-Syncretism*, In *The Cultural Heritage of India*, Vol. IV, The Ramakrishna Mission Institute of Culture, Calcutta, 1956.

Bailey, F.G., *Tribe, Caste and Nation*, Oxford University Press, 1960.

Bailey, F.G., *Caste and the Economic Frontier, A Village in Highland Orissa*, Manchester University Press, 1957.

Basham, A.L., *The Wonder that was India*, London, 1954.

Baudhayana Dharmasutra

Bayly, C.A., *The New Cambridge History of India*, Vol. II, Cambridge University Press, 1988.

Bateille, Andre, *Caste, Class and Power, Changing Patterns of Stratification on a Tanjore Village*, Berkeley, University of California Press, 1965.

Bateille Andre, *Castes: Old and New*, Asia Publishing House, 1969.

Bhagwata Gita

Bhattacharjee, Jogendra Nath, *Hindu Caste and Sects*,

Calcutta, 1896.

Bose, Subhas Chandra, *The Indian Struggle, Part II, Netaji's Life and Writings, 1920-34*, Calcutta, Thacker Spink & Co., 1948.

Bose, Subhas Chandra, *The Indian Struggle, 1920-42*, Asia Publishing House, 1964.

Bose, N.K., ed., *Data on Caste: Orissa*, Calcutta, Anthropological Survey, 1960 (Memoir No. 7).

Bose, N.K., Caste in India, *Man in India*, Vol. XXXI, No. 3-4, 1951.

Bose, N.K., Some Aspects of Caste in Bengal, *Journal of American Folklore*, LXXI, July-September, 1958.

Bose, N.K., *Some Aspects of Caste in Bengal*, In *The Social Organization of Indian Civilization*, edited by Milton Singer, American Folklore Society, Philadelphia, 1959.

Bougle, Celestin: *Essais Sur le regime des castes*, Paris, Alcan, (1st ed. 1908), 1927.

Brahmanya

Braibanti, Ralph and Spengler, Joseph J., ed., *Administration and Economic Development in India*, Cambridge University Press, 1963.

Buchanan, Daniel H., *The Development of Capitalist Enterprises in India*, New York, 1934.

Buhler, G., *Laws of Manu*, Oxford, 1886.

Buhler, G., *Sacred Laws*, Oxford, 1879-82.

Chandra, Bipan, The Struggle against Caste and Casteism, *The Telegraph*, May 14, 1991.

Chaturvedi, J.P., The Fragmentation of a nation, *The Telegraph*, March 19, 1991.

Coondo, R., *Dr. Ambedkar, the Iconoclast, In Dr. Ambedkar, Pioneer of Human Rights* ed. Bodhisattva Publication, New Delhi, 1977.

Das, Bhagwan, *Introduction to the Cultural Heritage of India*, Vol. IV, The Ramakrishna Mission Institute of Culture,

Calcutta, 1956.

Davis, Kingsley, *The Population of India and Pakistan*, Princeton University Press, Princeton, 1951.

Denzil, Ibbetson, *Punjab Castes*, Lahore, 1916.

Dubois, Abbe, *A Description of the People of India*, 1817.

Dumont, Louis, *Homo Hierarchicus*, Weidenfold and Nicolson, London, 1970.

Dushkin, Lelah, *The Policy of the Indian National Congress Toward the Depressed Classes: An Historical Study*, Master's thesis, University of Pennsylvania, 1957.

Dutt, Bhupendra Nath, *Sudras in Indian Social Polity*, Calcutta, 1944.

Dutt, N.K., *Origin and Growth of Caste in India*, Vol. I, London, 1931.

Dutt, N.K., *Origin and Growth of Caste in India*, Vol. II, Firma K.L. Mukhopadhaya, Calcutta, 1968.

Elliot, Carolyn M., *Caste and Faction among the Dominant Caste: The Reddies and Kammas of Andhra*, In *Caste in Indian Politics* ed. Orient Longman Ltd., 1970.

Encyclopaedia of Religion and Ethics, First Edition, Edinburgh, II.

Farquhar, J.N., *An Outline of the Religious Literature of India, London*, Oxford University Press, 1920.

Farquhar, J.N., *Modern Religious Movements in India*, Lahore, 1943.

Fuchs, Stephen, *Rebellious Prophets*, Asia Publishing House, 1965.

Furnivall, J.S., *Colonial Policy and Practice*, London, 1948.

Fick. Richard, *The Social Organization in North-East India in Buddha's Time*, Calcutta, 1920.

Galanter, Marc, *Competing Equalities*, Oxford University Press, 1984.

Gandhi, M.K., *An Autobiography or the story of My Experience with Truth*, Navajiban Publishing House, 1948.

Gandhi, M.K., *For Workers against Untouchability*. Navajiban Publishing House, 1954.

Gandhi, M.K., *The Removal of Untouchability*, Navajiban Publishing House, 1954.

Gandhi, M.K., *Young India*, December 20, 1920.

Gautama Dharmasutra

Ghose, Benoy, *Iswar Chandra Vidyasagar, Builders of Modern India.* Ministry of Information and Broadcasting, Government of India, 1971.

Ghurye, G.S., *Caste and Race in India*, Popular Prakashan, Bombay, fifth edition, 1990.

Gilbert, W.H., *Peoples of India*, Washington, 1944.

Gopalaswamy, Prof. K.V., *Brahmarshi Raghupati Venkatratnam Naidu Guru, Moral and Social Reformer—Life and Times*, In *Great Indian Social Reformers and Philanthropists*, edited by Prof. G.V.L.N. Sarma, Sri A.S. Chetti Sanmana Sangham, Narsapur, Andhra Pradesh, 1975.

Gough, Kathleen, E., *Caste in a Tanjore Village*, In *Aspects of Caste in South India, Ceylon and North-West Pakistan*, edited by E.R. Leach, Cambridge, Cambridge University Press, 1960.

Gould, Harold A., *Sanskritization and Westernization, A Dynamic View, The Economic Weekly*, June 24, 1961. Vol. XIII.

Hardgrave, Robert L. Jr., *The Dravidian Movement*, Popular Prakashan, 1965.

Hardgrave, Robert L. Jr., *Political Participation and Primordial Solidarity: The Nadars of Tamilnad*; In *Caste in Indian Politics* (ed.), Orient Longman Ltd., 1970.

Hasan, S. Nurul, Caste System in Medieval Muslim Society, *The Telegraph*, April 1, 1991.

Hill, S.C., *Origin of the Caste System in India*, XIII, I.A., March-October, 1930, Bombay, 1930.

Hocart, A.M., *Caste—A Comparative Study*, Methuen & Co., London, 1950.

Hutton, J.H., *Caste in India*, Oxford University Press, 1946.

Indian Annual Register, 1922-1947.

Irschick, Eugene, *Politics and Social Change in South India: The Non-Brahmin Movement and Tamil Separatism*, 1916-29, Ph.D. Thesis, Department of History, The University of Chicago, 1964.

Issacs, Harold R., *India's Ex-Untouchables*, New York, John Day, 1965.

Jain, Meenakshi, The myth of caste tyranny, *Indian Express*, September 26, 1990.

Jain, Meenakshi, Establishing Yadav Raj, *Indian Express*, October 30, 1990.

Jain, Meenakshi, A myth the British created, *Indian Express*, October 5, 1990.

Jayaram, R., *The Times of India*, February 11, 1968.

Jha, M.L., *Untouchability and Education*, Namita Publications, Meerut, 1973.

Jinarajadas, C., *What Theosophists Believe*, In *The Cultural Heritage of India*, Vol. IV, The Ramakrishna Mission Institute of Culture, Calcutta, 1956.

Joshi, Barbara R., *Democracy in Search of Equality: Untouchable Politics and Indian Social Change*, Hindustan Publishing Corporation (India), Delhi, 1982.

Kabir, Humayun, *Islam in India*, In *The Cultural Heritage of India*, Vol. IV, The Ramakrishna Mission Institute of Culture, Calcutta, 1956.

Karve, Iravati, *The Hindu Society—A New Interpretation*, Poona, Decan College, 1961.

Kashyap, Anirban, *Communalism and Constitution*, Lancers Books, 1988.

Keer, Dhananjoy, *Dr. Ambedkar: Life and Mission*, Popular Prakashan, Bombay, 1962.

Keith, A.B., *Cambridge History of India*.

Kerr, James, *The Domestic Life, Character and Customs of the Natives of India*, 1865.

Ketkar, S.V., *History of Caste in India*, Rawat Publications, Jaipur, 1979.

Kothari, Rajani (ed.), *Caste in Indian Politics*, Orient Longman Ltd., 1970.

Kautilya Arthasastra

Lal, K.S., *Indian Muslims, Who Are They?* Voice of India, 1990.

Lathe, A.B., *Memoirs of His Highness Shri Sahu Chattrapati Maharaja of Kolhapur*, Bombay, 1924.

Macnicol, Dr. N., *Indian Theism*, Oxford University Press, 1915.

Mahabharat

Manor, James, *The Evolution of Political Arenas and Units of Social Organization: The Lingayats and Okkaligas of Princely Mysore*, In *Dimensions of Social Change in India*, edited by M.N. Srinivas, S. Seshaish and V.S. Parthasarathy, Allied Publishers, Mysore, 1977.

Manucci, Niccolas, *Storica do Mogor or Mogul India*, 1653-1708, W. Irvine, 4 vols., John Murray, London, 1906.

Manu Smriti

Markendya Purana

Martin, Orans, *The Santhal, A Tribe in Search of a Great Tradition*, Detroit, 1965.

Mayer, Adrian C., *Caste and Kinship in Central India*, Berkeley, 1960.

Mazumdar, D.N., *Races and Cultures of India*, Asia Publishing House, 1958.

Mazumdar, D.N., and Madan, T.N., *An Introduction to Social Anthropology*, Asia Publishing House, 1956.

Mazumdar, Dr. R.C., *History and Culture of the Indian People*, Vol. X, Bharatiya Vidya Bhavan, 1951.

Mazumdar, Dr. R.C., *Evolution of Religion-Philosophic Culture in India, In The Cultural Heritage of India*, Vol. IV, The Ramakrishna Mission Institute of Culture, Calcutta, 1956.

Mazumdar, R.C. Roychaudhuri, H.C., and Datta, K., *An Advanced History of India*, London, 1963.

Mehta, Haroobhai and Patel, Hasmukh, ed., *Dynamics of Reservation Policy*, Patriot, Publishers, New Delhi, 1985.

Miller, Eric J., Caste and Territory in Malabar, *American Anthropologist*, LVI, June, 1954.

Mokkapati, Shivajee, *Justice Mahadeo Gobind Ranade*, In *Great Indian Social Reformers and Philanthropists*, edited by Prof. G.V. L.N. Sharma, Sri A.S. Chetti Sanmana Sangham,

Narsapur, Andhra Pradesh, 1975.

Muller, D.J., *Jurisdiction of Courts in matters relating to rights and powers of castes*, 1901.

Nag, Kalidas, *The Brahmo Samaj*, In *The Cultural Heritage of India*, Vol. IV. The Ramakrishna Mission Institute of Culture, Calcutta, 1956.

Natarajan, S., *A Century of Social Reform in India*, Asia Publishing House, 1959.

Nath, Raj Mohan, *Sankara Deva and the Vaisnava Movement in India*, In *The Cultural Heritage of India*, Vol. IV, The Ramakrishna Mission Institute of Culture, Calcutta, 1956.

Nehru, Jawaharlal, *The Discovery of India*, Second Edition, Signet Press, Calcutta, 1946.

Nesfield, J.C., *Brief View of the Caste System of the North-West Provinces and Oudh*, Allahabad, 1885.

Padgaonkar, Dileep, Ambedkar and Gandhi, *Times of India*, April 14, 1990.

Pancavimsa

Pandit Champuti, *The Arya Samaj*, In *The Cultural Heritage of India*, Vol. IV, The Ramakrishna Mission Institute of Culture, Calcutta, 1956.

Paranjpe, A.C., *Caste, Prejudice and the Individual*, Lalwani Publishing House, Bombay, 1970.

Paranjpe, A.C., *The Life History of Dr. Ambedkar*, In *Dr. Ambedkar: Pioneer of Human Rights*, ed., Boddhisattava Publication, New Delhi, 1977.

Paraskara Gruyasutra

Parvathamama, C., *Religion and Social Change: A Study of Tradition and Change in Virsasaivism*, In *Dimensions of Social Change in India*, edited by M.N. Srinivas, S. Seshaish and V.S. Parthasarathy, Allied Publishers, 1977.

Pillai, G.K., *Origin and Development of Caste*, Kitab Mahal, Allahabad, 1959.

Pillai, S. Satchidanandam, *The Saiva Saints of South India*, In *The Cultural Heritage of India*, Vol. IV, The Ramakrishan Mission Institute of Culture, Calcutta, 1956.

Panikkar, K.M., *Hindu Society at Cros: Roads*, Bombay. 1955.

Ram, Jagjivan, *Caste Challenge in India*, Vision Books, New Delhi, 1980.

Ramarao Adik, *Brahmanism without Casteism*, Bombay, 1961.

Rangacharya, V., *Historical Evolution of Sri-Vaisnavism in South-India*, In *The Cultural Heritage of India*, Vol. IV, The Ramakrishna Mission Institute of Culture, Calcutta, 1956.

Rao, C.V. Subba, *Life and Times of Sir K.V. Reddi Naidu*, Rajahmundry, 1957.

Rao, Hayavadana, *Indian Caste System*, Bangalore, 1931.

Rao, M.S.A., *Tradition, Rationality and Change (Essays in Sociology of Economic Development and Social Change)*, Popular Prakashani, Bombay, 1972.

Rao, V.R.K.V., *Some Thoughts on Social Change in India*, edited by M.N. Srinivas, S. Seshaish and V.S. Parthasarathy, Allied Publishers, 1977.

Ray, S., *From Phooley to Ambedkar: The Unaccomplished Revolution, In Dr. Ambedkar: Pioneer of Human Rights*, ed., Boddhisattva Publication, New Delhi, 1977.

Rice, S., *The Origin of Caste*, Asiatic Review, Vol.XXV, 1929.

Risley, H.H., *The Tribes and Castes of Bengal*, Calcutta, 1891.

Risley, H.H., *The People of India*, W. Thacker Co., London, Second Edition, 1915.

Roychaudhuri, H.C., *The Early History of the Vaisnava Sect*, Calcutta, 1920.

Roy, Sarat Chandra, *The Hill Bhuiyas of Orissa*, Ranchi, 1935.

Roy, Sarat Chandra, *Caste, Race and Religion in India, Man in India*, Vol. XIV, 1934, Parts I-III, Vol. XVII, 1937, Vol. XVIII, Part IV of 1938.

Saberwal, Satish, *States and Entrepreneurship: The Ramgharia Case, In Dimensions of Social Change in India*, edited by M.N. Srinivas, S. Seshaish and V.S. Parthasarathy, Allied Publishers, 1977.

Sachau, E.C., *Alberuni's India*, London, 1914.

Sachidananda, *The Harijan Elite*, Thomson Press (India) Limited, 1977.

Sadasivaiah, H.M., *A Comparative Study of Two Virasaiva Monastries: A Study in Sociology of Religion*, Prasaranga, Mysore, 1967.

Saksena, R.N., Factor in Social tensions, *Seminar*, No. 70.

Sharma, Prof. G.V.L.N., ed., *Great Indian Social Reformers and Philanthropists*, Sri A.S. Chetti Sanmana Sangham, Narsapur, Andhra Pradesh, 1975.

Seminar No. 70.

Sen, Kshitimohan, *The Medieval Mystics of North India*, In *The Cultural Heritage of India*, Vol. IV, The Ramakrishna Mission Institute of Culture, Calcutta, 1956.

Sen, Sukumar, *The Nath Cult*, In *The Cultural Heritage of India*, Vol. IV, The Ramakrishna Mission Institute of Culture, Calcutta, 1956.

Sharma, B.N.K., *The Vaisanava Saints of Karnataka*, In *The Cultural Heritage of India*, Vol. IV. The Ramakrishna Mission Institute of Culture, Calcutta, 1956.

Sharma, Dr. Brijendra Nath, *Social and Cultural History of Northern India c1000-1200 A.D.*, Abhinava Publications, New Delhi, 1972.

Sharma, Dasaratha, *The Early Chauhan Dynasties*, Delhi, 1959.

Sharma, N.K., *Southwestern Journal of Anthropology*, XVII, (Summer, 1961).

Sharma, R.S., *Sudras in Ancient India*, Motilal Banarasidas, 1958.

Sherring, M.A., *Hindu Tribes and Castes*, Calcutta, 1881.

Shinde, V.R., *The Problem of Untouchability* (Marathi)

Singer, Milton, *The Social Organizations of Indian Civilization* (ed.), American Folklore Society, Philadelphia, 1959.

Singh, Tarlok, *The Village Panchayat and the Pattern of Village Development*, 1955.

Singh, Teja, *The Religion of the Sikh Gurus*, In *The Cultural Heritage of India*, Vol. IV, The Ramakrishna Mission Institute of Culture, Calcutta, 1956.

Singh, Yogendra, *The Changing Pattern of Social Stratification in India*, In *Dimensions of Social Change in India*, edited by M.N. Srinivas, S. Seshaiah and V.S. Parthasarathy, Allied Publishers, 1977.

Sinha, Dr. R.K., *Alienation Among Scheduled Castes*, Manas Publications, Delhi, 1986.

Sinha, Sasadhar, *Indian Independence in Perspective*, Asian Publishing House, Bombay, 1964.

Sirsikar, V.M., Use in Politics, *Seminar No. 70*.

Sivakumar, Chitra, *Higher education, Social Stratification and Social Change in Mysore in the 1960s*, In *Dimensions of Social Change in India*, edited by M.N. Srinivas, S. Seshaiah and V.S. Parthasarathy, Allied Publishers, 1977.

Sovani, N.V., *Non-economic Aspects of India's Economic Development*, In *Administration and Economic Development in India*, edited by Ralph Braibanti and Joseph J. Spengler, Cambridge University Press, 1963.

Sovani, N.V., *Journal of World History*, II. 1954.

Srinivas, M.N., *Religion and Society among the Coorgs of South*, India Clarendon, London, 1952.

Srinivas, M.N., *Social Change in Modern India*, Allied Publishers, 1966.

Srinivas, M.N., *Sanskritization and Westernization*, In *Society in India*, edited by Aiyappan and Ratnam, SSA Publications, 1956.

Sriramamurti, Dr. P., *Sri Kandukuri Veeresalingam Pantulu*, In *Great Indian Social Reformers and Philanthropists*, edited by Prof. G.V.L.N. Sharma, Sri A.S. Chetti Sanmana Sangham, Narsapur, Andhra Pradesh, 1975.

Sudhitattam

Suman, R.D., *Dr. Ambedkar, Pioneer of Human Rights*, ed., Bodhisattva Publications, New Delhi, 1977.

Stein, B., *Social Mobility and Medieval South Indian Hindu Sects*, In *Social Mobility in Caste in India*, edited by J. Silverberg, 1968.

Taittiriya Aranayaka

Tekur, S.M., *Bharat Ratna Sir Mokshagundam Visvesvarva*, In *Great Indian Social Reformers and Philanthropists*, edited by Prof. G.V.L.N. Sharma, Sri A.S. Chetti Sanmana Sangham, Narsapur, Andhra Pradesh, 1975.

Tilman, Robert O., *The Influence of Caste on Indian Economic Development*, In *Administration and Economic Development in India*, edited by Ralph Braibanti and Joseph J. Spengler, Cambridge University Press, 1963.

Vajasanevi Samhita

Vasistha Dharmasutra

Vayu Purana

Vedic Index, by A.A. Macdonell and A.B. Keith, 2 vols., 1912.

Venkatarangiya, Prof. M. In *Great Indian Social Reformers and Philanthroposists*, edited by Prof. G.V.L.N. Sharma, Sri A.S. Chetti Sanmana Sangham, Narsapur, Andhra Pradesh, 1975.

Vishnu Purana

Vivekananda, Swami, *The Complete Works of—*, Vol. 1-8, Advaita Ashrama, 1990.

Vratyata-prayascitta-nirmaya

Vrihannardiya Purana

Weber Marx, *From Marx Weber Essays on Sociology*, edited by H.H. Garth and C.N. Mills, London, 1948.

Wilson, J., *Indian Castes*, 1877.

Yajnavalkya Smriti

Zaidi, A.M. and S.G., *The Encylopaedia of Indian National Congress*, Volumes 1 to 12, S. Chand & Co., New Delhi, 1979-81.

Zelliot, Eleanor, *Dr. Ambedkar and the Mahar Movement*, Ph.D. dissertation, University of Pennylsavania, 1968.

Zelliot, Eleanor, *Learning the use of Political Means: The Mahar Movements*, In *Caste in Indian Politics*, edited by Rajani Kothari, Orient Longman Ltd., 1970.

Index

174 G 918

THE SCHEDULED CASTES IN INDIA

VOL. II

THE SCHEDULED CASTES IN INDIA

VOL. II

S.K. Chatterjee

GYAN

GYAN PUBLISHING HOUSE

NEW DELHI-110 002

THE SCHEDULED CASTES IN INDIA (VOL. II)
(Anthropology, Tribal Studies, Sociology)

ISBN : 81-212-0511-5 (Set)

ISBN : 81-212-0536-0 (Vol. II)

Published in 2008 in India by
Gyan Publishing House
5 Ansari Road
New Delhi-110 002

All rights reserved. No part of this book may be reproduced in any manner without written permission

Printed at Vishal Kaushik Printers Delhi - 110093

CONTENTS

PREFACE VOL. II

The Scheduled Castes, their privileges and safeguards occupy a prominent place in the Constitution of India. In the Constitutions of other countries there are provisions for safeguards for religious and racial minorities. There are also provisions for representations of political minorities so that the political views of every segment of population are reflected in the Legislatures. But in no other country there are provisions for safeguards for a substantial section of population of the same religious community. As the institution of caste is a unique feature of the Indian social system, so the special privileges and safeguards for a section of population on account of their social disabilities is a unique feature of the Indian Constitution. In no other country such a system exists.

In a study of this nature the first and foremost consideration must be to find out what was the intention of the Framers of the Constitution. We have discussed the entire progress of framing of all the Articles of the Constitution relating to the Scheduled Castes. The study commenced with the memorandum of the Constitutional Adviser, prepared in 1947, the discussions and recommendations at the various committee stages, the suggestions and comments offered by eminent personalities and organisations on the provisions as brought out in the Draft Constitution and views of the Constitutional Adviser on these suggestion, the stand taken by the Drafting Committee and finally, the deliberations in the Constituent Assembly. This detailed narration was thought necessary to get a clear idea about the background of framing of these provisions of the Constitution. The debates in the Constituent Assembly give us a glimpse into the working of the mind of the Framers—what they thought of the issues then, why a particular provision was incorporated, what were the arguments advanced in favour of or against a particular provision and the relevancy of these arguments in the backdrop of the present situation.

We have also discussed the relevant Sections of the Government of India Act, 1935, because some of these constitutional provisions owed their origin in the said Act. Each chapter concludes with a critical assessment of the provision.

A study of this nature will remain incomplete if the historical perspective of the framing of these constitutional provisions and the Depressed Classes movements from the pre-independent period are not touched upon. The first chapter has been devoted to this.

Who are the Scheduled Castes for whom safeguards and privileges have been provided for in the Constitution of India? The Framers did not answer this question. They refrained from stipulating criteria for preparation of the list of Scheduled Castes. Instead, they shaddled the executive with the burden of specifying the Scheduled Castes. The term 'Scheduled Castes' was first coined for the Government of India Act, 1935 to denote the former Depressed Classes, i.e., Untouchables, though all the castes scheduled in the Order issued under the 1935 Act were not necessarily untouchables, at least as defined by the Lothian Committee in 1932. Since the Constitution abolished untouchability and made its practice an offence, a question was raised as to who should be treated as Scheduled Castes. Though the Framers decided to overlook this question they were considerably seized with the question of providing safeguards for the Scheduled Castes. Some Members of the Constituent Assembly thought that there was no need for any safeguards for the Scheduled Castes and that the Scheduled Castes should not be treated as a separate category. But Austin's 'Oligarchy', i.e., Pandit Nehru, Sardar Patel, Maulana Azad and Rajendra Prasad, gradually round the Ambedkarian theory that granting of safeguards for the Scheduled Castes was necessary for removal of 'grievous social disabilities' and improvement of their 'standards of education and material well-being'. With the tacit support, approval and even blessings of the 'Oligarchy' it was not difficult for Ambedkar to incorporate in the Constitution special provisions for the Scheduled Castes.

A distinct line of division amongst the Members of the Constituent Assembly on the question of Scheduled Castes rights and position was discernible. The caste Hindus were against classification of the Scheduled Castes as a separate minority and pleaded for treating them as an integral part of the Hindu community. But the leaders of the Scheduled Castes never cherished any desire of completely merging with the Hindu society. All along they pressed for reservation according to their numerical strength and even demanded that quota for Harijans in the Cabinet should be statutorily reserved, the Governorship and Presidentship should be rotated and similar reservation be provided in respect of Local Bodies. (Is it a matter of coincidence that these have since been accepted and given recognition either in the Statute or through convention?)

The debates in the Constitutent Assembly leading to the incorporation of various constitutional safeguards clearly indicate that whatever might have been the views of the Members on these constitutional safeguards, they, irrespective of caste and community affiliations, were sincerely concerned for the uplift of the Scheduled Castes and Backward Classes in all spheres of life—social, educational, cultural and political, and that too very quickly, so that shorn of disabilities and discriminations they could take their rightful and legitimate share in all the activities of the society in their own right, as an equal partner.

I am thankful to my friends and well-wishers who helped me in various ways in completing this study. I am grateful to Sri B.P. Garg of Gyan Publishing House for publishing this book within a very short time.

Salt Lake, **S.K. Chatterjee**
Calcutta

5

Introduction

The Rising of 1857 opened the eyes of the British Rulers to the reality that a united India would always be a threat to the very existence of the British Empire. So they assiduously pursued a policy not only of dividing the Indians but also of further broadening and sharpening the existing cleavages and chasm in this multi-lingual, multi-religious, multi-racial country. They realised that the safety of the Empire lay in ensuring that the Indians were never allowed to remain united. India became a veritable playground for the practical application of its "Divide and Rule" theory. Their efforts in this direction took a concrete shape in the Constitution of 1909 when, on the recommendation of Lord Minto, the then Viceroy of India, the Muslims were granted recognition as a separate entity by providing them separate electorates. This device proved to be very successful in preventing unity among Indians and hence it was elaborated in the course of all subsequent efforts at constitution making. Step by step the recognition of communal claims and communal interests became a part of the basic policy of the British Government in India. So whenever the Indians' demand for the establishment of popular government and representative institutions was conceded, it was accompanied by a corresponding emphasis on the obligation of the British Government to protect the minorities from the oppression and exploitation at the hands of the majority. As the demand for independence gained momentum so also increased the number of minorities who came to be recognised as being in need of protection of the British Government, through separate representation in the Legislatures, reserved quotas in the public services, and in various other ways. In course of time, the Sikhs, the Anglo-Indians, the Indian Christians, the Depressed Classes (the Scheduled Castes were known as such then), the backward and hill tribes—all these communities were treated as minorities in need of protection. In fact, the concept of minorities was so expanded as to include even the prosperous European commercial and mercantile community in India as needing separate representation in the Legislatures.

Apart from patronising the religious community interests with a view to splitting the Indians horizontally on the basis of religion, the British Government actively pursued a policy to precipitate vertical division of the Hindus, who constituted about 70-75% of the total population. In a caste-ridden society what better weapon could it be but caste. Not unexpectedly, the British Government exploited this unique feature of the Hindu society to its full advantage. In this regard they followed a dual policy. Apprehensive of the fact that caste could be a focal-point for challenging their authority, they formulated a policy of dis-integrating the caste-based Hindu society and of initiating a process of transition from a caste-based society to a class-based society. At the same time they made the caste rigid by extending several benefits and privileges to a section of people solely on the basis of caste. Thus, during their 200-year rule, specially after 1857, whatever measures they initiated in administrative, legislative, economic, educational and above all, in political fields, were aimed at a achieving these objectives.

This policy took a definite shape by the mid-20s when separate entity of the Depressed Classes was conceded and seats in the Legislatures were reserved for them, even though to be filled by nomination. The Depressed Classes were given due recognition as a separate community when Dr. B.R. Ambedkar and Rao Bahadur Srinivasan were nominated by the British Government to represent the Depressed Classes in the Round Table Conferences in London in 1930-32. It may be recalled that on the question of representation in the Legislatures, the delegates to the Round Table Conference were unable to reach an agreed solution and the British Prime Minister, Ramsay MacDonald, thus announced what is known as the Communal Award in August, 1932. This Award accorded representation through separate electorates to Muslims, Sikhs, Indian Christians, Anglo-Indians and Europeans. Seats were reserved for the Marathas in selected constituencies in Bombay. Special seats were also allotted to women, labour, commerce and industry, mining and planting, and landholders. The demand of Ambedkar and Srinivasan of treating the Depressed Classes as a separate minority community was also conceded and the Depressed Classes were given seats to be filled by election from special constituencies in which they alone could vote, though they were also entitled to vote in the general constituencies. On the question of separate electorates for the Depressed Classes, Mahatma Gandhi undertook his historic fast which resulted in the Poona Pact whereby a system of providing reserved seats for the Depressed Classes with joint electorates was agreed upon. 151 seats were allotted to them, which was about double the number proposed in the Communal Award.

The Constitution of 1935 created a new caste known as "Scheduled Castes" which became a permanent feature of the Hindu caste system. The Hindus became broadly divided into Scheduled Caste Hindus and non-Scheduled Caste Hindus. Earlier there was upward mobility within the caste system. Now this mobility practically stopped. Not only caste became rigid and static but a downward mobility within the caste system was not altogether unwelcome. The questions relating to the Scheduled Castes were brought under the purview of the popular governments under the 1935 Act subject to the special powers of the Governor. In so far as the public services were concerned again separatism was encouraged through a complicated system of rostering of vacancies for a number of monorities, Scheduled Castes included. These policies went on to foster and encourage a feeling of insecurity among the minorities and an expectation for a protective framework, not very much different from what the British Rulers in India had devised from time to time.

In spite of the efforts of the Britishers to divide the people on the basis of caste and creed, in the elections held in 1937 under the 1935 Act the Indian National Congress was returned in impressive majorities and was able to form government in seven, later increased to eight, out of the eleven Provinces.[1] On the other hand, the success of the communal and sectarian parties and organisations at the hustings was poor. Of the 151 seats kept reserved for the Scheduled Castes in the Provincial Legislatures, the Congress captured 78 seats and the remaining 73 went to non-Congress parties, the bulk of which was in the Provinces of Bengal, Central Provinces and Bearar, Bombay and Punjab. In Bombay, Ambedkar's Independent Labour Party secured 11 out of the 15 seats reserved for the Scheduled Castes while in C.P. & Berar, 13 of the 20 seats went to non-Congressmen and followers of Ambedkar.[2] Ambedkar, like other Depressed Classes leaders, cherished a fond hope that the Congress would not inter-meddle in the elections of the Scheduled Castes to the seats reserved for them. But when the Congress not only fielded candidates in those reserved seats to prove that the Congress represented the Scheduled Castes and that the Scheduled Castes believed in the Congress, but also secured 51% of the seats, Ambedkar sought to project, like the Muslim League, that the 73 seats captured by the non-Congressmen, were filled by "true and independent representatives of the Untouchables" and that in point of effective representation, the Untouchables got less than what the British Prime Minister had given them.[3]

The failure of the Muslim League in the polls further hardened the attitude of its leaders. The problem of Hindu-Muslim relations thereafter assumed increasingly formidable proportions until in March, 1940 the League adopted the famous Pakistan resolution which stated that no constitutional plan would be workable or acceptable to the Muslims unless it recognised the basic principle that geographically contiguous units should be demarcated into regions so constituted that the areas in which Muslims were numerically in a majority were grouped to constitute "Independent States". In all these activities, the League was not without support from the British Government.

Over the question of India's participation in the Second World War and obtaning immediate independence the Congress ministries resigned in October, 1939. Eager to include India's support in the war effort the British Government sent the Cripps Mission in March, 1942 but it returned empty handed. The sudden end of the Second World War and the formation of the anti-imperialist Labour Government in Great Britian in July, 1945 brightened the prospect of India's independence. A series of talks and negotiations ensued and the Cabinet Mission Plan unfold in May-June, 1946, contained the blue-print for the setting up of a Constituent Assembly to draft India's Constitution and some of the basic principles to which this Constitution would adhere.

Serious objections to the Cabinet Mission Plan were raised by the Muslim League and by Ambedkar, who had been inducted as a Member of the Viceroy's Council in July 1942, on the question of minority rights and safeguards. Though the British Government ultimately conceded the Muslim demand for the creation of Pakistan, even by partitioning Punjab, Bengal and Assam, it was not that much tolerant to Ambedkar's demand of according a separate racial and religious minority status to the Depressed Classes.

In the meeting with the Cabinet Delegation on April 5, 1946 Ambedkar said that he did not want Constituent Assembly at all as it would be dominated by the caste Hindus and the Scheduled Caste members would not be no more than a small minority which would always be outvoted even if a three-quarters or a two-thirds majority were required for the Assembly's decisions. All the assurances of protection which His Majesty's Government had given to the monorities would go by the board. Moreover, there would be an immense amount of corruption in the Assembly—members would be bought over to vote against the interests of their communities. He thought that if India became independent it would be one of the greatest disasters that could happen. Before they left, the British must ensure that the new constitution guaranteed to the Scheduled Castes the elementary human rights of life, liberty and the pursuit of happiness, and that it restored their separate electorates and gave them the other safeguards which they demanded. At present disillusionment was driving his followers towards terrorism and communalism. He was on trial with them for the efficacy of constitutional methods.

Lord Pethic-Lawrence, a member of the Delegation, said that up to now Indian politics had been dominated by two issues, the question of winning independence from British rule and the Hindu-Muslim problem. Once these were out of the way party divisions would probably be on economic issues. Surely the Scheduled Caste would have a better chance of getting their rights by allaying themselves with the left wing than by relying on the British who were about to hand over power. In reply Dr. Ambedkar reiterated that so long as there were joint electorates, Scheduled Castes voters would be so few that Hindu candidates could safely ignore their wishes. Caste Hindus would never support Scheduled Caste candidates. Admittedly under the present system they had to vote for Untouchables in the final elections; but their object in doing so was never to favour their own candidate but merely to outvote the candidate put up by his own Federation. Separate electorates were fundamental, since without them the Scheduled Castes would never have their own representatives.[4]

In a letter written to Lord Wavel on May 3, 1946 in protest against the omission on the part of the Cabinet Mission to invite a representative of the Scheduled Castes to their Conference in Simla, Ambedkar again followed up his contention that the demands of the Scheduled Castes for (1) separate electorates, (2) proper representation in the Central Executive which should be 50% of the representation granted to the Muslims and (3) undertaking from parties to accept certain general principles in regard to the safeguarding of the interests of the Scheduled Castes in the future constitution as a condition precedent for an interim Government, were such that they did not require the consent of other parties, much less of the Hindus, in as much as they did not trench upon their legitimate rights.[5] Just 2 days prior to the announcement of the Cabinet Mission Plan on May 16, 1946, Ambedkar made a personal appeal to Alexander, another Member of the Cabinet Mission, who "came from the under-privileged classes in Great Britain" to safeguard the position and interests of the Untouchables "who had helped the British to conquer India" and not allow power to pass into the hands of those who were, in fact "enemies of the Untouchables".[6]

Cabinet Mission Plan came in for sharp criticism by the All-India Scheduled Castes Federations for not prescribing representation of the Scheduled Castes by separate electorates and for not providing separate settlement for them. The Federation even threatened to resort to direct action and its President was authorised "to constitute a Council of Action charged with the duty of examining the lines of direct action and to determine the one most effective and fix the time for launching the same".[7] Significantly, this resolution was adopted about two months ahead of the resolution of "Direct Action" taken by the Muslim League.

In the elections held in July, 1946 for the composition of the Constituent Assembly, only one seat, that of Ambedkar's, was secured by the Scheduled Castes Federation from Bengal, another was bagged by the Unionist Party in Punjab while the rest 29 Scheduled Caste members belonged to the Congress.[8] This pitiable performance by Ambedkar's organisation convinced the British Government of the futility of conceding Ambedkar's demand that only his organisation was the true representative of the Scheduled Castes. Moreover, the decision of the Labour Ministry to hand over power to the Indians at any cost prompted them not to act in any manner which 'would be interpreted as interferences with the Constituent Assembly which was what they were most anxious to avoid' or would arouse a controversy which might result in the Congress opposing any such move.[9] So the British Government politely turned down the request of Ambedkar that unless the Scheduled Castes were declared as an important minority there was the danger of their being relegated to the position of a social group within the Hindus as distinguished from a minority,[10] because the British Government thought they were not in a position to secure representation of the Ambedkar's organisation in the Minority Advisory Committee.[11] So Ambedkar's effort to project himself as the only undisputed leader of the Scheduled Castes, on the lines of Jinnah, floundered on the rock of British apathy. In all likelihood, it would have been a different story had the Conservative Government been in power at the relevant point of time.

II

The suggestions of the Cabinet Mission for the setting up of the Constituent Assembly were:

(a) to allot to each province a total number of seats proportional to its population, roughly in the ratio of one to a million, as the nearest substitute for representation by adult suffrage;

(b) to divide this provincial allocation of seats betweeen the main communities in each Province in proportion to their population;

(e) to provide that the representatives allotted to each community in a province would be elected by the members of that community.

The Cabinet Mission added:

"We think that for these purposes it is sufficient to reognise only three main communities in India: General, Muslim and Sikh; the "General" community including all persons who are not Muslims or Sikhs. As the smaller minorities would, upon population basis, have little or no representation, since they would lose weightage which assures them seats in the provincial Legislatures, we have made the arrangements set out in paragraph 20 below (formation of the Advisory Committee on Minority Rights Fundamental Rights, etc,) to give then a full representation upon all matters of special interest to the minorities."[12]

According to this plan, elections to the Constituent Assembly were held in three communal divisions, viz., Muslim, Sikh and General. The omnibus group 'General' included all communities except Muslim and Sikh. The Cabinet Mission Plan fixed the total number of Members of the Constituent Assembly at 389—one per million on an average. Of them, 292 were to be elected by the Provincial Legislative Assemblies, 4 to represent the Chief Commissioner's Provinces and 93 to be selected to represent the Indian States. The 296 seats of the British Indian territory were divided amongst the three communities as follows: General—204, Muslim—78 and Sikh—4

In the elections to the Constituent Assembly held in July, 1946, almost all the political parties took part. In fairness to the Congress it must be admitted that it gave representations to all shades of opinion and to all minority groups in the Constituent Assembly. It selected men from all communities, even men who never served the Congress. It even selected men who had actively opposed it in the political sphere.[13] Out of the 296 seats, Congress secured 206 seats (202 General, 3 Muslim, 1 Sikh), Muslim League 73 (Muslim), Unionist Party 3 (2 General and 1 Muslim), Akali Party-3 (Sikhs), Communist-1 (General), Scheduled Castes Federation-1 (General), Backward Tribes-2 (General), Commerce and Industry-2 (General), Landlords-3 (General), Shahid Jirha-1 (Muslim) and Krishak Proja-1 (Muslim).

The members of the Constituent Assembly, apart from representing the political parties, also represented various communities and interests. An analysis of the communities to which the members from the British India belonged revealed the following fact:[14]

Hindus	163
Scheduled Castes	31
Muslims	80
Anglo-Indians	3
Indian Christians	6
Parsees	3
Backward Tribes	6
Sikhs	4
	296

(There were 13 women members including one from the Muslim Community among them).

Among the members of the Constituent Assembly were the Presidents of the Indian National Congress, the Muslim League, the Hindu Mahasabha, the Anglo-Indian and Domiciled European Association, the Indian National Trade Union Congress, the Depressed Classes League, the All-India Scheduled Castes Federation, the All-India Pasi Mahasabha, the All-India Adibasi Mahasabha, the All-India Women's Conference, the All-India Landholders' Association, and the Servants of India Society. Most of them were returned on Congress ticket. Later, when Ambedkar who was returned from Bengal as a candidate of the Scheduled Castes Federation, lost his membership because of fresh election in West Bengal after partition, he was provided with a seat from Bombay by the Congress.

The Congress obtained overwhelming majority in General seats while the Muslim League had a similarly decisive success with the Muslim seats. The 'brute' majority of the Congress in the Constituent Assembly made the Muslim League hardened its stand over entry in the Assembly. It resorted to a Direct Action Day on August 16, 1946. The intransigence of the League put a hurdle to the implementation of the Cabinet Mission Plan. Ultimately, the British Government accepted the League demand of partition of the country into three segments. After partition, the strength of the Assembly came down to 324 to be filled up as follows—British Indian Provinces 235 (General 200, Muslim 31, Sikh 4) and Indian States 89.

From among the Indian States, Hyderabad, entitled to 16 seats, did not send its representatives at all. In returning the members, the Princely states did not follow a communal pattern. Where States were merged in Provinces, the Speaker of the Legislative Assembly of the Province was authorised to hold elections and bye-elections wherever necessary and notify the person or persons elected or nominated. Where States were united to form Unions of States and in the case of Hyderabad, Mysore, Jammu & Kashmir, the Rajpramukh or the Ruler of the States, and in the case of the States constituted into Chief Commissioner's provinces, the Chief Commissioner, was entrusted with this function.

III

The Cabinet Mission recommended a basic form for the Constitution including clauses for rights and protection of the minorities. The Cabinet Mission's statement of May 16, 1946. visualized a Union of India in which the powers of the Centre would be limited to foreign affairs, defence and communications; all other subjects as well as all residuary powers were to vest in the Provinces. This idea of autonomous units, with extensive powers and a relatively weak Centre was admittedly a concession to communal apprehensions. It was, in the view of the Cabinet Mission, a compromise proposal offered in the hope of avoiding "a separate and fully independent sovereign State of Pakistan". Against Pakistan of any dimensions—whether of the size contemplated by the Muslim League or in a modified form—the Cabinet Mission found "weighty administrative, economic and military considerations". The plan propounded by the Mission was proposed as an alternative to the demand of the Muslim League for the partition of India; and in putting forward their proposals the Cabinet Mission had in mind what they described as the "very real Muslim apprehension that their culture and political and social life might become submerged in a purely unitary India, in which the Hindus with their greatly superior numbers must be a dominating element". The Cabinet Mission's statement playing upon the apprehensions of the Muslims contained far-reaching safeguards for the minorities. It was suggested that a provision should be made in the new Constitution that any question raising a major communal issue in the Legislature should require for its decision a majority of the representatives, present and voting, of each of the two major communities as well as a majority of all the members present and voting. The statement also visualized provisions in the nature of a bill of rights as a partial answer to the issue of minority rights and proposed setting up by the Constituent Assembly at preliminary stage of a committee on the rights of citizens, minorities and tribal and excluded areas. This committee was to contain due representation of the interests affected and its function was, inter alia, to report to the Union Constituent Assembly upon the provision to be made for the protection of minorities. The Cabinet Mission made it clear that the cession of sovereignty to the Indian people on the basis of a constitution framed by the Assembly would be conditional on adequate provisions being made for the protection of minorities.[15]

When the Constituent Assembly met on December 9, 1946, the Muslim League boycotted the Assembly and did not send any representatives; the great majority of the members present represented the Indian National Congress.

In the first two sessions held between December 9, 1946 and January 25, 1947 two very important resolutions were adopted in the Assembly. One was a resolution regarding the Aims and Objects of the Constituent Assembly and the other was regarding the formation of the Advisory Committee on Fundamental Rights, Minority Rights, etc. In the Objectives Resolution moved by Jawaharlal Nehru in the Constituent Assembly on December 13, 1946, it was stated that in the Constitution to be drawn up for the future governance of India

> adequate safeguards shall be provided for minorities, backward and tribal areas and depressed and other backward classes.[16]

A resolution for the setting up of an Advisory Committee on Fundamental Rights, Minorities and Tribal and Excluded and Partially Excluded Areas was moved by Govind Ballabh Pant in the Constituent Assembly on January 24, 1947. As already stated, the representatives of the Muslim League were not participating in the deliberations of the Constituent Assembly at this stage. The prevalent feeling among the members present was that notwithstanding the absentee members, the Assembly and its committees should proceed with their respective tasks; at the same time all care should be taken to ensure that the Muslim League was also given the fullest opportunity effectively to participate in the framing of the Constitution should that body decide at any stage to join the Assembly and its committees. There was also the further anxiety to ensure that the committee should be so constituted as to ensure full discussion of the claims of all minorities, irrespective of their numerical strength.

With these two objects in view the resolution for the constitution of the Advisory Committee, as finally adopted by the Assembly, provided that the committee would initially consist of fifty members elected by the Assembly. Of these, seven were to be representatives of the Hindus of Bengal, the Punjab, the North-West Frontier Province, Baluchistan and Sind, where they were in a minority. Seven members were representatives of the Scheduled Castes; six were Sikhs, four Indian Christians, three Anglo-Indians, and three Parsis. There was one representative each of the plains tribes of Assam, the tribal area of the North-West Frontier Province, and the tribal areas of Baluchistan. Three members were representatives of the excluded and partially excluded areas; and there were twelve general names. The resolution authorized the President of the Assembly to nominate not more than twenty-two additional members, seven of whom were to be the representatives of the Muslims of Madras, Bombay, the United Provinces, Orissa and Assam.

The Advisory Committee was initially constituted with 50 members. Three more members were nominated by February 27 and another on April 10. The Muslim members took part in the deliberations after July 14, 1947. In course of time some of the members were dropped being preoccupied with other work and new members were added in their place. According to Austin, there were as many as 64 members on the Advisory Committee as of May, 1949.[17]

At the first meeting of the Advisory Committee held on February 27, 1947, Sardar Vallabhbhai Patel was unanimously elected chairman and five sub-committees, including the Fundamental Rights Sub-Committee and the Minorities Sub-Committee were set up.

The Fundamental Rights Sub-Committee was composed of the following members:

Acharya J.B. Kripalani, M.R. Masani, K.T. Shah. Rajkumari Amrit Kaur, Alladi Krishnaswamy Ayyar, K.M. Munshi, Sardar Harnam Singh, Maulana Abul Kalam Azad, B.R. Ambedkar and Jairamdas Daulatram.[18] Subsequently Mrs. Hansa Mehta was nominated to this Sub-Committee on March 24, 1947,[19] and Sardar K.M. Panikkar on April 10, 1947.[20] J.B. Kripalani was elected chairman of the Sub-Committee in its first meeting held on February 27, 1947.[21]

Initially the Minorities Sub-Committee consisted of the following 26 members:

(1) Jagjivan Ram, (2) Maulana Abul Kalam Azad, (3) B.R. Ambedkar, (4) Sardar Jogendra Singh, (5) Dr. S.P. Mukherjee, (6) Sardar Ujjal Singh, (7) Sardar Harnam Singh, (8) Bakshi Sir Tek Chand, (9) Dr. Gopi Chand Bhargava, (10) H.J. Khandekar, (11) P.R. Thakur, (12) Sir Homi Mody, (13) Dr. H.C.Mookherjee, (14) P.K.Salve, (15) S.H. Prater, (16) F.R. Anthony, (17) C.Rajagopalachari, (18) Rajkumari Amrit Kaur, (19) Jairamdas Daulatram, (20) R.K. Sidhwa, (21) Rup Nath Brahma, (22) M. Ruthnaswamy, (23) M.V.H. Collins, (24) Dr. Alban D'Souza, (25) K.M. Munshi, (26) Govind Ballav Pant.[22]

Six members of the Fundamental Rights Sub-

Committee, namely, Rajkumari Amrit Kaur, K.M. Munshi, B.R. Ambedkar, Jairamdas Daulatram, Harnam Singh and Maulana Abul Kalam Azad were members of the Minorities Sub-committee also. Subsequently, the following members were added: Hifzur Rehman, Ali Zaheer, Abul Qayum Ansari, Khaliquzzaman, Ismail Chundrigar, Muhammad Saadulla, Kasturbhai Lalbhai, Kameshwar Singh of Darbhanga, Seth Govind Das, Lakshmi Kant Maitra and Thakurdas Bhargava.[23]

Salve, Brahma, Ruthnaswamy and Collins were not members of the Constituent Assembly.

The personnel of the Sub-Committee represented all the minority interests as under :

Muslims-7, Scheduled Castes-4, Sikhs-3, Indian Christians-4, Anglo-Indian-3, Parsis-2, Plains Tribal-1, and Hindus-13. It was truly a body composed of representatives of all minorities to safeguard the interests of all minorities to their satisfaction. The Sub-Committee elected Dr. H.C. Mookherjee, a respected Christian leader from Bengal as its Chairman.

IV

Having discussed the composition of the Constituent Assembly, the socio-political interests represented, their broad communal divisions, etc., and the formation of the Advisory Committee along with its two important Sub-Committees, let us examine the methodology followed in the drafting of the Constitution. For some time the Assembly did not go into detailed work because there was a slight hope that the Muslim League would join. When partition became inevitable, the Assembly went ahead with its task of framing the Constitution. Much of the actual drafting of the Constitution was done by the various Committees and Sub-Committees like the Advisory Committee, the Union Powers Committee, the Union Constitution Committee, the Provincial Constitution Committee, set up for the purpose of formulation of their proposals regarding the different provisions to be included in the Constitution. Each Committee went into the details of its subject-matter and came up with their reports containing suitable draft paragraphs. The reports of the different Committees came up for discussion in the Assembly as and when they became ready. The Assembly, after discussion, effected necessary changes, if required. At the end of August, 1947, a Drafting Committees was constituted to prepare a Draft Constitution on the basis of the reports on which the Assembly could come to a decision as well as those which could not be considered by the Assembly becasue of shortage of time. The work of drafting the Constituion was undertaken by the Secretariat of the Constituent Assembly in August, 1947, and the first draft prepared by the Secretariat and the Constitutional Adviser was ready by October, 1947. The Drafting Committee sat from day to day from October, 1947, scrutinising each clause of this Draft until its own revised text was ready in Feburary, 1948. This Draft Constitution was circulated amongst all sections of people including the members of the Assembly eliciting comments, suggestions, amendments etc.

The discussion on the Draft Constitution took place in several stages from November 4, 1948 to November 25, 1949. There was first a general discussion mainly on the principles of the Constitution, then a clause by clause considerations. Thereafter, the Drafting Committee had to redraft the Constitution incorporating all the amendmends adopted by the Assembly and giving final shape to the Constitution. This revised Draft Constitution came up for a general discussion. The discussions at the third reading stage were brief and of a general nature.

As already pointed out, the most crucial work of providing Fundamental Rights to the citizens and safeguards for the minorities, which included not only religious minorities and racial minorities but also that section of the Hindu population brought under the rubric of "Scheduled Castes" fell on the Advisory Committee. The modality followed in regard to the formulation of the recommendations of the Advisory Committee was that the Fundamental Rights Sub-Committee first prepared its own report regarding the various clauses on Fundamental Rights and then sent it to the Advisory Committee. The Advisory Committee, in turn, sent that report to the Minorities Sub-Committee to examine whether any of them required to be amplified or amended for the specific purpose of protecting minority rights. The Advisory Committee thereafter discussed the recommendations made by the Sub-Committee on Fundamental Rights together with the report of the Minorities Sub-Committee thereon and thereafter submitted its own reports on Fundamental Rights. The Advisory Committee submitted its report on justiciable fundamental rights on April 23, 1947 and another report on fundamental right and Directive Principles on August 25. 1947.[24] The report of the Minorities Sub-Committee on minority rights was however not sent to the Fundamental Rights Sub-Committee for its comments before the same was discussed in the full meeting of the Advisory Committee.

The Minorities Sub-Committee after preliminary discussion at its meeting on February 27 and 28, 1947, decided,[25] to circulate amongst its members a questionnaire drafted by Munshi, which was in the following terms:

(1) What should be the nature and scope of the safeguards for a minority in the new Constitution?

(2) What should be the political safeguards for a minority

  (a) in the Centre?

  (b) in the Provinces?

(3) What should be the economic safeguards for a minority

  (a) in the Centre

  (b) in the Provinces?

(4) What should be the religious, educational and cultural safeguards for a minority?

(5) How is it proposed that the safeguards should be eliminated. in what time and under what circumstances?

Replies to this questionnaire and other memoranda on the subject were invited by March 31, 1947. Replies to the questionnaire and memoranda received from members of the Sub-Committee included those sent by Rajkumari Amrit Kaur, M. Ruthnaswamy, R.K. Sidhwa, Homi Mody, H.J. Khandekar, P.K. Salve, Jagjivan Ram, S.P. Mookherjee, Frank Anthony, S.H. Prater, Jairamdas Daulatram, Ujjal Singh, Harnam Singh, and R.H. Brahma. Besides these, memoranda were received from other individuals and organisations like the All-India Adi Hindu Depressed Classes Association, Jain Swetambar Conference, representatives of the Jain community and K.T. Shah. As the Muslim League was not participating in the proceedings of the Assembly at this stage, no memorandum on behalf of the Muslim community was presented, though a letter was received from Hifzur Rehman and Abdul Qaiyum Ansari.[26]

Since Ambedkar submitted an extensive note on the subject of minorities and fundamental rights to the Sub-Committee on Fundamental Rights, he did not submit any separate memorandum to the Minorities Sub-Committee. This he did before he had become the Law Minister and piloted the Draft Constitution. As a leader of the Scheduled Castes, he was primarily concerned with the political and social safeguards for the Scheduled Castes, and with ensuring that new Constitution provided adequately for their uplift. By way of political safeguards, he suggested the establishment of non-parliamentary irremovable executives both in the Union and in the units. He proposed that the Scheduled Castes should have minimum representation according to their population ratio in the Legislatures, Ministries, in municipalities and local boards. These representatives were to be elected through separate communal electorates. In the Ministries of the Union and of the units the representatives of the Scheduled Castes and other minorities were to be elected by the members of the Legislature belonging to each minority community by the method of proportional representation by means of the single transferable vote. Ambedkar suggested further that the Scheduled Castes should have a minimum share of the posts in the various public services in proportion to their population and that this reservation should be made all along the line—in the Union services, the services of the units and in the services of municipalities, local boards and other local authorities. On every Public Service Commission and other selection committees the Scheduled Castes were to have at least one representative.

On the social side, Ambedkar suggested stringent punishment for social boycott and for promoting, instigating or threatening social boycott. Ambedkar's suggestions for the amelioration of the conditions of the Scheduled Castes included generous provision of funds in the budgets of the Governments of the Union and of the units for higher education, secondary and college education, and for education abroad of this community; the settlement of Scheduled Castes in separate villages; and the setting up of a Settlement Commission for this purpose. Finally to watch over the progress of these measures, he wanted an office of Superintendent of Minority Affairs to be created, with the same status as the Auditor-General, whose duty would be to prepare an annual report on the Union and the States; and on any transgressions of safeguards or miscarriage of justice arising out of communal bias by the Governments and their officers. These reports were to be placed before the Union and the State Legislatures and discussed by them.

Jagjivan Ram, a prominent leader of the Secheduled Castes and a Minister in the Central Government, emphasised that the guarantees should be directed to the protection of racial and religious minorities from "extinction" and the assimilation of minorities like the Scheduled Castes in the parent body by bringing them to a level equal with that of others in the community. Many of the safeguards could in his view be provided in the form of fundamental rights. The specific safeguards which he suggested for the Scheduled Castes were reservation of seats in proportion to their population in the Legislatures and in the Central and State Cabinets; and reservation of posts in services of all categories, civil and military, and in the judiciary. He also urged special ameliorative measures; a Housing Board to allot suitable plots and provide healthy houses; free education at all stages in all educational institutions; and generous stipends for higher and specialized education, both in India and abroad. Like Ambedkar, Jagjivan Ram also pleaded for the establishment of an independent Minorities Commission to deal with the welfare of minorities and to examine all cases of infringement of their rights, privileges and facilities. He suggested that the guarantee of religious and cultural freedom to racial and religious minorities should be a permanent feature of the Constitution; but the special provisions regarding Scheduled Castes could be eliminated when untouchbility itself was totally eliminated; when all Hindu temples were open to all the castes in Hindu society; when water or the food of the caste not considered "polluted" by the touch of any other caste: and Hindus of all castes could participate in all religious and social functions. Any resolution for the abolition of any of the safeguards for Scheduled Castes would require in its favour a two-thirds majority of all the members of the Scheduled Castes in all Assemblies of the units, and a similar two-thirds majority in the Union Legislature.

Other suggestions for safeguards for the Scheduled Castes were contained in a memorandum sent by the All-India Adi Hindu Depressed Classes Association and in the reply of Khandekar, a member of the Minorities Sub-Committee. The Depressed Classes Association formulated a long list of measures for the uplift of the Scheduled Castes; in particular it claimed reservation of seats in the various Legislatures in proportion to their population and asked that either elections to these reserved seats should be through separate electorates, or, if the principle of joint electorates was adopted, every candidate should, before he was declared elected, secure at least 40 per cent of the votes polled by members of the Scheduled Castes. Khandekar also gave a long list of general and specific suggestions, mainly on the lines of the proposals made by Jagjivan Ram; his main claim was that Scheduled Castes being in terms of population equal to Muslims, the reservation of seats in the Legislatures, Ministries, Judiciary and the public services should not be less favourable than the representation given to the Muslims. The safeguards provided that all concessions and privileges given to minority communities should be effective for a period of thirty years, after which the communities should be consulted as regards their modification.

No specific communal demands were put forward on behalf of Indian Christians and Parsis. Some of the prominent members of the Sub-Committee were against safeguards of any kind. Rajkumari Amrit Kaur and K.T. Shah may be mentioned in this regard.

It was against the background of these divergent views that the Minorities Sub-Committee met on July 21, 1947 to consider the political safeguards for minorities and their representation in the public services. By this time the question of partition had been decided and the Muslim League was also represented on the Sub-Committee.

The Sub-Committee in its report[27] on July 27 to the Advisory Committee concluded generally by a large majority that :

(1) there should be no separate electorates for elections to the Legislatures.

(2) as a general rule, there should be reservation of seats for the monority communities like the Anglo-Indians. Parsees, Plains' tribesmen in Assam, Indian Christians, Sikhs, Muslims and Scheduled Castes.

(3) such reservations would initially be for a period of ten years, the position to be reconsidered at the end of the period.

(4) no weightage should be given to any community.

(5) there should be no statutory reservation of seats for the minorities in the Cabinets.

(6) there should be reservation in the public services for the Scheduled Castes, Muslims, Sikhs, Plains' tribes in Assam, and Anglo-Indians. The Parsees and the Indian Christians did not ask for reservation in services.

(7) an independent officer to be appointed in the Centre

and in the Provinces to report on the working of the minorities' safeguards.

(8) a Commission to be set up to investigate into the conditions of the socially and educationally backward classes.

The report of the Minorities Sub-Committee was discussed by the Advisory Committee from July 28-31, 1947. It accepted the report with some modifications. Dealing with the quantum of representation to be given to individual minority communities, the Committee recommended that Muslims and Scheduled Castes should get reserved seats in proportion to their population; Indian Christians accepted reservation of seats in accordance with the population in the Centre and in Madras and Bombay; the Parsis withdrew their claim for any kind of statutory reservation; so far as the Anglo-Indian community was concerned, after much discussion, the representatives of the community were persuaded to withdraw claims for any statutory reservation of seats in the Legislatures, on the understanding that the President of the Union and the Governors of Provinces would have the power to nominate their representatives if they failed to secure any representation as a result of the general elections. The consideration of safeguards for the Sikh community was postponed; so was the case of tribesmen living in the plains of Assam, pending the report of the committee on the tribal areas and excluded and partially excluded areas of Assam.

The Committee also decided against any specific provisions for reservation of appointments in the public services; and it was in favour of a general provision on the lines suggested by Ali Zaheer that in the all-India and provincial services, the claims of minorities should be kept in view consistently with the efficiency of administration.[28]

The Committee agreed with the recommendations of the special sub-committee constituted to report on the position of Anglo-Indians in certain services and the grant of special educational facilities for them, that the reservation of appointments enjoyed by the Anglo-Indians in certain services should be continued for the time being but reduced gradually and cease to exist after ten years and that special assistance given to Anglo-Indian schools would be reduced gradually over a period of ten years; thereafter they would be treated in the same manner as other similar schools and included these recommendations in a supplementary report.[29]

The report of the Advisory Committee on minority rights and on Anglo-Indians were considered by the Constitutent Assembly on August 27 and 28, 1947 and were adopted with some minor amendments.

These decisions of the Constituent Assembly were incorporated in the Draft Constitution prepared by the Constitutional Adviser; it also included provisions to give effect to the recommendations of the two sub-committees on tribes—the sub-committee on tribal and excluded and partially excluded areas in Assam and the sub-committee on excluded and partially excluded areas in Provinces other than Assam.

These provisions were considered by the Drafting Committee on February 5 and 6, 1948. The Draft Constitution settled by this committee and published in February, 1948 contained a special part (Part XIV) under the title "Special Provisions relating to Minorities". This part contained ten articles setting out in detail and with meticulous care the decisions taken by the Constituent Assembly and the recommendations of the two sub-committees on tribal people (draft articles 292 to 301). Article 292 reserved seats in the House of the People for Muslims, the Scheduled Castes, the Scheduled Tribes, and in the States of Madras and Bombay for Indian Christians, in proportion to the population of these communities. Article 294 laid down a similar reservation for these communities in the Legislative Assemblies of Part I States—corresponding to the Provinces of the Dominion. In additon, seats in the Assam Legislative Assembly were also to be reserved for the autonomous districts of that State. Article 293 gave power to the President to nominate not more than two members of the Anglo-Indian community to the House of the People if he felt that it was not adequately represented. Article 295 contained a similar provision in relation to the State Legislatures. Article 296 required that, consistently with the maintenance of efficiency of administration, the claims of the minority communities should be taken into consideration in the making of appointments to public services and posts. Article 297 continued in force the reservation of posts for Anglo-Indians in the Railways, Castoms and Posts and Telegraphs Services of the Union on the same basis as immediately before August 15, 1947. Article 298 made elaborate provision regarding Government grants for the benefit of the Anglo-Indian community in respect of education. Article 299 provided for the appointment of a Special Officer for Minorities for the Union and one for each State, who would be charged with the duty of investigating all matters relating to the safeguards provided by the Constitution and required to make periodic reports to the respective Governments. These reports were to be placed before the appropriate Legislatures.

Article 300 empowered the President to appoint at any time a Commission to report on the administration of the Scheduled Areas and the welfare of the Scheduled Tribes. The appointment of such a Commission was made mandatory on the expiry of ten years from the commencement of the Constitution. Article 301 empowered the President to appoint a Commission to investigate the conditions of all socially and educationally backward classes within the territory of India and the difficulties under which they laboured, to suggest remedial steps and make recommendations as to the grants to be made by the Union for the purpose and the conditions subject to which such grants should be given.

A direction was contained in the Instrument of Instructions requiring the Governors to include in their Cabinets members of important minority communities, so far as this might be practicable, and a provision was also made that there should be a Minister in charge of tribal welfare in Bihar, the Central Provinces and in Orissa (Draft Article 144, (1).

That apart, special provisions for removal of social disabilities, prohibition of discrimination, equality of opportunity in matters of public employment were incorporated in the form of fundamental rights. Thus, Draft Article 11 abolished untouchability and clause 2 of Draft Article 19 threw open Hindu religious institutions to all classes or sections of Hindus. Draft Article 17 prohibited traffic in human beings and in forced labour whereas Draft Article 18 prohibited employment of children in factories. Draft Article 9 prohibited discrimination on grounds of religion, race, caste or sex. The principle of equality of opportunity and prohibition of discrimination on grounds of religion, race, caste, sex, descent, place of birth in the matter of public employment was contained in Draft Article 10, and, at the same time reservation of appointment or posts in favour of any backward class of citizens in the services under the state was provided for in the same darft article.

Draft Article 37 in the Directive Principles of State Policy cast a duty on the State for promotion of educational and economic interests of the weaker sections, and in particular of the Scheduled Castes and Scheduled Tribes and for their protection from social justice and all forms of exploitation.

The Draft Constitution of February 1948 was incomplete in one important respect. The position of the Provinces of East Punjab and West Bengal was uncertain on account of the large scale uprooting of people following the partition of India. Mainly because of this reason no decisions were taken on the minorities issues as they applied to these Provinces. The important question of safeguards for the Sikhs thus still remained to be discussed. A small sub-committee formed on February 24, 1948 to consider the position of the Sikhs and other minorities in East Punjab and the minorities in West Bengal submitted its report on November 23, 1948. This report of the sub-committee and the question of minority safeguards in East Pubjab and West Bengal were placed before the Advisory Committee on December 30, 1948, but consideration of these issues was again postponed.

At this meeting certain suggestions of a fundamental character on the question of minority rights were raised. Some members had given notice of resolutions seeking to do away with the reservations for all minorities. Referring to these notices, Vallabhabhai Patel, the Chairman of the Advisory Committee, suggested that the movers of such resolutions should confine their proposals to their own communities, as, in the absence of a general agreement, it would not be proper to force a minority to give up its right of separate representation. For example, if Muslims by general agreement among themselves felt that they did not want any reservation, their views would be accepted; but the proposal should come from them and not from a member of any other community.[30]

All these matters were considered by the Advisory Committee on May 11, 1949, and the recommendations of the committee were communicated to the President of the Assembly on the same date. The Advisory Committee's recommendations [31] recapitulated the previous decisions on the subject of minority rights and recalled the decision of the Constituent Assembly that seats were to be reserved in the Union Legislature for Muslims, Scheduled Castes and Indian Christians; in all the State Legislatures for Muslims and Scheduled Castes; and for Indian Christians in Madras and Bombay. At the meeting of the committee on December 30, 1948, according to the report, some members felt that conditions having vastly changed since the Advisory Committee had made its recommendations in 1947, it was no longer appropriate in the context of free India to reserve seats for Muslims, Christians, Sikhs or any other religious minority. Although the abolition of separate electorates had removed much of the poison from the body politic, the reservation of seats for religious communities, it was felt, would lead to a certain degree of separation and to that extent was contrary to the conception of a secular democratic State; and some members gave notice of resolutions to recommend to the Constituent Assembly the abolition of reservation of seats in the Legislatures for any community in India. The report observed how a decision on the issue was postponed so that representatives of the minorities on the committee should have adequate time both to gauge public opinion among their people and to reflect fully on the amendments that had been proposed, so that a change, if effected. would be one sought voluntarily by the minorities themselves and not imposed on them by the majority community.

The report added that at the adjourned meeting held on May 11, the resolution for the abolition of all reservation for minorities other than Scheduled Castes found whole-hearted support from an overwhelming majority of the members of the Advisory Committee. So far as the Scheduled Castes were concerned, it was recognised that their peculiar position would make it necessary to give them reservation for a period of ten years.

The proposal of the Advisory Committee was therefore that reservations should be provided only for Scheduled Castes and Scheduled Tribes; this was due to the backward position of these communities, which made it necessary that their representatives should be member of the Legislatures and actively participate in the political life of the country. In view of the special position of the Anglo-Indians, the provision enabling the President and the Governors to nominate members of this community was also retained.

Another matter of interest was also mentioned by Patel. The Constituent Assembly had always recognized that the Scheduled Castes were a backward section of the Hindu community who were handicapped by the practice of untouchability. This evil practice of untouchability was not recognized by any other religion and the question of any Scheduled Castes belonging to a religion other than Hinduism did not therefore arise. But, the Sikhs had made a demand that some of their backward sections—the Mazhabis, Ramdasias, Kabirpanthis and Siklagars-should be included in the list of Scheduled Castes. This was accepted by the Advisory Committee. Patel recognized that this was a political decision; but for the sake of securing their goodwill, he urged the Assembly to agree to this concession.

After a lengthy discussion the proposals of the

Advisory Committee were adopted by the Assembly with an amendment moved by Thakurdas Bhargava that no reservation would be operative for more than ten years.

In view of this changed decision of the Constituent Assembly, a number of consequential amendments were moved by Ambedkar on August 23-26, 1949 relating to draft articles coming under Part XVI.

Draft Articles 292 and 294 now provided reservation of seats for the Scheduled Castes and the Scheduled Tribes only in the House of People and the State Assemblies, respectively.

A new Draft Article 295A was moved by Ambedkar to lay down that the reservation of seats to Scheduled Castes and Scheduled Tribes would cease after ten years from the date of commencement of the Constitution.

The amended Draft Article 296 now restricted to the Scheduled Castes and Scheduled Tribes any special treatment in the matter of recruitment to the public services, but extending the scope of preference to Part III States (i.e., the Indian States) as well. Draft Article 299 relating to the appointment of special officers to investigate and report on minority safeguards was also ammended by the Drafting Committee in two important respects. In the first place, the jurisdiction of the special officers was limited to Scheduled Castes, Scheduled Tribes, Anglo Indians and other backward classes. The second change was that there was to be only one special officer to be appointed by the Union Government who would function for the Centre as well as for the States. The amended article was moved by Munshi on October 14, 1949.

Two new Articles 300A and 300B were moved by Ambedkar on September 17, 1949, empowering the President to issue a general notification, in consultation with the Governor or Ruler of a State, in the official gazette specifying the castes or tribes deemed to be Scheduled Castes or Tribes.

Draft Articles 293, 297 and 298 relating to Anglo-Indians were adopted by the Assembly without any amendment.

These articles were set forth as Articles 330-342 in Part XVI during revision. When the revised draft came up for discussion on November 16, Krishnamachari suggested in an amendment that for the word "minorities" wherever it occurred, the words "certain classes" be substituted. This was necessary, he pointed out, in view of the objection raised by some members to the use of the words "minorities" even in the heading of this Part and also the consequential use of this word elsewhere. The amendment was adopted by the Assembly, and the heading was changed to "Special provisions relating to certain classes".

After the commencement of the Constitution, Article 15 was amended to include a provision empowering the State to make special provisions for the advancement of any socially and educationally backward classes of citizens or for the Scheduled Castes and the Scheduled Tribes.

With this introductory background, we now propose to discuss the following provision of the Constitution relating to removal of social disabilities, promotion of educational and economic interest, reservation in services and political safeguards of the Scheduled Castes; and other backward classes:

Removal of Social Disabilities

(1) Abolition of untouchability (Article 17).

(2) Providing for social welfare and reforn or the throwing open of Hindu religious institutions of a public character to all classes and sections of Hindus (Article 25 (2) (b)).

(3) Prohibition of traffic in human beings and forced labour (Article 23).

(4) Prohibition of employment of children in factories (Article 24).

Promotion of Educational and Economic Interest

(5) Special provision for the advancement of any socially and educationally backward classes of citizens or for the Scheduled Castes and the Scheduled Tribes (Article 15(4)).

(6) Promotion of educational and economic interests of Scheduled Castes, Scheduled Tribes and other weaker sections (Article 46).

Reservation in Services

(7) Provision for reservation of appointments in posts in favour of any backward class of citizens (Article 16 (4)).

(8) Claims of Scheduled Castes and Scheduled Tribes to services and posts (Article 335).

(9) Public Service Commission not required to be consulted in certain matters (Article 320) (4)).

Political Safeguards

(10) Reservation of seats for Scheduled Castes and Scheduled Tribes in the House of the People (Article 330).

(11) Reservation of seats for Scheduled Castes and Scheduled Tribes in the Legislative Assemblies of the States (Article 332).

(12) Reservation of seats and special representation to cease after (fifty years) (Article 334).

Appointment of Special Officer (Now National Commission)

(13) Special Officer (Now National Commission) for Scheduled Castes. Scheduled Tribes, etc. (Article 338).

Appointment of Commission for Backward Classes

(14) Appointment of a Commission to investigate the conditions of backward classes (Article 340).

Definition

(15) Definition of Scheduled Castes (Article 341).

The entire process of framing of the foregoing constitutional provisions has been discussed in details. The chapter dealing with each area of safeguards and other related issues begins with an introductory resume and thereafter presents the discussions at the different stages till the relevant article in its final form finds its place in the Constitution. Since the commencement of the Constitution lively controversy centres around many of these provisions. It is, therefore, incumbent to look at the source materials which led to the incorporation of these measures in the Constitition. This calls for a closer look at the basic souce materials like memorandum and replies submitted by the members of the Constituent Assembly, individuals and organisations to the Fundamental Rights Sub-Committee and the Minorities Sub-Committee, the minutes and reports of these Sub-Committees, the recommendations of the Advisory Committee to the Constituent Assembly and the Assembly's reactions thereto, provisions incorporated in the Draft Constitutions prepared by the Constitutional Adviser and the Drafting Committee and the deliberations that took place in the Assembly on these provisions at different stages of their passage which have been discussed sytematically in each chapter.

The Indian Constitution is a history of the Indian Constituent Assembly, of how and why the members wrote their constitution as they did. It is also necessary to know the reactions of different socio-economic sections represented in the Constituent Assembly to these provisions relating to the Scheduled Castes and Backward Classes that finally emerged. It has been our endeavour to bring out whatever was said by the founding fathers in extenso. The proceedings in the Assembly give us an idea as to how the framers looked at the problems of the Scheduled Castes and Scheduled Tribes and its solution and what was the immediate compulsions for retaining the protective safeguards for the Scheduled Castes and Scheduled Tribes, especially when the religious minorities voluntarily withdrew their claim to reservations and other safeguards. That is the reason why the debates in the Constituent Assembly on these provisions either at the Committee stage or at the subsequent stages have been reproduced unedited. Even though the views expressed in interpretation of the consitutional provisions are not a legally recognised aid to interpretation of the constitutional provisions, yet they do provide valuable insight into the minds of the founding fathers and persepective to view these problems.

The minutes and reports of the different Sub-Committees and Committees together with the proceedings in the Constituent Assembly would reveal the intentions, expectations and apprehensions of the framers with regard to these protective measures and what was actually achieved. This study is aimed at placing relevant materials and facts as they were so that it does not become difficult to reach a conclusion without being influenced by the analysts and the commentators, who often tend to project their own views on the subject.

Since this study is confined to the issues related to castes, those provisions of the Constitution exclusively dealing with Scheduled Tribes and its allied matters have not been discussed.

We shall now discuss each of these provisions separately in the subsequent chapters.

Notes and References

1. Kashyap, Anirban, *Communalism and Constitution*, Lancers Books, New Delhi, 1988, p. 26.
2. *Dr. Babasaheb Ambedkar: Writings and Speeches*, Government of Maharashtra, 1991, Vol. 10, p. 7.
3. *Ibid.*, Vol. 9, *What Congress and Gandhi have done to the Untouchables*, p. 95.
4. *The Transfer of Power*, Nicholas Mansergh, Editor-in-Chief; published by His Majesty's Stationery Office, London, 1970; Vol. VII, No. 58, pp. 144-47.
5. *Dr. Babasaheb Ambedkar: Writings and Speeches*, Vol. 10, *op. cit.*, p. 487.
6. *Ibid.*, pp. 492-99.
7. *The Transfer of Power*, *op. cit.*, Vol. VII, No. 454, pp. 808-12.
8. Rao, Shiva Rao, *The Framing of India's Constitution*, the Indian Institute of Public Administration, New Delhi, 1966, p. 298.
9. *The Transfer of Power*, *op. cit.*, Vol. VIII, No. 288, pp. 466-68.
10. *Ibid.*, No. 142, pp. 221-23.
11. *Ibid.*, No 250, pp. 411-12.
12. Paragraph 18 of the Cabinet Mission's Statement of May 16, 1946, Kashyap, *op. cit.*, pp. 38-39.
13. *Ibid.*, p. 43.
14. Rao, *op. cit.*, Vol. 1, p. 298.
15. Cabinet Mission Statement of May 25, 1946, Rao, *Ibid*, Vol. 1, p. 258.

16. *Constituent Assembly Debates* (henceforth *CAD*), Vol. I, dated 13-12-46, p. 59.
17. Austin, Granville, *The Indian Constitution: Cornerstone of a Nation*, Oxford University Press, Bombay, 1966, pp. 333-34.
18. Rao, *op. cit.*, Vol. II, p. 65.
19. *Ibid.*, p. 110.
20. *Ibid.*, p. 171.
21. *Ibid.*, p. 114.
22. *Ibid.*, pp. 65-66.
23. *Ibid.*, Vol. V, p. 747.
24. *CAD*, Vol. III, pp. 437-44 and Vol. V, pp. 373-76.
25. Rao, *op. cit.*, Vol. II, pp. 389-92.
26. *Ibid.*, pp. 309-86.
27. *Ibid.*, pp. 396-400.
28. *CAD*, Vol. V, pp. 243-49.
29. *Ibid*, pp. 250-51.
30. Rao, *op. cit.*, Vol. IV, pp. 597-98.
31. *CAD*, Vol. VIII, pp. 310-15.

6

Abolition of Untouchability (Article 17)

Removal of untouchability from the Indian society, particularly the Hindu society, was an issue which was agitating the Indians from the early 20s. So when the occasion for framing a Constitution for India by the Indian themselves came, the question of incorporating a provision for the abolition of the age-old social evil of untouchability met with general approval. The only concern of the framers was how to draft it in a better form.

The Fundamental Rights Sub-Committee had before it the Notes and Draft Articles on Fundamental Rights prepared by K.M. Munshi, Draft on Fundamental Rights submitted by Harnam Singh and B.R. Ambedkar's Momorandum and Draft Articles on the Rights of States and Minorities, besides the Notes of B.N. Rau, the Constitutional Adviser, and of K.T. Shah. Clause 4(a) of Article III of Munshi's draft declared:

> Untouchability is abolished and the practice thereof is punishable by the law of the Union,[1]

while Harnam Singh's draft contained the following provision:

The recognition of untouchability shall be a crime in India.[2] Clause 1 of Article II of Section I of Ambedkar's draft had laid down that

Any privilege or disability arising out of rank, birth,

> person, family, religion or religious usage and custom is abolished.[3]

He also proposed in Clause 3 of Article II of Section II that the social boycott, promoting or instigating a social boycott shall be declared to be an offence,[4] because social boycott was always held over the heads of the untouchables by the caste Hindus as a sword of Damocles. The provisions relating to boycott were taken by him bodily from the Burma Anti-Boycott Act. 1922.[5] The Fundamental Rights Sub-Committee. after considering Munshi's draft in conjunction with other drafts, decided on March 29, 1947, to provide for abolition of untouchability,[6] and recommended in clause 6 of its draft report to be submitted to the Advisory Committee on Minorities, Fundamental Rights, etc., that "Untouchability is abolished and the practice thereof shall be an offence."[7]

The Constitutional Adviser noted on April 8, 1947 that what was exactly meant by the practice of untouchability would have to be defined in the law meant to implement this provision.[8]

On April 14, 1947, the Sub-Committee decided to add the words "in any form" after the word "untouchability".[9] The recommendation of the Sub-Committee to the Advisory Committee, therefore, was in the following words:

> Untouchability in any form is abolished and the practice thereof shall be an offence.[10]

The recommendations of the Fundamental Rights Sub-Committee were sent to the Minorities Sub-Committee for examination whether any of them required modification, amplification etc. from the minorities' point of view. The Minorities Sub-Committee had by this time before it the notes and memorandum submitted by its members on minorities' rights and safeguards. Jagjivam Ram, a leader of the Scheduled Castes, in his memorandum dated April 3, 1947, suggested that observance of untouchability in any shape or form by any person in public places, places of public worship, public institutions, and places established or maintained at public cost and for the use of the public should be regarded as a cognizable offence.[11] The memorandum of H.J. Khandekar, also a member belonging to the Scheduled Castes, also contained a similar suggestion in identical wording.[12]

The Minorities Sub-Committee considered this clause of the Fundamental Rights Sub-Committee on April 17, 1947. Dr. Syama Prasad Mookherjee and P.R. Thakur wished to have a definiton of "untouchability" to make it clear that it did not cover non-Hindus. Khandekar pleaded that "private untouchability" should also be abolished.[13] In its meeting on April 18, 1947, the Minorities Sub-Committed approved this clause without any modification.[14]

The recommendations of the Fundamental Rights Sub-Committee together with the recommendations of the Minorities Sub-Committee on this clause were considered by the Advisory Committee on April 21, 1947. P.R. Thakur found this clause rather very vague. He felt that it could not possibly mean untouchability in any form. To a Hindu, a Mohammedan or a Christian was an untouchable and they would remain so till doomsday. He thought that what was meant was untouchability within the Hindu fold. Jagjivan Ram commented that in the ordinary sense of the term, untouchability was a practice which prevailed in the Hindu society; but he wanted it to be made clear about the aim of the Committee; whether it was to abolish untouchability among the Hindus, among the Christians, among the Muslims and among the Sikhs, whether the intention was to abolish *inter se* untouchability among the various communities or whether it was to abolish inter-communal untouchability. [15] It was generally agreed that the purpose of the clause was to abolish untouchability in all its forms—whether it was untouchability within a community or between various communities. K.M. Panikkar, elucidating the point, observed that there were some Christians who suffered from the same disabilities as the Hindu untouchables. That is to say, depressed classes who had been converted to Christianity in Travancore, Cochin and Malabar in the South, and that what was therefore really intended was the abolition of the various disabilities arising out of untouchability. He explained:

> If somebody says that he is not going to touch me, that is not a civil right which I can enforce in a court of law. There are certain complex of disabilities that arise from the practice of untouchability in India. Those disabilities are in the nature of civil obligations or civil disabilities and what we have attempted to provide for is that these disabilities that exist in regard to the individual, whether he be a Christian, Muslim or anybody else, if he suffers from these disabilities, they should be eradicated through the process of law.[16]

Regarding the object of the clause, Rajagopalachari felt that there was a very definite legal meaning to it, namely that the law will not hereafter recognize untouchability in any form as bringing into existence any right or disability.

He suggested a slight amendment of the clause making "the imposition of any disability of any kind of any such custom of "untouchability" as offence".[17] Redrafted in the light of the views expressed by Panikkar and Rajagopalachari, it appeared as clause 6 in the Interim Report of the Advisory Committee.

> "Untouchability" in any form is abolished and the imposition of any disability on that account shall be an offence.[18]

This report of the Advisory Committee was introduced in the Constituent Assembly on April 29, 1947, for consideration when Rohini Kumar Chaudhry brought an amendment for defining untouchability as follows:-

> 'Untouchability' means any act committed in exercise of discrimination on grounds of religion, caste or lawful vocation of life mentioned in clause4.

In support of his amendment Chaudhury said: "In the fundamental rights, it has been laid down that untouchability in any form should be an offence punishable by law. That being so it is necessary that the offence should be properly defined. As it stands, the word 'untouchability' is very vague. It should be defined in the manner in which I have put it, or in some other better form which may be decided upon by the House."

Lending support to Chaudhury's amendment Dr. S.C. Bannerjee observed: "The word `untouchability' actually requires clarification. We have been accustomed to this word for the last 25 years, still there is a lot of confusion as to what it connotes. Sometimes it means merely taking a glass of water and sometimes it has been used in the sense of admission of 'Harijans' into temples, sometimes it meant inter-caste dinner, sometimes inter-caste marriage. Mahatma Gandhi who is the main exponent of `untouchability', has used it in various ways and on different occasions with different meanings. So when we are going to use the word 'untouchability', we should be very clear in our mind as to what we really mean by it. What is the real implication of this word? I think we should make no distinction between untouchability and caste distinction, because as Mr. Thakur has said, untouchability is merely a symptom, the root cause is caste distinction and unless and until the root cause, that is caste distinction is removed, untouchability in some form or other is bound to exist and when we are going to have an independent India, we should expect everyone to be enjoying equal social conditions. It is incumbent on us that we should be very clear as to make it explicit that in the future independent India, there should be no distinction between man and man in the social field. In other words, caste distinction must be abolished. Of course there is difficulty as to whether we can make it justiciable or not. I have thought over it for a long time. I do really believe that in place of untouchability, some other word, such as, 'caste distinction' should be used or the word 'untouchability' should be clearly defined so as to leave no doubt in the mind of any one as to what we really mean by it."

K.M. Munshi opposed this amendment because "the definition is so worded that if it is accepted, it will make any discrimination even on the ground of place of birth or caste or even sex untouchability. Clause 4 does not deal with untouchability at all. It deals with discrimination regarding services and various other things. It may mean discrimination even between touchables and touchables, between people of one province and another. The word "untouchability' is mentioned in clause 6. The word untouchability' is put purposely within inverted commas in order to indicate that the Union legislature when it defines 'untouchability' will be able to deal with it in the sense in which it is normally understood. The present amendment will be extending the scope of the definition of untouchability."

In concurring with Chaudhury's amendment Dhirendra Nath Datta stated that "whether the definition suggested by Mr. Rohini Kumar Chaudhury is accepted or not, it is necessary that there should be some definition put in. Here it is said that 'untouchability' in any form is an offence. A magistrate or a judge dealing with offences shall have to look to the definition. One magistrate will consider a particular thing to be untouchability, while another magistrate may hold a different thing to be untouchability, with the result there will be no uniformity on the part of the magistracy in dealing with offences. It will be very difficult for the judge to decide cases. Moreover, untouchability means different things in different areas. In Bengal, untouchability means one thing, while in other provinces, it means an entirely different thing. So, unless a definition is put in, it would be impossible for the judiciary to deal with offences coming under untouchability. Whether you accept the amendment of Mr. Rohini Kumar Chaudhury or not, some definition must be there. This question may be left to the Drafting Committee to find out some suitable definition of the word `untouchability'. I strongly feel that unless there is a definition, it cannot be dealt with as an offence. We all feel that untouchability should be made an offence and it should be done away with. I also feel with my friend Mr. Thakur that the root cause of untouchability, namely, the caste system in Hindu society should be abolished altogether. Unless the caste system is abolished, untouchability will persist in some form or other. It has been said times without number by our leaders that unless Hindu society is drastically reformed by abolishing the caste system, it is bound to perish. Caste system should be abolished. So, if we are to deal with 'untouchability' as an offence, there should be some definition and I hope it would be left to the Drafting Committee to frame suitable definition so that it will be placed before the House for discussion. With these words I support the amendment."

When the President of the Constituent Assembly pointed out that the Union Legislature would under clause 24 define that word 'untouchability' so that the courts might prescribe proper punishment, Chaudhury withdrew his amendment.[19]

Later, when the Constituent Assembly took up clause 6 on abolition of untouchability, three amendments were moved by H.V. Kamath, S. Nagappa and P. Kunhiraman. Kamath proposed for insertion of the word "unapproachibility" after the word "Untouchability" and of the words "and every" after the word "any", 'because in some parts of India the practice of unapproachibility besides untouchability used to obtain some years ago in some places like Malabar specially'. Inclusion of the word "unapproachibility" would make the clause more comprehensive, he felt. Nagappa suggested substitution of the words, "imposition of any disability" by the words "observance of any disability", so that if the untouchability was observed by any person it must be an offence. Kunhiraman wanted to add the words "punishable by law" after the word "offence".

Sardar Vallabhbhai Patel, the mover of this clause, considered all these amendments to be unnecessary. Regarding Kamath's amendment he pointed out that if untouchability was provided for in the fundamental rights as an offence, all necessary adjustments would be made in the law that might be passed by the Legislature and it was neither right nor wise to provide for such necessary corollaries. Untouchability in any form was a legal phraseology, and no more addition was necessary. In regard to Nagappa's amendment he stated that one would be guilty if he observed a man imposing a disability on another. He did not think such extreme things should be provided for.

The removal of untouchability was the main idea, and if that was made illegal or an offence, it was quite enough. As regards Kunhiraman's amendment, Patel observed that offence was an offence; it was not necessary to provide that offence should be punishable by law.

In view of Patel's stand on these amendments, Kamath and Kunhiraman withdrew their amendments and Nagappa's amendment was negatived, and the clause, as suggested by the Advisory Committee, was adopted.[20]

In the Constitutional Adviser's Draft Constitution prepared in October, 1947, the amendment moved by Kunhiraman was in effect accepted and the words "which shall be punishable in accordance with law" were added after the word "offence".[21]

The Drafting Committee revised this clause on October 30,[22] on October 31[23] and again on November 1,[24] 1947 and finally settled it in the following form:

> Untouchability is abolished and its practice in any form is forbidden. The enforcement of any disability arising out of 'untouchability' shall be an offence which shall be punishable in accordance with law.

It appeared as Article 11 in the Draft Constitution published by the Drafting Committee on February 21,1948.[25]

When this Draft Constitution was circulated for eliciting comments, suggestions etc., R.R. Diwakar and S.V. Krishnamoorthy Rao suggested that after the word "untouchability" the words "i.e., the custom which taboos the touch of a person or his belongings because he is born in a particular caste or belongs to a particular religion" be inserted. To this suggestion, the Constitutional Adviser's comments were that this amendment sought to define "untouchability". It would be difficult to define "untouchability" precisely. Under Article 11 the practice of untouchability in any form is forbidden. The law which had to be enacted under Article 27 (under Article 35) for prescribing punishment for offences in respect of untouchability would define the various forms in which it was practised. It would therefore be better not to attempt to define the expression in the Constitution.

S. Nagappa suggested that in the first line of Article 11, for the word "untouchability" the words "untouchability as defined by the State" be substituted. The Constitutional Adviser observed that the law prescribing punishment for offences in respect of untouchability would define the various forms in which untouchability was practised. Hence, this amendment was not necessary.

Besides these amendments from members, several representations were also received in the office of the Constituent Assembly mainly containing the criticism that Article 11 as drafted was very wide in so far as it forbade the practice of untouchability in any form. The representations also pointed out that apart from "communal" untouchability, which was objectionable, there was another form of untouchability in religious matters, for example, on occasions like births, deaths, etc. Commenting on such representations, the Constitutional Adviser once again pointed out that Parliament would have to enact auxiliary legislation under Article 27 (Article 35) which would doubtless attempt a definition of "untouchability".[26]

When draft article 11 came up for consideration before the Constituent Assembly on November 29, 1948, Naziruddin Ahmed moved an amendment for substitution of draft Article 11 by the following:

> No one shall on account of his religion or caste be treated or regarded as an untouchable; and its observance in any form may be made punishable by law

because "the original article 11 is a little vague. The word untouchability has no legal meaning, although politically we are all well aware of it; but it may lead to a considerable amount of misunderstanding as in a legal expression. The word 'untouchable' can be applied to so many variety of things that we cannot leave it at that. It may be that a man suffering from an epidemic or contagious disease is an untouchable; then certain kinds of food are untouchable to Hindus and Muslims. According to certain ideas women of other families are untouchables. Then according to Pandit Thakurdas Bhargava, a wife below 15 would be untouchable to her loving husband on the ground that it would be 'marital misbehaviour'. I beg to submit, Sir, that the word 'untouchable' is rather loose. That is why I have attempted to give it a better shape; that no one on account of his religion or caste be regarded as untouchable. Untouchability on the ground of religion or caste is what is prohibited."

No other amendment was moved. During general discussion of this article V.I. Munishswamy Pillai, Dr. Monomohan Das, Santanu Kumar Das and Shrimati Dakshayani Velayudhan—all belonging to the Scheduled Castes—welcomed it as a historic measure intended to abolish the social inequality, the social stigma and the social disabilities in the society, which had long been a shame and disgrace to Indians. Though there was no dissenting voice, Prof. K.T. Shah pointed out that the lack of any definition of the term 'untouchability' would make it open for busybodies and lawyers to make capital out of a clause like this, contrary to the intention of the Drafting Committee. Ambedkar, the mover of this clause, however, did not reply to the debate or to Naziruddin Ahmed's amendment and the suggestion of Shah. The amendment was negatived and the Draft Article, as moved, was adopted by the Constituent Assembly amidst shouts of "Mahatma Gandhi ki Jai."[27]

At the time of revision this draft article was renumbered as Article 17.

The main argument against this article, as we have seen, was its vaguencss, specially because of non-definition of the term 'untouchability'. Untouchability, like God, was rather difficult to define though everybody could understand what it connoted and the framers, therefore, took cover under the protective umbrella of Article 35 (a)(ii). It may be noted that Article 35 empowers Parliament to make laws for prescribing punishment for the acts which are declared to be offences under Part III (Fundamental Rights) of the Constitution. In exercise of this power, Parliament has enacted in 1955 the Untouchability (Offenes) Act, 1955 which received the assent of the President on May 8, 1955, prescribing punishment for the practice of untouchability and for the enforcement of any disability arising therefrom and for matters connected therewith. In 1976 the title of the Act was changed to the 'Protection of Civil Rights Act', 1955. This Act also refrains from defining 'untouchability'.

Though the expression 'untouchability' has not been defined either in the Constitution or in the Protection of Civil Rights Act, it is generally used with reference to those persons who are born in those castes and communities that are classed as Harijans or outcastes. It refers to the social disabilities historically imposed on certain classes of people solely by reason of their birth in certain castes which preclude them from any kind of intercourse with people belonging to the so-called higher classes or castes. The expression may also be so interpreted to include persons who are made untouchable even though they might have been born in a higher caste. In Hindu Dharmashastras there was always a sharp distinction between 'Jathi Chandalas' (Born Untouchables) and 'Karma Chandalas' (those who became Chandalas on account of their own bad conduct). If a person born in a higher caste is effectively ex-communicated he becomes for all practical purposes an 'untouchable' and has no place in the society in which he is born in consequence of which all the other members of his caste exclude him from joining in any social or religious ceremony or usage. Article 17 prohibits this form of untouchability also.[28]

The 1955 Act declares certain acts as offences, when done on the ground of untouchability', and prescribes the punishments therefore, e.g.,

(a) refusing admission to any person to public institutions, such as hospital, dispensary, educational institution, hostel;

(b) preventing any person from worshipping or offering prayers in any place of public worship or bathing in or using the waters of any sacred tank, well, spring or watercourse;

(c) subjecting any person to any disability with regard to access to any shop, public restaurant, hotel or public entertainment or with regard to the use of any reservoir, tap or other source of water, road, cremation ground, public conveyance, dharmashala, sarai or musafirkhana or any other place where 'services are rendered to the public'.

The sweep of the Act has been enlarged in 1976, by including within the offence of practising untouchability, the following—

(i) insulting a member of a Scheduled Caste on the ground of untouchability;

(ii) preaching untouchability, directly or indirectly;

(iii) justifying untouchability on historical, philosophical or religious grounds or on the ground of any tradition of the caste system or on any other ground.

The penal sanction has been enhanced by providing that (a) in the case of subsequent convictions, the punishment may range from one to two years' imprisonment; (b) a person convicted of the offence of 'untouchability' shall be disqualified for election to the Union or a State legislature.

If a member of a Scheduled Caste is subjected to any such disability or discrimination, the Court shall presume, unless the contrary is proved, that such act was committed on the ground of 'untouchability'. In other words, in such cases, there will be a statutory presumption of an offence having been committed under this Act.

In India the untouchables, even before the commencement of the Constitution, has the right to vote, to acquire property etc., which shone by contrast to conditions prevailing in South Africa and the anti-Negro pockets of America. The Harijan untouchable problem of India was a social one. The Adidravidas, Harijans, Chandalas, whichever appellation is given to these untouchables, were considered for long as outside the four *varnas* and their social aloofness was enjoined in every village community due to various causes. The sin of such birth had no social redemption. So the Constitution-makers resolved to declare that 'untouchability' is abolished, i.e., in toto. Article 17 knocks the whole problem of untouchability at the very bottom and throws it out lock, stock and barrel. Article 17 does not stop with a mere declaration but announces that this forbidden 'untouchability' is not to be henceforth practised in any form. If it were so practised it shall be dealt with as an offence punishable in accordance with the law.

Article 17 fulfils at least in law the dream of Gandhiji who worked hard for the eradication of the social evil of untouchability. The Act of 1955, as amended in 1976, has given a realistic and effective shape to the prohibition of untouchability enshrined in the Constitution.

Notes and References

1. Rao, *op. cit.*, Vol. II, p. 74.
2. *Ibid.*, p. 82.
3. *Ibid.*, p. 86.
4. *Ibid.*, p. 91.
5. *Ibid.*, pp. 104-06.
6. *Ibid.*, p. 131.
7. *Ibid.*, p. 138.
8. *Ibid.*, p. 148.
9. *Ibid.*, p. 164.
10. *Ibid.*, p. 172.
11. *Ibid.*, p. 334.
12. *Ibid.*, pp. 325-26.
13. *Ibid.*, pp. 200-01.
14. *Ibid.*, p. 204.
15. *Ibid.*, p. 226.
16. *Ibid.*, pp. 226-27.
17. *Ibid.*, p. 227.
18. *Ibid.* p. 297.
19. *CAD*, Vol. III, dated 29-4-47, pp. 413-14.
20. *Ibid.*, pp. 434-35.
21. Rao, *op. cit.*, Vol. III, p. 8.
22. *Ibid.*, p. 377.
23. *Ibid.*, p. 378.
24. *Ibid.*, p. 379.
25. *Ibid.*, p. 522.
26. *Ibid.*, Vol. IV, pp. 32-33.
27. *CAD*, Vol. VII, dated 29-11-48, pp. 665-69.
28. *Hadibanow Behra v. Benamali Sahu*, *AIR* 1961 Ori 33.

7

Right to Freedom of Religion (Article 25(2) (b))

One of the disabilities that the Depressed Castes suffered was that they were denied access to Hindu temples. They were required to stop outside the temple proper in the compound and satisfy themselves that they had had a glimpse of the idol of God. The movement to abolish this disability gained momentum in the 30s. At a public meeting of the Hindus which was held in Bombay on September 25, 1932, following the signing of the Poona Pact on September 24, a resolution was adopted, which, interalia, called for early removal of all social disabilities imposed by custom on the so-called untouchable classes, including the bar in respect of admission to temples. This resolution was followed by a spurt in the activities on the part of caste Hindus to throw open temples to the untouchables. Satyagrahas were also offered at different places for admission of untouchables to temples. The Maharaja of Travancore issued a proclamation on November 12, 1936 opening the Travancore Temple to the untouchables. Temples entry was proclaimed in a few progressive princely states as well. In 1938, for the first time in British India, governments intervened to secure the opening of temples when Bombay and Madras passed temple entry acts. When Independence came in 1947, the exclusion of untouchables from Hindu temples was made a statutory offence throughout most of India. When the Constituent Assembly met for framing the future Constitution of India, it was quite natural that the question of conferring constitutional right on the untouchables for temple-entry should have been considered by it.

Strangely enough, only Munshi's Note and Draft Articles on Fundamental Rights submitted on March 17, 1947 conferred in sub-clause (7) of Article XII special rights on all Hindus without any distinction of caste or denomination of access to and worship in all public Hindu temples, choultries, dharmashalas, bathing ghats, and other places, without any discrimination against or imposing any disability on any person on the ground that he belonged to an impure or inferior caste or menial class.[1]

No other member, even Dr. Ambedkar, raised the issue of temple-entry by the untouchables in their Notes on Fundamental Rights.

The Fundamental Rights Sub-Committee decided on March 29, 1947 that sub-clause (7) of Article XII of Munshi's draft should be taken up with the clauses dealing with untouchability.[2] This sub-clause was, however, not considered by the Fundamental Rights Sub-Committee thereafter, and, therefore, no such provision figured in the Sub-Committee's report sent to the Advisory Committee on April 16, 1947.

At the time of examination of the Fundamental Rights Sub-Committee's report by the Minorities Sub-Committee on April 17-19, 1947, its members had before them a letter circulated by Munshi on April 16, 1947 in which he further elaborated the provisions mentioned by him earlier:

6. (a) Notwithstanding any custom or usage or prescription, all Hindus without any distinction of caste or denomination shall have the right of access to and worship in all public Hindu temples, choultries, dharmasalas, bathing ghats, and other religious places.

(b) Rules of personal purity and conduct prescribed

> for admission to and worship in these religious places shall in no way discriminate against or impose any disability on any person on the ground that he belongs to impure or inferior caste or menial class.[3]

The Minorities Sub-Committee, however, did not deliberate on this recommendation of Munshi, and, therefore, did not suggest anything on this matter in its report to the Advisory Committee sent on April 19, 1947.

The Advisory Committee, while deliberating on the recommendations of the Fundamental Rights Sub-Committee together with those of the Minorities Sub-Committee on April 21-22,1947, had no occasion to go in for insertion of a clause on the lines advocated by Munshi. It was however, agreed that Messrs Rajagopalachari and S.P. Mukherjee should submit a draft proviso to clause 13 permitting social legislation which might affect religious practice,[4] but the same was never submitted.

On May 1, 1947, when the Constituent Assembly was discussing clause 13 of the Advisory Committee's report regarding Rights relating to religion, Munshi moved an amendment for addition of the following words after the last Explanation:

> and for throwing open Hindu religious institutions of a public character to any class of section of Hindus.

Munshi stated that "after the Explanation above was drafted it was thought that the practice of religion referred to should not be of such a character as will interfere with the right of the Legislature to legislate on social questions. The question arose with regard to the throwing open of all temples to all classes of Hindus, whether it would be religious practice. In order to prevent any such construction of clause, it was decided that the throwing open of Hindu religious institutions shall not be held to contravene the practice of Hindu religion."

H.J. Khandekar observed that "in case Mr. Munshi's amendment to this clause is accepted, it may be necessary to have a definition for 'places of public worship'. Unless this is done it may be difficult for people to know which is a place of public worship. Even where admission to people of all classes is given, depressed classes are not allowed. Even when there is a written record that a certain temple is open to worship by depressed classes the pujaris obstruct and say that that temple is a private one and, therefore, not open to depressed classes. So, Sir, if there is definition of "places of public worship" there will be no difficulty. I suggest, therefore, that there should be a definition for "places of public worship"...I want a definition for "religious institutions of a public character".

There was no further discussion on this clause. Sardar Patel accepted Munshi's amendment and the amended Explanation 3 of clause 13 which read as follows was adopted:

> The freedom of religious practice guaranteed in this clause shall not debar the state from enacting laws for the purpose of social welfare and reform and for throwing open Hindu religious institutions of the public character to any class of section of Hindus.[5]

This provision was slightly changed by the Constitutional Adviser while incorporating it as clause 20 (2) in the Draft Constitution prepared by him, which was as follows :

> Nothing in this section shall preclude the State from making laws for social welfare and reform and for throwing open Hindu religious institutions of a public character to any class or section of Hindus.[6]

This sub-clause was revised by the Drafting Committee on November 1, 1947 in the following form :

(2) Nothing in this section shall preclude the State from making any law

* * * *

(b) for social welfare and reform or for throwing open Hindu religious institutions of a public character to any class or section of Hindus.[7]

This clause that finally emerged as Article 19 (2) (b) in the Draft Constitution prepared and circulated by the Drafting Committee on February 21, 1948, read as follows:

(2) Nothing in this article shall affect the operation of any existing law or preclude the State from making any law—

* * * *

(b) for social welfare and reform or for throwing open Hindu religious institutions of a public character to any class or section of Hindus.[8]

When this Draft Constitution was circulated for obtaining suggestion, comments etc., B. Pattabhi Sitaramayya suggested that in clause (2) (b) of article 19 for the words "any class or section" the words "all classes and sections" be substituted. Constitutional Adviser's note on this suggestion was that the expression "any class or section of Hindus" used in sub-clause (b) of clause (2) of article 19 would not prevent the making of any law for throwing open Hindu religious institutions of a public character to all classes and sections of Hindus. There was, however, no objection to that amendment: discrimination on the ground of caste etc., was already forbidden by Article 19.

Tajamul Husain suggested that the words "of Hindus" in sub-clause (b) of clause (2) of Article 19 be deleted. The Constitutional Adviser observed that this amendment would not prevent the making of any law throwing open Hindu religious institutions of public character to members of any other religious community, such as Muslims or Christians.

The Editor of the Indian Law Review and some other members of the Calcutta Bar suggested that in sub-clause (b) of clause (2) of Article 19, (a) the word "Hindus" should be omitted; and (b) for the words "of Hindus" the words "of persons professing that religion" be substituted. The Constitutional Adviser's observance on this suggestion was that clause (2) of Article 19 was based on the decision of the

Advisory Committee on Fundamental Rights as adopted by the Constituent Assembly.

The Drafting Committee decided in October, 1948 that for the word "preclude" in clause (2) of article 19 the word "prevent" be substituted.[9]

Article 19 was considered by the Constituent Assembly on December 3 and 6, 1948. Ambedkar moved an amendment for substitution of the word "preclude" by the word "prevent" in clause (2) for the purpose of keeping symmetry in the language that had been used in other articles.[10]

Two more amendments relating to sub-clause (b) of clause (2) were moved—one by Prof. K.T. Shah and another by Shrimati G. Durgabai, Shah's amendment was for addition of the words "Jain, Buddhist, or Christians" after the words "or throwing open Hindu". The amended clause would have read—"for social welfare and reform or for throwing open Hindu, Jain, Buddhist, or Christian religious institutions of a public character to any class or section of Hindus". Shah observed that "I do not see why this right or obligation should be restricted only to Hindu Religious institutions to be thrown open to public. I think the intention of this clause would be served if it is more generalised, and made accessible or made applicable to all the leading religions of this country, whose religious institutions are more or less cognate, and who therefore may not see any violation of their religious freedom, or their religious exclusiveness, by having this clause about throwing open their places of worship to the public. I think, Sir, that the freedom of religion being guaranteed by this Constitution, and promised as one of the Fundamental Rights, the possibility of all religious institutions being accessible and open for all communities is a very healthy sign, and would promote harmony and brotherhood amongst the peoples following various forms of beliefs in this country, and therefore I think, Sir, that this amendment at any rate should find acceptance from those who have sponsored this clause.[11]

Shrimati Durgabai moved an amendment for substitution of the words "any class or section" by the words "all classes and sections" because "the clause as it stands is restricted in its scope, and the object of my amendment is to secure the benefit in a wider way and to make it applicable to all classes and sections. Though we are not able to make a sweeping reform or a more comprehensive reform in this direction, I feel that no distinction of any kind should be made btween one class of Hindus and another. Now, with regard to the Hindu religious institutions of a public character, we are all aware that there are various classes of these institutions, such as temples, religious maths, and educational institutions or Pathasalas conducted by these institutions, or attached to these institutions. So far as temples are concerned, I am sure that all of us are aware that almost all of the provinces, including some States, have already passed law throwing open temples to all classes or sections of Hindus. But I am equally sure that some distinction does still exist in regard to the other forms of religious institutions, such as Pathsalas, educational institutions and others managed or conducted by these religious institutions. As I have already explained, my object is to enlarge the scope of this clause, and to include within it all classes and sections of Hindus. If my amendment is accepted, then that object will be fulfilled. As I have already explained, there should not be any distinction between one class and another class of Hindus."[12]

During general discussion of this clause Munshi said that he entirely agreed with Prof. Shah that the word "Hindu" used in this section should be widely defined. As a matter of fact, the Hindu Bill which was before the House then in its legislative capacity had defined 'Hindu' so as to include the various sub-sections, but it would be "more appropriate to have this definition in the interpretation clause than in this."[13]

None else discussed these amendments or spoke on this sub-clause. Ambedkar accepted the amendment moved by Shrimati Durgabai and these two amendments, that is those moved by Ambedkar and Shrimati Durgabai, were adopted.[14]

Subsequently, at the time of revision in November, 1949, the Drafting Committee renumbered this article as Article 25 and effected two changes—some consequential drafting changes in Sub-clause (b) of Clause (2) and added a new Explanation—Explanation II—to honour the commitment made by Munshi to give a broad-based definition of 'Hindu'.

The modified sub-clause and the new Explanation figured in the revised Constitution as follows:

> (2) Nothing in this article shall affect the operation of any existing law or prevent the State from making any law—
>
> * * * *
>
> (b) *providing* for social welfare and reform or *the* throwing open of Hindu religious institutions of a public character to all classses and sections of Hindus.
>
> * * * *
>
> Explanation II: In sub-clause (b) of clause (2), the reference to Hindus shall be construed as including a reference to persons professing the Sikh, Jaina or Buddhist religion, and the reference to Hindu religious institutions shall be construed accordingly.[15]

The words in italics in sub-clause (b) and the entire Explanation II were new additions. These additions and alterations did not attract any further discussion in the Constituent Assembly.

Various social reform movements in the pre-partition days worked for obliteration of all distinctions between man and man solely on the basis of caste and called for removal of all social disabilities hindering the progress of the untouchables. The Indian National Congress, the All-India Hindu Mahasabha and other organizations were committed to remove all obstacles which stood in the way of integration of the so-called untouchables with the Hindu mainbody. Efforts to remove untouchability and help its victims proliferated in the wake of the Poona Pact of 1932. As a result, even before the Constitution came into force, attempts were made by different State legislatures, from time to time, to remove the social disabilities attached with the caste like admission into Hindu temples, which was a very emotive issue in the twenties and the thirties, and to bring equality before law irrespective of race, caste and creed. Mention may be made of the following:

The Travancore-Cochin Removal of Social Disabilities Act, 1925.

The Hyderabad Harijan (Removal of Social Disabilities) Regulation, 1938F.

The Madras Removal of Civil Disabilities Act, 1938.

The Mysore Removal of Civil Disabilities Act, 1943.

The Orissa Removal of Civil Disabilities Act, 1946.

The Bombay Harijan Removal of Social Disabilities Act, 1946.

The Central Provinces and Berar Scheduled Castes (Removal of Civil Disabilities) Act, 1947.

The Central Provinces and Berar Temple Entry Authorisation Act, 1947.

The United Provinces Removal of Social Disabilities Act, 1947.

The East Punjab (Removal of Religious and Social Disability) Act, 1948.

The West Bengal Hindu Social Disabilities Removal Act, 1948.

The Saurastra Harijan (Removal of Social Disabilities) Ordinance of 1948.

The Mysore Temple Entry Authorisation Act, 1948.

The Bihar Harijan (Removal of Civil Disabilities) Act, 1949.

The Madhya Bharat Harijan Ayogta Nivaran Vidhan of 1949.

The Coorg Scheduled Castes Removal of Civil and Social Disabilities) Act, 1949.

The Coorg Temple Entry Authorisation Act, 1949.

The Travancore-Cochin Temple Entry (Removal of Disabilites) Act, 1949.

Sub-clause (b) of Clause (2) of Article 25 gives a constitutional guarantee that all laws enacted before the commencement of the Constitution (a) for social welfare and reform or (b) for throwing open of Hindu religious institutions of a public character to all classes and sections of Hindus would not be invalidated. This sub-clause also entitles the States to legislate on matters of (a) social welfare and reform or (b) for throwing of Hindu religious institutions of a public character to all classes and sections of Hindus. For the purpose of this sub-clause only, Hindus would mean Sikhs, Jains and Buddhists as well. Thus, if religious beliefs and practices conflict with matters of social reform or welfare on which the State wants to legislate such religious beliefs and practices will have to yield to the higher requirements of social welfare and reform.[16] Such legislation however cannot affect the fundamentals of any religion.

'Social reform' connotes the concept of eradication of practices or dogmas which stand in the path of the country's onward progress as a whole *but do not form the essence of religion.* Thus, the State may prahibit bigamy amongst the Hindus because the need of having a natural son by marrying a second wife on the failure of the first wife to get a son was not of the essence of Hindu religious belief, as the purpose might be served by taking an adopted son. Prohibition of deleterious practices such as the "Suttee" or the system of "Devadasi" is also justified by the present clause.[17]

It has, however, been held by a majority of the Supreme Court that the banning of excommunication which is made solely on *religious* grounds cannot be considered to promote welfare and social reform because it is a right belonging to a religious denomination under Article 26(b); but it may be so where the law bars excommunication on non-religious grounds, e.g., for the breach of some obnoxious social rule or practice, or as a punishment for the crime punishable under the law of the land.[18] In short, the expression 'social welfare and reform' does not enable the Legislature to 'reform' a religion out of existence or identity. It does not extend to the basic and essential practice of religion, which is guaranteed by Article 25 (1) itself.[19]

The Supreme Court has laid down that legislation throwing open the religious institutions of the Hindus must not be very wide in its application. The right conferred by this clause is not of an absolute character. It is a right of every member of the Hindu public to enter into a public temple for worship. It does not, however, mean that such temple must be kept open *at all hours* or that any member of the Hindu public must be allowed to perform *those services* which are open only to those specially initiated, according to the ceremonial law governing the temple.[20] It stated; "It is a traditional custom universally observed not to allow access to any outsider (i.e., a person not connected with the spiritual functions) to particularly sacred parts of a temple, as for example, the place where deity is located. There are also fixed hours of worship and rest for the idol when no disturbance by any member of the public is allowed."[21] Moreover, Article 25(2) (b) is to be construed harmoniously along with the right guaranteed by Article 26(b), without rendering the latter nugatory.[21]

Explanation II expands the connotation of the word "Hindu" to include Sikhs, Jains or Buddhists, for the purposes of Article 25(2) (b) and consequently, their religious institutions of a public character should be thrown open to all sections of the Hindu instead of being confined to members of their own sects or denominations.

This sub-clause has put all classes and sections of Hindus on an equal footing so far as right to admission into a temple is concerned. The object appears to be to remove all traces of discrimination and inequality among the various sections of the Hindu social fabric. The Article confines its sphere only to public institutions, which are declared to be so either by grant or user, It would not affect private endowments or institutions of the Hindus, Jains, Sikhs and Buddhists.

Notes and References

1. Rao, *op. cit.*, Vol. II, p. 79.
2. *Ibid.*, p. 130.
3. *Ibid.*, p. 202.
4. *Ibid.*, p. 290.
5. *CAD*, Vol. III, dated 1-5-47, pp. 485-86.
6. Rao, *op. cit.*, Vol. III, p. 10.
7. *Ibid.*, p. 332.
8. *Ibid.*, p. 524.
9. *Ibid.*, Vol. IV, pp. 41-42.
10. *CAD*, Vol. VII, dated 6-12-48, p. 826.
11. *Ibid.*, p. 828.
12. *Ibid.*, pp. 828-29.
13. *Ibid.*, p. 837.
14. *Ibid.*, pp. 838-39.
15. Rao, *op. cit.*, Vol. IV, p. 758.
16. *State v. Narsu Appa*, 55, Bom. L.R. 729.
17. Basu, D.D., *Shorter Constitution of India*, Tenth Edition, Prentice Hall of India, New Delhi, 1988. p 202.
18. *Saifuddin v. State of Bombay*, A. 1962 S.C. 853.
19. *Ibid.*
20. *Venkataramana v. State of Mysore*, (1958) S.C.R. 895: A 1958 S.C. 255: *Yajanpurushadji v. Madras*. A. 1966 S.C. 1119.
21. *Commr., H.R.E. v. Lakshmindra*, 1954, S.C.A. 415.

8

Prohibition of Traffic in Human Beings and Forced Labour (Article 23)

It is now known that there was no class of agricultural labour as such in the rural areas in pre-British India. The policy of the British Government on land tenure created a new class of landlords and drove millions into the ranks of tenants and agricultural labourers. The decay of cottage and rural industries also swelled the ranks of agricultural labourers. Agricultural labour consisted of communities belonging to the backward classes, and a good percentage of Scheduled Castes and Scheduled Tribes were among them. They formed the most vulnerable sections of the population and their conditions of living were far from satisfactory. They were steeped in debt and were reduced to the rank of bonded labour.

Before the Indian Penal Code was enacted in 1860, slavery was dealt with by the Indian Slavery Act, 1843. Nevertheless, the bonded labour system prevailed. Rural indebtedness is one of the main causes for its continuation. The system has existed in almost all parts of the countryside where feudals and rich cultivators exploited the landless poor. Under this system of forced labour, a debtor either by an agreement, written or oral, or under a customary or social practice was bonded either free of charge or for a very nominal charge to render service by himself or through one of the members of his family to his creditors for any economic consideration till the repayment of the principal or the interest thereon.

This being the condition of a sizeable section of the population, the framers, quite naturally, were concerned with protecting them from the exploitation of their oppressors. They had before them the thirteenth Amendment of the American Constitution which lays dow: "Neither slavery nor involuntary servitude except as punishment for crimes whereof the party shall have been duly convicted, shall exist in the United States, or any place subject to their jurisdiction."

The right against exploitation was mentioned in the drafts prepared by B.R. Ambedkar, K.M. Munshi and K.T. Shah. While clause 9 of Article II, Section I of Ambedkar's draft provided that 'subjecting a person to forced labour or to involuntary servitude shall be an offence',[1] Clause 3 of Article VII of Munshi's draft contained more elaborate provisions for the abolition of 'every form of slavery or traffic in human beings or compulsory labour other than public service equally incumbent upon all or as part of the punishment pronounced by a court of law' and for 'punishment by the law of the Union if such form of traffic or labour is enforced'.[2] Clauses 39 and 40 of Shah's draft had laid down that

> Slavery of any kind is forbidden. No rights which would amount to property of any kind in human beings, or enslavement of one individual by another, or by groups or corporations, shall be recognised. All human beings in the Union of India are and shall be free and equal before the law.
>
> All labourers attached to land and working thereon in any degree of servile condition shall be deemed to be free workers, remunerated for their toil by wages at prescribed or agreed rates. All forced labour or begar of any kind is fobidden.[3]

Clauses 25 and 26 of the said draft recognized the right of the Central and State Governments to conscript by law all the man-power of the country for the purpose of national defence of the country, social service or for meeting a sudden emergency or natural calamitv or for maintaining peace and tranquility.[4]

When the subject was first considered in the Fundamental Rights Sub-Committee on March 27, 1947, it was agreed that a clause in the following form should be included :

> Every form of slavery or traffic in human beings is abolished and contravention of this prohibition shall be an offence.

It was also agreed that *begar* (a form of forced labour) should be prohibited. As regards other forms of forced labour the sub-committee decided by a majority vote that provision should be included prohibiting such labour, but subject to certain exceptions. It was decided by 5 votes to 4 that they should cover specified forms of public service other than service in the armed forces. Masani, Rajkumari Amrit Kaur, Jairamdas Daulatram and Shrimati Hansa Mehta stated that they would submit a minute of dissent. A separate vote was taken on the proposal whether military service should also be excepted. The proposal was lost by 5 to 4. The dissenting members said that they would submit a minute of dissent.[5]

On a suggestion of Munshi, the decision of the Subcommittee regarding compulsory military service was considered afresh on March 28,1947. The proposal to insert a prohibition of compulsory military service was put to vote and carried by 5 against 3. At the instance of Dr. Ambedkar a separate vote was taken on the question whether compulsory military training as distinguished from military service should be exempted. This was lost by 5 against 4. It was decided to insert a provision on the lines of the American clause against "slavery and involuntary servitude" and also a specific provision prohibiting conscription for military service. With regard to this latter provision, Munshi wanted to insert a clause on the following lines: "No person who has any conscientious objection should be compelled to join the armed forces or to undergo military training." This amendment was not agreed to. But the sub-committee agreed by majority to add a clause exempting compulsory service under any general scheme of education.[6]

Provisions against exploitation, as finally drafted by the sub-committee, were reproduced as clause 15 in the draft report of the sub-committee prepared on April 3, 1947 as follows:

1 (a) Slavery,

(b) traffic in human beings.

(c) the form of forced labour known as *begar*,

(d) any form of involuntary servitude except as a punishment for crime whereof the party shall have been duly convicted.

are hereby prohibited and any contravention of this prohibition shall be an offence.

Explanation.—Compulsory service under any general scheme of education does not fall within the mischief of this clause.

(2) Conscription for military service or training, or for any work in aid of military operation is hereby prohibited.[7]

Commenting on this draft report, Rajkumari Amrit Kaur pointed out that she and Shrimati Hansa Mehta had recorded their vote against compulsory service in any form during the discussions and they still adhered to that position. They were, therefore, not in favour of the "explanation" as given under clause 15.[8] B.N. Rau, the Constitutional Adviser, observed that the provision relating to slavery and involuntary servitude in sub-clause (1) were based on the Thirteenth Amendment of the U.S. Constitution. The prohibition of begar was added to them and any contravention of the general prohibition contained in the clause made an offence. For the prohibition of conscription for military service or training contained in sub-clause (2) there was no precedent available. On the other hand, some of the constitutions e.g., the Swiss (Article 18, para 1), the Czechoslovakian (Article

127, para, para 1) and the Chinese (Article 20) Constitutions contained provisions imposing compulsory military service on their citizens.[9] K.T. Shah suggested the substitution of "national or social services' in place of "education" in the Explanation. If conscription was justified and permitted for education, there was no reason why it should not be permitted for matters relating to public health or in times of civil calamities. Making a strong plea for social and economic planning on a national scale and for so developing all available resources as to provide work for every able and qualified citizen, Shah emphasized that it would not be possible for an independent sovereign India to make up the leeway in the social and economic field from which she suffered unless the Constitution allowed power to the State to conscript all available man and woman power in the country.[10]

The sub-committee, meeting on April 14-15, 1947, adopted clause 15 without any change except for a verbal modification replacing the word "mischief" by the word "purview" in the Explanation to subclause (1), though Sardar Panikkar thought that sub-clause (c) was open to the objection that it did not take into account different types of begar.[11]

In their minutes of dissent, appended to the final report of the sub-committee, Rajkumari Amrit Kaur and Shrimati Hansa Mehta reiterated their opposition to compulsory service in any form: giving to the State powers of compulsion in any sphere of life was against all tenets of democracy. They suggested the creation of a paid social service for the spread of education and other nation-building activities. In a country where there was no lack of man-power, they felt, compulsion was particularly out of place.[12] Alladi Krishnaswami Ayyar and Ambedkar, taking the contrary view, suggested the deletion of clause 15(2) prohibiting for military service. It was one thing not to have recourse to conscription as a matter of policy but quite another for a nation or a State to deny to herself the power to conscript if and when occasion arose. No country, however peaceful and non-violent in its intention or philosophy, could escape the necessity of compulsory military service for defending itself and its liberty when attacked by another nation. A ban on compulsory military service would be nothing but wilful self-immolation.[13] Alladi Krishnaswami Ayyar said that war might be forced on India much against her will and, in sheer self-defence. she might have to raise an army appropriate to the occasion.[14] Shah said that while education certainly was amongst the foremost of the needs of nation-building for which conscription would be fully justified, that should not make the claims of other items in nation-building or social service like health any the less urgent.[15]

The recommendations of the Fundamental Rights Sub-Committee, sent to the Minorities Sub-Committee for amplifications, alterations, modifications, etc., were considered by the Minorities Sub-Committee on April 17-19, 1947. By this time it had received the notes, memoranda, etc., submitted by its members on minority rights, safeguards, etc. Only two members—H.J. Khandekar and Jagjivan Ram, both belonging to the Scheduled Castes—had asked for declaring forced labour as a cognizable offence. Khandekar suggested that "forced labour should be regarded as a cognizable offence"[16] Jagjivan Ram also suggested that "all *begar* and compulsory forced labour in whichever form existing anywhere shall cease and shall be dealt with as a cognizable offence."[17] All-India Adi-Hindu Depressed Classes Association demanded that "no form of forced labour shall be permitted".[18]

In view of general acceptability of the provision recommended by the Fundamental Rights Sub-Committee, the Minorities Sub-Committee in its meeting on April 17, 1947, agreed not to offer any comment on this provision.[19] The Interim Report sent by the Minorities Sub-Committee to the Advisory Committee on April 19, 1947, therefore did not contain any recommendation on this clause.[20]

Clause 15 of the Fundamental Rights Sub-Committee's report was taken up for consideration by the Advisory Committee on April 21 and 22, 1947. Sub-clause (1) was adopted without any midification except for the omission of the word 'slavery'. This omission was made at the suggestion of Rajagopalachari who considered it improper to adopt the laws of America enacted at the time when slavery was prevalent. Since there was difference of opinion over the provisions as contained in the Explanation to sub-clause(1) and in sub-clause (2), a small committee consisting of Shrimati Hansa Mehta, Rajagopalachari and G.B. Pant was constituted by the Chairman of the Advisory Committee to consider the matter and prepare a suitable draft.[21] This special sub-committee redrafted the Explanation to sub-clause (1) and omitted sub-clause (2). The recommendations of the special sub-committee were accepted.[22]

The redrafted provisions, as adopted by the Advisory Committee and reproduced as clause 11 in its interim report submitted to the President of the Constituent Assembly on April 23, 1947, were as follows :

11. (a) Traffic in human beings and

(b) forced labour in any form including *begar*, and involuntary servitude except as a punishment for crime whereof the party shall have been duly convicted,

are hereby prohibited and any contravention of this prohibition shall be an offence.

Explanation: Nothing in this sub-clause shall prevent the State from imposing compulsory service for public purposes without any discrimination on the ground of race, religion, caste or class.[23]

When this clause came up for discussion in the Constituent Assembly on May 1, 1947, Munshi moved an amendment. He suggested substitution of clause 11 by the following:

> Traffic in human beings, and begar and other forms of forced labour are prohibited, and any contravention of this provision shall be an offence.

He suggested that the Explanation be dropped as it became unnecessary in view of the shortening of the whole sentence. The object was to deal in one sentence with both subjects. Briefly explaining its scope, Munshi said that if there was any short of forced labour like begar, it would be prohibited. Traffic in human being would be prohibited. But the other forms of labour e.g., labour for educational purposes or for any other purpose of public service would be regulated by legislation.[24]

While members like Shrimati Dakshayani Velayudan and B. Das expressed happiness for giving relief to the underdogs who were subjected to economic exploitation, members like Ambedkar, P.K. Sen, M. Ananthsayanam Ayyangar, held the view that the omission of the Explanation would not be wise. On the other hand, Alladi Krishnaswamy Ayyar held the view that there was no need for retaining the Explanation, since the clause as redrafted would not preclude military conscription. On a suggestion of Ambedkar, the clause was referred to the ad hoc committee appointed by the President of the Assembly earlier for considering the citizenship clause.[25] This committee reported the next day: in its view the Explanation was necessary in order that the wording "forced labour" might not have a controversial interpretation. On a suggestion from Munshi, the President decided to hold over further consideration of the clause.[26] The Constituent Assembly, however, did not get any chance to consider this clause until the Draft Constitution came up for consideration.

Clause 11 figured as Clause 18 in the Constitutional Adviser's Draft Constitution as follows:

> Traffic in human beings and begar and other similar forms of forced labour are prohibited and any contravention of this provision shall be an offence punishable in accordance with law:
>
> Provided that nothing in this section shall prevent the state from imposing compulsory service for public purposes without any discrimination on the ground of race, religion, caste, or class.[27]

The Drafting Committee meeting on November 1,

1947, made some minor drafting changes to this Clause which appeared as Article 17 in the Draft Constitution prepared by the Drafting Committee:

> 17. (1) Traffic in human beings and *begar* and other forms of forced labour are prohibited and any contravention of this provision shall be an offence punishable in accordance with law.
>
> (2) Nothing in this article shall prevent the State from imposing compulsory service for public purposes. In imposing such service the State shall not make any discrimination on the ground of race, religion, caste or class.[28]

None offered any comments, suggestions, etc., when the Draft Constitution was circulated for eliciting opinion.

Draft Article 17 came up for consideration in the Constituent Assembly on December 3, 1948. As many as seven amendments were moved—two by Prof. K.T. Shah, and one each by Damodar Swarup Seth, Giani Gurmukh Singh Musafir, Sardar Bhopindar Singh Man, H.V. Kamath and Kazi Syed Karimuddin. Karimuddin sought to substitute Article 17 by the following so as to enable jail authorities to extract work from prisoners:

> Neither slavery nor involuntary servitude such as *begar* except as a punishment for crime shall exist within the Union State.[29]

K.T. Shah wanted to extend the scope of this article by the substitution of the words "Traffic in human beings or their dedication in the name of religion to be Devadasis or be subject to other forms of enslavement and degradation and *begar*" in place of "Traffic in human beings and *begar*". In commending the motion Shah pointed out that although, as commonly understood, 'traffic in human beings' meant only slavery as it was practised in olden countries and until recently even in the so-called civilized countries of Europe and America, it also covered what was known as white slave traffic, namely, the buying and selling of young women for export or import from one set of countries to another; and their permanent enslavement or servitude to an owner or proprietor of an establishment of commercialized vice probably for life. He mentioned the devadasi system, i.e., dedication, in the name of religion, of young women to be devadasis, and as such devoted to immoral traffic almost from an immature age.[30] In another amendment shah proposed, what he called a very small but important amendment, seeking to add the word "only" after the words "discrimination on the ground" in clause(2).[31]

Gurumukh Singh Musafir wanted the addition of the words "including prostitution" after the words "human beings" in clause (1)[32] while Damodar Swarup Seth suggested the addition of the words "Servitude and serfdom in all forms as well as" at the beginning of clause (1).[33]

Bhopindar Singh Man's amendment was for payment of adequate compensation for any compulsory service imposed by the State,[34] while Kamath sought to substitute the words "social or national" in place of the word "public", because he felt national service and social service had a wider and a higher and a more comprehensive connotation than `public service.[35]

During the debate on the Draft Article, several members welcomed it as a charter of liberty for the downtrodden people who had so far suffered from the imposition of forced labour in one form or other at the hands of Princes and zamindars. Gurumukh Singh Musafir referred to two points: (1) that the curse of prostitution should be specially abolished, and (2) that provision must be made for compensation being paid for compulsory service.[36] Shrimati G. Durgabai referred to the system of devadasis and said that the worst form of this custom had existed in Madras for a long time but that it had already been prohibited there under a law and whatever relics of the system still remained were bound to disappear in course of time; and no specific provision in this regard was necessary in the Constitution.[37] B.Das suggested that particular attention be paid to the prohibition of traffic in women.[38]

Raj Bahadur, while welcoming the article, said:

> As a man coming from an Indian state, I know what this *begar*, this extortion of forced labour, has meant to the down-trodden and dumb people of the Indian States. If the whole story of this begar is written, it will be replete, with human misery, human suffering, blood and tears. I know how some of the Princes have indulged in their pomp and luxury, in their reckless life; at the expense of the ordinary man, how they have used the down-trodden labourers and dumb ignorant people for the sake of their pleasure. I know for instance how for duck shooting a very large number of pople are roped in forcibly to stand all day long in mud and slush during cold chilly wintry days. I know how for the sake of their game and hunting people have been roped in large numbers for beating the lion so that the Princes may shoot it. I have also seen how poor people are employed for domestic and other kinds of labour, no matter whether they are ailing or some members of their family are ill. These people are paid nothing or paid very little for the labour extorted from them. This is not the whole story. As I said in the beginning, it would make really a terrible reading if the whole story is told. I know that very often these tyrannies are perpetrated upon poor people by the petty officials. Not only do these petty officials perpetrate such tyrannies but they also extort bribes from the labourers who want to escape the curse of this *begar*... This article frees the poor, down-trodden and dumb people of the Indian States from this curse of *begar*. This *begar* has been a blot on humanity and has been a denial of all that has been good and noble in human civilization. Through the centuries this curse has remained as a dead weight on the shoulders of the common man like the practice of slavery.[39]

Renuka Ray wanted early abolition of all forms of traffic in women including the devadasi system either by legislation or by consitutional provision.[40]

S. Nagappa pointed out that

> This practice of *begar* is prevalent in my own part of the country, especially among the Harijans. I am glad that the Drafting Committee has inserted this clause to abolish begar. Whenever cattle die; the owner of the cattle wants these poor Harijans to come and remove the dead cattle, remove the skins, tan them and make chappals and supply them free of cost. For this, what do they get? Some food during festival days. Often this forced labour is practised even by the government. For instance, if there is any murder, after the postmortem, the police force these people to remove the dead body and look to the other funeral processes. I am glad that hereafter this sort of forced labour will have no place. Then this is practised in zamindaries also. For instance, if there is a marriage in the zamindar's family, he will ask these poor people, especially the Harijans, to come and white wash his whole house, for which they will be given nothing except food for the day. This sort of forced labour is still prevalent in most parts of the Presidency. Another thing that I want to bring to the notice of the House is that whenever that big zamindar's lands are to be ploughed, immediately he will send word for these poor people, the Harijans, the previous day, and say; "All your services are confiscated for the whole of tomorrow, you will have to work throughout the day and night. No one should go to any other work." In return, the zamindar will give one morsel of food to these poor fellows. This sort of forced labour is in practice in the 20th century in our so-called civilised country.[41]

Dealing with the various amendments, T.T. Krishnamachari said that the basic principle sought to be enshrined in the draft article was that of ensuring certain rights to the individual so that he would be ennobled; not to import into the article reform of all the abuses which society had inherited from the past. The Constitution had necessarily to provide for matters where vested interests were likely to seek the perpetuation of anti-social customs for purposes of economic gain. Referring particularly to *begar* he said that some form of forced labour existed in practically all parts of the country, whether it was called *begar* or by any other name. They were trying to root out this evil and by putting it among the fundamental rights it would hasten legislation to wipe out evils of this kind as this would become an obligation on the State. But there was no point in trying to include the reform of all abuses which society was heir to, and it would be a blot on the fair name of India to enact in the Constitution a ban on social abuses against which public opinion was already sufficiently well mobilized, and which could be wiped out by ordinary legislation and therefore were bound to disappear in course of time.[42]

Concluding the debate, Ambedkar rejected all the amendments except the one moved by K.T. Shah for the inclusion of the word "only" after the words "discrimination on the ground "in clause (2) of the article. Replying to Kamath, he said that the words "social and national" were not necessary since the word "public" was wide enough to cover both. With regard to the suggestion regarding compensation for compulsory service, he felt it was not desirable to put such a fetter on the authority of the State. Compulsory service demanded by the State would be restricted to hours of leisure and, in any case, was to be demanded from all without any discrimination.[43] All the amendments, except the one accepted by Ambedkar, were rejected by the Assembly and Draft Article 17, as amended, was adopted.[44]

At the revision stage Draft Article 17 was renumbered as Article 23 of the Constitution.

Constitutions of countries like Burma, Japan and the Federal Republic of Germany have provisions prohibiting 'forced labour' or 'involuntary servitude'. Article 19 of the 1948 Constitution of Burma states:

> (1) Traffic in human beings and (2) forced labour in any form and involuntary servitude except as a punishment for crime whereof the party shall have been duly convicted, shall be prohibited.
>
> Explanation—Nothing in this section shall prevent the State from imposing compulsory service for

> public purposes without any discrimination on grounds of birth, race, religion or class,

Article XVIII of the Japanese Constitution of 1946 states:

> No person shall be held in bondage of any kind. Involuntary servitude, except as punishment for crime is prohibited.

Article 12 of the Constitution of the Federal Republic of Germany enunciates:

> (1) All Germans have the right of tree choice of occupation, place and employment and place of training. The pursuit of occupation may be regulated by legislation.
>
> (2) No one shall be forced to do a particular job except in virtue of an established general obligation to perform a public service lying equally upon all.
>
> (3) Forced labour is only permissible where a sentence of imprisonment is ordered by a court.

Article 4 of the United Nations Declaration of Human Rights states;

> No one shall be held in slavery or servitude; slavery and the slave trade shall be prohibited in all their forms.[45]

Article 23 of the Indian Constitution is very much on the same lines as Article 19 of the Burmese Constitution. The Burmese Article, however, goes further and clearly states that forced labour and involuntary servitude may be imposed as punishment for a criminal offence.

The scope of Clause (1) in Article 23 extends not only to the prohibition of forced labour and *begar* but also to the wider category 'traffic in human beings'. This term connotes not only "slavery" but also traffic in women for immoral or other purposes. This clause is applicable to citizens as well as aliens.

Under Article 23 Clause (1) the categories of traffic in human beings, begar and other forms of forced labour, if contravened, shall be an "offence punishable in accordance with law". Such laws are invited to be made by the

Constitution. By Article 35 Clause (2) Parliament alone, and not the Legislature of a State, shall have the power for prescribing punishment for acts declared to be offences under Part III of the Constitution. There is a further mandatory duty on Parliament to make laws as soon as may be after the commencement of the Constitution, prescribing punishment for the acts referred to in the sub-clause.

Article 23 prohibits traffic in human beings, begar and other forms of forced labour but authorises the State to impose compulsory service for public purposes. The Constitution does not use the word 'slavery', which in its ancient form may not so much be a problem in every state today. Instead it uses the more comprehensive expression 'traffic in human beings' which includes a prohibition not only of slavery but also of traffic in women or children or the crippled, for immoral or other purposes.[46] Parliament has passed the Suppression of Immoral Traffic in Women and Girls Act in the year 1956. The Allahabad High Court laid down that such a law will be valid and would not be inconsistent with the provisions of fundamental rights to carry on any trade, etc.[47]

This Article also prohibits forced labour in any form which is similar to 'begar', i.e. an act of compelling a person to render gratuitous service where he was lawfully entitled either not to work or to receive remuneration for it. 'Forced labour' is a wide expression, which would be attracted whenever a person is *compelled* to give his labour or service, even though remuneration be paid for it. The same would be the result where the labourer is obliged to work at wages less than the minimum wages.[48] This Article is enforceable not only against the State but also against private persons indulging in such practice.[49] It has been held that withholding of pay of a government employee as a punishment is not valid in view of Article 23 which prohibits begar.[50] A civil servant must be paid his salary so long as he continues to be in service.

The guarantee in Article 23 is so fundamental that even the custom whereby each house-holder of a village offers a day's free labour to the headman or khullakpa of the village for his being headman and for his settlement in the village was struck down as offending Article 23(1).[51] The element of compulsion lurks in such a custom. The khullakpa renders public service as the village officer and must hence be treated as a public servant. The free service to the headman will be a sort of a tax which he has no authority to levy. Only the state can levy taxes under Article 265, and the only authority who can compel a citizen to render service is the State as provided in Article 23(2).

Begar was legally sanctioned in certain parts of India. Certain provisions of the Indian Criminal Tribes Act also sanctioned forced labour. As a result of the provision of Article 23, as many as twelve Central and State laws that sanctioned forced labour under certain circumstances became void, and as many as 26,500,000 people, mostly hillmen, got relief from forced labour.[52]

Since the mere constitutional provision of Article 23 could not abolish the social evil of forced labour, Parliament passed in 1976 the Bonded Labour System (Abolition) Act, 1976 exempting completely the liability to pay the bonded debt. Thousands of bonded labours have been set free after the implementation of this legislation but there are some areas where this practice is still in force. The creditors adopt all means to circumvent the law. If this social evil is to be eradicated completely follow-up action is meeded by the Government in right earnest. It has been held that Article 23 has to be read with the Directives in Articles 39(c), 41, 42. So read, the State should not only identify bonded labourers but also provide for their rehabilitation. Failure to do so would constitute violation of Articles 21 and 23.[53] In an application under Article 23, the Court may direct rehabilitation of the bonded labourers or payment to them of minimum wages.

Since most of the bonded labourers belong to that category of people classified as 'Scheduled Castes and Scheduled Tribes', it devolves primarily on the State and secondarily on the political parties and the social and welfare organisations wedded to the cause of uplift of the social and economic conditions of weaker sections of the society, including the SC/ST, to work unitedly and conjointly for the eradication of this social evil, cutting across party ideologies and barriers, for realisation of the ideal of fraternity, 'assuring the dignity of the individual and the unity of the nation' so very eloquently adumbrated in the preamble to our Constitution.

Notes and References

1. Rao, *op. cit.*, Vol. II, p. 87.
2. *Ibid.*, p. 77.
3. *Ibid.*, p. 53.
4. *Ibid.*, pp. 51-52.
5. *Ibid.*, pp. 125-26.
6. *Ibid.*, p. 128.
7. *Ibid.*, p. 140.
8. *Ibid.*, p. 146.
9. *Ibid.*, p. 149.
10. *Ibid.*, p. 156.
11. *Ibid.*, p. 165.
12. *Ibid.*, p. 178.
13. *Ibid.*, p. 183.
14. *Ibid.*, p. 180.
15. *Ibid.*, pp. 193-94.
16. *Ibid.*, p. 326.
17. *Ibid.*, p. 332
18. *Ibid.*, p. 383.
19. *Ibid.*, p. 201.
20. *Ibid.*, pp. 207-09.
21. *Ibid.*, pp. 255-56.
22. *Ibid.*, p. 264.
23. *CAD*, Vol. III, p. 442.
24. *Ibid.*, dated 1-5-47, p. 479.
25. *Ibid.*, pp. 480-84.
26. *Ibid.*, dated 2-5-47, p. 531.
27. Rao, Vol. III., *op. cit.*, p. 10.
28. *Ibid.*, p. 331, pp. 331, 524.
29. *CAD.*, Vol. VII, dated 3-12-48, p. 804.
30. *Ibid.*, pp. 804-05.
31. *Ibid.*, p. 807.
32. *Ibid.*, p. 805.
33. *Ibid.*, p. 804.
34. *Ibid.*, p. 806.

35. *CAD.*, Vol. VII, dated 3-12-48, pp. 806-07.
36. *Ibid.*, pp. 807-08.
37. *Ibid.*, p. 808.
38. *Ibid.*, pp. 808-09.
39. *Ibid.*, pp. 809-10.
40. *Ibid.*, p. 810.
41. *Ibid.*, pp. 810-11.
42. *Ibid.*, pp. 811-12.
43. *Ibid.*, pp. 812-13.
44. *Ibid.*, pp. 813-14.
45. Ramachandran, V.G., *Fundamental Rights and Constitutional Remedies*, Vol. II, Second Edition, 1982, Eastern Book Company, Lucknow, pp. 328-29.
46. *Raj Bahadur* v. *Legal Remembrancer*, AIR 1953 Cal 523.
47. *Sharma v. U.P., AIR 1959 All 57.*
48. *People's Union v. Union of India,* A. *1982 S.C. 1473.*
49. *Sanjit v. State of Rajasthan, A. 1983 S.C. 328.*
50. *Suraj v. M.P. AIR 1960 M.P. 303.*
51. Rai Weinao Kahaosan Tangkhul v. Rui Weinao Sumiraj Shailli Khullakpa, AIR 1961 Manipur I.
52. Tope, T.K., *The Constitution of India*, Popular Prakashan, Bombay, 1971, p. 116.
53. *Neeraja v. State of M.P., A 1984 S.C. 1099.*

9

Prohibition of Employment of Children in Factories, Etc. (Article 24)

Exploitation of children, though reprehensible, prevailed in the past and is still prevailing in one form or the other in many areas of this country. A large number of children have to work for a living, either because they have to support themselves, being orphams, or have dependent disabled parents or they have to supplement the meagre income of their parents. Besides, a number of children have to stay at home to look after their little brothers and sisters and do the household work while their parents go away to work. Children are exploited by adults either in the workplace, through low wages and long hours, or outside by unscrupulous elements seeking to gain by forcing them into undesirable occupations. The Indian Factories Act of 1881 forbade employment of children under seven years, limited hours of work to nine and provided for four holidays a month. The Indian Factories Act of 1891 raised the minimum age for child workers to nine generally and fourteen for some kinds of heavy and hazardous work. Subsequent legislations increased the minimum age for child labourers to twelve and even to fifteen for various industries, the lowest being for plantations. The Employment of Children Act of 1938 was enacted prohibiting the employment of children below fifteen years in any occupation: (1) connected with the transport of passengers, goods or mails by railway; (2) involving handling of goods within the limits of any 'port'. The Indian Factories (Amendment) Act, 1940 also prohibited employment of children in unhealthy and dangerous surroundings and conditions.

The framers had first-hand knowledge about the miserable and pitiable working conditions of the child labourers and how they were exploited by their unscrupulous employers, They, therefore, felt the necessity of providing for ample provision in the Constitution to afford protection to these economically disadvantaged children from exploitation.

Curiously enough neither Ambedkar, nor Prof. K.T. Shah nor Harnam Singh in their drafts on fundamental rights voiced any concern for child labour. Only Munshi in Article VII(5) of his draft declared:

> Child labour in all forms is prohibited and employment of children for any purpose whatever shall not be permitted except under conditions prescribed by the law of the Union.[1]

B.N. Rau, the Constitutional Adviser, in Clause 7 of Part A of his Preliminary Notes dealing with fundamental principles of State Policy suggested:

> The State shall ensure that the strength and health of workers, men and women, and the tender age of children shall not be abused and that they shall not be forced by economic necessity to take up occupations unsuited to their sex, age or strength.[2]

Jagjivan Ram, in his reply to the questionnaire to the Minorities Sub-committee suggested inclusion of the following provision in the fundamental rights :

> Special protection shall be extended to women and young persons engaged in occupations injurious to health.[3]

The Fundamental Rights Sub-committee considered

clause (5) of Article VII of Munshi's draft on March 27, 1947 and adopted it in the following amended form:

> Employment of children under 14 years of age in mines, factories and hazardous employment shall not be permitted.[4]

This appeared as sub-clause (3) of Clause 15 of the Sub-committee's Draft Report to be submitted to the Advisory Committee.[5]

While commenting on this Draft Report, the Constitutional Adviser pointed out that the principle of prohibition of employment of children in mines, factories or other hazardous jobs embodied in sub-clause (3) was based on the Indian National Congress declaration of 1933 and on the Yugoslavian Constitution (Article 23, paragraph 2).[6]

Sub-clause (3) of Clause 15 of the Fundamental Rights Sub-committee's report sent to the Advisory Committee on April 16,[7] was considered by the Minorities sub-committe in its meeting on April 17, 1947 when it agreed to offer no comment on this clause.[8]

Clause 15(3) of the Fundamental Rights Sub-committee's report was taken up for consideration by the Advisory Committee on April 21, 1947 when the Chairman of the Advisory Committee appointed a small committee consisting of Shrimati Hansa Mehta, C.R. Rajagopalachari and G.B.Pant to look into the matter and prepare a suitable draft.[9] This Committee suggested the following day that sub-clause (3) relating to prohibition of child labour be made an independent clause with the addition of a new Explanation.[10]

The redrafted provisions, as adopted by the Advisory Committee and reproduced as clause 12 in its interin report sent on April 23, 1947 were as follows:

> No child below the age of 14 years shall be engaged to work in any factory, mine or any other hazardous employment.

> Explanation—Nothing in this clause shall prejudice any educational programme or activity involving compulsory labour.[11]

The Constitutent Assembly took up clause 12 for discussion on May 1, 1947 when Munshi moved an amendment for deletion of the explanation as it had nothing to do with the clause.[12] There was no discussion on this clause and the amended clause was adopted.[13]

Clause 12 was reproduced in the Constitutional Adviser's Draft Constitution as clause 19 with minor drafting changes:

> No child below the age of fourteen years shall be employed to work in any factory or mine or engaged in any other hazardous employment.[14]

The Drafting Committee did not make any change in this clause[15] which was incorporated as Article 18 in the Draft Constitution prepared by the Drafting Committee and ciruclated on February 21, 1948.[16]

This Draft Article, when put to circulation, however, did not elicit any comment from any quarter.

This Article came up for consideration before the Constituent Assembly on December 3, 1948. Damodar Swarup Seth moved an amendment seeking to include a clause for the prohibition of employment of women in mines or in industries during night. This amendment was supported by Prof. S.L. Saxena who also pleaded for raising the age of children to sixteen, because particularly on account of our climate, children were weak at the age of fourteen. Ambedkar did not accept the amendment and it was negatived by the Assembly. Article 18 was adopted without any modification.[17]

At the revision stage it was renumbered as Article 24 of the Constitution.

Article 24 prohibits employment of children below the age of fourteen years in (1) any factory, (2) or mines or (3) in any other hazardous employment. It is to be noted that the prohibition imposed by this Article is absolute and does not admit of any exception for the employment of a child in a factory or mine or in any hazardous employment, e.g., in a railway or a port or a construction industry. It has been held that this right of a child is enforceable even in the absence of implementing legislation and in a 'public interest' proceedings.[18]

Article 24, however, does not prohibit, in general, employment of children outside the above three categories in any innocent or harmless job which is not hazardous. What is secured by Article 24 is the health and safety of the child. Section 67 of the Factories Act, 1948 prohibits employment of a child who has not completed fifteenth year. There is a similar provision in Section 45 of the Mines Act, 1952. The Child Labour (Prohibition and Regulation) Act of 1986 is aimed at prohibiting the employment of children below fourteen years in 'certain hazardous employment'. But, as in other areas, there is a yawning chasn between what the Government says and what it does.

Article 39 (e) lays down that the State shall, in particular, direct its policy towards securing that the health and strength of workers, men and women, and the tender age of children are not abused and that citizens are not forced by economic necessity to enter avocations unsuited to their age or strength. Article 39(f) directs the State to ensure that children are given opportunities and facilities to develop in a healthy manner and in conditions of freedom and dignity and that childhood and youth are protected against exploitation and against moral and material abandonment. Article 45 directs the State to provide, within a period of ten years from the commencement of the Constitution, for free and compulsory education for all children until they complete the age of fourteen years. But out of an estimated 180 million children just over 40 million attend schools today. For the vast majority of these children, going to school or playing with friends is a luxury to dream of. They are children without childhood. Abandoned by parents or driven by poverty, they find themselves scraping out an existence alongside adults in this cruel, unfriendly world. They are engaged in all sorts of vocations—from ragpicking to shoe shining, from teashop boys to domestic helps, and from roadside acrobatics to begging. They work day and night, mostly in unsafe and unhealthy conditions, and have not heard of such things as minimum wages acts or child labour being illegal. These children come from all castes, class or creed. For them the fine distinctions between one religion and another, 'high' castes and 'low' castes and 'forward' class and 'backward' class do not exist. They are merely fighting for their existence in this vast world.

Economic need is the main cause of child labour. Most of them come from poverty-stricken families who take up any available employment irrespective of caste affiliations or skills. Apart from cheapness of child labour, the amenability of children to discipline and their easy acceptance of deprivation make them easier to control.[19] They are forced to live in servitude. They are found in various hazardous professions like carpet industry, glass factories, stone querries and brick klins.

In both Europe and the USA, concern over sensitive issues such as child labour and bonded labour in the Third World has been on the increase in the recent years. Recently, at the world's largest carpet fair, DOMOTEX '93 in Germany, the Federal Association for Oriental Carpets raised the issue of employment of child labour in carpet industry in India and proposed that if the European market refused to buy carpets made by children the Indian manufacturers would be forced to dismiss their minor employees. The German importers were even ready to pay two per cent to five per cent hike if the working conditions were improved and adult labour was employed. There have been proposals by non-governmental organisations in Europe and the USA to ban import of hand-woven carpets and certain leather products made in India because the customers feel 'guilty' of using the products which involve inhuman exploitation. Already a significant initiative has been taken by Indian carpet manufacturers in Mirzapur in U.P., the largest carpet manufacturing pocket in India, to do away with child labour in the carpet inustry. The recent furore raised in the international fora over employment of child labour in carpet industry has, no doubt, caused damage to India's image in the international market.[20]

Notwithstanding the constitutional provisions, the various legislations like the Juvenile Justice Act of 1986 which came into force on October 2, 1987, replacing the obsolete Children's Act, 1960 and superseding at least 25 different corresponding laws in various States and Union Territories and other enactments, and the UNICEF Declaration of Children's Rights in 1989, the children continue to be exploited. All these have failed to provide a deterrent to the use of children as a labour force. Child labour still goes on to a certain extent even in the organized sector by hoodwinking, suborning or bribing officials. Laws are broken openly and with impunity in the unorganized and infomal sector, particularly where the Factories Act does not apply, such as bidi, mica, shellac, rice and oil mills, The law regarding adoption of children, it has been observed, has led to their being misused as slaves in some inhuman homes. They are also employed in begging and criminal activities.[21] India's child labour force exceeds 30 million. The Census Report of 1981, however, computes it at 13.59 million, 5.55 per cent of the total labour force of the country. Even if the total abolition of child labour is not possible, it must be conceded that the legislations lack teeth and have been honoured more in the breach than in observance.

Notes and References

1. Rao, *op. ctt.*, Vol. II, p. 77.
2. *Ibtd.*, p. 34.
3. *Ibtd.*, p. 332.
4. *Ibtd.*, p. 126.
5. *Ibtd.*, p. 140.

6. Rao, *op. cit.*, Vol. II, p. 149.
7. *Ibid.*, p. 173.
8. *Ibid.*, p. 201.
9. *Ibid.*, p. 256.
10. *Ibid.*, p. 264.
11. *Ibid.*, p. 298.
12. *CAD.*, Vol. III, dated 1-5-47, p. 484.
13. *Ibid.*, p. 485.
14. Rao, *op. cit.*, Vol. III, p. 10.
15. *Ibid.*, p. 330.
16. *Ibid.*, p. 524.
17. *CAD.*, Vol. VII, dated 3-12-48, pp. 814-15.
18. *People's Union v. Union of India, A. 1982 S.C. 1473.*
19. Karlekar, Kalyani, Children at work, *The Statesman*, January 2, 1993.
20. *The Statesman*, February 12, 1993.
21. Ghosh, S.K., *Protection of Minorities and Scheduled Castes*, Ashish Publishing House, New Delhi, 1980. p. 82.

10

Special Provision for the Advancement of any Socially and Educationally Backward Classes of Citizens or for the Scheduled Castes and the Scheduled Tribes (Article 15(4))

Article 15 forbids the State from discriminating against any citizen on grounds only of religion, race, caste, sex, place of birth or any of them. An exception to the rule against discrimination is, however, provided in clause (3) which does not prevent the State from making any special provision for women and children. Subsequently, after the commencement the Constitution, the Constitution was amended in June, 1951, by the Constitution (First Amendment) Act, 1951 to provide for another exception in clause (4) to enable the State to make special provision for the advancement of any socially and educationally backward classes of citizens or for the Scheduled Castes and the Scheduled Tribes.

Article 15 owes its origin to Article 9 of the Draft Constitution, which again originated from the first report of the Advisory Committee on Minorities, Fundamental

Rights, etc., submitted on April 23, 1947. The Committee recommended for inclusion in the Constitution certain rights which are fundamental in nature and are enforceable by appropriate legal process. Under the broad heading Rights of Equality, clauses 4 to 7 were included. Clause 4 of the report had the following provision:

4 (1). The State shall make no discrimination against any citizen on grounds of religion, race, caste or sex.

(2) There shall be no discrimination against any citizen on any ground of religion, race, caste or sex in regard to—

(a) access to trading establishment including public restaurants and hotels,

(b) the use of wells, tanks, roads and places of public resort maintained wholly or partly out of public funds or dedicated to the use of the general public:

Provided that nothing contained in this clause shall prevent separate provision being made for women and children.[1]

This clause was debated[2] in the Constituent Assembly on April 29, 1947. Certain amendments were accepted after due deliberations but none of the members did ever speak about any provision on the line of clause (4) of Article 15. On the other hand, everybody wanted to ensure that the clause was as non-discriminatory as possible.

This clause was incorporated in the Draft Constitution as Article 9 which read as follows:

(1) The State shall not discriminate against any citizen on grounds only of religion, race, caste, sex or any of them.

In particular, no citizen shall, on grounds only of religion, race, caste, sex or any of them, be subject to any disability, liability, restriction or condition with regard to—

(a) access to shops, public restaurants, hotels and places of public entertainment, or

(b) the use of wells, tanks, roads and places of public resort maintained wholly or partly out of the revenue of the State or dedicated to the use of the general public.

(2) Nothing in this article shall prevent the State from making any specific provision for women and children.[3]

When on November 29, 1948, the Constituent Assembly took up the consideration of Draft Article 9, it had before it about four dozen amendments of which notice had been given by the members. Most of them were either not moved or disallowed as being verbal. The amendments that were actually moved had one thing in common—to make the article as much non-discriminatory as possible. The underlying idea was to ensure that the citizens were not discriminated on grounds of caste, sex, birth etc. Sectarain or denominational exclusiveness was thought to be a blot on democratic equality and all members were demanding in unison to dismantle the barrier and the tendency of exclusiveness, in whatever form it might be.[4]

Only Prof. K.T. Shah brought an amendment for extending some advantage or safeguards to the Scheduled Castes and backward tribes. His amendment was for addition of the words 'or for Scheduled Castes or backward tribes, for their advantage, safeguard or betterment' at the end of clause (2) of article 9. The intention was to give special facilities to the Scheduled Castes and the Scheduled Tribes for some time so that real equality of citizens be established. He argued:

> In regard to the Scheduled castes and backward tribes, it is an open secret that they have been neglected in the past; and their rights and claims to enjoy and have the capacity to enjoy as equal citizens happens to be denied to them because of their backwardness. I seek therefore by this motion to include them also within the scope of this sub-clause (2), so that any special discrimination in favour

> of them may not be regarded as violating the basic principles of equality for all classes of citizens in the country. They need and must be given, for some time to come at any rate, special treatment in regard to education, in regard to opportunity for employment, and in many other cases where their present inequality, their present backwardness is only a hindrance to the rapid development of the country.
>
> Any section of the community which is backward must necessarily impede the progress of the rest; and it is only in the interest of the community itself, therefore, that it is but right and proper we should provide facilities so that they may be brought up-do-date so to say and the uniform progress of all be forwarded.
>
> I have, of course, not included in my amenament the length of years, the term of years for which some such special treatment may be given. That may be determined by the circumstances of the day. I only want to draw your attention to the fact that there are classes of our citizens who may need. through no fault of theirs, some special treatment if equality is not to be equality of name only or on paper only, but equality of fact. I trust this will commend itself to the House and the amendment will be accepted.[5]

Negativiting this amendment of Prof. Shah, Dr. Ambedkar pointed out that his amendment would have 'just the opposite effect'. Elaborating this point he said: "The object which all of us have in mind is that the Scheduled Castes and Scheduled tribes should not be segregated from the general public. For instance, none of us, I think, would like that a separate school should be established for the Scheduled Castes when there is a general school in the village open to the children of the entire community. If these words are added, it will probably give a handle for a State to say, 'well, we are making special provision for the Scheduled Castes'. To my mind they can safely say so by taking shelter under the article if it is amended in the manner the Professor wants it. I therefore think that it is not a desirable amendment."[6]

None else spoke on this amendment and the House ultimately negatived it.[7]

Draft Article 9 which was renumbered as Article 15 at the time of revision thus became one of the Fundamental Rights enshrined in the Constitution.

But within sixteen months of the commencement of the Constitution, this Article was subjected to an amendment for addition of clause (4) to it stipulating that "nothing in this article or in clause (2) of Article 29 shall prevent the State from making any special provision for the advancement of any socially and educationally backward classes of citizens or for the Scheduled Castes and the Scheduled Tribes." The need to amend this Article arose to meet the judgment of the Supreme Court which held that any reservation for backward classes in educational institutions was invalid because of the provisions in clause (2) of Article 29 which provided that "no citizen shall be denied admission into any educational institution maintained by the State or receiving aid out of State funds on grounds only of religion, race, caste, language or any of them."

On May 12, 1951, Pandit Jawaharlal Nehru, the Prime Minister, introduced in the Parliament (Lok Sabha and Rajya Sabha did not come into being then) the Constitution (First Amendment) Bill not only for addition of clause (4) to Article 15, but also for amendments in Articles 85, 87, 174, 176, 341, 342, 372, 376, substitution of a new clause (2) for original clause (2) of Article 19 and addition of a new sub-clause to clause (6) of the same Article and addition of new Articles 31A and 31B along with a new Schedule called the Ninth Schedule.

The Bill was debated in the Parliament at different stages—first while considering the motion for referring the Bill to the Select Committee, then while considering the motion for taking into consideration this Bill, as amended by the Select Committee, then during clause-wise discussion when amendments were moved and discussed, and lastly during the general discussion of the Bill.

So far as our study is concerned, we propose to

confine only to that portion of the deliberations having a bearing on clause (4) of Article 15 at these four stages.

On May 16, 1951, Pandit Nehru moved a resolution in the Parliament for referring the Bill to a "Select Committee consisting of Prof. K.T. Shah. Sardar Hukam Singh, Pandit Hirday Nath Kunzru, Dr. Syama Prasad Mookerjee. Shri Naziruddin Ahmed, Shri C. Rajagopalachari, Shri L. Krishnaswami Bharati, Shri Awadheswar Prasad Sinha, Shri T.R. Deogirkhar, Dr. B.R. Ambedkar, Shri V.S. Sarwate, Shri Mohanlal Gautam, Shri R.K. Sidhva, Shri Khandubhai K.Desai, Shri K. Hanumanthaiya, Shri Raj Bahadur, Shrimati G. Durgabai, Shri Manilal Chaturbhai Shah, Shri Dev Kanta Borooah, Shri Satya Narayan Sinha and the Mover with instructions to report on Monday the 21st May, 1951,"[8]

The discussion on the motion to refer the Bill to the Select Committee continued for three days—on May 16, 17 and 18, 1951 after which the motion was adopted.[9] Many Members like Dr. S.P. Mookerjee, Prof. Ranga, Kameshwar Singh, Pandit Thakur Das Bhargava, Pandit Kunzru, Shrimati Renuka Ray, Kamath, Syamnandan Sahaya, Deshbandhu Gupta, Kala Venkatrao, Hussain Imam, M.P. Mishra, Pandit Krishna Chandra Sharma, Shankaraiya, Sarangdhar Das, Dr. Ambedkar, Ethirajulu Naidu, Ramalingam Chettiar, J.P. Srivastava, K.K. Bhattacharya, Chaudhuri Ranbir Singh, Himatsingka, Ghule, R.K. Chaudhuri participated in the discussions. But all of them did not deliberate on the provisions of the proposed clause (4) of Article 15, rather the Members were more concerned with the proposed amendments to Article 19 and the new Articles 31A and 31B. Only nine Members spoke on the provisions of the proposed amendment to Article 15 at this stage. The main criticisms against the proposed amendment were that in the absence of a definition of the "backward classes" this provision might be abused when attempts would be made to bring in new communities under this class by the backdoor and that the very purpose of the amendment would be defeated unless clause (2) of Article 29 was also amended.

Now let us see what the Members had actually stated in the Parliament on this provision at this stage

Shri Jawaharlal Nehru

...In article 15 it is sought to add certain words. Perhaps it might appear that these words might almost be considered redundant. Nevertheless it has been considered desirable to add them and I am not quite sure if a slight further addition would not even be better to make it quite clear.

The real difficulty which has come up before us is this. The Constitution lays down certain Directive Principles of State Policy and after long discussion we agreed to them and they point out the way we have got to travel. The Constitution also lays down certain Fundamental Rights. Both are important. The Directive Principles of State Policy represent a dynamic move towards a cerain objective. The Fundamental Rights represent something static, to preserve certain rights which exist. Both again are right. But somehow and sometime it might so happen that that dynamic movement and that static standstill do not quite fit into each other.

A dynamic movement towards a certain objective necessarily means certain changes taking place: that is the essence of movement. Now it may be that in the process of dynamic movement certain existing relationships are altered, varied or affected. In fact they are meant to affect those settled relationships and yet if you come back to the Fundamental Rights they are meant to preserve, not indirectly, certain settled relationships. There is a certain conflict in the two approaches, not inherently, because that was not meant, I am quite sure, but there is that slight difficulty and naturally when the courts of the land have to consider these matters they have to lay stress on the Fundamental Rights than on the Directive Principles of State Policy. The result is that the whole purpose behind the Constitution, which was meant to be a dynamic Constitution, leading to a certain goal step by step, is somewhat hampered and hindered by the static element being emphasised a little more than the dynamic element and we have to find out some way of solving it.

The amendment which I seek to move is, to be quite

frank with the House, not a solution of the basic problem which will come up before the House in various shapes and forms from time to time. But it does lay stress on one small aspect of it.

May I also point out and try to remove a possible misconception that might be in the minds of some honourable Members. They might think that this is perhaps a devious method to bring in some kind of a communal element in the consideration of this problem. I want to make it perfectly clear that so far as Government are concerned they do not wish to have any truck with communalism in any form. But you have to distinguish between backward classes which are specially mentioned in the Constitution that have to be helped to be made to grow and not think of them in terms of this community or that. Only if you think of them in terms of the community you bring in communalism. But if you deal with backward classes as such, whatever religion or anything else they may happen to belong to, then it becomes our duty to help towards educational, social and economic advance. Naturally that advance is not meant to be, if I may say so, at the expense of the others. We want to pull people up and not pull them down. But sometimes in this intervening period difficulties arose, because we have not got enough provision, let us say, for giving a certain type of education, technical or other. The question arose whether we should give some reasonable encouragement and opportunity for that education to be given to members of the backward classes, which otherwise, without that encouragement and opportunity, they may not get at all, so that they remain where they are and we cannot pull them up. Therefore the object of this amendment is to lay stress on this.

The House may remember article 29(2) which says that no one by reason of his religion, etc., should be kept out of an educational institution. That is a fundamental thing by which this Constitution stands and we must stand by it. There is no question of going behind that. What I submit is, respecting that we have also to respect that fundamental directive of this Constitution and the fundamental aims of our policy, that we must encourage and help those who are backward to come up and give them proper training and proper opportunities of social and economic advance.

The essential difficulty is this. The whole conception of the Fundamental Rights is the protection of individual liberty and freedom. That is a basic conception and to know where from it was derived you have to go back to European history from the latter days of the 18th century; roughly speaking, you may say from the days of the French Revolution which spread on to the 19th century. That might be said to be the dominating idea of the 19th century and it has continued and it is a matter of fundamental importance. Nevertheless, as the 19th century marched into the 20th century and as the 20th century went ahead, other additional ideas came into the field which are represented by our Directive Principles of State Policy. If in the protection of individual liberty you protect also individual or group inequality, then you come into conflict with that Directive Principle which wants, according to your own Constitution a gradual advance, or let us put it another way, not so gradual but more rapid advance, whereever possible to a State where there is less and less inequality and more and more equality. If any kind of an appeal to individual liberty and freedom is construed to mean as an appeal to the continuation of the existing inequality then you get into difficulties. Then you become static, unprogressive and cannot change and you cannot realise that ideal of an egalitarian society which I hope most of us aim at.

These problems arise and I have mentioned them to the House, not because they arise out of the little amendment that I propose but at the back of these problems they are there and we have to come to grips with them. If this particular amendment can be somewhat varied I should welcome it. I do not stick to that particular wording. In the Select Committee or elsewhere some few words may perhaps make the meaning clearer which I have sought to put before the House and I would personally welcome it...[10]

Pandit Thakur Das Bhargava

In articles 16 and 340 the words "backward classes" are used. I do not know the exact connotation of the words. I know what is meant by the Scheduled Castes and Scheduled Tribes, but I do not know who these people are who are known by the term backward classes. In the Constituent Assembly I wanted to define the word by including the Scheduled Castes and such other classes as were recommended by the Commission to be appointed by the President under article 340. Unfortunately my amendment was not accepted. I adhere to the view that the Scheduled Castes are the real backward classes. There might be a few other classes which may be on the same level but which are not in the Schedule. Beyond that I do not know what is meant by backward classes. So far as backwardness is concerned all the Brahmins of India are backward economically. I think the Rajputs, who are considered as one of the most influential classes in India are very backward socially because they observe purdah and previously resorted to infanticide. In Article 340 we have used the words "socially and culturally backward" and my fear is that if these words are allowed without being defined we may be confronted with difficulties...

Dr. Deshmukh (Madhya Pradesh)

A Commission is going to be appointed to investigate it.

Pandit Thakur Das Bhargava

I know it and I will advert to it later. It is quite right that those classes who are considered by the Commission to be backward should be included and I have no objection. But supposing the Madras Government notification about the reservation of seats in universities, etc. is sought to be maintained by the backdoor method and some classes who are not backward are brought in as backward, then I am very much against this.

Dr. Deshmukh

It is not the intention.

Pandit Thakur Das Bhargava

The Mover of the Bill was pleased to say that our

Government is committed to bringing about a classless society. We all stand by it. But if by this backdoor method the Government of Madras wants seats reserved for the non-Brahmins, including other classes, I am opposed to it.

Dr. Deshmukh

Is it the Brahmin in you speaking?

Pandit Thakur Das Bhargava

I respect the Brahmins and I respect the other classes also. But I want that the really backward classes alone should be given the protection. Give them all that you can and even if you want that property should be given to them I am quite ready to agree. But at the same time it would be quite wrong to bring in those classes which are not backward by virtue of an ambiguous phrase and introduce confusion and uncertainty. As regards reservation of seats I was of opinion that under Article 16 you can very easily include it, as you have already included reservation of appointments for the backward classes. These words "economically, educationally and socially" throw open a very wide field and I want to know which way we are going, how far we are going and where exactly we are going. Whatever can be done for the Scheduled Castes should be done and I do not want to be misunderstood in this regard. We would be failing in our duty if we do not do all that we possibly can for the weaker and Scheduled Classes. During the last three years we have done quite a bit but that is not sufficient. We should give them proprietary rights on their houses and every student should get a stipend or scholarship to go up to the highest standard and they should also be given jobs. But I do not want that communalism should be introduced by the backdoor methods. I know that the Government do not want it. At the same it is not the Central Government that is going to implement it. But it is the Provincial Ministers who will give effect to it and I do not know what they may or may not do. As a matter of precaution I am uttering this warning, though I am not opposed to the proposed amendment.[11]

Shri Kamath (Madhya Pradesh)

. As regards the proposed amendment to article 15, it is rather inconsistent with Article 29 of the Constitution. Article 29(2) of the Constitution, which is not sought to be amended, says:

> "No citizen shall be denied admission into any educational institution maintained by the State or receiving aid out of State funds on grounds only of religion, race, caste, language or any of them."

I wonder how the ingenuity of Dr. Ambedkar and other legal advisers to Government will reconcile the proposed amendment to Article 15 with clause (2) of article 29 as it still stands in the Constitution.

The amended Article 15(3) will read as follows:

> "Nothing in this article shall prevent the State from making any special provision for women and children or for the educational, economic or social advancement of any backward class of citizens."

The background to this amendment is very well known. I need not go into the history of the Communal G.O. (the Government Order) issued by the Madras Government and later held *ultra vires* and invalid by the Supreme Court. To obviate any difficulties arising out of the Supreme Court's judgment this amendment has been brought before the House. But I submit that so long as article 29(2) be wholly inconsistent with that article, and I do not know what will happen to it in the Supreme Court if it were to go before the Supreme Court again. Two fundamentally inconsistent articles will be incorporated in the Constitution and it will militate against the consistency of the whole provision as it is sought to be brought before the House in this amendment to Article 15...[12]

Shri Syamnandan Sahaya

...If you take up the amendments, one gets lost and begins thinking if the matter has really received serious consideration. The first amendment regarding Article 15 leaves us in serious doubts. In the first place, the amendment seeks to introduce a new phrase 'backward class'. I do not know if the phrase 'backward class' has been defined anywhere, and if it has not been, it will create a position extremely difficult to fulfil the objectives which the present Government and the Congress had for a long time. We have already made provisions in the Constitution with reagard to Scheduled Castes and Scheduled Tribes. Now we propose to make this change with regard to backward classes.

Dr. Deshmukh

There is provision for backward classes also in the Constitution.

Shri Syamnandan Sahaya

In the Directives.

Mr. Chairman

The provision enables the Government to appoint a committee.

Shri Syamnandan Sahaya

If there is already a provision in the Constitution, then what is the amendment for. I suppose it is only there to meet the requirements of a certain Provincial Government.

Dr. Deshmukh

The purpose is not being fulfilled.

Shri Syamnandan Sahaya

That is what some people may think and there are others again who think that the provision in the Constitution is sufficient. If you read the clause to which the amendment is proposed...

Mr. Chairman

The Prime Minister made it clear yesterday in his speech that what is added to Article 15(3) is only to give effect to what is laid down in the Directive Principles and also the provision enabling the President to appoint a committee. He further clarified the position by saying that it was to enable the backward classes to make progress and not to allow any other communal point of view to enter into it.

Shri Syamnandan Sahaya

The term backward classes has first to be defined. The President has the power to appoint a commission. If the President had already appointed the commission and if the commission had reported and if as a result of that report we found that these backward classes were not included in the Scheduled Castes or Scheduled Tribes and their number was so large as to necessitate such a provision then we might have agreed to amend the Constitution. At present we are not aware of what is meant by backward classes. When we talk in terms of backward classes we know that it generally refers to Scheduled Castes and Tribes. By calling a new set of people as backward classes you want to bring in new communities by the backdoor.

Some Hon. Members

No. no.

Shri Syamnandan Sahaya

I am entitled to my opinion and you are entitled to yours. I do not know what particular conditions obtain in different parts of the country but I do not see that there is any special case...

Shri Rudrappa

We want an explanation from the hon. Member as to what is meant by backdoor.

Shri Kesava Rao

For information of the hon. Member...

Mr. Chairman

Is he giving information or does he want information?

Shri Kesava Rao

The hon. Member said that there was no definition of backward classes. The President has already notified the backward classes.

An Hon. Member

A Commission is going to be appointed.

Shri Syamnandan Sahaya

I do not follow what the hon. Member has said. As far as I know it is not defined anywhere. An amendment is proposed to be made in clause 15(3) which reads:

> "Nothing in this article shall prevent the State from making any special provision for women and children."

To that it is proposed to add "or for the educational, economic or social advancement of any backward class of citizens". When the clause is thus amended we are faced also with another provision in Article 29(2) which lays down:

> "No citizen shall be denied admission into any educational institution maintained by the State or receiving aid out of State funds on grounds only of religion, race, caste, language or any of them."

On the top of these there is the directive policy about it in Article 46. Article 46 lays down:

> "The State shall promote with special care the educational and economic interests of the weaker sections of the people, and, in particular, of the Scheduled Castes and Scheduled Tribes, and shall protect them from social injustice and all forms of exploitation."

I would ask the House through you to consider what anomalies and complicated situation this amendment will create. We say now in this amendment that we shall make special arrangements for the educational, economic and social advancement of what are called "backward classes". At another place we say in clause (2) that we shall not discriminate with regard to admissions to colleges on the ground of caste, religion, etc. Then we have also a directive in Article 46 that where necessary Government will take special steps to see that the weaker sections are encouraged to improve. Then again, as Dr. Deshmukh said, the President has got the power to appoint a commission to look into the question of backward classes. In view of all this, where is the justification for this amendment? Let us first of all know what are the requirements, and of which section in the country, before we are asked to amend the Constitution. I submit this amendment is more with a view to meet a certain judgment which has been passed by the Supreme Court with regard to admission to colleges. But if that is the purpose of this amendment, then I submit that it does not cure the trouble; as long as Article 29 (2) is there there can be no discrimination in the matter of admission of students to colleges aided by Government or entirely financed by them.

Dr. Deshmukh

Suggest an amendment of that.

Shri Syamnandan Sahaya

That is quite a different matter, but so long as that Article 29(2) is there this amendment would make confusion worse confounded and that is why I have been trying to tell the House not to accept it.[13]

If we analyse the different provisions of this Bill, we will find,—at least I have the apprehension—that even after passing these amendments, perhaps the object which the Government has in view may not be fully met...I voice that apprehension today also. Look at the very first amendment of Article 15. The judgment of the Supreme Court relates to clause (2) of Article 29, we leave clause (2) of Article 29 as it is, but amend Article 15. I do not know how far the purpose of the Government will be fulfilled. I know it is difficult to amend clause (2) of Article 29.[14]

Shri Shankaraiya (Mysore)

The Prime Minister in his speech has given an account of the conditions prevailing in the country, particularly in South India and he has been fully aware of the serious consequences that would arise if things are not settled in proper time. Being aware of those consequences, he has proposed this amendment to Article 15(3), by providing that equal opportunities be given to the minority communities, especially the backward communities or the backward classes, so to say, for economic and educational advancement. But, the only point that I wish to bring to the notice of the House is that this amendment will not serve the purpose we have in view, if it is not specifically laid down. In view of the decision of the Supreme Court on the communal G.O. of the Madras Government, under Article 29 (2), no restrictions could be placed with regard to admission to colleges on grounds of community, caste or religion. This has led to a good deal of upheaval and a sort of agitation in the minds not only of the elderly people, but even of the younger generation, particularly the student community. In order to prevent this, I would request the hon. Prime Minister to seriously consider this matter and see that the proposals that are laid down are fully effective. Even if the proposed amendments are carried, the purpose will not be served. It is a legal question. I would like to explain it. The proposed amendment is of a general nature. It runs like this:

> "for the educational, economic or social advancement of any backward class of citizens:

This is a general clause. No doubt, it gives facilities to them. But, this general clause will be qualified to the extent that an Article 29(2) stands there. So long as the general provision is there, it will be interpreted subsquently that any State Government or the Central Government may provide all facilities for their advancement in the educational and economic field; but it will be qualified to the extent that Article 29 (2) is not altered or modified. When a specific article is there, like Article 29(2), it will have precedence and it must be enforced. Even though there is a general clause, that general provision is subject to Article 29(2). So long as Article 29(2) is there, no Government can try to act or pass any order or devise any means whereby the difficulty that has now arisen on account of the decision of the Supreme Court could be obviated. The purpose, in view in the Bill, will not be achieved if Article 29(2) were to remain operative and it will be very difficult for the backward classes to get educational facilities. If they are deprived of these facilities and if they do not get admission into the colleges, what will be the consequences? I would like to bring this to the notice of the House. If they do not succeed in getting admission into these institutions, especially the technical colleges and institutions, then the very purpose of giving them these facilities would be defeated. Also Article 16(4) which provides for equal opportunity for appointments will also be a dead letter. At the time of appointment there will be a dearth of candidates from among the backward classes and hardly anyone among them can be appointed. So I submit equal opportunities should be given to the backward classes to get into the colleges and this can be effected by inserting a provision even in the present Bill to the following effect, namely that notwithstanding any other article in the Constitution and notwithstanding Article 29(2), equal opportunities should be given. If the present measure is qualified in some manner as I have just suggested, that will serve the purpose and enable the backward class students to get access into these institutions. Otherwise it will be open to the High Court to again say that so long as Article 29(2) is there, this general clause 15(3) will not help in the matter. This will not solve the problem, and as I said, Article 16(4) will remain a dead letter.

Another effect will be this. We are now in the country which has yet to make advance in the economic and industrial fields. Progress of the country in these fields will depend to a very great extent on the extent of training we give to our people in technical fields and on the extent of their technical knowledge. If the people of backward classes are denied access to the technical colleges and are deprived of the opportunity of getting this technical knowledge, the backward communities will be entirely dependent on others and will be at their mercy. So greater opportunities should be given to them.

I would like to bring to the notice of the hon. Prime Minister that the matter is not so simple as it may appear and that it is deeply agitating the minds of the people, especially in the southern part of the country. Even though the Congress may not carry on any communal propaganda, there are people who try to take advantage of the present situation and who want to exploit it. Therefore it is highly desirable that this question should be tackled properly and the country is not driven into communal feelings and rancour, if I may say so. This possible danger should be guarded against.

I would like to bring to the notice of the hon. Prime Minister that these communal feelings have already entered the portals of the universities, not only among the students but even among the professors, teachers and others. It is high time that we do something to prevent this sort of thing. Because if the mind of the younger generation is poisoned on account of this, the country will be lost and the potential danger to the country will be far greater. It is not only the Madras Government that is concerned with this but the whole of South India-the States of Mysore, Travancore-Cochin and even Bombay are all affected by this. I will not be wrong if I say that this feeling is bring spread and propaganda is being carried on in Northern India too. So I would request that this enabling provision should be included in the Bill if any relief is to be given, and that it shall be duly effective. I would request the Select Committee to bear this in mind, the serious consequences that will follow and hence bestow their best attention to the matter.

With regard to the conditions, I do not want to beg the question again as it would lead to all sorts of undesirable results. Therefore it is for the good of the country that such things are being tackled. I would like to dispel a feeling that has been prevalent and that is this: it is not a communal question but it is a question of distinction or inequality that has been existing in the different classes in South India. It is only those who are interested in it that are giving it a communal colour in order to retain their vested interests and rights. Whatever may be the circumstances that have led to the present position, I would request that we should not allow it to be exploited by anybody in the country but it should be prevented and the larger interests of the country should be looked into and fuller opportunities should be given to all classes and communities. There is a question as to who are the backward classes. With regard to that there is Article 340 and the President has got power to appoint a commission and the terms of reference of that commission could include all the details. It may be immediately appointed and it can ascertain the opinion of the people, find out the social conditions and report. This commission's report need not be final for all times. It can be reviewed periodically and these backward communities could be reclassified off and on, as and when, circumstances require by taking into consideration the progress and the development they have made and I would request that this article can be easily availed of. This is not of very serious consequences but it would lead to the greater harmony in the country. Therefore, I would request the Prime Minister to consider this matter and see that Article 29(2) is not exploited again and present amendment even though introduced will not be carried to the Supreme Court for interpreting again. If at all we are legislating, let us be definite on the point and see that all reliefs are given. With this request, I support this Bill.[15]

The Minister of Law (Dr. Ambedkar)

In the course of the debate yesterday, my friend Pandit Hirday Nath Hunzru said that Government had done great injustice to the House by not explaining the necessity and the purpose of the various clauses in this Bill, and that some one on the side of Government—and he referred particularly to me—should have got up to discharge that duty to the House.., However, as Pandit Kunzru expressed the wish of many Members of this House, I thought it incumbent on my part to intervene in this debate and to clarify the position so as to dispel the two arguments which had been used in the course of the debate, that there was no necessity for the amendment of the Constitution; and secondly, that Government could wait and give the country and the public larger and longer time and should not rush through the measure. In the observations that I propose to make, I will take the Bill clause by clause, and try to explain the necessity for making the changes which the Bill proposes to make.

I will begin with clause 2 of the Bill. Clause 2 of the Bill proposes to amend article 15. The necessity for the amendment of article 15 has arisen on account of the judgments recently delivered by the Supreme Court in two cases which came up before them from the Madras State. One case was Madras Vs. Shrimati Champakalal

Dorairajan, and the other case was Venkatraman Vs. the State of Madras. In the case of Venkatraman the article involved was Article 16, clause (4) and in the case of Shrimati Champaklal the article involved was Article 29 clause (2). In the one case the question involved was the reservation for backward classes in public services and in the other case, the question involved was the reservation for backward classes in educational institutions. The question turned upon what is known in the Madras Presidency and elsewhere as the Communal G.O. The argument on which the Communal G.O. of the Madras Government was declared to be void and invalid was this. It was said by the Supreme Court that Article 29, clause (2), did not have a saving clause like clause (4) attached to Article 16. As the House will remember under clause (4) of Article 16, a special provision is made that Article 16 shall not stand in the way of the Government making a suitable provision for representation of backward classes in the services. Such a provision, of course is not to be found in Article 29. With regard to Article 16, clause (4), the Supreme Court came to the conclusion that it involved discrimination on the ground of caste and therefore, it was invalid. I have carefully studied both these judgments of the Supreme Court and with all respect to the judges of the Supreme Court, I cannot help saying that I find this judgment to be utterly unsatisfactory.

Shri Naziruddin Ahmad (West Bengal)

Sir, on a point of order. Is it in order for any Member to express disrespect to the highest judiciary in the land? It is the custom in Parliament not to speak disparagingly about the courts.

Dr. Ambedkar

There is no disparagement of the learned judges at all.

Mr. Speaker

I myself felt that the word should not have been used but I think what the hon. Law Minister meant was that the judgment was unsatisfactory from the point of view of what the Government proposed to do.

Dr. Ambedkar

The judgment does not appear to be in consonance with the articles of the Constitution. That is my point.

Mr. Speaker

I am afraid the hon. Minister will not be in order to pass any such strictures on any judgment expressed by the Supreme Court.

Dr. Ambedkar

I am very sorry.

Mr. Speaker

I was thinking whether what he expressed was not capable of a different interpretation viz., that the judgment was unsatisfactory from the point of view of what the Government proposed to do.

The Minister of Home Affairs (Shri Rajagopalachari)

Will the hon. Speaker forgive my intervention? I think really what the hon. Law Minister meant is that a doubt has arisen on account of the judgment.

Mr. Speaker

Let us now proceed.

Dr. Ambedkar

My view is that in Article 29, clause (2), the most important word is 'only'. No distinction shall be made on the ground only of race, religion, or sex. The word 'only' is very important. It does not exclude any distinction being made on grounds other than those mentioned in this article and I respectfully submit that the word 'only' did not receive the same consideration which it ought to have received.

Then with regard to Article 16, clause (4), my submission is this that it is really impossible to make any reservation which would not result in excluding somebody who has a caste. I think it has to be borne in mind and it is one of the fundamental principles which I believe is stated in Mulla's last edition on the very first page that there is no Hindu who has not a caste. Every Hindu has a caste— he is either a Brahmin or a Mahratta or a Kunby or a Kumbhar or a carpenter. There is no Hindu—that is the fundamental position—who has not a caste. Consequently, if you make a reservation in favour of what are called backward classes which are nothing else but a collection of certain castes, those who are excluded are persons who belong to certain castes. Therefore, it is impossible to avoid reservation without excluding some people who have got a caste. On these points I do not think personally that the judgment is a very satisfactory judgment. In this connection I would like to state, notwithstanding what the House and some Members are saying, that I have often in the course of my practice told the presiding judge in very emphatic terms that I am bound to obey his judgment but I am not bound to respect it. That is the liberty which every lawyer enjoys in telling the judge that his judgment is wrong and I am not prepared to give up that liberty. I have always told the judges before whom I practised that that is my view of the matter. Now the point has to be borne in mind that in Article 46 of the Directive Principles an obligation has been laid upon the Government to do everything possible in order to promote the welfare and the interest of what are called the weaker sections of the public by which I understand to mean the backward classes or such other classes who are for the moment not able to stand on their legs—the scheduled castes and the scheduled tribes. It is therefore incumbent not merely on the Government but upon this Parliament to do everything in its hands to see that article 46 is fulfilled and if that fulfilment is to come, I cannot see how one can escape an amendment so as to prevent Article 29, clause (2), and Article 16, clause (4) being interpreted in the way in which it has been interpreted and being made to block the advancement of the people who are spoken of as the weaker class. That is the necessity for amending Article 15...[16]

Shri Ethirajulu Naidu (Mysore)

...I now propose to deal with Article 15(3) which is sought to be amended. May I say that we are very much indebted to the hon. Prime Minister for raising this very human and national problem into a higher plane and lifting it from the morass of communal and caste politics which has gathered round it; for, lifting it out of this sphere and putting it on that psychological plane, enables us to look at this problem in its real perspective without the prejudices and other disturbing factors that may otherwise gather round it. I do not want to tread on anybody's corns. But I would say this: for historical or other reasons a situation has arisen in most States where one or two sections have intellectually advanced far beyond the rest of the community. Out of that other consequences flow—their predominance in the services, in the educational institutions, their ability to secure seats in technical colleges and professional colleges, etc. This creates a vicious circle. Just as rivers flow into the ocean, the forward classes get more and more forward and the backward classes recede further backward. Therefore, a conscious effort is necessary if the backward classes are to be pulled up. It may be partly due to their lethargy, and partly due to circumstances over which they have no control. The Prime Minister has often said that the future lies in the hands of engineers and technicians and that the days of the lawyers are over. But I am more concerned with the first part of his statement that the future lies in the hands of engineers. technicians, doctors and scientists. And unfortunately it so happens that it is in these institutions that accommodation is limited. In regard to this I can do no better than quote the words of the Prime Minster himself, uttered when he moved the motion. In his own way he said that there was a static state of things and if we are to move forward, as we propose to do, a certain amount of dynamic effort is necessary. And then he continued:

> "But sometimes in this intervening period difficulties arose, because we have not got enough provision, let us say, for giving a certain type of education, technical or other. The question arose whether we should give some reasonable encouragement and opportunity for that education to be given to members of the backward classes, which otherwise, without that encouragement and opportunity, they may not get at all, so that they remain where they are and we cannot pull them up.

Therefore, the object of this amendment is to lay stress on this."

Now, that being so, how is that purpose to be achieved? It is sought to be achieved by amending Article 15(3). I would bring it to the notice of the members of the Select Committee that that does not serve the purpose. The judgment of the Supreme Court was based on an interpretation of clause (2) of Article 29, and they went further and said that in that light it was unnecessary to consider the provisions of Articles 14 and 15. I have got a copy of that judgment, and that is what they say. When they base their decision on an article of the Constitution and we find that the intention of the Constituent Assembly was something different, the appropriate thing to do would be to amend that article on which the judgment is based. I would therefore suggest—it may not be too late—I would suggest it to the Select Committee and I would press it on the Prime Minister as well as the Government that Article 29(2) itself may be amended so that there may be no doubt left as to the intention that is sought to be achieved. Or, alternatively, I would suggest that Article 15(3) may be amended in such a way as to override the effect of Articles 14 and 15 and clause(2) of Article 29. That view has been expressed by my hon. friend Mr. Kamath, Mr. Symnandan Sahaya and Mr. Shankaraiya and other hon. friends who have spoken before me. There is a conflict in amending Article 15(3) without amending Article 29(2). It may again be a case of our meaning one thing and not expressing it clearly, and again the matter may be taken to the courts. I am further heartened in this matter because the Prime Minister while speaking about this amendment more than once expressed himself that he would welcome an addition to these words or a change so that the intention may be made clear.

Before I conclude I would express one sentiment. It is not a matter of putting the wording of a clause in a particular way or amending an article in a particular way. The primary purpose is to adjust these human relationships which unfortunately are now in conflict on account of these factors. Constitutions and laws must change to meet this supreme need. We who claim to represent the masses cannot remain indifferent to their aspirations, indifferent to their progress, and allow them to remain in their backward condition and at the same time claim to represent them or to demand their support.[17]

Shri Ramalingam Chettiar (Madras)

...I will first say a few words about the amendment relating to the question of the Communal G.O. as it is callled in the Madras State. I was never an admirer of the Communal G.O. I may say at once. But at the same time the principle underlying that Communal G.O. is a matter which will have to be considered very deeply, and I am very glad to say that the Constitution as framed embodies the principle that underlines the Communal G.O. The first provision that it has made is for social justice. There ought to be justice among all the communities. You cannot prefer or give an advantage to one community as against the other. The second principle that is enunciated is that the weaker sections of the community should be helped to come up. That again is an unexceptionable provision which will have to be borne in mind making provisions for the advancement of the several sections of the community. And thirdly, it has also been recognised in Article 16 of the Constitution that the unrepresented communities in the services should be given preference so that they may have their due share in the administration of the country. These are all principles which are unexceptionable. But unless they are given effect to in the spirit in which they have been framed, there will be no sort of social justice in the country. The question is whether the provisions that are made in the other clauses carry out the principles that are enunciated.

This question of discrimination mentioned in clause 15 is put very widely and whether or not it really contravenes the other clauses in the Bill and what it really means are all matters that have to be considered carefully. The matter has gone up to the Supreme Court and the Supreme Court has stated that this applies both to giving some preference to the education of the backward classes and also for giving some special representation to unrepresented classes in the services. As I said in the beginning, I am not a supporter of the Communal G.O. as framed. The chief difficulty of the Communal G.O. is that it specifies the proportion of appointments or the proportion of admissions that will have to be made. If, on the other hand, the provision that is made relates to some preference being given to those classes which are backward. I think that principle cannot be attacked in view of the principles already contained in the Constitution itself. The question now is the Government has found it necessary to amend article 15 to meet the difficulties that have been raised by the Supreme Court.

The question is whether the amendment that is proposed is adequate to meet the difficulties that have been felt. The two difficulties that have been met with are (1) admission to educational institutions and (2) the representation of the unrepresented classes in the services. These are the two matters about which the Supreme Court has expressed itself and this present amendment is intended, as was explained, to meet those difficulties. I should think that the amendment as proposed will not meet the difficulties. It is not framed in such a way as to meet the difficulties at all. In the first place the amendment says: "or for educational, economic or social advancement of any backward class". What do you mean by the "backward class"? It is not defined anywhere. The Governments also in the States have got their lists of backward communities for different purposes. They sometimes are satisfactory and sometimes they are not. What is contemplated in the Constitution itself is not a question of merely 'backward classes' in the sense that there are lists of backward communities in the several States and they will have to be helped. What is provided for in the Constitution is, as I said, those communities which are not represented in the services are mentioned in Article 16. Whether they are backward communities or they are forward communities is a question that will always be in doubt. For instance, a person belonging to the Vaisya caste who may be rich, but whose caste will be educationally very backward and probably none of whose members will be represented in the State services, will that person be considered as a backward person or not? If you are going to do social justice, it cannot be done merely by saying that if he is rich in one matter, he need not have any share in the Government of the country. That is not a position which will be either good for the country or safe in the interests of the general advancement of the country.

What is meant by this discrimination and all these differences and things like that? When we are talking about this, we are talking merely in terms of the marks obtained in the examinations. Is that the proper standard? When there is a question raised, for instance, in Madras, that Brahmins are discriminated against, all that is said is that some Brahmin boys who got more marks in an examination have not been admitted and that some boys belonging to other communities who got less marks have been admitted. Is that the proper test? There are technical colleges all over the country. What has been the result of the training that we have been giving in these technical colleges? I can speak for Madras. Take for instance, the agricultural college. There have been so many thousands of boys who have been turned out of the college. How many of them have taken to agriculture? Are these degrees in the agricultural colleges considered merely as a passport for service in the civil departments? For purposes of manufacturing merely clerks, are we going to give preference to persons who have got more marks, for instance, in mathematics or in some other subject, for admission to the agricultural college and therby deflect all the money that you are spending for enabling these boys to get jobs in the civil departments? Should you not discriminate in favour of those boys who are likely to make use of the special technical knowledge they are given by taking to agriculture? Similarly with reference to the engineering college. For instance, most of the boys who pass from the engineering college only find employment in the civil services of the State. Those who are acquiring the technical knowledge during their education are not using that special knowledge for the purpose of advancing the interests of the country or entering into the particular professions for which they are being trained.

So, it seems to me that the tests that we are applying are not the proper tests. It ought to be a test with reference to the use to which the knowledge they gained in the technical colleges is likely to be utilised. That ought to be the test and if that is going to be the test, the mere test of marks in an examination—very often it has nothing to do with the technical college to which admission is sought—will not be the proper way of dealing with the thing. So it seems to me what ought to be done is a matter of liberalising these admissions, not with reference to the marks obtained in the Intermediate or the B.A. or the Schools Final but with reference to the possibility of the students who are seeking admission utilising the knowledge they gained for the purposes for which they are going to be trained. If there is going to be a liberalisation in that way, probably it will meet at least half of the difficulty that is met with at the present moment.

So it seems to me that the present amendment that is proposed will not meet the difficulties of the situation. It will have to be considered seriously whether the amendment to article 15 alone will solve the difficulties that we are meeting with and whether we ought not to amend the other articles, for instance, the article relating to admission to educational institutions and to appointments in such a way that the difficulties we are experiencing will be met properly and not have the effect of a sort of white wash like the amendment that is being proposed. I hope the Select Committee will seriously consider the problems they have to meet and they will frame the amendments in such a way that the problems are met and not merely bring a sort of a white-washing amendment and just as a salve to the conscience of the people who are dealing with it.[18]

Ch. Ranbir Singh

..The other issue concerns the granting of concessions to the backward classes. In this country the backward classes constitute from 80 to 85 per cent. of the total population. The public opinion, should you desire to know it, is very clear on this point. If, however, you mean to elicit the exploiters' opinion, then that too is quite clear. They are not in favour of this amendment. As things stand, the exploiters form a very small minority while the exploited constitute a large majority in this country. So far as an accurate viewpoint is concerned, it has been placed before the House by our respected leader hon. Shri Jawaharlal Nehru and as far the opinion of the exploiting section is concerned, every hon. Member of the House is quite aware of that....[19]

Shri Jawaharlal Nehru

...May I now go back to Article 15? I tried to make clear on the last occasion when I spoke that in what we were trying to add there was really not the slightest attempt at changing the Constitution or amending it in any real sense. It was to lay a certain emphasis on something which had been adequately emphasised in other parts of the Constitution, but again because some doubts had arisen; it is perfectly true that those doubts had arisen in another connection. Although there is a connection, nevertheless it is another matter. Looking at that narrow issue that arose in Madras, for my part this amendment, I should like to say, is not intended to be a communal amendment, or to help in any way a communal approach to this problem. We must distinguish between the communal approach and the approach of helping one of our weaker, backward brothers and sisters. And, if I may say so, although it is my amendment, thinking about it I do not particularly like the words "backward class of citizens", and I hope the Select Committee may find a better wording. What I mean is this: It is the backward individual citizen that we should help. Why should we brand groups and classes into backward and forward?

Several Hon. Member

That is the point

Shri Jawaharlal Nehru

However, it is a fact that certain groups or classes

are backward, but I do not wish to brand them as such or treat them as such.

Shri Sidhwa

The order itself says. "communal".

Shri Jawaharlal Nehru

In this connection, may I say that perhaps a group or class which deserves greater sympathy from this House are tribal folk, whether in the North-East Frontier tract or in Central India or elsewhere. We have many of our colleagues in this House representing the scheduled castes and they help us not only in our work but keep us up to the mark in regard to the necessities of the scheduled castes, but we have very few persons in this House to speak for the scheduled tribes. Therefore, it should be the peculiar concern and care of this House to look after the interests of the scheduled tribes and their advancement in every way, and when we add these words to Article 15, or may be any other words in addition to them, we certainly include the scheduled tribes...[20]

After this reply of Pandit Nehru, the motion to refer the Bill to the Select Committee was adopted.[21]

In the Select Committee the proposed amendment to Article 15 underwent some changes. Many members, even Pandit Nehru, the Mover of the Bill, were not happy with the wording of the proposed amendment which was for insertion of the following words at the end of clause (3) of Article 15: "or for the educational, economic or social advancement of any backward class of citizens". Honouring the views of the Members that the clause should be couched in such a language as to ward off the effect of clause (2) of Article 29, the Select Committee redrafted it and made it an independent clause as follows:

> Nothing in this article or in Article 29 shall prevent the State from making any special provision for the advancement of any socially and educationally backward class of citizens or for the Scheduled Castes and Tribes.

The Report of the Select Committee to amend the

Constitution of India was presented to the Parliament on May 25, 1951, by the Prime Minister[22] who on May 29, 1951 moved a resolution in the Parliament for taking into consideration this Bill, as amended by the Select Committee.[23] The debate that followed lasted three days—May 29, 30 and 31, 1951. Fourteen Members participated in the deliberations at this stage. Though the Members were more concerned with the amendments to Article 19, nine of them seized this opportunity to express their opinion on the desirability of the proposed amendment to Article 15. While generally welcoming this amendment, the Members again apprehended that this provision might be abused for party reasons. Prof. Shah criticised this amendment for laying a new emphasis on "class consciousness", or backwardness of certain classes, rather than of citizens as a body.

The relevant portion of the debate having a bearing on this provision of the Constitution is reproduced below:

Shri Jawaharlal Nehru

...Now I come to deal with those three specific articles to which a great deal of argument has been attached. There is Article 15(2) or 15(4) as it is proposed to make it, that is to say, the clause which says that nothing in Article 15(2) or in Article 29(2) should come in the way of our making special provisions for certain groups or classes etc. which are not defined exactly but indicated there. I wonder if the House remembers that when I referred to this during the earlier stages of this Bill I mentioned that by an oversight the Bill as printed then had left out a small but rather important matter, that is, in clause relating to Article 15 we had said at that time in the printed Bill that nothing in Article 15(2) will come in the way etc. What we had intended saying—in fact what we had decided to say was that "nothing in article 15 or in Article 29(2)" but unfortunately owing to a slight error, the words "Article 29(2)" were left out. I mention this clearly merely to indicate that this was not an afterthought on our part. It was an error for which I take full share. It was not an after thought to include Article 29(2) because we had decided about it previous to putting it in the Bill. There were two views in regard to Article 29(2). It was the view of many eminent people that Article 29(2) in this particular context does not affect the matter at all. It does not come in the way at all, and yet, in another context Article 29(2) had been referred and because of the certain doubt in people's minds that although the best opinion was that it does not come in the way, nevertheless, there was a hesitation or doubt and we thought that that doubt should be removed.

Without going into the details of this article or of the amendment proposed I wish to say a few words about—shall I say—our basic ideas on this subject. Why have we done this and why has it been thought that these articles come in the way of doing something that we wish to do? The House knows very well and there is no need for trying to hush it up, that this particular matter in this particular shape arose because of certain happenings in Madras. Because the Government of the State of Madras issued a G.O.—I do not know the details of it—by making certain reservations etc. for certain classes or certain communities—rather for all communities—and the High Court of Madras said that this G.O. was not in order, was against the spirit or letter of the Constitution etc. I do not for an instant challenge the right of the High Court of Madras to pass that order. Indeed from a certain point of view it seems to me, if I may say so with all respect, that their argument was quite sound and valid. That is to say, if communities as such are brought into the picture, it does go against certain explicit or implied provisions of the Constitution. Nevertheless, while that is quite valid and we bow to the decision of the High Court of Madras in that matter, the fact remains that we have to deal with the situation where for a variety of causes for which the present generation is not to blame, the past has the responsibility, there are groups, classes, individuals, communities, if you like, who are backward. They are backward in many ways—economically, socially, educationally—sometimes they are not backward in one of these respects and yet backward in another. The fact is therefore that if we wish to encourage them in regard to these matters, we have to do something special for them. We come up against this difficulty that we talk on the one hand in our Directive Principles of Policy of removing inequalities, in raising people up in every way—socially, educationally, economically, reducing the distances which separate groups or classes of individuals from each other, we cannot make a fool a wise-man or make a wise-man a fool, individuals are clever or not clever, individuals are tall or short, thin or fat and nobody tries to have similar rotundity either in the mind or body but we do wish to give the same opportunities to everyone so that he can take full advantage of those opportunities and grow to the full stature as far as that stature allows it and if anything comes in the way of achieving this, we should remove that. It is not an easy matter, it is not a thing to be done quickly and suddenly when we have a vast population.

Yet, again, there is one Member who has pointed out in his minute of dissent that when we talk of people or groups as backward, whom are we thinking of. Because 80 per cent.—I do not know what percentage it is—are backward in all these respects. That is perfectly true and yet we have to tackle the problem. It is not good saying that because 80 per cent are backward, so we must accept the position. We have to give them opportunities—economic opportunities, educational opportunities and the like. Now in doing that we have been told that we come up against some provisions in the Constitution which rather lay down some principles of equality or some principles of non-discrimination etc. So we arrive at a peculiar tangle. We cannot have equality because in trying to attain equality we come up against some principles of equality. That is a very peculiar position. We cannot have equality because we cannot have non-discrimination because if you think in terms of giving a lift up to those who are down, you are somehow affecting the present status quo undoubtedly. Therefore you are said to be discriminating because you are affecting the present *satus quo*. Therefore if this argument is correct, then we cannot make any major change in that respect because every change means a change in the *status quo*, whether economic or in the sphere of public or private activity. Whatever law you may make, you have to come to grips with this subject in some other way.

Take another very important approach of ours, that is, in our attempt gradually or rapidly to realize an egalitarian society or some society where these differences are not great, apart from national or physical differences etc., in our attempt to do that, we want to put an end to or try to put an end to all those infinite divisions that have grown up in our social life or in our social structure—we may call them by any name you like, the caste system or religious divisions etc. There are of course economic divisions but we realize them and we try to deal with them not always very satisfactorily. But in a structure that has grown up—quite apart from the religious point of view or the philosophical aspect of it—this is the structure of society with its vast numbers of fissures or divisions etc. Now, to get rid of that in order to build, not only to give opportunity to each individual in India to grow but also to build up a united nation where each individual does not think so much of his particular groups or caste but thinks of the larger community—that is one of our objectives. On the other hand while that may be our objective, the fact remains that there are these larger numbers of divisions and fissures in our social life, though I think they are growing less. We are gradually obliterating all those hard and fast laws that divide them but nevertheless the process is slow and we cannot ignore the present. We cannot ignore existing facts. Therefore one has to keep a balance between the existing fact as we find it and the objective and ideal that we aim at. If we stick to the existing fact alone, then we are static and unchanging and we give up all the objectives we have or the Directive Principles of Policy that are laid down in the Constitution. That of course we cannot do, and must not do. On the other hand if we talk only about those Directive Principles etc. ignoring existing facts, then we talk logic and we may talk fine sense even in a way but it has no relation to facts and it becomes artificial, it becomes slightly adventurish and therefore not realistic enough.

So we have to find a middle way, that is keeping with the objective or the ideal in view, taking steps which gradually carry us in that direction and yet not ignoring the existing facts with which we have to deal. We have to deal with them anyhow, even if you have to deal with it in the sense of fighting against the existing situation.

These were the difficulties and the House will understand that in grappling with this problem one can lay emphasis on this aspect or that aspect of it, because both aspects are important and the real difficulty comes in finding a balance between the two. It is very easy to say to any Member that it is a simple problem which requires an aye or nay. This is good or that is bad. But normally the problems we have to face cannot be answered easily by ayes and nays. We have to consider them in the total context of things. We have to consider them in their relation to a hundred other things and thereby bring the ideal into some relation to the actual. These were the matters at the back of our minds as we discussed this matter from hour to hour in the Select Committee.

I think I may say with perfect truth that every single Member of the Select Committee recognised the desirability of giving these opportunities for growth to those who in any sense may be considered backward. There was no doubt in any Member's mind but what some Members were afraid of in doing so was, might not this be abused, might this be utilised for the accentuation of the very class or communal divisions which have done us so much injury and which we have been trying to get rid of. This fact troubled and rightly troubled their minds as it must trouble the House and each one of us. So we tried to find a middle way and I submit that the wording we have adopted in this article is more or less a successful way of meeting this difficulty and finding the middle way.

You must have read an earlier paragraph in the report which says:

"Some apprehensions have been expressed in respect to this amendment. The Select Committee is of the view that this provision is not likely to be, and cannot indeed be, misused by any Government for perpetuating any class discrimination against the spirit of the Constitution, or for treating non-backward classes as backward for the purpose of conferring privileges on them."

We have said so and we earnestly hope that if and when this provision is passed it will not be misused. Nobody can guarantee against misuse or some kind of special or undesirable use by any authority of any provision you may make. We can only try our best to create the conditions where this would not be so. What I wish to assure this House about is this, that we are alive to the possibility of this kind of thing being used for a particular purpose to which we are opposed. And may I say also that when we talked with certain persons, including the Chief Minister of Madras Government, they also told us that they realised our difficulty, they appreciated it and they had no desire to function exactly in that way which people feared. So I would commend this particular amendment of Article 15 to the House...[24]

Prof. K.T. Shah (Bihar)

...You will agree that the Constitution is, whatever its stability in times of emergency or revolution, a sacred thing, with which we have to work. Changes, therefore, in its very basic articles should not be undertaken very lightly. For instance, this question of special provision for the so-called "backward classes of citizens" is liable, not only to a misdirection of the entire system of Constitutional life we hope to live in this country, but it is liable even to be abused for party reasons. I hold, therefore, the view that, if you really think of this country's millions, educationally, socially or economically deficient, backwardness is the rule, and forwardness is the exception, if at all. It was I who has said that it is something like 80 per cent. of the population which is illiterate; and if you take women only, perhaps 95 per cent is illiterate. On this matter we have got a whole Chapter of Directive Principles of Policy, which though not "justiciable", are certainly intended to embody the intention of Government, and enshrine our ideals of the life to be in this country. We have yet to give concrete shape to those heads which would change the "backwardness" into something like a normal, reasonable standard of living and working for the masses of our people. In this connection, may I add that we are passing through an age when idealism is very much at a discount; and those who are charged with holding ideals are usually ridiculed as lacking in a sense of practical statesmanship. I plead guilty to that. I am afraid that no matter what ridicules showered upon me may be, no matter what the prophets of realism may insist upon—I shall remain incorrigible in this regard. It is therefore, impossible for me to overlook the force of the ideals embodies in the Chapter on Directives of Policy. My greatest regret is that this Government has not yet been able to implement substantially, or even upto a reasonable extent, many of the great things promised in this Chapter, so that the Chapter remains so much paper promises, or eye-wash; and that, in reality, these prophets of realism and practical wisdom do not insist upon giving effect to any of these, notwithstanding their claims for realism in this regard.

The amendment now proposed to be made is, thus, not only offending against all the grandiose promises which were equally held out to all, but lays a new emphasis on "class consciousness", or backwardness of certain classes, rather than of citizens as a body. This, in my opinion, is highly objectionable. We shall consider that matter when the amendment comes up specifically on that subject. But I cannot help feeling that, notwithstanding the actual language embodied,—which includes a reference to both Articles 15 and 29(2)—what is stated in the amendment is positive, not negative, whereas 29(2) lays it down in negative terms that no citizen shall be barred from any educational institutions on grounds of race, cread, class, etc. In this amendment we are proposing—and please do not misunderstand me. I am not against the basic idea of this amendment,—we are authorising and permitting special provision being made for "backward classes of citizens" educationally or socially. The word "economically" does not find any place here. I will try to place the matter more clearly before the House when the time comes. But here I must add that the educational, social and material development of the "backward classes" is a sacred obligation, which none of us deny. The hon. Prime Minister was only just when he said that every Member of the Select Committee, and I am sure every Member of this House, shares that desire with him. But when you think of it with the background of the history that we have had, we cannot but recognise that it would be the word "classes" that would be stressed, and not the "citizens". It is, therefore, my regret that the amendment does not really carry the intention, either of the Chapter of Directives, or of the sponsor of the Bill into effect in that regard.

The greatest need in this country at the moment is bread; and according to the calculation that I have personally made two out of three citizens of this country do not get even one meal out of three that are necessary to keep body and soul together; and that, too, of the coarsest, the poorest and the scantiest. If 3,600 calories are supposed to be necessary, according to the experts of the League of Nations, for keeping the human body in a condition to work efficiently, we in this country hardly get 1,200 on an average. And believe me, the term "average" is very misleading; it is a fallacious idea. The average is not the actual or real for vast masses of our country. It is the flat level, the average, over millions of this country, where perhaps one per cent owns and monopolises one-third of the total wealth of the country, and two-third may not get even half the "average" for each of them. The average of 1,200 calories would mean less than 600 per day for each one of 67 per cent of the population. If, as the Planning Commission has told us, the average per capita income in this country in 1948-49 was Rs. 265, the actual per capita income for 25 crores, perhaps, of our people would work out at less than Rs. 12 per month, a very poor, misleading, insufficient standard of living. Your Chapter of Directives has declared that a normal standard of living shall be secured for all. Here you are providing, by a specific amendment of the Constitution, special facilities for what you expressly state as "backward classes of citizens". That would naturally draw attention, focus attention, upon "classes" rather than upon "citizens"; and, if I may say so, throws the larger problem that is facing us, the people and the rulers of this country, somewhat in the background, to the advantage only of certain classes which may be more vocal but to the disadvantage of the masses as a whole...[25]

Shri Naziruddin Ahmad

..Without going into details I should submit with regard to the amendment of Article 15 that though on principle it is very good and an attractive looking thing, yet believe there is considerable amount of Madras politics behind it. It is an open secret..

Dr. Deshmukh

It is an all-India problem, my dear friend.

Shri Naziruddin Ahmed

Quite so, but it arose from Madras politics. It is an open secret that there is a good deal of discussion and also passion attached to this. Though the article as it now stands is not open to much theoretical objection I think the House should express its desire that it should be properly and fairly worked. The objections were so insistent that even the Select Committee has added a note of warning providing some consolation to those who might be affected by it. Things are not what they really seem.[26]

Rev. D'Souza (Madras)

...I now come to a point of very great importance to those of us who know conditions in the Madras province—I refer to the amendments to Article 15 making provision for a certain degree of assistance to backward groups, or as they are called, classes or communities. I have again absolutely no doubt that when the Constitution was framed and discussed and passed, it was the intention of all without any exception that some provision should be made for the uplifting of backward classes so that they might come to a degree of contentment and live in happy cooperation with those whom they consider to be the more fortunate citizens of this country.

There was no doubt whatever about what was to be done for what are called scheduled castes and scheduled tribes. Having been in touch with this question—to put it very plainly with the well-known frequently referred to Government Order of the Madras Government—and having had considerable experience of admission in colleges during the last eighteen or twenty years, I was aware of the gravity of that problem and the difficulty of solving it by a very simple formula. Sympathising as I do profoundly with those who maintain that talent should not be penalised, that the best brains in the province and in the country should be made available for professional, for technical or for Government service, nevertheless, I realise that owing to a play of historic circumstances, to the evolution of social history of our country, there were groups, there were classes, there were, may be, individuals—in whatever manner you may describe them as communities or as castes without bringing in the notion of religion, but only of race—who could not get the chance which they deserved and who in the long run might be deprived of all social and economic equality without which legal equality would be useless.

I realised the difficulty of this and in practice even when the Government Order did not rigidly apply to private institutions, such as those with which I was associated, we tried to enforce the spirit of it, meeting nevertheless the legitimate demands of the other school of opinion also, I believe from the example of private institutions a workable solution and a formula could be arrived at in which the difficulties would be overcome and the unacceptable features of the earlier order might be modified.

Therefore, when this discussion took place, some of my Madras friends asked me: "Do you think that this Article 29(2) is going to prevent us from applying that Government Order?" My impression was as I told them, that I did not believe that was possible, because the spirit of the Constitution, taken as a whole, whatever may be the wording of this clause, the implication of the Constitution, the general bearing of it, the Directive Principles as well as the specific provisions made for the scheduled castes and the scheduled tribes, included in its scope the spirit of the Madras Government Order also as it had come to be accepted in its broad outline. I knew there was some difference of opinion in my province in regard to the application of it in this or that particular aspect in which really deserving people were not helped and perhaps less deserving people by a mere mechanical enumeration got the help which was intended to be given to really derserving people. These things can be adjusted. But I believe this amendment which has been introduced does give the hope of what I may call an agreed solution by which the controverted portion of the earlier order which were not acceptable to a very large section in the province might be modified, and the just desires and claims, and the need for their satisfaction which the backward elements really do deserve, might be recognised. Before we harden and crystalise and fossilise into a ligalistic interpretation of the Constitution, the larger objective of a more homogeneous political community based on social and economic eqality, must be achieved. That I understand is the purpose of this amendment and therefore I think that we should subscribe to it, vote for it with full conviction, as I shall certainly do.

One point more I may be permitted to bring out on this important occasion, when by a happy chance I have the good fortune of presenting to a fuller House than I ever remember to have secured on any earlier occasions. Some objection seems to have been raised to the wording of this clause. Objection has beeen made to the wording of this because the word 'communities' comes back. I understand the difficulty. The word 'communities' implies something communal, and in our country the word 'communal' has meant religious differences and animosities. It has been the source of great suffering and tragedy in the country, and is likely to be a possible source of future tragedies. Therefore it is perfectly right that those who wanted to introduce the amendment should take away all notion of religious differences from it and confine it to the economically backward groups and families. I understand this. I would therefore make an appeal to the House to consider this, although you may use the word 'caste' or 'community' for practical purposes, do not, I pray, use it as implying specific religious beliefs. On this subject, I have received repeated representations and have had the honour and privilege of transmitting these representations to the hon. the Prime Minister and to the President. And we have received the assurance that even among the scheduled castes the mere fact of religion, which does not make any difference in their social and economic condition, should not stand in the way of their receiving the ameliorations which have been promised by the Constitution. And I was proud and happy that the spirit of the Constitution should have been so interpreted by our most honoured leader and by our President. I appeal to this House to see to it that the spirit of those declarations may be applied integrally and sincerely by the Provinces so that this great step forward in the political homogeneity of our country may be carried out, that if there are backward classes or minorities, they may be recognised on a linguistic or racial or cultural basis. It is impossible to overlook the fact of "backwardness", it will persist for a long time, but in this matter religious differences and cleavages must be ignored; race or culture may certainly be recognised to determine the groups which need assistance but no distinction should be made in regard to religious conviction which is a matter of personal conscience. I therefore request my respected friends, the representatives of the scheduled castes who are present here not to oppose these concessions and help being given to their kinsmen who till yesterday were with them and who today share the same conditions in regard to social and personal relationships, the same economic and educational conditions as they themselves, not to refuse these concessions and help to those who, by a personal decision have chosen Christianity for their faith. Christianity is one of the religions of our land. It has flourished here for two thousand years, from the very dawn of its history; it has contributed its own share to the culture of our land, an element genuinely Indian and destined to be part of Indian culture till the end of time.

I have said these things with a certain amount of feeling. I wished to have an opportunity of expressing this, and at the same time of expressing my deep satisfaction that it is along the spirit that I have indicated that these amendments have also been framed, and it is my earnest hope that along these same lines this amendment will be interpreted and applied more and more widely as days go on...[27]

Dr. S.P. Mookerjee

...With regard to Article 29(2) I do not wish to speak in details. The Prime Minister said yesterday and we all agreed with him that there is complete unanimity of opinion inside this House and in fact in the country as a whole that everything possible should be done to give the fullest possible facilities to the backward classes. That is a principle on which we stand. There can be no question or dispute about it. If we allow the backward classes or those who are educationally, socially or economically far behind other classes or people to continue as they are, it will be disastrous, not for them but for the entire country. But that has to be done and in a manner which will obtain the utmost support of the entire people of this country. The fear is that if you amend Article 15 in a way which will make it possible to make discrimination or discriminate in a way which may not really help those who are backward but may do something else or prevent people who belong to some castes, who are more intelligent or advanced, from getting what is due to them, then difficulties and controversies are bound to arise. Here is a question of arriving at some such formula which will make it possible for us to help the backward people as also to see that it is not abused. The Select Committee in its report has mentioned this point, but I would like if the clause can itself be amended in an agreed manner so that this point of view can be specifically mentioned there. Unfortunately, it has been left in the hands of any State. If the power could have been given to the President to see to it that this is not abused, well, that would have been some guarantee; or, if you say that reasonable provision should be made—not a question of special provision—then also no State will venture to go out of its way and do something which will be against the interest of the general public as a whole...[28]

Pandit Thakur Das Bhargava

...In regard to Article 15 I would submit that that change which Government has made is also a salutary one. We in this House made provisions in regard to scheduled castes and scheduled tribes and backward classes, and we want that all these pople may come up to the standard of the rest of the country. How can that be done unless they get educational facilities and seats in the Universities? That is the only ladder by which they can get up to the coveted place. If a special provision is made for securing seats to these people, Article 29(2) will not be offended. Suppose 25 per cent of the seats are secured to the scheduled castes and scheduled tribes and backward classes. Out of the rest 75 per cent no distinction will be made between the other classes. That is the right view, I think, I am rather afraid that this provision may be misused by non-backward people to get into reserved seats. But I should trust to the sense of the Central Government and the Local Governments in this respect. I was anxious and I proposed while I was in the Constituent Assembly that 'backward classes' should be defined in a manner that sheduled castes and scheduled tribes and some of those who were just above the level of the scheduled castes and tribes were included in it. But at that time I did not succeed. I hope that the definition now given in this clause will be taken as a good one, because it indicates that only socially and educationally backward classes coming under article 340 of the Constitution are to be included and no others.

I am rather doubtful whether you will be able to do much, and I am rather critical of the action of the Government in this respect. My own feeling is that Government has done very little for the scheduled castes and backward classes during the last four years. I wish something more were done. I wish that all that they can possibly do was done. The period provided for achieving the object is ten years and if during four years we have not done anything how will we succeed in seeing that they rise up in the social and educational standard of this country? My submission is rather than fighting for words let us all try and let the whole country declare that all jobs in this country for the coming five years will be given to such deserving people belonging to the scheduled castes, scheduled tribes and backward classes as can be found. That seems to me to be the way to do it. I wish that the Commissioner was at once appointed and that he began to function. I am glad to find that something has been done in the States, but whatever we wanted has not been done so far...[29]

Prof. S.N. Mishra (Bihar)

..By introducing an amendment to Article 15 we are in a way giving formal recognition to the sublime ideal of Sarvodaya, according to which those who are on the lowest rung of the social ladder must be helped towards progress and advancement in different spheres of life[30]... Then I come to Article 15. Let us not forget that there are millions of people submerged in poverty, filth and squalor, and something special and urgent has to be done for them if they are not to remain like that for ever. But when we proceed and want to do something, the doctrine of 'non-discrimination' or the doctrine of equality begins to operate. That is what we are faced with at the present moment and what the Government of Madras was faced with in many cases. But I would like to ask the House as to what exactly is the meaning of equality? What exactly is the meaning of non-discrimination? Does it mean that there should be absolutely no distinction between the sick and the healthy and that we should not accord special treatment and special diet for the return of the sick to normalcy of health? A certain amount of suspicion has been aroused in this connection, however. And probably not without reason. That suspicion is that the remedy may degenerate into the disease itself and those who are real claimants may be elbowed out of the queue and ulterior considerations may prevail. As the Prime Minister referred yesterday there is just a possibility, if we are not very careful, just and cautious, that the accentuation of class distinction or caste distinction might take place. But if we have our standard as vigilant as the Prime Minister who always thinks about a just and equalitarian Social order, there need be no apprehension on that score...[31]

Dr. Deshmukh (Madhya Pradesh)

...So far as Article 15 was concerned, it should not be understood that the situation has arisen only in Madras and the amendment has been proposed only to remove those difficulties. If what has happened in Madras can be any lesson to us, it will have to be realised and borne in mind that similar difficulties are bound to arise in other parts also. It may be that people in other parts—the backward classes—are not yet so conscious as to assert their wishes and are prepared to put up with a whole-sale exploitation on uncertain grounds of merit and denied any opportunity of education and advancement. But that cannot remain so very long. Thanks to the freedom we have attained people are getting conscious of their rights and in the name of justice and equality that we have preached in the Preamble and our desire to help the weaker and backward classes to come forward it is very necessary that adequate chances should be afforded to these people at least to get education. If we want them to do this, if we have sympathy for them—and it has been now fairly established in the House that every Member of the House has great sympathy for the backward elements in the society—then it is our duty to see that they get a chance to go to the best institutions and receive education which will put them on certain level of advancement and progress. I hope there will be no speech which will try to minimize the importance of this amendment or try to take away the force of it. I would have certainly liked a little stronger expressions used so as to obviate any fear or suspicion that this again may be questioned and there might be delay in enforcing what we have agreed to. My intention in proposing certain amendments or suggesting certain other phraseology was merely intended to see that a difficulty which has arisen in the past will not recur and the desirable facilities which we want to convey to these classes will not be denied to them. I would also like to say that the suspicions of the Select Committee expressed in the Report are absolutely ill-founded. I think many people do not know what is exactly happening regarding backward classes. There have already been schedules prepared by each State Government and if we compare them you will find that the social advancement and educational progress of these people is in no way better than the castes and communities which are included in the scheduled castes and scheduled tribes. If anything, they are more backward in some respects at least. I quite realise that a caste here or there might have got certain advantages which they do not deserve. For that the remedy is not to condemn what is being done for a large number of people who deserve it. The remedy is to take out those castes and deprive them the facilities. But if we try to oppose this amendment, then you are undoing something for which you have sympathy, which would not be a proper thing to do. I do not wish to illustrate the matter in any detail for want of time. If one looks at the schedules prepared by the State Governments at the instance of the Central Government a cursory glance will convince one that the facilities afforded to these classes are amply deserved. I have been a member of the scheduled castes, scheduled tribes and backward classes scholarship board for two years and I know from experience that the people who are getting the scholarships amply deserve them. Along with me on the board were the representatives of the scheduled castes and scheduled tribes and backward classes and they also know and are convinced that these boys who belong to the other communities were fully deserving such facilities along with the scheduled castes and tribes. I hope therefore that there will be no criticism so far as this amendment is concerned. I also express the hope that this amendment will fully meet the requirements of the situation. In fact so far as the other backward classes are concerned very little has been done for them so far. I am very glad to say that people are becoming more and more eager to help the scheduled castes and tribes, but the same eagerness is unfortunately wanting with regard to the other classes. I must express my gratitude to Maulana Azad because it was he who took a decisive stand and gave scholarship facilities to these backward classes for the first time in the history of India. These castes never organised themselves as separate entities from the Hindu community and they did not form their own Depressed Classes League. It was for this reason that they have been left behind. Much has yet to be done for them and I hope by this amendment we will start doing something more for them than has been done so far.[32]

After a formal reply of Pandit Nehru during which he did not say anything on the amendment to Article 15, the motion that the Bill to amend the Constitution, as reported by the Select Committee, be taken into consideration, was carried by a majority of 246 to 14 of the House on May 31, 1951.[33]

Clause-wise discussion of the Bill took place immediately thereafter on June 1 and 2, 1951. Clause 2 relating to amendment of Article 15 was taken up for discussion on June 1, when as many as 14 amendments were moved which are listed below. The first three amendments were moved by Prof. S.L. Saksena, the next three by Sardar Hukam Singh, the next on by Dr. S.P. Mookerjee, the next four by Prof. K.T. Shah, the next one by Hussain Imam and the last two by Kamath. Naziruddin Ahmad's amendment was the same as the second amendment moved by Saxena. The amendments moved were:

(1) In page 1, omit clause 2.

(2) In page 1, line 8, for "socially and educationally backward classes" *substitute* "socially, economically and educationally backward classes."

(3) In page 1, line 9, *add* at the end "during the first ten years since the commencement of this Constitution."

(4) In page 1, line 6, *omit* "or in clause (2) of article next 29."

(5) In page 1, lines 8 and 9, for "any socially and educationally backward classes of citizens or for the Scheduled Castes and the Scheduled Tribes "*substitute*" such

backward classes as are referred to in Articles 340, 341 and 342 of the Constitution."

(6) In page 1, line 8, *after* "socially" *insert* economically".

(7) In page 1, line 7, *for* "special" *substitute* "reasonable."

(8) In page 1, line 7, *after* "provisions for the" *insert* "economic, social, educational."

(9) In page 1, line 8, *after* "specially" *insert* a comma and "economically, or".

(10) In page 1, line 8, for "classes of "*substitute*" or deficient".

(11) In page 1, line 8, after "advancement" insert "employment and reservation of seats in educational institutions".

(13) In page 1, *after* line 9 *add*: "provided that such provision does not impose unreasonable restrictions upon the right to equality of opportunity guaranteed to all citizens by the Constitution."

(14) In page 1, *after* line 9 *add*: "provided that such provision does not entail undue or unreasonable discrimination against other classes of citizens."

The amendment in serial No. 1 was ruled out of order by the Speaker as it was the negative of the original and the remaining thirteen amendments were discussed by the House.[34] The debate was opened by M.A. Ayyangar and was closed by Nehru.

Shri M.A. Ayyangar (Madras)

I shall say a few words both on the clause as also on the amendments. In my opinion, backward classes must be a first charge along with Scheduled Castes and Tribes on the attention of the State as a whole and on the Government. If in the original Constitution as framed all those provisions have not been introduced which have been intended for safeguarding and uplifting the Scheduled Castes and Scheduled Tribes, we thought that a Commission would be appointed by the President and in accordance with the recommendations of the Commission steps would be taken as early as possible. I am sorry to note that still no Commission has been appointed by the President. Till such a Commission has been appointed, various steps have to be taken. The courts have found that there are some difficulties not only with respect to the Scheduled Castes but also in respect of other backward classes. In so far as there are any restrictions on the powers of the Government under the Fundamental Rights preventing any special provisions being made for the uplift of the backward classes, I entirely agree with the Government that the provisions ought to be relaxed and there must be sufficient latitude for the State Governments to introduce provisions so as to enable the backward classes, as early as possible, to come up to the level of the other classes.

Now it is suggested that this might introduce religion, caste and other things by the back door. On that score, I felt at one stage that Article 15 need not be amended and that it would be better to amend Article 29. Article 29 relates to education and special provisions may be made for the reservation of seats in schools and colleges, etc. In article 16, there is already provision for the reservation of posts for backward classes wherever in the opinion of the State they are not adequately represented. So far as article 340 is concerned, the President can appoint a Commission to investigate into the social and educational backwardness of these communities and to make adequate provision for bringing up these to the level of the others. Therefore, I thought that these three provisions in Articles 16, 29 and 340 were sufficient, and that Article 15 need not be touched because Article 15 says that no discrimination shall be allowed on grounds of religion, race, caste, creed, etc. and this amendment might indirectly bring in once again race, religion, caste, etc. As soon as the President appoints the Commission and the Commission reports. I am sure that these backward classes would be such as are indicated by the Commission's report or the President's order. That is what is also referred to in the Report of the Select Committee. Therefore, there need not be any apprehension on the ground that indirectly other communities, castes and creeds will be brought in and that these provisions will be enlarged or circumvented so as to benefit any privileged classes that do not require any special treatment. I am satisfied that that recommendation in the Select Committee Report will be followed by the State Governments. There is no good in making aspertions on the State Governments. These are provincial subjects and therefore the State Governments have to be relied upon to carry out these behests and the directions in the Constitution.

I would have liked that so far as this provision in article 15(4) is concerned, the word "reasonable" might have been put there. But, whether the word 'reasonable' is there or not, this provision cannot be a cent per cent provision for the backward classes ignoring the claims of all the others. In the very nature of things, there must be reasonable provisions. I am sure the courts will interpret, whether the word "reasonable" is there or not, that provision means reasonable provision, not leaving out the rest. So, I am not very particular that the word 'reasonable' should be added.

So far as social and educational backwardness is concerned, I thought 'economic' might be added so that rich men may not take advantage of this provision. In my part of the country there are the Nattukkottai Chettiars who do not care to have English education, but they are the richest of the lot. They have all the business houses and factories. You can compare them to the Marwari community in the north. If these people do not want English Education, should there be special reservation for them? Therefore, I thought the word 'economic' should also be added. Both the hon. Prime Minister and Home Minister thought that this provision should be brought in line with Article 340 and therefore used deliberately 'socially and educationally' and avoided the word 'economic'. I am sure this will serve the purpose. I am happy at the clause as it has emerged from the Select Committee, though I would like to have some changes here and there. I hope the clause will be interpreted in the light in which it is intended and in the light of the directions given in the Report of the Select Committee.

Mr. Speaker

Prof. Shibban Lal Saxsena. I am going in the order of the amendments.

Prof. S.L. Saxsena

...My second amendment is that for "socially and educationally backward classes", "socially, economically and educationally backward classes" be substituted. Then I have another amendment that the words "during the first ten years since the commencement of the Constitution" be added at the end.

This amendment I consider to be a most dangerous amendment. It cuts at the very root of the principles which we have accepted to be the basis of our democracy. Equality has been the one important principle which we have adopted. We have also set ourselves against untouchability. But, I think through this clause we are introducing a new kind of untouchability—untouchability of those who so far were the backward classes. That is the result of this amendment. I feel that this Constitution should not be disgraced by having such an amendment as this. I feel that there is nobody in this House today who does not want that the backward classes, who are low in the scale of education, to be brought up. I am in full agreement with them. But what I feel is that this amendment will be used for people who are neither backward nor who need any special provisions.

I was surprised when the Prime Minister said that this amendment would bring some people up. I thought that the real purpose of this amendment is to nullify the judgment of the Supreme Court. The House will realise that the article, as it is in the Constitution, enunciates a very salutary rule. I do not think that an amendment of the Constitution is the proper method of circumventing the judgment. While I know that the House is going to pass the amendment, I have suggested two amendments: One that the word "economically" be added and another that the operation of this provision may be limited to ten years. We all want that the really backward classes who are poor and who cannot get opportunities to come up and raise themselves should all be helped. And for this it is very necessary that the word "economic" should be there. There may be classes which taken as a whole may be backward, but the individual who claims these privileges or benefits may be a millionaire and have all the opportunities he wants by reason of his wealth. But still this clause will help him. If you want that these benefits or privileges should go to those who are really in need of them, then you must have the word "economic" in this clause. I do not understand the objection to this addition of the word "economic". It is said that in Madras there are very rich people who call themselves backward classes or sub-castes of some castes and who get all these benefits to themselves. I think the clause should not be allowed to stand as it is, otherwise it will be a dangerous thing. If it is allowed to pass in its present form, it will mean that any class which has entrenched itself in power may use this clause to advance its own particular class and I do not think our Constitution should be burdened with such privileges to particular classes. I personally think that if the word "economic" is there it will serve to benefit those who are really backward and who need to be helped. I do not know why this healthy amendment is not being accepted by the Government. Mr. Ananthasayanam Ayyangar himself has just now said that the word "economic" should be there, the purpose being that those who will benefit from it should be the persons who are really backward, and who without this provision, will not be able to come forward. I think this word should be added and if that is done, the sting will be taken away from this clause.

Dr. Deshmukh

If their backwardness disappears, the concessions will also disappear.

Prof. S.L. Saksena

If you continue these privileges, these disabilities or this backwardness will never disappear, because crutches will never enable the backward classes to come up. At present they need to be helped because they are backward and so our Constitution has wisely provided that these privileges or concessions should be there for ten years to enable then to rise up. But we should not perpetuate these inequalities. Unless we place such a time-limit it will be nothing but perpetuation of these inequalities for ever in the Constitution. I therefore think the period should be limited to ten years as I have suggested and it should be extended only to those who are socially and economically backward.

I think these are healthy amendments which I hope the Prime Minister will accept.

Prof. K.T. Shah

My amendments are also on the same lines as those of Prof. Saksena and I will not repeat the arguments that he has already advanced, except in two particulars which he has not touched. I am quite certain that the backwardness which really needs to be remedied is backwardness of an economic character. This affects a very large proportion of the people of this country and we hope they will be affected and helped by the so called Chapter on Directive Principles. If for instance the article in the Constitution which assures compulsory universal elementary education is implemented, then many of these questions would not arise. Therefore I feel that the most important thing to do is to implement our Chapter on Directive Principles and not because you are not able to do so, to revive that which we had sought to abolish by our Constitution. I say that because the definition of classes will be really nothing but a definition of birth. It just happens that you are born in a certain class or group and that class is regarded as a backward class, no matter what its advancement may be in social or other respects. I think we have some experience, for instance, of the Punjab Land Alienation Act where agricultural classes are defined and the Punjab Members will perhaps tell the House how that has worked. Classes are called by a particular name not bacause they carry on this occupation or profession but because they happen to be born in certain families or certain groups. Therefore the retention of this word "class" would mean, in my opinion, the negation of the spirit of the Constitution, and my amendment, therefore, seeks to substitute the word "citizen" for it, and also the word "deficient".

Another point that I would like to bring to the notice of the House is that nothing in this will prevent the State from making special provisions. Under Article 29 you have not debarred anybody from any educational institutions on the ground of birth or sex and so on. And that will still stand, in spite of this amendment. You have to make adequate arrangements for effectively bringing up the backward classes and you have to define these classes according to Articles 340, 341 and 342. Unless and until you take precise measures to bring up these backward classes, they will remain where they are. Therefore, I have suggested in my amendment that the words "backward classes" should be eliminated and they should be substituted by the word "deficient". I have also suggested that as an alternative rather than a conjuctive expression should be there, that is to say, for "Scheduled Castes and Scheduled Tribes", the spirit of the Constitution has to be maintained and also the intentions of the Chapter on Directive Principles which you are now trying to sidetract, or you are, at any rate, salving your conscience and putting them aside on the ground of inability, for the time being. You tell the so-called backward classes that special arrangements will be made to them, though actually your ability to do so is very limited. Let us be honest. Let us accept this amendment. We must remove the backwardness, especially backwardness arising out of or created by social customs and traditions and our history. Every effort must be made to remove this sort of backwardness. But this clause does not work in that direction. That is not the direction in which this clause will lead you. Therefore I have proposed my amendments and I commend them for the acceptance of the House.

Sardar Hukam Singh

...So far as my first amendment is concerned, my objection is rather technical. I find that reference has been made to Article 29 as well now and this has been done by the Select Committee. The hon. Prime Minister said that even in the first instance this was kept in mind and it was only an error that it was not included. Whatever that might be, my fears are that in an implied manner we are going to amend clause (2) of Article 29 as well because under the present amendment the application of Article 29(2) is being restricted. So even if we did not say expressly, that article is also sought to be amended. I fear that would be out of our scope and would not be permissible.

As for my second amendment, it has also been argued by two friends of mine who have preceded me. So far as the idea underlying the clause is concerned, I am in perfect agreement. I also find that there is need that those backward classes should be brought up to the standard of average citizen. They need our sympathy and support. But the difficulty is that with the amendment—we are not definite who will be eligible for this support—it would be possible for the State legislatures or the executive to corrupt those lists as they want. We have defined what our intention was when we made the Constitution that the Scheduled Castes, Scheduled Tribes as well as other backward classes, who were suffering from such disabilities, socially, economically or educationally, should be helped and I support that wholeheartedly but the clause as it stands now and as emerged from the Select Committee does not make it clear and my apprehension is that it will be left to the party in power in the various States what lists they prepare and perhaps it might be used for political purposes as well. The real needy might not be given the assistance that they deserve and others not backward in one respect or other may be aided under that guise. So we have Articles 340, 341 and 342. If we adhere to them—and they lay down that the President has to declare under Articles 341 and 342 the lists of Scheduled Castes and Scheduled Tribes and backward classes and an officer has to be appointed to prepare the lists—then the various Legislatures and the executives in the States might confine themselves to aiding really needy persons who might deserve the aid.

In my third amendment I have said that the word 'economically' should be inserted. You yourself, Sir, have argued that there may be persons who may be educationally and socially considered to be backward and yet they may be very advanced economically. In that prospect we should not deprive those who are really economically backward and if my amendment is accepted the scope would be limited to helping the really needy.

I therefore commend my three amendments for the acceptance of the House.

Dr. S.P. Mookerjee

The amendment which I have moved seeks to substitute the word 'special' by the word 'reasonable'. With regard to this matter, there is complete unanimity in the House that adequate provision must be made for the advancement of the interest of those who are today backward but the question is how to make a suitable provision in the Constitution which will prevent an abuse of such a provision. Now this point has been touched in the report of the Select Committee and it has been suggested there that it is hoped that nothing will be done which may lead to an abuse of this clause. As you are aware, this matter came up in connection with the recent judgment of the Supreme Court with regard to what is called the communal G.O. of Madras. Now the communal G.O. has been quoted in the text of the judgment and it appears therefrom that this was really not a provision for the advancement of the educational interest of backward communities as such but there was a provision for non-Brahmin Hindus—six, backward Hindus-two, Brahmins—two, Harijans—two, anglo-Indians and Indians Christians one, Muslim—one. This was the ratio to be followed for every 14 seats to be filled for admission to Medical College and the Engineering College. In other words, supposing for every 14 seats there are more than two capable and qualified Harijan candidates, even they would not be admitted and they will have to make room for others who come under this category of backward Hindus or non-Brahmin Hindus. From my discussion with Members I gathered that it was nobody's intention to justify the communal G.O. That is good. That is reassuring but the amendment which is sought to be made today in the Constitution leaves scope to the State Government to pass a similar provision like the communal G.O. of Madras if it so chooses. No doubt the Select Committee says that this should not be done and there should not be any abuse made, and that those who are really backward should be helped in every possible way. There is no objection to that. In fact the more we give them educational facilities, the greater will be the chance of doing away with these artificial barriers.

Mr. Deputy Speaker

Have they not already committed themselves to what classes come under 'backward classes' in the communal G.O.?

Dr. S.P. Mookerjee

That may not be covered under the amendment which we are passing. At any rate, that is a debatable point. One attempt we made in the Select Committee was to confine the definition of backward classes to Article 340. There a procedure had been laid down indicating that the President would appoint a Commission and the Commission would enquire into the conditions of certain classes or castes of people in the country and if after a comprehensive report it was thought necessary that certain facilities should be given, such facilities could be provided for. But that reference has been omitted from the clause as it is now before us today. What I seek, therefore, to do is practically to implement the spirit of the observations which are made in the Select Committee Report. No doubt the Government of India may in a friendly way suggest to the State Governments that they should not proceed in a particular way which may mean abuse of the powers which are being given to the State Governments. But there will be no legal force behind it. On the other hand if you say that the provisions made shall be reasonable, that will act as a very salutary check in respect of any efforts which may be made by any State Government. The provision should be so made that it would not take away the legitimate rights of others who may be more qualified but who may not get opportunities, or extend the facilities to such sections of the people who are not really backward but who, for political reasons, have got to be supported and strengthened. Now that is a dangerous tendency. I know that this is a delicate matter and I do not wish to say anything which may give the impression that any section of the House is opposed to the central idea of providing facilities to those who are backward. If my amendment is accepted in the form in which I have moved it or in the form of Mr. Kamath's amendment, I do not think there will be any objection from any quarter except from those who may in their heart of hearts consider it desirable that a provision like the Madras communal G.O. should be revived. If you say "reasonable" the communal G.O. cannot apply, If you do not want to see it revived, then why not accept my amendment and set all doubts at rest? That is the object of my amendment.

Shri Hussain Imam

I am a believer in being explicit and perfectly clear about my intentions. The law and especially the Constitution should not be ambiguous and capable of interpretation in different ways. It is because of this that we have today to face this amending Bill. Had we made our intention clear in the way in which we wanted it there would have been no need for this measure.

I entirely agree with the Prime Minister that in order to establish equality it will be necessary to deny certain privileges to those who are in enjoyment of them. It is on this basis that the Zamindari Abolition Act is being passed. If so, I ask why should it not be perfectly all right that those who are educationally or economically or due to statutory actions backward, things should be reserved for them? I feel that the intention of the Government, however laudable it may be, is very much clouded by non-explicit words. I am afraid it will again lead to litigation and the judiciary will have to interpret it with the result perhaps that the intention of the Government may not be carried out. For this purpose I have tried to clarify the matter by providing for reservation, as apart from rotation. The difficulty with the Madras G.O. was that it provided for a system of rotation. Instead of that what we might do is to reserve something for those who are backward and the rest should be open to competition in which both the backward and forward will come in according to merit. It is for this purpose that I have moved my amendment so that you may provide for the minimum by means of a statutory guarantee both in appointments and educational institutions and for the rest in order to avoid discrimination you may throw it open to everybody on sheer merit. There should be no rotation but reservation cum open competition. I therefore appeal to the House to modify the wording in whatever manner they think proper so that the intention of the Government may be explicitly indicated and all ambiguity removed and thus obviate the necessity for further amendment.

Shri Kamath

Let me make it clear at the very outset that I yield to none in my desire to see that the backward classes and the Scheduled Castes and Tribes attain a high level in educational and economic standards in this country and I would even look forward to the day when the stigma attaching to Scheduled Castes and Scheduled Tribes or backward classes will disappear for ever from our constitutional vocabulary and parlance.

The idea underlying this amendment to Article 15 is laudable and unexceptionable but, I am afraid, in practice, if left to the State Governments without central direction, the power is likely to be abused. The Prime Minister himself in his speech the other day appeared to labour under an apprehension when he said that the High Court of Madras was perhaps after all not wrong in holding the communal G.O. of the Madras Government as invalid and *ulra vires* of the Constitution. He said:

"I do not for an instant challenge the right of the High Court of Madras to pass the order. Indeed, from a certain point of view it seems, if I may say so with all respect, that their argument was quite sound and valid. That is to say, if communities as such are brought into the picture, it does go against certain explicit or implied provisions of the Constitution."

Then he went on to say that conditions have brought about this amendment and how certain classes have been kept in a certain state of depression, if I may say so, I am against dubbing a class wholesale as a backward class just as I have objection to listing certain castes or tribes as Scheduled and placed in a separate category. Circumstances may justify this provision, but on grounds of principle it is open to objection.

The Prime Minister was right in saying the other day that it would be more proper to refer to backward individuals and not classes as a whole or in a lump. Consider my friend Dr. Ambedkar. Will anybody dare say that Dr. Ambedkar is a backward individual or belongs to a backward class? Latterly he has been crusading for Buddhism...

Dr. S.P. Mookerjee

That is a sign of being forward.

Shri Kamath

My friend Dr. Mookerjee says that it is a sign of being forward. Dr. Ambedkar is educationally, socially and economically far more forward than myself..

Shri J.R. Kapoor

Those who do not belong to the Forward Bloc are backward.

Shri Kamath

The Scheduled Castes under the Constitution are entitled to protection. Will anybody say that Dr. Ambedkar needs protection at the hands of anybody?

Shri Rathnaswamy (Madras)

We do not go by individuals but by community.

Shri Kaamath

Dr. Ambedkar, if he will pardon me for saying it, is so aggressive that others may need protection from him. Fortunately his aggression is confined so far to words and not to deeds.

Dr Deshmuch

Deeds he has left behind.

Shri Kamath

Consider again my friend Dr. Deshmukh, who is the President of the All-India Backward Classes Association. I do not know whether he styles himself as a member of the backward classes. But will yield to him any day as regards intellectual superiority, social charm or educational qualifications.

I agree with the Prime Minister's remark the other day that it is wrong to dub or brand a whole class as backward. Dr. Deshmukh is the President of the Backward Classes Association and yet he may not belong to the backward classes.

Look at the other aspect of the problem. The Brahmins are supposed to be very forward, at any rate not backward. Dr. Ambedkar said the other day that every Hindu has got a caste—but I do not think that is why he has embraced Buddhism where all classes and even Scheduled Castes disappear. That apart, the Brahman are supposed to be the most superior among the *chaturvarnas*, though what Dr. Ambedkar said the other day is not quite correct, that the Hindu *smritis* and *shastras* perpetuate this *chaturvarnas*. Even the *Gita* which he quoted perhaps mentions only *guna* and *karma* and not *janma*. Anyway, that is beside the point. But today you will find many Brahmanas who are cooks and even *chaprasis*, and Scheduled Caste and backward class individuals occupying the position of ambassadors and Ministers and political leaders, presidents of various political organisations, and high posts in Government.

Dr. Deshmukh

What is the percentage?

Shri Kamath

What is the percentage of Brahmanas too? How many Brahmanas work as cooks and chaprasis all over India today? How many Brahmans are also illiterate today?

Therefore my point is this: I am all for making provision for backward classes, wholeheartedly in favour of making provision for backward classes and Scheduled Tribes. Let me make it quite clear. But in practice this might lead to abuse unless it is laid down, as you, Sir, have suggested, that the provision made for them should be reasonable—Dr. Mookerjee also supported that idea—

or, as I have suggested in my amendment, that such provision does not impose unreasonable restrictions upon the right to equality of opportunity guaranteed to all citizens by the Constitution, or, if that is not acceptable, the other one which suggests that such provision shall not entail undue or unreasonable discrimination against other classes of citizens.

The Home Minister answering a question the other day in the House about Scheduled Caste appointments, I believe, said appointments are made consistently with the necessity to maintain efficiency in the services. And even our constitution provides for that. Article 335 says that consistently with the maintenance of efficiency of administration, members of Scheduled Castes and Scheduled Tribes should be given their due share in the making of appointments to services and posts under Governments. If this clause be accepted as it is, it is likely that premium may be put upon a caste or a community as against efficiency or merit of an individual. I am sure the Prime Minister, the Home Minister, and Dr. Ambedkar, all of them and the whole House, are anxious to avoid that premium should be put upon a caste or a community or a class. Merit or efficiency must be the guiding consideration—not the sole, but the main consideration. But, nevertheless it may happen, if this clause is accepted as it is, that you might introduce what I might call 'casteism' or 'classism'—if communalism is not acceptable—by the backdoor, and that might lead to various irregularities, to use the mildest word, so far as admission to educational institutions or appointment to Government posts are concerned. Therefore, I would plead, with all the earnestness at my command, that the clause be accepted with a qualifying proviso that this will not militate against the right to equality of opportunity guaranteed to all citizens not merely in the Preamble but also in article 16 and several articles of the Directive Principles of State Policy. If that is not done, I am afraid that this clause again may be challenged in a court of law, and owing to mutual inconsistencies of the various articles of the Constitution—15, 16, 29, etc.,— I for one am afraid that even this clause may be held invalid and *ultra vires* of the Constitution.

Shri Naziruddin Ahmad

Sir, I have only a few words to say because my most important arguments have already been given to the House by you in better words than mine. We want really to help the backward people, but it is necessary that they should be socially, educationally as well as economically backward. If they are merely socially backward, or educationally backward, they may not be economically so. I submit that these three words should be used cumulatively and not disjunctively. Then I would also support your suggestion, Sir, that the word "economically" should also be there.

Coming to the amendment of Prof. Shah, I think instead of the word "class" the word "citizen" should be more appropriate. We want to help the really backward persons. We should not have the term backward "classes". It may be that if we characterise a particular class as backward, there may be a case of two brothers of that class one of whom may be advanced and the other backward. So, the approach should rather be from the individual than from the class. Therefore, I would place the word "economical" in addition, and also substitute "citizen" in place "classes".

Shri Jawaharlal Nehru

I regret that I am unable to accept any of the amendments put forward—not that I do not sympathise with the great deal that has been said. Indeed, I think it might well be said that with the object of this amendment of the Constitution there is practically unanimous agreement here. The only difference comes in sometimes, to a slight extent about its scope, and to a greater extent in regard to certain apprehensions that it arouses. It was for this reason that even in the Select Committee's Report we draw attention to these fears and apprehensions and said that we were quite sure that the Select Committe is of the view that this provision is not likely to be, and cannot indeed be, misused by any Government for perpetuating any class discrimination or for treating non-backward classes as backward for the purpose of conferring privileges on them. I realise that by putting in a paragraph in a Select Committe Report we do not necessarily legally or constitutionally govern anybody or prevent anybody from doing something. That is true, but in the nature of things you have to give a certain latitude in certain directions.

One of the main amendments or ideas put forward is in regard to the addition of the word "economically". Frankly, the argument put forward, with slight variation, I would accept, but my difficulty is this that when we chose those particular words there, "for the advancement of any socially and educationally backward classes", we choose them because they occur in Article 340 and we wanted to bring them bodily from there. Otherwise I would have had not the slightest objection to add "economically". But if I added "economically" I would at the same time not make it a kind of cumulative thing but would say that a person who is lacking in any of these things should be helped. "Socially" is a much wider word including many things and certainly including economically. Therefore, I felt that "socially and educationally" really cover the ground and at the same time you bring out a phrase used in a slightly similar context. Therefore, we adhered to that, although I entirely agree with what Prof. Shah and Prof. Shibbanlal Saksena said about people who are economically backward being helped.

Prof. Shah said something about our approaching this question in a more positive way, that is to say, by implementing the Directive Principles of Policy and by trying to uplift backward classes in the sense of nurturing them by special treatment. I completely and whole heartedly agree with that approach and that is the only correct appraoch to this problem laid down by the Constitution and laid down by commonsense. The only difficulty again arises that many correct things cannot be done suddenly and normally. Take this matter of educational advancement. The obvious way to proceed is to build more educational institutions and to give admission to every person who wants that particular type of training and who is competent to profit by it. It is quite desirable, but for lack of room in our colleges and other institutions for that higher education, we are not able to do it. We want every person to have a house to live in. But unfortunatley, let us say in the city of Delhi or elsewhere, we have to apportion houses and give priority to some people. Some people have to live in tents for some time, or some people have to live even in the open for some time. But the object is that everyone should have a house and everyone should have a place in an educational institution to be trained up to the limit of his or her capacity.

Again I think it was Dr. Syama Prasad Mookerjee who said that these provisions should be used in a reasonable manner. Yes, undoubtedly, of course. I do not know how the putting in of those words here is going to help, because the idea is bound to be there. If a thing is used unreasonably, then it is wrong—if it is used merely to perpetuate, to give unfair advantage to some. After all the whole purpose of the Constitution, as proclaimed in the Directive Principles, is to move towards what I may say a casteless and classless society. It may not have been said precisely in that way; but that is, I take it, its purpose; and anything that perpetuates the present social and economic inequalities is bad.

So, I would beg the House not to accept the amendments to the amendment suggested to this article, because while there is much in them with which we agree they do not really clarify or help the situation. It is one of a slight conflict between existing things and what we want them to be. We want to approach that ideal. If we merely talk of the ideal we do not deal with the practical; if we merely talk of the practical and foget the ideal we become static and forget the Directive Principles of Policy. We have to aim in that direction and move towards it keeping our feet on this ground. I think after careful consideration that the words that the Select Committee has recommended to this House are appropriate for the occasion and the House will accept them as such.

Shri J.R. Kapoor

May I ask one question of the Prime Minister?

Several Hon. Members

No questions now.

Mr. Deputy Speaker

The hon. Prime Minister's speech is crystal clear—I do not think any further explanation is necessary.

I shall now put amendment to the House, except those which are withdrawn.[35]

Dr. S.P. Mookerjee withdrew his amendment while Kamath and Prof. Shah withdrew their second amendments. The other amendments were negatived by the House. Clause 2 was adopted by the House by a majority of 243 to 5 votes. It may be noted that Dr. S.P. Mookerjee, Prof. S.L. Saksena, Kamath and Naziruddin Ahmed abstained from casting their votes.[36]

Each of the remaining eleven clauses relating to amendments of various articles of the Constitution was similarly taken up individually, considered and discussed along with their respective amendments and thereafter finally adopted by the House.

The last stage of passage of the Constitution (First Amendment) Bill was reached when after the clause-wise discussion and adoption, the motion "That the Bill, as amended, be passed" moved by Pandit Nehru was taken up by the House on June 2, 1951. At this stage, i.e. the third reading of the Bill, as many as eleven Members including the Mover expressed their opinion on the necessity and urgency of enacting the Bill. Only Seth Govind Das, T.N. Singh and Dr. Venkataraman, while welcoming the Bill, chose to speak on this provision relating to amendment to Article 15 as well, which, in their opinion, was necessary for the amelioration of the condition of the downtrodden and backward class of people. This is what they had stated:

Seth Govind Das (Madhya Pradesh)

..Now, if we look to the various things dealt with in this Bill we find, firstly, that something has been said for the backward classes. Everything can have both good and bad aspects. We shall be able to go ahead a great deal if confiding in the assurances given to us by hon. Prime

Minister we try to work into action this clause without any scepticism, without any suspicion and without any fear. Fears have been expressed here, and they have been expressed by several of those belonging to upper classes, that the State Governments would not properly observe it and would misuse it. After all, the State Governments are also your own Governments. Why should you have such scepticisms, suspicion and fear from the State Governments? I am sure our State Governments would make proper use of this clause[37]

Shri T.N. Singh (Uttar Pradesh)

...The third important point in this Bill relates to backward classes. I do not know why any heat need be created on this account. After all the Constitution has provided that those who are backward should be allowed to come up—the Scheduled Tribes and Scheduled Castes and the backward classes. They have been kept back for long due to customs and habits and traditions and to enable them to make up the leeway, they must be allowed special facilities. But it has been found that the Constitution itself stood in the way of this being done, in the matter of educational facilities and the like and so the necessary changes have now been brought about...[38]

Shri Venkataraman (Madras)

...There is the amendment to Article 15 which has been made at the instance and is very largely due to the pressure or influence from Madras. There is a feeling both in this House as well as elsewhere that by this amendment we are trying to get over the decision of the Supreme Court. If we carefully analyse the facts relating to the communal G.O., its history and its past, we will realise that this amendment is necessary in the interests of the social welfare of all the people in that State. In the year 1926 the independent ministry of Madras introduced this communal G.O. It was then supported by two members who were originally in the Congress but who had crossed the floor. But then for nearly fifteen or twenty years it has been in existence and our concept of social justice has been changing in the meanwhile. When the hon. Home Minister was the first Premier of Madras under the first Congress Government, he extended this principle of the communal G.O. to recruitment to the judiciary. I am sure you will agree, Sir, that the hon. Home Minister is perhaps one of the rarest men who has the courage of his conviction, and if he did not feel that that principle was a true reflection of social justice I am quite positive he would not have extended it to recruitment to the subordinate judiciary.

Subsequently when we were framing the Constitution we thought it was no longer necessary to have any provision for the advanced classes and that it would be quite sufficient if we made provision only for the backward classes. If you look into Article 16 you will find that provision has been made for reservation of seats for the backward classes in the matter of appointments to services. Article 16(4) makes it possible for the State Governments to reserve seats for these backward classes in the services. But when we come to Article 29, clause (2), we find such a reservation has not been made—either by oversight, or—I do not know why. Nobody would deny that it is absolutely necessary to make some provision for the purpose of giving adequate educational facilities to the backward classes and provide reservation of seats for the purpose, but when we actually come to Article 29 we find that clause (2) of that article makes it almost impossible for the State to reserve seats for the backward classes. The present amendment brings the law under Article 29 on the same par with that under Article 16(4) where we have accepted the principle. Therefore, this amendment makes no further change and there is absolutely no need for apprehension of any kind. In the case which came up before the Supreme Court—not the one which most of the Members have read and quoted from, but the other one of Venkataramana versus the State of Madras (No. 318 of 1950) the Supreme Court said that in the circumstances it is impossible to say that classes of people other than Harijans and backward Hindus can be called backward classes. Therefore, there is no need for either the members of the Select Committee or even the Prime

Minister to give an assurance in this House that this provision cannot be abused. There is a decision of the Supreme Court and if it is abused by the Government of Madras it will certainly be questioned before the Supreme Court. Therefore, to raise imaginary fears and imaginary doubts and then to cast a slur or aspersion on the State Governments is wholly unnecessary, because you have adequate protection, even as the law now stands and even according to the judgement delivered by the Supreme Court, to prevent any abuse of this clause...[39]

After a forceful reply of Pandit Nehru when he scathingly attacked the dissentients of the Amendment Bill, the House adopted the notion by a majority of 228 to 20 votes.[40]

On receiving the assent of the President on June 18, 1951, the Bill became law with effect from that date.

This is how and why clause (4) of Article 15 finds it place in the Constitution. This amendment of Article 15 and Article 29(2) was found necessary on account of the decisions of the Madras High Court in *Shrimati Champakam Dorairajan v. State of Madras* which on appeal was affirmed by the Supreme Court. This case arose from the fact that the Justice Party, while in power in the Madras Presidency in the 1920s, acted as the watchdog of Non-Brahmin interests and issued orders known as communal G.O. reserving seats in medical and other educational institutions for different communities according to a fixed ratio on the basis of religion, race and caste. The ratio and precedence was this:- out of every fourteen seats, six were allotted to Non-Brahmin Hindus, two to Backward Hindus, two to Brahmins, two to Harijans, one to Anglo-Indian and Indian Christian and one to a Muslim. This order of preferential treatment of Non-Brahmins was issued by the Justice Party to make up for the advantages which the Brahmins had secured over them in the fields of education and employment. The Supreme Court held that the communal G.O. infringed Article 29(2) and was therefore void. The effect of Article 14 and 15 was not considered in the decision but it was opined that clause (2) of Article 29 guarantees the Fundamental Right of citizens to get admission to any State maintained or aided educational institution and any discrimination in that behalf on account of merely religion, race, caste or language is rendered ultra vires of Article 29(2). To the argument that as Article 46 charges the State with promoting the educational interest of the weaker sections of the people and so the communal G.O. is valid, the Supreme Court firmly laid down that Article 29(2) is not controlled by Article 46 and that the Constitution does not intend to protect the interest of the backward classes in the matter of admission to educational institutions.

In Venkataraman v. State of Madras the Supreme Court had again occasion to declare the Madras communal G.O. ultra vires of Article 16(4) as it reserved posts for different communities according to their race, caste and religion, though Article 16(4) permitted reservation only to Backward Classes.

The result of this opinion of the Supreme Court was that Parliament enacted the Constituion First Amendment Act. 1951, for insertion of clause (4) to Article 15.

Clause (4) is an exception to the general rule laid down in clauses (1) and (2) of Article 15. It is also in the nature of an exception to clause (2) of Article 29. The first clause of Article 15 postulates that the State shall not discriminate as between citizen and citizen on grounds only of race, caste, sex, place of birth or any of them. The second clause prohibits citizens themselves as well as the State from making any such discrimination with regard to access to shops, hotels, etc., and all places of public entertainment or public resort, well, tanks, roads, etc. The word 'State' in Article 15 takes its connotation from Article 12 in a distributive sense including the Government and the Parliament of India, the Government and the Legislatures of the State concerned, and all local or other authorities within India or under control of the Government of India. The first clause of Article 15 enumerates the prohibited grounds in any matter which is within the control of the State. The second clause prohibits both the State and the private individual whoever may be in control of the public places mentioned in that clause. The third clause gives power to the State to specially protect women and children. The fourth clause has been added so as to give special recognition to backward classes, scheduled castes and scheduled tribes and extend them an exemption from Article 15 and Article 29(2).

Though discrimination on the ground of caste only is prohibited by clause (1) of Article 15, it would be permissible under clause (4) for the State to make special provision for three categories of persons—

(1) socially and educationally backward classes of citizens,

(2) scheduled castes, and

(3) scheduled tribes.

The special provision may be by way of reservation of seats for them, or to grant them fee concession, in public educational institutions.

This amendment brings Articles 15 and 29 in line with Articles 16(4), 46 and 340. Though the amendment would vailidate reservation for the backward class, scheduled castes and scheduled tribes, it would not support the distribution of seats according to communities so as to discriminate between classes who are not backward *inter se*, in short, the amendment would not sanction any communal order.

Though the object of this clause was to negate the verdict of the Supreme Court, Pandit Nehru, the Mover of the Bill, projected it as an endeavour to bring out explicitly what was implicit in the Constitution. The Philosopher in Nehru took pains to explain the static-dynamic concept adumbrated in the Constitution. But apart from Article 46, there are as many as thirteen other Directives which could have been implemented without any amendment of the Constitution and if some of them at least were implemented, a new India would have emerged. Take for instance, the right of every citizen to have an adequate means of livelihood (Article 39), the right to work, to education and to public assistance in cases of unemployment, old age, sickness and disablement (Article 41), free and compulsory education for children upto fourteen years of age (Article 45), to quote only a few. If the purpose was really to honour the 'dynamic' move towards a certain objective represented by the Directive Principles of State Policy, what prevented then in implementing them? Singling out only an Article for implementation that too by amending an Article of the Fundamental Rights Chapter of the Constitution, while neglecting and sidetracking others revealed the true character of the powers-that-be. It was simply to put the people in perpetual strife and conflict for small loaves and fishes and to put a premium on 'backwardness' the meaning of which was, however, not clear to anybody. Many Members sounded a note of warning that this provision would be abused and misused if 'backward classes of citizens' remained undefined. Even the Select Committee, while reporting on the Constitution Amendment Bill, wisely sounded a note of caution thus:

> Some apprehensions have been expressed in respect of this amendment. The Select Committee is of the view that this provision is not likely to be and cannot indeed be misused by any Government for perpetuating any discrimination against the spirit of the Constitution, or for treating non- Backward Classes as backward for the purpose of conferring privileges upon them."

Nehru was rather apologetic for amending this Article. He tried to give the inpression that he did not mean what was being read into the amendment. He said that backward classes were to be thought of not in terms of this community or that. They might belong to any religion, but so far as their educational, social and economic advancement were concerned, it was the duty of every body to help them. Though their advance was not meant to be at the expense of others, there not being enough educational institutions for imparting technical and other education at the moment, special provision need be provided for the members of the backward classes. But he himself was not sure who were they. He thought that it was the backward citizens who should be helped. Why should groups or classes be branded into forward or backward he questioned. But Dr. Ambedkar, his Law Minister and the main Architect of the Constitution had no such illusion. He knew who would be beneficiaries of this amendment. He gave out that the backward classes were nothing but a collection of certain castes, or such other classes who were for the moment not able to stand on their legs, i.e., the scheduled castes and the scheduled tribes. He was more than sure that it was solely on the basis of caste that this provision would be applied. But, strangely enough, Ambedkar was against incorporation of a similar provision for the scheduled castes and backward tribes when suggested by Prof. Shah in the Constitutent Assembly barely two and a half years ago, because that would have 'just the opposite effect' of segregating the scheduled castes and the scheduled tribes from the general public and hence would defeat the very purpose of that provision. What an irony of fate that the same Ambedkar had no qualms in negating the concept of 'casteless society' within sixteen months of the commencement of the Constitution.

There was a persistent demand for an economic criterion for the enumeration of the backward classes. M.A. Ayyangar, the then Deputy Speaker of the Parliament, Sardar Hukam Singh, Prof. K.T. Shah, Prof. S.L. Saxsena and Naziruddin Ahmad pleaded in vain in the Parliament for such a criterion. Nehru was also inclined to have such a qualifying word but he could not do so because the wording of the amendment of Article 15 had been borrowed literally from Article 340 which also speaks of 'socially and educationally backward classes'. As we will see later in Chaper 20 the Framers hardly applied their mind while adopting Article 340 in the Constituent Assembly. In any case, if Nehru was convinced of the utility and necessity of such a qualifying word in Article 15, why did he not go for consequential amendment in Article 340 as well? After all, if there be any drafting fault who else to be blamed except Nehru and his team who drafted the Constitution, shaped it and hammered it in the Constituent Assembly and were piloting the Constitution First Amendment Bill in the Parliament? What stood in the way of rectifying a past mistake? Had he been little bold in doing so, the country could have been saved from 'blood-bath' and 'caste-war' witnessed in the 80s and 90s. His argument that the term 'socially' was a much wider word which included 'economically' as well, did not stand the scrutiny by subsequent judgements.

A term was imported in the Constitution without defining it. Whenever faced with the demand for defining it the Framers took shelter behind Article 340 which provided for instituting a Commission to investigate the conditions of backward classes. A Commission charged with the duty of investigating the conditions of 'socially and educationally backward classes' would enumerate them and submit its recommendations for improving their condition was yet to be appointed but that did not deter the authority to amend the Constitution in anticipation of its recommendations. Was it to nourish the vote bank they were out to create? The concept of 'backward classes' was imported in Madras by the Justice Party, known for its regional and castist outlook, and the invalidation of the order passed by that Party, instead of reversing the trend, made it an All-India phenomenon. Was it necessary to follow the British policy of dividing the people in so many compartments, segments, castes, classes, etc., for all time to come? Did it help the country ultimately?

Notes and References

1. *CAD*, Vol. III, p. 440.
2. *Ibid.*, dated 29-4-47, pp. 426-33.
3. Rao, *op. cit.*, Vol. III, p. 521.
4. *CAD*, Vol. VII, dated 29-11-48, pp. 650-64.
5. *Ibid.*, dated 29-11-48, pp. 655-56.
6. *Ibid.*, dated 29-11-48, p. 661.
7. *Ibid.*, dated 29-11-48, p. 664.
8. *Parliamentary Debates* (Part II-Proceedings other than Questions and Answers), Vol. XII, 1951 (15th May, 1951 to 6th June, 1951), Third Session (Second Part) of Parliament of India, 1951 dated 16-5-51, Column 8814.
9. *Ibid.*, dated 18-5-51, Cols. 9088-89.

10. *Parliamentary Debates* (Part II-Proceedings other than Questions and Answers), Vol. XII, 1951 (15th May, 1951 to 6th June, 1951), Third Session (Second Part) of Parliament of India, 1951, Column 8814. dated 16-5-51, Cols. 8820-23.
11. *Ibid.*, dated 17-5-51, Cols. 8892-94.
12. *Ibid.*, dated 17-5-51, Cols. 8917-18.
13. *Ibid.*, dated 17-5-51. Cols. 8928-30.
14. *Ibid.*, dated 17-5-51, Cols. 8938-39.
15. *Ibid.*, dated 17-5-51, Cols. 8998-9001.
16. *Ibid.*, dated 18-5-51, Cols. 9004-9007.
17. *Ibid.*, dated 18-5-51, Cols. 9037-9039.
18. *Ibid.*, dated 18-5-51, Cols. 9040-9043.
19. *Ibid.*, dated 18-5-51, Col. 9054.
20. *Ibid.*, dated 18-5-51, Cols. 9084-9085.
21. *Ibid.*, dated 18-5-51, Cols. 9088-89.
22. *Ibid.*, dated 25-5-51, Col. 9307.
23. *Ibid.*, dated 29-5-51, Cols. 9612.
24. *Ibid.*, dated 29-5-51. Cols. 9615-9619.
25. *Ibid.*, dated 29-5-51, Cols. 9640-9642.
26. *Ibid.*, dated 29-5-51, Col. 9655.
27. *Ibid.*, dated 30-5-51, Cols. 9688-9691.
28. *Ibid.*, dated 30-5-51, Cols. 9709-9710.
29. *Ibid.*, dated 30-5-51, Cols. 9719-20.
30. *Ibid.*, dated 30-5-51, Col. 9730.
31. *Ibid.*, dated 30-5-51, Cols. 9734-9735.
32. *Ibid.*, dated 30-5-51, Cols. 9775-9776.
33. *Ibid.*, dated 31-5-51, Col. 9801.
34. *Ibid.*, dated 1-6-51, Col. 9815.
35. *Ibid.*, dated 1-6-51, Cols. 9816-9832.
36. *Ibid.*, dated 1-6-51, Cols. 9832-37.
37. *Ibid.*, dated 2-6-51, Col. 10051.
38. *Ibid.*, dated 2-6-51, Cols. 10072-10073.
39. *Ibid.*, dated 2-6-51, Cols. 10080-81.
40. *Ibid.*, dated 2-6-51, Col. 10103.

11

Promotion of Educational and Economic Interests of Scheduled Castes, Scheduled Tribes and Weaker Sections (Article 46)

Ambedkar stipulated in Clause 1 of Part II of Article II-Section IV of his draft submitted on March 24, 1947 that the United States of India should undertake the following special responsiblities, among others, for the betterment of the Scheduled Castes:

(1) Governments--Union and State—shall be required to assume financial responsibility for the higher education of the Scheduled Castes and shall be required to make adequate provisions in their budgets. Such provisions shall form the first charge on the Education Budget of the Union and State Governments.

(2) The responsibility for finding money for secondary and college education of the Scheduled Castes in India shall be upon the State Governments and the different States shall make a provision in their budgets for the said purpose in proportion to the population of the Scheduled Castes to the total budget of the States.

(3) The responsibility for finding money for foreign education of the Scheduled Castes shall be the responsi-

bility of the Union Government and the Union Government shall make a provision of rupees ten lakhs per year in its annual budget in that behalf.

(4) These special grants shall be without prejudice to the right of the Scheduled Castes to share in the expenditure incurred by the State Government for the advancement of primary education for the people of the State.[1]

Ambedkar in the Explanatory Notes appended to the draft pointed out that

> This is not a new demand. Clause 9 of Poona Pact guarantees that an adequate sum shall be earmarked for the education of the Scheduled Castes. It does not define the quantum. All that the demand does is to define the quantum of the liability the State should take. In this connection reference may be made to section 83 of the Government of India Act, 1935, which relates to the education of the Anglo-Indians and Europeans and to the grants made to the Aligarh and Banaras Hindu Universities by the Central Government.[2]

Harnam Singh's draft had laid down that

> The State shall provide special educational facilities to enter public services for Backward Classes, such as Scheduled Castes, the Aboriginal Tribes, the Mazhabis, Ramdasis and Kabirpanthis and shall protect them from social injustice and all forms of exploitation: Provided that all such facilities shall be available to any member of these castes and tribes regardless of religious denomination to which he may belong.[3]

Clause 4 of part A of the Constitutional Adviser's Preliminary Notes on fundamental principles of State policy declared the following objective of the State:

> The State shall promote with special care the educational and economic interests of the weaker sections of the people and, in particular, of the Scheduled Castes and the aboriginal tribes, and shall protect

them from social injustice and all forms of exploitation.[4]

The Fundamental Rights Sub-Committee in its meeting on March 31, 1947, decided to include the above clause of the Constitutional Adviser's Notes in the Fundamental Rights. It was also decided that the word 'and' in the second sentence should be omitted and the expression 'in particular of the Scheduled Castes and the Scheduled tribes' should be enclosed in brackets.[5] But in the Draft Report prepared by the Fundamental Rights Sub-Committee on April 3, 1947, clause (4) of Rau's Notes figured as clause 43 without any modification.[6]

While commenting on this clause of the Draft Report the Constitutional Adviser observed that this provision was peculiarly needed in India. There was an analogous provision in Article 169 of the Chinese Constitution, which provided for the education and economic advancement of the various peoples of China in the frontier regions.[7]

The Fundamental Rights Sub-Committee meeting on April 15, 1947, accepted clause 43 without any change,[8] which appeared as clause 41 in the report submitted to the Advisory Committee on April 16, 1947.[9]

This report of the Fundamental Rights Sub-Committee was thereafter examined by the Minorities Sub-Committee for modifications, amplifications etc. The Minorities Sub-Committee had by then received the replies to the questionnaire issued to its members on minorities as well as the memoranda from different organizations. Jagjivan Ram, a leader of the Scheduled Castes, demanded that

(i) Provision shall be made by every Provincial Government for the free education of the students of the Scheduled Castes at all stages in all types of educational institutions maintained, aided or recognised by Government or local bodies.

(ii) Provision shall be made in the budget of every Provincial Government for adequate sums of money each year for ameliorative measures for the Scheduled Castes.

(iii) Provision shall be made in the budget of the Central Government for adequate sums of money each year for granting stipends to Scheduled Castes students for higher and specialised training in science, arts, etc., in India and abroad.

(iv) Provision shall be made for proportionate representation of the Scheduled Castes in Senates, Syndicates, Courts, etc., of Universities and on governing bodies of all educational institutions.[10]

H. J. Khandekar's memorandum on minorites also contained similar demands couched more or less in identical language.[11] Momorandum of the Working Committee of the All India Adi-Hindu Depressed Classes Association demanded that there should be provisions for earmaking a definite sum in the budgets of the Provincial and Central Governments for the secondary, university and advanced education of the Scheduled Castes.[12] B.N. Brahma's memorandum on the safeguards for the Plains Tribal People of Assam laid down that

> In Assam the Plains tribal people are the most backward people in education. Over and above the general provisions in the provincial annual budget where the tribal people should have their due share, specific sums should every year be set apart as earmarked provisions from the public funds for the educational and cultural developments of these people in the areas where they preponderate. There should be reservation of sufficient number of scholarships both for technical and general education on population basis for the tribes in the plains in schools and colleges. There should be special officers, and a board or a committee to advise and look after the education of these tribal people. More schools should be opened in tribal areas. Adequate and sufficient aids should be given to the schools in tribal areas. In the areas where it is found necessary the tribal people in the plains should be allowed the option of introducing their mother-language or vernacular as medium of instruction at least in the primary schools.[13]

The joint memorandum of Sardar Ujjal Singh and Sardar Harnam Singh suggested that

> The State shall provide special educational facilities and also facilities to enter public services for backward classes such as the Scheduled Castes, Aboriginal Tribes, the Mazhabis, Ramdasis and Kabir Panthi Sikhs and shall protect them from social injustice and all forms of exploitation. All such facilities shall be available to any member of these castes and tribes who embraces Sikhism.[14]

P.K. Salve in reply to the questionnaire stated that the State should provide for free and compulsory education of poor boys and girls in primary and secondary schools and in special schools for technical education. In case of aptitude higher education should be provided free to boys and girls in poor circumstances.[15] Homi Mody felt that any discrimination in the economic sphere based on communal consideration was to be strongly deprecated, both because it would be detrimental to the economic advance of the country and because such discrimination might work to the disadvantage of the members of the minorites. Every person would have the right to enter any educational institution, without discrimination of any kind, as he or she might choose. Opportunities for education and training should be available to all who possessed the requisite qualifications.[16]

M. Ruthnaswamy suggested that the right of each of the national, religious and cultural minorities to have the promotion of their religious and secular culture suitably and adequately provided for. Legal provision should therefore be made in the constitution of the Centre, the Provinces and the States that their budgets should provide for the cultural advancement of these minorities by

(i) grants-in-aid to schools and other educational institutions maintained by these religious communities and in which their religion was taught;

(ii) special grants for the promotion of the education, in all grades and kinds of education (including university and technical) of educationally backward minorities—such aids should continiue till these communities came up to the general level of educational progress in the country;

(iii) schools for minorities, where their religion and their culture would be cultivated, should be maintained by the government in areas where the majority of the population belonged to a cultural or religious minority.[17]

In view of these diverse suggestions of its members, the Minorities Sub-Committee in its meeting of April 18 decided not to offer any comment on the recommendation of the Fundamental Rights Sub-Committee[18] and, therefore, the Interim Report of the Minorities Sub-Committee to the Advisory Committee on April 19 did not contain suggestion on this clause.[19]

The Advisory Committee in its meeting held on April 22, 1947, decided to postpone consideration of the clauses in Part II of the recommendations of the Fundamental Rights Sub-Committee relating to the directive principles of state policy and finally authorized the Chairman to submit a report on their behalf to the Constituent Assembly after it was considered by a sub-committee consisting of Pandit Govind Ballabh Pant, Sir Alladi Krishnaswami Ayyar, Dr. B.R Ambedkar and K.M. Munshi.[20] The Advisory Committee included clause 41 of the Fundamental Rights Sub-Committee's report as clause 9 in its supplementary report submitted to the President of the Constituent Assembly on August 25, 1947, without effecting any change.[21]

This report was introduced in the Constituent Assembly on August 30, 1947, i.e. on the very day of prorogation of the Assembly. The recommendations could not naturally be considered in the Assembly. There was only a general discussion on the report[22] before passing it on to the Drafting Committee for incorporation in the Draft Constitution.

Clause 9 was reproduced, with only minor drafting changes, in the Constitutional Adviser's Draft Constitution of October, 1947, as clause 38 [23] and in the Draft Constitution prepared by the Drafting Committee as Article 37:

> The State shall promote with special care the educational and economic interests of the weaker sections of the people and in particular, of the Scheduled Castes and the Scheduled Tribes, and shall protect them from social injustice and all forms of exploitation.[24]

When this Draft Constitution was circulated for eliciting suggestions, comments, etc., R.R. Diwaker and S.V. Krishna-moorty Rao suggested that in article 37, after the words "special care the "word "cultural" be inserted, for the words "of the "weaker" the words "of the backward", and for the words "protect them from social" the words "protect them from social and economic" be substituted. On this, the Constitutional Adviser commented that the expression "weaker sections" occurring in the Draft has been taken from Article 45(4)1 of the Irish Constitution. The emphasis was not so much on their backwardness as on their lack of strength to resist exploitation. If the State promoted their economic interests with special care and protected them from all forms of exploitation, they would necessarily be protected from "economic injustice". The Constitutional Adviser observed that while, therefore, there was no great objection to the amendments suggested, they would seem to be unnecessary.[25]

This Article was taken up for consideration in the Assembly on November 23, 1948. There was not much of a discussion on this Article. Only one amendment was moved by Sardar Hukam Singh for substitution of the words "Backward communities of whatever class or religion" for the words "Scheduled Castes". In commending the motion for acceptance he said:

> "Scheduled Castes" has been defined in Article 303 (w) of this Draft Constitution as castes and races specified in the Government of India (Scheduled Castes) Order, 1936. In that Order, most of the tribes, castes and subcastes are described and include

Bawaria, Chamar, Chuhra, Balmiki, Od, Sansi, Sirviband and Ramdasis. It would be conceded that they have different faiths and beliefs. For instance, there are considerable numbers of Sikh Ramdasis, Odes, Balmiki and Chamars. They are as the backward as their brethren of other beliefs. But, so far, these Sikh backward classes have been kept out of the benefits meant for Scheduled Castes. The result has been either conversion in large numbers or discontent.

I do realise that so far as election to legislatures was concerned, there could be some justification as the Sikhs had separate representation and the Scheduled Castes got their reservation out of General Seats. There is the famous case of S. Gopal Singh Khalsa who could not be allowed to contest a seat unless he declared that he was not a Sikh. Such cases have led to disappointment and discontent on account of a general belief that some sections were being discriminated against.

Now the underlying idea is the uplift of the backward section of the community so that they may be able to make equal contribution in the national activities. I fully support the idea. I may be confronted with an argument that at least there is the first part of the article which provides for promotion "of educational and economic interests of weaker sections of the people." So far it is quite good and it can apply to every class. But, as the "weaker sections" are not defined anywhere, the apprehension is that the whole attention would be directed to the latter part relating to 'Scheduled Castes' and 'weaker sections' would not mean anything at all. Even the article lays the whole stress on this latter portion by centralising attention through the words 'in particular' of the 'Scheduled Castes'.

I may not be misunderstood in this respect. I do not grudge this special care of the State being directed towards "Scheduled Castes". Rather, I would support even greater concessions being given and more attention being paid to backward classes. My only object is that there should be no discrimination. That is not the intention of the article either. But, as I have said, so far the "Scheduled Castes" have been understood by general masses to exclude the members of the same castes professing Sikh religion. We should be particular in guaranteeing against any misconstruction being placed or any discrimination being exercised by those who would be responsible for actual working of it. Under the present article, it is the "educational and economic interests" that are to be promoted and therefore it should be made clear that it is to be done for all backward classes, and not for persons professing this or that particular religion or belief.[26]

A.V. Thakkar wanted to move an amendment which asked for the inclusion of the backward castes among Hindus and among Muslims...(in the weaker sections?) when Ambedkar intervened to say that both these amendments dealing with the backward classes, etc., would be more appropriate to the Schedule and could be better considered when the Schedule was being dealt with. He therefore suggested postponement of the consideration of these amendments.

Thakkar, therefore, did not move his amendment and Sardar Hukam Singh withdrew his amendment. There was no further discussion on this Article and the Article was added to the Constitution.[27]

Draft Article 37 was renumbered as Article 46 at the revision stage.

This is how this provision finds its place in the Constitution. As could be seen from the foregoing, there was hardly any discussion worth mentioning either at the Committee or in the Constituent Assembly on the provision of this Article. The Article, as recommended by the Constitutional Adviser, was finally adopted by the framers.

This Article merely declares the objective of the State and, like other Directives, does not confer any justiciable rights. It enjoins on the State to (1) devote special care to promote the educational and economic interests of the

(a) Weaker sections of the people,

(b) Scheduled Castes, and

(c) Scheduled Tribes.

(2) protect them from, (a) social injustice and (b) all forms of exploitation.

Whereas Scheduled Castes and Scheduled Tribes have been defined in the Constitution, "weaker sections of the people" have not been defined anywhere in the Constitution. As a result it has to be decided by the court in each case. It is a question of just backwardness. Such minorities exist in a small percentage even in the so-called high caste Brahmins.

Article 46 is of significance in India where society has not advanced uniformly and where there are what are called educationally and economically backward sections. This Article embodies the concept of 'distributive justice' which connotes, inter alia, the removal of economic and educational inequalities and rectifying the injustice resulting from the dealings or transactions between unequals in society. The idea behind enunciating this principle in the Constitution was no doubt lofty. But in their eagerness to do something positive for the 'weaker sections', the framers forgot to take the elementary precaution against the future 'power brokers'. The tragedy of modern power politics in public life is that interested persons bolster up the claims not only of their kith or kin but also of those on whom they can rely as their 'vote bank', on the sad plea of 'weaker sections of the people' with little or no justification for the same. Article 46 is not there to be exploited by the scheming power seekers but is designedly meant to foster the true claims and further the interests of the really 'weaker sections' of the society. This Article is not to be allowed to be exploited by people who do not deserve such protection. If the latter tendency is encouraged by fissiparous political interests at State level the advancement of India as a whole as welfare state will be long delaved as the really backward will long stand neglected.

The Article should not be allowed to be misused in applying the doctrine to perpetuate the benefits to only a particular section of people, however vocal they might be, for retaining what they have already secured for them and in the process depriving the genuine weaker sections among the people. Nor should it be a handy weapon in the hands of the power-seekers to maintain their hold over a section of people in the name of giving them certain benefits to which they are not socially, economically, educationally or morally entitled and thus ensure their patronage during elections.

The ambiguous expression 'weaker sections' is said to include Scheduled Castes and Scheduled Tribes. Dr. Ambedkar, while explaining the necessity and purpose of addition of a new clause(4) to Article 15 for which the Constitution (First Amenedment) Bill, 1951 was introduced, told the Parliament in May, 1951 that the expression 'weaker sections' meant 'backward classes' or such other classes who for the moment could not stand on their own feet—the scheduled castes and the scheduled tribes.[28] Sir B.N. Rau, the Constitutional Adviser, who drafted this provision, however, had a different perception. He explained that the emphasis was not so much on the backwardness as on the lack of strength to resist exploitation.[29] This is indeed multiplying ambiguities. A greater exactitude. by defining the expression 'weaker sections' and even the avoidance of such an expression might have been wholesome. The legal interpretation of this expression may bring about confusion because, after all, it has been left to the court to interpret what is meant by the expression 'weaker sections'. The Constitution-makers have rightly thought it fit in the interests of the society as a whole that the 'weaker sections of the people' should be afforded certain protection. But by leaving the expression undefined in the

Constitution, they have given enough handle to the self-seekers to exploit this provision of the Constitution.

Notes and References

1. Rao, *op. cit.*, Vol. II, pp. 94-95.
2. *Ibid.*, p. 111.
3. *Ibid.*, p. 82.
4. *Ibid.*, p. 34.
5. *Ibid.*, pp. 136-37.
6. *Ibid.*, p. 142.
7. *Ibid.*, p. 150.
8. *Ibid.*, p. 168.
9. *Ibid.*, p. 176.
10. *Ibid.*, p. 334.
11. *Ibid.*, p. 326.
12. *Ibid.*, p. 382.
13. *Ibid.*, pp. 372-73.
14. *Ibid.*, p. 368.
15. *Ibid.*, p. 329.
16. *Ibid.*, pp. 323-24.
17. *Ibid.*, p. 315.
18. *Ibid.*, p. 204.
19. *Ibid.*, pp. 208-09.
20. *Ibid.*, p. 292.
21. *CAD*, Vol. V, p. 376.
22. *Ibid.*, dated 30-8-47. pp. 333-48.
23. Rao, *op. cit.*, Vol. III, p. 14.
24. *Ibid.*, p. 528.
25. *Ibid.*, Vol. IV, p. 55.
26. *CAD*, Vol. VII, dated 23-11-48, pp. 552-53.
27. *Ibid.*, p. 553.
28. *Parliamentary Debates* (Part II-Proceedings other than Questions and Answers), Volume XII, 1951 (15th May, 1951 to 6th June, 1951), Third Session (Second Part) of Parliament of India, 1951, Column 9007.
29. Rao. *op. cit.*, Vol. IV, p. 55.

12

Reservation in Services for any Backward Class of Citizens [(Article 16(4)]

The basic principle of equality of opportunity and prohibition of discrimination on grounds of religion, race, colour, caste or language, in the matter of public employment, was contained in the drafts submitted by Munshi, Ambedkar, Harnam Singh and K.T. Shah. Clause 5 of Article III of Munshi's draft declared:

> All citizens are entitled to equal opportunity:
>
> (a) in matters of public employment and office of power and honour:
>
> (b) in the exercise of trade, profession or calling; and
>
> (c) in the exercise of franchise according to the law of the Union;
>
> and no citizen shall be denied the right on grounds of religion, race, colour, caste or language[1]

while clause 6 of Article II, Section I of Ambedkar's draft stripulated that:

> No citizen shall be disqualified to hold any public office or exercise any trade or calling by reason of his or her religion, caste, creed, sex or social status.[2]

Shah had laid down in clause 2 of his draft that:

> Every citizen of India has, and is hereby guaranted equal rights and opportunity in respect of education, training, health and employment in any post, office, or capacity, irrespective of any differences of birth, sex, wealth, creed or colour.[3]

and Harnam Singh provided in clause 8 of his draft that:

> No subject of the Indian Republic shall on grounds of religion, caste, creed, place of birth or descent be ineligible for office in any part of the Indian Republic or be prohibited on any such ground from acquiring, holding, or disposing of property or carrying on any occupation, trade, business or profession in any part of the Indian Republic. (Vide section 298 of the Government of India Act, 1935).[4]

The Sub-committee on Fundamental Rights discussed the subject on March 24, 1947, and decided to include the following provision in clause (5) :

> There shall be equality of opportunity for all citizens:
>
> (a) in matters of public employment;
>
> (b) in the exercise or carrying on any occupation, trade, business or profession, and no citizen shall, on grounds only of religion, place of birth, descent, race, caste, language or sex be ineligible for public office or be prohibited from acquiring, holding or disposing of property or exercising or carrying on any occupation, trade, business or profession within the Union.[5]

This appeared as clause 5 (1) (b) of the Draft Report of the Sub-committee prepared on April 3, 1947.[6]

In his explanatory notes on the draft clauses, B.N. Rau pointed out that sub-clause 1(b) was actually adapted from section 298 of the Government of India Act, 1935.[7]

When the sub-clause was considered by the sub-committee on April 14 and 15, 1947, it was decided that clause 5 (1) (b) should be an independent clause. Alladi Krishnaswami Ayyar referred to enactments like the Religious Endowments Act which restricted certain appointments to Hindus, and suggested that it would be necessary to protect such provisions. This suggestion was accepted and the provision was redrafted as an independent clause[8] and appeared in the report of the sub-committee submitted to the Advisory Committee on April 16, 1947 as clause 5:

> There shall be equality of opportunity for all citizens:
> (i) in matters of public employment;
> (ii) in the exercise or carrying on of any occupation trade, business or profession:
>
> and no citizen shall on any of the grounds mentioned in the preceeding section be ineligible for public office or be prohibited from acquiring, holding or disposing of property or exercising or carrying on any occupation,. trade, business or profession within the Union. Nothing herein contained shall prevent a law being made prescribing that the incumbent of an office to manage, administer or superintend the affairs of a religious or denominational institution shall be a member of a particular religion, persuasion or denomination[9]

The Sub-committee on Minorities decided, at its meeting on April 17, first of all to examine the draft clauses recommended by the Fundamental Rights Sub-committee in its report of April 16 in order to see whether any of them required to be amplified or amended for the specific purpose of protecting minority rights.[10] In its meeting on April 18, the Sub-committee decided that a provision might have to be added to clause (5) to meet the claims of minorities to special representation in the services[11] and this recommendation was included in the interim report of the Sub-Committee on Minorities sent to the Advisory Committee on April 19, 1947.[12]

The Advisory Committee first discussed this clause along with the recommendations of the Minorities Sub-committee on April 21, 1947. At the outset Alladi Krishnaswamy Ayyar objected to the affirmative assertion in the first part of the clause on the ground that the claims of minorities could be adequately met without an additional sub-clause if the affirmative expression was changed into a negative one as in section 298 of the 1935 Act and suggested deletion of first paragraph 5 (i) and 5 (ii). Munshi, on the other hand, stressed the view of the Sub-committee on Fundamental Rights that the general principle regarding equality of opportunity to all must be asserted in the affirmative first, and if any exception was to be provided in favour of backward communities, that should be done by incorporating a separate sub-clause to that effect. Disagreeing with Alladi Krishnaswamy Ayyar, Ambedkar pointed out that even among the members of the same minority there might be complaints of partiality, of provincial favouritism or personal favouritism. Guranteeing of equality of opportunity between members of the same minority might become essential. He favoured the addition of a proviso enabling the Government to reserve for the minorities a certain proportion of posts in the public services. K.M. Panikkar was against an unqualified declaration of equality of opportunity in the matter of public employment. In many of the Indian States and most of the Provinces there was a well-established policy of giving preference to the people of the State or Province in the matter of public employment; and in some Provinces conditions existed where local people had but an inadequate share in the employment provided by the State, and special preference to such people might even be a necessity. The clause as drafted declared all such preferences illegal in respect of employment not only in the Union but also in the units. Panikkar thought that "to provide that there shall be equality of opportunity in the matter of public employment whether in the unit or in the Union without reference to local conditions is utterly impracticable", Rajagopalachari observed that the caluse would rouse all-round resentment if it was going to mean that there would be no reservation made in favour of the people of any particular unit. Ambedkar felt that the clause as it stood did not prevent any unit from prescribing additional conditions for employment. It was finally decided to refer the clause for redrafting to the ad hoc committee consisting of Rajagopalachari, Ambedkar, Sardar Panikkar and Munshi.[13]

When the clause as redrafted came before the Advisory Committee on April 22, 1947, discussion centred round the respective merits of certain phrases used in the exception clause which, as recommended by the ad hoc committee, read:

> Nothing herein contained shall prevent the State from making provision for reservations in favour of classes not adequately represented in the public services.

Ambedkar suggested the deletion of all the words after the word "reservations" and in their place the insertion of the words "in public services in favour of classes as may be prescribed by the State". If the words "not adequately represented" were retained he felt, any reservation made by the State would be open to challenge in a court of law on the ground that the classes in whose favour reservation was made happened to be in fact already adequately represented. Ambedkar was opposed to this matter being the subject of judicial interpretation.

In an attempt to meet Ambedkar's argument and at the same time to retain the spirit of the draft provision as recommended by the ad hoc committee, Munshi suggested the use of the words: "classes which in the opinon of the State are not adequately represented". The modification was accepted by Ambedkar. A fear was expressed by Ujjal Singh that the words "not adequately represented" in the clause might be interpreted to mean that no minority community would be given representation in the services on a scale higher than what it would get on a population basis. He pointed out that this would be unfair to the Sikhs for whom 20 per cent of public appointments were at the time reserved in the Punjab though they formed only 13 per cent of the population. Rajagopalachari, among others, considered that there were no genuine grounds for Ujjal Singh's apprehensions because the clause would not prevent the State from giving a greater proportion.

Other expressions on the respective merits of which considerable discussion took place were "minorities",

"minorities and classes", "minorities and backward classes", and "classes including minorities" suggested by various members of the committee as alternatives to the expression "classes" used by the ad hoc committee. Claiming in the committee that actually he was the person responsible for the change to "classes" from "minorities", Panikkar observed that "minorities" in India had come to have a specific meaning, i.e., to denote religious or political minorities-Muslims, Sikhs, etc. "There may be", he said, "among the majority, among the Hindus for example, many classes who have not adequate representation in the services". The cases he had in mind were those of small communities like the Namboodiris in the south and Garhwalis in the north. The Chairman also intervened to clarify that "classes" included "minorites" and that the draft as it stood was satisfactory.[14]

The entire provision as accepted by the Advisory Committee appeared as clause 5 in its interim report sent to the Constituent Assembly on April 23, 1947:

> There shall be equality of opportunity for all citizens in matters of public employment and in the exercise of carrying on of any occupation, trade, business or profession.
>
> Nothing herein contained shall prevent the State from making provision for reservations in favour of classes who, in the opinion of ths State, are not adequately represented in the public services.
>
> No citizen shall on grounds only of religion, race, caste, sex, decent, palce of birth or any of them be ineligible for public office or be prohibited from acquiring, holding or disposing of property or exercising or carrying on any occupation, trade, business, or profession within the Union.
>
> Nothing herein contained shall prevent a law being made prescribing that the incumbent of an office to manage, administer or superintendent the affaris of a religious or denominational institution or the member of the Governing Body thereof shall be a member of that particular religion or denomination.[15]

This clause was taken up for discussion in the Constituent Assembly on April 30, 1947, when Munshi moved the following amendment:

In clause 5 paragraph 1 may be marked '(a)', and paragraph 3 may be marked '(b)'.

Paragraph 3 may be placed immediately after paragraph 1. Delete from paragraph 1 the words 'and in the exercise of carrying on of any occupation, trade, business or profession', and from paragraph 3 the words 'or be prohibited from acquring, holding or disposing of property or exercising or carrying on any occupation, trade, business, or profession within the Union'.

While commending this amendment for acceptance, Munshi said: "This amendment is intended to classify the two heads of rights under two different clauses. As the House will be pleased to see, clause 5 deals not only with public employment but also with occupation, trade, business or profession, and the right acquire, hold and dispose of property. The same right occurs once again in clause 8 and proviso has been put in at the end of cluase 8 permitting Government by law to restrict this freedom under certain circumstances. It was felt that these two clauses were overlapping, and for the purpose of having a proper logical division, clause 5 is now being only restricted to public employment, while freedom to carry on occupation, trade, business or profession and freedom to acquire, hold and dispose of property have been transferred to clause 8 (e). The result of all this change is that this clause will stand only with regard to public employment, and the right with regard to trade, occupation, etc., and with regard to property will come under clause 8 (c)."

Mahavir Tyagi suggested the addition of the following proviso after the first para:

Provided that a Unit may frame rules whereunder in the matter of public employment it may give preference over others to such citizens as are bona fide or domiciled residents of its own territory.

After pointing out the desirability of the units having the right to give preference in the matter of public employment to its residents. Tyagi said that if in the proceedings of this House it was recorded that the right of allowing privileges to its domiciles would vest in every province and in matters of employment it should be able to allow privileges to its residents over those of other provinces, then he need not move any amendment. On this point Patel, the mover of this clause, explained that the clause did not deprive the Provinces of their right to legislate in matters of public employment: it simply removed the ineligibility of a citizen. Patel also accepted the amendment moved by Munshi and the Assembly accepted the amended clause.[16]

This clause was reproduced as clause 12 in the Constitutional Adviser's Draft Constitution with some monor alterations:

12.(1) There shall be equality of opportunity for all citizens in matters of employment under the State.

(2) No citizen shall, on grounds only of religion, race, caste, sex, descent, place of birth or any of them, be ineligible for any office under the State.

(3) Nothing in this section shall prevent the State from making any provision for the reservation of appointments or posts in favour of any particular classes of citizens who, in the opinion of the State, are not adequately represented in the services under the State.

(4) Nothing is this section shall affect the operation of any law which provides that the incumbent of an office in connection with the affairs of any religious or denominational institution or any member of the governing body threof shall be a person professing a particular religion or belonging to a particular denomination.[17]

D.P. Khaitan, a member of the Drafting Committee,

in a separate note suggested that the word 'domicile' be added after the words 'place of birth' in clause (2) and the words 'being minorities' be added after the words 'citizens' in clause (3).[18]

The Drafting Committee considered this cluase on October 30, 1947,[19] and on October 31, 1947 [20] and decided to approve this clause subject to the substitution of the words 'backward class' for the words 'particular classes' in sub-clause (3) thereof. This clause appeared as Article 10 of the Draft Constitution prepared by the Drafting Committee in February. 1948.[21]

When the Draft Constitution was circulated for eliciting opinion, a number of amendments were received. R.R. Diwakar and S.V. Krishnamoorthy proposed the addition of the words "economically or culturally" after the words "or posts in favour of "in sub-clause (3). To this suggestion, B.N. Rau commented that while there could be no great objection to the amendment, it was unnecessary. T.A. Ramalingam Chettiar and the Madras Legislative Council suggested the deletion of the word `backward' from sub-clause (3). B.N. Rau's comment on this was that if the word "backward" be omitted from clause (3) then it would be open to a State to reserve appointments or posts in favour of any class of citizens who were not adequately represented in the services under the State. It was, however, for the Constituent Assembly to decide whether the scope of this clause should be so extended. Upendranath Barman proposed that in clause(3) before the word "backward" the words "the Scheduled Castes or" be inserted. B.N. Rau noted that this amendment involved a question of policy. He however pointed out that the Advisory Committee on the subject of Minority Rights in their report which was adopted by the Constituent Assembly during August 1947 session did not recommend any reservation of posts for the Scheduled Castes in the all-India and provincial services. Atul Chandra Gupta, an Advocate of Calcutta High Court suggested limiting reservation to a period of fifteen years in order to avoid the growth of a vested interst in backwardness. To this proposal, R.N.Rau noted that this amendment involved a question of policy.[22]

This Article came up for consideration before the Constituent Assembly on Novermber 30, 1948. As many as sixteen amendments were moved—two on clause (1), nine on clause (2), four on clause (3) and one on clause (4). Mohamed Tahir's amendment to article 10 as modified by Ananthasayanam Ayyangar sought to provide—

(i) that in cluase (1), for the words "in the matters of employment", the words "in matters relating to employment or appointment to office" be substituted;

(ii) that in clause (2), after the words "ineligible for any" the words "employment or" be inserted.[23]

Jaspat Roy Kapoor moved that in clause (2), after the word "birth" the words "or residence" be inserted.[24] Kapoor's amendment, however, brought in another amendment moved by Alladi Krishnaswami Ayyar. It sought to add a fresh clause after clause (2) to enable Parliament to make

> any law prescribing, in regard to a class or classes of employment or appointment to an office under any State for the time being specified in the First Schedule or any local or other authority within its territory, any requirement as to residence within that State prior to such employment or appointment.[25]

Ananthasayanam Ayyangar moved another amendment which sought the insertion of the words "or discriminated against" after the word "ineligible" in clause (2).[26] These are the four amendments which were accepted by Ambedkar.

Amongst the other amendments which were not accepted by Ambedkar, one by Lokanath Mishra suggested the deletion of clauses (2), (3), and (4). The deletion of clause (3) was also proposed by Damodar Swaroop Seth. Pandit Hirday Nath Kunzru proposed that the reservation of seats for backward classes should be restricted to a period of only ten years, while Aziz Ahmed Khan sought for the omission of the word "backward" from clause (3) of the draft article.[27]

During the general discussion on the clauses the use of the word "backward" proved controversial. Some members supported its omission on the ground that the scope of the word was likely to be misconstrued by the State thereby adversely affecting the claims of minority groups for adequate representation in the services. On the other hand, members belonging to the backward classes came forward, one after another, generally to welcome the provision in clause (3) of the draft article. Most of the members belonging to the Scheduled Castes and Tribes, expressed their apprehension, regarding the scope of the word "backward" and pressed for a clarification so that the word "backward" might apply only to them. K.M. Munshi, while referring to the fears expressed by members belonging to the Scheduled Castes, said:

> In view of the conditions in our country prevailing in several Provinces, we want to see backward classes, classes who are really backward, should be given scope in the State services;...the word "backward" signifies that class of people—does not matter whether you call them untouchables or touchables belonging to this community or that—a class of people who are so backward that special protection is required (for them) in the services..[28]

In his reply, Ambedkar accepted the four amendments, mentioned earlier, and referring to the controversy regarding the use of the word "backward" in clause (3), said that the Drafting Committee had to reconcile opposing points of view to produce a "workable proposition which will be accepted by all." If this was borne in mind, it would be seen that no better formula could be produced than the one embodied in clause (3). He added:

> Unless you use some such qualifying phrase as "backward" the exception made in favour of reservation will ultimately eat up the rule altogether...That I think...is the justification why the Drafting Committee undertook on its own shoulders the responsibility of introducing the word "backward" which,

> I admit, did not originally find a place in the fundamental right in the way in which it was passed by this Assembly.

Ambedkar referred, finally, to two questions raised during the debate : first, regarding the definition of "backward community" and the second, regarding the justiciability of clause (3) of the draft article. Regarding the former he said :

> Any one who reads the language of the draft itself will find that we have left it to be determined by each local government. A backward community is a community which is backward in the opinion of the Government.

As for the latter, he said :

> It is rather difficult to give a dogmatic answer. Personally I think it would be a justiciable matter.[29]

On being put to vote, all the amendments, except those accepted earlier by Ambedkar, were negatived by the Assembly and draft article 10, as amended, was adopted to be added to the Constitution.

The relevant portions of debate, relating to clause (3) only, are reproduced below verbatim.

Shri Lokanath Misra (Orissa : General)

Sir, I beg to move :

"That clauses (2), (3) and (4) of Article 10 be deleted."

On this matter I need not make a long speech. To my mind clause (1) covers all cases and clause (2) is definitely in clause (1), and clause (3) which refers to reservation of appointments to backward classes is really unnecessary because it puts a premium on backwardness and inefficiency. Everybody has a right to employment, food, clothing, shelter and all those things, but it is not a fundamental right for any citizen to claim a portion of State employment, which ought to go by merit alone. It can never be a fundamental right. If we accept that as one, it may be generous but this generosity will itself be a degradation to those people who are favoured with it...

Shri Damodar Swarup Seth (United Provinces : General)

Sir, I beg to move :

"That clause (3) of Article 10 be deleted.

Sir, the reason for my submission is that though the clause on the face of it appears to be just and reasonable, it is wrong in principle. Who will not believe it, Sir, that reservation of posts or appointments in services for the backward classes means the very negation of efficiency and good Government? Moreover, it is not easy to define precisely the term 'backward'; nor is it easy to find a suitable criterion for testing the backwardness of a community or class. If this clause is accepted, it will give rise to castism and favouritism which should have nothing to do in a secular State. I do not mean that necessary facilities and concessions should not be given to backward classes for improving their educational qualifications and raise general level of their uplift. But, appointments to posts should be only left to the discretion of the Public Service Commission, to be made on merit and qualification, and no concession whatever should be allowed to any class on the plea that the same happens to be backward.

Pandit Hirday Nath Kunzru (United Provinces : General)

Mr. Vice-President, Sir, I beg to move :

"That in clause (3) of article 10, for the words 'shall prevent that State from making any provision for the reservation' the words 'shall, during a period of ten years after the commencement of this Constitution, prevent the State from making any reservation' be substituted."

Sir, I am not in principle against the protection of the interests of classes that are at present unable to look after themselves unaided; but this article, as it is, presents several difficulties, In the first place, the word 'backward' is not defined anywhere in the Constitution. There is another article in the Constitution, namely article 301, that provides for the appointment of a Commission to enquire into the condition of the backward classes. But, it is stated there that only those classes will come within the purview of the enquiry that are educationally or socially backward. There too there is no enumeration of the classes to which the enquiry will refer. This article is even more indefinite. Whether any class is backward or not, should be left to the law courts to decide. It is therefore our duty to define the term 'backward' so that there may be no dispute in the future about its meaning.

My second point, Sir, is this. While granting protection to communities that have been left behind in the race of life, is it desirable that any special provisions laid down for them should operate indefinitely? Or is it desirable both in the interest of the backward classes and the State that any special provisions made for these classes should be of limited duration? If this article remains as it is and if reservation of appointment or posts can be made in favour of any backward class indefinitely, the State might come to think that it had done its duty by these classes by making this provision. I think and I believe that the House, if left to itself, would agree that it is desirable that the operation of such a provision should come under review from time to time so that we may be able to see whether the State had taken such steps as were necessary in order to lift these classes from their present position and enable them to compete on terms of equality with the other classes.

Sir, my third argument is that the provision with regard to the reservation of seats in the legislatures for the minorities, which must include the depressed classes and the scheduled tribes, according to the draft constitution is to be of limited duration. Now nobody can deny at the present time that a provision of this kind is necessary for these classes and it must be obvious to everybody here that representation in the legislature is of far greater importance than representation in services. If a community is represented in the legislature, its representatives can voice its demands from time to time and can see that any injustice done to that community either in the matter of appointment to posts or in any other matter is rectified. But if it ceases to be represented in the legislature whatever protection might be granted to it in this or that matter, it will be in a far more helpess condition than if it were deprived of any other special aid. Now it has been provided in the Constitution that the reservation of seats for the minorities which include the scheduled tribes and depressed classes, who must according to any definition be regarded as backward, is limited to ten years. Article 305 lays down that the provision for the reservation of seats for the minorities according to their population shall continue in force unchanged for ten years and no more. On the expiration of ten years from the commencement of the Constitution this "provisions shall lapse unless its operations is extended by an amendment of the Constitution." Now is it not desirable that a similar limitation should be laid down in clause (3) of article 10? Indeed it can be applied with greater force to article 10 than to the reservation of posts for the minorities in the Central and Provincial Administrations. If clause (3) of Article 10 is to be in conformity with the scheme for the protection of the interests of the backward classes, I submit that it is not merely desirable but necessary that the amendment that I have proposed should be made.

Lastly, Sir, I should like to know what is the relationship between clause (3) of Article 10 and Article 296. Article 296 provides that the claims of minority communities shall be taken into consideration consistently with the maintenance of efficiency in the administration in the making of apointments to services and posts in connection with the affairs of the Union or of a State for the time being specified in Part I of the First Schedule. Now in so far as clause (3) of Article 10 applies to all States specified in the First Schedule, the difference between it and Article 296, which applies only to States in Part I of the First Schedule, is clear. But beyond that it is far from clear what the relationship between these two articles is. Article 296 relates to minorities. The claims of the minority communities can be taken into consideration in making appointments to services only on the ground that they are backward. Though it is the word 'minority' that is used in Article 296 and the exrpession 'backward classes' is used in Article 10(3), it seems to me that in fairness to the country protection can be granted to any class, whether you call it a backward class or a minority, only on the ground that it is backward and if left to itself, would be uanble to protect its interests. This shows the need for clearing up the connection between the two articles that I have just referred to. Apart from this, I should like to know whether if clause (3) of article 10 is passed, it would be possible for sections within the various communities to ask for special protection for themselves in the matter of appointments to services or posts. It may be that if clause (3) of Article 10 were passed, it will not be possible for State to make any reservations in the services for minorities as such. But will it not be a temptation to sections of these and other communities to claim that they are backward in order to get the protection of clause (3) of article 10? Sir, I submit that we should have a system that would not encourage fissiparous tendencies and under which it will not be to the interest of any class to claim that it is backward. It is desirable therefore to limit the operation of any special protection that we may grant—protection of whatever kind—that its duration should be limited, so that the legislature may from time to time be able to see how it has worked and how the State has discharged its duty towards the protected classes. Unless this is done, I venture to think that article 10 would not be in conformity with the intention of the constitution to remove all those conditions on account of which special protection is necessary. We are all aware that when the Report of the Minorities Committee was considered by the House, the entire House was anxious that reservations of whatever kind should be done away with as quickly as possible. It was recognized that for the time being they were necessary, but it was insisted on that whatever protection might be considered necessary now, should be granted temporarily only, and no community or class might be tempted to claim special advantages for itself. On these grounds, Sir, I venture to put forward my amendment, though I have no doubt whatsoever, that it will not find favour with my friend Dr. Ambedkar.

Mr. Aziz Ahmad Khan (United Privubces: Muslim)

Mr. President, I propose:

"That in clause (3) of Article 10 the word `backward' be omitted."

Sir, I would like to submit that at the time when the Minority Report was submitted to this House, the word "backward" was not there and we had finally decided that it is unnecessary to include the word "backward". Moreover, if you look at the Draft Constitution, you will find that there are several articles of such a nature that in case this amendment is not accepted, those articles become opposed to Article 10; I refer to Articles 296 and 299.

I have listened with attention the speech just delivered by Shri Kunzru. His object was to emphasise that under the new conditions created in India, if any protection is to be given, it could be given only to those particular classes of people who are educationally or culturally backward. Only such people require protection and not the minorities. In his opinion, no class or group as such requires any protection under the existing conditions. In my opinion, however, only those people require protection who have misgivings that in case protection is not given, their rights will not be preserved. I think that in case state services are monopolised by one particular class, then others might think that their existence has been ignored. This very idea will become a source of creating unpleasantness in the country. To my mind, therefore, this amendment is essential. I am of the opinion that in the new set up which we have to make in the country, we should neither create nor multiply differences. Nevertheless, it is a fact that due to the changes which we are introducing in the country, there are minorities who require protection. Safeguards should be provided for them and this can be done easily.

Sir, by Article 296 such a safeguard has been provided and in Article 299 also a similar provision has been made. I would like to submit that if as a matter of fact we are shaping this country in such a manner that there should not remain any difference, then it is necessary that there should not be any inpediment that might create a feeling in the mind of an individual who has educational and citizenship qualifications that his claims are being ignored. Therefore, if this Article is not amended, then there will be doubts and misgivings among the minorities that they are being ignored. I do not say that it is necessary to recruit 20 per cent Sikhs, 15 per cent Christians or 15 per cent Muslims in the public services of our country. I want only this much that if the Sikhs, the Muslims, the Christians and similar other groups living in the country, have educational and other requisite qualifications, then their claims should not be overlooked. Therefore, I think if this word be deleted from this article, then we shall not be accused of overlooking the claims of any particular class. To my mind if the word 'backward' is deleted, then the hand of the Government will be strengthened in such a way that it will enable the Government from time to time to make adequate arrangements in case the claims of any particular group are overlooked in public services. I think that this article would fetter the powers of the Government so tightly that they will not be able to remove the defects and the differences which exist today and they will continue. On these grounds, I hope that the House will accept this amendment which is certainly in consonance with the Minority Committee's Report.

Mr. Vice-President

Before we start the general discussion, I would like to place a particular matter before the honourable Members. The clause which has so long been under discussion affects particularly certain sections of our population—sections which have in the past been treated very cruelly—and although we are today prepared to make reparation for the evil deeds of our ancestors, still the old story continues, at least here and there, and capital is made out of it outside India. Every time we seek to place discussions in the international sphere on a high plane, it is at once thrown in our teeth that we have been treating certain sections of our brethren in a very unjustifiable way. I would therefore very much appreciate the permission of the House so that I might give full freedom of discussion on this particular matter to our brethren of the backward classes. Do I have the permission?

Honourable Members

Certainly

Mr. Vice-President

I will first call upon Mr. Gurung.

Shri Ari Bahadur Gurung (West Bengal: General)

Mr. Vice-President, I thank you very much for the opportunity given me to speak on this occasion. I am particularly happy to note the provision in clause 3 of this article which says:

Nothing in this article shall prevent the State from making any provision for the reservation of appointments or posts in favour of any backward class of citizens who, in the opinion of the State, are not adequately represented in the services under the State.

Sir, may I take it that the word 'backward' includes three categories of people, namely Scheduled Castes, and Tribes and one particular class which is not included so far, under the term 'backward' although it is educationally and economically backward? If I may say so, Sir, 90 per cent, if not more of the Indian people are educationally and economically backward; the meaning of the word 'backward' seems to be vague to me. I feel I shall be failing in my duty to a particular section of the Indian people, viz., the Gurkhas, if I do not voice their feeling at this stage.

The Gurkhas, I must bring to the notice of the House, are three millions, if not more, domiciled in India. They are educationally and economically backward. I feel that the Gurkhas who are domiciled in India should have the same privilege as other backward communities in India. Sir, it is a known fact that the Gurkhas have played their part in the preservation of the independence of India and are now actually fighting in Kashmir after fighting in Hyderabad. They have had their share of the work in the preservation of India's independence. I assure the House that the Gurkhas who are now domiciled in India owe their full allegiance to the Indian Government. There had been a deep rooted suspicion in the minds of many that the Gurkhas owe their allegiance to the Government of Nepal. Today, on the floor of the House, I assure you that the Gurkhas who are domiciled in India owe allegiance to the Government of India and not to the Government of Nepal. These Gurkhas will not hesitate to shed their last drop of blood to preserve the independence that we have got.

There has been a very good gesture since the 15th August, 1947 regarding the Gurkhas. When the Britishers were ruling in India, the Gurkhas were given only Viceroy's Commissions in the Army, but since 1948, many Gurkhas have been given emergency commissions as officers and I understand some of them have risen to the rank of Colonels too. This grant or recognition has been a very good gesture.

Now this clause in article 10 makes a provision in favour of the backward classes of citizens who in the opinion of the State are not sufficiently represented in the services of the State. Today, I feel that the Gurkhas who had their opportunity to serve in the army and are educated, with this provision, may be taken to the civil side of the administration. I hope that the Gurkhas who have shown their bravery and valour in the army would show equal intelligence and integrity in the civil departments.

Shri R.M. Nalavade (Bombay:General)

Mr. Vice-President, Sir, I am very glad to express the support of the depressed classe to Article 10 which is now under discussion. In this article, particularly in clause (3) there is provision made for reservation in the services for the backward classes. But the words 'backward classes' are so vague that they could be interpreted in such a way as to include so many classes which are even educationally advanced. They are found mentioned in the list of backward classes. If the words 'Scheduled Castes' might have been used it would have been easier for the depressed classes to get adequate representation in the services. Our experience in the provinces, though there are provisions for reservation in the services, is bitter. Even though the depressed classes are educated and qualified, they are not given chances of employment under the Provincial Government. Now that we have provided for this in the Constitution itself, there is no fear for the Scheduled Castes. According to this clause we can be adequately represented in the provincial as well as in the Central Services. I therefore support this clause on behalf of the depressed classes.

Dr. Dharam Prakash (United Provinces : (General)

Mr. Vice-President, it is an undoubted fact that "backward" class has not been defined so far and there is no possibility of its being defined in the near future. In fact there is no community which does not have a section of people which is backward, whether economically or educationally or socially. Thus there are backward people in every community. Personally I believe that if there is to be any reservation for backward classes in the services it is very necessary to see as to what is the present position and what is to be the future of a particular class which has been backward for centuries, whether religiously or economically or socially. This view needs careful consideration.

The first objectionable feature of this clause is that it can be instrumental in bringing about a great crisis even in the present circumstances. Every honourable Member knows that our national government has inherited an administrative machinery which always had a very narrow communal, provincial or religious outlook. Even now it is an undeniable fact that whenever the question of reservation in services arises, the people of any province holding a majority of posts or the person holding any office are led by provincial or individual interests in making appointments. If the person concerned belongs to the province of the officer he is favoured from the provincial point of view. If he belongs to his community, he is favoured from the communal point of view and if he belongs to his caste, sub-caste or section, he is favoured from that point of view. The officer does not take into consideration the merit of the candidate but only sees whether he can serve his interest. Therefore he encourages such people alone to join the services. It cannot be expected of this machinery of the old pattern, which is moving at its present speed with great effort, that it will act impartially in making appointments to the services. This is a great danger and to remove it, I think, it is necessary to clarify impartially as to who are the backward classes. This may remove the difficulty. The atmosphere in the country today is such as compels us to demand reservation not in the services but also in the Legislatures. Otherwise I am of the opinion that in a country, which has become free and the constitution of which is being framed with full freedom, there is no necessity for reservation. But the great difficulty which forces us to make a demand for reservation is that there is no such generosity and impartiality in our society as a society needs for its welfare nor is there any possibility of its being there in the near future. Therefore, as it has been suggested by the amendment, I submit that the words 'backward class' should be substituted by 'depressed class' or 'scheduled class' because the latter have a definite meaning. Among the scheduled castes have been included a number of those classes which are accepted by all to be backward. Therefore, I support this amendment in the form that the words 'backward class' should be substituted by the words 'scheduled caste'. I think that reservation in services too is necessary for them for some time. Otherwise I do not even like to have any reservation in the legislatures. I personally hold the view that in this free country it is not proper to make reservation for Hindus, Muslims, Christians and Sikhs on the ground that they are minorities. But in so far as that section of Hindus is concerned who are called Harijans, and they are really backward—it appears to be appropriate that there should be reservation for some time. That too should be for some time only. When they reach the same level of culture as other sections of the population have, I would be the first person to oppose any reservation whatsoever for them. So long as they do not attain that position, I favour reservation. Therefore, I submit that with the addition of these words reservation in services will prove to be useful instead of being harmful.

Shri Chandrika Ram (Bihar : General)

Mr. President, I rise to express my support for Article 10. Several amendments have been moved for inserting the words "Scheduled Castes" after the words "Backward Classes" in this Article, I would like this to be done. Members are perhaps aware of the fact that the question of reservation for Depressed Classes and Scheduled Castes was discussed by the Advisory Committee but it was lost by a single vote. Otherwise there would have been legally binding provisions for reservation in services for the Harijans. But as it is, I find that people are wondering why the expression "Backward Classes" has been put in this article and why is it that "Backward Class" has not been properly defined. The members of the House who have had occasion to go through the Census Reports specially of the years 1921 and 1931, would have found that the expression `Backward Class' has, in a way, been defined therein. So far as I think, and this opinion is borne out by these Reports, our society is divided into three sections—the highest consisting of that section of our society which is known as 'Caste Hindus' and the lowest of the section known as Scheduled Castes or Harijan, while the third occupying a middle position between these two and consisting of a large portion of our people is what may be termed as the Backward Class. I am sorry that this backward class for whose cause Honourable Pandit Hirday Nath Kunzru has pleaded, has not been given reservation in Legislatures, that is neither in the assemblies nor in the councils. I may cite Bihar as a case in point. According to the Census Report, the backward class constitutes a major section of the population of the province. But you will find that with the only exception of Ahir community no other community has been given representation in the Council or Assembly of the province. Their population in the province is about five millions. There are altogether 152 seats in the Assembly and 30 seats in the Council; but in both the Houses the Backward Class has got only two seats. No doubt they are not treated as untouchables. Moreover from the educational and economic point of view they are in a much better condition than the other communties. If a community, however, is to progress and occupy a high position in society it is essential that it must possess political rights. If a community, howsoever, large it may be within a society and whatever pre-eminence it may have reached in the matter of its culture, does not possess political rights and have also no political representation in the Council and the Assembly, I am afraid, I cannot see how it can have the same status as the other communities in the eyes of the State. I, therefore, think that just as we have provided for reservations for the Harijans in Services, in Assemblies and in Councils, it would be proper on our part to make similar provision for backward classes also for whom Pandit Hirday Nath Kunzru has argued so feelingly. We have provided so many privileges to Harijans on the ground that they are backward and I fail to understand why the same argument should not be applied for providing reservations for the backward classes. I think that this is a view requiring serious consideration. We are framing a constitution for our country by which we intend, and this has been specifically stated in the preamble, to secure to all citizens 'Justice, social, economic and political'. But I think that we are actually denying political rights to a large section of our countrymen who constitute in my opinion, a majority of the population. We profess to be providing equal opportunity to all but in fact we are denying this to the backward classes. Therefore, if we really mean to secure equal opportunity to all we should, in Article 10, not only provide for reservation of appointments or posts in favour of backward class of citizens but should also provide for reservation of seats in Legislatures for them. I would like to answer the objection of many members against the retention of the words 'backward class' in this article.

Particularly my socialist friends Seth Damodar Swarup

Seth and Pandit Lokanath Misra have moved amendments seeking deletion of the word 'backward class'. The first observation I would like to make in this connection is that I do not understand why Sethji who is a member of the Socialist Party, which, as is well-known, desires to secure representation for every section of the population, should be raising an objection against the provision in this clause which is for the benefit of the 'Backward Class'. To those who think that no backward class exists in the country, I would only say that they are blind to the facts of the history of our country, to the progressive society of today and to the conditions obtaining at present. I therefore commend wholeheartedly the labours of the Drafting Committee in this respect.

Shri P. Kakkan (Madras : General)

Mr. Vice-President, Sir, I am very glad to support Article 10. The poor Harijan candidates hitherto did not get proper appointments in Government services. The higher officers selected only their own people, but not the Harijans. Sir, even in the matter of promotions, we did not get justice. The Government can expect necessary qualifications or personality from the Harijans, but not merit. If you take merit alone into account, the Harijans cannot come forward. I say in this House that the Government must take special steps for the reservation of appointments for the Harijans for some years. I expect that the Government will take the necessary steps to give more appointments in Police and Military services also. For example, in Kashmir the poor Harijans are fighting with great vigour. I say in this House that the Harijans must be given more jobs in this Government and be encouraged by the Government.

Shri V.I. Muniswamy Pillay (Madras :General)

Mr. Vice President, Sir, in the first two clauses of Article 10, it has been made clear that all citizens will have a general right for the services, but when we come to clause (3), by putting the word 'backward' which has already been pointed out by one of the honourable members, it has not been defined properly. So this throws me in confusion, whether the communities that were left out early in the administration for their due share have been provided for. Sir, in the great upheaval of making a Constitution for this country, I feel that the communities that have not enjoyed the loaves and fishes of the services should not be left out. It is for this purpose, I gave notice of an amendment and a further amendment signed by more than fifty members has been presented to this House, but for reasons well-known to you, Sir, I could not move that amendment. But I wish to make it clear that unless there is an assurance that these communities—I specially mean the Scheduled Castes—are given a chance, unless there is an assurance that these communities will at all times be taken into account and given enough and more chances in appointments, their uplift will still stand over. The other day, Sir, our Honourable Deputy Premier, Sardar Patel, has clearly said that not only justice must be done to the Harijans, but their case must be treated with generosity. It is in that view and spirit I request that a clear indication should be given by this House that the interests of the Scheduled Castes will be looked after. Sir, some honourable Members feel that reservation is not necessary. I think this is unwholesome thinkng, because so long as the communal canker remains in the body politic, I feel there will be communities coming up for reservation; but the case of the Scheduled Castes is not pleaded on a matter of communalism, because they have been left in the lurch and due to their lack of social, economic and educational advancement for years and decades it is necessary, and I also feel that their case must be presented in this House vehemently, so that we may get justice at all times. At the same time I may tell this House that it is not the object of any of the leaders of the Harijan community to perpetuate the communal bogey in this land for ever, but so long as they remain so backward in getting admission into the services, it is highly necessary that they must be given some protection. Sir, in the past, the Government of India had made provision experiencing their inadequacy in the services; and even in my own province the Government of Madras have issued a communal G.O. and thereby have given chances for the

Harijans. Apart from that all those people who have been recruited from the Scheduled Castes have proved worthy of the choice. If I may say so, Sir, even in the Military, we know that in Kashmir they have played their part most efficiently and the very existence of the Chairman of the Drafting Committee here shows the ability that the Scheduled Castes possess.

Shri T. Channiah (Mysore)

Mr. Vice-President, Sir, the retention of the word 'backward' in clause (3) of Article 10 has created some doubt among honourable members from the Madras province. It is a fact, of course, Sir, that the word 'backward' has not been specifically defined in the Draft Constitution. Honourable Members coming from Northern India have been puzzled to note that honourable members coming from the south are very particular about this word 'backward'. In Northern India, for instance, the honourable Members from Northern India are aware that there is a clear distinction between Hindus and Muslims; that much they understand very clearly. They also know that among the Hindus there are classes of people who are agricultural classes, and also people who are engaged in artisan works. They also belong to the backward class. In South India, Sir, the term 'backward classes' is very distinct. The Backward classes in South India, as I am aware, are either socially backward or educationally backward. The only classes who do not fit in this context, namely, clause (3) of article 10 are those who are economically forward. They feel that the word backward, if retained, will come in the way of their interest, namely, entertainment of these classes in the services. Therefore, Sir, the backward classes of people as understood in South India, are those classes of people who are educationally backward, it is those classes that require adequate representation in the services. There are other classes of people who are socially backward; they also require adequate representation in the services The economically forward class of people are really disinterested in the word 'backward' appearing in clause (3) of article 10.

To give a clear picture of this, Sir, I would like to state what obtains in Mysore. There are two classes of vacancies, A and B classes. For the A class vacancies, both the Brahmins and the Non-Brahmins are competent to apply, whereas for the B class vacancies, only the backward classes are entitled to compete. Sir, these backward communities suffer from two disabilities, namely, social disabilities and educational disabilities. It is from these two points of view, that the State Government has specifically provided the appointments in the B class. Therefore, Sir, it is but right that the word 'backward' appearing in clause (3) of Article 10 should be retained. As the Honourable Dr. Ambedkar has rightly said, the retention of the word 'backward' will be very appropriate also for this reason, namely, that clauses (1) and (2) of Article 10 would be null and void if this word 'backward' is not retained in clause (3) of Article 10. I am really sorry that the honourable Pandit Kunzru should have felt that the backward class should be given this opportunity only for a period of ten years. Sir, I want this reservation for 150 yeras which has been the period during which opportunities have been denied to them.

Shri Santanu Kumar Dass (Orissa: General)

...The evil effects of foreign rule in our country prevent us from immediately deleting all provisions relating to reservations from Constitution. So long as these conditions continue in our country we will continue to demand reservations in the services for the Harijans and the scheduled castes, for these are covered by the term 'backward class'. We will go on scrutinising the number of Harijans, Muslims and Christians in the services...At present there is reservation in the elections and therby we get a chance to discuss our problems here. But if there was no such reservation it would not be possible for us to come here as we would not be able to win in the general election. I, therefore, submit that there should be reservation in services and elections. There is one thing more: It has been said that reservation should be kept for ten years. Why only for ten years? If we get equal rights within two years all would be on the same level after that period and there would be no need for reservations. With these words I suppport the article.

Shri H.J. Khandekar

Mr. Vice-President, Sir, I have come here to support Article 10 which is being discussed in the House. Before supporting it, I congratulate the friend who in the Drafting Committee has inserted this word 'backward' in Article 10 clause (3). If this word 'backward' had not been here, the purpose of the scheduled caste would not have been served as it should be. The condition of the scheduled castes has been explained by many friends who made their speeches in the House. The condition is so deplorable that though the candidates of the scheduled castes apply for certain Government posts, they are not selected for the posts because the people who select the candidates do not belong to that community or that section. I can give so many instances about this because I have got the experience from all provinces of the country that the scheduled caste people though they are well qualified do not get opportunity and fair treatment in the services. It would have been better if the word 'scheduled caste' as has been proposed by an amendment by my friend Mr. Muniswamy Pillay would have been inserted in this article. Because the term 'backward' is so vague that there is no definition of this word anywhere, I do not agree with my friend Mr. Chandrika Ram saying that the definition of the word 'backward' is given in the Census report. That is the definition of the word 'scheduled caste' and a list of the castes included in the scheduled caste. But I think the friend who has inserted this word in this article is aiming at the community known as the scheduled caste and when this Constitution is passed and when the article comes into operation, I hope that the Executive who will operate this clause or this Constitution will also aim at the community known as scheduled castes. Our revered leader Thakkar Bapa is in the House. He has been working for this community for about sixteen years as the General Secretary of the Harijan Sewak Sangh. He knows the difficulties of this community socially, economically, educationally, religiously and even politically. If I may say here leaving aside all these aspects, and if we consider the aspect politically, this community is not represented anywhere if no reservation of seats are given to that community.

Mr. Vice-President

You had better confine yourself to the article under discussion, How does politics enter into the picture at all?

Shri H.J. Khandekar

Therefore, if I leave aside the political aspects of the community and come to the social, educational, economical and religious aspects, the condition of the scheduled caste in this respect also is more deplorable than that of any man living in this country. I may say, that if a candidate of the scheduled caste applies for a particualr post in the Government of India or in the Provincial Governments he is ordinarily ignored. There are commissions for recruiting these candidates. There is a Federal Public Service Commission, there are provincial Commissions; and while recruiting—you know, Sir, we people are educationally backward and we cannot come in competition with the other communities—if the qualifications for the Harijan candidates are not relaxed, our candidates will not be able to compete with the candidates of the Brahmin community or the so-called Savarna Hindus. Then if our candidates go to the F.P.S.C. or the Provincial Commissions they will not be successful in the selections as these commissions are not represented by us. I therefore think that while bringing this clause into operation, the F.P.S.C. or the Provincial Commissions should be instructed to relax the qualifications in connection with the Harijan candidates or the Scheduled Caste candidates and there should also be Harijan representatives on these commissions. Moreover, Sir, I know and the House and you too, Sir, know that the Government of India—I mean the present Government of India—has issued a circular about the service for the Scheduled Caste. They have said that in higher services 12½ per cent of the seats are reserved for the scheduled caste and in the lower services 16½ per cent are reserved for them.

Sir, if you just see how the recruiting of scheduled castes candidates is going on in practice, you will find that not even 1 per cent. of these candidates has been recruited in the higher services and in the lower services of the Government of India. Look at the Provincial Governments that have been run by our popular ministeries. Even in those provinces, the schedulecd castes have no adequate representation in the services. I, therefore, would have been very glad if after or before the word 'backward', the word "scheduled castes" had been inserted, because this term "backward" is a vague one and while making the selections, communalism will arise and the commissions, I do not blame them, will be helpless. As was said here by certain friends of mine, communalism is going on, and provincialism is going on and other things are also going on and I am afraid if these things are continued, even if this clause is brought into operation, the scheduled castes will never get a chance, as the word 'backward' would be interpreted in such a way that we people would get no chance in the services because the people of other castes will also claim to be backward and get the chances on reserved posts. Therefore, Sir, before resuming my seat, I would request you to see that the machinery which will operate this clause should be so pure, that no discrimination of any sort should be made between scheduled castes and other people who come under the category of backward classes.

Mr. Mohamed Ismail Sahib (Madras : Muslim)

Mr. Vice-President, Sir, this word 'backward' I cannot understand in the context in which it is put here in clause (3) of Article 10. If one reads the clause without this word, then one can quite clearly and easily understand its meaning. But when the word 'backward' is inserted, it obscures the meaning a great deal. The word 'backward' has not been defined at all anywhere in this Constitution. But I may tell you it has been defined in certain places. In Madras it has got a definite and technical meaning. There are a number of castes and sub-castes called backward communities. The Government of Madras have counted and scheduled more than 150 of these classes in that province and in that province when you utter the word 'backward', it is one of those 150 and odd communities that is meant, and not any community that is generally backward. And I may also say that those 150 and odd communities constitute almost the majority of the population of that Provinces, and everyone of these communities comes from the Hindus—the majority community. In that list the scheduled castes are not included and if you include the scheduled castes also in the class of those backward communities, then all of them put together, will form decidedly the majority of the whole population of that province. I want to know whether by inserting the word 'backward' here you mean the same backward classes as the Madras Government means, I want to know the meaning of the word. I submit that it should not in any way be taken to mean that the backward classes as those of the minority communities such as Muslims, Christians and the shceduled castes people are excluded from the purview of this clause. As a matter of fact, there are backward people amongst the non-majority people as well, The Christians are backward. As a matter of fact they are not adequately represented in the services of the province. So also the Muslims, and also the Scheduled Castes. If any provision is made, it has to be made for such really backward people. It may be pointed out that such a provision is made in Article 296 under the minorities rights. But there the article does not speak of the reservation for those people in the services as this clause (3) does. Therefore, it is here, and that in the fundamental rights that such a provision ought to be made for such minorities as the Muslims, Christians and the Scheduled Castes.

Then, Sir, I am oppsed to the amendment moved by Pandit Kunzru. He says that the Government shall have the right or option of providing for reservation only for a period of ten years. Sir, the measure or yard-stick in any such matter should not be the period of time. The backwardness of the people is the result of conditions which have been persisting and in existence for several centuries and ages, and these will not die off easily. So the measure really should be the steps that are being taken to liquidate that backward condition, and it should be the forwardness of the people which has resulted as a consequence of those steps. Therefore, when these people advance and have come forward as much as any other community in the land, then these very reservations would automatically disappear. I feel that no period need be stipulated at all for this purpose. That period might be less than ten years, or it may be more than ten years, according as the backwardness persists or disappears. The measure, as I said, should be the effect and result of the steps that are bring taken for removing and eliminating those conditions which go to make the backwardness.' I would now request the mover of the motion to at least remove the word 'backward' and make it clear to the House that here, when the clause speaks of reservation, it means also minority communities, who stand in need of such reservations.

Sir, there is only one more point which I have to touch upon. When we speak of reservations and rights and privileges, the bogey of communalism is being raised. Sir, communalism does not come in because people want their rights. When people find that they are not adequately represented, they rightly feel that they must have due representation and then such a demand comes up. It comes because of their non-representation in the srevices, and because of their discontent. When such discontent is removed, the unity of hearts comes in. It is the unity of hearts and not any attempt at a physical unity that will do good to the country and to the people. The differences will be there, but there must be harmony and that is what we all really want, and that harmony can be brought about only by creating contentment amongst the people. And reservation in services is one of the measures we can adopt to bring about contentment among the people. You can then say to the people, "Look here, you have your proper share in the services and you have nothing to complain." When people themselves find that they are given as good an opportunity as others, harmony will be there and the so-called communalism will not come in at all. There are countries which have followed the procedure which I am advocating and quite effectively, they have eliminated communalism. Therefore, I say that one of the ways of removing disharmony and producing harmony, is to make provision for the people's representation in the services and to make them feel that they have got a real share and an effective share in the governance of the country.

Sardar Hukam Singh (East Punjab : Sikh)

Mr. Vice-President, Sir, the point that I want to press before this House has already been touched upon by one or two Members. The Honourable Pandit Kunzru has said that he wants to enquire what relation there is between Article 10 and Article 296. Certainly if we take Article 10, clause (1), it is laid down there that "there shall be equality of opportunity for all citizens in matters of employment under the State". That would mean that when posts are to be filled, that would be done by open competititon and the topmost men would be taken in. That is quite all right; that should be the procedure.

But when we look at articles 296 and 297, those two articles lay down that claims of all minorities shall be taken into consideration :—

"Subject to the provisions of the next succeeding article the claims of all minority communities shall be taken into consideration, consistently with the maintenance of efficiency of administration, in the making of appointments..."

To me it seems that there is some conflict between these two articles. If we are to fill up these posts by open competititon and on merit, certainly we cannot give recognition to the claims of all minorities. Then the best men would be taken in and if some members of the minorities do happen to suceed, that would not be on the consideration of their claims as minorities but that would be under Article 10 as equal citizens of the State. If they get those posts in open competition, it is all right; but if they are not adequately represented by that method, then what Article 296 implies is, that special consideration shall be shown to them to see that their representation is made up.

Sir, there can be only one of these two things—either there can be clear equal opportunity or special consideration. Article 10 says there shall be equality of opportunity, then it emphasises the fact by a negative clause that no citizen shall be discriminated on account of religion or race. It is quite good, but when no indication is given whether this would override Article 296 or Article 296 is independent of it, we are certainly left in the lurch. What would be the fate of the minorities?

In cluase (3) this new phrase "backward class" of citizens has been introduced. We had heard of "depressed class", "scheduled castes", but this "backward class of citizens", so far as our part of the country is concerned, we have never seen used in any statute. Just now we have been told that "backward classes" have been defined in the Province of Madras; that may be, but that is not within my knowledge. Whereas this new term has made apprehensive the members of the scheduled castes and they have pressed here that it should be made clear that it only applies to them, if it is for their benefit, at the same time it has made the minorities apprehensive whether they are being included, as Pandit Kunzru said, whether "backward classes" would include those minorities as well, whether if they are not adequately represented any concession would be shown to them; and if they are not to be included in this phrase then what would be their fate under Article 296. Unless we reconcile these two Articles—296 and 10—the safeguards that are being provided in Article 296 become illusory and there is apprehension in our minds as to whether that article would be to our benefit at all.

Shri K.M. Munshi

Mr. Vice-President, Sir, the oriticism that has been placed before the House so far has revolved round two points. The first point is the scope of amendment No. 82 moved by my honourable friend Shri Alladi Krishnaswami Ayyar; the second is about the word "backward"....There is one point of view which I would like to place before the House. I happen not to belong to the Scheduled Castes; and I am putting that point of view, which possibly may come better from me than my Honourable friend Dr. Ambedkar. Certain members of the Scheduled Castes have expressed a doubt whether by the use of the word "backward classes" their rights or privileges or opportunities will be curtailed in any manner. I cannot imagine for the life of me how, after an experience of a year and a half of the Constituent Assembly any honourable Member of the Scheduled Castes should have a feeling that they will not be included in the backward classes so long as they are backward. I cannot also imagine a time when there is any backward class in India which does not include the Scheduled Caste. But the point I want to draw the attention of these Members to is this. Look at what has been going on in this House for the last year and a half. Take Article 11. From the first time the draft was put before the subcommittee of the Minorities Committee—the Fundamental Rights Committee—there has not been a single member of the non-Scheduled Castes who has ever raised any objection to it. On the contrary, we members who do not belong to the Scheduled Castes, have in order to wipe out this blot on our society, been in the forefront in this matter. Not only that, but Article 296 and even this particular proviso has been put in and supported fully by members of other communities and have been supported by the whole House. There need, therefore, be no fear that the House, as constituted at present or hereafter, will ever make a distinction or discriminate against the Scheduled Castes. That fear, I think, is entirely unfounded. What we want to secure by this clause are two things. In the fundamental right in the first clause we want to achieve the highest efficiency in the services of the State—highest efficiency which would enable the services to function effectively and promptly. At the same time, in view of the conditions in our country prevailing in several provinces, we want to see that backward classes, classes who are really backward, should be given scope in the State services; for it is realised that State services give a status and an opportunity to serve the country, and this opportunity should be extended to every community, even among the backward people. That being so, we have to find out some generic term and the word "backward class" was the best possible term. When it is read with Article 301 it is perfectly clear that the word "backward" signifies that class of people—does not matter whether you call them untouchables or touchables, belonging to this community or that—a class of people who are so backward that special protection is required in the services and I see no reason why any member should be apprehensive of regard to the word "backward".

Pandit Hirday Nath Kunzru

This is begging the question. To argue like this is to argue in a circle.

Shri K.M. Munshi

Well, I have not been able to trace the circle so far, in spite of my learned friend's attempt to make me do it.

An Honourable Member

Who are those backward classes?

Shri K.M. Munshi

Article 301 makes it clear that there will be a Commission appointed for the purpose of investigating what are backward classes. Some reference has been made to Madras. I may point out that in the province of Bombay for several years now, there has been a definition of backward classes, which includes not only Scheduled Castes and Scheduled Tribes but also other backward classes who are economically, educationally and socially backward. We need not, therefore, define or restrict the scope of the word 'backward' to a particular community. Whoever is backward will be covered by it and I think the apprehensions of the Honourable Members are not justified.

Shri T.T. Krishnamachari

Mr. Vice-president, Sir, I am afraid I am in a position of disadvantage, coming as I do after Mr. Munshi, whom the House knows as a very learned lawyer. I now see that his technique in advocacy is to confuse the judge, as—if I had heard him aright—he must have confused the minds of those Members of this House who had some doubts in regard to the provisions of Article 10. Sir, I was reading recently in a newspaper the comments on this Constitution by a celebrated authority—Prof. Ivor Jennings, Vice-Chancellor of the Ceylon University—and he characterises this chapter of fundamental rights as a paradise of lawyers. And, as a piece of loose drafting, Article 10 takes the palm. My own view, if I may be permitted to state it, is that this article had better not find a place in this Chapter on Fundamental Rights.

...I now come to clause (3). Quite a number of friends objected to the word 'backward' in this clause. I have no doubt many of them have pointed out that when this House took a decision in this regard in this particular matter on a former occasion the word 'backward' did not find a place. It was an after-thought which the cumulative wisdom of the Drafting Committee has devised for the purpose of anticipating the possibility of this provision being applied to a large section of the community.

May I ask who are the backwrd class of citizens? It does not apply to a backward caste. It does not apply to a Scheduled Caste or to any particular community. I say the basis of any future division as between 'backward' and `forward' or non-backward might be in the basis of literacy. If the basis of division is litcracy, 80 per cent of our people fall into the backard class citizens, who is going to give the ultimate award? Perhaps the Supreme Court. It will have to find out what the intention of the framers was as to who should come under the category of backward classes. It does not say 'caste'. It says 'class'. Is it a class which is based on grounds of economic status or on grounds of literacy or on grounds of birth? What is it?

My Honourable Friend Mr. Munshi thinks that this word has fallen from heaven like manna and snatched by the Drafting Committee in all their wisdom, I say this is a paradise for lawyers. I do not know if the lawyers who have been on the Cimmittee have really not tried to improve the business prospects of their clan and the opportunities of their community or class by framing a constitution so full of pitfalls... my feeling is that this article is very loosely worded. That the word 'backward' is liable to different interpretations is the fear of some of my friends, though I feel that there is no need for such fear because I have no doubt it is going to be ultimately interpreted by the Supreme authority on some basis, caste, community, religion, literacy or economic status. So I cannot congratulate the Drafting Committee on putting this particular word in; whatever might be the implication they had in their mind. I cannot help feeling that this clause will lead to a lot of litigation...

The Honourable Dr. B.R. Ambedkar

...My friend Mr. T.T. Krishnamachari, has twitted the Drafting Committee that the Drafting Committee, probably in the interests of some members of that Committee, instead of producing a Constitution, have produced a paradise for lawyers. I am not prepared to say that this Constitution will not give rise to questions which will involve legal interpretation or judicial interpretation. In fact, I would like to ask Mr. Krishnamachari if he can point out to me any instance of any Constitution in the world which has not been a paradise for lawyers. I would particularly ask him to refer to the vast storehouse of law reports with regard to the Constitution of the United States, Canada and other countries. I am therefore not ashamed at all if this Constitution hereafter for purposes of interpretation is required to be taken to the Federal Court. That is the fate of every Constitution and every Drafting Committee. I shall therefore not labour that point at all. ...Now, Sir, to come to the other question which has been agitating the members of this House, viz., the use of the word "backward" in clause (3) of Article 10, I should like to begin by making some general observations so that members might be in a position to understand the exact import, the significance and the necessity for using the word "backward" in this particular clause. If members were to try and exchange their views on this subject, they will find that there are three points of view which it is necessary for us to reconcile if we are to produce a workable proposition which will be accepted by all. Of the three points of view, the first is that there shall be equality of opportunity for all citizens. It is the desire of many Members of this House that every individual who is qualified for a particular post should be free to apply for that post, to sit for examinations and to have his qualifications tested so as to determine whether he is fit for the post or not and that there ought to be no limitations, there ought to be no hindrance in the operation of this principle of equality of opportunity. Another view mostly shared by a section of the House is that, if this principle is to be operative—and it ought to be operative in their judgment to its fullest extent—there ought to be no reservations of any sort for any class or community at all, that all citizens, if they are qualified, should be placed on the same footing of equality so far as the public services are concerned. That is the second point of view we have. Then we have quite a massive opinion which insists that, although theoretically it is good to have the principle that there shall be equality of opportunity, there must at the same time be a provision made for the entry of certain communities which have so far been outside the administration. As I said, the Drafting Committee had to produce a formula which would reconcile these three points of view, firstly, that there shall be equality of opportunity, secondly that there shall be reservations in favour of certain communities which have not so far had a 'proper look-in' so to say into the administration. If honourable Members will bear these facts in mind—the three principles, we had to reconcile,—they will see that no better formula could be produced than the one that is embodied in sub-clause (3) of article 10 of the Constitution; they will find that the view of those who believe and hold that there shall be equality of opportunity, has been embodied in sub-clause (1) of Article 10. It is a generic principle. At the same time, as I said, we had to reconcile this formula with the demand made by certain communities that the administration which has now—for historical reasons—been controlled by one community or a few communities, that situation should disappear and that the others also must have an opportunity of getting into the public services. Supposing, for instance, we were to concede in full the demand of those communities who have not been so far employed in the public services to the fullest extent, what would really happen is, we shall be completely destroying the first proposition upon which we are all agreed, namely, that there shall be an equality of opportunity. Let me give an illustration. Supposing, for instance, reservations were made for a community or a collection of communities, the total of which came to something like 70 per cent of the total posts under the State and only 30 per cent are retained as the unreserved. Could anybody say that the reservation of 30 per cent as open to general competition would be satisfactory from the point of view of giving effect to the first principle, namely, that there shall be equality of opportunty? It cannot be in my judgement. Therefore the seats to be reserved, if the reservation is to be consistent with sub-clause (1) of Article 10, must be confined to a minority of seats. It is then only that the first principle could find its place in the Constitution and effective in operation. If honourable Members understand this position that we have to safeguard two things, namely, the principle of equality of opportunity and at the same time satisfy the demand of communities which have not had so far representation in the State, then, I am sure they will agree that unless you use some such qualifying phrase as "backward" the exception made in favour of reservation will ultimately eat up the rule altogether. Nothing of the rule will remain. That I think, if I may say so, is the justification why the Drafting Committee undertook on its own shoulders the responsibility of introducing the word "backward" which, I admit, did not originally find a place in the fundamental right in the way in which it was passed by this Assembly. But I think honourable members will realise that the Drafting Committee which has been ridiculed on more than one ground for producing sometimes a loose draft, sometimes something which is not appropriate and so on, might have opened itself to further attack that they produced a Draft Constitution in which the exception was so large, that it left no room for the rule to operate. I think this is sufficient to justify why the word "backward" has been used.

With regard to the minorities, there is a special reference to that in Article 296, where it has been laid down that some provision will be made with regard to the minorities. Of course, we did not lay down any proportion. That is quite clear from the section itself, but we have not altogether omitted the minorities from consideration. Somebody asked me: "What is a backward community"? Well, I think, any one who reads the language of the draft itself will find that we have left it to be determined by each local Government. A backward community is a community which is backward in the opinion of the Government. My honourable Friend Mr. T.T. Krishnamachari asked me whether this rule will be justiciable. It is rather difficult to give a dogmatic answer. Personally I think it would be a justiciable matter. If the local Government included in this category of reservations such a large number of seats; I think one could very well go to the Federal Court and the Supreme Court and say that the reservation is of such a magnitude that the rule regarding equality of opportunity has been destroyed and the court will then come to the conclusion whether the local Government or the State Government has acted in a reasonable and prudent manner. Mr Krishnamachari asked, "Who is a resonable man and who is a purdent man? These are matters of litigation." Of course, they are matters of litigation, but my honourable Friend, Mr. Krishnamachari will understand that the words "reasonable persons and prudent persons" have been used in very many laws and if he will refer only to the Transfer of Property Act, he will find that in very many cases the words "a reasonable person and a prudent person" have very well been defined and the court will not find any difficulty in defining it. I hope, therefore, that the amendments which I have accepted, will be accepted by the House.[30]

At the revision stage, this Article was renumbered as Article 16 without any alteration or modification in substance and clause (3) become cluase (4) of Article 16.

So, this is how clause (4) of Article 16 was enacted, which, in course of time, became one of those provisions of the Constitution where "the exception ate up the rule altogether".

Sardar Ujjal Singh first suggested in the Minorities' Sub-committee meeting of a provision that would not debar rules being made for giving special consideration to *minority communities* in recruitment to public services. The Minorities' Sub-Committee, therefore, recommended for a proviso to meet the claims of *minorities* to special representation in services. The reasons for having such a provision might have been the existence of a similar clause in Section 298 of the Government of India Act, 1935, itself, on which this provision was largely based.

In the Advisory Committee meeting Munshi first used the word "backward communities" while defending the proposal of the Minorities' Sub-committee. Ambedkar, who was then a member of the Advisory Committee only, favoured reservations in favour of certain minorities. He suggested a clause like "Nothing herein contained shall prevent the Government from prescribing a certain proportion of posts of public service for the *minorities.*" Ambedkar was in favour of using the term 'minority'. bcause he all along considered the depressed classes as a minority and was fighting for a share of posts in the government services for them. It was only the other day, to be specific in August, 1943, that he could prevail on the Central Government, as a member of the Governor-General's Executive Committee, to issue a G.O. specifically reserving $8^1/_3\%$ of posts in Central Government services for the Scheduled Castes (erstwhile depressed class).

But Sardar Patel, Chairman of the Advisory Committee, had a different perception of this provision. He thought that clauses of this nature would only be applicable if there was one Union of the whole of India, provided the

May 16th document stood as it was. But supposing the Muslim League insisted on a division of the country and wanted a portion of the Punjab and a portion of Bengal, in those areas these fundamental rights would not apply. The Land Alienation Act and such other Acts would stand there. If there was to be one Union, there would be no difficulty; but the possibility of the League not coming in would have to be taken into consideration when framing the fundamental rights. But Ambedkar contradicted him, because, whether they came or not, these fundamental rights would be useful for the 'willing areas'. If they did not come in, negotiations would have to be opened for entering into some sort of reciprocal arrangements.[31]

In the hand of a Committee, of which Ambedkar was a member and who actually drafted this cluase, the word 'minorities' was dropped and the word 'classes' was introduced instead. All these changes took place between April 21 and April 30, 1947, when it was more or less known that the transfer of power to the Indians was imminent. The outbreak of large-scale communal riots in several parts of Northern India and the sharply adverse comments of the Muslim League on the Objectives Resolution adopted by the Constituent Assembly convinced everybody that the transfer of power would have to be hastened in order to prevent further deterioration of the situation, which meant not only a division of India but a division of some Provinces, as well, on the basis of religion. This might have hardened the attitude of the framers towards the minority community, i.e., the Muslims, which resulted in changing of the word 'minorities' to 'classes.

The Constitutional Adviser introduced the phrase "any particular classes of citizens" in place of the word "classes" in his Draft Constitution and the Drafting Committee changed the word "particular" to "backward" in October, 1947. Thus, ultimately "backward class" finds its place in the Constitution that we have today.

As we have seen, the Members belonging to the Scheduled Castes, who were given a special opportunity by the Vice-President of the Constituent Assembly to express their views on the subject, as it concerned them intimately, welcomed this provision of clause (3) of Draft Article 10 [Article 16(4)]. Though they knew fully well that the word 'backward', in the absence of a definition to the contrary, would include the Scheduled Castes, pressed for a clarification so that the word 'backward' might apply to them only. To be sure that the 'backward class' included 'Scheduled caste', they in fact, suggested that the words 'backward classes' be substituted by the words "Scheduled Castes" or "depressed classes" or the words "Scheduled Castes" added after the words "backward classes". One of them could not even suppress his feeling and congratulated the friend in the Drafting Committee (meaning Dr. Ambedkar?) who was instrumental for inserting the word "backward" in the clause.

Mohamed Ismail pointed out that in Madras the word "backward" bore a "definite and technical meaning according to which more than a hundred and fifty communities—all belonging to the Hindu majority community—came under this lable and, with the addition of the Scheduled Castes, decidedly constituted the majority of the whole population of the Province. If that was the meaning of the word "backward", Mohamed Ismail apprehended, the backward classes in the minority communities such as the Christians and Muslims would be totally excluded from the purview of the clause.

Ambedkar was rather apologetic for including the word "backward" in this clause. But he also could not define what he meant by this word and ultimately said that "a backward community is a community which is backward in the opinion of the Government". Munshi, another member of the Drafting Committee, thought that "the word backward signifies that class of people—does not matter whether you call them untouchables or touchables belonging to this community or that a class of people who are so backward that special protection is required for then in the services". T.T. Krishnamachari, who later became a member of the Drafting Committee, launched a scathing attack on the Drafting Committee for incorporating this provision in the Constitution. He also wondered what would be the basis for determining backwardness in a country where 80 per cent of the people fell into that category on ground of illiteracy alone. He felt that ultimately the Supreme Court of the country would have to define backwardness on some basis—caste, community, religion, literacy or economic status.

The framers incorporated a provision in the Constitution without defining the term "backward" or laying down the criterion for testing the backwardness of a community or class. As a result backwardness assumed a new dimension in our body politic which divided the people on the basis of "forward" and "backward" community forever. This clause encouraged fissiparous tendencies for the obliteration of which the framers talked so much. Even the colonial British Government which seized every opportunity to give a phillip to the disintegrating and fissiparous forces did not venture to include a clause of this dimension in the 1935 Act. Section 298 of the Government of India Act, 1935 which provided that "no subject of His Majesty domiciled in India shall on grounds only of religion, place of birth, descent, colour or any of them be ineligible for office under the Crown in India, or be prohibited on any such grounds from acquiring, holding or disposing of property or carrying on any occupation, trade, business or profession in British India", and an exception in clause (3) conferring special responsibility on the Governor-General or on a Governor for the safeguarding of the legitimate interests of *minorities*. Even then it has been held that clause (3) has no bearing on the question of appointments to offices mentioned in this Section.[32] But the framers in their wisdom had incorporated an exception which was so large that it practically left no room for the rule to operate and almost ensured the destruction of the fundamental right of equality of opportunity enshrined in Article 16 (1) and (2) of the Constitution.

The absurdity arising out of not defining 'backward classes' is seen in a Mysore case.[33] In this case the old order of the Mysore Government dated 16-5-1921 that the term 'backward communities' should be understood as including all communities other than Brahmins who are not adequately represented in services was sustained as there was no constitutional definition for the term 'backward classes'.

There is nothing to prevent classes other than Scheduled Castes and Scheduled Tribes and even Non-Hindus such as Chrisitians and Sikhs, from being included in the list of 'Backward Classes' and the authority to do it is the State and it appears court could not question the discretion of the State in this regard. Since neither the Constitution nor law described the procedure for identification of backward classes, it was left to the State to adopt such procedures that it thought fit. When the Constitution allows this unfettered power to the State, courts cannot possibly attempt to substitute their own view on it. Possibly only a gross abuse of the State's power, anounting almost to a fraud on the Constitution, may invoke the interference of the judiciary. Ordinarily the latter will not interfere. It, therefore, appears that to leave the term 'Backward Classes' unenumerated in a Schedule has led to certain abuses by the executive or scheming party politicians who have majority in their side to create such 'classes' to suit their own ends.

The Framers had not provided categorical answers to the basic questions of reservation for whom, and for how long. Unlike reservation of seats in the Legislatures, there is no time limit of this reservation. As it stands, this reservation will go on till eternity. Pandit Kunzru's attempt in the Constituent Assembly to limit the operation of this provision to a period of ten years did not get any support. The Framers refused to face facts; unless the system changes, no amount of reservations or Government concessions can improve the lot of the really backward. By providing for reservation of appointment or posts in favour of backward classes indefinitely, they thought that they had done their duty towards this section of people. They conveniently forgot that if the country was to move forward, it was to move forward as a nation, as 'Indians', and not as so many Brahmins, so many non-Brahmins, so many Scheduled Castes, so many 'forward classes' and so many 'backward classes'. Since this constitutional provision has put a premium on 'backwardness' of a community, there is now even a mad race for inclusion in the list of 'Backward Classes'. Reservation of posts is never going to solve the problem of 'backwardness' of the community or to advance the 'backward classes', because only a few, that too only those more advantaged among them, will get jobs and this will only further accentuate the differences even among the members of the backward classes, because within the enumerated 'Backward Classes' each component individual can invoke the 'equal protection' clause of Article 14. Any attempt to dislodge the disavantaged group/section of the Backward Classes from the position of power and authority, as a consequence of entry in 'services', is often resisted, even violently. The recent directive of the Supreme Court[34] to identify and exclude the 'creamy layers' of the Backward Classes could have corrected the imbalance to some extent, had it been implemented in true spirit. By accepting the recommendations of the committee, constituted in pursuance of the directive of the Supreme Court, that the 'creamy layer' would be restricted to those earning Rs. one lakh and above per annum, the Central Government might have carried out the orders of the Supreme Court in letter but surely not in spirit. In a country where around 25% of the people live below the poverty level, the gross income of most of the workforce, specially in the unorganised sector, does not ecceed Rs. 10,000 per annum and not even 1% of the Government servants earn Rs 1 lakh and above per annum, the prudence of such a yardstick can easily be questioned. One is prone to conclude that it was a conscious effort to whittle down the verdict of the Supreme Court. The lot of the really backward will not improve and they remain as they were.

The Supreme Court in its judgement in the *Mandal case*[35] has also directed the Union of India, the State Governments and the Union Territories to constitute

Commissions to act on representations for inclusion in, and exclusion from, the list of Backward Classes. These Commissions will be permanent in nature. Quite predictably, the Supreme Court has refrained from giving any guidelines for enumeration of the Backward Classes. This is the job of the executives, and more pertinently of the legislatures. Now that a term has been imported in our Constitution without defining it, these Commissions will face an uphill task in enumerating the Backward Classes. Will they be enumerated on the basis of caste, community, sect, literacy, income, social position, adequacy of employment in Government services, employment opportunities, size of family or what? Will they be categorised region-wise or even sub-sect-wise? Was it really necessary to incorporate a term without assessing its true import? It is better to remember that even Ambedkar at the initial stage of framing of the Constitution did not insist on using such a word and, in fact, suggested that reservations should be 'in favour of classes as may be prescribed by the State'. Though he demanded reservations for a section of Hindu, known as Schedled Castes, he did not favour the creation of any other layer in the society excepting those already existing. In their eagerness to project themselves as true champions of the cause of the 'backward sections of people', the Framers created more divisions in the society, then what they possibly could conceive of. They talked of integrating the country, but by their deed and actions, as it seems, strengthened the divisive forces in the body politic. Will it be improper to say that the same old 'Divide and Rule' policy was at the back of their mind?

Notes and References

1. Rao, *op. cit.*, Vol. II, p. 74.
2. *Ibid.*, p. 86.
3. *Ibid.*, p. 49.
4. *Ibid.*, p. 81.
5. *Ibid.*, p. 118.
6. *Ibid.*, p. 138.
7. *Ibid.*, p. 148.

8. Rao, *op. cit.*, Vol. II, pp. 164, 167.
9. *Ibid.*, pp. 171-72.
10. *Ibid.*, p. 200.
11. *Ibid.*, p. 204.
12. *Ibid.*, p. 208.
13. *Ibid.*, pp. 223-26.
14. *Ibid.*, pp. 258-63.
15. *CAD*, Vol. III, pp. 440-41.
16. *Ibid*, dated 30-4-47, pp. 445-51.
17. Rao, *op. cit.*, Vol. III, p. 8.
18. *Ibid.*, p. 215.
19. *Ibid.*, p. 325.
20. *Ibid.*, p. 328.
21. *Ibid.*, pp. 521-22.
22. Rao, *op. cit.*, Vol. IV. pp. 31-32.
23. *CAD*, Vol. VII, dated 30-11-48. pp. 673-74, 676.
24. *Ibid.*, p. 676.
25. *Ibid.*, p. 677.
26. *Ibid.*, p. 679.
27. *Ibid.*, p. 673, 679, 681.
28. *Ibid.*, p. 697.
29. *Ibid.*, pp. 699-02.
30. *Ibid.*, pp. 673-02.
31. *Op. cit.*, Vol. II, p. 225.
32. Anand, C.L. *Constitutional Law and History of Government of India*, The University Book Agency, Allahabad 1990, p. 735.
33. *B.S. Kesava Iyengar v. State of Mysore*, AIR 1956 May, 20.
34. *The Statesman*, November 17, 1992.
35. *Indra Sawheny v. Union of India*, AIR 1993 SC 477.

13

Claims of Scheduled Castes and Scheduled Tribes to services and posts (Article 335)

The Advisory Committee constituted on February 27, 1947 the Minorities Sub-Committee whose mission was, as Sardar Vallabhbhai Patel put it, to safeguard the interests of all minorities to their satisfaction. The personnel of the Sub-Committee included all the minority interests. Members belonging to the Scheduled Castes and Scheduled Tribes were also represented on it. The members of the Sub-Committee were asked to send their views on the question of providing adequate political, economic, religious, educational and cultural safeguards for the minorities.

Ambedkar's note on the subject of minorites and fundamntal rights provided for right to the Scheduled Castes for representation in the services in clause 3 of Part I of Article II, Section IV:

(a) The quantum of representation of the Scheduled Castes in the Services shall be as follows:

(i) In the Union Services—In proportion to the ratio of their population to the total population in India or British India as the case may be.

(ii) In the State and Group Services—In proportion to their population in the State or Union.

(iii) In the Municipal and Local Board Services.—In proportion to their population in the Municipal and Local Board areas:

Provided that no minority community is allowed to claim more than its population ratio of representation in the services.

(b) Their right to representation in the Services shall not be curtailed except by conditions relating to minimum qualifications, education, age, etc.

(c) The conditions prescribed for entry in services shall not abrogate any of the concessions given to the Scheduled Castes by the Government of India in their Resolutions of 1942 and 1945.

(d) The method of filling up the vacancies shall conform to the rules prescribed in the Government of India Resolutions of 1942 and 1946.

(e) On every Public Services Commission or committee constituted for filling vacancies, the Scheduled Castes shall have at least one representative.[1]

Jagjivan Ram, a prominent leader of the Scheduled Castes and a Minister in the Central Government, suggested that the political safeguards for the Scheduled Castes should include reservation of seats in services of all categories, civil including judiciary and military, and in local bodies, proportionate to their population.[2]

H.J. Khandekar suggested that the Scheduled Castes, being in terms of population equal to Muslims, the reservation of seats in the public services should not be less favourable than the representation given to Muslim.[3]

The All-India Adi Hindu Depressed Classes Association demanded representation of the Scheduled Castes in proportion to their population in the public services.[4]

R.N. Brahma wanted that the Plains Tribal people of Assam should have their legitimate and due shares in Central services and in Provincial Government services on the basis of their population.[5]

Sardar Ujjal Singh and Sardar Harnam Singh in their memorandum demanded that Sikhs should have reserved for them 5 per cent of the Central Services or at least $8^1/_3$ per cent reserved for small communities according to the existing arrangement should be split up on the basis of population of these communities to ensure a separate share for the Sikhs. In the Punjab 25 per cent, in North-West Frontier Province 10 per cent and proportionate share of the existing reservation of 10 per cent in the United Provinces representation in the services were demanded. In the defence services the proportion of Sikhs should not be lower than what they already enjoyed.[6]

Dr., Shyama Prasad Mukherjee recommended that during the transitional period 50 per cent posts in all public service should be recruited purely on merit as the result of open competitive examination, and the remaining 50 per cent filled on population basis by selecting the best candidates from each community. Communal inequalities, if any, in the first half should not be made up from the other half. This latter percentage should be reduced after every five years, by progressive stages and entirely done away with after twenty years.[7]

Memoranda were submitted on behalf of the smaller minorities. The memoranda submitted on behalf of the Anglo-Indians demanded a preferential claim to a percentage of appointments in the Railways, in the Customs and in the Post and Telegraph Departments, in view of the fact that in the past members of the community were dependent on the public services, particularly in these departments, for their existence, and any sudden upsets would seriously prejudice the community's economy.[8]

Homi Mody, on behalf of the Parsis, said that his community had never asked for any special privileges, but their position was that if other minorities were accorded special representation anywhere, the Parsis should also receive treatment at least equal to that given to one of the smaller minorities.[9]

Rajkumari Amrit Kaur was against safeguards of any kind. M. Ruthnaswamy advocated representation of national religious and cultural minorities like Muslims, Sikhs, Indian Christians and Anglo-Indians in all departments of the administration in the central and states, according to population.[10]

The Muslim League was not participating in the proceedings of the Assembly; and no memorandum, on behalf of the Muslim community was presented.

The Minorities Sub-Committee met on July 21-27, 1947, to consider the political safeguards for the minorities and their representation in the public services. By this time the question of partition had been decided and the Muslim League was also represented in the Sub-Committee.

The decisions reached at the meetings of the Sub-Committee were embodied in the report drafted and approved on the day of its last sitting, i.e. on July 27, 1947.

The report of the Sub-Committee on the subject of reservation for the minorities in the public services to the Advisory Committee is reproduced below:

(1) The sub-committee voted on the general propostion that there shall be reservation in the public services for the different communities mentioned in groups A, B and C of paragraph 3(3),

It was agreed that the provisions, if any, regarding reservations should appear in a schedule to the Constitution Act and should have the force of a directive of Government policy. The decisions were as follows:

(i) Agreed by a majority of votes (16 to 1) that there shall be reservation in the services for the Scheduled Castes.

(ii) Agreed by a majority of votes (9 to 7) that there shall be reservation in the services for Muslims.

(iii) Agreed by a majority of votes (6 to 1) that there shall be reservation in the services for Sikhs.

(iv) Agreed by a majority of votes (12 to 1) that there shall be reservation in the services for plains tribes in Assam.

(v) Agreed by a majority of votes (12 to 3) that there shall be reservation in the services for Anglo-Indians.

Note: The Parasees and the Indian Christians did not ask for reservation in services.

(2) Mr. Ali Zaheer moved the following resolution:

This committee recommends that in the Provincial as well as Central services, the claims of all the minorities should be kept in view in making appointments to such services consistently with the consideration of efficiency of administration. The committee further recommends that suitable provision to this effect may be embodied in some form in the Constitution or in some other way.

When this proposition was put before the sub-committee, Chaudhuri Khaliquzzaman raised the point that the proposition was out of order in view of the decision already taken in para (1) above. The Chairman did not accept this view.

Nine members voted for Mr. Ali Zaheer's proposition and 9 against.

(3) The sub-committee then considered the question as to whether seats should be reserved even for posts for which competitive examinations are held. The decisions were as follows:

(i) Agreed by a majority of votes (11 to 6) that there should be reservation for Scheduled Castes in services to which recruitment was made by competitive examination.

(ii) Decided by a majority of votes (8 to 7) that there should be no reservation for Muslims, Sikhs and tribesmen.

Note: Anglo-Indians did not want reservation in services of this category. Parsees and Indian Christians did not want reservation in any services, whether filled by competition or otherwise.

(4) Chaudhuri Khaliquazzaman, before these propos-

als were put to vote, raised a point of order that as the sub-committee had already decided on reservation in the services for certain communities in unqualified terms, it was not in order now to break up the proposition into compartments and vote on each of them separately. The Chairman did not accept this view on the ground that it had from the very beginning been understood that these matters would be considered separetely. On this ruling being given, Ch. Khaliquzzaman and the Hon'ble Mr. Ismail Chundrigar abstained from taking part in the voting on the above propositions.

Subsequently, Maulana Hifzur Rahman also raised the same point of order, and the Chairman again ruled it out.

(5) The next question examined was on what basis reservation should be made in those cases in which the committee had decided in favour of reservation. It was proposed that reservation should be on the basis of population. This was rejected by the sub-committee by a majority of 9 to 8 votes.[11]

Rajkumari Amrit Kaur, in her minute of dissent, recorded her opposition in the matter of reservation in the services. She held that anything in the nature of privileges for any special class or section of society was wrong in principle; and when it was given on the ground of religion, it was doubly wrong, for all religions stood for the brotherhood of man and none for separatism. Moreover, such reservations and special privileges would militate against the declared objective of the Indian Union, which was to establish a classless society. Special privileges and protection, she feared, would lead to the fragmentation of the Indian nation. She even questioned the legal existence of the depressed classes the moment the new Constitution came in. She said :

Once untouchability is abolished and its practice made a criminal offence who are the Scheduled

> Castes? They have always been and will now, I submit, become legally one with most of the backward and ignorant poor Hindus of this country. They need straightaway all the necessary facilities and oportunities for raising their standards of education and life in general.[12]

The report of the Minorities Sub-Committee was discussed by the Advisory Committee for four days, from July 28 to 31.

On July 30, 1947, Ali Zaheer moved the same resolution which he moved in the Minorities Sub-Committee earlier on claims of all the minorities to services and discussion on that resolution was postponed till the next day.[13]

On July 31, Muniswamy Pillai moved the following amendment to Syed Ali Zaheer's amendment, namely, that the words "consistently with the consideration of efficiency of administration" be deleted. Chaudhuri Khaliquzzaman moved the amendment that seats should be reserved in the public services for minorities on the population basis. Dr. Ambedkar asked that the case of the Scheduled Castes might be treated separately. So far as they were concerned, seats should be reserved for them on the population basis. Subject to this he was prepared to accept Syed Ali Zaheer's resolution. Frank Anthony moved the following amendment:

> Owing to the complete dependence of the economy of the Anglo-Indian community on their position in certain services and their existing educational facilities, a sub-committee consisting of the following members be appointed to submit a report: Pandit Pant, Mr. Munshi, Mrs. Hansa Mehta, Mr. Prater, and Mr. Anthony.

After discussion, the amendments were put to the vote and lost with the exception of Mr. Anthony's which was carried. Syed Ali Zaheer's original resolution was also carried.[14]

The Advisory Committee sent its report to the President of the Constituent Assembly on August 8, 1947.

On the subject of representation in services of the minority communities, the Advisory Committee reported that

> A proposal was made to us that there should be a constitutional guarantee of representation in the public services of the minority communities in proportion to their population. We are not aware of any other constitution in which such a guarantee exists, and, on merits, we consider, as a general proposition that any such guarantee would be a dangerous innovation. At the same time, it is clear to us that consistently with the need of efficiency in administration, it is necessary for the State to pay due regard to the claims of minorities in making appointments to public services. We recommend, therefore, that as in the case of appointments to Cabinets, there should be in some part of the Constitution or the Schedule an exhortation to the Central and Provincial Government to keep in view the claims of all the minorities in making appointments to public services consistently with efficiency of administration.[15]

It, therefore, recommended in clause 9 of its recommendation that

> Due share to all minorities guaranteed:
>
> In the all-India and Provincial Services, the claims of all the minorities shall be kept in view in making appointments to these services consistently with the consideration of efficiency of administration.
>
> Note: Appropriate provision shall be embodied in the Constitution or a Schedule thereto to this effect.[16]

The report of the Advisory Committe on minority rights was considered by the Constituent Assembly on August 27 and 28, 1947. Introducing the report, Sardar Vallabhbhai Patel informed the House that on the question of representation in the services

> The general standard that we have accepted is that ordinarily competitive posts must go by merit and if

> we are to depart from this, the general administration would suffer immensely. It is well-known that since this departure has been introduced in the matter of services our administration has suffered considerably. Now that we begin afresh, we must see that where we have to fill some administrative posts of a higher level, these posts have to be filled by competition, i.e., by competitive examination and competitive tests. We have made some concessions in the matter of certain communities which require a little help.[17]

Cause 9 was considered by the Constituent Assembly on August 28. Mahavir Tyagi moved an amendment for dropping of the word "guaranteed" occurring in the marginal note. The President also observed that it might be left out from the heading.

There was hardly any discussion on this clause. Only Chandrika Ram requested Sardar for an assurance that there would be full protection for the minorities in the provincial services as well and that what was contained in the clause would find a place somewhere in the constitution. Clause 9 was thereafter adopted by the Assembly.[18]

This decision of the Constituent Assembly was incorporated in the Draft Constitution prepared by the Constitutional Adviser in October, 1947, as clause 226:

> Claims of minority communities to services and posts—Subject to the provision of the next succeeding section the claims of all minority communities shall be taken into consideration, consistently with the maintenance of efficiency of administration, in the making of appointments to services and posts in connection with the affairs of the Federation or a Province.[19]

Clause 226 was considered and revised by the Drafting Committee on February 5, as follows:

> Subject to the provisions of the next succeeding article the claims of all minority communities shall be taken into consideration, consistently with the

> maintenance of efficiency of administration, in the making of appointment to services and posts in connection with the affairs of the Union or of a State for the time being specified in Part I of the First Schedule.[20]

The Drafting Committee also decided that the heading of Part XII in which clause 226 was placed by the Constitutional Adviser should be changed to "Special provisions relating to minorities."[21]

In the Draft Constitution settled and published by the Drafting Committee in February, 1948, this provision appeared as Article 296 in Part XIV—Special provisions relating to minorities.[22]

When this Draft Constitution was circulated for eliciting suggestions, comments, etc., K. Santhanam, M. Ananthasayanam Ayyangar, Shrimati G. Durgabai and T.T.krishnamachari suggested substitution of the article by the following:

> Subject to the provisions of the next succeeding article, only individual merit and qualifications shall be taken into consideration in the making of appointments to services and posts in connection with the affairs of the Union or of a State for the time being specified in Parts I and II of the First Schedule;
>
> Provided, however, that the claims of Scheduled Castes and Scheduled Tribes and educationally backward sections of the population for a fair share of representation shall be taken into consideration consistently with the maintenance of efficiency of administration.

The Constitutional Adviser's comments on this suggestion were that the effect of this amendment would be to exclude the Muslims and the Indian Christian community from the protection afforded to the minorities by Article 296. The words "a fair share of representation" in the redraft of this article suggested by this amendment were vague. Article 296 was based on the recommendation of the Advisory Committee on Minority Rights which had been adopted by the Constituent Assembly. This amendment involved a departure from the decision of the Constituent Assembly and should therefore be left to the Constituent Assembly for final decision.

S. Nagappa, H.J. Khandekar, Dharam Prakash, Yashwant Rai, Chandrika Ram. V.C. Kesava Rao, T. Channaya and Shrimati Dakshayani Velayudhan suggested that for the words "Part I" the words "Parts I, II and III" be substituted and the follwing be added at the end:

> but in the case of Scheduled Castes there shall be reservation in services and posts on their population basis with a requisite minimum qualification for the service or post.

The Constitutional Adviser noted that the amendment sought (a) to extend the application of Article 296 to appointments to services and posts in connection with the affairs of any State specified in Parts II and III of the First Schedule; and (b) to provide for special reservation for members of the Scheduled Castes possessing the requisite qualifications in respect of services and posts in proportion to their population. As regards (a), the Constitutional Adviser pointed out that the Advisory Committee was also of opinion that the provisions relating to the claims of minorities to public services and posts should be made applicable to all States including States in Part III of the First Schedule and to give effect to the views of the Special Committee an amendment had been suggested to omit the words "for the time being specified in Part I of the First Schedule" from Article 296 and the first part of this amendment would not therefore be necessary. As regards (b), the Constitutional Adviser pointed out that the Advisory Committee on Minority Rights had not recommeded any special provision to be included in the Constitution for reservation in respect of services and posts for the Scheduled Castes and so the second part of this amendment should be left to the Constituent Assembly for final decision.

Tajamul Hussain suggested that Article 296 be deleted. On this amendment, the Constitutional Adviser observed that Article 296 was based on the recommendation of the Advisory Committee on Minority Rights which had been adopted by the Constituent Assembly. This amendment involved a departure from the decision already taken by the Constituent Assembly and should therefore be left to the Constituent Assembly for final decision.

The Drafting Committee decided that in Article 296 the words "for the time being specified in Part I of the First Schedule" be omitted. The background for moving this amendment was that the Special Committee was of opinion that the provisions relating to the claims of minorities to public services and posts should be made applicable to all States including the States in Part III of the First Schedule.[23]

Before the Draft Article 296 could be taken up for consideration by the Constituent Assembly, the Assembly took a momentous decision on May, 25, 1949, with the consent of all the minorities, to abolish reservations on communal grounds. Draft Articles 292 and 294 were adopted in the assembly on August 23 providing reservation of seats for the Scheduled Castes and Scheduled Tribes in the House of People and in the State Assemblies, respectively.

After the adoption of the Draft Article 292 and 294, Draft Article 296 came up for discussion on August 26, 1949. Before Ambedkar could formally move an amended article restricting to the Scheduled Castes and Scheduled Tribes any special treatment in the matter of recruitment to the public service, objection was raised to this proposal by Naziruddin Ahmed and Sardar Hukam Singh, especially on the ground that the amendment was not in accordance with the previous decisions of the Assembly and was grossly in violation of the agreement with the minorities who had consented to give up reservation of seats in the legislatures and not reservation in the services. T.T. Krishnamachari contended that since the Muslims and the Indian Christians were no longer to be treated as minorities the new article was perfectly in order. Ambedkar said that in view of the fact that the Advisory Committee had come to the conclusion on the consent of the two minorities—Muslims and Christians—that they were not to be treated as minorities and that the House had also accepted that the only minorities to be provided for in this manner were the Scheduled Castes and Scheduled Tribes, the Drafting Committee was bound by the decision of the House and to alter the article in terms of such decision. The President felt that since matters relating to minorities had always been decided with their consent, the difference of opinion should be ironed out in private discussion and till then the article should stand over.[24]

The consideration of Draft Article 296 was again postponed on September 9, as some members had got notice of certain amendments to the article too late.[25]

Ambedkar finally moved the amended Article on October 14, 1949 when an acrimonious debate followed. Sardar Bhupindar Singh Man raised a point of order that in accordance with the decisions of the Minorities Committee certain decisions were taken. These decisions were partially modified with regard to reservation of seats in the legislatures only. As regards reservation in the services, it was allowed to remain intact. So unless a special resolution was moved the present House was not competent to go back upon its own decisions. Naziruddin Ahmed also raised a similar point of order. The President ruled that under Rule 32, if one-fourth of the Member present and voting were in favour of reopening, the question can be reopened. On obtaining opinion of the House, this matter was reopened.[26]

Hukam Singh moved an amendment making it clear that in regard to appointments to the public services, the Constitution should require the Central and State Governments to give special consideration to all minorities, and not only to Scheduled Castes and Scheduled Tribes, as was now proposed by the Drafting Committee. He added an explanation specifying Muslims, Christians, Sikhs, Anglo-Indians and Parsis as the recognised minorities. In an impassioned speech, Hukam Singh complained that step by step the protection and safeguards to minorities had been whittled down, until only two provisions were left—consideration for appointment to the public services and inclusion within the scope of functions of the special officer on minorities. He alleged that the pledges given to the Sikhs from time to time were being violated; and he urged the Assembly "to go slow"; he appealed to the majority to win the confidence of the minorities by "positive actions and not by slogans"—the positive action suggested being apparently the retention of the direction to be given to the Central and State Governments to ensure proper representation in the public services for all minorities.

Brajeshwar Prasad moved an amendment to ensure that the maintenance of efficiency of administration should be the only consideration in the making of appointment to services and that the President alone would be vested with powers to appoint persons of the Scheduled Castes and Scheduled Tribes.

Guptanath Singh moved an amendment seeking to include "educationally and socially backward castes" within the ambit of this Article as well. Kamath's amendment was verbal in nature.

During general discussion only two members spoke. While R.K. Sidhva supported the ammedment moved by Ambedkar, it fell on the shoulder of Vallabhbhai Patel to give replies to all the comments of the Members. He said that the question of representation in the public services was specifically raised in the Advisory Committee and it was agreed that neither this nor any other matter would be raised. He also said that the Sikhs were not backward in any respect—in trade. commerce, industry or anything else. He therefore appealed to them to "forget that psychology". He also appealed to the Muslims to drop claims for minor provisions.

After this, the following article, as moved by Ambedkar, was adopted by the Assembly:

Claims of Scheduled Castes and Scheduled Tribes to

services and posts—The claims of the members of the Scheduled Castes and the Scheduled Tribes shall be taken into consideration, consistently with the maintenance of efficiency of administraion, in the making of appointments to services and posts in connection with the affairs of the Union or of a State.

This is the full text of the deliberations[27] in the Constituent Assembly:

Sardar Hukam Singh (East Punjab: Sikh)

Mr. President, Sir, I beg to move:

"That with reference to amendment No. 3163 of the List of amendments, for Article 296, the following be substituted:-

> 296. Subject to the provisions of the next succeeding article the claims of all minority communities shall be taken into consideration, consistently with the maintenance of efficiency of administration, in the making of appointments to services and posts in connection with the affairs of the Union or of a State for the time being specified in Parts I & III the First Schedule.
>
> Explanation:—Among others Muslims, Christians, Sikhs, Anglo-Indians and Parsees shall be recognised as minority communities"

And then there is the alternative amendment as well, but I do not propose to move it. I leave it here.

Sir, as has already been pointed out, the original draft that was put before this House was different, and radically different I would say, from the one that is being proposed now. It read like this:

> "296 Subject to the provisions of the next succeeding article the claims of all minority communities shall be taken into consideration, consistently with the maintenance of efficiency of administration, in the making of appointments to services and posts in connection with the affairs of the Union or of a State for the time being specified in Part I of the First Schedule."

My object is very clear. What I want is to restore the original proposal that had already been accepted by this House. I cannot understand why the Drafting Committee has thought it fit to bring about this change. So far as that article stood in its original form, it was considered as a safeguard for the minorities, and I must say that it was only a solemn affirmation of bonafides on behalf of the majority, and a mental satisfaction to the minority. Otherwise it had not very much value. That right was not justiciable in any court of law and it could not be enforced anywhere else as well. It had no binding force. But in spite of that, it is being taken away now. I must, at the same time, make myself clear that so far as I can think out, it was no blot on our secularism and it did not soil our nationalism as well. The minorities have always been advised to repose full confidence in the majority. Article 296 as originally framed, in my opinion, was that complete reposal of confidence by the minorities in the majority and nothing beyond that. The only thing that the members of the minority could do at any time, in cases of violation was that the attention of the majority could be drawn to the fact, that there was some pledge or an undertaking; and that is also being removed.

Sir, before I proceed further, I must make an appeal to the honourable Members on two points here. It is very unfortunate that the Sikhs for the present cannot persuade themselves to have implicit faith in the party in power. They have reasons for that, for they think that the past is a record of repudiated promises and broken pledges. Suppose, for the sake of argument, that I am wrong, that this is incorrect, and that the present leaders can be trusted to do justice to everybody; then is there any guarantee that the present leaders will continue for all time to come? Are there not indications, even now apparent, that men with different ideals and aims might come to power very soon? This House should take a detached view and not consider the fear of the minorities as necessarily a disparagement of the present party or of its leaders.

Then my second point is that the honourable

Members should place themselves in the position of the minorities and then try to appreciate those fears that they have expressed from time to time.

Sir, I might be accused of communalism when I sound this discordant note. But I hold that this nationalism is an argument for vested interests. Even the aggressiveness of the majority would pass off as nationalism, while the helplessness of the minority might be dubbed as communalism. It is very easy for the majority to preach nationalism to the minorities; but it is very difficult to act up to it. The original draft of Articles 296 and 299 was a result of the recommendations of the Minorities Committee, dated the 8th August, 1947, as accepted by the Constituent Assembly on 27/28th August of that year, and there were four definite provisions, four definite clauses for these safeguards. The first was joint electorates with reservation of seats. This was embodied in 292. Then as regards Cabinet it was provided that there would be no reservation, but a Schedule would be provided as Instrument of Instruction, that was schedule 4; and then the claims of minorities to be kept in view in appointments to services, that was section 296: and then a Commission for minorities, that was embodied in Article 299.

As for the Sikhs, Sir, I must make a special mention, because I think they are very unfortunate in this respect. When the question of safeguards for minorities was decided in 1947, the question as regards the Sikhs was kept pending as it was said that the result of the partition was not known very clearly then. I may say that before that date, the "Award" had been given. The Sikhs were leaving the West Punjab under circumstances which are well known to everybody here. They had willingly suffered themselves to be vivisected and they elected to remain with India. They were marching on foot, leaving behind everything that they loved. They were not coming alone. They had saved and brought seven districts to the Indian Dominion. The full significance of leaving open the question of Sikh minority on 28th August cannot fully be understood when we look at these events. If the Sikhs were not to be treated in some special way, where was the need for consideration of that question then? If the Sikhs were to be given reservation on population basis, just as any other minority had been given, what was to be awaited after August? What number migrated to India was not material at all. But it was considered that might be too great a blow at that time to bear for this unfortunate community. So the question was kept pending and the Sikhs thought that they would get special consideration on account of their sufferings.

Then came the next stage for the Minorities Sub-Committee to make a report and that is dated 23rd November 1948. That time was considered opportune for telling them that nothing special could be done for them, perhaps because more than a year had elapsed since that calmity came. But even then there was one satisfaction offered to the Sikhs. Though special safeguards were denied, pious platitudes were offered instead. The Sub-Committee observed:

> "It seems scarcely necessary for us to say that in dealing with this problem we are acutely aware of the tragic sufferings which the Sikh community suffered both before and after the Partition of the Punjab. The holocaust in West Punjab has deprived them of many valuable lives and great material wealth. Moreover, while in this respect the Hindus suffered equally with the Sikhs, the special tragedy of the Sikhs was that they had to abandon many places particularly sacred to their religion. But while we fully understand the emotional and physical strain to which they have been subjected, we are clear in our mind that the question remitted to us for consideration must be settled on different grounds."

Then comes the third stage. The report is placed before the Minorities Committee and the resolution adopted is that the system of reservation for minorities other than Scheduled Castes in Legislatures be abolished.

I have to apologise to the members of the other minorities. They had their reservation. But, as soon as the Sikhs came in, they had to give up that as well. The

Committee recommended that statutory reservation of seats should be abolished. I want to place more emphasis on that, because it is clearly the recommendation of the Sub-Committee as well as the resolution of Minorities Committee that the statutory reservation of seats in Legislatures should be abolished. There is nothing boyond it. This recommendation was accepted on 26th May 1949.

Now, the position was that there was reservation in legislatures under Article 292. That has gone now. Article 292 stands amended in that sense.

Then there was the Fourth Schedule of Instrument of Instructions. That has also gone, as decided by us on 11th October. But the remaining two clauses embodied in Articles 296 and 299, which we have just decided to reopen, reflect the decision of the Constituent Assembly. So far as I can see there is absolutely no reason for that change that is intended to be brought about now.

The second point is that the Minorities Committee never recommended any change in these two articles. My third point is that the minorities themselves never agreed to give up these safeguards at any time. It was given out now and then that the safeguards would only be taken back if the minorities themselves thought and were convinced that it is to their own interests. But I submit here that so far as these two Articles 296 and 299 are concerned, the minorities themselves never agreed to give up these safeguards at any time. The Minorities Committee observed in their report that the Committee are fully alive to the fact that decisions once reached should not be changed lightly. Then I ask, why is this change being brought about so lightly and so casually? So my prayer is that these amendments that have now been brought forward by Dr. Ambedkar must be rejected and my amendment may be accepted and the original safeguards restored.

There is one very important factor that has gained currency during the last three or four days. It concerns the Sikhs alone. It has been given out that the Sikh representatives on the Minorities Committee gave an undertaking in writing that they would not put forward any further demands for any safeguard in the Constitution if, that was a very big if—their backward classes the Mazhabis, Ramdasis, Kapirpanthis and Sikligars were recognised and calculated as Scheduled Castes. That may be true. In May last, as I have said, the position was that these two Articles 296 and 299 had been accepted by the Constituent Assembly. The reservation was there also, but they agreed on that date that they would give it up. The Instrument of Instructions is gone. So far as I have been able to ascertain from the preceedings of the Minorities Sub-Committee, I do not find any mention anywhere that 296 and 299 were referred to or that the minorities were asked to give up this as a whole. The Minorities Committee decided to abolish reservation only in the legislature. I must point out here that there is no reservation in Articles 296 and 299. The Minorities Committee did not díscuss anything else. Clauses (3) and (4) of the safeguards contained in Article 296 and 299 were never discussed. They had already been passed.

Now, Sir, I appeal to you to see how the representatives of the Sikhs know that they would be altered at the last moment? If I do desire to retain those decisions, I am not asking for any further safeguards for the Sikh community. I am only raising my voice against those safeguards being taken away from us, safeguards which had already been given. And, if any body in going back on the undertaking or on his word, then it is the Drafting Committee or the party in power and not the Sikhs.

Then there is another point that is also very relevant as far as this question is concerned. Supposing for the sake of argument we grant that the Sikh representatives agreed to forego every safeguard, is it to be understood that they did so because they were very keen to have their backward classes included in the Scheduled Castes? Is then their anxiety for that to be exploited and the opportunity utilised to get them to give up all other safeguards? I do not believe it. but suppose that was alse true, I do realise this also that there was much opposition from the Scheduled Castes against such inclusion and Sardar Patel had to secure this to the Sikhs with great difficulty. The Sikhs are thankful to him. But what has happened to that concession secured at the sacrifice of all other demands, as is alleged? In the first place a restriction was placed that this concession was confined to East Punjab only. It was not extended to the Patiala Union. How strange! Was there any justification for this discrimination on the basis of religion? If reservation was denied to religious minorities, and the Scheduled Castes were to get it for their backwardness then is there any justification to deny this concession to similar backward sections suffering from identical disabilities simply because they profess the Sikh religion? Would this be secularism? This much-coveted demand secured at such a heavy price and given so grudgingly and reservedly has become uncertain. Schedule X which was to enumerate the Scheduled Castes is deleted and Article 300A empowers the President after consultation with the Governor or the Ruler to specify the castes or races to be Scheduled castes. Sir, it will be realised that again the Sikhs shall have to strive and strive hard to persuade the Governor to advise the President to include these castes in the list of Scheduled Castes. My anxiety is that the Sikhs are left with nothing now. They have no further safeguards. What shall they offer to the Governor to advise the President to secure these safeguards? So, my submission is that even if there was any undertaking, that should be no consideration because what was secured in lieu of that has already gone.

The Sikhs are told, when they remind the congress of their past pledges in 1929, 1946 and again in 1947 that circumstances have changed. The Sikhs were recognised as one of the three main communities in the Cabinet Mission Plan of which this Constituent Assembly is the creature. The only changed circumstances is that the Muslims have got Pakistan. Does it stand to reason that because the Muslims have secured Pakistan, therefore the Sikhs have ceased to be a minority? Is this a logical conclusion? I will be failing in my duty if I do not point out what our feelings are. Pakistan resorted to crude and positive violence to eliminate their minorities. We are using a subtle, indirect and peaceful way of resolving the same question. True to our traditions, we are of course non-violent. I appeal to the House to go slow. I request the majority to win the confidence of the minorities by positive actions and not by mere slogans. This change in Article 296 has caused consternation in the minds of the minorities affected thereby. I request that the whole draft be allowed to remain as in my asmendment.

It has also been given out that our leaders consider that our original draft of 296 would disfigure the whole Constitution. Sir, I fail to understand that. If the mention of Anglo-Indian and Scheduled Castes or Scheduled Tribes does not disfigure this Constitution to any extent, the mention of Sikhs surely would not further disfigure it. But if in spite of my appeals, this House is not inclined to accept any amendments for restoring the old draft, then my last appeal is for the acceptance of another amendment, which is No. 256.

> "That with reference to amendment No. 23 of List II (Second Week), the following clause be added to Article 296:-
>
> (2) Nothing in this article or in Article 10 of the Constitution shall prevent the State from making any provision for the reservation of appointments or posts in favour of any minority community which, in the opinion of the State, is not adequately represented in the services under the State."

The Centre may be aware of every detail of everything occurring in the States; yet some liberty shall have to be left to the man on the spot. If for the smooth working of the administration and for creating cordial relations between the different communities, the State decides on some adjustment in the services, then there should be no bar under the Constitution. Some dignitaries think that there is no such bar at present, but my fears are that article 10 would be a bar for any option or adjustment—when it says that there shall be equality of opportunity for all citizens in matters relating to employment or appointment to office under the State. I might have understood that it would not bar such an option if such clause (3) of Article 10 had not specifically provided that:-

> "Nothing in this article shall prevent the State from making any provision for the reservation of appointments or posts in favour of any backward class of citizens who, in the opinion of the State, are not adequately represented in the services under the State."

My Amendment No. 256 runs on the same lines as this clause (3). Why I did not move it at the time that Article 10 was being considered here is that because 296 was already there, there was no need then, but now because 296 is going to be altered, therefore I feel that this option must be left and it should be made clear that if a State wants to make any adjustments so far as the different communities are concerned, it will be free to make that.

I have seen certain reports in the Press that the East Punjab Government have been advised by the legal advisers of the Government of India that they cannot consider the claims of any section in the services, and that has increased my fears, and I am now convinced that unless we leave some option or choice to the States, it would not be possible for them to make any adjustment even if they wanted to do. I make my appeal to the House again. I am not asking for any reservation in this Constitution. I am not disfiguring it. I claim only for an indication of the goodwill of the majority. If that is also denied, it may prove the last straw on the camel's back so far as the confidence of the minorities is concerned.

Shri Brajeshwar Prasad (Bihar: General):

Sir, I move:

"That in Amendment No. 15 (with your permission, Sir, I want to say No. 15 instead of No. 23)—of List II (Second Week), for the proposed Article 296, the following be substituted :-

'296. (1) The maintenance of efficiency of administration shall be the only consideration in the making of appointment to services and posts in connection with the affairs of the Union or of a State.

(2) Parliament may by law prescribe the conditions under which the President may, if he deems necessary, appoint members of the Scheduled Tribes and the Scheduled Castes to services and posts in connection with the affairs of the Union or of a State.

(3) The provisions of clause (2) of this article shall apply in relation to such other backward classes as the President may on receipt of the report of a Commission appointed under clause (1) of article 301 of this Censtitution by order specify as they apply in relation to members of the Scheduled Castes and the Scheduled Tribes.

(4) Parliament shall have the power to repeal, extend or modify any or all of the provisions of this article from time to time."

The Honourable Shri K. Santhanam:

(2) and (3) are inconsistent with (1)

Shri Brajeshwar Prasad:

No. Let me explain how it is not inconsistent. If it is inconsistent, the Chair will give its ruling.

Mr. President:

He has raised the point. I have to consider it.

Shri Brajeshwar Prasad:

Let me first explain. If he has raised a point of Order, I will explain whether it is consistent or not. Clause (1) says that there shall be only one consideration before the Public Service Commission, namely, the efficiency of administration and the merit of the individual candidate. The Public Service Commission shall not take into consideration the claims of the minority communities. The Public Service Commission shall not be swayed by any other consideration at the time of making appointments.

As a matter of political expediency, I have vested powers into the hands of the President and the President alone to appoint persons of the Scheduled Tribes and the Scheduled Castes. The Public Service Commission must be free from political entanglements. I do not know how (2) and (3) are inconsistent with (1). I await your ruling before I proceed with my speech.

Mr. President:

The way in which it has been put is making it inconsistent. You can make it consistent by putting in the word "provided".

Shri Brajeshwar Prasad:

Of course, I am not a draftsman, Sir, nor am I an able lawyer like Mr. Santhanam.

Mr. President:

However, I would not overrule your amendment.

Shri Brajeshwar Prasad:

As far as clause (4) is concerned, the purpose is to make the whole article very flexible, so that with the growth of education and with the economic improvement in the standard of living, Parliament shall have the power to do away with this article at any time it likes. I am opposed to Amendment No. 15 as it has been moved by the Drafting Committee, because I do not want that any other extraneous considerations should be brought in at the time of making appointments. I am afraid that if the claims of all these communities are taken into consideration, the whole fabric of the State will be jeopardized.

I am quite clear in my own mind that there are no minorities in this country, therefore the claims of no minorities can be taken into consideration. There are backward communities. There are people who have been suppressed and oppressed for centuries. It is their claims and their claims alone that shall be taken into consideration. The burden of making such appointments must fall upon the shoulders of the President and the President alone. I feel that if we introduce the provision that the claims of the communities like tribals and Scheduled

Castes should be taken into consideration, we shall be burdening the shoulders of the members of the Public Service Commission with a task for which they are not equal. What are the claims of the minority communities? What are the claims of the Scheduled Castes and Scheduled Tribes? Can any man endowed with ordinary intelligence and commonsense reconcile the irreconcilable claims of these communities?

The claim has been made that we demand parity. Another section demands that we should have representation in the services in proportion to our population. A third demand has also been made on the floor of this House that because we have been suppressed and oppressed for centuries, therefore the members of the Caste Hindu community must be made to make penance., If we are going to make penance for the sins that we have done against these people, then we shall have to hand over the entire machinery of the State into the hands of the Tribals and the Scheduled Castes. Are these claims going to be considered by the Public Service Commission? I think that it is wrong to blame any community for a historical wrong. History alone is responsible for all the wrongs that have been inflicted upon the Scheduled Castes and the Tribals. It is the Age—the Time Spirit—which alone can be held responsible.

Shri H.V. Kamath:

Who makes history?

Shri Brajeshwar Prasad:

Let me explain. History is made by the wrong doer and the oppressed. It was wrong on the part of the wronged to submit to oppression. If objection is raised that they were not in a position to organise, we also will say that it was due to lack of political consciousness, due to lack of social sense, that these things were perpetrated. It was the institution, it was society itself that was responsible. It was the time spirit and the time spirit alone that was responsible for the wrongs done to the Scheduled Castes and the Tribals. The Caste Hindus are not responsible for any wrong. We have also suffered, because Caste Hindus have also been exploited by people living in this country and wrong have been committed and perpetrated upon us. For conturies, India was under foreign subjection. It was subject to foreign intervention and foreign oppressions from times immemorial. The Caste Hindus have never flourished. It is wrong, it is atrocious to throw all blame and responsibility on the Caste Hindus, they have been victims of circumstances. I cannot accept the proposition that the Caste Hindus have perpetrated any wrong on anybody.

I would like also to emphasise that this article ought to have been placed in the Directive Principles of the State policy. It is merely a pious declaration. If it is merely a pious declaration, it should have been placed in the Chapter relating to Directive Principles of the State policy.

I think there is another reason why I oppose this article. It is that we have done the utmost that we could do for raising the economic, moral and the material condition of these people. We have passed the Chapter relating to Fundamental Rights. We have passed article 10. We have made provision for reservation of seats in the Central and provincial legislatures. We have laid down provision for adult franchise. We have made the basis of a secular State. What more do you want? Do you want to disintegrate the State?

I am quite clear in my own mind that if we do not take a bold stand at this moment and clearly lay down the principle that the basis of a secular State shall not be allowed to be corrupted by any other consideration, the future of this country is dark. I hold the opinion that those persons are clamouring for these seats, for reservation, for consideration, represent a handful of people, constituting the cream of the Harijan society. They constitute the politically powerful group among the Tribals and the Scheduled Castes. I do not think that these claims and demands touch the broad classes of people within the Scheduled Castes and Tribals. Job-hunting does not affect the problems that confront us as far as the question of Scheduled Castes and Tribes is concerned. It is by assimilating ourselves and by integrating all the communities in one nation that there can be any peace and progress in this country. I do not want that the politics of the Muslim League should be re-enacted again on the political arena. The whole purpose of my amendment is to strengthen the foundations of the State. It has been the central theme of the speeches that I have delivered here in this Assembly. I have moved my amendment so that the interests of the State may be protected.

Shri Guptanath Singh (Bihar: General):

Shri, I move:

"That in Amendment No. 15 above, in the proposed Article 296, for the words "The claims of the members of the Scheduled Castes and the Scheduled Tribes' the words 'The claims of the members of the Scheduled Castes, the Scheduled Tribes and such other castes who are educationally and socially backward' be substituted."

Before making my observations on the amendment, I should like to make it clear at the very outset that I am dead against all sorts of mischievous methods of communalism, caste-ism and such other "isms".

Shri R.K. Sidhva:

And yet you move an amendment for the backward classes?

Shri Guptanath Singh:

Yes Mr. Sidhva. But have patience. This communalism has proved to be a curse to the country. It has become a national nuisance. We have reaped the cruel consequences of this kind of thing. Still, we are going to continue such things. I want that this demon of distinction and differentiation between man and man should not be allowed to flourish further in free India. But the present structure of society is such that we have been forced and our leaders have been forced to accept the principle of pretection and reservation. I know we have done it in no happy mood. We desire that these things should be abolished for ever. But some of the sections of Indian society—our Harijan friends, our Adibasi breathren—have been oppressed for centuries and they have been tyrannised for ages that is why they are demanding these reservations. That is well and good. They should get the reservations and as much reservation as may be possible to make them equal to other sections of society and bring them on the same level. Then and then alone these distinctions and differentiations between man and man can be domolished.

But there are other sections in the country, whose conditions are not better than the conditions of these friends, the Harijans and the Adibasis. In some parts of the country their conditions are worse than some of our Harijan and Adibasi Friends. I wish to bring to your notice that even among the Brahmins, who claim to belong to the highest rank of humanity, there are untouchables. You will be surprised to know that even among Brahmins there are untouchables and they are regarded inferior even to other non-Brahmin castes. What is the meaning of this? This is utter nonsense. Some men are regarded as superior and some are regarded to be inferior! In human society such distinctions and discriminations should not be maintained. But our society is maintaining them. It is a matter of misfortune for our society. Therefore, some of these friends demand reservation, protection, safeguards and securities.

I know, Sir, and you also know that protection and control are sources of corruption. I will cite you two instances. The Central Government were pleased to award some scholarships to persons belonging to the Scheduled Castes and Scheduled Tribes as well as to socially and educationally backward people, and among those backwards people one caste is called 'Kisans'. You see, the general meaning of the word 'kisan' is farmer, and a farmer may be any man, whether he is a Brahmin or a Kayasth or somebody else. But this term has been used in the United Provinces in a restricted sense. A man belonging to a farming class and who is very backward is called a kisan. You will be surprised to know, Sir, that some of the students belonging to very advanced classes applied for scholarships on the ground that their forefathers were kisans and even today they are cultivators, and therefore they think they should get the scholarships.

Similarly, once some Brahmins applied to the Harijan fund for scholarship claiming themselves to be Harijans. Thus controls and reservations beget corruption and should not be encouraged. But as society is bigoted we must reap the consequences. The present structure of our society begets or creates these things and a kind of distrust, doubt and fear has been created in the minds of the oppressed classes. They fear that they will not get their share in the administrative services and therefore they are demanding it. Though they have been assured their rights in the Fundamental Rights and in the general directive principles, they are still persisting in demanding reservation.

I want to bring to your notice how the words "educationally and socially backward" came into the Constitution. Article 10, sub-clause (3) reads:

> "Nothing in this article shall prevent the State from making any provision for the reservation of appointments or posts in favour of any backward class of citizens who, in the opinion of the State, are not adequately represented in the services under the State."

So though we have granted them every thing, there is still distrust in the minds of the people.

I want to cite an instance. In a neighbouring province of Bihar a very brilliant student personally known to me, who had passed M.Com. from the Benaras Hindu University, applied for a post. He appeared before the Public Service Commission in his province recently. Perhaps the members of the Public Service Commission did not know that the wretched fellow belonged to a very backward class. He had stood first throughout his career. A month after his appointment a letter came from the government of that province informing him that his services had been terminated. He wrote to the Government and his department to know the case and suggesting that if he was guilty he should be prosecuted and tried. Government refused to give any information regarding his case. This should be a matter of shame for the Government of that province.

Similarly during the British regime in our glorious Bihar one gentleman belonging to a very backward farming or cultivating class was rejected as a deputy collector. Simply because he belonged to a very backward community... (Interruption). Have patience and hear me Mr. Sidhva. You had your chance to speak. You will be glad to know that this gentelman is the principal of a first class degree college in Bihar. The selection committee rejected him as a deputy collector but he is a brilliant scholar and efficient educational administrator.

I want to bring to your notice one more instance.....

Mr. President:

Is it any use giving instances of this kind? They must be occurring all over.

Shri Guptanath Singh:

All right Sir, I would not give. I want, Sir, that those classes who are the backbone of Indian society—the agricultural, pastoral or artisan classes—though they are not counted as Scheduled Castes or Tribes, should be given some opportunities to serve in government services. You have already accepted the proposal to appoint a commission to study and investigate their conditions. If you insert words to the effect that these wretched people will be given some chance it would be better for the country. They will prove to be most honest and efficient national servants.

When I tabled this amendment one day it was accepted by the drafting committee some days after—Dr. Ambedkar was pleased to include my suggested words in his own Amendment No. 23. He realised the lacuna and accepted my amendment substantially. After that Mr. Munshi also accepted the principle contained in my amendment. But I do not know why they kept mum today when you asked them to move their subsequent amendments. They are masters and they can do as they please. I would appeal to them to consider the appropriateness of these words. They should include these words also in this article.

I hope they will consider the points I have raised and prove to the agricultural and pastoral classes whose condition is worse than that of the Harijans and Adibasis, that they are going to do something for them and assure them that they would get their opportunities to serve the country. I hope, the caravan of communalism will now be stopped, the cobra of casteism will be killed and immediate steps will be taken to make this glorious land of free India heaven for the humanity suffering from inequality for several cennturies.

Shri H.V.Kamath:

Mr. President, Sir, I move:-

"That in Amendment No. 23 above, in the proposed Article 296, for the words 'shall be taken into consideration, consistently with the maintenance of efficiency of administration, the words 'shall, consistently with the maintenance of efficiency of administration, be taken into consideration' be substituted."

Sir, as you observed this is a purely formal amendment but I think that it is a more correct construction of the proposed sentence in the article and I would recommend it earnestly to the Drafting Committee for what it is worth. But, Sir, may I by your leave make some observations on the amendment moved today by Dr. Ambedkar?

Mr. President: Yes.

Shri H.V. Kamath:

Today, Sir, we have taken another step forward in the building of our common Indian nation-hood. Over two years ago this Assembly resolved that so far as the legislatures of this country were concerned, the minority communities should have reservation so far as their seats in these bodies were concerned, but in view of the fact that great events, perhaps tragic in some respects but events fraught with destiny occurred soon thereafter, Sardar Vallabhbhai Patel, a little over two months ago moved in this House, and this House accepted his proposition, that so far as the Muslims and Sikhs were concerned, reservation in legislatures for them should go. That was a wise decision taking us one step forward in our march to nation-hood. Today again we are taking another decision which marks another stride in our onward march, and that is that we propose to abolish reservation for the minority communities, the Muslims and Sikhs so far as reservation for them in the services of the State is concerned. The only exception that we made on that day, two months ago when Sardar Patel moved his proposition in the House is again the only exception that we make today, that is, with regard to the Scheduled Castes and Tribes. Members and even friends outside may dispute the wisdom of this course, but practical politics and statemanship is guided not always by absolute ideal considerations; our policy and our course are often guided by expediency and the exigencies of the prevailing situation. The situation today dictates to us this course.

My honourable Friend, Mr. Brajeshwar Prasad referred to the plight of the Scheduled Castes and Tribes and remarked in passing that History alone is responsible for the condition of the Harijans today, and that the Caste Hindus cannot be held responsible. I for one do not propose to go into this intricate question as to who is responsible and who is not responsible. I do not want to apportion blame. After all if Mr. Brajeshwar Prasad says that history is responsible and later on said after examining further causes that the time spirit was responsible, I venture to suggest that the divine force or whatever supreme force operates in this universe was responsible; the elan vital or the evolutionary force as you may call it, is responsible for what is happening in the world. He said that Caste Hindus were oppressed by foreign exploiters, but we see that these foreign exploiters have been vanquished by another force and that force has been attacked by another third or fourth force. As some English cynic has said: "In this world there is one flea which is preyed upon by another bigger flea and that bigger flea is again preyed upon by a third flea". One is never quite sure about what is going on in the unviverse. Some grand precess is unravelling itself and I do not propose to go into the vexed question of who oppressed whom and how it all came about.

I only wish to say this much, Sir, that with the passing of this article today the only class of people of this country who might be lightly apprehensive will be as my honourable Friend Mr. Guptanath Singh observed, those who are called the backward class of citizens. I do not wish to say who is backward and who is not backward, who are pastoral classes and who are agricultural classes or which other class is backward, but we have used that very term in the Constitution—backward classes, socially and educationally backward classes. They perhaps will be somewhat apprehensive about their future, as to what their share will be as regards the services in the State, but I wish to dispel their misapprehension by referring to the Fundamental Rights in Article 10 in Chapter 3 of the Constitution. Clause (3) of Article 10 provides :

> "Nothing in this article shall prevent the State from making any provision for the reservation of appointments or posts in favour of any backward class of citizens who, in the opinion of the State, are not adequately represented in the services under the State."

This is not a mere directive principle of state policy; this is in Chapter III on Fundamental Rights. When this is guaranteed to them, no backward class of citizens need be apprehensive. If there is no representation for them in the services they can take the Government to task on that account. I think this would be an adequate safeguard for them so far as their share in the services is concerned. I hope that this Article 10 guarantees that right to them, and so they need have no dispute or quarrel with the article before the House today.

Before I close, I only wish to express the hope that, before ten years have expired from the commencement of the Constitution, in this country of ours which has had an ancient history, this country of ours which is ancient, but ever young, there will be not merely no backward classes, socially and educationally backward classes left, but that all the classes will come up to a decent normal human level, and also that we shall do away with this stigma of any caste being scheduled. This was a creation of the British regime which happily has passed away. We have taken many strides forward in removing or doing away with the numerous evils that were associated with the British regime. This is one of the few that still remain. I hope, Sir, that ere long, this stigma too will disappear from our body politic, and we shall all stand before the world as one single Indian community.

Shri R.K.Sidhva:

Sir, I am very glad that the Honourable Dr. Ambedkar has moved Amendment No. 15 and the other amendments relating to backward classes have been dropped. My amendment, as just now stated, related to the deletion of the clause relating to backward classes.

Sir, I have been trying to understand what is the definition of backward classes. In Article 301, we have stated that those who are socially and educationally backward would be known as backward classes. Today, in this country, 88 per cent of the people are illiterate. They do not know even the A B C or the alphabet of their own mother tongue. Only 12 per cent of the people are literate in this country. Socially also they are backward. Am I to understand that 88 per cent of the people are backward? Article 301 definitely states that those who are socially and educationally backward will come under that article. How can we then say that the whole country, 88 per cent. of the people are to be known as backward classes? My honourable Friend, Mr. Guptanath Singh, went to the length of saying that the peasant belongs to the backward class. He mentioned the illustration of the Brahmin as a backward class. I know of an illustration and I shall give it. This was all created for the purpose of getting position and power and nothing else. Some ten years age, a person wanted to get into the services as a Subordinate Judge. He belonged to Pushkar Brahmin cemmunity. He set up a theory that the Pushkar Brahmins belonged to the backward classes. He had merely to take the signatures of 500 persons and present it to the Chief Judge. The Judge was guided by the signatures and as there was no Pushkar Brahmin in the service as Judge, he appointed him.

I may also tell the House that thirty years ago, the Parsees were considered as a backward class by the Bombay Government. You know, Sir, that we are a far advanced community. Thirty years ago, 80 per cent of us were educated; today 99 per cent are educated. Still, thirty years ago, the Bombay Government declared that the Parsees were a backward class. It is only those people who want to get into the services that use their influence and class themselves as a backward class. This is what was happening in the British regime. Some people who wanted to get into the services used their influence and classified themselves as backward classes, whereas really the masses of the people who are really the backbone of the country, they are not given any representation in the services. (Interruption).

Shri Guptanath Singh

You talk much but do not know the masses; I know the minds of the masses.

Shri R.K.Sidhva:

I do not want to argue with you. What I was saying was that there has been injustice done to a small section of our own people. I know there has been fovouritism going on and let me tell you favouritism will go on for ever unless a real Ram Rajya comes into being. Some sort of favouritism will prevail even in the best of Government. So far as the Scheduled Classes are concerned, I have never conceded that the Scheduled Castes are a community. I have considered them as a class of people whom really great injustice has been done in the past by the Hindu community. Therefore, we want to do something to see that they come up to standard of their own brethren. If they were to classify themselves into a separate community, I would opppose it. I do not consider them as separate. So far as the Scheduled Tribes are concerned, they are not untouchables. For instance, there are the

Bhils; they are not untouchables. They are only backward. They have also been brought under Scheduled Tribes. These people require attention at the hands of the special officer that is to be appointed.

I do feel that our Article 301 is a real stigma on our Constitution. I wish Article 301 should go. I do not want backward classes at all to be mentioned in our Constitution. It is a slur upon our intelligence. For those who are educationally backward, we have provided in the Directive Policy that within ten years every man, woman or child should be made literate. When educationally every person is advanced, who will call them backward? There will be no backward classes. Socially, they become advanced. If a man is educated, I have seen he improves his position in society and social affairs. Therefore, the fundamental thing is education and we have provided for that in the Directive Policy. I would have wished it to have come in the Fundamental Rights. Within ten years, there shall not be a single person who shall be illiterate. Of course, there are certain difficulties in the way. I am sure our present Government are going to see that every man is made literate within a period of ten years, and we shall be proud that every person can read in his own mother tongue.

I, therefore, oppose the amendment proposed by Mr. Guptanath Singh. It has no meaning. It has meaning only when we want to favour some body and therefore we want to classify them as backward classes. The article as moved by Dr. Ambedkar is sufficient for our purposes. When a time limit is not mentioned, I am quite sure that within a short period these Scheduled Classes will go and they will come up to the level of the other people and we shall see that there is no mention of these Scheduled Classes in our Constitution hereafter. With these words, I strongly support the proposition and I oppose any kind of reservation or even the mention to reserve posts in services in the Constitution. We have done away with reservation in the legislatures. With what face shall we say that there should be reservation in the services?

It looks so awkward. Our leader, Sardar Patel, made it very clear the other day when he brought the question of representation in the Legislatures, and today my Friend Sardar Hukam Singh has put in Parsees also that they want special rights. Sir, my community has never asked for special rights in any Legislature or in the services. They have come by merits and I can assure you whatever number they are in the Government of India—there are some Parses in services of the Government of India—they have come by merit and not by favour. The majority community realise it and we leave it to them. We know they can appreciate it. Merit alone should count in our future Constitution and nothing else. I place great stress upon this. This method has been started by the British Government of favouring one community or the other. Sir, we have given our President the power to classify who are the backward classes. Mushroom association in the name of backward class will be formed and the President will be put in an awkward position; many communities will try to influence them. I am sorry that this clause is there but I only expect that article 301 will remain a dead article in this Constitution and shall never be operated upon. With these words I strongly support the original proposition and oppose all amendments.

The Honourable Sardar Vallabhbhai J.Patel : (Bombay: General).

Sir, I had no intention to speak on this article, but when I heard that a definite insinuation was made in this House, that because the Congress Party has a majority in this House, therefore it does not care for the promises given to the Sikhs and they are breaking the promises given them—I have to speak. I am very sorry to hear this charge from the Sikhs or a representstive of the Sikhs. Sardar Hukam Singh made this point. At another place on another occasion I had made it clear to him and yet he seems to have raised the same question. Now I wish only to answer that charge. For the other things I do not think I need go into discussion or say anything about it. But when it is alleged that Congress is breaking its promises given to the Sikhs, one after another, I wish to understand the position

We are—he alleges—breaking the promises—broke the

promise given in 1929, one in 1946 and another in 1947. I do not know what promises he refers. If he refers to 1929 and then again to the Partition of India and Pakistan, I wish to point out to him that there was not a single Sikh voice against the Partition; on the other hand they were probably in the forefront in demanding partition of the Punjab. After the butchery and the bloodshed that took place in Rawalpindi and Multan, the Sikhs were terribly upset and naturally distressed and they had considerable sympathy from the Congress. At that time there were other tragedies happening in other parts of the country and then came the conflagration in Lahore, Amritsar and other parts of the Punjab. It was at that time with the concurrence of the Sikhs,—unanimously, with one voice they agreed,—we agreed to the Partition of India. Now to turn round and charge us with a breach of faith is a charge which I cannot understand and it is not right for the Sikh community—a brave community like the Sikhs—to fling these charges at us. Who were we to agree to the partition of India and Partition of the Punjab if the Sikhs were opposed? We could never have done that. Because they also said that it was best in the interest of India that we should agree to partition on condition that the Punjab was partitioned—that we agreed to it. Now that is about 1929 promise.

Then again he says about 1946. If he refers to the Minorities Committee recommendations, I can understand it. I propose to explain it in detail as to what has taken place. But I do not know what he means by 1946 promise. If I can have any concrete expression of a promise given by Congress leaders, I might, and if so I do not think there is any one Congressman who will go against that promise. I have not however understood the psychology of the Sikh leaders—some of them—who often charge everybody with breach of faith, and always complain of minorities being ill-treated.

Look at the army. Are they not very heavily overweighted? What have we done? we are under their protection and we trust them and not a single army officer is disloyal to us. Why do you create this feeling for nothing?

What is it that you want?

When the Minorities Committee in the Advisory Committee passed its first decisions, I was appointed Chairman and I took all the minorities with me and the decisions of the Minorities Committee and the Advisory Committee were almost unanimous. This House appreciated the work of these Committees and congratulated me on that. Time went on and the minorities themselves began to feel that we should reconsider our decision and, headed by the great patriotic Christian leader, they brought in a Resolution that they want to give up the reservations. And what reservations?—Not this petty reservation of minorities in the services—but the big reservations in the Assemblies, both in the Centre and in the Provinces.

They agreed to have joint electorates and to have nothing to do with this communal separatism. When they desired that, I called a meeting of the minorities Committee and the Advisory Committee. At their instance decisions were taken. The Sikh stand has always been that "if all minorities agreed, we are also agreeable. We do not want any special arrangement. We do not want any advantage. We are able to stand on our own legs". That was their stand throughout, in the Congress and outside the Congress.

When this resolution was brought, and this question was about to be considered, the Sikh representatives of the Punjab came to me and they said so far as the Scheduled Caste Sikhs are concerned, they should be treated separately and given the same advantage that was being given to the Hindu Scheduled Castes. The Scheduled Castes objected to a man that these are not Scheduled Castes, and if they are Scheduled Castes, then they are not Sikhs. Therefore, they said, "you cannot give them separate treatment. There are forcible conversions being made from the Scheduled Castes to the Sikhs for this purpose." That was their grievance. On the other side, the Sikhs said that they had converted so many and it was not by force. "They have come to our fold," they said, "and if you do not recognise those concessions, then they will all go back to the Scheduled Caste Hindus and we will lose."

Now, it was against our conviction to recognise a separate Sikh caste as untouchables or Scheduled Castes, because untouchability is not recognised in the Sikh religion. A Scheduled Caste Sikh community has never been in the past recognised. But as the Sikhs began to make a grievance continuously, against the Congress and against us, I persuaded the Scheduled Castes people with great difficulty to agree to this, for the sake of peace. I persuaded the other members of the Advisory Committee on the condition, which is in writing, by the representatives of the Sikhs, that they will raise no other question hereafter.

Then in the Advisory Committee, when this question came, Sardar Ujjal Singh raised the question, "What about the Services?" I said, "your representatives have given in writing that no other question hereafter is to be raised." Giani Kartar Singh was also in the Advisory Committee, and he got up and said, "No, we will settle it in the Provinces. It is not to be raised here."

What is the use of charging the Congress with having broken promises? Do not break the promises that you have given, and do not charge others with breach of promises. If you now say, as Sardar Hukam Singh says, that these people were anxious to serve an advantage for the Scheduled Caste Sikhs and they may have agreed to this, but it is a mistake, then if it is a mistake, reconsider your position, and I shall reconsider mine. Take away that concession and remove it, and you get your pound of flesh, if you want it.

What is it that you get in the Services? Even at present, what do the Sikhs do? What do other communities do? So far as the Services are concerned, for all major posts or all posts which go by competitive examinations there is no reservation on communal grounds. They go to the Public Service Commission. You are quarrelling or asking for the minor posts—Chaprasis and clerks. Is it the Sikh position now that we have not get enough Sikh Chaprasis and clerks? Are you going to raise the community in that manner? If that is so, tell me, and if you leave what you have got for the Scheduled Castes, I shall persuade the Constituent Assembly to give you what you want, but you will repent afterwards.

You say, in PEPSU it is not the arrangement. But this is not the House to hear that complaint. If there is any such complaint, send it to us. We shall consider about it. But do not go behind your pledged words and charge other people with breach of promises or pledges. We are not the people to break pledges. Every sympathy and every consideration will be shown to the Sikh community because it is located in a particular area; it is a small community, and it is brave, virile and it can stand on its own against anybody. Do not break that spirit by continuously saying, "We are injured, we are helpless, we are in a minority, we are helpless, we cannot do anything."

That kind of psychology will injure the community itself and not others, and injuring the community means injuring the nation. It is not as a representative of the majority community that I give this advice, but as a well-wisher of the Sikh community. I advise you not to create this atmosphere by saying continually, "we are badly treated, badly treated". If you do, then it is the Sikh community that will be hurt.

When the Advisory Committee took this decision to give up reservation, we clearly understood the position and all communities clearly understood it. When the decision of the Advisory Committee came before this House for its acceptance, I made it clear that this Constitution of India, of free India, of a secular State will not hereafter be disfigured by any provision on a communal basis. It was accepted with acclamation.

It is said that if you make any arrangements in the provinces then the provisions of the Constituent Assembly with regard to fundamental rights will come in the way. Let me tell you, nothing comes in the way where arrangements are made by mutual agreement, and without mental reservations. That provision in the fundamental rights is provided for an individual who is injured. But if you make domestic arrangements in the Punjab between community and community for the small posts, then who is going to question that? But first create an atmosphere for adjustment of such things in your Province. It is the continued atmosphere of quarrel between two communities that has created distrust among them, and that creates difficulties. You will have our support and sympathy continuously in that Province because that Province has suffered most. It is injured and the wounds have not yet healed. It is for us all, and for you particularly, to help us in healing the wounds. Therefore, let us make a united effort to raise the morale of that Province, the strength of that Province, which really is at the top of India, where the border is. Then you will have no complaint at all.

After all, what is the Sikh community backward in? Is it backward in trade? Is it backward in industry, or commerce or in anything? Why do you consider yourselves to be backward? Therefore, forget that psychology. If there is any injustice done, then come to us, we will see that no injustice is done.

Sardar Hukam Singh said, "We trust the present leaders. What about the future?" I say, you must have the courage to trust the future and not the present leaders. What will happen when the present leaders are gone? Will Sardar Hukam Singh be living here? Why raise this issue? We must trust that if the present leaders go, we will have better leaders in the future. If we have trust in the future our country, we may trust that in the future our country will produce leaders who will make a name in the history of the world. We have shown it today. We will do it in the future. That is India. India produced a Mahatma in a State where slavery was rampant. He went to a country where people could not walk on the foot-path, where people could not travel even in the III class with safety, where we were all treated as untouchables even now we are treated as untouchables there. There he made a name and fame all over the world, and presented a new weapon to the world. Then he came here. Here he raised the Sikhs, the Muslims, the Hindus, Scheduled Castes, everybody. He gave us freedom. Do you think that we are going to raise the morale of our country or the reputation of our country or the fame of our country by breaking promises? No. We have all agreed that we must trust each other.

I know that the atmosphere so far as the Muslims are concerned is not quite as happy as it should be. But there are reasons for that. The Congress is not responsible for this. If there had been no Partition, perhaps we would have been able to settle our differences. But there was Partition. This Partition by agreement brought about subsequent events. But, since Partition, whatever is being done on the other side is having a reaction here for which we have to struggle day and night.

You do not know the immense difficulties of a secular State being governed peacefully in such conditions. Now, the world is in such a condition that we cannot take any independent action of our own accord. Even though there is injustice done, we have to wait, pause, ponder and consider, because there is an Organisation known as the U.N.O. who day and night watch the situation all the world over and try to see how peace could be maintained. I do not wish to say anything about the work of the U.N.O., because I know nothing about it. But the other part of the country known as Pakistan misses no opportunity of defaming and blackmailing us all over the world, whether there is occasion for it or no occasion for it. So we have to be specially careful. They break promises and charge us with breach of faith: and yet we cannot solve it without reference to the other countries or without any regard for its reaction in other countries.

Therefore we have to be very careful. Do not add to our difficulties by creating internal difficulties in which there will be disputes between the communities. Help us and it will be to your advantage and it will be to the advantage of the whole country. You will have no cause for regret if you drop the claims for minor provisions for small minorities in regard mainly to service questions. Fight over issues beneficial to the whole country. Let us do that. Let us prepare the ground for that. You have big interests involved in two provinces. Though the problems in Bengal are different, as in the Punjab they have also certain problems. These problems can be settled not by the Centre, but by the provinces themselves. So, for God's sake, those who are interested in the well-being of the country should create a different atmosphere and not an atmosphere of distrust and discord.

My only point in coming to reply here was to meet the charge that has been levelled against the Congress. I am sorry to bear it. Neither I nor any Congressman has done anything here in the Centre to give cause to the Sikh Community to distrust us. We shall never give cause for that in spite of what you may do. Therefore for the last time in this Constituent Assembly, as responsible Members of Parliament, I appeal to you. By all means ask for what you want or what you like. But do not blame other people for your own faults. I desire now to give you this undertaking that if you still feel that the advantage that was taken from us is not worth it, you throw it away and, if you think this is better, I will give it to you. You consider the matter amongst yourselves, amongst the Sikh community and decide. But do not try to have it both ways. One section first comes and gets certain advantages and gives promises to a certain section of the community and thereafter another section comes and charges us with not having given it certain other advantages which it is anxious to have. That is not the way to do things. You may unite and decide what you want. It is not our fault if you have not done so. After all, what is it that you want? You want an insignificant thing, but granting it would mean putting a blot on the Constitution. We agreed about certain things on that day and everybody was pleassed with it. Therefore be satisfied with what you have done and there will be no cause for regard. (Applause).

At the revision stage the draft article was renumbered as Article 335.

Article 335 reminds us of the demands of the leaders of various minority organisations, specially of the Muslim League and the Depressed Classes Associations, during the pre-partition days for an adequate share in the

Central and Provincial Government services. Jinnah's famous 14-point character of demands of 1929 contained a demand that there should be constitutional provision giving the Muslims an adequate share along with the other Indians in all the services of the State and in local-governing bodies, *having due regard to the requirements of efficiency.*[28] Ambedkar, who was fighting for the rights of the Depressed Classes as a minority, in his joint memorandum to the Round Table Conference in 1931, asked for establishment of a Public Service Commission in each Province charged with the duty of recruiting services in such a manner as would secure due and adequate representation of all communities and of regulating from time to time priority in employment in accordance with the existing extent of the representation of the various communities in any particular service concerned.[29] The Document, known as the Minorities Pact, to which Ambedkar was a signatory, amongst others, produced during the Round Table Conference jointly by Muslims, Depressed Classes and a section of Indian Christians, Anglo-Indians and Europeans for a settlement of the communal problem, also suggested that recruitment to the Public Services should be made through the Public Service Commission in such a way as to secure a fair representation to the various communities *consistently with the considerations of efficiency and the possession of the necessary qualifications*. There should be generous treatment to the Depressed Classes in the matter of recruitment to Public Service and the opening of enlistment in the Police and Military Service.[30]

Inspite of the known proclivities of the British Government to use any issue to create fissures in the Indian body politic, the 1935 Act did not contain any specific provision to meet the demands of Jinnah, Ambedkar and others. Only two provisions of the 1935 Act met their demands partially. Clause (2) of Section 255 relating to Subordinate Judicial Services expressly provided that appointments to that service should be made by the Governor in accordance with such regulations as might from time to time be made by him as to the number of persons in the said services who belonged to the different communities in the Province.. Similarly Clause (2) of Section 242 provided that in framing rules for recruitment to superior railway services the Federal Railway Authority should have due regard to the past association of the Anglo-Indian community with railway service in India, and should give effect to any instructions which might be issued by the Governor-General for the purpose of securing, so far as practicable, to each community in India a fair representation in the railway services of the Federation.

Subject to the provisions of Section 242 and 255, the position with regard to appointment in Provincial and Federal Governments was governed by Clause (1) of Section 298 which laid down that "no subject of His Majesty domicled in India shall on grounds only of religion, place of birth, descent, colour or any of them be ineligible for office under the Crown in India". Clause (1) of Section 298 virtually repeated the language from the earlier statutes of 1833, 1915 and 1919 relating to the Constitution of India. The meaning of this clause was that there should be no governing castes in British India. That whatever other tests of qualification might be adopted, distinction of race, descent, and religion should not be of the number.[31]

Where a Provincial Government framed rules for reservation of offices on communal and class basis, it might be suggested that the Governor had the power to make such rules under Section 52(1) of the Act in the exercise of his special responsibility mentioned in Clause (b), viz., 'the safeguarding of the legitimate interests of minorities'. That apart, under the second paragraph of the Instrument of Instructions the Governor was charged with the responsibility "to secure a due proportion of appointments in services to the several Communities". It may be contended that the Instrument of Instructions was merely a prerogative document issued by the king and could not override or supersede an express provision of the Constitution contained in Clause (1) of Section 298 of the Act. In any case, if the Governor adopted measures for reservation of offices on the basis of religion and class, it was contended, his action could be challenged in the courts of law.[32]

The British Government, however, reserved a certain percentage of posts in Government services for the religious minorities as well as for the Depressed Classes (Scheduled Castes) by executive fiats issued in 1934, 1943 and 1946.

Having secured reservation for them in government services from the Britishers, the leaders of these communities pressed for continuation of the same facilities in free India as well. They asked for a constitutional guarantee of representation in the public services of the minority communities in proportion to their population. While conceding that no such guarantee existed in any other constitution, the Constituent Assembly gave its approval to the proposition that claims of all the minorities to central and state government services should be taken into consideration, on August 28, 1947, i.e. when the country was realing under the holocaust of partition. In course of time. 'minorities' were replaced by the 'Scheduled Castes and Scheduled Tribes'. Thus, though the Constitution refrains from stipulating any communal orientation in the matter of appointment to Government services, it could not impose any restrictions on the 'caste divide'. Perhaps the framers in their wisdom thought that this sort of constitutional provision would act as an harbinger of a 'casteless society' which they cherished to usher in.

Notes and References

1. Rao, *op. cit.*, Vol. II, p. 94.
2. *Ibid.*, p. 333.
3. *Ibid.*, p. 325.
4. *Ibid.*, p. 383.
5. *Ibid.*, p. 372.
6. *Ibid.*, pp. 366-67.
7. *Ibid.*, p. 339.
8. *Ibid.*, pp. 346-47, 349.
9. *Ibid.*, pp. 322-24.

10. Rao, *op. cit.*, Vol. II, p. 314.
11. *Ibid.*, pp. 399-400.
12. *Ibid.*, pp. 401-402.
13. *Ibid.*, p. 409.
14. *Ibid.*
15. *CAD*, Vol. V, p. 246.
16. *Ibid.*, p. 249.
17. *Ibid.*, dated 27-8-47, p. 200.
18. *Ibid.*, dated 28-8-47, pp. 278-79.
19. Rao, *op. cit.*, Vol. III, p. 94.
20. *Ibid.*, p. 478.
21. *Ibid.*, p. 474.
22. *Ibid.*, pp. 631-32.
23. *Ibid*, Vol. IV, pp. 361-62.
24. *CAD*, Vol. IX, dated 26-8-49, pp. 701-3.
25. *Ibid.*, dated 9-9-49, p. 1171.
26. *Ibid.*, Vol. X, dated 14-10-49, pp. 229-32.
27. *Ibid.*, dated 14-10-49, pp. 232-51.
28. Chatterjee, S.K. *The Scheduled Castes in India*, Vol. I, Chapter IV.
29. *Ibid.*, Appendix C.
30. *Ibid.*, Appendix D.
31. Anand, *op. cit.*, p. 734.
32. *Ibid.*, p. 737.

14

Public Service Commission not Required to be Consulted in Certain Matters [Article 320(4)]

Though there was a provision in the Government of India Act, 1919 for the establishment of a Public Service Commission in India,[1] no such Commission was set up after the passing of the Act.

The establishment of a Public Service Commission was revived by the Lee Commission (the Royal Commission on Superior Services in India, 1924). As a result, a Public Service Commission was set up under the Central Government of India in 1926, with advisory functions confined primarily to the All-India Services and Class I Central Services, its scope covering recruitment, disciplinary appeals, memorials and representations about grievances, claims for compensation and general questions of conditions of service. So far as provincial services were concerned, provision was made to enable the Commission to perform such functions as the Provincial Government or the Governor might invite it to undertake. But hardly ever was its assistance so invoked by a Province. Madras (in 1930) was the first and until 1937 the only Province to have a Commission of its own.[2] The Government of India Act of 1935 provided for a separate Commission for each Province as well as one for the Centre; provision was also made so that two or more Provinces might agree to have a joint Commission. The Government policy, particularly at the Centre, till 1947, had consistently been in favour of increasing the status and authority of the Commission and of extending the range of its powers.

The members of the Constituent Assembly had thus before them fairly well-established traditions in this matter. The Union Constitution Committee and the Provincial Constitution Committee did not find it necessary to go into this matter in any great detail; they continued themselves with recommending that provisions regarding the Public Service Commission should be on the lines of those in the Government of India Act, 1935. There was, however, one noticeable difference: the Union Constitution Committee had recommended that the appointment of the Chairman and the members of the Commission should be made by the President on the advice of his Ministers,[3] while the Provincial Constitution Committee had suggested that the appointment of the Chairman and the members of each Provincial Public Service Commission should be vested in the Governor in his discretion.[4] The Assembly accepted the recommendation of the Provincial Constitution Committee without any change[5] and that of the Union Constitution Committee with a minor change,[6] in respect of formation of the Public Service Commission. The President was no longer required to appoint the Chairman and the members of the Commission "on the advice of his ministers".

In accordance with the reports of these two Committees, as approved by the Constituent Assembly, the Constitutional Adviser in his Draft Constitution of October, 1947, included provisions for the Public Service Commissions in clauses 219-233, which closely followed those in the 1935 Act.[7]

The Government of India Act, 1935, contained the following provision in clause (4) of Section 266 which dealt with the functions of the Public Service Commission:

> Nothing in this section shall require a Public Service Commission to be consulted as respects the manner in which appointments and posts are to be allocated as between the various communities in the Federation or a Province or, in the case of the subordinate ranks of the various police forces in India, as respect any of the matters mentioned in paragraphs (a), (b), and (c) of subsection (3) of this section.

A provision on this line was included by the Constitutional Adviser in sub-clause (4) of clause 221:

> Nothing in this section shall require a Public Service Commission to be consulted as respects the manner in which appointments and posts are to be allocated as between the various communities in the Federation or a Province.[8]

This sub-clause was accepted by the Drafting Committeè with some minor drafting changes on January 30, 1948,[9] and figured as clause (4) of Draft Article 286 in its Draft Constitution[10] of February, 1948.

When this Draft Constitution was circulated for eliciting comments, suggestions, etc., K. Santhanam, M. Ananthasayanam Ayyangar, Shrimati G. Durgabai and T.T. Krishnamachari suggested that clause (4) of Article 286 be deleted. The Constitutional Adviser's comments in this suggestion were that this amendment involved a question of policy. If the amendment was accepted, then the following consequential amendment would be necessary:

> In clause (3) of Article 286, the words "and to the provisions of the next succeeding clause" be omitted.

Gopal Narain and Ram Chandra Gupta suggested the substitution of clause (4) of Article 286 by the following:

> (4) Every Public Service Commission shall furnish an annual report on the business conducted during the year, and other affairs of the Commission, to the President or the Governor of the State, as the case may be, who shall cause it to be laid before Parliament in the case of the Union Commission and before the Legislature of the State in the case of the State Commission.

The Constitutional Adviser observed that this amendment sought to delete clause (4) of Article 286 and to insert a new clause (4) in its place with regard to submission of annual reports by the Public Service Commissions as to the work done by them and the laying of such reports before the appropriate Legislature. The deletion of existing clause (4) of Article 286 involved a question of policy. As regards the new clause (4) of Article 286 proposed by this amendment, the Constitutional Adviser pointed out that an amendment for the insertion of a new Article 288-A had been separately proposed to give effect to a similar suggestion made by the Chairman and members of the Federal Public Service Commission and the Chairmen of the Provincial Public Service Commissions. This amendment would not therefore be necessary.[11]

This clause was taken up by the Constituent Assembly on August 23, 1949 for consideration when an amendment was placed before the Assembly by Ambedkar which changed the clause as follows:

(4) Nothing in clause (3) of this article shall require a Public Service Commission to be consulted as respects the manner in which appointments and posts are to be reserved in favour of any backward class citizens in the Union or a State.[12]

It may be noted that the Constituent Assembly had already decided to make provision for the reservation of appointments in favour of backward class of citizens [Art. 16(4)], and the other article enjoining that the claims of members of the Scheduled Castes and Scheduled Tribes should be taken into consideration, consistently with the maintenance of good administration, in the making of appointments to Government posts (Article 335) was yet to be adopted by the Assembly, though this change in policy was more or less known.

This clause aroused some lively controversy. Three amendments were moved—one each by Dr. P.S. Deshmukh, Naziruddin Ahmed and Sardar Hukam Singh. Deshmukh wanted not only to extend the principle adumbrated in clause (4) to all classes for the purpose of bringing about a just and fair representation in public services of the Union or a State but also sought to lay down that the various classes should be represented in the public services according to their numbers in the Union or a State. The purpose of this amendment, he explained, was to secure a just and fair representation for all classes in the public services of the Union and the States and not leave it to bare competition and to the sweet choice of the Public Service Commissions. He mentioned the position particularly in Madras where the various communities were arranged in various groups and each group was given representation in Government services on the basis of its population. He said that eighty per cent of the people took no part so far as the "civilized things of life" were concerned, and there was an iron curtain between them and the rest: unless every community, especially the larger and the more populous communities advanced equally and the advanced communities afforded them opportunities of development, the progress of India would be impossible. He expressed apprehension that if the clause stood as drafted, the backward classes were likely to suffer.

Naziruddin Ahmad proposed deletion of clause (4) because there was no reason why the backward classes should be totally excluded from the purview of the Public Service Commissions. Hukam Singh's amendment sought to include an Explanation in the clause to define Backward Classes as those who are "backward economically and educationally".

Phool Singh and Prof. Yashwant Rai supported the amendment of Deshmukh while Kamath, Raj Bahadur and H.N. Kunzru opposed the amendment. Ambedkar pointed out that the provincial governments by Article 10 (Article 16) were left free to make provisions for the backward classes. He, therefore, felt that there was no fear that the interests of the backward classes or the Scheduled Castes would be overlooked in the recruitment to the services.

When the clause and the amendments were put to vote, Deshmukh withdrew his amendment while the amendments moved by Naziruddin Ahmed and Hukam

Singh were negatived by the House and the amendment as moved by Ambedkar was adopted.[13]

The deliberations, in the Constituent Assembly relating to clause (4) of Draft Article 286 are reproduced below:

Dr. P.S. Deshmukh (C.P. & Berar: General)

> Sir, I move: "That in amendment No. 12 of list I (Fifth Week) of Amendments to Amendments, at the end of clause (4) of the proposed Article 286 the full-stop be substituted by a comma and thereafter the following be added:-
>
> or for the purpose of the bringing about a just and fair representation of all classes in Public Services of the Union or a State."

There is also an alternative Amendment, i.e. No. 88 which I would like to move also:

"That in Amendment No. 12 of List I (Fifth Week) of Amendments to Amendments, after clause (4) of the proposed Article 286, the following clause (5) be inserted, and the existing clause (5) be renumbered as clause (6):-

> (5) Nothing in clause (3) of this article shall require a Public Service Commission to be consulted as respects the manner in which appointments are made and posts reserved for purposes of giving representation to various classes according to their numbers in the Union or a State."

These two Amendments, Nos. 86 and 88, are as I said alternatives, and if one is accepted, I would not press the other, although I personally would urge that No. 86 which is more specific would be preferable.

The purpose of this amendment is to secure a just and fair representation of all classes in the public services of the Union and the State, and not leave it to bare competititon and according to the sweet choice of the Public Services Commissions themselves. Now, if we examine the systems of recruitment to the public services, we know that as a matter of fact certain provinces, because the public of those provinces were more alive to their rights, agitated that they were not having any share in the administration of their province and as a result of their agitation, the Governments of those provinces had to yield. This has happened particularly in that enlightened and advanced province of Madras where the various communities were grouped in various groups and each group was gives, according to the basis of its population, representation in the government services. This has workd very well, with the resultt that Madras has become one of the most advanced provinces in the whole of India. That is the reason why we find Delhi being crowded by Madrasis, because their standard of education has gone up due to the fact that all the communities have advanced equally with the others and not disproportionately as elsewhere. There you do not have the disproportionate advancement which you find in the other provinces where the suppressed communities have always been content with their lot, where they have not agitated to get more places in the government and where the advanced communities have never been charitable to consider their claims or to give them any help. This has happened particularly in the province of Central Provinces & Berar where we find that even today in the whole department of education there is hardly a person belonging to any other community except one particular community. There are departments after departments were ninety per cent and more of the incumbents come from a specific community.

Sir, if this is not communalism, what is communalism? And these people who now fill every place in the department see to it that anybody else, who wants to come in, is effectively prevented from doing so. Is this not communalism? A community which is only 3 to 5 per cent of the population, is it destined to govern the whole province so far as every department is concerned? Would it not be charitable to give at least a few places to the other people who have never been given what they have been asking for? Those Members of this House who are taken in by the sweet name of merit and efficiency, I can tell them that in efficiency neither Madras not Bombay has suffered to that extent that it will be detrimental to the country. There might have been a slight falling-off of the standard, but that much we have always tolerated.

When we were not able to compete with the British people we asked for places for Indians from the British. We wanted increased recruitment in the I.C.S. We struggled for it and we have passed resolutions to this effect even at the Sessions of the Indian National Congress. But when the same thing is done by other people we call it communalism. I submit there is ample room for doing justice to all. In Madras or Bombay where this principle has been practised, it has not led to any ruin of efficiency or to any very great danger or damage to the administration. If that is our experience, there is no reason why other provinces should not be wise also before the event and try and give sympathetic consideration to the other sections of the populations. The contention is on behalf of more than 85 per cent of the population and so it cannot be called communal. If you do not want to name the communities, or castes, there are other devices by which you can do it. But I submit, this demand ought to be considered more sympathetically, and since we have adopted the basis of population for representation, the basis of population should also be followed so far as recruitment is concerned.

I have urged what I wished to without specifying any community, without trying to go against any particular community. All that I want is that Parliament and the Legislatures should be free to see that there is a fair proportion of representation for all classes and communities in India. I had not specified that any single community should be given preference or priority—I want that there should be a fair distribution so that the unity and freedom of India will be real and genuine. It appears to me that the development in India has been lop-sided, one-sided. About 80 per cent of the people take no part so far as your cultural affairs are concerned, so far as the civilized things of life are concerned. There is a black-out so far as they are concerned; an iron curtain between them and the rest; unless every community, especially the larger and more popular communities advance equally and the advanced communities afford them opportunities for development, the advancement of India will be impossible. All that I demand is fairness and justice for the millions of people who are not in a position to come forward and compete with you, and in saying so I do not introduce any communalism, I do not introduce any discrimination. These things have been tried, they worked well and there is no reason why they should not work well on a larger scale.

..All that I wish to add is because the "backward classes" are likely to be defined in a very limited and restricted manner, it is not the claim of only the Scheduled Castes that they are backward, it is not the tribal people alone who should be considered backward; there are millions of others who are more backward than these and there is no rule nor any room so far as these classes are concerned. In those communities education is at a low ebb. In the whole of India there is 15 per cent of literacy. If you analyse it you will find about half a dozen communities have got literacy to the extent of 90 per cent and the others are illiterate to the extent of 98 per cent. There are communities whose populations may be millions but whose literacy standard may not go beyond 5 per cent.

There is no use to look at England or at America. I am surprised that my honourable Friend Shri Lakshminarayan Sahu, the great sponsor of the cause of the agriculturists, should come forward to propound a different view and not take these facts into consideration. (An Honourable Member: "Better fight for the education of the illiterates"). The heavens are fighting for the education of illiterates. We know how precious little is being done so far as that is concerned. You cannot do that in a day. That method by itself would not do. You could have as well told that to the Scheduled Castes themselves that by and by they will be educated and by and by the advanced classes will come to their senses and untouchability will automatically disappear. So do not agitate do not demand anything. It will all come to you may be in a hundred years hence. "You need not ask for reservations". I am afraid that advice cannot satisfy any one. We should know that the same demand the same insistent demand is there and will be there whether you like it or not, and the more you want to prevent or suppress it the more insistent and irresistible it will become.

Mr. Naziruddin Ahmad (West Bengal: Muslim)

Sir I beg to move...

"That clause (4) of the proposed article 286 be deleted."

...This clause relates to appointments reserved for backward classes, in respect of which it says that the Public Service Commission need not be consulted. This again raises a very important question of principle. There is a doubt as to the exact import of clause(4). We are passing the Constitution in such a great hurry that it is impossible to give detailed and proper consideration, but I presume—as many honourable Members will do—that clause (4) seeks to take out of the jurisdiction of the Public Service Commission matters relating to appointments of the backward classes. I concede that backward classes require special treatment. No one would grudge that. That very fact that they are backward requires that their case should be treated with some amount of sympathy and statesmanship. In fact, the backward classes are backward educationally, morally, financially and in other respects.

Dr. P.S. Deshmukh

Morally they are better.

Mr.Naziruddin Ahmad

Yes. I stand corrected. Dr. Deshmukh's suggestion that they are morally better is certainly right. It was an unconscious error of mine which led to the statement. So I am thankful for the correction. Educationally and in other respects they are really backward. In this respect, they require some amount of special treatment. The special treatment which I would suggest would be that with regard to those classes some minimum standard of efficiency should be laid down for a job, because we cannot demoralize the efficiency of the public services. Supposing there is a backward class candidate who has a minimum qualification needed for the job in hand and there is another class of candidate who has superior qualifications, in that case the backward class candidate may be accepted because he has to be protected and has the necessary minimum qualification. In this way the backward classes will have some protection.

But there is no reason why they should be totally excluded from the purview of the Public Service Commission. The Commission may be given the choice of selecting backward class candidates from those possessing minimum qualifications to the exclusion of candidates of other classes possessing superior qualifications. In this way we can serve the backward classes and the Commission can ensure efficiency of candidates. So I suggest that their cases should go to the Commission for their recommendation but directions should be given as to the sufficiency of certain qualifications for the service in question. So I see no justification for excluding these classes from the jurisdiction of the Commission.

..The other amendment of Dr. Deshmukh requiring fair representation of the different classes is one which deserves acceptance. In fact although distinctions between classes and communities have been done away with, there may be some remnants here and there and the decision of the Commission with regard to fair representation of different classes would be welcome and it would be above criticism. So this amendment, I submit, should be accepted..

Sardar Hukam Singh

Mr. President, Sir, I beg to move:

"That after clause (4) of the proposed Article 286, the following Explanation be added:-

> Explanation-Backward class of citizens would mean and include class or classes of citizens backward economically and educationally."

These words "backward classes" have been used in our Draft Constitution in the various articles that we have passed. Now, in clause (4) of this Article 286, it is said that,

> Nothing in clause (3) of this article shall require a Public Service Commission to be consulted as respects the manner in which appointments and posts are to be reserved in favour of any backward class of citizens in the Union or a State."

I wholeheartedly support this clause. This is a very wholesome provision, but my difficulty is that the term "backward classes of citizens" is not defined anywhere in the whole Constitution. This phrase has been used in some places and, in my humble opinion, it does not convey any definite meaning. It is so loose and vague that it might be interpreted differently by different Governments or by different authorities. In Article 10(3) it is stated:

> "Nothing in this article shall prevent the State from making any provision for the reservation of appointments or posts in favour of any backward class of citizens who, in the opinion of the State, are not adequately represented in the services under the State."

The second phrase is found in Article 37 and there the words used are different. It runs as follows:

"The State shall promote with special care the educational and economic interests of the weaker sections of the people, and in particular, of the Scheduled Castes and the Scheduled tribes, and shall protect them from social injustice and all forms of exploitation."

The Scheduled Castes and the scheduled tribes have been defined in the interpretation clause under Article 303, but there is no definition of those backward classes. Here the words used are "weaker sections". I feel some difficulty whether these weaker sections mean the same thing as backward classes or these would have a different meaning so far as Article 37 is concerned.

Then I wish to bring to the notice of the House the following

> "The State shall promote with special care the educational and economic interests of the weaker sections."

Then we have passed another section namely Article 301. There it is provided that:

> "The President may by order appoint a Commission consisting of such persons as he thinks fit to investigate the conditions of socially and educationally backward classes within the territory of India and the difficulties under which they labour and to.."

Here also the Commission that is to be appointed shall investigate the conditions of socially and educationally backward classes. Here the word "economically" is absent. It is not provided as to who would decide who are the backward classes. I endorse the remarks of my honourable Friend, Dr. Deshmukh that there are regions in this vast country and there are classes of persons who are as backward as the Scheduled Castes and unless we provide for the development of their interests and bring them forward along with the other sections, when they could compete with other sections of the community, they would remain backward and the country would not grow harmoniously. Therefore, I submitted yesterday, it is very essential that we should define here who would be the backward classes. This must be defined at some place at least. We can provide that the President shall have authority to appoint a Commission which would prepare a schedule, as there is one for the Scheduled Castes and Scheduled Tribes, or a special tribunal should be appointed or some officer deputed to go into the conditions of these citizens and then decide: otherwise if that is not done; there would be difficulty and some persons might be suffering from certain difficulties in a certain region; they might not be looked after as backward classes while persons in similar conditions might be given advantages and their development might be looked after in another region. Therefore, I have by this explanation only tried to give some kind of definition. It is not conclusive and it is not exhaustive; it does not say who the backward classes are but it only indicates that backward classes must include backward economically and educationally.

I have not included the word "socially" purposely

because I thought perhaps most of the classes who were backward socially might be included in Scheduled Castes and scheduled tribes and even though some are left out, the object can be achieved by amendment of that schedule. Therefore, my purpose here is that it should be made clear that backward classes should mean and include all those persons and all those classes who are left behind and cannot keep pace with the other section of the community because they are economically and educationally backward in this respect. I request my honourable Friend, Dr. Ambedkar to remove this difficulty of mine whether a definition would be provided somewhere to define who would be the "backward classes" under this Constitution because this phrase has been used in so many places.

Mr. President

..The amendments and the articles are now open for discussion.

Shri H.V. Kamath (C.P. & Berar: General)

..Article 286, as it originally stood, provided,—I invite the attention of the House to clause (4) of the original ariticle,— "Nothing in this article shall require a Public Service Commission to be consulted as respects the manner in which appointments and posts are to be allocated as between the various communities in the Union or a State." This has been suitably and wisely modified so as to refer only to the backward class of citizens and not to the various communities. In this view, I am sorry I am not able to agree with the proposition that has been adumbrated by my honourable Friend Dr. Deshmukh. Though it is difficult not to be in sympathy with the general view he has expressed, I feel, constitutionally there is a difficulty, in so far as the incorporation of that proposition in this article is concerned. The House will recollect, Dr. Deshmukh I am sure is well aware, that this Assembly long ago adopted article 10 in the Chapter on Fundamental Rights, which provides, firstly, that there shall be equality of opportunity for all citizen in matters of employment under the State, secondly that no citizen shall on grounds only of religion, race, caste, sex, descent, place of birth or any of them, be ineligible for any office under the State. The only exception to this provision, is that we have already adopted, "Nothing in this article shall prevent the State..

Dr. P.S. Deshmukh

What I have suggested would be the right fulfilment of the fundamental rights; it would be in no way contradictory.

Shri H.V.Kamath

I am sorry Dr. Deshmukh did not hear all I had to say and chose to interrupt before I concluded my say in the matter. I was pointing to clause (3) of Article 10 which lays down that nothing in this article shall prevent the State from making any provision for the reservation of appointments or posts in favour of any backward class of citizens, but not for *any community*. The class referred to explicity in the Clause (3) of Article 10 which is an exception to the general rule propounded, is any backward class of citizens. Now, if Dr. Deshmukh seeks to include not merely these backward classes of citizens—I for one hate this very term "backward class"; it connotes a stigma which I hope we, in this country, will do away with at the earliest possible opportunity; I hope that ere long no class of citizens will be called backward in our country.

Dr. P.S. Deshmukh

It is only descriptive.

Shri H.V. Kamath

I do hope that all citizens will be equally backward or equally forward and there would not be any particular class of citizens to be dubbed as backward.

Chaudhri Ranbir Singh (East Punjab: General)

This is not so today.

Shri H.V. Kamath

I say in the future. I hope Chaudhuri Ranbir Singh listens to me patiently and makes his remarks when the time comes. I do not mind interruptions; but I hope he will hear me first and than make any interruption.

Now, Dr. Deshmukh suggests that we should incorporate in this Article 286 his Amendment No. 86, adding "or for the purpose of bringing about a just and fair representation of all classes in Public Services of the Union or a State", and his amendment No. 88, adding, "nothing in clause (3) of this article shall require a Public Service Commission to be consulted as respects the manner in which appointments are made and posts reserved for purpose of giving representation to various classes according to their numbers in the Union or a State". Unfortunately, this provision if accepted by the House, will militate against what the House has already adopted in Article 10 providing for reservation only to backward classes. I wish article 10 had been adopted in a different manner, but Article 10 having been adopted already in the form in which it was adopted, it is too late now, unless that is revised so to make a provision in this fashion, firstly to give representation to all classes as well as the second one; otherwise it will conflict with Article 10 (1) (2) and (3) which we have already adopted. I for one would not mind even weightage being given to those people who are really backward for the transitional period, but a constitutional provision of this nature in this article would militate against the article which we have already adopted. It can be safely left to be regulated by Parliament. I am sure the future Parliament in this country will deal fairly and squarely with all communities, and there should be no difficulty about leaving the matter of making provision in this regard to the future Parliament.

...Further, I feel that as for the subject matter in clause (4) of this article, the Public Service Commission might be consulted as regards the reservation of appointments and posts for backward citizens. When posts are reserved for a particular class, of course I am not sure whether there would be weightage in the services for these classes—if there is, well and good—but if there is reservation on some basis either of population or some other, then the number is first fixed—so much for this class, so much for that etc.

Now, Sir, suppose the President takes it into his

head that so many posts should be filled by nomination. There should be a certain proportion for nomination, as it used to be, for instance, in the case of the I.C.S. in the olden days, that so many posts will be filled by nomination and so many by open competition. Here also the President will have to decide what proportion will be recruited by nomination and what proportion by open competition. Unless this number is decided, it will be difficult for the President to finally fix the relation between nomination and competition. Therefore, in that connection he will have to consult the Public Service Commission, and there is nothing wrong, or derogatory to the dignity of the President, if he thus consults the Commission as to the number of posts which have to be reserved. Considering the importance that we have attached to the Commissions in our Constitution, it would have been better that the Commission should be consulted about this matter also, besides the matters mentioned in clause (3) of Article 286...

Shri Phool Singh (United Provinces: General)

Mr. President, Sir, I rise to give my support, my whole-hearted support to the two amendments moved by Dr. Deshmukh. The other point of view expressed in this House is for giving greater powers to the Public Service Commission, and the opponents hold that efficiency and merit should be the only tests in recruitments. It is not a fight for a few loaves and fishes for those who are ultimately to be appointed to these posts. Self-Government, means government of the people, and if the legistures are to be manned by the toiling masses, to make good laws, the proper execution of these good laws depends upon the services, and hence the importance of the services. Much has been made of merit in this case; but equal merit pre-supposes equal opportunity, and I think it goes without saying that the toiling masses are denied all those opportunities which a few literate people living in big cities enjoy. To ask the people from the villages to compete with those city people is asking a man on bicycle to compete with another on a motor-cycle, which in itself is absurd. Then again, merit should also have some reference to the task to be discharged. Mr. Tyagi interrupted Dr. Deshmukh by saying that it is a fight for the illiterates. I think, however sarcastic that remark may be, he was probably right. Self-Government means a government by the people, and if the people are illiterate, a few leaders have no right to ursup all the power to themselves. This cry, this bogey of merit and fair-play is being raised by those who are in an advantageous position and who stand to suffer if others also come into the picture.

Sir, I can quote numerous instances where a mess has been made by those who claim to be efficient enough. To give an example. The U.P. Government legislated that petty proprietors should not transfer their land without the permission of the court. Now it depended upon the court. If the Magistrate happened to be a man who came from a poor family, he was very conscientious and would not permit the transfer. But in the case of those who are either themselves money-lenders or big capitalists, or who had nothing to do with the masses, it only meant the expenditure of a few more rupees to be given to the Peshkar. I can give another instance. In U.P. as late as last year, one very big official got the canal stopped at the time when the harvest was about to ripen. This resulted in the loss of many lakhs maunds of good rice. This is what happens if you appoint people who can compete in examinations, but who have nothing to do with the task in hand, who know nothing about the task that is going to be allotted to them. Sir, efficiency, I say, should have something to do with the task that the man is called upon to discharge.

A few years back I complained that all the commodities that the grower had to sell are being controlled, whereas he is offered no facility whatsoever in the production of food grains. I quoted the example of cane-crushers. Cane crushers could be had at Rs. 20 before the war. During the war its hire went up to Rs. 250 though everything else was being controlled. My complaint went up to the Government and then to the Secretariat. It was, I may tell you, the month of October, and everybody in this House know that the crushing season does not start before November. The Secretariat reported that all the cane-crushers had already been let out. There were no cane-crushers left to be hired. This will always happen when you man the services with people who do not know their jobs.

It is not a question of competition. If you want to run the country properly, if the administration is to be efficient as my friends want it to be, then you must have people in the job who know something about the job and who come from the masses. Otherwise the administration will lose touch with the masses. That is why in almost all the countries of the world fresh blood is being recruited to services constantly and a judge's son does not necessarily become a judge or the deputy collector's son does not necessarily become a deputy collector. The practice should be that those, who have been in the services for a long time should be asked to go and settle in the villages while men from the villages should be called to run the administration because they alone know the difficulties of the masses, they alone can feel for the masses and they alone can interpret their sentiments...

Prof. Yashwant Rai (East Punjab: General)

Mr. President, Sir, I have come here to support the amendments moved by Dr. Deshmukh.

After two thousand years the Harijans of this country had begun to entertain the hope that they too would get the same rights as others did. In spite of the fact that twelve to seventeen per cent of posts have been reserved for us in the services, injustice is done even now.

It was as the result of Dr. Ambedkar's efforts that some students were sent to foreign countries and the Central Government spent a lot of money on them. Such examples as I am going to state prove that injustice is being done even now. A Harijan youngman who has come back after obtaining the degree of M.A., M.Ed. was getting a salary of Rs. 180 per month before going abroad, but I regret to say that on his return no Public Service

Commission selected him for any better job, and he is even now rotting on a salary of Rs. 220 per month only, although on this student alone the Central Government spent an amount of forty thousand rupees.

In the circumstances, I cannot believe that the Federal Public Service Commission or other Commissions will not do injustice in the case of Harijans. I believe that there will certainly be injustice in their case. We see that in the subordinate services the principle of providing friends and relatives alone is followed. Recommendations are made for relations. I have seen that even the Ministers speak to the Members on the phone in regard to their candidates and secure interviews for them. In the circumstances, I think that until some special provision is made under this clause, there will always be injustice in the case of Harijans and backward communities. I want to impress that there should be some representatives of the Harijans on the Federal Public Service Commission and the Commissions which are formed in the States and provinces so that they may watch over the interests of the candidates who apply for different posts and who may prevent any injustice being done to Harijans.

After thousands of years the Harijans for the first time under the leadership of Mahatma Gandhi and thanks to Swami Dayanand felt encouraged to take to education and they began to hope that untouchability would be eradicated from society and that they would enjoy equal rights with others. If we want to achieve these objects and to form a classless society, we should include a provision to that effect in the Constitution. Mr. Kamath has said that in Article 10 of the Fundamental Rights it has been stated that there shall be equality of opportunity for all irrespective of caste, creed and colour. We see that untouchability has been abolished under the clause regarding untouchability. But this has had no effect in the rural areas. You can find for yourselves that in the rural areas 85 per cent of the people, who will have to follow this Constitution, are uneducated.

Therefore, if you want to give equal status to those communities which are backward and depressed and on whom injustice has been perpetrated for thousands of years and if you want to establish Indian unity, so that the country may progress and so that many parties in the country may not mislead the poor, I would say that there should be a provision in the Constitution under which the educated Harijans may be provided with employment. I have examples of high-caste matriculates holding the same posts as Harijan M.A.'s. Therefore in the circumstances as demand for the repesentatives of Harijans in the Public Service Commissions and for a special provision for them is not an unreasonable one.

Shri S. Nagappa (Madras: General)

...I am very much thankful to the Honourable Dr. Ambedkar and the Drafting Committee for bringing in this particular provision, viz., "appointments and posts are to be reserved in favour of any backward class of citizens in the Union or a State". Now, as my Friend Mr. Kamath has pointed out, what is the basis of the reservation? Whether it is population or some other basis must be prescribed. I would prefer, in order to be just and equitable, that the reservation should be on population basis.

Another thing is that "backward classes" include so many classes. I would request Dr. Ambedkar to state clearly who all come under this category. I think he has in mind Scheduled Classes, Scheduled Tribes and other backward classes. If there are any others I would request him to explain now.

From this clause I see that certain categories of jobs are excluded. While it may be necessary from the point of view of the administration to so exclude them, the executive must bear in mind that in the clause there is reservation for the backward classes and that the spirit of this clause must be translated in action by the executive and a certain proportion of such posts also is given to the backward classes...I would request my Honourable Friend, Dr. Ambedkar, to be good to explain as to what "backward classes" mean, who are the people who come under that category. I would request him to be good enough to explain this.

Shri Raj Bahadur

Mr. President, Sir, the discussion on this article has brought into the forefront certain vital question of principle as well as of national policy. It appears to me that clause (4) of Article 286 is only a painful reminder to us of the cancer from which our body-politic has suffered for such a long time—I mean to refer to the curse of caste system. The amendments Nos. 86 and 87 moved by my Friends Dr. Deshmukh and Sardar Hukam Singh, are also pointers in the same direction. It has to be recognised without any hesitation that there has been injustice and inequity in the distribution of jobs and services amongst the different classes and castes in our country. As I submitted the other day, there has been a certain amount of favouritism and nepotism on the part of those who happened to be in power. But apart from that certain psychological conditions and traditions that have prevailed throughout our history are also responsible for this alleged injustice.

Nevertheless I would submit, Sir, that we should rather go to the root of the evil. The remedy for the evil does not lie in providing a few jobs or posts in services of the State to persons living in rural areas or to persons living in urban areas. The remedy perhaps lies elsewhere. We can, however, trace the cause of these injustices or inequities to the evil of caste system, the evil that was responsible for our prolonged slavery, the evil that has resulted in our degeneration, morally and politically, the evil that has resulted in creating so many watertight compartments, the evil that has created other evils like untouchability etc. It is only a symptom of that evil that all communities are not represented in the services in an equitable or just manner. To ask for representation, however, on class or caste basis in the services is to remedy that disease only superficially. But we have got to cure the disease from its very roots.

I would submit, Sir, that if we want the best sort of Government in our country, then we must have the best men possible to man our services,—the best men available, the most deserving and the most honest men that we can lay our hands upon. We cannot gamble with our freedom. We cannot afford to gamble with the peace, progress and tranquility of our nation, by simply trying to provide jobs for a few persons belonging to certain classes either in the urban or in the rural areas.

My main objection to the amendment proposed by Dr. Deshmukh does not therefore, proceed from any lack of sympathy for the injustice—which I recognise—from which certain classes of people have been suffering from. My objection is based on the ground that the proposed amendments obviously seek to perpetuate the evil from which we have been suffering and which we want to eradicate. The amendments clearly recognise representation on the basis of castes and classes in the services of the State. It is high time that we do away with such representations. It is time that we recognise that our safety, the safety of our freedom, the safety of our country lies in our unification, in making our nation a homogeneous whole. I would submit that if, for the sake of argument, we recognise the principle that appointments should be made on the basis of castes and classes, let us think where it would lead us. It is obvious that in that case we would shift the centre and focus of our loyalty and allegiance. It would shift from that to the nation as a whole, to loyalty and allegiance to the interests of a group or a class or caste. Our allegiance to the nation would become only secondary. Our primary allegiance would be to class or caste. This is an evil from which we have suffered so long, an evil that led to the partition of the country. This would also kill all incentive for progress. If you say that representation in the services should be on the basis of caste or class, then you remove all incentives to self-development. All incentive for efficiency will be lost.

Dr. P.S. Deshmukh

I did not say that representation should be on the basis of caste or class.

Shri Raj Bahadur

Your amendment says: "or for the purpose of bringing about a just and fair representation of all classes in Public Services of the Union or a State."

There you recognise the principle of repesentation in the services on the basis of class. If you do that, all incentive to efficiency, goes. When this incentive to progress and efficiency goes, the whole nation degenrates. In such a case we would also remain infected with the evil of separatism and with the evil of group or class prejudices.

I would submit, Sir, that this evil would go even further than that and would permeate into all aspects of our national life. Elections would then be fought not on the basis of loyality or service to the nation, not on the basis of the will and capacity for sacrifice for the cause of the nation, but on the basis of class loyality. Can we afford to do that? I respectfully submit that we cannot. We have had enough of it, and it is time that we try to remove all class or caste distinctions. My honourable Friend Shri Phool Singh, while supporting Dr. Deshmukh's amendment, quoted instances where people got into jobs for which they were not fit. I submit that in quoting those instances he went against his own viewpoint. That only shows that people have been appointed on considerations other than merit. To say that the people of the urban areas alone are good or the people of the rural areas alone are good is not correct. We find good and bad people everywhere. We find efficient and inefficient people in all classes and in every walk of life. To brand one as entirely good and another as entirely bad is not wisdom. On the other hand it is sheer non-sense in my opinion. No man is entirely good or bad. One of our famous poets has said:

In man whom men condemn as ill,
I find so much of goodness still,
In man whom man proclaim divine,
I find so much sin and blot,
That I hesitate to draw a line,
Between the two where God has not.

We are all mixtures of good and evil. We are all mixtures of efficiency and inefficiency, of perfection and imperfection. God alone is perfect. Hence we should better do away with all sorts of class prejudices and caste loyalties. That is the only way in which we can strengthen our nation.

We are responsible not only to the present generation but also to posterity, the coming generations. If we try to perpetuate class distinctions, the evil from which we have been suffering so long, I think we would not be acting faithfully to our posterity. As such I find myself in total disagreement with the principles underlying the amendments moved by my honourable Friend, Dr. Deshmukh.

I want to add one word more, Sir, about certain remarks that have fallen about the discriminations and handicaps which are being experienced by the rural communities and by the Scheduled Castes. I have already submitted, that we have got to recognize that these inequalities do exist, but I submit that they are simply symptoms of the disease and if we want to do away with these inequalities or injustices, we must not try or proceed to cure those symptoms of the disease, we must try to get to the disease itself, we must try to go to the root of the evil and kill the evil itself, instead of simply fumbling our way here or there for superficial remedies. I would submit that these jobs, services, posts and seats in the Legislature have always served as "apples of discord" for our nation. We must beware of that apple of discord. We must try to make this country into one compact and strong unified nation. We must try to see that fissiparous tendencies and all sorts of causes which are responsible for our disunity must be eliminated. I would therefore request Dr. Deshmukh and Sardar Hukam Singh to withdraw their amendments.

So far as Sardar Hukam Singh's amendment is concerned, I submit, Sir, that to me it appears that this amendment defeats the very purpose with which it has been moved. His amendment reads: "Backward class of citizens would mean and include class or classes of citizens backward economically and educationally". "Backward classes" may mean anything, backward educationally, economically, socially or otherwise. Why try to specify or restrict its meaning here? I think in its present form it is a much wider term and should be left as it is. I submit that it is time that we should try to eliminate all sorts of class distinctions and class prejudices. The real remedy to my mind is that we should try to strike at the very root and at the very foundation of this caste system. We should try to exterminate it as early as practicable, by an effective piece of legislation so that no class distinctions, discriminations, or caste or communities are recognized any further in any form, and further make it compulsory that a person born in one particular so-called caste shall not marry himself or his sons or daughters in that particular caste. It should be made penal for him to marry in his own so-called caste. For the present this appears to me to be the only remedy. By enacting a piece of legislation alone we can do away with this evil of caste system. The evil cannot be erdicated by superficial remedies.

Shri M. Ananthasayanam Ayyangar (Madras: General)

..Then as regards the manner in which these Public Service Commissions are to work, the first requisite is that all appointments shall be made in the interests of public administration on merit and merit alone. But, having regard to the conditions of our country, there must be some provision in favour of those persons who are not even economically and socially advanced and may not be able to come up to the mark. There must be some limitation no doubt. With regard to appointments which require enormous skill and capacity, certainly, these rules cannot be relaxed, because public interests demand otherwise. Take, for instance, the case of an eminent surgeon; merely because he belongs to a particular community, he ought not to be taken for that job. There are other classes of jobs where such enormous technical skill and capacity may not be necessary, in which case there must be distribution. A hard and fast rule cannot be laid down in the Constitution. Therefore, some provision has been made in favour of the backward classes. There are some communities which have been taken to trade; take, for instance, the Marwari community. They are rich; they have taken to trade. Is it open to them under the existing circumstances to say that they have not received proper representation in the services? In reality public service has no attraction for them, Two or three members of a family engage themselves in business and become millionaires. It is true not one of them is in the public service. To avoid giving representation to the richer classes, the term "backward classes" has been introduced instead of the word "community". Though the term "backward classes" has not been defined, I am sure a Commission appointed by the President will determine who are the backward classes. There are backward classes in every community. Therefore, greater attention has to be given to these backward classes. Whether or not a certain class of people are backward does not depend upon the caste, or community. There is one rich class; there is a poor class. Some classes have economic advantages; some classes have not. The term backward classes is sufficiently comprehensive. To find out who are the backward people, under Article 301 a Commission will be appointed to go into this matter and I believe whosoever is found as such will come under this clause for whom special reservations are sought to be made. Under Article 10 of the Fundamental Rights, it is said that no discrimination shall be made; but discrimination is allowed to afford special help in favour of the backward classes who will be hereafter found to be so or whose names will, after investigation by a Commission, be declared as such. I believe Dr. Deshmukh will be sufficiently satisfied; when the matter comes up before the Commission, it will be time enough to place the case of the various sub-communities and other classes before it so that justice may be done to all of them who are in need of special help...

Pandit Hirday Nath Kunzru (United Provinces: General)

...Sir, the articles that we are considering have been subjected to a certain amount of criticism. My honourable Friend Dr. Deshmukh finds that the articles do not protect the rights of all classes of the population. He is not satisfied with the provision in Article 286 regarding the reservation of posts for any backward class of citizens without consultation with the Public Service Commissions.

He wants that this principle should be extended and that it should apply to all classes. Indeed, he goes further than this and wants that the State should, without consulting the Public Service Commission, lay down that the various classes shall be represented in the Public Services according to their numbers in the Union or the State. This amendment has been dealt with so fully by a number of speakers that I do not think that I need dwell at length on it. But I should like to add my voice to that of those speakers who have opposed this amendment. We are all desirous that the public services should be recruited in such a manner as to give satisfaction to the public as a whole, but it would be..

Dr. P.S. Deshmukh

That is all I want.

Pandit Hirday Nath Kunzru

I am glad to know that this is all that my Friend Dr. Deshmukh wants. But his amendment has been drafted in such a way as to create a very serious danger. I mean, that if it is acted upon, the public interests will suffer seriously. Steps can be taken to see that interests of no community are ignored; but it will be most undesirable to require the executive to lay down that every class be represented in the public services according to its numerical strength. We all know that education is not widely spread in this country. There is, therefore, a large majority of people who are uneducated. Can we, seriously speaking, ask in this state of things, that all the classes should be represented in accordance with their population? If it were a question of representation in the legislature, this argument would have force. But where important business of the State requiring knowledge and judgment has to be carried on from day to day, we should appoint people only on the ground of merit. We cannot appoint them merely on the ground that their appointment will give satisfaction to certain classes; for if that were done, the very classes that want adequate share in the public services would be the first to suffer, for they have to gain more by the efficiency of the administration and the impartiality of the officers than the members of the more advanced classes. I am, therefore, compelled to oppose Dr. Deshmukh's amendment. I have hardly any doubt that the House will not accept it.

The Honourable Dr. B.R. Ambedkar

...The only point that remains for me to say anything about is the question that is raised about the Scheduled Castes and the Backward Classes. I think I might say that enough provision has been made, both in Article 296 which we have to consider at a later stage and in article 10, for safeguarding the interests of what are called the Scheduled Castes, the Scheduled Tribes and the Backward Classes. I do not think that any purpose will be served by making a provision whereby it would be obligatory upon the President to appoint a member of what might be called either a Scheduled Caste, or Scheduled Tribe or a member belonging to the backward classes.

Shri A.V. Thakkar

Other backward classes.

The Honourable Dr. B.R. Ambedkar

The function of a member of the Public Service Commission is a general one. He cannot be there to protect the interests of any particular class. He shall have to apply his mind to the general question of finding out who is the best and the most efficient candidate for an appointment. The real protection, the real method of protection that has been adopted, namely, to permit the Legislature to fix a certain quota to be filled by these classes. I am also asked to define what are backward classes. Well, I think the words "backward classes" so far as this country is concerned is almost elementary. I do not think that I can use a simpler word than the word "Backward classes". Everybody in the province knows who are the backward classes, and I think it is, therefore, better to leave the matter as has been done in this Constitution, to the Commission which is to be appointed which will investigate into the conditions of the state of society, and to ascertain which are to be regarded as backward classes in this country.

Shri A.V. Thakkar

May I ask whether it will not take several years before that is done?

The Honourable Dr. B.R. Ambedkar

Yes, but in the meantime, there is no prohibition on any provincial government to make provisions for what are called the backward classes. They are left quite free, by Article 10. Therefore, my submission is that there is no fear that the interests of the backward classes or the Scheduled Castes will be overlooked in the recruitment to the services. As my Friend Pandit Kunzru has said, the articles I have presented to the House are certainly a very great improvement upon what the articles were before in the Draft Constitution. We have, if I may say so for myself, studied a great deal the provisions in the Canadian law and the provisions in the Australian law, and we have succeeded, if I may say so, in finding out a *via media* which I hope the House will not find any difficulty in accepting.[14]

The Draft Article was again referred to the Drafting Committee, along with the other Draft Articles, with instructions to carry out such renumbering of the articles, clauses and sub-clauses and such revision as might be necessary, and to recommend such formal or consequential or necessary amendments to the Constitution as might be required. The Draft Constitution as revised by the Drafting Committee was submitted to the President of the Constitutent Assembly on November 3, 1949. In this Draft, where words were substituted or new words were inserted, they were indicated in italics.

Clause (4) of Draft Article 286, which was renumbered as clause (4) of Article 320 in revision, was modified by the Drafting Committee with the addition of the following words "the members of the Scheduled Castes or Scheduled Tribes or". The revised Article was as follows:

> Nothing in clause (3) shall require a Public Service Commission to be consulted as respects the manner in which appointments and posts are to be reserved in favour of *the members of the Scheduled Castes or*

> *Scheduled Tribes* or any backward class of citizens in the Union or a State.[15]

Notice of amendments of this clause was given by the Drafting Committee as well as by other members of the Assembly. All the amendments were considered by the Assembly on Novermber 14 when Pandit Thakurdas Bhargava moved an amendment for deletion of the words suggested by the Drafting Committee because those were against the verdict of the Assembly. Dr. P.S. Deshmukh pleaded for a reciprocal provision for the backward classes in Article 335. V.I. Muniswamy Pillai and H.J. Khandekar, both belonging to the Scheduled Castes, and Jaipal Singh, a tribal leader of Bihar, supported the amendment suggested by the Drafting Committee while R.K. Sidhva advocated the application of this provision for the Scheduled Castes only. Mahavir Tyagi felt that once a matter had been decided after protracted deliberations and heated discussions in the Assembly it should not be raked up again. K. Santhanam explained that the purpose of this amendment was to keep the Public Service Commission out of all controversy, if reservation became necessary by the application of Article 335. Kunzru argued that even if it be held that the amendment of clause (4) of Article 320 was unnecessary, it was in accord with or it was consequential to the power given to the state by Article 16.[16]

In view of the controversy, the Drafting Committee met some of the members of this connection[17] and eventually the following amended clause was placed before the Assembly by T.T. Krishnamachari on Novermber 15 for acceptance:

> Nothing in clause (3) shall require a Public Service Commission to be consulted as respects the manner in which any provision referred to in clause (4) of article 16 may be made or as respects the manner in which effect may be given to the provisions of Article 335.[18]

The Assembly finally accepted this provision on Novermber 16, 1949.[19]

The deliberations in the Constitutent Assembly on

this clause on Novermber 14 and 15, 1949, were as follows:

Pandit Thakur Das Bhargava

Sir, I move:

"That in clause (4) of a article 320, the words "the members of the Scheduled Castes or Scheduled Tribes or" be deleted."

If you will kindly refer to Article 320, clause (4) it would appear that it says:

"Nothing in clause (4) shall require a Public Service Commission to be consulted as respects the manner in which appointments and posts are to be reserved in favour of the members of the Scheduled Castes or Scheduled Tribes or any backward class of citizens in the Union or States". These words "members of the Scheduled Castes or Scheduled Tribes or" have been added newly. Previously, these words did not exist. Now, so far as reservation is concerned, we find mention of this reservation in article 16, where it is said in clause (1) "There shall be equality of opportunity for all citizens in matters relating to employment or appointment to any office under the State," and in clause (4), "Nothing in this article shall prevent the State from making any provision for the reservation of appointments or posts in favour of any backward class of citizens which, in the opinion of the State, is not adequately represented in the Services under the State". A perusal of these two sections would establish that as a matter of fact, there is only provision for this reservation in respect of the backward class of citizens which in the opinion of the State is not adequately represented in the services of the State. There is absolutely no provision for reservation so far as members of the Scheduled Castes and Scheduled Tribes are concerned. The safeguard given by law to this class is contained in Article 335 which says: "The claims of the members of the Scheduled Castes and Scheduled Tribes shall be taken into consideration, consistently with the maintenance of efficiency of administration, in the making of appointments to services and posts in connection with the affairs of the Union or of a State." Therefore, one thing is absolutely clear, that no reservation was meant to be made for the members of the Scheduled Castes or Scheduled Tribes as such. I remember that in the Sub-Committee of the Minorities Committee, this matter came up and then we decided that there should be no reservation at all. Now, as if by the backdoor, by smuggling, this reservation for the Scheduled Castes and Scheduled Tribes is being inserted in clause (4) of Article 320. My submission is when there is a positive command of the Constitution to the members of the Public Service Commission which they must obey that the claims of the members of the Scheduled Castes and Scheduled Tribes must be considered consistently with the maintenace of efficiency of administration, this provision would be useless, and also, in a manner, I should say, this takes away the effect of Article 335 to an extent. I am therefore, anxious that so far as the Scheduled Castes and Scheduled Tribes are concerned, their claims must be considered with regard to all appointments and not only with regard to reserved appointments. Because, if they are reserved, it means that the claims of other people for these appointments will not be considered, and their claims only will be considered. The likelihood is that their claims will be confined only to the reserved posts and in regard to other posts, their claims will not be considered.

Now, as the House knows, the provision contained in article 16 clause (4) is a short of a negative provision to counterpoise the equality of opportunity for all citizens, some of whom are very much developed and others not so developed, and provision is made that the State is not prevented from making any provision for the reservation of appointments or posts. I do not know whether the State is going to reserve any posts. Supposing no posts are reserved, this provision will neither benefit the backward classes nor any other class. When reservation of posts has not been decided by this House, I do not think we are justified in having in this clause (4) a contingency for which reservation could be made. When the House has decided once for all that no reservation is to be made, then these words would give rise to the impression that reservation is possible.

I am anxious that whatever rights have been given by the Constitution that should be enjoyed by the members of the Scheduled Castes and Scheduled Tribes and no more or no less. In regard to Article 335, I beg to submit that this is a very positive and extensive provision. If I were a member of the Public Service Commission, I would like to give every post to the members of the Sheduled Castes & Scheduled Tribes consistently with the maintenance of efficiency of administration for at least five or ten years so that they may have been.

Shri T.T. Krishnamachari

Will the honourable Member please say how article 335 could be implemented?

Pandit Thakur Das Bhargava

Can it only be implemented by reservation? If that is so, why did we not so decide? We decided against that; we were against that. The Drafting Committee is smuggling in some provision which is against the verdict of the Assembly. Why was this point not raised before? I think reservation is entirely a wrong thing. Under Article 335, their claims can certainly be considered. After all, a Commission is to be appointed and welfare officers are going to be appointed. The President has to see whether the rights of these communities are safeguarded. I have no reason to believe that Article 335 will not be implemented. It must be implemented; but this is not the way to implement it.

Shri V.I. Muniswamy Pillay (Madras : General)

Mr. President, Sir, I think it is an irony of fate that hurdles of this sort are sought to be placed even in regard to the meagre facilities that have been adopted in this House. I do not agree with my honourable Friend Pandit Thakurdas Bhargava's amendment since the implementation of Article 335, which was formerly Article 296, is sought in this clause (4) of Article 320. Sir, if I were to tell him, the backward communities which he refered to is not a comprehensive term or adopted by all the provincial

Governments in India. In Madras, backward communities refer to certain sections of the people and the Scheduled Castes and Scheduled Tribes form a separate class from the backward communities. If it is the idea of my enlightened friend that the backward classes alone must remain in the Constitution for any reservation, the Scheduled Castes and Scheduled Tribes will not find reservation for appointments either in Madras or in some other provinces. So, I feel what the Drafting Committee has done for implementing and also making it clear what obtains in Article 335 in clause (4) of Article 320 is correct. My friend was saying that no reservation was made: but if he studies Article 335, there is reservation in services for Scheduled Castes and Scheduled Tribes. This clause (4) gives power of consultation with the Public Service Commission which is ultimately the authority that will be advising the Governors and the President of the Union on what basis the members of Scheduled Castes or Scheduled Tribes are to be taken in services. So I feel very strongly that if my honourable Friend's amendment is accepted, it will mean that the Scheduled Castes or Tribes will not count for reservation in the services. So I oppose this amendment.

Shri Mahavir Tyagi

Sir, I propose that this may be held over. It is very controversial.

Mr. President

I would allow discussion of this. Those who wish to speak may speak now. Voting will be taken at the end, of course.

Dr. P.S. Deshmukh

I am glad the importance of this article is being appreciated by many honourable Members. It is certainly very very important. I for one do not oppose the changes made by the Drafting Committee in this article, but I would appeal to the Members and to the representatives of Scheduled Castes and Tribes that they should not also object to the insertion of the words "backward classes" in Article 335. It was very unjustly and unfairly ommitted from that article and it was no gain to anybody, especially to Members representing the Scheduled Castes or Tribes. Just as in this Article 320, we propose to add the words "the Members of the Scheduled Castes and Scheduled Tribes" and retain the words "Backward classes of citizens", similarly the words "backward classes" should be added to Article 335. That will be entirely fair and consistent and if that is accepted, I would strongly oppose the amendment that has been just moved. If, for the purpose of even carrying greater assurance to Members of Scheduled Classes, it is necessary to mention certain safeguards specifically, I do not think we should fight shy of it. We are trying too much to ask people to have faith in our liberal intentions and generous motives but in many respects it is better to come down to practical politics and embody what we mean in a concrete shape, understandable by the ordinary citizen. If for that purpose the Drafting Committee has suggested the addition of the two classes of communities in Article 320, I for one would not quarrel with it. But I would appeal to the House and to everybody that the words "backward classes" should be added to Article 335. There is a little history so far as this article is concerned and the omission is, I believe, as accidental as some other things that have happened in regard to the provisions in the Constitution. Backward classes were omitted from article 335 in this way. The omission was never contemplated. Mr. Munshi had attempted amendments of the proposed article several times, but in none of them "backward classes" was omitted. But suddenly at a very late stage, when unfortunately I happened to be out of Delhi, I discovered that these words happen to be omitted. The best solution which is acceptable to everybody is that the proposed addition to Article 320 should stay and honourable Members of this House should insist that the words "backward classes" should be added to Article 335 and the *status quo* maintained which was deliberate, intentional and which was really the demand of everybody, especially of Members representing the backword classes and also, if I may say so, of the representatives of the Scheduled Castes and

Tribes. There has never been any conflict of interests between the various groups of communities and I hope the Scheduled Castes and the Scheduled Tribes will not bring about this conflict which will be of evil consequences to the whole nation. I would, therefore, appeal that whatever has been embodied in article 320 should now stay and in Article 335 the word "backward"...

Mr. President

There is no Amendment for 335.

Dr. P.S. Deshmukh

I have given an amendment to that effect somewhat late. I was away from home and I was not able to table it in time but as soon as I got it, I sent the amendment in. I would beg of you that this amendment of mine may be permitted. It is No. 530. I have said "that in Article 335 after the word "members", the words "backward classes" be inserted."

Shri H.J. Khandekar (C.P. & Berar: General)

Mr. President, Sir, I stand here to oppose the amendment moved by my Friend, Mr. Thakur Das Bhargava. The draft that has been put forward by the Drafting Commitee is with certain reasons. Because this House has adopted Article 335 last time as Article 296 and in order to give effect to that article, this Article 320 has been submitted to the House. According to Article 335 the seats have been reserved for members of the Scheduled Castes in services and posts, but that article does not give power to the Public Service Commission or the Federal Public Service Commission. We had to bring that article into effect and for this purpose this amendment has been moved by the Drafting Committee and then only the F.P.S.C. or P.S.C. of the States will consider the claims of the Scheduled Caste. I am very sorry to say that such amendments as have been moved by Shri Bhargava regarding the Scheduled Castes are being moved at this stage to bury down the Harijans. There are certain people in the country from the caste Hindus—I am not of course criticising them—but I would like to tell certain facts that they do not want to give any faciiities to us. Certain members of the Hindu society will only be satisfied when the Scheduled Castes and Scheduled Tribes are buried. I think, Sir, these amendments are brought with these motives. I, therefore, feel very sorry and pity for such caste Hindu friends. With these words, I oppose the amendment moved by my Friend Mr. Bhargava.

Shri R.K. Sidhva

Mr. President, all along during the discussions and start of this Constitution I have held the view that if anybody deserves protection or special rights or privileges, it is the Scheduled Castes only and I hold today the same view that none but the Scheduled Castes should have a special right for the reasons that I frequently stated that we have done certain injustice to that class and for the purpose of undoing that injustice, we specially gave them this protection. I have all along extended my support to this on this ground. I am not in favour of giving any protection to the so-called backward classes. Backward classes were introduced by the British Government, and I do not want that blot to be continued in this Constitution. Backward classes exist in all communities and in the directive policy and the fundamental policy we have decided that within ten years everyday shall be made literate, and with literacy nobody will remain backward. I would like to know what is the meaning of "backward class".

An Honourable Member:

Those not in service.

Shri R.K. Sidhva

With education such service also will automatically come in. When proper education has been provided for, automatically their rights to entry into the services will also come in. Therefore, I do not approve of my Friend Dr. Deshmukh's proposal to introduce the words "backward class" in Article 313 which we have after full consideration decided should not be there. Therefore, I say that the amendment of the Drafting Committee is a perfectly correct one and that is the only amendment which we should support, without any other amendment. I do not think anyone in this House would take away the powers or the rights which we have given to the Scheduled Castes. My Friend, Pandit Thakur Das Bhargava, said— I do not think he means it—that the word should be deleted. I strongly oppose it. Why should it be deleted when we have fundamentally accepted it in our Constitution. Therefore, I support the amendment of the Drafting Committee and I oppose any kind of amendment. Although the words "Backward class" are there, I am obliged to reluctantly accept it, and if I had my way, I would have said that there shall be no such thing as "backward classes". Within the next five years, I would make them all literate, so that they may be able to occupy any place in our society. We have to undo what has been done during the past 150 years, and we have to undo it as early as possible. Sir, with these words I strongly support the Drafting Committee's amendment.

Shri Mahavir Tyagi

Sir, I do not know whether I am really right in interpreting the procedure of the third reading of such Bills. As far as I know, in the Legislative Assembly of the Province, the third reading is only...

Shri R.K. Sidhva

This is not a third reading.

Shri Mahavir Tyagi

What reading is it then? The second reading has been finished and only such amendments as are of a consequential nature or as accrue from our past decisions are to come at this stage. If, however, matters which were closed after protracted deliberations and heated discussions, were to be raked up again at this stage, I am afraid, your time limit for the discussion and decisions will be rather very unfair. Sir, my submission is that all such matters, which were once discussed and closed here, and which were also discussed among Members mutually, either in the shape of different parties or groups, and particularly such matters which were as a result of compromise resolved as unanimous decisions, were to be reopened for discussion, I assure you, Sir, that it will take a very long time and it will not be possible for you with due fairness, to finish the discussions according to the schedule which you have kindly prescribed. I submit that the amendment under discussion was neither consequential nor was there any necessity for introducing the question of reservation of offices or posts for Scheduled Castes, here. Sir, the House has expressed itself a number of times in the past that our people do not want any reservations for anybody. And particularly in the case of the Scheduled Castes, the House had agreed, after heated discussions and passed Article 335, as it is at present numbered, to the effect that "the claims of the members of the Scheduled Castes and the Scheduled Tribes shall be taken into consideration, consistenly with the maintenance of efficiency of administration in the making of appointments to services and posts in connection with the affairs of the Union or a State". That was quite enough and that was the last word unanimously agreed upon by the House. And the Members of the Scheduled Castes were also satisfied with this article. Why introduce the same communal virus into another article? Is not one enough? To bring it here again means raking up the old controversy again. That representation of Scheduled Castes shall be so and so, the manner of giving it shall be such and such, that the rules of giving this representation in the services or posts to the Scheduled Castes shall not be made in consultation with the Public Services and so on. All this, I say is absolutely unnecessary, and surely it does not benefit the Scheduled Castes people at all. Even Article 335 was a matter of controversy, and it was opposed. Some of us felt that the special reservation was forced against their wishes. But then we were told that it was only a directive article, and that it directs the policy of future Governments, the House agreed to have it only as a directive. And now you want to bring it in another article. The Constitution is in your hands and you can introduce controversial matters in any article and it will be discussed here as a basic proposal and then amendments will come in. Sir, I submit that you might kindly rule such matters as out of order. Matters once, twice and thrice discussed cannot be brought in again.

How long can the House go on discussing these matters?

Shri Jaipal Singh (Bihar: General)

Mr. President, Sir, I feel I must come forward to congratulate the Drafting Committee for having made a point more clear than it might have been, had they not introduced the amendment in clause (4) of Article 320. I must confess that I have been very much surprised by the amendment that my honourable Friend, Pandit Thakur Das Bhargava, has been pleased to place before the House. My memory is not very weak. Not many months ago, he was the one who congratulated himself and the House for atoning for what had not been done for centuries; but, now, some-how or other, he swallows his words and tries to accuse the Drafting Committee and the Scheduled Castes and the Scheduled Tribes and any other backward classes of aligning ourselves as a communal group. The hint has already been made by my predecessor just now. Sir, we are not asking for this from any communal angle. We do not want anything. If you do not want to give it, do not give it. We are not asking for it. Do not give with your right hand and take away with your left. I have said every time that it has been my privilege to come and plead for the most backward group in our country, and made it quite emphatic and quite clear that I am not here with a beggar's bowl. If you give it, give it without any mental reservations.

As far as I can see, all that the Drafting Committee has done is to elucidate what were the intentions in the Fundemental Rights and the directive principles of the Constitution. Beyond that they have not gone. My friends will be the first to admit that the Scheduled Castes and the Scheduled Tribes are among the backward classes. Well, they have already accepted in their previous speeches and the previous consideration stage that the Backward Classes have to be brought up to the general level. How else can you do it unless there is some way of implementing that intention? We have had enough for words. We have had them for centuries and centuries. In this Constitution we are providing the wherewithals for materialising those intentions. You have appealed to us not to talk at length. I have no desire to do so; all that I say is—be generous and mean it.

The Honourable Shri K. Santhanam

I am afraid the scope of this particular clause has been widely exaggerated by almost every speaker. It does not prescribe by itself any kind of reservation or any privilege which has not been given by the other articles of the Constitution. What all it attempts to do is to decide whether the Public Service Commissions shall have anything to do with either the reservation of the Backward Class or of the Scheduled Tribes. If by the application of article 335 such reservation becomes necessary. No one will contend that in attempting to apply 335, in considering the claims of scheduled castes, no reservation will be made. If any one comes to that conclusion that no reservation shall be made, I believe that 335 cannot be implemented to any extent. But whether in any particular service the Scheduled Castes should be represented and to what extent—all that may be a matter of argument, consideration and discretion. But to say that at no point whatsoever any reservation shall be made, is, I think, wholly inconsistent with either the letter or spirit of Article 335.

Assuming that in some matters some kind of reservation will have to be made, the question here is whether it shall be done by the rules of the Public Service Commissions or by the Government directly. That is the short issue of this particular clause. It is our policy that the Public Service Commissions should be kept out of all these communal and other considerations.

Pandit Thakur Das Bhargava

May I know if the provisions of 335 are not binding upon the Public Service Commissions? They must take it into consideration.

The Honourable Shri K. Santhanam

Here the point is whether the rules to be made should be by the Public Service Commissions or by the Government. We do not want the Public Service Commissions to be brought into these matters. It only says that "nothing in clause 3 shall require the Public Services to be consulted".

Shri Mahavir Tyagi

Why not make it clear. Was it incumbent on the Government to consult the Public Services Commission, that you want to have an exemption?

The Honourable Shri K. Santhanam

My honourable Friend, Mr. Tyagi, is altogether wrong in thinking that this is a new insertion. This is purely consequential to Article 335.

Shri Mahavir Tyagi

I want to put one question. Is there any compulsion on us that we must approach the Public Service Commissions for rules?

The Honourable Shri K. Santhanam

If he reads clause (3), he will find that for all these matters, the Public Service Commissions should be consulted. Therefore, if clause (4) were not there, then the Public Service Commissions would be involved in the controversy regarding the manner in which reservations should be carried out. We do not want our Public Service Commissions to be brought in. If any reservations are to be made, that should be done purely at the discretion and judgment of either the Central or Local Government. It is only to prevent the Public Service Commissions from being brought into the controversy that clause (4) is brought in. Without it, if at any time reservations become necessary, consultation with the Commission is also necessary and the public will begin to blame the Public Service Commissions either for the manner or the extent of the reservations. It is only to preserve the purity of the Public Service Commissions that this is inserted, and so whatever objections one may have to reservation is quite a different matter. One may contend that no Government should interpret 335 as giving them reservations. That is a matter for the Superme Court and for anyone to argue out. It is not possible for the Drafting Committee or for this Assembly to assume that no reservations can be made under article 335 and, therefore, this preservation of the purity of the Public Service Commissions need not be undertaken. As a matter of fact, if the Drafting Committee had not put this forward they would have failed in their duty.

Pandit Hirday Nath Kunzru (United Provinces : General)

Mr. President, the question before us has been discussed by those who have favoured the amendment made in clause (4) of Article 320 by the Drafting Committee with reference to Article 335. I think, Sir, that we should refer to clause (4) of Article 16 before we refer to any other article. It says: "Nothing in this article shall prevent the State from making any provision for the reservation of appointments or posts in favour of any backward class of citizens which in the opinion of the State is not adequately represented in the services under the State. "Under this clause, it is not necessary for the Central Government or the Government of a State to consult the Public Service Commissions with regard to the reservation of posts for any or all of the Backward Classes. The question then before us reduces itself to the proposition whether the Scheduled Castes and the Scheduled Tribes should be included among the Backward Classes or not. Now it may be said that these classes have been specially mentioned in various parts of the Constitution and that, therefore, they should not be included among the Backward Classes. It is hard for me to accept any such interpretation. The Scheduled Castes and the Scheduled Tribes have been specifically mentioned in several places because they are believed to be more backward than the classes called backward according to the official terminology of the Provincial Governments. That is the only reason, I believe, why they have been selected for special mention in several articles. It seems to me, therefore, that even if clause (4) of Article 320 were not amended in the manner that it has been by the Drafting Committee, a State would not be under any compulsion to consult the Public Service Commissions with regard to the reservation of posts for the Scheduled Castes or the Scheduled Tribes. Article 335 has been referred to but that is of limited application. All that it says is that...

Pandit Balkrishna Sharma

May I draw the attention of the honourable Member to one point? He says the Government is not in duty bound to consult the Public Service Commission, but if he would only refer to Article 320 (3) (a) there he will find that the Public Service Commission should be consulted on all matters relating to the methods of recruitment to civil service and for civil posts, and this might be interpreted as involving the Public Service Commission in a sort of a controversy regarding the reservation of seats for Scheduled Castes, Scheduled Tribes and other Backward Classes. In order to avoid that contingency, "that amendment has been brought in".

Pandit Hirday Nath Kunzru

I am aware of the provisions of clause (3) but what I meant to say was that the provisions of clause (3) must be regarded as subject to the provisions of clause (4) of Article 16 which embodies a fundamental right.

The Honourable Shri K. Santhanam

It is really supplementary.

Pandit Hirday Nath Kunzru

In any case what I have tried to say is that the amendment made in clause (4) of Article 320 does not confer any power on the State with regard to the reservation of posts for any Backward Class that it did not have before.

Sir, I was referring to Article 335. It merely says that the claims of the members of the Scheduled Classes and the Scheduled Tribes shall be taken into consideration consistently with the maintenance of efficiency of administration, etc. It may be found on examination that it is not possible to take the claims of the members of these classes into consideration without reserving a certain proportion of posts for them. Therefore, in my opinion, the more important article that we should consider in this connection is Article 16. Article 335 seems to me to be of more limited application than Article 16. We may draw an inference from Article 335 that the State has the power to reserve posts for the Scheduled Castes and the Backward Tribes but I think that clause (4) of Article 16 lays down very clearly and in express terms that the State has the power to make reservations of appointments or posts in favour of any backward class of citizens. Even if it be held that the amendment of clause (4) of Article 320 is unnecessary, it is clear that it is in accord with or that it is consequential to the power given to the State by Article 16.

Mr. President

We shall continue the discussion tomorrow.[20]

Shri T.T. Krishnamachari (Madras : General)

May I mention, Sir, that the Drafting Commmittee met some of the Members who had tabled the amendments to Article 320 yesterday and also others who were interested in it and a new amendment has been tabled to Article 320 which finds a place in today's list? Its number is 559. If the House will defer discussion on this particular article and take it up when that amendment is moved, perhaps it might be more beneficial and will save time.

Mr. President

Do I understand that this form was acceptable to other Members?

Shri T.T. Krishnamachari

It was acceptable to the Members who moved the amendments and spoke yesterday. In any case, this article can be discussed when we take up that particular amendment.[21]

Mr. President

I take it as moved.

Amendment moved:

"That for clause (4) of Article 320, the following clause be substituted:-

(4) Nothing in clause (3) shall require a Public Service Commission to be consulted as respects the manner in which any provision referred to in clause (4) of Article 16 may be made or as respects the manner in which effect may be given to the provisions of Article 335.'

Dr. P.S. Deshmukh

What have you done with Amendment 559 to Article 320, Sir?

Mr. President

I have taken it as moved. You are referring to Amendment No. 559. Do you want to speak, Dr. Deshmukh?

Dr. P.S. Deshmukh

Yes, Sir. I am sorry to say that this new amendment does not appear to be at all satisfactory. First of all, Sir, it is very circuitous in its drafting. It is like a definition known as circular. The amendment reads:

Nothing in clause (3) shall require a Public Service Commision to be consulted as respects the manner in which any provision referred to in clause (4) of article 16 may be made or as respects the manner in which effect may be given to the provisions of Article 335.

If this amendment is considered satisfactory by the representatives of the Scheduled Castes and Scheduled Tribes, I would at least beg of them that my Amendment to 335 may be accepted. If that is done, then the whole thing would be clearer; otherwise it will restrict the scope of this article so far as the backward classes are concerned if not have the effect of excluding them; because, from 335 already the word backward class has been by a mistake omitted and that was the reason why I proposed that the word should be added to 335.

Mr. President

You are referring to Amendment 530.

Dr. P.S. Deshmukh

Yes, Sir. So if we have the amendment now, moved by Mr. T.T. Krishnamachari I would at least request my Friend Mr. T.T. Krishnamachari whether he would accept my amendment which seeks to add backward classes to 335. If this is done then of course I would have no objection because this will bring the whole matter on all fours with the other articles on the subject: Otherwise it will be very curious because in Article 16 (4) we have the word "backward class" whereas in 335 there is no mention of backward class, and we have only two groups—the Scheduled Castes and the Schduled Tribes. It would be absolutely incongruent and inconsistent. If my Friend, Mr. T.T. Krishnamachari would like this amendment to be accepted, I would be prepared to accept his provided he has no objection to the inclusion of backward class in 335: otherwise we would be saying one thing with respect to one provision but we would be including only the word backward class without mentioning Scheduled Castes or Scheduled Tribes. If this amendment is accepted it would mean that there is no mention of the Scheduled Castes or Scheduled Tribes either in 16 (4) or in 320. But in Article 335 there is nothing else but Scheduled Castes and Scheduled Tribes and no mention of backward class. I would like in the alternative, if my Friend is not prepared to accept my amendment, that this matter may be postponed because we may probably discuss the question this evening.

Shri T.T. Krishnamachari

I may mention that 16 (4) is an enabling provision in regard to special representation for backward classes. 335 is an enabling provision is regard to taking into consideration the claims of Scheduled Tribes and Scheduled Castes. These two enabling provisions are brought together in this particular clause. It has merely been made permissible for the Governments not to consult the respective Public Service Commissions in these cases because of the mandatory character of the provision in clause (3) which requires the Public Service Commission to be consulted on every matter. So there is no question of any injustice being done either to the Scheduled Castes and Scheduled Tribes or to the backward classes or any preference being given to one over the other. I do not think my honourable Friend need have any fear that the rights of the backward classes have been taken away or anything has been done to their detriment.

Dr. P.S. Deshmukh

I do not feel at all convinced by my Friend's explanation. Article 16 (4) reads:

Nothing in this article shall prevent the State from making any provision for the reservation of appointments or posts in favour of any backward class..."

Backward class has been used as a general term as will be evident from the speech made by Dr. Ambedkar when the House was considering Article 16. It includes not only Scheduled Castes and Scheduled Tribes but also other educationally and economically backward communities. Now, my honourable Friend curiously enough wants to play between 16 (4) and 335. His contention is absolutely astounding. He does not want to give the same privileges which have been given to the Scheduled Castes and Scheduled Tribes so far as reference to the Public Service Commission is concerned, although according to Article 16 (4) these three groups of people are supposed to get the benefit of this protection. If the reservation is made and the phrase "appointments and posts" is present in Article 16 (4), I think it is absolutely wrong to take the view which he is taking. I know the point of view from which my Friend is looking at the whole thing. I think he will be doing a real disservice to the backward classes and in a sort of underhand way harming their interests, because when 16 (4) was provided it was for backward classes as a whole without any reference to a particular group or groups. From that point of view I request that this matter be left over for the present. It would be very wrong not to add the word "backward classes" to 335.

Pandit Thakur Das Bhargava

May I put one question to my honourable Friend? How is it wrong if the Scheduled Castes and Scheduled Tribes are given more rights than the "backward classes"? They should be given more rights. Are they not more backward?

Dr. P.S. Deshmukh

I do not claim to get more rights or less rights than the backward classes. All I want is equal rights. If "backward classes" was to include not only Scheduled Tribes and Scheduled Castes as well as the economically and educationally backward other castes, and if you are now going to exclude the backward classes simply because they have not formed themselves into one group or agitated I have nothing to say; but if you are going to drive them to that situation I do not think it will be good for the nation or for you. So I should very much like that the intention to include the backward classes as additional and apart from the Scheduled Castes and Scheduled Tribes should not be given up in this way. Originally, there was no intention of even specifying these two groups and my honourable Friend who interrupted just now was the best and most vehement exponent that the word should be "backward classes" only— the other groups should not be separately and specifically referred to.

Shrimati G. Durgabai (Madras: General)

On a point of order, the Drafting Committee has not made any change in Article 335. Therefore, I do not think any amendment would arise.

Mr. President

Let him finish.

Dr. P.S. Deshmukh

So my friend is really speaking against his own contention.

Pandit Thakur Das Bhargava

It is the decision of the House. I want that all the amenities may be extended to all backward classes, but the decision of the House is against my friend's present contention.

Dr. P.S. Deshmukh

If he is prepared to admit that it is in spite of himself, I can understand; but when he wants to lend support to the fact that it is not necessary to retain "backward classes", he is arguing against himself.

Mr. President

We have had enough discussion on this article yesterday also and today.[22]

The redrafted amendment of the Drafting Committee

was put to vote and adopted by the Assembly on November 16, 1949.[23]

Clause (4) of Article 320 owes its origin to Sub-section (4) of Section 266 of the Government of India Act, 1935. It may be remembered that the British Government had pursued a policy of reserving a certain percentage of direct appointments to Government services on the pretext of redressal of communal inequalities and issued an elaborate order in 1934 apportioning percentage of vacancies to various communal groups with detailed instructions issued indicating the manner in which the apportionment was to be effected. These reservations were always treated as matters of Government policy and not to be referred for the advice of bodies like the Public Service Commissions, so that they could pursue their policy of dividing the people even in matters of state appointments with impunity. The existence of the "communal roster" of appointments necessitated the incorporation of such a provision in the Government of India Act of 1935. Subsequently, taking advantage of this provision in the Act of 1935, the British Government extended their policy of reserving a certain percentage of posts in Government services to the Scheduled Castes in 1943.

So the framers had this provision before them when they considered different provisions of the future Constitution of India and, initially, in their wisdom thought of retaining the same provision in the Constitution even though they were quite aware of the fact that this sort of provision in the 1935 Act had enabled the Government of the day to perpetuate cleavages in our body politic which ultimately divided the people so much that the country had to be partitioned on the basis of community and that it would have the same effect in future as well.

As the process of constitution-making advanced, the question of communal representation in legislatures, and by implication, in services, was considered to be not congenial for the interests of the concerned groups themselves and was therefore dropped, but the same was not true so far as the Scheduled Castes, Scheduled Tribes and Backward classes were concerned. The principle of equality of opportunity in respect of state appointments was generally accepted but two exceptions were allowed—one enabling the State to make provision for the reservation of appointments in favour of backward classes of citizens (Article 16 (4)) and the other enjoining that the claims of members of the Scheduled Castes and Scheduled Tribes should be taken into consideration, consistently with the maintenance of good administration, in the making of appointments to Government posts (Article 335).

Having provided for these two exceptions, there was no other alternative but to have a provision of this nature which was incorporated in the Constitution after three drafting changes. The idea behind inclusion of this provision was to ensure that the Government was not deterred in any way from implementing the policy of reservation of appointments and posts, if the state ultimately decides so to do, in favour of three categories of persons—Scheduled Castes, Scheduled Tribes and Backward Classes, though who would constitute the Backward Classes remained undefined in the Constitution.

The "great improvement effected upon the 1935 Act" is that instead of "various communities", we are now concerned with "caste, class and race". This clause makes it clear that the Public Service Commission has no right to be consulted in the matter of taking into consideration the claims of Scheduled Castes and Scheduled Tribes to services and posts as well as in the matter of reservation of posts for backward classes nor can it itself make any such reservation. It ensured that there should be no hindrance, hurdle and obstruction to the implementation of the policy of reservation in the services on the basis of caste, class and race, as if the partition of the country on the basis of religion was not enough to gird our loins against other distintegrating tendencies manifested in allegiance and loyalties based on caste, class and race.

Notes and References

1. Section 96-C of the Government of India Act, 1919.
2. Rao, *op. cit.*, Vol. V, p. 725.
3. *CAD*, Vol. IV, p. 727.
4. *Ibid.*, p. 598.
5. *Ibid.*, dated 21-7-47, p. 702.
6. *Ibid.*, dated 29-7-47, pp. 908-09.
7. Rao, *op. cit.*, Vol. III, pp. 90-93.
8. *Ibid.*, p. 93.
9. *Ibid.*, p. 459.
10. *Ibid.*, p. 629.
11. *Ibid.*, Vol. IV, pp. 351-52.
12. *CAD*, Vol. IX, dated 23-8-49, p. 598.
13. *Ibid.*, pp. 630-32.
14. *Ibid.*, pp. 602-30.
15. Rao, *op. cit.*, Vol. IV, p. 865.
16. *CAD*, Vol. XI, dated 14-11-49, pp. 494-502.
17. *Ibid.*, dated 15-11-49, p. 503.
18. *Ibid.*, pp. 547-49.
19. *Ibid.*, dated 16-11-49, p. 601.
20. *Ibid.*, dated 14-11-49, pp. 494-502.
21. *Ibid.*, dated 15-11-49, p. 503.
22. *Ibid.*, dated 15-11-49, pp. 547-49.
23. *Ibid.*, dated 16-11-49, p. 601.

15

Reservation of Seats for Scheduled Castes and Scheduled Tribes in the House of People (Article 330)

Having lived and worked under the shadow of the 1935 Act in which minority rights and safeguards figured as one of the most important features, the framers could not easily shake off the past and initially followed the same general principle of reservation of seats for the religious, racial and other minorities adumbrated in that Act. One of the terms set out in the questionnaire sent to the members of the Sub-committee on Minorities in February, 1947, therefore, was: What should be the political safeguards of a minority (a) in the Centre, and (b) in the Provinces? The replies received on this point were quite illuminating.

M. Ruthnaswamy suggested that:

> Provision for the adequate representation of such minorities in the Central, Provincial or State Ministries and all departments of the administrations—the fairest proportion would be according to population.[1]

Homi Mody said that:

> So far as Parsees are concerned, they have never asked for any special privileges, but their position is

> that if other minorities are accorded representation anywhere, it is but fair that Parsees should receive treatment at least equal to that given to any of the smaller minorities.[2]

P.K. Salve argued that:

> Election by joint electorates with reservation of seats for a period of ten years. This should apply also to local bodies. The franchise shall be on the basis of universal adult suffrage. The minorities should enjoy equal rights with others before the law and should not, because of their religion or caste or sex, be subject to any public disqualification or discrimination in respect of political, civic, economic, cultural or religious rights.[3]

S.H. Prater, a member belonging to the Anglo-Indian community, suggested that provision should be made in the new Constitution for the representation in the Cabinet at the Centre and in the Provinces of the small minorities which were accorded representation in the legislatures because of the need of associating the minorities with legislative and administrative measures proposed by the Executive which might materially affect their interests. There should be reservation of seats for minorities in the Central Legislature or Legislatures, if bicameral legislatures were established and in the Provincial Legislatures. Under the 1935 Act seats were reserved for the Anglo-Indian community in the Council of State, Federal Assembly and in the Provincial Legislatures. These reservations should be maintained or increased when necessary. Provision should be made to secure representation of the community in all Provinces. Weightage was especially important to the smaller minorities whose interests were likely to be disregarded and overwhelmed by the political power and influence of the major elements of the population.[4]

The representatives of the Jain community in their memorandum submitted in March/April, 1947, demanded that

> The actual safeguards for ensuring the rights and

privileges of the Jain community should be on parallel lines to those provided for the other minorities. The Jains should be given special representation in the administrative, executive, judicial, diplomatic, foreign and military services of the nation, of course, subject to the Government rules and regulations which shall be applicable thereto. They should also be given special representation in the Central and Provincial Legislatures, local self-governing bodies, as well as in all the official committees set up from time to time by the Central and Provincial Governments.[5]

Ujjal Singh and Harnam Singh in their memorandum on Minorities demanded that:

In the Central Legislature, 6 per cent of the seats shall be reserved for the Sikhs both in the Upper and the Lower Houses.

At least one Sikh shall always find a seat in the Cabinet of the Union.

In Sind, Baluchistan, United Provinces, Delhi, Bengal, Bombay, Central Provinces, Bihar and Assam, the Sikhs shall be recognised as a separate minority and provisions shall be made for their representation in the Legislatures of the said provinces. In the North-West Frontier Province the Sikhs shall have representation of 10 per cent in the Legislature.

The Punjab shall be divided into two separate autonomous units, but in case division of the Punjab into two separate autonomous units is not possible under the State Paper of May 16, 1946, the Punjab shall be divided into two sub-provinces, North-West Punjab and South-East Punjab. Each sub-province shall have its own Legislature and Cabinet to deal with its own affairs. In this set-up, affairs of joint concern, if any, shall be dealt with by a Joint Legislature comprising an equal number of members elected by the sub-provincial Legislatures. The weightage to the Sikhs in the Joint Legislature shall be on the lines adopted for Muslims at the Centre.

> In the passing of any bill, motion, or resolution affecting exclusively a single community, members of other communities shall not have a right of vote. The executive head will be advised by the Cabinet of North-West Punjab in affairs relating to North-West Punjab, by the Cabinet of the South-East Punjab in affairs solely of the South-East Punjab and by the Joint Cabinet in affairs of joint concern.
>
> In the Cabinet constituted for the administration of affairs of joint concern, the representation of the Sikhs shall be at least 25 per cent.
>
> In North-West Frontier Province and Baluchistan, a Sikh Minister shall be appointed by rotation with a Hindu Minister.
>
> In United Provinces one Minister for smaller minorities shall be appointed.
>
> The Cabinet shall be chosen on the Swiss model, all the legislatures and Cabinets having the same fixed term.[6]

H.J. Khandekar, a member belonging to the Scheduled Caste suggested that

> Reservation of seats in Legislatures, Executive Governments, Judiciary, and the Services for Scheduled Castes proportionate to their population taking into consideration that they are as equal as Muslims with such weightage as may be given to other communities. Out of the seats reserved for ladies in the general constituencies, seats should be reserved for Scheduled Castes ladies also. The seats reserved in the Legislatures should not in any case be less than what have been allotted at present.
>
> In local bodies as well there should be reservation on the above lines. The post of head executive should rotate by turn among the Scheduled Castes as well.[7]

Jagjivan Ram, a leader of the Scheduled Castes, put the same demands more elaborately as follows:

> Seats shall be reserved for the Scheduled Castes proportionate to their population in Legislatures,

> Cabinets, Ministries and local bodies. The post of the executives shall rotate by turn among the several communities represented in the local body concerned.
>
> Scheduled Castes have never demanded weightage for themselves and have always insisted that no weightage should be given to any community. If weightage is to be given to any community it should come from the share of the majority community and the Scheduled Castes should also get proportionate weightage. If representation is to be given to special interests it should come from the share of the majority and not of the minorities. Election to all seats reserved for the Scheduled Castes in Legislatures and local bodies shall be by the system of (i) joint electorate with the caste Hindus: (ii) adult franchise; and (iii) distributive voting in plural constituencies.
>
> Scheduled Castes shall be free to contest unreserved seats in elective bodies and compete for unreserved seats in services and executives.[8]

The Working Committee of the All-India Adi-Hindu Depressed Classes Association demanded that there should be provision for

> Representation of the Scheduled Castes in proportion to their population:
>
> (i) in the Central and the various Provincial Legislatures,
>
> (ii) in the Central and Provincial executives,
>
> (iii) in municipalities and all statutory local bodies.
>
> Their representation in the Central and the various provincial legislatures by:
>
> (a) adult suffrage,
>
> (b) by separate electorates or by reservation of seats in joint electorates provided that a candidate to be declared elected must secure 40 per cent of the total number of votes recorded by members of the Scheduled Castes.[9]

R. N. Brahma in his memorandum on the safeguards for the Plains Tribal people of Assam demanded that:

The Plains tribal people in Assam demand their proportionate representation in the Central Legislature on population basis and also representation in the Central executives for the Plains tribal people. They also demand seats in the Central Cabinet.

The Plains tribal people in Assam demand proportionate re-presentation on population basis in the provincial Legislatures with weightage of at least 25 per cent of the total seats allotted.[10]

Dr. S. P. Mookerjee suggested that:

An adequate share for the minorities in the legislatures and other self-governing authorities should be secured by joint electorate and reservation of seats for recognised minorities. If any weightage is to be given it should be on a uniform basis in the Centre and in the Provinces. In no Province should any weightage be given to the majority community, nor the minority be given less representation than is due to it on population basis. Reservation of seats should cease after twenty years or earlier, if the communities concerned agree. The executive governments in the Provinces and at the Centre during the period referred to in clause (a) shall be of a composite nature reflecting the proportion of each community in the various legislatures, and enjoy the confidence of the minority community or communities concerned.[11]

The franchise shall be on the basis of universal adult suffrage. Elections to legislatures, provincial and union, and to all local self-governing bodies shall be through joint electorates, with reservation of seats for minorities according to population unless a particular minority does not wish to have any seats reserved for them.[12]

Ambedkar's note on the subject of minorities and fundamental rights provided for right to the Scheduled Castes for representation in the Legislatures and in the Executive in clauses 1 and 2 of part I of Article I of Section IV:

The Constitution of the United States of India shall guarantee to the Scheduled Castes the following rights:

Clause I—Right to representation in the Legislature (1) Quantum of Representation—(a) (i) The Scheduled Castes shall have minimum representation in the Legislature—Union and State—and if there be a group constitution then in the group Legislature equal to the ratio of their population to the total population, provided that no other minority is allowed to claim more than what is due to it on the basis of its population.

(ii) The Scheduled Castes of Sind and the N.W.F. Province shall be given their due share of representation.

(iii) Weightage where it becomes necessary to reduce a huge communal majority to reasonable dimensions shall come out of the share of the majority. In no case shall it be at the cost of another minority community.

(iv) Weightage carved out from the share of majority shall not be assigned to one community only. But the same shall be divided among all minority communities equally or in inverse proportion to their

(1) economic position,

(2) social status, and

(3) educational advance.

(b) There should be no representation to special interests. But if the same is allowed it must be taken out of the share of representation given to that community to which the special interest belongs.

(2) Method of Election—

(A) For Legislative Bodies

(a) The system of election introduced by the Poona Pact shall be abolished.

(b) In its place, the system of *Separate Electorates* shall be substituted.

(c) Franchise shall be adult franchise.

(d) The system of voting shall be cumulative.

(B) For Local Bodies

The principles for determining the quantum of representation and the method of election for municipalities and local bodies shall be the same as that adopted for the Union and State Legislatures.

Clause 2—Right to Representation in the Executive

(1) The Scheduled Castes shall have minimum representation in the Executive—Union and State—and if there be a group constitution then in the group Executive equal to the ratio of their population to the total population provided that no minority community is allowed to claim more than its population ratio.

(2) Weightage where it becomes necessary to reduce a huge majority to reasonable dimensions shall come out of the share of the majority community. In no case shall it be at the cost of another minority community.

(3) Weightage carved out from the share of the majority shall not be assigned to one community only. But the same shall be divided among all minorities equally or in inverse proportion to:

(i) their economic position,

(ii) social status, and

(iii) educational advance.[13]

The Muslim League was not participating in the proceedings of the Constituent Assembly then and no memorandum on behalf of the Muslim community was presented.

The Minorities Sub-Committee met on July 21, 1947, to consider the political safeguards for minorities. By this time the question of partition had been decided and the Muslim League was also represented in the Sub-Committee. Discussions in the Sub-Committee continued till July 27. The issues involved, inter alia, were (1) representation in the Legislatures; joint vs separate electorates and weightage; and (2) reservation of seats in the Cabinets. Unanimous decision could not be reached on many points, and in fact the voting on several items was very close. On some points the voting was equal and where voting was equal, the Chairman of the Sub-Committee did not consider it necessary to exercise his casting vote, since in any case these matters were to be discussed by the Advisory Committee. The report of the Sub-committee submitted on July 27 contained only a summary of the conclusions of the Sub-Committee and also mentioned the result of the vote on each issue.

The report of the Sub-Committee on the subject of representation in the Legislatures; joint vs separate electorates and weightage and reservation of seats in the Cabinets was as follows:

> Representation in Legislatures: (1) The Sub-committee decided by a majority of 28 to 3 that there should be no separate electorates for elections to the Legislatures.
>
> It was understood, in arriving at this decision, that it was open to the sub-committee to decide on any one of the several methods of joint electorates that could be devised.
>
> (2) As a general principle, there should be reservation of seats for different recognised minorities in the various Legislatures. This was carried by a majority of 26 to 3.
>
> The reservation shall be for 10 years, the position to be reconsidered at the end of that period.
>
> (3) The sub-committee considered what minorities and in which provinces may be given the right of reserved seats. For this purpose, the recognised minority communities were considered in three groups as shown below:
>
> A—*Population less than 1½ per cent in the Indian* Dominion omitting States
>
> 1. Anglo-Indians.

2. Parsees.
3. Plains tribesmen in Assam.

B—Population not more than 1½ per cent

4. Indian Christians.
5. Sikhs.

C—Population exceeding 1½ per cent

6. Muslims.
7. Scheduled Castes.

(4) Sir Homi Mody advanced the claim of his community for adequate representation in the Central and Provincial Legislatures. While the committee was of opinion that adequate representation should be provided for in response to this claim, it welcomed Sir Homi's request to have more time to think over the matter and therefore the matter was left over for decision by the Advisory Committee.

(5) The sub-committee than examined the demand put forward by representatives of the Anglo—Indian community but thought it advisable that the question of both the minorities in 'A' group should be decided at the same time by the same body, viz., the Advisory Committee to whom the matter was decided to be referred.

(6) The representatives of the Indian Christians stated that so far as their community was concerned they did not like to stand in the way of nation-building. They were willing to accept reservations proportionate to their population in the Central Legislature and in the Provincial Legislatures of Madras, Bombay, Assam and East Punjab. In the other Provinces, they would have the liberty of seeking election from the general seats. They made it plain, however, that if any weightage was given to any minority in groups 'B' and 'C', they would demand similar weightage though, on principle, they were against weightage being given to any community. The sub-committee accepted this

position and decided to commend it to the Advisory Committee. Rajkumari Amrit Kaur dissented from the views of the other Christian members as she was opposed both to reservation and weightage for any community. A copy of her minute of dissent is attached.

(7) In view of the peculiar and uncertain position of the East Punjab and the position of the Sikhs, the sub-committee decided by a majority of votes (15 to 4) that the question of their representation be referred to the Advisory Committee.

(8) The sub-committee decided by 9 to 4 votes that no weightage be given to any minority in groups 'B' and 'C'.

(9) It was decided by a majority of 8 to 2 that cumulative voting should not be permissible.

(10) The committee examined the proposal that a minority candidate standing for election for a reserved seat should poll a minimum number of votes of his community before he is declared elected. 7 members of the sub-committee voted for this proposal and 7 against it, and it was decided to refer it to the Advisory Committee.

(11) It was proposed that members of a minority community who have reserved seats should have the right to contest unreserved seats as well. This was accepted by the sub-committee in the case of both the Scheduled Castes and other minorities.

Mr. Thakur Das Bhargava made the point and the sub-committee agreed that the position of the communities in East Punjab is so balanced that the whole question of East Punjab should be considered in the Advisory Committee independently of the decisions of the sub-committee.

(12) Dr. Ambedkar suggested that candidates of a majority community should, before being declared elected, poll a minimum number of votes from among voters of the minority communities in their constituencies. This was lost by a large majority, only Dr. Ambedkar voting for it.

4. *Reservation of seats in the Cabinet:*

The sub-committee considered that (a) no statutory provision should be made for reservation of seats for the minorities in Cabinets and that (b) a convention on the lines of paragraph VII of the Instrument of Instructions issued to Governors of provinces under the Government of India Act, 1935, be provided in a schedule to the Constitution.

The first proposition was carried by 8 votes to 7 and the second by 12 votes to 3.

A proposal to delete the words "important" in paragraph VII of the Instrument of Instructions was lost by 9 votes to 8.

Mr. Khandekar has submitted a minute of dissent a copy of which is attached to the report.[14]

In his minute of dissent, Khandekar expressed the apprehension that notwithstanding the declaration of the practice of untouchability as an offence, it could not be safely expected that in all spheres of life and particularly in the matter of sharing power, justice would be done to the Scheduled Castes. Till the Scheduled Castes found that a distinct change in the outlook and attitude of the caste Hindus had taken place and the untouchability was removed root and branch, the case of the Scheduled Castes of giving statutory reservation in the Cabinets both at the Centre and in the Provinces should be considered as a special case.[15]

Rajkumari Amrit Kaur, while dissenting with the decision of the Sub-Committee to provide for reservation of seats in Legislatures and in the services for the minorities which included Scheduled Castes as well, pointed out that to perpetuate any such privilege in the Constitution of a free India would be against the ideal for which the Indian Union stands pledged to work, namely a classless society where there shall be no high nor low, no rich nor poor, and would also keep alive the flame of communalism which is destroying the very fabric of our national life. I question the legal existence of the depressed classes the now, I submit, become legally one with most of the backward and ignorant poor Hindus of this country. They need straightaway all the necessary facilities and opportunities for raising their standards of education and life in general.

No minority will get facilities and opportunities of service through reservation of seats for a handful of their representatives in Legislatures or the services. If such are conceded by statute they will not only further weaken the community concerned but will also lower the standards of efficiency and good governance".[16]

The report of the Minorities Sub-Committee along with the dissenting notes of Khandekar and Rajkumari Amrit Kaur came up before the Advisory Committee on July 28, 1947 for consideration. The discussion lasted four days. The Committee endorsed almost all the conclusions reached by the Sub-Committee which was arrived at after an exhaustive discussion in the Committee.

The Advisory Committee by an overwhelming majority came to the conclusion that the system of separate electorate must be abolished in the new Constitution. In order that minorities might not feel apprehensive about the effect of a system of unrestricted joint electorates on the quantum of their representation in the Legislature, it was recommended as a general rule that seats for the different recognized minorities should be reserved in the various legislatures on the basis of their population. This reservation should be initially for a period of 10 years; the position to be reconsidered at the end of that period. The members of a minority community who had reserved seats should have the right to contest unreserved seats as well. As a matter of general principle, the Committee was opposed to weightage for any minority community.

The recommendations of the Advisory Committee, where they were not unanimous, were taken by vary large majorities composed substantially of members belonging to minority communities themselves. The recommendations relating to representation in Legislatures and representation of minorities in Cabinets were as follows:

Representation in Legislatures

1. *Electorates*: All elections to the Central and Provincial Legislatures will be held on the basis of joint electorate :

> Provided that as a general rule, there shall be reservation of seats for the minorities shown in the schedule in the various legislatures on the basis of their population:
>
> Provided further that such reservation shall be for 10 years, the position to be reconsidered at the end of the period.

Schedule

Group A: Population less than: 1½ per cent in the Indian Dominion, omitting States.

1. Anglo-Indians
2. Parsees.
3. Plains tribesmen in Assam.

Group B. Population not more than 1½ per cent.

4. Indian Christians.
5. Sikhs.

Group C: Population exceeding 1½ per cent.

6. Muslims.
7. Scheduled Castes.

2. (a) *Anglo-Indians*: There shall be no reservation of seats for the Anglo-Indians, but the President of the Union and the Governors of Provinces shall have power to nominate their representatives in the Centre and the Provinces respectively if they fail to secure adequate representation in the legislatures as a result of the general election.

(b) *Parsees*: There shall be no statutory reservation in favour of the parsee community, but they would continue to remain on the list of recognized minorities:

Provided that if as a result of elections during the period prescribed in proviso 2 to para 1 above it was found that the Parsee community had not secured proper representation, their claim for reserved seats would be reconsidered and adequate representation provided should the separate representation of minorities continue to be a feature of the Constitution.

Note : The above recommendations represent the view taken by the representatives of the Parsee community.

3. (a) *Indian Christians*: There shall be reserved representation for Indian Christians in proportion to their population in the Central Legislature and in the Provincial Legislatures of Madras and Bombay. In other Provinces, they will have the right to seek election from the general seats.

   (b) *Sikhs*: The question of minority rights for the Sikhs will be considered separately.

   (c) *Muslims and Scheduled Castes*: There shall be reservation of seats for the Muslims and Scheduled Castes in the Central and Provincial Legislatures on the basis of their population.

4. *Additional rights to minorities*: The members of a minority community who have reserved seats shall have the right to contest unreserved seats as well.

5. *No weightage*: The minorities for whom representation has been reserved will be allotted seats on their population ratio, and there shall be no weightage for any community.

6. *No condition for a minimum number of votes of one's own community*: There shall be no stipulation that a minority candidate standing for election for a reserved seat shall poll a minimum number of votes of his own community before he is declared elected.

7. *Method of voting*: There may be plural member

constituencies but cumulative voting shall not be permissible.

Representation of Minorities in Cabinets.

8. *No reservation for minorities*: (a) There shall be no statutory reservation of seats for the minorities in Cabinets but a convention on the lines of paragraph VII* of the Instrument of Instructions issued to Governors under the Government of India, Act, 1935 shall be provided in Schedule to the Constitution.

*VII. In making appointments to his Council of Ministers our Governor shall use his best endeavours to select his Ministers in the following manner, that is to say, to appoint in consultation with the person who in his judgment is most likely to command a stable majority in the legislature those persons (including so far as practicable members of important minority communities) who will best be in position collectively to command the confidence of the legislature. In so acting, he shall bear constantly in mind the need for fostering a sense of joint responsibility among his Ministers.[17]

This report of the Advisory Committee on minority rights submitted to the President of the Constituent Assembly on August 8, 1947, was considered by the Assembly on August 27 and 28, 1947, i.e., after India gained independence. The partition of the country, however, had no effect on the outcome of the decision of the Constituent Assembly. Introducing the minority report, Sardar Vallabhai Patel said:

Sir, on behalf of the Advisory Committee I beg leave to place this Report on Minority rights before the House. It has been drafted after considering the report of the Minority Committee and after considering all the points raised with regard to the safeguards for different minorities in this country. You all know that the question of safeguards for minorities has been discussed several times and considered in various committees, and there is no new point to be discussed. In one committee or other for several years past this question has been discussed, sometimes very minutely, sometimes generally. Sometimes its discussion has taken an acute form and sometimes it has resulted in a bitter controversy. But I am happy to say that this report has been the result of a general concensus of opinion between the minorities themselves and the majority: Therefore, although it is not possible to satisfy all, you will see that this report has been the result of agreement on many points; and wherever there has been disagreement the recommendations have been carried by a very large majority, so that except perhaps on one point the report is practically an agreed report. It may be that there are some who are not satisfied on some points, but we have to take into consideration all points of view and feelings and sentiments of the minorities, big and small. We have tried as far as possible to meet the wishes of all the minorities. The minorities among themselves are also divided; there are conflicting interests among them. We have not tried to take advantage of these differences among the minorities themselves; we have tried to see that the minorities also instead of being divided among themselves try to present a united front in order to safeguard their interests. But there are certain points on which the minorities cannot be united because there are minorities within minorities. So it is a difficult proposition. We have tried to solve this difficult problem without any bitterness and without any controversy which would create any ill-feeling or hitch; and I hope that this House also will be able to dispose of this question in a friendly spirit and in an atmosphere of goodwill. Let us hope that we will leave the legacy of bitterness behind and forget the past and begin with a clean slate. There is much that is happening round us which requires us to dispose of our business as quickly as possible; and we should do nothing in this House which will add to our difficulties or to the difficulties of our neighbours who are at present involved in bitter strife and when our hearts are bleeding with the wounds that are being inflicted on one of our best provinces in India. Therefore I trust that in this House in considering this question which affects all the minorities we will introduce no heat or argument which may lead to such controversy as would have a repercussion outside. I hope that we shall be able to dispose of this matter quickly and in a friendly spirit.

You will remember that we passed the Fundamental Rights Committee's Report which was sent by the Advisory Committee; the major part of those rights has been disposed of and accepted by this House. They cover a very wide range of the rights of minorities which give them ample protection; and yet there are certain political safeguards which have got to be specifically considered. An attempt has been made in this report to enumerate these safeguards which are matters of common knowledge, such as representation in legislatures, that is, joint versus separate electorates. This is the question which has raised controversy for almost a decade and we have suffered and paid heavily for it. But fortunately we have been able to deal with this question in such a manner that there has been unanimity on the point that there should be no more separate electorates and we should have joint electorates hereafter. So that is a great gain.

Then again on the question of weightage we have agreed that there should be no weightage and with joint electorates the communities should be represented according to the proportion of their population. Then we have thought fit to agree to reservation in proportion to the population of the minorities. Some of the minorities gladly surrendered that right, and said that they wanted neither weightage nor separate electorates but in the general upheaval that is taking place they want to merge themselves in the nation and stand on their own legs. I congratulate those who have taken that stand but I also sympathise with those who still want some help to come up to the standard which we all expect of the nation. We have now also decided that in the public services a certain amount of reservation for certain communities is necessary—particularly the Anglo-Indian community and the scheduled castes in certain respects deserve special consideration. We have made recommendations in this respect. I am glad to say that in this matter also there is unanimity between us and the communities whose interests are affected.

Then we have also provided for some sort of

administrative machinery to see that whatever safeguards are provided are given effect to, so that it may not be felt by the communities concerned that these are paper safe-guards. There should be continuous vigilance and watch kept over the safeguards that have been provided in the working of the Government machinery in different provinces, and it shall be the business of the officer or administrative machinery concerned to bring to the notice of the legislatures or the Government the defects or drawbacks in the protection of the rights of minority communities.

We have divided the minorities according to their strength or according to their population. In the Schedule the three parts are set out and dealt with separately because they require separate consideration in proportion to their strength.

The Anglo-Indians have special rights or rather special privileges or special concessions which they have been enjoying in certain types of services, such as the railways and some one or two other services. Now, suddenly to withdraw these concessions and to ask them to abandon these claims or these concessions and to stand with the general standard would put them perhaps in a difficult position. They may not be prepared for that at present and it is better that we give them time for adjustment. They now know that they have to prepare themselves for this. They have ample notice and I am glad to say that they have agreed that they take this notice. The gradual reduction of these concessions has been agreed to by them. Similar concessions have been given to them in the matter of education. In certain educational institutions they get special grants. These educational institutions are open also to students of other communities, but they are generally meant for the Anglo-Indian community and they get certain concessions in the matter of financial assistance. It is proposed to continue this assistance for some time and by a process of gradual reduction to prepare them for a stage when they can be prepared to come to the general level of the other communities and to share the financial burdens, obligations and difficulties.

So there also we have solved this problem by agreement.

Then about representation in the Legislatures. In their case it is difficult. It is a small community of a lakh of people or more, but very substantially small, spread all over India and not located in a particular Province. It is difficult for them to get seats in a general election. Therefore, if they fail in getting representation by the normal process of election in some Provinces or in the Centre, provision has been made for their being nominated, if they are not properly or adequately represented, and that power of nomination is given to the Governor or the Governor-General, as the case may be.

Then in other cases, that of the Parsis, they have themselves voluntarily abandoned any concessions that may be given to them and wisely they have done so. Besides, it is well-known that though small, it is a very powerful community and perhaps very wise. They know that any concessions that they may get would perhaps do more harm to them than any good, because they can make their way anywhere, and make their way in such a manner that they would get more than they would get by any reservation or by any separate process of elections. Either in the legislature or in the service, they stand so high in the general standard of the nation that they have disclaimed any concessions and I congratulate them on their decision.

Then comes the Christian community. This community is more populous in two or three provinces; and in other Provinces they are not so located as to have any direct representation by the process of election. Still they have agreed to have reservation according to their population and to abandon the claim for separate electorate; there is no other safeguard that they have claimed.

We have, so far as the Cabinet representation is concerned also adopted the formula that exists today in the 1935 Act which is considered constitutionally proper and, therefore, it has also been accepted unanimously.

Then comes representation in the services. The general standard that we have accepted is that ordinarily competitive posts must go by merit and if we are to depart from this, the general administration would suffer immensely. It is well-known that since this departure has been introduced in the matter of services our administration has suffered considerably. Now that we begin afresh, we must see that where we have to fill some administrative posts of a higher level, these posts have to be filled by competition, i.e., by competitive examination and competitive tests. We have made some concessions in the matter of certain communities, which require a little help.

On the whole, this report is the result of careful sifting of facts on both sides.

One thing I wish to point out. Apart from representation in the Legislature and the reservation of seats according to population, a provision has been made allowing the minorities to contest any general seat also. There was much controversy about it, both in the Advisory Committee and in the Minorities Committee; but it has been passed by a majority. There was also another point which was a matter of controversy, and that was on behalf of the Muslim League and a section of the Scheduled Castes. The point was raised that a certain percentage of votes should be considered necessary for a successful candidate. This was a matter of controversy and amongst the Scheduled Castes themselves a very large majority sent me a representation yesterday saying they were against this. But in the Advisory Committee it was discussed and it was thrown out by a large majority.

Now, this is in substance the Report. But it is possible that when we take the Schedule item by item, it may be necessary to modify the Report as and when the items are considered and passed. Therefore, as the President has urged, we may take the Schedule item by item and the Report may be modified accordingly as and when the items are passed.[18]

Discussion mainly centred round the issue of joint or separate electorates. B. Pocker Sahib Bahadur, a Muslim Leaguer from South India, moved an amendment for continuing separate electorates for the Muslim community. Chaudhuri Khaliquz-zaman, President of the All India Muslim League, supported him. This move was opposed by M.A. Ananthasayanam Ayyangar, Mahavir Tyagi, T. Prakasham, Gobind Ballabh Pant and Sardar Vallabhbhai Patel.[19] G.B. Pant strongly opposed the proposal as suicidal for the minorities themselves. He warned them:

If you have separate electorates for the minorities, the inevitable result is that the majority becomes isolated from the minorities, and being thus cut off from the minorities, it can ride roughshod upon them.[20]

Commenting on the attitude of the Muslim League Vallabhbhai Patel, the Chairman of the Advisory Committee, said:

> When I agreed to reservation on the population basis, I thought that our friends of the Muslim League would see the reasonableness of our attitude and allow themselves to accommodate themselves to the changed conditions after the separation of the country, But I now find them adopting the same methods which were adopted when separate electorates were first introduced in this country, and in spite of ample sweetness in the language used there is a full dose of poison in the method adopted.[21]

The amendment was rejected by the Assembly.

Munshi moved two amendments to define the Scheduled Castes as a 'section of the Hindu community.' The first amendment was for insertion of the words 'and the section of the Hindu community referred to in paragraph 1A hereof' after the word 'schedule' occurring in the first proviso and the second amendment was for deletion of the words '7. Scheduled Castes' from the 'Schedule' and for addition of the following para after that:

> '1A. The section of the Hindu community referred to as Scheduled Castes as defined in Schedule 1 to the Government of India Act, 1935 shall have the same rights and benefits which are herein provided for minorities specified in the Schedule to para 1.'

Giving reasons for these amendments Munshi said:

The object of this amendment is to clarify the position of the so-called Scheduled Castes. The word 'minorities' so far as international treaties and international law is concerned, is only restricted to racial, linguistic and religious minorities. The Harijans, generally known as Scheduled Castes, are neither a racial minority nor a linguistic minority, nor certainly a religious minority. Therefore in the interest of exact phraseology this amendment was found necessary. It was only, as members of the House will remember, when the Government of India Act was moved that the definition of 'minorities' was so extended by Sir Samuel Hoare as to include every minority which the Governor thought fit to consider as minority. This is a very very mischievous extension of the term and my amendment seeks to clarify the position that so far as the Scheduled Castes are concerned, they are not minorities in the strict meaning of the term; that the Harijans are part and parcel of Hindu community, and the safeguards are given to them to protect their rights only till they are completely absorbed in the Hindu community.

Another reason is this, and I might mention that reason is based on the decisions which have already been taken by this House. The distinction between Hindu Community other than Scheduled Castes and the Scheduled Castes is the barrier of untouchability. Now, by the Fundamental Rights which we have accepted, untouchability is prohibited by law and its practice is made a criminal offence under the law of the Federation. We have also accepted in the Fundamental Rights that no public place should be prohibited to anyone by reason of his birth. So far as the Federation is concerned, we have removed the artificial barrier between one section of the Hindu Community and the other.

In view of those facts, any safeguard as a minority, so far as the Scheduled Castes are concerned, is illogical and will possibly prevent their complete absorption in the Hindu fold. I therefore submit that the amendment which I am moving clearly defines the position.[22]

Prof. Shibban Lal Saksena moved an amendment for deletion of the words "7. Scheduled Castes" from the schedule. The purpose of that amendment was that scheduled castes should not be classed as a separate minority but should be treated as an integral part of the Hindu community. [23]

Sardar Vallabbhai Patel accepted the amendments moved by Munshi.[24]

H.D. Khandekar moved an amendment suggesting that the representation of the Scheduled Castes should be according to 1931 census. Introducing this amendment, he said:

India's population is increasing day by day. If we review the period between the census of 1911 and that of 1941, we discover that India's population has reached the figure of 40 crores. I want to place before you a fact which you all know that the Scheduled Castes belong to the lower strata which is in no way behind higher classes, in respect of increasing its numbers. If one child is born to a caste Hindu then four are born to a Scheduled Caste Hindu but it is very sad and surprising that the population of Harijans has been decreasing since 1931. I do not know why it is so. When we sought the reason for it we discovered that in 1941 Census in the provinces of Bengal and Bihar, some of our Muslim brethren got the Scheduled Castes registered as Muslim on the one hand and Caste Hindus got them registered as Hindus on the other. And this is the reason why ever since the 1931 Census our population has been continuously declining and in the 1941 Census the strength of Scheduled Castes was less than in the 1931 Census by 2 crores. Therefore I have to place this amendment before you, because the minorities are getting their rights in the provincial and Central Assemblies according to their numerical strength, and if we get our rights according to 1941 census then our representation will be much less. The reason is that according to 1931 census we are few but even that is tolerable as compared to the 1941 census, when the latter was taken the war was on and it is possible that the census might not have been taken correctly, especially of the Scheduled Castes. Caste Hindus got Scheduled Castes registered as Hindus and the Muslims got them registered as Muslims. Therefore, I suspect that the 1941 census is absolutely wrong. Not only I but the whole Harijan community throughout the country loudly proclaimed that our strength as shown in the 1941 Census was wrong and that our representation should not be based on that figure. Now there is no way out except that the mover of this resolution may give us an assurance that census will be taken again, in which case I will be prepared to withdraw my amendment. If the census had been taken fairly then our strength would have been much more, but as regards 1941 census, I suspect that it is not a correct census so far as we are concerned. From this standpoint I put this amendment before you, I am aware that every member of this House has great sympathy for Scheduled Castes. I have heard many speeches. Many leaders sympathise with us, but that is of no use, if it is merely verbal. People say and I also affirm that we are a part and parcel of the Hindu community. If you oppose this amendment of mine, it will only mean that you are not prepared to give us anything more than what we are getting according to the 1941 census. When you say that they are Hindus and that a few seats less or a few seats more does not make much difference, than I will request that if under the 1931 census we get a few seats more, the House should not hesitate to give us those seats. Therefore, I request the Honourable Mover that he may accept my amendment and give to the Scheduled Castes rights according to 1931' census.[25]

Pandit Chaturbhuj Pathak, objecting to this amendment, pointed out:

> If instead of 1941 census we give representation to the minorities on the basis of 1931 census, it will have its repercussions on other minorities as well. He has stated that there have been mistakes in the taking of Census because in some places they have

> been registered as Muslims and at other places they have been registered as Caste Hindus. Because the Muslims have increased their numbers in this way, they would also like to increase their representation according to 1941 Census. And if the forthcoming census which will take place after 4 years is correct and according to it the strength of the Scheduled Castes increases, Mr. Khandekar will be tempted to suggest that they (Harijans) should be given representation not according to 1931 census, but according to 1951 census. I fail to see how this will be appropriate.[26]

This amendment was not accepted by Sardar Patel because "it would not be proper to make a special exception for the Scheduled Castes, that their reservation should be on the basis of one census and that reservation for other minority communities should be on the basis of another census. It would not be proper and it would be an invidious distinction. I do not understand why he wants to do that. Probably he wants to exclude some of those who have been included in the Scheduled Castes in 1931. I do not think it is proper to do so at this stage. In the resolution that I have moved, there is no mention of any census. We have simply said 'on the basis of their population.' Therefore it should be kept as it is. No injustice is being done to any community, and uniformity is also desirable and necessary,"[27] This amendment was by leave of the Assembly, withdrawn by Khandekar.[28]

The Constituent Assembly was meeting at a time when the effect of the Radcliffe Award on the population structure of the Provinces of East Pubjab and West Bengal could not be accurately gauged, because of a large-scale migration of populations taking place across the frontiers of East Punjab and West Bengal. The Assembly accordingly decided, on a motion moved by Munshi, to postpone consideration of minority rights in the political field to be provided in the Constitution for the Sikhs in East Punjab.[29] The Assembly also agreed to the suggestion of the representatives of West Bengal to postpone consideration of the proposal that members of minority communities in that Province would have the right to contest general seats in addition to the seats reserved for them on their population strength. [30]

Another attempt was made during the discussion of the report to introduce the principle of separate communal voting. S. Nagappa, a member of the Scheduled Castes, on behalf of Dr. Ambedkar and two other members of the Scheduled Caste community, moved an amendment that a candidate from that community should, before being declared elected to a reserved seat, be required to poll 35 percent of the votes polled by the community[31] and a similar amendment was moved in respect of all minorities by K.T.M. Ibrahim.[32] Shrimati Dakshayani Velayudan[33] and H.J. Khandekar,[34] both belonging to the Scheduled Castes community, opposed the amendment of Nagappa, who it may be pointed out, resurrected in a different form the earlier proposal of Dr. Ambedkar made before the Minorities Sub-Committee that the candidates of a majority community should, before being declared elected, poll a minimum number of votes from among voters of the minority communities in their constituencies, a proposal which could muster only one vote, that of Dr. Ambedkar, in the Minorities Sub-Committee[35] and was ultimately withdrawn by Dr. Ambedkar in the Advisory Committee meeting.[36] Sardar Patel summarily rejected this amendment and asked the Scheduled Castes to join the mainstream. He said:

> So those representatives of the Scheduled Caste must know that the Scheduled Caste has to be effaced altogether from our society, and if it is to be effaced, those who have ceased to be untouchables and sit amongst us have to forget that they are untouchables or else if they carry this inferiority complex, they will not be able to serve their community. They will only be able to serve their community by feeling now that they are with us. They are no more Scheduled Castes and therefore they must change their manners and I appeal to them also to have no breach between them and the other group of Scheduled Castes. There are groups amongst themselves, but everyone tries according to his own light. We are now to begin again.

> So let us forget these sections and cross-sections and let us stand as one, and together.[37]

The proposal of Ibrahim received support of Muslim Members like Kazi Syed Karimuddin[38] and Naziruddin Ahmad.[39] Vallabhbhai Patel was severly critical of this suggestion of Ibrahim; he saw in this amendment a further attempt at sowing the seeds of communal disruption. He pointed out that the formula of separate electorates was evolved in order to prevent the separation of the country, as a sort of half-way house, to be dropped afterwards when the nation became one. "Now", he said, "the separation of the country is complete and you say, let us introduce it again and have another separation... If the process that was adopted, which resulted in the separation of the country, is to be repeated then I say: Those who want that kind of thing have a place in Pakistan, not here. Here, we are building a nation and we are laying the foundations of One Nation, and those who choose to divide again and sow the seeds of disruption will have no place, no quarter, here, and I must say that plainly enough... I once more appeal to you to forget the past. Forget what has happened. You have got what you wanted. You have got a separate State and remember, you are the people who were responsible for it, and not those who remain in Pakistan. You led the agitation. You got it. What is it that you want now? I don't understand..."[40] Nagappa, in the face of stiff opposition from members of his own community withdrew his amendment and Ibrahim's amendment was rejected by the House.[41]

The report of the Minorites Rights relating to representation in Legislatures and in Cabinets, as adopted by the Constituent Assembly, was as follows:

Representation in Legislatures

1. *Electorates:* All elections to the Central and Provincial Legislatures will be held on the basis of joint electorates:

Provided that, as a general rule, there shall be reservation of seats for the minorities shown in the Schedule and the section of the Hindu community referred to in paragraph

I-A hereof in the various Provincial Legislative Assemblies on the basis of their population:

Provided further that such reservation shall be for 10 years, the position to be reconsidered at the end of the period.

Schedule

Group A.—Population less than ½ percent in the Indian Dominion omitting Indian States.

1. Anglo-Indian
2. Parsees.
3. Plains tribesmen in Assam, other than tea garden tribes.

Group B.—Population not more than 1½ per cent.

4. Indian Christians.
5. Sikhs.

Group C.—Population exceeding 1½ percent.

6. Muslims

I-A. The section of the Hindu community referred to as Scheduled Castes as defined in Schedule I to the Government of India Act, 1935, shall have the same rights and benefits which are herein provided for minorities specified in Schedule to paragraph 1.

2. (a) *Anglo-Indians*: There shall be no reservation of seats for Anglo-Indians, but the President of the Union and the Governors of Provinces shall have power to nominate their representatives in the Centre and the Provinces respectively if they fail to secure adequate representation in the legislatures as a result of the general election.

(b) *Parsees*: There shall be no statutory reservation in favour of the Parsee community, but they would continue to remain on the list of recognized minorities:

Provided that if as a result of elections during the period prescribed in proviso 2 to para 1 above it was found that the Parsee community had not secured proper representation, their claim for reserved seats would be reconsidered and adequate representation provided should separate representation of minorities continue to be a feature of the Constitution.

Note: The above recommendations represent the view taken by the representatives of the Parsee community.

3. (a) *Indian Christians:* There shall be reserved representation for Indian Christians in proportion to their population in the Central Legislature and in the Provincial Legislatures of Madras and Bombay. In other Provinces, they will have the right to seek election from the general seats.

(b) *Sikhs:* In view of the special situation of East Punjab, the whole question relating to it will be considered later.

(c) *Muslims*: There shall be reservation of seats for the Muslims in the Lower Houses of the Central and Provincial Legislatures on the basis of their population.

3-A. The section of the Hindu community referred to as Scheduled Castes as defined in Schedule I to the Government of India Act, 1935, shall have the same rights and benefits which are herein provided for the minority community specified in paragraph 3(c).

4. *Additional right to minorities:* The members of a minority community who have reserved seats shall have the right to contest unreserved seats as well.

In view of the special situation of West Bengal, the question relating to it will be considered later.

5. *No weightage:* The minorities for whom representation has been reserved will be allotted seats on their population ratio, and there shall be no weightage for any community.

6. *No condition for a minimum number of votes of one's own community:* There shall be no stipulation that a minority candidate standing for election for reserved seat shall poll a minimum number of votes

of his own community before he is declared elected.

7. *Method of voting:* There may be plural member constituencies, but the voting shall be distributive, that is each voter will have as many votes as there are members and he should give only one vote to a candidate.

Representation of Minorities in Cabinets

8. *No reservation for minorities:* There shall be no statutory reservation of seats for minorities in Cabinets but a convention on the lines of paragraph VII of the Instrument of Instruction issued to Governors under the Government of India Act, 1935, shall be provided in a Schedule to the Constitution.

These decisions of the Constituent Assembly on the problem of minorities were incorporated in the Draft Constitution prepared by the Constitutional Adviser in October, 1947. The provision for reservation of seats for Muslims, the Scheduled Castes, Scheduled Tribes and the Indian Christians in the Parliament was incorporated as a proviso to sub-sub-clause (a) of a sub-clause (5) of Clause 60 as follows:

5 (a) The House of the People shall consist of not more than five hundred representatives of the people of the territories of the Federation directly chosen by the voters on the basis of adult suffrage in territorial constituencies delimited by or under Acts of the Federal Parliament and until they are so delimited, in the territorial constituencies specified in the Fourth Schedule to this Constitution:

Provided that seats shall be reserved in the House of the People for—

(i) the Muslim community and the Scheduled Castes;

(ii) the Scheduled Tribes in every Governor's Province; and

(iii) and the Indian Christian community in the Provinces of Madras and Bombay,

according to the scale prescribed in clause (b) of this

sub-section:

Provided further that if the President is of opinion that the Anglo-Indian community is not adequately represented in the House of the People, he may nominate not more than two members of the community to the House of the People.[42]

Sub-clasue 5(a) of Clause 60 without the two provisos was revised on December 4, 1947,[43] December 5, 1947,[44] December 6,1947,[45] and January 22, 1947[46] and ultimately figured as Clause (5) of Article 67[47] of the Draft Constitution prepared and circulated by the Drafting Committee in February, 1948.

The first proviso to sub-clause 5(a) of Clause 60 relating to reservation of seats for the Muslim community, Scheduled Castes, Scheduled Tribes and the Indian Christians and the second proviso regarding the representation of the Anglo-Indian community in the House of People were made independent Articles by the Drafting Committee in its meeting on February 5, 1948[48] which ultimately appeared as Articles 292 and 293 respectively in the Draft Constitution prepared and circulated by the Drafting Committee in February, 1948. Article 292 read as follows:

Seats shall be reserved in the House of the People for—

(a) the Muslim community and the Scheduled Castes;

(b) the Scheduled Tribes in every State for the time being specified in Part I of the First Schedule; and

(c) the Indian Christian community in the States of Madras and Bombay,

according to the scale prescribed in sub-clause (b) of clause (5) of article 67 of this Constitution.[49]

When the Draft Constitution was circulated eliciting comments and suggestions on different provisions of the Constitution, many suggestions were received on Article 292. Govind Das suggested that (i) article 292 be deleted and consequential changes be made in the numbering of subsequent articles, and (ii) that for article 292 the following be substituted:

Seats shall be reserved in the House of the People for the Scheduled Tribes in every State for the time being specified in Part I of the First Schedule according to the scale prescribed in sub-clause (b) of clause (5) of article 67 of this Constitution.

Govind Das and Thakurdas Bhargava suggested that (i) in article 292 after the words "Seats shall be reserved" the words "for ten years from the commencement of the Constitution" be inserted.

(ii) that the following be added at the end of article 292: and in case the communities for whom the seats have been so reserved fail to return the full quota of membership the deficiency shall be made up by nomination by the President.

(iii) that the following provisos be added to article 292: Provided that members of the communities for whom seats are reserved under article 292 shall not be chosen from general constituencies and members of communities other than those for whom seats are reserved shall not be chosen from reserved constituencies;

Provided that no member of any community for whom seats are so reserved will be competent to stand for any seat other than those reserved for the community.

(iv) that Article 292 be renumbered as clause (1) of Article 292 and after the said clause as so renumbered the following be added as clause (2):

(2) Such reserved seats shall be filled by those members of the communities concerned who are returned by general elections and the President shall nominate as many members from the community concerned as are required to make up the deficiency. The President shall on subsequent occasions of shortage similarly in the quota reserved for the community concerned make up the shortage by nomination.

The Constitutional Adviser's comments on these suggestions were that Article 292 followed the decisions of the Advisory Committee (with regard to the reservation of seats in the House of the People) as adopted by the Constituent Assembly during its August 1947 session. The provision that reservations shall remain in force for ten years has been included in Article 305 of the Draft Constitution. It has also been decided by the Constituent Assembly that the members of minority communities having reserved seats should have the right to contest unreserved seats as well. The total number of reservations under Article 292 for the House of the People would work out to about 137. If power were given to the President to nominate members of the minority communities so as to make up for any deficiency resulting from the general election, the number of nominations might be so large as seriously to interfere with the democratic character of the House. It might also result in the total number of members of the House of the People being increased to more than 500 and would thus contravene the provisions of sub-clause (a) of clause (5) of Article 67 of the Draft Constitution. The Drafting Committee did not therefore accept these amendments.

K. Santhanam, M. Ananthasayanam Ayyangar, Shrimati. G. Durgabai and T.T. Krishnamachari suggested that in paragraph (a) of Article 292, the words "the Muslim community and "be deleted and (ii) that in Article 292, paragraph (c) be omitted. To this suggestion the Constitutional Adviser noted that these amendments involved questions of policy.

Tajamul Husain suggested that Article 292 be deleted; or, alternately, that in clause (a) of Article 292 the words "the Muslim community and" be deleted. The Constitutional Adivser's comments on these suggestions were that Article 292 followed the decision of the Advisory Committee (with regard to the reservation of seats in the House of the People) as adopted by the Constituent Assembly during its August 1947 session. This amendment which sought to delete Article 292 and the alternative amendment which sought to delete the words "the Muslim community and" from clause (a) of Article 292 thus both involved questions of policy.

Atul Chandra Gupta, an Advocate of Calcutta High Court suggested that Article 292 should be deleted. The Constitutional Adviser noted that this article was based on the decision already taken by the Constituent Assembly. The proposal to delete it involved a question of policy.

The Drafting Committee decided that Article 292 be renumbered as clause (1) of Article 292 and

(a) in the said clause as so renumbered the words "according to the scale prescribed in sub-clause (b) of clause (5) of Article 67 of this Constitution" be omitted;

(b) after the said clause as so renumbered, the following new clause be added:

(2) The number of seats reserved in any State for any community under clause (1) of this article shall bear, as nearly as may be, the same proportion to the total number of seats allotted to that State in the House of the People as the population of the community in that State bears to the total population of that State.

Explanation: All the Scheduled Castes in a State shall be deemed to be a single community for the purposes of this clause and so also all the Scheduled Tribes in a State.

As an explanatory note to this suggestion the Constitutional Adviser observed that the note under amendments to article 67 might be seen. In view of the amendments suggested in clause (5) of Article 67 to make it clear that the provisions with regard to the calculation of the number of representatives to be allotted to each constituency in sub-clause (b) of that clause and also the provisions of sub-clause (c) of that clause would not apply to constituencies having seats reserved for the purposes of Article 292 of the Constitution, the proposed amendments should be necessary in Article 292.

The Drafting Committee decided in October, 1948 to sponsor the amendments. The Committee also decided that in sub-clause (b) of Article 292 the words "(except the Scheduled Tribes in the tribal areas of Assam)" in brackets be inserted. A new clause "(d) the Scheduled Tribes in autonomous districts of Assam" was added after clause (c).[50]

The Draft Constitution of February, 1948, was however, incomplete in an important respect. The position of the Provinces of East Pubjab and West Bengal was uncertain on account of the large scale uprooting of people following the partition of India. Mainly because of this reason no decisions were taken on the minorities issues as they applied to these Provinces. The important question of safeguards for the Sikhs thus still remained to be discussed. A meeting of the Advisory Committee was held on February 24, 1948 to consider the position of the Sikhs, the rights of the minorities in the East Punjab and reservation of seats for minorities in West Bengal. The Committee accepted the suggestion made by Dr. Ambedkar that in order to come to a peaceful and expeditious decision a small committee consisting of Vallabhbhai Patel, Jawaharlal Nehru, Rajendra Prasad, K.M. Munshi and Dr. Ambedkar be constituted where the whole matter might be thrashed out.[51]

The Committee met on November 23, 1948 and presented its report on the same day. It was in favour of reservation of seats for the Sikhs, as for other minorities, with joint electorates. It recommended that no special provision should be made for the Sikhs other than the general provisions already approved for other minorities. The committee also thought that there were no reasons why the arrangements already approved by the Assembly for other Provinces should not be applied to West Bengal.[52]

The members of the Sikh community sharply reacted to these recommendations of the Sub-Committee. The Sikh members of the East Punjab Assembly presented a memorandum in which they made the following claims:

1. The Sikh backward classes, viz. Mazhabis, Kabirpanthis Ramdasias, Baurias, Sareras and Sikligars, should be placed on par with Hindu Scheduled Castes in the matter of political rights.

2. In the matter of language, script and culture, either zonal arrangements should be provided in the Constitution or settled immediately by executive action.

3. Sikh minorities outside East Punjab should receive similar treatment as had been or might be granted to other minorities in the matter of political rights.[53]

In a letter addressed to Vallabhbhai Patel on December 17, 1948, Giani Kartar Singh suggested certain steps whereby, without separate electorates or weightage, it would be possible to satisfy Sikh feelings. This letter pointed out that the substance of the report of the sub-committee was based on a discussion of the demands of the Akali Dal alone; and the more moderate suggestions made by the Sikh legislators of East Punjab had not been considered. Giani Kartar Singh laid particular emphasis on three points. The first was the question of representation of the Sikhs in the Central and Provincial Cabinets. He referred to a convention which was established with Vallabhbhai's approval regarding the composition of the Cabinet in East Punjab; and he expressed the fear that if this was not mentioned, there was the danger of an impression gaining ground that the convention had been dropped. He then referred to the fact that the whole question of Sikhs throughout India had been entrusted to the sub-committee and wanted it to be clarified whether the reservation of seats on a population basis would apply also to Legislatures other than in East Punjab. The third point raised related to the exclusion of Gurgaon district from East Punjab and the making of regional arrangements in the matter of education, culture, language etc. on the basis of the Punjabi-speaking areas and the Hindi-speaking areas within the Province. He thought that this proposal would have the additional merit of killing the demand for a linguistic Province.[54]

The report of the sub-committee and the question of minority safeguards in East Punjab and West Bengal were placed before the Advisory Committee on December 30, 1948, but consideration of these issues was again postponed.

At this meeting certain suggestions of a fundamental

character on the question of minority rights were raised. Some members had given notice of resolutions seeking to do away with reservations for all minorities. Referring to these notices, Vallabhbhai Patel, the Chairman of Advisory Committee, suggested that the movers should confine their proposals to their own communities, as in the absence of a general agreement it would not be proper to force a minority to give up its right of separate representation. For an example, if the Muslims by general agreement among themselves felt that they did not want any reservation, their view should be accepted; but the proposal should come from them and not from a member of any other community.[55]

On May 10, a meeting of the Sikh Members of the East Punjab Legislative Assembly and of the Constituent Assembly was held and the following proposals were unanimously adopted in regard to the safeguards for Sikh minorities to be provided in the Constitution. These proposals had the support of almost all the members who could not be present at the meeting.

1. The Sikh Backward Classes, viz. Mazhabis, Kabirpanthis, Ramdasis, Baurias, Sikligars etc. should be given the same privileges in regard to representation in the Legislatures and other political concessions in the East Punjab and PEPSU as may be provided for the Scheduled Castes. For this purpose, either these classes may be included in the schedule of Scheduled Castes enumerated in the Draft Constitution or seats may be reserved for them on population basis out of the quota reserved for Sikhs.
2. In the East Punjab, seats should be reserved for Sikhs according to their population with right to contest additional seats.
3. In the Provinces other than the East Punjab and the Centre, the Sikh minorities where they are entitled to representation on the strength of their numbers should have seats reserved for them and where adequate numbers are not returned by election, their strength should be made good by nomination.

4. The Sikhs will be prepared to give up reservation in the East Punjab if Sikh and Hindu Scheduled Castes are lumped together and seats reserved for them on the strength of their population.
5. In case these proposals are not accepted, the whole question of safeguards for Sikh minorities may be referred to arbitration in accordance with the assurances given by the Congress.[56]

These proposals of the Sikh Members were also considered by the Advisory Committee along with others on May 11, 1949 and the recommendations of the Advisory Committee were communicated to the President of the Constituent Assembly on the same day. Recapitulating the previous decisions of the Advisory Committee on the subject of minority rights which were accepted by the Constituent Assembly during the August 1947 session and had been embodied in Part XIV of the Draft Constitution, the report stated that at their meeting held on the 30th December, 1948,

> some members of the Committee felt that, conditions having vastly changed since the Advisory Committee made their recommendations in 1947, it was no longer appropriate in the context of free India and of present conditions that there should be reservation of seats for Muslims, Christians, Sikhs or any other religious minority. Although the abolition of separate electorates had removed much of the poison from the body politic, the reservation of seats for religious communities, it was felt, did lead to a certain degree of separatism and was to that extent contrary to the conception of a secular democratic State. Dr. H.C. Mookherjee, Mr. Tajamul Hussain, Shri Lakshmi Kanta Maitra and certain other members gave notices of resolutions seeking to recommend to the Constituent Assembly that there should be no reservation of seats in the Legislatures for any community in India. Shri V.I. Muniswamy Pillai gave notice of an amendment to the said resolutions seeking to exclude the Scheduled Castes from the purview of the said resolutions. At that meeting I (Vallabhbhai Patel) pointed out that if the members of

a particular community genuinely felt that their interests were better served by the abolition of reserved seats, their views must naturally be given due weight and the matter allowed to be reopened. At the same time I was anxious that the representatives of the minorities on the Committee should have adequate time both to gauge public opinion among their people and to reflect fully on the amendments that had been proposed, so that a change, if effected, would be one sought voluntarily by the minorities themselves and not imposed on them by the majority community. Accordingly the Committee adjourned without taking any decision and we met again on the 11th May, 1949. At this meeting, the resolution of Dr. H.C. Mookherjee found wholehearted support of an overwhelming majority of the members of the Advisory Committee. It was recognised, however, that the peculiar position of the Scheduled Castes would make it necessary to give them reservation for a period of ten years as originally decided. Accordingly the Advisory Committee, with one dissenting voice, passed the said resolution as amended by Shri V.I. Muniswamy Pillai in the following form:

> That the system of reservation for minorities other than Scheduled Castes in Legislatures be abolished.

It was further decided that nothing contained in the said resolution shall affect the recommendations made by the North-East Frontier (Assam) Tribal and Excluded Areas Sub-committee and Excluded and Partially excluded areas (Other than Assam) Sub-Committee with regard to representation of tribals in the Legislatures. The committee also decided that the resolution should not affect the special provision made for the representation of Anglo-Indians in the Legislature.

The committee also accepted the unanimous proposal made by the Sikh representatives that the following classes in East Pubjab, namely Mazhabis, Ramdasias, Kabirpanthis and Sikligars, who suffer the same disabilities as other members of the Sched-

ten years as originally decided. Accordingly the Advisory Committee, with one dissenting voice, passed the said resolution as amended by Shri V.I. Muniswamy Pillai in the following form:

> That the system of reservation for minorities other than Scheduled Castes in Legislatures be abolished.

It was further decided that nothing contained in the said resolution shall affect the recommendations made by the North-East Frontier (Assam) Tribal and Excluded Areas Sub-committee and Excluded and Partially excluded areas (Other than Assam) Sub-Committee with regard to representation of tribals in the Legislatures. The committee also decided that the resolution should not affect the special provision made for the representation of Anglo-Indians in the Legislature.

The committee also accepted the unanimous proposal made by the Sikh representatives that the following classes in East Pubjab, namely Mazhabis, Ramdasias, Kabirpanthis and Sikligars, who suffer the same disabilities as other members of the Scheduled Castes, should be included in the list of Scheduled Castes so that they would get the benefit of representation given to the Scheduled Castes. Subject to this change and to the above-mentioned resolution, the report of the special sub-committee appointed by the Advisory Committee was approved.

As a result of the above decisions, the resolutions seeking to do away with the rights of minorities to contest general seats in addition to reserved seats in Assam and West Bengal, of which notices had been given by some members of the committee, were withdrawn.

The Committee are fully alive to the fact that decisions once reached should not be changed lightly. Conditions have, however, vastly changed since August 1947 and the Committee are satisfied that the minorities themselves feel that in their own in-

> terests, no less than in the interests of the country as a whole, the statutory reservation of seats for religious minorities should be abolished. The Committee accordingly recommend that the provisions of Part XIV of the Draft Constitution should be amended in the light of the decisions now taken.[57]

The report of the Advisory Committee was considered by the Constituent Assembly on May 25-26, 1949 when Vallabhbhai Patel explained the important decisions of the Advisory Committee. He said that the vast majority of the minority communities had them selves realised after great reflection the evil effects in the past of such reservation on the minorities themselves, the general opinion in the Advisory Committee was that this reservation so far as the Scheduled Castes were concerned should be continued for a period of ten years and the voting for abolition of communal reservation and for reservation for Scheduled Castes was practically unanimous, only one member out of about forty members of the Advisory Committee voting against the proposal.

Referring to the demand of the Sikhs for inclusion of certain classes in the category of Scheduled Castes he said:

> The Sikhs themselves have thought that certain classes of people amongst them, who have been recent converts, and who were originally Scheduled Caste Hindus, are suffering from the disabilities which the Scheduled Caste Hindus are suffering from for the fault of the Hindu community. The Sikhs are suffering for the fault of the Sikh community and nobody else. Really, as a matter of fact, these converts are not Scheduled Castes or ought not to be Scheduled Castes; because in the Sikh religion, there is no such thing as untouchability or any classification or difference of classes. But, as unfortunately in this country the Hindu religion is suffering from the evil effects of certain customs and prejudices that have crept into the society, so also, the reformed community of the Hindus, called the Sikhs, have also in course of time suffered from degeneration to

a certain extent. They are suffering from a complex which is called fear complex. They feel that if these Scheduled Castes who have been converted to Sikhism are not given the same benefits as the Scheduled Castes have been, there is a possibility of their reverting to the Hindu Scheduled Castes and merging along with them. So, the House will realise, and I do not propose to conceal anything from the House, that religion is only a cloak, a cover, for political purposes. It is not really the high-level Sikh religion which recognises this class distinction. The Sikhs, today, it should be recognised, have suffered from various causes and we have to regard with considerable tenderness of feeling in taking into consideration their existing state of mind and provide as far as possible to meet with that situation. And so when these proposals were brought to us, in fact, I urged upon them strongly not to lower their religion to such a pitch as to really fall to a level where for a mess of pottage you really give up the substance of religion. But they did not agree. Therefore, the utmost that we can do, is to advise those people in their community who were wanting these safeguards to go into the classification of Scheduled Castes. These people have now agreed to be lumped into the Scheduled Castes; not a very good thing for the Sikh community, but yet they want it, and feel, for the time being, we would make that allowance for them. Theoretically the position is logically correct. They will be all Scheduled Castes, the Ramdasis, and three or four others whatever they are, they will all be called one Scheduled Castes. The Sikhs may call them Scheduled Caste Sikhs. After all, in the eye of religion, in the eye of God and in the eye of all sensible people they are one. These advantages are there reserved for a class of people, and therefore, although there was stout opposition from the Scheduled Castes people, who also naturally feared, and who have a justifiable fear complex that if they agreed to this, or if the House accepts this position, there is really a danger of forcible conversion from their class to the

Scheduled Caste Sikhs, we have accepted it. Now our object is, or the object of this House should be, as soon as possible and as rapidly as possible to drop these classifications and differences and bring all to a level of equality. Therefore, although temporarily we may recognise this it is up to the majority community to create by its generosity a sense of confidence in the minorities; and so also it will be the duty of the minority communities to forget the past and to reflect on what the country has suffered due to the sense of fairness which the foreigner thought was necessary to keep the balance between community and community. This has created class and communal divisions and sub-divisions, which in their sense of fairness, they thought fit to create, apart from attributing any motives. We on our part, taking this responsibility of laying the foundations of a free India which shall be and should be our endeavour both of the majority—largely of the majority—and also of the minority community, have to rise to the situation that is demanded from all of us, and create an atmosphere in which the sooner these classifications disappear the better. Therefore, I will appeal to the House, particularly to the Scheduled Castes, not to resent or grudge the concession that is made in the case of Sikhs, and I concede that this is a concession. It is not a good thing, in the interest of the Sikhs themselves. But till the Sikhs are convinced that this is wrong, I would allow them the latitude, consistent with what we think to be our principles of just dealings. So far as the other communities are concerned, I feel that enough time was given when we met in February in the Advisory Committee, when these proposals were brought forward on behalf of the minorities, particularly the Muslims, enough time was given to consult their own constituencies, their communities and also other communities. It is not our intention to commit the minorities to a particular position in a hurry. If they really have come honestly to the conclusion that in the changed conditions of this country, it is in the

> interest of all to lay down real and genuine foundations of a secular State, then nothing is better for the minorities than to trust the good-sense and sense of fairness of the majority, and to place confidence in them. So also it is for us who happen to be in a majority to think about what the minorities feel, and how we in their position would feel if we were treated in the manner in which they are treated. But in the long run, it would be in the interest of all to forget that there is anything like majority or minority in this country and that in India there is only one community.[58]

A lengthy discussion took place on these proposals of the Advisory Committee.[59] Three Muslim members of the Assembly expressed their opposition to Patel's motion for the abolition of reservations to all except Scheduled Castes and Scheduled Tribes: and each of them suggested a different alternative. Muhammad Saadulla from Assam, a member of the Drafting Committee, wanted the continuance of reservations for a period of ten years. Though he was personally not enamoured of reservation, the Muslim members of his party in the Assam legislature had given him a unanimous mandate to claim reservation for the Muslims, and he felt that reservation would have a "tremendous psychological effect" on the Muslim community. He also made the interesting statement that only four members of the Muslim community were present at the meeting of the Advisory Committee on May 11 and that only one of them supported the proposal for the abolition of reservations, thereby challenging Patel's claim of unanimity. Saadulla mentioned in particular that Abul Kalam Azad was neutral to this issue.[60]

Muhammad Ismail from Madras not only opposed the motion but wanted a reversion to the previous position of separate electorates. He moved an amendment that the Assembly should approve and confirm the reservation of seats on the population basis for Muslims and other minority communities in the Central and Provincial Legislatures and that these seats would be filled by members elected by constituencies of voters belonging to the respective minorities. He maintained that separate electorates were the only means of bringing about harmony among the people.[61]

Z.H. Lari urged the removal of reservations for all communities and suggested instead the introduction of a system of proportional representation and cumulative voting through multi-member constituencies.[62]

These amendments were opposed not only by members who were Christians, Anglo-Indians, Sikhs, Scheduled Castes and Caste Hindus but also by Muslim members like Naziruddin Ahmad, Begum Aizaz Rasul, Muhammad Ismail Khan, Tajamul Hussain, Maulana Hasrat Mohani and Col. B.H. Zaidi. In a forthright speech Sardar Patel gave a resume of what had happened at the Advisory Committee meeting. He said:

> ...it was Mr. Tajamul Husain from Bihar who stood up and moved an amendment that reservations must go. He was challenged in the Committee whether he had consulted the other members of the Muslim community, and he quoted chapter and verse from the representatives of the Provinces whom he had consulted. Yet we did not want a snap vote. I said that I would advise the Advisory Committee to hold over the question and ask all members of the minority communities to consult their constituencies and find out what they really wanted. Nearly four months after that we met and unfortunately Mr. Saadulla was not present or he did not appear and so the opinions that he had gathered remained with him. He did not even communicate them to us. He said that there was only an attendance of four there of whom (I do not know whether he has consulted Maulana Azad or not) he says that Maulana Azad remained neutral. He claims to know Maulana Azad's mind more than I can do. But I can tell him that Maulana Azad is not a cipher; he has a conscience. If he felt that it was against the interests of his community he would have immediately said so and protested. But he did not do so, because he knew and felt that what was being done was right. There-

> fore if Mr. Saadulla interprets his silence as neutrality he is much mistaken, because Maulana Azad is a man who has stood up against the whole community all through his life and even in crisis. He has not changed his clothes and I am sure if he has claimed or worked for partition and if he had ever believed that this is a country of two nations after the partition he would not have remained here: because he could not stay here if he believed that his nation was separate.[63]

Lari wanted abolition of reservation for the Scheduled Castes as well. His motion was, however, not accepted by the House. Pandit Thakur Das Bhargava moved an amendment that the provision for reservation of seats and nominations would last for a period of ten years from commencement of the Constitution, which was accepted by the House. Dr. H.C. Mookherjee who along with Tajamul Husain was instrumental in reversing the previous decision of the Advisory Committee, was also critical for giving this benenfit to the Scheduled Castes and the Scheduled Tribes and said

> personally I have the greatest possible objection to reservation for backward groups in the political sphere. I do admit that they deserve our sympathy and that they require economic safeguards but I do not see any reason why they should demand political safeguards. I do not see why a person belonging to a backward community should feel that his grievances cannot be placed before the legislatures unless he elects somebody in whom he has faith. Such an attitude to my mind shows that he has not as yet, as a member of a minority community, made up his mind to become a part and parcel of the nation. Still I do submit to the wisdom of our leaders and I support the Resolution, only because I hope the House will accept the amendment moved by Pandit Thakur Das Bhargava, to the effect that these reservations should have a definite time limit, that once for all we shall see their end at the end of ten years from the time that the Constitution comes into operation.[64]

> Nehru also echoed the same sentiment when he said: frankly I would like this proposal to go further and put an end to such reservations as there still remain. But again, speaking frankly, I realise that in the present state of affairs in India that would not be a desirable thing to do, that is to say, in regard to the Scheduled Castes. I try to look upon the problem not in the sense of a religious minority, but rather in the sense of helping backward groups in the country. I do not look at it from the religious point of view or the caste point of view, but from the point of view that a backward group ought to be helped and I am glad that this reservation also will be limited to ten years.[65]

But the most severe criticism came from Mahavir Tyagi who pleaded for extending this benefit to the "Scheduled Classes" instead of "Scheduled Castes", so that class and not caste could be taken into consideration for protecting the minorities. He said:

When the idea of giving separate reservation to the scheduled castes was first introduced, the intention was that it should last only for twenty years. After that period they were expected to become absolutely one with the Hindus. It was in the year 1933 and now it is 1949. So it is only a few years less than twenty. According to the old scheme of the British Government reservation for the Scheduled Castes should go in 1952, why are we now giving it a further lease of ten years? Again, Sir, if we look at the list of Scheduled Castes, there are so many included in it. We have had the experience of separate reservation for Scheduled Castes. Facts must be faced as they are. The term "Scheduled Castes" is a fiction. Factually there is no such thing as "Scheduled Castes". There are some castes who are depressed, some castes who are poor, some who are untouchables, some who are downtrodden. All their names were collected from the various provinces and put into one category, "Scheduled Castes". In spite of the category being a fiction, it has been there for so many years. Let us look at the way these castes are represented. There are hundreds of castes included in the

List, but if you look at their representation, in every province you will find that only one or two castes are represented. Those who have got predominance are mostly Chamars, I would say. In the U.P. it is the case. It is the case in the Punjab also. I want to know how the Koris or the Pernas or the Korwas or the Dumnas have benefited by the reservation. It is all a fiction, Sir. How is Dr. Ambedkar a member of the Scheduled Caste? Is he illiterate? Is he ill-educated? Is he an untouchable? Is he lacking in anything? He is the finest of the fine intellectuals in India and still he is in the list of scheduled castes. Because he is in the list and because he is a genius, he will perpetually be a member and also a Minister, he will always be their representative. Moreover, Sir, he has lately married a Brahmin wife. He is a Brahmin by profession and also because his in-laws are Brahmins. Then they are others like my Friend, Professor Yashwant Rai. What does he lack? There are thousands of Brahmins and Kshatriyas who are worse off than these friends belonging to the scheduled castes. So by the name of Scheduled Castes, persons who are living a cheerful life, and a selected few of these castes get the benefit. This is no real representation. No caste ever gets any benefit out of this reservation. It is the individual or the family which gets benefited. So, Sir, while we are doing away with representations and reservations, while we are doing away with this caste system, why should we allow it even for ten years? Does not our past experience show that out of the hundred and one scheduled castes only a few get any representation? Then why are so many castes linked with the chariot wheel of the Scheduled Castes? They are simply voters; they do not get any benefit and even if any member of a caste in India comes up and gets elected how does the Community benefit. I do not understand. I could understand if instead of castes, classes were given reservations. To say that it should be a casteless society; I can understand. Society can be casteless, but society cannot be class-less. So long as the country does not decide to make the society class-less, classes must exist and therefore, classes must have their representation. Sir, to make the whole nation one party, I am afraid, will not be a practical idea. Minorities must exist and must be provided for. There will be no peace so long as minorities are not provided for. I do not believe in the minorities on community basis, but minorities must exist on economic basis, on political basis and on an ideological basis and those minorities must have protection. In this sort of a wholesale decision, the minorities will get little representation. I would suggest that in the place of the Scheduled Caste, the landless labourers, the cobblers or those persons who do similar jobs and who do not get enough to live, should be given special reservations. But allowing caste representations, let us not re-inject the poisonous virus which the Britisher has introduced into our body politic. I would suggest, Sir, that instead of the so-called Scheduled Caste, minorities be protected, if you like, on class basis. Let cobblers, washermen and similar other classes send their representatives through reservations because they are the ones who do not really get any representation. As a matter of fact even after passing the motion which Sardar Patel has put before us, I am afraid the tiller of the soil will not as the conditions are get any representation. The villager is nowhere in the picture. It is the urban citizen alone who gets the protection. It is not the toilers of the soil but the soilers of toil who are benefited. Persons who irrigate paper with black ink get the representation and not those who irrigate the land. These literate mediocrities create fear and do nothing productive, but these tillers of the soil and producers of wealth are mostly those who are illiterate and therefore they are deprived of their due share of representation. Thus the nation is perpetually mis-represented by men of law, literature and letters. The 'Pen' rules over the 'Plough'. The creators of wealth are those who are without education and those persons will remain as such. They were slaves before and will remain slaves today and even after your passing this Constitution. If you want to help those down-trodden classes, then Sir, the best thing would be to keep some safeguards for them. We should forge a law which bring those illiterates into this House. As a matter of fact there is hardly a single

Kisan member of the Constituent Assembly of the type of which 80 per cent of Kisans live in India. Unless those very Kisans come here as they are, India will not be properly represented. I therefore, submit, Sir, that the Scheduled Castes should now go and in place of Scheduled Castes, the words "Scheduled Classes" be substituted so that we may not inadvertently perpetuate the communal slur on our Parliaments. In fact the Untouchables had only some social disabilities. Now all the Governments have passed enactments removing those social disabilities and among those persons who come here as the representatives, I fear, there is not one who has any social disability about him. The Scheduled Caste man can marry a Brahmin girl and there is no disability. I say, Sir, in the name of Scheduled Castes a few individuals are getting the benefit. Let the House dispassionately consider the situation as it is, take advantage of the experience that we have gained for the last so many years of what the "Scheduled Castes" have actually meant. And then make up our mind as to whether or not we could substitute this communal representation by giving reservations to classes who would mostly be the same voters but with a better title and healthier outlook.[66]

The Constituent Assembly adopted the proposal of the Advisory Committee that reservations be provided only for the Scheduled Castes and the Scheduled Tribes and that the President and the Governors would nominate members of the Anglo-Indian community to Legislatures as also the amendment of Pandit Thakur Das Bhargava that no reservation would be operative for more than ten years.[67]

In view of this changed decision in the matter of reservation of seats relating to minorities, Ambedkar moved an amended Article 292 on August 23, 1949 providing reservation of seats in the House of the People for Scheduled Castes and Scheduled Tribes, separately mentioning the Scheduled Tribes in the autonomous districts of Assam and those outside. The revised draft also laid down that the number of seats reserved would be according to the population.

Several amendments were proposed to this article. N.C. Lasker moved an amendment suggesting that the population proportion generally adopted for reservation of seats should not apply to the Scheduled Castes of Assam, because their number in Assam after partition might not give them any representation. This point was countered by Kuladhar Chaliha, who said that in spite of all his sympathy for the Scheduled Castes in Assam, their entitlement to reservation of seats would depend on their population strength. Chaliha cited the cases of other communities who, on account of the smallness of their numbers, would not be entitled to reservation.

Jaspat Roy Kapoor suggested that the reserved seats should be allowed to constituencies having larger number of Scheduled Castes and Scheduled Tribes population.

Sardar Hukam Singh wanted it to be expressly stated that Scheduled Castes and Scheduled Tribes would be entitled to contest "unreserved seats". Ambedkar affirmed that this was the intention and that while Article 292 was not the appropriate place for a provision of this kind, he assured the Assembly that a provision to this effect would find a place in the law relating to elections.

V.I. Muniswamy Pillai's amendment was that the population should be estimated as actually existed or known by a fresth census because the census of 1941 was a gross under-enumeration of Scheduled Caste population. It may be noted that Khandekar, who made a similar suggestion in the 1947 August session, did not participate in the discussion this time. Ambedkar, however, did not make any definite commitment but promised that either a fresh census would be taken or that an estimate of the population strength would be made on the basis of the strength of voters, a process which he described as a rough and ready estimate of the population.

Thakurdas Bhargava moved an amendment designed to secure that in Assam the Scheduled Tribes would not have the right to contest general seats, because in Assam, where seats not reserved for any particular community would be less than 50 per cent, the reserved classes should not be allowed to infringe on the rights of the unreserved classes.

As usual, all the amendments were either withdrawn or negatived by the House, and the amended Article 292 moved by Ambedkar was adopted.

The deliberations of the framers on this article may be seen below:

The Honourable Dr. B.R. Ambedkar:

I move that for Article 292, the following be substituted: "292 (1) seats shall be reserved in the House of the people for:-

Reservation of seats for Scheduled Castes and Scheduled Tribes in the House of the people

(a) the Scheduled Castes;
(b) the Scheduled Tribes except the Scheduled Tribes in the tribal areas of Assam;
(c) the Scheduled Tribes in the autonomous districts of Assam.

(2) The number of seats reserved in any State for the Scheduled Castes or the Scheduled tribes under clasue (1) of this article shall, save in the case of the Scheduled Castes in to the total number of seats allotted to that State in the House of the People as the population of the Scheduled Castes in that State or of the Scheduled Tribes in that State or part of that States as the case may be, in respect of which seats are so reserved bears to the total population of that State":-

This Article 292 is an exact reproduction of the decisions of the Advisory Committee in this matter and I do not think any explanation is necessary.

Mr. President:

This represents the decision which was taken at another session of this House when we considered the Advisory Committee's report. This puts in form the decision then taken. We have several amendments to this here. I will take them now.

Prof. Nibaran Chandra Laskar (Assam: General):

Mr. President, Sir, I shall move No. 24. I am not moving No. 23. I move:

"That in amendment No. 22 above in clause (2) of the proposed Article 292, after the words, brackets and figures "under clause (1) of this article shall" the words 'save in the case of the Scheduled Castes in Assam' be inserted."

If my amendment is accepted, then clause (2) of the Article 292 will read thus:

"The number of seats reserved in any State for the Scheduled Castes or the Scheduled Tribes under clause (1) of this article shall, save in the case of the Scheduled castes in Assam bear, as nearly as may be, the "same proportion to the total number" of seats allotted to that State in the House of the People as the population of the Scheduled castes in that State or of the scheduled tribes in that State or part of that State, as the case may be, in respect of which seats are so reserved bears to the total population of that State."

I wholeheartedly support the proposed amendment of Dr. Ambedkar with a very slight modification as mentioned in my amendment. During the last session of the Constituent Assembly, the historic decision was made to abolish the reservation of seats for minorities except in the case of Scheduled Castes and scheduled tribes. I offer my heartfelt thanks to the Members of the Constituent Assembly who were good enough to support the report of the Minorities Sub-Committee and granted these privileges to the Scheduled Castes and scheduled tribes. I shall be failing in my duty if I do not say that the Scheduled Castes and scheduled tribes in the country will remain grateful to the Honourable Prime Minister and Honourable Deputy Prime Minister, the Chairman of the Minorities Sub-Committee, who really felt the demands and grievances of the scheduled Castes and Scheduled tribes and who had to face strong opposition for their cause. It is through their grace the Schedule Castes and tribes are getting these political rights.

I believe that any reservation will go against the principle of democracy, but the circumstances such as political unconsciousness, backwardness in education and the very poor economic condition of the Scheduled Castes compel them to demand for these privileges. If Dr. Ambedkar's amendment is accepted, then the Scheduled castes or scheduled tribes will get reservation of seats. But it has been stated as a fundamental concept of the Constitution that the representation for the House of the People would be on the basis of one seat to at least 5 lakhs of people, and it will be considered according to the preceding census just before the election. Therefore, I have great doubts in my mind whether the Scheduled Castes in Assam will get the benefit of this privilege. Unfortunately, the district of Sylhet which was a part of Assam has been annexed to Pakistan by referendum, and thereby about three lakhs of Scheduled Castes people went over to Pakistan and the population of the Scheduled Castes which was 6,76,566 before partition, has come down after partition to 3,77,025 according to 1941 census, although I question the authenticity of the census figures of 1941. Now, I shall try to prove it. On the figure as given in 1941 census, the Scheduled Castes cannot claim as of right any seat in the House of the People. Therefore, by my amendment I want to have an exception to be made to give scope to the Scheduled Castes to approach before the Election Commission or whatever that authority may be to place their legitimate demands. First of all, I shall show to the House that the figures of 1941 census are incorrect, inaccurate and fallacious. In the whole of Assam the total population is only about one crore. I shall take only the major communities. In Vol. IX of the Census Report of 1941 the following figures are given about the variation of communities from 1931-41:- Among Hindus there is a decrease of 12 per cent. and among Muslims there is an increase of 24 per cent. The Tribes have increased by 184 per cent. In the Brahmaputra Valley there has been an increase in the Tribals of 477 per cent. and in the Surma valley 2266 per cent. From these figures the House can see the inaccuracy of the census figures of 1941: While there is a general increase of 18 per cent in the province of Assam, among the Tribals there is an increase of 184 per cent and among the Hindus there is a decrease of 12 per cent.

In the Minorities Sub-Committee Report, some 9 lakhs of garden labourers, considered as Tribals in the 1941 Census have been shown as general population. If the Census figure is correct, then there is no justification for taking out 9 lakhs of garden labourers from the fold of the Tribals and showing them as general. By this the strength of the Scheduled Castes has been reduced. I shall prove that their number is more than 10 lakhs now. Leaving aside the gradual decrease of the number of the Scheduled Castes from 1911 to 1931, if we take the garden labourers numbering 9 lakhs who are included in general population, then we can easily get the number of Scheduled Castes. Then what Communities do the garden labourers belong to? I can prove from records that 80 per cent of them are Hindus and 80 per cent. of these Hindus belong to Scheduled Castes.

Shri A.V. Thakkar:

We are unable to follow the speaker.

Prof. Nibaran Chandra Laskar:

There has been a tendency from 1911 onwards amongst the Scheduled Castes to change their communities, because they were very much afraid that the caste-name generally prohibited them from getting into any Government services. Therefore the community began to decrease gradually. In 1911 the strength of the Scheduled Castes was 13 lakhs, in 1921 it was 14 lakhs and in 1931 it came to about 6 lakhs and in 1941 it came to 4 lakhs. As for instance, the strength of the Scheduled Patni community in 1911 it was 1,11,000 but in 1921 the strength came down to 45,000. With regard to this Community the Census Superintendent in his report of 1921 Vol. III Part I page 154 says." It was suggested by one of the Leaders (himself a Brahmin) that a caste which was looked down upon could not hope to improve its status without a better name." This shows that Scheduled Castes were made to decrease by the leaders not belonging to their own communities.

I would like to draw the attention of the House today to the Census Report of 1921, Vol. III, Part I; and in page 154 of that report a table was given with variation in caste, tribe, etc., since 1881 and from this table I shall give certain instances of gradual decrease of the depressed classes.

Patni population in 1911 was 1,11,000.

Patni population in 1921 was 45,000.

Nandiyal population in 1911 was 68,000.

Nandiyal population in 1921 was 18,000.

Rajbansi population (they are considered as Scheduled Caste in Bengal) in 1911 was, 133,000.

Rajbansi population (they are considered as Scheduled Caste in Bengal) in 1921 was, 92,000.

Now I would like to draw the attention of the House to the Census Report of 1931, Vol. III, Part I, page 219, wherein it is stated :-

"The total for the exterior castes, i.e., Scheduled Caste of Sylhet is therefore 392,000 at a minimum and for Cachar 80,000 and the total for the whole of the Surma Valley is 472,000 at a minimum. For Assam and Surma Valley together the total is 655,000 and for the whole province is 657,000."

The Census Superintendent made certain remarks also with regard to the Patni community in that page of that Report. He said "the Census figures give 9,000 only in the District of Cachar and the correct figures are at least 40,000. In Sylhet the figure for the Patni community is given as 43,000 only and there are at least 70,000. The total population for the depressed classes for the whole Province is 6,57,000."

In 1921, the strength of the Scheduled Castes was 12 lakhs. Then, there is a big gap in 1931. Because the garden labourers were considered as depressed classes in 1921 but in 1931 they were separated from the depressed classes and considered as a single caste, that is the garden cooly caste. That is why, in the census of 1931, their strength came down from twelve lakhs to six and a half lakhs. In article 155 of that Report dealing with the difficulties of return of caste, the Census Superintendent said: "When it comes to castes like the Kayasths, Mahisyas, and Patnis, I confess that the figures appear to me to be worthless and not worth the trouble of collecting." In the same page, he again said: "When we came to castes like the Patnis in the Surma Valley, we find that at each successive census their numbers have been melting away in a most mysterious fashion." That shows that the 1931 census could not give the accurate or correct figures of the Scheduled Castes people, and also indicated a gradual decrease in the number of the Scheduled Castes.

Now, Sir, what were the causes of this decrease? There were two causes. The first is that, between 1911 and 1931, the Scheduled Castes could not get scent of the divide and rule policy of the British Government, the award of the Simon Commission and the provisions of the Government of India Act, 1935. Therefore, there was a tendency to raise the social status by removing the caste designation. The second reason is, that there was a tendency to realise their social status by changing their caste names and the Scheduled Castes took the help of certain leaders who did not belong to their own Communities or of the Puranas or the Shastras. These leaders made them Caste Hindus only in name; but they could not make them free from untouchability. This accounts for the gradual decrease in the Scheduled Castes people.

Then, I would like to draw the attention of the House to the position of the garden labourers. The 1911 census figures show that the strength of the garden labourers was 5,07,058. They mostly belonged to the depressed classes. I refer to article 73, page 57 of the Census report of 1921, Vol. III, part I, in which it is stated the total garden labour population is 9,22,000. Over 7,82,000 or 85 per cent are Hindus. (Vide 1931 census Report Vol. III, Part I, page 222): "these garden labourers were considered as garden cooly castes and their total population given in the report was 14 lakhs in which the number of Hindus was 13,16,000." According to the 1941 census, these garden cooly castes changed their status and they were considered as garden tribes. They were included in the Scheduled Tribes and thus increased the population of Scheduled Tribes from 16 lakhs to 28 lakhs. Thus, the status of the garden labourers has been changed gradually. Up to 1921 they belonged to the depressed classes; then they were promoted to garden cooly caste in 1931, then they were considered as garden Tribes in 1941.

Now, fortunately nine lakhs of them are going to be recognised as general, i.e., Caste Hindus. If we consider that out of 11,34,000 (vide 1941 census report) of the garden labourers 80 per cent (of this population) are belonging to the Hindu Community, then, the strength of the garden labourers comes to a total of about 10 lakhs Hindus. I strongly feel that 80 per cent of these Hindus garden coolies belong to the Scheduled Castes; thus we get about 8 lakhs of Scheduled Castes from the Garden labourers. If we add these with the total population of Scheduled Castes of 1941 census then, I can claim rightfully that the Scheduled Castes population is sure to be about 11 lakhs even according to 1941 census. Therefore, if a real census is taken before the election, I can assure the House that we shall get about 11 to 12 lakhs of Scheduled Castes in the province of Assam.

Before the partition, one seat was allotted in the Constituent Assembly to the Scheduled Castes from Assam. After the partition also, this community was treated with exceptional generosity by the members of the Assam Legislative Assembly and one seat was allotted to them in the Constituent Assembly.

Mr. President:

Is it your argument that because they happen to be eleven lakhs, there should not be any reservation of seats?

Prof. N.C. Laskar:

There should be, but I have some doubts in my mind; therefore, I want some clarifications.

Mr. President

What are you driving at? Is it because they happen to be eleven or twelve lakhs in the province they should not have reservation of seats?

Prof. N.C. Laskar:

I would like to say that according to the 1941 census their numbers are about four lakhs. I have great doubts, in my mind whether this population can claim any seat in the House of the people. Therefore, by my amendment I want some exception to be made for the Scheduled castes of Assam so that they get representation in the House of the People.

Mr. President:

Whatever their population may be, reservation of seats will be in proportion to their number.

Prof. N.C. Laskar:

I have already proved before the House that the census figure of 1941 is not correct. I demand a regular census before election and if not, some exceptions to be made for this community before elections. I would like to say that for granting one seat in the Constituent Assembly even after the partition, I am very much grateful to the Honourable Premier of Assam and the Congress Parliamentary Party of the Assam Legislative Assembly. I feel that they realised the real strength of the Scheduled Castes in Assam and therefore granted one seat in the Constituent Assembly.

Then, Sir, in the amendment of Dr. Ambedkar, it is stated that:

"The Scheduled Castes or the Scheduled Tribes shall bear, as nearly as may be, the same proportion to the total number of seats allotted to that State...as the population of the Scheduled Castes in that State or of the Scheduled Tribes in that State..."

The insertion of the words" as nearly as may be" cannot remove my doubts, the meaning of the words "as nearly as may be" seems to be vague. The Election Commission may make out a common formula such as, "no seat should be allotted to a community having a population of less than 4,50,000." Thereby we cannot claim any seat in the House of the People. Therefore I want some exception in the provision of this article.

The language that has been used in my amendment is not my language. It is the language of the Drafting Committee. Mine is not a "solitary example". Exceptions have already been given to other communities also. By the provision of Article 293 some exceptions are being made for the Anglo-Indian community, and again by Article 149 some exceptions are being made for the people of the tribal areas and Shillong constituencies of Assam. In Clause (3) of Article 149 it is stated:

"The representation of each territorial constituency in the Legislative Assembly of a State shall be, on the basis of the population of that constituency as ascertained at the last preceding census of which the relevant figures have been published and shall, save in the case of the autonomous districts of Assam and the constituency comprising the cantonment and municipality of Shillong, be on a scale of not more than one representative for every seventy-five thousand of the population".

The Shillong constituency contains a population of about 12000. Exception is also being made for that Shillong constituency under the provisions of this Constitution, and therefore, I think my demand in my amendment is legitimate.

I cannot check temptation in giving some facts about the present situation of the Cachar district in Assam which contain about one-third of the Scheduled Caste population of Assam, which narrowly escaped from the grip of Pakistan by Radcliffe award and which district I belong to. After the partition, the total population of this district is 10,24,581. Of these, Scheduled Castes are 1,17,205, Hindus are, 2,82,646, and Muslims 4,34,205. There are also refugees who have come from Eastern Pakistan to Assam. The total population will be about 55,000. The Muslim influx in this district is not less than that.

I shall now deal with the present position of the major communities of Cachar district. First of all, I shall take up the case of Hindus. About fifty per cent of these caste Hindus are untouchables. They are mainly belonging to Manipuries, Naths communities. There are some communist elements in my district. On the last Assembly election the Communist candidates from this district polled the largest number of votes amongst the Communist candidates in the whole of India, and therefore I cannot say that the Communist movement has been checked in my district. Some reactionaries of the Muslim community created also some troubles in my district. On the twelfth day after the assassination Mahatmaji, small children started a silent procession and it was intercepted with lathi charge by some Muslims and the offenders were convicted in the court. Again in my district, I can quote another instance after partition. A cow was slaughtered on the land of the Hindus just in front of a Kali temple. The offenders were caught hold and the case tried in the Law Court and the offenders were convicted. Therefore you can imagine, Sir, that there are some Muslim disruptive elements also in my district. As regards the Scheduled Castes there are some followers of Mr. J.N. Mandal also. After Partition, the President of the Assam Scheduled Caste Federation appeared before the Boundary Commission with memorandum to get Cachar included in Pakistan. Then just before the referendum, Mr. J.N. Mandal of Syllhet District, the Honourable Minister of Pakistan Government, was invited by the Scheduled Caste Federation and Mr. Mandal in a meeting requested the Scheduled Castes to vote for Pakistan.

But in the last election all the Scheduled Caste seats were captured by the Congress in Assam. Each seat was contested by the Scheduled Castes Federation but was badly defeated by the Congress. I do not know, if the Honourable Dr. Ambedkar has in his mind any prejudice against the Scheduled Castes of Assam. I hope he will kindly wash it off from his mind. Because I believe that he loves Scheduled Castes more than I do. He did much for the Scheduled Caste and hope he will do much more. Therefore I request him to accept my amendment. If any privileges are not given to Scheduled Castes people of Assam, then these poor innocent people of Assam may be handled by some other reactionary groups. Therefore in consideration of the geographical position and political and strategic condition of Assam, I appeal to the House to accept my amendment. With these words, Sir, I move.

Shri Jaspat Roy Kapoor (United Provinces: General):

Mr. President, Sir I beg to move:

"That in amendment No. 22 above, at the end of the proposed Article 292, the following proviso be added:-

> 'Provided that the constituencies for the seats reserved for the Scheduled Castes or Scheduled Tribes shall comprise, so far as possible such contiguous areas where they are comparatively more numerous than in other areas.

If this is not acceptable to the House, I move alternatively that the following proviso be added:-

> "Provided that reserved seats shall be allotted to such constituencies as contain comparatively larger number of Scheduled Castes or Scheduled Tribes members than in other constituencies.

Sir, I am sure that everyone of us here today is very happy at the amendment which has been moved by the Honourable Dr. Ambedkar. By his amendment he is replacing the old draft of Article 292. This is one of those few amendments which is going to have a far reaching consequence for the great good of the country. It is based on the agreement which has been arrived at in the Minorities Committee, between the major and the different minority communities of this country. By that agreement our Muslim friends and our Christian friends as also our Sikh breathen have agreed to give up reservation of seats in the different legislatures. I would like to take this opportunity to congratulate them all for this wise and bold decision that they have taken in the larger interest of the country. I would particularly like to congratulate my Muslim breathren because for so many years past they have had separate electorates and separate representation and they had begun to think that therein only lay their salvation and that without separate electorate and separate representation it would not be possible for them to safeguard their interests. We know they were grossly mistaken but then all the same because of the clever tactics of the British Government, this thing had been instilled in their minds and they always felt convinced about the propriety of this separate representation. It is a very fortunate day for us and for this country that they have now come to realise that such a system is certainly not in their interest. I congratulate them once again for this wise and bold decision. They have now thrown the responsibility of safeguarding their interests on the major community and it is now for the major community to show by their conduct, by their actions, by their dealings towards the Muslim brethren to convince them that they were in the wrong in the past and that they are right now, that their interests are safe when they forget to think themselves as a separate community and that their interest is the same as the interest of the major community or rather that the interest of every community and every citizen of the country lies in the interest of the country as a whole.

The major community has already begun to realise what a tremendous responsibility has been thrown on its shoulders. I know of several places where members of the majority community have realised their responsibility. I would hereafter very much prefer not to refer to any community as major or minor community and I am sure after the adoption of this article and the coming into being of this constitution we should forget the sting of communities as major or minor communities. Because the more we talk in this way the more we remind the people that we are not one Nation and that they are different communities with different interests. I have often felt that when we address meetings and say Hindu and Muslim "Bhaiyon", and when we appeal to them that the Hindus, Muslims and Christians should come together—I have always felt that we remind them by that appeal that they are so many different communities who need being brought together. It is much better that we do no refer them as Hindus, Muslims and Christians in our meetings and publications. The members of the majority community have already begun to realise that a heavy responsibility has been cast on them by their Muslim brethren. They have now thrown themselves at our mercy—if I could put it like that and therefore, we now owe it to our Muslim breathren and we owe it more to ourselves to prove by our conduct and actions that the trust that they have reposed in us will not be betrayed, that this step has not been a wrong one and that they have everything to gain thereby. The majority community is out to make specific efforts to see that in the elections—municipal and otherwise, that are to take place shortly in some places the Muslims may be elected not only in proportion to their number but even more, if possible.

Of course the task is not an easy one. It would have been easier before partition. It has been made more difficult by partition, because partion has been brought about because of the existence of separate electorates and separate representation. The canker in our political system leading to the partition of the country and the consequent tragedy therafter has left behind bitter memories, and it will take sometime before these bitter memories are wiped out but all responsible members of the major community are keenly alive to the responsibility that has now been cast on their shoulders, and they have already begun to take active steps to see that in the elections that will take place hereafter their Muslim brethren's interests are amply safeguarded.

I would also like to congratulate our Christian friends who have also given up their contention of separate representation and reservation of seats. In the past the Christians had hardly ever demanded separate representation. They have all along been nationalists to their core, but somehow when this Draft Constitution was under preparation some of them thought that since Muslims, Scheduled Castes and even Sikhs and probably even Parsees were thinking of having separate seats reserved they might as well take advantage of this and claim a few seats in the legislatures. Happily they gave it up, which of course I know was hardly ever put with any seriousness. The credit in a great measure for this must go to my honourable and reverend Friend Dr. H.C. Mookherjee who adorned this Chair in your absence, Sir. I have developed very great regard and affection for Dr. H.C. Mookherjee. I have known how hard he worked to persuade the other communities to give up claiming reservation of seats, and if he has not succeeded in persuading the Scheduled Castes Members to give up this claim, the fault is not surely his.

As I am thinking of Dr. Mookherjee I cannot forget to mention my Friend Mr. Sidhva over there. He was perhaps thinking why I am forgetting him but I had not forgotten him. I was thinking that at the end I would congratulate him and not only him but the great Parsee Community to which he belongs, not only for giving up the claim of reservation but for something more and that is for never having thought of it at all. Their is an example worth emulating. The Parsee community is neither a majority community nor a minority community. It is, if I may say so, a baby community, and though a baby may well always claim special treatment and special nursing, this baby community has never thought of any special protection. What is the result? We find Parsees being represented not only represented but even overwhelmingly representated, looking to their small number, in this country, not only in the legislature but in every walk of life, be it social, industrial, commercial, banking or any others. They have always been patriots whose example is worth emulating. On this occasion I cannot forget mentioning the sacred names of Dadhabhoy Naoroji of reverned memory, the late Sir Pherozeshah Mehta, the late Shri Dinshaw Wacha whose names go down in history as the makers of modern India, as the harbingers of freedom in this country and to their sacred memory I bow my head in reverence. I congratulate and express my great appreciation for the patriotic attitude which this baby community has always adopted in this country.

Last of all, Sir, I would like to refer to my Sikh brethern. They also deserve our congratulations for having fallen in the line with the other minority communities. As a matter of fact our Sikh brethren should never have thought of being a minority community. They have always been part and parcel of the Hindu community.

Only for a few loaves and fishes of office or seats in the legislatures they allowed themselves to be tempted to claim separate representation. I say they are always a part and parcel of the Hindu community, in spite of what any Sikh friend of mine might say to the contrary. There has always been interdining; there has always been inter-marriages between the Hindus and Sikhs, though these inter-marriages have become less common now ever since our Sikh brothers have begun to say that they are entirely separate from the Hindus. I hope there will be a change in their attitude also and we shall have occasion hereafter to welcome this changed attitude on their part. Our Sikh brethren have always been not only part and parcel of the Hindu community, but they have always been the sword-arm of the Hindus and of the country as a whole. Hereafter we are going to forget thinking in terms of Hindus, Muslims and Sikhs as such and they shall continue to be the swordarm of India. To them we shall look up for the defence of the country and for keeping our enemies out of our boundaries.

But, Sir, I wish I could similarly congratulate my Scheduled Caste friends, but then, unfortunately today there is no such occasion. They still think that they cannot safely fall in with other minority communities in this country. As I said about Sikhs, so also the Scheduled Castes people are not a minority community which have a separate entity from the Hindus; they are blood of our blood and flesh of our flesh. Why should they think that they are in any way separate from the rest of the Hindu community? We do not wish to impose on them our judgement and our views. We will leave it to them to realize in course of time that they are not in the right when they demand reservation of seats; and the other communities of this country in as short a time as possible by their conduct must convince the members of the Scheduled Castes that their interest are as safe in the hands of the rest of India as in their own hands. The rest of India must, therefore, make specific efforts to remove this apprehension in the minds of the Scheduled Castes, so that even before the period of ten years they may themselves come forward with suggestion that they do not want any reservation of seats. My amendment is in that direction. Now that they have demanded reservation of seats, let us give it to them. Let us not only give it to them but let us make such provisions which may ensure a representation of theirs to their satisfaction. My amendment suggests that constituencies which are reserved for the Scheduled Caste members should be such as contain a larger number of Scheduled Caste voters than in other constituencies so that it may be easier for the Scheduled Castes to send to the legislatures such persons as are of their confidence. The larger the number of the members of the Scheduled Castes in a constituency the easier will it be for them to elect member of their choice. Their choice if it not be actually the determining and deciding factor, at least it should have a great voice, a very influential voice in the selection or the election of candidates. This is my object in moving this amendment.

Again I say, it is for the Scheduled castes themselves to see whether this amendment of mine is to their advantage or not. My intention is to suggest to them that they might accept it, for I consider it to be in their interest and in whatever lies their interest, lies the interest of the rest of communities of this country. Should they feel that they have nothing to gain by accepting this amendment, or that they have something to lose thereby, I shall readily withdraw this amendment, because I do not want to press any amendment which, though moved with a view to safeguard their interests, and to give them something more than what they have for themselves, does not meet with their approval. With these words, Sir, I place this amendment of mine for the consideration of the House or I should rather say particularly for the consideration of my Scheduled Caste friends, but if they do not want it, it should not be there.

Mr. President:

I may point out to honourable Members that the articles which we are now considering represent decisions which we have taken after two days' debate and it is not necessary to repeat that debate again. So Members might confine themselves to the amendments, or if they have any different views they might express them, but we need not go over the same ground that we covered during the debate which lasted two days.

Sardar Hukam Singh (East Punjab: Sikh):

Sir, I am not moving amendments Nos. 29 to 31. I beg to move: "That in amendment No. 22 of List I (Fifth, Week) of amendments to amendments, at the end of the proposed Article 292, the following Explanation be added:

'Explanation.-The members of the Scheduled Castes and the Scheduled tribes mentioned in sub-clauses (a), (b) and (c) of clause (I) above shall have the right to contest unreserved seats as well".

At the outset, I might submit that the Explanation proposed in this amendment is not a new idea. It was already there in the recommendations of the Minorities Advisory Committee and that recommendation was also placed, and I am sure, agreed to, by this sovereign body on the 27th and 28th August, 1947. In my opinion it was a wholesome provision. I do not know why it has been dropped in this draft. Of course things were different when the original was put before this Constituent Assembly and all religious minorities had been given reservation of seats. They have now voluntarily agreed not to have them. My community is also one of those religious minorities. The Sikhs are not sorry for having come to that decision. They think that it is the right decision for the benefit of the minorities themselves.

But Mr. Kapoor has referred to one or two things, to which I must beg permission to reply. He has said that the minorities,—and he has given very good counsel,—should cease to think in terms of minorities and majorities and that we should all consider ourselves as one whole community. I do agree with him there and I can assure my honourable Friend that the Sikhs do want to be and will try to be welded into one whole. I have also heard several times slogans here in this House and outside as well that there are no minorities now. I wish it were so. But my submission is that so far we have this question, the minorities are there. Mere wise counsels and slogans will not eliminate them. It is something else, something better, that is required to bring about the objective, the goal that we desire to reach. For that purpose, I cannot do better than read passage form the introductory remarks of our learned Friend Dr. Ambedkar when he introduced this Draft Constitution. He gave very sound counsel to the majority and the minorities and I think those words have much significance and they stand even today as the only solution of this problem.

He said then that the minorities have loyally accepted the rule of the majority which is basically a communal majority and not a political majority. It is for the majority to realise its duties not to discriminate against minorities. Whether minorities will continue or will vanish must depend upon the habit of the majority. The moment the majority loses the habit of discriminating against minority the minorities can have no ground to exist. They will vanish, but that depends entirely upon the attitude of the majority.

I cannot improve upon it. My only submission to Mr. Kapoor is that this is the only solution and if the majority behaves and conducts itself in a manner that minorities feel secure, then certainly they will vanish in a certain period of time. So far as the Sikhs are concerned—I cannot speak for the others-they have certain natural apprehensions and these slogans and these wise counsels will only increase those apprehensions. They feel that it is the future alone that could tell them whether their fears are well-founded or not.

Now I come to the merits of this amendment of mine. I think the original object was that, because we were taking a jump over from the separate electorates to unadulterated joint electorates, the Minorities Committee recommended that lest the minorities might feel apprehensive of the sudden change they must be assured some seats by reservation and a minimum number of seats should be secured to them. It could not be the object of the Minorities Committee or this Assembly that the maximum should be limited. If this additional right is not given then the only effect is that the maximum number is being limited and not that the minimum be secured.

My second point is that this feeling of separation should go. We are accepting this reservation of seats as an unavoidable evil for the present, though it is only for the Scheduled Castes and the scheduled tribes. I am not directly concerned with it, but I do feel that if we want this feeling of separatism to go, then it is necessary that side by side with this reservation there should be a feeling in the minds of these classes as well that they are a part of the whole and that they can stand for those seats as anybody else. If after ten years suddenly we were to go to the other side, then this might not be accepted with equanimity ant there might be certain bickerings.

The third point want to submit is that this additional right would not materially affect the numerical strength of the majority. So far as I can make out it is only a psychological gesture; otherwise there is very little chance that the minority for whom these seats have been reserved shall secure additional seats to any considerable extent. But why should there be a feeling in their minds that a close preserve is thing maintained by the majority for itself and it is to their benefit that such seats are being reserved? In my humble submission there is no harm absolutely if that additional right which was contemplated in the beginning is given to them and they are allowed to contest the seats that are not reserved for them.

Shri V.I. Muniswamy Pillay (Madras : General):

Mr. President, Sir, I rise to move the two amendments that I have given notice of. I move.

"That in Amendment No. 22 of list (Fifth week) of Amendments to Amendments, in clause (2) of the proposed Article 292, after the words 'as the population' the words 'actually exists or known by a fresh census' be inserted."

I do not wish to take much of the time of the House since the reports of the Advisory Committee have been dealt with thread-bare in this House. I would, however, like to bring to the notice of the Drafting Committee certain factors which will go a long way to assure the Scheduled Castes of the seats that ought to be allotted to them under the scheme for reservation. The reason for my suggesting that the population must be taken as it exists today, or determined by a fresh census is because in the 1931 census the total population of Scheduled Castes was computed to be 50 millions, but in the census of 1941 it is shown as nearly 44 millions. I do not know how it is possible for a community like the scheduled Castes to dwindle in the course of ten years. In August 1947 when the report of the Minorities Committee was considered in this august Assembly my honourable Friend, Mr. Khandekar, who happens to be the President of the Depressed Classes League of India, urged that a census should be taken before the allocation of seats, or that our numerical strength should be taken before the allocation of seats, or that our numerical strength should be fixed on the basis of the 1931 census. We are prepared to accept representation either on the basis of the 1931 census or on a new census which will be taken in 1951. But the figures of the census of 1941 are utterly wrong so far as the Scheduled Castes are concerned. Any representation on that basis would be grossly unjust to us.

Secondly, due to the division of the country there has been a great influx of Harijans from the East Bengal to West Bengal and also from the West Punjab to East Punjab. It is a well known fact that lakhs of people of my community have had to emigrate to India due to the partition and various other causes. This matter should be taken note of by the Drafting Committee.

The third point I wish to make is that the 1935 Act and the orders thereon give power to the various Provincial Governments to include such of the communities as are considered to be backward and take them in the list of Scheduled Castes. From 1941, many communities have been taken on to the list of the Scheduled Castes, and as a matter of fact my Friend Shri Thakkar Bapa has given notice of a few communities that should be taken on the list. Taking these into consideration I feel that the population of the Scheduled Castes will be more than what it was in 1941. It will therefore be necessary that a census should be taken as early as possible for the purpose of computing the number of seats so that the Scheduled Castes may feel satisfied that they have secured their political rights.

Another thing which I would like to submit to this august Assembly is in regard to determining the seats for the Scheduled Castes on the population basis. This House has granted adult franchise. Those that were minors in 1941 would have become adults during these ten years, and unless a correct census is taken it cannot be said that the population of the Scheduled Castes has been correctly computed. This is one of the important reasons, because the article clearly says:

"The same proportion to the total number of seats allotted to that State in the House of the People as the population of the Scheduled Castes in that State or of the Scheduled Tribes in that State or part of that State, as the case may be, in respect of which seats are so reserved bears to the total population of that State."

All those who were minors in 1941 would have become adults at present and so it is imperative that they must be included in the population list. Hence a fresh census for this purpose is necessary.

The other day my honourable Friend Dr. Ambedkar said that there is no reservation in the Upper House. As I read the report I could not come to that conclusion at all. I feel strongly that a large number of Scheduled Castes must get into the Lower House, if there is no reservation in the Upper House, so that our position may be safer.

I would also like to state that by reservation which is envisaged in this article it should not be taken to perpetuate the seclusion of this community for all time. I know the real Gandhian spirit has been applied in this article, so that other communities may rise up to the occasion; and whether it be for ten more years the other communities must exhibit a very brotherly love towards this unfortunate community known as the Scheduled

Castes, so that after this period they themselves may come forward and say that they require no reservation.

With regard to my second amendment, which I move "determining constituencies where the Scheduled Castes are in largest number in each district", my honourable Friend Mr. Jaspat Roy Kapoor has given us enough and more reasons why it is necessary that determining of seats or constituencies for the Scheduled Castes must be in contiguous areas, where the largest number of them inhabit. The reason is that in years past the seats were allotted in such places where the caste Hindus and other communities predominated and hence the Harijan was not given free scope to exercise his franchise as also to see that the best of the community were returned. It is for this reason that I have given notice of this amendment as well. I hope that the Drafting Committee will either accept my amendment or that of Mr. Kapoor.

With these words I support the motion moved by Dr. Ambedkar.

Mr. President:

Mr. Sahay's amendment will also have to stand over. Pandit Thakur Das Bhargava has expressed a desire to move some of his amendments. I would like to know which of them he proposes to move.

Pandit Thakur Das Bhargava (East Punjab: General):

Sir, I wish to move Amendments No. 237, 236 and 234 in the Consolidated List up to the 10th July, 1949.

I beg to move:

"That in Amendment No, 225, above at the end of the proposed Article 292 the following proviso be added:

> 'Provided that the members of the scheduled tribes in Assam will not have the right to contest general seats."

"That in Amendment No. 225, above, after clause (2) of proposed Article 292, the following new clause be added:

> (3) The reservation of seats shall, as far as possible be secured by single member territorial constituencies."

"That in Amendment No. 225, above, in clause (2) of the proposed Article 292, but before the Explanation, the following proviso be inserted:

> "Provided that for the calculation the balance of the proportion is more than half of what it requires to obtain one seat, one seat shall be allotted and if it is less than half it shall be ignored."

I accept the interpretation which Friend. Mr. Nagappa just put on the general articles which we have passed already. According to the relevant article which the House has already passed every person has a right to stand for the general seats, which means that persons for whom seats are being reserved shall also have the right to contest general seats unless there is a provision to the contrary.

It is quite true that democracy means one person one vote. When the House agrees to reservation of seats for certain classes it really gives them concession, an unavoidable concession under the circumstances in which we are placed. This is the right solution of the difficulty. I do not know whether any member of the Scheduled Castes wants that seats be reserved for them. All that he wants is that he should come up to the general standard of the other communities in this land and for this purpose there are other means in which this could be brought about. Since these classes think as also others that they will not be returned in the general constituencies it is best that we have agreed to reservation of seats for them. I have no doubt that if they are allowed to contest general seats we are certainly doing a wrong thing. We are departing from a principle but all the same I think that if this right is allowed to the Scheduled Castes no harm is being done. If psychologically they are happy over it, let them have that happiness. I do not think there will be a single seat in the whole of India from the general seats to which a member of the Scheduled Castes will be returned.

I will be happy if many of them are returned. I want that the members of the Scheduled Castes should enjoy the confidence of the other classes. I would be happy if many of them are returned defeating the other candidates. I do no grudge them this right. I am sure that after the lapse of ten years many of them will say: "We tried to see if other classes support us. We have not been supported. Therefore there is a case for the continuance of the reservation." Then this argument will not be open to them. As they have accepted the extreme limit of 10 years with open eyes.

In regard to the Scheduled Castes of Assam, the case is peculiar. In Assam, as I have bèen told, there are 20 per cent. Muslims, 32 per cent scheduled tribes and those who are not reserved form about 48 per cent of the population. If there is a big majority for those that are not reserved, I do not mind giving persons who have seats reserved right to contest the general seats. But in relation to the people whose numbers are less than half, this kind of right is certain to give valid ground for grouse.

Kazi Syed Karimuddin (C.P. & Berar: Muslims):

Muslims and others for whom seats are not reserved will get more than 60 per cent.

Pandit Thakur Das Bhargava:

My Friend's 60 per cent adds more weight to my argument. I submit that reservation of seats being not a desirable thing, reservation for classes is calculated to induce a feeling of separateness and exclusiveness and would stand against the amalgamation of classes. In this view also it will not be fair to give these classes who have been favoured with this undemocratic right the right to contest other seats thus reducing still further the strength of those who have not been given reserved seats. Sir, everyone has got a right to be represented by a person of his choice. By reserving seats to certain classes you are depriving people of their right to be represented by persons of their choice. I can understand the argument that you are taking away the rights of others also. Those persons belonging to the Scheduled Castes may also choose to be represented in the legislatures by persons of their choice. And it may happen that they may place more faith on particular candidates from the unreserved classes. So reservation as a matter of fact deprives all people of their right to choose. It should be therefore our endeavour to see that the evils of this reservation do not harm the interests and the legitimate rights of the others. Therefore I say that in the case of Assam, where the unreserved people are less than 50 per cent., it is but fair that you do not allow the reserved classes to infringe upon the rights of the unreserved people.

Now I come to my second Amendment 236:

"That in amendment No, 225 above, after clause (2) of the proposed Article 292, the following new clause be added:

(3) The reservation of seats shall, as far as possible, be secured by single-member territorial constituencies".

If there are plural constituencies my humble submission is that the representation secured is not fair. Those candidates who have to stand for plural member constituencies will not fully represent those for whom they stand in the same effective manner in which those who represent single-member constituencies will represent those for whom they stand. In the case of the Scheduled Caste men those who will stand to represent them would be persons quite unknown except in their own neighbourhood. Therefore to ask them to stand for plural-member constituencies will mean that people who vote for them will be absolute strangers to them. This is also true of the other unreserved classes, because people are not generally known far beyond their immediate neighbourhood. As a matter of fact a person who is popular in his own district has no right to stand for another district. He may be unknown there. Therefore representation by means of plural-member constituencies is no right at all.

Moreover, when you consider the question of expenditure for canvassing an electorate of 750000 people spread over a vast area you will understand the difficulty and the trouble of the candidate. Similarly I submit that if there are single-member constituencies people living in the constituency will be deprived of their right to choose their particular candidate in so far as only persons from a particular tribe will be allowed to stand. If these are plural-member constituencies the trouble will be greater. Considering all these, neither in the interests of the classes for whom seats are reserved nor in the interests of the others there should be plural-member constituencies. I would appeal to the House to accept this suggestion of mine and make it a part of the Constitution that, as far as possible, this representation of the Scheduled Castes also should not be from plural-member constituencies, but from single-member constituencies.

Now I come to my third Amendment, viz.,

"That in Amendment No. 225 above, after clause (2) of the proposed Article 292, but before the Explanation, the following provision be inserted: .

"Provided that for the calculation the balance of the proportion is more that half of what it requires to obtain one seat, one seat shall be allotted and if it is less than half it shall be ignored."

It is a rule of mathematics and an equitable rule too. I do not want to say anything further about it. This is a just proposition.

Mr. President

The Amendments moved by Pandit Bhargava are, Nos; 234, 236 and 237 of the list of Amendments of 10th July, 1949.

Shri Kuladhar Chaliha (Assam : General):

Mr. President, I shall confine my remarks firstly to the motion moved by my Friend Professor Laskar. I feel deeply sympathetic to his case, but then we are faced with a difficult situation. If you take the figures of population of Assam his case will not stand scrutiny. First, we find that we have there 34 lakhs of tribal population and 17 lakhs of Muslims, leaving the general population in a sort of minority. According to the 1941 census the total population of Assam (Divided) was about 74 lakhs. As such, it is very difficult to give representation in the House of the People on the basis of population which is only 3¼ lakhs of Scheduled Castes. There are other communities in Assam such as Ahoms. They are three lakhs odd. The

Ahoms were the ruling community and therefore they will have as much right to claim a seat : Then we have Mataks and Morans who are also 3½ lakhs, Chutias about 1¼ lakhs, seats for them also to be created and carved out of the general community which, as I have said, is a minority. I feel that Mr. Laskar's community deserves our sympathy and I hope Mr. Laskar will have a seat in the House. But our position is such that it is impossible for us to concede his point. We have grown a convention in our part of the country to see that as far as possible all communities are represented. The Congress Committee has observed this for a very long time and they will make sure that in spite of the fact that the number of his community is small, there is a chance in the next five years for him to come into the House of the People.

Mr. Laskar has also found fault with census figures. The Congress was not in power in 1941. It is true that most of the figures for the tribals have been inflated. Some of the Scheduled Castes were said to have been converted to tribal religion because they were addicated to drink, and others were said to have been converted to Hinduism, and the increase is 184 per cent. But that is not the fault of the Congress. If there is an increase of the tribal population God alone is to be blamed and none else. I hope in the next census, such sort of things will not occur, and that things will be just and equitable.

As regards Pandit Thakur Das Bhargava's amendment, Sir, I agree with him. The general constituencies of Assam are in minority. Those who claim reservation should not further trangress into the domain of the general population and should have no right to seek seats there. Fortunately in Assam we have been carrying on happily, making adjustments, and I am sure that the minorities will show us the tolerance which we expect of them and we will show them that tolerance which they expect of us as well.

With these words, Sir, I oppose Mr. Laskar's amendment and I give my qualified support for Pandit Thakur Das Bhargava's amendment. Also I am at one with Rev.

Nichols Roy in his views that the seats reserved for the tribals should not be deprived on one ground or another and the tribals should not be divided as proposed in another amendment.

Mr. President

Mr. Jaipal Singh.

Shri M. Ananthasyanam Ayyangar (Madras : General);

The question may now be put.

Shri Jaipal Singh (Bihar : General):

Mr. President, Sir, it is most unfortunate that this House has not had an opportunity to discuss the recommendations made by the two Tribal Sub-Committees. I know we had a debate of two days to consider the report of the Minorities Committee in regard to whether the Scheduled Castes and the Muslims were to get any reservation of seats or not. At that time all the discussion was confined to the Muslim problem. Only when I raised the question of our reports, you were pleased to say, Sir, that this House would have an opportunity in the future to discuss the reports. However, if it is the wish of the House that without any discussion the articles which deal with the scheduled tribes will be taken up in this House, I have no personal quarrel except that it is very unfortunate that the two Chairmen of these two Sub-Committee should not have an opportunity to explain to the Members why their recommendations have taken a particular pattern.

Take for example the recommendations of the Sub-Committee of which I myself was a member and over which the venerable social reformer the Honourable Mr. Thakkar presided. In due course we will have to discuss certain provisions that have been recommended by this Sub-Committee. Why these recommendations have been made will have to be explained by someone. I should have thought that it would be very much better if a discussion had taken place which would have put the Members wise as to the investigations that have been carried out, as to why the Sub-Committee had come to certain conclusions, as why, for example, I had to submit a minority minute of dissent, as to why my Friend, Mr. Devendra Nath Samanta, had to agree with me in regard to my minute of dissent, etc. All these things would have been thrashed out in *extenso* in the discussion so that the Members would have appreciated the difficulties of the Sub-Committee on the tribal problems before they participated in the discussion and before they exercised their vote for or against any of the recommendations.

Having said that, Sir, I would like to congratulate Dr. Ambedkar for his new amendment which he has presented to us today. As I have said before, if there is any group of people who have got a right to rule over India, they are the Adibasis. They are first-rate Indians and all the others are second-rate, third-rate, fourth-rate Indians; I think that situation has to be appreciated when we take up questions like the reservation of seats. Sir, we are not begging anything. I do not come here to beg. It is for the majority community to atone for their sins of the last six thousand odd years. It is for them to see whether the original inhabitants of this country have been given a fair deal by the late rulers. But the future can be brightened up. What has happened in the past, let it be a matter of the past. Let us look forward to a glorious future, to a future where there shall be justice and equality of opportunity.

One honourable Member said that he was glad that the Muslims and the Christians had given up something, given up the reservation of seats. Sir, the Adivasis are not giving up anything because they never had anything. It seems very surprising that people should talk of democracy when their whole conduct has been anti-democratic in the past. What have the general community done for these backward people in the past? Has there been anything in the statue to prevent them from putting up the Adivasis in more seats than were due to them according to their population? Take Bihar. There are 5.1 million Adibasis in Bihar, but only 7 Adivasi M.L.As. Did the Congressmen put up a single Adivasi for a general seat? No. Take the Central Provinces and Berar. There were before the merger of the States 2.9 million Advasis; but there was only one seat for the Adivasis. After the merger, there would be an addition of something like 2.8 million more, a large majority of whom would be Adivasis, I can say the same thing about every province. Even in a province like Bombay, where without the merged States, there was an Adivasis population of 1.6 million, which would be added to on account of the merger by a figure that may double itself from out of the 4.4 million that have been put within the province, there is only one seat reserved. And also in province where the Premier has been a very ardent worker amongst the Advasis for many years. He was the President of the Adivasi Seva Mandal there and it was a privilege for me to see something of the work he did before he became the Premier. After he became the Premier, he could not devote so much time for that work.

Even in a province where you have such a sympathetic leader of the dominant party, you find no generosity whatever. People talk of democracy. Let them search their hearts. Is there anything that prevented them from bringing out these people from their jungle fastnesses into the legislature? How do they explain their niggardliness, in fact their apathy, hostility to bring these people to the legislature and other forums of public life? It is essential that these people should be compelled to come out of their jungle fastnesses. It is for that reason reservation is very very necessary. If you want unity in this country, we must all get together.

Sir, in this connection, I would like to quote something that you said about nine years ago when you were the chairman of the Reception Committee of the 53rd session of the Indian National Congress at Ramgarh. I am not quoting anything out of its proper context. I think what you said is very relevant to prove what I have been endeavouring to say. You said:

"That portion of Bihar where this great assemblage is meeting today has its own peculiarities. In beauty, it is matchless. Its history, too, is wonderful. These parts are inhabited very largely by those who are regarded as the original inhabitants of India. Their civilisation differs in many respects from the civilisation of other people. The discovery of old articles shows that this civilisation is very old. The Adibasis belong to a different stock (Austrick) from the Aryas and people of the same stock are spread toward the south-east of India in the many islands to a great distance. Their ancient culture is preserved in these parts to a considerable extent, perhaps more than elsewhere. It is not, however, as if the Aryas and the Adibasis never mingled with one another. As a matter of fact, there have been considerable intermixture and exchange. Aryas have taken many things from them and they have taken many things from the Aryas. With all this, however, they have kept themselves apart. It is the opinion of experts that the colour and facial expression of the Biharis, the formation of their skulls and even their language exhibit clear unmistakable marks of their influence. Having, however, once cast their influence on the Biharis, the Adibasis have made much of our culture and our speech their own."

There has been this peculiarity. In certain parts of India, what is called inter-mixture and inter-mingling has been fairly considerable with the result that the process of absorption into the Hindu fold has been very great. On the other hand, in particular areas, this has not been the case. There has however developed somehow a hostility between the ancient people and the new-comers. When the Aryan hordes came into this country, naturally they were unwelcome because they were intruders. But, they began to pour in streams one after another and pushed the peopie that were there, the aboriginals, the Advasis, further and further away. The Arya-speaking people settled in the rich Gangetic valley and ousted the Advasis who had to retreat to the jungle fastnesses because the Aryas found them inhospitable. That is roughly the history as to why the Adivasis are today found only in the mountainous tracts, because these tracts were inhospitable, were inclement to the Arya people.

Now, that, of course, is no longer the case. Nothing is isolated. We can get everywhere and therefore, intercourse on a fresh scale, on a much more intensive scale, will take place in the future. Another reason for the hostility and bitter feeling against the *dikus*, as we call the new-comers—diku means new-comer—has been the fact that the new-comer has always exploited that simple, ignorant Adivasis; he has looted him of his land; he has expropriated him of his many rights; he has taken away the jungle freedom from him. This the Adivasis rightly resents. All this hostility that has gone on for thousands and thousands of years must be done away with. I am very glad indeed that in the new Constitution there is not going to be anything like separate electorates. I welcome the fact that the Adivasis will be elected from the joint general electorates. I also welcome the fact that the House, as a whole, is unanimous that the Advasis must be compelled to come into the Government of the provinces as well as at the Centre. The result of this Article 292 will be, whereas in the past we had seven M.L. As from Bihar, now we shall have something like 51. There must be 51 because there will be 51 seats reserved for them. There may be more if the political parties would be generous enough to give more seats than is due to the Adivasis according to their population figures. Like that, in the Central Provinces, where as there is only one Adivasi M.L.A, there may be as many as thirty. In Assam, according to the population, there are 2.4 million Advasis; at present there are only nine seats reserved for them. Well, I am not one who was ever an admirer of the census figures. Ever since the Hindu Mahasabha became a millitant political orginisation, the census figures have never been reliable or accurate. We have yet to get to a stage where we want to get scientific facts in a honest way. Take for instance, the Central Provinces. You compare the figures of Adibasis there, say in 1941; take the censuses of 1921, 1931 and 1941. You find in between 1911 and 1941 the figure gets reduced by 18 lakhs. I know particularly that the Adivasis are not a dying race and yet somehow or other one minute the Gonds are enummated as Hindus and the next minute they come back as Adivasis; and that type of cooking of figures and misenumeration has gone on at every census and the sooner this country becomes honest about it and tries to find out statistics in an honest way, without any religious bias, the better it will be. At the last Session of the Indian Science Congress, the scientists said--there are people who want to know and who are not moved by religious or political bias—that there were in this country not less 30 million Adivasis. In 1941 census the figure is of course only 24.8 million. You may multiply that by 5 or not, but, the fact is that any section of our society that is economically and politically backward must have safeguards and provisions which will enable it to come up to the general level.

That is the only reason, Mr. President, why I do support the reservation of seats for Scheduled Castes and the scheduled tribes and for no other reason. I am not at all optimistic that in the short space of ten years, which means two general elections, Adibasis will have come to the level of the rest of India and therefore at the end of ten years reservation of seats should be done away with. I am not one who will be so bold as to believe in such a miracle. Things are going to move as fast as we would like them to move. I would have preferred that this matter should have been reviewed at the end of ten years to find out whether Adibasis and Scheduled Castes in the two general elections that will take place during the ten years had made good, whether they had been able to assert themselves in the Councils and take their share in the national life of the country. When that had been made, then I think the Parliament could decide whether or not these reservations should be done away with or continued for a further period of say ten or fifteen or twenty-five years. I would have preferred it that way but if there is any suspicion in the minds of non-Scheduled Caste people or non-Adibasis, I would not insist on it. The generous thing would have been to give them ample scope to come into all the Councils in the provinces and at the Centre and not to limit them only to two general elections.

Some people harp on separatism being implied in reservation of seats. Some people have a kink and they like to explain everything away by attributing separatism to any difference of opinion. It has become the fashion in this country to call every rebel a communist. Similarly, those of us who desire that the backward groups in our society should be compelled to come by the front door and not by backdoor and the front door is open reservation, are dubbed as separatists. It does not lie in the mouth of people to talk of separatism when 30 million Adibasis have been treated as political untouchables over centuries. It does not lie in the mouth of those people to tell Adibasis what democracy is. Adibasi society is the most democratic element in this country. Can the rest of India say the same thing? Can people who have for centuries been living under the Caste system honestly and genuinely say that they can have democratic outlook? It takes time. In Adibasi society all are equal, rich or poor. Everyone has equal opportunities and I do not wish that people should get away with the idea that by writing this Constitution and operating it we are trying to put a new idea into the Adibasi society. What we are actually doing is you are learning and taking something as you, Mr. President, said, Non-Adibasi society has learnt much and has still to learn a good deal. Adibasis are the most democratic people and they will not let India get smaller or weaker. It is not they who are responsible for the partition. Adibasis claim the whole of India. So I would like that Members should look at it from that generous angle and not be so condescending. You are clearing your own conscience, having expropriated them from their lands, having made laws whereby you have driven them out of their rights. What is the position today? Why are there about ten lakhs of people in Assam crimped away from Chhattisgarh, Orissa and Bihar and they are running from place to place with no sense of security? It is because non-Adibasis have taken away their lands, cheated them and they continue to cheat.

Now it is very necessary in the interest of this country, for its great future, that every element of India, be it backward or forward, should get together and pull in the same direction and for that we must see to it that the backward sections come up. Reservation is very necessary for the backward people whether they are Adibasis or whether they are Scheduled Castes, or Jains or Muslims. Once you acknowledge that something has got to be done, some fulcrum has to be pushed in to tilt them up to a higher level, then the question of separatism does not arise at all. Therefore I, as an Adibasi representative, am not ashamed to accept this principle of reservation. I regret it is there only for ten years, because I am convinced that India is not going to become heaven, that everybody is not going to become a graduate in ten years or that everybody will get politically educated. What is necessary is that the backward groups in our country should be enabled to stand on their own legs so that they can assert themselves. It is not the intention of this Constitution, nor do I desire it, that the advanced community should be carrying my people in their arms for the rest of eternity. All that we plead is that the wherewithal should be provided as has been provided in Article 292, so that we will be able to stand on our own legs and regain the lost nerves and be useful citizens of India.

There is much more to be said, but I understand that some of the amendments have been deferred to another occasion and, therefore, I would not say much at this stage. But I am sure and I may assure non-Adibasis that Adibasis will play a much bigger part than you imagine, if only you will be honest about your intentions and let them play a part they have a right to play.

Shri R.V. Dhulekar (United Provinces: General):

What does he exactly want?

Shri Jaipal Singh:

I want Mr. Dhulekar to behave just as he used to when he was a student in St. Columbia's College, Hazaribagh, when he mixed freely with the Adibasis and spoke of them as being the finest citizens in India. But at the present moment, the Adibasis have been put into a water-tight compartment. I know there are people who will say that the British put them into zoos. We have now an Indian National Government. Is the zoo not still there? Popular ministries have been heard of in this country for the last twelve years; what have they done in any way to remove this stigma? Have they done anything? During the

Sub-Committee's tour—wherever we went—Provincial Governments came out with eleborate reports of the heavenly things they were doing for the Adibasis to fight their poverty and the evil disease in their midst, and how all that was going to be removed. One provincial Prime Minister told me that he had set aside Rs. 20 lakhs for ameliorative measures for the Adibasis in a particular district. I asked him how much he had spent in the last eight months. He said: "We still have our plans but we hope it will be ready on paper!" What happens is just paper and paper: all window-dressing, We want concrete work among these people. Some people think that by opening a few schools and giving some scholarships they will be making a tremendous change among the Adibasis. It is economic betterment that the backward people need. Once they are economically better, they will be able to educate themselves.

I would like to, if I may, tell the provincial Prime Ministers who are here and in whose provinces there are large numbers of Adibasis, that no good will come out of the lakhs and lakhs that they profess to earmark for welfare and other work among the Adibasis and other backward people in their provinces, unless there is the missionary spirit behind it. I know in my own province of Bihar that all welfare work has a political background. In Bihar, unfortunately, there have been three conflicting militant groups, one pulling eastwards towards Bengal, one pulling southwards towards Jharkand and one pulling northwards towards the Himalayas. Now, in order to kill the eastwards and southwards groups, lakhs and lakhs of rupees are being spent, all in the name of welfare among the backward people. Evidence is there, Mr. President, of leading Congressmen in Manbhum, in Palamau, in Ranchi, in Hazaribagh and other districts.....

Shri Biswanath Das (Orissa: General): Are all these matters relevant to the subject matter of the discussion?

Mr. Naziruddin Ahmad (West Bengal: Muslim):

Every truthful statement in this connection is certainly relevant.

Shri Jaipal Singh:

Lakhs of rupees are being spent, not for the direct benefit of the people, but for the employment of armies of welfare workers and the money gets swallowed up in the payment of wages and salaries, and motor cars and propaganda vans. The actual result to the Adibasi is nil. It is very much like the Grow More Food campaign, if for the amount of money that we spend in this campaign one more grain was grown, it would have been a success. But it seems to be the other way round.

The idea of the generosity of the Members as a whole in recognising the necessity of giving reservation of seats to the Scheduled Castes and the scheduled tribes was that these people, who as you have said at Ramgarh have somehow or other kept apart, will now be compelled to come into the inner circle and do their best and contribute their share for the betterment of this country. I know there is fear in certain quarters. There is fear in Assam: there was fear in West Bengal. When Mr. Khaitan moved his amendment, or rather gave notice of his amendment—he is no longer in our midst—I discussed with him why he wanted no reservation of seats for the Scheduled Castes in West Bengal. He was quite honest about it. He said, if the Scheduled Castes combined with any minority group, then the upper class people were nowhere. Some such apprehension has been indicated from a Member from Assam. I know perfectly well that it is not a question that you have reserved so many seats for Adibasis therefore you should not give them any of the general seats. That is not the general issue. Let us be honest. What the upper classes in Assam fear is that if the Scheduled Castes and the Adibasis were to combine, and if these two groups were given the right to contest also the general seats, then the upper classes might not remain in power.

That is the truth of the matter as I see it and I deeply beg of everyone not to think in terms of fear. Let us not be afraid of our fellowman because, if we do not trust him, we have no right that he should trust us. We have been living under different circumstances in the past. Now the

eight lakhs of them are in hills area and the remaining eight lakhs are in the tea gardens. The tribals in the tea gardens are included in the general population, with the result that the only people who will have reserved seats will be the eight lakhs in the plains area and the eight lakhs in the hills area. As regards the eight lakhs of tribals living in the plains area the Working Committee of the Assam Provincial Congress Committee have agreed to allow them to stand as candidates from the general constituencies and my honourable Friend the Premier of Assam himself has said that he does not want that there should be any limitation on any tribals of the plains to stand for the general seats.

Therefore, Sir, I oppose Pandit Bhargava's amendment regarding preventing the tribals of Assam from standing as candidates from the general constituencies.

Sardar Bhopinder Singh Man (East Punjab: Sikh):

As a number of amendments have been moved, it seems to me that some time be given to oppose those amendments.

Mr. President:

As I said we have discussed this very proposition for two full days in this House, and every section of the House had full opportunity of expressing itself on the general principles, Now it is those very principles which are sought to be embodied in the resolution which has been placed before the House by Dr. Ambedkar. I do not think any further discussion will help the Members. I therefore call upon Dr. Ambedkar to speak.

The Honourable Dr. B.R Ambedkar:

Mr. President, Sir, a great many of the points which were raised in the course of the debate on this article and the various amendments are, in my judgement, quite irrelevant to the subject matter or this article. They might well be raised when we will come to the discussion of the electoral laws and the framing of the constituencies. I, therefore, do not propose to deal with them at this stage.

There are just three points which, I think, for a reply. One point is the one which is raised by Mr. Laskar by his amendment. His amendment is to introduce the words "save in the case of the Scheduled Castes in Assam". I have completely failed to understand what he intends to do by the introduction of these words. If these words were introduced it would mean that the Scheduled Castes in Assam will not be entitled to get the representation which the article proposes to give them in the Lower House of the Central Parliament, because if the words stand as they are, "save in the case of the Scheduled Castes in Assam" unaccompained by any other provision, I cannot see what other effect it would have except to deprive the Scheduled Castes of Assam of the right to representation which has been given to them. If I understand him correctly, I think the matter, which he has raised, legitimately refers to article 67B of the Constitution which has already been passed. In that article it has been laid down that the representation in the Lower House at the Centre shall be not less than one representative for every 7,50,000 people or not more than one representative for a population of 5,00,000. According to what he was saying—and I must confess that it was utterly impossible for me to hear anything that he was saying—but if I gathered the purport of it, he seems to be under the impression that on account of the division of Sylhet district the population of the Scheduled Castes in Assam has been considerably reduced and that there may not be any such figure as we have laid down, namely, 7,50,000 or 5,00,000 with the result that he feels that the Scheduled Castes of Assam will not get any representation. But I should like to tell him that the provision in article 67(5) (b) does not apply to the Scheduled Castes. It applies to the constituency. What it means is that if a constituency consists of 7,50,000 people, that constituency will have one seat. It may be that within that constituency the population of the Scheduled Castes is much smaller, but that would not prevent either the Delimitation Committee or Parliament from allotting a seat for the Scheduled Castes in that particular area. His fear, therefore, in my judgement, is utterly groundless.

Then I come to the amendment moved by Sardar

Hukam Singh in which he suggests that provision ought to be made whereby the Scheduled Castes and the Scheduled tribes would be entitled to contest seats which are generally not reserved for the Scheduled Castes or the Scheduled tribes. He said that the Drafting Committee has made a deliberate omission. I do not think that is correct. It is accepted that the Scheduled Castes and the scheduled tribes shall be entitled to contest seats which are not reserved seats, which are unreserved seats. That is contained in the report of the Advisory Committee which has already been accepted by the House. The reason why that particular provision has not been introduced in article 292 is because it is not germane at this place. This proposition will find its place in the law relating to election with which this Assembly or the Assembly in its legislative capacity will have to deal with. He therefore need have no fear on that ground.

With regard to the point raised by my Friend Mr. Pillai that the population according to which seats are to be reserved should be estimated by a fresh census, that matter has been agitated in this House on very many occasions. I then said that it was quite impossible for the Government to commit itself to taking a fresh census but the Government has kept its mind open. If it is feasible the Government may take a fresh census in order to estimate the population of the Scheduled Castes or the scheduled tribes in order to calculate the total representation that they would be entitled to in accordance with the provisions of Article 292. The Government is also suggesting that if in any case it is not possible to have a fresh census, they will estimate the population of these communities on the basis of the voters' strength which may be calculated from them, in which case we might be able to arrive at what might be called a rough and ready estimate of the population. I do think it is possible for me to go beyond that.

All the other amendments I oppose.[68]

After this speech of Ambedkar, N.C.Laskar, Sardar Hukam Singh and V.I. Maniswamy Pillai withdrew their amendments and the other amendments were negatived by the House. The amended article 292, as moved by Dr. Ambedkar, was adopted by the House.[69]

At the revision stage it was renumbered as Article 330.

The framers of the Constitution aimed at the progress of the country as a whole and in their wisdom thought that if for a limited period of time, special protection was given to the Scheduled Castes and the Scheduled Tribes, they would be able to march in tune with the advanced sections of the society.

There is provision for reservation of seats for them but no weightage. The members of the Scheduled Castes and Scheduled Tribes are elected by the general electorate. There is no special electorate for them.

The original scheme of reservation of seats for all religious and racial minorities and a 'section of Hindu community known as Scheduled Castes' was jettisoned mid-way when the representatives of all the religious communities, due to the endeavour and persuasion of Dr. H.C. Mookherjee and Tajamul Husain—two farsighted and nationalistic leaders belonging to two religious communities—Indian Christian and Muslim, decided on their own to ask for abolition of the principle of representation on the basis of religious minorities. The leaders of the Sikh community bargained for and accepted the same principle in regard to their own community when the depressed classes belonging to the Sikh community were given the status of Scheduled Castes for enjoying the same privileges and safeguards accorded to Hindu Scheduled Castes. It may be noted that this change of policy did not receive the same amount of support from at least a section of Muslim Leaguers and there was even an insinuation that not only all the Muslim Members of the Advisory Committee were not present in the crucial Advisory Committee meeting but all of them did not support this move when this principle was discussed and adopted. In the Constituent Assembly, as we have seen, many Muslim Members did rise above their own community feeling and extended support to abolition of reservation of seats on communal basis.

But the Scheduled Castes Members in the Advisory Committee did not fall in line. They insisted and the Advisory Committee acquiesced, on reservation of seats for them on population basis. Curiously enough, not a single Scheduled Caste Member voiced his concern in the Constituent Assembly for the continuance of this policy of representation for them, as if they could not see anything beyond their own sectarian interests. Alas, there was no Tajamul Husain amongst them who could convince others not to follow a policy which would perpetuate seclusion of their community for all time. Even leaders like Dr. Ambedkar and Jagjivan Ram could not rise above petty communal interests. Gandhiji in 1932 agreed to the Poona Pact with a view to keeping the Scheduled Castes within the fold of Hinduism. He was dead against branding them as a separate community, far less as a minority community. But Dr. Ambedkar and his cohorts were all along asking for a separate entity for the Scheduled Castes outside the Hindu community and they more or less achieved their goal when the British Prime Minister accepted the Scheduled Castes as a separate community in his famous Communal Award. Though in the face of stiff resistance, Dr. Ambedkar had to settle for reservation of seats for the Scheduled Castes with joint electorate and sign the Poona Pact, but he was very unhappy and gave vent to his feelings that he had to sign the Poona Pact much against his wishes. But in free India, when all religious communities, seeing the futility of the policy of reservation of seats on communal basis, opted for abolition of the same, no such move was initiated either by Dr. Ambedkar or any other leader of the Scheduled Castes. Rather they insisted on their representation as a separate community. And the farmers, true to their stand that no change affecting the members of the minorities including the Scheduled Castes would be effected unless they themselves asked for the same, did not go for abolition of the policy of separate representation for the Scheduled Castes.

Perhaps being wise at the vivisection of the country on the basis of religion, which was construed as a direct fall-out of the policy of communal representation, the framers had no compunction in reversing their own previous decision on reservation of seats for the religious minorities, specially the Muslims, even though some of the Muslim Members did object to this change. They, however, could not take the same liberty with the Scheduled Castes, though many, like Nehru, were convinced that no reservation should be given to them on the basis of community. Or was the presence of Dr. Ambedkar as the Chairman of the Drafting Committee a positive set-back for the pro-changers? It is better to remember that in the December 30, 1948 meeting of the Advisory Committee Ambedkar raised a point of order that the political safeguards for the minorities having been accepted by the Constituent Assembly they were not within the reach of the Advisory Committee and that if it was the desire of the Committee to discuss the matter *de novo* the proper procedure was to move amendments to the provisions contained in the Draft Constitution. Vallabhbhai Patel, chairman of the Advisory Committee, however, ruled that there was no bar to a discussion and that the Committee also could recommend reconsideration of the whole matter.[70] Ambedkar made this futile attempt, perhaps apprehending that the benefits, privileges and safeguards secured for the Scheduled Castes would be similarly done away with. In any case, if the leaders of the Scheduled Castes, especially Dr. Ambedkar, as chairman of the Drafting Committee, had the courage, sagacity and prescience, they could have easily fallen in line with the leaders of other communities and saved India from a perpetual cleavage on the basis of caste. That this policy of reservation for a section of community solely on the basis of caste would perpetuate casteism, separateness, exclusiveness and divisiveness, would not only stand against integration of the county but also go against the national interest, was recognised even by those who stood for special privileges and safeguards for the Scheduled Castes, but they made convenient pretensions that this provision was intended to be of a temporary duration—just sufficient to enable them to come up to the level of the general body of citizens. The period of ten years prescribed in the Constitution was extended to fifty years by subsequent amendments on the ground that the object of the safeguard had not yet been fulfilled. That this provision is still continuing in free India even after 48 years of Independence only strengthens the hands of those who thought that separate representation would not help in removing the disabilities which were basically social in character. Political safegaurds, instead of making real efforts for bringing them in the mainstream, have perpetuated separateness and divisiveness, as apprehended by many. As a matter of fact, by providing reservation of seats for some people who have been categorised solely on the basis of caste, has not helped in ushering in a 'caste-less' society cherished by the framers. Rather, it has brought in a 'casteist', society to last for eternity.

Notes and References

1. Rao, *op. cit.*, Vol. II, p. 315.
2. *Ibid.*, p. 323.
3. *Ibid.*, p. 329.
4. *Ibid.*, pp. 351-52.
5. *Ibid.*, p. 375.
6. *Ibid.*, pp. 365-66.
7. *Ibid.*, p. 325.
8. *Ibid.*, p. 332.
9. *Ibid.*, p. 382.
10. *Ibid.*, p. 371.
11. *Ibid.*, p. 338.
12. *Ibid.*, p. 340.
13. *Ibid.*, pp. 93-94.
14. *Ibid.*, pp. 397-98.
15. *Ibid.*, pp. 400-01.
16. *Ibid.*, pp. 401-02.
17. *CAD.*, Vol. V, pp. 248-49.
18. *Ibid.*, pp. 198-200.
19. *Ibid.*, pp. 211-26.
20. *Ibid.*, p. 224.
21. *Ibid.*, p. 270.
22. *Ibid.*, pp. 227-28.
23. *Ibid.*, p. 235.
24. *Ibid.*, p. 233.
25. *Ibid.*, pp. 228-29.
26. *Ibid.*, p. 232.

27. *CAD.*, Vol. V, p. 233.
28. *Ibid.*, p. 234.
29. *Ibid.*, p. 240.
30. *Ibid.*, pp. 254-58.
31. *Ibid.*, pp. 259-61.
32. *Ibid.*, pp. 261-63.
33. *Ibid.*, pp. 263-64.
34. *Ibid.*, pp. 266-68.
35. Rao, *op. cit.*, Vol. II, p. 398.
36. *Ibid.*, p. 408.
37. *CAD*, Vol. V, p. 272.
38. *Ibid.*, pp. 265-66.
39. *Ibid.*, pp. 269-70.
40. *Ibid.*, pp. 271-72.
41. *Ibid.*, pp. 272-73.
42. Rao, *op. cit.*, Vol. III, pp. 22-23.
43. *Ibid.*, p. 352.
44. *Ibid.*, p. 354.
45. *Ibid.*, p. 358.
46. *Ibid.*, p. 419.
47. *Ibid.*, p. 540.
48. *Ibid.*, p. 477
49. *Ibid.*, p. 630.
50. *Ibid.*, Vol. IV, pp. 354-56.
51. *Ibid.*, p. 590.
52. *Ibid.*, pp. 590-94.
53. *Ibid.*, p. 594,
54. *Ibid.*, pp. 595-97.
55. *Ibid.*, p. 598.
56. *Ibid.*, pp. 598-99.
57. *CAD*, Vol. VIII, pp. 311-12.
58. *Ibid.*, pp. 271-72.
59. *Ibid.*, pp. 274-354.
60. *Ibid.*, pp. 303-05.
61. *Ibid.*, pp. 274-82.
62. *Ibid.*, pp. 282-90.
63. *Ibid.*, pp. 351-52.
64. *Ibid.*, p. 298.
65. *Ibid.*, p. 331.
66. *Ibid.*, pp. 344-45.
67. *Ibid.*, pp. 354-55.
68. *CAD*, Vol. IX, pp. 633-58.
69. *Ibid.*, pp. 658-59.
70. Rao, *op. cit.*, Vol. IV, p. 598.

16

Reservation of Seats for Scheduled Castes and Scheduled Tribes in the Legislative Assemblies of the States (Article 332)

In Chapter 15 we have seen that the Minority Sub-committee in its report submitted on July 27, 1947 had concluded that as a general principle there should be reservation of seats for different recognised minorities in the various legislatures. The Advisory Committee endorsed this view of the Minority Sub-committee and stated in its report submitted to the President of the Constituent Assembly on August 8, 1947 that as a general rule there should be reservation of seats for the minorities in the various legislatures on the basis of their population. This report of the Advisory Committee on minority rights was considered by the Constituent Assembly on August 27 and 28 when all the recommendations of the Advisory Committee were generally adopted with minor amendments.

The decision of the Constituent Assembly on reservation of seats for the Muslims, the Scheduled Castes, the Scheduled Tribes and the Indian Christians in the legislatures was incorporated in the Draft Constitution, prepared by the Constitutional Adviser in October, 1947, in two different sections. The provision relating to reservation of seats in the Parliament was included in Clause 60 figuring in Part IV under the Federal Parliament, while that relating to Provincial Legislatures was incorporated in Clause 130 occurring in Part V under the Provincial Legislature. Sub-Clauses (3), (4), (5), (7) and (8) of Clause 130 had the following provisions:

(3) Seats shall be reserved for—

(a) the Muslim community, the Scheduled Castes and the Scheduled Tribes (except the Scheduled Tribes in the autonomous districts of Assam) in the Legislative Assembly of every Province;

(b) the Indian Christian community in Legislative Assemblies of the Provinces of Madras and Bombay; and

(c) the autonomus districts in the Legislative Assembly of the Province of Assam;

according to the scale prescribed in sub-section (6).

(4) (a) The number of seats reserved for any community in the Legislative Assembly of any Province shall bear, as nearly as may be, the same proportion to the total number of seats in that Assembly as the population of the community in the Province bears to the total population of the Province.

Explanation. All the Scheduled Castes in a Province shall be deemed to be a single community for the purposes of this clause and so also all the Scheduled Tribes in a Province.

(b) The number of seats reserved for an autonomous district in the Legislative Assembly of the Province of Assam shall bear to the total number of seats in that Assembly a proportion not less than the population of the district bears to the total population of the Province.

(5) Notwithstanding anything contained in this section the Governor of a Province may, if he is of

opinion that the Anglo-Indian community is not adequately repersented in the Legislative Assembly of the Province, nominate such number of members of the community to the Legislative Assembly as he considers appropriate.

(7) The constituencies for the seats reserved for any autonomous district of the Province of Assam shall not comprise any area outside that district.

(8) No person who is not a member of a Scheduled Tribe in any autonomous district of the Province of Assam shall be eligible for election to the Legislative Assembly of the Province from any constituency of that district except from the constituency comprising the cantonment and municipality of Shillong.[1]

Clause 130 without sub-clauses (3), (4), (5), (7) and (8) was revised by the Drafting Committee on Junuary 24, 1948.[2] The Drafting Committee decided on February 5, 1948 to insert new clauses 225-A to 225-D and to include them in Part XII of the Constitution. Clause 225-C incorporated the provisions of sub-clauses (3), (4), (7) and (8) of Clause 130 of the Constituional Adviser's Draft Constitution with minor drafting changes while Clause 225-D incorporated the provisions of sub-clause (5) of Clause 130 of the Constitutional Adviser's Draft.[3] Clauses 225-C and 225-D ultimately appeared as Articles 294 and 295 respectively in the Draft Constitution finalised by the Drafting Committee in February, 1948. Article 294 read as follows:

(1) Seats shall be reserved for—

(a) the Muslim community, the Scheduled Castes and the Scheduled Tribes (except the Scheduled Tribes in the autonomous districts of Assam) in the Legislative Assembly of every state for the time being specified in Part I of the First Schedule; and

(b) the Indian Christian community in the Legislative Assemblies of the States of Madras and Bombay;

according to the scale prescribed in clause (3) of Article 149 of this Constitution.

(2) Seats shall be reserved also for the autonomous districts in the Legislative Assembly of the State of Assam.

(3) The number of seats reserved for any community in the Legislative Assembly of any State for the time being specified in Part I of the first Schedule shall bear, as nearly as may be, the same proportion to the total number of seats in that Assembly as the population of the community in the State bears to the total population of the State.

Explanation: All the Scheduled Castes in a state shall be deemed to be a single community for the purpose of this clause and so also all the Scheduled Tribes in a State.

(4) The number of seats reserved for an autonomous district in the Legislative Assembly of the State of Assam shall bear to the total number of seats in that Assembly a proportion not less than the population of the district bears to the total population of the State.

(5) The constituencies for the seats reserved for any autonomous district of the State of Assam shall not comprise any area outside that district.

(6) No person who is not a member of a Scheduled Tribe of any autonomous district of the State of Assam shall be eligible for election to the Legislative Assembly of the State from any constituency of that district except from the constituency comprising the cantonment and municipality of Shillong.[4]

When this Draft Constitution was circulated eliciting comments, suggestions, etc., many suggestions were received.

Govind Das suggested that (i) Article 294 be omitted and consequential changes be made in the numbering of the subsequent Articles; (ii) for clause (1) of Article 294 the following be substituted:

> (1) Seats shall be reserved for the Scheduled Tribes (except the Scheduled Tribes in the autonomous district of Assam) in the Legislative Assembly of every State for the time being specified in Part I of the First Schedule according to the scale prescribed in clause (3) of Article 149 of this Constitution.

and (iii) clause (3) of Article 294 be omitted and the subsequent clauses be renumbered accordingly.

Thakurdas Bhargava and Govind Das suggested that (1) the following proviso be added to clause (1) of Article 294.

> Provided that members of communities for whom seats are reserved under Article 294 shall not be chosen from general constituencies and members of communities other than those for whom seats are reserved shall not be chosen from reserved constituencies:
>
> Provided that no member of any other communities for whom seats are so reserved will be competent to stand for any seat other than those reserved for the community.

(ii) the following be added at the end of Article 294:

and in case the communities for whom the seats have been so reserved fail to return the full quota of membership the deficiency shall be made up by nomination by the Governor.

(iii) to Article 294, the following new clause be added:

> (7) Such reserved seats shall be filled by those members of the communities concerned who are returned by general elections and the Governor shall nominate as many members from the community concerned as are required to make up the deficiency. The Governor shall on subsequent occasions of shortage similarly in the quota reserved for the community concerned make up the shortage by nomination.

and (iv) in clause (1) of Article 294, after the words "Seats shall be reserved" the words "for ten years from the commencement of this Constitution" be inserted.

To these seven suggestions, the Constitutional Adviser noted that Article 294 followed the decisions of the Advisory Committee (with regard to the reservation of seats in the Legislatures of the States) as adopted by the Constituent Assembly during the August 1947 session. The provision that such reservation should remain in force for ten years had been included in Article 305 of the Draft Constitution. It had also been decided by the Constituent Assembly that the members of minority communities having reserved seats should have the right to contest unreserved seats as well. The remarks on amendments under Article 292 would apply to these amendments also *mutatis mutandis*. The Drafting Committee also did not accept any of these amendments.

H.J. Khandekar, Dharam Prakash, Yashwant Rai, Chandrika Ram, S. Nagappa, V.C. Kesava Rao, T. Channaya and Srimati Dakshayani Velayudhan suggested (i) that for paragraph (a) of clause (i) of Article 294, the following be substituted.

(a) the Muslim community, the Scheduled Castes and the Scheduled Tribes (except the Scheduled Tribes in the autonomous districts of Assam) in Parts I, II and III of the First Schedule; and

and (ii) that in clause (3) of Article 294, for the words "Legislative Assembly" the words "Legislature and local bodies", and for the words "Part I" the words "Parts I, II and III" be substituted.

S. Nagappa suggested that in paragraph (a) of clause (1) and in clause (3) of Article 294, for the words "specified in Part I" the words "specified in Parts I, II and III" be substituted.

To these three suggestions, the Constitutional Adviser's comments were that these amendments were not very clear. Apparently the intention was that the reservation of seats for the Muslim community, the

Scheduled Castes and the Scheduled Tribes provided for in sub-clause (a) of clause (1) of Article 294 should be made applicable not only in the case of the Legislative Assemblies in States in Part I of the First Schedule but also in the case of local bodies in such States and the Legislative Assemblies and local bodies in States in Parts II and III of the First Schedule. As had already been pointed out, the provisions regarding reservations contained in Article 294 followed the decisions of the Advisory Committee as adopted by the Constituent Assembly. The Special Committee also considered this question and was of the view that the provisions relating to reservation of seats to minorities should be made applicable to all elections to the Legislatures or in the case of Legislatures having two Houses, in the Lower Houses of the Legislatures of States including the States in Part III of the First Schedule and to give effect to the views of the Special Committee necessary amendments had been suggested in Article 294 separately. The Scheduled Tribes had been defined in sub-clause (x) of clause (1) of Article 303 in relation only to States in Part I of the First Schedule. Accordingly, the question of reservation of seats for Scheduled Tribes in States in Parts II and III of the First Schedule would not arise. The amendments suggested to give effect to the views of the Special Committee would meet the point regarding the reservation of seats for the Muslim community and the Scheduled Castes in States in Part III of the First Schedule raised in this amendment. Necessary amendments had been also suggested in article 294 for reservation of seats for the Muslim community and the Scheduled Castes in the Legislative Assemblies of States in Part II of the First Schedule if the recommendations of the *ad hoc* Committee on the Chief Commissioners' Provinces regarding separate Legislatures for such States were accepted. The question of reservation of seats in local bodies should be left to be regulated by Acts of the appropriate Legislatures relating to such bodies. These amendments were not therefore necessary.

K. Santhanam, M. Ananthasayanam Ayyangar, Shrimati G. Durgabai and T.T. Krishnamachari suggested,

(i) that in paragraph, (a) of clause (1) of Article 294, the words "the Muslim community" be deleted and (ii) that in Article 294, paragraph (b) of clause (1) be deleted. The Constitutional Adviser observed that these two amendments involved questions of policy.

Tajamul Husain suggested that Article 294 be deleted, or, alternatively, that in sub-clause (a) of clause (1) of Article 294, the words "the Muslim community" be deleted. To this suggestion, the Constitutional Adviser noted that article 294 followed the decision of the Advisory Committee (with regard to the reservation of seats in the Legislatures of the States) as adopted by the Constituent Assembly during the August 1947 session. Both the amendments which sought to delete Article 294 and the alternative amendment which sought to delete the words "the Muslim community" from sub-clause (a) of clause (1) of Article 294 involved questions of policy.

The Drafting Committee decided (i) that for clause (1) of Article 294 the following clause be substituted:

(1) Seats shall be reserved for—

(a) the Muslim community and the Scheduled Castes in the Legislature of every State for the time being specified in Part I or Part III of the First Schedule;

(b) the Scheduled Tribes (except the Scheduled Tribes in the autonomous districts of Assam) in the Legislature of every State for the time being specified in Part I of the First Schedule; and

(c) the Indian Christian community in the Legislatures of the States of Madras and Bombay.

Explanation: In this clause and in clause (3) of this article the expression "Legislature" means, where the Legislature is bicameral, the Lower House of the Legislature.

(ii) that for the clause (3) of article, the following clause be substituted.

(3) The number of seats reserved for any community in the Legislature of any State under clause (1) of this article shall bear, as nearly as may be,

the same proportion to the total number of seats in the Legislature as the population of the community in the State bears to the total population of the State.

Explanation: All the Scheduled Castes in a State shall be deemed to be a single community for the purposes of this clause and so also all the Scheduled Tribes in a State.

Giving reasons for bringing in these amendments by the Drafting Committee, the Constitutional Adviser noted that the Special Committee was of opinion that the provisions relating to reservation of seats for minorities should be made applicable to all elections to the Legislature or where there were two Houses of the Legislature to the Lower House of the Legislature in all States including the States in Part III of the First Schedule and these amendments were suggested to give effect to the views of the Special Committee.

In October, 1948, the Drafting Committee decided to sponsor its amendments.[5]

But before the Drafting Committee could sponsor its amendments to Draft Article 294 for consideration of the Constituent Assembly, a momentous event took place. That was in relation to reservation of seats for the minorities. The Constituent Assembly, agreeing with the proposal of the Advisory Committee, decided on May 25-26, 1949, to do away with all reservations for the minorities except that reservations be provided only for the Scheduled Castes and Scheduled Tribes which would be operative for ten years. This has been discussed in Chapter 15.

In view of this changed decision of the Constituent Assembly in the matter of reservation of seats relating to minorities, Ambedkar moved a revised Article 294 on August 24, 1949, immediately after the Assembly had adopted the provision relating to reservation of seats for the Scheduled Castes and Scheduled Tribes in the House of People. (Article 330). The most important feature of the revised draft of Article 294 was that reservations were now confined to State Assemblies communally to Scheduled Castes and Scheduled Tribes, and territorially to the autonomous districts of Assam, the number of seats reserved was proportionate to the population; no person who was not a member of a Scheduled Tribe of an autonomous district of Assam would be eligible for election from that district (except from the constituency representing the cantonment and municipality of Shillong); and reservation of seats for Scheduled Castes and Scheduled Tribes was provided in all the States mentioned in Part I and Part III of the First Schedule (that is, all the Provinces and all the Indian States except those constituted into Chief Commissioners' Provinces).

Since the Assembly had adopted a similar provision relating to the House of People, there was no obstruction to the passage of this article which was not even much deliberated upon. Only six members, apart from Ambedkar, participated in the discussion. Though no amendment was moved there was criticism against this provision. Khandekar a leader of the Scheduled Castes, thought that the reservation that had been provided would not do any good to the Harijans. It would have been helpful to them if the reserved seats were given in constituencies where they were in a majority. He also felt that the conditions of the Harijans could not improve within a span of the next 10 years. Tyagi more or less repeated his previous argument that the policy of reservation would promote separatist tendency in the country and that only the elite amongst the Scheduled Castes would reap the benefit of this policy. Kishori Mohan Tripathi wanted to know as to how reservation of seats would apply to areas, like Chattisgarh, having an overwhelming majority of tribal people. Naziruddin Ahmad and Rev. J.J. Nichols-Roy supported this article while Brajeshwar Prasad lent qualified support to it.

This is what they actually stated in the Assembly:

The Honourable Dr. B.R. Ambedkar

Sir, I move:

That for Article 294, the following be substituted :—

'294(1) Seats shall be reserved for the Scheduled Castes and the Scheduled Tribes, except the Scheduled Tribes in the tribal areas of Assam, in the Legislative Assembly of every State for the time being specified in Part I or Part III of the First Schedule.

(2) Seats shall be reserved also for the autonomous districts in the Legislative Assembly of the State of Assam.

(3) The number of seats reserved for the Scheduled Castes or the Scheduled Tribes in the Legislative Assembly of any State under clause (I) of this article shall bear, as nearly as may be, the same proportion to the total number of seats in the Assembly as the population of the Scheduled Castes in the State, or of the scheduled tribes in the State or part of the state, as the case may be, in respect of which seats are so reserved bears to the total population of the State.

(4) The number of seats reserved for an autonomous district in the Legislative Assembly of the State of Assam shall bear to the total number of seats in that Assembly a proportion not less than the population of the district bears to the total population of the State.

(5) The constituencies for the seats reserved for any autonomous district of the State of Assam shall not comprise any area outside that district except in the case of the constituency comprising the cantonment and the municipality of Shillong.

(6) No person who is not a member of a Scheduled Tribe of any autonomous district of the State of Assam shall be eligible for election to the Legislative Assembly of the State from any constituency of that district except from the constituency comprising the cantonment and municipality of Shillong.

This article is exactly the same as the original article as it stood in the Draft Constitution. The only amendment is that the provision for the reservation of seats for the Muslims and the Christians has been omitted from clause (1) of Article 294. That is in accordance with the decision taken in this Assembly on that matter.

Shri Brajeshwar Prasad

Mr. President, Sir, I rise to give my qualified support to the article, Sir, I am convinced in my own mind that the Scheduled Castes do not form a minority in this country. They are not distinct or separate in any way whatsoever from the rest of the people of this country. Numerically they form a considerable section of the population. Moreover, I am convinced that the problems confronting the Scheduled Castes are in no way of a political character. The problems are primarily educational and of an economic character. They are of a cultural character. We want to raise the cultural level of these down-trodden and oppressed people. I do not see how their representation in the legislatures will in any way alter the material and the moral level of these people. Representations here and there will provide opportunities for a handful of leaders but it will not in any way materially alter their economic or their educational level. Better lay down in the Constitution that a fixed percentage in the budget, both Central and Provincial, shall be exclusively devoted for their welfare. I am a lover of those people who have been suffering and my whole attempt is to somehow liquidate their backwardness. I do not want by any back-door method to suppress or to deprive them of their just rights. If you want to give them representation, by all means give them. I am not opposed to their representation as such but I feel that this will be inadequate it will not solve their problems. I want that for the tribals and for the Scheduled Castes provision must be made in the Constitution, not in the directive principles. It should be laid down clearly in express terms that educational and free education shall be imparted to them. There is only one country in the world where free education is imparted up to the university stage and that is Ceylon. I hope in the future with the growth and development of our economic resources it will be possible for us to provide the same facilities to our citizens. I want that for the tribals and for the Harijans provision must be made in the Constitution that free agricultural lands should be given to them. If we cannot give any one of these, I am quite clear in my own mind that by giving them a few seats here and there, their economic condition and their educational level will in no way be improved.

A friend of mine, an honourable Member of this House, has said that there are people who are opposed to the reservation of seats on the ground that it promotes fissiparous tendencies. I have very great regard and very great respect for that honourble gentleman. I know that he is a representative of the tribal people. I think he will realize that it promotes fissiparous tendencies and weakens the foundation of the State. I am a great friend of these people, I want to help them. I am prepared to incur the displeasure of those who are closely associated with me on this question. May I ask how 50 persons in a legislature where there will be 200 or 300 non-tribals, achieve anything substantial for the tribals? They will raise a terrible hue and cry but nothing substantial will be achieved. All those things that we consider to be necessary and desirable for the economic advancement and the moral uplift of the tribals should be decided here and now and laid down in the Constitution.

I would like at this stage to raise the point which I had raised a few days back. We have not decided the constitution of the tribal people. Now to say here that seats shall be reserved for the tribal people in the legislature is rather premature. It is quite possible that when we discuss the Schedules relating to the tribal areas, we evolve a Constitution entirely different from what has been proposed.

Lastly, I would say that I am opposed to the introduction of the principle of elections in the tribal areas. This will disrupt the life of the tribal people. It is a fissiparous tendency and they have got a system of society which is entirely different from ours. It is more or less a corporate society which emphasises group consciousness. The principle of elections emphasises individualism and the principle of competition. The tribal people being ignorant, being backward, being down-trodden, will be exploited by powerful groups during the times of election. I hold that the principle of election is not at all suitable to these people. With these words, I support the article.

Mr. Naziruddin Ahmad :

...The only point I wanted to submit was that a few of the sentiments given expression to in this House should be objected to. I must make my position perfectly clear. I was a member of a minority community. I have now shaken off that minority feeling and I speak as a perfectly independent man having no axe to grind. I feel that the Scheduled Castes and the Scheduled Tribes some times require protection. My honourable Friend Mr.Brajeshwar Prasad remarked that a few members selected in the legislative assemblies will not improve their lot. I seriously contest this proposition. Theirs is a life of misery and exploitation. They are exploited on account of their ignorance and backwardness. If a few members are selected by them, they will ventilate their grievances, will focus public attention on their grievances and difficulties and that would lead to their redress. If a few seats given to the Scheduled Castes will not improve their lot, I ask how can a large number of members coming from the non-Scheduled classes be of any service to them? That argument should be of no avail. I believe this representation means representation of the weak. It is for their protection. My honourable Friend's contention that the benefits of democracy cannot be given to the Scheduled Castes, I should think, must also be contested. Democracy is a blessing. Democracy alone can lift these unfortunate Scheduled Castes and Scheduled Tribes from their miserable lot.

I do not desire to say anything more. I fully support the article. But, my honourable Friend who preceded me while trying to support the article actually advanced arguments which went against it.

Shri Krishorimohan Tripathi (C.P. & Berar States):

Mr. President, Sir, I have just come to seek clarification from Dr. Ambedkar.

The proposed Article 294 says in clause (1):

"Seats shall be reserved for the Scheduled Castes and the Scheduled Tribes, except the Scheduled Tribes in the tribal areas of Assam, in the Legislative Assembly of every State for the time being specified in Part I or Part III of the First Schedule".

When I look at Part III of the First Scheduled, in division B, it is stated, "All other Indian States which were within the Dominion of India immediately before the commencement of this Constitution". Most of these States have now either formed into Unions or have merged into the provinces. Among the latter category come some of the States which I represent here. These States taken together and known as the Chattisgarh States, have a tribal population of roughly 50 per cent., that is, about 14 lakhs out of the total population of nearly 30 lakhs. I want to know from Dr. Ambedkar as to how reservation of seats will apply to these States which have now merged in the province of C.P. I will quote, for example, the State of Bastar; it has a tribal population of 4,78,970 out of a total population of 6,33,888. The State of Udaipur which forms part of the newly formed district of Raigarh contains 72 per cent, of tribals out of its total population. The State of Jashpur contains 73 per cent of tribals out of its population. These States have got tribal population in contiguous areas. Each State by itself can claim reservation for itself. I would therefore like to know from Dr. Ambedkar as to how these States are to be treated in respect of reservation of seats as also other advantages accruing to tribals under this Constitution.

The Honourable Rev. J.J.M. Nichols-Roy:

Mr. President, I rise to support this article as moved

by Dr. Ambedkar. I had given notice of an amendment; but that amendment has been included in this amendment which has been moved by Dr. Ambedkar. I am very glad that that has been incorporated here.

I just want to make a statement in regard to the statement made by Mr. Brajeshwar Prasad regarding tribal people. There are different kinds of tribal people. In Assam, we have got tribals who are very democratic. These democratic institutions which we have here in this Constitution will suit them very well. They are used to this kind of democratic institutions; I do not know where they are. Whatever I have known, the tribal people are very democratic-minded. There may be Scheduled Castes and Scheduled Tribes in some other parts of India where the people are very down-trodden and not looked after, and democratic institutions may not suit them. As far as the tribals are concerned, as Mr. Jaipal Singh has already stated, they are very democratic, and in Assam they are so. For that reason I believe that this right and privilege given to them of sharing in the democratic instituons in the whole of India is a very good thing indeed.

Shri H. J. Khandekar (C.P. & Berar: General):

Mr. President I stand to support Article 294 moved by Dr. Ambedkar. This article provides for reservation of seats for the Scheduled Castes and Scheduled Tribes. As a member of Scheduled Castes, I would like to submit that the reservation which is being provided for us is no favour to us. The members of the Scheduled Castes have for thousands of years, suffered cruelties and oppression in various forms at the hands of their brethren belonging to castes other than their own. Now reservation is being provided for us as a compensation for the atrocities we have suffered, and therefore I do not deem this provision as any great favour to us. The article that was originally drafted to provide for reservation, contained provisions for the reservation of seats to Muslims also, on the basis of their population. But for some reasons this provision has now been dropped. I think reservation ought to have been provided for Muslims as well. Though, I do not belong to the Muslims community, I would like to say that from the political point of view.......

Mr. President :

I think, you should not take up this question because it has already been discussed.

Shri H.J. Khandekar:

I would like to say only one sentence in this connection.

Mr. President:

Even one sentence will re-open the matter.

Shri H.J. Khandekar:

I hold that politically it was a mistake. However, I shall not touch that question as I do not belong to the community concerned. To resume my point, reservation is being provided to Harijans only for ten years. But from the experience that I have of the Scheduled Castes and other communities of the country, I feel certain that the condition of the Harijan cannot improve within the next ten years. Continously from 1927 to the time of his death Mahatma Gandhi made every effort physically, mentally and financially, for the uplift of the Harijans, but even within a period of twenty or thirty years no appreciable improvement as was expected, could be brought about in their conditions. I am unable, therefore, to accept that within a period of ten years for which reservation is being provided for them, a complete reform or change can be brought about in their condition.

I, therefore, think that if, along with reservation in respect of Legislatures, a similar reservation is provided in respect of Local bodies—municipalities, and District Boards too, it will help much to improve their lot. But no mention of such a provision has been made here. If you look at the conditions obtaining in each and every province of the country, you will find that politically their condition, even today, is very deplorable. If any Harijan stands for election to any local body and tries to secure the votes of the Caste Hindus, I have myself been witness to it, he is never able to get their votes and is unable therefore to get elected. As for the future, I am sure no candidate belonging to Scheduled Castes or Scheduled Tribes would ever be returned to these bodies in elections. This is the state of affairs obtaining in our country today, and it is in view of this state of affairs that you have accepted our demand for the reservation of seats. I think if you provide reservation in respect of local bodies also, Harijans will be able to benefit considerably.

Secondly, if any one thinks that the provision of reservation would cause an all-round improvement among the Harijans, I would say, he is sadly mistaken. There are many avenues in which Harijans will have to make improvement. They have to make much progress and require much help to be able to come on a par with other communities of the country. Reservation of seats alone will not do much. We were exploited in the past; and we are being exploited to day and even in future, after the Constitution is pased, we should be exploited by members of the other castes. Divisions will be created amongst us. In a constituency where caste Hindu voters have a majority over Harijans if one section of the Scheduled Castes, say for example chamars have a majority over the other Scheduled Castes, our caste Hindu friends will not enter into an alliance with the chamars but they will support the minorities of the Scheduled Castes in the constituency and thus suppress the majority section of the Scheduled Castes. This will be the ultimate outcome of this provision of reservation. This is bound to happen because the Harijan voters are not in majority in any constituency.

What I mean to say is this, that this provision of reservation will be helpful to Harijans only when they are given reserved seats in constituencies where they are in a majority. Otherwise in the name of Harijans, showboys only would be returned to Legislatures as is the case today in the Central and Provincial Legislatures. So by this provision, I am afraid you are not going to do any good to Harijans; rather you would be doing them harm.

I want to tell you one thing more, and it is, that you should provide for the same type of reservation in the

Cabinet as you have provided in the Provincial legislatures so as to enable the Harijans to promote their advancement. However, I have seen it and you might have also seen it, and it is a matter of regret that whenever the interest of a caste Hindu and that of a Scheduled Caste man clashes, it is the Scheduled Caste man who suffers. This is the situation in the country and no sensible man can deny it. To give an instance, if you look at the cabinet of a province where twenty-four to twenty-five per cent of the people are Harijans you will find that there is only one Harijan in the cabinet. But it is a matter of regret that in a province where the caste Hindus, that is to say the Brahmins, are in a minority and in such a small minority as two per cent of the population, ten ministers out of twelve are Brahmins. Would you not consider this an injustice?

Pandit Balkrishna Sharma (United Provinces : General):

Down with the Brahmins !

Shri H.J. Khandekar:

That you can say that non-Brahmins can say. Very well, they can be downed.

I mean to say that if you had provided for reservation for Harijans in the cabinet it would have prevented the injustice that is being perpetrated on the Harijans and Scheduled Tribes. It is a matter of regret that that article is no longer under discussion. Some people have remarked that barring the seats reserved for Harijans, they should not be allowed to contest the election for other general seats. But I want to tell you that if you do not allow the Harijans to contest the elections for general seats, you will never be able to bridge the gulf that has been created between the Harijans and the caste Hindus.

Mr. President:

As you were not present in the House you could not listen to the previous debate. Had you listened to it, you would not have said such things.

Shri H.J. Khandekar:

I was not present and I did not listen to it. But I want to say that if we have to level the breach between us and the Caste Hindus, the same treatment should be meted out to us as is asked for by us. However, the treatment that is meted out to us is one that suits people blinded with self-interest. If I cite examples where self-interest was sught to be promoted, it will take the whole of the day and even to- morrow. I do not want to threaten anybody but I want to tell the caste Hindus in this House and outside that they should remember one thing. It is that if you want to atone for the atrocities perpertated by you on the Harijans, you should bring them up to your level by granting them whatever they ask for. If you do not do this, the Harijans will intensify the movements they have launched for their progress, which you do not desire they should make, and through these movements they shall effect an improvement in their lot though I cannot predict what may happen in the country as a result thereof. I am not holding out any threat. Members of parties seeking to exploit the situation for their own benefit move about amongst the Harijans of India and propagate such views as might go against the interests of this country. I warn you of this situation and urge you to grant to Harijans whatever facilities they ask for to come to your level.

I shall place before you one more example. Hundreds of Harijans applied recently for Indian Administrative Service and Indian Police Service and they were interviewed. But it is to be regretted that none of them was selected for the posts. The reason stated is that none of them was fit for the posts. You are responsible for our being unfit today. We were suppressed for thousands of years. You engaged us in your service to serve your own ends and suppressed us to such an extent that neither our minds nor our bodies and nor even our hearts work, nor are we able to march forward. This is the position. You have reduced us to such a position and then you say that we are not fit and that we have not secured the requisite marks. How can we secure them?

You just look at the position in which we are placed. The condition of our village boys is very bad today. They do not get the facilities enjoyed by the sons of well-placed men. How can you then expect our boys to compete with those who enjoy all sorts of facilities. You do not know under what conditions our students receive education in schools. The Government does not show any consideration to them. I know of a Harijan boy of C.P. who lives in Delhi. He studies in the Pusa Institute. He is a poor boy and his parents are dead. He is in such circumstances that for the last one month he has had no money to pay his fees. His monthly expenses amount to Rs. 105/ including the sum of Rs. 75/- which he has to pay towards fees etc. every month. A week back he received a notice that he should deposit his fees for being permitted to prosecute his studies. The only recourse for this poor boy, who has no money to meet the expenses of food, clothes and fees, is either to beg or to steal. He has no other remedy. The other alternative before him is to leave the school but then he would be ruined completely. Yet it did not strike the mind of any government official that either he should be exempted from paying fee or some other kind of help might be given to him. This boy submitted many applications to the government, but as yet nobody has replied to him. Under such troubles and hardships how can that boy compete with the other boys who have all facilities available to them?

You have given us privileges for ten years. After that period you will tell us that you helped us in all respects. I would then ask you, in what respect you helped us. Will you prepare some scheme for the uplift of Harijans in these ten years? Have you prepared any scheme for education of Harijans up to this day? Have provincial governments earmarked some money for the uplift of the Harijans?

Mr. President:

A period of ten years has been provided in this article. Other things are covered by other articles. You can say these things then. At present I shall not allow you to take up this issue.

Shri H.J. Khandekar:

I mean that our students do not get those facilities which other students get and hence they cannot stand in competition with others. The government has never thought of our uplift. Very often we have requested that to safeguard our interests there should be at least one Harijan Minister appointed in every province and one at the centre also who should work for the uplift of the Harijans. Had such Ministers been appointed in every province and Centre, who could have thought over the difficulties of the Harijans, there would have been a lot of improvement by this time. In every province such resolutions were passed and were sent to the Government by the Harijans from all the places requesting that these resolutions should be given effect to, but it is very painful to note that those persons have not as yet received a written acknowledgement of the receipt of their resolutions. This is the value and importance attached to the uplift of the Harijans. Such an attitude reveals that you want to please them with sweet words. In India there are many who talk sweetly and the Harijans are very easily taken in. They serve their selfish purpose. Except Mahatma Gandhi and ten or twenty other persons there is none to think of the uplift of the Harijans in the true sense.

Mr. President:

You are talking of the provinces.

Shri H.J. Khandekar:

I am talking of many provinces, and whatever I say is based on my personal experience. I have got an experience of about twenty or twenty-five years. I have been witnessing even up to this day that nothing good had been done for the Harijans. You have appointed Harijan ministers in the provinces but they are all your men. Then article about reservation provided by you is not going to safeguard our interests. In this way all the problems of Harijans would not be solved.

Mr. President:

It appears that you have been continuously absent.

Shri H.J. Khandekar:

I was not absent from this Assembly for a day, I was present all along even if someone marks me absent. I was here in my seat all the while.

Mr. President:

But I would like to tell you that you can speak on the question which is under consideration. You cannot be permitted to discuss the question of all the Harijans. Nothing would be gained by that. If you are a member of any provincial assembly you can raise this question there. Others also, who get an opportunity of speaking here, should restrict themselves to this article only. It is useless to talk of other things here.

Shri H.J. Khandekar:

I am speaking on this article. I want to submit that I do not believe that the reservation that has been provided will do any good to the Harijans. I say that this reservation can bring no good to the Harijans. But the painful aspect of the problem is that those, who believe in the uplift of the Harijans and also know that they suffer in many ways, are in favour of this article. But I feel that this article of reservation provides no scope for the uplift of the Harijans.

There are differences amongst our sub-castes. This article provides scope for creating all kinds of differences amongst the sub-castes of the Harijans. It has got a scope for ousting the Harijans who are a majority in a province. Every community will have some percentage. You know that there is one community in majority in Bombay. None has paid any attention to it. There are ten or twelve persons who can enter the legislature of Bombay province through reservation. Those members of the minority community who come from that fold will be ousted. Up to this present day there are only two or three men of the minority community in the Bombay Legislature. Even now there are members of such minority communities who are not even two per cent of the Harijans. I submit that when this article is implemented the Harijans would move still more backward rather than forward. I submit to you, Sir, that it would neither be beneficial to the country nor the Congress government nor even to the Harijans.

That is what I mean and after explaining it I support the article and resume my seat.

Shri Mahavir Tyagi (United Provinces: General):

Mr. President, I rise to lend my support to this article. I would like to submit, that the question of reservation for the Scheduled Castes was raised in this land during the British regime in pursuit of a policy which was then followed by them. By raising the same question in respect of Muslims the Britishers created a division between the Hindus and Muslims of the country—a policy which ultimately culminated in the creation of Pakistan. 'Divide and rule' was the policy of the alien rulers in India in those days. It was in pursuit of this policy that in the Round Table Conference the English politicians made attempts for the first time to establish the system of separate representation for the Scheduled Castes by creating a division between them and the caste Hindus. At this, Mahatma Gandhi declared his resolve to fast unto death if attempts were made to create another party of Scheduled Castes in India. As a result of this, they could not be separated from the Hindus and the system of separate electorates could not be adopted for them as was done for the Muslims. But seats were reserved for them on the basis of their population. Mahatma Gandhi settled this question with Dr. Ambedkar and gave an award which offered the Scheduled Castes more seats than what were given to them by the Round Table Conference. It was then felt that justice must be done to the Scheduled Castes.

The statement made by my Friend Mr. Khandekar that prior to this award no representative of the Scheduled Castes was ever elected, is a fact. According to the agreement reached between Mahatmaji and Dr. Ambedkar in regard to this question, representatives of the Scheduled Castes were to be elected by a common electorate but a certain number of seats were reserved for them and the number of seats so reserved was greater than what was given to them in the Round Table Conference. This agreement, has since then been in operation.

Now when after fourteen years we are again going to decide that seats will be reserved for them, we must not lose sight of the experience gained in the past in this respect. I would like to draw the attention of the house to the past experience with regard to this question. The reservation of seats has benefited us in many ways. Firstly, it has created an awakening among the Scheduled Castes; it has brought among them a spirit of self-progress: it has made others to realise that the members of the Scheduled Castes are citizens, equal to them and that they too should be entitled to all the rights that citizen should have. It has also developed amongst us a habit to sit together and decide the future of the country and to discuss the important and grave problems of the country mutually. This helps a lot in our affairs.

But we have to see what will in fact be the advantage of such a reservation. My Friend Mr. Khandekar has just now complained that the majority community does not allow minority community to send its representatives. This is a fact. In this respect I too belong to a minority community. The strength of my community in my district consists of myself, my daughters and a policeman. They are all five in number. Still, whenever there is an election in my district, I am returned. But this is not the general rule. Those who are not elected on the basis of service to the country, are returned on the strength of their relations. Whoever has a large number of relations, is returned. In the district of Meerut, where the Jats are in a majority, only a Jat candidate can come out successful. A Brahmin cannot be elected there. Therefore, this is not a question of Scheduled Castes only but is so in the case of other Castes also. This, of course, is very unfortunate for this country. Even if we confine our attention to the

Scheduled Castes alone we find that they also suffer from the same malady. Twenty seats have been reserved for the Scheduled Castes in our province and there are perhaps eight seats for them in the Punjab. If we undertake a study of the caste composition of the members filling the seats and if Shriyut Khandekar does the same in regard to the seats reserved for the Scheduled Castes all over India it will be found that excepting two or three Mahars, including my Friends Mr. Khandekar and Dr. Ambedkar, the majority of seats have gone to Chamars because among the Scheduled Castes they have a majority. If you look at the Ministers also, you will see that excepting Dr. Ambedkar there is no Scheduled Caste Minister who is a non-Chamar.

Some Honourable Members:

In Bihar, there are

Shri Mahavir Tyagi:

Yes, excepting Bihar, in all other places these people alone are ministers. May I ask whether the four hundred communities are taking advantage of the Scheduled Castes seats? Out of these four hundred communities only two or three communities are taking advantage of the seats reserved for Scheduled Castes. In Bombay the Mahars are in a majority but owing to joint elections some other members of the community have been returned and this has given cause to Mr. Khandekar to complain. I am opposed to this type of mentality. The Scheduled Castes have been formed by combining together four to five hundred communities but if a majority section and a minority section are found among them, it would mean that the seats reserved for Scheduled Castes would go to the majority section. Even if we reserve a number of seats in India for the Chamars the result would be the same as we have achieved by reserving seats for Scheduled Castes because in our province the Chamars are in a majority and they alone get the majority of votes. Every party too puts forward a candidate on the consideration whether he has a large number of relations, so that matters may be facilitated. Therefore all the Scheduled Caste people do not benefit by reservation. There are five hundred to six hundred Scheduled Castes and we are not familiar even with their names. Indeed, it will never be posssible for them to get representation in the Assembly.

This means that we provide seats for Scheduled Castes to benefit those who have a large number of relations. The advantage of joint elections, to which my Friend Mr. Khandekar objects, would be that caste Hindus would be able to extend justice to those Scheduled Castes people who are in a minority. They would realise that the Chamars have a majority in the district and that those people who are in a minority have no chance of winning an election, although their candidates are well qualified for being returned to the Legislative Assembly. They would help these candidates and make up the deficiency of votes in their favour. What I mean to say is this, that the advantage of other caste people participating in the elections for Scheduled Caste seats would be that besides those who are in a majority among the scheduled Caste, even those who are in a minority among them would be able to fight elections and win them. This is my reply to the objection that has been raised. We should keep in view the interests of all the Scheduled Castes specified in the Schedule and not only of those which are in a majority.

I would like to draw the attention of the House to another aspect of this problem. The reservation that has been provided for the Scheduled Castes uptill now, is producing, the effect; among others, of the formation of a separate kind of group of the Scheduled Castes. And if this practice is continued for some time more the leaders of the Scheduled Castes will act in the same way as the Muslim Leaguers did. They can become ministers and members of the Assembly as long as the reservation of their seats is continued. Under such circumstances the separatist tendency cannot be brought to an end in this country. I, therefore, feel that there should be no kind of reservation.

In my province of U.P., the Panchayat Election has just been held. It may be a surprise to the House that the election of these Panchayats was a joint one. In our eastern districts more than half of the Panchayats are such wherein the members of the Scheduled Castes have been elected as Sarpanch. This is the result of the Gram Panchayat election held through the government and the members of the Scheduled castes elected as Sarpanch. It is wrong to think that the minorities are not enjoying the privileges in the political spheres. Had I been a leader of a minority community I could have very easily demonstrated to you that in a House consisting of one hundred members I could form a ministry with the backing of my twenty followers in the legislature. I hold this belief because I am confident that the remaining eighty members of the House would be divided into a number of parties and I could, therefore, lend my support to one of these parties and thereby enable it to be dominant in the Legislature. By this bargain I could easily obtain the premiership for myself. The fact is that all the world over the ministers enter into such bargains and are thereby able to secure their ends. There are different groups in the majority, and the minority always secures advantages for itself by favouring one group or the other. It is therefore wrong to say that the minority group does not secure advantage for itself. In the same way the minority pushes its candidate in general elections too and it is a clear misunderstanding that the minorities cannot take part in election.

My own idea was that there should be no reservation. On the other hand, the provision of reservation makes me feel that there has been a litle of injustice to the Sikhs. They have been living separate for many years and this right to reservation has been denied to them. Similarly Christians have also been denied this right. All the other minorities generously accepted to give up this right. I therefore fail to see why this reservation should be kept. I believe that even without reservation the members of the Scheduled Castes can gain seats in proportion to their population. You will see after ten years that they will gain seats in a greater proportion. I would like to repeat it again that in election importance should be attached to the capabilities of the candidate and not to the caste of the candidate. It should be considered as to who has served the country in a better way and who can represent the country in a better way. Unfortunately people having good knowledge of English gain success. It is a misfortune that nobody thinks for those Brahmans who are even poorer than the members of the Scheduled Castes. Similarly there are Kashtriyas, Rajputs and some persons and families among all the other castes, who do not get any opportunity to gain education and wealth. There is no provision for them in this Constitution. They are poor and illiterate and can neither become representatives nor ministers. Unfortunately the conditions are such that those, who have English education and have adopted English methods, are the representatives of India. Only such persons can gain representation. It pains me greatly that there is no scope in this country for the illiterates. I say that until the rein of administration is held by non-English-knowing illiterate persons and until a majority of illterate persons comes in Government Service, India would not be able to feel the glow of freedom. The educated persons are demoralised. And in the present regime the administration of India is in the hands of those who are devoted to English culture and language and are demoralised. Just as with other castes, in Scheduled Castes also there is no opportunity for their real representatives even after the removal of the British regime. Persons like Dr. Ambedkar, who are capable in all respects, will come forward from the Scheduled Castes. To what Scheduled Castes does Dr. Ambedkar belong to, who is the Pandit of the Pandits? He only takes advantage of the Scheduled Castes. At the same time Dr. Ambedkar can come into the Legislature from any part of the country by virtue of his own merits.

I therefore, see no advantage, as I have already stated, in reservation. The true representatives do not enter the Legislatures even through reservation. This may be attained only when we change our mentality, and elect persons according to our old Indian custom based on honesty, ability, conscientiousness, service to humanity and intelligence. We have been so much entangled in the English language that one who has attained even an alphabetical knowledge of this language attains the right of being the representative of the country. Even after saying so much I feel that this provision is good. They will get opportunities for ten years more and after that period it will automatically come to an end and there would be joint elections.[6]

No other member participated in the discussion. Since no amendment was moved on this article, which as the President of the Constitutent Assembly pointed out, was "one of the articles which represent the decisions arrived at a previous session and I do not think much discussion is necessary", Dr. Ambedkar did not say anything in reply. The President of the Assembly thereafter put the revised article before the Assembly which adopted it.[7]

At the revision stage this draft article was renumbered as Article 332.

Once the Constitutent Assembly had opted in favour of reservation of seats in the House of People only for the Scheduled Castes and the Scheduled Tribes, there was no other alternative but to provide for representation of the Scheduled Castes and the Scheduled Tribes in the State Legislative Assemblies in proportion to their population as well. In the Constitutions of other countries there are provisions for representation of political minorities so that the political views of every segment of population are reflected in the Legislatures. There are also provisions for representation of religious and racial minorites but in no other country there are provisions for reservation of seats for a substantial section of people of the same religious community on the basis of the strength of their castist population. As the institution of caste is a unique feature of the Indian social system so the representation of a large number of people belonging to two religious communities—Hindus and Sikhs—in the legislatures is a unique feature of the Indian Constitution. In no other country such a system exists.

Identity of communities on any basis in political arena gives rise to a sense of separateness which in course of time tends to create a chasm which is very difficult to bridge. At least this is the lesson of history so far as the Indian sub-continent is concerned. Separate representation of religious communities ultimately led to the partition of India. But the framers refused to draw lessons even from the immediate past history and in their collective wisdom provided for separate representation for a section of people which have tended to foster divisiveness and separateness in the Indian body politic. If the idea of the framers was to inculcate the spirit of togetherness and belonging on community basis, the composition of which rested solely on the Government and not on the society, this sort of constitutional provision is, no doubt, the ideal one. But the fallacy is that they did it in the garb of obliterating hierarchical differentiations in the society. They put forward a thesis that unless representation was accorded to this section of people their uplift would be at peril. They conveniently overlooked the fact that in a democracy with adult franchise, once the people elect their representative he is supposed to be above all partisan, sectarian and communal interests and is expected to work for all sections of people, within the parametre of party policy and programme, irrespective of caste, creed and sex. If uplift of a section of population was dependant on their separate representation in the legislatures, local bodies etc., on the basis of their population strength, all countries would have emulated the Indian model. In one breath it was claimed that social disabilities had to be removed at all cost and in the next moment steps were taken to perpetuate it, so much so that the social disability instead of a debilitating factor has become a boon in disguise for the power-brokers to hold their reign supreme over the gullible people. This policy was evolved primarily to cash on the existing social differentiations. That it continued to thrive by widening the chasm and cleavages and prolonging the differences in the body politic is brone out by the fact that that this 'temporary' provision has become a 'permanent' feature of our constitutional system for obvious reasons. The situtation has been so created that it would be difficult for the people to wriggle out from the vicious atmosphere of caste politics, for all time to come and building of a unified nation free from caste or sectarian motivation would be a far cry.

Notes and References

1. Rao, *op. cit.*, Vol. III, pp. 50-51.
2. *Ibid.*, pp. 433-34.
3. *Ibid.*, pp. 477-78.
4. *Ibid.*, pp. 630-31.
5. *Ibid.*, Vol. IV, pp. 357-60.
6. *CAD*, Vol. IX, dated 24-8-49, pp. 663-73.
7. *Ibid.*, dated 24-8-49, pp. 673-74.

17

Reservation of Seats and Special Representation to Cease after ten years (Fifty years) (Article 334)

In chapter 11 we have observed that the Minority Sub-Committee in its report submitted on July 27, 1947 had stated that as a general principle there should be reservation of seats for different recognised minorities in the various Legislatures for ten years, the position to be reconsidered at the end of that period. This recommendation of the Minority Sub-Committee was endorsed by the Advisory Committee in its report sent to the President of the Constituent Assembly on August 8, 1947. This report of the Advisory Committee was adopted by the Constituent Assembly after due deliberations on August 27 and 28, 1947.

This decision of the Constituent Assembly on continuance of the reservation for a period of ten years was incorporated in the Draft Constitution prepared by the Constitutional Adviser in October, 1947 as a proviso to Clause 232 occurring in part XIII—Amendment of the Constitution in the following terms:

> Provided further that the provisions of this Constitution relating to the reservation of seats for the Muslim Community, the Scheduled Castes, the Sched-

> uled Tribes, the Indian Christian community or the Sikh community either in the Federal Parliament or in any Provincial Legislature shall not be amended within the period of ten years from the commencement of this Constitution and shall cease to have effect on the expiration of that period unless continued in operation by an amendment of the Constitution in the manner provided in this section.[1]

The Drafting Committee revised this Clause on February 6, 1948,[2] February 9 [3] and February 10, 1948 [4] and ultimately included it in Part XVI relating to Amendment of the Constitution as an independent Article— Article 305 as follows:

> Notwithstanding anything contained in Article 304 of this Constitution, the provisions of this Constitution relating to the reservation of seats for the Muslims, the Scheduled Castes, the Scheduled Tribes or the Indian Christians either in Parliament or in the Legislature of any State for the time being specified in part I of the First Schedule shall not be amended during a period of ten years from the commencement of this Constitution and shall cease to have effect on the expiration of that period unless continued in operation by an amendment of the Constitution.[5]

When this Draft Constitution was circulated eliciting comments, suggestions, etc., many suggestions were received on this Draft Article.

K. Santhanam, M. Ananthasayanam Ayyangar, Shrimati G. Durgabai and T.T. Krishnamachari suggested that the words "the Muslims", "or the Indian Christians" and "unless continued in operation by an amendment of the Constitutions" be deleted. To this suggestion, the Constitutional Adviser commented that this amendment also involved a question of policy. If this amendment was accepted, then it should be redrafted as follows:

(1) In Article 305, for the words "the Muslims, the Scheduled Castes, the Scheduled Tribes or the Indian Christians" the words "The Scheduled Castes or the Scheduled Tribes" be substituted.

(2) In Article 305, the words "unless continued in operation by an amendment of the Constitution" be omitted.

S. Nagappa suggested that for the words "for the time being specified in part I" the words "for the time being specified in Parts I, II and III" and for the words" amended during a period of ten years" the words "amended during a period of fifteen years be substituted." The Constitutional Adviser noted that the Special Committee was of opinion that the provisions relating to reservation of seats for minorities should be made applicable to all elections to the Legislatures, or, in the case of Legislatures having two Houses, to the Lower Houses of the Legislatures, of all States including the States in Part III of the First Schedule. Accordingly, the first part of this amendment might be accepted, but it should be redrafted as follows:

> In Article 305, the words "for the time being specified in Part I of the first Schedule" be omitted.

He further mentioned that the second part of the amendment which sought to extend the period for which the reservation should remain in force from ten years to fifteen years involved a question of policy.

H.J. Khandekar, Yashwant Rai, Chandrika Ram, S. Nagappa, V.C. Kesava Rao, Dharam Prakash, T. Channaya and Shrimati Dakshyani Velayudhan suggested that for the words "Part I" the words "Parts I, II and III" and for the words "ten years" the words "fifteen years" be substituted respectively. The Constitutional Adviser's comment on this amendment was that it was the same as the earlier amendment of Nagappa.

P.M. Velayudapani suggested that for the words "ten years" the words "fifteen years" be substituted and the words "and shall cease to have effect on the expiration of that period unless continued in operation by an amendment of the Constitution" be deleted. The Constitutional Adviser pointed out that Article 305 followed the decision of the Advisory Committee on Minority Rights as adopted by the Constituent Assembly. Both the Drafting Committee and the Special Committee had considered this amendment and had expressed the view that the amendment proposed involved a question of policy the decision of which should be left to the Constituent Assembly.

To the suggestion of Tajamul Husain that Article 305 be deleted, the Constitutional Adviser noted that this amendment involved a question of policy.

The Drafting Committee decided that the words "for the time being specified in Part I of the First Schedule" be omitted. In justification of this decision of the Drafting Committee, the Constitutional Adviser noted that the Special Committee was of opinion that the provisions relating to reservation of seats for minorities should be made applicable to all elections to the Legislatures or where there were two Houses of the Legislatures, to the Lower Houses of the Legislatures of all States including the States in Part III of the First Schedule. The proposed amendment gave effect to that suggestion.

The Drafting Committee decided in October, 1948 to sponsor its amendment.[6]

Draft Article 305 was, however, never taken up for consideration by the Constituent Assembly. Consequent to the decision of the Constituent Assembly on May 25-26, 1949 that the benefit of reservation should be restricted to the Scheduled Castes and the Scheduled Tribes only and that too for a period of 10 years, the relevant Draft Articles underwent drastic changes. Soon after the adoption of revised Draft Articles 292 and 294 (Articles 330 and 332 respectively) by the Constituent Assembly on August 24, 1949, Dr. Ambedkar moved a motion for insertion of new Draft Article 295-A (Article 334), which was adopted by the Assembly with some changes. Later, on September 17, 1949, on a motion of Krishnamachari, Draft Article 305 was deleted.[7]

The new Draft Article 295A moved by Ambedkar laid down that the reservation of seats for the Scheduled Castes and the Scheduled Tribes would cease after ten years from the date of commencement of the Constitution. This was in accordance with the decision already taken by the Assembly. But a number of clarificatory amendments were moved. Thakurdas Bhargava's amendment suggested that the special provision for the nomination of Anglo-Indians should also cease after ten years. T.T. Krishnamachari moved an amendment to add a proviso to the effect that the abolition of reservations at the end of ten years would not affect the representation of the House of the People or the Legislative Assembly of a State until the dissolution of the then existing House or Assembly. He explained that there was a lacuna in the article proposed by Ambedkar in that the period of ten years might terminate at a time when these bodies had just begun their life after a general election or were half-way through their life. The amendment would ensure that the membership of the House and the representation therein would continue unchanged till the next general election.

A great deal of anxiety was expressed by S. Nagappa, V.I. Muniswamy Pillai and Monomohan Das, all belonging to the Scheduled Castes, that the period of ten years would be quite an insufficient period and that reservations might be necessary even thereafter.

Ambedkar accepted the amendments suggested by Bhargava and Krishnamachari. On the question of the period for which reservation of seats for Scheduled Castes and Tribes would be necessary, he himself was prepared to press for a longer period; but the ten years' period was the result of a general agreement among the parties, accepted by the Assembly, and it would not be right to go back on these provisions at that stage. If at the end of ten years the conditions of the Scheduled Castes and Tribes had not improved or they wanted a further extension of the period, "it would not be beyond their capacity or their intelligence to invent new ways of getting the same protection which they were promised here. "In reply to a query about Scheduled Tribes, Ambedkar was willing to give a far longer time; but all those who had spoken about the reservations to Scheduled Castes and Scheduled Tribes had been specific that reservations should end after ten years. While faithfully carrying out the mandate of the Constituent Assembly, Ambedkar left his audience in no doubt that his own conviction was that reservations would be needed for a longer period; and he quoted Burke's famous saying "large empires and small minds go ill together."

With the amendments accepted by Ambedkar, the Draft Article was adopted by the Assembly.

The deliberations in the Constituent Assembly on this important provision of the Constitution are as follow:

The Honourable Dr. B.R. Ambedkar:

Sir, I move :

"That after Article 295, the following new article be inserted:-

"295-A. Notwithstanding anything contained in the foregoing provisions of this Part, the provisions of this Constitution relating to the reservation of seats for the Scheduled Castes and the Scheduled Tribes either in the House of the people or in the Legislative Assembly of a State shall cease to have effect on the expiration of a period of ten years from the commencement of this Constitution."'

This is also in accordance with the decision of the House. I do not think any explanation is necessary.

Mr. President:

There are certain amendments to this. Amendment No. 39 has been given notice of by three Members.

Shri Yudhisthir Mishra (Orissa States):

Sir, I move :

"That in amendment No. 38 above, in the proposed new Article 295-A, the words 'and the scheduled tribes' be deleted."

The effect of my amendment will be that the provision of this Constitution regarding reservation of seats for the Scheduled Tribes both in the Centre and in the

Provinces shall not cease to have effect even after the lapse of ten years from the commencement of this Constitution. The purpose of this new Article 295-A is not to allow reservation of seats to Scheduled Castes and tribes after a period of ten years from the date of the commencement of this Constitution. My amendment seeks to provide that the reservation of seats for the tribes should not be limited to ten years only.

We decided in the last session of the Constituent Assembly, in a motion tabled by the Honourable Sardar Patel, that the system of reservation of seats for minorities other than the Scheduled Castes in the legislatures be abolished and that the reservation of seats for the Scheduled Castes shall be limited to ten years only. The communities referred to in this resolution are Muslims, Sikhs, Scheduled Castes and Indian Christians. It was held that in the context of a free and independent India, and according to the present conditions, there should not be any reservation of seats for religious communities. Therefore, it did not affect the reservation of seats for the scheduled tribes. Sir, in the report of the Advisory Committee dated 11th May 1949 submitted by Sardar Patel to this House on the subject of political safeguards for minorities, it has been specifically stated that nothing contained in the resolution passed by the Minorities Advisory Committee shall effect the recommendations made by the North-East Frontier (Assam) Tribal and Excluded Areas Sub-Committee with regard to the tribals in the legislatures. It was also laid down that the resolution would not affect the special provision made for the representation of Anglo-Indians in the legislatures.

Now, Sir, in their report, the Advisory Committee for Tribal and Excluded Areas have suggested some protection for the tribes, and no limitation, as far as I remember, was fixed as regards the period for which such protection should be provided. It is of course surprising to me how the Drafting Committee in its recent amendment or in its new Article 295-A has put in a time-limit. We have passed new Article 215-B which provides for the administration and control of the tribal areas in any State, according to the provision of the Schedule V and Schedule VI of the Draft Constitution. This provision in 215-B is a permanent feature of the Constitution which will not cease to be operative even after a lapse of ten years.

Then again, in the Vth and VIth Schedules in the Draft Constitution, a Tribal Advisory Committee has been provided to advise the Government of the States in all matters pertaining to the administration of the scheduled tribes and the welfare of the tribal people in all States. Now, three-fourths of the Tribal Advisory Committee will consist of the elected representatives of the scheduled tribes in the legislature of the States. If there is no reservation for the tribes, how are you going to give effect to the provisions of this Constitution as far as the provisions laid down in the Schedule V of the Draft Constitution are concerned? So far as the tribal people are concerned, due to their social, educational and political backwardness, I am sure very few of them will be returned to the Assembly if reservation is abolished. I feel that even after the lapse of ten years we shall not be able to remove the backwardness of the tribes. I hold that the standards of education and material well-being of the Scheduled tribes are lower in most cases than even those of most of the Scheduled Castes. That is clear from the representation of the scheduled tribes in this House in comparison with the representation that the Scheduled Castes have been able to secure. Even the representative character of this House, as far as the interests of the scheduled tribes are concerned has been challenged by some people. I recently received some letters and telegrams from the tribal people of the Orissa States that the representatives in this House are not entitled to make any Constitution for them and that even if a Constitution is made, they are not bound by it. This is due to the apprehension in their minds that they will receive proper justice unless we go and try to understand their feelings as far as reservation of seats are concerned. Therefore we should think twice before abolishing reservation of seats for the tribal people after the lapse of ten years. I feel that the scheduled tribes will not be able to attain the same social standard as the other people within ten years. So I submit that the time-limit should be removed. I hope this amendment will receive due consideration at the hands of the Drafting Committee.

Shri S. Nagappa (Madras: General):

Mr. President, Sir, I beg to move:

"That in amendment No. 38 above, at the end of the proposed new Article 295-A, the following proviso be added:-

Provided the people for whom seats in the Legislatures have been reserved are brought to the level of other advanced classes of people educationally, socially and economically."

My intention in moving this amendment is not to extend the period of reservation, but to see that Government takes effective care that, within this ten years' period, the people for whom seats have been reserved are brought to the level of other advanced classes. As it is, in the various provinces there are ministries which are in charge of Harijan uplift, but in the Centre, I do not find such a ministry and I would request the Government to create a Ministry of that sort and see that a Harijan is kept in charge of this Ministry and a plan is chalked out for ten years so that these people are brought to the level of other advanced classes, educationally, economically and socially. In order to achieve this object, I would request the Central Government to set apart 5 per cent of its revenues in order to give grants to the Provincial Government as they have been doing in the case of rural water-supply or in the case of medical relief to the rural areas. So also, in order that these people are brought to the level of the other people we must have such definite plans and schemes. Unless and until such schemes are chalked out and are worked out, I do not think it will be possible for us to bring these down-trodden people to the level of the other advanced communities within the short period of ten years.

The Harijan movement was started in the year 1932 with the blessings and active co-operation of our revered leader Mahatmaji. All these days we did it and we have been doing it with the public co-operation and by constant propaganda in order to see that the Harijans are also treated equally along with others. No doubt, Sir, it has brought about some psychological change in the minds of people who are modern; who are civilized, who are educated, who can understand things, who can move with the times, but as regards people who are not educated, who are still orthodox type of people, who believe in the old theory, to those people especially in the rural areas, it has not brought any change. Indeed I am thankful to the Central Government as well as to the various Provincial Governments for having been good enough to include an article in this Constitution and having brought suitable legislation in various provinces in order to see that untouchability is made an offence and that too a cognizable offence, but still to my knowledge, it is not worked out in the same spirit with which it has been enacted. Well, Sir, the proof of the pudding is in the eating. We must see that what we have enacted, every word of it, every letter of it, with all the spirit behind it must be transmitted into action, not in the cities, not in the towns, but in the villages. In order to achieve this object at least five per cent of the Central revenues should be set apart; there should be a Ministry in charge of these people in the Centre to consolidate the work that is being done in the various provinces and States.

Another thing that would go a long way in bringing these people to the level of the other advanced classes is education. As it is, in our country illiteracy happens to be the highest. After all, the literate population may be 12 to 15 per cent. If you take the Harijans alone, I think it will be 1 per cent or 2 per cent. Every year we must watch what percentage is converted to literacy and we must give a great fillip to this movement for the spread of education. Education is the key of all-round development. Unless and until they are educated, you may not be in a position to bring them to the level of the other advanced people.

I would request you to make elementary education compulsory to these people. I know that large tracts of waste land are available in this country. But, unfortunately, these people are not allowed to cultivate the land. I would request the Government to have a definite plan, especially the Ministry of Agriculture and Food. They must go on alloting these lands to these people in order to produce more food and in order to elevate the economic condition of these people.

In order to raise these people economically, multi-purpose co-operative societies must be organised all over the country and you should see that each society has a definite plan in order to see that a particular thing is done in a particular time. We see the strike mentality is spreading among the workers. There is a mentality of profit-making among the capitalists. As a result of the strike mentality of the labourers and as a result of the profit-making mentality among the capitalists, the country is suffering as production is going down. I would suggest solution for this : that is, make the worker the owner of the factory. You may ask, how to make him the owner? It is a very simple thing. For instance, we may take it that a worker earns about Rs. 2 a day. Suppose, in a mill the investment is Rs. 40 lakhs and 4,000 people are working in that mill. If you go on deducting at the rate of two annas in the Rupee that every labourer earns, for every labourer you will be saving four annas a day, and for 4,000 people it means Rs. 1,000. In course of time, you will be able to make up the capital invested in the factory. You may give that money to the capitalist and then you may say to the workers, "Well, this is your own from today; go along and produce whatever you like." The capitalist will get back his money and he may invest it in some other industry. The country will be developed industrially. I would particularly request the Honourable the Minister for Labour to hear this carefully and see that this is done at an early date. If the Honourable the Minister for Labour takes it into his head, he can do it and the production could be increased to many more times its present output. He can make the country above want if he has a mind to do so. There is no use of this profit-sharing or any other sharing. You must make the worker feel that it is his own factory. If you bring about that conciousness, he will put his heart and soul into the task. By simply saying that you will get 50 per cent of the profit and this and that, you cannot increase production.

Mr. President:

I am sure you are making a good suggestion which will receive due consideration. But, these suggestions are out of place so far as this article is concerned.

Shri S. Nagappa:

Certainly I think this is the best way in which we can bring the condition of these people to the level of the other people economically.

My amendment is that this reservation should last for ten years, provided the Government takes this actually into its head and sees that these people are brought to the level of the advanced classes. I am not simply agitating, I want to give constructive suggestions and in order to give suggestions I have to express these things elaborately. You must have a definite scheme. You must at least take up 100 young men from this community and send them to foreign countries to make them experts technically, as was done under the Bevin Boys' Scheme or any other scheme. You must send them to foreign countries, and make them techincal experts. There must be a definite quota or a definite scheme for each year. There is no use of saying that everything will be done and leaving it in the air that we will do this and that. You must start with a definite scheme. I come to understand that there is a Scholarship Board; but to my surprise, the amount that is set apart at its disposal is very limited, when the applications that have come for scholarship are taken into consideration. About 60 or 70 per cent of the applications have had to be rejected because there are not enough funds at their disposal. I would request the Government to see that every application that is sent to this Scholarship Board is granted and every student that seeks

Government help is given help and that too in time, and he should be allowed to make the best use of the good-will of the Government to his best ability.

When these people are equipped with all the qualifications necessary, it is again a problem for them to get themselves absorbed in responsible positions, because there are so many hurdles for them to cross. The Services Commission is one of the bottlenecks for these poeple. In order to see that the interests of these people are safeguarded, in every Provincial Service Commission there should be at least one member belonging to these people. In the Central Commission also, there should be one. Only then, will these people advance further.

Another most important thing is that these people are well-fitted for any military job. They have enough stamina; they can withstand any amount of physical strain. These people must be recruited in large numbers to the Military not merely as sepoys alone, but to responsible posts also. At the end of five years, you should appoint a commission to go round the country and take into consideration what advance these people have made during the last five years, and whether the advance is commensurate with the scheme that we have on hand and if the advance has not been sufficient, what suggestions could be made to go further.

Another most important thing is this. In the Constitution we have provided that equal opportunity should be given to all irrespective of caste, creed and colour, religion or race. Well, it sounds well, so far as we read it. But we must see that it is translated into action. While making appointment to responsible jobs like Governors, Ambassadors, High Commissioners, Trade Commissioners and other like cases, you must take into consideration the claims of these people. We are an independent contury for the last two years; I am surprised to find not a single Governor, nor a single ambassador from these people.

Sardar Hukam Singh (East Punjab: Sikh):

On a point of Order, Sir. Why should colour be emphasised now? Because all Indians are of one colour.

Shri S. Nagappa:

So far as my honuourable Friends from the North are concerned, they may have a uniform colour, but for us, South Indians, who are nearer the Equator we have a different colour. Whether we are black or brown, we have an Indian colour. We are Indians irrespective of our colour. You have been good enough to enact that we should give equal opportunity for one and all. It must be acted upon in the same spirit. Can you give one example of a Scheduled Caste man being a Governor in this country? You are adding insult to injury. What opportunity you have provided for those people? Can you say, out of those whom you have selected either as Cabinet Ministers or other officers, have they failed? They have been doing work more than others. Why do you brand them as inefficient? Somehow or other you want to by-pass our claim. Do not utter it hereafter. The most important means by which you can bring in the rural population to an economic level at the earliest opportunity is by providing them facilities in order to encourage themselves commercially, provide them lands and give them licenses for controlled commodities and send them to countries which have advanced commercially.

Another thing is you are abolishing the zamindari system all over the country. It is a good sign of advancement but what is going to happen? If the Zamindars are sent out, the chota Zamindars are created, i.e., those who are supposed to be the agriculturists. They do not till the land and it is the mazdoor who tills the land. You make them owners of the lands, give lands to these people or let it be given to co-operative societies and give them Government loans and modern machinery to cultivate the lands.......

Shri L. Krishnaswami Bharathi (Madras: General):

It is relevant?

Shri S. Nagappa:

It is relevant for the elevation of Hari jans. So I would

request the Government to bear in mind that we have agreed to the reservation......

An honourable Member:

There is no Government.

Shri S. Nagappa:

I am suggesting to the future Government as to how it should conduct its affairs. We are enacting a Constitution for our future Government. These are the implications that are implied in it. So I would request that the honourable Members would be good enough to acccept my amendment. You must realise that greater responsibility is now lying on your shoulders. You have to bring us to that level by which we will be able to say that we do not want reservations. We cannot go on begging for a favour. As it is, we are making the Government to commit itself for the future advancement of this country and of this community. I would request the honourable Members to support this amendment. I would particularly request Dr. Ambedkar who belongs to the same community to accept this. Sir, I thank you very much.

Shri V.I. Muniswamy Pillay (Madras: General):

Mr. President, I beg to move:

"That in Amendment No. 38 of list I (fifth Week) of Amendments to Amendments, in the proposed new Article 295-A after the words 'ten years' the word 'or longer period if the parliament so decides at a later date' be inserted"....

My Friend, Mr. Nagappa moving his amendment has explained to the House the difficulties under which the Scheduled Castes are labouring today. Now, my view or rather my request to this House is that the period of ten years that has been accepted on the report of the Advisory Committee is a premature one. It is clearly seen in Article 299 that the Drafting Committee has brought an article whereby it clearly says that

"It shall be the duty of the Special Officer for the

Union to investigate all matters relating to the safeguards provided for minorities under this Constitution in connection with the affairs of the Union and to report to the President upon the working of the safeguards at such intervals as the President may direct, and the President shall cause all such reports to be laid before Parliament."

Under this clause I feel that this House will do well to prolong the period of ten years until the Special Officers have investigated into the matters connected with the minorities and a report is made to the President. The President according to this article has to place this matter before Parliament. It is this that I wish, that after a period of ten years the Special Officers' report can go before the President who in turn can place it before Parliament. The Parliament can review the whole thing and see whether the Scheduled Castes have advanced so well that the reservation ought to be taken away. I think by this House accepting ten years will be putting the cart before the horse. We do not know what will be the position of the Scheduled Castes after this period of ten years. If there is real advancement among them, if they have progressed in all ways, then we need not have anything further, this reservation can go at the end of that period. But if their position is the same as it is now, or if it is worse, if they have made less progress than we expect, then it is highly necessary that this period should be prolonged.

Sir, I have got several other reasons also why it is necessary that this period should be extended. We may remember that in the year 1947, when the report of the Advisory Committee came up for discussion in this House and for its decisions, several recommendations were made. But I do not think either the Government of India at the Centre, or the Provincial Governments have taken the clue from the discussions that took place here on these recommendations and they have not done much by way of amelioration of the condition of the Scheduled Castes. Even in the Constituent Assembly (Legislative) a resolution was adopted and all Members who were sympathetic towards the Scheduled Castes took part in the discussion of that resolution and then an assurance was given that everything will be done for the welfare of the Scheduled Castes. May I know what steps have been taken? I know, as a matter of fact, that only in the U.P. and in Madras in a less degree, they have taken steps to do something for the amelioration of the Scheduled Castes. In Madras they have set up a committee and after two years' labour, and after debating the subject in the Legislature, very lately, the Government has come to the rescue and they have started a department called the Hari jan Uplift Department and only this year this Department started functioning, with a small amount—to start with.

What I would request is that if the Government or this House is definitely to have only this period of ten years for reservation, then they must have a dynamic plan for the uplift of the Harijans, and in this connection, I hope it will not be too much, if I suggest to the Government of India that they must have a separate Minister and a separate portfolio for Harijan Uplift, as has been done in the Province of Madras. Unless this is done, and unless the Government takes a keen interest and shows to the Hari jans that their position will definitely be improved during the course of the next ten years, it is no use accepting this period of ten years now. In this House it has been possible to review the whole position and also to change things that have been adopted previously. Therefore, it will not be wrong if this House, after hearing us, decides that this period of ten years may be prolonged, as required in my amendment. With these few remarks I support the motion of the Honourable Dr. Ambedkar,

Dr. Monomohon Das (West Bengal: General)

Mr. President, Sir, I move:

"That in Amendment No. 38 of List I (fifth week) of amendments to Amendment at the end of the proposed new Article 295-A the following be added:

'Unless Parliament' by law otherwise provides."

If my amendment is accepted, then the new article proposed will read as follows :-

"Notwithstanding anything contained in the foregoing provisions of this part the provision of this Constitution relating to the reservation of seats for the Scheduled Castes and the Scheduled Tribes either in the House of the People or in the Legislative Assembly of a State shall cease to have effect on the expiration of a period of ten years from the commencement of this Constitution, unless Parliament by law otherwise provides."

The proposed new article of Dr. Ambedkar declares that the safeguards which have been granted to the Scheduled Castes and the Scheduled tribes will come to an end at the expiration of ten years. But my amendment proposes that these safeguards will come to an end at the end of ten years, but if the Parliament after consideration of the situation then of the Scheduled Castes and the Scheduled tribes, thinks that these provisions for reservation of seats should be continued, for some further period, then these reservations of seats, these political concessions granted to the Scheduled Castes and the scheduled tribes will continue and not come to an end.

It is not very pleasant for a man to stand before his colleagues and friends and beg for concessions for himself or his community, especially when one knows that the majority in the House is not favourbly disposed towards the grant of such concessions, especially when he knows that his pleadings and entreaties for concessions for a down-trodden community are sure to meet with unkind, unfriendly and unsympathetic criticisms. But in spite of all this, when I take into consideration the great magnitude and importance of this article, when I take into consideration the great bearing that this article will have upon the future political life of millions of the Scheduled Caste people and the scheduled tribes, I am inclined to think that I shall be greatly failing in my duty to these people whom I claim to represent here, if I do not place before you their grievances.

Sir, the problem of the Scheduled Castes and the Scheduled Tribes is not a new one. The British rulers, in the latter part of their regime, recognised this problem and made some provisions for it. It is true that they made those provisions not out of genuine love for the Scheduled Castes and the Scheduled Tribes, not for the welfare of those classes, but they did it for the benefits that they themselves hoped to acquire from them. The Indian National Congress became conscious of this problem at the instance of Mahatma Gandhi. Mahatmaji found that millions of peoples in this country were groaning under inhuman oppression for thousands of years. The distinction between man and man, the distinction between one class and another did not escape the notice of Mahatma Gandhi. This diabolical contrivance to enslave humanity did not escape the discerning eye of Mahatmaji and he declared to the people of India that emancipation of the country from a foreign yoke will be nothing but a mockery to the millions of down-trodden Scheduled Castes and Scheduled Tribes of this land, if we fail to tear away, if we fail to break down this diabolical contrivance for enslaving humanity.

Sir, so long as Mahatmaji was living, we the people of this land, we the oppressed and down-trodden people of this land found in him a court of appeal; not only we, but everyone who has aggrieved or oppressed or down-trodden, found in him a court of appeal. Whenever we thought that some injustice had been done to us, we knew that if we could approach him, we would get not only justice but more than justice. We knew that if we could convince him of the righteouness of our case, then we would get not only our due, but more than our due. Sir, that court of appeal is no longer amongst us, and to our great misfortune, today we find that after his departure, the attitude in this country towards the Scheduled Castes and the Scheduled Tribes is gradully becoming definitely stiffened. So long as he was here amidst us, we the Scheduled Castes and the Scheduled Tribes were treated with some sympathy, and with a touch of feeling, but now after his demise, we find that we are treated as rivals, political opponents, as co-sharers, as co-partners.

The Advisory Committee on Minorities in their report

dated the 8th August, 1947, clearly stated that there will be reservation of seats for the Scheduled Castes and the Scheduled Tribes for a period of ten years. At the end of ten years this position was to be reconsidered. This formula was accepted by the Constituent Assembly during its session of August, 1947. But in their subsequent meeting on 11th May, 1949 the Advisory Committee on Minorities abolished the reservation of all other minorities except the Scheduled Castes and the Scheduled Tribes. The reservation of seats for Scheduled Castes and Scheduled Tribes was retained for ten years as originally decided, but nothing was said about the reconsideration of the problem at the end of ten years. I beg to lay emphasis upon these words that nothing was said about the reconsideration of the question at the end of ten years. This silence on the part of the Advisory Committee on Minorities about the question of reconsideration of this problem has been construed to mean that the Advisory Committee is against reconsideration at the end of ten years. In their report the Minorities Committee say that they have given this political concession to the Scheduled Castes and Scheduled Tribes because "the standards of education and material well-being of the Scheduled Castes, even on Indian standards, are extremely low and moreover they (the scheduled castes) suffer from grievous social disabilities". Therefore it is evident from the Report of the Minorities Committee that it is on account of the extremaly low educational and economic conditions of the Scheduled Castes and the grievous social disabilities from which they suffer that the political safeguard of reservation of seats had been granted to them.

Now, I ask the honourable Members of this House, do they believe that in the next ten years the economic and educational conditions of the Scheduled Castes and the scheduled tribes are going to be improved to such an extent that there will be no necessity of these political safeguards for those communities? I ask my honourable Friends do they really believe that the grievous social disabilities under which these classes of people have been suffering for thousands of years will be removed in the coming ten years? I ask the honourable Members of this House are they prepared to give us a guarantee to that effect.

A very pertinent question has been raised by our esteemed Friend Mr. Brajeshwar Prasad in yesterday's meetings. My Friend Mr. Brajeshwar Prasad shed much tears I should say over the pitiable conditions of the Scheduled Castes and the Scheduled Tribes. But he failed to see what part this reservation of seats would play towards the amelioration of the conditions of these classes. He thought that it will lead to the exploitation of these classes and it will give rise to fissiparous tendencies among them. If by "exploitation" he means econoimic exploitation, then I cannot understand how a few seats in the Central Legislature or in the Provincial Legislature will lead to the exploitation of the Scheduled Castes and the Scheduled Tribes. If he mean by "exploitation" political exploitation, then I must remind him that a leader who has more capacity to appeal to our sentiments and reasoning is more able to exploit us. It is a matter of common knowledge with the Members of this House as to how many times we have been compelled to revise our decision by the convincing and eloquent reasonings of Dr.Ambedkar or our Prime Minister. So, if by "exploitation" he means that the political leaders will bring these Scheduled Castes and Scheduled Tribes under their own influence, I will say to him that this is the case everywhere.

About the fissiparous tendencies, everyone of us knows that a hundred illiterate people come to a common conclusion more easily than a hundred educated, cultured men. It is a commom knowledge that in the present times, in a family consisting of father, mother and two sons we see the father is a Congressman, the mother is a Hindu Mahasabhite, the older son is a Socialist and the younger son is a Communist. So, fissiparous tendencies are found more among the educated and cultured classes than among these classes.

I next come to the question, what part does reservation of seats play towards the amelioration of our grievanes?

In the golden days of yore when civilization was not so advanced as it is now, physical strength was the only potent weapon for protection of life and property and protection from traynny and oppression. With the advancement of civilisation and with the advancement of modern scientific instruments and weapons we find that physical prowess is of no avail towards these ends. It is political strength, it is political power, it is the part in the administration of the country, it is the influence you wield, it is the voice you have got in the administration of your State—it is these things that will give you protection of your life and property and protection from tyranny and oppression. Therefore, I think the view expressed by my friend Mr. Brajeshwar Prasad is diametrically opposed to truth.

I appeal to the honourable Members of this House, why do you grudge a few seats in the Central or in the Provincial Legislature to the Scheduled Castes and Scheduled Tribes? In this House containing more than three hundred members there may be at the maximum thirty to forty members belonging to the Scheduled Castes and Scheduled Tribes. What have they done to you—what disadvantage have they created for you? They simply come here and watch the proceedings of the House, practically taking no part in its proceedings except when their own interests are going to be trampled down by the decisions of this House. I appeal to you to take these Members into your confidence. Then you will see that they will strengthen your hands and not weaken them. I appeal to you to treat them as your younger brothers and you will find that they are with you and not against you.

My amendment proposes to reconsider the situation at the expiration of ten years. If at the end of ten years it is found that the conditions of the Scheduled Castes and the Scheduled Tribes have changed to such an extent that no safeguard is necessary, then the Parliament will do away with it. I fail to understand why there is this hurry, why there is this indecent haste to close all doors of reconsideration of the problem at the end of ten years. Let the future take its own course. After all, what is there to be afraid of for the majority community? If you are in thumping majority today in the Indian Parliament you will be so tomorrow, the day after tomorrow and for all times to come. Whatever may be the form of Government, whatever political parties may come to power, the majority will always remain a majority and it will have the minority under its feet, at its mercy. So, what is there to be afraid of the Scheduled Castes?

In the Report of the Advisory Committee it has been said "the Committee was always anxious that the representatives of the minorities should have adequate time to reflect fully so that a change, if effected, would be sought voluntarily by the minorities themselves and not be imposed upon by the "majority community". If that be the case, if that be the attitude of the Advisory Committee on Minorities, why then should this provision of consideration be deleted without the consent of the representatives of the Scheduled Castes and the Scheduled Tribes? I am sanguine that there is not a single Member from the Scheduled Castes or the Scheduled Tribes in this House who can give the consent to such a proposal of deleting this stipulation that there will be consideration of their question at the end of ten years.

I feel, Sir, that justice has not been done in this case and the will of the majority is going to be imposed by force upon us—the minority—against our will. Therefore, I appeal to the honourable Members of this House that my amendment which proposes to reopen the whole question at the expiration of ten years, and which is in no way against the decision of the Advisory Committee, may be accepted by this House.

Mr. Naziruddin Ahmad:

Mr. President, Sir, I beg to move:

"That in amendment No. 38 of List I (Fifth week) of Amendment to Amendments, at the end of the proposed new Article 295-A, the following be added:-

and a general election shall be held thereafter."

It seems to me that there is an ambiguity in the article. 'The article says that the reservations of seats for the Scheduled Castes and Scheduled Tribes in the House of the People at the Centre and in the Lower Houses in the States shall cease to have effect at the expiration of a period of ten years from the commencement of this Constitution. I think there is some amount of lurking ambiguity in the expression though the idea is quite clear. I submit a question which should be considered. At the next election I believe....

Shri T.T. Krishnamachari (Madras: General):

Mr. President, if it will help to shorten my friend's remarks, may I mention that the Drafting Committee has an amendment to fit into the contingency that he envisages?

Mr. Naziruddin Ahmad:

Where is that amendment?

Mr. President:

I was just going to point out amendment No. 114 which covers the point which the honourable Member has raised.

Mr. Naziruddin Ahmad:

The idea must have been misappropriated or stolen from my amendment. I am very grateful for it—it is a great compliment paid to me.

The point is that the expiration of ten years from the commencement of the Constitution and the expiration of the House of the People or of the States Assemblies may not coincide. It may be that for various reasons the second election is held in the ninth year of the passing of the Constitution. Then there would remain only one year for the completion of ten years but there would be an unexpired period of four years for the Legislature to expire. What is ambiguous is that on the expiration of ten years the duration of the Assemblies might not have expired. The question would be whether on the expiration of ten years the elected Legislature would cease to function entirely and there would be a fresh election or whether there would be no more election but the body elected will continue for the unexpired period of its normal life. It is to clear up that ambiguity that I have tabled the amendment. I am glad however that the error has been noticed. The difficulty of the Drafting Committee is that though in the usual number of cases they are prepared to accept good ideas, sometimes they do not like to admit their mistakes; it is on this account that many good amendments have not been accepted. But we shall look up to the Third Reading which, I hope, would be another eleborate Second Reading on account of the many errors we have passed over.

Pandit Thakur Das Bhargava (East Punjab: General):

Sir, I beg to move:

That in amendment No. 38 of List I (Fifth Week) of Amendments to Amendments in the proposed new Article 295-A after the word 'Constitution' the brackets and letter '(a)' be inserted and after the word 'State' the following be inserted:-

(b) relating to the representation of the Anglo-Indian community either in the House of the People or in the Legislative Assemblies of the States through nomination.

In regard to this amendment, I would beg the House to consider that the present proposal contained in Article 295A only refers to the reservation for Scheduled Castes and the Scheduled Tribes. It does not refer to Articles 293 or 295. When 293 and 295 were adopted and a decision was reached among the various members of the Minorities Committee, this nomination was given to the Anglo-Indian Community in place of reservation. The first proposal was that the Anglo-Indian Community will be given reservation like the Scheduled Castes and the Scheduled Tribes but as that involved weightage, ultimately it took the shape of nomination. It was absolutely clear from the very beginning that the Anglo-Indian community will get this reservation through nomination only for ten years. It was never agreed that they will get it for all time; and when we did not move our amendments to articles 293 and 295 it was under the belief that as a matter of fact this community also will get this reservation through nomination for ten years. Therefore, if only the agreement is to be implemented, then even ten years should be the time fixed for this nomination. If there is no such agreement then I would place other reasons before the House. I was also a member of the Minorities Committee and I remember that when the decision was arrived at it was made absolutely clear that this will be only for ten years. I have consulted some of the prominent Members who took part in arriving at this decision and I am reliably informed that this was the intention when the agreement took place. Because we did not want to disturb the agreement among our leaders we refrained from moving amendments, it is therefore only fair that this reservation be extended for ten years only. If we look at the reasons why this reservation is given to the Anglo-Indian community, even on other grounds except agreement, these provisions for nomination should not inure for a period longer than ten years.

The Anglo-Indain community is one of those most advanced communities in India which can hold its own against other communities who have got smaller numbers. I am glad that our leaders considered the claims of this community and dealt with them in a generous way as admitted by Mr. Anthony himself. But all the same, I believe that in regard to the House of the People this is the only community which gets a seat through nomination. There is no other provision for any community through nomination and we do not want that our Constitution should be disfigured by a provision of this nature. The Anglo-Indian community has been to a great extent protected by the provisions of Articles 297 and 298. In regard to those provisions also, instead of ten years they are getting twelve and more. I do not grudge any sort of provision for any community on fair and reasonable grounds; but all the same when the other communities come forward. When the Scheduled Castes and Scheduled Tribes come forward for our consideration, their claims are based on an entirely different footing; if they want much more representation, I can understand their position and we should not grudge to give them what they want. But so far as an advanced community is concerned, there is absolutely no reason why this community should be favoured so unduly that these provisions may inure for all time. You may say that this is only a discretionary provision, but when a discretion is given, in particular circumstances, it becomes an obligation and a duty.

I, therefore, submit that there is no reason why we should agree to accept these provisions for a longer period than ten years, and I have no doubt in the matter that if the Anglo-Indian community behaves well—and I know from my own experience they will do so—we know our Friend Mr. Anthony; he is a *persona grata* with most Members of the House—and there is no reason why he should not succeed in the General Elections if he stands after ten years. The whole complexion of India shall have changed by that time. Otherwise, I do not see why there is no great force in the amendments which have been moved by Members of the Scheduled Castes and Scheduled Tribes. After ten years we shall have a society in which the present distinctions shall cease or shall not have the same force as there is today. If we do not expect that, if we proceed on the basis that they will remain, then my humble submission is that there is no reason why we should not have to extend the period of ten years in the case of other communities also.

I am rather astonished at the amendments moved by some of my Friends belonging to the Scheduled Castes. On the day when the Minority Report was discussed in the House, I moved an amendment then that these reservations and nominations should be for ten years and the amendment was accepted. Along with that, there was an amendment by Mr. Nagappa himself and in those very terms. Now he comes forward and brings another proposition. I do not think he has the right to do so. He is stopped from doing so, as he himself and other Members agreed that this reservation will continue for ten years. As I submitted yesterday—I do not want to repeat the same arguments today—this reservation denogates from the enjoyment of the full electoral rights by the people in general. It is harmful to the general community and to the Scheduled Castes also.

Therefore, my humble submission is when we agree to deprive ourselves of the exercise of full electoral rights, it is just to placate our friends and at the same time to do them the justice which they fully deserve. We ourselves are guilty of having brought them to this level. It is upto us to see that they are not left in the lurch and they advance with the other communities. While this period of ten years is a challenge to the depressed classes to come up to the level of the other people, it casts an obligation upon the whole country and upon all the communities living in India, because now not only Hindus, but the Muslims and the Sikhs and all other communities are on the general list. Now it becomes our solemn duty that we should see that within these ten years, we behave in such a manner that these people of the Scheduled Castes and the Scheduled Tribes come up to our standards. What is the use of Articles 301, 296, 299 and 10 if the community does not rise to the height to which it is expected to rise? It will be our duty in future to see that our Central Government and the governments of the provinces do their duty by our brethren—the Members of the Scheduled Castes and the Scheduled Tribes.

Mr. Nagappa indicated some of the ways in which it should be done. This is not the occasion and I shall not take up the time of the House in giving some of those ways in which we should behave, but all the same I must say that apart from the Governments, it is the duty of everyone of us who have given our pledges and who support and swear by this Constitution, to see that within the coming ten years, we bring all these classes up to our standard. If we do not do that, if we do not do our duty, I do not know with what face we can deny these very right to them for another ten years; and that would be a most serious thing, because it would deprive all of us including the Scheduled Castes of the elementary rights of the exercise of full electoral rights. Therefore, I would submit that from today we should resolve, after passing this, that when we make it ten years we mean to make it ten years, but at the same time our duty becomes all the greater and therefore we should begin from today to discharge our duty in the right fashion. This duty will not be discharged by passing a resolution here or passing a resolution there. Unless the economic position is bettered, unless we are willing to make them feel like human beings which they do not do today, our duty will not have been performed.

I would, in this connection, submit that all these Governments should pass a law in which they may be given full rights of ownership in their houses in the villages where they are not enjoying them today. Like all others, fundamental rights are open to them, but I know in many villages these Scheduled Castes are not enjoying fundamental rights. Therefore we should see that they enjoy fundamental rights. Similarly, I would submit that in 301 the Commission should be forthwith apppointed as soon as the Constitution comes into force and when the Commission makes its report, we should see that the Report is implemented. Therefore my humble submission to the House is that when we pass this clause it becomes our duty to see that this particular clause is backed up by the force of all our resolves and determination to do our duty by our Scheduled Castes and Scheduled Tribes brethren.

Shri T.T. Krishnamachari:

Mr. President, Sir, I move:

"That in Amendment No. 38 (List I) to the proposed Article 295A the following proviso be added:-

'Provided that nothing in this article shall affect the representation in the House of the People or in the Legislative Assembly of a State until the dissolution of the then existing House or Assembly as the case may be'."

Sir, this amendment is self-explanatory and in moving it, I would like to say at once that the Drafting Committee does not claim any originality or copy-right for it. If the incentive for this amendment has been the amendment moved by Mr. Naziruddin Ahmad, we are prepared to give him full credit, but anyway it was felt by the Drafting Committee that there was a lacuna similar to the one pointed out by Mr. Naziruddin Ahmad, as, if it happens that a period of ten years falls at a time when the House has just begun its life or it is half-way through its life or in any stages of its life, the representation in that House—the membership of that House—should not be affected by the wording of Article 295-A moved by Dr. Ambedkar. The House will undoubtedly understand that this fits into the scheme in a better way than the amendment of Mr. Naziruddin Ahmad.

I would like to add one word in regard to the remarks made by Pandit Thakur Das Bhargava. He has attempted to be logical. I felt, as he was speaking, that he was trying to direct a heavy machinegun against a small mosquite. This provision of two nominated seats in the House of the People, if the President thinks it necessary to so nominate and a few seats in the Lower House of a State if the Governor so thinks fit, is merely a permissive provision. It is not an obligatory or mandatory provision. If the Anglo-Indain community is not given these seats by nomination they could not go to a court of law on the ground that the Constitution has provided for nominations, and that has been ignored by the Authorities. Full discretion to nominate or not is given to the President or to the Governor of the State concerned. Why therefore bring in all these arguments and all this logic against a purely permissive provision?

So far as the Anglo-Indians are concerned, it is doubtless true that they are not large in numbers. It is also true, as pointed out by Pandit Thakur Das Bhargava, that special provision has been made in Articles 297 and 298 in regard to the services and in regard to the educational facilities of this community respectively. That being so, he asks why any provision should be made for the continuance of this political privilege. I would ask him not to exercise his mind on a small matter of this kind which is purely left to the discretion of the executive of the day both in the Centre and in the Provinces. I would also ask him to take note of one idea that, while the Scheduled Castes are members of the Hindu community and are part and parcel of ourselves, and only the economic level of their existence deters them from assuming a position of equality with the others—the Anglo-Indains happen to be a distinct community. Because of the fact that we are supposed, in the years to come, to go farther and farther from the European civilization to which we were subjected in the years of our slavery. The difference in the way of life of the Anglo-Indian community and in the way of life of the other communities of our country will be more and more glaring hereafter and the possibility of assimilation of the Anglo-Indian community in the body-politic will be difficult. It all depends on whether our standards of living approximate to the ideas obtaining in the West or whether we propose to go back on the level we have attained. All these are problems in regard to which we do not know which way they will ultimately take. If would be cruel to ask these people to completely merge themselves in the body-politic of our country, if the future standards of life are if even anything less than our present standards.

This concession, which has been generously made by the Minorities Committee on page 35 of the Appendix to their Report, says:

"In regard to the Anglo-Indians there should be no reservation of seats. But the President of the Union and the Governors of the Provinces shall have power to nominate representatives to the Centre and the Provinces respectively if they fail to secure adequate representation in the Legislature as a result of the general election."

Actually it will happen that if Mr. Anthony gets returned to the Central Legislature no other person will have perhaps any chance. The President has no chance for exercising his discretion so far as nomination is concerned and has to be guided by the views of the Ministry. Similarly in the provinces, it is purely a permissive thing to fill a lacuna or a contingency in which the majority community might completely neglect the Anglo-Indian community. I think this concession need not be restricted for a period of ten years. It is not an obligatory provision, similar to the reservation provided for other communities.

I, therefore, suggest that my honourable Friend Pandit Thakur Das Bhargava will not press his amendment. This is a very small matter. There is nothing wrong in allowing the Anglo-Indian community of India this very doubtful privilege which is conferred ex-gratia by the executive of the day for a period longer than ten years if it be necessary. I hope he will not press his amendment.

Shri Chandrika Ram (Bihar : General) :

Mr. President, Sir, I am here to support the article as moved by Dr. Ambedkar as subsequently amended by Shri T.T. Krishnamachari. The only consideration for the Members of the Scheduled Castes in this House and outside is that this period of ten years is very small. This is a fact that within this short period the Scheduled Castes may not come up to the standard of other communities. This is based upon the fact that the provincial governments as well as the Central Government are not doing things as they should. We know from personal experience over the last twelve to fifteen years that when for the first time Congress Ministries came to power nothing practical or appreciable was done for the amelioration of the depressed classes which are backward economically, socially and educationally. This is a question of faith. We do not want even ten years. If they like, the Central and provincial Governments can do a lot for these people within the next five years. But the question of good faith is not there.That is the fear of the Scheduled Castes Members who have moved so many amendments for the extension of the period from ten to fifteen years and more.

We know so much about the work done by the Father of our Nation, Mahatma Gandhi and we are all followers of that great man. But when we look to the actual working in the provinces and in the Centre we find nothing done. It is all very good to say that there must be a separate portfolio for the backward classes and that there must be a Minister and Parliamentary Secretary from the backward classes. My feeling is that if you appoint some Ministers and create some posts and give some portfolios to Scheduled Castes and tribes you can improve the condition of those people. I know the working of the last Ministries in the provinces. In the province of Bombay there were no Ministers or parliamentary secretaries from the Scheduled Castes, but the welfare work done there was far more and better than that done in any other provinces in the country. So that without having special Parliamentary Secretaries or Ministers or special officers a good deal can be done for the Scheduled Castes. We know that the centre has two very important Ministers like Dr. Ambedkar and Mr. Jagijivan Ram. But we know, too, that in the Scheduled Castes Board there are 3,000 applicants, but only 625 scholarships. What is the use of having Ministers and Parliamentary Secretaries if you do not have money? The whole question is that you must have money. If the provincial Ministers and the Central Ministers who are all followers of Mahatma Gandhi have sufficient funds at their disposal, without creating any posts or portfolios, they can do the work for the Scheduled Castes very well and raise them to the general level of society.

Therefore, it is a question of faith, a question of confidence and a question of goodwill. I would like to say that if this work is not done during this period it may be that the scheduled classes will go against the Hindu society and against the general community. Therefore there may not be any general improvement which we envisage within ten years. I do not care much for the period; I care much for the work. I know that even in the last 25 or 30 years Mahatmaji and other people who have been working for this cause in this country, could not make much progress regarding removal of untouchability. You know in the rural areas, it is as bad today as it was before and I know among the educated classes in towns and the people with English education, there has been a change and it is this fact that has given us encouragement. And we know that the Provincial Governments are passing some enactments to remove this disability. It is a good thing for us, for the country and for this august Assembly that we have passed article 11 to remove untouchability for ever. But only passing a legislation for the purpose, or appointing ministers and allocating some portfolios will not do. If the whole amount of work has to be done, it is to be done by having funds at our disposal and my appeal to both Central and Provincial Governments is to allot enough funds, so that educationally they may be raised and economically their condition may be bettered. Regarding their social disability we know that in social matters, we should not hurry. In social matters it is all a matter of change of heart. I know that persons who are prepared to hang themselves for the cause of the country, they are not ready to remove this untouchability from their houses or from the members of their family, because it is a social custom, it is a social manner from time immemorial; it has come into the blood of these caste—Hindus and the Hindu society as a whole because these have been written in many books of Shastras, Vedas and all that.

Therefore regarding social matters we have to wait and both sides have to wait. There cannot be a social revolution at once because India is a vast country and vast numbers of people are living here having different ideas and different faiths. We know there are those faiths where this untouchability is a crime, like Sikhism, Buddhism and among the Muslims as well. Therefore, in a social matter we have to wait; we have to work and we have to go on slowly. Regarding their economic condition we have to do a little more. As yet, they have not done anything. As a matter of fact there is no programme before us as to what should be done first. Even in doing things we must have priority. For the Harijans we have no plan and no programme and no actual policy to work. Therefore my suggestion was this that the Government of India should appoint a Commission or a Committee at once and that Commission or Committee should go into the entire matter of the social, educational and economic field of the Harijans and should suggest ways and means and make recommendations so that the Governments in the Provinces or at the Centre just after the election start work on definite lines as suggested by the Commission in their report. That was my suggestion. The question of period is not very important to me.

As I said before, the question of funds at the disposal of the Government and the question of faith and good-will and good wishes are very important. Otherwise we, the Members representing the Scheduled Caste community, we do want that even this concession for ten years should go if our conditions are improved very much within this period. We shall be glad to remove this caste and communities, Scheduled Castes, Harijans, Achuths and all that if our social conditions are bettered within this period. We have faith in our leaders, we have faith in the future and even if our condition is not bettered during this period, we have hope and faith that after ten years the members of your community, the members of the Assembly and Council, the members of the Government, the Provinces and Centre will look to this matter and examine these questions and if another period is required they will give. Therefore, we are not very anxious about having the period but we are anxious to have the funds at our disposal and we are anxious to have the goodwill of the people belonging to the majority community, belonging to the Caste Hindu society.

Shri Jagat Narain Lal (Bihar: General):

Mr. President, the principle of reservation generally is one which has done much harm to our country. I do not wish to dilate on it, and if we have accepted this principle of reservation in the case of the Scheduled Castes and the aboriginals, it is because there is a very strong case for them. If there is any case, the case is for these two classes of people in our country. The proposal that the period should terminate after ten years and there should be no reservation after that is certainly a desirable one. But at the same time, I wish to add my own humble voice to that of the previous speaker, and I wholeheartedly share the sentiments which he has expressed in this

House. If we really want to raise the Scheduled Castes to that level in which the other communities in this country find themselves, we have to be very earnest about the matter. If the Provincial Governments or for the matter of that, the Central Government feel satisfied that they have set apart a certain sum, that they have appointed certain officers and that they have thereby discharged their duty and obligation, it would not be proper. We have seen speaker after speaker rising from among the Scheduled Castes,—Members here—speakers who share our national feeling, who are equally patriotric, but who feel for their brethren and for the troubles and sufferings to which they are being put in the interior particularly. I, therefore, suggest that the Central Government and the Provincial Governments, if they are really serious that this period of ten years should not be extended and that within ten years we should sincerely and honestly discharge our obligations to these two classes of our countrymen who have remained very much backward so long, we should be really very earnest about the matter and I would suggest that the Government should whip up the Provincial Government and if possible at the end of every year or every two years watch how much progress has been made in the matter. If, Sir, within these ten years by the combined efforts of the Governments, of the upper classes and of the Schedule Castes, we have not been able to raise them up to the level to which we would like all communities of this country, all classes of people of this country to be raised we cannot have any case for terminating that period of reservation. And therefore, while on the one hand, I support this proposal that during this period of ten years alone seats should be reserved and that no reservation should continue in this country after that, I very strongly support the plea made out by the previous speaker. Mr. Chandrika Ram and certain other speakers that every possible effort should be made both by Government, by the people, by various organization in this country to see that the Scheduled Castes and the aboriginal tribes also are raised to that level to which we find all other communities in this country raised so far.

So far as the Anglo-Indian community is concerned, I feel, as Pandit Thakur Das Bhargava feels, that it is a most enlightened community, a most advanced community in this country. If there is to be any reservation for them, it is because they are in a minority. On that ground, we can find so many other communities in this country which are in a very great minority. No community, however small in this country, should ever think of claiming representation or having representation in the legislatures or anywhere on the ground of being in a minority. Service and capacity alone should be the passport. I feel that if there are really members among the Anglo-Indian community advanced as they are, who are equally imbued with the spirit of service to this country, and to the people, they will continue to have representation and this country will not deny that representation to them. I would like them to depend upon their service and capacity and ability more than on any reservation being continued in the Constitution giving them representation in the Legislature and here and there. These are the few words that I want to submit on this article.

Shri Upendranath Barman (West Bengal : General)

Mr. President, Sir, three Scheduled Caste MCAs in this House have moved separate amendments. From those amendments, it is quite clear to the House that even at this stage, the Scheduled Castes are very much apprehensive of their future even after the 10th year of the coming into force of this Constitution. I do not like to comment either way on their proposals but I simply submit to this august House that this is a genuine apprehension in the mind of the Scheduled Castes, and therefore I appeal to the House to take stock of the whole position.

I myself have got different views in the matter. I know very well that if there is no real sympathy, if it be only lip sympathy, not only ten years but twenty years will be of no avail. So long as the advanced community in this country simply realise that they have done some wrong to their brethren, and that it is now their duty to give some help, I think we shall not get what we really want and what the country really needs. I should appeal to them to think entirely in a different light. Who are the Scheduled Castes and Scheduled Tribes? Do they not constitute 85 or 90 per cent of India's population? Many of my friends have times without number expressed concern for the rural people. To my mind, the term rural people is synonymous with the sum total of the Scheduled Castes and Scheduled Tribes and the backward classes. You are leaving behind 85 or 90 per cent of the total population in a backward condition. Unless you level up this 85 per cent of the population, is it possible for India to advance a step further, that is expected of free India now? I think not. This is not my personal view. I can cite one of the greatest men of India, our late revered poet, Rabindranath Tagore. In an exasperated mood, he cried aloud in his poem "My unfortunate country"; in fact the theme of that poem is this, that unless and until you level up this 90 per cent of your population, you can never rise up, because what he says is, those you have left behind they are dragging you down. If you understand from that angle of vision that unless you level up the 80 or 90, or whatever that may be, per cent of the population, you cannot rise up yourself; you cannot progress as you want to. I think it would be really action by which this unfortunate condition of this country could be improved.

That is one aspect of the matter which I would like to place before my honourable Friends who are advanced. My next appeal is to my Scheduled Caste brethren and it is this. We have seen that since 1932, these Scheduled Castes have been recognised as a separate community and certain advantages were being conceded to them by the then Government. After that, when the 1935 Act came, they were recognised as a differen tentity and several provisions have been made for our uplift in the Act itself. But, from 1935 or 1937, up till now, it is now more than a decade that has passed, and I ask, how much have we really improved? Excepting a fraction of our community who had somehow got a chance of getting education, all the rest of our brethren remain in the same static condition. Under this process, even our present Government gave us some latitude, gave us some concessions in the way of scholarships and stipends, a Minister here or a Parliamentary Secretary there. But, I do not think that the whole lot of the Scheduled Castes has been greatly improved. I think there is a fund of sympathy in the mind of our advanced brethren because they understand more than we understand ourselves. And it is for us to drink deep upto that fountain and put our legitimate claims before the Government, before the public and also before our august Organisation. If even after that, our legitimate claims and demands are not conceded, then it would be our duty to stand on our own legs and try our level best to get our just share.

After all, I want to consider our position in India as a family consisting of our brothers. The eldest brother somehow got the opportunity for education, public life and other kinds of experience and is far advanced. The other three brothers are left in the dark and they are lagging behind. Unless and until the other three brothers understand their equal rights along with the eldest, I do not think that the eldest brother will really feel that it is his duty to do justice to his other brothers, because man is essentially selfish and what is true of a man is mostly true of a class also. So long as there are class distinctions in this country there is no solution and once the class distinctions go, all this trouble will go. I do not know when they will go. Even after two years of independence, I do not find either from the Government or from the Congress organisation itself any active and vigorous step to drive away this curse, which we every day admit to be a curse. So that hope is to be left now. We have to assert our rights. We are, after all, children of the same soil and if our eldest brother is doing some job we are also doing some other job and according to the law of the land we have equal rights to whatever assets our motherland has conferred upon us. So if we assert our right, then we can stand on our own legs. Revolt—I purposely use the word 'revolt' because when justice is not done, it is only by revolt that justice can be done and once we stand on our rights and are determined to get it, I know there will be no difficulty in getting that justice conceded, because after all, this Constitution of India as it is being framed by this Constituent Assembly has given us one fundamental right viz., adult franchise. If we find that our interests are not being served by the intelligent section of this country, then what we have to do is to choose our own men and according to adult franchise, I have no doubt that we shall overwhelmingly preponderate in any assembly or council. We can therefore take the Government in our own hands and do justice to others and to ourselves.

So we should not be entirely crying for mercy and justice but we should not only ask for justice to ourselves but also strive to lever up our own condition. For that purpose if we find that certain communities are not co-operating, then our next duty would be to take the Government in our own hands. But that would be an unfortunate position. What I mean is this, that we should do our own duty and then accuse those who are at the helm of affairs for not doing full justice to us. In that context, I should submit that this ten years' limitaton is perhaps right. So long as we think that the advanced community will do everything for us I think there would be some diffidence in our minds and out of that diffidence we shall not strive to attain what is justly due to us. But once it is fixed that ten years is limit, then from tomorrow we shall have to think out how to do our part in the play. We have got adult franchise and the right to choose our men in Government. I think there will be no obstacle in our way. But if we fix a period indefinitely, much energy which is needed for the purpose will not be coming. Therefore I am for supporting the article that has been presented by Dr. Ambedkar as subsequently amended by him and would ask my Scheduled Caste brothers to co-operate with the advanced community and get justice from them in whatever direction we need, but failing which I would ask them to unite and snatch away the justice that is due to us.

Shri Jadubans Sahay: (Bihar: General)

Mr. President, with your permission I shall devote myself to the analysis of the amendment moved by Shri Yudhisthir Mishra so far as it relates to scheduled tribes.

So far as the Scheduled Castes are concerned, enough has been said and I should not take the time of the House by adding more to what has already been said. So far as the amendment of Shri Yudhisthir Mishra is concerned the effect of that will be that after even 10 years the reservation of seats to the scheduled tribes will continue. I say most respectfully that this approach is rather wrong, from the point of view of the tribes. Our approach to this problem should not be from the point of view of the backwardness of the tribes. We know that the tribes are backward and we know for centuries past they have been exploited. We know also that economically and politically they are backward; but our approach should be not what the tribes would do for themselves, but what we should do for them. I have faith in myself and the organisation to which I belong and I have faith in the present democratic set up of Government and I can say that within the course of ten years, if you are not able to elevate and to ameliorate the conditions of the tribes, then woe be to us, not the tribes. It was said by Dr. Kunzru once that this Constitution and the letters embodied and printed in the book of this Constitution will not avail much if there are not men honest enough to execute them.

Shri Brajeshwar Prasad (Bihar : General)

Sir, may I say that Mr. Sahay should speak in the mike. He is not audible.

Shri Jadubans Sahay:

I was saying that what is embodied in the Constitution will not bring relief by itself. The letters, the printed cold letters will not bring relief either to the tribal or to any part of the down-trodden citizens of this country. It requires a band of workers, a band of people imbibing in themselves the vigour, the spirit, the message as also the gospel of Mahatma Gandhi. We have I confess, travelled a long way and have not been able to do what we think we should achieve for the tribes. It is not a test for the tribes, really it is a test for us—this period of ten years and therefore I will appeal to my friends not to approach this problem from the view of tribes.

It was said yesterday—I will not take up the time of the House by following or analysing the criticisms made yesterday—I will not go into that because the time at my disposal is short but I must say that the irresponsible statements and baseless allegations which were made yesterday could not advance the cause of the aboriginals. We know, I confess, that for eight decades down to this decade charges have been levelled against us. We plead guilty and we are ready to do what we can, but simply by abusing us you will not help any one. It will throw a cold douche in the hearts of those who are there to work for the tribes.

It was asked, what good the Bihar Government as well as other Governments have done to them? I will not try to convince those who refuse to be convinced; but given time, I will give you some figures. During the course of three years, you will be surprised to know, a grant of rupees one crore has been spent over the construction of irrigation bunds for the five districts of Chota Nagpur. Is that politics? Bunds were constructed so that the aboriginals could irrigate their fields and thus grow two blades where they could only grow one. But yesterday Mr. Singh said that this is politics. If it is politics, then in spite of what Mr. Singh says, we would stick to that politics, the politics of constructing more bunds. As our Premier said only a few days back, every village of the aboriginals should have a bund to irrigate their fields, because the problem of the aboriginals is their economic poverty. They cannot get industries and factories all at once. But if bunds are constructed for them, then they can get enough water to irrigate their lands. If we do this, then you will see that within ten years these people will be quite different from what they are. We do not claim to have done much for them, but for what we do in our province we claim that we are swiftly travelling towards the solution of this problem.

Not only have we constructed bunds, we have also taken steps for the removal of the money-lenders from among the aboriginals. We have also opened hostels—52 of them in three years, for the aboriginal boys. For irrigation bunds we have spent a crore of rupees though for the rest of Bihar we would have spent not more than fifty lakhs or less. Indeed this is a sort of complaint by the people there, though they do not mean it seriously, but they joke, that everything seems to be for the aboriginals, that the Finance Minister is loose with his money when the aboriginals are concerned, that our Revenue Minister is concerned much more with the uplift of the aboriginals than with other problems. We can only beseech you to give us some time, and we have laid down this period of ten years so that during this period we may go rapidly and not slacken our progress. Otherwise, we might think, that the aboriginals are going to get this reservation and so we need not go fast with our work of bringing them up to the level that we want them to reach. It was said yesterday that from the epic age, ever since the Aryans came to this land we have only neglected and done nothing for the aboriginals. I can only say that during the last fifty years, during the British rule, they did not achieve even as much as we have claimed to have progressed during the last three years. What was my friend doing, Sir, who was so vociferous yesterday in criticising us? What was he doing during the British rule? Recruiting soldiers, when we were fighting for the aboriginals. Even now if I......

Mr. President:

I will ask the honourable Member not to digress about this.

Shri Jadubans Sahay:

I bow, Sir. Even now, without meaning any offence to anyone, I will simply say if the Government only proceeds rapidly, for a period of three years, we can work wonders with the aboriginals. Only the heart is required, and the money. Bihar is a poor province; but in spite of our poverty, in spite of the fact that Bihar is the poorest province in India, we can claim that we have done more than what was done under the British and even under our own rule under the 1937 regime. So I plead with my friends to give us these ten years. This period of ten years will be a period of test for us. It will not be a test for the tribals, for the oppressed people of Chota Nagpur or the oppressed people of any other part of India, but it will be a test for the non-aboriginals. It is a challenge to us. It is a challenge to the social workers in India, and we accept that challenge. We only request you to give us this ten years' time.

Shri B.L.Sondhi (East Punjab: General)

The question may be put.

Mr. President:

Closure has been moved.

The question is:

"That the question be now put."

The motion was adopted.

Mr. President:

Dr. Ambedkar.

The Honourable Dr. B.R. Ambedkar (Bombay: General):

Mr. President, Sir, there are just four amendments about which I would like to say a few words. I will first take the amendment of my Friend Mr. Bhargava, and say that I am prepared to accept his amendment, because I find that although in the general body of the report that was made to this House, no mention as to time-limit was made to the proposal for allowing representation to Anglo-Indians by nomination, I find that in the subsequent debate which took place on that report, there is an amendment moved by my Friend Pandit Bhargava which is very much in the same terms as the amendment which he has now moved, and I find that amendment of his was accepted by the House. I, therefore, am bound to accept the amendment that he has moved now.

Next, with regard to the question raised by Mr. Naziruddin Ahmad, one part of it has been, I think, met by the amendment moved by my Friend Mr. Krishnamachari which I also accept. I am not at all clear in my own mind at the present stage whether the words in the clause mean that the time-limit should begin to operate from the commencement of the Constitution or whether from the date of the first election to the new Parliament. But all I can say at this stage is that that is matter which the Drafting Committee will consider and if it is necessary, they will bring about some amendment to carry out the intention that the period should be from the date of first meeting of the first Parliament.

With regard to the other arguments which have been used by my Friends Mr. Muniswami Pillai and Mr. Monomohon Das, I am sorry it is not possible to accept that amendment. Their proposal is that while they are prepared to leave the clause as it is, they propose to vest Parliament with the power to alter this clause by further extension of the period of ten years. Now first of all we have, as I said, introduced this matter in the Constitution itself, and I do not think that we should permit any change to be made in this, except by the amendment of the Constitution itself.

I would like to say one or two words on the remarks of Members of the Scheduled Castes who have spoken in somewhat passionate and vehement terms on the limitation imposed by this article. I have to say that they have really no cause for complaint, because the decision to limit the thing to ten years was really a decision which has been arrived at with their consent. I personally was prepared to press for a larger time, because I do feel that so far as the Scheduled Castes are conerned, they are not treated on the same footing as the other minorities. For instance, so far as I know the special reservation for the Mussalmans started in the year 1892; so to say, the beginning was made then. Therefore, the Muslims had practically enjoyed these privileges for more or less sixty years. The Christians got this privilege under the Constitution of 1920 and they have enjoyed it for 28 year. The Scheduled Castes got this only in the Constitution of 1935. The commencement of this benefit of special reservation practically began in the year 1937 when that Act came into operation. Unfortunately for them, they had the benefit of this only for two years, for from 1939 practically up to the present moment, or upto 1946, the Constitution was suspended and the Scheduled Castes were not in a position to enjoy the benefits of the privileges which were given to them in the 1935 Act, and it would have been quite proper, I think, and generous on the part of this House to have given the Scheduled Castes a longer term with regard to these reservations. But, as I said, it was all accepted by the House. It was accepted by Mr. Nagappa and Mr. Muniswamy Pillai, and all these Members, if I may say so—I am not making any complaint—were acting on the other side, and I think it is not right now to go back on these provisions. If at the end of the ten years, the Scheduled Castes find that their position has not improved or that they want further extension of this period, it will not be beyond their capacity or their intelligence to invent new ways of getting the same protection which they are promised here.

Shri A.V. Thakkar (Sourashtra)

What about the Scheduled tribes who are lower down in the scale?

The Honourable Dr. B.R. Ambedkar

For the scheduled tribes I am prepared to give far longer time. But all those who have spoken about the reservations to the Scheduled Castes or to the Scheduled Tribes have been so meticulous that the thing should end by ten years. All I want to say to them, in the words of Edmund Burke, is "Large Empires and small minds go ill together."

Mr. President

I shall now take up the amendments one by one.[8]

At this stage,Yudhisthir Misra, S. Nagappa, V.I. Muniswamy Pillai, Naziruddin Ahmed withdrew their amendments. Dr. Monomohan Das refused to withdraw his amendment but it was negatived by the House. The revised Draft Article along with the amendments of Bhargava and Krishnamachari was thereafter adopted by the House.[9]

At the revision stage it was renumbered as Article 334 when some minor drafting changes were effected.

Unlike the general authorization of special treatment and the provision for reserved posts in government service, the reserved seats in legislatures are subject to a constitutional time limit. It was originally provided that such reservations should expire ten years after the commencement of the Constitution. In 1959 these provisions were extended for another ten years,[10] in 1969 for another ten,[11] in 1980 for another ten[12] and in 1990 for yet another ten years.[13]

This Article is an exception to the general provision of reservation of seats for the Scheduled Castes and the Scheduled Tribes in the House of the people and in the Legislative Assemblies and of nomination of the Anglo-Indian community in the House of the people and in the Legislative Assemblies stipulated in Articles 330, 332, 331 and 333 of the Constitution respectively. Articles 330, 331, 332, and 333 will become inoperative as soon as this Article expires. The intentions of the framers were to extend this benefit to a section of people for a limited period only and even the greatest champions of their cause never dreamt of making this provsion a permanent feature of the Constitution. Rather they were against it because, they thought, that would foster separateness and divisiveness and isolate them from the mainstream. Had their intentions been otherwise, there was no need of incorporating this specific provision in Part XVI of the Constitution to negate the effects of four other provisions of the same part. The idea was to give a fillip to a section of people, albeit for a temporary period, though the modality might be questioned. In any case, the provisions of Articles 330 to 333 are temporary in nature which will cease to have any effect on the expiration of the period provided for in Article 334; it is, however, a different matter that the period never expires as it is always extended by amending this provision of the Constitution.

In the name of bringing about a psychological change in the attitude of the people and ameliorating the economic and educational conditions of the Scheduled Castes as well as doing them justice, this provision has been included in the Constitution. If this sort of provision could help bring a section of population, put under the rubric of Scheduled Castes, to the level of other advanced classes, educationally, economically and socially, it would not have been in operation for the last 45 years, with no sign of its abrogation in the near future. On the other hand it has only accentuated the divide. When the 'Communal Award' was pronounced by the British Prime Minister in 1935 providing for, amongst others reserved seats for the Scheduled Castes, it was condemned by all and sundry because of its disintergrating tendencies. It is a pity that the same set of people, while framing the future Constitution of India, not only faltered and wavered but allowed themselves to be carried away by partisan interests. In the case of British it is understandable. They did it with a missionary zeal, of dividing the people on any pretext. But the framers were not imbued with this spirit. Why they could not rise to the occasion to purge the society of communal forces? Can it be easily explained?

Ambedkar knew it very well that once a provision of such a nature could be incorporated in the Constitution, "it will not be beyond their (Scheduled Castes community) capacity or their intelligence to invent new ways of getting the same protection which they are promised here". What a prophetic statement!

Notes and References

1. Rao, *op. cit.*, Vol. III, p. 99.
2. *Ibid.*, p. 485.
3. *Ibid.*, pp. 490-91.
4. *Ibid.*, p. 493.
5. *Ibid.*, p. 639
6. *Ibid.*, Vol. IV, pp. 375-76.
7. *CAD*, Vol. IX, dated 17-9-49, p. 1669.
8. *Ibid.*, dated 24-8-89, pp. 674-97.
9. *CAD*, Vol. IX, dated 17-9-49, pp. 697-98.
10. *The Constitution (Eighth Amendment) Act.*

11. *The Constitution (Twenty-third Amendment) Act.*
12. *The Constitution (Forty-fifth Amendment) Act.*
13. *The Constitution (Sixty-second Amendment) Act.*

18

National Commission for Scheduled Castes, Scheduled Tribes, etc. (Article 338)

One of the points included in the questionnaire issued to the members of the Minorities Sub-Committee in March 1947 was about the machinery to be set up to ensure that the safeguards of the minorities were effective. The replies of the members to this item were either for setting up of a Minority Commission or for entrusting the judiciary with this responsibility. Jagjivan Ram, H.J. Khandeker, R.K. Sidhva, P.K. Salve, S.P. Mookherjee, S.H. Prater, Ujjal Singh and Harnam Singh were in favour of a Minority Commission while M. Ruthnaswamy and Homi Modi suggested the second course.

Jagjivan Ram suggested that

> There shall be an independent Minorities Commission to deal with those rights which are not enforceable by a court of law, in the Centre and in every Province.
>
> Its composition shall be as follows:
>
> 1. One judge of the Supreme Court (of the Provincial High Court in the case of a Province) who will be ex-officio chairman of the commission.
>
> 2. Three members of the Legislative Assembly elected by the members of the minority community in the Assembly concerned.

3. Three members of the minority communities nominated by the Government.

The commission shall have power—

(a) to call for any information from the Government.

(b) to call for any person, official or non-official, to appear before it and give evidence.

(c) to examine laws or rules which operate against a minority or minorities.

(d) to examine acts of omission or commission on the part of the executive in administration of the privileges and facilities granted to the minorities and submit report to the Government.

Procedure : The commission shall examine on its own initiative or on application from any person of the aggrieved community, in the matter of any infringement of the rights, privileges or facilities of the minorities, and submit its findings with a recommendation to the Government. The Government shall, thereupon, take steps, legislative or administrative, as the case may be, to give effect to the recommendations of the commission.[1]

Khandekar's suggestion was couched more or less in identical language.[2]

Sidhwa advocated a minority commission as outlined by Babu Rajendra Prasad in his Book "India Divided," to ensure that the safeguards, provided in the Constitution for minorities were fully adhered to.[3]

Salve favoured the establishment of a Minority Commission with adequate and full representatives of minorities. In questions exclusively pertaining to any minority special consideration be given to the view of the minority.[4]

S.P. Mookherjee suggested that

There shall be a permanent Minorities Commission under the Union Government which in consultation with that Commission, shall immediately after the first operation of this Constitution frame the necessary rules and procedure for protecting these rights.

> In every Province also there shall be a permanent Minorities Commission, consisting of the representatives of the minorities concerned to advise the Provincial Government and Legislature in regard to the protection of the interests and rights of the minorities. If the Provincial Government fails to protect the rights of the minorities, the commission may ask for the intervention of the Union Government.
>
> No citizen of the Indian Union shall be debarred from approaching the Federal Court for relief against the infringement of any of the aforesaid rights.
>
> In case any Provincial Government fails to implement any of these rights, or in case any decision of the Minorities Commission either at the Centre or in the Province, or any decision on an appeal from an aggrieved person is not duly executed by the proper provincial authority in that behalf, then and in every such case, as far as only as the circumstances of each case require, the Union Government may make remedial laws for the due protection of such rights.[5]

Prater, a member belonging to the Anglo-Indian community, held the view that

> Should a Union Government be established for the whole of India as envisaged in the Cabinet Mission's Plan, the protection of the minorities might be effected by a convention established between the Union Government and the Federating Provinces and States and placed under international guarantees. In the alternative Minority Offices, Mixed Commissions and an Arbitral Tribunal with functions such as already indicated may be set up in required areas. This regional machinery must be supplemented by right of appeal to the Supreme Federal Court, direct or through the 'Minority Offices'.[6]

In their joint memorandum Ujjal Singh and Harnam Singh proposed that

> The Constitution Act shall provide the establishment at the Centre and in each of the Province of independent Minority Commission which shall be composed

of a representative of each of the communities concerned.

The functions of the Commission shall be:

(a) to keep constant watch over the interests of the minority communities in the area;

(b) to call for such information from the Government concerned as the Commission may consider necessary for the discharging of its functions;

(c) to review periodically—for example once every six months—the policy pursued in legislation and administration by the Legislature and the Executive in regard to the implementing of non-justiciable fundamental rights and other minority rights assured by the Constitution to the minority community and to submit a report to the Government concerned.

The recommendations of the commission shall be considered by the Cabinet concerned as soon as possible. In case any of the recommendations are not accepted wholly or in part, the report shall be referred to the Federal Court and the decision on such report taken by the Federal Court shall be binding on the Government concerned.[7]

Sardar Harnam Singh's note to the Fundamental Rights Sub-Committee sent on March 18, 1947, had also recommended the same provision.[8]

The Memorandum sent by the representatives of the Jain community to the Minorities Sub-committee in March/April, 1947, stipulated that

a permanent commission consisting of accredited representatives of the various minorities should be set up both at the Centre and in the Provinces. All legislation affecting the minorities should require the prior consent of those commissions before such legislation is introduced and also should be approved by it. Any member of the commission may demand that legislation affecting his own community should require the consent of that particular community. In case of dispute between the legislature and the

> commission the matter should be referred to the Federal Court and its precedents should be binding on both the legislature and the community concerned. It is suggested that in any Central Judicial machinery that may be set up there should be a special section which alone would be competent to decide both questions of law and fact with regard to the minorities.[9]

That apart, Ambedkar's Memorandum and Draft Articles on the Rights of States and Minorities sent on March 24, 1947, to the Fundamental Rights Sub-Committee demanded that

> There shall be appointed an Officer to be called the Superintendent of Minority Affairs.
>
> His status shall be similar to that of the Auditor-General appointed under section 166 of the Government of India Act of 1935 and removable in like manner and on the like grounds as a judge of the Supreme Court.
>
> It shall be the duty of the Superintendent to prepare an annual report on the treatment of minorities by the public, as well as by the Governments, Union and State, and of any transgressions of safeguards or any miscarriage of justice due to communal bias by Governments or their officers.
>
> The annual report of the Superintendent shall be placed on the Table of the Lagislatures, Union and State, and the Government, Union and State, shall be bound to provide time for the discussion of the report.[10]

It may be noted that all these replies and memoranda were received in March/April, 1947, when the partition of the country on the basis of Two Nation Theory was not finalised.

The Minorities Sub-Committee discussed the question of an administrative machinery to ensure protection of minority rights in its meetings held on July 21-27, 1947 when the division of the country was a certainty and a date was even fixed. The Sub-Committee submitted its report to the Advisory Committee on July 27, 1947. In the report the Minority Sub-Commitee commented that

> There were four proposals before the sub-committee as regards the administrative machinery to ensure protection of minority rights. Mr. Khandekar moved a proposal for a Minority Commission whose findings should be mandatory on Government. This was lost by a large majority. Mr. Anthony proposed a Minority Commission with the right only to make a report. This also was lost. Dr. Ambedkar suggested that there should be an independent officer appointed by the President at the Centre and by the Governors in the Provinces to report to the Union and Provincial Legislatures respectively about the working of the safeguards provided for the minorities. This was accepted by a majority of 16 to 2 votes. The proposal that the officer should be independent of the executive like the Auditor-General or the judge of a High Court was negatived by a majority of 9 to 6. In view of the voting on this proposal of Dr. Ambedkar there was no voting on Mr. C. Rajagopalachari's proposal that a sub-committee of the Legislature concerned, together with an adequate secretariat staff, should be charged with preparing a report for submission to the Legislature.[11]

The Advisory Committee considered the report of the Minorities Sub-Committee on July 28-31, 1947. In the meeting held on July 31, Munshi moved that an officer should be appointed by the President at the Centre and by the Governors in the Provinces to report to the Union and Provincial Legislatures about the working of the safeguards provided for the minorities. This was carried.[12]

The Advisory Committee in its report to the President of the Constituent Assembly on August 8, 1947, noted that

> The minorities' representatives in the committee naturally attached importance to the provision of administrative machinery for ensuring that the guarantees and safeguards provided for the minori-

ties both in the Constitution and by executive orders are in fact implemented in practice. After considerable discussion, we have come to the conclusion that the best arrangement would be for the Centre and for each of the Provinces to appoint a special Minority Officer whose duty will be to enquire into cases in which it is alleged that rights and safeguards have been infringed and to submit a report to the appropriate legislature.[13]

It, therefore, recommended in clause 11 of the summary of recommendations that

An Officer be appointed by the President at the centre and by the Governors in the Provinces to report to the Union and Provincial Legislatures respectively about the working of the safeguards provided for the minorities.[14]

Clause 11 of the Advisory Committee's recommendations was considered and adopted by the Constituent Assembly on August 28, 1947 without any debate.[15]

Keeping this decision of the Assembly in mind, the Constitutional Adviser incorporated this provision in his Draft Constitution of October, 1947, as Clause 229 :

(1) There shall be a Special Officer for minorities for the Federation who shall be appointed by the President, and a Special Officer for minorities for each Province who shall be appointed by the Governor of the Province.

(2) It shall be the duty of the Special Officer for the Federation to investigate all matters relating to the safeguards provided for minorities under this Constitution in connection with the affairs of the Federation and to report to the President upon the working of the safeguards at such intervals as the President may direct, and the President shall cause all such reports to be laid before the Federal Parliament.

(3) It shall be the duty of the Special Officer for a Province to investigate all matters relating to the safeguards provided for minorities under this Consti-

tution in connection with the affairs of the Province and to report to the Governor of the Province upon the working of the safeguards at such intervals as the Governor may direct, and the Governor shall cause all such reports to be laid before the Provincial Legislature.[16]

The Drafting Committee made some minor drafting changes on February 5, 1948,[17] and incorporated it as Draft Article 299 in the Draft Constitution prepared and circulated in February, 1948 as follows:

(1) There shall be a Special Officer for minorities for the Union who shall be appointed by the President, and a Special Officer for minorities for each State for the time being specified in Part I of the First Schedule who shall be appointed by the Governor of the State.

(2) It shall be the duty of the Special Officer for the Union to investigate all matters relating to the safeguards provided for minorities under this Constitution in connection with the affairs of the Union and to report to the President upon the working of the safeguards at such intervals as the President may direct, and the President shall cause all such reports to be laid before Parliament.

(3) It shall be the duty of the Special Officer for a State so specified to investigate all matters relating to the safeguards provided for minorities under this Constitution in connection with the affairs of the state and to report to the Governor of the State upon the working of the safeguards as the Governor may direct and the Governor shall cause all such reports to be laid before the Legislature of the State.[18]

When this Draft Constitution was circulated for eliciting comments, suggestions, etc., Tajamul Husain suggested that Article 299 be deleted. The observation of the Constitutional Adviser on this suggestion was that Article 299 was based on the recommendation of the Advisory Committee on Minority Rights as adopted by the Constituent Assembly during the August 1947 session.

This amendment which sought to delete Article 299 involved a departure from the decision of the Constituent Assembly and should therefore be left to the Constituent Assembly for final decision. The Drafting Committee decided in October, 1948 to insert the words "each House of" after the words "laid before" in clause (2) of Article 299.[19]

The Assembly took up this Article for consideration on June 16, 1949, but could not proceed with it as it was held over.[20] On August 26, 1949, Dr. Ambedkar introduced an amended Article providing for a Special Officer for minorities only at the Centre and the original provision for a minority officer both at the Centre and in each of the Provinces was dispensed with. As the number of minorities had been considerably reduced it was not desirable to have a cumbrous provision like that for having an officer in each province, he pointed out. The purpose of the original article would be carried out if the Centre appointed an officer and made him report to the President, he said. Dr. Monmohan Das raised a point of order as it was not settled then as to who these minority communities were. Sardar Hukam Singh pointed out that if Article 296 (Article 335) was to remain as it was drafted then there would be no other safeguard for any other minority except the Scheduled Castes. That being so, he pleaded to take up this article side by side with the other article which dealt with Scheduled Castes, Scheduled Tribes etc. Naziruddin Ahmad pointed out that if Article 296 was carried, this article would be meaningless. M. Anantyasayanam Ayyangar observed that there was no definition of 'Minorities' in the whole of the Draft Constitution. Unless they were specified, its interpretation would be left to the jurisdiction of courts. Since the Special Officer was to be appointed for two or three minorities, like Scheduled Castes, Scheduled Tribes, Anglo-Indians, it was better to specify them. Unless this is done, any minority would come forward and ask for this or that right, he felt. Pandit Hirday Nath Kunzru pointed out that the words 'minority communities' were used in both the Articles— 296 (Article 335) and 299 (Article 338) and the two articles were inter-connected. The decision on Article 296 would affect the decision about Article 299. So Article 299 would have to be reconsidered in the light of the decision on Article 296.Though the President of the Constituent Assembly and T.T. Krishnamachari were keen to continue the discussion on this article, in view of the insistence of these members, the consideration of this article was held over.[21]

The discussion of this article was held over for the third time on September 9, 1949, because some Members got notice of certain amendments to this article too late.[22]

The Constituent Assembly finally considered this article on October 14, 1949, after the adoption of Article 296. Munshi, on behalf of the Drafting Committee, introduced a revised article containing changes in two important respect. In the first place, the jurisdiction of the Special Officer was limited to Scheduled Castes, Scheduled Tribes, Anglo-Indians and other backward classes. The second change was that there was to be only one Special Officer to be appointed by the Union Government who would function for the Centre as well as for the States.

As many as six amendments were moved by R.K. Sidhva, Kuladhar Chaliha, Sardar Bhupinder Singh Mann, H.V. Kamath, Brajeswar Prasad and Sardar Hukum Singh. Sidhva's amedment was for deletion of that category of persons coming under other backward classes. Chaliha wanted to empower the Parliament to approve, modify or add to the report of the Special Officer. Kamath suggested that action on the report of the Special Officer should be taken by the Parliament and not by the President. Prasad made the article more elaborate and comprehensive regarding its composition, powers, etc. The controversy, however, principally centred round the demand of Mann and Hukam Singh that the jurisdiction of the officer should extend to matters pertaining to all minorities, including Muslims, Christians and Sikhs. Munshi replying to the debate emphasized that the safeguards which the Special Officer was to investigate would be the political safeguards for the protection of certain well-defined sections of citizens; and since specific political safeguards were now confined to the Scheduled Castes, Scheduled Tribes and Anglo-Indians, and certain backward classes, the Special Officer would deal only with these safeguards and these communities. The amendments were negatived and the article as proposed by Munshi was adopted.

This is what transpired in the Assembly:

Shri K.M. Munshi (Bombay General)

Sir, I move—

"That with reference to Amendment No. 63, for Article 299, the following be substituted:-

'299. (1) There shall be a Special Officer for the Scheduled Castes and the Scheduled Tribes to be appointed by the President.

(2) It shall be the duty of the Special Officer to investigate all matters relating to the safeguards provided for the Scheduled Castes and Scheduled Tribes under this Constitution and report to the President upon the working of those safeguards at such intervals as the President may direct, and the President shall cause all such reports to be laid before each House of Parliament.

(3) In this article, the reference to the Scheduled Castes and Scheduled Tribes shall be construed as including the reference to such other backward classes as the President may on receipt of the report of a Commission appointed under clause (1) of Article 301 of this Constitution by order specify and also to the Anglo-Indian community."

I need not say anything more on this amendment. The Special Officer is intended to look after the political safeguards that have already been given by other articles in the Constitution. I therefore, move the amendment.

Shri R.K. Sidhva

Sir, I move :

"That in Amendment No. 64 above, in clause (3) of the proposed Article 299 the words 'to such other backward classes...

Backward classes have gone. Mr. Munshi has put it only the Scheduled Castes and Scheduled Tribes. If this is so, I do not want to move my amendment.

Mr. President

Clause (3) of Mr. Munshi's amendment says—

"In this article, the reference to the Scheduled Castes and Scheduled Tribes shall be construed as including the reference to such other backward classes as the President may on receipt of the report, etc."

Shri R.K. Sidhva

Then I move my amendment, Sir.

"...as the President may on receipt of the report of a Commission appointed under clause (1) of article 301 of this Constitution by order specify and" be deleted.

Sir, I do not want to speak at length because I have touched upon this point in my previous amendment. I know there is the article 301 which specifies backward classes. I am not quite sure that it will be easy for the President to find out who are the backward classes. I do feel that this backward classes article will remain a dead article, because I know that people who will come in the name of the backward classes will come only for their own personal position and personal aggrandisement to insert themselves as backward classes to win their own personal ends. I know people would come in the name of backward classes only to get a few posts, leaving the poor masses of that community in the lurch. I am therefore strongly opposed to the inclusion of the term 'backward classes'. Article 301 says 'investigate the conditions of socially and educationally backward classes'. Now, what does that mean? 80 per cent, of our people are illiterate. Are they all backward? Sometimes people who are illiterate have a far better sense of argument than the literate people.

Therefore, Sir, I contend that there is no such class as a backward class. The Britishers wanted to dub many as backward classes and then play them up to the whole world and say that India consists of so many backward classes and so they do not deserve freedom. I do not want this term "backward classes" perpetuated in our Constitution. The sooner we do away with this, the better for our country, the better for our position in the world. Beyond the Scheduled Castes and the Scheduled Tribes, I do not want any kind of reservation for anybody. If there is any class which feels that their interests have not been justly represented in the services, they should go to the proper authorities and find the remedy. After hearing Sardar Patel, I do not think there will be any injustice to any class of people who really deserve some kind of sympathy and justice. If there is any injustice, then our leaders are there who will look after their interests. With these few words, I commend my amendment for the acceptance of the House.

Shri Kuladhar Chaliha (Assam: General)

Sir, I move:

"That in Amendment No. 63, above at the end of clause (2) of the proposed Article 299, the word 'for its approval, modification or addition' be added."

Sir, the article merely says that such reports shall be laid before each House of the Parliament. We should positively mention there what the powers of the Parliament are in this regard. As such, these additional words will make the clause a little clearer than it is. My own experience is that many such reports are laid before the House, but very few people take care either to look into it or give effect to it. So, in order to be more specific, I have added these words. I trust the Drafting Committee and Dr. Ambedkar will see that it is changed. I commend my amendment to the acceptance of the House.

Sardar Bhopinder Singh Mann

Sir, I move:

"That in Amendment No. 63 above, in clause (1) of the proposed Article 299, after the word 'by the President' the word 'and a Special Officer for minorities for each State for the time being specified in Parts I and II and Part III of the First Schedule who shall be appointed by the Governor or Rajpramukh of the State, as the case may be' be added."

"That in Amendment No. 63 above, in clause (2) of the proposed Article 299, after the words 'under this Constitution and' the words 'their representation in different legislatures and services of the country' be inserted.

"That in Amendment No. 63 above, at the end of the Explanation to the proposed Article 299, the words 'Muslim, Christians, and Sikhs' be added."

My first amendment states that the Minority Officers as originally proposed to be appointed in the States should be permitted to continue. I feel that a Minority Officer appointed at the Centre will be at too distant a place to investigate and see the daily working of the Constitution. If Minority Officers are not there, this safeguard contained in Article 299 will not be effective. After all, it is the daily life and daily administration and governance that count more than anything. I request that Minority Officers in the States should continue and there should not be merely one officer appointed at the Centre.

My other two amendments state that there should be Minority Officers to investigate, not only the safeguards contained in the Constitution, but also to look into matters pertaining to all minorities and see how they have fared so far as representation in legislatures is concerned or securing of services in the administrative machinery is concerned. There seems to be some confusion about minorities. Certain friends say that because the Minorities Advisory Committee resolved that there will be no political reservations in the legislatures, there will henceforth be no minorities in the country. It takes my breath away how a paper resolution can do away with minorities, and that too, in so short an interval as just a year or so.

The position of this Constituent Assembly, as I understand from its previous decisions, is that they agreed that this country has got minorities. They classified these minorities into three groups—Group A, Group B and Group C. Not only that, I hold here another pamphlet published by the Ministry of Information and Broadcasting. They corroborated the same view and say the basis of these minorities is their religion. They mention the Minorities in the Indian Union as the Muslims, the Sikhs, the Christians, the Parsis and the Anglo-Indians. Now, to agree basically against this contention is to go behind their own words.

A happy sort of atmosphere has been brought about and the minorities henceforward repose their confidence in the good sense of the majority—not that they are wiped out altogether from our country. We march forward in the hope that no injustice will be done, but from that it should not be argued that henceforward the minorities cease to exist. After all, safeguards are just the instruments securing the due share of minorities in the governance and administrative machinery of the country. If we are assured that no injustice will be done so far as governance or administrative machinery is concerned, naturally we will not ask for any political safeguards in the Assemblies or elsewhere.

It is a very daring experiment. I wish it success wholeheartedly. I am quite sure that it will succeed. It should succeed. I shall be very happy indeed if the fears of the minority communities are ultimately proved to be false. But to enable the experiment to succeed, I say that the cases of all the minorities should be reviewed and Minority Officers should be appointed for all the Minorities. After all, you are not giving anything. You are not giving any quota or any share or reserving anything. You only say that these Minorities Officers will be reviewing the case of these minorities and Scheduled Castes. I take your word.

You are taking a great responsibility upon your shoulders. You promise that you will give us no cause for anxiety. Then may I ask Dr. Ambedkar why he feels shy of reviewing the cases of all the minorities? I am quite sure you will be very just, you will be very fair and that the minorities will get their due share. Then, where is the harm if all these cases are reviewed periodically and brought before the Assembly and the Parliament? It would give us a constitutional opportunity of reviewing our position. I shudder to think of the alternative, which will be only to raise some sort of agitation and din it into your ears that an injustice has been done to us. Instead of resorting to certain unconstitutional methods, this provides a constitutional door. I believe there will be no injustice whatever, but that is no reason why these constitutional doors should be closed.

In all earnestness I plead before you—kindly do not abrogate these articles, kindly do not re-open what has already been conceded. I shall be failing in my duty if I do not represent to you that the abrogation of these articles 296 and last of all of 299 will have very widespread and serious repercussions so far as my community is concerned. You are taking away that mental assurance that you have all along given to us. You had said, "Do not worry, there will be somebody all the time observing the working of the Constitution". Now you take that away. You say, "Justice or Injustice, case or no case, your case will not be reviewed." I think it will be injurious to that psychological atmosphere and mental assurance that you had given. I think by taking away this machinery by which the working of the Constitution so far as minorities are concerned will be observed, you are taking away our last hope of securing a hearing and of approaching the Parliament in a constitutional manner and getting our cases periodically reviewed. I believe, Sir, it will not be disfiguring the Constitution, as the popular slogan goes.

In the end I must refer to a certain assurance which is said to have been given by some representatives of my community. It has created a certain impression, and I beg to differ from Sardar Patel and to say that it has created a false impression. Actually, so far as the assurance is concerned, (I do not controvert the facts) I have asked those representatives about the assurance and I have got a copy with me containing the assurance. I have to remove the misunderstanding because it is creating a false impression in my community and elsewhere and hence there is the charge that the Sikhs are going back upon the undertaking they had given. In view of the fact that articles 296 and 299 had been agreed to by the House as recommended by the Advisory Committee, and the draft wording of which has been the same for the last one year and in addition to that they have agreed that Scheduled Castes will be included, the Sikh representatives said that henceforward they were not asking for any further assurance. But having got that assurance, if you now turn back and reopen the case in this House and thereby recede on articles 296 and 299, certainly our pledges cannot be thrown at our face to effect that we are going back on them. Let me read the actual wording of the agreement. If there is anything else that should be in it, let that be produced, so that this false impression can be removed. It runs :

'We, the Sikh Members of the East Punjab Assembly, beg to refer to the report of the Sub-Committee of the Minorities Advisory Committee and to say that in so far as this relates to the problems of the Sikh community, the following points should be conceded in addition to the recommendations made in the said report....

You agreed to certain recommendations made by Minorities Advisory Committee, which are clear and emphatic and so far as the sharing in the services is concerned, it is said that it will be conceded and a specific article relating to it will be incorporated in the draft Constitution. You also say that a Minority Officer for all the Minority Communities will be appointed. You conceded it and we gave the assurance that we will not be asking any further safeguards in addition to what already had been conceded.

Shri R.K. Sidhva

What order? What was conceded?

Sardar Bhopinder Singh Mann

What you conceded and you have not yet abrogated. You conceded it in August 1947.

Shri R.K. Sidhva

There were subsequent developments.

Shri Bhopinder Singh Man

I shall refer to that too. After this there was another

report of the Advisory Committee dated 11th May 1949. If my friend were to read it carefully, not a single reference is there so far as these two resolutions are concerned. So far as the reservation in the Assembly is concerned, that has been taken away. So far as the other decisions, as regards the services and the Minority Officer for reviewing the cases of the minority communities are concerned, they stand and here I request my friend to produce a single sentence or line in the subsequent report submitted by the Advisory Committee and as approved by this House to show that in any case article 296 and article 299 have been abrogated.

Shri R.K. Sidhva

I have been a Member of the Minorities Committee from the very inception and I have no recollection of this question having come up so prominently as my friend relates it now.

Sardar Bhopinder Singh Mann

It is not my fault if my friend misses the point. But unfortunately, it is there incorporated in black and white. For me it is a very important point. You...

Mr. President

What is the document you have been reading from? You referred to some sort of pledge.

Sardar Bhopinder Singh Mann

I was referring to certain assurances which were said to have been given by Sikh Members that henceforward they would not be opening any case and would not be bringing forward any matter or any other safeguards and I say this, in spite of Sardar Patel's speech. As a matter of fact this has gone into the press as if there was some such assurance to give up all the minority rights.

Mr. President

Have you got that document with you?

Sardar Bhopinder Singh Mann

I have read it.

Mr. president

I did not quite follow. If you read out that whole document to which Sardar Patel was referring....

Sardar Bhopinder Singh Mann

I have this copy with me. If there is any other document, then I stand corrected with regard to what I have read.

Mr. President

I think you had better read it out so that Sarder Patel or anyone else can have a chance of finding out whether this is the document.

Sardar Bhopinder Singh Mann

I have said I have no direct knowledge of that document. With regard to the document that those Sikh representatives gave, I have ascertained from them that this is the document containing the assurances that they gave.

Mr. President

Let us have the document.

Sardar Bhopinder Singh Mann

Yes, the document reads as follows :

"We, the Sikh Members of the East Punjab Assembly, beg to refer to the report of the sub-committee of the Minorities Advisory Committee and to say that in so far as this relates to the problems of the Sikh community, the following points should be conceded in addition to the recommendations made in the said report :-

1. The Sikh Backward Classes, namely, Mazhbis, Kabirpanthis, Ramdasias, Bawrias, Sareras and Sikligars, should be placed at par with the Scheduled Castes in the matter of their political rights. This can be done by —

(a) including these classes in the Scheduled Castes enumerated in the Draft Constitution; or

(b) by abolishing the reservation of seats for all minorities including the Scheduled Castes in East Punjab; or

(c) reserving seats for the said Sikh Backward Classes

out of the quota of seats reserved for Sikhs. The estimated population strength of these classes among the Sikhs is roughly ten per cent; these classes would get ten per cent of the quota of Sikh seats.

2. In the matter of language, script and culture, either zonal arrangements should be provided in the Constitution, or, settled immediately by executive action.

3. Sikh minorities outside East Punjab should receive similar treatment as has been or might be granted to other minorities in the matter of political rights.

We would, respectfully suggest that for the elucidation of our case we should be given a hearing before the final decision is taken. We may add that we have no other communal safeguards to ask for so far as provision in the Constitution is concerned and that satisfaction along the lines suggested will go a long way to win over the Sikh masses for the national cause."

Shri R.K. Sidhva

Who has signed it?

Sardar Bhopinder Singh Mann

The Sikh members and Sikh representatives signed it. The question is that we have to win over the confidence of the minorities. I do repeat here that it is going back upon certain things which you conceded yourself.

Shri R.K. Sidhva

There is nothing in the article to say that we are going back.

Mr. President

Let me have a copy of the document. I shall have it ascertained from Sardar Patel whether it is the representatives' document or whether there is any other document and then I shall communicate it to you.

Sardar Bhopinder Singh Mann

Mr. Sidhva knows perfectly well that in the light of the President's decision today that it is a reopening of the case......

Mr. President

So far as the question of reopening is concerned the case was put on the basis that a decision has already been taken and I said that even if decision has been taken it can be reopened. By reopening I did not mean going back on anything that has been done. Reopening only meant that objection was taken on the ground that a certain decision had been taken and this decision which we are going to take now would be inconsistent with that; and I held that even if it was so, it can be taken up, if 25 per cent of the Members were in favour of reconsidering the question.

Shri H.V. Kamath

Sir, I move:

"That in Amendment No. 63, at the end of clause (2) of the proposed Article 299, the words 'for such action as Parliament may deem necessary' be inserted.

It is likely that when the report is presented to the President by the Special Officer appointed under this article, Parliament may consider it necessary or even essential that in view of the advance or the progress registered by the Scheduled Castes and Tribes it would be in the best interests of the country to abolish totally the distinction called Scheduled Castes and Tribes and there will be one big unified Hindu community. If this action were to be necessary, it cannot be left to the President alone. It is Parliament which has been invested with power in this Constitution to take the decision. Constitutional safeguards have been guaranteed to the Scheduled Castes and Tribes under this Constitution and it is only Parliament that can take a fundamental decision of this nature. Therefore, I desire that the report presented to Parliament should not be taken up for action by the President but the action taken shall be by the Parliament and not the President.

There is another Amendment No. 75 which was in respect of Amendment No. 63. But unfortunately that amendment has been substituted by Amendment No. 64 just moved by Mr. Munshi. But my amendment would apply in a modified form to this amendment as well. In that Amendment (No. 63) with regard to the explanation in that article...

Mr. President

There is no explanation in Amendment No. 63.

Shri H.V. Kamath

Instead of explanation we have got clause (3) in Amendment No. 64. That amendment proposes reservation to the Anglo-Indian Community as such. A specific reference to the Anglo-Indian Community is, in my humble judgment out of place. We have provided safeguards for the Scheduled Castes and Tribes......

Mr. President

As a matter of fact I think that the substance of No. 75 has been taken in clause (3). Clause (3) of Amendment No. 64 does not include the Anglo-Indian community now.

Shri H.V. Kamath

It does, Sir. The last words are "the Anglo-Indian community" and I want that to be deleted.

Mr. President

Yes, I see.

Shri H.V. Kamath

The reference to Scheduled Castes and Tribes is construed as meaning also backward classes as the President may by order specify after receiving the report of the Commission. The Anglo-Indian community is neither a backward class nor a Scheduled Caste. I do not know how it can be lumped together with these two classes—Scheduled Castes and backward communities. The only safeguard that will be provided to the Anglo-Indian community is representation in the House of the People and State Legislatures through nomination, in case the President or the Governor thinks that that community is not adequately represented in those legislatures, and that too for a period of ten years. After that the safeguard automatically lapses.

As regards the safeguard given to the Anglo-Indian

community regarding reservation in the services, the Anglo-Indian community, not being a backward community at all, is even today, over-represented in some services, far in excess of its proportion to the population. Therefore I feel that in this clause (3) reference to the Anglo-Indian community is absolutely unnecessary. The Anglo-Indian community is not all a religious community: it is at best, or at worst, a racial community and it has a racial basis. I think we should not give encouragement to racial communities in this country. If at all they want to join any minority they would join the Christian community in India. They have no right to exist as a separate Anglo-Indian community. I hope that necessary changes will be made in clause (3) of this article.

Shri Brajeshwar Prasad

Sir, I move:

"That in Amendment No. 63 of List II (Second Week), for the proposed Article 299, the following be substituted:

'299. (1) There shall be Special Officer for the Scheduled Castes and Scheduled Tribes to be appointed by the President.

(2) The special officer in consultation with the President may appoint a special officer for each State who shall work exclusively under his superintendence, direction and control.

(3) The special officer appointed either for the Union or for a State shall not be a member either of the Scheduled Tribes, the Scheduled Castes or of such other backward classes as the President may on receipt of the report of a commission appointed under clause (1) of Article 301 of this Constitution by order specify.

(4) The salaries, allowances and pensions payable to the special officer for the Union and to the special officer for each State shall be expenditure charged on the revenues of India.

(5) It shall be the duty of the special officer for the Union to make annual recommendations as to the steps that should be taken by the Union and by each State to

improve the economic, educational and cultural level of the Scheduled Tribes, the Scheduled Castes or of such other backward classes as the President may on receipt of the report of a commission appointed under clause (1) of Article 301 of this Constitution by order specify and as to the sums that should be separately allotted in the annual budget of the Union Government and of each State Government for the purpose; and the President shall cause all such recommendations to be laid before Parliament.

(6) Parliament shall have the power to reject or accept in whole or in parts any of the recommendations contained in the Report.

(7) All State Governments shall be bound to make annual allotment in their budgets of such sums as Parliament may deem to be necessary for the purpose of giving effect to the recommendations contained in the Report of the special officer for the Union.

(8) Until the appointment of the commission and consideration of its Report by the President under clause (1) of Article 301 of the Constitution the backward classes shall consist of such castes and communities as may be determined by the President.

(9) The President may delegate the power to the special officer for the Union to supervise and give effect to all or any recommendations made by the commission appointed under Article 301 and accepted by the President.

(10) All appointments to be made under clause (1) of this Article shall be made from the following category of persons :-

(a) Doctors,

(b) Scientists,

(c) Sociologists and

(d) Anthropologists.

(11) Parliament shall have the power to repeal or amend any or all of the provisions of this Article'."

Sardar Hukam Singh

Mr. President, Sir, I beg to move :-

"That in Amendment No. 63 above, in the explanation to clause (2) of the proposed Article 299, after the word `means' the words `the Muslims, the Christians, the Sikhs, the Parsees, the Anglo-Indians' be inserted."

Sir, I would not go over the ground that has already been covered.....

Shri K.M. Munshi

May I rise to point of Order? The words of my Amendment No. 64 only refer to "all matters relating to the safeguards", that is only where safeguards are provided by the Constitution. No safeguards have been provided for the Muslims, Christians, Sikhs and Parsees. The only safeguards in the Constitution so far accepted are with regard to Anglo-Indians and the Scheduled Castes and Scheduled Tribes. Therefore, Sir, my submission is that there are no safeguards for the other communities and this amendment is out of order.

Sardar Hukam Singh

Under the Constitution there are safeguards.

Shri K.M. Munshi

There are no safeguards for these communities.

Sardar Hukam Singh

Under Article 23 there are safeguards for minorities. That is also included in the Constitution.

Shri K.M. Munshi

Article 23 is fundamental, cultural right for which the safeguard is the Supreme Court and not the Special Officer.

Mr. President

The Special Officer may be called upon to report as to how that has worked. You can go to the Federal Court or to the Supreme Court and get its decision whether a particular article of the Constitution has been broken, but then the Officer may also report whether a particular article in the Constitution has been given effect to and so that is what Sardar Hukam Singh wants.

Shri K.M. Munshi

Sir, that is not a safeguard. It is not, with great respect, a safeguard. 'Safeguard' means a political safeguard for a community which has been provided, but fundamental right belongs to every citizen and if his right is infringed, the only remedy that he has is to go to the Supreme Court. Supposing an officer is invested with the power to investigate into it, it has no value.

Mr. President

It has a certain value for administration purposes and the Government can take note of the report of an officer that a particular right which has been conferred is not being observed or is not being respected. The Administration can take note of that and can deal with that.

Sardar Hukam Singh

If the violation is not taken to the Federal Court, then, would it not be the duty of the Government to see whether the minorities are being fairly treated or not or whether they are getting the justice or not?

I am not afraid of the answer. I cannot go over the ground already covered and I would submit only one or two things. Even if my request and my amendment under 296 has been rejected, then it is all the more necessary that under 299 the Special Officer should be invested with the powers and authority to go into details of the safeguards and rights of all minorities and it should not be restricted to these Scheduled Castes and Scheduled Tribes alone. We have been told here that we should trust our leaders and we should trust the future. This is all right and everything conceded. Granting that everybody is honest the Government wants to do justice to every community, what then unless the Government know whether anything amiss has been done, whether any unfair treatment has been meted out, whether any pledges have been violated or whether fair treatment is being meted out to everybody? Unless the Government has some source of knowing it, how will it be in a position to redress the wrongs? Therefore, my submission is that even if it was considered that it was not necessary to include these minorities and to specify them under 296, it is very essential that the officer if he is to be appointed ought to go into these things to find out and report on the working of the Constitution so far as all the minorities are concerned, and it should not be restricted to one or two classes only.

I take this opportunity of answering one thing that has already been said. I put a question, but that has not been answered. I request the Honourable Mr. Munshi to answer that. I was told by the Honourable Sardar that if the Sikhs are sorry, then they can return what they have got and they can have the safeguards if they want. That was my complaint. I should like to know what they have got. We are told that four backward classes have been included. Where are they included in any Schedule? That is what I want to know. There was a schedule and we had to sacrifice everything for getting those four backward classes included in that Schedule. This Schedule is absolutely gone now. Under Article 300-A, it is left to the President to consult the Governor and then to specify who would be the Scheduled Castes. I have paid the price, as I am told. I have sacrificed everything that I had, but I have got nothing in the Constitution. This is my complaint and that shall be answered.

Mr. President

These are all the amendments we have got Does any Member wish to say anything?

Honourable Members

No, Sir.

Shri K.M. Munshi

Sir, I have very few words to say in reply. As regards the amendment of my honourable Friend, Mr. Chaliha, he will see that the Special Officer's report is a kind of expert's report which comes before the Parliament. The Parliament certainly will have a right to discuss it. Any member can raise a debate on it, but surely a report of an expert, who has collected facts, cannot be modified or added to by a legislature. It only contains the materials placed before the Parliament for its decision and therefore, I submit, Sir, that amendment No. 71 is really inappropriate.

With regard to amendment No. 80 of honourable Mr. Kamath, I am really surprised that he wants the deletion of the words "and also to the Anglo-Indian community". By sections 297 and 298 the Constitution has given specific safeguards to the Anglo-Indian community and the whole object of this Article 299 is to see that the working of such of the political safeguards given to some of the communities as have been accepted by the Constitution should be properly investigated into and placed before the Parliament. If the Anglo-Indian community has certain safeguards, then it is the function of this officer to scrutinise their working.

Then as regards amendment No. 74 where the honourable Sardar Hukam Singh wants to introduce the Muslims, the Christians, the Sikhs and the Parsees in addition to Anglo-Indians, I am of opinion, Sir, with great respect that the safeguards contemplated by Article 299 are not fundamental rights which are attached to every citizen. They are only 'safeguards', safeguards meaning political safeguards for the protection of certain well defined sections of the citizens. Otherwise, it would involve the special officer going into the working of all the fundamental rights given by the Constitution. So far as I understand my amendment, it only means that the Scheduled Castes, the Scheduled Tribes, the Anglo-Indian community and the backward classes who are, under the fundamental right Article 10, given specific safeguards, and the officer should examine whether they have been properly worked or not. That being this thing, it is not possible for me to accept the words "Muslims, Christians, Sikhs" etc. mentioned in amendment No. 74.

Sir, I have only one word more to say with regard to Sardar Bhopinder Singh Mann's Amendment No. 67.

Shri H.V. Kamath

What about amendment 72?

Shri K.M. Munshi

As regards amendment No. 72, it is not necessary to put in the words suggested, viz., "for such action as Parliament may deem necessary". Once the report is before the Parliament, as I stated already, a debate can be raised on it and a resolution can be moved. It is implied; it is not necessary to add these words.

Sardar Bhopinder Singh Man by his Amendment No. 67, wants that there should be a special officer in each State. Well, if the special officer envisaged in this article requires assistance of other officers, they will be appointed. But there is no need for appointing a separate officer for each State. That would only complicate matters. The object is to see whether the whole thing is worked on one principle throughout the country. We do not want separate officers in each State as permanent guardians. The honourable the Mover of the amendment has also introduced the word 'minorities' in it. We have removed the word 'minorities' from Article 296 and it is entirely inappropriate in 299. In passing, he tried to reply to what Sardar Patel had already said. I shall deal with only one point to which he referred and which I think I should refer. I was a member of the Committee appointed for the purpose of looking into the Sikh question. From the beginning of the Advisory Committee and the Minorities Committee, I had something or other to do with all the stages of the negotiations. I can assure the House that at the time when the Advisory Committee met on the last occasion, there was no question of providing safeguards for any religious minority. The negotiations proceeded on the footing that except the backward classes who are economically and socially backward, and the Scheduled Castes and Tribes who have a special claim of their own, no other minority should be recognised in the Constitution. The honourable Member read some statements made by certain Sikhs. Unfortunately, in the short time at my disposal I have not been able to reclaim the different documents; but of one thing I can assure the House. When the matter came up before the Advisory Committee, the Sikh members withdrew every sort of claim for any safeguards whatever in consideration of the Sikh scheduled classes being placed among the Scheduled Castes and given the privileges, which the latter were entitled to. Any cry raised now that they did not do so is an afterthought.

I do not want to say anything more about it and the kind of allegations which have been made are entirely unwarranted. Even with regard to the Muslim community, the debate centred round the question of representation. But it was understood that even so far as they were concerned also, the claims as regards service were given up. They were not expressly mentioned in the report. The basis of that decision was that we should not recognize in the Constitution any religious minority of this nature. That was the basis. I submit it is too late to go back upon this.

Sardar Hukam Singh

My question has not been answered. Have these four Sikh classes been included in the Scheduled Castes?

The Honourable Dr. B.R. Ambedkar

Of course, they will be.

Shri K.M. Kamath

The President is empowered to issue, under Article 300-A, a list of Scheduled Castes. In that, these Scheduled Castes will find a place.

Sardar Hukam Singh

Where is the guarantee that the President will include these people in that list? We have given up all safeguards to secure this in the Constitution. That has not been done.

Shri K.M. Munshi

The President has that power. The President is sure to keep to the pledge which has been given. This decision finds a place in the Advisory Committee's Report that the Sikh Scheduled Castes will form part of the Scheduled Castes and provided with the safeguard under Article 296 which we have already passed. There is no question of going back upon that pledge, you may take it from me. I repeat the Sikh Scheduled Castes will be included in the list of Scheduled Castes and Scheduled Tribes in the Punjab.

Mr. President

I will now put the amendments to vote, one by one...[23]

At the revision stage this article was renumbered as Article 338 of the Constitution.

This Article envisaged the appointment of a Special Officer to investigate into the working of the safeguards enshrined in the Constitution for the (1) Scheduled Castes, (2) Scheduled Tribes, (3) Backward Classes and (4) Anglo-Indians. It may be noted that the Constitution has provided special privileges, benefits and safeguards only to these four categories of persons and the Special Officer was responsible to investigate and report to the President on the working of those safeguards.

The post of the Special Officer was initially filled on November 18, 1950 in pursuance of this provision of the Constitution and he was designated as Commissioner for Scheduled Castes and Scheduled Tribes. Since then he has submitted, following investigation into the working of the various constitutional safeguards, many reports to the President containing his suggestions and recommendations which helped in the evolution of viable policies for achieving the objectives of those constitutional provisions. Though the Commissioner was charged with the duty of investigating all matters relating to the safeguards provided for four categories of persons, his report revealed that he was primarily concerned for the Scheduled Castes and the Scheduled Tribes.

When the Janata Government was in power at the Centre in 1977-79, it decided that considering the magnitude of the problem relating to the safeguards provided for the Scheduled Castes and Scheduled Tribes, in addition to the functioning and authority of the Special Officer, those matters should appropriately be entrusted to a high level Commission consisting of persons of eminence and status in public life. The functioning of the

Commission would not be lessening the authority of the Special Officer.

The Government of India, Ministry of Home Affairs, accordingly resolved to constitute a Commission for the Scheduled Castes and Scheduled Tribes vide their Resolution No. 13013\9\77-SCT. I dated July 21, 1978 consisting of a Chairman and not more than four other Members including the Special Officer.

The functions of the Commission broadly corresponded with the functions of the Special Officer appointed under Article 338 of the Constitution and were as follows:

(i) To investigate all matters relating to safeguards provided for Scheduled Castes and Scheduled Tribes in the Constitution. This would, inter alia, include a review of the manner in which reservations stipulated in public services for Scheduled Castes and Scheduled Tribes are in practice, implemented.

(ii) To study the implementation of Protection of Civil Rights Act, 1955, with particular reference to the objective of removal of untouchability and invidious discrimination arising therefrom within a period of five years.

(iii) To ascertain the socio-economic and other relevant circumstances accounting for the commission of offences against persons belonging to Scheduled Castes or Scheduled Tribes with a view to ensuring the removal of impediments in the laws in force and to recommend appropriate remedial measures including measures to ensure prompt investigation of the offences.

(iv) To enquire into individual complaints regarding denial of any safeguards provided to any person claiming to belong to Scheduled Castes or Scheduled Tribes.[24]

It would appear that the Commission's main functions related to important safeguards provided for the Scheduled Castes and Scheduled Tribes, working of the Protection of Civil Rights Act and investigation into cases of atrocities on Scheduled Castes and Scheduled Tribes. The Resolution also provided that the Commission might ascertain the socio-economic and other relevant circumstances accounting for the commission of offences against them.

While setting up this Commission the intention of the Government of India was to vest this Commission with constitutional status and consequently merge the organisation of the Commissioner for Scheduled Castes and Scheduled Tribes with that of this Commission. With that intention the Government of India had formulated the Constitution (46th Amendment) Bill, 1978, subsequently called the Constitution (51st Amendment) Bill, 1979 which fell through for lack of prescribed majority in the Parliament.[25]

The propriety to set up, by an executive order, a separate Commission for Scheduled Castes and Scheduled Tribes in July 1978 alongside the Commissioner for the Scheduled Castes and Scheduled Tribes appointed by the President as a constitutional obligation under Article 338 of the Constitution might very well be questioned. The anomaly inherent in a situation when two parallel set-ups, one of which enjoying constitutional status, were called upon to discharge similar functions without at the same time not intended to infringe upon the authority of each other was quite obvious. The appropriate course should have been to first amend the relevant Article of the Constitution and then set up the Commission in terms of the Constitution rather than creating by an executive order a machinery supposed to be apparently independent and to act as a judge and auditor of the performance of the State with regard to the various constitutional safeguards guaranteed to the members of the Scheduled Castes and the Scheduled Tribes. Both the Commissioner for Scheduled Castes and the Commission for Scheduled Castes and Scheduled Tribes, therefore, harped on the necessity for giving top priority to the amendment of the Constitution in all their reports submitted since 1978.

It was, however, during the tenure of the National Front Government, the second non-Congress Government at the Centre in 1989-91, that the Constitution was amended to give constitutional recognition to the Commission, rechristened as the National Commission for

Scheduled Castes and Scheduled Tribes by the Congress Government in 1987,[26] by abolishing the office of the Special Officer. The Constitution (Sixty-Eighth Amendment) Bill, 1990, popularly known as the "Ram Dhan Bill" because of the interest and initiative taken by Ram Dhan, the proposed Chairman of the National Commission for Scheduled Castes and Scheduled Tribes, was debated in the Lok Sabha on May 28-30, 1990 and in the Rajya Sabha on May 31, 1990 and ultimately became the Constitution (Sixty-Fifth Amendment) Act, 1990 on obtaining the ascent of the President on June 7, 1990. This Amendment Act establishes a 7-member National Commission for Scheduled Castes and Scheduled Tribes including a Chairperson and a Vice-Chairperson by amending Article 338 of the Constitution.

There was hardly any criticism against the provisions of the amended Article but it was cautioned that unless a process of implementation of the safeguards was evolved, this constitutional provision by itself would not do anything because the complaint was not that no safeguards were envisaged in the Constitution or in the normal laws of the land, but the complaint was that the implementation had not been successful. It was wondered whether the present law would be able to ensure that there was successful implementation and no continuance of the past failure.[27] It was also observed that mere legislation would not even touch the fringe of the problems of Scheduled Castes unless there was a basic change in the attitude of the people of the country and unless punitive measures were taken whenever there was a violation of the minimum safeguards guaranteed in the Constitution.[28] The Special Officer under Article 338 had to some extent a reporting role. He could investigate a matter and send his report to the President. But he had got no direct authority to implement something or redress something. His role was advisory reporting.[29] The Commission's role is similar to that of the Special Officer but with wide-ranging powers. Instead of a single officer, the Commission would be a multi-member one. In order to make the Commission more powerful and meaningful, the Chairperson would have the status of a Cabinet Minister while the Vice-Chairperson would have the status of a Minister of State. Earlier the Special Officer was only of the rank of a Secretary. The Commission would not only enquire into the complaints but also examine them. It enjoys the same powers as are enjoyed by a Commission constituted under the Commission of Inquiry Act. It would also send its representatives to participate in the meetings held by the Planning Commissions of various States and the Central Planning Commission while preparing plans for their respective spheres. The Commission has been given full authority to go into cases of atrocities, socio-economic matters, matters relating to reservation and the like.[30]

The tenor of the debate, however, gave an impression that the members expected some sort of ombudsman type of role from the Commission to look into all types of problems confronting the SC & ST people—be they socio-economic, socio-religious, socio-cultural, political, educational and the like. It was thought that the Commission should protect them from all sorts of atrocities, eliminate proverty, untouchability and even abolish their backwardness,[31] monitor whether the States were properly spending the funds provided to them for the welfare of SC & ST,[32] ensure that the SC & ST people who worked as daily wage labourers in different States got the just and minimum wages and were not tortured for launching agitations for better wages,[33] and also not only ensure their progress but also bring them into the mainstream of the country.[34]

To the objection raised for providing for the office of Vice-Chairperson, it was given out that it was a Scheduled Castes and Scheduled Tribes Commission. Problems of Scheduled Castes and Scheduled Tribes were different from each other. Since it was not the intention to give lesser importance to the problems of either of them an arrangement was evolved under which if in one term the Chairperson was appointed from the people belonging to the SC, the Vice-Chairperson should be from the people belonging to ST and in the second term the position would be *vice-versa.* In that there would be no possibility of discrimination and no controversy would arise, rather they would supplement each other[35]. It was also suggested that the Commission should consist of members who belonged to SC & ST because others could not protect the interest of the SC\ST people.[36]

Article 338, as amended, stands as follows:

National Commission for Scheduled Castes and Scheduled Tribes—

(1) There shall be a Commission for the Scheduled Castes and Scheduled Tribes to be known as the National Commission for the Scheduled Castes and Scheduled Tribes.

(2) Subject to the provisions of any law made in this behalf by Parliament, the Commission shall consist of a Chairperson, Vice-Chairperson and five other Members and the conditions of service and tenure of office of the Chairperson, Vice-Chairperson and other Members so appointed shall be such as the President may by rule determine.

(3) The Chairperson, Vice-Chairperson and other Members of the Commission shall be appointed by the President by Warrant under his hand and seal.

(4) The Commission shall have the power to regulate its own procedure.

(5) It shall be the duty of the Commission—

(a) to investigate and monitor all matters relating to the safeguards provided for the Scheduled Castes and Scheduled Tribes under this Constitution or under any other law for the time being in force or under any order of the Government and to evaluate the working of such safeguards;

(b) to inquire into specific complaints with respect to the deprivation of rights and safeguards of the Scheduled Castes and Scheduled Tribes;

(c) to participate and advise on the planning process

of socio-economic development of the Scheduled Castes and Scheduled Tribes and to evaluate the progress of their development under the Union and any State;

(d) to present to the President, annually and at such other times as the Commission may deem fit, reports upon the working of those safeguards;

(e) to make in such reports recommendations as to the measures that should be taken by the Union or any State for the effective implementation of those safeguards and other measures for the protection, welfare and socio-economic development of the Scheduled Castes and Scheduled Tribes; and

(f) to discharge such other functions in relation to the protection, welfare and development and advancement of the Scheduled Castes and Scheduled Tribes as the President may, subject to the provisions of any law made by Parliament, by rule specify.

(6) The President shall cause all such reports to be laid before each House of Parliament along with a memorandum explaining the action taken or proposed to be taken on the recommendations relating to the Union and the reasons for the non-acceptance, if any, of any of such recommendations.

(7) Where any such report, or any part thereof, relates to any matter with which any state Government is concerned, a copy of such report shall be forwarded to the Governor of the State who shall cause it to be laid before the Legislature of the State along with memorandum explaining the action taken or proposed to be taken on the recommendations relating to the State and the reasons for the non-acceptance, if any, of any such recommendations.

(8) The Commission shall, while investigating any matter referred to in sub-clause (a) or inquiring into any complaint referred to in sub-clause (b) of clause (5), have all the powers of a civil court trying a suit and in particular in respect of the following matters, namely:-

(a) summoning and enforcing the attendance of any person from any part of India and examining him on oath;

(b) requiring the discovery and production of any document;

(c) receiving evidence on affidavits;

(d) requisitioning any public record or copy thereof from any court or office;

(e) issuing commission for the examination of witnesses and documents;

(f) any other matter which the President may, by rule, determine.

(9) The Union and every State Government shall consult the Commission on all major policy matters affecting Scheduled Castes and Scheduled Tribes.

(10) In this article, references to the Scheduled Castes and Scheduled Tribes shall be construed as including references to such other backward classes as the President may, on receipt of the report of a Commission appointed under clause (1) of Article 340, by order specify and also to the Anglo-Indian community.

The Constitution (Sixty-Fifth Amendment) Act, 1990 came into force from March 12, 1992.

Clause (2) of amended Article 338 empowers the President to frame rules for the conditions of service and tenure of office of the Chairperson, Vice-Chairperson and other Members of the Commission. Accordingly, the National Commission for Scheduled Castes and Scheduled Tribes Chairperson, Vice-Chairperson and Members (Conditions of Service and Tenure) Rules, 1990 was framed and issued on November 3, 1990 under Resolution No. GSR 891(E) of the Ministry of Welfare (Department of Welfare), Government of India. As regards qualifications of the Members, Chairperson and Vice-Chairperson, it was stipulated that

(1) The Members shall be appointed from amongst persons of ability, integrity and standing who have had a record of selfless service to the cause of justice for the Scheduled Castes and Scheduled Tribes.

(2) The Chairperson shall be appointed from amongst eminent socio-political workers belonging to the Sched-

uled Castes or Scheduled Tribes, who inspire confidence amongst the Scheduled Castes and Scheduled Tribes by their very personality and record of selfless service.

(3) The Vice-Chairperson and not less than three other Members shall be appointed from amongst persons belonging to the Scheduled Castes and Scheduled Tribes.

(4) At least one other Member shall be appointed from amongst women.

The term of office of every Member should be for three years while the first Chairperson shall hold office for a term of five years.

The office of the Chairperson should be rotated in such a manner that in a block of three terms of office, a person belonging to the Scheduled Castes shall hold office for two terms and a person belonging to the Scheduled Tribes shall hold office for one term. When the Chairperson is a person belonging to the Scheduled Castes, the Vice-Chairperson shall be a person belonging to the Scheduled Tribes and if the Chairperson is a person from the Scheduled Tribes, the Vice-Chairperson shall be from the Scheduled Castes.

This Rule was framed and issued on November 3, 1990, that is, when the National Front Government was already reduced to a minority following the withdrawal of support from the Ministry by the BJP on October 23, 1990,[37] and immediately prior to its formal defeat on the floor of the Lok Sabha on November 7, 1990.[38] The propriety of issuing such a Rule by a minority Government, which had by this time put the country into turmoil by dividing the people on the basis of 'forward' caste and 'backward' caste, simply for clinging to power, may very well be questioned. At the time of deliberations in the Lok Sabha on the setting up of the National Commission for Scheduled Castes and Scheduled Tribes, Members demanded that in the appointment of Members of the National Commission, priority should be given to their sense of duty, dedication, sense of social values and their commitment for the progress of the country. They should not be appointed to this important position due to the support of any political party. In fact a provision to that effect should have been made in the Act itself, it was felt.[39] But a Government accused of directly promoting caste divisiveness in the country for its very survival, had altogether a different view. Having succeeded in conferring constitutional status and power on a multi-member National Commission, it now devolved on it to ensure that the composition of the Commission should be such as would serve its very purpose. It, therefore, narrowed down the field of choice not only by political consideration but by caste consideration also. Apart from gaining political mileage by reserving these constitutional posts exclusively for Scheduled Castes and Scheduled Tribes, it used it as a vehicle to sell its thesis that none but the members of the Scheduled Castes and Scheduled Tribes would work for the cause of Scheduled Castes and Scheduled Tribes in right earnest, forgetting what could be the logical fallout of such a theory in a multi-lingual, multi-racial, multi-religious, caste-ridden society.

The framers of the Constitution in their wisdom provided certain safeguards, benefits and privileges for a section of people. Having done that, they set up a constitutional machinery to ensure that those constitutional safeguards were not infringed upon. During the last forty-two years from the commencement of the Constitution, that constitutional machinery was known as Commissioner for Scheduled Castes and Scheduled Tribes. Now that a more powerful multi-member Commission, composed of members belonging to Scheduled Castes and Scheduled Tribes, has been set up. it has to be observed keenly how its functioning would help the Scheduled Castes and Scheduled Tribes achieve what they could not so far. It is the desire of everybody that this National Commission will bring about a change in the social condition of a large segment of population and integrate them with the general milieu of the society for all time to come. It is also their hope that the National Commission will create a climate in the society when this canker of casteism will not be perpetuated any longer and 'scheduling of caste' will be done away with. Let us hope and pray that if would succeed.

Notes and References

1. Rao, *op. cit.*, Vol. II, pp. 334-35.
2. *Ibid.*, p. 325.
3. *Ibid.*, p. 322.
4. *Ibid.*, p. 330.
5. *Ibid.*, p. 340.
6. *Ibid.*, pp. 360-61.
7. *Ibid.*, p. 369.
8. *Ibid.*, pp. 83-84.
9. *Ibid.*, p. 376.
10. *Ibid.*, p. 91.
11. *Ibid.*, p. 400.
12. *Ibid.*, p. 410.
13. *CAD*, Vol. V, p. 247.
14. *Ibid.*, p. 249.
15. *Ibid.*, p. 281.
16. Rao, *op. cit.*, Vol. III, p. 95.
17. *Ibid.*, p. 478.
18. *Ibid.*, p. 633.
19. *Ibid.*, Vol. IV, p. 362.
20. *CAD*, Vol. VIII, dated 16-6-49, p. 941.
21. *CAD*, Vol. IX, dated 26-8-49, pp. 703-06.
22. *Ibid.*, dated 9-9-49, p. 1171.
23. *CAD*, Vol. X, dated 14-10-49, pp. 251-64.
24. Para 4 of the *Government of India, Ministry of Home Affairs, Resolution No. 13013/9/77-SCT-I dated 21-7-78, quoted in the Eighth Report of the Commission for Scheduled Castes and Scheduled Tribes*, April, 1985- March, 1986, p. 3.
25. *Second Report of the Commission for Scheduled Castes and Scheduled Tribes*, April, 1979- March, 1980, p. 2.
26. Ram Dhan, Lok Sabha Debates, Ninth Series, Vol. VII, No. 51, dated 29-5-1990, Col. 117.
27. Piyare Lal Handoo, *Ibid.*, Col. 143-44.
28. Kusum Krishna Murthy, *Ibid.*, Col. 114.
29. A.K. Roy, *Ibid.*, Col. 165-66.

30. Ram Vilas Paswan, *Ibid.*, Vol. VI, No. 50, dated 28-5-1990, Col. 116-17.
31. Ram Lal Rahi, *Ibid.*, Vol. VII, No. 51, dated 29-5-1990, Col.142.
32. Matilal Hansda, *Ibid.*, Vol. VI, No. 50, dated 28-5-1990, Col. 138.
33. *Ibid.*, p. 139.
34. Ram Vilas Paswan, *Ibid.*, Vol. VII, No. 51, dated 29-5-1990, Col. 164.
35. *Ibid.*, Vol. VII, No. 52, dated 30-5-1990, Col. 140.
36. *Ibid.*, Col. 138.
37. *The Statesman*, 24-10-1990.
38. *Ibid.*, 8-9-1990.
39. Matilal Hansda, Lok Sabha Debates, Vol. VI, No. 50, dated 28-5-1990, Col. 140.

19

Appointment of a Commission to Investigate the Conditions of Backward Classes (Article 340)

The necessity of having a Commission for a. periodic investiga-tion into the conditions of socially and educationally backward classes was first raised by K.M. Munshi in the Minorities Sub-Committee meeting held on July 21-27, 1947. None else felt such a necessity earlier. Munshi proposed and the Minorities Sub-Committee agreed that there should be provision for the setting up of a statutory commission to investigate into the conditions of socially and educationally backward classes, to study the difficulties under which they laboured and to commend to the Union or the unit Government, as the case may be, the steps that should be taken to eliminate these difficulties and the financial grants that should be given and the conditions that should be prescribed for such grants. This decision of the Minorities Sub-Committee was embodied in its report sent to the Advisory Committee on July 27, 1947.[1]

The Advisory Committee met on July 28-31, 1947 to consider the various recommendations of the Monorities Sub-committee. On July 31,1947, Munshi moved a proposition in terms of the above recommendations of the

Minorities Sub-Committee and it was carried in the meeting.[2] The Advisory Committee in its report to the President of the Constituent Assembly on August 8, 1947, stated, inter alia, that

> In particular, we think it is a fundamental duty of the State to take special steps to bring up those minorities which are backward to the level of the general community. We recommend accordingly that a Statutory Commission should be set up to investigate into the conditions of socially and educationally backward classes, to study the difficulties under which they labour and to recommend to the Union or the Unit Government, as the case may be, steps that should be taken to eliminate their difficulties and suggest the financial grants.that should be given and the conditions that should be prescribed for such grants.[3]

and included it as one of its recommendations in clause 12 of the summary of recommendations.[4]

Clause 12 of the Advisory Committee's report was considered by the Constituent Assembly on August 28, 1947. This provision, which its mover, Sardar Patel, described as "an administrative provision for the benefit of the oppressed and the backward classes," was adopted by the Assembly without any debate.[5]

This decision of the Constituent Assembly was incorporated in the Draft Constitution prepared by the Constitutional Adviser in October, 1947, as Clause 230:

> (1) The President may, by Order, appoint a Commission consisting of such persons as he thinks fit to investigate the conditions of socially and educationally backward classes within the territories of the Federation and the difficulties under which they labour and to make recommendations as to the steps that should be taken by the Federation or any unit to remove such difficulties and to improve their condition and as to the grants that should be given for the purpose by the Federation or any unit and

the conditions subject to which such grants should be given, and the order appointing such Commission shall define the procedure to be followed by the Commission.

(2) A Commission so appointed shall investigate the matters referred to them and present to the President a report setting out the facts as found by them and making such recommendations as they think proper.[6]

The Drafting Committee revised it on February 5, 1948,[7] and incorporated it as Draft Article 301 in its Draft Constitution as follows:

(1) The President may by order appoint a Commission consisting of such persons as he thinks fit to investigate the conditions of socially and educationally backward classes within the territory of India and the difficulties under which they labour and to make recommendations as to the steps that should be taken by the Union or any State to remove such difficulties and to improve their condition and as to the grants that should be given for the purpose by the Union or any State and the conditions subject to which such grants should be given, and the order appointing such Commission shall define the procedure to be followed by the Commission.

(2) A Commission so appointed shall investigate the matters referred to them and present to the President a report setting out the facts as found by them and making such recommendations as they think proper.

(3) The President shall cause a copy of the report so presented, together with a memorandum explaining the action taken thereon to be laid before Parliament.[8]

On this provision in this Draft Article, H.J. Khandekar, Dharam Prakash, Chandrika Ram, Yashwant Rai, S. Nagappa, V.C. Kesava Rao, T.Channaya and Shrimati Dakshayani Velayudhan, all belonging to the Scheduled Castes, suggested that in clause (1) of article 301 for the words "educationally backward classes" the words "educationally and economically backward particularly Scheduled Castes classes" be substituted. The Constitutional Adviser, however, commented that article 301, at it stood, follows the language of the decision of the Advisory Committee on Minority Rights as adopted by the Constituent Assembly.[9]

Draft Article 301 was taken up for consideration by the Constituent Assembly on June 16, 1949. H.V. Kamath moved as many as six amendments, some of which were of a drafting nature. In one amendment he suggested that the President would not be required to explain the action taken on the report and instead Parliament would take further action after considering the report. Ambedkar also moved an amendment for laying the report before each House of Parliament. There was hardly any discussion in the Assembly. Only Pandit Thakur Das Bhargava and Prof. Shibban Lal Saksena participated in the debate. Bhargava characterised this article as the soul of the Constitution as the article sought to complete the process of bringing the depressed classes to normal standards. He called for maintenance of a register of all backward classes including the depressed classes and suggested that once their disabilities and difficulties, as indicated by the Commission, were removed and they had reached normal standards, they should be taken out of the backward class category so that their backwardness was not "crystalized and perputated". Prof. Saksena hoped that the Commission would define the terms `depressed classes' and `backward classes' in their report.

As usual, the amendments of Kamath were negatived and that of Ambedkar was adopted. Article 301, as amended, was thereafter added to the Constitution. The discussions in the Assembly on this provision are reproduced below.

Shri H.V. Kamath:

Mr. President, Sir, I move Amendments Nos. 3191, 3195, 3196, 3197, 3198 and 3200 standing in my name.

I move:

"That in clause(1) of Article 301, the words 'consisting of such persons as he thinks fit' be deleted."

In my judgment these words are wholly superfluous. I may even go to the length of saying that they cast a reflection upon the wisdom of the President. The President when he appoints certain persons, certainly appoints such persons as he thinks fit for the job with the commission of which those persons are charged. It is absolutely pointless and purposeless to say here that he may "appoint a Commission consisting of such persons as he thinks fit". It may stop after "appoint a Commission." This adequately and sufficiently conveys the meaning intended in this portion of the article.

Then I move:

"That in clause (1) of article 301, for the word 'difficulties' the word 'disabilities' be substituted."

Bearing in mind what we have already adopted in this House I think the word "disabilities" convey the idea far better than the word "difficulties". If we turn to the Chapter on Fundamental Rights we find that the second part of article 9 refers to "any disability, liability, restriction, condition" etc. The word "difficulty" nowhere occurs in that very important article which seeks to abolish discrimination on grounds of religion, race, caste or sex. We have passed that article. The word "difficulty" is to my mind hardly a constitutional term. I have read several constitutions of the world, but I find that it finds no place in constitutional terminology or parlance. The word "disability" is a far more appropriate word than the word "difficulty". I am sure Dr. Ambedkar, steeped as he is in constitutional lore and constitutional learning, will have no difficulty in accepting this amendment.

I move my next amendment :

"That in clause (1) of article 301, for the words 'grants should be given", the words 'grants should be made,' be substituted."

This is a purely verbal amendment. I do not wish to press home, but I leave it to the collective wisdom of the Drafting Committee which I am sure will come into play at the appropriate• time.

Then I move:

"That in clause (1) of Article 301, for the word 'and' the words 'as well as' be substituted."

That portion of the article reads thus as it has been moved before the House:

"The President may by order appoint a Commission...to remove such difficulties and to improve their condition and as to the grants that should be given for the purpose by the Union or any State and the conditions subject to which such grants should be given..."

I think the meaning would be more exactly expressed by the phrase "as well as" than by the single word 'and' here. That also I leave to the wisdom of the team of wisemen which this House has appointed to draft the Constitution.

I next move Amendment No. 3198—

"That in clause (2) of Article 301, for the words 'a report setting out the facts as found by them and' the words 'a report thereon' be substituted."

The clause as it stands reads thus:

"A Commission so appointed shall investigate the matters referred to them and present to the President a report setting out the facts as found by them and making such recommendations as they think proper."

If my amendment is accepted by the House the clause will read as follows:

"A Commission so appointed shall investigate the matters referred to them and present to the President a report thereon making such recommendations as they think proper."

This is only with a view to avoid cumbersome language and style and secure brevity and precision, but not at the sacrifice of any substantial meaning.

Lastly, I move my Amendment No. 3200 which runs thus:

"That in clause (3) of Article 301, the words 'together with a memorandum explaining the action taken thereon' be deleted and the following words be added at the end :-

'For such further action as may be necessary'.

This clause of the article as it now stands runs thus:

"The President shall cause a copy of the report so presented together with a memorandum explaining the action taken thereon to be laid before Parliament".

My amendment seeks to modify it in this regard and if it is accepted by the House, the clause will read as follows:

"The President shall cause a copy of the report so presented to be laid before Parliament for such further action as may be necessary."

This is a drafting amendment, plus an amendment of substance. There are two parts to it. The first relates to the manner in which the President shall cause a copy of this report to be laid before both the Houses of Parliament. The clause, as it is now, makes it incumbent upon the President to affix a memorandum to the copy of the report to be laid before Parliament. It does not seem to be wise to lay down the manner in which the report should be presented to Parliament by the President. If the President deems it necessary to submit a memorandum along with the report he will certainly do so. The President will be a wise man. I am sure we will not have as President a man who is not wise or who is incompetent to do his duties in the interests of the nation. If the President thinks it necessary to affix a memorandum to the report he will do so. Why should we lay down in the Constitution things in such minute detail? It is just a tremendous trifle to say that he must add a memorandum to the report. That is the first aspect of my amendment.

The second part of my amendment relates to the sequel to the submission to Parliament by the President of this report by the Commission. I think, Sir, that the House is agreed on this point that Parliament, our sovereign Parliament of Free India, shall have a definite say, a substantial voice in whatever policy is going to be adopted or action taken with regard to the welfare of the socially and educationally backward classes in our country. This article has relation to the conditions of socially and educationally backward classes in the Indian Union. Parliament, I am aure, will be entitled to ask that any action taken with regard to the welfare of its backward people must be in conformity with the policy that will be formulated by it. Therefore, I am anxious that with a view to having this implemented, when the report comes before Parliament, further action should be taken by Parliament and not by the President. The President will if need be, communicate to Parliament his own reactions to the report, but should not be final authority to take action thereon. Parliament must have the last word on the action to be taken on that report. Therefore, this last amendment of mine seeks to make that quite clear, absolutely fool-proof and knave-proof, as Dr. Ambedkar might say, and make it impossible for the President to divest Parliament of this inherent right to take action on the report of the Commission submitted by the President to Parliament. Therefore I have suggested the addition of the words "for such further action as may be necessary". It may be that within the next ten years there may be no socially or educationally backward classes in our country. I look forward to that day even before the expiry of ten years. We have the example of Soviet Russia before us. Russia abolished illiteracy and brought even the lowest strata of the population to a fairly decent level in ten or fifteen years. Can we not, with our ancient heritage and our background of cultural and spiritual genius aspire to something better and to bring all these backward classes within less than ten years to a socially and educationally higher level? I hope, Sir, that within ten years we will have advanced a good deal towards redeeming these fallen and so-called backward people and we shall have no occasion to appoint a Commission for the submission of a report.

I shall be very happy if that day comes in less than ten years. But, as it is, the Constitution provides for the appointment of a Commission. Then let Parliament consider and deliberate on the report submitted by the Commission to the President and let Parliament take such action as it deems fit or necessary in this matter, so that within the ten-year period, when a Commission has been appointed and its report comes before Parliament, Parliament may chalk out a programme for the uplift and redemption of these educationally backward classes, and carry it out. I trust that after the first ten-year period has expired, there will be no need for the President again to appoint a Commission of this nature to enquire into the conditions of the backward classes in our country. Sir, I move these various amendments and commend them for the acceptance of the House.

The Honourable Dr. B.R. Ambedkar

Sir, I move:

"That in clause (3) of Article 301, for the word 'Parliament' the words 'each House of Parliament' be substituted."

Mr. President

The article and the amendments are now open to discussion.

Pandit Thakur Das Bhargava

Sir, I consider that Article 301 is one of the most important articles of this Constitution. Left to myself, I would call it the soul of the Constitution. So far as the Depressed Classes are concerned, we have only reserved some seats for them. The rest we have not done, and this Article 301 seeks to complete the process of bringing them up to normal standards. This article places upon the entire nation the obligation of seeing that all the disabilities and difficulties of the Depressed Classes are removed and therefore it is really a charter of the liberties of the backward classes and in a sense this is an oath taken by the House, an oath to see that within the coming years we will provide all the facilities which can be provided by the nation for expiating our past sins. Now, Sir, in this country there are backward classes some of whom have had reservation given to them so far as representation is concerned, but the other classes have not been given such reservations but they are equally backward. I would therefore have liked a register to be made of all the backward classes including the present Depressed Classes, and after the Commission had found out what their difficulties and disabilities were and a programme chalked out for providing facilities to every member of these backward classes. If a particular class was economically very backward, provision could be made that with regard to their houses in the villages, they were given not only the residential rights but rights of disposal of their properties. If we chalk out a programme after the Commission has investigated their disabilities, we will be taking a great step towards the removal of those disabilities. There are many disabilities pertaining to them which the House fully knows and I need not go into them at this stage. What I want to say is that so far as these classes are concerned, we should see to it that these classes do not continue in the category of backward classes after they have come up to normal standards so that their backwardness is not crystalized or perpetuated. After they have reached normal standards, they should be taken away from this category. If any community continues in backwardness, socially, culturally or educationally, then it should not be a question of ten years or fifteen years but up to the time they are brought up to normal standards, facilities should be given and continued for them.

My next submission is that the article says, "The President may by order appoint, etc" I have given notice of an amendment in this regard for substituting the word 'shall' for 'may' and even if the word 'may' is used in the article, I think it should be the obligations of the President to appoint such a Commission. Even though the word 'may' has been used, it must be construed as 'shall'. Therefore I have no doubt that the President shall appoint such a Commission and the Commission after making investigation into the conditions of these classes, shall have to suggest in what particular manner the steps suggested should be implemented. The article here simply says that he shall cause a copy of the Report to be placed before Parliament. The obligations of the Parliament are not given in Article 301. I understand there is provision for them in 299 which has been held over. I do not want to speak now on that article, but what I want to submit is this: Now the safeguards for minorities have been taken away, for instance for the Muslims and the Sikhs. The only responsibility of the Parliament are the Scheduled Castes and the backward classes. In regard to these classes, special officers are to be appointed to see whether the fundamental rights which have been given to them under this Constitution and the special facilities which are sought to be provided for them after the investigation of the Commission are enjoyed by these people or not. These classes are not only the responsibility of the Central Parliament but of the State Legislature as well. But I submit they are the special obligation of the Central Legislature. This Article 301 is only the material form of the Objectives Resolution. This article only gives the mechanism by which the Objectives Resolution is carried out. We should provide in this article that it shall apply not only to the communities for whom reservation has been made but also to those for whom no reservation has been made but who are all the same backward.

Sir, I feel great happiness in supporting Article 301.

Prof. Shibban Lal Saksena

Mr. President, Sir, I whole-heartedly support this article. I only wish to point out two things in this regard. The first thing is according to the scheme of the Constitution, this Commission will be appointed at the very outset of the commencement of the Constitution. That means that as soon as our Constitution comes into existence, the President shall appoint the Commission to investigate into the conditions of the socially, educationally and culturally backward classes and then make its report on how to remove their backwardness. We are using the expression 'the backward classes' in several places in the Constitution, but we have not defined them anywhere in the whole Constitution. I hope this Commission which will specially investigate the conditions of the backward classes all over the country will be able to tell us what is meant by the term "backward classes". When the Commission reports to the Parliament, I hope they will define the terms "backward classes" and "depressed classes" in their report.

I also support the amendment of Mr. Kamath for the addition of the words "for such further action as may be necessary". That means that when the report is made, the House must consider the ways and means of removing the backwardness of these people. I think, therefore, that this amendment is necessary.[10]

At the revision stage this article was renumbered as Article 340 of the Constitution.

Thus was framed an Article whose impact on the body politic has proved rather disastrous. The framers first imported the phrase 'backward class of citizens' in clause (4) of Article 16. They, however, did not take upon themselves the responsibility of defining them or, should we say, was incapable of defining them, and , therefore, had to leave it to this Commission to find out who they are. In every society, more so in the Indian society where the dissimilarities and inequalities are so glaring, there has to be 'backward' and 'forward' classes in relation to certain aspects of human behaviour and development—education, culture, knowledge, health, money, position, status, power and the like. The framers never explained what they actually meant by backwardness, what are the criteria and degree of backwardness and how it is to be measured. They never indicated whom they had in view and why. Did they confuse 'caste' with 'class'? Is it an ascribed or an achieved status? And will the status stick on perpetually like caste? Is there no way of coming out of the quagmire of backwardness? Did these and other related questions baffle them as well?

In this Article the framers have used the phrase "socially and educationally" without indicating what was actually meant by "social and educational" backwardness. The debate in the Constituent Assembly do not give any indication of what they wanted to convey and what were the compulsions behind coinage of certain phrases without making clear their true import. They took this matter rather casually and did not give it the attention it deserved. They were apparently not aware of the fact that they conceived of a Commission whose reports might put the country in flames and split the society more or less vertically on the basis of "caste" and not on the basis of "class". Will it be uncharitable if one concludes that they themselves were confused and perplexed at the attempt of dividing the polity and, therefore, were in a hurry to leave the field in favour of a Commission without opening their heart and without giving vent to their own perception of the proposition? Otherwise, how one explains the reticence on the part of the framers to discuss the pros and cons of a provision giving constitutional power to an authority which they were afraid of doing themselves? Their silence made the position worse confounded leading to varied interpretation of the term used by them. Or, it might be that the absence of any guidance from the 1935 Act further aggravated their confusion.

Notes and References

1. Rao, *op. cit.*, Vol. II, p. 400.
2. *Ibid.*, p. 410.
3. *CAD*, Vol. V, p. 247.
4. *Ibid.*, p. 249.
5. *Ibid.*, p. 281.
6. Rao. *op. cit.*, Vol. III, pp. 95-96.
7. Ibid., p. 479.
8. *Ibid.*, pp. 633-34.
9. *Ibid.*, Vol. IV, p. 363.
10. *CAD*, Vol. V III dated 16-6-49, pp. 943-47.

20

Definition of Scheduled Castes [Article 341 and Article 366(24)]

The Draft Constitution prepared by the Constitutional Adviser in October, 1947, sought to give a definition of the Scheduled Castes in Sub-clause (2) of the Interpretation clause 231 as follows:

> For the purposes of this Constitution the castes, races or tribes, or parts of or groups within castes, races or tribes specified in Parts I to IX of the Eleventh Schedule to this Constitution shall, in the Provinces to which those parts respectively relate, be deemed to be scheduled castes so far as regards members thereof resident in the localities specified in relation to them respectively in those parts of that Schedule:
>
> Provided that—
>
> (a) no Indian Christian shall be deemed to be a member of a Scheduled Caste;
>
> (b) in West Bengal no person who professes Budhhism or a tribal religion shall be deemed to be a member of a Scheduled Caste.[1]

Castes to be considered as Scheduled Castes in the provinces of Madras, Bombay, West Bengal, the United Provinces, East Punjab, Bihar, the Central Provinces and

Berar, Assam and Orissa were specified separately in Parts I to IX of the Eleventh Schedule.[2] The Castes included is this Schedule varied from Province to Province and were nothing but verbatim reproduction of the lists issued under the Scheduled Castes Order of 1936 of the Government of India.

The Drafting Committee meeting on February 13, 1948, decided that the Eleventh Schedule should be omitted and a definition of the expression "Scheduled Castes" should be inserted in the Interpretation Clause and that the said expression should have the same meaning as in the Government of India (Scheduled Castes) Order, 1936.[3]

The definition of the expression "Scheduled Castes" was accordingly incorporated in sub-clause(w) of the revised Interpretation Clause 231 as follows:

> "Scheduled Castes" means in relation to any State for the time being specified in Part I of the First Schedule such castes, races or tribes or parts of or groups within castes, races or tribes as are specified in the Government of India (Scheduled Castes) Order, 1936, to be Scheduled Castes for the purposes of the Fifth and Sixth Schedules of the Government of India Act, 1935 in relation to the corresponding Province.[4]

This sub-clause figured as sub-clause (w) of Article 303 of the Draft Constitution prepared and circulated by the Drafting Committee in February, 1948.[5]

The definition Article 303 was taken up by the Constitutent Assembly on September 16 and 17, 1949, when almost all the Draft Articles had been discussed and adopted by the House. Sub-clause (w) of clause (1) of Draft Article 303 was considered on September 17, 1949 when Dr. Ambedkar moved an amendment for substitution of sub-clause (w) and also introduced new Draft Article 300A and 300B. Ambedkar explained that the object of the new articles was to eliminate the necessity of burdening the Constitution with long lists of Scheduled Castes and Scheduled Tribes. It was now proposed that the President, in consultation with the Governor or Ruler of a

State, should have the power to issue a general notification in the official gazette specifying the castes or tribes deemed to be Scheduled Castes or Tribes. This procedure became necessary also because the lists previously compiled covered only what were then the Provinces of the Dominion of India; and with the inclusion of the territories of the Indian States within the framework of the Constitution, it became necessary to define the Scheduled Castes and Tribes in these territories as well. The two new articles enabled this to be done, the only limitation being that if any elimination was subsequently to be made from the list initially notified, or if any addition was to be made, this could be done only by Parliament. Pandit Thakur Das Bhargava moved an amendment to enable the President to include or exclude proper classes from the purview of the notification after a period of ten years from the commencement of the Constitution. This amendment was negatived by the House. Only Muniswamy Pillai spoke welcoming this new Article, and thereafter the new Article as well as the amended sub-clause (w) were adopted by the House. This is what actually transpired in the House:

The Honourable Dr. B.R. Ambedkar

Sir, I move:

"That with reference to Amendment No. 147 of list IV (Eighth Week), for sub-clause (w) of clause (1) of article 303, the following sub-clause be substituted:-

'(w) 'Scheduled Castes' means such castes, races or tribes or parts or groups within such castes, races or tribes as are deemed under Article 300A of this Constitution to be Scheduled Castes for the purposes of this Constitution."

The only change is, the word 'specified' has been changed to 'deemed'.

Shall we take up the two other articles which has been tables?

Mr. President

Yes.

New Articles 300A and 300B

The Honourable Dr. B. R. Ambedkar

Sir, I move :

"That after Article 300, the following articles be inserted:-

300A (1) The President may, after consultation with the Governor or Ruler of a State, by public notification specify the castes, races or tribes or parts of or groups within castes, races or tribes, which shall for purposes of this Constitution be deemed to be Scheduled Castes in relation to that State.

(2) Parliament may be law include in or exclude from the list of Scheduled Castes specified in a notification issued by the President under clause (1) of this article any caste, race or tribe or part of or group within any caste, race or tribe, but save as aforesaid a notification issued under the said clause shall not be varied by any subsequent notification.

The object of these two articles, as I stated, was to eliminate the necessity of burdening the Constitution with long lists of Scheduled Castes and Scheduled Tribes. It is now proposed that the President, in consultation with the Governor or Ruler of a State should have the power to issue a general notification in the Gazette specifying all the Castes and tribes or groups thereof deemed to be Scheduled Castes and Scheduled Tribes for the purposes of the privileges which have been defined for them in the Constitution. The only limitation that has been imposed is this: that once a notification has been issued by the President, which, undoubtedly, he willl be issuing in consultation with and on the advice of the Government of each State, thereafter, if any elimination was to be made from the List so notified or any addition was to be made, that must be made by Parliament and not by the President. The object is to eliminate any kind of political factors having a play in the matter of the disturbance in the Schedule so published by the President.

Pandit Thakur Das Bhargava

Sir I move:

"That in Amendment No. 201 of List V (Eighth Week) in clause (2) of the proposed new Article 300 A the following be added at the end:—

'for a period of ten years from the commencement of this Constitution'."

...I agree with the principle that for ten years to come no variation of the notification originally made by the President should be possible. Because now that special privileges of reservation, etc., have been given to the Scheduled Castes, I do not like the idea that the Executive, President or Governor or any other person may be able to tamper with that right, but after a period of ten years, when this privilege will no longer be available to the Scheduled Castes, there will be no difference between the Scheduled Castes and other backward classes which will be declared under article 301 of the Constitution. At that time there will be no meaning in taking away this power from the President in consultation with the Governor. Therefore my humble submission is that the proposed amendment be accepted to make the point absolutely clear and free from ambiguity. Unless we add these words for a period of ten years from the commencement of this Constitution, you will be taking away the power of the President to include or exclude proper classes from the purview of the notification which will be issued under 300A and B. After the first ten years the privileges which will be open to these classes are probably under Article 10 and under Article 296 and 299. I do not know of any other privileges which have been specifically given to these Scheduled Castes. Whereas I am, very insistent and conscious that these provisions should not be tampered with, I do like that these castes may not become stereotyped and may not lose the capacity of travelling out of the schedule when the right occasion demands it. I, therefore, submit that if you put these words you will be making the whole thing elastic and the President will have the power of including or excluding after the lapse of ten years such tribes or castes within the notification.

Shri V.I. Muniswami Pillai

Mr. President, I come to support the amendments that have been moved by the Honourable Dr. Ambedkar. These amendments deal with the definition of Scheduled Castes. As far as I can see he has made it clear that, according to the second part of it, the President on the 26th January, 1950 will publish a list of such communities that come under the category of Scheduled Castes. But I would like to inform this House of the background which brought out the special name of Scheduled Castes. It was the untouchability, the social evil that has been practised by the Hindu Community for ages, that was responsible for the Government and the people to know the section of people coming under the category of Hindus and who were kept at the outskirts of the Hindu society. Going backwards to 1916 it was in that year when Government found that something had to be done for the untouchable classes, (when they said untouchable classes, they were always understood to be Hindus,) and they had to be recognised. In Madras there were six communities that came under this classification. During the Montago-Chelmsford reforms they were made ten. In 1930 when the great epoch-making fast of Mahatma Gandhi came about, then only the country saw who were the real untouchable classes. And in the 1935 Act, the Government thoroughly examined the whole thing and as far as the Province of Madras is concerned they brought 86 communities into this list or category, though there were some touchable classes also. Now, after further examination the Provincial Governments have drawn up a list and I think according to the amendment mover's suggestions, all those communities that come under the category of untouchables and those who profess Hinduism will be the Scheduled Castes, because I want to emphasise about the religions. I emphasise this because of late there have been some movements here and there; there are people who have left Scheduled Castes and Hinduism and joined other religious and they also are claiming to be Scheduled Castes. Such convert cannot come under the scope of this definition. While I have no objection to Government granting any concessions to these converts, I feel strongly that they should not be clubbed along with Scheduled Castes.

Sir, I am grateful to the Drafting Committee and also to the Chairman of that Committee for making the second portion of it very clear, that in future, after the declaration by the President as to who will be the Scheduled Castes, and when there is need for including any other class or to exclude anybody or any community from the list of Scheduled Castes that must be by the word of Parliament. I feel grateful to him for bringing in this clause, because I know, as a matter of fact, when Harijans behave independently for asserting their right on some matters, the Ministers in some Provinces not only take note and action against those members, but they bring the community to which that particular individual belongs; and thereby not only the individual, but also the community that comes under that category of Scheduled Castes are harassed. By this provision, I think that danger is removed.

I strongly oppose the amendment moved by Pandit Bhargava. The reason is that he wants to have the ten years period for observing these amendments. But he has entirely forgotten that under another article that we have already passed, or will pass the Constitution provides for the appointment of a Special Officer at the Centre and also various officers in all the Provinces to go into the various disabilities of these communities and to submit a report to the President who will then be able to know whether the Scheduled Castes have reached a stage when the facilities now given to them could be withdrawn. I do not think that the reasons that he has advanced are fair and square for the uplift of the Harijans.

With these few words, I support the amendment.

Mr. President

Does anyone else wish to speak? Do you wish to say any thing

Dr. Ambedkar?

The Honourable Dr. B.R. Ambedkar

I do not accept the amendment of Pandit Thakur Das Bhargava.

Mr. President

Then I put the amendments.[6]

The amended sub-clause (w) of clause (1) of Article 303 and new Article 300A were adoped and the amendment moved by Pandit Bhargava was negatived by the House.[7]

At the revision stage, these were renumbered as clause (24) of Article 366 and article 341 respectively.

Article 341 specifically empowers the President to issue notification specifying the castes, races or tribes which would be treated as Scheduled Castes for the *purposes of the Constitution.* The Presidential notification cannot, however, notify an All-India Scheduled Caste. It can declare a particular caste or even a group within a particular caste as Scheduled Caste only in relation to a particular State. It is also open to the President to declare that castes etc. or parts thereof shall be deemed to be Scheduled Castes not only in the entire State but in a particular part of a State and not in another part. There can never be a list of All-India Scheduled Castes under the Constitution.

The power under this Article is absolute. The Courts have no power to go behind these Orders or question the validity of the President's determination that a particular caste etc. is a Scheduled Caste. It is, therefore, useless to refer to Gazetteers or glossaries for establishing that a caste is a 'Scheduled Caste,' though not mentioned in the President's Order. The only limitation is that the President can issue this Order only once after consultation with the Governor of the State concerned. Once an Order has been issued, it cannot be modified or varied by a subsequent notification by the President. This can only be done if it is issued under a law made by Parliament.

This Article does not stipulate which castes, races or tribes would be included in the notification for the purposes of declaring them as Scheduled Castes. It is the Presidential notification issued under this Article which determines permanently, unless modified subsequently by an Act of Parliament, who are to be deemed to be members of the Scheduled Castes for the purposes of the Constitution. The term "Scheduled Castes" is of recent origin. It had no place in our lexicon till 1935 when it was imported for the first time in the 1935 Act to mean "such castes, races or tribes or parts of or groups within castes, races or tribes, being castes, races, tribes, parts, or groups which appear to His Majesty in Council to correspond to the classes of persons formerly known as "the depressed classes", as His Majesty in Council may specify."[8] The power to specify any caste etc., as a Scheduled Caste vested in His Majesty in Council and whether any caste etc., corresponded to the erstwhile "Depressed Classes" rested with it.

Who were the Depressed Classes and what should be their status in the Indian polity? There were two diametrically opposite views. Ambedkar thought that the untouchables, otherwise known as Depresssed Classes, were outside the *varna* system of Hindu Society, and hence should be treated as a separate minority. The Gandhian view was that those unfortunate people who were subjected to certain disabilities due to the practice of untouchability were very much a part and parcel of the Hindu society and all efforts to be made to remove the stigma of untouchability and the consequent disabilities. The attempt to treat them as a separate community led to the signing of the famous Poona Pact in 1932. A number of seats, about 19% of the total general seats, in the Provincial and Federal Legislatures, were reserved for them. Once the seats were earmarked for the representation of the Depressed Classes, it fell on the administration to ascertain their number after classifying and categorising them. The question of "scheduling of caste" brooked no delay. The twin criteria of untouchability and unapproachability were not adhered to for determining the Depressed Classes. Rather other extraneous factors like social, political, economic and educational position of the castes were taken into consideration to determine whether those castes were below the general level of development and if so, were included in the list of Scheduled Castes to give them special representation to protect their interest. So it was no longer the untouchability and unapproachability but the level of social, political, economic and educational position of a caste which determined whether it merited inclusion in the list of Scheduled Castes.[9]

Notwithstanding the demand of Ambedkar the Scheduled Castes were considered to be that section of the Hindu community which was subject to certain social disabilities like untouchability and Munshi explicitly described the Scheduled Castes as a "section of the Hindu community" by introducing an amendment in the Constituent Assembly on August 27, 1947, at the time of consideration of the Report on Minority Rights [10] which provided for certain safeguards for Minorities which included Scheduled Castes as well. Munshi contended that the Scheduled Castes were neither a racial minority nor a linguistic minority nor a religious minority but were part and parcel of the Hindu community. The distinction between Hindu community other than Scheduled Castes and the Scheduled Castes was the barrier of untouchability. Untouchability was prohibited by law and its practice was made a criminal offence. Similarly it was accepted that no public place should be prohibited to anyone by reason of his birth. Since the artificial barrier between one section of Hindu community and the other had thus been removed, he preferred the description 'a section of the Hindu community referred to as Scheduled Castes' instead of the term 'Scheduled Castes.'[11] This amendment of Munshi was accepted by the House.[12]

As the Constitution conferred certain special privileges and benefits on that class of citizens, known as Scheduled Castes, demands were raised in the Constitutent Assembly for inclusion in the list of Scheduled Castes of the backward classes belonging to religions other than Hindu as well. The main argument was that if this section of people, who were ex-untouchables of the Hindu community, was not considered as Scheduled Castes, they might seek reconversion to Hindu religion for being treated as Scheduled Castes for enjoying the privileges and benefits conferred on them. The leaders of the Sikh community gave up their demand for reservation of seats in the East Punjab in lieu of recognition of the Sikh Backward Classes, viz., Mazhabis, Kabirpanthis, Ramdasias, Baurias, Sikligars etc. as Scheduled Castes.[13] The demands of the leaders of the other religions were, however, not conceded.

What should be the criteria for recognition as Scheduled Castes was never explained in the Constituent Assembly. The framers did not reveal their mind as to what castes they wanted to include in the list of Scheduled Castes. The Scheduled Castes Order of 1936 became very handy to the framers and they never applied their mind as to the pros and cons of wholesale application of that order, which was basically issued to meet the immediate necessity of drawing up an electoral college created under the 1935 Act primarily for dividing the Hindu community, in free India as well when adult franchise was introduced and the special privileges and benefits were accorded to that congeries of castes, known as Scheduled Castes, for their uplift in the social and economic ladder of the society. Or did they realise that they were creating a permanent caste in the Hindu society and that too in the name of obliteration of caste from our society?

Notes and References

1. Rao, *op. cit.*, Vol. III, p. 98.
2. *Ibid.*, pp. 187-93.
3. *Ibid.*, p. 504.
4. *Ibid.*, p. 506.
5. *Ibid.*, p. 637.
6. *CAD*, Vol. IX, dated 17-9-49, pp. 1636-39.
7. *Ibid.*, pp. 1639-40.
8. Section 26(1) of Schedule I of the Government of India Act, 1935.
9. See Chapter IV "Growth and Development of Caste during the British Period" in *The Scheduled Castes in India*, Vol. I by the Author.
10. *CAD*, Vol. V, pp. 243-49.
11. *Ibid.*, dated 27-8-47, pp. 227-28.
12. *Ibid.*, dated 27-8-47, pp. 229-38.
13. *CAD*, Vol. X, p. 266.

21
Perception

The problem of minorities had bedeviled Indian politics for a long time. It was in fact one single factor, above all others, that held up the progress of the country towards freedom and independence. The consequence of recognising a division of interests on communal lines was soon realized by the Britishers. Step by step the recognition of communal claims and communal interests became part of the basic policy of the British Government in India. Having succeeded in dividing the Indian polity on religious lines, the Britishers followed the same mechanism for dividing other segments of population as well. In a traditional hierarchical society like Indian what better means could it be but caste. So soon after the initial demands for self-rule and constitution-making by the Indians came up, it was met with a equally challenging problem relating to the Depressed Classes (Scheduled Castes were known as such then) since the 20s. It cannot be gainsaid that the 'high caste' people stands guilty for creating social barriers and divisions but the British aggravated these evils in order to establish and consolidate their imperialistic hold on the gullible people and thereby created a sense of hatred and ill-feeling between the Indians. They never made any attempt to solve the complicated problems which they had themselves created; on the contrary intensified them. They created a gulf between the Brahmans and the non-Brahmans, between the Brahmans and the Depressed Classes and even between the non-Brahmans and the

Depressed Classes. The Britishers played their game under the cover of safeguards. With the help of it they allowed themselves to cling to power.

While the mechanics of protection was followed throughout the British rule none of the constitutional reforms set a goal for integration of the diverse people and the removal of their social problems. Under the Government of India Act, 1935, an elaborate arrangement ensuring seats to the religious minorities, Scheduled Castes and the aboriginal and backward tribes, women, etc. was in force in the Provincial Legislatures and, in general, safeguarding the legitimate interests of minorities was a special responsibility of the Governor-General and the Governors. Creation of separate electorates was the mechanism in operation for all such sections while for the Scheduled Castes some general seats were reserved as agreed to under the Poona Pact. As regards representation in the Cabinets relevant clauses contained in the Instruments of Instructions for the Governor-General and the Governors took care of it. An elaborate system of 'communal roster' for appointment in government services of different communities was in vogue. In this prospective the nature and scope of safeguards was naturally agitating the minds of the different sections concerned the utmost.

Once an euphoria could be raised about 'minority status' and 'minority safeguards', it was inevitable that any plan for transfer of power to Indians should be dependent on the constitutional provisions for the minorities. Though the Britishers did not concede to the demands of a section of Scheduled Castes of giving them minority status, the British Government viewed it as a problem which would merit due consideration in the hands of the Indian National Congress. The Indian National Congress also felt that widest scope should be given to the Scheduled Castes for development and participation in the fullest measure in the *political, economic and cultural life of the nation.*

So when the Advisory Committee was constituted to draft provisions for the protection of minority rights, not only seven representatives of the Scheduled Castes were included in the Advisory Committee, but four of these seven representatives were also included in the 26-member Minorities Sub-Committee.

It was quite natural that removal of social disabilities, emancipation of the Harijans and creation of a congenial atmosphere which would give them freedom and equality of status and a chance of developing socially, economically and culturally received top priority of the iramers. They wanted to usher in a caste-less, exploitation-free society where all sections of people, irrespective of religion, caste, sex, descent, place of birth should receive equal opportunity for their development in all spheres of life. With that end in view they included in the fundamental rights provisions for abolition of untouchability, throwing open of Hindu temples to all castes in Hindu society, prohibition of traffic in human beings, forced labour and child labour. It is needless to say that all these measures which are aimed at improving the social and economic conditions of the downtrodden people obtained unanimous support of the Framers. If there was any difference of opinion that was in the matter of making these provisions more effective and fool-proof.

The Framers prohibited discrimination against any citizen on ground of religion, race, sex or place of birth. They also provided for equality of opportunity for all citizens in matters related to appointment in government services and prohibited discrimination against any citizen on grounds of religion, race, caste, sex, descent, place of birth, residence, in respect of employment made under the State. They also ensured that there was one electoral roll for all citizens and that there was no ineligibility for inclusion in any such roll on grounds of religion, race, caste or sex. All these provisions were aimed at removing all traces of discrimination and inequality among the various sections of the Hindu social fabric, abolishing the social disabilities imposed on certain classes of people solely by reason of their birth in certain castes which precluded them from any kind of intercourse with people belonging to the so-called higher classes or castes and ushering in a society where no person would claim an advantageous position solely on caste consideration.

The Framers also paid attention to the removal of economic and educational inequalities and rectifying the injustice resulting from the dealings or transactions between unequals in society. They laid emphasis on the uplift of the weaker sections of the community so that they might be able to make equal contribution in the national activities. With that end in view the Framers stipulated that the State should promote with special care the educational and economic interests of the weaker sections of the people, and in particular of the Scheduled Castes and the Scheduled Tribes and should protect them from social injustice and all forms of exploitation. In the larger interest of the society the Framers have rightly provided for certain protection to the weaker sections of the people. But by leaving the expression 'weaker sections of the people' undefined in a written constitution, they have afforded enough scope to the self-seekers to exploit this constitutional provision in their own petty self interest.

But when the question of providing safeguards for the minorities was taken up, the scramble for extracting maximum advantages began. The dilemma of the Minorities Sub-Committee whose strength was meanwhile increased to 37 with the inclusion of Muslim and other members, is best manifested in its report. The majority of the Minorities Sub-Committee, to be precise 24 in the enlarged Sub-Committee, represented Muslim, Indian Christian, Anglo-Indian, Sikh, Parsee, Scheduled Caste and Scheduled Tribe communities and they failed to reach any unanimous decision on minority rights. The Sub-Committee, therefore, refrained from submitting any recommendation and its report contained only a summary of the conclusions and also mentioned the result of the vote on the issues of electorates, representation in legislature, reservation of seats in the Cabinet, reservation in services, etc. The Advisory Committee, however, submitted its recommendations on the line of majority opinion in the Minorities Sub-Committee and the Assembly, after a brief deliberation, accepted these recommendations. Separate electorates which had divided the people so much so that the country had to be partitioned ultimately were given up in favour of joint electorates because it was thought that the joint electorates would give equal opportunity for the caste Hindus and the minority communities to come and work together for a better India.[1] But representation of all religious communities as well as of the Scheduled Castes to the legislatures according to the proportion of the population was assured. The demand raised by the leaders of the Muslim League and a section of the Scheduled Castes that a certain percentage of votes of their own community should be necessary for a successful candidate was, however, not entertained because it would have perpetuated separate electorates in another name and form.[2] Claims of the minorities to the services were assured and an instruction to the Governor was contained in the Instrument of Instructions to ensure representation of minorities in the Cabinet. All these provisions were incorporated in August, 1947, just immediately after partition.

By the time the Draft Constitution finalised by the Drafting Committee was circulated eliciting opinion, a section of the leaders of the minority communities was questioning the necessity of these safeguards. Tajamul Hussain asked for deletion of the 'Muslim community' from the minority groups. Leaders of the Indian Christian and Parsee communities were also not in favour of any reservation for them as a minority. So when the Advisory Committee was seized with the question of providing safeguards to the Sikhs and other minorities of West Bengal and East Punjab, the minority groups based on religion pressed for withdrawal of minority safeguards. The lead came from Dr. H.C. Mookherjee, a respected Christian leader, and Tajamul Hussain, a Shia Muslim leader of Bihar, who could convince other leaders of the minority communities of the futility of such safeguards which would only perpetuate communal divide. The Assembly ultimately decided not to provide any safeguards for the minorities. Even the claim for representation to services of the minorities was also withdrawn, in the face of stiff opposition of leaders of the Muslim League and the Sikh community, because" this Constitution of India, of free India, of a secular State will not hereafter be disfigured by any provision on a communal basis."[3] So the word 'minority' was omitted from the relevant articles.

But the same thing was not true so far as the Scheduled Castes were concerned. The Framers knew that the Scheduled Castes were not a minority because "the word 'minorities' so far as international treaties and international law is concerned, is only restricted to racial, linguistic and religious minorities. The Scheduled Castes are not minorities in the strict meaning of the term and any safeguard to the Scheduled Castes as a minority is illogica."[4] But that did not deter them from according safeguards to the Scheduled Castes like that of other 'minorities', because, as Naziruddin Ahmad said, "it is not a question of logic or argument but it is a question really of creating in each sect or community a feeling of confidence and security that by a particular scheme, it would be treated justly and fairly."[5] Once they were included in the 'minority group' for the purpose of providing safeguards there was no way of withdrawing those safeguards unless they themselves had asked for it. The Cabinet Mission Plan stipulated that "any question raising a major communal issue in the Legislature should require for its decision a majority of the representatives present and voting of each of the two major communities as well as a majority of all the members present and voting".[6] The Framers not only followed this principle for deciding communal issues affecting the Hindus and the Muslims but extended it in respect of all other communal groups as well. Once they had accepted this as a policy they could not possibly deviate from this set principle unless the 'minority' group concerned had asked for its withdrawal. The safeguards covering the religious minorities could be withdrawn because the Framers could prevail on them but no such move was forthcoming in the case of the Scheduled Castes. None of the representatives belonging to the Scheduled Castes did venture to ask for its deletion. They could not come out of the mental make-up created by the movement which led to the signing of the Poona Pact and the events thereafter.

A distinct line of division amongst the members on the question of Scheduled Castes rights and position was discernible. The Caste Hindus were against classification of the Scheduled Castes as a separate minority and pleaded for treating them as an integral part of the Hindu community.[7] But the Scheduled Castes leaders were for their categorisation as a separate political, economic and social minority,[8] as a minority having a separate political entity.[9] They agreed that great mischief was done in 1932 by Ramsay Macdonald because it was he who sowed the seed of disunity and destruction by giving the communal award[10] but in the same breath it was demanded that quota for Harijans in the Cabinet should be statutorily reserved,[11] the Governorship and Presidentship should be rotated[12] and similar reservation be provided in respect of Local Bodies.[13] Actually the demand for separate electorates for the Scheduled Castes was articulated by Ambedkar from the time of the Round Table Conference till July, 1947. The Poona Pact provided for primary electorates and cumulative voting which indirectly meant separate electorates.[14] Though Ambedkar did not press his demand for separate electorate in the Minorities Sub-Committee meetings, but the impact of Ambedkar's message to the Scheduled Castes community that they were not even Hindus, that they wished to have a colony separate from the Hindus, that they were not within the fold of Hindu religion, had a disastrous effect on the society. It created a sort of discord between Caste Hindus and the Scheduled Castes and it had gone to the extent that the Harijans even did not wish to converse with Hindus.[15] The Scheduled Caste leaders followed the Ambedkar line of thinking that in political power lay the key for their elevation.[16] It was said that reservation of seats would militate against the principle of democracy and adult franchise but the Scheduled Castes line of thinking was that the circumstances such as political unconsciousness, backwardness in education and the very poor economic condition of the Scheduled Castes compelled them to demand for these privileges.[17] It was necessary not only to allay the fear in the minds of the Scheduled Castes that the Hindus were getting into power and that Hindu Raj was coming into force[18] but also to atone for the atrocities perpetrated on the Harijans[19] and to compensate for the atrocities the Scheduled Castes had suffered at the hands of other castes for thousands of years.[20] They knew that safeguards would not improve the status of the Harijans[21] but even then insisted on it because it was their experience that the conditions of the Harijans classified amongst Caste Hindus during the census were not the same as that of the Caste Hindus and they were still in the same deplorable state.[22] They thought that it would give them an opportunity to be equal, to feel like equals and enable them to take due share in the administration of the country.[23] It would also free them from exploitation and give them a chance of developing socially, economically and culturally.[24]

There was a lone dissenter in Shrimati Dakshayani Velayudan who did not believe that the 70 million Harijans were to be considered as a minority.[25] She pointed out that joint electorates and reservation of seats also was a kind of separate electorates but it had to be accepted as a necessary evil because the British Imperialism had left some marks on the Indians who were always feeling afraid of one another.[26] She was, like Rajkumari Amrit Kaur, against any kind of reservation in any place whatsoever.[27] What was needed was the immediate removal of social disabilities, she felt.[28] Pillai, however, had a different perception. Since the Scheduled Castes suffered from disabilities, they should be given all the advantages as a minority, he asserted.[29] Curiously enough, the five-member Special Sub-Committee consisting of Sardar Patel as Chairman, and Pandit Nehru, Dr. Rajendra Prasad, Munshi and Ambedkar as members, constituted to report on the minority problems affecting East Punjab and West Bengal in its report presented to the Advisory Committee on

November 23, 1948, did not accept the demands of the Sikh community but at the same time stated that special safeguards were given only to the Scheduled Castes "whose standards of education and material well-being are, even on Indian standards, extremely low and who, moreover, suffer from grievous social disabilities."[30] The motive of the Sub-Committee in singling out the Scheduled Castes for justifying the granting of safeguards to them while negating the demands of the Sikhs, especially when it was not within its terms of reference may very well be questioned. It appeared that while Austin's 'oligarchy' had made up its mind of not granting any safeguards to the religious communities, it had already veered round the Ambedkarian theory that granting of safeguards to the Scheduled Castes was necessary for removal of "grievous social disabilities" and improvement of "standards of education and material well-being". Otherwise how one explains the fact that while the safeguards originally meant for the 'minorities' were withdrawn, the same were retained for the Scheduled Castes, that too because a resolution to that effect was moved in the Advisory Committee by Pillai. Without the tacit support, approval and even blessings of the 'oligarchy', this resolution would have met with a natural death, as was the fate of innumerable such proposals. While eager to remove all sorts of communalism from the body politic, they perhaps overlooked the danger the country would face if communalism based on caste was allowed to perpetuate. Or was it not a clever ploy to obtain the *imprimatur* of the 'oligarchy' beforehand that no matter what happened to the religious minorities, the Scheduled Castes would continue to enjoy the safeguards and privileges? This commitment from them made the task easier for Ambedkar to retain these provisions in the Constitution.

The Framers contended that to continue the safeguards and perpetuate the divisions would not be a wise course, for safeguards could not remove the existing disparities and divisions because the ground could not be made even by providing pits and mounds.[31] By providing constitutional safeguards for Harijans, the word 'Harijans' would be perpetuated contrary to the intentions of the Framers of forming a classless society.[32] This would 'possibly prevent their complete absorption in the Hindu fold.'[33]

The Framers predicted that a larger representation could not be a guarantee of safety. On the contrary, the tussle for representation would create conflict.[34] The Scheduled Castes had been formed by combining together four or five hundred communities and only two or three communities out of them, who formed the majority section, took advantage of the benefits. All the Scheduled Caste communities did not benefit by the reservation policy.[35] It was warned that it would provide opportunities for a handful of leaders but it would in no way materially alter the economic or educational level of the Scheduled Castes.[36] Dr. H.C. Mookherjee observed: "This reservation business comes from the upper middle classes—people who have political ambitions—self-seekers after power, self-seekers after position, and in fact, people who want to take advantage of their position in the different legislatures for their own selfish purposes".[37]

The Framers were concerned that this reservation policy would promote fissiparous tendencies and weaken the foundation of the State.[38] Reservation for classes was calculated to induce a feeling of separateness and exclusiveness and would stand against the amalgamation of classes.[39] The giving of facilities here and there does not help raise a man up. It does create an inferiority complex in the man.[40] It was warned that it was no use to gamble with the freedom of the country, with the peace, progress and tranquility of our nation by simply trying to provide jobs for a few persons belonging to certain classes either in the urban or in the rural areas. It was pointed out that if appointments were made on the basis of castes and classes then there would be a shift of the centre and focus of the loyalty and allegiance from the nation as a whole to that of the interests of a group or a class or castes. The allegiance to the nation would become only secondary; the primary allegiance would be to class and caste. It was also prophesied that this evil from which the country had suffered so long and which led to the partition of the country, would go even further than that and would permeate into all aspects of our national life. Elections would then be fought not on the basis of the loyalty or service to the nation but on the basis of class loyalty.[41] It was implored that if a bold stand was not taken and a principle was not laid down that the basis of a secular state should not be allowed to be corrupted by any other consideration, the future of the country would be dark.[42] It was even warned that the leaders of the Scheduled Castes would act in the same way as the Muslim Leaguers did.[43] But the Framers had to yield to the pressures of the Scheduled Caste Members in giving the facilities they insisted upon.

Contrary to popular belief it may be remembered that all the safeguards and privileges extended to the Scheduled Castes are permanent in nature. There is a time stipulation only in the matter of reservation of seats in the Legislatures. It was initially meant for ten years which has since been extended to fifty years by constitutional amendments. But even the Framers thought that all the safeguards were temporary in nature which would continue "till they are completely absorbed in the Hindu community."[44]

It was the pious hope of the Framers that class and communal divisions and sub-divisions created by the Britishers to keep the balance between community and community would wither away as soon as possible and as rapidly as possible and an atmosphere would be created in which classifications and differences would disappear,[45] and a day would come when reservation could be taken away.[46] Even Pillai thought that by reservation it should not be taken to perpetuate the seclusion of the Scheduled Castes for all time.[47] Radhakrishnan's advice was to make it clear that it was not the intention of the House to have the minorities perpetuated and the disruptive elements should be put to an end to.[48] Dr. Mookherjee entreated that the reservations should have a time limit and that once for all there should be an end to it at the end of ten years from the time the Constitution came into operation[49] and Bharathi pleaded that there should be a time limit for all these peace or compromise moves and it should be made clear that after the lapse of a certain specified period all these special provisions must go.[50] Kunzru suggested that reservations of whatever kind should be done away with as quickly as possible. Even if it was considered necessary for the time being, it should be granted temporarily only, so that the population of the country might become fully integrated and no community or class might be tempted to claim special advantages for itself.[51] Maulana Hasrat Mohani thought that there was absolutely no need of reservations after provisions were made for joint electorates and adult franchise.[52] Bhargava pointed out that the reservation derogated from the enjoyment of the full electoral right by the people in general. It was harmful to the general community and to the Scheduled Castes also.[53] Dr. Mookherjee was more candid. He said: "In my view the Scheduled Castes do not require representations."[54] Nehru would have liked to put an end to such reservations as remained but he could not do away with it in the present state of affairs to India in regard to the Scheduled Castes which would be limited to ten years.[55] But Ambedkar knew that this ten-year period was a mere device to get over with the opposition to the proposal because once this provision found its place in the Constitution, it would not be "beyond their (Scheduled Castes') capacity or their intelligence to invent new ways of getting the same protection which they are promised here.[56]

The Scheduled Castes Members never cherished any desire of completely merging with the Hindu society. All along they asked for reservation according to their numerical strength[57] and made it an issue in the Constituent Assembly when their population in Bihar, Punjab and Bengal registered a decrease in the 1941 census. Since all representations in the legislatures and services were to be according to population, they wanted that their population should not be allowed to suffer any diminution in number.[58] As a matter of fact, a reverse mobility in the Hindu society ensued. The 'low caste' people no longer aspired for an upward mobility in the society, because such a mobility did not attract them any further. Instead, from 1941 many communities had been taken on to the list of Scheduled Castes by the various Provincial Governments and many more wanted to be taken on the list.[59]

The Constitution of 1935 for the first time created a separate caste known as 'Scheduled Castes' by scheduling certain castes for the purposes of electoral arrangements and other privileges. The castes which *appeared* to correspond to the classes of persons formerly known as Depressed Classes were no doubt included in the list but other castes whose level of *social, political, economic and educational* development was below the general level of development were also included in the Scheduled by the District Officers and the Commissioners of Divisions. Earlier a sort of social stigma was attached to 'Depressed Classes' but this shift in the criteria for inclusion removed that stigma. The Framers emulated the British policy and refrained from stipulating the criteria for preparation of the list of 'Schedule Castes'. They left it to the executive to *specify* the castes, races and tribes which shall for the purposes of this Constitution be deemed to be Scheduled Castes in relation to a particular State. Any subsequent variation in the list can only be effected under a law made by Parliament.

Now a demand for inclusion in the list mounted. The Sikh representatives in the Constituent Assembly demanded that the Hindu Scheduled Caste converts to the Sikh religion should be treated as Scheduled Castes so that they could also enjoy the benefits and privileges extended to their counterpart. That demand was also accepted by the Framers. Now there are Scheduled Castes both among the Hindus and the Sikhs.

And this is not all. Not only the Framers did not discard the British policy of scheduling of castes and thereby creating a new 'castes' in the society, but they created another layer in the society by innovating the term 'backward class', which even the Britishers in their heydays could not conceive of. Nehru imported this term in the Objectives Resolution in December, 1946 and Munshi followed it up in the Minorities Sub-Committee meeting in July, 1947 for providing a constitutional machinery to investigate into their conditions. The Drafting Committee on its own introduced this term for making provision for reservation in services for "certain communities who have not so far have a proper look-in into the administration."[60] Later, within one and a half years of the commencement of the Constitution, the Constitution was amended to enable the State to make special provision for the advancement of the socially and educationally backward classes of citizens. But who are the "backward class"? The Framers also did not know who they were. The meaning of the word "backward" seemed vague to them and they, therefore, pressed for its clarification and definition. The founding Fathers' idea about them differed widely. Nehru himself was not sure who they were. He was, however, not in favour of branding groups or classes as backward or forward. Backward classes were to be thought not in terms of this community or that. It was the backward citizens who should be helped, he said.[61] D'Souza also harped on the desirability of giving special safeguards to backward groups on consideration of individual needs and deficiencies and not on the basis of a communal or religious classification.[62] The class character of the backwardness was also highlighted by Ayyangar. He felt that to avoid giving representations to the richer classes, the term backward classes had been introduced instead of the word community. Whether or not a certain class of people was backward did not depend upon the caste or community, he asserted.[63] Contrary to Nehru's emphasis on the *individual* character of backwardness, Ambedkar laid stress on the *caste or community* character of backwardness. He thought that they were nothing but a collection of certain castes or such other classes who were for the moment not able to stand on their own legs[64] and that it was for the local government to determine who were they because a backward community was a community which was backward in the opinion of the government.[65] Munshi thought that the word 'backward' signified that class of people who were so backward that special provision was required for them in the services,[66] and Kunzru considered a class to be backward, if left to itself, would be unable to protect its interest.[67]

The Members belonging to the Scheduled Castes community thought that, inspite of its vagueness, the Scheduled Castes were definitely included within the Backward Classes and Munshi allayed their apprehensions by observing that he could not imagine a time when there was any backward class in India which did not include the Scheduled Castes.[68] Bhargava felt that the backward classes included depressed classes as well[69] and Kunzra advised that scheduled tribes and depressed classes should be regarded as backward.[70] But Chandrika Ram, a Member belonging to Scheduled Caste community, thought that the backward class occupied the middle position in the society—between the highest, the Caste Hindus and lowest, the Scheduled Castes.[71]

Since it was not easy to define precisely the term 'backward' or to find a suitable criterion for testing backwardness of a community,[72] the Framers refrained from defining the 'backward class' and left the task to the Commission to be constituted for investigating into the conditions of the backward classes.

The Framers did not indicate who they should be but said that social and educational backwardness should be taken into consideration. The economic criterion was also aired by the Framers. Members like Hukum Singh, M.A. Ayyangar, Prof. Shah, Prof. Saksena and Naziruddin Ahmed pleaded in vain in the Parliament at the time of passage of the First Constitution Amendment Bill for inclusion of such a criterion. Left to himself, Nehru would have included the economic condition of the class as a yardstick, but the adoption of the phraseology occurring in other Articles prevented him from taking such a step.[73] The consequence of leaving a term undefined in the Constitution is, as it should be. There is now a virtual scramble for inclusion either in the list of Scheduled Castes or in the list of Backward Classes for enjoying the constitutional benefits and safeguards provided for them, thereby giving rise to, as predicted, "casteism and favouritism which should have nothing to do in a secular State.[74]

The debates in the Constituent Assembly leading to the incorporation of various constitutional safeguards clearly indicate that whatever might have been the views of the Members on these constitutional safeguards, they, irrespective of caste and community affiliations, were sincerely concerned for the uplift of the Scheduled Castes and Backward Classes in all spheres of life—social, educational, cultural and political, and that too very quickly, so that, shorn of disabilities or discriminations, they could take their legitimate share in all the activities of the society in their own right, as an equal partner. Theirs is a life of misery and exploitation. They are exploited on account of their ignorance and backwardness. The backwardness of the people is the result of conditions which have been persisting and in existence for several centuries and ages. The Framers knew that these backwardness would not die off easily. So the measure really should have been for liquidating that backward condition,[75] so that they no longer remain victims of educational or economic backwardness or are haunted by social stigma. The problems are primarily educational and of an economic character. They are of a cultural character too. So what was required was to raise the educational, cultural and economic level of these downtrodden and oppressed people.[76] The Framers knew that unless this section of population reached the same level of culture as other sections of the population,[77] or were brought to a certain standard or their economic condition was bettered, the duty towards them would not have been performed.[78]

In their wisdom the founding fathers thought that the economic, social and cultural conditions of the Scheduled Castes would not improve unless these safeguards were provided for them. This principle of reservation for that section of population which form part of the Hindu community, follow the same culture and same religion and are also of the same racial stock, no doubt goes against the national interest, because it fosters a sense of divisiveness, separateness and exclusiveness. This principle of two standards for enjoying certain facilities—that too because one belongs to a certain caste or community, is making even a new-born babe aware of the vicious caste system in a 'caste-less' State the Framers thought of ushering in. This policy is not only not good from the point of view of justice and fairplay but it would not be in the interests of the community as a whole.[79] This also throws up many pertinent questions. Actually for whom the reservations are made? Who are they? Who are the beneficiaries? Whether these safeguards will cover all castes and sub-castes coming under the broad category of Scheduled Castes or only that section of the Scheduled Caste population whose economic, educational and cultural level did not improve? What are the yardstick for measuring it? How has it changed the life style of the common man? Did the Framers honestly believe that the economic and educational conditions of the Scheduled Castes would improve by these measures? How long will it continue? In perpetuity? And lastly, will it be conducive to national integration, unity and cohesiveness?

In the fitness of things, this section of population for whom these safeguards have been provided should have marched with time and achieved a certain level of progress, socially, educationally and culturally, which should have enabled, them, if not all, atleast a section of them, to come out of the 'seclusion' imposed by these safeguards and merge with the mainstream, as contemplated by the Framers. The mere fact that a large segment of population—since increased to 16.33% according to the 1991 census from 14.67% in 1961—still cherishes the desire to be categorised as Scheduled Castes for the purposes of certain benefits and privileges and that even that section of the Scheduled Castes population which have progressed and advanced in the social ladder are not willing to give up their claims to these privileges in favour of their less advantaged brethren, is a reason enough to delve deep into the matter and find out what has gone wrong. If this section of population, notwithstanding these safeguards, still thinks that they are still much below the general level of development in the social, educational, cultural, political and economic spheres and that their position has not improved materially even within the last forty eight years of independence, it will only prove that something is amiss somewhere—either these constitutional provisions are not meant to achieve these objectives or some other measures were called for, which the founding fathers conveniently overlooked. They thought that they had done their duty by this section of population by providing these constitutional safeguards. They faltered and prevaricated when correct decisions were called for. In the process, they created a big chasm in the body politic on the basis of caste. They might have been guided by the 'expediency and the exigencies of the situation'[80] but the wisdom of the course chartered by them which has only broadened the cleavages and further strengthened the fissiparous and disintegrationist tendencies, may very well be questioned. Was it necessary to put the country in perpetual strain and conflict for gaining some immediate political advantages? The country-wide violent agitations in the wake of the Mandal Report were not only against the implementation of the Mandal Report but also in protest against the Reservation policy as a whole—a policy which cannot cure the malady but help spread it has got to be looked into afresh.

The legacy of the policy formulated by the Founding Fathers continued during the time of their successors as well, because they were very quick to perceive the immense political gain if the policy was perpetuated. As the natural heir to the British system of administration, they inherited the British policy of 'Divide and Rule' as well. Instead of drawing a lesson from the past mistakes and taking corrective measures they are still experimenting with it and have, in fact, taken it to the grassroot level by amending the Constitution which allows the States to reserve seats in the three-tier Panchayati Raj Institutions for the Scheduled Castes according to their population. While the Founding Fathers were content to reserve seats for the Scheduled Castes only in the State and Union Legislatures, their successors have taken it to the village level. Though they talk of a 'caste-less society' and of the ill-effects of the caste-system, they work for its continuance, because, in their heart of hearts they know that there is a definite advantage if such a system is continued. If they are really concerned for ushering in a 'caste-less society' they would have definitely removed all vestiges of caste-system and would not have worked for dividing the society on the basis of caste, that too created by them. They are so much at variance in their professed ideals and its actual implementation that one shudders to think what is in store for us. Only the future can tell what would be the effect of their recent experiment.

Notes and References

1. Pillai, *CAD*, Vol. V, dated 27-8-47, p. 203.
2. Khandekar, *Ibid.*, dated 28-8-47, p. 266
3. Patel, *Ibid.*, Vol. X, dated 14-10-49, p. 248.
4. Munshi, *Ibid*, Vol. V, dated 27-8-47, p. 227.
5. Naziruddin Ahmed, *Ibid.*, Vol. VIII, dated 25-5-49, p. 298.
6. Para 15(2) of the *Cabinet Mission Statement* of May 16, 1946.
7. Saksena, *CAD*, Vol. V, dated 27-8-47, p. 235.
8. Nagappa, *Ibid.*, Vol. VIII, dated 25-5-49, p. 292.
9. P.R. Thakur, *Ibid.*, Vol. I, dated 19-12-46, p. 139
10. Nagappa, *Ibid.*, Vol. V, dated 27-8-47, p. 206.
11. Nagappa. *Ibid.*, Pillai, *Ibid.*, Vol. V, dated 27-8-47, p. 203.
12. Nagappa, *Ibid.*, p. 206.
13. Khandeker, *Ibid.*, Vol. IX, dated 24-8-49, p. 666.
14. Khandekar, *Ibid.*, Vol. V, dated 28-8-47, p. 267.
15. Khandekar, *Ibid.*, p. 266.
16. Monmohan Das, *Ibid.*, Vol. IX, dated 25-8-49, p. 684.
    Pillai, *Ibid.*, dated 27-8-47, p. 203.
17. Laskar, *Ibid.*, dated 23-8-49, p. 634.
18. Pillai, *Ibid.*, Vol. V., dated 27-8-47, p. 204.
19. Khandekar, *Ibid.*, Vol. IX, dated 24-8-49, p. 668.

20. Khandekar, *Ibid.*, Vol. IX, dated 24-8-49, p. 666.
21. Dakshayani Velayudan, *Ibid.*, Vol. I, dated 19-12-46, p. 152.
22. Khandekar, *Ibid.*, Vol. V, dated 27-8-47, p. 233.
23. Nagappa, *Ibid.*, Vol. II, dated 20-1-47, p. 284.
24. Devendranath Samanta, *Ibid.*, dated 21-1-47, p. 294.
25. Velayudan, *Ibid.*, Vol. I, dated 19-12-45, p. 152.
26. *Ibid.*, Vol. V, dated 28-8-47, p. 264.
27. *Ibid.*
28. Velayudan, *Ibid.*, Vol. I, dated 19-12-46, p. 152.
29. Pillai, *Ibid.*, Vol. V, dated 27-8-47, p. 229.
30. *Ibid.*, Vol. VIII, p. 315.
31. Dhulekar, *Ibid.*, Vol. II, dated 21-1-47, p. 303.
32. Chaudhuri Ranbir Singh, *Ibid.*, Vol. VII, dated 6-11-48, p. 289.
33. Munshi, *Ibid.*, Vol. V, dated 27-8-47, p. 228.
34. Dhulekar, *Ibid.*, Vol. II, dated 21-1-47, p. 303.
35. Tyagi, *Ibid.*, Vol. IX, dated 24-8-49, p. 671.
36. Brajeswar Prasad, *Ibid.*, p. 663.
37. Mookherjee, *Ibid.*, Vol. VIII, dated 25-5-49, p. 299.
38. Brajeswar Prasad, *Ibid.*, Vol. IX, dated 24-8-49, p. 644.
39. Bhargava, *Ibid.*, p. 648.
40. Krishna Chandra Sharma, *Ibid.*, Vol. VIII, dated 1-6-49, p. 517.
41. Raj Bahadar, *Ibid.*, Vol. IX, dated 23-8-49, pp. 622-23
42. Brajeswar Prasad, *Ibid.*, Vol. X, dated 14-10-49, p. 239.
43. Tyagi, *Ibid.*, Vol. IX, dated 24-8-49, p. 672.
44. Munshi, *Ibid.*, Vol. V, dated 27-8-47, p. 227.
45. Patel, *Ibid.*, Vol. VIII, dated 25-5-49, p. 272.
46. D'Souza, *Ibid.*, Vol. V, dated 27-8-47, p. 232.
47. Pillai, *Ibid.*, Vol. IX, dated 24-8-49, p. 647.
48. Radhakrishnan, *Ibid.*, Vol. V, dated 28-8-47, p. 283.
49. Mookherjee, *Ibid.*, Vol. VIII, dated 25-5-49, p. 298.
50. Krishnaswami Bharati, *Ibid.*, Vol, VII, dated 9-11-48, p. 366.
51. Kunzru, *Ibid.*, dated 30-11-48, p. 681.
52. Hasrat Mohani, *Ibid.*, dated 4-1-49, p. 1255.
53. Bhargava, *Ibid.*, Vol. IX, dated 25-8-49, p. 687.
54. Mookherjee, *Ibid.*, Vol. VIII, dated 25-5-49, p. 299.
55. Nehru, *Ibid.*, Vol. VIII, dated 26-5-49, p. 331.
56. Ambedkar, *Ibid.*, Vol. IX, dated 24-8-49, p. 697.

57. Khandekar, *Ibid.*, Vol. II, dated 21-1-47, p. 299.
58. Laskar, *Ibid.*, Vol. IX, dated 23-8-49, pp. 634-35.
59. Pillai, *Ibid.*, dated 24-8-49, p. 646.
60. Ambedkar, *Ibid.*, Vol. VII, dated 30-11-48, p. 701.
61. Nehra, *Parliamentary Debates*, Vol. XII,1951, Third Session, (Second Part) of Parliament of India, 1951, dated 18-5-51, Cols. 9084-85.
62. D'Souza, *CAD*, Vol. VIII, dated 25-5-49, p. 307.
63. Ayyangar, *Ibid.*, Vol. IX, dated 23-8-49, p. 626.
64. Ambedkar, *Parliamentary Debates*, Vol. XII,1951, Third Session, (Second Part) of Parliament of India, 1951, dated 18-5-51, Cols. 9006-7.
65. Ambedkar, *CAD*, Vol. VII, dated 30-11-48, p. 702.
66. Munshi, *Ibid.*, p. 697.
67. Kunzru, *Ibid.*, p. 681.
68. Munshi, *Ibid.*, p. 696.
69. Bhargava, *Ibid.*, Vol. VIII, dated 16-6-49, p. 946 and dated 1-6-49, p. 513.
70. Kunzru, *Ibid.*, Vol. VII, dated 30-11-48, p. 680.
71. Chandrika Ram, *Ibid.*, p. 687.
72. Damodar Swarup Seth, *Ibid.*, p. 679.
73. Nehru, *Parliamentary Debates*, Vol. XII, 1951, Third Session (Second Part) of Parliament of India, 1951, dated 1-6-51, Cols. 9831-2.
74. Seth, *CAD*, Vol. VII, dated 30-11-48, p. 679.
75. Ismail Sahib, *Ibid.*, p. 693.
76. Brajeswar Prasad, *Ibid.*, Vol. IX, dated 24-8-49, p. 663.
77. Dharam Prakash, *Ibid.*, Vol. VII, dated 30-11-48, p. 687.
78. Bhargava, *Ibid.*, Vol. IX, dated 25-8-49, p. 688.
79. K.C. Sharma, *Ibid.*, Vol. VIII, dated 1-6-49, p. 516.
80. Kamath, *Ibid.*, Vol. X, dated 14-10-49, p. 243.

Index

I-511435B

THE SCHEDULED CASTES IN INDIA

VOL. III

THE SCHEDULED CASTES IN INDIA

VOL. III

S.K. Chatterjee

GYAN

GYAN PUBLISHING HOUSE

NEW DELHI-110 002

THE SCHEDULED CASTES IN INDIA (VOL. III)
(Anthropology, Tribal Studies, Sociology)

ISBN : 81-212-0511-5 (Set)

ISBN : 81-212-0537-9 (Vol. III)

Published in 2008 in India by
Gyan Publishing House
5 Ansari Road
New Delhi-110 002

All rights reserved. No part of this book may be reproduced in any manner without written permission

Printed at Vishal Kaushik Printers Delhi - 110093

CONTENTS

PREFACE VOL. III

This is the third volume on the "Scheduled Castes in India". The origin and growth of caste system in India upto the British period was discussed in the first volume. The second volume was devoted to the study on the framing of the discriminatory constitutional provisions. This volume deals with the genesis, growth and demographic pattern of the Scheduled Castes. These four volumes together complete the project on the "Scheduled Castes in India".

Many official bodies estimated the depressed population during the period 1916-32. In the absence of an official definition the officers of the Government as well as the different official bodies, while estimating their number, generally included the 'Untouchables' in this category. As their perception of the degree, criteria and manifestations of untouchability varied widely, so did their estimates of depressed population. What was, however, more important than the estimates of depressed population was the identification of castes to be included in this category. Many official bodies like the Indian Central Committee, the Simon Commission and even the 1921 Census Commissioner estimated the depressed population but refrained from mentioning the castes considered depressed by them. Though both the Indian Central Committee and the Simon Commission relied on the provincial Governments' reports, there was a difference in their population figures. I tried to procure the relevant papers, correspondences, etc., of the Indian Central Committee and of the Simon Commission in order to find out which castes were considered depressed by them and why there was anomaly in their population estimation, but failed.

It has also been noticed during this study that soon after the publication of the Indian Franchsic (Lothian) Committee's report in 1932, the Bengal Government was asked by the Government of India in early 1933 to send their recommendations for inclusion of castes in the "Schedule of Castes". The Bengal Government invited suggestions representations, etc., from the caste Associations and general public in this regard. The District Officers and the Divisional Commissioners were also asked to send their reports. These representations, reports, etc., were scrutinised in the Reforms Department of the Government, which functioned under Mr. Gilchrist, the Reforms Officer. The Reforms Officer put up these reports, etc. along with his recommendations to the Member of the Governor's Executive Council who took the final decision. This process was completed in 1933 itself and the provincial Government's report was sent to the Government of India by the end of 1933. The Government of India, in turn, forwarded this report alongwith similar reports of the other provincial Governments to His Majesty's Government in London and His Majesty in Council, on the basis of these reports, issued the Government of India (Scheduled Castes) Order, 1936.

I could locate the Bengal Government's papers and tried to obtain the relevant papers of the remaining provincial Governments but failed. I feel the study would have been more penetrating if these papers were available.

Now that the National Commission on Scheduled Castes and Scheduled Tribes has started functioning, it may not be difficult for it to take up the responsibility of procuring the relevant papers, correspondences, reports, etc., on this subject from the concerned State Governments and the Central Government and of preserving them in a systematic manner. This would of immense help not only to the researchers and the academicians but to the Administrators and the political leaders as well for taking decisions on policy matters.

The Scheduled Castes Orders and the Scheduled Tribes Orders have been amended many times. It is very difficult to keep track of them unless all the relevant amendments are handy. Appendix I is expected to fill up this void both in regard to the Scheduled Castes and the Scheduled Tribes.

Annexture Tables III to XI will give an idea about the position accorded to different castes as also the estimates of the Untouchable/Depressed population by the official bodies during the period 1911-1936, i.e., till the issuance of the Scheduled Castes Order of 1936. A mere glance at these Tables will help clear many misgivings.

The Main Table lists out the castes scheduled under different Orders/Acts since 1936 and also contains the total population of each Scheduled Caste as revealed at the time of the 1961, 1971 and 1981 Censuses. Since the 1991 Census figures have not yet been published the same could not be incorporated in this Table.

The Census reports have been relied on for the population figures. As is well-known, the Census figures have certain limitations which may not be of any consequence in a macro-level study. This would, however, be more evident in micro-level studies. Since there is no other alternative but to depend on the Census figures for undertaking any demographic study of this nature, it is better to keep this fact in view.

In completing this study I have received help and cooperation from many persons. My wife has been a constant source of inspiration and encouragement to me. I owe a special debt of gratitude to my publisher, Sri B.P. Garg of the Gyan Publishing House for bringing out the book in time.

Salt Lake
Calcutta

S.K. Chatterjee

22

Genesis of Scheduled Castes

The Constitution of India uses the following terms for classification of certain categories of citizens:

(1) Socially and educationally backward classes of citizens [Article 15(4)],

(2) Backward class of citizens [Article 16(4)],

(3) Weaker sections of the people [Article 46],

(4) Other backward classes [Article 338(3)],

(5) Socially and educationally backward classes [Article 340], and

(6) Scheduled Castes and Scheduled Tribes.

The Constitution has attempted to give a definition of the Scheduled Castes and the Scheduled Tribes in Article 341 and Article 342,respectively, and has refrained from defining the other groups detailed above.

Article 341, as amended says:

(1) The President may with respect to any State or Union territory, and where it is a State, after consultation with the Governor thereof, by public notification, specify the castes, races or tribes or parts of or groups within castes, races or tribes which shall for the purposes of this Constitution be deemed to be Scheduled Castes in relation to that State or Union territory, as the case may be.

(2) Parliament may by law include in or exclude from

> the list of Scheduled Castes specified in a notification issued under clause (1) any caste, race or tribe, or part of or group within any caste, race or tribe, but save as aforesaid a notification issued under the said clause shall not be varied by any subsequent notification.

Article 341 closely resembles Section 26(1) of the First Schedule of the Government of India Act, 1935, which defines Scheduled Castes as follows:

> The 'Scheduled Castes' means such castes, races or tribes or parts of or groups within castes, races, or tribes, being castes, races, tribes, parts or groups which appear to His Majesty in Council to correspond to the classes of persons formerly known as "the depressed classes", as His Majesty in Council may specify.

It may be remembered that the term 'Scheduled Castes' was used for the first time in the 1935 Act and in pursuance of the provisions in the 1st, 5th and 6th Schedules of the Act, the Government of India (Scheduled Castes) Order, 1936 was issued delineating the castes and tribes to be treated as the 'Scheduled Castes' for the purposes of the Act in the respective provinces. The Founding Fathers initially contemplated to provide in the Constitution a Schedule listing therein the Scheduled Castes, State-wise. The Constitutional Adviser in his Draft Constitution, prepared in October, 1947, adhered to this 1936 Order of the Government of India and put these castes in the Eleventh Schedule of the Draft Constitution, Province-wise.[1] The Drafting Committee, however, simplified the procedure and instead of enumerating all the Scheduled Castes in a Schedule of the Constitution, simply stipulated that the expression Scheduled Castes should mean those as were specified in the Government of India (Scheduled Castes) Order, 1936, in relation to the corresponding provinces.[2]

But towards the fag end of the Constituent Assembly sessions, on September 17, 1949, on a motion moved by Dr. Ambedkar, the chairman of the Drafting Committee, a new Article (Article 341) was inserted empowering the President to issue a general notification, in consultation with the Governor or Ruler of the State, specifying the castes, races or tribes which should be deemed to be Scheduled Castes for the purposes of the Constitution. "The object of the Article was to eliminate the necessity of burdening the Constitution with long lists of Scheduled Castes."[3] This procedure became necessary also because the lists previously compiled covered only what were then the Provinces of the Dominion of India and with the inclusion of the territories of the Indian States within the framework of the Constitution it became necessary to define the Scheduled Castes in these territories as well.[4]

The 'Scheduled Castes' under the 1935 Act meant such castes, races or tribes which corresponded to the classes of persons formerly known as 'Depressed Classes'. Though the term 'Depressed Classes' was used by different official bodies and the Government as an euphemism for the word 'Untouchables', it lacked any official definition because of the difficulty in giving a proper definition to such ill-defined a group as the 'Depressed Classes' of the community. The Government of India also "have consistently avoided themselves making any precise classification of the groups forming what are called the depressed classes, if only on the ground that owing to the social disabilities to which members of the depressed classes are exposed it would be in the highest degree undesirable that any official authorisation might appear to extend to such classification. The fluidity of social distinctions and the efforts of the classes lowest in the scale, aided by social reformers to improve their status made it the more desirable that Government should abstain from doing any thing which would tend to give rigidity to these distinctions. There has accordingly been no official definition of any castes or tribes of the community as depressed classes and the question whether or not any group of the community is socially depressed or treated as untouchable is a matter of local custom."[5]

In the absence of any official definition of the 'depressed classes', Government officials and the official bodies, while preparing the list of depressed classes, generally included the 'untouchables' in the list of 'depressed classes', according to their own concept of 'untouchability'. As very aptly pointed out by Ambedkar, untouchability is not a legal term. There is no exact legal definition of untouchability whereby it could be possible to define who is an untouchable and who is not. Untouchability is a social concept which has become embodied in a custom and as custom varies so does untouchability.[6] This difficulty in giving a proper definition to the term 'untouchability' and the 'untouchables' however, did not deter the official bodies from identifying the depressed classes and estimating their number.

Emergence of the term 'Depressed Classes'

From 1911 onwards Depressed Classes and its population assumed a centre stage position in the political and social arena of the country. The question of depressed classes came into prominence in 1916 when in pursuance of a resolution in the Imperial Legislative Council the Government of India addressed local Governments to ascertain their views on the subject of the amelioration of the condition of the depressed classes. In the said letter they stated that some definition was required of the term "depressed classes". Apart from incidental references to the humbler sections of the community whose condition was largely due to poverty the tenor of the discussion in the Imperial Council was to include in this expression:

(i) Criminal and wandering tribes,
(ii) Aboriginal tribes, and
(iii) Untouchables.

The Government of India asked that the 'heads' to be adopted by the local Governments should be—

(a) depressed classes (i.e. "untouchables"),

(b) aboriginal and hill tribes, and

(c) criminal tribes,

and that the actual castes or tribes in each group should be enumerated.

In pursuance of this directive the provincial Governments (except Assam and Punjab) furnished the lists and figures of the depressed classes to the Government of India, whose total population was 27.4 millions.[7]

The next important reference is to be found in the Seventh Quinquennial Review of the Progress of Education in India for the years 1912-17. This Review was prepared by Sir Henry Sharp, who was at the time Educational Commissioner under the Government of India. In the Report the depressed classes were specifically dealt with from the point of view of educational assistance and progress. In that Review statistics were given separately of :—

(a) aboriginal or hill tribes,

(b) depressed classes, and

(c) criminal tribes.

A list of castes and tribes constituting the depressed classes was given. In paragraph 505 of his report, Sharp expressed his views as follows on the classes of the depressed community:

> The depressed classes, like the tribes just described (i.e., the aboriginals,) are often the original inhabitants. But they differ from the hill tribes in having preferred a life of servitude to exile into inhospitable regions. Thus they have lost their distinctive habits and languages and have become a recognized part of the general community. The rules of caste (probably invented and developed for this very end) have however kept them distinct from the invaders and the tasks assigned to them are menial and regarded as degrading. They form the unclean castes, whose touch or even whose shadow is pollution. But a wider significance is often

> attached to the expression so that it includes communities which, though not absolutely outside the pale of caste, are backward and generally poor and despised and also certain classes of Muhammadans. Some have interpreted it as simply educationally backward. The task of definition is made difficult by doubt as to where the line should be drawn and the elastic condition of such classes as dwell on the borderland of respectability. Sometimes a whole community declares itself to be depressed with a view to reaping special concessions of education or appointment. Sometimes a caste or a sub-caste hitherto regarded by all as depressed, totally repudiates the description and declares itself as good as its neighbours. On the whole the tendency is for the lower castes to edge themselves here and there into a higher scale by the assumption of new names and privileges. Further complicating facts are that many of these downtrodden castes come into the fold of Christianity and that a caste reckoned as untouchable or depressed in one locality is not necessarily so in another.[8]

Sharp's comments serve to illustrate the difficulty of arriving at any correct definition of so vague a term as "the depressed classes". His estimates of the depressed classes population in British India of 31.5 millions were apparently based on the Census Report of 1911, but we are without any precise information of the particular data on which he relied when reaching a decision whether to include or to exclude any particular caste. In Assam, as distinct from other provinces, hill or aboriginal tribes living in the plains were specifically included in the same category as the depressed classes.

The next reference to this question is found in the Report of the Franchise Committee (Southborough Committee), 1918-19. This Committee, established to advise on the franchise under the 1919 reforms, gave population figures in respect of each Governor's province and divided the Hindus into

(1) Brahmins,
(2) non-Brahmins, and
(3) Others.

In footnotes to each appendix a statement was given of the basis on which the grouping of "Others" was made. The Madras group was stated to consist of the main Panchama or untouchable castes, for instance, the Paraiyans, Pallans and Valluvans in the Tamil districts, the Malas and Madigas in the Telugu districts, the Cherumans of Malabar and the Holeyas of South Canara. In Bombay, including Sind, the group was stated to consist of castes which were ordinarily denied access to a Hindu temple vide page 66, Part I, of the Bombay Census Report, 1911 with a note that the castes were generally described as "untouchables". In Bengal, Bihar and Orissa, the term "Others" was stated to include the castes and tribes constituting more than 1 per mille of the total population and classed as Hindus in the Census, which were denied access to the interior of ordinary Hindu temples and fell within categories 7, 8, 9 or 10 at page 232, part I, Census Report of Bengal, Bihar, Orissa and Sikkim, with a note that these castes and tribes were generally described as 'untouchables'. For the United Provinces the Committee gave a reference to Groups XI and XII at pages 231 and 232, Part I, of the United Provinces Census Report, 1901, as 'untouchable' castes. The group in the Punjab was stated to consist of castes not ordinarily admitted to a Hindu temple, vide page 109, Part I, Punjab Census Report, 1911. In the Central Provinces and Berar the group was stated to include castes who were denied access to a Hindu temple, as 'untouchables', vide page 74, Part I, Central Provinces and Berar Census Report, 1911. In Assam the group was stated to include castes which caused pollution by touch and which buried their dead vide page 41 of Part I of the Assam Census Report, 1911 and it was stated that these castes were generally described as 'untouchables'.

The figures collected by the Franchise Committee yielded a figure of 42.2 millions for this group of "Others", as a third Hindu group, formed in the manner described above and apparently identified by the Committee with the "depressed classes".[9]

Depressed Classes in the Census

The next important reference to this question is in the Census Report of 1921. But before discussing the 1921 Census Report, it is better to have a look at the previous Census Reports. The first general census of India was taken in the year 1881. Beyond listing the different castes and creeds and adding up their numbers so as to arrive at the total figure of the population of India the Census of 1881 did nothing. It made no attempt to classify the different Hindu castes either into higher and lower or touchable and untouchable. The second general census of India was taken in 1891. It was at this census that an attempt to classify the population on the basis of caste, race and grade was made by the Census Commissioner for the first time. But it was only an attempt.

The third general census of India was taken in 1901. At this census a new principle of classification was adopted, namely, "classification by social precedence as recognised by native public opinion". This census of 1901 did not result in fixing the total population of the Untouchables at any exact figure. This was due to two reasons. In the first place no exact tests were applied to determine who was an Untouchable. Secondly, a class of the population which was economically and educationally backward but not Untouchable was mixed up with those who were actually Untouchables.[10]

The Census Commissioner of 1911 went a step further and decided that instead of raising the question whether the members of particular castes should be regarded as genuine Hindus or not, a list should be prepared of the castes and tribes contributing more than 1 per mille to the total population and returned and classed as Hindus, which *qua* castes did not conform to certain standards or were subject to certain disabilities, viz.

(1) deny the supremacy of the Brahmans;
(2) do not receive the *mantra* from a Brahmana or other recog-nised Hindu guru;
(3) deny the authority of the Vedas;
(4) do not worship the great Hindu gods;
(5) are not served by good Brahmanas;
(6) have no Brahman priests at all;
(7) have no access to the interior of the ordinary Hindu temples;
(8) cause pollution (a) by touch, (b) within a certain distance;
(9) bury their dead; and
(10) eat beef and do not reverence the cow.[11]

It may be recalled that the separation of the Untouchables from the Hindus was insisted upon by the Muslims in a memorial to the Government dated January 27, 1910 in which they claimed that their representation in the political bodies of the country should be in proportion to the population of Touchable Hindus and not Hindus as a whole because they contended that the Untouchables were not Hindus.

Therefore this attempt of the Census Commissioner of grouping together castes on the basis of these tests was perceived by the Hindus as aiming at separating the Depressed Classes from the Hindus and thereby reducing the strength of the Hindu community and its importance. It was even said that this attempt of the Census Commissioner was the result of a conspiracy between the Musalmans and the British Government to divide and weaken the Hindu community. It was alleged that what was behind this move was not a genuine desire to know the population of the Untouchables but the desire to break up the solidarity of the Hindu community by separating the Untouchables from the Touchables. Many protest meetings were held all over the country by the Hindus and this plan of the Census Commissioner was condemned in the strongest terms.[12]

Be that as it may, the Census of 1911 which estimated the population of those coming under any one of the 10 categories as 42.57 millions, marks the beginning of the assessment of the population of the Untouchables.

In the Census of 1921 the Census Commissioner, J.T. Marten, found it incumbent on himself to try to obtain some statistical estimate of the number of the depressed classes. He observed that it had been usual in recent years to speak of a certain section of the community as the "depressed classes', and he referred to the attempt made by Sharp in his Quinquennial Review of the Progress of Education in India, 1912-17, discussed earlier, to prepare a list of the castes and tribes constituting this section of the community.

The question before Marten, as Census Commissioner then, was whether he would use the opportunity of the new Census of 1921 to verify the classification made by Sharp of the depressed classes. Marten explained in his report that he recognised that there was undoubtedly some danger of giving offence by making in a public report social distinctions which might be deemed invidious; but in view of the lists already prepared (i.e., the lists prepared by the Franchise Committee and Sharp's list), and owing to the fact that the "depressed classes" had, especially in South India, attained a class consciousness and a class organization, were served by special missions, "raised" by philanthropic societies and officially represented in the legislatures under the Reforms Scheme, Marten considered it necessary to face the facts and attempt to obtain some statistical estimate of their numbers. Notwithstanding the fact that Marten found that "the term has no final definition, nor is it certain exactly whom it covers", he refrained from giving any guideline to the Provincial Superintendents but asked them "to let me have an estimate based on census figures of the approximate strength of castes who were usually included in the category of 'depressed'." He received lists of "some sort" from all provinces and states except the United Provinces, where what Marten described as "the extreme delicacy of official sentiment" shrank from the task of attempting even a rough estimate. Marten stated that the figures given were not based on exactly uniform criteria, as a different view was taken of the position of the same groups in different parts of India, and he had occasion in some instances to modify the estimates on the basis of figures of Sharp's lists and of information from the 1911 Census report and tables. The estimates were further subject to the general defect that the total strength of any caste was not recorded.

From the statistics received the Census Commissioner prepared an estimate of 52,680,000 persons, what he described as *minimum* numbers which might be considered to form the "depressed classes" of the Hindu community, and added a note that these figures must be taken as a *low and conservative* estimate since they did not include all those who should have been included. i.e.,

(1) the full strength of the castes and tribes concerned, and

(2) the tribal aborigines more recently absorbed in Hinduism, many of whom were considered impure.

He then observed that "we may confidently place the numbers of these depressed classes, all of whom are considered impure, at something between 55 and 60 millions in India proper." Of the 52½ millions for which the Census Commissioner gave actual figures less than 43½ millions were to be found in British India.[13]

Depressed Classes and other Committees

The Reforms Enquiry Committee of 1924, popularly known as the Muddiman Committee, relied on the Census figures of 1921 in its report.[14]

The Moral and Material Progress Report on India for the year 1925-26 reported that there "are said to be no fewer than 60 millions" of depressed classes in India.[15]

This wide variation in the figures of the Depressed Classes population estimated by the different official agencies —approximately 30 millions by Sharp in 1912-17, 55-60 millions for the whole of India by the Census Commissioner in 1921 and 60 millions in the Moral and Material Progress Report for 1925-26 was pointed out by Lala Lajpat Rai in the Legislative Assembly on February 16. 1928. Later, while participating in a debate in the Legislative Assembly on February 23, 1928, G.S. Bajpai, the then Secretary to the Government in the Department of Education, Health and Lands, stated that he wished to correct the figure of 60 millions quoted by Lala Lajpat Rai in his speech. He stated that he had calculations made in the light of available material and that according to his calculation, the so-called depressed or untouchable classes (and he was careful to explain that he did not include the backward classes generally) in the Governor's provinces, excluding Burma and Assam, number 28 ½ millions. Bajpai's calculations had been compiled in the Department of Education, Health and Lands after reference to the annual and quinquennial reports of the Directors of Public Instruction of the various provinces, to the census figures, and to the special reports of the provincial Governments sent in 1917-18.[16]

The next reference to the number of Depressed Classes population was made in the House of Commons on March 26, 1928, by Wellock when he asked the Under Secretary of State for India what was the most recent estimate of the number of depressed classes in British India. The Government asked for time and on April 23, 1928 Earl Winterton in his reply stated that "the Government of India inform me that the latest census figures indicate 43 millions as the number of members of the so-called depressed classes, and that from information provided in provincial educational reports they estimate that of these some 29 millions are 'untouchables'. Neither term is capable of very precise definition, consequently these figures are somewhat indefinite."[17]

In reply to another question the Home Member to

the Government of India informed the Legislative Assembly on September 4, 1928 that "the class generally considered as depressed beside or in addition to the untouchables are hill tribes, aboriginals and criminal tribes" and a list of castes which were generally, according to local usage and custom, regarded as untouchable was laid on the table of the Legislative Assembly.[18]

It may be noted that there was no material difference between the two Government lists of 1917 and of 1928. In 1917, the Provincial Governments identified 104 castes as depressed, i.e., untouchables. In 1928 this figure went up to 106. Chuckler in the Madras list of 1917 was omitted from the 1928 list and the new additions were Bhangi in the Bihar list and Chamar and Chuhra in the Punjab list. It may be remembered that the Punjab Government did not furnish any list in 1917 as the "idea of pollution by mere touch was rapidly dying out". Like the 1917 list, the 1928 list did not speak of any untouchable caste in Assam.

Simon Commission and Depressed Classes

The Depressed Classes and its population continued to dominate the political scene of the late 20s. The Simon Commission, constituted in 1927 to report on the constitutional changes which might be considered desirable was confronted with the question of reservation of seats for the Depressed Classes. Sixteen of the eighteen Depressed Classes Associations, while testifying to the Commission, asked for separate electorates for the Depressed Classes. Ambedkar, as leader of the Bahiskrit Hitakarini Sabha told the Simon Commission that the Depressed Classes should be treated as a distinct minority because they were outside the pale of Hindu society and claimed far greater political protection than any other community in India because of educational backwardness, economic and social barriers. As a matter of demand for political protection, representation on the same basis as the Mohammadan community was asked for Reserved seats, if accompanied by adult franchise or separate electorate in the absence of adult franchise and certain safeguards regarding the education of Depressed Classes and the entry in public services were claimed by him.[19]

The Commission in its report submitted in May, 1930, recommended reservation of seats for the Depressed Classes in all the eight British Indian Provinces. While rejecting the proposal for a separate electorate for the Depressed Classes, it pointed out that a separate electorate for the depressed classes meant, as a preliminary a precise definition of all who were covered by the term, and the boundary would be in some cases difficult to draw. It meant stigmatising each individual voter in the list, and militated against the process which was already beginning, and which needed to be in every way encouraged—that of helping those who were depressed to rise in the social and economic scale.[20]

While admitting the difficulty of giving a definition of the Depressed Classes which should apply to all Provinces,[21] it recommended the appointment of a Franchise Committee one of whose tasks was "to frame for each province a definition of Depressed Classes (which may well vary, sometimes even between parts of the same province) and to determine their numbers so defined."[22] The Commission, however, adopted the definition "causes pollution by touch or by the approach within a certain distance" and "after studying various figures and analysing the evidence put before" it, made "the best estimate" that total population of the 'untouchables' in British India was 43.6 millions, with a stipulation that there was a wide margin of possible error in the case of Bengal, the United Provinces and Bihar and Orissa, accounting for a Depressed Classes population of 11.5, 12.0 and 5.0 millions respectively, that is out of an estimated population of 43.6 millions, there was the possibility of a wide margin of error in regard to 28.5 millions.[23] Since the Commission was not sure of its own estimation, it recommended that "when the definitions are settled and the correct totals ascertained the number of seats to be reserved for depressed classes should be settled".[24]

Before the submission of the Simon Commission Report, two other Committees identified the number of Depressed Classes in 1929. The Hartog Committee, constituted to review the growth of education in India, submitted its report on March 8, 1929. In Chapter X of its report dealing with Education of the Depressed Classes, it stated that the use of the term "depressed classes" had given rise to some difficulties. In the Chapter on the Education of the Depressed Classes in the Memorandum on the Progress of Education in India prepared by the Government of India, it was made clear that the Chapter dealt with

> "those members of the Hindu community who are regarded as outcastes or 'untouchables' and who have in consequence suffered from serious social disabilities in the matter of education and general advancement."

Taking the definition of the depressed classes in that form, the Committee found that the figures for these classes were not directly ascertainable from the Census of 1921. It, therefore, made a calculation of its own and gave a figure of 29.76 millions, which "are based on the classification of tribes and castes regarded as 'untouchable' in the papers laid by the Government of India before the Legislative Assembly in 1928". It also added that the majority of the quinquennial Reviews included under the depressed classes only those who were regarded as 'untouchables'.[25]

Again, in 1929, the Indian Central Committee, set up under the chairmanship of Sir Sankaran Nair to advise the Simon Commission, found that there had been considerable difference of opinion on the question of the population numbers of those communities to be considered as 'depressed' and accepted the figures of 44.5 millions supplied by the several governments.[26] Observing that the term 'depressed classes' was frequently used in a loose sense to connote not only members of the communities classed as 'untouchable', but criminal tribes, aboriginals and other backward communities, the Indian Central Committee, decided to "confine the term to those who are classed as 'untouchable', leaving it to the local governments to draw up lists of the castes which fall within this category."[27]

Though there was not much difference in the estimates made by the Indian Central Committee and by the Simon Commission, there was a wide difference in their attitude and approach to this question. The Indian Central Committee wanted to confine the Depressed Classes to the Untouchables only but accepted the figures furnished by the Provincial Governments without any demur. It neither gave any definition of the 'Untouchables' nor bothered to check up whether the Provincial Governments followed its own criterion of the Depressed Classes while estimating its population. The Simon Commission, on the other hand, had given a definition of the 'Depressed Classes' and yet gave sufficient warning that there was a wide margin of error in its estimation of Depressed Classes population, specially in the provinces of Bengal, the United Provinces and Bihar and Orissa.

So, immediately prior to the 1931 census, a number of agencies estimated the Depressed Classes population. All these agencies, however, attempted at estimating the Depressed Classes population according to their own criteria of untouchability. The total population classed as depressed, therefore, varied primarily because of lack of uniformity in identifying the criteria of untouchability and in following any general principle in this regard. The variation in the figures arose largely from a difference in the meaning and application given to what was at all times a rather vague term. Though there was no difference of opinion in the inclusion of only the untouchables in this category, the difference of opinion was manifest in regard to the degree of untouchability and consequently on the question as to who should be treated as Untouchables.

Depressed Classes in the 1931 Census

At the time of the 1931 Census it was realised that some more definite figures of depressed classes population should be obtained than the estimate hitherto employed. Both for social and for political reasons it was obviously necessary to know the number of these classes not only in India as a whole but also in different provinces. The matter was of importance not only with reference to their representation in the body politic, but also with reference to any social work that would be undertaken towards raising them from their backward position.[28]

Hutton, as Census Commissioner for 1931, found that the definition to be used in arriving at the figure of depressed classes population was a very difficult matter. He, therefore, in the most elaborate attempt to specify criteria by which to identify untouchable groups, proposed a series of tests which revolved round the incidence of disabilities:

(1) Whether the caste or class in question can be served by Brahmin or not.

(2) Whether the caste or class in question can be served by the barbers, water-carriers, tailors, etc., who serve the caste Hindus.

(3) Whether the caste or class in question pollutes a high-caste Hindu by contact or proximity.

(4) Whether the caste or class in question is one from whose hands a caste Hindu can take water.

(5) Whether the caste or class in question is debarred from using public conveniences, such as roads, ferries, wells or schools.

(6) Whether the caste or class in question is debarred from use of Hindu temples.

(7) Whether in ordinary social intercourse a well-educated member of the caste or class in question will be treated as an equal by the high-caste men of the same educational qualifications.

(8) Whether the caste or class in question is merely

depressed on account of its own ignorance, illiteracy or poverty and but for that, would be subject to no social disability.

(9) Whether it is depressed on account of the occupation followed, and whether but for that occupation it would be subject to no social disability.[29]

Hutton also issued instructions to the Provincial Superintendents not to include non-Hinduised, hill and forest tribes as well as criminal tribes in the depressed classes.[30]

The existence of multiple criteria permitted regional variation by giving the Census Superintendents scope for discretion. Each provincial Superintendent was instructed to draw up his own list, taking these tests into account, "and to reckon as depressed only those castes who definitely suffer from serious social and political handicap on account of their degraded position in the Hindu social scheme."[31] The final reckoning, then did not apply Hutton's tests pure and simple. Excluded were some castes which were theoretically untouchables but who, by virtue of prosperity and vigorous organization, "have built up for themselves a strong position which obviates the need for any special measure for their social, political or religious protection".[32] Conversely, some groups were included even though theoretically they were not untouchables. For instance, the Bengal list included several criminal tribes and aboriginals and consisted of thirty-one groups.[33] Dushkin observes that in Orissa, Bihar and Bengal local Census Superintendents utilized "ad hoc" criteria, in addition to those given by Hutton, to include Hinduised tribals, nomadic and criminal tribes. Their numbers were negligible except in Bengal where these "ad hoc" castes made up over a quarter of the population on the final list.[34] The total of depressed classes reported by the Provincial Census Superintendents was 407 with a population of 40.8 millions but the Census Commissioner did not concur with the Provincial Census Superintendents in all cases. He identified 351 of them as depressed classes (exterior castes) having a population of 39.1 millions in British India and another 11.1 millions in the States and Agencies-making a total of 50.2 million.[35]

Lothian Committee and Depressed Classes

None, however, bothered about the exact population of the Depressed Classes and none questioned the accuracy of the census figures of the Depressed Classes till the discussions in the Round Table Conference, convened in London in 1930-32 to iron out the differences and objections over the framing of a new constitution of India crystalised towards making adequate provision for the representation of the Depressed Classes, if necessary through separate electorates, mainly at the instance of Dr. Ambedkar. In consequence of the recommendations made by the Franchise Sub-Committee of the Round Table Conference as well as by the Simon Commission, discussed earlier, Indian Franchise Committee, popularly known as the Lothian Committee, was appointed after the close of the second session of the Round Table Conference, in December 1931. One of the terms of the committee was to come to some conclusion on the total population of the Untouchables in British India for making adequate provision for the representation of the Depressed Classes in the legislature. The Committee started its work early in January, 1932. For doing its work, the Committee took the help of the Provincial Governments and of the Provincial Franchise Committees, consisting of non-officials, specially constituted for this purpose, province by province.

Before the time of the Lothian Committee the population of the Untouchables had no value. But, as very rightly pointed out by Ambedkar, after the Round Table Conference the Hindus had come to know that the Untouchables were demanding separate allotment of their share of representation, that such share must come out of the lump which the Hindus had been enjoying in the past and that the measure of the share must depend upon the population of the Untouchables.[36]

Now the number of the Untouchables became a bone of contention between the protagonists and detractors of separate electorates for the Untouchables. The report and recommendations of the Lothian Committee, therefore, assumed great importance. Now that the "depressed classes" were to be recognised as a distinct element of population for political purposes, the Lothian Committee felt it necessary to have a more precise classification of them. It, therefore, considered that "the term depressed classes should not include primitive or aboriginal tribes, nor should it include those Hindus who are only economically poor and in other ways backward but are not regarded as untouchables."[37] The Committee was "of opinion that the term should be applied only to those who are untouchables",[38] that is those satisfying the tests of untouchability, mentioned under heads 7 and 8 of the 10 tests of disabilities categorised during the 1911 Census operation, which was found by the Committee to be the generally accepted tests of untouchability, namely,

"(7) are denied access to the interior of ordinary Hindu temples,

(8) cause pollution,

(a) by touch,

(b) within a certain distance."

The Committee made it clear that its "proposals in regard to the 'depressed classes' should extend only to those castes who are included in these categories."[39]

The Lothian Committee received conflicting estimates from a number of quarters. The Provincial Governments supplied figures totalling 37.44 millions. The Provincial Franchise Committees, set up to advise the Indian Franchise Committee, produced figures that totalled less than half of the local Governments' estimates (18.67 millions).[40] The dissenting members of the Franchise Committee, namely, S.B. Tambe, C.Y. Chintamani and R.R. Bakhale minimised the number even further to 14.42 millions.[41] The Franchise Committee itself was unable to arrive at a firm figure.[42]

It is better to remember that the Franchise Committee on its own did not make any estimate of the depressed classes population. It depended entirely on the information and reports received from the provincial Governments and the provincial Franchise Committees. After considering the reports from these two agencies as also the replies to its questionnaire, it accepted the figures as 'substantially correct', where there was general agreement between the provincial Committees and local Governments, as happened in the case of Madras, Bombay, the Central Provinces, and Assam.[43] In this context the Indian Franchise Committee observed that "in the three provinces, Madras, Bombay and the Central Provinces, the distinction between the depressed and other classes of the Hindu community is clearly defined, and there is general agreement between the provincial Committees and local governments in regard to the numbers and castes to be included. We are also satisfied from the replies which we received to our questionnaire and from the statements of witnesses who appeared before us that the numbers for these three provinces are not disputed by other communities in these provinces. The Census estimates of 1931 closely correspond to the numbers given to us by the committees. In view of this unanimity we are ourselves prepared to accept the figures given to us as substantially correct, and believe that they are not likely to be open to serious criticism."[44] But unanimity in views did not mean that the figures of Depressed Classes population were extracted only for that segment of population which came within the definition settled by the Indian Franchise Committee. But, as pointed out, the Committee did not bother to check up whether the figures furnished by the Governments of Bombay and Madras conformed to its own definition of the term "depressed'.[45] The Madras Government had for purposes of their own defined the term "Adi-Dravida" in the Madras Local Boards and the Madras District Municipalities Acts, 1920 and the provincial Government as well as the provincial Committee viewed that this definition of "Adi-Dravida" would be suitable for the definition of 'depressed classes' as well. Nine communities—

Chakkiliyans, Cherumans, Holeyas, Malas, Madigas, Pallans, Paraiyans, Tottiyans and Valluvans — were included within the term "Adi-Dravida" under these Acts. Again by a notification issued under G.O. No. 1541-L & M dated May 7, 1931, i.e., after the publication of the Simon Commission Report and before the constitution of the Indian Franchise Committee, a supplementary list of another 21 communities was included in this category.[46] Since the depressed classes in Madras had already been scheduled by notification under the Madras Local Boards Act of 1920 and since the Indian Franchise Committee thought that there was no controversy in regard to the official classification in that province, it accepted the unanimous estimate furnished by the local Government and the provincial Committee.

The estimates of the Bombay Government were based on the investigations of a Committee of officials and non-officials appointed by that Government in 1930 to report on various economic and social problems affecting the depressed classes in that Presidency.[47] This Committee was appointed long before the definition of the term "depressed classes" was settled by the Lothian Committee, but the figures furnished by the Bombay Government had not been examined in the light of the Lothian Committee's definition of the term. Even then, as the provincial committee also agreed with the estimates of the provincial Government, the Indian Franchise Committee accepted the provincial Government's estimates.

In the Central Provinces the Census Superintendent, whose report was accepted both by the provincial Committee and the provincial Government, applied the same tests as those accepted by the Lothian Committee. As a result some castes were listed as untouchables in certain districts or even in a part of a district only. The Indian Franchise Committee in accepting this report observed that for electoral purposes these castes should be treated in those districts as belonging to the depressed classes, and if the same conditions prevailed elsewhere, the same principle should be applied.

In Assam, both the provincial Committee and the provincial Government accepted the recommendations of Mullan, the then Census Superintendent of Assam, with regard to inclusion of communities in this category and therefore, their recommendations were the same. So there was no difficulty for the Franchise Committee to accept this unanimious opinion of these two bodies.

In Bihar and Orissa there was practical agreement in regard to the castes which should be included in the term "depressed". The Bihar Government did not furnish any figure and instead, referred to the note of their Chief Secretary in which the position of the depressed classes in the province was explained. The Chief Secretary pointed out in his note that the criteria adopted in 1911 led to the inclusion of a large number of aboriginal tribes who were really outside the Hindu religion. These tribes were excluded by him from his list. He also mentioned of some tribes which were included in the list of depressed classes in the 1931 census. Though he mentioned that 'probably the only castes which are regarded as causing pollution' were Dom, Halalkhor and Hari, he estimated the depressed classes population between 5 to 6 millions.[48] The Provincial Franchise Committee on the other hand went by the 1931 census which included 31 castes in the Depressed Classes list. The Census Superintendent admitted that there were 8 tribes in this list of depressed classes which should have been excluded from the list in view of the definition of the term given by the Indian Franchise Committee,[49] and the Provincial Committee excluded these 8 tribes from the Depressed Classes list. It also excluded the Christians, Muhammadans and Amimists from the Depressed Classes and estimated that the total population of the depressed classes was 4,344,585.[50] The Indian Franchise Committee on verification found that this estimate of the provincial committee was an accurate one based on the census figures of 1931 and therefore accepted this figure.[51] The dissenting members of the Franchise Committee, however, were not prepared to accept the figure of 4.3 millions as the total of depressed classes population in Bihar and Orissa and thought that the three castes of Dom, Halalkhor and Hari, which were mentioned by the Chief Secretary as the only castes regarded as causing pollution, were the only depressed classes. They numbered 400,000.[52]

In regard to Bengal, Uttar Pradesh and Punjab, there was no general agreement between the local Government and the provincial Committee in regard to the number who should be classed as depressed, and the Indian Franchise Committee, therefore, failed to give any estimation of the number and castes to be included as depressed classes in these three provinces.

The greatest divergence of opinion was revealed in the United Provinces. The Government of U.P. in their first report observed that the schedule of depressed classes should include the classes the total population of which was 6,773,814.[53] In their final reply they observed that "Government are informed that the chairman of the Indian Franchise Committee has given a definition to the chairman of the provincial committee which would confine the depressed classes to those who cause 'pollution by touch or approach as it exists in this province', If so, the actual number would be reduced to 459,000 and on that definition it would be impossible to secure representation for other than those restricted classes. At the same time the local Government feel that it is necessary to take into consideration classes other than those so defined."[54] The majority of the provincial Committee came to the conclusion that only those classes should be called "depressed" which were untouchable. Judged by this test, the problem of untouchability was non-existent in the province except in the case of Bhangis, Doms and Dhanuks, whose total population, including those sections which were touchables, was only 581,000. The Depressed Classes members in the provincial Committee questioned the correctness of the definition, but stated that if it was to be regarded as final, they agreed that only the three classes mentioned fell under the definition "depressed".[55] The dissenting members of the

Indian Franchise Committee also concurred with this estimate.[56]

The Government of Punjab gave an estimate and also a list of eleven (11) castes, numbering 1.3 millions, who were classed as depressed in the province.[57] This number included the Ad-Dharmis who claimed that they were not Hindus now, and the Ramdasis who were said to be Sikhs. In their final report, the majority of the provincial committee were of the opinion that only Chuhras and Chamars could be regarded in the Punjab as in any sense untouchables, while a minority of two members accepted the estimate given by the Government. The Committee was unable to give even an approximate estimate of the number of depressed classes who would come on the electoral roll under their proposal.[58] The dissenting members of the Franchise Committee excluded the Ad-Dharmis who vehemently urged that they were not Hindus and the Ramdasis, who were Sikhs, from the depressed classes population of 1.3 millions estimated by the provincial Government and calculated the number of depressed classes as 1 million.[59] In view of the disagreement between the provincial Committee and the Government, and of the doubtful position of the Ad-Dharmis and Ramdasis, the Lothian Committee considered that a further investigation should be made with the help of the list of castes given in 1911, and that a final list should be drawn up of the castes which satisfied the test indicated earlier.[60]

In Bengal, the position was so complicated that neither the provincial Government nor the provincial Committee could furnish any estimate of the depressed classes population. The Government of Bengal stated that the list of castes to be included in the depressed classes was under revision, but forwarded a list of those castes which were classed as depressed, with a corresponding list taken from the 1931 census indicating the omissions and additions which had been proposed. The 1921 list contained 40 castes accounting for a population of 11.2 million, while the 1931 list had 85 castes but returned a population of only 8.07 million. They stated that the decision of the Government regarding these additions would be arrived at after ascertaining the views of the castes concerned, but that it would be impossible for coming to final conclusions in time for submission to the Franchise Committee. They, therefore, adopted the 1921 list and based their replies on numbers which were classed as depressed in 1921.[61] The provincial Committee, on the other hand, stated that according to the criteria laid down by the Lothian Committee there was only one caste in Bengal, numbering 72,000, which satisfied the tests. The depressed class member on the committee dissented from this view and submitted a separate note in which he gave a list of over 80 castes, which agreed with the Government list.[62] The dissenting members of the Franchise Committee pointed out that no final figure was received from the Bengal Government. In fact, the figures supplied by them from time to time varied. The majority of the Bengal Provincial Franchise Committee put the number of depressed classes at 70,000. The evidence tended to show that there was very little of untouchability existing in the province. They, therefore, accepted the majority opinion of the provincial committee and estimated the depressed classes population as 70,000.[63] The Indian Franchise Committee in its report pointed out that a few days before the report was signed, a telegram was received from the local Government to the effect that up to the date of telegram the revised figure for depressed classes in the province was 10.3 millions. This total included the Rajbansis, numbering 1,804,371, who had themselves asked for exclusion, and who,it was generally agreed, should be excluded. Certain hill tribes should also be excluded. The balance would number about 7.5 millions. The Committee, therefore, recommended that the local Government should examine the varying figures and arrive at a final estimate of the number after completing the enquiries in regard to the castes which should either continue on or be taken off the 1911 list in accordance with their social position at that time.[64]

Communal Award and Depressed Classes

After the submission of the Lothian Committee's report, the British Prime Minister announced on August 4, 1932 the now famous Communal Award, assigning a number of special seats for the depressed classes. These seats would be filled by election from special constituencies in which only members of the depressed classes electorally qualified would be entitled to vote. The number of seats assigned to them was 61 excluding Bengal for which the number of seats would not exceed 10.[65] The Poona Pact, signed on September 24, 1932 which modified the Communal Award to the extent that the depressed classes would be part of the general electorate, however, increased the number of seats reserved for the depressed classes to 148, which was further raised to 151 in making adjustments of seats for Bihar and Orissa.[66] Once the seats had been fixed it devolved on the Provincial Governments to find out who would be entitled to be returned from these seats. This necessitated preparation of the "Scheduled Castes" lists, province by province. It was like putting the cart before the horse. The Simon Commission had specifically recommended that once the correct totals of Depressed Classes had been ascertained according to settled definitions, the number of seats should be settled.[67] Contrary to the Simon Commission's recommendation, the seats were fixed without ascertaining the numbers.

In paragraph 9 of the Communal Award it is stated:

> The precise definition in each province of those who (if electorally qualified) will be entitled to vote in the depressed classes constitutencies has not yet been finally determined. It will be based as a rule on the general principles advocated in the Franchise Committee's report. Modification may, however, be found necessary in some provinces in Northern India where the application of the general criteria of untouchability might result in a definition unsuitable in some respects to the special conditions of the province.

Effect of Poona Pact

Now trouble started over this modification of the Lothian Committee's twin criteria of Depressed Classes. In accordance with the discretion given to them by the British Government, the Provincial Governments were asked to prepare a "Schedule of Castes" for electoral purposes. If the Provincial Governments had strictly adhered to the Lothian Committee's twin criteria of untouchability, the number of castes considered depressed would have been much less and consequently their population. But the Communal Award, as modified by the Poona Pact, had already fixed the number of seats for the Depressed Classes in the Legislatures. So for electoral purposes the Provincial Governments started modifying the lists of Depressed Classes, thereby including in the lists even those castes, which were not depressed according to the definition of the Lothian Committee. In preparing the "Schedule of Castes" the Provincial Governments not only did not follow the recommendations of the Lothian Committee but went beyond the discretion allowed to them by the Communal Award. The Communal Award envisaged that modification to the general principles advocated in the Lothian Committee's report would be necessary in some provinces in Northern India only. But the Provincial Governments not only of the Northern India but also of other provinces as well including Bombay and Madras Presidencies and the Central Provinces, where, as was generally believed, 'there was little dispute about who were the untouchables',[68] took liberty in adding to this Schedule such castes which were not enumerated as depressed in the Census reports or even mentioned by any other official bodies earlier. The position is best illustrated if we have a look at Annexure Tables I and II.

Stepping into the Arena of Scheduled Castes

The estimates of depressed population by various official bodies in 1917-41 are presented in Annexure Table I. This Table gives an impression that there was little dispute about who were the untouchables in the southern and western India — in Madras and Bombay Presidencies and the Central Provinces. The dispute was about the northern and eastern India. It was more pronounced in Bengal, the United Provinces, Bihar and Orissa and Punjab and in a lesser degree in Assam. These figures in Annexure Table I will lead one to agree with the observations of the Simon Commission that "in provinces where the effects of untouchability are most seriously felt, the figures are likely to be fairly precise, but in other parts of India, where the treatment meted out to depressed classes is not so severe, there is a margin of possible error."[69]

If instead of relying only on the depressed population estimated by these bodies, one takes into consideration the castes which go to account for these figures, a different picture will emerge. Annexure Table II gives both the number of castes considered depressed as also their population estimated by various official bodies during the period 1911-36.

Annexure Table II reveals that the number of castes which fell under any one of the 10 categories in the 1911 census was 187 and their population was 42.5 millions in India excluding the United Provinces and Madras. Needless to say, all the 10 categories were not considered depressed by the Lothian Committee. Only those coming under categories 7 and 8 were treated as depressed by the Lothian Committee. Of these 187 castes, only 87 fell under categories 7 and 8 and their population in British territories was only 17,812,774. That was in 1911.

In 1917 the Provincial Governments at the instance of the Government of India, prepared a list of depressed classes, i.e., untouchables. All the Provincial Governments except Assam and Punjab submitted this list along with an estimate of their population. This list accounted for 104 castes with a population of 27.4 millions. The number of castes under the depressed classes increased marginally in the hand of the Provincial Governments, compared to that of the 1911 Census. It, however, did not mean that all the 87 castes falling under categories 7 and 8 in the 1911 Census were considered depressed, i.e., untouchables by the Provincial Governments. As many as 40 castes out of these 87 castes were not listed as depressed by the Provincial Governments.

Sharp also prepared a list of depressed classes more or less during this time and mentioned it in his Quinquennial Review for the years 1912-17. He not only indicated the population of the depressed classes but also in most cases furnished the names of the castes considered depressed by him. Only in the case of the U.P. it was not given. There was not much difference between Sharp's lists and the Government lists except in the case of Madras. Sharp, however, furnished lists of depressed classes for Assam and Punjab as well.

The Franchise Committee in 1919 also estimated the depressed population. The Committee, however, did not specifically mention the castes considered depressed by it but quoted the Census Reports on which these estimates were based. It furnished a figure of 42.2 millions with province-wise break-up. By back calculation the castes could be identified in some provinces but in others it could not be arrived at. There was wide discrepancy in Bihar, where its estimate exceeded the Census figures substantially and in Bombay, where it was much less. It is not clear how the Committee could arrive at these figures for these two provinces. In absence of the particulars of the castes taken into consideration by this Committee it is difficult to say which castes were actually considered depressed by it. In any case, their total number would be more than 127.

In the 1921 Census many Provincial Census Superintendents did not indicate in their reports who were the depressed classes. Only the Census Superintendents of Madras, the Central Provinces and Berar, Bengal, and Bihar and Orissa did specify the castes considered depressed/untouchables and their population. But the Census Commissioner did not accept their lists. He modified the estimates on the basis of figures of Sharp's lists and of information from the 1911 Census report and tables. Though he estimated a population of 43.3 millions for these 8 provinces which included figures for the States as well, he refrained from mentioning the castes which accounted for these population and the area from which those were extracted.

In 1928 the Government of India laid on the table of the Assembly a list of castes considered untouchables by it. The list mentioned 106 castes which closely followed the previous list of 1917. There was only one change this time. 2 castes were found untouchable in Punjab. Like the previous report, there was none in Assam this time also.

The Hartog Committee relied on this information of the Government of India and estimated the population of the depressed classes as 29.76 millions, which indicated that there was a fall in the population of the depressed classes in all the provinces except Bihar and Madras compared to the 1917 figure.

Both the Indian Central Committee and the Indian Statutory Commission estimated the depressed classes population based on information furnished by the Provincial Governments but did not mention the castes which were considered depressed by them.

The Provincial Census Superintendents in 1931 identified 407 castes as depressed including 46 which were depressed. i.e., untouchables only in some parts of the provinces of Assam and the Central Provinces and Berar, but the Census Commissioner reduced it to 351 which included 41 that were depressed only in some parts of the provinces of Assam and the Central Provinces and Berar. It is better to remember that before the finalisation of the 1931 Census report the Lothian Committee's recommendations on identification of depressed classes in different provinces as well as its definition of depressed classes was known to the Census authorities. But except in the Central Provinces and Berar, in no other provincial report, a reference was made to the definition of the depressed classes as finally settled by the Committee. In the Central Provinces and Berar where the Lothian Committee's definition of depressed classes was followed, the enumeration of the depressed classes was done according to the areas in which a caste was reported to be untouchable. As a result, even those returning as small a population as 3, 6, 12 or 41 from an area as small as a tehsil or a district of the province were categorised as depressed. The number of castes thus found to be untouchable in only a part of the province was not a few. They were 29 out of the 38 castes treated as untouchables. In Assam, it was not taken to such a proportion, where it was done broadly on the basis of two distinct areas-Surama valley and Assam valley.

The controversy over the inclusion of a caste in the list of depressed classes reached its peak in 1932 when different estimates were furnished to the Lothian Committee. While the Provincial Governments supplied figures totalling 37.44 millions initially, which later dwindled to 30.22 millions, the Provincial Franchise Committees produced figures that ranged between 18.67 millions and 17.37 millions. The dissenting members of the Franchise Committee minimised the number even further to 14.42 millions. Though none of them indicated specifically the castes treated as depressed, from the figures furnished by them the number of castes as well as the castes themselves could be identified. It appears that it would be ranging between 149 and 161 in the case of the Provincial Governments (except Bombay and Madras), between 95 and 86 in the case of the Provincial Franchise Committees (except Bombay and Madras) and it would be 66 in the case of the dissenting members of the Indian Franchise Committee (except Bombay and Madras).

In 1936, when the Government of India (Scheduled Castes) Order was issued, many castes which were never considered as depressed by any other body were included. The total number of castes listed in the Schedule was

450, including 86 which were considered scheduled only in a part of the respective provinces. Since no separate list of tribes was prepared in 1936, many tribes found place in this Schedule. After the commencement of the Constitution, the Scheduled Tribes became a separate entity and many of them were shifted to the Scheduled Tribes list. Some castes were descheduled also in course of time. Similarly, some castes which were considered depressed by different bodies at some point of time during the period 1911-31 but did not find place in the 1936 Order, were later included in this Schedule, though their number was not too many.

In fine, in 1911 the Census authority could identify 87 castes in the Indian provinces except Madras and U.P., which satisfied the twin criteria of untouchability accepted by the Lothian Committee in 1932. The number of untouchable castes/depressed classes increased to 104/106 in 1917 and to at least 127 in 1919. The number again came down to 106 in 1928 but showed four-fold increase at the hands of the Census Superintendents in 1931 which was reduced to 351 by the Census Commissioner. Their number ranged between 161 and 66 in 1932 when the Lothian Committee was called upon to define and estimate their number but it again soared to 450 in 1936. It, however, did not mean that all these castes were common in all the estimates. As we will see in the next chapter, a caste treated as untouchable/depressed by one body was not considered as such by another body. Which castes were considered as depressed by which body during the period 1911-36 and which of them ultimately landed in the 1936 list or in the subsequent lists can best be found if the case of each province is taken up separately.

Notes and References

1. Rao, B. Shiva, *The Framing of India's Constitution*, The Indian Institute of Public Administration, New Delhi, 1967, Vol. III, pp. 187-93.
2. *Ibid.*, p. 637.
3. Dr. Ambedkar, *Constituent Assembly Debates*, (henceforth *CAD*), Vol. IX, dated 17-9-49, p. 1637.
4. Rao, *op. cit.*, Vol. V, pp. 779-80.
5. *Report of the Indian Statutory Commission*, 1930, Vol. V, pp. 1340-41.
6. *Dr. Babasaheb Ambedkar: Writings and Speeches*, Vol. 5, Unpublished Writings, Government of Maharashtra, 1989, p. 229.
7. *Report of the Indian Statutory Commission*, 1930, Vol. V, pp. 1341-47.
8. *Progress of Education in India, 1912-17*, Seventh Quinquennial Review, 1919, Vol. I, pp. 204-6.
9. *Report of the Franchise Committee (Southborough Committee)*, 1919, Vol. I, Paragraph 11 and Appendices I to VIII, pp. 19-80.
10. *Dr. Babasaheb Ambedkar: Writings and Speeches*, Vol. 5, *op. cit.*, pp. 6-7.
11. *Census of India*, 1911, Vol. I, Part I, Para 155, p. 117.
12. *Dr. Babasaheb Ambedkar: Writings and Speeches*, Vol. 5, *op. cit.*, pp. 230-32.
13. *Census of India*, 1921, Vol. I, Part I, Para 193, p. 225.
14. *Report of the Reforms Enquiry Committee (Mudiman Committee)*, 1924, Para 64, p. 56.
15. *The Moral and Material Progress Report on India for the year 1925-26*, p. 237.
16. *The Legislative Assembly Debates (Official Report)*, Vol. I., (1st February to 7th March, 1928), Second Session of the Third Legislative Assembly, 1928, p. 721.
17. *Parliamentary Debates, Official Report, Fifth Series*, Volume 216, Fourth Volume of Session, 1928, dated April 23, 1928, Cols. 601-602.
18. *The Legislative Assembly Debates (Official Report)*, Volume III, (4th September to 15th September, 1928), Third Session of the Third Legislative Assembly, 1928, pp. 2-3.
19. *Report of the Indian Statutory Commission*, 1930, Vol. XVI, pp. 27-37.
20. *Ibid.*, Vol. II, Para 79, p. 65.
21. *Ibid.*, Vol. I, Para 58, p. 40.
22. *Ibid.*, Vol. II, Para 80, p. 67.

23. *Ibid.*, Vol. I, Para 58, pp. 40-41.
24. *Ibid.*, Vol. II, Para 80, p. 67.
25. *Interim Report of the Indian Statutory Commission (Hartog Committee)* 1929, pp. 217-18.
26. *Report of the Indian Central Committee*, 1929, Para 76, p. 44 and Appendix III, p. 86.
27. *Ibid.*, Para 75, p. 43.
28. Hutton. J.H., *Caste in India*, Oxford Cambridge Press, 1946, p. 193.
29. *Ibid.*, p. 194.
30. *Ibid.*, p. 196.
31. *Ibid.*, p. 197.
32. *Ibid.*, p. 196.
33. *Census of West Bengal. 1951*, Caste and Tribes of West Bengal, pp. 4-5.
34. Dushkin, Lelah, *The Policy of the Indian National Congress Toward the Depressed Classes : An Historical Study*, Master's thesis, University of Pennsylvania, 1957, pp. 91-95.
35. Hutton, *op. cit.*, p. 199.
36 *Dr. Babasaheb Ambedkar: Writings and Speeches*, Vol. 9, pp. 76-77.
37. *Report of the Indian Franchise Committee (Lothian Committee)*, 1932, Vol. I, para 282, p. 109.
38. *Ibid.*, Para 283, p. 109.
39. *Ibid.*, Para 286, p. 110.
40. *Ibid.*, p. 119.
41. *Ibid.*, p. 219.
42. *Ibid.*, p. 179.
43. *Ibid.*, pp. 111-14, 179.
44. *Ibid.*, pp. 111-12.
45. *Ibid.*, Para 11, p. 217.
46. *Ibid.*, Vol. II, p. 14.
47. *Ibid.*, Vol. I, p. 112.
48. *Ibid.*, Vol. III, pp. 158-62.
49. *Census of India, 1931*, Vol. VII, Part I, p. 285.
50. *Report of the Indian Franchise Committee*, 1932, Vol. III, pp. 226-27.
51. *Ibid.*, Vol. I, pp. 112-13.
52. *Ibid*, pp. 217-18.
53. *Ibid.*, Vol. II, Para 16, p. 298.
54. *Ibid.*, p. 376.

55. *Ibid.*, p. 398.
56. *Ibid.*, Vol. I, p. 218.
57. *Ibid.*, Vol. III, pp. 49-50.
58. *Ibid.*, p. 63.
59. *Ibid.*, Vol. I, p. 219.
60. *Ibid.*, p. 118.
61. *Ibid.*, Vol. II, pp. 214-15.
62. *Ibid.*, Vol. I, p. 117.
63. *Ibid.*, p. 219.
64. *Ibid.*, pp. 117-18.
65. *Para 9 of the Communal Award, 1932.*
66. *Dr. Babasaheb Ambedkar: Writings and Speeches*, Vol. 9, p. 94.
67. *Report of the Indian Statutory Commission*, 1930, Vol. II, Para 80, p. 67.
68. *Ibid.*, Vol. I, p. 41.
    Report of the Indian Franchise Committee, 1932, Vol. I, p. 111.
    Galanter, Marc, *Competing Equalities*, Oxford University Press, 1984, p. 125.
69. *Report of the Indian Statutory Commission*, 1930, Vol. I, Para 58, p. 41.

23

Transformation of Depressed Classes to Scheduled Castes in Pre-independent India

The formation of the Muslim League in 1906 not only heigh-tened communal politics in the country but also accentuated the demand for a separate entity for the untouchables, i.e., the depressed classes. As a result, the depressed classes and their number gradually obtained greater attention from the Britishers. The 1911 Census, without directly mentioning the Untouchables or the depressed classes, sought to find out the castes which were subject to certain social and religious disabilities. Along with the identification of those castes, their numbers were also extracted in each of the British provinces, except Madras and U.P., including both the British territories and the States. In the British territory, it was done upto the district level and in case of the states, it was extracted for each individual States. In Madras, the Census Superintendent did not identify the depressed classes because he thought that the disabilities mentioned in the Census Commissioner's instructions were experienced by all sections of Hindus irrespective of their position in the social scale. In U.P. very few were found who did not fulfill any of the prescribed tests. There was, however, no compilation of figures by the Census Commissioner in 1911.

By the time the 1921 Census was undertaken the term "depressed" carved out its place in the official lexicon. Only 4 provincial Census Superintendents identified the Depressed Classes and extracted their population while the remaining 5 did not even bother to mention them in their reports. The Census Commissioner, however, modified the reports received from the Superintendents and furnished figures for each of the British Provinces and the States. The provincial figures, however, included those for the British territory as well as the States. But the Census Commissioner did not mention the castes considered depressed by him.

The 1931 Census gave a detailed classification of Depressed Classes both in the provincial Census Reports as well as in the Census Commissioner's Report. The population, in most cases, were extracted up to the district level for the British territory and for the individual States, in case of the States included in the provincial report.

The classification of Depressed Classes in these three Census reports did not follow a uniform pattern, specially because of absence of an accepted definition of Depressed Classes. As a result, the castes treated as Depressed in these Census reports varied widely. Apart from the Census reports, many official bodies also furnished reports on Depressed Classes and their population.

In between the 1911 Census and 1921 Census, three reports-that of the provincial Governments, Sharp, the Educational Commissioner and the Franchise Committee (Southborogh Committee) mentioned about the Untouchable castes/depressed classes. They based their reports primarily on the 1911 Census. What they did were either addition to or substraction from the Census list of certain castes, according to their own perception of 'untouchability'.

In between the 1921 Census and 1931 Census, at least four reports dwelt with Untouchables/depressed classes. These were the Government list of 1928 and the reports of the Hartog Committee, the Indian Central Committee and the Indian Statutory Commission. The Government list mentioned the castes and the Hartog Committee relied on this list of the Government and estimated the depressed population according to the 1921 Census. Both the Indian Central Committee and the Indian Statutory Commission depended on the provincial Governments' reports for estimating the depressed classes population but refrained from mentioning the castes considered depressed by them.

In 1932 the Indian Franchise Committee (Lothian Committee) gave a definition of the depressed classes and also estimated their population in some cases, without verifying whether the population estimated by them were for those who conformed to their own definition of depressed classes or not.

Finally the 1935 Act put at rest all doubts by empowering His Majesty in Council to include any caste in the "Schedule of Castes" and in pursuance of this power, the Scheduled Caste Order was issued in 1936.

It is to be remembered that the Census reports provided the basic materials regarding population of the castes. It was left to the various official bodies to include whichever castes they thought fit in their lists of depressed classes, but for their population they had to depend on the Census reports. Some of these official bodies, in estimating the depressed classes population, confined themselves to the British Territory only while the remaining ones covered the entire province including both the British Territory and the States.

Any discussion as to how a caste ultimately landed in the Scheduled Castes Order of 1936 will, therefore, have to take into consideration the following reports :

1911 Census

Government list of 1917

Sharp's list of 1917

Franchise Committee's report in 1919

1921 Census

Government list of 1928

Hartog Committee's report in 1929

Indian Central Committee's report in 1929

Indian Statutory Commission's report in 1930

1931 Census

Lothian Committee's report in 1932

1936 Order under the 1935 Government of India Act.

Though most of these bodies treated 'depressed classes' and 'untouchables' as synonymous, as was the general concept then, the lists differed widely. The castes considered depressed by one of them were not treated as such by another, even if the reports followed one another in quick succession. Their idea and concept of untouchability differed and so were the lists. A clearer picture will emerge if each of the provinces is considered, one by one.

Assam

The 1911 Census identified 19 castes satisfying one or more of the 10 tests evolved in 1911. Their total population was 975,459. But only 4 of them (Chamar, Dhobi, Dom and Muchi) were stated to cause pollution by touch. Their total population was 131,189. No caste, however, could be classified which was denied access to the interior of Hindu temples.[1]

The Government of Assam did not furnish any list of depressed classes, i.e., untouchables to the Government of India in 1917 as "the depressed classes or untouchables could scarcely be said to have any representatives in the province." The Government of Assam stated that in the Assam Valley Hinduism was a plant of comparatively recent growth. The high Hindu castes were poorly represented in the division. The Hindus of the Assam Valley for the most part belonged to racial castes, such as Ahom, Koch, Chutiya, whose position in any orthodox system of

Hinduism was very questionable. In consequence, there were no peoples in the division corresponding to the untouchables of other parts of India. The conditions in the Surma Valley were not quite so dissimilar from those prevailing in the rest of Eastern Bengal, but the higher castes were less powerful and the abundance of waste land enabled the lower castes to rise to a position denied to them in more densely populated districts.[2]

Sharp's list of depressed classes, prepared in 1917, included no less than 163 different tribes and castes who were entered as "depressed classes and aboriginals living in the plains" as distinguished from "Hill or aboriginal tribes living in the hills" They ranged from the Khawas who numbered 100 in the province to the Ahoms who numbered 197,340. As distinct from other provinces, hill or aboriginal tribes living in the plains were specifically included in the same category as the depressed classes in Assam. The total population of the 'depressed classes' was estimated by Sharp to be 2,701,144.[3]

The Franchise Committee in 1919 gave a figure of 292,533 of those castes included in the group 'Others'. In Assam the group was stated to include castes which caused pollution by touch and which buried their dead, i.e., those coming under categories 8 and 9 in the 1911 Census.[4] It may be noted that the Jugis and the Bairagis, though did not cause pollution by touch, were included in the group 'Others' by the Franchise Committee because they followed the practice of 'burying their dead'. Altogether six castes were identified by this Committee.

The 1921 Provincial Census Superintendent did not identify the depress classes, and therefore, did not furnish their population in his report. But the Census Commissioner gave a figure of 2 million as the population of the depressed classes of Assam. He, however, did not mention the castes/tribes actually put in that category by him.[5]

The dilemma about locating the untouchable castes, however, persisted in the official quarter and no untouchable caste could be identified for incorporation in the 1928 list of untouchables prepared by the Government.

The Hartog Committee relied on the Government list of untouchables prepared in 1928 for estimating the depressed classes population in the provinces and as no untouchable caste was identified in the province of Assam, it reported that in regard to the depressed classes population in Assam there was 'practically none'.[6]

The indian Central Committee in 1929 accepted the provincial Government's figure of 1.55 million as the depressed classes population in the province. The Indian Statutory Commission, a year later, however, estimated the depressed classes population as 1 million. Apparently, the castes/tribes considered depressed by the 1921 Census Commissioner were not accepted as such by the Indian Central Committee and those considered depressed by the Indian Central Committee were not recognised as depressed by the Indian Statutory Commission, if the figures are any indication. More important than the population figures, which was in any case based on the Census figures, was the castes/tribes actually considered depressed by the Census Commissioner, the Indian Central Committee and the Indian Statutory Commission during the decade 1921-30, which none of them, incidentally, specified.

The provincial Census Superintendent in 1931 classed 19 castes, including 17 for parts of the province-4 in the Assam Valley and 13 in the Surama Valley, as exterior and estimated their population in round thousands as 656,000. The Census Commissioner classified 17 castes as exterior, including 12 for parts of the province — 2 in the Assam Valley and 10 in the Surama Valley. He retained all but 6 of the 19 castes of the provincial list (except Bania, Mali, Dhupi, Dholi, Kaibartta and Sweeper castes) and included 4 new ones — Bhangi, Bhuimali, Tea Garden Coolies and Others. His estimates of exterior caste population of 1,829,009 excluding 1,421 for Assam States differed widely from the provincial estimates because of inclusion of Tea Garden Coolie castes returning a population of more than 1.2 million within the exterior castes population.[7] A peculiar feature which merits special mention is the exclusion of 2 castes (Chamar and Dom) considered polluting in the 1911 Census from the 1931 Census list of Exterior Castes and the retention of another with a slightly modified nomenclature (Dhoba as Dhobi).

In reply to the questionnaire issued by the Indian Franchise Committee in 1932, the Assam Government intimated that in Assam the term 'Depressed Classes' had not the same significance as in some other parts of India. In Assam the term 'depressed classes' would include (1) aboriginal tribes, (2) ex-tea garden coolies (amongst whom animists predominate) settled in Assam, and (3) also those Hindu castes classed as 'exterior', and also referred to the note submitted by C.S. Mullan, the Superintendent of Census of Assam in 1931, to the Indian Franchise Committee.[8] This note of Mullan was more or less the reproduction of his note on exterior castes incorporated in the 1931 Census Report for Assam in which the estimate of exterior castes population was given as 0.656 million. The provincial Franchise Committee also endorsed the views expressed in the above note of Mullan and reported that the majority in the Committee were of opinion that the castes mentioned as 'exterior' in that note might be treated as belonging to the depressed classes in the restricted sense in which the term was used in Assam.[9] The Indian Franchise Committee also considered the castes designated "exterior castes" in Assam as the depressed classes in Assam and accepted the estimate of their population as calculated by Mullan.[10] The dissenting members of the Franchise Committee also indicated the same population figure in their note.[11]

The 1936 Scheduled Castes Order listed 22 castes, including 17 for parts of the Province-3 in the Assam Valley and 14 in the Surama Valley. It included all the exterior castes listed as such either by the Census Superintendent or the Census Commissioner in 1931 except four (Jugi, Sweeper castes, Tea Garden Coolies and Others) and included 3 new ones (Bansphore, Lalbegi and Mehtor). Annexure Table III will indicate the position accorded to different castes from 1911 till 1936. Of the 4 polluting castes identified in 1911 2 have been excluded (Chamar and Dom) and 2 retained (Dhoba as Dhobi and Muchi) in the 1936 order. Of the remaining 15 castes of the 1911 list as many as 12 have been excluded and only 3 have been retained (Brittial Bania, Hira and Namasudra), though none of them was considered to be causing pollution in 1911. Of the 6 castes included in the 'Other' group by the Franchise Committee in 1919, 4 have been excluded (Bairagi, Chamar, Dom and Jugi) and 2 (Dhoba as Dhobi and Muchi) have been retained. The 22 castes figuring in the 1936 list were included as follows :

5 castes from the 1911 list
(Brittial Bania, Dhoba as Dhobi, Hira, Namasudra and Muchi),

12 Castes from the 1931 provincial Census report
(Bania, Dhupi, Dholi, Dugla, Jhalo, Malo, Kaibartta, Jalia Kaibartta, Mahara, Mali, Patni and Sutradhar).

2 castes from the 1931 Census Commissioner's list
(Bhangi and Bhuimali)

3 were added only in 1936
(Bansphore, Lalbegi and Mehtor).

Total 22

Assam is one of the few provinces where the provincial Census Superintendent conducted detailed study in 1931 about the social position of the exterior castes. The reports received from his officers indicated that Bania, Dhobi, Dugla, Hira, Kaibartta, Mali, Muchi, Namasudra and Patni were considered 'untouchable' by Hindus who neither admitted them into their places of worship nor took water touched by them. Jhalo and Malo were fishing castes and for that very reason were exterior. The Sutradhars were principally boat-builders and makers of plough; they were not *jal-chal* and were educationally very backward.[12] This report of the Census Superintendent, perhaps, led the Indian Franchise Committee to conclude that the exterior castes though not literally 'untouchable' were yet 'unclean' castes, and the main test that distinguished them from others was that water touched by them was not acceptable by others. Moreover, these castes, though within the Hindu fold, were not allowed access to temples in which the high castes worshipped.[13]

As the social position of these exterior castes was not the same throughout the province, 17 of the 22 castes listed in the 1936 order were considered scheduled for a part of the province-3 in the Assam Valley and 14 in the Surama Valley only. But from 1950 onwards this area restriction was withdrawn and all of them became "scheduled" for the entire province.

Bengal

The castes considered depressed in Bengal varied from year to year and from one official body to another. The 1911 Census could identify 37 castes which satisfied one or more of the 10 tests formulated in 1911. The total population was 11,493,413.[14] Of these 37 castes, only 18 fell within categories 7 and 8, i.e., the two tests accepted by the Lothian Committee in 1932. They accounted for 6,398,481 persons in the entire province and 5,930,436 in the British territory.[15]

The Bengal Government list of Depressed Classes, i.e., untouchables in 1917 contained 21 castes with a population of 6,742,913.[16] The Bengal Government list retained all the 18 castes coming under categories 7 and 8 in the 1911 Census and included three new castes (Dosadh, Oroan and Munda). Dosadh did not figure in the 1911 list of 37 castes and both Oroan and Munda were said to cause pollution by touch or approach. It may be mentioned that no other castes besides these 20 castes, included in the Bengal Government list, were identified as causing pollution by touch or within a certain distance in the 1911 Census.

Sharp's list furnished with the Quinquennial Report for 1912-17 contained the same 21 castes as that in the Bengal Government list and also accounted for the same number.[17]

The Franchise committee (Southborough Committee) of 1919 stated that the castes and tribes constituting more than 1 per mille of the total population and classed as Hindus in the Census, which were denied access to the interior of ordinary Hindu Temples and fell within categories 7,8,9 or 10 at p. 232, Part I, Census Report of Bengal, Bihar and Orissa, and Sikkim, 1911, were included within the term 'Others', as those castes and tribes were generally described as "untouchables". The Franchise Committee did not mention the castes so listed but gave their total population as 9,948,244.[18] On back calculation it is found that the Franchise Committee not only included the 18 castes coming under both the categories 7 and 8, but also 8 castes falling under category 7 only, (i.e., denial of access to temple) and 2 castes falling under category 8 only, (i.e., causing pollution). So, as it appears, 28 castes coming under either both the categories 7 and 8 or any one of them were brought under the "Others" group.

The provincial Census Superintendent included 40 castes under 'depressed classes' in the 1921 Census and their total population was estimated at 11,216,911.[19] The 1921 Census list of 'Depressed Classes' did not include (1) Dhoba and (2) Sunri who came under categories 7 and 8 in the 1911 Census and (3) Dosadh who was included in the Bengal Government list of 'Depressed Classes' in 1917. This list also did not include (4) Jugi or Jogi, (5) Kamar, (6) Shaha, (7) Sonar, (8) Sutradhar and (9) Kapali who were put in the term "Others" by the Franchise Committee in 1919. But the 1921 Census Commissioner made certain changes in the provincial Census Superintendent's list and in all probability excluded the Chasi Kaibarttas or Mahishya from the list to arrive at a figure of (11,216,911-2,208,670) 9 million.[20]

In 1928 September the Government of India laid on the table of the Legislative Assembly a list of castes which were generally, according to local usage and custom, regarded as untouchable. 21 castes were shown against Bengal.[21] Incidentally, this was the same list which was sent by the Bengal Government in 1917 to the Government of India. It meant that there was no change in the Government stand in regard to the castes considered untouchables.

The Hartog Committee in 1929 regarded these 21 castes as depressed and calculated their population as 6.64 millions,[22] according to the 1921 Census.

Both the Indian Central Committee in 1929 and the Simon Commission in 1930 accepted the provincial Government's estimate of depressed classes population of 11.5 millions.[23] It is to be noted that in spite of the fact that the Indian Central Committee wanted to confine the term "depressed" to the untouchables and the Simon Commission adopted the definition, "causes pollution by touch or by the approach within a certain distance", both these bodies accepted the provincial Government's figures of depressed classes population without raising any question for such wide difference in the "depressed classes" population, specially when the Government list prepared only a year earlier contained only 21 castes with a population of 6.64 millions. None of these bodies, however, indicated the castes considered depressed by them.

In Bengal, the 1931 Census Superintendent included 88 castes/groups in the Depressed Classes and categorised them in the following classes :—

	No. of castes
A. Untouchables	
(i) sweepers and scavengers	8
(ii) other untouchables	40
B. Groups of aboriginal derivation	18
C. Other Depressed Classes	22
Total	88

The 1931 Census excluded 10 castes which were listed earlier in the 1921 Census, all of which came under category 'C' above. The provincial Census Superintendent calculated a figure of 8,390,942.[24] Though the Census Superintendent had classified the Depressed Classes into three broad categories, there is nothing to indicate that he classified the untouchables group keeping in view the twin criteria of untouchability accepted by the Lothian Committee. As a matter of fact, the basis of inclusion in the 'untouchables' category has not been explained any where. Moreover, the inclusion of 'Groups of aboriginal derivation' and 'other depressed classes' in the "Depressed Classes" was not in conformity with the Lothian Committee's definition of the depressed classes.

The 1931 Census Commissioner, however, retained only 62 of them in his list of exterior castes (depressed classes) and estimated their population at 6,899,809.[25] The 26 castes excluded by the Census Commissioner were from the following categories of the Census Superintendent's list :—

A. (ii) other untouchables	—	8
B. Groups of aboriginal derivation	—	17
C. Other depressed classes	—	1
Total		26

The Lothian Committee in 1932 asked the local Government and the Provincial Franchise Committee to furnish a list of castes and sub-castes together with an estimate of their numbers, which in their opinion were depressed in Bengal, applying the criteria of untouchability and unapproachability. The Government of Bengal failed to furnish any list but forwarded a list of those castes which were classed as depressed in the 1921 Census with a corresponding list of the 1931 Census.[26] Later, on April 16, 1932, they sent a telegram to the Lothian Committee intimating that revised figure for the depressed classes in the province in the 1931 Census was 10.3 millions.[27] The Lothian Committee found that this total included the Rajbansis, numbering 1,804,371, who had themselves asked for exclusion, and who, it was generally agreed, should be excluded. The Committee observed that certain hill tribes should also be excluded. The balance, according to it, would be about 7.5 millions.[28] The Provincial Franchise Committee, on the other hand, stated that according to the criteria laid down by the Lothian

Committee, there was only one caste in Bengal, numbering 72,000, which satisfied the tests.[29] The dissenting members of the Lothian Committee also concurred with this view of the provincial Committee.[30] In view of this wide disagreement in the figures, the Lothian Committee recommended that "in Bengal a list of castes was drawn up during the 1911 census which satisfied the criteria of untouchability which we have adopted as a general definition. The local Government will, no doubt, examine the varying figures which have been given to us, and we think that there should now be no difficulty in arriving at a final estimate of the numbers after the local Government have completed their enquiries in regard to the castes which should either continue on or be taken off the list in accordance with their social position at the present time. We, therefore, suggest that on the line already indicated by us a complete classification should be made of the depressed classes in the province as soon as all the information required by the local Government has been collected."[31]

The Government of Bengal being saddled with the task of preparing a list of "Scheduled Castes" in 1933, took into consideration not only the 88 Depressed Classes identified by the Census Superintendent in 1931 but also the 10 castes listed in the 1921 Census but left out in the 1931 Census. From this list of 98 Depressed Classes, the Bengal Government prepared in January, 1933, a provisional list of 86 castes to be designated as "Scheduled Castes" on the "basis of the social and political backwardness of these castes and the necessity of securing for them special representation in order to protect their interest" and circulated the said list to different caste associations, individuals, etc., with a view to obtaining their views regarding inclusion in or exclusion of any caste from the provisional list.[32] In Bengal, for some time past, most of the castes had been trying to show that they were really Brahmans, Kshattriyas or Vaisyas or identical with one or other of the castes mentioned in Manu or Yajnavalkya and preferred their claims before the Census authorities for being treated as such. Thus Vaidyas, Napits,

Karmakars, Kamis, Namasudras and Swarnakars all claimed to be Brahmanas; Aguris, Bagdis, Jhalo Malos, Kayasthas, Kurmis, Mahisyas, Nats, Pods, Pundaris, Hadis, Kahars, Kalwars, Koiris, Rajbanshis, Sunris, and even Oroans claimed to be Kshattriyas; Baruis, Bhuimalis, Dhobas, Kapalis, Shahas and Sankharis all claimed to be Vaisyas. Jalia Kaibarttas and Patnis claimed to be Mahisyas; Patikars and Khens claimed to be Kayasthas while Tiyars claimed to be Rajbanshis.[33] The *Census Report of Bengal*, 1931, after discussing at length most of these claims, rejected them and included most of these castes in the Depressed Classes. Again, when the Bengal Government issued this communication in 1933 seeking opinion for inclusion in or exclusion from the list of "Scheduled Castes" in respect of these 86 castes, representations were received from many caste associations and individuals for their exclusion from this list. But not much importance was laid on these representations. Instead, the District Officers and the Commissioners of the Divisions were asked to determine the social, political, economic and educational position of these castes in order to determine whether the castes were below the general level of development and so deserved special representation to protect their interests.[34] The reports received from them formed the basis for arriving at a decision in regard to this list.

The Bengal Government after carefully considering the representations received from public bodies, caste associations and individuals as well as the recommendations of the Divisional Commissioners and the District Officers, decided that 76 castes should be included in the list of "Scheduled Castes for Bengal".[35] The British Government made only a minor change in the list-it omitted `Sutradhar' and included `Sunris' instead.

Since in 1936 no separate list of Scheduled Tribes was prepared, many tribes were included in the Scheduled Castes Order of 1936 as well. The process of transferring them to the Scheduled Tribes list started from 1950 with the conferment of separate status on them in the Constitution of India. In the 1950 Order 4 tribes (Mech, Munda, Oroan and Santal) from this list were included in the Scheduled Tribes list, another 10 (Mahli, Malpahariya, Bhumij, Garo, Ho, Kora, Lodha, Nagesia, Rabha and Hajang) in the 1956 order and 1 (Bediya) more in the 1976 order. So, altogether 15 tribes from the original list of 76 'Scheduled Castes' of 1936 have been transferred to the Scheduled Tribes list so far. That apart, 3 more castes (Asur, Birhor and Korwa) of the 98 castes/groups prepared in 1933 have since been listed as Scheduled Tribes. Some castes included in the 1936 Order were, however, omitted from the subsequent Orders and again included in the list of Scheduled Castes/Scheduled Tribes. A chart indicating the position accorded to these castes/ tribes as Untouchables/Depressed Classes/Scheduled Castes/Scheduled Tribes by the various official bodies and the Constitutional Orders during the period 1911-1936 may be seen in Annexure Table IV.

Annexure Table IV makes a very interesting reading.

(A) Of the 37 castes identified in the 1911 Bengal Census as satisfying one or more of the 10 tests, 4 castes (Baishnab, Chakma, Chasadhoba and Subarnabanik) did not figure in any other reports subsequently, 4 (Jugi or Jogi, Kamar, Shaha and Sonar) were included only in the 1919 Franchise Committee's report, 1 (Kalu) in both the census reports of 1921 and 1931 as well as the 1919 Franchise Committee's report, 1 (Kapali) in the Census report of 1931 as well as in the 1919 Frnachise Committee's report and 1 (Tripara) only in the 1931 Census report, but none of these 11 castes figure in the 1936 list of Scheduled Castes.

Another caste (Sutradhar) which was also included in the 1919 Franchise Committee's report, was recommended by the Bengal Government in 1933 for inclusion in the list of "Scheduled of Castes", but this proposal was turned down by His Majesty's Government.

The remaining 25 castes were included in the 1936 list of Scheduled Castes. Of them, 18 answered the twin criteria of untouchability accepted by the Lothian Committee and were all along considered as Depressed/Untouchables. 3 of these 18 (Bhumij, Kora and Santal) were later transferred to the Scheduled Tribes list. 2 castes (Munda and Oroan) considered only polluting in the 1911 Census were similarly considered Depressed/Untouchables and later shifted to the Scheduled Tribes list. 3 castes (Koch, Jaliya Kaibartta and Patni), which were identified as being not served by good Brahmin in 1911, became 'depressed' in the 1921/1931 Census and later 'Scheduled' Castes. Malos, identified for not being served by good Brahmins in the 1911 Census became 'depressed' in the 1921 Census but not in the 1931 Census but was ultimately included in the 1936 list of 'Scheduled Castes'. Rajbanshis, identified for not being served by good Brahmin as well as for denial of access to Hindu temples in 1911, were included in the 'depressed classes' list in the 1921 Census but not in the 1931 Census. The Lothian Committee felt that they were going to be excluded from the Depressed Classes list in view of the representations of the caste-members. But in the final reckoning landed themselves in the Scheduled Castes list.

(B) Of the 28 Castes included in the 'Others' group by the Franchise Committee in 1919, 7 did not find place in the 1936 list of Scheduled Castes — 4 did not figure in any other subsequent reports, 2 figured in the census reports and another was recommended by the Bengal Government for inclusion in the Scheduled Castes list but was rejected by His Majesty's Government.

(C) The Government list of Untouchables prepared in 1917 and in 1928 remained unchanged but there was a slight drop in their population, based on the corresponding census figures:

Year	*No. of caste*	*Population according to*	*Per cent*
1917	21	1911 Census — 6.74 millions	100.00
		1921 Census — 6.64 millions	98.5
1928	21	1931 Census — 6.46 million	95.8

This decrease in the 'Untouchable' population was in spite of an overall increase of 10.7% in population during these two decades. This was so because some members of these castes at the time of enumeration chose to return themselves as members belonging to those castes which were not considered depressed/untouchables and hence, there was a perceptible drop in the population of the Depressed Classes/Untouchables. This also demonstrates the effect of the reformist movement on the upward mobility of individual caste members as well as the efforts of the individual caste groups to rise up in the social scale.

(D) The provincial Census Superintendents tended to include more castes/groups of castes in the category of Depressed Classes (in the 1911 Census the word 'Depressed' was not specifically used) but this was not met by a corresponding increase in the 'Depressed Classes' population. On the other hand, their number registered a downward fall. Another phenomenon was the exclusion of 'certain doubtful cases' from the Census Superintendents' list of Depressed Classes by the successive Census Commissioners :

Census	*By the Census Superintendent*		*By the Census Commissioner*	
	No. of Caste	Total Population	No. of Caste	Total Population
1911	37	11.4 million	x	x
1921	40	11.2 million	39	9.0 million
1931	88	8.4 million	62	6.9 million

(E) 77 castes listed in the Schedule in 1936 figured in the following reports for the first time :

25 were included in the 1911 Census,
(Bagdi, Bauri, Bhuimali, Bhuiya, Bhumij, Chamar, Dhoba, Dom, Hari, Jalia Kaibartta, Kaora, Koch, Kora, Mal, Malo, Muchi, Munda, Namasudra, Oroan, Patni, Pod, Rajbanshi, Santal, Sunri and Tiyar)

1 was included in the 1917 Government list,
(Dusadh)

8 were included in the 1921 Census,
(Hadi, Hajang, Lohar, Garo, Khaira, Kasta, Mech and Nuniya), and

43 were included in the 1931 Census
(Agariya, Baheliya, Baiti, Bediya, Beldar, Berua, Bhatiya, Bind, Binjhia, Doai, Dhenuar, Ghasi, Gonhri, Halalkhor, Ho, Jhalo Malo, Kadar, Kan, Kandh, Kanwar, Kandra, Kapuria, Karenga, Kaur, Khatik, Konai, Kotal, Lalbegi, Lodha, Mahli, Mahar, Mallah, Malpahariya, Musahar, Mehtar, Nagesia, Nat, Paliya, Pan, Pasi, Rabha, Rajwar and Turi).

Total 77

(F) The 1911 Census listed the castes according to the 10 tests and, as pointed out earlier, 4 of these 25 castes were included in 1911 because no good Brahmin served them and another because no good Brahmin served them as also was denied access to the interior of Hindu temples.

(G) The 1921 Census Commissioner did not give any definition of the Depressed Classes but asked the Census Superintendents to list those who were "usually included in the category of depressed". Of the 8 castes from the 1921 Census report, Hajang, Garo and Mech were tribals.

(H) Before the publication of the Census report for 1931 the Lothian Committee's definition of 'Depressed Classes' was known to the Census authority. But they not only did not follow that criteria but evolved their own methodology of grouping of the "Depressed Classes" under three broad categories, mentioned earlier, without explaining the criteria for inclusion in the categories of "Untouchables" and "Other Depressed Classes". The Census Superintendent included as many as 54 new castes under these different groups in the 1931 Census, but could not extract the population figure of as many as 5 of them (Asur, Birhor, Dalu, Korwa and Kurariar). He might have followed the 9-point tests of the Census Commissioner, but it may be remembered that only 2 of them (Sl.

3-whether the caste or class in question pollutes a high-caste Hindu by contact or proximity, and Sl. 6-whether the caste or class in question is debarred from use of Hindu temples) satisfied the twin criteria of the Lothian Committee. Unlike the 1911 Census, the 1931 Census did not indicate to which categories of these 9 tests these new 54 castes as well as the 34 castes retained from the earlier Censuses fell. We are, therefore, denied of the opportunity of ascertaining whether all the 48 castes included in the 'Untouchables' category satisfied the twin criteria of untouchability. We also do not know what category or categories of castes were included in the "Other depressed classes".

The Census Commissioner, however, did not approve of all these cases being included in the list of Depressed Classes (exterior castes). He rejected 21 cases because they were primitive tribes and another 2 because they were admittedly 'doubtful'. He specifically mentioned the cases of Khandait, Sukli, Rajbanshi and Kurmi, none of whom was, however, included in the 1931 provincial Census Superintendent's list of Depressed Classes. While Suklis had definitely protested against their inclusion, the attitude of Rajbanshis had been equivocal. Kurmis whom the local Government were including in their list of Depressed Classes, were not even a doubtful case, he said. In his report the Census Commissioner included 62 castes in the list of exterior castes (Depressed Classes) with a total population of 6,930,631 including 30,822 in Bengal States.[36]

(I) The list of Scheduled Castes of 1936 contained 43 castes which were shown in the category of Untouchables in Group A in the 1931 Census. Apart from the fact that many of them did not meet the twin criteria of the Lothian Committee, many of these castes themselves did not like to be included in the list of Depressed Classes, much less in the list of Scheduled Castes. For instance, Bhuimali, included in the list of Untouchables under "sweepers and scavengers" category in the 1931 Census, represented to the Census authority in 1931 for treating them as

"Vaishyamali". But the Census authority did not treat them as such. Their second attempt was in 1933 at the time of preparation of the "Schedule of Castes" when as many as 6 representations were submitted for their exclusion from the list of Scheduled Castes. But the Government decided to keep them in the list of Scheduled Castes.

Namasudras, Bagdis, Pods, Sunris, Dhobas and Hadis, who were mentioned in the "other untouchables" category advanced their claims for higher status in the 1931 Census and also represented before the provincial Government in 1933 not to include them in the Schedule. Namasudras claimed to be treated either as "Namabrahman" or "Namabrahma" during the Census operation in 1931. But they were included in the "other untouchables" category. They again represented to the Government in 1933 for exclusion from the list of Scheduled Castes. (There were 4 representations for exclusion and 7 for inclusion). Since the protests against inclusion were based on social claims, the Government considered them valueless.

Bagdis claimed during the Census operation in 1931 for treating them as Byagrya Kshattriya or simply Kshattriya. It was rejected. Again, in 1933 there were 6 representations for their exclusion from the list of Scheduled Castes on the ground that they were Byagrya Kshattriyas. They were, however, retained in the Scheduled Castes list.

Pods preferred their claim for the higher status of Paundra, Paundra Kshattriya, or Padmaraj in the 1931 Census and also submitted representations to the Provincial Government for exclusion from the list of Scheduled Castes. (There were 15 representations for exclusion and 2 for inclusion). They were, however, retained in the Scheduled Castes list.

Sunris had been included in the "other untouchables" category in the 1931 Census, ignoring their claim for the higher status of Kshattriya, Saundik Kshattriya or Sondia Kshattriya. Again in 1933 they represented to the Government for not including them in the list of Scheduled Castes. (There were 11 representations for exclusion against 1 for inclusion). The provincial Government recommended in 1933 for their exclusion from the 'Schedule of Castes' because their percentage of literates was not bad - 12.7% - and the representations for exclusion were fairly widespread. But His Majesty's Government overruled their recommendation and included them in the 1936 list.

Dhobas preferred their claim for the higher status of Vaishya in the 1931 Census and also submitted 4 representations to the Government in 1933 for their exclusion from the list of Scheduled Castes. But they were included in the "other untouchables" category in the 1931 Census and also in the 1936 list of Scheduled Castes.

Hadis requested the Census authorities in 1931 for considering them as Haihai Kshattriya and also submitted 3 representations to the Government in 1933 for excluding them from the Scheduled Castes list. But they were included in the "other untouchables" category in the 1931 Census and also as Scheduled Caste in the 1936 list. But from 1950 they were not being separately counted as Scheduled Caste, mainly because 99.80% of them hailed from the Mymensingh district, in East Bengal, now Bangladesh. Incidentally, Hadis were not considered as untouchable in the Census of 1911 or by the Bengal Government in 1917 and in 1928. They were included for the first time in the 1921 Census as a Depressed Class.

The castes mentioned as 'other depressed classes' in the 1931 Census were also included in the 1936 list of Scheduled Castes. Among them Jaliya Kaibartta and Jhalo Malos claimed higher status in the 1931 Census and also pressed for exclusion from the 'Schedule of Castes'. Jaliya Kaibarttas claimed the higher status of Mahishya or Rajbanshi in the 1931 Census and also represented before the Government (there were 10 representations for exclusion and 4 for inclusion) not to include them in the 'Schedule of Castes', but their representations were not accepted.

Jhalo Malos claimed to be recognised as Malla Kshattriya or Jhalla Kshattriya in the 1931 Census and also requested the Government not to include them in the list of Scheduled Castes. (There were 10 representations for exclusion against 1 for inclusion). In spite of their representations, they were listed as Scheduled Castes.

These 9 castes, which claimed for higher status to the Census authority during the 1931 Census operations and also represented to the Bengal Government for exclusion from the list of Scheduled Castes, constituted about 67.80% of the total Depressed Classes population of the 1931 Census (4,678,402 out of 6,899,803 estimated by Hutton, the Census Commissioner).

(J) There were claims to new names in the 1931 Census as well, ostensibly in their effort to gain higher social status. Thus, Tiyar, Patni and Chamar, all included in the "Other untouchables" category and Nat and Rajbanshi, included in the "other depressed classes" category in the 1931 Census claimed the new names of Rajbanshi, Lupta Mahishya or Mahishya, Satnami, Bratya Kshattriya and Kshattriya, respectively. None of them, however, requested the Bengal Government in 1933 for their exclusion from the Scheduled Castes list.

(K) The Bengal Government all along relied on the Provincial Census Superintendents' reports on the Depressed Classes, ignoring the fact that the Census Commissioners modified their reports. Thus, in the 1921 Census the Census Superintendent identified 40 castes as depressed with a population of 11.2 millions. But the Census Commissioner reduced the number to 9 millions ostensibly omitting Chasadhoba accounting for a population of 2.2 millions. The Bengal Government not only relied on this Provincial Census report but asked the Indian Franchise Committee to accept the figure of 11.2 millions as the tentative Depressed Classes population.

Again when the Census Commissioner of 1931 reduced the Census Superintendent's figure of Depressed Classes to 6.9 millions after omitting "doubtful cases", the

Bengal Government never took this fact into consideration and as a matter of fact, ignored it altogether.

(L) It may be noted that contrary to the recommendations of the Lothian Committee, the 1911 list of castes was not made the basis for preparation of 'Schedule of Castes'. The said list was never consulted. On the other hand, the Bengal Government were guided by the social precedence of these castes as determined by Risley in 1901. That much water had flown down the Ganges during these 30 years when the social conditions of many of these castes had improved perceptibly either due to their own endeavour or due to other pressing factors, were not taken into consideration.

(M) For examination of merit of individual castes for their inclusion in the "Schedule of Castes", the Bengal Government tabulated the various information relating to the individual castes. In that Table a column was inserted showing therein which castes were considered depressed by the Bengal Government in 1917. As many as 27 castes were shown to have been actually mentioned under this category, whereas only 21 castes were actually mentioned under this category. Thus, 6 castes (Bediya, Garo, Hadi, Hajang, Koch and Lodha) were said to have been classified as depressed in 1917 by the Government, whereas as Annexure Table IV indicates, they were never included in that category. Moreover, the list of Untouchables laid on the table of the Legislative Assembly in September, 1928 was also not taken into account by the Government.

So the "Schedule of Castes" prepared in 1936 did not reflect the will and aspirations of the people belonging to a particular caste. Even when they represented against their inclusion, that was not honoured because the District Officers and the Commissioners of the Divisions found them "socially, politically, economically and educationally" backward and that was the reason for their inclusion. So it was not the untouchability but the "social, political, economic and educational" backwardness, as perceived by the Government Officers, which merited their inclusion in the list. This list was, therefore, not a list of

"Depressed Classes" in the sense in which that term was used by the Indian Franchise Committee in 1932 or was viewed by the political leaders or the social reformers, and no caste was excluded from the list of "Schedule of Castes" merely because it failed to satisfy the Franchise Committee's twin criteria of untouchability. This list is, strictly speaking, not a list of 'Untouchable' castes but a list of castes whose "social, political, economic and educational" development were considered by the Government officials and the provincial Government to be such as to warrant their inclusion in the list. A number of seats in the legislature having been provided for in the 1935 Act for a section of undefined people, known as Depressed Classes, the Government was duty bound to find out the persons who should be clubbed together for this purpose. "Scheduled Castes" were a new political creation[37] for the purpose of special electoral arrangement contemplated by the Communal Award and the Government of the day did everything possible to honour the commitment.

Bihar and Orissa

In the 1911 Census the Census Commissioner decided that instead of raising the question whether the members of particular castes should be regarded as Hindus or not, a list should be prepared of the castes and tribes contributing more than 1 per mille to the total population and returned and classed as Hindus, which *qua* castes did not conform to certain standards or were subject to certain disabilities. In accordance with the Census Commissioner's instructions inquiries were made in each district by the Census Superintendent regarding the castes which would come within any one or more of the 10 categories, ennuciated by the Census Commissioner, and as many as 37 castes were identified as falling under one or more of the 10 categories. The total population of these castes for the entire province including the states was 13,672,131, which included both the Hindus as well as the Animists.[38]

If we consider only those castes falling in categories

7 and 8, then their number would come to 22 having a population of 9,081,299 in the entire province including the states and those for the British Territory and for the Hindus only was 5,830,058.[39]

The list of Depressed Classes, i.e., untouchables prepared by the Government in 1917, however, included 19 castes accounting for a population of 1,109,724. But all of them were not considered depressed, i.e., untouchable throughout the British territory. From the population figures furnished against each caste it appears that only 5 of them (Dom, Hari, Halalkhor, Mehtor and Turi) were considered untouchables throughout the British territory while the remaining 14 were treated as untouchables only in the Orissa Division of the province and only Hindus were considered depressed in those areas.[40] The Government list, however, did not include all the castes which fell in categories 7 and 8 in the 1911 Census. Out of the 22 castes listed under these categories in 1911, as many as 13 (Bhuiya, Ho, Kalwar, Kora, Munda, Musahar, Oroan, Pasi, Santal, Savar, Sunri, Tiyar and Dusadh) were not included in the Government list and only 9 were included. The remaining 10 of the Government list were new additions. Incidentally, none of them came under any of the 10 categories in the 1911 Census.

Sharp's list of Depressed Classes appearing in the Quinquennial Review for the years 1912-17 contained only 22 castes- all the 19 castes of the 1917 Government list and 3 more (Bhangi, Kewat and Kaibartta). Of the new additions, only Kewat figured in category-5 of the 1911 list, i.e., not served by a good Brahmin. In the report the caste-wise population was not given and a total figure of 1,236,300 was mentioned. Though Sharp did not indicate the population of each caste, he indicated the areas for which this population was extracted. They were :

6 throughout the province,
(Bhangi, Dom, Halalkhor, Hari, Mehtor and Turi)

2 in Orissa Division
(Kandra and Pan)

3 in the districts of Cuttack, Puri, Balasore and Sambalpur of Orissa Division
(Chamar, Dhoba and Muchi)

8 in the districts of Cuttack, Puri and Balasore of Orissa Division
(Bauri, Ghusuria, Gokha, Kela, Mahuria, Siyal, Kaibartta and Kewat)

1 in the districts of Angul and Sambalpur of Orissa Division
(Ghasi)

1 in the district of Angul of Orissa Division
(Ahir-Gaura)

1 in the district of Sambalpur of Orissa Division
(Ganda)

Total 22

It indicates that out of the 22 castes listed as depressed, Orissa or parts of it accounted for 16 of them.[41] It may be noted that the population of these castes in the areas mentioned, according to the 1911 Census, exceeds the figure given by Sharp.

The 1919 Franchise Committee included in their term 'Others' the castes and tribes contributing more than one per mille of the total population and classed as Hindus in the Census who were denied access to the interior of ordinary Hindu temples and fell within categories 7,8,9 or 10 at p. 232 of Part I, Census Report of Bengal, Bihar, Orissa and Sikkim, 1911 and it was noted that these castes and tribes were generally described as untouchables. A figure was also mentioned—9,382,321, but its caste-wise break-up was not mentioned. It is really difficult to say which castes were included and for which area.[42]

In the 1921 Census, P.C. Tallents, the Census Superintendent for Bihar and Orissa, identified 22 castes or tribes as 'causing pollution by touch or within a certain distance' and felt that tribes like Kandhs, Kharias and Kheriwars, which seemed to be no more respectable than the Mundas and Oroans, should have been included. He also offered a very interesting definition of the depressed classes, which appeared to him to include a wider range of castes and tribes than the untouchables. He stated that it should be taken to include the Hindu 'untouchables', *plus* the Animists *plus* the Hindu members of tribes which were largely Animistic. As a matter of fact, in his figure of the 'untouchables' calculated to be 8,825,000, he included the Animists as well as the Hindus.[43] The total population of these 22 depressed classes came to 8,808,012 for the entire province including the British territory but the Census Commissioner reduced it to 8 millions after some 'minor adjustment's.[44] He, however, did not specify the castes considered depressed by him. Incidentally, the Census Superintendent's list of 'untouchable castes' more or less coincided with the 1911 list of castes falling under categories 7 and 8. The only difference was that Nuniya, who was listed in the 1911 Census for not being served by a good Brahmin became 'untouchable', in the 1921 Census and Pan was omitted.

The 'untouchables' list prepared by the Government in 1928 listed 20 castes-one caste more than the 'Depressed Classes' list prepared by the Government in 1917. The newly added caste was Bhangi.[45] It may be noted that 8 of these castes were considered 'untouchables' by the Census Superintendent in 1921 and the remaining 12 were not treated as 'untouchable' by the Census Superintendent.

The Hartog Committee in 1929 accepted this untouchables' list as the list of Depressed Classes for the province and calculated their population as 2.53 millions.[46] As it appears, this committee did not consider all of these castes depressed throughout the province because 8 of them, i.e., those considered 'untouchable' in the 1921 Census alone accounted for a population of 2.51 millions in the province. It is quite likely that this Committee followed Sharp's classification of depressed classes as being 'depressed' in only a part of the province, but it is not possible to identify the areas for which they were treated as such by it.

Both the Indian Central Committee in 1929 and the Indian Statutory Commission in 1930, on the basis of the provincial Government's report, estimated the depressed classes population at 5 millions, but the castes considered depressed by them were not indicated.[47]

In the 1931 Census the Provincial Census Superintendent treated 31 castes as falling within the category of depressed classes. Their total population was 6,510,192 including 631,864 for the States. Though the Indian Franchise Committee's definition of the depressed classes and their views on inclusion of castes in that list was known to the Census authority before the final publication of the Census report, 8 castes or tribes (Bauri, Bhogta, Bhuiya, Bhumij, Ghasi, Pan, Rajwar and Turi) were included in the depressed classes list although, according to the Census Superintendent they were "more closely akin to those of the primitive tribes than to those of the depressed Hindus", because the lists of primitive tribes and depressed classes "were not compiled solely with a view to the particular problem confronting the Franchise Committee."[48] Be it noted that the Census Superintendent did not include 8 tribes (Ho, Khond, Kharia, Kora, Munda, Oroan, Santal and Savar) although they were included in the 1911 Census and also in the 1921 Census list of 'untouchables' (except Khond and Kharia), because they were "aboriginal tribes which were regarded as being on a different footing from the Hindu castes."[49] All of them except Kharia were later included in the Scheduled Tribes lists since 1950.

Of these 31 castes, 10 (Ghusuria, Godra, Gokha, Irika, Kandra, Kela, Mahuria, Mangan, Pan and Siyal) were confined almost entirely to Orissa, while 12 (Kanjar, Kurariar, Chaupal, Bhogta, Dosadh, Halalkhor, Lalbegi, Mochi, Musahar, Nat, Pasi and Rajwar) were almost peculiar to the districts of Bihar. The remaining 9 (Bauri, Bhuiya, Bhumij, Chamar, Dhobi, Dom, Ghasi, Hari and Turi) were common to both Orissa and Bihar.[50]

The Census Commissioner retained all of them except Rajwar (133,935) in his list of exterior castes. Of the total of 6,376,257 in his list of exterior castes not more than 631,864 were found in the Bihar and Orissa States, leaving not more than 5,744,393 in British districts.

Among the 31 castes in the Census Superintendent's list, only 12 were considered depressed/untouchables in the 1911 Census as well as in the 1921 Census [Bauri, Bhuiya, Chamar, Dhobi, Dom, Dusadh, Hari, Kandra, Muchi, Musahar, Pan and Pasi (Pan was not included in the 1921 Census)] and the remaining 19 did not figure in the previous Census lists of depressed classes.

Non-compliance with the Indian Franchise Committee's definition of the depressed classes in the preparation of the list of depressed classes by the Census authority no doubt made the task of the Franchise Committee difficult, but this 1931 list of 'depressed classes' was taken into account by all the bodies including the provincial Government for projecting their estimates of the depressed classes population.

In their First Memorandum the Government of Bihar and Orissa refrained from submitting replies to the questionnaire prepared by the Indian Franchise Committee. In their second Memorandum the provincial Government did not give any figure of the depressed classes but referred to the note of M.G.Hallet, their Chief Secretary in which the position of the depressed classes in the province was explained and which they stated would give all the information available.[51] During the Census of 1911 a complete classification was made under the ten categories and, in the note mentioned, the Chief Secretary proceeded to discuss each of those castes with reference to present conditions, and stated that the depressed classes in the province amounted to between 5 and 6 millions. He added that the problem of the depressed classes did not exist in an acute form in the province where the conditions were very different from those which obtained in Southern India. The Chief Secretary pointed out in his note that the criteria adopted in 1911 led to the inclusion of a large number of aboriginal tribes, e.g., Ho, Munda, Oroan, Santal, Ganda, Khond, etc., who were really outside the

Hindu religion as well as of some castes which were high in the social scale and were often men of education, wealth and property, e.g., Kalwars and Sunris. In regard to the 1931 Census, the Chief Secretary pointed out that this list contained some tribes which were probably in origin aboriginal and whose main habitat was in the aboriginal tracts of Chota Nagpur, like Bhuiya, Bhumij, Bauri, Ghasi, Rajwar or Turi or even the wandering tribes like Kanjaria of Purnea and Nats of Purnea and Patna Divisions, some of whose members were criminals. He concluded by saying that "if we include the major castes of Chamars and Mochis (about 1,300,000), Dhobi (414,000), Dusadh (1,300,000), Doms, Halalkhors and Haris about 400,000, Pasis 172,000 and from Orissa Pans 418,000, we have between 5 and 6 millions which is a fairly large percentage of the total population....."[52].

The Bihar and Orissa provincial Franchise Committee in their provisional Memorandum sent on February 9, 1932 intimated that it was difficult to give an exhaustive list of the castes or sects who came under the definition of depressed classes. The only classes which could be called depressed were Musahars, Dusadhs, Chamars, Doms and Mehtors. The problem of depressed classes was not so acute in Bihar as in Bombay or South India.[53] In their final Memorandum sent on March 19, 1932, the Provincial Franchise Committee stated that the depressed classes were enumerated in the 1931 Census but "some of the classes in this list, e.g., Bauri, Bhogta, Bhuiya, Bhumij, Ghasi, Pan, Rajwar and Turi have also been classed as aboriginals during the Census. There may be also other classes who are regarded as depressed in different local areas of the province. The degree of untouchability of the depressed classes varies in different parts of the province. In some districts, members of certain sects and sub-sects of depressed classes are denied access to wells and temples. In others, the same sects and sub-sects are denied access to temples but not to wells. There are places where the children of the depressed classes are allowed to attend ordinary schools. The classes which are commonly regarded as untouchable are Chamar, Dusadh, Dom,

Halakhor, Hari, Mochi, Musahar, Pan and Pasi."[54] The provincial Franchise Committee added that of the 31 castes classed as depressed in the 1931 Census, the population of the 8 castes, mentioned earlier, who were classed as aboriginals as also the Christians, Muhammadens and Animists included within the depressed classes population should be excluded from the total of the depressed classes population to give the total population of the depressed classes as 4,344,585.[55]

In view of the general agreement between the Chief Secretary's list of castes and that of the Provincial Committee, the Indian Franchise Committee had no difficulty in arriving at a final figure for this province. The Franchise Committee observed that the estimate given by the provincial Committee was an accurate one based on the Census figures of 1931 and the total of 4.3 millions was found to be correct on verification. Hence the Committee accepted "this as the estimate of the number of depressed classes in that province who fall under the definition which we have accepted."[56] This is the only instance when the Indian Franchise Committee gave a definite opinion regarding the population of the depressed classes. As to the rationality of their estimates, the Indian Franchise Committee later explained that the Censuses of 1911, 1921 and 1931, the local Franchise Committee and the Chief Secretary to the Government of Bihar and Orissa "are all unanimous in declaring that eight castes, the Dom, Chamar, Dusadh, Musahar, Pasi, Mochi, Pan and Hari, satisfy the two tests referred to in paragraph 285 of our report. These castes number 3,973,953. Our estimate of 4,300,000 includes also about 400,000 persons for minor castes, whose numbers individually are small."[57]

The dissenting members of the Indian Franchise Committee, however, disagreed with this estimate of 4.3 millions. Referring to the note of the Chief Secretary in which it was stated that Dom, Halalkhor and Hari were probably the only castes which were regarded as causing pollution, they concluded that "in the circumstances, we are not prepared to accept the figure of 4,300,000 as the total of depressed class population in Bihar and Orissa. The evidence which we recorded and the evidence contained in the written statements tends to establish that there are very few classes which can be called 'depressed'. We think that the three castes mentioned by the Chief Secretary are the only depressed classes. They number 400,000."[58]

The acceptance of the list of castes as depressed and their numbers by the Indian Franchise Committee did not mean that the Government would go by its recommendations. By the time the list of 'Scheduled Castes' was issued in 1936 Bihar and Orissa were bifurcated and separate lists were issued for these two provinces.

Bihar

The Bihar list contained 22 castes. All these 22 castes were among the 31 castes listed in the 1931 Census. The 9 castes not finding place in the Bihar list were included in the Orissa list to which we will refer to later.

Of the 22 castes listed as "Scheduled" in Bihar, 14 were Scheduled throughout the province and 8 in parts of the province. Incidentally, all these 8 castes considered scheduled in parts of the province were excluded by the Indian Franchise Committee from the list of Depressed Classes accepted by them, because they were aboriginals in origin. But this recommendation of the Indian Franchise Committee had no impact on the Government's decision.

Annexure Table V will indicate the position accorded to the various castes by different agencies since 1911. It will appear that the 22 castes 'scheduled' in 1936 were mentioned for the first time in the reports as follows :

13 were mentioned in the 1911 Census,
(Bauri, Bhuiya, Bhumij, Chamar, Dhobi, Dom, Dusadh, Hari, Muchi, Musahar, Pan, Pasi and Rajwar)

3 in the 1917 Government list, and
(Ghasi, Halalkhor and Turi)

6 in the 1931 Census
(Bhogta, Chaupal, Kanjar, Kurariar, Lalbegi and Nat).

Total 22

It will appear from Annexure Table V that

(A) Of the 13 castes taken from the 1911 Census list, Bhumij and Rajwar were included in the 1911 list for not being served by good Brahmans as family priests. None of them were mentioned as depressed till the 1931 Census and the 1931 Census Commissioner even deleted Rajwar from his list of exterior castes. The remaining 11 were in categories 7 and 8 in the 1911 Census. All these 11 except 4 (Bhuiya, Dusadh, Musahar and Pasi) were considered depressed/untouchable all along while Bhuiya, Dusadh, Musahar and Pasis were treated as depressed in the Census of 1921 as well as of 1931.

(B) Of the 22 castes identified as falling in categories 7 and 8 in the 1911 Census, all but five figured either in the 'Scheduled Castes' list or in the 'Scheduled Tribes' list-11 in the Scheduled Castes list and 6 in the Scheduled Tribes list. The exceptions were Ganda, Kandra, Tiyar, Kalwar and Sunri. The first three, however, appeared in the Orissa list while Kalwar and Sunri did not find place in either list.

(C) Of the castes treated as untouchables in 1917 and in 1928 by the Government, all of them except one (Ahir Gaura) were included in the Scheduled Castes lists of either province-10 in the Bihar list and 8 in the Orissa list.

(D) All the 22 castes except 3 (Ahir Gaura, Kaibartta and Kewat) in Sharp's list figured in the Scheduled Castes lists of either province.

(E) Of the castes listed as untouchable in the 1921 Census, 16 figured either in the Scheduled Castes list or in the Scheduled Tribes list, 3 in the Orissa Scheduled Castes list and 3 (Kalwar, Nuniya and Sunri) were not included in any list.

(F) All the castes classed as depressed in the 1931 Census were listed in the 1936 Schedule-22 in the Bihar list and the 9 not included in the Bihar list were included in the Orissa list. It may be remembered that during the 1931 Census 10 castes were almost exclusively confined to Orissa region, but in the 1936 list one of them, Pan, was included for the Bihar region as well.

(G) As already mentioned, the 1936 Order included all the 8 aboriginal castes much against the recommendation of the Indian Franchise Committee and they continued to remain in the Scheduled Castes list since then.

(H) Castes having very insignificant population were among the new castes included in the 1931 Census. For instance, Lalbegi and Kurariar, whose population were only 105 and 631 respectively, in the 1931 Census were included in the Scheduled Castes list of 1936.

Orissa

Till the 1935 Act became operative all classification and enumeration of the depressed classes/untouchables in the Bihar and Orissa province was done jointly and not separately. Only consequent to the bifurcation of this province the Scheduled Castes Order was issued separately for this province.

In the 1936 Order as many as 62 castes/sub-castes were 'scheduled', 9 of them along with other castes/sub-castes. Of these 62, no less than 13 were considered 'scheduled' in parts of the province. It will appear from Annexure Table VI that quite a large number of them were not even mentioned in any earlier reports. Of them, 1 (Bhuiya) was transferred to the Scheduled Tribes list in 1950 and another (Bhumij) to the Scheduled Tribes list in 1956 while only one (Pradhan) was descheduled in 1956.

Annexure Table VI will indicate the position accorded to different castes in various Censuses and other reports since 1911. The castes scheduled in 1936 were first mentioned by the earlier bodies/census reports as follows:

11 in the 1911 Census,
(Bauri, Bhuiya, Bhumij, Chamar, Dhobi, Ganda, Dom, Hari, Kandra, Muchi and Pan)

8 in the 1917 Government list,
(Ghasi, Ghusuria, Gokha, Kela, Mahuria, Mehtar, Siyal and Turi)

1 in the Quinquennial Report of Sharp,
(Bhangi)

3 in the 1931 Census
(Godra, Irika and Mangan)

39 in the 1936 list
(Adi-Andhra, Audhelia, Bariki, Basor, Bavuri, Burud, Chachati, Chandala, Dandasi, Dewar, Dhoba, Dombo, Gadagali, Ghasia, Godari, Haddi, Jaggali, Katia, Kodalo, Kori, Madari, Madiga, Mala, Mang, Mehra, Mahar, Mochi, Nagarchi, Paidi, Painda, Pamidi, Panchama, Panka, Pano, Pradhan, Relli, Sapari, Satnami and Valmiki).

Total 62

(A) Of the 11 castes finding place in the 1936 list from the 1911 Census report, Bhumij was included in the 1911 Census for not being served by good Brahmans as family priests. It was also not mentioned as depressed by any other authority till the 1931 Census. The remaining 10 were in categories 7 and 8 in the 1911 Census.

(B) All the 22 castes which were identified as causing pollution in 1911 except two were included either in the Scheduled Castes lists or in the Scheduled Tribes list. 10 were included in the 1936 Order, 3 (Dusadh, Pasi and Tiyar) in the 1950 Order and one (Musahar) in the 1956 Order while 6 (Ho, Kora, Munda, Oroan, Santal and Savar) were in the Scheduled Tribes list since 1950. Only Kalwar and Sunri did not find any place anywhere.

(C) Of the 37 castes listed in 1911 for satisfying one or more of the 10 tests, as many as 24 have since figured either in the Scheduled Castes list or in the Scheduled

Tribes list. Apart from the 11 castes included in the 1936 Order, Dusadh, Pasi and Tiyar, which were considered polluting in the 1911 Census, and Beldar which was listed for 'not receiving the mantra from a Brahman or other recognised Hindu *guru*' and for 'not being served by good Brahmans as family priests', were added to the Scheduled Caste list in 1950, and Musahar which satisfied the twin criteria of untouchability in the 1911 Census, was included in the Scheduled Castes list in 1956. Similarly, 8 castes (Ho, Kharia, Kharwar, Kora, Munda, Oroan, Santal and Savar) which were listed in 1911 for satisfying any one of the 10 tests, were later included in the Scheduled Tribes list in 1950. The remaining 13, most of whom were listed for 'not being served by good Brahmans' did not find place in any list.

(D) Of the castes considered untouchable by the Government in 1917 and in 1928, all except 2 (Ahir Gaura and Halalkhor) figured in the Scheduled Castes list.

(E) Of the 22 castes in Sharp's list, all but 4 (Ahir Gaura, Halakhor, Kaibartta and Kewat) were included in the Scheduled Castes list of the Province.

(F) Of the castes considered 'untouchable' in the 1921 Census only 3 (Kalwar, Nuniya and Sunri) were not included in any list.

(G) Of the 31 castes listed as depressed by the Census Superintendent in the 1931 Census, 20 were included in the 1936 Order, another 3 (Dusadh and Pasi in 1950 and Musahar in 1956) in subsequent Scheduled Castes Orders and the remaining 8 (Bhogta, Chaupal, Halakhor, Kanjar, Kurariar, Lalbegi, Nat and Rajwar) were not included in any Scheduled Castes Order pertaining to this State. These castes, were, however, found to be exclusively in the Bihar region during the 1931 Census.

(H) Apart from the castes which were confined exclusively to the Orissa region, some castes which were almost peculiar to the Bihar region till the 1931 Census figured in the Orissa Scheduled Castes list as well, though most of them subsequently, like Dusadh, Musahar and Pasi.

(I) Of the 8 castes which were excluded from the depressed classes list by the Indian Franchise Committee in 1932 because of their aboriginal lineage, 6 (Bauri, Bhumij, Ghasi, Bhuiya, Pan and Turi) figured in the 1936 list and also in the subsequent lists, except two, Bhuiya and Bhumij, transferred to the Scheduled Tribes list in 1950 and 1956, respectively.

(J) All the three castes (Godra, Irika and Mangan) which came into the picture only from the 1931 Census returned a very insignificant population-762, 322 and 184, respectively.

(K) In no other province so many castes-39 in all-were put in the Schedule which no other body had ever considered depressed/untouchables. Transfer of areas from the Vizagapa-tam and Ganjam Agencies in the then Presidency of Madras to this Province at the time of its formation in 1936 might be one of the reasons for this new additions. Of the 39 castes included in the Schedule, as many as 23 (Adi-Andhra, Bariki, Bavuri, Chachati, Chandala, Dandasi, Dombo, Godagali, Godari, Haddi, Jaggali, Kodalo, Madari, Madiga, Mala, Paidi, Painda, Pamidi, Panchama, Pano, Relli, Sapari and Valmiki) were listed in the Schedule for the Madras Presidency as well. Since these castes were peculiar for the transferred areas from the Madras Presidency and not in the entire Province, they should have been made scheduled for a part of the Province, i.e., only for the ceded areas from the Madras Presidency, as was done in other provinces. But this principle was followed in reverse in this Province. While 21 were scheduled for the entire Province and only 2 (Dombo and Pano) for parts of the Province, the areas for which these two were made non-scheduled were no other than the transferred areas from the Madras Presidency!

Another 15 (Audhelia, Basor, Burud, Dewar, Ghasia, Katia, Mang, Mahar, Mehra, Mochi, Nagarchi, Panka, Pradhan, Satnami and Kori) were in the list of Scheduled Castes for Madhya Pradesh. But in that Province these castes (except five) were scheduled only for an area and not for the entire Province. But in Orissa, where these castes had no existence even a year earlier, all of them except four — Ghasia, Kori, Nagarchi and Pradhan — were put in the schedule for the entire Province.

United Provinces

Richard Burn as Superintendent of Census Operations in the North-Western Provinces and Oudh in 1901, in accordance with the instructions of the Census Commissioner that a scheme should be drawn up as nearly as possible in the order of social precedence recognised by public opinion, made investigations regarding the position of castes in the social hierarchy. He divided the Hindus into the following thirteen groups according to the social precedence of the castes :

Group 1	...	Brahmins.
Group II	...	Castes allied to Brahmins.
Group III	...	Kshattriya.
Group IV	...	Castes allied to Kshattriyas.
Group V	...	Vaishya or Bania.
Group VI	...	Castes allied to Vaishyas or Banias.
Group VII	...	Castes of good social position distinctly superior to that of the remaining groups.
Group VIII	...	Castes from whom some of the twice-born would take pakki and all would take water.
Group IX	...	Castes from whose hands some of the twice-born would take water, while others would not.
Group X	...	Castes from whose lotah the twice-born cannot take water, but who are not untouchable, (a) with respectable occupations,

		(b) with occupations considered more or less degrading, and
		(c) suspected of criminal practices.
Group XI	...	Castes that are untouchable, but that do not eat beef.
Group XII	...	The lowest castes who eat beef and vermin and are considered filthy.
Group XIII	...	Miscellaneous
		(a) Possibly wrongly recorded as Hindus instead of Muhammadans
		(b) Foreigners
		(c) Miscellaneous
		(d) Faqir.[59]

Unlike other provinces, E.A.H. Blunt, the 1911 Census Superintendent of the United Provinces, did not draw up the list of castes after classifying them according to the 10 tests enunciated by the Census Commissioner. Instead, he devised his own 9 tests of 'Hinduism' which were as follows :

(1) Admission of Brahman supremacy.

(2) Being served by good Brahmans as family priests.

(3) Being served by inferior Brahmans as family priests.

(4) Utilising the services of Brahmans in any of their traditional capacities.

(5) Receipt of the *mantra* from a Brahman or other recognised Hindu guru.

(6) Worship of the great Hindu gods.

(7) Permission to enter Hindu temple.

(8) Death ceremonies, whether burial or cremation.

(9) Customs in the matter of eating beef and veneration of the cow.

He, however, did not classify the castes satisfying

these tests. He selected certain representative castes and after discussing how each of them conformed to these tests, concluded that "very few in this province are the members of those, who, while returning themselves as of the Hindu religion, do not fulfill any of the prescribed tests. It is very rare indeed that no *test* at all is fulfilled by any tribe ... Whether reckoned as Hindu or Hinduised or non-Hindu, there is very little doubt that there is not a tribe or caste in the province which would not be strict Hindu in all essentials if it was allowed to be so."[60] Since the castes were not identified in the 1911 Census even according to these 9 tests, we are denied of the opportunity of knowing which castes answered these tests. It may be noted that in the Census Superintendent's 'chief tests' of Hinduism, the test of causing pollution by touch or approach did not figure.

In 1917 the United Provinces Government prepared a list of Depressed Classes, i.e., untouchables. There were 20 castes in this list returning a population of 8,374,542 for the province including the British territory.[61]

Sharp in his Quinquennial report for 1912-17 did not specify the castes included in his list of Depressed Classes but indicated the same population.[62] It is, therefore, assumed that he also considered the same 20 castes as depressed.

Since the classification of castes according to the Census Commissioner's 10-point test or even according to the Census Superintendent's own 9-point test was shunned away in the 1911 Census, the Franchise Committee in 1919 could not fall back on that classification. It, therefore, included the castes mentioned in Groups XI and XII of the 1901 Census as 'untouchables' in the group 'Others'. In Group XI, i.e., Castes that are untouchable, but that do not eat beef, there were 24 castes with a population of 3,454,096 and in Group XII, i.e., the lowest castes who eat beef and vermin and are considered filthy, 13 castes were listed having a population of 6,594,821. The total population of these 37 castes, which included all the 20 castes classed as depressed by the provincial Government in 1917, according to the 1901 Census, was 10,048,917,[63] and the population of these castes estimated by the Franchise Committee in 1919 was 10,118,435,[64] a marginal increase from the 1901 Census figure. Though population of many of these castes was not extracted in the 1911 Census, it appeared that the population of the castes brought under the group 'Others' related to the British territory only.

The 1921 Census Superintendent followed the foot-step of his predecessor in office in the matter of identification of the 'depressed classes'. He not only did not enumerate the depressed classes, but also, what Marten, the 1921 Census Commissioner, described as "the extreme delicacy of official sentiment" shrank from the task of attempting even a rough estimate of that. The Census Commissioner, however, on his own, estimated the depressed population in the United Provinces at 9,000,000, but refrained from specifying the castes constituting this figure.[65]

The untouchable list prepared by the Government in 1928 had on its roll the same 20 castes which were considered depressed, i.e., untouchable by the provincial Government in 1917.[66]

The Hartog Committee in 1929, adhering to this list of untouchables, estimated the depressed classes population to be 7.89 millions.[67] Since the 1921 Census did not tabulate the caste-wise population figure of many castes, it is not known whether Hartog's estimate covered the entire province or only the British territory. In any case, there was some decrease in the population of these castes during this period.

The same year, the Indian Central Committee, on the basis of the provincial Government's report, predicted a figure of 13 millions for the depressed classes[68] and the Indian Statutory Commission, a year later, in 1930, reduced it by 1 million.[69] None of them, however, specified the castes considered depressed by them.

In the 1931 Census,[70] A.C. Turner, the Census Superintendent, classified the depressed in two groups —

A — Untouchable and depressed

B — Touchable but depressed.

Group A consisted of the following three categories :

	No. of Castes	*No. of persons in British territory*
(1) Tribes and castes who are untouchable and depressed on account of their unclean habits chiefly in the matter of diet.	40	2,840,078
(2) Vagrant tribes	19	110,447
(3) Those who follow unclean occupations	7	8,253,323
Total	66	11,203,848

In Group B was included those castes and tribes, which whilst not causing pollution to high caste Hindus by personal contact, were nevertheless considered depressed. The Touchable but depressed classes were divided into two categories :

(1) Degraded tribally through their habits and customs	5	118,433
(2) Depressed on account of their traditional occupations	4	1,269,244
	9	1,387,677
Total of Groups A and B comes to	75	12,591,525

The 1931 Census Commissioner concurred with the report of the provincial Census Superintendent and included all of them in his list of exterior castes except the 4 castes categorised in Group B(2) returning a figure of 1,269,244. He also did not include Pasia, grouped with Bahelia in Group A(1) in his list of exterior castes. So, according to the Census Commissioner, there were 70 exterior castes having a population of 11,322,281. This population was, however, for the British territory only. He also observed that a number of quasiaboriginal tribes were included in his list as they were reported to be completely detribalised and their social position was indistinguishable from that of other depressed castes included.[71]

The classification of so many castes-75 according to the Census Superintendent and 70 according to the Census Commissioner—as depressed in the 1931 Census resulted in the inclusion of Touchables, Vagrant tribes, quasi-aboriginals, etc., Not only the Indian Franchise Committee's definition of depressed classes was not honoured, even the much wider instruction of the Census Commissioner himself was not followed. It exposed the difficulty of defining and hence enumerating the depressed classes.

The same difficulty persisted when the Indian Franchise Committee in 1932 undertook the task of defining and estimating the depressed classes population. Various estimates received by it revealed the greatest divergence of opinion.

The Government of the United Provinces in their first report sent on March 20, 1932 to the Indian Franchise Committee observed that the "schedule of depressed classess" to be drawn up for the use of the Governor should at least include the following classes :

Dhanuk	127,581
Chamars in rural areas estimated at	4,187,770
Bhangi group	349,053
Kolarian group	125,356
Dom group	109,906
Pasi group	1,446,155
Hill Dom	326,012
Vagrant tribes	111,981
Total	6,773,814

This list was based on the information furnished by Blunt in his note.[72] There were altogether 41 castes in these groups.

In their final reply sent on April 8, 1932, the provincial Government observed as follows :

> Government are informed that the Chairman of the Indian Franchise Committee has given a definition to the Chairman of the Provincial Committee which would confine the depressed

> classes to those who cause 'pollution by touch or approach as it exists in this province'. If so, the actual number would be reduced to 459,000 and on that definition it would be impossible to secure representation for other than those restricted classes. At the same time the local Government feel that it is necessary to take into consideration classes other than those so defined.[73]

Blunt, who as the Census Superintendent of the United Provinces in 1911 did not consider it feasible to draw up a list of castes satisfying the 10 tests of the Census Commissioner or even those meeting his 9 tests and therefore failed to estimate their population, now as Member of the Executive Council of the United Provinces, in an exhaustive note prepared in March, 1932 for the benefit of the Indian Franchise Committee, estimated the 'untouchables' at 9,181,315. He, however, did not confine himself to the interpretation of untouchability adopted by the Indian Franchise Committee. In paragraph 16 of his note he remarked :

> In theory, the following practices would make a tribe or caste permanently untouchable, at all events to a Brahmin :—
>
> (i) the following of some unclean profession, such as scavenging ;
>
> (ii) the keeping of pigs, or the eating of unclean food, such as pork or beef ;
>
> (iii) vagrancy, unless there is a settled home to which the tribe or caste occasionally returns.
>
> Reports received in connection with the census of 1931 from the districts, show that the average Brahman still regards these practices as carrying with them a theoretical stigma of untouchability, even though that stigma, as already explained may now be lightly regarded. There is, moreover, a marked and growing tendency to make untouchability a personal and not a caste

> attribute. Formerly, every person born into a caste, the members of which followed some degrading practice, was treated as permanently untouchable. At the present day, any caste, or any section of a caste, or any individual who has abandoned the practice which made him untouchable, becomes touchable. The village Chamar, for instance, will remain untouchable so long as he handles dead animals, but the Chamar who has become a saddler (zingar) or a cobbler (mochi) or a groom (syce), is not. This has happened even amongst Bhangis, for there is a case recorded of a municipal latrine-cleaner, who having first risen to the rank of jamadar of scavengers, subsequently abandoned that occupation altogether, and is now no longer regarded as untouchable by his fellow-citizens. And all recent evidence suggests that, at the present day the castes that would, as a whole, be treated as untouchable are very low-the Bhangi, the Dom, and the wandering tribes; and these would be untouchable not only to the Brahman but to all orthodox Hindus. The whole idea of untouchability, in fact, is now disappearing.[74]

In spite of these observations, Blunt estimated the depressed classes population at 9,181,315 and mentioned the groups of castes and castes included by him under his classification in the list given in Appendix II of his note.[75]

A third estimate of 12.6 millions was given by the Census Commissioner.[76] It was the same estimate which was furnished by the Census Superintendent in his Census report, discussed earlier.

It may be noted that all the three estimates given to the Franchise Committee-those by the provincial Government in their first report, by Blunt and by the Census Commissioner— were made without taking into consideration the definition of the depressed classes accepted by the Indian Franchise Committee. The number was reduced to a mere 459,000 by the provincial Government in their second report when they took into consideration the definition of the Franchise Committee.

The United Provinces Franchise Committee, was, however, in agreement with the Indian Franchise Committee that the term 'depressed classes' should be confined to those who were untouchables. It was of opinion that only those classes should be called 'depressed' which were untouchable. Judged by this test, the problem of untouchability was non-existent in these provinces except in the case of Bhangis, Doms and Dhanuks whose total population including those sections which were touchable, was only 581,000. The two depressed class members questioned the correctness of the Indian Franchise Committee's ruling, but stated that if it was to be regarded as final, they agreed that only the three classes mentioned above fell under the definition of 'depressed'.[77]

Though the Indian Franchise Committee could not arrive at any estimate of the depressed population or their composition,[78] the dissenting members of the Indian Franchise Committee, while estimating the number of the depressed classes in the province to be 0.6 millions, observed :

> The only classes, which, according to the definition of our Committee, would fall under the category of depressed classes in the United Provinces, are three, namely, Bhangis, Doms and Dhanuks, as stated by the Provincial Franchise Committee. The two members of the depressed classes on the Provincial Committee agreed that these were the only three castes which come within our Committee's definition of depressed classes. The number of these castes is 581,000. There is thus agreement between the depressed class representatives, the Provincial Committee and the local Government, and the matter, in our opinion, should be concluded here. But a note by Mr. Blunt, which was prepared before our second visit to the United Provinces and

> before our definition was communicated to the Provincial Committee and the local Government, has been brought in and this has confused the issue. But it is a material circumstance that Mr. Blunt, who is a member of the Government, has not dissented from their reply. The last sentence of paragraph 16 of Mr. Blunt's note shows that the only classes which strictly fall within our definition of depressed classes were Bhangis and Doms. His note, in this light, is not really inconsistent with his subsequent opinion. In our opinion, the discussion of Mr. Blunt's note is irrelevant. The issue raised by the Provincial Committee and the local Government about some other classes as requiring special treatment is outside the scope of enquiry in connection with the depressed classes. It opens a very large question and is outside the terms of reference to this committee.[79]

Notwithstanding this wide disagreement with the classification of the depressed classes, in the 1936 order as many as 61 castes were scheduled.

Annexure Table VII will indicate the position accorded to the castes considered depressed/untouchable/exterior/scheduled by the different bodies during the period 1901-1936. In the 1911 and 1921 Censuses no lists of depressed classes were drawn up. The two Government lists of 1917 and 1928 contained the same 20 castes while the 1919 Frnachise Committee's list included 17 more. 5 of the castes considered depressed/untouchable by the Government and the Franchise Committee (Raj, Rangsaz, Rangraz, Saiqalgar and Sunkar) were, however, not included in the 1931 Census list of Depressed Classes or in the Scheduled Castes Orders issued since 1936. Balai and Tarmali considered depressed/untouchable both by the Government and the Franchise Committee and Musahar and Dusadh, considered depressed only by the Franchise Committee, though included in the 1931 Census list, were not included in the 1936 Order. The first three were included in the Scheduled Castes Order of 1956 and the last one in the 1950 Order.

The 61 castes scheduled in the 1936 order figured for the first time in the following reports :

45 in the 1901 Census

(Agariya, Aheriya, Badhik, Baheliya, Bajgi, Balahar, Bansphor, Barwar, Basor, Bawariya, Beldar, Bengali, Berya, Bhuiya, Bhuiyar, Boriya, Chamar, Dabgar, Dhangar, Dhanuk (Bhangi), Dharkar, Dhobi, Dom, Domar, Gharami, Ghasiya, Habura, Khairaha, Kanjar, Kapariya, Kharot, Kharwar, Khatik, Kol, Kori, Korwa, Majhawar, Nat, Panka, Parahiya, Pasi, Patari, Saharya, Sansiya and Tharu).

10 in the 1931 Census

(Badi, Bajania, Banmanus, Bhantu, Chero, Gual, Kalabaz, Karwal, Sanaurhiya and Shilpkar).

6 in the 1936 order

(Balmiki, Hari, Hela, Lalbegi, Rawat and Turaiha)

Though the Census reports since 1901 were commenting on the difficulties of identifying the 'untouchables' and two successive Census Superintendents—that of 1911 and of 1921 —in fact, failed to identify them and even in 1932, Blunt, an ex-Census Superintendent of the province, conceded that "the whole idea of untouchability in fact, is now fast disappearing", when the time came for scheduling of castes, it is amazing that a large number of castes were enlisted.

(A) While it was the general consensus that 'untouchability was fast disappearing' in the United Provinces, this process suffered a jolt in the mid-30s. Castes which were not untouchable even in 1901 became 'scheduled' in 1936. As many as 18 castes figured in the 1936 order that were identified as not untouchable in the 1901 census, the details of which are as follows :—

Group X — Castes from whose lotah the twice-born cannot take water, but who are not untouchable :

(a) with respectable occupations 1
(Tharu)

(b) with occupations considered more or less degrading 12
(Beldar, Bhuiya, Bhuiyar, Ghasiya, Kharot, Khairaha, Kharwar, Kol, Majhawar, Pankla, Parahiya and Patari)

(c) suspected of criminal practices 5
(Badhik, Barwar, Bawariya, Kapariya and Sansiya).

(B) In the 1901 Census 24 castes were included in Group XI (Castes that are untouchable, but that do not eat beef). Of them 16 figured in the 1936 Order, Dusadh in the 1950 Order, Balai and Tarmali in the 1956 Order and the remaining 5 (Raj, Rangraz, Rangsaz, Saiqalgar and Sunkar) did not find place in any list.

(C) In the 1901 Census 13 castes were included in Groups XII (The lowest castes who eat beef and vermin and are considered filthy). Of them, 11 landed in the 1936 list, another (Musahar) in the 1956 list and Bhangi was excluded.

(D) Till the 1931 Census Bhangis alone were considered depressed/untouchable, but in the 1936 Order Bhangis were excluded from the list and in its place the communities, 7 in all, composing it were included.

(E) Of the 20 castes considered untouchable by the Government in 1917 as well as in 1928, 12 were included in the 1936 Order, 2 (Balai and Tarmali) in the 1956 Order, 1 (Bhangi) was dropped in preference to its seven constituent communities and the remaining 5 (Raj, Rangsaz, Rangraz, Saiqalgar and Sunkar) were omitted from the 1931 Census list of depressed classes as well as the Scheduled Castes Order of 1936.

(F) In the 1936 Order not only aboriginal castes but 18 vagrant or wandering tribes were also included in the Schedule. In Bengal, groups of aboriginal derivation were also included in the 1936 Order but those were gradually transferred to the Scheduled Tribes Lists from 1950 onwards, but in the United Provinces they continued to remain in the Scheduled Castes lists because no Scheduled Tribes list was prepared for the United Provinces immediately after the commencement of the Constitution of India. Even when the Scheduled Tribes list was notified in 1967, none of these tribes was transferred to that list.

(G) A number of castes having an insignificant population were included in the 1936 list like Sansiya (886), Kapariya (803), Dabgar (657), Korwa (467), Kharot (356), Karwal (108), Badi (34) and Sanaurhiya (31).

(H) Like all provinces, claims to higher social status were articulated during the 1931 Census in the United Provinces as well. But in this province the number of such claimants was unusually large. Representations were received for treating them either as Brahman or Kshattriya or Vaishya or Rajput or for allowing them to return themselves in new names. Of the 63 castes preferring such claims, 10 were included in the Depressed Classes list in the 1931 Census. But unlike the other provinces, their requests were conceded in certain cases. For instance, Bhar (claiming the status of Jaduvanshi Kshattriya), Kumhar (claiming the status of Balkhariya Thakur, Rajput, Vaishya or Jaiswar) and Luniya (claiming the status of Chauhan Rajput or Thakur) were never included in the Scheduled Castes lists and Aheria (claiming the status of Hara Rajput), though included in the 1936 order was excluded from the Scheduled Castes list since 1950. This is a special feature in this province.

Punjab

In the 1911 Census 24 castes were identified whose touch was considered to pollute food and water and who were denied access to the interior of Hindu temples. These castes totalled 2,268,831 but the author of the report, Rai Bahadur Pandit Hari Kishan Kaul, stated that the strength of such of them, who would pollute a high caste Hindu by touching him would not be more than 1 million.[80] It may be mentioned that this figure of 2,268,831 was extracted for the entire Punjab province including Native States for the Hindu population only. The corresponding figure for the British territory only was 1,774,031.[81]

In view of the fact that the idea of pollution by mere touch was rapidly dying out, the Punjab Government did not submit any list of Depressed Classes, i.e., untouchables to the Government of India in 1917 and quoting the authority of Pandit Hari Kishan Kaul, the Census Superintendent of 1911, stated that in 1917, it would be nearer the mark to say that about half a million persons in the province were regarded as capable of conveying such pollution, while it must be remembered that only a comparatively small section of the population so regarded them.[82]

Sharp in his Quinquennial Report for the period 1912-17 identified only 10 castes as depressed with a population of 2.1 millions.[83] He, however, did not follow the 1911 classification and included as many as 6 (Dhobi, Ghosi, Marecha, Mahtam, Od and Ramdasis) castes in his list which were outside the 1911 list. In regard to the Depressed Classes population Sharp deviated from the usual practice of restricting it to the Hindu population only. Instead, he calculated the Depressed Classes population by adding up the population of all religious communities-Hindu, Muslim and Sikh-belonging to each of these 10 castes residing in British territory only. That is the reason why his figure exceeded the corresponding figure in the 1911 Census which related to Hindu population only.

The Franchise Committee in 1919, as usual, did not indicate the castes it grouped within the term "others". It only stated that the group consisted of castes not ordinarily admitted to a Hindu temple and referred to p.190(109?) of Part I, Census Report of Punjab, 1911. It also indicated a figure-1,738,701.[84] In all probability, it included almost all the major Depressed Classes including Chamar and Chuhra in this category — if population figures were of any indication.

The 1921 Census Superintendent did not identify the

depressed classes in his report. The 1921 Census Commissioner, on his own calculated that there were 2.8 millions Depressed Classes population in Punjab,[85] but the castes were not mentioned in his report.

Though the provincial Government failed in 1917 to furnish any list of Depressed Classes, i.e., untouchables, in 1928 two castes-Chamar and Chuhra-were included in the list of untouchables.[86] The Hartog Committee in 1929 considered only these two castes as depressed and calculated their population at 1.70 millions.[87]

Inspite of the fact that only in 1928 two castes were listed as untouchables, it did not preclude the provincial Government from intimating the Indian Central Committee in 1929,[88] and the Indian Statutory Commission,[89] a year later, that the Depressed Classes population mentioned in the Census of 1921 might be taken as the Depressed Classes population for the province. Both these bodies also accepted this figure furnished by the provincial Government without any verification as to whether the castes whose population was given as 2.8 millions in the 1921 Census actually conformed to their own definition of Depressed Classes, which, as defined by both of them, were untouchables only.

The 1931 Census Superintendent identified 12 castes as depressed and estimated their total population in British territory as 1,310,709. Another 20 castes were also identified by him as untouchables but all of them were numerically unimportant. An estimate of their population made on the basis of the 1921 figures indicated their population to be 131,300. Thus the population of these 32 castes was 1,442,009.[90] The 1931 Census Commissioner, however, retained only 10 of the 12 major castes (except Od and Ramdasis) in his list of exterior castes.[91]

In reply to the questionnaire issued by the Indian Franchise Committee in 1931, the Punjab Government in their Memorandum reported that they considered that the tribes to be regarded as untouchables should be those selected under the orders of the Census Commissioner, namely, the 12 castes including the Ad-Dharmis included in the Provincial Census Superintendent's report in 1931, mentioned earlier, accounting for a population of 1,310,709.[92]

The Provincial Franchise Committee could not arrive at any agreed estimate. In their final report, the majority of the provincial Committee was of the opinion that only Chamar and Chuhra could be regarded in the province as in any sense untouchable. The Committee was unable to give even an estimate of the number of the depressed classes. A minority of two members accepted the estimate given by the Government.[93]

In view of this disagreement in the estimates of the Depressed Classes and their population, the Lothian Committee also could not furnish any figure of Depressed Classes population and recommended that "a further investigation should be made with the help of the list of castes given in 1911, and that a final list should be drawn up of the castes which satisfy the test indicated above."[94]

The dissenting members of the Lothian Committee pointed out that the local Government's estimate of the depressed classes population included Ramdasis, who were Sikhs, and Ad-Dharmis, who themselves urged not to be considered as Hindus. As the enquiry was confined to untouchables in the Hindu Community, the dissenting members questioned the justiciability of including those who were non-Hindus and gave their estimate of Depressed Classes population at 1 million.[95]

The distinction between clean and unclean castes was much less rigid in Punjab than in other parts of India, probably as a result of Muhammadan and Sikh influences. Even then, when the "Schedule of Castes" was drawn up for the province of Punjab in 1936, the list included 30 castes, all of which except 3 figured in the 1931 Census Superintendent's list of depressed classes.

Annexure Table VIII will indicate the position accorded to the castes by different bodies during the period 1911-1936. It will appear from the Table that these castes were mentioned for the first time in the following reports:

19 In the 1911 Census
(Barar, Bawaria, Bhanjra, Chamar, Chanal, Chuhra, Dagi and Koli, Dhanak, Dhumna, Gagra, Gandhila, Khatik, Kori, Megha, Pasi, Sansi, Sarera and Sapela)

3 In Sharp's report
(Marecha, Od and Ramdasi)

6 In the 1931 Census
(Ad-Dharmi, Bazigar, Bengali, Nat, Perna and Sirkiband)

2 In the 1936 list
(Balmiki and Marija)

Total 30

Annexure Table VIII reveals that

(A) Of the 24 castes classed in categories 7 and 8 in the 1911 Census, 19 were included in the 1936 Order, 2 (Batwal and Mazhbi) in the 1950 Order and the rest 3 (Gedri, Jaiswara and Mochi) did not find place in any list.

Only 2 of them (Chamar and Chuhra) were all along considered depressed/untouchable by all the bodies.

(B) Of the 6 new castes included in his list of depressed classes by Sharp in 1917, 3 (Dhobi, Ghosi and Mahtam) were not treated as depressed by any other body and did not figure in the Scheduled Castes lists. The remaining 3 (Marecha, Od and Ramdasi) were included in the list of depressed classes by the Census Superintendent in 1931 but the Census Commissioner did not concur with his classification and specifically omitted Od and Ramdasi from his list and did not mention Marecha, that being a minor caste. But all these three ultimately found place in the 1936 list.

(C) Of the 32 castes (12 major and 20 minor) treated as depressed by the Census Superintendent in 1931, all the 12 major castes were included in the 1936 list. Among the 20 minor castes, 15 were included in the 1936 list, 1 (Mazhbi) in the 1950 list and the remaining 4 (Gedri, Daoli (Doala), Kehal and Rihar) did not figure in any list.

(D) The rigidity of untouchability was so much less in Punjab that the different bodies and agencies considered it difficult to classify those who were untouchables. Successive reports, however, veered round to the fact that Chamar and Chuhra, the two most populous castes among the Depressed Classes, could at best be considered depressed and in 1928 the Government also listed them in the untouchable category. After the Lothian Committee defined the term 'depressed' in no uncertain term, it devolved on the Government to classify only those castes which answered those tests. The Government simply adhered to the list of depressed classes of the Provincial Census Superintendent. It may be mentioned that as many as 20 of them were not even put in the list of Depressed Classes by the Provincial Census Superintendent himself. He only mentioned them in a footnote and estimated their population on the basis of the 1921 Census because their population was not extracted by him in 1931.

In 1911 it was rather difficult to classify the real untouchables and in 1917 no untouchable caste could be identified because the idea of pollution was rapidly dying out and in 1928 only two castes could be listed as untouchables, but within 7 years the position changed so perceptibly that 30 castes could be put in the "Schedule of Castes" in 1936. The provincial Census Superintendent's list of 32 castes was relied upon for drawing up the Schedule without taking into consideration the fact that the Census Superintendent, while preparing his list, did not adhere to the Lothian Committee's definition of untouchability, thus giving a decent burial to the recommendation of the Lothian Committee.

Central Provinces and Berar

J.T. Marten as Census Superintendent of the Central Provinces and Berar in 1911 identified the castes and tribes satisfying the tests mentioned by the Census Commissioner. He could enumerate as many as 43 communities falling into one or more of the 10 categories. Of them, Banjara, Baiga, Bhaina, Bhil, Bhuinhar, Binjhwar, Bharia,

Chadar, Dhanwar, Gond, Gowari, Halba, Karwa, Kol, Korku, Nagasia, Oroan and Barwara were tribes.[96] The total population of these 43 communities which included Hindus, Animists and Musalmans living in the entire Province including the Feudatory States was 7,790,530.

Of them, only 13 castes satisfied both the tests of untouchability, i.e., fell in categories 7 and 8 and their total population for the entire Central Provinces and Berar was 3,060,232 and of the Hindus in the British territory was 2,705,214.[97]

The Government list of Depressed Classes, i.e., untouchables, prepared in 1917 also mentioned the same 13 castes and the same population[98] as was enumerated for the entire Province.

Sharp in his Quinquennial Review for 1912-17 listed 14 castes as depressed — the 13 castes identified by the Government as depressed and 1 more, i.e., Mahar and gave a figure which was less than those for the 13 castes even — 3,012,289 for the 14 castes as against 3,060,232 for the 13 castes.[99] Since he did not furnish the caste-wise break-up of the population, and since the population of Mahars was not extracted in the 1911 Census, it is difficult to say how he arrived at that figure. If the population of the Feudatory States was omitted, the figure would come to only 2,705,214, excluding Mahars.

The 1919 Franchise Committee included in the group 'Others' all those who were denied access to a Hindu temple vide p. 73, Part I, Central Provinces Census Report, 1911 and also mentioned a figure — 3,769,338 in its report.[100] This, incidentally, is the population figure of 26 castes/tribes which fell in category 7 (denial of access to temple), according to the 1911 Census.

Unlike many other provincial Census Reports, the 1921 Central Provinces and Berar Census Report made a specific mention of the castes which were untouchables and also gave their population figure. It identified 14 castes as untouchables. The list deviated marginally from the 1917 Government list of Depressed Classes. Only 1 caste —

Ghasia — was omitted and 2 new ones — Mala and Madgi — were added. The total population of the 14 untouchable castes including the Animists for the whole of the Central Provinces and Berar was 2,965,859.[101]

The 1921 Census Commissioner, however, modified the Census Superintendent's figure and increased it to 3,300,000 in his report[102] without indicating the castes considered depressed by him.

The Government list of untouchables prepared in 1928, however, did not follow the 1921 Census list of untouchables and, as was done in case of other provinces, adhered to the previous list of 1917 without any change.[103]

The Hartog Committee followed the 1928 Government list of untouchables and indicated a figure — 3.01 million as the population of the depressed classes,[104] which compared to the 1921 Census Superintendent's figures appeared to be on the higher side by 0.02 million.

The Indian Central Committee in 1929 estimated the depressed classes population as 2.67 million.[105] It is one of those very rare occasions when the Indian Central Committee's estimate was less than that of the Hartog Committee. In the absence of the list of castes considered depressed by the Indian Central Committee, it would be an exercise in futility to find out which castes were actually treated as depressed by it.

The Indian Statutory Commission's estimate of the depressed classes population in 1930 of 3.3 million[106] was exactly the same as was estimated by the Census Commissioner in 1921. Like the Census Commissioner, the Statutory Commission also did not specify the castes considered depressed by it.

Before the finalisation of the 1931 Census Report the definition of the "depressed classes" finally settled by the Indian Franchise Committee was known to the Provincial Census Superintendent. He, therefore, requested the Deputy Commissioners to include in the returns for their districts only those who were regarded as 'untouchable' in the sense indicated by the Indian Franchise Committee. The Census Superintendent divided the depressed classes broadly in two categories— (1) those regarded as untouchable throughout the British districts of the province, and (2) those, although not universally regarded as untouchable, were treated as unclean in certain divisions or even in certain districts of a division and the statistics were abstracted according to the areas in which a caste was reported to be untouchable.[107] The Provincial Census Superintendent identified 41 castes including 3 castes grouped with another (Burud with Basor, Mahar with Mehra and Bhangi with Mehtar). Of them as many as 29 were treated as untouchable only in some parts of the province, might be even in a district or Tehsil of a district. These have been marked with asterisk in Annexure Table IX. (Wherever a caste is asterisked, the implication is that in some parts of the province it was treated as depressed and in other parts it was not treated as such). The Census Superintendent gave the figure of 3,180,075 as the total of the depressed classes in the Central Provinces and Berar, both in Chapter XII of his report and in Provincial Table II and in Appendix II to his report. But when the population figure of each caste was added it gave a figure of 3,071,078 which included the States' number of 252,732, the remaining 2,818,346 being in the British territory.

The 1931 Census Commissioner did not interfere with the list of untouchables prepared by the Census Superintendent. He only effected some alterations in the total figure. As the provincial figure included those returning tribal religions as well, the Census Commissioner took as the total of the Exterior Castes (Depressed Classes) the sum of those returned as Hindu by religion and made a corresponding change in the caste-wise figure, the total of which came to 3,071,078. The distribution of this depressed population between the British districts and the States of the province was 2,818,346 and 252,732 respectively.[108]

Like the earlier Censuses, the 1931 Census also witnessed the determined attempts on the part of the

Sudras to obtain equality with the higher castes, to gain a share of their privileges, and in many cases, to claim descent from the twice-born, specially from the Brahman and the Kshattriya. The claim for higher status or to have their communities recorded under fresh names was, however, more pronounced in the 1931 Census than the earlier ones. Thus, in the 1931 Census, Nai, Bhat, Panchal, Vidurs or Krishnapakshi and Joshi claimed to be classified as Nai or Kulin Brahman, Brahm Bhat Brahman, Vishwa Brahman, Parashar Brahman and Jyotishi Brahman respectively: Kalar, Kurmi, Jaiswara, Lunia, Khangar, Kunbi, Mali, Teli, Bonari-Kunbi and Gadhewal wanted to return themselves as Haihaya Kshattriya, Kurmi Kshattriya, Jaiswara Kshattriya, Lunia Kshattriya, Khangar Kshattriya, Kshattriya Maratha, Kshattriya Mali, Kshattriya Teli, Lonari Kshattriya, and Gadhewal Kshattriya respectively and even Gond claimed to be classified as Raj Gond Kshattriya Surajwansi and Kalal preferred the claim to be treated as Shivhara Vaisya. Several castes which had hitherto classified as lower castes or untouchables claimed Rajput origin. Lodhi, Katia and Chippa claimed to be classified as Lodhi Rajput, Renhia Rajput and Rajput Chippa respectively. Mahars wanted to call themselves as Kshattriya Mahar or Kashyap Rajput while Dhimars claimed to be returned as Renkwar Rajput or Kashyap Rajput. Claims to new names were preferred by Rathor — Teli, Burud, Pardhan and Chamar who asked to be returned as Rathor, Lingayat Burud, Gond and Satnami respectively. The intention of some of the applications was to avoid an alleged stigma from incorrect identification with castes of similar names in other districts.[109] These claims, however, had no impact on the classification of the castes by the Census authority, specially those listed as untouchables or depressed.

The census classification of the depressed classes which was 'the result of correspondence with district authorities and investigations extending over a period of 18 months', was relied upon by the Central Provinces Government in its reply sent to the Indian Franchise Committee on February 26, 1932 regarding the Depressed

Classes. The provincial Government also submitted a 'complete list of the depressed classes' whose total number was 2,965,490.[110] This was the same list which was drawn up by the 1931 Census Superintendent with only a minor change-Dhimar was omitted and Kanjar was added instead. There was a slight variation in the total population as well. The Provincial Franchise Committee did not raise any objection to the provincial Government's estimate of the depressed classes and their number. The Indian Frnachise Committee also accepted the provincial Government's estimate because the tests applied were the same as those accepted by it.[111]

The dissenting members of the Indian Franchise Committee did not agree that the classes which were listed as untouchables, not throughout the whole province but in certain districts, should be treated in those districts as belonging to depressed classes, because 'this is unsound in principle and unsafe in practice'. They, therefore, thought that classes which were listed as untouchable in only a part of a province should not be treated as such for electoral purposes.[112] But their estimate of the depressed classes population was the same as was given by the provincial Government.[113]

The Scheduled Castes Order of 1936 more or less followed the Census classification of 1931. Only two castes — Balai and Koli — were added to the 1931 Census list. So altogether 43 castes figured in the 1936 Order. Of them, 33 were considered scheduled in a part of the province only as against 29 in the 1931 Census. This change was due to the fact that Koli and Balai, the newly added, were untouchable in only a part of the province and Mahar and Mehra, which were shown in the 1931 Census as untouchable throughout the province were actually touchable in two tehsils of Hosangabad district and untouchable in the rest of the province. This mistake was rectified in the 1936 Order.

In the listing of untouchables/depressed classes a distinct pattern is discernible. From 1917 to 1928, the number of untouchable castes/depressed classes varied between 13 and 26. The Franchise Committee's list included as many as 12 tribes (Baiga, Banjara, Bhaina, Bharia, Bhil, Bhuinhar, Binjwar, Dhanwar, Korku, Korwa, Nagasia and Oroan), which did not figure in any other list or even in the Scheduled Castes lists. 9 of them (except Banjara, Bharia and Bhuinhar) were, however, included in the Scheduled Tribes list of 1950. So actually the number ranged between 13 and 14. But the number jumped up to 41 in the 1931 Census which claimed to have classified the untouchables strictly according to the twin criteria of untouchability adopted by the Lothian Committee and to 43 in the 1936 Order. Of these 43, 8 (Chauhan, Dhimar, Jangam, Kaikari, Mala, Nagarchi, Ojha and Panka) were excluded from the Scheduled Castes list since 1950 and another Pardhan was shifted to the Scheduled Tribes list in 1950.

Annexure Table IX will indicate the position accorded to different castes by the various bodies since 1911. It will appear from the said Table that the 43 castes listed in the 1936 Order were mentioned for the first time in the reports as follows.

16	In the 1911 Census (Balahi, Basor, Chadar, Chamar, Dhobi, Ganda, Ghasia, Katia, Koli, Kori, Kumhar, Mang, Mehra, Mehtar, Panka, and Pardhan)
1	In the Quinquennial report of Sharp (Mahar)
2	In the 1921 Census (Madgi, Mala)
23	In the 1931 Census (Audhelia, Bahna, Bedar, Bhangi, Burud, Chauhan, Dahayat, Dhanuk, Dewar, Dhimar, Dohor, Dom, Holiya, Jangam, Kaikari, Khangar, Khatik, Mochi, Nagarchi, Ojha, Pardhi, Rajjhar and Satnami)
1	In the 1936 Order (Balai)
Total 43	

Annexure Table IX reveals that

(A) Of the 16 castes enlisted from the 1911 Census, all except 3 (Chadar, Koli and Pardhan) fell in categories 7 and 8 in the 1911 Census and were all along considered as depressed/untouchables/scheduled. From them only Panka was descheduled in 1950.

Chadar was identified in the 1911 Census for being denied entry in Hindu temples and for burying their dead, Koli for burying their dead while Pardhans for burying their dead as well as for not revering the cow. Of them, only Pardhan was shifted to the Scheduled Tribes list in 1950.

(B) Of the remaining 27 castes in the 1911 list, Beldar, which was classified for burying their dead was included in the 1956 order, 15 castes were included in the Scheduled Tribes list (Baiga, Bhaina, Bhil, Binjwar, Dhanwar, Gond, Halba, Kawar, Kol. Kolam, Korku, Korwa, Nagasia, Oroan and Sawara) and the remaining 11 did not find place in any list. Of these 11, Bhoyar, Dhanagar, Gowari, Koshti, Mana, Rujwar, Rangari and Wanjari were classified for indulging in the practice of burying the dead and the other 3 (Banjara, Bharia and Bhuinhar) though tribes, had the same characteristics.

(C) All the castes considered depressed/untouchable by the Government in 1917 and in 1928 and by Sharp in 1917 were retained in the 1936 list.

(D) Similarly, all the 26 castes of the 1919 Franchise Committee's list, except 12 which were tribes, were included in the 1936 list.

(E) All the 14 castes considered untouchable by the 1921 Census Superintendent were included in the 1936 list. But those 2 which were included for the first time in the 1921 Census were descheduled-Mala in 1950 and Madgi in 1956.

(F) All the 41 castes considered untouchable, even in parts of the Province, in the 1931 Census were included in the 1936 Order. Of the 22 which were considered untouchable for the first time in the 1931 Census, 6 (Chauhan, Dhimar, Jangam, Kaikari, Nagarchi and Ojha) were descheduled in 1950.

(G) The 1931 Census classification on which the Scheduled Castes Order of 1936 was based became a role model for the rest of India. The classification of castes according to the areas in which a caste was reported to be untouchable resulted in abstraction of statistics for an area even as small as a sub-division. The apprehensions of the dissenting members of the Indian Franchise Committee, though expressed in a different context, that 'this would be unsound in principle and unsafe in practice' came to be true. It was not possible to exclude such persons of that very class in another district from the list of 'Scheduled Castes' for long. By 1976, the division of such persons on the basis of area was largely done away with in most of the States.

The reason for this classification, even for a small area, as given out by the Census Superintendent, was that "the castes concerned are strong in the districts where they are treated as impure, while their numbers are comparatively small and they are little known in other districts."[114] But one fails to understand how castes having as small a population as 3,6,12 or 41 could be strong in a district. Dhanuk, considered Scheduled Caste in Sugar district except in the Damoah subdivision thereof, returned a population of only 3; Bahna considered Scheduled Caste in Amraoti district accounted for a population of only 6; Jangam which was treated as Scheduled Caste in only Bhandara district had a population of 12; Pardhi, a Scheduled Caste only for Narsinghpur sub-division of Hoshangabad district accounted for a population of 41. If they could be regarded as pure when they moved into other parts of the country, how is it that such a small number of persons could be considered as 'strong' and therefore, 'untouchable' in only a district or even a part of a district?

The Census authority was so much keen to reflect the 'fact' of untouchability in its report that it identified as many as 9 castes in one district or part thereof and another 5 in only 2/3 districts or part thereof, but the same consideration was not shown to the claims of certain castes like Dhimar, Katia, Khangar or Mahar to the higher status of Kshattriya or Rajput or to the fact that the untouchability of Khangars was 'slowly lessening in degree',[115] that the Mahars having 'made greatest advance socially and economically' would have 'broken the age-long bonds of servility and untouchability' 'before the year 1941 has passed',[116] or that 'a Brahman of the highest section would not hesitate in taking water from the hand of a Dhimar'.[117] The Census authority, no doubt, followed the twin criteria of untouchability while enumerating the 'Untouchables', later known as 'Scheduled Castes', but it is debatable how much of it was followed in letter and how much in spirit.

Bombay

The 1911 Census Superintendent, in accordance with the instructions of the Census Commissioner, identified as many as 28 castes which satisfied one or more of the 10 tests. Their total population for the whole of Bombay province including Bombay States was 6,371,318. This list included 13 communities which fell in category 1, i.e., those denied supremacy of the Brahman. The Census Superintendent noted that those who denied supremacy of the Brahman were on the borders of Hinduism and Animism.[118]

In the Bombay province there was no caste which caused pollution within a certain distance but the touch of 7 castes was unclean and none of these castes were allowed within the interior of the ordinary Hindu temples. Their total population was 2,145,256 for the whole of Bombay and 1,481,840 for the British territory only.[119]

The Bombay Government's list of Depressed Classes., i.e., untouchables, prepared in 1917, mentioned 14 castes, but in the list Mahar, Holiya and Dhed were put in one group, Chambhar, Chamar or Mochi in another group and Mang and Madig in one group. The remaining 6 were, however, mentioned singly. The total population of

1,635,896 for these 14 castes[120] was for British territory only.[121] All the 7 castes falling in categories 7 and 8(a) in the 1911 Census were included in this Government list.

Sharp also mentioned the same 14 castes and the identical population in his Quinquennial Review for 1912-17.[122]

The Franchise Committee in 1919 included in the group 'Others' those castes 'which are ordinarily denied access to a Hindu temple' and a reference was given to page 66, Part I, of the Bombay Census Report, 1911. It refrained from mentioning the individual castes but gave their total population as 577,216.[123] It is difficult to state which of the 7 castes identified during the 1911 Census for being denied access to the interior of the ordinary Hindu temples the Committee had actually in mind, because the total population of these 7 castes for the British territory only was 1,481,840 and for the whole of Bombay province 2,145,198, according to the 1911 Census, mentioned earlier.

The 1921 Census Superintendent did not identify the depressed classes, but the Census Commissioner furnished a figure of 2.8 millions for the Depressed Classes population[124] but the castes accounting for this population were not mentioned.

The 1928 Government list of untouchables included the same 14 castes[125] identified as depressed in 1917 and the Hartog Committee, which accepted this list of untouchables, gave a population of 1.46 millions.[126] This population was based on the 1921 Census and was limited to British territory only.[127]

The provincial Government furnished both the Indian Central Committee and the Indian Statutory Commission with relevant data concerning depressed classes and their population. The India Central Committee accepted the depressed classes population of 1.48 millions[128] and the Indian Statutory Commission estimated the depressed classes population to be 1.50 millions.[129] Both these estimates exceeded the Hartog Committee's estimates, though marginally. In the absence of caste-wise break-up of these population, it is difficult to say which castes were actually included in these two reports.

The 1931 Census Superintendent separated the Hindu community into 5 divisions and the population was arranged by these divisions :—

(1) Hindu — Advanced,
(2) Hindu — Immediate,
(3) Hindu — Primitive,
(4) Hindu — Other Backward, and
(5) Hindu — Depressed.

In Appendix F of Part I of the Report, details of the castes/tribes along with their areas of habitation, traditional or habitual occupation of each of these five divisions were given.

So far as the Depressed Classes were concerned, it may be pointed out that the Government of Bombay had appointed a committee, known as Starte Committee, specially for the purpose of identifying the units to be treated as depressed. The recommendations of this committee formed the basis of identification of the depressed classes by the provincial Census Superintendent and therefore, he thought that there was every reason to believe that the census list was exhaustive.[130] As many as 39 castes were mentioned as depressed, but in some cases, more than one caste or sub-caste had been put in one group. For instance, Chambhar, Mochi, Mochigar and Sochi were placed in one group and their population was extracted together. Mahar, Holiya, Dhed and Wankar were put in the same group and their population was abstracted accordingly. Similarly, Kolcha was clubbed with Kolgha, Madig with Mang, Maghval with Menghwar, Halalkhor with Bhangi, Chuhar with Chuhra, Kotwal with Kotwalia, Shenva with Shindhava and Halsar with Haslar and their population was shown under the respective group. The total population of the depressed classes was estimated at 1.750,424.[131]

Though the Depressed Classes list was based on the recommendations of the Starte Committee and accordingly mentioned in Appendix F, population of 11 of them was, however, not extracted individually but was tabulated under the omnibus group 'Others'.

The 1931 Census Commissioner also accepted the Census Superintendent's list of Depressed Classes as well as their population figure without raising any question. But the Census Commissioner did not specifically mention about those 11 castes whose population had not been extracted individually by the Census Superintendent but put in the group 'Others'.[132]

The listing of the Depressed Classes according to the Starte Committee's report and their enumeration by the Census authority in 1931 were accepted by the Provincial Franchise Committee, the Provincial Government and also by the Indian Franchise Committee in 1932. The Provincial Franchise Committee informed the Indian Franchise Committee that the term 'depressed classes' should be confined to the untouchable classes as shown in Schedule I of Appendix II of the Starte Committee's report.[133] The Provincial Government also concurred with the Provincial Franchise Committee that the expression "Depressed Classes" should be interpreted to mean the untouchable classes only. This definition, it was informed, had also been accepted by Dr. Ambedkar and many other representatives of the Depressed Classes and had also been recommended by the Depressed Classes and Aboriginal Tribes Committees appointed by the local Government. They also intimated the Indian Franchise Committee that the population of the Depressed Classes (untouchables) was 1,750,424.[134]

The India Franchise Committee observed that the estimates of the Bombay Government were based on the investigations of a Committee of Officials and non-Officials appointed by that Government in 1930 to report on various economic and social problems affecting the depressed classes in that Presidency. They, therefore, accepted the Provincial Government's figure of depressed classes without any hesitation.[135] The supposed pit-fall in the wholesale acceptance of this list of Depressed Classes without any verification was, however, pointed out by the dissenting members of the Indian Franchise Committee. They stated that the Starte Committee was appointed by the Bombay Government long before the Indian Franchise Committee had defined the term 'depressed classes' to investigate and report on certain matters concerning what they called the depressed classes. The figures furnished by the Government of Bombay had not been examined in the light of the Indian Franchise Committee's definition of the term, but their correctness had not been questioned.[136] They, nevertheless, accepted the depressed classes population figure for the province as furnished by the Bombay Government.[137] It may be pointed out that there is a small discrepancy in the Census figure and the Bombay Government figure. The Census furnished a figure of 1,750,424, whereas the Bombay Government's figure was 1.70 millions. Thus there was a discrepancy of 50,424. It is, however, not known whether this was the result of rounding up to a million.

Since the Census list of depressed classes was exhaustive, being based on the recommendations of the Starte Committee report, and since the same was accepted by the Lothian Committee, inspite of the fact that the same was not drawn up following the twin criteria of untouchability fixed by it, there should have been no difficulty in preparing the 'Schedule of Castes' for the purposes of the 1935 Act.

But when the Scheduled Castes Order of 1936 was issued, it deviated from the 1931 Census list substantially. Out of the 39 castes specified in the 1931 Census, as many as 7 castes (Ager, Halalkhor, Kotwal, Kotwalia, Holiya, Wankar and Wansfoda) were excluded and 15 new castes, (Asodi, Bakad, Chakrawadya-Dasar, Daka-leru, Dhegu-Meghu, Halleer, Holaya, Kotegar, Lingadar, Mini-Madig, Nadia, Samagar, Shinghdav, Shingadya and Vankar) were added to take the total to 47. Grouping of castes which was a peculiar phenomenon in this province continued. As many as 9 castes were grouped with others (Chuhar with Chuhra, Mochigar and Samagar with Chambhar, Halsar with Haslar, Kolcha with Kolgha, Madig with Mang, Maghval with Menghwar, Shenva with Shindhava and Shinghdav with Shingadya).

Of the 47 castes included in the 1936 list, 12 were descheduled in 1956 (Charawadya-Dasar, Chena Dasaru, Chuhar, Chuhra, Daka-leru, Garode, Kotegar, Shindhaya,- Shingdav, Shingadya, Sochi and Timali) and 3 were shifted to the Scheduled Tribes lists- Koli-Dhor in 1950 and Kolcha and Kolgha in 1956. Of the castes not included in the 1936 list even though figured in the 1931 Census list of depressed classes, 3 were inducted in the Scheduled Castes lists subsequently-Ager in 1950 and Halalkhor and Holiya in 1956 and another (Kotwalia) in the 1956 Scheduled Tribes list.

Annexure Table X depicts the position accorded to different castes by the various bodies since 1911. It will appear therefrom that the 47 castes included in the 1936 Scheduled Castes Order were mentioned for the first time in the following report :

5 In the 1911 Census
(Bhangi, Dhed, Mahar, Mang and Mochi)

7 In the 1917 Government list
(Chambhar, Dhor, Khalpa, Kolgha, Madig, Shindhava and Turi)

20 In the 1931 Census
(Bhambi, Chalvadi, Chena-Dasaru, Chuhar, Chuhra, Garode, Halsar, Haslar, Hulsavar, Kolcha, Koli-Dhor, Maghval, Menghwar, Mang Garudi, Mochigar, Mukri, Shenva, Sochi, Timali and Vitholia)

15 In the 1936 Order
(Asodi, Bakad, Chadrawadya-Dasar, Dhaka-leru, Dhegu-Megu, Halleer, Holaya, Kotegar, Lingader, Mini-Madig, Nadia, Samagar, Shingdav, Shingadya and Vankar).

47

It will appear from Annexure Table X that :

(A) In the 1911 Census 28 castes were identified for meeting any one of the 10 tests. They are broadly of the following categories :—

Category 1	13
Category 5	3
Categories 7-8	7
Category 9	3
Category 10	2
	28

Those coming under category 1, i.e., denied supremacy of the Brahmin, were on the borders of Hinduism and Animism. 8 (Bhil, Chodhva, Dhodia, Dubla, Katkari, Naikda, Thakur and Varli) of them were later included in the Scheduled Tribes list in 1950 and the remaining 5, as also all those belonging to categories 5, 9 and 10 did not find place in any list.

As regards the 7 castes which fell in categories 7 and 8, in the 1911 Census, all of them were all along considered depressed/untouchable but two of them — Chamar and Holiya — did not figure in the 1936 list. This omission was rectified in the 1956 Order.

(B) All the 14 castes classed as depressed/untouchable by the Government in 1917 and 1928 and by Sharp in 1917 were included in the 1936 Order except two — Holiya and Chamar — who were later included in 1956.

(C) Of the 39 castes considered depressed in the 1931 Census, as many as 36 were included either in the Scheduled Castes lists or in the Scheduled Tribes lists. Only 3 (Kotwal, Wankar and Wansfoda) did not figure in any list. In 1956, 7 castes included in the Scheduled Castes list were descheduled.

(D) 15 new castes landed in the 1936 Order even though not mentioned as depressed/untouchable by any body earlier. Of them, 5 were descheduled in 1956.

(E) A large number of castes — 12 — were descheduled

in 1956. Of them, 7 (Chena Dasaru, Chuhar, Chuhra, Garode, Shindhaya, Sochi and Tamil) were in the 1931 Census list of depressed classes and 5 (Chakrawadaya Dasar, Dakaleru, Kotegar, Shingdav and Shingdaya) were included for the first time in the 1936 Order.

(F) The grouping of castes and sub-castes, which started in the Bombay province in 1917, became, in course of time, especially since 1950, an all-India phenomenon, though more marked in Western and South-Western India.

(G) Another trend which was emulated by the other States in independent India, was the inclusion of a large number of castes/sub-castes in the Schedule by the Government themselves, even though none of the earlier committees including the official bodies and the Census authority did recommend for conferring such status on them. The assumption of such wide power by the Government made them the real "Ballal Sens" in modern India.

Madras

It is the popular belief that there was little dispute about who were the untouchables in the South. Annexure Table XI however, depicts another picture.

Madras was the second province, the other being the United Provinces, which failed to classify the castes according to the 10-point test formulated by the 1911 Census Commissioner. During the 1911 Census, the Census Superintendent, J. Chartres Molony, did not draw up the list of castes satisfying those tests, including the two tests which became important later because of their adoption by the Lothian Committee as the criteria for determining the Depressed Classes, viz., denial of access to Hindu temples and causing pollution by touch or proximity, because he thought that "right of entrance to a temple or shrine is in no wise an essential of Hinduism. Such right is not conceded to the Shanan, who claims to be a Kshatriya and whose Hinduism no one disputes; nor in certain cases will it be allowed to the Brahman, as such, should he lack the ordinations or consecrations requisite for the practical or better, ritualistic observances of religion." And "similarly may these other tests be tried and found wanting. A Brahman does not, it is true, receive water from the hands of a Paraiyan, but neither will he drink from the hands of a Sudra. Sudra again does not invariably drink with Sudra, nor Brahman with Brahman. Pollution caused by touch or proximity has been publicly rejected, in theory, as an essential of religion by sundry eminent Hindus; in fact, by many more, not less pious if less vocal, in the daily practice of the railway."[138]

The Government list of Depressed Classes, i.e., untouchables, prepared in 1917 had 17 castes with a total population of 6,484,776.[139] But Sharp's list prepared more or less at the same time retained only 5 of them accounting for a population of 5,686,342.[140] Sharp relied on the 1911 Census figures for the whole of the province, whereas the figures in the Government list related to the British Territory only.[141] This was the reason for the anomaly that had crept in these two population figures.

Since the 1911 Census did not classify the castes according to the 10-point tests, the Franchise Committee in 1919 could not draw on that classification. It identified 7 castes which included all the main Panchama or untouchable castes, for instance, the Paraiyans, Pallans and Valluvans in the Tamil districts, the Malas and Madigas in the Telugu districts, the Cherumans of Malabar and Holeyas of South Canara. This list included all the 5 castes of Sharp's list and 2 more (Cheruman and Valluvan). The population figure of 6,377,168 given in the report[142] exceeded the population figure of 6,004,230, abstracted for these castes for the entire province in the 1911 Census.[143]

But neither the list of untouchables prepared by the Government in 1917 nor the identification of the castes by the Franchise Committee in 1919 put to rest all doubts regarding the depressed classes. As a matter of fact, even the provincial Government was not sure as to who they were. In 1920, the Madras Government enacted the Madras Local Boards Act, 1920 (Madras Act XIV of 1920) which defined the term "Adi-Dravida" in clause (1) of Section 3 as "any person professing the Hindu religion and belonging to any of the following communities, namely, the Paraiyans, Pallans, Valluvans, Malas, Madigas, Chakkiliyans, Tottiyans, Cherumans and Holeyas or to any other community that may be prescribed". These 9 castes together with the Adi-Dravidas were considered to be depressed. These 10 castes included all the 7 castes mentioned by the Franchise Committee and only 8 castes from the 1917 Government list. 2 new castes (Adi-Dravida and Tottiyan) were added to the list of depressed classes for the first time. So within 3 years the provincial Government changed its view on the castes to be considered depressed and excluded as many as 9 castes from its own list.

But the identification of these 10 castes as depressed in a statute by the provincial Government did not mean that other governmental agencies would accept the list as final. Within a year of its enactment, the 1921 Census was conducted. The Provincial Census Superintendent specified 9 castes as depressed but he did not include in his list all the 10 castes mentioned in the Madras Local Boards Act, 1920. He omitted 2 (Valluvan and Tottiyan) and included a new one-Semman. The population of these 10 depressed classes was estimated by him to be 6,372,074.[144] Since the Census Commissioner also furnished the same population figure in his report[145] it is presumed that he also concurred with the Census Superintendent's classification of depressed classes.

Again in 1928, a list of untouchables was prepared by the Government. This list mentioned 16 castes. It retained all the 17 castes of the 1917 list except one-Chuckler.[146] So there was not much difference between these two untouchables lists prepared by the Government. Only one caste, Chuckler, was dropped in 1928. Chuckler, however, did not figure in any other report since 1917. This list did not encompass all those included in the 1920 statute or in the 1921 Census. Three castes-Tottiyan (mentioned in the statute), Adi-Dravida (mentioned in the statute as well as in the 1921 Census) and Semman (mentioned in the 1921 Census) did not find place in the Government list of untouchables. One fails to comprehend how there could be so much divergence in these four reports — the two Government lists of untouchables on the one hand and the list in the 1921 Census as well as in the 1920 Statute on the other.

The Hartog Committee in 1929 followed the list of untouchables prepared in 1928 and the population extracted was 6,529,560[147] which was naturally above the 1921 Census figure of 6.37 millions because the 1921 Census was limited to only 9 castes whereas the Hartog Committee dealt with 16 castes.

The Indian Central Committee in 1929[148] and the Indian Statutory Commission in 1930[149] accepted the Government figure of Depressed Classes population, which was 6.5 millions, that is, the same as was estimated by the Hartog Committee.

So between 1917 and 1930, there were minor additions and alterations in the list of castes considered depressed — the upper limit was 17 and the lower limit was 5. But the position changed perceptibly with the brightening of prospect of the Depressed Classes being considered as a separate entity after the First Round Table Conference in November, 1930—January, 1931. The number of castes to be classed as depressed started increasing.

The Adi-Dravida group of castes increased to 31 by Government Notification No. 1541-L & M dated 7th May, 1931 issued under the Madras Local Boards Act, 1920 and the 1931 Census Superintendent listed 86 castes under the Depressed Classes, which included 12 castes which were considered both Depressed Classes as well as Primitive Tribes. These castes totaled 7,299,400, including 65,296 for Madras States.[150] In this list of 86 castes did not figure 2 (Kota and Chuckler) of the 1917 Government list and 1 (Tottiyan) of the 1920 Statute.

The Census Commissioner did not interfere with this provincial list of Depressed Classes. He estimated the same population which included 65,296 for Madras States other than Cochin and Travancore.[151]

In 1932, the Indian Franchise Committee was constituted to define the 'depressed classes' and estimate their population. The Government of Madras informed the Indian Franchise Committee on February 22, 1932, that the definition of the term Adi-Dravidas as given in clause 3(1) of the Madras Local Boards Act, 1920 would be suitable for the definition of the depressed as well: It also informed that under this section a supplementary list of communities had been notified by the Government in G.O. No. 1541 — L & M dated the 7th May, 1931. The Government proposed that a similar list should be issued in respect of the separate electorates for the Legislative Council. "This would cover all those known or hitherto regarded as 'untouchables' and the Government consider that only such communities should be included in the category of 'Depressed Classes' for special treatment".[152] The Madras Provincial Franchise Committee also agreed with this view of the local Government. The Committee informed the Indian Franchise Committee that "the definition of Adi-Dravida in the Local Boards Act as supplemented by the notification in G.O. No. 1541-L & M dated 7th May, 1931 sufficiently covers, in the opinion of the Committee, those who are the depressed classes. It covers all the sections and sub-sections of the untouchables".[153]

The Indian Franchise Committee observed that in Madras as also in Bombay and the Central Provinces, the distinction between the depressed classes and other classes of the Hindu community was clearly defined, and there was general agreement between the provincial Committee and the provincial Government in regard to the numbers and castes to be included. The Committee was also satisfied that the number for the province was not disputed by other communities in that province and the Census estimates of 1931 closely corresponded to the numbers given to it by these two bodies. In view of this unanimity and in view of the fact that the depressed classes in Madras had already been scheduled by notification under the Madras Local Boards Act of 1920 and as the Franchise Committee understood that there was no controversy in the province of Madras in regard to the official classification, it accepted the figure of 7.1 million as depressed classes population in the province given by the local government and the provincial Committee.[154]

The dissenting members of the Indian Franchise Committee pointed out that "the Madras Government had for purposes of their own local Act to define the term 'depressed classes' and the figures which they have given are not necessarily the total population of those who should form the depressed classes according to our definition."[155] But they also accepted the population of depressed classes in that province as given by the provincial Government and the provincial Committee.[156]

The Indian Franchise Committee, the Provincial Frachise Committee and the provincial Government, all were very emphatic that only the castes already scheduled under the 1920 Act should be considered depressed in the province. But the provincial Government and the Provincial Franchise Committee furnished a figure of 7.1 millions as the depressed classes population in the province and the Indian Franchise Committee accepted that figure whereas the total population of the 31 castes scheduled under the 1920 Act was 6,108,353, according to the 1931 Census and not 7.1 million, as projected. The acceptance of the population figure of 7.1 million implied that not only the 31 castes already scheduled but some more unspecified castes were also considered depressed. In any case, the number of castes should be more than 31 castes whose total population was 6.1 million and below 86 whose total population was 7.3 million.

When the Scheduled Castes Order of 1936 was issued it included all the 86 castes mentioned in the provincial Census Superintendent's list of Depressed Classes. Altogether 9 of them have since been transferred to the Scheduled Tribes List (Aranadan, Kattunayakan, Kudiya, Kuraman and Paniyan in 1950 and Koraga, Kurichchan and Malasar in 1956 and another Valmiki to the Scheduled Tribes List of Andhra Pradesh in 1956), 8 castes were descheduled (Battada, Dombo and Relli in 1950 and Hasla, Kadan, Kodalo, Kudubi and Painda in 1956) and another 12 were shifted to the Andhra Pradesh Scheduled Castes list in 1956 (Bariki, Bavuri, Byagari, Chachati, Dandasi, Ghasi, Godari, Haddi, Mala Dasu, Matangi, Paky and Pamidi).

An analysis of the 86 castes included in the Scheduled Castes list of 1936 indicates that these castes were mentioned for the first time as Depressed Classes as follows :

15 were first mentioned in the Government list of 1917
(Bavuri, Chakkiliyan, Cheruman, Dandasi, Haddi, Holeya, Koraga, Madari, Madiga, Mala, Nayadi, Pallan, Panchama, Paraiyan and Valluvan).

1 in the Madras Local Boards Act, 1920
(Adi-Dravida),

1 in the 1921 Census
(Semman),

15 in the 1931 Government Notification
(Baira, Bakuda, Bellara, Chalavadi, Godda, Kanakkan, Maila, Moger, Mundala, Nalakeyava, Pambada, Paravan, Raneyar, Relli and Vettuvan), and

54 in the 1931 Census
(Adi-Andhra, Adi-Karnataka, Ajila, Aranadan, Arunthuthiyar, Bandi, Bariki, Battada, Byagari, Chachati, Chamar, Chandala, Devendrakulathan, Dombo, Ghasi, Godagali, Godari, Gosangi, Hasla, Jaggali, Jambuvulu, Kalladi, Kadan, Karimpalan, Kattunayakan, Kodalo, Koosa, Kudiya, Kudubi, Kudumban, Kuravan, Kurichchan, Kuruman, Mala Dasu, Malasar, Matangi, Mavilan, Muchi, Pagadai, Paidi, Painda, Paky, Pamidi, Paniyan,

Panniandi, Pano, Pulayan, Puthirai Vanan, Samagara, Samban, Sapari, Thoti, Tiruvalluvar and Valmiki).

Total 86

As is evident from Annexure Table XI, Madras's contribution in the "Scheduling of Castes" is simply unique. The phrase `Depressed Classes' as Blunt says, found its way, probably from Madras, into the United Provinces[157] and elsewhere, about 1920.

Annexure Table XI reveals that :

(1) Madras refused to classify the castes according to the tests evolved by the 1911 Census Commissioner as the Census Superintendent considered that those were not 'essentials of Hinduism'. We are, therefore, denied of the opportunity of knowing which among these 86 castes scheduled in 1936 satisfied the twin tests of untouchability in 1911.

(2) Madras is the only province which listed certain castes in a Statute and also made provision in the same Statute to include "any other community that may be prescribed". The Statute made the Government sole arbiter in the matter of inclusion of any caste in the list. Vesting the Government with this sort of wide power in the matter of "Scheduling of Castes" became the trend-setter in India.

(3) The Government itself was not very sure as to who should be brought under this category. It classified 17 castes as Depressed i.e., untouchable, in 1917, but in the 1920 Act put only 10 castes in that category. Of these 10, 2 (Adi-Dravida and Tottiyan) were not in the Untouchables list of 1917. Again in the 1928 list of untouchables all the castes of the 1917 list except one were retained and these two new castes of the 1920 Act did not figure therein. In 1931, when the 1920 list was enlarged to accommodate 31 castes, the Government, curiously enough, did not think it fit to include 3 castes (Dandasi, Kota and Panchama) considered depressed by the Government since 1917.

(4) The 1931 Census Superintendent listed 54 new castes in the category of Depressed Classes. There is, however, nothing to indicate that he followed the Lothian Committee's definition of Depressed Classes while classifying the new ones or retaining the older ones.

(5) A large number of castes — 29 — returning a very insignificant population were included in the list of Depressed Classes in the 1931 Census and ultimately in the 1936 list of Scheduled Castes. For instance, 5 returned a population below 100 [Panniandi (54), Arandan (60), Puthirai Vanan (74), Bellara (87) and Painda (92)], 2 between 100 and 200 [Chamar (140) and Gadda (146)], 8 between 200 and 500 [Tiruvalluvar (207), Gosangi (244), Pambada (335), Hasla (368), Godari (419), Pamidi (424), Sapari (462) and Kadan (491)] and 14 returned a population between 500 and 1000 [Nayadi (520), Bandi (553), Samban (557), Battada(558), Matangi (623), Adi-Karnataka (644), Ajila (659), Pagadai (771), Moger (773), Bakuda (806), Koosa (818) Paravan (826), Kudumban (827) and Godagali (969)].

(6) The provincial Government in its memorandum to the Indian Franchise Committee in 1932 stated that the term 'Adi-Dravida' as given in the 1920 Act would be suitable for the definition of the depressed classes. It referred to the castes scheduled in the 1920 Act and stated that those were the depressed classes. The Indian Franchise Committee accepted that list without verifying whether those castes conformed to its own definition of depressed classes.

(7) The Indian Franchise Committee not only did not check up whether the castes listed in the schedule were the depressed classes according to its own definition of untouchability but it also accepted the population figure of 7.1 million without even bothering to check up which were the castes accounting for this population. As stated earlier, the 31 castes scheduled under the 1920 Act (population of 1—Tottiyan — was not extracted in the 1931 Census) accounted for a population of 6.1 million. The Indian Franchise Committee did not consider it necessary

to find out which were the castes making up this one million of population.

(8) Since the Lothian Committee itself did not bother to ensure that its own definition of Depressed Classes was honoured by the Provincial Government, the Provincial Government cannot perhaps be faulted if it did not ensure that only those castes answering the Lothian Committee's twin criteria of untouchability were included in the list of Depressed Classes. Even then, when the Lothian Committee settled the definition of 'Depressed Classes' once for all, it devolved on the Provincial Government to identify the castes satisfying this twin criteria of untouchability. Not only it did not take any step in that regard but, on the other hand, accepted the 54 new castes added to the list of Depressed Classes only in the 1931 Census, as if all of them satisfied the Lothian Committee's definition. So many castes, evidently, could not form the Depressed Classes, according to the definition of the Lothian Committee, specially when the Census Superintendent 25 years earlier found it difficult to identify castes satisfying these two tests of untouchability.

Methodology in Scheduling of Castes

In the classification of Scheduled Castes in 1936 certain trends which emanated mainly in the Southern Provinces of Bombay, Madras and the Central Provinces and Berar, became an all-India phenomena, specially in independent India.

(1) In the Central Provinces and Berar, castes were classified according to the areas in which a caste was reported to be untouchable. Once a caste was considered 'untouchable' and therefore, 'scheduled' for an area, even as small as a sub-division of only one district, it was not possible to exclude such persons of that very class in other areas from the list of 'Scheduled Castes' for long. In course of time these castes became scheduled in the entire State. This model was first experimented in the Central Provinces in the 1931 Census. In Assam classification of castes according to the areas in which a caste was

considered untouchable was also resorted to in the 1931 Census but there was a difference between these two provinces. In Assam it was confined to two valleys — Brahmaputra Valley and Surma Valley and the population was extracted accordingly. The Central Provinces model was followed in the 1936 Order not only in the Central Provinces but in Bihar, Orissa, U.P., Bombay and Madras, though the number of castes considered scheduled for a part of the Province was very insignificant in the Provinces of U.P. and Bombay, only 3. This model continued to be followed in independent India and reached its peak in the 1956 Order. Since 1976 almost all the castes considered scheduled for a part of the State were treated as scheduled for the entire State. There are only a few exceptions.

(2) In the Bombay Province, grouping of castes and sub-castes was first resorted to by the Government in 1917, which in course of time, specially since 1950, became an all-India phenomenon, though more marked in Western and South-Western India.

(3) Another trend which was emulated by other States in independent India was the inclusion of a large number of castes/sub-castes in the Schedule by the Governments themselves. This was followed by the Orissa and Bombay provincial Governments in 1936 when as many as 39 and 15 castes, respectively were added to the Scheduled Castes lists [New castes were also added to the Scheduled Castes list in 1936 in U.P. (6), Assam (3), Punjab (2) and Central Provinces (1)], even though none of the earlier Committees including the Census authority did consider them depressed/untouchable.

(4) Madras was the only province where certain castes were scheduled in an Act. Government was vested with the power of inclusion of any caste in the Schedule in future as well. Government became the sole authority in the matter of 'Scheduling of Castes'. This became a trend-setter in India.

(5) Bengal's contribution in the matter of 'Scheduling

TABLE I

Names of Province	Total No. of castes considered depressed/ untouchables during the period 1911-32	Total No. of castes included in the 1936 Scheduled Castes Order	Total No. of castes since shifted to the Scheduled Tribes lists from the 1936 list	Total No. of castes since descheduled from the 1936 list	Total No. of castes inclu-ded in the subsequent Scheduled Castes lists which were not included in the 1936 list	Total No. of castes not included in the 1936 list but included in the subsequent Scheduled Tribes lists Total No. of	castes never considered for inclusion in the Scheduled Castes lists or in the Scheduled Tribes lists
Assam	40	22	-	-	-	-	18
Bengal	108	77	15	9	2	3	26
Bihar	59	22	-	-	3	8	26
Orissa	98	62	2	1	5	8	23
U.P.	89	61	-	3	4	-	24
Punjab	41	30	-	-	2	-	9
C.P.	71	43	1	10	2	15	11
Bombay	78	47	3	12	6	9	16
Madras	89	86	9	7	-	1	2
Total	673	450	30	42	24	44	155

of Castes' was no less significant. Instead of following the criteria of 'untouchability' and 'unapproachability', the Government included in the 'Schedule' those castes whose 'social, political, economic and educational backwardness' was considered by the Government to be such as to merit their inclusion in the Schedule.

As we have seen, a large number of castes were identified by various bodies as depressed/untouchables at different point of time during the period 1911-1932— some of them even once by a single authority and a considerable number of them did not figure in the Scheduled Castes Order of 1936 or in the subsequent Scheduled Castes/Scheduled Tribes Orders. Table I will give a complete picture.

Out of the 450 castes scheduled in 1936, 42 have since been descheduled and 30 shifted to the Scheduled Tribes lists. Again, out of those castes not considered for inclusion in the 1936 list, 24 have since been scheduled and another 44 have been included in the Scheduled Tribes list. So, out of the 673 castes treated as depressed/ untouchables during the period 1911-32 (1901 in the case of the United Province), 402 are in the Scheduled Castes list, 74 in the Scheduled Tribes list, 42 were included in the Scheduled Castes list of 1936 but since descheduled and the remaining 155 were never considered for inclusion in the Scheduled Castes lists/ Scheduled Tribes lists, the largest number being in the Northern and Eastern Provinces (126 out of 155).

Table I explodes the myth that in the South there was little dispute about who were the untouchables/depressed. In the Bombay Presidency and Central Provinces, a large number of castes — 149 — were categorised as depressed/untouchables by one or more of the official bodies before finally selecting 90 of them as scheduled. Again, the largest number of castes descheduled from the 1936 list was from the South, as many as 29 out of the 42 descheduled. If there was little or no dispute about the identity of the untouchables in the South, unanimity or at least little divergence in the classification of depressed

TABLE II

	1901 Census	1911 Census	Govt. list	Sharp	Franchise Committee	Madras Local Boards Act, 1920	1921 Census	Govt. Notification	1931 Census	Newly added in 1936	Total
Period	1901	1911	1917	1917	1919	1920	1921	1931	1931	1936	
Names of Province	No. of caste	No. of caste	No. of caste	No. of caste	No. of caste	No. of caste	No. of caste	No. of caste	No. of caste	No. of caste	No. of caste
Assam		5							14	3	22
Bengal		25	1				8		43		77
Bihar		13	3						6		22
Orissa		11	8	1					3	39	62
U.P.	45								10	6	61
Punjab		19		3					6	2	30
C.P.		16		1			2		23	1	43
Bombay		5	7						20	15	47
Madras			15			1	1	15	54		86
Total	45	94	34	5	—	1	11	15	179	66	450

classes/untouchable castes would have been manifest. But non-inclusion of a large number of castes considered depressed/untouchables during the period 1911-32 in the 1936 list and descheduling of 29 castes subsequently in the post-1936 period only shows that it was as much difficult in the South as anywhere else to identify the untouchables.

If we consider the castes scheduled in 1936 then it will be observed that these castes were mentioned for the first time in the reports as indicated in Table II.

Table II is a pointer to the fact that as the stigma of untouchability started petering out due to various factors — social, religious, economic, administrative and political — it was matched with a corresponding effort to rope in more and more castes within the ambit of 'untouchables'. As the rigidity of untouchability became less pronounced, as the 'lower castes' claimed higher status for them in the society and stepped up their attempts to obtain equality with the 'higher castes', which were more marked in the 20s, there was an effort to segregate a sizable section of Indians from others, to raise a barrier around them, albeit in the name of their social, economic, educational and political development, so that they can never integrate themselves with the other sections of people. Ruling power saw in them a potential weapon to keep the Hindus divided, the communal forces used them to perpetuate the communal divide on the basis of caste, the elite among the so-called 'untouchables' utilised them as a stepping stone for garnering more power—political, social and economic —and a new power center emerged which rivetted round the forces of casteism. The cumulative effect of all these factors and forces was the inclusion of a large number of castes as 'untouchables' and later in the 'schedule' in the early 30s. Thus, of the 450 castes scheduled in 1936, as many as 260, i.e., 58% came into this category only from 1931 onwards and 128, i.e., about 50% of the new comers were from the South which was acclaimed to be a place where the line of demarcation between 'touchables' and 'untouchables' was clearly drawn for a long time. Incidentally, in the South, out of the 176 castes included in the 1936 list, 128, i.e., more than 72% was from the 1931-36 period.

In order to perpetuate their rule in India by hook or by crook the British Government pursued the 'Divide and Rule' policy ruthlessly and intelligently. In pursuance of this policy, the Britishers evolved the policy of disintegrating the Indian society on any pretext possible — religion, caste, language, region and the like, thus preventing the growth of Indian Nationalism and a united Nationhood. The Indian political leaders were supposed to be well aware of the calamitous and far-reaching effect of the British policy. So when the Britishers left India for good, everybody in the country thought that a new India would emerge, at least the foundation of the nascent Nation would be strong, where there would be no distinction between man and man on the basis of religion, caste, race, language and so on, where people would not be known by their caste. But the Birtish policy had so much entrenched itself into the Indian mind that when the time came to frame a Constitution for a free and new India, our framers could not shake off the British legacy and as a matter of fact, followed in their footstep. The policy of dividing the people on the basis of caste was followed by the Framers with equal zest and passion, if not more. The British policy is understandable because the Britishers had to achieve their goal at any cost. But what is not easily comprehended is the policy of dividing and sub-dividing the people on the basis of caste in free India as well, specially when the Framers had vowed to usher in a casteless society.

Notes and References

1. *Census of India, 1911*, Vol. III, Part. I, Para 51, pp. 40-41.
2. *Report of the Indian Statutory Commission, 1930*, Vol. V, p. 1348.
3. *Ibid.*, p. 1352.
4. *Report of the Franchise (Southborough) Committtee, 1919*, Appendix VIII, p. 75.
5. *Census of India, 1921*, Vol. I, Part I, p. 225.

6. *Interim Report of the Indian Statutory Commission (Hartog Committee)* 1929, pp. 217-18.
7. *Census of India, 1931*, Vol. I, Part I, p. 474.
8. *Report of the Indian Franchise Committee*, 1932, Vol. III, p. 320.
9. *Ibid.*, p. 327.
10. *Ibid.*, Vol. I, p. 179.
11. *Ibid.*, p. 219.
12. *Census of India, 1931*, Vol. III, Part I, pp. 208-19.
13. *Report of the Indian Franchise Committee, 1932*, Vol. I, p. 113.
14. *Census of India, 1911*, Volume V, Part I, pp. 232-33.
15. *Ibid.*, Part II, Table XIII, pp. 152-89.
16. *Report of the Indian Statutory Commission, 1930*, Vol. V, p. 1345.
17. *Ibid.*, p. 1351.
18. *Report of the Franchise Committee, 1919*, Vol. I, Appendix III, p. 37.
19. *Ibid., 1932*, Vol. II, pp. 220-21.
20. *Census of India, 1921*, Vol. I, Part I, para 193, p. 225.
21. *The Legislative Assembly Debates (Official Report) 1928*, Vol. III, pp. 2-3.
22. *Interim Report of the Indian Statutory Commission (Hartog Committee)* 1929, pp. 217-18.
23. *Report of the Indian Central Committee, 1929*, p. 367.
    Report of the Indian Statutory Commission, 1930, Vol. I, para 58, pp. 40-41.
24. *Census of India, 1931*, Vol. V, Part I, pp. 502-13.
25. *Census of India, 1931*, Vol. I, Part I, p. 475.
26. *Report of the Indian Franchise Committee, 1932*, Vol. II, 214-15 and pp. 220-21.
27. *Ibid.*, p. 263.1
28. *Ibid.*, Vol. I, p. 117.
29. *Ibid.*
30. *Ibid.*, p. 219.
31. *Ibid.*, p. 117.
32. *Resolution No. 122 A.R. dated the 16th January, 1933 of the Government of Bengal, Appointment (Reforms) Department in File No. 1-R-2(4) of 1993.*
33. *Census of India, 1931*, Vol. V, Part I, para 449, p. 426.
34. *Letter No. 1790-1820—A.R. dated 4th April, 1933 of the Government of Bengal, Appointment (Reforms) Department in File No. 1-R-2(14) of 1933.*
35. *D.O. No. 322—A.R.D. dated the 19th September, 1933 from the Reforms Officer, Government of Bengal to the Reforms Commissioner, Government of India, in File No. 1-R-2(50) of 1933.*

36. *Census of India, 1931*, Vol. I, Part I, p. 475.
37. *Note by D.R. Prentice, Member of the Executive Council of the Governor of Bengal in File No. 1-R-2 of 1933 dated the 15th June, 1933.*
38. *Census of India, 1911*, Vol. 5, Part I, pp. 232-33.
39. *Census of India, 1911*, Vol. 5, Part III, Table XIII, Part A, pp. 98-123.
40. *Ibid.*
41. *Progress of Education in India, 1912-17*, Vol. II, Appendix XIII, p. 93.
    Report of the Indian Statutory Commission, 1930, Vol. V, p. 1351.
42. *Report of the Indian Franchise Committee, 1919*, Appendix VI, p. 61.
43. *Census of India, 1921*, Vol. VII, Part I, p. 234.
44. *Ibid., 1921*, Vol. I, Part I, para 193, p. 225.
45. *The Legislative Assembly Debates (Official Report), 1928*, Vol. III, pp. 2-3.
46. *Interim Report of the Indian Statutory Commission, (Hartog Committee) 1929*, pp. 217-18.
47. *Report of the Indian Central Committee, 1929*, p. 367.
    Report of the Indian Statutory Commission, 1930, Vol. I, para 58, pp. 40-41.
48. *Census of India, 1931*, Vol. VII, Part I, para 7, p. 285.
49. *Ibid.*, para 9, p. 286.
50. *Ibid.*, Part II, Tables XVII-XVIII, pp. 136-39 and 142-43.
51. *Report of the Indian Franchise Committee, 1932*, Vol. III, p. 154.
52. *Ibid.*, pp. 158-62.
53. *Ibid.*, p. 129.
54. *Ibid.*, p. 188.
55. *Ibid.*, p. 227.
56. *Ibid.*, Vol. I, p. 113.
57. *Ibid.*, pp. 233-34.
58. *Ibid.*, p. 218.
59. *Census of India, 1901*, Vol. XVI, Part I, pp. 216-33.
60. *Ibid., 1911*, Vol. XV, Part I, pp. 123-24.
61. *Report of the Indian Statutory Commission*, 1930, Vol. V, pp. 1345-46.
62. *Ibid.*, p. 1351.
63. *Census of India, 1901*, Part I, Subsidiary Table I, p. 252.
64. *Report of the Franchise Committee, 1919*, Appendix III, p. 45.
65. *Census of India, 1921*, Vol. I, Part I, para 193, p. 225.
66. *The Legislative Assembly Debates (Official Report), 1928*, Vol. III, pp. 2-3.

67. *Interim Report of the Indian Statutory Commission (Hartog Committee), 1929*, p. 218.
68. *Report of the Indian Central Committee, 1929*, pp. 86 and 367.
69. *Report of the Indian Statutory Commission, 1930*, Vol. I, pp. 40-41.
70. *Census of India, 1931*, Vol. XVIII, Part I, pp. 634-38.
71. *Ibid., 1931*, Vol. I, Part I, p. 479.
72. *Report of the Indian Franchise Committee, 1932*, Vol. II, p. 298.
73. *Ibid.*, p. 376.
74. *Ibid.*, p. 308.
75. *Ibid.*, pp. 328-30.
76. *Ibid.*, Vol. I, p. 116.
77. *Ibid.*, Vol. II, p. 398.
78. *Ibid.*, Vol. I, p. 179.
79. *Ibid.*, pp. 218-19.
80. *Census of India, 1911*, Vol. XIV, Part I, para 132, pp. 109-11.
81. *Ibid.*, Part II, Table XIII, pp. 230-90.
82. *Report of the Indian Statutory Commission 1930*, Vol. V, p. 1348.
83. *Ibid.*, p. 1351.
84. *Report of the Franchise Committee, 1919*, Appendix V, p. 53.
85. *Census of India, 1921*, Vol. I, Part I, para 193, p. 225.
86. *The Legislative Assembly Debates (Official Report), 1928*, Vol. III, pp. 2-3.
87. *Interim Report of the Indian Statutory Commission (Hartog Committee)*, 1929, p. 218.
88. *Report of the Indian Central Committee, 1929*, p. 367.
89. *Report of the Indian Statutory Commission, 1930*, Vol. I, pp. 40-41.
90. *Census of India, 1931*, Vol. XVII, Part I, p. 374.
91. *Ibid., 1931*, Vol. I, Part I, p. 478.
92. *Report of the Indian Franchise Committee, 1932*, Vol. III, Para 17, pp. 49-50.
93. *Ibid.*, Para 15, p. 63.
94. *Ibid.*, Vol. I, p. 118.
95. *Ibid.*, p. 219.
96. *Census of India, 1911*, Vol. X, Part I, pp. 73-74.
97. *Ibid.*, Part II, Table XIII, pp. 113-51.
98. *Report of the Indian Statutory Commission, 1930*, Vol. V, p. 1347.
99. *Ibid.*, p. 1352.
100. *Report of the Franchise Committee, 1919*, Appendix VII, p. 69.
101. *Census of India, 1921*, Vol. XI, Part I, para 192, p. 158.
102. *Census of India, 1921*, Vol. I, Part I, para 193, p. 225.

103. *The Legislative Assembly Debates (Official Report), 1928*, Vol. III, pp. 2-3.
104. *Interim Report of the Indian Statutory Commission, (Hartog Committtee), 1929*, p. 218.
105. *Report of the Indian Central Committee, 1929*, p. 367.
106. *Report of the Indian Statutory Commission, 1930*, Vol. I, pp. 40-41.
107. *Census of India, 1931*, Vol. XII, Part I, p. 365.
108. *Ibid., 1931*, Vol. I, Part I, pp. 476-77.
109. *Ibid., 1931*, Vol. XII, Part I, pp. 354-55.
110. *Report of the Indian Franchise Committee, 1932*, Vol. III, pp. 259-60.
111. *Ibid.*, Vol. I, p. 112.
112. *Ibid.*, p. 217.
113. *Ibid.*, p. 219.
114. *Census of India, 1931*, Vol. XII, Part I, p. 387.
115. *Ibid.*, p. 393.
116. *Ibid.*, p. 394.
117. *Ibid.*, 390.
118. *Census of India, 1911*, Vol. VII, Part I, para 137, p. 65.
119. *Ibid.*, Part II, pp. 231-60.
120. *Report of the Indian Statutory Commission, 1930*, Vol. V, pp. 1344-45.
121. *Census of India, 1911*, Vol. VII, Part II, pp. 231-60.
122. *Report of the Indian Statutory Commission, 1930*, Vol. V, p. 1351.
123. *Report of the Franchise Committee, 1919*, Vol. I, p. 29, Appendix II.
124. *Census of India, 1921*, Vol. I, Part I, para 193, p. 225.
125. *The Legislative Assembly Debates (Official Report), 1928*, Vol. III, pp. 2-3.
126. *Interim Report of the Indian Statutory Commission (Hartog Committtee)*, 1929, p. 218.
127. *Census of India, 1921*, Vol. VIII, Part II, pp. 176-88.
128. *Report of the Indian Central Committee, 1929*, p. 367.
129. *Report of the Indian Statutory Commission, 1930*, Vol. I, pp. 40-41.
130. *Census of India, 1931*, Vol. VIII, Part I, p. 333.
131. *Ibid.*, Part II, p. 434.
132. *Census of India, 1931*, Vol. I, Part I, p. 476.
133. *Report of the Indian Franchise Committee, 1932*, Vol. II, pp. 71 and 157.
134. *Ibid.*, pp. 125-26.
135. *Ibid.*, Vol. I, p. 112.

136. *Ibid.*, p. 217.
137. *Ibid.*, p. 219.
138. *Census of India, 1911*, Vol. XII, Part I, paras 22 and 24, p. 51.
139. *Report of the Indian Statutory Commission, 1930*, Vol. V, pp. 1341-44.
140. *Ibid.*, p. 1350.
141. *Census of India, 1911, Vol. XII*, Part II, pp. 112-14, Table XII.
142. *Report of the Franchise Committee, 1919*, Vol. I, p. 19, Appendix I.
143. *Census of India, 1911*, Vol. XII, Part II, pp. 112-14.
144. *Ibid., 1921*, Vol. XIII, Part I, p. 158.
145. *Ibid., 1921*, Vol. I, Part I, para 193, p. 225.
146. *The Legislative Assembly Debates (Official Report), 1928*, Vol. III, pp. 2-3.
147. *Interim Report of the Indian Statutory Commission (Hartog Committee)*, 1929, pp. 217-18.
148. *Report of the Indian Central Committee, 1929*, p. 367.
149. *Report of the Indian Statutory Commission, 1930*, Vol. I, pp. 40-41.
150. *Census of India, 1931*, Vol. XVII, Part II, p. 306.
151. *Census of India, 1931*, Vol. I, Part I, pp. 477-78.
152. *Report of the Indian Franchise Committee*, 1932, Vol. II, p. 14.
153. *Ibid.*, p. 28.
154. *Ibid.*, Vol. I, pp. 111-12.
155. *Ibid.*, p. 217.
156. *Ibid.*, p. 219.
157. *Ibid.*, Vol. II, p. 306.

24

Scheduling of Castes: Emerging Pattern

The Constitution of India in Article 341 empowers the President of India to specify the castes, races and tribes to be included in the list of Scheduled Castes in relation to a particular State or Union Territory. Once such a list is notified with respect to any State or Union Territory, the said list cannot be varied by a subsequent notification. It requires the sanction of Parliament. Parliament is to enact a law for including in or excluding from the list of Scheduled Castes any caste, race or tribe. Article 342 of the Constitution vests the President of India with similar power in regard to the tribes or tribal community to be included in the list of Scheduled Tribes.

Listing of Scheduled Castes in different Orders

After the commencement of the Constitution, statutory lists of Scheduled Castes were notified for the first time under the Constitution (Scheduled Castes) Order, 1950 on August 8, 1950, specifying the castes, races or tribes deemed to be Scheduled Castes in relation to 16 Parts A and B States [Jammu and Kashmir and Vindhya Pradesh, two Part B States were not included in this Order], and the Constitution (Scheduled Castes) (Part C States) Order, 1951 was issued on September 20, 1951 in relation to 10 Part C States [Vindhya Pradesh was included in this Order]. Another Order, the Constitution

(Scheduled Tribes) Order, 1950 was issued on September 6, 1950, in accordance with the power vested in the President of India under Article 342(1) of the Constitution, specifying the tribes or tribal communities included in the Scheduled Tribes list in relation to 14 Parts A and B States and the Constitution (Scheduled Tribes) (Part C States) Order, 1951 was issued on September 20, 1951 in relation to 7 Part C States. Apart from these Orders, Presidential Orders under Articles 341 and 342 were issued in 1956 for the State of Jammu and Kashmir, in 1959 for the Andaman and Nicobar Islands, in 1962 for Dadra and Nagar Haveli, in 1964 for Pondicherry, in 1967 for U.P. (for S.T. only), in 1968 for Goa, Daman and Diu, in 1970 for Nagaland, in 1978 for Sikkim and in 1989 for Jammu and Kashmir (for S.T. only). These lists have been modified or amended or supplemented from time to time under Acts of Parliament.

The first amendment to the Order of 1950 was effected under the Andhra State Act, 1953 when the Madras Presidency was bifurcated to create the separate State of Andhra Pradesh and a portion of Bellary district (excluding 3 taluks) was transferred to Mysore State. The 1950 Madras list was made applicable to the States of Madras and Andhra Pradesh and the ceded areas (Bellary district) of Mysore State.

Again in 1954 when Bilaspur, a Part C State, was merged with Himachal Pradesh, another Part C State, the Scheduled Castes (Part C States) Order, 1951 was amended under the Himachal Pradesh and Bilaspur (New State) Act, 1954 to include some new castes in the Himachal Pradesh Scheduled Castes list.

When the Constitution came into being in 1950, the States which formed the Union of India were classified into three categories and enumerated in Parts A, B and C of the First Schedule of the Constitution. All the nine British Indian Provinces were included in Part A, the Indian States in Part B and the Chief Commissioners' Provinces in Part C. At the time of commencement of the Constitution, the number of these States was 9, 9 and

10 respectively, making a total of 28. Besides these 28 States of different category, there was another category, viz., a territory specified in Part D of the First Schedule. The reorganisation of States in 1956 reduced the Parts A, B, C and D categories of States/territories into two only. Instead of three categories of States there was only one class of States and the number of such States became 14. The category 'territory in Part D' was replaced by the 'Union Territories' and this class was to include not only the Andaman and Nicobar Islands which were previously in Part D but also some of the erstwhile Part C States like Delhi, Manipur, Himachal Pradesh and Tripura.

The reorganisation of States and creation of new States in 1956 as also the demand for inclusion of more castes/tribes in the lists of Scheduled Castes/Scheduled Tribes necessitated the enactment of the Scheduled Castes and Scheduled Tribes Orders (Amendment) Act, 1956, and consequently, the issuance of a fresh Scheduled Castes and Scheduled Tribes Lists (Modification) Order, which came into force with effect from October 29, 1956. In the 1956 Order, 13 States and 4 Union Territories were covered. A separate Order was issued for the State of Jammu and Kashmir. There was no Scheduled Castes in the remaining two Union Territories of Andaman and Nicobar Islands and Lakshadeep.

Thereafter a few Orders specifying the Scheduled Castes/Scheduled Tribes in respect of a few individual States/Union Territories were also issued. For instance, the bifurcation of the Bombay State in 1960 into Maharashtra and Gujarat States and the reorganisation of Punjab into 2 States — Punjab and Haryana —and a Union Territory — Chandigarh — and transfer of an area to the Union Territory of Himachal Pradesh under the Punjab Reorganisation Act, 1966, called for modification of the SC/ST Order in respect of these States/Union Territories, which was effected under the provisions of these two Acts. Under the Assam Reorganisation (Meghalaya) Act, 1969, Garo Hills and United Khasi and

Jaintia Hills district of Assam were taken out on April 2, 1970 to form the autonomous State of Meghalaya. Mizo district was also taken out of Assam to form a full-fledged Union Territory with effect from January 21, 1972. The North-East Frontier Agency was also formed into a Union Territory known as Arunachal Pradesh. The Union Territories of Manipur and Tripura and the autonomous State of Meghalaya were granted full statehood. The creation of new States/Union Territories in the North-Eastern Areas made it necessary to issue fresh SC/ST lists in relation to these newly created States/Union Territories. This was done under the North-Eastern Areas (Reorganisation) Act, 1971. That apart, a few Constitutional Orders were also issued in the 60s for the Union Territories of Dadra and Nagar Haveli in 1962, Pondicherry in 1964 and Goa, Daman and Diu in 1968.

Later, the Scheduled Castes and Scheduled Tribes (Order) (Amendment) Act, 1976 came into force. The main purpose of this Amendment Act was to remove area restrictions in respect of most of the Scheduled Castes and Scheduled Tribes. The 1976 Order covered 19 States i.e., 16 States/Union Territories covered by the 1956 Order and the three newly created States of Gujarat, Haryana and Meghalaya. By this time twenty-two States came on the political map of India. The three States not covered by this amendment Act were Jammu and Kashmir, Nagaland and Sikkim. The Jammu and Kashmir Order issued separately in 1956 remained unaltered. Nagaland had no Scheduled Castes and Sikkim's list was issued in 1978. The Amendment Act of 1976 also did not include the Scheduled Castes/Scheduled Tribes in respect of the Union Territories of Mizoram, Arunachal Pradesh, Goa (all since attained statehood), Daman and Diu, Delhi, Dadra and Nagar Haveli, Pondicherry and Chandigarh, which were guided by the Orders issued already in respect of each of them.

After 1976, the status of some has undergone change from a Union Territory to that of a State and jurisdictional changes have also taken place in relation to a

Union Territory. The Union Territories of Mizoram and Arunachal Pradesh attained statehood with effect from February 20, 1987. The Union Territory of Goa, Daman and Diu was reorganised under the Goa, Daman and Diu Reorganisation Act, 1987. Under this Act, Goa district of the Union Territory of Goa, Daman and Diu was accorded the status of a State and the districts of Daman and Diu continued to form a Union Territory. Moreover, a Presidential Order had to be issued in relation to the newly added State of Sikkim and another Order in relation to the State of Jammu and Kashmir for the Scheduled Tribes only. The following Orders were, therefore, issued after 1976 :

(1) a Constitutional Order for the newly added State of Sikkim,

(2) fresh Orders for Mizoram and Arunachal Pradesh on attaining statehood under the Mizoram State Act, 1986, and the Arunachal Pradesh State Act, 1986, respectively,

(3) fresh orders for the State of Goa and the Union Territory of Daman and Diu under the Goa, Daman and Diu Reorganisation Act, 1987,

(4) a Constitutional Order for the State of Jammu and Kashmir for the Scheduled Tribes only.

Since 1950 the following Orders have been issued :

Scheduled Castes

(1) The Constitution (Scheduled Castes) Order, 1950, C.O. 19.

(2) The Constitution (Scheduled Castes) (Part C States) Order, 1951, C.O. 32 [Since renamed as the Constitution (Union Territories) Scheduled Castes Order, 1951].

(3) The Scheduled Castes and Scheduled Tribes Lists (Modification) Order, 1956 issued under No. SRO 2477A dated the 29th October, 1956 modifying (1) the Constitution (Scheduled Castes) Order, 1950, (2) the Constitution (Scheduled Castes) (Part C States) Order, 1951, (3) the Constitution (Scheduled Tribes)

Order, 1950 and (4) the Constitution (Scheduled Tribes) (Part C States) Order, 1951.

(4) The Constitution (Jammu and Kashmir) Scheduled Castes Order, 1956, C.O. 52.

(5) The Constitution (Dadra and Nagar Haveli) Scheduled Castes Order, 1962, C.O. 64.

(6) The Constitution (Pondicherry) Scheduled Castes Order, 1964, C.O. 68.

(7) The Constitution (Goa, Daman and Diu) Scheduled Castes Order, 1968, C.O. 81.

(8) The Scheduled Castes and Scheduled Tribes Order (Amendment) Act, 1976.

(9) The Constitution (Sikkim) Scheduled Castes Order, 1978, C.O. 110.

Scheduled Tribes

(1) The Constitution (Scheduled Tribes) Order, 1950, C.O. 22.

(2) The Constitution (Scheduled Tribes) (Part C States) Order, 1951, C.O. 33 [Since renamed as the Constitution (Union Territories) Scheduled Tribes Order, 1951].

(3) The Scheduled Castes and Scheduled Tribes Lists (Modification) Order, 1956.

(4) The Constitution (Andaman and Nicobar Islands) Scheduled Tribes Order, 1959, C.O. 58.

(5) The Constitution (Dabra and Nagar Haveli) Scheduled Tribes Order, 1962, C.O. 64.

(6) The Constitution (Scheduled Tribes) (Uttar Pradesh) Order, 1967, C.O. 78.

(7) The Constitution (Goa, Daman and Diu) Scheduled Tribes Order, 1968, C.O. 81.

(8) The Constitution (Nagaland) Scheduled Tribes Order, 1970, C.O. 88.

(9) The Scheduled Castes and Scheduled Tribes Order (Amendment) Act, 1976.

(10) The Constitution (Sikkim) Scheduled Tribes Order, 1978, C.O. 110.

(11) The Constitution (Scheduled Tribes) (Amendment) Act, 1987 (in relation to the State of Meghalaya).

(12) The Constitution (Jammu and Kashmir) Scheduled Tribes Order, 1989.

Whenever a new State/Union Territory is formed or the boundary of a State is changed, a fresh SC/ST list in relation to that State/Union Territory/ceded areas had to be issued. Since any change in the lists mentioned in the above Presidential Notifications could only be effected under an Act of Parliament, the said SC/ST lists were modified/amended by the following Acts :

(1) The Andhra State Act, 1953 (in relation to the States of Madras, Andhra and Mysore),

(2) The Himachal Pradesh and Bilaspur (New State) Act, 1954 (in relation to the State of Himachal Pradesh),

(3) The Bombay Reorganisation Act, 1960 (in relation to the States of Maharashtra and Gujarat),

(4) The Punjab Reorganisation Act, 1966 (in relation to the States of Haryana and Himachal Pradesh and the Union Territory of Chandigarh),

(5) The North-Eastern Areas (Reorganisation) Act, 1971 (in relation to the States of Meghalaya, Manipur and Tripura and the Union Territories of Mizoram and Arunachal Pradesh),

(6) The State of Mizoram Act, 1986 (in relation to the State of Mizoram),

(7) The State of Arunachal Pradesh Act, 1986 (in relation to the State of Arunachal Pradesh), and

(8) The Goa, Daman and Diu Reorganisation Act, 1987 (in relation to the State of Goa and the Union Territory of Daman and Diu).

All the Orders relating to the Scheduled Castes/ Scheduled Tribes, mentioned above, including the one issued in 1936 may be seen in Appendix I.

It will appear from the Orders that a number of castes have been added to the list of 1936 and many castes have been transferred to the Scheduled Tribes lists or were altogether deleted. There are instances where the castes deleted earlier were reinducted. The latest position of the Scheduled Castes in relation to 19 States and of the Scheduled Tribes in 16 States and in the Union Territory of Andaman and Nicobar Islands is in accordance with the 1976 Order. The remaining 6 States (Jammu and Kashmir, Nagaland, Sikkim, Mizoram, Arunachal Pradesh and Goa) and 6 Union Territories (Chandigarh, Dadra and Nagar Haveli, Daman and Diu, Delhi, Lakshadeep and Pondicherry) are not covered by this Order. They are guided by the individual Order issued earlier or later, as the case may be.

No caste has been notified as Scheduled Caste for Nagaland, Andaman and Nicobar Islands and Lakshadeep and no Tribe has been notified as Scheduled Tribe for Haryana, Punjab, Chandigarh, Delhi and Pondicherry.

Number of Scheduled Castes under Different Orders

In the 1936 Order which related to 9 British Indian Provinces 417 Castes [actually 450 castes if we count the castes listed with others against the same serial number separately and not jointly. Henceforth, the figures in bracket will indicate the actual number of castes, treating each of the castes/sub-castes, etc., which are grouped together as a separate entity]. Of them, 74(86) were considered scheduled for a part of Provinces.

The number of castes scheduled in the Orders of 1950 and 1951 increased to 821(927). Of them, only 22(25) were considered scheduled for a part of the States.

The number of castes notified as Scheduled Castes under the Orders of 1956 shot up to 1119(1590). A large number of them, as many as 704(1048), were considered scheduled for a part of the States. This was because of merger of areas from the neighbouring States and amalgamation of Parts B and C States with Part A States for formation of linguistic States in 1956.

The Orders issued in between 1956 and 1976 for the newly created States and Union Territories like Maharashtra, Gujarat, Haryana, Himachal Pradesh,

Meghalaya, Tripura, Manipur, Mizoram, Arunachal Pradesh, Goa, Daman and Diu, Chandigarh, Dadra and Nagar Haveli and Pondicherry listed 376(633) Scheduled Castes.

In the 1976 Order 941(1492) castes figured. In 1976, the lists were amended mainly to remove area restrictions in respect of most of the Scheduled Castes. In the 1976 Order there were only 25(27) castes which were considered scheduled for a part of the States.

The 1976 Order did not cover the State of Jammu and Kashmir and the Union Territories of Mizoram, Arunachal Pradesh, Goa, Daman and Diu, Chandigarh, Dadra and Nagar Haveli, Delhi and Pondicherry, which were guided by the earlier Orders. While in the case of Jammu and Kashmir, the Constitution (Jammu and Kashmir) Scheduled Castes Order, 1956 is applicable, in the case of Delhi, the 1956 (Modification) Order is relevant. In the case of Dadra and Nagar Haveli and Pondicherry the Constitution (Dadra and Nagar Haveli) Scheduled Castes Order, 1962 and the Constitution (Pondicherry) Scheduled Castes Order, 1964 have to be referred to, while in the case of Chandigarh, the Punjab Re-organisation Act of 1966 is still valid. The Union Territories of Mizoram and Arunachal Pradesh were guided by the North-Eastern Areas (Reorgani-sation) Act, 1971 and Goa, Daman and Diu was guided by the Constitution (Goa, Daman and Diu) Scheduled Castes Order, 1968. The number of castes considered scheduled in relation to these States/Union Territories was 141(200). So, the total number of Scheduled Castes in the States/Union Territories in 1976 was 941(1492) plus 141(200)= 1082(1692).

After 1976 the Union Territories of Mizoram and Arunachal Pradesh attained statehood and in the relevant Acts of 1986 (the State of Mizoram Act, 1986 and the State of Arunachal Pradesh Act, 1986) the same set of castes was retained in the respective schedule. Goa became a State in 1987 when the same set of castes was retained for the State of Goa as well as the Union

Territory of Daman and Diu in the Goa, Daman and Diu Reorganisation Act, 1987. Another Constitutional Order was issued for the State of Sikkim in 1978. These are the only changes which took place after 1976. So there was no appreciable increase in the total number of Scheduled Castes after 1976. In 1996, their total number stands at 1082(1692) + 9(12)=1091(1704).

These are the castes which figure in the Orders issued under Article 341 of the Constitution or under different Acts of Parliament. After 1976 some more Orders were issued by the Government of India which substantially enlarged the number of castes grouped with others by adding more castes as equivalent names and name of synonyms and sub-castes/tribes of the existing Scheduled Castes and Scheduled Tribes in different States. The Government of India Order, however, took ample care to emphasise that "the above list is not intended or shall not be treated as an alteration or amendments of the Schedules to the Presidential Order specifying Scheduled Castes and Scheduled Tribes in relation to ..... State, as any alterations or amendments of the lists of Scheduled Castes and Scheduled Tribes contained in the Presidential Orders can be made only by Parliamentary legislation." Whatever it is, for all practical purposes, considerable addition to the castes grouped with others was effected through these Orders. The orders issued in 1979-81 added 57 castes/sub-castes in 7 States [Karnataka (14), Jammu and Kashmir (5), Haryana (13), Gujarat (8), Andhra Pradesh (4), Bihar (10) and Orissa (3)]. Some more castes/sub-castes were added afterwards. A specimen of such Orders may seen as Appendix II.

Some State Governments have also added new castes/sub-castes to the existing lists in the name of issuing clarification as to which communities having particular 'surname' should be construed as belonging to a particular caste. For instance, in West Bengal an Order was issued directing that communities using the surnames of Hela, Balmiki, Bansfor, Bhangi should be construed as belonging to the 'Methor' caste because "these persons using such surnames, but engaged in clearing night-soil are by profession and/or caste 'Methor'." In an earlier Order, it was said that 'Morangia' should be construed as belonging to 'Rajbanshi' community. This type of Orders also substantially increased the number of castes/sub-castes grouped with others. A specimen of such Order is given as Appendix III.

In this study, these additions either by the Government of India or by the State Governments have not been taken into account. Only the castes scheduled in the Orders issued under Article 341 of the Constitution or under an Act of Parliament have been considered.

Position in Different Units

Table III in the next pages indicates the number of castes scheduled under different Orders in the Provinces/States/Union Territories since 1936.

This table reveals that in the Eastern and North-Eastern States except Orissa and Punjab [i.e., the erstwhile Northern and Eastern Provinces under the 1935 Act, viz., Assam, Bengal (now West Bengal), Bihar and U.P.] the number of castes included in the Schedule did not vary too much during the period 1936-76. Once a caste was identified and listed in the 1936 Order there was not much dispute about its continuance. Whatever might be the dispute or 'wide margin of error', that was prior to its inclusion. Once the list was prepared, it stabilisied at a certain figure. The increase was within the range of 10 to 15 percent.

Assam started with 22 castes (i.e., if the castes and sub-castes included in the same group are counted separately) in 1936 and settled at 25 in 1976, i.e., an overall increase of 14%. Even Meghalaya and Mizoram, which were carved out of Assam, and Arunachal Pradesh, i.e., the erstwhile NEFA, accounted for the same set of castes. Tripura had 36 castes in its list, first prepared in 1951, which was reduced to 33 in 1976.

West Bengal began with 77 in 1936 which dwindled

TABLE III

Number of castes scheduled under different orders, 1936-96.

Names of Units	1936 Order	1950 Order	1951 Order	1953/54 Order	1956 Order	Between 1960-71	1976 Order	1978-87 Order	Number in 1996
Assam	15(22)	15(22)			16(25)		16(25)		16(25)
	10*(17*)								
Meghalaya						16(25)	16(25)		16(25)
Mizoram						16(25)			16(25)
Arunachal Pradesh						16(25)			16(25)
Bihar	22(22)	24(27)			23(30)		23(30)		23(30)
	8*(8*)	3*(3*)			2*(2*)		1*(1*)		1*(1*)
Bombay	38(47)	38(49)			99*(193*)	77*(165*)	59(149)		59(149)
(Maharashtra)	2*(2*)	2*(2*)					1*(1*)		1*(1*)
Saurastra		15(15)							
Kutch			6(6)						
Gujarat						46*(106*)	30(91)		30(91)
Himachal Pradesh			30(38)	37(48)	52(71)	64(96)	56(99)		56(99)
Bilaspur			9(11)						
Jammu & Kashmir					13(16)				13(16)
Madhya Pradesh	39(43)	25(32)			83*(143*)		47(104)		47(104)
	31*(33*)	16*(19*)					4*(4*)		4*(4*)
Madhya Bharat		19(22)							

(*Continued on next page*)

TABLE III

Names of Units	1936 Order	1950 Order	1951 Order	1953/54 Order	1956 Order	between 1960-71	1976 Order	1978-87 Order	Number in 1996
Bhopal			16(17)						
Vindhya Pradesh			10(14)						
Manipur			15(22)		7(9)	7(9)	7(9)		7(9)
Madras	86(86)	77(82)		77(82)	79(89)		76(86)		76(86)
(Tamil Nadu)	12*(12*)				73*(80*)		15*(17*)		15*(17*)
Andhra Pradesh				77(82)	60(77)		59(77)		59(77)
					56*(71*)				
Hyderabad		32(37)							
Mysore		6(7)		81(87)	142*(207*)		101(166)		101(166)
(Karnataka)				79*(85*)			2*(2*)		2*(2*)
Coorg			11(11)						
Travancore-Cochin		30(32)			70(77)		68(75)		68(75)
(Kerala)					64*(68*)		2*(2*)		2*(2*)
Orissa	53(62)	92(114)			94(124)		93(123)		93(123)
	10*(13*)				1*(1*)				
Punjab	27(30)	34(39)			37(59)		37(59)		37(59)
					4*(8*)				
Pepsu		34(39)							

(Continued on next page)

TABLE III

Name of Units	1936 Order	1950 Order	1951 Order	1953/54 Order	1956 Order	between 1960-71	1976 Order	1978-87 Order	Number in 1996
Haryana						37(59) / 4*(8*)	37(59)		37(59)
Rajasthan		44(45)			142*(230*)		59(133)		59(133)
Ajmer			40(40)						
Sikkim								4(5)	4(5)
Tripura			36(36)		37(38)	37(38)	32(33)		32(33)
U.P.	61(61) / 1*(1*)	64(65) / 1*(1*)			66(70) / 2*(2*)		66(70)		66(70)
West Bengal	76(77)	58(59)			62(81) / 50*(57*)		59(79)		59(79)
Chandigarh						36(56)			36(56)
Dadra and Nagar Haveli						4(5)			4(5)
Delhi			41(46)		36(49)				36(49)
Goa						5(7)		5(7)	5(7)
Daman and Diu								5(7)	5(7)
Pondicherry						15(17)			15(17)
Total	417(450) / 74*(86*)	607(686) / 22*(25*)	214(241)		1119(1590) / 704*(1048*)	376(633) / 4*(8*)	941(1492) / 25*(27*)		1091(1704) / 25*(27*)

* indicates parts of the state.

figures in bracket indicates the actual number of castes, treating each caste/sub-caste grouped together as a separate entity.

to 59 in 1950 but increased to 81 in 1956 because of the merger of a district from Bihar in 1956, and ultimately ended with 79 in 1976. The number did not increase abnormally during the period 1936-76, as happened in the Southern and Western Indian States, because the increase due to merger of areas from Bihar in 1956 was largely offset by transfer of a number of castes from the Scheduled Castes list to the Scheduled Tribes list.

Bihar started with 22 in 1936, accounted for 27 in 1950 and remained contended with 30 in 1956 as well as in 1976.

U.P. began with 61 and ended with 70 in 1976.

Manipur and Jammu and Kashmir also fit in with this pattern. As a matter of fact, Manipur started with 22 in 1951, i.e., the same set of castes as that of Assam but ultimately retained only 9 in its list. In Jammu and Kashmir, there was no variation in the list once notified in 1956.

The Southern, Western, North-Western and Central India depict another picture. These States (Kerala, Karnakata, Tamil Nadu, Andhra Pradesh, Madhya Pradesh, Maharashtra, Gujarat and Rajasthan) accounted for a sharp rise — both vertically and horizontally — in the number of castes listed as Scheduled; the number increased from 369(409) in 1950 to 675(1017) in 1956, and ultimately settled at 499(881) in 1976. It may be remembered that the geographical boundary of all these States changed materially in 1956 due to formation of linguistic States when the contiguous linguistically homogeneous areas were amalgamated. So when these areas were merged either with the existing neighbouring States or with the newly created States, the ceded areas also brought with them the castes listed as 'Scheduled' in these areas. Inspite of this, the number would not have registered such a sharp rise had not the number of castes listed as scheduled in the earlier Orders showed a substantial increase in the Order of 1956. This happened not only in the case of Parts B and C States which ceased to exist with the formation of linguistic States in 1956 but also in the Part A States.

Madhya Pradesh had 43 castes in its list in 1936. In 1950 it came down to 32. Another 53 castes (Madhya Bharat 22, Vindhya Pradesh 14 and Bhopal 17) were scheduled in 1950/51 in these areas which later merged with Madhya Pradesh in 1956. So their effective number would be 85 in 1951. It soared to 143 in 1956 and ultimately settled at 104 in 1976.

In the Bombay Presidency 47 castes were scheduled in 1936, which went up to 49 in 1950. In 1950/51, 15 castes were scheduled for the State of Saurastra and 6 in Kutch, which later merged with Bombay in 1956. 37 castes were listed in Hyderabad and 32 in Madhya Pradesh. Since the Marathi-speaking areas from these States were also merged with the Bombay Presidency the total number of castes for these areas would be 139 in 1950/51. But in the 1956 Order Bombay accounted for an astronomical number of 193 castes and with the bifurcation of the State in 1960 came down to 165 for Maharashtra and 106 for Gujarat, which were further reduced to 149 and 91 respectively in the 1976 Order. In both these States a large number of castes — even 25/30 — have been put under a single entry, thus making an artificial reduction in the serial number while the actual number was much more. In Bombay, as many as 149 castes were placed in 59 groups while in Gujarat 91 castes were put in 30 groups.

Madras started with 86 in 1936 which came down to 82 in 1950. Though the State was bifurcated in 1953 when Andhra Pradesh State was created with the Telugu-speaking areas, the number remained the same for both these States. In 1956 it soared to 89 and ultimately stabilised at 86 in 1976.

Andhra Pradesh was a part of Madras in 1950. When the State was formed in 1953 with the Telugu-speaking areas, it had the same set of Scheduled Castes as that of Madras. In 1950, 37 castes were scheduled for Hyderabad, the major portion of which was merged with Andhra Pradesh in 1956. In the 1956 Order 77 castes were scheduled and the same number continued in later years as well.

Same is the position in Kerala, Mysore and Rajasthan, the States formed after independence. Kerala had 32 castes in its list in 1950, which soared to 77 in 1956 and ultimately settled at 75 in 1976.

Mysore (Karnataka) had only 7 castes in its list in 1950. With the merger of a district from Madras State in 1953 the total number became 87. Coorg, which was later merged with Mysore in 1956, had 11 castes. In 1956 the number increased to 207 and came down to 166 in 1976.

Rajasthan had 45 castes and Ajmer 40 castes in the lists in 1950/51. The number increased to 230 in 1956 and was brought down to 133 in 1976.

The number increased sharply in these States in 1956 not only for merger of areas from the neighbouring States which had a substantially different set of Scheduled Castes but also for additions of new castes in the existing lists for both these States as well as the ceded areas. Table IV may help clear the position.

It will appear from Table IV that in almost all the States, viz., Travancore-Cochin, which later became Kerala, Mysore, Coorg which was merged with Mysore, Bombay, Saurastra (merged with Bombay), Madhya Pradesh, Bhopal and Vindhya Pradesh (both merged with Madhya Pradesh), Madhya Bharat (merged with Madhya Pradesh and Rajasthan), Rajasthan and Ajmer (merged with Rajasthan) showed a substantial increase in the number of Scheduled Castes in the 1956 Order compared to the one issued in 1950. The only exceptions were Madras and Andhra Pradesh, that too because the Order issued in 1953 did not take into consideration the fact that the Telugu-and Tamil-speaking areas had Scheduled Castes which were not common in both the areas. Hyderabad and Kutch, however, did not register any increase. It is, therefore, no wonder that these States accounted for such a phenomenal increase in the 1956 Order.

TABLE IV

Names of States	No. of castes scheduled in		Reorganisation in 1956		Total number of castes listed as S.C. in the 1956 Order
	1950 Order		Areas excluded 1956 Order	Areas included (No. of Scheduled Castes shown in bracket)	
1	2	3	4	5	6
Travancore-Cochin	30(32)	30(36)	(a) entire State except 5 Taluks merged with Kerala (b) 5 Taluks merged with Madras		
Kerala				(a) entire Trancore-Cohin State except 5 Taluks—30(36) (b) Malabar district and Kosargad Taluk of South Kanara district of Madras—46(50)	70(77)
Madras	77(82)	57(65)	(a) Malabar district and Kosargad Taluk of South Kanara district to Kerala (b) South Kanara (except Kosargad Taluk) district and Kallegal Taluk to Mysore	(a) existing State excluding the areas transferred—57(65) (b) 5 Taluks from Travancore-Cochin—28(33)	79(89)

(Continued on next page)

TABLE IV

1	2	3	4	5	6
Mysore	6(7)	15(16)		(a) existing state—15(16) (b) South Kanara (except Kosargad Taluk) district and Kallegal Taluk of Madras—58(62) (c) Trichur, Bidar and Gulbarga districts of Hyderabad—32(37) (d) Four Kannada-speaking districts of Bombay—25(80) (e) Coorg—12(12)	142(207)
Coorg	11(11)	12(12)	Merged with Mysore		
Hyderabad	32(37)	32(37)	(a) Trichur, Bidar and Gulbarga districts to Mysore (b) Marathwada districts to Bombay (c) Residuary Telegu-speaking areas to Andhra Pradesh		

(Continued on next page)

TABLE IV

1	2	3	4	5	6
Andhra Pradesh	77(82)	32(44)		(a) existing State—32(44) (b) residuary Telegu-speaking areas of Hyderabad—32(37)	60(77)
Bombay	38(49)	25(78)	(a) Four Kannada-speaking districts to Mysore (b) Abu Road Taluk of Banaskantha district to Rajasthan	(a) existing State—25(78) (b) Marathwada districts from Hyderabad—32(37) (c) Vidarbha areas of Madhya Pradesh —21(50) (d) Saurastra—15(22) (e) Kutch—6(6)	99(193)
Saurastra	15(15)	15(22)	merged with Bombay		
Kutch	6(6)	6(6)	merged with Bombay		
Madhya Pradesh	25(32)	24(55)	(a) Vidarbha areas to Bombay	(a) existing State—24(55) (b) Bhopal State—19(24) (c) Vindhya Pradesh State—15(27) (d) Madhya Bharat (except Sunel Tappa) State—25(37)	83(143)

(Continued on next page)

TABLE IV

1	2	3	4	5	6
Vindhya Pradesh	10(14)	15(27)	merged with Madhya Pradesh		
Bhopal	16(17)	19(24)	merged with Madhya Pradesh		
Madhya Bharat	19(22)	25(37)	(a) entire area except Sunel Tappa merged with Madhya Pradesh (b) Sunel Tappa merged with Rajasthan		
Rajasthan	44(45)	55(74)		(a) existing State—55(74) (b) Abu Road Taluk from Bombay—24(77) (c) Sunel Tappa enclave from Madhya Bharat —25(37) (d) Ajmer—38(42)	142(230)
Ajmer	40(40)	38(42)	merged with Rajasthan		

A third picture emerges in the Punjab and Orissa. It may be remembered that unlike the Southern and Western Indian States, no new area was merged with these States at the time of reorganisation of States in 1956 whose list of Scheduled Castes differed with that of these States. Even then, the number of castes included in the list of Scheduled Castes almost doubled in both these States.

Punjab had 30 castes in its list in 1936 which increased to 39 in 1950. PEPSU had the same set of Scheduled Castes which was merged with Punjab in 1956. Even then, the number soared astronomically to 59 in 1956 and remained static since then. Within a period of 20 years (1936-1956) the number of castes listed as Scheduled nearly doubled, whereas the Provincial Government in 1928 could identify only 2 untouchable castes in Punjab, because the rigidity of caste system was practically non-existent in Punjab.

Haryana, which was carved out of Punjab in 1966, has the same set of 'Scheduled Castes' and the Union Territory of Chandigarh has only 1(3) less.

Orissa's case is very peculiar. In the 1936 Order there were 62 castes in the list. Though the substantial increase in 1936 was mainly for merger of areas from the Madras Presidency, but not a single one was treated as scheduled for that part of the erstwhile Madras Presidency. Again, in 1950 it swelled to 114 and ultimately settled at 123 in 1976, i.e., an increase of 100% in the last 40 years (1936-1976) although there was no change in the boundaries of this State which were fixed in 1936.

In 1956, a large number of castes were scheduled for a small area of the States including the transferred areas. As a matter of fact, as many as 704(1048) castes were scheduled for a part of the States and of them, 644(977) related to the Southern, Western and Central India. It may be mentioned that the scheduling of castes even for a small area like a sub-division originated in Madhya Pradesh in 1931, which in course of time spread to the whole of India. With the withdrawal of area restriction in 1976 a caste considered scheduled for a particular area became scheduled for the entire State. In the whole of India only 25(27) castes are now being treated as scheduled only for a part of the States of Bihar (1), Maharashtra (1), Kerala (2), Karnataka (2), Madhya Pradesh (4) and Tamil Nadu [15(17)].

Exclusion from and inclusion in of castes in Schedules

The above resume may give an impression that a caste once scheduled always remained as such. But it was not so. There was exclusion as well as inclusion. Many castes suffered exclusion from the list by way of transfer to the Scheduled Tribes Lists and descheduling. That apart, the withdrawal of area restriction in 1976 led to rationalisation and simplification in the system of listing of castes in the schedule. A number of castes/ sub-castes or groups of castes/sub-castes which were listed separately in the earlier segmental lists became automatically redundant, a similar one having already found a place in the list from another segmental list. Moreover, so long the words 'or' and 'and' were used in the groups of castes. In the 1976 Order these words were done away with and coma(,) was used instead. This enlarged the scope of including more castes in the groups of castes without in any way increasing the serial numbers in the lists of Scheduled Castes, and resulted in the merger of castes/sub-castes into bigger groups. All these led to considerable reduction in the number of castes/sub-castes — both in the serial number in the Schedule as well as in the effective number without actually excluding any caste/sub-caste from the lists.

The inclusion of castes/sub-castes in the Schedule was effected in two ways — some castes/sub-castes were put individually under separate serial number while some were simply added to the existing ones. Though technically both were fresh scheduling, there was a slight difference in that those coming under the second category did not increase the serial number in the Schedule, only increased the effective strength of castes.

Appendix IV mentions the castes which were actually excluded and included in 16 States from 1950 onwards. Apart from the twelve States, viz., Assam, West Bengal, Bihar, Orissa, U.P., Punjab, Haryana, M.P., Maharashtra, Gujarat, Tamil Nadu and Andhra Pradesh, which formed the nine British Indian Provinces under the 1935 Act, 4 other States, i.e., Kerala, Mysore (Karnataka), Rajasthan and Himachal Pradesh merited similar consideration because in these States also a number of castes were scheduled, descheduled or grouped together before finally settling in 1976. The Scheduled Castes lists in relation to these 4 States were first notified in 1950, which underwent modification in 1956 and 1976. But in the case of Mysore (Karnataka) the list suffered another amendment in 1953 while in the case of Himachal Pradesh the list was amended twice-once in 1954 and again in 1966.

Annexture Table XII gives the figures in a tabulated form.

Transfer to the Scheduled Tribes list

Altogether 32(33) castes have since been transferred to the Scheduled Tribes list as follows :

1950	12(12)
1956	16(17)
1976	4(4)
	32(33)

Of them, 12(12) were in Bengal,

4(4) in Orissa,
9(9) in Madras (Tamil Nadu),
1(1) in Andhra Pradesh,
3(3) in Kerala,
1(1) in Madhya Pradesh, and
2(3) in Bombay (Maharashtra).

32(33)

Descheduling

Altogether 205(243) castes/sub-castes have been descheduled so far since 1950 :

1950	38(38)
1956	108(120)
1960	17(24)
1976	42(61)
	205(243)

In 1950 the largest number of descheduling was in West Bengal and Madhya Pradesh — 28(28).

In 1956, 108(120) castes/sub-castes were descheduled. Of them, as many as 87(91) were in the States of Madras, Andhra Pradesh and Mysore. It may be remembered that in 1953, when Andhra Pradesh was formed and a part of Bellary district was transferred to Mysore State from Madras (undivided) State, the Madras (undivided) list was made applicable to the States of Madras (divided), Andhra Pradesh and the ceded areas of Mysore State. But in the 1956 Order Andhra Pradesh descheduled 46(46) castes, Madras (divided) 17(19) and Mysore 24(26) castes. The descheduling of so many castes within 3 years lends credence to the fact that much thought was not given to the lists while notifying the same in 1953. It was not considered necessary to examine which of these castes should pertain to the new areas. Another point which deserves mention is that of the castes descheduled in these three States, 5 [Byagari, Kadan, Kodalo, Kudubi and Painda] did not figure in any of these 3 States' lists. This brings to the fore the question as to why these were at all put in the Schedule in 1936 itself.

All the castes descheduled in 1960 related to the reconstituted Maharashtra State. As these castes were listed for the particular areas not included in Maharashtra State, these were descheduled from the State's list.

In 1976 42(61) castes were descheduled. Of them, 37(56) were from the two States of Mysore (Karnataka) and Rajasthan. In Karnataka, of the 14(17) castes descheduled, as many as 8(8) were from the Madras (undivided) list, first included in 1953. The rest were from the other ceded areas. So altogether, 32(34) [24(26) + 8(8)] castes out of the 75(80) castes of the Madras (undivided) list have so far been descheduled in this State.

In Rajasthan, 23(39) castes were descheduled. These were from the ceded areas from the erstwhile Bombay State [13(27)], Madhya Bharat [8(9)] and other areas.

Rescheduling

Of the 38 castes descheduled in 1950, 11 were reinducted in 1956 itself and one more in 1976, taking the total to 12. All of them, however, necessarily did not figure individually in the lists. Some were included as a constituent of a wider group. They are :

2 (Halalkhor and Nat) in West Bengal
[both were included in 1956 and 1976]

5 (Dhobi, Khatik, Kumhar, Koli and Ganda) in Madhya Pradesh
[first four were included in 1956 and all five in 1976]

2 (Khatik and Kori) in U.P.
[both were included in 1956 and 1976]

2 (Khalpa and Dhed) in Bombay (Maharashtra)
[both were included in Maharashtra in 1956 and 1976]

1 (Relli) in Andhra Pradesh
[included in Andhra Pradesh in 1956 and 1976]

There were no reinduction from those descheduled in 1956 and 1976.

Grouping of Castes

Grouping of castes was first resorted to by the Bombay Provincial Government in 1917, when in reply to a question from the Government of India, the provincial Government put (1) 'Mangs or Madigs', (2) 'Mahars, Holiyas or Dheds' and (3) 'Chambhar, Chamars or Mochis' in three groups and indicated their population accordingly. This pattern was followed in the 1936 Order when a number of castes were grouped together in Assam, Orissa, M.P., Punjab, Bombay and Bengal, but most of them [31 out of 32] were in the 2-caste group and only 1 in the 3-caste group. In the 1950 Order the same policy was pursued and the number of groups increased substantially but the majority (65) were in the 2-caste group, 6 in the 3-caste group and only 3 in the 4-caste group. This time it was, however, not confined to only 5/6 States but spread to almost all the States.

As the years rolled by, more and more castes were put in the same group — thus dispensing with the separate identity of these castes and in the process, reducing the serial number of castes listed in the Schedule while at the same time ensuring that no caste was left out of the 'Schedule'.

The process is simple enough. For instance, in the earlier Orders, 'Chamar' and 'Muchi' were put separately in the lists of Scheduled Castes. So they were allotted two serial numbers. Now, 'Chamar' and 'Muchi' were put against one serial number. So the serial number was reduced by one while the effective number did not suffer any diminution. In Annexure Table XII under the column 'merger' this has been indicated as 1(0), i.e., one reduction in serial number but no reduction in the effective strength. Similarly, when 'Chamar', 'Muchi' and 'Satnami' were merged in one group, the position was indicated as 2(0), i.e., reduction in the serial number by two but no reduction in the effective number. The position will be clear if one consults the Main Table, placed at the end of all Tables.

In the 1956 Order every 5th (243 out of 1119) caste listed in the Schedule had more than 1 caste against the same entry. Secondly, the number of castes put in a group was not a mere 2, 3 or 4 but much more than that — 5, 6, 7, 8, 9, 10, or even 21, 22. In the 1976

Order it became a phenomenon. Every 4th caste had more than 1 caste against the same entry and the number of castes grouped together swelled to 10, 12, 16, 23, 29, 30.

Table V will give an idea about the number of castes put in a group in the 1936, 1950/51, 1956 and 1976 Orders. There were Orders in between but those are not tabulated for the sake of brevity.

If a caste is grouped with another it can be argued that they are synonyms or the generic names of the same caste. They are not a separate entity by themselves and hence put together in one single entry. This argument does not necessarily hold good in respect of all the castes put in the 2-caste groups or the 3-caste group. Even if this argument is accepted in respect of the 2-caste or 3-caste groups, can the same argument be treated as valid in respect of inclusion of so many castes [10, 12, 16, 22, 23, 29 or 30] in one single group? If they were synonyms or generic names, a question may easily be raised as to why many of them were given a separate entity in the 1936 Order as well as in the 1950 Order. As a matter of fact, as many as 59 castes [4 in 1950, 24 in 1956, and 31 in 1976] were merged with others in this manner over the years.

Moreover, castes/sub-castes were added to the existing ones, which meant no change in the serial number of the Schedule but accretion in the effective strength of castes. As many as 137 castes/sub-castes were thus added as follows :

1950	15
1956	104
1960	1
1966	11
1976	6
	137

So, actually 196 [59 + 137] castes have thus been included in the Schedule without according them individual

TABLE V

	Groups of castes of																
	2	3	4	5	6	7	8	9	10	12	16	21	22	23	29	30	Total
1936	31	1															32
1950/51	65	6	3														74
1956	163	42	19	3	3	3	1	2	4			2	1				243
1976	164	44	22	8	4	1	3		3	1	1			2	1	1	255

identity. These, however, do not take into account the groups of castes which have been included in the respective Orders from the very beginning.

The number of caste-groups in the States under the various Orders may be seen in Annexure Table XIII. It will appear from this Table that bunching of a large number of castes against one single entry is a feature noticeable mainly in five States — Maharashtra, Gujarat, Rajasthan, Madhya Pradesh and Karnataka. This is mainly due to the influence of Bombay (undivided) in the scheduling of castes in these States. For instance,

(1) Bahmbi group is found in the States of Maharashtra (29), Gujarat (23), Rajasthan (30), M.P.(16) and Karnataka (23);

[The figure in bracket indicates the number of castes grouped together.]

(2) Bhangi group is found in the States of Maharashtra (10), Gujarat (10), Rajasthan (12), M.P. (5) and Karnataka (10);

(3) Mahyavanshi group is found in the States of Maharashtra (4), Gujarat (6), Rajasthan (5) and Karnataka (4);

(4) Mang group is found in the States of Maharashtra (8), Rajasthan (3), M.P. (8) and Karnataka (3);

(5) Meghwal group is found in the States of Maharashtra (2), Gujarat (3) and Rajasthan (4);

(6) Halsar group is found in the States of Maharashtra (4), Gujarat (4) and Karnataka (4);

(7) Shenva group is found in the States of Maharashtra (4) and Gujarat (5);

(8) Basor group is found in the States of Maharashtra (4) and M.P. (6).

This leads us to another question — the expansion of Scheduled Castes from one region to another.

Expansion of Scheduled Castes

Till 1952, the geographical boundary of the States coincided with that of the British Indian Provinces and the Indian States. The merging of the Princely States with the States in 1947-49 did not alter the boundary of the Indian Provinces/Indian States which came to be known as States in independent India. The first State to emerge in independent India was Andhra Pradesh which was formed in 1953 by splitting up Madras State when a part of Bellary district was also transferred to Mysore State. Since then, a number of States have been created by reorganisation of existing States/Union Territories, the major one being in 1956, when, in pursuance of the recommendations of the States Reorganisation Commission, the boundaries of many States, specially in the Southern Peninsula and Western India were substantially altered. As the Scheduled Castes had to be listed for each State individually, whenever an area from a State was transferred to another State, the castes treated as scheduled in that area were also made scheduled in the new State for the ceded areas only. In this process, many castes were added to the schedule of the newly created/ constituted States. In the 1956 Order, these castes were considered scheduled only for the ceded areas. This area restriction was withdrawn in1976 and the castes which were treated as scheduled for an area only now became scheduled for the entire State. In this way the castes once considered scheduled in only one State became scheduled also in those States to which new areas were added.

A look at Table IV will indicate that this outflow and inflow of Scheduled Castes from one State to another took place as follows :

- (I) one stream from Madras spread to (1) Kerala, (2) Andhra Pradesh and (3) Karnataka;
- (II) another stream from Hyderabad covered the States of (1) Andhra Pradesh, (2) Karnataka and (3) Maharashtra;
- (III) the Bombay stream moved to (1) Karnataka, (2) Gujarat and (3) Rajasthan;
- (IV) the Madhya Bharat stream extended to (1) Madhya Pradesh and (2) Rajasthan;

(V) Madras was influenced by Kerala because of inflow of Scheduled Castes along with the ceded territory;

(VI) Maharashtra was similarly influenced by Madhya Pradesh because of inflow of Scheduled Castes along with the ceded territory.

The maximum number of streams converged at Karnataka (3), followed by Maharashtra (2) and Rajasthan (2).

That apart, two other streams are also in evidence :

(VII) the Bihar stream spread to West Bengal and Orissa; and

(VIII) the Punjab stream which not only covered (1) Haryana, and (2) Chandigarh, which were part of undivided Punjab, but (3) Himachal Pradesh and (4) Delhi as well.

Because of the influence of these streams and sub-streams, a large number of Scheduled Castes are now common in many of these States. It was held earlier that a caste was untouchable only in a particular area and not in the entire country. A caste was untouchable in a particular area because the degree, concept and manifestation of untouchability varied from area to area. It was also thought that there was 'little or no dispute as to who were untouchables and in which areas, specially in the Southern India'. But the outflow and inflow of Scheduled Castes from one area to another set at naught, at least partially, these widely accepted views.

Another question which merits indepth study is the relation between culture and language and the 'Scheduling of Castes'. An area from one State was merged with another State because of cultural and linguistic homogeneity and geographical contiguity. But this homogeneity had nothing to do so far as 'Scheduling of Castes' was concerned. The 'Scheduling of Castes' was not dependent on 'culture and language' but on their enlistment by the State Government. To bring home this point, the following case may be considered as a representative one.

Purulia district was merged with West Bengal from Bihar in 1956 because the people spoke the same language and were culturally akin to Bengal. But so far as the listing of Scheduled Castes was concerned, Purulia was influenced by Bihar and not by West Bengal. Bantar was a Scheduled Caste in Bihar and so also in Purulia, but not in West Bengal. So when Purulia became a part of West Bengal, Bantar became a Scheduled Caste in West Bengal as well, initially for Purulia district and later for the entire State. Thus, listing of Scheduled Castes depended not on the linguistic and cultural pattern of an area but on the Government in whose hand lies the power.

Due to this expansion of Scheduled Castes from one region to another, a large number of Scheduled Castes are common in these States' lists. This is evident more in those States which were submerged by the eight streams/sub-streams, mentioned above. The names of castes which are common in these States may be seen in Appendix V. The synopsis is given in a tabulated form.

Thus, Tamil Nadu has common list with four States (Kerala, Andhra Pradesh, Karntaka and Pondicherry);

Kerala has common list with four States (Tamil Nadu, Andhra Pradesh, Karnataka and Pondicherry);

Pondicherry has common list with four States (Tamil Nadu, Kerala, Andhra Pradesh and Karnataka);

Andhra Pradesh has common list with eight States (Tamil Nadu, Kerala, Karnataka, Pondicherry, M.P., Maharashtra, Gujarat and Rajasthan);

Karnataka has common list with eight States (Tamil Nadu, Kerala, Andhra Pradesh, Pondicherry, M.P., Maharashtra, Gujarat and Rajasthan);

Madhya Pradesh has common list with five States (Andhra Pradesh, Karnataka, Maharashtra, Gujarat and Rajasthan);

Maharashtra has common list with five States

TABLE VI (A)

Number of Scheduled Castes common with

	Bihar	West Bengal
Bihar		
West Bengal	22(29)	
Orissa	11(13)	16(20)

TABLE VI (B)

Number of Scheduled Castes common with

	Punjab	Himachal Pradesh
Punjab		
Haryana	same	
Chandigarh	same	
Himachal Pradesh	36(56)	
Delhi	15(19)	18(23)

TABLE VI (C)

Number of Scheduled Castes common with

	Tamil Nadu	Kerala	Andhra Pradesh	Karnataka	M.P.	Maharashtra	Gujarat
Tamil Nadu							
Kerala	60(67)						
Andhra Pradesh	19(23)	13(14)					
Karnataka	45(49)	37(38)	43(53)				
Pondicherry	14(15)	10(11)	7(8)	11(12)			
Madhya Pradesh			6(7)	8(14)			
Maharashtra			31(37)	42(98)	21(51)		
Gujarat			6(7)	21(71)	8(13)	24(77)	
Rajasthan			7(8)	11(52)	22(34)	17(58)	12(53)

(Andhra Pradesh, Karnataka, M.P., Gujarat and Rajasthan);

Gujarat has common list with five States (Andhra Pradesh, Karnataka, M.P., Maharashtra and Rajasthan);

Rajasthan has common list with five States (Andhra Pradesh, Karnataka, M.P., Maharashtra and Gujarat).

Earlier also there were certain castes which were common in the Schedules of these States, like Chamar, Muchi/Mochi, Dom and the like, but it never reached such a proportion. It is like inundation of the neighbouring areas by a lake which bursts at its seam.

Number of Castes in the Schedules

We have seen that according to the Orders which are current there are 1091(1704) Scheduled Castes in all the States/Union Territories taken together. It, however, does not mean that there are 1091(1704) Scheduled Castes in the country. For instance, Pasi is a Scheduled Caste in Bihar, Gujarat, Haryana, Himachal Pradesh, Madhya Pradesh, Maharashtra, Orissa, Punjab, Rajasthan, Uttar Pradesh, West Bengal, Chandigarh and Delhi, thus it has been counted 13 times. Likewise, Adi Andhra is a Scheduled Caste in Andhra Pradesh as well as in Karnataka, Kerala, Orissa, Tamil Nadu and Pondicherry and therefore, has been treated as a caste six times. The number of Scheduled Castes in the country would be much less if the Scheduled Castes which are common in more than one State are counted only once and not so many times as figuring in so many States' lists. If the States of Bombay, Madras, Punjab, Assam and Goa, Daman and Diu were not split up and remained undivided, then the total number of Scheduled Castes in all the States/Union Territories taken together would have been 922(1407). This would have been further reduced to 594(890) if all the Scheduled Castes which have been found common in the various States, as listed in Appendix V, were counted only once. Needless to say, the number would have decreased appreciably if all the

Scheduled Castes which are common in all the States'/ Union Territories' lists were identified and then deleted to arrive at an All-India figure. This is, no doubt, a complicated task and in any case is only of academic interest because the Scheduled Castes lists have to be notified in relation to each unit separately. In all our analysis the individual State's list has been adhered to.

25

Scheduled Caste Population: Emerging Pattern

The previous chapter was devoted to the discussion on 'scheduling of castes'. In this chapter it is proposed to have a detailed discussion on the population of the Scheduled Castes.

Enumeration in Different Censuses

Listing of a caste in the "Schedule" is intimately connected with its enumeration in the decennial censuses. It may be remembered that the words "Scheduled Castes" became a part of census lexicon only from the 1941 census. In the Indian censuses prior to 1931, information was collected and published for each individual caste and tribe separately. In the 1931 census, tabulation of figures for individual castes was limited to :

(i) Exterior Castes;

(ii) Primitive Castes;

(iii) All other castes with the exception of:

- (a) those whose members fell short of four per thousand of the total population; and
- (b) those for which separate figures were deemed to be unnecessary by the local Government.

As we have already noticed, most of the exterior castes of the 1931 Census found a place in the 1936 Order, which, for the first time, listed the Scheduled

Castes for each of the Nine British Indian Provinces. The 1941 Census, however, did not furnish the population of each individual "Scheduled Caste" in the British Indian Provinces. 'Group Totals' were tabulated for "Scheduled Castes", "Tribes" and "Anglo-Indians". Separate totals were furnished only for a few selected individual tribes.

Though the 1936 Order refrained from categorising the "Scheduled Castes" in the Indian States, the 1941 Census did furnish the 'Group Totals' of the 'Scheduled Castes' in the Indian States as well. It is, however, not understood how the Census Authority, in the absence of specific lists in relation to these Indian States, could enumerate the 'Scheduled Castes' in the Indian States and also furnish their total population figures. Since separate totals for each of the individual 'Scheduled Castes' in the Indian States were not indicated in the 1941 Census report, the castes considered 'Scheduled' in the Indian States by the Census Authority could not be identified.

The vivisection of the country in 1947 saw the emergence of two independent nations. Not only the Muslim-majority provinces of the NWFP, Sind and Baluchistan, but the Muslim-majority areas of the provinces of Assam, Bengal and Punjab also went to Pakistan. Consequently, there was change in the total population as well as in the 'Scheduled Castes' population in that portion of Assam, Bengal and Punjab which formed part of India. Moreover, the population of the Indian States which either were merged with the existing provinces (now States) or remained as a separate entity had to be taken into account.

The 1951 Census, pursuant of the policy of the Government of India to discourage community distinction based on castes, marked a complete departure from the traditional recording of Race, Tribe or Caste. The only relevant question on Caste or Tribe incorporated in the Census Schedule was to enquire if the person enumerated was a member of any 'Scheduled Caste', or any 'Scheduled Tribe' or any other 'Backward Class' or if he was an 'Anglo-Indian' and only group totals of such communities were given. The data was published in the following three Tables :

(i) Table I — Scheduled Castes — giving the distribution of the members of Sche-duled Castes by livelihood classes, by rural-urban and sex break up;

(ii) Table II — Scheduled Tribes — giving the distribution of the members of the Scheduled Tribes by the characteristics as mentioned above; and

(iii) Table III — Anglo-Indians — giving the population for India, each Zone and State/Union Territory by sex break up.[1]

In the 1951 Census the 'Scheduled Castes' population was extracted according to the Orders issued in 1950-51 in relation to 9 Part A, 8 Part B and 9 Part C States. But like its predecessor, the 1951 Census also did not furnish the population of each individual 'Scheduled Caste' in relation to these Parts A, B and C States. Only 'Group Totals' were furnished.

In 1956 the States were reorganised and a fresh Order listing the Scheduled Castes in relation to these States was issued. In 1960 Bombay was bifurcated into Maharashtra and Gujarat and the lists of Scheduled Castes again underwent modification in relation to these two States. In the 1961 Census, the Scheduled Caste population was extracted as per the revised Orders. This time it was felt that group totals alone would be too meagre to guide in the implementation of measures adequately for the amelioration of the special groups of the socially and economically handicapped according to the directive principles of State policy. Therefore, special detailed tabulation of social, economic, demographic and educational data pertaining to each Scheduled Caste and Scheduled Tribe separately was found necessary. Accordingly, in all, seven tables relating to each Scheduled Caste were prepared and published as follows :

(1) Industrial classification of persons at work and non-workers by sex for (each) Scheduled Caste.

(2) Age and marital status for (each) Scheduled Caste.

(3) Education in urban areas only for (each) Scheduled Caste.

(4) Education in rural areas only for (each) Scheduled Caste.

(5) Religion for (each) Scheduled Caste.

(6) Sample households engaged in cultivation classified by interest in land and size of land cultivated in rural areas for (each) Scheduled Caste.

(7) Persons not at work classified by sex, type of activity and educational levels for (each) Scheduled Caste.[2]

These tables at the State and Union Territory level have been published in Volume I : India, Part V-A(i) Special Tables for Scheduled Castes. Tables at the district level have been published in separate volume for each State and Union Territory.

But an innovation was made in the 1961 Census. The enumerators were provided with a set of synonyms and generic names of the Scheduled Castes and Scheduled Tribes so that a person who returned his caste or tribe by any synonym or generic name was enumerated as Scheduled Caste or Scheduled Tribe, irrespective of whether such synonym or generic name found a place in the notified list.[3] The 1961 Census figure, therefore, went beyond the population figure of the listed castes.

In the 1971 Census, however, in view of the

Supreme Court Judgment on the subject in Bhaiya Ram Munda Vs. Anirudh Patar (A.I.R. 1971 S.C. 2533) the notified list of Scheduled Castes and Scheduled Tribes applicable to each State and Union Territory had to be strictly followed and the synonyms or generic names of such communities could not be recognised for purpose of enumeration as Scheduled Caste or Scheduled Tribe. There was, therefore, a possibility that despite specific instructions to enumerators to make all efforts to elicit the correct name of the caste or tribe, some persons might have returned themselves by some synonym, local name or generic name and suffered omission from the enumeration as a member of a Scheduled Caste or a Scheduled Tribe.[4]

In the 1971 Census, the Scheduled Caste population of the newly created States/Union Territories were also tabulated along with the existing ones. This time also the population of each individual Scheduled Caste was tabulated and six comparable tables for Scheduled Castes have been prepared and published :

1 Industrial classification of persons at work and non-workers by sex for (each) Scheduled Caste —Rural.

2 Industrial classification of persons at work and non-workers by sex for (each) Scheduled Caste — Urban.

3 Age and marital status for (each) Scheduled Caste.

4 Education in urban areas only for (each) Scheduled Caste.

5 Education in rural areas only for (each) Scheduled Caste.

6 Persons not at work classified by sex, type of activity and educational level for (each) Scheduled Caste.[5]

Like 1961, in 1971 also these tables at the State and Union Territory level have been published as Series I-India, Part V-A(i) Special Tables for Scheduled Castes.

Tables at the district level have been published in separate volumes for each State and Union Territory.

In 1976, the Scheduled Castes Orders were again modified mainly to do away with the area restriction. Bunching of castes, which was started in 1936 and followed in all subsequent Orders, reached its zenith in 1976. The 1981 Census was undertaken as per the 1976 Order.

As in 1961 and 1971 censuses, comparable tables for individual Scheduled Caste have been prepared and published for the 1981 Census :

1 Industrial category of main workers, marginal workers, non-workers and seeking/available for work by sex for Scheduled Castes (for each Scheduled Caste separately).

2 Industrial category of work of marginal workers of Scheduled Castes by seeking/available, non-seeking/available for work and sex (for each Scheduled Caste separately).

3 Marginal workers and non-workers by sex, type of activity and educational level for Scheduled Castes (for each Scheduled Caste separately).

4 Marginal workers of Scheduled Castes by main activity cross-classified by industrial category of marginal workers and sex (for each Scheduled Caste separately).

5 Age and marital status of Scheduled Castes-All areas (for each Scheduled caste separately).

6 Educational levels of Scheduled Castes-Urban areas (for each Scheduled Caste separately);

7 Educational levels of Scheduled Castes-Rural areas (for each Scheduled Caste separately).[6]

These tables have been published in separate volumes (Part-IX Special Tables for Scheduled Castes) for each State and Union Territory at district level. All India volumes containing data upto State and Union Territory level have not yet been published.

Comparable tables for individual Scheduled Caste for the 1991 census are yet to be published.

Another point which deserves mention is the enumeration of a large number of persons as unclassified/ unspecified in all the censuses since 1961. In spite of specific instructions on the subject, it was found by the Census authority that in some individual slips of Scheduled Castes and Scheduled Tribes, the name of caste or tribe was not entered and returns in general terms as 'Harijan', 'Adivasi', 'Achhut', etc., were found. The Census authority thought that there was no doubt that the person so returned did belong, in fact, to a Scheduled Caste/Scheduled Tribe. Such returns were clubbed together and shown under "unclassified", separately for the Scheduled Castes and Scheduled Tribes in the 1961 Census[7] and were treated as "unspecified" Scheduled Castes/Scheduled Tribes in the 1971 Census.[8] But in the 1981 Census, the general terms, like Harijans/ Girijan/or Achhut/Adivasi were not reckoned as belonging to Scheduled Caste or Scheduled Tribe, as the case might be. In such cases, the name of the caste/tribe was ascertained fully and if that name found place in the list furnished to the enumerator, he/she was treated as Scheduled Caste or Scheduled Tribe, as the case might be. If the person merely claimed to be a Scheduled Caste or Scheduled Tribe, but said that he/she did not belong to any of the notified communities applicable to the area, he/she was not reckoned as belonging to a Scheduled Caste or a Scheduled Tribe.[9] But, in spite of this clear instructions of the Census Commissioner, in the 1981 Census, "All Scheduled Castes" included the figures of "Unclassified" as well.

Total Population as well as the Scheduled Caste Population since 1941

Having discussed the procedure adopted for enumeration and tabulation of the population figures of the Scheduled Castes in successive census operations, let us now have a look at the population figures themselves. Table VII gives the total population as well as the

Scheduled Caste population in India as enumerated in the censuses since 1931. The 1931 figure has been calculated according to the 1936 Order. Both the 1931 and 1941 figures pertain to undivided India. In 1981, census could not be held in Assam because of the disturbed condition prevailing there at the time of the 1981 census operations. The projected population of Assam has, however, been given in the census report of 1981. Accordingly, the Scheduled Caste population has been projected assuming that the decadal growth rate of the Scheduled Caste population was the same as that of the total population in that State.

In 1991, census could not be conducted in Jammu and Kashmir due to the disturbed condition in that State. As the projected population of Jammu and Kashmir in the 1991 Census has since been indicated in the Census report of 1991, Series I, Paper 2 of 1992, the Scheduled Caste population has been calculated assuming the decadal growth rate (28.92%) being the same for the Scheduled Caste population also.

It will appear from Table VII that the Scheduled Caste population declined appreciably in the 1941 Census, i.e., immediately after the 1936 Order listing the castes as 'Scheduled' was issued. It registered a steady increase since 1951, with the exception in 1971 when it decreased marginally compared to that of 1961. This may be attributed to the Supreme Court Judgment in the Bhaiya Ram Munda case in obedience to which the Census of 1971 had to be undertaken strictly adhering to the list of Scheduled Castes applicable to each State/Union Territory. The synonyms or generic names of communities considered Scheduled Castes for the purpose of enumeration in the 1961 Census could not be recognised as Scheduled Castes in the 1971 Census.

The steady increase in the Scheduled Caste population is, however, not uniform in all the States/Union Territories. The Scheduled Caste population as well as the percentage of Scheduled Caste population to total population of the State/Union Territory in all the States/

TABLE VII

Period	Total population	Total Scheduled Caste population	Percentage of Scheduled Caste population to total population	Source
1931	25,67,57,818*	3,99,12,634*@	15.54	a
1941	29,58,08,722*	3,99,20,807*	13.49	b
1951	35,67,00,000	5,13,43,898	14.40	c
1961	43,92,34,771	6,44,49,275	14.67	d
1971	54,81,59,652	8,00,05,398	14.60	e
1981	68,51,84,692**	10,60,27,207**	15.47	f
1991	84,63,02,688***	13,88,64,477***	16.41	g

* only British Indian provinces in undivided India.

** includes projected population of Assam.

*** includes projected population of Jammu and Kashmir.

@ approximately.

Source :

a. Annexture Table II.

b. Census of India, 1941, Vol. I, Pt. I (Tables), Table XIII, p. 98.

c. Census of India, 1951, Paper 4 of 1953, p. 3.

d. Census of India, 1961, Vol.I, Part V A(1), p. xlviii.

e. Census of India, 1971, Series I, Paper 1 of 1975, pp. 2-4.

f. Census of India, 1981, Series I, Paper 2 of 1984, p. 6, and pp. 14-16.

g. Census of India, 1991, Series I, Paper 2 of 1992, p. 86.

Union Territories since 1961 has been tabulated in Annexure Table XIV. While in the all-India projection, there was a marginal drop in the Scheduled Caste population in 1971, it was not reflected in the Scheduled Caste population figures of many States/Union Territories. Whereas in the States of Kerala, Karnataka, Tamil Nadu, Andhra Pradesh, Madhya Pradesh, Rajasthan, Himachal Pradesh, Manipur and Orissa, there was a commensurate decrease in the Scheduled Caste population as compared to its share in the total population of these States, in the States of Assam, Tripura, West Bengal, Bihar, U.P., Jammu and Kashmir, Punjab, Gujarat, Maharashtra, and in the Union Territories of Delhi, Pondicherry and Dadra and Nagar Haveli, the increase in the growth of the Scheduled Caste population continued unhindered.

As a matter of fact, the steady increase in the Scheduled Caste population is perceptible in the latter States in all the censuses. In the case of the former States, the increase was picked up in the latter censuses of 1981 and 1991 except in the State of Himachal Pradesh where the share of the Scheduled Caste population in the total population never reached the 1961 level and in the State of Kerala, it fell again marginally in 1991 compared to that of 1981.

Decadal growth

Table VIII indicates the total population of India since 1901 and its decadal growth percentage along with the comparative figures of the Scheduled Caste population.

The Scheduled Caste population as also the total population in the British Indian provinces in the 1931 and 1941 censuses are available. While the figure of total population in the truncated India in the 1941 Census and beyond has been tabulated and furnished in the 1981 Census Report, the Scheduled Caste population in 1931 and 1941 in the truncated India have not been indicated. Hence for facility of comparison, the 1931 and 1941 Scheduled Caste population figures have not been taken into account.

TABLE VIII

Population of India, 1901-1991

Year	Population	Decadal growth rate percentage	Source	Scheduled Caste population	Decadal growth rate percentage
1901	238,396,327	-	a		
1911	252,093,390	5.75	a		
1921	251,321,213	-0.31	a		
1931	278,077,238	11.00	a		
1941	318,660,580	14.22	a		
1951	361,088,090	13.31	a	51,343,898	
1961	439,231,771	21.51	a	64,449,275	25.52
1971	548,159,652	24.80	a	80,005,398	24.14
1981	685,184,692*	25.00	a	106,027,207*	32.52
1991	846,302,688**	23.51	b	138,864,477**	30.97

* includes the projected population of Assam.

** includes the projected population of Jammu and Kashmir.

Source :

a. Census of India, 1981, Series I, Paper 2 of 1984, p. 3.

b. Census of India, 1991, Series I, Paper 1 of 1992, p. 86.

It will appear from Table VIII that the decadal growth rate of Scheduled Caste population since 1961 was more than the total population growth rate except in 1971 when it was marginally less for the reasons stated earlier. The overall increase of the population from 1951 to 1991 was 234.38% whereas the Scheduled Caste population increased by 270.46% during the same period. Since the jurisdiction of many States changed and new States came into being in 1956 and thereafter, for purposes of a meaningful comparison, it is better to confine to the period of 1961-1991. It has the added advantage in that the population figure of each and every Scheduled Caste was tabulated since the 1961 Census [The 1991 Census figure is, however, not yet published]. During the period 1961-91, the total population increased by 192.47% while the Scheduled Caste population increased by 215.46%. This increase in the Scheduled Caste population was, however, not distributed equitably in all the States/Union Territories.

From Table IX placed on next page, it will appear that the growth rate was below the All-India average in Tamil Nadu (176.56%), Orissa (185.58%), U.P. (190.35%), Bihar (193.26%), Kerala (201.11%), and Andhra Pradesh (212.96%), whereas it was very high in Delhi (525.52%), Maharashtra (393.27%), Tripura (376.79%) and Himachal Pradesh (354.21%), followed by Manipur (277.74%), Dadra and Nagar Haveli (277.16%), Karnataka (236.40%), West Bengal (233.38%) and Pondicherry (230.94%). The increase in Assam (227.79%), Rajasthan (226.44%), Madhya Pradesh (226.35%), Jammu & Kashmir (225.67%), Gujarat (223.83%), and Punjab (219.84%) is, however, not so phenomenal.

Barring West Bengal, the other Eastern States of Orissa, Bihar and U.P. witnessed a less-than-all-India-average growth. All the North-Eastern States, viz., Manipur, Tripura and Assam (Meghalaya and Mizoram included) experienced a sizable increase. Similarly, there was a very high increase in Delhi and Himachal Pradesh and a marginal increase in Rajasthan and Punjab. It is a

TABLE IX

Growth rate of Scheduled Caste population, 1961-91

Name of units	Population in 1961	Base	Population in 1991	Percentage increase
India	64,449,275	100	138,864,477	215.46
Andhra Pradesh	4,973,616	100	10,592,066	212.96
Arunachal Pradesh			4,052	
Assam	732,756	100	1,659,412	227.79 *
Meghalaya	--		9,072	
Mizoram	--		691	
Bihar	6,504,966	100	12,571,700	193.26
Gujarat	1,367,255	100	3,060,358	223.83
Himachal Pradesh	369,916	100	1,310,296	354.21
Jammu and Kashmir	284,131	100	641,200	225.67
Karnataka	3,117,232	100	7,369,279	236.40
Kerala	1,434,817	100	2,886,522	201.11
Madhya Pradesh	4,253,024	100	9,626,679	226.35
Maharashtra	2,226,914	100	8,757,842	393.27
Manipur	13,376	100	37,150	277.74
Orissa	2,763,858	100	5,129,314	185.58
Punjab	4,139,106	100	5,742,528	219.84 **
Haryana			3,250,933	
Chandigarh			105,977	
Rajasthan	3,359,640	100	7,607,820	226.44
Sikkim			24,084	
Tamil Nadu	6,067,327	100	10,712,266	176.56
Tripura	119,725	100	451,116	376.79

(Continued on next page)

TABLE IX

Growth rate of Scheduled Caste population, 1961-91

Name of units	Population in 1961	Base	Population in 1991	Percentage increase
Uttar Pradesh	15,399,881	100	29,276,455	190.35
West Bengal	6,890,314	100	16,080,611	233.38
Dadra and Nagar Haveli	985	100	2,730	277.16
Delhi	341,555	100	1,794,836	525.52
Goa, Daman & Diu			28,255	
Pondicherry	56,846	100	131,278	230.94

* includes Meghalaya and Mizoram.

** includes Haryana and Chandigarh.

matter of study whether the influx of migrants from East Pakistan, now Bangladesh, and West Pakistan, had anything to do with this increase in these two pockets. What is, however, very difficult to explain is the abnormal increase in Maharashtra.

In the three Southern States of Kerala, Tamil Nadu and Andhra Pradesh, the decrease was quite perceptible, even though these States accounted for a sharp rise in the number of castes listed as Scheduled.

Distribution of Scheduled Caste population

This now takes us to the question of distribution of Scheduled Caste population among the States and Union Territories. It would be evident from Annexture Table XV which gives the distribution percent of total population as well as of the Scheduled Caste population in States and Union Territories during the period 1961-91, that the distribution of percentage of Scheduled Caste population among the States/Union Territories was not in conformity with the distribution of percentage of total population. As the States' share of the total population increased in the States of Gujarat (from 4.70% to 4.88%), Haryana (from 1.83% to 1.95%), Himachal Pradesh (.31% to .61%), Jammu and Kashmir (.81% to .91%), Madhya Pradesh (7.37% to 7.82%), Maharashtra (9.01% to 9.33%), Rajasthan (4.59% to 5.20%), West Bengal (7.95% to 8.04%), Manipur (.18% to .22%), Tripura (.26% to .33%), Dadra and Nagar Haveli (.01% to .02%), Delhi (.61% to 1.11%), Pondicherry (.08% to .10%), Chandigarh (.05% to 0.8%) and Sikkim (.04% to .05%) during the period 1961-91, there was an increase in their share of Scheduled Caste population as well in all these States/Union Territories except in Haryana where it decreased marginally (from 2.37% to 2.35%) and in Meghalaya and Pondicherry where it remained static. Again, while during the same period share of the total population decreased in the States of Andhra Pradesh (from 8.19% to 7.86%), Assam (from 2.70% to 2.65%), Bihar (10.58% to 10.21%), Punjab (2.47% to 2.40%), Karnataka (5.37% to 5.31%), Kerala (3.85% to 3.44%), Orissa (3.99% to

3.74%), Tamil Nadu (7.67% to 6.60%), U.P. (16.79% to 16.44%) and in the Union Territory of Goa, Daman and Diu (.16% to .15%), there was a decrease in their share of Scheduled Caste population in all these States except in the States of Assam (from 1.14% to 1.20%) and Karnataka (from 4.84% to 5.33%) where it increased marginally and in Goa, Daman and Diu where it remained static. So, Haryana, Assam and Karnataka are the exceptions to the general trend of increase/decrease in the percentage of Scheduled Caste population when there was an increase/decrease in their share of total population.

Again, this increase or decrease in the percentage of Sche-duled Caste population in the States/Union Territories was not commensurate with the corresponding increase or decrease in the percentage of total population during the period 1961-91. In some States/Union Territories the Scheduled Caste population increased or decreased more than the corresponding increase or decrease in the total population while in some States/Union Territories it was the other way round. Among the States/Union Territories where the increase in the percentage of Scheduled Caste population was more than the increase in the percentage of the total population, Maharashtra heads the list. The total population registered an increase of 103.55% whereas the Scheduled Caste population increased by 183.24%. The other States/Union Territories are Sikkim (general population increased by 125% : the Scheduled Caste population increased by 200%), Tripura, (126.92% : 173.68%), Manipur (122.22% : 150%), Chandigarh (160% : 200%), Delhi (181.97% : 243.40%), West Bengal (101.13% : 108.69%) and Gujarat (103.83% : 104.24%). The States where increase in the Scheduled Caste population could not keep pace with the increase in the total population are Madhya Pradesh (106.11% increase in the total population : 105.61% increase in the Scheduled Caste population), Jammu and Kashmir (112.35% : 104.55%), Rajasthan (113.29% : 105.56%), Himachal Pradesh (196.77% : 166.66%), Pondicherry (125% : 100%) and Meghalaya (116.60% : 100%). The only State where the Scheduled Caste population registered a negative growth was Haryana (106.55%: 99.16%).

Similarly, among the States where the ratio between the decrease in the total population and the decrease in the Scheduled Caste population are not commensurate mention may be made of the following where the Scheduled Caste population did not decrease in the same proportion as that of the total population and in two cases, it registered an increase: Karnataka (total population decreased to 98.88% : the Scheduled Caste population increased to 110.12%), Assam (98.15% : 119.94%), Goa, Daman and Diu (93.75% : 100%), Andhra (total population decreased to 95.97% : Scheduled Caste population decreased to 99.22%), Punjab (97.17% : 99.52%) and Kerala (89.35% : 93.72%), whereas in the following States the decrease in the percentage of the Scheduled Caste population was more than the decrease in the percentage of total population : U.P. (97.92% : 88.58%), Orissa (93.73% : 86.48%), Bihar (96.50% : 90.00%), and Tamil Nadu (86.05 : 82.27%).

The study of the proportion of Scheduled Caste population among the States/Union Territories, as revealed in the censuses, makes quite an interesting reading. According to the 1991 Census, Uttar Pradesh, which accounted for 16.44% of the country's population, had a considerable high share of 21.18% of the country's Scheduled Caste population. Bihar, on the other hand, shared 10.21 percent of the country's total population but its share of the Scheduled Caste population was relatively less, 9.09 percent. The third most populous State of Maharashtra accounted for 9.33 percent of the country's population whereas only 6.34 percent of the country's Scheduled Caste was enumerated in the State. The next most populous State of West Bengal registered 8.04 percent of the country's population but 11.63 percent of the country's Scheduled Caste population were found in that State. Of the major States having 1 crore plus population at the time of the 1991 Census, the share of the country's total population was less than the share of the country's Scheduled Caste population in Tamil Nadu (6.60 percent of the country's population: 7.75 percent of the country's Scheduled Caste population), Karnataka (5.31% : 5.33%), Rajasthan (5.20% : 5.50%), Punjab (2.40% : 4.16%) and Haryana (1.95% : 2.35%).

Annexure Table XV also reveals that in U.P. which accounted for 21.18% of the country' Scheduled Caste population in the 1991 Census its Scheduled Caste population was 21.04 percent of the total population of the State, while in West Bengal which accounted for 11.63% of the country's Scheduled Castes in the 1991 Census, its Scheduled Castes comprised 23.62% of the State's total population. The position in some other States are : Tamil Nadu (7.75 : 19.15), Orissa (3.71 : 16.20), M.P. (6.97 : 14.55), Kerala (2.09 : 9.92), Karnataka (5.33 : 16.38), Punjab (4.16 : 28.31), Haryana (2.35 : 19.75), Bihar (9.09 :14.55), Maharashtra (6.34 : 11.09), Gujarat (2.21 : 7.41), Assam (1.20 : 7.40), and Andhra Pradesh (7.66 : 15.92). The position in other States/Union Territories has been detailed in Annexure Table XV. It will appear from this Table that this trend as noticed in the 1991 Census was observed in the previous censuses of 1961, 1971 and 1981 as well.

The ratio between the percentage of the Scheduled Caste population in the 1961 Census and in the 1991 Census shows that the maximum increase was in the State of Maharashtra where it was 196.98% and the minimum was in the State of Himachal Pradesh where it was 92.55%. The position in the other States/Union Territories has been indicated in Annexure Table XV. It will appear that among the major States, apart from Maharashtra, West Bengal (118.59%), Karnataka (123.73%), Assam (119.94%), Andhra Pradesh (115.20%), Punjab (114.57%), Gujarat (111.76%) and Madhya Pradesh (110.73%) registered a two digit increase. In urban areas like Delhi and Chandigarh it was quite high — 148.25% and 146.11% respectively.

It may be noted that in all these States except Andhra Pradesh and Punjab the ratio between the percent distribution of the country's Scheduled Caste population in the 1961 Census and the 1991 Census has registered an increase, though not commensurate with the increase in the States' Scheduled Caste population ratio. So far as the increase in the percent distribution of total population during the same period is concerned, Andhra Pradesh, Assam and Punjab (the period is 1971-1991) showed a decreasing trend while the remaining five States registered a minimal increasing trend. Both the Union Territories of Delhi and Chandigarh registered an overwhelming increasing ratio both in regard to the percent distribution of the country's Scheduled Caste population as well as the country's total population during this period (in the case of Chandigarh the period was 1971-91).

Another feature which deserves special mention is the preeminent position enjoyed by the States of West Bengal and U.P., where about 1/3rd of the country's Scheduled Caste population live. Though their share dwindled to 32.91% in 1991 from 34.01% in the 1961 Census, it was still higher than the 1951 Census figure of 31.50%. Incidentally, these are the two States where, according to the Simon Commission in 1930, there was 'wide margin of possible error' so far as the untouchable population was concerned.

Caste-wise analysis

If we examine the population distribution of individual community among the Scheduled Castes, broad variations between their numbers are noticed. This variation in population is found with the highest of 129 lakhs in U.P. to the lowest of 1 in Mizoram in the 1981 Census. For the purpose of convenience and getting into close view of the situation, it will be better to classify the different castes or groups of castes according to their population sizes. If we categorise them on the basis of their relative population strength like 1,00,000 or 10,000 or 1,000 or even 100, then the actual position would not be reflected because the population vary tremendously from State to State, depending on the size of the State and the density of the population. So, instead of categorising them according to their population number, it is better to classify the castes or groups of castes according to its share in the State's Scheduled Caste population. Accordingly, the castes/groups of castes have been brought under six different categories. Those communities with a population of 10% or more of the total Scheduled Caste population of the State have been brought under 'very large' group. The communities with a population between 10% and 1% of the State's Scheduled Caste population are put under 'large' group. 'Small' communities are those returning a population between 1% and .1% while 'very small' communities are those having a population ranging between .1%-.01%. The communities accounting for a population between .01% and .001% are categorised as 'negligible' while those less than .001%, i.e., less than 1 per lakh of Scheduled Caste population in a State are classed as 'most negligible'.

The number of castes coming under these six different categories as also its share in the unit's total Scheduled Caste population in each State/Union Territory in the censuses of 1961, 1971 and 1981 are indicated in Annexure Table XVI.

Most Negligible category

Annexure Table XVI indicates that in one extreme of the population distribution is the 'most negligible' category. A number of castes returned a very insignificant population, even less than 1 per lakh of the States' Scheduled Caste population. 70 such castes were identified in the 1961 Census, 83 in the 1971 Census and 35 in the 1981 census in the States mentioned in table X.

It may be noted that bulk of them were from the southern and western States of Kerala, Tamil Nadu, Andhra Pradesh, Maharashtra and Gujarat. They contributed 57 castes in the 1961 Census, 60 in the 1971 Census and 28 in the 1981 Census.

TABLEX

	1961 census	1971 census	1981 census
Andhra Pradesh	2	2	1
Gujarat	3	8	3
Haryana	-	-	1
Himachal Pradesh	-	4	2
Karnataka	16	14	7
Kerala	3	6	2
Madhya Pradesh	1	2	-
Maharashtra	12	8	-
Orissa	4	6	4
Punjab	2	2	-
Rajasthan	3	7	-
Tamil Nadu	21	21	15
Tripura	1	1	
Uttar Pradesh	2	1	
West Bengal	-	1	
Total	70	83	35

Very Large category

On the other hand, it is found that only a few castes/ groups of castes constitute the majority of the units' Scheduled Caste population. They come under 'very large' category, i.e., those returning a population of 10% and above and their number ranged between 1 to 4 in the States/Union Territories accounting for more than 65% of the total Scheduled Caste population in the units. In Andhra Pradesh 3 castes accounted for a population of 90.24% in the 1961 Census, 90.82% (again 3 castes) in the 1971 Census while 2 castes constituted 81.25% of the total Scheduled Caste population in the 1981 Census. The corresponding figure for the other States/ Union Territories are as follows (the number of castes are noted in bracket) : Assam 69.18% (3 castes) in the 1961 Census, 65.27% (2 castes) in the 1971 Census and none in the 1981 Census as the census was not under-taken; Bihar 71.13% (3 castes); 71.14% (3 castes) and 69.27% (3 castes); Gujarat 70.50% (4 castes); 58.73% (3 castes) and 82.88% (3 castes); Jammu and Kashmir 86.89% (3 castes), 85.32% (3 castes) and 84.81% (3 castes); Kerala 57.57% (3 castes); 57.84% (3 castes) and

44.67% (2 castes); Karnataka 50.89% (2 castes); 47.65% (2 castes) and 55.61% (3 castes); Madhya Pradesh 56.87% (3 castes); 44.99% (2 castes) and 52.25% (1 caste); Maharashtra 73.72% (5 castes); 60.91% (4 castes) and 83.16% (3 castes); Manipur 85.07% (2 castes); 83.07% (2 castes) and 92.66% (3 castes); Orissa 46.01% (3 castes); 31.50% (2 castes) and 53.57% (4 castes); Punjab 82.15% (4 castes); 83.19% (4 castes) and 84.24% (4 castes); Rajasthan 40.57% (1 caste); 51.48% (2 castes) and 47.29% (2 cases); Tamil Nadu 82.49% (4 castes); 85.74% (4 castes) and 76.05% (3 castes); Uttar Pradesh 70.87% (2 castes); 68.44% (2 castes) and 69.67% (2 castes); West Bengal 56.64% (4 castes); 52.19% (4 castes) and 60.99% (4 castes); Delhi 52.33% (2 castes); 50.88% (2 castes) and 56.52% (2 castes); Himachal Pradesh 62.10% (2 castes), 60.06% (2 castes) and 66.51% (3 castes), Tripura 76.81% (4 castes), 90.59% (2 castes) and 82.23% (4 castes); Dadra and Nagar Haveli 98.79% (2 castes), 97.60% (2 castes) and 90.44% (2 castes); and Pondicherry 89.41% (2 castes), 84.83% (2 castes) and 89.58% (2 castes).

61 castes/groups of castes came in this category from 21 States/Union Territories in the 1961 Census, 73 from 26 States/Union Territories in the 1971 Census and 74 from 27 States/Union Territories in the 1981 Census, the national average being 2.90 castes covering 67.85% of the population in the 1961 Census, 2.81 castes accounting for 65.23% of the population in the 1971 Census and 2.74 castes covering 67.32% of the population in the 1981 Census. Thus, there was a marginal decrease in the average number of castes — from 2.90 to 2.74 during the period 1961-81 while the percentage of population covered by them also decreased to 67.32% from 67.85% during the same period.

The castes/groups of castes coming under this category along with their population in each State/Union Territory in the three censuses of 1961, 1971 and 1981 are presented in Annexure Table XVII. Annexure Table XVII reveals that more or less the same castes/groups of castes figured in this category in almost all these censuses. There were, however, some exclusions or inclusions in some States because the strength of these castes/groups of castes either decreased or increased warranting their exclusion from or inclusion in this category. The formation of bigger groups due to merger of castes/groups of castes led to increase in the strength of some castes/groups of castes, specially in the 1981 Census. Only Bhangi group of castes in Gujarat and Ganda in Orissa were not included in this category in the 1971 Census but their position was restored in the 1981 Census. 7 castes/groups of castes, however, could not retain their position in the 1981 Census. They were : Adi Andhra in Andhra Pradesh, Kuravan, Sidhanar in Kerala, Adi Dravida in Karnataka, Chakkiliyan in Tamil Nadu, Mali in Tripura, and Brittial Bania, Bania and Kaibartta, Jaliya in Meghalaya.

Similarly, eleven new castes/groups of castes were added to this category — Dhoba in Tripura and Megh, Meghwal in Rajasthan since the 1971 Census, Patni in Manipur, Dhoba, Dhobi in Orissa, Banjara, Lambani and Bhovi in Karnataka, Lohar in Himachal Pradesh, Mehtar, Bhangi in Meghalaya, Dhupi, Dhobi, Muchi, Rishi and Namasudra in Arunachal Pradesh in the 1981 Census.

A point which deserves mention is the predominance of one or two castes or groups of castes in the all-India arena. Though there is no all-India list of Scheduled Castes, certain castes/groups of castes are found in more or less every State/Union Territory. Chamar group of castes, which, inter alia, included Muchi, Jatava, Bhambi, Chambhar and the like, form the largest block in the all-India field. It is no wonder that this group of castes figures in the 'very large' group in 17 States/Union Territories, in the 'large' group in 5 States/Union Territories, in the other intermediary groups in 3 States and has no representation in 2 units (Sikkim and Pondicherry) in the 1981 Census. This group of castes alone accounted for 27.88% of the country's Scheduled Caste population in the 1961 Census, 27.18% in the 1971 Census and 26.46% in the 1981 Census. If the four southern States of Kerala, Tamil Nadu, Pondicherry and Andhra Pradesh, where this group of castes has not many followers, are left aside, then the share of this group of castes in the Scheduled Caste population of the remaining States/ Union Territories comes to 34.60% in the 1961 Census, 33.38% in the 1971 Census and 36.05% in the 1981 Census. It is quite interesting to note that in Uttar Pradesh, 'Chamar, Dhusia, Jhusia, Jatava', treated as one group, accounted for more than half of the total Scheduled Caste population of the State (55.06 percent to be exact) in the 1981 Census. Similarly, in Madhya Pradesh 'Chamar, Chamari, Bairwa, Bhambi, Jatav, Mochi, Regar, Nona, Rohidas, Ramnami, Satnami, Surjyabanshi, Surjyaramnami, Ahirwar, Chamar Mangan, Raidas' together accounted for 52.25 percent of the Scheduled Caste population of the State. In Haryana also 'Chamar, Jatia Chamar, Rehgar, Raigar, Ramdasi, Ravidasi' accounted for 52.65 percent of the Scheduled Caste population of the State in that census.

In the four southern States of Kerala, Karnataka, Tamil Nadu and Andhra Pradesh and in the Union Territory of Pondicherry the three 'Adi' groups of castes (Adi Andhra, Adi Dravida and Adi Karnataka) accounted for 25.98% of these units' Scheduled Caste population in the 1961 Census, 27.47% in the 1971 Census and 30.51% in the 1991 Census.

Both in regard to these 'Adi' groups of castes and 'Chamar' group of castes, there is a marked increase in their population in the 1981 Census, compared to the two previous censuses, though there was a decrease in the case of 'Chamar' groups of castes in the 1971 Census.

Large Category

It is quite interesting to note that in the case of those units where the percentage of population in the 'very large' category hovered around 50% of the units' population, the population under 'large' category was quite enormous — more or less the same population as that of

TABLE XI

Distribution of Schedule Castes under categories I and II (very large and large), 1961-1981

Names of units	1961		1971		1981	
	No. of caste	Percent of unit's S.C population	No. of caste	Percent of unit's S.C. population	No. of caste	Percent of unit's S.C. population
Andhra Pradesh	5	93.05	4	91.94	5	92.05
Arunachal Pradesh	—		4	99.38	11	92.28
Assam	11	98.55	10	97.71	—	
Bihar	12	95.90	12	96.08	12	97.22
Gujarat	10	93.98	10	88.86	7	94.40
Himachal Pradesh	12	92.65	11	87.92	13	93.09
Haryana	—		9	94.06	10	96.06
Jammu & Kashmir	7	98.08	7	97.35	7	97.62
Karnataka	9	87.28	10	85.14	9	87.90
Kerala	14	91.51	14	90.58	15	91.79
Madhya Pradesh	15	89.10	17	89.61	13	91.79
Maharashtra	12	93.44	12	91.11	8	91.51
Manipur	5	99.51	6	99.73	6	98.96
Meghalaya	—	—	11	94.19	10	96.34
Mizoram	—	—	—		14	77.03
Orissa	16	90.49	14	82.76	15	89.24
Punjab	11	96.61	10	93.31	11	96.46
Rajasthan	12	83.67	14	87.74	14	91.49
Sikkim	—	—	2	34.74	4	99.94
Tamil Nadu	10	93.73	10	96.09	6	93.35

(Continued on next page)

TABLE XI

Distribution of Schedule Castes under categories I and II, 1961-1981

Names of units	1961		1971		1981	
	No. of caste	Percent of unit's S.C population	No. of caste	Percent of unit's S.C. population	No. of caste	Percent of unit's S.C. population
Tripura	9	95.09	9	96.69	8	95.93
Uttar Pradesh	9	92.44	9	90.62	8	90.57
West Bengal	17	86.89	16	90.62	15	89.78
Chandigarh	—	—	10	88.62	11	93.63
Dadra & Nagar Haveli	2	98.79	3	100.00	4	96.66
Delhi	9	86.23	9	84.42	11	94.20
Goa, Daman & Diu	—	—	5	94.20	5	96.06
Pondicherry	6	97.69	6	93.12	6	98.10
Total	214	91.75	254	90.21	258	90.78
National average	10.19	91.75	9.41	90.21	9.56	90.78

'very large' category. If these two categories (very large and large) are added, then the castes coming under these two categories would account for more than 90% of the units' total Scheduled Caste population. The population necessarily did not remain static in all the censuses held in 1961-81 and therefore, variation in the number of castes coming under these two categories as well as their share in the units' Scheduled Caste population, though minor, was noticed in the last three censuses, as Table XI will illustrate.

Only one State, Mizoram, accounted for 77.03% of the population under these two categories in the 1981 Census. A large number of population was placed under 'unspecified' category in this State and that was the reason why the population under these two categories registered such a percentage.

In all the other States except Karnataka, Orissa and West Bengal it crossed the 90% mark in the 1981 Census.

The percent of the country's Scheduled Caste population coming under these two categories hovered between 91.75% in the 1961 Census and 90.78% in the 1981 Census. Though the national average of castes covered by these two categories fell to 9.56% in the 1981 Census from 10.19% in the 1961 Census, their share in the total number of Scheduled Castes increased to 24.20% in the 1981 Census from 21.47% in the 1961 Census.

Intermediary categories

The overwhelming majority of the communities amongst the Scheduled Castes of the country — about 72% — belonged to the remaining three categories of 'small', 'very small' and 'negligible', i.e., those returning a population between .1% to .001% of the units' Scheduled Caste population, whereas the population they represented were a mere 6.59%.

Non-enumeration

It may be noted that the population of each and

every Scheduled Caste was not extracted in all the censuses. A number of them was not enumerated in the Censuses — specially those conducted earlier to 1981, because not a single member of these castes could be found during the Census operations. Table XII indicates the number of Scheduled Castes whose population was not extracted in the censuses during the period, 1961-81. Even in the 1981 Census as many as four castes were found which did not have even a single member. They were Mahara in Meghalaya, Sutradhar in Mizoram, Padanaan in Tamil Nadu and Khadit in Tripura.

TABLE XII

	1961	1971	1981
Arunachal Pradesh	x	10	x
Gujarat	5	x	x
Himachal Pradesh	1	4	x
Karnataka	27	27	x
Kerala	4	x	x
Madhya Pradesh	5	4	x
Maharashtra	8	8	x
Manipur	1	x	x
Meghalaya	x	4	1
Orissa	3	3	x
Mizoram	x	x	1
Rajasthan	41	33	x
Tamil Nadu	11	3	1
Tripura	5	8	1
Chandigarh	x	14	x
Dadra and Nagar Haveli	x	1	x
Delhi	2	x	x
Total	113	119	4

Inclusion of castes in the Schedule (1) whose population was such as not to warrant their enumeration or (2) even if extracted, was 'most negligible' only tended to inflate the number of castes in the Schedules. This happened mainly in the Southern and Western States of Rajasthan, Gujarat, Maharashtra, M.P., Karnataka, Kerala and Tamil Nadu, which witnessed inclusion of a large number of castes in the Schedules from 1956 onwards.

Unclassified/Unspecified Category

A large number of persons belonging to the Scheduled Castes were treated as 'Unclassified' in the 1961 and 1981 Censuses and as 'Unspecified' in the 1971 Census. Their number was 1,200,215 in the 1961 Census, 2,516,504 in the 1971 Census and 2,753,739 in the 1981 Census and constituted 1.864% of the country's total Scheduled Caste population in the 1961 Census, 3.145% in the 1971 Census and 2.628% in the 1981 Census. Notwithstanding the clear instruction of the Census authority not to enumerate any population in this category in the 1981 Census, enumeration of population in this category could not be completely dispensed with. The number in the 1981 Census would have been much less had not 1,453,897 Scheduled Caste population of three Districts of Tamil Nadu (Tiruchirappalli, Pudukkottai and Tirunelveli) whose individual slips were destroyed by floods, been included in this class. If these Unclassified/Unspecified population were tabulated against the individual Scheduled Caste to which they rightly belonged, population-size of many of the individual Scheduled Caste would have given a completely different picture.

The unit-wise population of this class of population is as follows :

TABLE XIII

	1961	1971	1981
Andhra Pradesh	18,648	40,772	124,600
Arunachal Pradesh	x	x	161
Assam	x	x	x
Bihar	121,973	98,770	13,975
Gujarat	28,360	127,954	75,882
Haryana	x	37,797	16,770
Himachal Pradesh	1,144	29,906	2,626
Jammu & Kashmir	x	1,241	354
Karnataka	66,717	189,378	144,505
Kerala	29	6,559	4,381
Madhya Pradesh	25,910	57,928	45,584
Maharashtra	9,354	96,633	64,950
Manipur	x	6	67

(Contd. to next page)

TABLE XIII

	1961	1971	1981
Meghalaya	x	208	39
Mizoram	x	x	29
Orissa	13,560	226,414	69,742
Punjab	3,068	160,130	74,218
Rajasthan	263,673	189,488	87,280
Sikkim	x	6,003	13
Tamil Nadu	205,430	60,683	1,460,799
Tripura	x	10	178
U.P.	109,998	375,282	534,252
West Bengal	309,721	749,196	25,710
Chandigarh	x	2,402	1,115
Dadra and Nagar Haveli	x	x	68
Goa, Daman and Diu	x	957	925
Delhi	22,630	56,115	4,293
Pondicherry	x	2,672	223
Total	1,200,215	2,516,504	2,753,739
Percent of total Scheduled Caste population	1.864%	3.145%	2.628%

Main Table

As we have seen, the increase or decrease in the total Scheduled Caste population of a State/Union Territory was not reflected in the growth of the population of individual Scheduled Caste. Some Scheduled Castes increased at a higher rate while some registered a decrease. There were instances where not a single member of a caste was found during the Census operations. The population-size of the castes also varied tremendously. Statistics of each Scheduled Caste/group of Scheduled Castes for each State/Union Territory for the years 1961-1981 are presented in the Main Table. In the 1941 and 1951 Censuses population of individual Scheduled Caste were not tabulated and published (except in West Bengal) and those for the year 1991 are yet to be published and are not expected to come out earlier than the latter part of 1995 or early 1996. In the absence of data regarding population of individual Scheduled Castes in the Censuses of 1941, 1951 and 1991, population figure of individual Scheduled Caste/group of Scheduled Castes could not be tabulated in the Main Table for these years. The population figure for the years 1961-1981 has only been incorporated in this Table. The population, as explained, varied due to jurisdictional changes, withdrawal of area restriction, clubbing together of Castes and inclusion of new castes under different Orders. For facility of comparison, the castes or groups of castes listed as Scheduled in the different Orders/Acts during the period 1936-91 are noted on the left hand side of the Table, while the corresponding population enumerated in the Censuses of 1961-1981 have been shown on the right hand side.

Consolidation of certain castes

There is a tendency towards consolidation of castes in the higher two categories — categories I and II — both in regard to their share in the total number of Scheduled Castes as well as in the total Scheduled Caste population, as the Table XIV will reveal.

In 1961 21.47% of the castes enumerated were in categories I and II, in 1971 it increased to 22.90% and in 1981 it increased further to 24.20%. This increase was pronounced in both the categories I and II. So far as their share in the total Scheduled Caste population was concerned, 91.75% of the total Scheduled Caste population were in these two categories in the 1961 Census, which fell marginally to 90.21% in the 1971 Census but again increased to 90.78% in the 1981 Census.

In regard to the castes in the intermediary categories of III, IV and V, there was a decreasing trend. In 1961 they were 71.41% of the total Scheduled Castes, which decreased to 69.53% in the 1971 Census. In the 1981 Census the same decreasing trend would have been maintained but for the shift of about 4% from category VI to these intermediary categories. Their share in the total population varied between 6.64% in the 1971 Census to 6.38% in the 1961 Census. The 1981 figure was 6.59%.

TABLE XIV

	1961			1971			1981		
	No. of caste	Percent of total caste	Percent of total S.C. population	No. of caste	Percent of total caste	Percent of total S.C. population	No. of caste	Percent of total caste	Percent of total S.C. population
Category I	61	6.12	67.88	73	6.58	65.25	74	6.94	66.39
Category II	153	15.35	23.87	181	16.32	24.96	184	17.26	24.39
Category III	298	29.89	5.55	323	29.13	5.84	297	27.86	5.73
Category IV	271	27.18	.79	292	26.33	.76	304	28.52	.81
Category V	143	14.34	.04	156	14.07	.04	170	15.95	.05
Category VI	71	7.12	.001	84	7.57	.0016	37	3.47	.001
Categories I & II	214	21.47	91.75	254	22.90	90.21	258	24.20	90.78
Categories III to V	712	71.41	6.38	771	69.53	6.64	771	72.33	6.59
Category VI	71	7.12	.001	84	7.57	.0016	37	3.47	.001
Total	997	100.00	98.13	1109	100.00	96.8516	1066	100.00	97.371
Unclassified/ Unspecified			1.86			3.145			2.628

This tendency towards consolidation of certain castes/groups of castes was to some extent the result of the rationalisation in the system of listing of Scheduled Castes in the 1976 Order. The other factor might be the reversal of the process of higher mobility within the castes, so very evident in the first four decades of this century.

Linkage between caste and population

Table XII revealed that many castes were included in the Schedules without giving much thought about the existence of caste members in the State. This happened not only in the pre-Independence period but in the post-Independence period as well, as borne out by the fact that it was not possible to trace out even a single member of many a caste in successive census operations. The reorganisation of States in 1956 led to the listing of castes in the Schedules for the ceded areas only. With the withdrawal of area restriction in 1976 these castes became scheduled for the entire State. Many castes/sub-castes were added to the existing ones over the years.

Though a large number of castes have been scheduled over the years in the manner stated above, the numerical strength of many of them are quite minimal. It has already been pointed out that cultural and linguistic homogeneity or geographical contiguity has hardly any effect on the caste system, which is primarily conditioned by the custom, tradition, manner and mode of living, habitat, economic condition and the like of an area. That is the reason why a caste found in an area may not be found in a contiguous area even though there is not much cultural or linguistic difference. Every caste, whether scheduled or not, has some peculiarities, some small differences which vary from area to area, region to region. Moreover, the concept, criterion, degree and manifestation of untouchability differed so widely from area to area that no attempt was ever made to prepare an all-India list of Untouchables/Depressed Classes. That is also the main reason why the list of Scheduled Castes is prepared unit-wise. The listing of many common castes in the States' Schedules also could not remove this regional barrier. The demographic pattern also establishes this fact.

In the 1981 Census, out of the 1066 castes enumerated, 771 castes, i.e., 72.33% of the total enumerated castes, covered only 6.59% of the country's Scheduled Caste population while 258 castes, i.e., 24.20% of the total enumerated castes, accounted for 90.78% of the country's Scheduled Caste population. So many castes (72.33%) accounting for so little a population (6.59%) goes to show that even though castes have been added in the Schedules over the years, not many of them have any sizable following. Castes are basically regional in character and the inclusion of a caste in the Schedule does not change its basic character.

Dominant castes

All the 258 castes accounting for 90.78% of the country's Scheduled Caste population cannot, however, be considered as numerically dominant castes among the Scheduled Castes. Only 74 of them, listed in Annexure Table XVII, can be classified as such because each one of them accounts for at least 10% of the respective State's Scheduled Caste population. Among these 74 castes/ groups of castes, the 'Chamar' group of castes can be said to be the dominant caste in the all-India arena (except Southern and North-Eastern States) because it figures in almost all the States' (except Sikkim and Pondicherry) lists and accounts for 36.05% of the country's Scheduled Caste population (except Southern States) in the 1981 Census. Similarly, the 'Adi Groups' of castes can be said to be the dominant castes in the Southern States. Barring these two groups of castes, the other castes/groups of castes have no all-India character. A glance at Annexure Table XVII will reveal that the remaining castes/groups of castes are dominant primarily in one or two States. Again, the sphere of dominance of most of these castes is not evenly spread throughout the States, but is mostly localised. A caste may be dominant in one area of the State while another in an altogether different area. For instance, Rajbanshis are a dominant caste in the two districts of Coochbehar and Jalpaiguri in the State of West Bengal while the Pods are a dominant caste in the district of 24 Parganas in the same State. This is more or less the all-India pattern with regard to other Scheduled Castes also.

Mobility of the castes

We have seen in Chapters I and II that the census operations had witnessed the determined attempts on the part of many 'lower castes' to obtain equality with the 'higher castes', to gain a share of their privileges and in many cases, to claim a descent from the twice-born, specially from the Brahman and the Kshattriya. The claim for higher status, or to have their communities recorded under fresh names, was, however, more pronounced in the 1931 Census than the earlier ones. This process was called the Sanskritization process or the Brahminisation process. All the Census Superintendents had commented on this phenomenon in their Census Reports. Let us now examine the position of some of the castes which had persistently claimed higher status in the Census operations but whose claims were not conceded by the Census authority or the provincial Governments, and therefore, were ultimately included in the lists of Scheduled Castes.

In Bengal Bagdi, Bhuimali, Dhoba, Jalia Kaibartta, Jhalo Malo or Malo, Namasudra, Pod, Rajbanshi, Sunri and Tiyar communities represented before the Census authority that they should be enumerated as Vaishyamali, Byagra Kshattriya, Vaishya, Mahishya or Rajbanshi, Malla Kshattriya or Jhalla Kshattriya, Nama Brahmna or Namobrahmo, Poundra or Poundra Kshattriya or Padmaraj, Kshattriya, Kshattriya Saundik or Kshattriya Sandia or Kshattriya, and Rajbanshi respectively and also demanded of the provincial Government that they should be excluded from the list of the Depressed Classes and consequently from the list of the Scheduled Castes. It was almost conceded by the Lothian Committee in 1932 that the Rajbanshi community would not be included in

TABLE XV

Year Source	1901 a	1911 a	1921 a	1931 a	1941 a
Bagdi	970,270	973,791	850,163	937,606	635,308
Bhuimali	13,218	14,659	17,156	19,286	21,058
Dhoba	100,122	98,184	95,923	92,639	70,342
Jalia Kaibartta	74,061	98,835	135,277	122,003	72,724
Jhalo Malo or Malo	46,058	49,793	38,069	35,332	33,730
Namasudra	174,888	160,304	165,027	161,804	134,748
Pod	351,373	393,168	431,327	476,589	453,524
Rajbanshi	939,291	1,218,346	1,165,141	1,209,612	826,640
Sunri	114,652	102,799	82,766	73,978	60.008
Tiyar	148,729	157,396	135,540	71,620	28,845
Total	2,932,662	3,267,275	3,116,389	3,200,469	2,336,927

(Continued on next page)

TABLE XV

Year	1951	1961	1971	1981
Source	a	b	c	d
Bagdi	904,361	1,096,885	1,291,127	1,831,565
Bhuimali	19,399	39,181	45,059	47,521
Dhoba	70,570	154,791	191,063	251,737
Jalia Kaibartta	83,969	117,384	204,679	318,344
Jhalo Malo or Malo	46,595	68,757	89,918	154,557
Namasudra	324,723	729,057	980,524	1,692,233
Pod	593,093	875,525	975,352	1,536,197
Rajbanshi	742,619	1,201,717	1,353,919	2,258,760
Sunri	45,153	106,870	166,418	252,331
Tiyar	41,978	39,633	79,786	82,108
Total	2,872,460	4,429,800	5,377,845	8,425,353
Percent of total Sceduled Caste population	61.16%	64.29%	61.00%	70.02%

Source : a — Castes and Tribes of West Bengal, Census of West Bengal, 1951, pp. 95-114.

b — Census of India, 1961, Vol. I, India, Part V-A (1), pp. 286-92.

c — Census of India, 1971, Series 1, Paper 1 of 1975, pp. 89-92.

d — Census of India, 1981, Series 23, Part IX(i), pp. 8-62.

the list of Scheduled Castes. All these communities, however, figure in the Scheduled Castes list. A glance at the population figure (relating to the West Bengal portion only) of these castes during the period 1901-1981, incorporated in Table XV, will indicate that a downward trend in their population was registered by Dhoba and Sunri communities constantly from 1911 to 1951, by Jhalo Malo or Malo and Tiyar communities from 1921 to 1941, and by Jalia Kaibartta and Namasudra communities from 1931 to 1941. Bagdi and Rajbanshi communities showed a wavy curve but definitely registered a downward fall in the 1941 Census while the Pod community showed a steady rising trend till 1931 and registered a fall in the 1941 Census. One thing, however, was common in regard to each of these nine castes, that is, each one of them registered a fall in the 1941 Census, i.e., immediately after the 1936 Order listing them as Scheduled Caste was issued. The only exception was Bhuimali which registered a steady increase from 1901 to 1941. The total population of all these castes showed a wavy curve till the 1931 Census and in the 1941 Census registered a sharp fall. Even in the 1951 Census their total population was less than that of the 1901 Census. In the 1951 Census, they accounted for 61.16% of the State's total Scheduled Caste population which increased to 70.02% in the 1981 Census.

In U.P. Bawaria, Beldar, Chamar, Dhobi, Kanjar and Kori communities pressed their demand for according them the higher status of Brahman, Kshattriya or Bindwar Vaishya, Jatav or Rajput Jatav, Chhattri, Kanjarmana, and Kush Kulin Rajput or Tenturai Vaidya or Jaiswar, respectively. Chamar was the dominant caste amongst them and accounted for 49.22% of the Province's total Scheduled Caste population, according to the 1931 Census. Some more castes were added with the 'Chamar' group of castes under subsequent Orders and this group of castes constituted 56.44% of the State's Scheduled Caste population in the 1961 Census, 54.45%in the 1971 Census and 55.06% in the 1981 Census. The 'Chamar' group of castes along with the other five castes, mentioned above, contributed 61.58% of the State's Scheduled Caste population according to the 1931 Census, 67.44% in the 1961 Census, 66.40% in the 1971 Census and 67.66% in the 1981 Census. Unlike West Bengal population figure of these castes for the entire period of 1901-1981 are available and therefore, no discussion could be made as to how they figured in those Censuses. Only those of 1901, 1931, 1961-1981 are available and incorporated in Table XVI.

It is curious that in the two States of West Bengal and U.P. where there was a wide margin of error in regard to Depressed (Scheduled Caste) population, and which, incidentally, accounted for more than 1/3rd of the country's Scheduled Caste population, the castes which persistently demanded for their exclusion from the list of Depressed Classes and therefore, from the list of Scheduled Castes as well, but were retained in the list at the instance of the Government of the day, not only contributed the majority of the State's Scheduled Caste population [70.02% in West Bengal and 67.66% in U.P., both according to the 1981 Census], but their share in the total Scheduled Caste population registered an increasing trend in all the Censuses (except 1971) and it is quite likely that the same trend will continue in the 1991 Census as well. This increasing trend in their population explains the fact that the splinter groups which sought higher mobility by assuming new names and thus maintained some distance from their parent community so long, have gradually started coming back to their original fold. Having understood the futility of doing so they are no longer keen to maintain their separate identity.

The same trend is evident in Bihar as well. Dusadhs claimed the higher status of Gahlot Rajput but were denied the same. This community was the second major community amongst the Scheduled Castes in Bihar, only next to Chamar, and the same position is still maintained, as revealed by their population in the successive Censuses :

TABLE XVI

Year	1901	1931	1961	1971	1981
Source	a	b	c	d	e
Bawaria	839	15,956	2,905	3,757	4,893
Beldar	46,520	44,117	59,247	80,626	94,185
Chamar	5,890,639	6,097,113	8,693,327	10,121,421	12,914,218
Dhobi	609,445	656,913	888,466	1,156,243	1,423,574
Kanjar	18,198	23,211	31,335	44,176	50,752
Kori	990,027	916,472	710,241	909,537	1,381,588
Total		7,753,782	10,385,521	12,315,760	15,869,110
Percent of total Scheduled Caste population		61.58%	67.44%	66.40%	67.66%

Source : a — Census of India, 1901, Vol. XVI, Part I, pp. 250-54.

b — Census of India, 1931, Vol. XVIII, Part I, pp. 634-38.

c — Census of India, 1961, Vol.I, Part V, A(i), pp. 274-80.

d — Census of India, 1971, Series I, Paper 1 of 1975, pp. 86-89.

e — Census of India, 1981, Series 22, Part IX(i), pp. 10-70.

1911	1,189,274	
1921	1,167,686	
1931	1,290,936	
1961	1,724,553	26.51% of the State's S.C. population
1971	2,105,413	26.48% -do-
1981	2,655,832	26.19% -do-

In Madhya Pradesh, Katias demanded to be named as Renhia Rajputs, Khangars as Khangar Kshattriyas and Mahars as Kashyap Rajputs or Kshattriya Mahars. Their demands, however, were not conceded by the Census authority and they continued to be treated as Depressed and later, as Scheduled Castes. Their population enumerated in different Censuses are given in table XVII.

TABLEXVII

Year	Katia	Khangar	Mahar with Mehra	Source
1911	40,637	–	1,114,510	a
1921	37,950	–	1,170,737	b
1931	24,510	7,650	1,255,703	c
1961	29,433	5,640	246,614	d
1971	37,779	9,629	352,278	e
1981	95,647	96,529	577,240	f

Source: a - Census of India, 1911, Vol. X, Part II, pp. 113-151.
b - Census of India, 1921, Vol. XI, Part I, p. 158.
c - Census of India, 1931, Vol. XII, Part I, p. 365.
d - Census of India, 1961, Vol. I, India, Part V-A(i), pp. 202-208.
e - Census of India, 1971, Series I, Paper 1 of 1975, pp. 60-63.
f - Census of India, 1981, Series II, Part IX(1), pp. 10-36.

The Katias and the Khangars increased appreciably in the 1981 Census while the Mahar group of castes showed a steep fall in the 1961 Census, which might be due to transfer of the Vidbhara region to the Maharashtra State at the time of reorganisation of States in 1956.

It is quite likely that similar trend would be found in all other States if the relevant data are processed and tabulated.

The higher mobility within the caste witnessed in the first four decades of this century was aimed at elevating the social position of the caste by the Sanskritization process. This mobility, which was vertical in nature and socio-religious in character, has not only been stalled but has been completely reversed, so much so that not only the splinter groups have started joining the main groups, but even those castes which pressed for and achieved higher status in the social scale due to their efforts or were not included in the list of 'Scheduled Castes' due to their own representations, have now staked their claim for being listed as a Scheduled Caste and, if it is not at all possible to be enlisted as such, then to be classified at least as a member of the Other Backward Classes. This process has been set in motion mainly for obtaining higher position in the political echelon as well as for getting economic and other benefits and privileges enshrined in the Constitution. This is no doubt a mobility towards achieving political and economic power and is basically horizontal in nature. It is to be seen whether the replacement of the socio-religious mobility by the politico-economic mobility helps in starting the process of secularisation of the caste system or whether this mobility, being dependent on the caste system for its very survival, meets with the same fate as that of the Westernisation process.

Notes and References

1. *Census of India*, 1961, Vol. I, Part V-A(1), p. 1.
2. *Ibid.*, pp. I-II.
3. *Ibid.*, 1971, Series 1, Paper 1 of 1975, p. (V).
4. *Ibid.*
5. *Ibid.*, 1971, Series 1, Part V-A(1), p. VII.
6. *Ibid.*, 1981, Series 1, Part IX(i), pp. III-IV.
7. *Ibid.*, 1961, Vol. I, Part V-A(1), p. II.
8. *Ibid.*, 1971, Series 1, Paper 1 of 1975, p. (V).
9. *Ibid.*, 1981, Series 1, Paper 2 of 1984, pp. 2-3.

Index

THE SCHEDULED CASTES IN INDIA

VOL. IV

THE SCHEDULED CASTES IN INDIA

VOL. IV

S.K. Chatterjee

GYAN

GYAN PUBLISHING HOUSE

NEW DELHI-110 002

THE SCHEDULED CASTES IN INDIA (VOL. IV)
(Anthropology, Tribal Studies, Sociology)

ISBN : 81-212-0511-5 (Set)

ISBN : 81-212-0538-7 (Vol. IV)

Published in 2008 in India by
Gyan Publishing House
5 Ansari Road
New Delhi-110 002

All rights reserved. No part of this book may be reproduced in any manner without written permission

Printed at Vishal Kaushik Printers Delhi - 110093

CONTENTS

MAIN TABLE

List of Scheduled Castes in different Orders/Acts and population of each Scheduled Caste in the 1961, 1971 and 1981 Censuses.

Main Table

Scheduled Castes in different Orders and their population in the 1961 1971 and 1981 Censuses.
SC denotes Scheduled Castes.
ST denotes Scheduled Tribes.
* means part of a Province/State

ANDHRA PRADESH

	Scheduled Castes in				Population in		
	1953 Act	1956 Order	1976 Order		1961 Census	1971 Census	1981 Census
1	2	3	4		5	6	7
Caste				Total	4,973,616	5,774,548	7,961,730
Adi Andhra	SC	SC*	SC		595,008	616,319	698,860
Adi Dravida	SC	SC*	SC		37,459	39,118	105,382
Adi Karnataka	SC						
Ajila	SC						
Anamuk		SC*	SC		3,071	876	76
Aray Mala		SC*	SC		3,152	1,828	1,395
Arunthathiyar	SC						
Arundhatiya		SC*	SC		85,220	52,628	78,496
Arwa Mala		SC*	SC		4,218	5,518	22,937
Baira	SC						
Bakuda	SC						
Bandi	SC						
Bariki	SC	SC*	SC		9,905	8,016	11,844
Bavuri	SC	SC*	SC		887	667	756

(Continued on next page)

1	2	3	4	5	6	7
Bellara	SC					
Beda Jangam		SC*	SC*	1,840	1,932	12,024
Budga Jangam						
Bindla		SC*	SC	5,111	11,910	13,659
Byagara		SC*	SC	5,903	14,023	14,120
Byagari	SC					
Chachati	SC	SC*	SC	6,829	8,274	5,244
Chakkiliyan	SC					
Chalvadi	SC	SC	SC	1,541	1,324	1,740
Chamar	SC	SC	SC	7,304	14,397	12,881
Muchi	SC					
Mochi						
Chambhar		SC*	SC	2,833	3,690	519
Chandala	SC	SC*	SC	34	89	184
Cheruman	SC					
Dakkal		SC*	SC	1,109	851	1,598
Dakkalwar						
Dandasi	SC	SC*	SC	5,581	5,574	5,410
Devendrakulathan	SC					
Dhor		SC*	SC	1,926	1,215	2,452
Dom	SC	SC*	SC	15,043	24,629	23,214
Dombara						
Paidi						
Pano						
Ellamalawar		SC*	SC	599	333	358
Yellammalawandlu						
Ghasi	SC	SC*	SC	1,725	1,456	1,872

(Continued on next page)

1	2	3	4	5	6	7
Hadi						
Relli Chachandi						
Godagali	SC	SC*	SC	1,690	1,723	2,212
Godari	SC	SC*	SC	702	591	834
Godda	SC					
Gosangi	SC	SC*	SC	65	66	7,653
Hasla	SC					
Holeya	SC	SC*	SC	371	687	675
Holeya Dasari		SC*	SC	154	246	620
Jaggali	SC	SC*	SC	2,489	3,121	983
Jambuvulu	SC	SC*	SC	9,549	18,545	22,335
Kadan	SC					
Kalladi	SC					
Kanakkan	SC					
Karimplan	SC					
Kodalo	SC					
Kolupulvandlu		SC*	SC	675	693	961
Koosa	SC					
Koraga	SC					
Kudumban	SC					
Kuravan	SC					
Kudubi	SC					
Kurichchan	SC					
Madari	SC					
Madiga	SC	SC	SC	2,147,879	2,514,948	3,572,622
Madasi Kurava		SC*	SC	416	1,152	3,550
Madari Kurava						

(Continued on next page)

1	2	3	4	5	6	7
Madiga Dasu		SC*	SC	4,223	4,543	5,450
Mashteen						
Mahar		SC*	SC	11,741	8,799	11,486
Mala	SC	SC	SC	1,745,466	2,113,393	2,894,643
Mala Dasari		SC*	SC	7,493	5,046	18,416
Mala Dasu	SC	SC*	SC	26,834	21,872	8,385
Mala Hannai		SC*	SC	101	56	120
Malajangam		SC*	SC	5,296	5,179	4,895
Mala Masti		SC*	SC	565	184	474
Mala Sale		SC*	SC	54,290	64,775	81,272
Netkani						
Malasar	SC					
Mala Sanyasi		SC*	SC	52	104	300
Maila	SC					
Mang		SC*	SC	11,456	7,859	8,007
Mang Garodi		SC*	SC	123	48	107
Manne		SC*	SC	46,344	50,255	64,668
Mashti		SC*	SC	824	1,120	2,992
Matangi	SC	SC*	SC	642	607	323
Mavilan	SC					
Mehtar		SC*	SC	3,126	3,659	4,553
Mitha Ayyalvar		SC*	SC	2,542	3,851	2,777
Moger	SC					
Mundala	SC	SC*	SC	515	319	840
Nalakeyava	SC					
Nayadi	SC					
Pagadai	SC					

(Continued on next page)

1	2	3	4	5	6	7
Paky	SC	SC*]	SC]	3,826]	3,859]	7,876]
Moti						
Thoti	SC	SC*		3,523	1,921	
Pallan	SC					
Pambada	SC	SC*]	SC]	952]	1,222]	2,333]
Pambanda						
Pamidi	SC	SC*	SC	4,593	3,833	5,647
Panchama	SC	SC*]	SC]	17,887]	22,636]	9,265]
Pariah						
Painda	SC					
Panniandi	SC					
Paraiyan	SC					
Paravan	SC					
Pulayan	SC					
Puthirai Vannan	SC					
Raneyar	SC					
Relli		SC*	SC	38,845	48,147	76,329
Samagara	SC	SC*	SC	779	1,151	1,845
Samban	SC	SC*	SC	4	581	3,233
Sapari	SC					
Sapru		SC*	SC	418	510	492
Semman	SC					
Sindhollu		SC*]	SC]	2,220]	1,808]	2,583]
Chindollu						
Tiruvalluvar	SC					
Valluvan	SC					
Valmiki	SC	ST	ST			

(Continued on next page)

1	2	3	4	5	6	7
Vettuvan	SC					
Panan	SC					
Unclassified/ Unspecified				18,648	40,772	124,600
Total No. of caste	77(82)	60(77) / 56*(71*)	59(77)	60	60	59
Source				a	b	c

Source: a — Census of India, 1961, Vol. I, India, Part V-A(1), SCT-II Part A, pp. 172-78.

b — Census of India, 1971, Series 1, Paper 1 of 1975, Appendix to Table C-viii Part A, pp. 45-47.

c — Census of India, 1981, Series 2, Part IX(i), SC I, pp. 10-46.

ARUNACHAL PRADESH

	Scheduled Castes in			Population in	
	1971 Act	1986 Act		1971 Census	1981 Census
1	2	3		4	5
Caste			Total	339	2,919
Bansphor	SC	SC			152
Bhuinmali	SC]	SC]			36]
Mali					
Brittial Bania	SC]	SC]			102]
Bania				4	
Dhupi	SC]	SC]			353]
Dhobi					
Dugla	SC]	SC]			7]
Dholi				1	
Hira	SC	SC		3	9
Jalkeot	SC	SC			34
Jhalo	SC]	SC]			75]
Malo					
Jhalo-Malo					
Kaibartta	SC]	SC]		326	769]
Jaliya					
Lalbegi	SC	SC			15
Mahara	SC	SC			13
Mehtar	SC]	SC]			214]
Bhangi					

(Continued on next page)

1	2	3	4	5
Muchi	SC]	SC]	1	328]
Rishi				
Namasudra	SC	SC	4	540
Patni	SC	SC		11
Sutradhar	SC	SC		100
Unspecified				161
Total No. of caste	16(25)	16(25)	6	16
Source			a	b

Source: a — Census of India,1971, Series 1, Paper 1 of 1975, p. 92.

b — Census of India, 1981, Series 25, Part IX, p. 8.

ASSAM

	Scheduled Castes in					Population in	
	1936 Order	1950 Order	1956 Order	1976 Order		1961 Census	1971 Census
1	2	3	4	5		6	7
Caste					Total	732,756	912,639
Bansphor	SC	SC	SC	SC		8,179	6,093
Bhuinmali ⎤ Mali ⎦	SC*	SC	SC	SC		26,396	22,175
Brittial Bania ⎤ Bania ⎦	SC*	SC	SC	SC		30,627	28,097
Dhupi ⎤ Dhobi ⎦	SC*	SC	SC	SC		19,589	20,801
Dugla ⎤ Dholi ⎦	SC*	SC	SC	SC		3,590	4,013
Hira	SC*	SC	SC	SC		25,856	32,624
Jalkeot			SC	SC		2,280	2,537
Jhalo ⎤ Malo ⎦	SC*	SC					
Jhalo ⎤ Malo ⎥ Jhalo Malo ⎦			SC	SC		15,503	32,988
Kaibartta ⎤ Jaliya ⎦	SC	SC	SC	SC		199,590	294,819
Lalbegi	SC	SC	SC	SC		35	45
Mahara	SC*	SC	SC	SC		581	899
Mehtar ⎤ Bhangi ⎦	SC	SC	SC	SC		4,198	7,296

(Continued on next page)

1	2	3	4	5	6	7
Muchi	SC*	SC	SC]	SC]	62,564]	40,786]
Rishi						
Namasudra	SC	SC	SC	SC	221,714	300,843
Patni	SC*	SC	SC	SC	85,587	85,910
Sutradhar	SC*	SC	SC	SC	26,467	32,713
Total No. of Caste	15(22) / 10*(17*)	15(22)	16(25)	16(25)	16	16
Source					a	b

Source: a — Census of India, 1961, Vol. I India, Part V-A(i), SCT-II, Part A, p. 178.

b — Census of India, 1971, Seriés 1, Paper 1 of 1975, Appendix to Table C-viii Part A, pp. 47-48.

BIHAR

	Scheduled Castes in					Population in		
	1936 Order	1950 Order	1956 Order	1976 Order		1961 Census	1971 Census	1981 Census
1	2	3	4	5		6	7	8
Caste					Total	6,504,966	7,950,652	10,138,368
Bantar		SC	SC	SC		45,048	53,264	66,026
Bauri	SC*	SC	SC	SC		76,057	95,260	103,114
Bhogta	SC*	SC	SC	SC		87,733	104,790	137,175
Bhuiya	SC*	SC*	SC*	SC		360,495	438,196	850,469
Bhumij	SC*	SC*	SC*	SC*		533	2,139	466*
Chamar	SC	SC	SC	SC		1,895,179	2,382,440	2,978,562
Mochi	SC	SC						
Chaupal	SC	SC	SC	SC		10,214	24,114	44,372
Dabgar		SC'	SC	SC		3,104	3,971	5,508
Dhobi	SC	SC	SC	SC		332,245	433,317	553,380
Dom	SC	SC	SC	SC		158,638	165,228	200,827
Dhangad								
Dusadh	SC	SC	SC	SC		1,724,553	2,105,413	2,655,832
Dhari								
Dharhi								
Ghasi	SC*	SC	SC	SC		55,034	73,611	84,756
Halalkhor	SC	SC	SC	SC		2,947	5,267	5,463
Hari	SC	SC	SC	SC		90,162	114,956	156,349
Mehtar								
Bhangi								

(Continued on next page)

1	2	3	4	5	6	7	8
Kanjar	SC	SC	SC	SC	445	3,152	1,780
Kurariar	SC	SC	SC	SC	312	1,711	4,449
Lalbegi	SC	SC	SC	SC	336	759	932
Musahar	SC	SC	SC	SC	1,007,340	1,168,447	1,391,000
Nat	SC	SC	SC	SC	12,154	17,431	24,897
Pan	SC*	SC	SC]	SC]	14,767]	27,531]	28,931]
Sawasi							
Pasi	SC	SC	SC	SC	260,087	333,765	463,601
Rajwar	SC*	SC	SC	SC	155,174	193,686	237,370
Turi	SC*	SC	SC	SC	90,436	103,434	133,134
Unclassified/ Unspecified					121,973	98,770	13,975
Total No. of caste	22(22) / 8*(8*)	24(27) / 3*(3*)	23(30) / 2*(2*)	23(30) / 1*(1*)	23	23	23
Source					a	b	c

Source: a — Census of India, 1961, Vol. I, India, Part V-A(i), SCT-II Part A, pp. 178-84.

b — Census of India, 1971, Series 1, Paper 1 of 1975, Appendix to Table C-viii A, pp. 48-49

c — Census of India, 1981, Series 4, Part IX(i), Table SC 1, pp. 10-28.

GUJARAT

	Scheduled Castes in		Population in		
	1960 Act	1976 Order	1961 Census	1971 Census	1981 Census
1	2	3	4	5	6
Total			1,367,255	1,825,432	2,438,297
Caste					
Ager	SC*	SC	19	15	151
Bakad	SC*	SC	227	310	303
Bant					
Bawa (Dhedh)	SC*	SC	3,187	5,178	12,823
Dedh-Sadhu					
Bhambi	SC*	SC	237,458	321,868	664,086
Bhambhi					
Asadaru					
Asodi					
Chamadia					
Chamar					
Chambhar					
Chamgar					
Haralayya					
Harali					
Khalpa					
Machigar					
Mochigar					
Madar					
Madig					
Telegu Mochi					

(Continued on next page)

1	2	3	4	5	6
Kamati Mochi					
Ranigar					
Rohidas					
Rohit					
Samgar					
Mochi	SC*			69	
Chamar	SC*		65,957	87,428	
Nalia					
Rohit					
Chamar	SC*		1,841	5,671	
Chamadia	SC*		1,235	298	
Bhangi	SC*		1,682	2,885	
Rukhi	SC*		41,609	48,399	
Bhangi					
Bhangi	SC*	SC	144,284	181,601	306,031
Mehtar					
Olgana					
Rukhi					
Malkana					
Halalkhor					
Lalbegi					
Balmiki					
Korar					
Zadmalli					
Chalvadi	SC*	SC	16	84	58
Channayya					
Chenna Dasar	SC*	SC	—	4	139

(Continued on next page)

1	2	3	4	5	6
Holaya Dasar					
Dangashia	SC*	SC	1,673	1,926	3,160
Dhor	SC*	SC	115	399	877
Kikkayya					
Kankayya					
Garmatang	SC*	SC	730	899	292
Garoda	SC*		5,685	7,591	
Garoda	SC*	SC	29,084	38,197	52,549
Garo					
Halleer	SC*	SC	-	13	28
Halsar	SC*	SC	8	4	154
Haslar					
Hulasvar					
Halasvar					
Holar	SC*	SC	17	11	170
Valhar					
Holaya	SC*	SC	-	34	92
Holer					
Lingadar	SC*	SC	8	9	94
Mahar	SC*	SC	2,668	4,806	9,281
Taral					
Dhegu Megu					
Mahyavanshi	SC*	SC	426,912	510,256	1,049,837
Dhed					
Vankar					
Maru Vankar					

(Continued on next page)

1	2	3	4	5	6
Vankar	SC*		155,199	239,917	
Dhedh					
Antyaj					
Mang	SC*	SC	941	1,257	2,765
Matang					
Minimadig					
Mang Garudi	SC*	SC	153	105	1,182
Meghval	SC*	SC	18,359	21,591	133,760
Menghvar					
Meghwal	SC*		131,420	127,458	
Mukri	SC*	SC		2	26
Nadia	SC*	SC	10,772	12,862	30,820
Hadi					
Hadi	SC*		6,521	9,215	
Pasi	SC*	SC	125	273	1,164
Shenva	SC*	SC	34,534	45,343	63,867
Chenva					
Sedma					
Rawat					
Senva	SC*		1,992	2,460	
Shemalia	SC*	SC	1	4	139
Thori	SC*	SC	73	167	3,222
Tirgar	SC*	SC	2,828	4,165	5,460
Tirbanda					
Turi	SC*	SC	9,775	11,834	12,846
Turi-Barot	SC*		226	362	

(Continued on next page)

1	2	3	4	5	6
Turi-Barot	SC*]	SC]	1,561]	2,508]	6,039]
Dhedh-Barot					
Unclassified/ Unspecified			28,360	127,954	75,882
Total caste	46*(106*)	30(91)	37	42	30
Source			a	b	c

Source: a — Census of India, 1961, Vol. I, India, Part V-A(i) SCT II-Part A, pp. 184-190.

b — Census of India, 1971, Series 1, Paper 1 of 1975, Appendix to Table C-VIII Part A, pp. 49-51.

c — Census of India, 1981, Series 5, Part IX(i), SC I, pp. 10-28.

HARYANA

	Scheduled Castes in			Population in	
	1966 Act	1976 Order		1971 Census	1981 Census
1	2	3		4	5
Caste			Total	1,895,933	2,464,012
Ad Dharmi	SC	SC		868	689
Balmiki	SC	SC		374,960	488,649
Chura					
Bhangi					
Bangali	SC	SC		325	674
Barar	SC	SC		532	957
Burar					
Berar					
Batwal	SC	SC		444	524
Bauria	SC	SC		23,851	31,296
Bawaria					
Bazigar	SC	SC		39,703	56,383
Bhanjra	SC	SC		7,669	3,700
Chamar	SC	SC		1,004,413	1,297,339
Jatia Chamar					
Rehgar					
Raigar					
Ramdasi					
Ravidasi					
Chanal	SC	SC		21	293
Dagi	SC	SC		25	50

(Continued on next page)

1	2	3	4	5
Darain	SC*	SC	19	65
Deha	SC*	SC	230	6,709
Dhaya				
Dhea				
Dhanak	SC	SC	206,783	269,436
Dhogri	SC*	SC	249	438
Dhangri				
Siggi				
Dumna	SC	SC	7,311	9,248
Mahasha				
Doom				
Gagra	SC	SC	96	58
Gandhila	SC	SC	270	331
Gandil Gondola				
Kabirpanthi	SC	SC	18,072	31,503
Julaha				
Khatik	SC	SC	23,346	32,259
Kori	SC	SC	24,351	34,303
Koli				
Marija	SC	SC	37	145
Marecha				
Mazhabi	SC	SC	55,564	71,152
Megh	SC	SC	8,420	11,265
Nat	SC	SC	3,583	3,991
Od	SC	SC	30,288	54,687
Pasi	SC	SC	3,372	6,746
Perna	SC	SC	167	550

(Continued on next page)

1	2	3	4	5
Pherera	SC	SC	46	24
Sanhal	SC	SC	37	35
Sanhai	SC	SC	427	59
Sansi	SC*]	SC]	13,977]	20,871]
Bhedkut				
Manesh			50	68
Sansoi	SC*	SC	3,644	4,716
Sapela	SC	SC	137	51
Sarera	SC	SC	3,599	6,355
Sikligar	SC	SC	1,250	1,511
Sirkiband	SC	SC		
Unspecified/ Unclassified			37,797	16,770
Total No. of caste	37(59) / 4[8](8*)	37(59)	37	37
Source			a	b

Source: a — Census of India, 1971, Series 1, Paper 1 of 1975, pp. 51-53.

b — Census of India, 1981, Series 6, Part IX, SC1, pp. 10-18.

HIMACHAL PRADESH

	Scheduled Castes in					Population in		
	1950 Order	1954 Act	1956 Order	1966 Act	1976 Order	1961 Census	1971 Census	1981 Census
1	2	3	4	5	6	7	8	9
Caste					Total	369,916	769,572	1,053,958
Ad Dharmi	SC	SC	SC	SC	SC	2,353	10,348	15,103
Badhi			SC	SC	SC	12,840	8,728	16,601
Nagalu								
Chuhra								
Chuhre		SC	SC	SC	SC	95	235	
Balmiki	SC	SC	SC	SC		2,820	14,075	19,764
Bhangi								
Chura								
Sweeper								
Bandhelia			SC	SC	SC	74	79	30
Bangali	SC	SC	SC	SC	SC	445	889	1,691
Banjara	SC	SC	SC	SC	SC	920	1,162	2,100
Bansi			SC	SC	SC	875	553	957
Barad			SC	SC	SC	679	603	2,883
Barar	SC	SC	SC	SC	SC	443	1,829	416
Burar								
Berar								
Batwal			SC	SC	SC	757	7,582	10,290
Bauria				SC	SC			88
Bawaria	SC	SC	SC			7	1	

(Continued on next page)

1	2	3	4	5	6	7	8	9
Bazigar	SC	SC	SC	SC	SC	27	663	1,144
Chamar	SC	SC	SC	SC	SC	70,597	224,574	286,668
Ramdasi	SC	SC						
Ravidasi								
Ramdasia	SC	SC						
Mochi	SC	SC						
Jatia Chamar								
Raigar								
Rehgar								
Chanal	SC	SC	SC	SC	SC	8,590	12,434	13,134
Dhobi		SC	SC	SC	SC	2,194	2,798	12,166
Chhimbe								
Dagi	SC	SC	SC	SC	SC	22	1,548	1,625
Darain				SC	SC		3,597	656
Darai			SC	SC	SC	691	628	6,385
Daryai								
Daule		SC	SC	SC	SC	719	597	2,101
Daole	SC	SC	SC	SC		346	650	
Dhaki	SC	SC	SC	SC	SC	3,324	3,463	4,557
Toori								
Dhanak				SC	SC		519	34
Dhaogri			SC	SC	SC	657	203	793
Dhuai								
Dhogri				SC	SC		2,331	2,993
Dhangri								
Siggi								

(Continued on next page)

1	2	3	4	5	6	7	8	9
Doom	SC	SC	SC	SC	SC	19,297	39,022	54,489
Doomna								
Dumna								
Mahasha								
Dumne		SC	SC	SC		3,956	5,120	
Bhanjre					SC			
Bhanjra	SC	SC	SC	SC		1,264	2,736	4,359
Gagra				SC	SC			6
Gandhila				SC	SC			6
Gandhil Gandola								
Hali			SC	SC	SC	6,778	6,761	20,022
Hesi	SC	SC	SC	SC	SC	1,306	1,235	2,037
Hese		SC						
Turi								
Jogi			SC	SC	SC	4,151	3,570	11,183
Julahe		SC	SC	SC	SC	6,264	12,987	
Julaha	SC	SC	SC	SC		17,778	64,158	10,838
Kabirpanthi								
Keer								
Kamoh			SC	SC	SC	391	362	249
Dagoli								
Karoack			SC	SC	SC	30	1	47
Khatik			SC	SC	SC	105	251	449
Kori								
Koli	SC	SC	SC	SC	SC	159,133	237,614	301,925
Lohar			SC	SC	SC	27,546	41,916	112,389

(Continued on next page)

1	2	3	4	5	6	7	8	9
Marija				SC	SC]			12]
Marecha								
Mazhabi	SC	SC	SC	SC	SC	12	118	221
Megh			SC	SC	SC	488	1,082	1,485
Nat	SC	SC	SC	SC	SC	57	151	232
Od	SC	SC	SC	SC	SC	584	497	639
Pasi	SC	SC	SC	SC	SC	151	109	226
Perna				SC	SC			21
Phrera	SC	SC	SC	SC	SC]	162	89	1,109]
Pherera				SC			375	
Rehar	SC	SC	SC	SC	SC]	1,691	956	2,383]
Rehara			SC	SC		48	966	
Sanhai				SC	SC		972	1,675
Sanhal				SC	SC		1	12
Sansi	SC	SC	SC	SC]	SC]	4	470]	464]
Bhedkut								
Manesh								
Sansoi				SC	SC		686	1.052
Sapela	SC	SC	SC	SC	SC	21	4	23
Sarde			SC]	SC]	SC]	371]	287]	9,668]
Sarere								
Siryare								
Sarera				SC			6,173	
Sarehde		SC	SC	SC		107	155	
Sikligar	SC	SC	SC	SC	SC	369	380	795
Sipi			SC	SC	SC	5,822	8,145	14,294
Sirkiband	SC	SC	SC	SC	SC		10	15

(Continued on next page)

1	2	3	4	5	6	7	8	9
Teli			SC	SC	SC	1,068	1,823	3,768
Thathiar Thathera			SC]	SC]	SC]	337]	395]	709]
Unclassified/ Unspecified						1,144	29,906	2,626
Total No. of caste	30(38)	37(48)	52(71)	64(96)	56(99)	51	60	56
Source						a	b	c

Source: a — Census of India, 1961, Vol. I, Part V-A(i)-SCT II, Part A, pp. 298-304.

b — Census of India, 1971, Series 1, Paper 1 of 1975, Appendix to Table C-VIII Part A, pp. 53-56.

c — Census of India, 1981, Series 7, Part IX, SC I, pp. 4-40.

JAMMU AND KASHMIR

	Scheduled Castes in		Population in		
	1956 Order		1961 Census	1971 Census	1981 Census
1	2		3	4	5
Caste		Total	284,131	381,277	497,363
Barwala	SC		10,839	14,202	18,882
Basith	SC		2,494	6,124	9,962
Batwal	SC		12,733	18,972	26,693
Chamar Ramdasia	SC		69,777	93,997	122,292
Chura	SC		1,040	2,228	2,538
Dhyar	SC		3,386	3,404	4,796
Doom Mahasha	SC		57,871	78,430	100,296
Gardi	SC		771	775	2,180
Jolaha	SC		128	285	371
Megh Kabirpanthi	SC		119,225	152,886	199,242
Ratal	SC		903	1,460	1,705
Saryara	SC		4,933	6,592	8,024
Watal	SC		31	681	88
Unclassified/Unspecified				1,241	354
Total No. of caste	13(16)		13	13	13
Source			a	b	c

Source: a — Census of India, 1961, Vol. I, Part V-A(1), Table SCT-II, p. 190.
b — Census of India, 1971, Series 1, Paper 1 of 1975, Appendix to Table C-viii, Part A, p. 56.
c — Census of India, 1981, Series 8, Part IX, SC-1, pp. 8-12.

KARNATAKA (MYSORE)

	Scheduled Castes in					Population in		
	1950 Order	1953 Act	1956 Order	1976 Order		1961 Census	1971 Census	1981 Census
1	2	3	4	5		6	7	8
Caste					Total	3,117,232	3,850,034	5,595,358
Adi Andhra		SC*	SC*	SC		22,871	30,514	29,516
Adi Dravida	SC	SC	SC*	SC		360,112	429,601	518,860
Adi Karnataka	SC	SC	SC*	SC		1,226,269	1,404,946	1,896,558
Adiya			SC*	SC*		516	588	865*
Ager			SC*	SC		3,636	3,978	4,815
Ajila		SC*	SC*	SC		532	692	1,301
Anamuk			SC*	SC		-	107	60
Aray Mala			SC*	SC		45	17	189
Arunthathiyar		SC*	SC*	SC		-	2	899
Arwa Mala			SC*	SC		23	-	171
Baira		SC*	SC*	SC		1649	2,522	4,223
Bakad				SC				990
Bant			SC*	SC*		920	1,128	1,746*
Bakuda		SC*	SC*	SC		1,189	2,015	1,525
Balagai			SC*	SC		6,206	3,589	12,813
Bandi		SC*	SC*	SC		10	10	2,958
Banjara	SC	SC*	SC*	SC		146,781	185,027	607,189
Lambani								
Bariki		SC*						
Bathada			SC*	SC		567	656	1,026
Bavuri		SC*						

(Continued on next page)

1	2	3	4	5	6	7	8
Beda Jangam			SC*	SC	5,141	13,676	3,035
Budga Jangam							
Bellara		SC*	SC*	SC	175	277	1,263
Bhangi			SC*	SC	19,384	76,979	25,536
Mehtar							
Olgana							
Rukhi							
Malkana							
Halalkhor							
Lalbegi							
Balmiki							
Korar							
Zadmalli							
Mehtar			SC*		981	555	
Bhambhi			SC*	SC	204,348	2,62,466	353,162
Asadaru							
Asodi							
Chamadia							
Chamar							
Chambhar							
Chamgar							
Haralayya							
Harali							
Khalpa							
Machigar							
Madar							
Madig							

(Continued on next page)

1	2	3	4	5	6	7	8
Mochi							
Telegu Mochi							
Kamati Mochi							
Ranigar							
Rohidas							
Rohit							
Samgar							
Muchi		SC*			37	67	
Chamar		SC*					
Chambhar			SC*		3,845	10,500	
Chamar			SC*		70	625	
Muchi							
Mochi			SC*		11,963	23,685	
Bhovi	SC	SC*	SC*	SC*	268,141	296,673	607,931
Bindla			SC*	SC	15	55	194
Byagara			SC*	SC	16,668	16,873	17,700
Byagari		SC*					
Chachati		SC*					
Chakkiliyan		SC*	SC*	SC	78	98	2,831
Chalvadi			SC*		5,298	10,813	
Chalavadi		SC*	SC*	SC			
Chalvadi			SC*		35,860	42,194	103,596
Channayya							
Chandala		SC*	SC*	SC	126	157	175
Chenna Dasar			SC*	SC	2,723	7,760	17,732
Holaya Dasar							
Cheruman		SC*	SC*				

(Continued on next page)

1	2	3	4	5	6	7	8
Dakkal			SC*	SC	40	26	141
Dokkalwar							
Dakkaliga			SC*	SC	273	363	282
Dandasi		SC*					
Devendrakulathan		SC*	SC*				
Dhor			SC*		5,650	8,892	
Dhor			SC*	SC	8,694	10,513	22,432
Kakkayya							
Kankayya							
Dom		SC*	SC*	SC	11	4	12,995
Dombara							
Paidi							
Pano							
Ellamalwar			SC*	SC	208	101	103
Yellammalwandlu							
Ghanti Chores			SC*	SC	503	711	3,020
Garoda			SC*	SC	1	89	129
Garo							
Ghasi		SC*					
Haddi							
Relli Sachandi							
Godagali		SC*	SC*				
Godari		SC*					
Godda		SC*	SC*	SC	721	644	1,280
Gosangi		SC*	SC*	SC	-	12	748
Halleer			SC*	SC	1,721	1,897	2,790
Halsar			SC*	SC	4,563	4,869	7,952

(Continued on next page)

1	2	3	4	5	6	7	8
Haslar							
Hulsavar							
Halasvar							
Handi Jogis			SC*	SC	5,299	7,828	9,631
Hasla		SC*	SC*	SC	1,392	628	1,446
Holar			SC*	SC	22	639	1,190
Valhar							
Holaya			SC*	SC	129,466	149,108	450,675
Holer							
Holeya		SC*	SC*		182,062	225,162	
Holeya Dasari			SC*	SC	2,474	3,823	2,873
Jaggali		SC*	SC*	SC	5	9	229
Jambuvulu		SC*	SC*	SC	37	649	4,082
Kadaiyan			SC'	SC	1	1	172
Kadan		SC*					
Kalladi		SC*	SC*	SC	66	9	511
Kanakkan		SC*					
Karimpalan		SC*	SC*				
Kepmaris			SC*	SC	189	301	153
Kolupulvandlu			SC*	SC	-	1	107
Kodalo		SC*					
Koosa		SC*	SC*	SC	7,597	6,817	8,227
Koracha	SC	SC*	SC'	SC	15,326	22,243	32,894
Koraga		SC*					
Korama	SC	SC*	SC*	SC	28,665	32,120	79,167
Kotegar			SC*	SC	1,261	1,192	16,675
Metri							

(Continued on next page)

1	2	3	4	5	6	7	8
Kudubi		SC*					
Kudumban		SC*	SC*	SC	326	516	147
Kuravan		SC*	SC*	SC	265	138	1,335
Kurichchan		SC*					
Lingader			SC*	SC	130	119	139
Machala			SC*	SC	185	409	99
Madari		SC*	SC*	SC	120	378	3,434
Madiga		SC*	SC*	SC	167,665	210,828	301,383
Mahar			SC*		26,237	18,402	
Mahar]			SC*]	SC]	29,381]	33,527]	50,620]
Taral]							
Dhegu Megu							
Mahyavanshi]			SC*]	SC]	72]	3]	719]
Dhed]							
Vankar]							
Maru Vankar							
Maila		SC*	SC*	SC	628	1,079	1,236
Mala		SC*	SC*	SC	4,371	4,266	10,149
Mala Dasari			SC*	SC	1,099	874	2,223
Mala Dasu		SC*					
Mala Hannai			SC*	SC	-	-	40
Mala Jangam			SC*	SC	26	344	291
Mala Masti			SC*	SC	-	-	34
Malasar		SC*					
Mala Sale]			SC*]	SC]	-	-	21]
Netkani]							
Mala Sanyasi			SC*	SC	—	—	778

(Continued on next page)

1	2	3	4	5	6	7	8
Mang			SC*		18,584	13,248	
Mang			SC*	SC	10,317	8,623	24,264
Mang Matang							
Minimadig							
Matangi		SC*					
Mang Garodi			SC*	SC	256	844	2,339
Mang Garudi			SC*		620	494	
Manne			SC*	SC	2	—	174
Masthi			SC*	SC	59	—	80
Mavilan		SC*	SC*	SC	—	16	51
Meghval			SC*	SC	20	60	22
Menghvar							
Mitha Ayyalvar			SC*				
Moger		SC*	SC*	SC	7,880	16,994	45,113
Mukri			SC*	SC	5,260	5,419	7,669
Mundala		SC*	SC*	SC	10,669	12,729	20,623
Nadia			SC*	SC	6	9	118
Hadi							
Nalkadaya			SC*	SC	309	1,210	483
Nalakeyava		SC*	SC*	SC	2,663	3,484	4,928
Nayadi		SC*	SC*	SC		65	1,434
Pagadai		SC*	SC*				
Painda		SC*					
Paky		SC*					
Pale			SC*	SC	5,437	6,358	11,325
Pallan		SC*	SC*	SC	21	14	745
Pambada		SC*	SC*	SC	248	243	683

(Continued on next page)

1	2	3	4	5	6	7	8
Pamidi		SC*					
Panan		SC*					
Panchama		SC*	SC*	SC	198	190	785
Pannadi			SC*				
Panniandi		SC*	SC*	SC	29	-	97
Paraiyan		SC*	SC*	SC]	145	268	2,307]
Paraya			SC*		—	49	—
Paravan		SC*	SC*	SC	1,051	1,332	2,227
Pasi			SC*				
Pulayan		SC*					
Puthirai Vannan		SC*	SC*				
Raneyar		SC*	SC*	SC	888	1,305	2,553
Samagara		SC*	SC*	SC	7,631	10,230	54,433
Samban		SC*	SC*	SC	1	—	71
Sapari		SC*	SC*	SC	2	—	21
Semman		SC*	SC*				
Shenva			SC*]				
Chenva							
Sedma							
Ravat							
Sillekyathas			SC*	SC	2,807	3,494	7,868
Sindhollu			SC*]	SC]	91]	—	41]
Chindollu							
Sudugadu Sidda			SC*	SC	2,093	3,466	7,669
Thoti		SC*	SC*	SC	266	803	1,184
Tirgar			SC*]	SC]	31]	—	173]
Tirbanda							

(Continued on next page)

1	2	3	4	5	6	7	8
Tiruvalluvar		SC*	SC*				
Turi			SC*				
Valluvan		SC*	SC*	SC	—	130	1,002
Valmiki		SC*					
Vathiriyan			SC*				
Vattuvan		SC*					
Unclassified/ Unspecified					66,717	189,378	144,505
Total No. of caste	6(7)	81(87) / 79*(85*)	142*(207*)	101(166) / 2*(2*)	100	100	101
Source					a	b	c

Source: a — Census of India, 1961, Vol. I, India, Part V-A(i), SCT-II, Part A, pp. 232-224.

b — Census of India, 1971, Series I, Paper 1 of 1975, Appendix to Table C VIII-Part A, pp. 67-71.

c — Census of India, 1981, Series 9, Part IX(i), Table SC-1, pp. 4-100.

KERALA

	Scheduled Castes in				Population in		
	1950 Order	1956 Order	1976 Order		1961 Census	1971 Census	1981 Census
1	2	3	4		5	6	7
Caste				Total	1,434,817	1,772,168	2,549,382
Adi Andhra		SC*	SC		203	1,607	7,353
Adi Dravida		SC*	SC		4,289	3,969	2,458
Adi Karnataka		SC*	SC		379	925	1,087
Ajila		SC*	SC		72	71	150
Arunthathiyar		SC*	SC		360	308	1,303
Ayyanavar	SC	SC*	SC		3,937	7,484	10,079
Baira		SC*	SC		464	596	668
Bakuda		SC*	SC		2,047	3,076	4,107
Bandi		SC*	SC		—	1	24
Bathada		SC*	SC		438	—	46
Bharatar	SC	SC*	SC		1,281	3,362	1,892
Bellara		SC*	SC		—	9	45
Boyan		SC*	SC*		1,768	2,697	1,028'
Chakkiliyan	SC	SC	SC		16,892	21,773	29,001
Chamar Muchi		SC*]	SC]		18]	47]	298]
Chandala		SC*	SC		40	49	90
Cheruman		SC*	SC		215,396	259,966	293,150
Domban	SC	SC*	SC		45	86	248
Eravalan	SC	ST	ST				
Gavara		SC*	SC		576	3,755	1,561

(Continued on next page)

1	2	3	4	5	6	7
Godagali		SC*	SC	-	7	37
Godda		SC*	SC	9	26	186
Gosangi		SC*	SC	1	36	769
Hasla		SC*	SC	64	57	6
Holeya		SC*	SC	3,404	2,753	2,031
Kadaiyan		SC*	SC	247	669	3,042
Kakkalan	SC	SC*	SC	2,830	3,708	5,487
Kalladi		SC*	SC	11,370	13,745	23,435
Kanakkan]	SC	SC*]	SC]	91,589]	105,010]	144,034]
Padanna]						
Karimpalan		SC*	SC	5,481	7,772	10,156
Kavara	SC	SC*	SC	1,869	2,203	8,327
Koosa		SC*	SC	-	1	268
Kootan]	SC]	SC*]	SC]	1,791]	1,644]	3,163]
Koodan]						
Kudumban		SC*	SC	417	387	3,368
Kuravan]	SC	SC]	SC]	144,442]	178,060]	218,048]
Sidhanar]						
Maila		SC*	SC	498	841	1,243
Malayan		SC*	SC*	9,549	9,715	11,661'
Mannan	SC	SC*	SC	15,667	22,202	51,902
Mavilan		SC*	SC	7,026	10,152	16,362
Moger		SC*	SC	5,383	10,857	19,665
Mundala		SC*	SC	217	284	291
Nalakeyava		SC*	SC	136	370	269
Nalkadaya		SC*	SC	436	541	833
Nayadi	SC	SC	SC	1,579	2,067	2,852

(Continued on next page)

1	2	3	4	5	6	7
Padannan	SC	SC*	SC	2,421	3,693	5,015
Palluvan	SC	SC*	SC	1,296	1,406	3,063
Pallan	SC	SC	SC	32,503	30,172	43,959
Pambada		SC*	SC	29	47	105
Panan	SC	SC*	SC	26,781	31,927	40,964
Panchama		SC*	SC	197	5	134
Paraiyan		SC	SC	130,165	152,787	189,241
Parayan	SC					
Sambavar						
Paravan	SC	SC*	SC	18,819	20,515	42,884
Pathiyan	SC	SC*	SC	5,939	7,548	9,508
Perumannan	SC	SC*	SC	4,702	5,528	34,940
Pulaya Vettuvan		SC*	SC	9,262	11,379	1,008
Pulayan	SC	SC*	SC	466,170	586,988	845,604
Cheramar						
Puthirai Vannan		SC*	SC	2,856	1,038	280
Raneyar		SC*	SC	-	2	148
Samagara		SC*	SC	165	155	247
Samban		SC*	SC	24	54	2,486
Semman		SC*	SC	8	19	1,142
Thandan	SC	SC*	SC	77,382	95,446	202,064
Thoti		SC*	SC	547	210	411
Ulladan	SC	SC*	ST	5,049	7,045	-
Uraly	SC	SC*	ST	809	1,829	-
Vallon	SC	SC*	SC	143	453	431
Valluvan	SC	SC	SC	9,364	11,395	13,488
Vannan	SC	SC*	SC	10,711	12,639	34,068

(Continued on next page)

1	2	3	4	5	6	7
Velan	SC	SC*	SC	33,581	42,216	58,796
Vetan	SC	SC*	SC	15,560	17,725	21,346
Vettuvan	SC	SC*	SC	28,095	40,500	111,436
Unclassified/ Unspecified				29	6,559	4,381
Total No. of caste	30(32)	70(77) / 64*(68*)	68(75) / 2*(2*)	66	70	68
Source				a	b	c

Source: a — Census of India, 1961, Vol. I, India, Part V-A (i), SCT-II, Part A, pp. 196-202.

b — Census of India, 1971, Series 1, Paper 1 of 1975, Appendix to Table C-viii Part A, pp. 56-59.

c — Census of India, 1981, Series 10, Part IX (i), SC 1, pp. 10-38.

MADHYA PRADESH

	Scheduled Castes in					Population in		
	1936 Order	1950 Order	1956 Order	1976 Order		1961 Census	1971 Census	1981 Census
1	2	3	4	5		6	7	8
Caste					Total	4,253,024	5,453,690	7,358,533
Audhelia	SC*	SC*	SC*	SC		1,680	1,662	2,794
Bagri			SC* ⎤	SC ⎤		71,756 ⎤	95,374 ⎤	149,080 ⎤
Bagdi			⎦	⎦		⎦	⎦	⎦
Bahna	SC*	SC ⎤	SC* ⎤	SC ⎤		1,275 ⎤	2,499 ⎤	1,835 ⎤
Bahana		⎦	⎦	⎦		⎦	⎦	⎦
Balai			SC*			359,570	441,393	
Balahi			SC*			37,474	54,675	
Balahi	SC* ⎤	SC ⎤	SC* ⎤	SC ⎤		56,922 ⎤	74,187 ⎤	715,435 ⎤
Balai	⎦	⎦	⎦	⎦		⎦	⎦	⎦
Banchada			SC*	SC		7,067	9,807	14,151
Barahar			SC* ⎤	SC ⎤		20,724 ⎤	23,555 ⎤	60,789 ⎤
Basod			⎦	⎦		⎦	⎦	⎦
Bargunda			SC*	SC		6,735	8,645	13,626
Basor	SC ⎤	SC ⎤	SC* ⎤	SC ⎤		59,680 ⎤	74,897 ⎤	164,630 ⎤
Burud	⎦	⎦	⎥	⎥		⎥	⎥	⎥
Bansor			⎦	⎥		⎦	⎦	⎥
Bansodi				⎥				⎥
Basar			SC*	⎥				⎥
Basor			SC* ⎤	⎥		50,153 ⎤	67,724 ⎤	⎥
Bansphor			⎦	⎦		⎦	⎦	⎦
Bansphor			SC* ⎤			7,155 ⎤	11,768 ⎤	

(Continued on next page)

1	2	3	4	5	6	7	8
Basor							
Bedar	SC*	SC*					
Bedia			SC*	SC	5,548	8,416	13,301
Beldar			SC*		116	1,140	
Beldar			SC*	SC	2,883	6,152	17,618
Sunkar							
Mehtar	SC	SC	SC*		41,199	55,482	
Bhangi							
Bhangi			SC*	SC	71,938	100,714	222,039
Mehtar							
Balmik			SC*		5,023	7,413	
Lalbegi							
Dharkar							
Mehtar			SC*		9,381	19,068	
Bhangi							
Dhanuk							
Bhanumati			SC*	SC	713	1,122	1,105
Chadar	SC*	SC*	SC*	SC	16,567	22,065	41,527
Chamar			SC*		451,121	516,282	
Ahirwar							
Chamar Mangan							
Mochi							
Raidas							
Chamar	SC	SC	SC*	SC	1,114,358	1,376,189	3,845,106
Chamari							
Mochi	SC	SC					
Nona							

(Continued on next page)

1	2	3	4	5	6	7	8
Rohidas							
Ramnami							
Satnami	SC	SC					
Surjyabanshi							
Surjyaramnami							
Chamar			SC*		853,326	1,077,561	
Bairwa							
Bhambi							
Jatav							
Mochi							
Regar							
Chamar			SC*		87,551	118,176	
Jatav							
Mochi							
Chauhan	SC*						
Chidar			SC*	SC	13,942	18,247	35,533
Chitar			SC*	SC	230	536	423
Dahait		SC*	SC*	SC	854	1,129	37,706
Dahayat	SC*						
Dahat							
Dewar	SC*	SC*	SC*	SC	4,474	4,715	6,568
Dhanuk	SC*	SC*	SC*	SC	21,524	32,963	49,391
Dhed			SC*	SC	168	536	883
Dher			SC*				
Dhimar	SC*						
Dhobi	SC*		SC*	SC*	10,461	15,645	22,318
Dohor	SC*	SC*	SC*	SC		2	10,836

(Continued on next page)

1	2	3	4	5	6	7	8
Dom	SC	SC	SC*		952	1,653	
Dom			SC*	SC	12,503	17,275	39,874
Dumar							
Dome			SC*		14	45	
Domar			SC*		4,209	15,385	
Doris							
Ganda	SC		SC*	SC	154,085	172,855	205,166
Gandi							
Ghasi		SC*	SC*	SC	58,912	61,175	76,320
Ghasia	SC						
Ghasia			SC*		1,584	1,995	
Holiya	SC*	SC*	SC*	SC	1,246	1,661	3,363
Jangam	SC*						
Kanjar			SC*	SC	2,373	4,588	8,553
Kaikadi		SC*					
Kaikari	SC*						
Katia	SC*	SC*	SC*	SC	29,433	37,779	95,647
Patharia							
Khatik	SC*		SC*	SC	25,221	35,107	75,068
Khatik			SC*				
Chikwa				SC	25,626	24,409	27,311
Chikvi							
Koli			SC*		7,319	13,054	
Katia							
Koli	SC*		SC*	SC	125,451	155,520	379,138
Kori	SC*	SC*					
Kori			SC*		29,476	40,946	

(Continued on next page)

1	2	3	4	5	6	7	8
Kotwal			SC*	SC*	3,171	5,053	8,363*
Khangar	SC*	SC*	SC*	SC	5,640	9,269	96,529
Kanera							
Mirdha							
Kuchbandhia			SC*	SC	385	1,239	5,699
Kumhar	SC*		SC*	SC*	69,979	112,009	121,874*
Madgi	SC*	SC*	SC*				
Mahar	SC*	SC*	SC*	SC	204,594	332,823	577,150
Mehara							
Mehar			SC*		6,880	10,061	
Mahar			SC*		5,200	9,394	
Mala	SC*						
Mang	SC	SC	SC*		163	306	
Mang			SC*	SC	1,596	2,468	17,738
Mang Garodi							
Mang			SC*		7,994	12,084	
Dankhni Mang							
Mang Mahasi							
Mang Garudi							
Madari							
Garudi							
Radhe Mang							
Meghwal			SC*	SC	5,439	6,855	11,944
Moghia			SC*	SC	150	224	21,489
Mushkhan			SC*	SC	180	612	417
Nagarchi	SC*						
Nat			SC*	SC	17,963	21,967	44,127

(Continued on next page)

1	2	3	4	5	6	7	8
Kalbelia							
Sapera							
Navdigar							
Kubutar							
Ojha	SC*						
Panka	SC*						
Pardhi	SC*		SC*	SC*	7,132	6,029	7,523*
Pasi			SC*	SC	7,434	11,067	30,310
Pardhan	SC*	ST	ST	ST			
Rujjhar	SC*	SC*	SC*	SC	1,096	1,207	1,721
Sansi			SC*	SC	1,525	3,362	3,430
Sansia			SC*				
Sansia			SC*		1,208	2,197	
Bedia							
Silawat			SC*	SC	6,752	10,474	23,832
Zamral			SC*	SC	2,661	3,435	3,961
Unclassified/ Unspecified					25,910	57,928	45,584
Total No. of caste	39(43) / 31*(33*)	25(32) / 16*(19*)	83*(143*)	47(104) / 4*(4*)	68	69	47
Source					a	b	c

Source: a — Census of India, 1961, Vol. I, Part V-A(i), Special Table for Scheduled Castes, SCT-II, Part A, pp. 202-208.

b — Census of India, 1971, Series I, Paper 1 of 1975, Appendix to Table C-VIII Part A, pp. 60-63.

c — Census of India, 1981, Series 11, Part IX(i), SC I, pp. 10-36.

MAHARASHTRA (BOMBAY)

	Scheduled Castes in						Population in		
	1936 Order	1950 Order	1956 Order	1960 Act	1976 Order		1961 Census	1971 Census	1981 Census
1	2	3	4	5	6		7	8	9
Caste						Total	2,226,914	3,025,761	4,479,763
Ager		SC	SC*	SC*	SC		3,897	4,048	3,846
Anamuk			SC*	SC*	SC		4	-	116
Aray Mala			SC*	SC*	SC		13	7	232
Arwa Mala			SC*	SC*	SC		-	-	241
Bahna			SC*	SC*	SC		28	-	303
Bahana									
Bakad	SC	SC	SC*	SC*	SC		250	119	736
Bant									
Balahi			SC*	SC*	SC		2,872	3,700	8,672
Balai									
Basor			SC*	SC*	SC		7,554	8,959	34,206
Burud									
Bansodi									
Bansor									
Bawa (Dhedh)			SC*						
Dedh-Sadhu									
Beda Jangam			SC*	SC*	SC		16	455	27,994
Budga Jangam									
Bedar			SC*	SC*	SC		339	831	25,139
Bhambi	SC	SC	SC*	SC*	SC		334,474	439,503	865,500
Bhambhi									

(Continued on next page)

1	2	3	4	5	6	7	8	9
Asadaru								
Asodi	SC	SC						
Chamadia								
Chamar								
Chamgar								
Haralayya								
Harali								
Khalpa	SC							
Chambhar	SC	SC						
Samgar								
Mochigar								
Machigar		SC						
Madar								
Telegu Mochi								
Kamati Mochi								
Ranigar								
Rohidas								
Rohit								
Madig	SC	SC						
Mang								
Mochi								
Chamar			SC*	SC*		81,429	116,482	
Chamari								
Mochi								
Nona								
Rohidas								
Ramnami								

(Continued on next page)

1	2	3	4	5	6	7	8	9
Satnami								
Surjyabanshi								
Surjyaramnami								
Samagara			SC*	SC*				
Mochi	SC*	SC*	SC*	SC*		4,808	4,230	
Chamar			SC*					
Nalia								
Rohit		SC						
Chambhar			SC*	SC*		70,615	95,849	
Chamar			SC*					
Chamadia			SC*					
Mehtar			SC*	SC*		1,586	1,461	
Bhangi	SC	SC	SC*	SC*	SC	42,040	58,958	133,386
Mehtar								
Olgana								
Rukhi								
Malkana								
Halalkhor								
Lalbegi								
Balmiki								
Korar								
Źadmalli								
Mehtar			SC*	SC*		18,353	24,025	
Bhangi								
Bhangi			SC*					
Rukhi								
Bhangi			SC*					

(Continued on next page)

1	2	3	4	5	6	7	8	9
Bindla			SC*	SC*	SC	2	22	303
Byagara			SC*	SC*	SC	1	7	358
Chakrawadya-Dasar	SC	SC						
Chalvadi			SC*	SC*				
Chalvadi	SC	SC	SC*]	SC*]	SC]	349]	1,001]	1,718]
Channayya								
Chenna Dasaru	SC	SC						
Chenna Dasar			SC*]	SC*]	SC]	141]	347]	613]
Holaya Dasar								
Holeya Dasari			SC*	SC*		16	100	
Chadar			SC*	SC*				
Chuhra	SC]	SC]						
Chuhar								
Dakkal			SC*]	SC*]	SC]	107]	53]	342]
Dokkalwar								
Dakaleru	SC	SC						
Dangashia			SC*					
Dhor			SC*	SC*		12,966	13,976	
Dhor	SC	SC	SC*]	SC*]	SC]	23,781]	32,320]	68,509]
Kakkayya								
Kankayya								
Dohor			SC*	SC*		4,741	4,673	
Dom			SC*]	SC*]	SC]	2,123]	5,413]	6,070]
Dumar								
Ellamalvar			SC*]	SC*]	SC]	514]	786]	12,484]
Yellammalawandlu								

(Continued on next page)

1	2	3	4	5	6	7	8	9
Ganda			SC*	SC*	SC	275	300	615
Gandi								
Garoda			SC*					
Garoda		SC	SC*	SC*	SC	209	114	352
Garo								
Garmatang			SC*					
Ghasi			SC*	SC*	SC	125	410	1,983
Ghasia								
Halleer	SC	SC	SC*	SC*	SC	201	—	241
Halsar	SC	SC	SC*	SC*	SC	68	74	123
Haslar								
Hulsavar	SC							
Halsavar								
Garode	SC	SC						
Holaya	SC		SC*	SC*	SC	1,781	276	14,927
Holer								
Holeya			SC*	SC*		4,343	5,019	
Holiya			SC*	SC*		2,302	2,490	
Holar			SC*	SC*	SC	27,602	39,355	52,203
Valhar								
Kaikadi			SC*	SC*	SC*	1,946	2,614	2,678
Katia			SC*	SC*	SC	328	60	3,207
Patharia								
Khangar			SC*	SC*	SC	1	5	858
Kanera								
Mirdha								
Khatik			SC*	SC*	SC	13,584	19,006	55,036

(Continued on next page)

1	2	3	4	5	6	7	8	9
Chikwa								
Chikvi								
Kolcha	SC	SC	ST	ST	ST			
Kolgha			ST	ST	ST			
Koli-Dhor	SC	ST	ST	ST	ST			
Kolupulvandlu			SC*	SC*	SC	222	71	517
Kori			SC*	SC*	SC	457	860	17,506
Kotegar	SC*	SC*						
Lingadar	SC	SC	SC*	SC*	SC	95	43	65,075
Madgi			SC*	SC*	SC	15,471	18,255	34,544
Madiga			SC*	SC*	SC	2,350	5,569	3,772
Mahar			SC*	SC*		244,341	266,530	
Mahar			SC*	SC*		79,572	163,391	
Mehra								
Mahar	SC	SC	SC*	SC*	SC	458,095	641,166	1,648,269
Taral								
Dhegu-Megu	SC	SC						
Mahyavanshi		SC	SC*	SC*	SC	11,999	9,100	13,555
Dhed	SC							
Vankar	SC	SC						
Maru Vankar								
Vankar			SC*					
Dhedh								
Antyaj								
Mala			SC*	SC*	SC	234	252	11,890
Mala Dasari			SC*	SC*	SC	6	55	1,011
Mala Hannai			SC*	SC*	SC	—	—	70

(Continued on next page)

1	2	3	4	5	6	7	8	9
Mala Jangam			SC*	SC*	SC	318	986	17,595
Mala Masti			SC*	SC*	SC	—	27	60
Mala Sale			SC*	SC*	SC	1	6	437
Netkani								
Mala Sanyasi			SC*	SC*	SC	12	44	769
Mang			SC*	SC*		285,660	353,176	
Mang			SC*	SC*	SC			
Matang						319,102	409,145	1,211,335
Mini Madig	SC	SC						
Mang			SC*	SC*		114,129	143,056	
Dankhni Mang								
Mang Mahashi								
Madari								
Garudi								
Radhe Mang								
Mang Garudi								
Mang Garudi	SC	SC	SC*	SC*	SC	7,838	9,853	19,183
Mang Garodi			SC*	SC*		277	288	
Manne			SC*	SC*	SC	122	78	1,752
Mashti			SC*	SC*	SC	2	52	107
Meghval	SC	SC	SC*	SC*	SC	9,031	16,738	29,310
Menghvar								
Meghwal			SC*					
Mitha Ayyalvar			SC*	SC*	SC	—	6	202
Mukri	SC	SC	SC*	SC*	SC	301	32	74
Nadia	SC	SC	SC*	SC*	SC	133	176	249
Hadi								

(Continued on next page)

1	2	3	4	5	6	7	8	9
Hadi			SC*					
Pasi			SC*	SC*	SC	1,354	2,757	11,995
Sansi			SC*	SC*	SC	4	62	526
Shindhava	SC]	SC]						
Shenva			SC*]	SC*]	SC]	321]	120]	501]
Chenva								
Sedma								
Ravat								
Senva			SC*					
Shinghdav	SC]	SC]						
Shingadya								
Shemalia			SC*					
Sochi	SC	SC						
Sindhollu			SC*]	SC*]	SC]		4]	181]
Chindollu								
Thori			SC*					
Timali	SC	SC						
Turi	SC	SC	SC*	SC*	SC	268	133	275
Turi Barot			SC*					
Turi Barot			SC*]					
Dhedh Barot								
Tirgar			SC*]	SC*]	SC]	61]	49]	1,154]
Tirbanda								
Vitholia	SC	SC						

(Continued on next page)

1	2	3	4	5	6	7	8	9
Unclassified/ Unspecified						9,354	96,633	64,950
Total No. of caste	38(47) / 2*(2*)	38(49) / 2*(2*)	99*(193*)	77*(165*)	59(149) / 1*(1*)	69	69	59
Source						a	b	c

Source: a — Census of India, 1961, Vol. I, Part V-A(i), pp. 220-32.

b — Census of India, 1971, Series 1, Paper 1 of 1975, Appendix to Table C-VIII, Part A, pp. 63-66.

c — Census of India, 1981, Series 12, Part IX(i), SC I, pp. 8-44.

MANIPUR

	Scheduled Castes in				Population in		
	1950 Order	1956 Order	1976 Order		1961 Census	1971 Census	1981 Census
1	2	3	4		5	6	7
Caste				Total	13,376	16,376	17,753
Bansphor	SC						
Bhuinmali	SC						
Mali							
Brittial Bania	SC						
Bania							
Dhupi	SC	SC	SC		65	262	186
Dhobi							
Dugla	SC						
Dholi							
Hira	SC						
Jhalo	SC						
Malo							
Kaibartta	SC						
Jalia							
Lalbegi	SC						
Lois		SC	SC		9,216	11,303	11,234
Mahara	SC						
Mehtar	SC						
Bhangi							
Muchi	SC	SC	SC		415	304	193
Ravidas							

(Continued on next page)

1	2	3	4	5	6	7
Namasudra	SC	SC	SC	2,163	2,300	2,423
Patni	SC	SC	SC	772	1,504	2,793
Sutradhar	SC	SC	SC	-	28	11
Yaithibi		SC	SC	745	669	906
Unspecified/ Unclassified				6		67
Total No. of castes	15(22)	7(9)	7(9)	6	7	7
Source				a	b	c

Source: a — Census of India, 1961, Vol. I, Part V-A(1), p. 304.

b — Census of India, 1971, Series 1, Paper 1 of 1975, Appendix to Table C-viii, Part A, p. 66.

c — Census of India, 1981, Series 13, Part IX, Table SC I, pp. 4-8.

MEGHALAYA

Act	Scheduled Castes in				Population in	
	1969 Act	1971 Order	1976		1971 Census	1981 Census
1	2	3	4		5	6
Caste				Total	3,887	5,492
Bansphor	SC	SC	SC		115	212
Bhuinmali	SC	SC	SC		323	201
Mali						
Brittial Bania	SC	SC	SC		386	115
Bania						
Dhupi	SC	SC	SC		165	313
Dhobi						
Dugla	SC	SC	SC			22
Dholi						
Hira	SC	SC	SC			48
Jalkeot	SC	SC	SC			8
Jhalo	SC	SC	SC		651	1,052
Malo						
Jhalo-Malo						
Kaibartta	SC	SC	SC		414	191
Jaliya						
Lalbegi	SC	SC	SC			30
Mahara	SC	SC	SC		70	—
Mehtar	SC	SC	SC		238	621
Bhangi						

(Continued on next page)

1	2	3	4	5	6
Muchi Rishi	SC]	SC]	SC]	651]	1,204]
Namasudra	SC	SC	SC	471	1,112
Patni	SC	SC	SC	177	54
Sutradhar	SC	SC	SC	18	270
Unspecified/ Unclassified				208	39
Total No. of caste	16(25)	16(25)	16(25)	12	15
Source				a	b

Source: a — Census of India, 1971, Series 1, Paper 1 of 1975, pp. 66-67.

b — Census of India, 1981, Series 14, SC 1, pp. 6-10.

MIZORAM

	Scheduled Castes in			Population in
	1971 Act	1986 Act		1981 Census
1	2	3		4
Caste			Total	135
Bansphor	SC	SC		8
Bhuinmali Mali	SC	SC		3
Brittial Bania Bania	SC	SC		2
Dhupi Dhobi	SC	SC		33
Dugla Dholi	SC	SC		4
Hira	SC	SC		3
Jalkeot	SC	SC		2
Jhalo Malo Jhalo-Malo	SC	SC		1
Kaibartta Jaliya	SC	SC		5
Lalbegi	SC	SC		3
Mahara	SC	SC		6
Mehtar Bhangi	SC	SC		10

(Continued on next page)

1	2	3	4
Muchi	SC]	SC]	15]
Rishi			
Namasudra	SC	SC	7
Patni	SC	SC	4
Sutradhar	SC	SC	-
Unclassified			29
Total No. of caste	16(25)	16(25)	15
Source			a

Source: a — Census of India, 1981, Series 31, Part IX, pp. 10-16.

ORISSA

	Scheduled Castes in					Population in		
	1936 Order	1950 Order	1956 Order	1976 Order		1961 Census	1971 Census	1981 Census
1	2	3	4	5		6	7	8
Caste					Total	2,763,858	3,310,854	3,865,543
Adi Andhra	SC	SC	SC	SC		8,313	10,584	3,621
Amant		SC]	SC]	SC]		12,656]	8,765]	9,866]
Amat								
Audhelia	SC	SC	SC	SC		-	12	15
Badaik		SC	SC	SC		3,763	7,821	10,291
Bagheti		SC	SC]	SC]		8,600]	14,940]	17,916]
Baghuti								
Bajikar		SC	SC	SC		36	195	203
Bari		SC	SC	SC		45	115	144
Bariki	SC	SC	SC	SC		26,996	13,129	12,357
Basor	SC]	SC]	SC]	SC]		68]	34]	178]
Burud								
Bauri	SC	SC	SC	SC		250,914	303,460	336,278
Bauro	SC'							
Bauti		SC	SC	SC		245	122	307
Bavuri		SC	SC	SC		4	2	50
Bedia		SC]	SC]	SC]		383]	1,026]	631]
Bejia								
Beldar		SC	SC	SC		914	1,268	2,440
Bhata		SC	SC	SC		3,332	3,346	4,508
Bhoi			SC	SC		36,302	30,645	69,545

(Continued on next page)

1	2	3	4	5	6	7	8
Bhuiya	SC*	ST	ST	ST			
Bhumij	SC*	SC	ST	ST			
Chachati	SC	SC	SC	SC	-	15	95
Chakali			SC	SC	639	157	215
Chamar	SC	SC	SC	SC	57,064	81,314	109,576
Mochi	SC	SC					
Muchi							
Satnami	SC	SC					
Chandala	SC	SC	SC	SC	4,466	4,244	5,581
Chandhai Maru			SC	SC	224	-	28
Cherua		SC	SC	SC	271	608	759
Chhelia							
Dandasi	SC	SC	SC	SC	50,250	47,048	50,437
Desua Bhumij		SC	ST	ST			
Dewar	SC	SC	SC	SC	19,323	3,637	4,250
Dhanwar		SC	SC	SC	718	1,147	1,135
Dharua		SC	ST	ST			
Dhoba	SC	SC	SC	SC	265,360	322,216	418,383
Dhobi							
Dom	SC*	SC	SC	SC	311,183	370,236	427,078
Dombo							
Duria Dom							
Dosadha		SC	SC	SC	156	101	455
Ganda	SC	SC	SC	SC	358,403	325,053	418,956
Ghantarghada		SC	SC	SC	2,754	3,358	5,205
Ghantra							
Ghasi	SC*	SC	SC	SC	54,647	56,330	77,132
Ghasia							

(Continued on next page)

1	2	3	4	5	6	7	8
Ghogia		SC	SC	SC	313	629	656
Ghusuria	SC	SC	SC	SC	2,272	4,590	5,127
Godagali	SC	SC	SC	SC	24	48	24
Godari	SC	SC	SC	SC	-	72	225
Godra	SC	SC	SC	SC	2,370	2,784	2,309
Gokha	SC	SC	SC	SC	66,739	82,206	116,226
Gorait		ST]	SC]	SC]	14]	342]	395]
Korait							
Gunju		SC]					
Ganju							
Hadi		SC]	SC]	SC]	91.819]	101,331]	133,625]
Haddi	SC]						
Hari							
Irika	SC	SC	SC	SC	192	158	270
Jaggali	SC	SC	SC	SC	4,182	4,394	4,626
Kandra	SC	SC]	SC]	SC]	212,039]	248,380]	316,367]
Kandara							
Karua		SC	SC	SC	2,410	3,799	4,208
Katia	SC	SC	SC	SC	3,357	1,144	1,200
Kela	SC	SC	SC	SC	7,764	14,611	13,344
Khadala		SC	SC	SC	37,686	30,730	51,055
Kodalo	SC	SC	SC]	SC]	505]	8,377]	330]
Khodalo							
Kori	SC*	SC	SC	SC	765	197	286
Kumbhar		SC					
Kuli			SC*		3,911	4,086	
Kummari			SC	SC	743	1,961	2,501

(Continued on next page)

1	2	3	4	5	6	7	8
Kurunga		SC	SC	SC	2,187	2,051	2,371
Laban		SC	SC	SC	1,018	1,151	1,099
Laheri		SC	SC	SC	3,093	3,713	5,102
Madari	SC	SC	SC	SC	1,635	1,644	1,940
Madiga	SC	SC	SC	SC	756	793	1,314
Mahuria	SC	SC	SC	SC	2,555	3,566	4,286
Mala	SC	SC	SC	SC	4,506	4,629	6,118
Jhala							
Malo							
Zala							
Mang	SC	SC	SC	SC	156	1	273
Mangan	SC	SC	SC	SC	805	883	983
Mehra	SC	SC	SC	SC	12,803	11,297	16,158
Mahar							
Mehtar	SC	SC	SC	SC	3,491	7,358	2,332
Bhangi							
Mewar		SC	SC	SC	243	232	540
Mundapotta		SC	SC	SC	879	527	1,318
Musahar			SC	SC	80	19	29
Nagarchi	SC*	SC	SC	SC	403	71	225
Namasudra			SC	SC	7,900	49,796	76,316
Paidi	SC	SC	SC	SC	550	-	343
Painda	SC	SC	SC	SC	275	892	964
Pamidi	SC	SC	SC	SC	125	52	64
Pan	SC*	SC	SC	SC	602,126	672,627	806,514
Pano							
Panchama	SC	SC	SC	SC	783	383	269

(Continued on next page)

1	2	3	4	5	6	7	8
Panika		SC	SC	SC	7,504	8,083	8,063
Panka	SC	SC	SC	SC	15	-	1,683
Pantanti		SC	SC	SC	32,875	43,013	27,210
Pap		SC	SC	SC	6,702	7,211	8,789
Pasi		SC	SC	SC	870	94	537
Patial		SC	SC	SC	41,371	23,481	34,769
Patikar							
Patratanti							
Patua							
Pradhan	SC*	SC					
Rajna		SC	SC	SC	254	13	704
Relli	SC	SC	SC	SC	4,548	4,742	6,353
Sabakhia		SC	SC	SC	556	966	1,079
Samasi		SC	SC	SC	688	906	1,214
Sanei		SC	SC	SC	937	574	1,005
Sapari	SC	SC	SC	SC	71	41	129
Sauntia			SC	SC	15,703	19,452	23,877
Santia							
Sidhria		SC	SC	SC	1,436	506	573
Sindhuria		SC	SC	SC	720	39	177
Siyal	SC	SC	SC	SC	10,351	13,965	18,666
Sukuli		SC					
Tamadia		SC	SC	SC	1,684	2,292	238
Tamudia		SC	SC	SC	6,917	5,590	4,743
Tanla			SC	SC	32,245	36,921	46,343
Tiar		SC	SC	SC	12,012	13,490	20,140
Tior							

(Continued on next page)

1	2	3	4	5	6	7	8
Turi	SC*	SC	SC	SC	3,807	4,698	7,374
Ujia			SC	SC	6,424	14,488	16,370
Valamiki		SC]	SC]	SC]	1,111]	1,423]	1,960]
Valmiki	SC						
Unclassified/ Unspecified					13,560	226,414	69,742
Total No. of caste	53(62) / 10*(13*)	92(114)	94(124) / 1*(1*)	93(123)	91	91	93
Source					a	b	c

Source: a — Cesus of India, 1961, Vol. 1, India, Part V-A(1), pp. 250-56.

b — Census of India, 1971, Series 1, Paper 1 of 1975, Appendix to Table C-viii Part A, pp. 71-75.

c — Census of India, 1981, Series 16, Part IX(i), Table SC I, pp. 4-72.

PUNJAB

	Scheduled Castes in					Population in		
	1936 Order	1950 Order	1956 Order	1976 Order		1961 Census	1971 Census	1981 Census
1	2	3	4	5		6	7	8
Caste					Total	4,139,106	3,348,217	4,511,703
Adi Dharmi	SC	SC	SC	SC		451,514	439,632	680,132
Balmiki	SC	SC	SC	SC		688,588	401,960	532,628
Chura								
Bhangi								
Bangali	SC	SC	SC	SC		1,008	498	1,600
Barar	SC	SC	SC	SC		4,423	1,911	4,761
Burar								
Berar								
Batwal		SC	SC	SC		11,479	6,210	9,367
Bauria			SC	SC		41,770	42,713	62,624
Bawaria	SC	SC						
Bazigar	SC	SC	SC	SC		78,932	75,092	120,250
Bhanjra	Sc	SC	SC	SC		3,702	1,907	3,557
Chamar	SC	SC	SC	SC		1,596,030	981,471	1,221,146
Jatia Chamar								
Rehgar								
Raigar								
Ramdasi	SC	SC						
Ravidasi								
Chanal	SC	SC	SC	SC		2,345	37	139
Dagi	SC	SC	SC	SC		380	29	54

(Continued on next page)

1	2	3	4	5	6	7	8
Koli		SC	SC	SC	70,743	2,057	5,652
Kori	SC						
Darain			SC*	SC	3,632	162	156
Deha			SC*	SC	994	1,524	4,783
Dhaya							
Dhea							
Dhanak	SC	SC	SC	SC	163,619	27,910	46,289
Dhogri			SC*	SC	1,415	46	265
Dhangri							
Siggi							
Dumna	SC	SC	SC	SC	95,609	91,685	124,929
Mahasha							
Doom							
Gagra	SC	SC	SC	SC	31	55	413
Gandhila	SC	SC	SC	SC	901	883	1,869
Gandil Gondola							
Kabirpanthi		SC	SC	SC	103,618	37,625	56,888
Julaha							
Khatik	SC	SC	SC	SC	21,988	5,943	8,932
Marija	SC	SC	SC	SC	36	218	649
Marecha							
Mazhabi		SC	SC	SC	664,161	962,546	1,366,843
Megh	SC	SC	SC	SC	44,185	52,608	78,405
Nat	SC	SC	SC	SC	1,982	43	466
Od	SC	SC	SC	SC	20,829	1,251	6,494
Pasi	SC	SC	SC	SC	2,064	1,713	5,593
Perna	SC	SC	SC	SC	227	4	75

(Continued on next page)

1	2	3	4	5	6	7	8
Pherera		SC	SC	SC	182	72	279
Sanhai		SC	SC	SC	1,515	180	73
Sanhal		SC	SC	SC	72	163	192
Sansi	SC	SC	SC]	SC]	38,286]	39,084]	61,986]
Bhedkut							
Manesh							
Sansoi			SC*	SC	124	601	320
Sapela	SC	SC	SC	SC	2,486	823	1,012
Sarera	SC	SC	SC	SC	10,122	5,969	10,238
Sikligar		SC	SC	SC	5,251	1,514	4,321
Sirkiband	SC	SC	SC	SC	1,790	1,948	14,111
Unclassified/ Unspecified					3,068	160,130	74,218
Total No. of caste	27(30)	34(39)	37(59) / 4*(8*)	37(59)	37	37	37
Source					a	b	c

Source: a — Census of India, 1961, India, Vol. I, Part V-A(i), SCT-II, Part A, p. 262.

b — Census of India, 1971, Series 1, Paper 1 of 1975, Appendix to Table C-viii Part A, pp. 76-77.

c — Census of India, 1981, Series 17, Part IX, Table SC I, pp. 6-18.

RAJASTHAN

	Scheduled Castes in				Population in		
	1950 Order	1956 Order	1976 Order		1961 Census	1971 Census	1981 Census
1	2	3	4		5	6	7
Caste *				Total	3,359,640	4,075,580	5,838,879
Adi Dharmi	SC	SC*	SC		1,573	467	780
Ager		SC*					
Aheri	SC	SC*	SC		1,947	1,495	2,736
Badi	SC	SC*	SC		1,287	4,474	5,698
Bagri	SC	SC*			18,564	19.004	
Bagri		SC*	SC				25,326
Bagdi							
Bakad		SC*					
Bant							
Bairwa		SC*	SC		8,836	139,942	429,625
Berwa							
Bajgar	SC	SC*	SC		3,372	6,717	3,085
Balai		SC*	SC		306,034	333,443	462,925
Bansphor	SC	SC*	SC		751	1,506	3,929
Bansphod		SC*			—	30	
Baori		SC*	SC		1,989	2,308	180,054
Bargi	SC	SC*			-	322	
Bargi		SC*	SC		3,557	3,654	3,725
Vargi							
Birgi							
Bawaria	SC	SC*	SC		83,104	51,212	32,003

(Continued on next page)

1	2	3	4	5	6	7
Bedia		SC*				
Bedia		SC*]	SC]	4,623]	1,011]	2,361]
Beria						
Bhand	SC	SC*	SC	4,303	8,345	12,058
Banchada		SC*				
Barahar		SC*]				
Basod						
Bargunda		SC*				
Bhanumati		SC*				
Bhangi	SC	SC*		153,117	132,949	
Bhangi		SC*]				
Mehtar						
Mehtar	SC	SC*		12,495	48,579	
Bhangi		SC*]	SC]		1,264]	263,565]
Mehtar						
Olgana						
Rukhi						
Malkana						
Halakhor						
Lalbegi						
Balmiki						
Korar						
Zadmalli						
Valmiki	SC	SC*		6,462	7,407	
Chura	SC	SC*		10,859	4,611	
Bidakia	SC	SC*	SC	749	347	245
Bola		SC*	SC	16,355	15,476	5,945

(Continued on next page)

1	2	3	4	5	6	7
Bambhi		SC*	SC	1,363,000	1,498,633	1,872,133
Chamar	SC					
Jatav						
Jatia	SC					
Mochi	SC					
Raidass						
Raigar	SC					
Ramdasia	SC					
Bhambi						
Bhambhi		SC*		—	988	
Asadaru						
Asodi						
Chamadia						
Chamar						
Chambhar						
Chamgar						
Haralayya						
Harali						
Khalpa						
Machigar						
Mochigar						
Madar						
Madig						
Telegu Mochi						
Kamati Mochi						
Ranigar						
Rohidas						

(Continued on next page)

1	2	3	4	5	6	7
Rohit						
Samgar						
Chamar		SC*				
Bariwa						
Bhambi						
Jatav						
Mochi						
Regar						
Chamar		SC*		70,531	82,255	
Jatava						
Jatia						
Mochi						
Raigar						
Bambhi		SC*		20,971	17,760	
Chandal		SC*	SC	218	607	1,105
Chidar		SC*				
Chalvadi		SC*				
Channayya						
Chennna Dasar		SC*				
Holaya Dasar						
Dabgar	SC	SC*	SC	1,276	985	1,166
Dhanak		SC*	SC	1,885	2,099	82,234
Dhanuk		SC*				
Dhankia	SC	SC*	SC	40,352	44,932	6,477
Dhobi		SC*	SC	5,812	5,195	104,252
Dholi		SC*	SC	4,934	4,791	72,282
Dome	SC	SC*	SC	22,645	7,137	3,692

(Continued on next page)

1	2	3	4	5	6	7
Dom		SC*		293	196	
Dhor		SC*				
Kakkayya						
Kangayya						
Gandia	SC	SC*	SC	264	186	159
Garancha Mehar	SC	SC*		1,666	2,937	
Gancha						
Gancha		SC*	SC	228	387	5,168
Garancha						
Garo		SC*	SC	11,553	15,201	28,888
Garura						
Gurda						
Garoda		SC*		136	139	
Garoda		SC*			65*	
Garo						
Gavaria		SC*	SC	5,116	9,158	30,268
Godhi	SC	SC*	SC	418	631	263
Halleer		SC*				
Halsar		SC*				
Haslar						
Hulsavar						
Halasvar						
Holar		SC*				
Valhar						
Holaya		SC*				
Holer						
Jingar		SC*	SC	1,637	1,793	12,327

(Continued on next page)

1	2	3	4	5	6	7
Kamad		SC*]	SC]	2,521]	5,229]	6,270]
Kamadia						
Kanjar		SC*	SC]	10,,714	15,767	21,001]
Kunjar	SC	SC*		31		
Kapadia Sansi	SC	SC*	SC	1,455	880	1,768
Khangar	SC	SC*	SC	262	2,453	4,320
Khatka	SC					
Khatik		SC*	SC	104,641	152,838	215,089
Koli		SC*]	SC]	133,997]	170,417]	265,767]
Kori						
Koli		SC*		14,201	20,451	
Kooch Band	SC	SC*	SC]	501	167	1,509]
Kuchband		SC*		4	968	
Koria	SC	SC*	SC	315	1,715	2,794
Kabirpanthi		SC*				
Kotwal		SC*				
Lingader		SC*				
Madari	SC]	SC*]	SC]	586]	1,046]	11,191]
Bazigar						
Bazigar		SC*		56	15	
Mahar		SC*				
Mahar		SC*]	SC]		3]	7,635]
Taral						
Dhegu Megu						
Dheda	SC	SC*	]	5,218	524	]
Mahyavanshi		SC*]	SC		7]	1,868
Vankar						

(Continued on next page)

1	2	3	4	5	6	7
Maru Vankar						
Dhed						
Dhed		SC*		68	25	
Majhabi	SC	SC*	SC	42,540	45,250	80,344
Mang		SC*	SC			241
Matang						
Minimadig						
Mang		SC*		1		
Mang Garodi			SC			
Mang Garudi		SC*				177
Meghwal		SC*		2,406	5,321	
Megh		SC*		312,020	599,644	889,300
Meghwal			SC			
Meghaval		SC*			1,924	
Menghvar						
Mehar	SC	SC*	SC	19,185	27,731	31,450
Mukri		SC*				
Nut	SC	SC*	SC	9,950	16,239	23,225
Nat		SC*		756	565	
Nat		SC*				
Kalbelia			SC			30,874
Sapera						
Kalbelia	SC	SC*		12,690	19,449	
Nadia		SC*				
Hadi						
Pardhi		SC*				
Pasi	SC	SC*	SC	186	406	943

(Continued on next page)

1	2	3	4	5	6	7
Rawal	SC	SC*	SC	4,656	5,383	12,649
Salvi		SC*	SC	3,319	7,584	19,409
Sansi	SC	SC*	SC	12,694	20,365	31,997
Satia		SC*	]	39	160	]
Santia		SC*	SC]	1,554	3,428	5,372]
Sarbhangi	SC	SC*	SC	445	326	613
Sargara		SC*	SC	45,680	54,3100	77,169
Singiwala	SC	SC*	SC	151	915	1,786
Shenva		SC*]				
Chenva		]				
Sedma		]				
Ravat		]				
Thori	SC	SC*		3,105	170	
Thori		SC*]	SC]	155,954]	221,583]	347,613]
Nayak		]	]	]	]	]
Tirgar	SC	SC*		1,159	1,985	
Tirgar		SC*]	SC]		12]	2,170]
Tirbanda		]	]		]	]
Turi		SC*	SC		29	2,041
Zamral		SC*				
Unclassified/ Unspecified				263,673	189,488	87,280
Total No. of caste	44(45)	142*(230*)	59(133)	73	81	59
Source				a	b	c

Source: a — Census of India, 1961, Vol. I, part V-A(i)-Table SCT-II, Part A, pp. 268-74.
b — Census of India, 1971, Series 1, Paper 1 of 1975, Appendix to Table C-VIII, Part A, pp. 77-81.
c — Census of India, 1981, Series 18, Part IX(i), Table SC 1, pp. 4-40.

SIKKIM

	Scheduled Castes in		Population in	
	1978 Order		1971 Census	1981 Census
1	2		3	4
Caste		Total	9,502	18,281
Damai (Nepali)	SC		1,166	5,980
Kami (Nepali)	SC]		2,135	11,438]
Lohar (Nepali)	]			]
Majhi (Nepali)	SC			246
Sarki (Nepali)	SC		198	604
Unspecified/ Unclassified			6,003	13
Total No. of caste	4(5)		3@	4
Source			a	b

@ Figures shown against Sikkim relate to the castes declared as scheduled castes under the Representation of Sikkim Subjects Regulation (1966). No caste or tribe has been scheduled under the Constitution in relation to Sikkim.

Source: a — Census of India, 1971, Series 1, Paper 1 of 1975, p. 81.

b — Census of India, 1981, Series 19, Part IX, Table SC 1, p. 4.

TAMIL NADU (MADRAS)

	Scheduled Castes in				Population in		
	1936 Order	1950 Order	1956 Order	1976 Order	1961 Census	1971 Census	1981 Census
1	2	3	4	5	6	7	8
Caste / Total					6,067,327	7,315,595	8,881,295
Adi Andhra	SC	SC	SC*	SC	18,269	32,156	50,391
Adi Dravida	SC	SC	SC*	SC	1,763,000	2,547,168	3,831,152
Adi Karnataka	SC	SC	SC*	SC	12,448	20,459	30,055
Ajila	SC	SC	SC*	SC	-	39	35
Arnadan	SC*	ST	ST	ST			
Arunthathiyar	SC	SC	SC*	SC	99,947	256,709	424,209
Ayyanavar			SC*	SC*	632	693	1,224*
Baira	SC	SC	SC*	SC	150	248	431
Bakuda	SC	SC	SC*	SC	50	113	198
Bandi	SC	SC	SC*	SC	37	70	486
Bariki	SC	SC					
Battada	SC						
Bavuri	SC	SC					
Bellara	SC	SC	SC*	SC	-	11	44
Bharatar			SC*	SC*	513	1,138	1,790*
Byagari	SC	SC					
Chachati	SC	SC					
Chakkiliyan	SC	SC	SC	SC	778,076	864,842	513,365
Chalvadi	SC	SC	SC*	SC	1	68	131
Chamar	SC	SC	SC*]	SC]	14]	10,585]	165]
Muchi	SC	SC					

(Continued on next page)

1	2	3	4	5	6	7	8
Chandala	SC	SC	SC*	SC	2	105	37
Cheruman	SC	SC	SC*	SC	1,884	1,014	1,673
Dandasi	SC	SC					
Devendrakulathan	SC	SC	SC*	SC	15,963	22,236	33,528
Dom		SC]	SC*]	SC]	1,977]	4,594]	892]
Dombara							
Paidi	SC						
Pano	SC*						
Domban			SC*	SC	26	31	7,311
Dombo	SC*						
Ghasi	SC	SC]					
Haddi	SC						
Relli Sachandi							
Godagali	SC	SC	SC*	SC	-	31	24
Godari	SC	SC					
Godda	SC	SC	SC*	SC	8	118	116
Gosangi	SC	SC	SC*	SC	85	7	157
Hasla	SC	SC					
Holeya	SC	SC	SC*	SC	1,826	1,003	1,521
Jaggali	SC	SC	SC*	SC	8	578	1,248
Jambuvulu	SC	SC	SC*	SC	10	12	131
Kadan	SC*	SC					
Kadaiyan			SC*	SC	1,750	2,418	4,847
Kakkalan			SC*	SC*	26	58	66*
Kalladi	SC	SC	SC*	SC	117	2,279	409
Kanakkan	SC	SC	SC*]	SC*]	96]	160]	176*]
Padanna							

(Continued on next page)

1	2	3	4	5	6	7	8
Karimpalan	SC*	SC	SC*	SC		4	9
Kavara			SC*	SC*	252	1,246	3,711*
Kattunayakan	SC*	ST	ST	ST			
Kodalo	SC	SC					
Koosa	SC	SC	SC*	SC		5	41
Koraga	SC	SC	ST	ST			
Koliyan			SC*	SC	5,680	7,013	7,509
Kootan]			SC*]	SC*]	49]	64]	147*]
Koodan]							
Kudumban	SC	SC	SC*	SC	247,822	113,888	54,814
Kuravan]	SC	SC	SC]	SC]	78,470]	76,642]	71,065]
Sidhanar]							
Kudiya	SC*	ST	ST	ST			
Kudubi	SC*	SC					
Kurichchan	SC*	SC	ST	ST			
Kuruman	SC*	ST	ST	ST			
Madari	SC	SC	SC*	SC	60,015	98,432	346,899
Madiga	SC	SC	SC*	SC	3,198	7,564	6,195
Maila	SC	SC	SC*	SC	1	6	47
Mala	SC	SC	SC*	SC	2,060	16,781	16,115
Malasar	SC*	SC	ST	ST			
Mala Dasu	SC	SC					
Mannan			SC*	SC*	16	234	274*
Mavilan	SC*	SC	SC*	SC	196	4	64
Matangi	SC	SC					
Moger	SC	SC	SC*	SC	13	186	89
Mundala	SC	SC	SC*	SC	4	23	26

(Continued on next page)

1	2	3	4	5	6	7	8
Nalakeyava	SC	SC	SC*	SC	2	2	7
Nayadi	SC	SC	SC	SC	107	329	360
Padannan			SC*	SC*		2	-
Pagadai	SC	SC	SC*	SC	19,299	26,186	17,863
Paky	SC	SC					
Pallan	SC	SC	SC	SC	950,266	1,326,745	993,070
Palluvan			SC*	SC	1	115	151
Pamidi	SC	SC					
Pambada	SC	SC	SC*	SC	12	543	624
Panan		SC	SC*	SC*	182	192	209*
Panchama	SC	SC	SC*	SC	278	950	76
Pannadi			SC*	SC	10,745	15,444	18,385
Painda	SC	SC					
Paniyan	SC	ST	ST	ST			
Panniandi	SC	SC	SC*	SC	642	2,831	2,695
Paraiyan	SC	SC	SC]	SC]	1,513,627]	1,533,482]	842,337]
Parayan							
Sambavar							
Paravan	SC	SC	SC*	SC*	1,550	1,684	1,643*
Pathiyan			SC*	SC*	30	-	23*
Perumanan			SC*				
Pulayan	SC	SC	SC*]	SC]	907]	1,679]	6,581]
Cheramar							
Puthirai Vannan	SC	SC	SC*	SC	9,696	10,543	17,962
Raneyar	SC	SC	SC*	SC	-	10	4
Relli	SC						
Samagara	SC	SC	SC*	SC	19	4	37

(Continued on next page)

1	2	3	4	5	6	7	8
Samban	SC	SC	SC*	SC	136,818	146,563	38,465
Sapari	SC	SC	SC*	SC	-	45	19
Semman	SC	SC	SC*	SC	176	1,234	992
Thandan			SC*	SC*	1,105	1,795	2,466*
Thoti	SC	SC	SC*	SC	41,129	12,337	4,536
Tiruvalluvar	SC	SC	SC*	SC	10,077	1,629	3,828
Vallon			SC*	SC		2	104
Valluvan	SC	SC	SC	SC	62,450	65,115	63,253
Valmiki	SC	SC					
Vannan			SC*	SC*	3,383	4,660	4,566*
Vattiriyan			SC*	SC	-	-	302
Velan			SC*	SC	8	606	318
Vetan			SC*	SC*	630	822	774*
Vethiyan			SC*	SC	3,541	7,415	2,706
Vettuvan	SC	SC	SC*	SC*	141	688	143*
Ulladan			SC*				
Uraly			SC*	ST	385	277	
Unclassified/ Unspecified					205,430	60,683	6,902 + 1,453,897 @
Total No. of caste	86(86) / 12*(12*)	77(82)	79(89) / 73*(80*)	76(86) / 15*(17*)	68	76	75
Source					a	b	c

Source: a — Census of India, 1961, India, Vol. I, Part V A(i), SCT II-A, pp. 214-20.
b — Census of India, 1971, Series 1, Paper 1 of 1975, Appendix to Table C-viii, Part A, pp. 81-85.
c — Census of India, 1981, Series 20, Part IX(i), Table SC I, pp. 8-44.
@ The caste-wise figures excludes three districts, namely, Tiruchchirappalli, Pudukkottai and Tirunalveli, which could not be keyed in because the individual slips were damaged by floods. However, the total S.C. population includes these three districts.

TRIPURA

	Scheduled Castes in				Population in		
	1951 Order	1956 Order	1976 Order		1961 Census	1971 Census	1981 Census
1	2	3	4		5	6	7
Caste				Total	119,725	192,860	310,383
Bagdi	SC	SC	SC		161	116	239
Baiti	SC	SC					
Bhuimali	SC	SC	SC		784	315	789
Bhunar	SC	SC	SC		4	475	90
Chamar	SC	SC]	SC]		3,640]	4,228]	6,833]
Muchi	SC						
Dandasi	SC	SC	SC		10	-	57
Dhenuar	SC	SC	SC		9	1	13
Dhoba	SC	SC	SC		10,887	19,953	34,314
Duai	SC	SC					
Dum	SC	SC	SC		155	143	283
Ghasi	SC	SC	SC		327	72	443
Gour	SC	SC	SC		3,523	2,877	3,720
Gunar	SC	SC					
Gur	SC	SC	SC		258	1,145	1,187
Gorang	SC	SC					
Jalia Kaibartta	SC	SC	SC		18,208	29,897	52,612
Kahar	SC	SC	SC		125	181	223
Kalindi	SC	SC	SC		40	30	34
Kan	SC	SC	SC		5	23	8
Kanda		SC	SC		1,226	1,202	1,813

(Continued on next page)

1	2	3	4	5	6	7
Kanugh	SC	SC	SC	1	15	81
Keot	SC	SC	SC	133	336	262
Khadit	SC	SC	SC	15	-	-
Kharia	SC	SC	SC	513	744	913
Khemcha	SC	SC		-	-	
Koch	SC	SC	SC	366	650	843
Koir	SC	SC	SC	118	100	63
Kol	SC	SC	SC	1.067	519	582
Kora	SC	SC	SC	15	26	14
Kotal	SC	SC	SC	51	-	43
Mahisyadas	SC	SC	SC	11,994	28,733	53,751
Mali	SC	SC	SC	15,362	21,134	28,643
Mehtor	SC	SC	SC	456	626	1,279
Musahar		SC	SC	52	7	237
Namasudra	SC	SC	SC	46,383	74,980	114,599
Patni	SC	SC	SC	1,687	2,228	3,268
Sabar	SC	SC	SC	2,150	2,904	3,000
Unclassified/Unspecified					10	178
Total No. of caste	36(36)	37(38)	32(33)	32	29	31
Source				a	b	c

Soruce: a — Census of India, 1961, Vol. I, Part V-A(1), SCT-II Part A, pp. 304-10.

b — Census of India, 1971, Series 1, Paper 1 of 1975, pp. 85-86.

c — Census of India, 1981, Series 21, Part IX, Table SC I, pp. 10-30.

UTTAR PRADESH

	Scheduled Castes in					Population in		
	1936 Order	1950 Order	1956 Order	1976 Order		1961 Census	1971 Census	1981 Census
1	2	3	4	5		6	7	8
Caste					Total	15,399,881	18,548,916	23,453,339
Agaria	SC	SC	SC	SC		10.261	12,555	12,276
Aheriya	SC							
Badi	SC	SC	SC	SC		1,724	4,711	4,481
Baheliya	SC	SC	SC	SC		27,629	41,454	57,470
Basiwar		SC	SC	SC		5,774	12,824	16,145
Baiga		SC	SC	SC		3,874	6,415	14,148
Bajgi	SC	SC	SC	SC		2,165	6,953	14,584
Bajania	SC	SC	SC	SC		671	1,223	1,510
Balahar	SC	SC	SC	SC		8,720	10,225	5,297
Balai			SC	SC		902	2,229	1,321
Balmiki	SC	SC	SC	SC		558,389	731,226	744,821
Bangali	SC	SC	SC	SC		1,388	26,152	31,952
Banmanus	SC	SC	SC	SC		8,848	10,077	13,570
Bansphor	SC	SC	SC	SC		14,853	18,721	18,530
Barwar	SC	SC	SC	SC		6,303	11,111	12,001
Basor	SC	SC	SC	SC		58,805	73,517	83,386
Bawariya	SC	SC	SC	SC		2,905	3,757	4,893
Beldar	SC	SC	SC	SC		59,247	80,626	94,185
Beriya	SC	SC	SC	SC		14,949	22,221	19,504
Badhik	SC	SC	SC	SC		9,972	12,240	7,014
Bhantu	SC	SC	SC	SC		7,903	8,649	6,663

(Continued on next page)

1	2	3	4	5	6	7	8
Bhoksa		SC					
Bhuiya	SC	SC	SC	SC	3,188	6,011	8,145
Bhuiyar	SC	SC	SC	SC	26,766	28,815	12,630
Boria	SC	SC	SC	SC	1,175	4,952	2,004
Chamar	SC	SC	SC	SC	8,693,327	10,121,421	12,914,218
Dhusia		SC					
Jhusia							
Jatava		SC					
Chero	SC	SC	SC	SC	12,779	15,401	17,239
Dabgar	SC	SC	SC	SC	3,754	3,761	3,202
Dhangar	SC	SC	SC	SC	8,705	24,072	20,127
Dhanuk	SC	SC	SC	SC	224,055	272,970	330,473
Dharkar	SC	SC	SC	SC	41,662	70,684	58,711
Dhobi	SC	SC	SC	SC	888,466	1,156,243	1,423,574
Dom	SC	SC	SC	SC	41,388	79,396	55,590
Domar	SC	SC	SC	SC	11,081	14,443	19,196
Dusadh		SC	SC	SC	93,021	110,105	141,177
Gharami	SC	SC	SC	SC	3	21	615
Gond		SC*	SC*	SC	38,356	45,811	204,638
Gual	SC	SC	SC	SC	314	44,250	7,491
Ghasiya	SC	SC	SC	SC	1,742	2,193	4,531
Habura	SC	SC	SC	SC	2,466	3,389	3,529
Hari	SC	SC	SC	SC	2,907	3,820	2,121
Hela	SC	SC	SC	SC	21,051	32,840	29,837
Kalabaz	SC	SC	SC	SC	1,965	5,618	5,347
Kanjar	SC	SC	SC	SC	31,335	44,176	50,752
Kapariya	SC	SC	SC	SC	3,147	7,163	6,872

(Continued on next page)

1	2	3	4	5	6	7	8
Karwal	SC	SC	SC	SC	36,282	46,767	12,154
Khairaha	SC	SC	SC	SC	901	1,120	809
Kharwar	SC	SC	SC	SC	30,366	35,965	56,477
Khatik	SC		SC	SC	305,326	390,566	496,944
Khorot	SC	SC	SC	SC	275	533	962
Kol	SC	SC	SC	SC	126,288	135,617	196,654
Kori	SC*		SC*	SC	710,241	909,537	1,381,588
Korwa	SC	SC	SC	SC	169,712	63,812	1,734
Lalbegi	SC	SC	SC	SC	11,316	14,908	1,374
Majhwar	SC	SC	SC	SC	69,133	43,447	12,978
Mazhabi			SC	SC	255	3,621	6,781
Musahar			SC	SC	88,119	104,725	126,018
Nat	SC	SC	SC	SC	51,155	78,777	93,530
Pankha	SC	SC	SC	SC	7,703	8,941	3,784
Parahiya	SC	SC	SC	SC	583	1,217	1,072
Pasi	SC	SC	SC]	SC]	2,221,136]	2,572,563]	3,425,929]
Tarmali							
Patari	SC	SC	SC	SC	917	1,412	1,257
Rawat	SC	SC	SC	SC	17,577	29,181	53,727
Saharya	SC	SC	SC	SC	11,786	12,483	21,902
Sanaurhiya	SC	SC	SC	SC	40	225	249
Sansiya	SC	SC	SC	SC	4,896	5,626	657
Shilpkar	SC	SC	SC	SC	465,870	513,719	514,877
Turaiha	SC	SC	SC	SC	2,071	4,420	11,969
Tharu	SC						

(Continued on next page)

1	2	3	4	5	6	7	8
Unclassified/ Unspecified					109,998	375,282	534,252
Total No. of caste	61(61) / 1*(1*)	64(65) / 1*(1*)	66(70) / 2*(2*)	66(70)	66	66	66
Source					a	b	c

Source: a — Census of India, 1961, Vol. I, India, Part V-A(i), pp. 274-80.

b — Census of India, 1971, Series 1, Paper 1 of 1975, Appendix to Table C-viii, Part A, pp. 86-89.

c — Census of India, 1981, Series 22, Part IX(i) —Table SC I, pp. 10-70.

WEST BENGAL (BENGAL)

	Scheduled Castes in					Population in		
	1936 Order	1950 Order	1956 Order	1976 Order		1961 Census	1971 Census	1981 Census
1	2	3	4	5		6	7	8
Caste					Total	6,890,314	8,816,028	12,000,768
Agaria	SC							
Bagdi	SC	SC	SC*	SC		1,096,885	1,291,127	1,831,565
Duley								
Bahelia	SC	SC	SC*	SC		1,263	2,189	4,602
Baiti	SC	SC	SC*	SC		8,269	7,410	10,034
Bantar			SC*	SC		435	637	2,086
Bauri	SC	SC	SC	SC		501,269	624,077	732,605
Bediya	SC	SC	SC	ST		4,380	7,471	
Beldar	SC	SC	SC*	SC		1,795	1,682	1,829
Berua	SC							
Bhatiya	SC							
Bhogta			SC*	SC		987	333	13,807
Bhuimali	SC	SC	SC*	SC		39,181	45,059	47,521
Bhuiya	SC	SC	SC*	SC		53,329	58,453	93,411
Bhumij	SC	SC	ST	ST				
Bind	SC	SC	SC*	SC		22,924	20,772	34,028
Binjhia	SC							
Chamar	SC	SC	SC	SC		396,591	507,759	711,024
Charmakar								
Mochi								
Muchi	SC	SC						

(Continued on next page)

1	2	3	4	5	6	7	8
Rabidas							
Ruidas							
Rishi							
Chaupal			SC*	SC	523	655	2,515
Dabgar			SC*	SC	72	93	460
Damai (Nepali)			SC*	SC	11,486	11,553	18,842
Dhenuar	SC						
Dhoba	SC	SC	SC	SC	154,791	191,063	251,737
Dhobi							
Doai	SC	SC	SC*	SC	14,191	4,770	8,054
Dom	SC	SC	SC	SC	151,818	174,367	231,595
Dhangad							
Dosadh	SC	SC	SC	SC	25,835	32,072	39,284
Dusadh							
Dhari							
Dharhi							
Garo	SC		ST	ST			
Ghasi	SC	SC	SC	SC	11,941	16,494	17,411
Gonrhi	SC	SC	SC*	SC	13,859	12,153	14,832
Hadi	SC						
Hajang	SC		ST	ST			
Halalkhor	SC		SC*	SC	326	479	1,348
Hari	SC	SC	SC*		125,880	161,357	
Hari			SC*	SC	14,080	17,470	267,465
Mehtar							
Bhangi							
Mehtor	SC	SC	SC*		30,8850	47,005	

(Continued on next page)

1	2	3	4	5	6	7	8
Ho	SC		ST	ST			
Jalia Kaibartta	SC	SC	SC*	SC	117,384	204,679	318,344
Jhalo Malo]	SC]	SC]	SC*]	SC]	68,757]	89,918]	154,557]
Malo]							
Kadar	SC	SC	SC*	SC	5,610	7,400	9,782
Kami (Nepali)			SC*	SC	26,148	31,590	42,493
Kandra	SC	SC	SC*	SC	25,430	42,294	65,183
Kanjar			SC*	SC	1,417	1,219	1,067
Kaora	SC	SC	SC*	SC	117,929	145,442	180,912
Karenga]	SC	SC	SC*]	SC]	11,332]	12,388]	21,129]
Koranga]							
Kastha	SC	SC					
Kaur	SC	SC	SC*	SC	2,394	5,841	20,860
Keot]			SC*]	SC]	23,174]	24,397]	45,282]
Keyot]							
Khaira	SC	SC	SC*	SC	67,913	63,513	77,605
Khatik	SC	SC	SC*	SC	2,716	1,415	4,862
Koch	SC	SC	SC*	SC	3,522	17,257	9,714
Konai	SC	SC	SC*	SC	43,101	59,223	71,423
Konwar	SC	SC	SC*	SC	3,895	1,469	2,841
Kora	SC	SC	ST	ST			
Kotal	SC	SC	SC*	SC	7,700	15,537	19,310
Kan	SC						
Kandh	SC						
Kapuria	SC						
Kurariar			SC*	SC	722	164	1,416
Lalbegi	SC	SC	SC	SC	845	1,384	1,179

(Continued on next page)

1	2	3	4	5	6	7	8
Lodha	SC	SC	ST	ST			
Lohar	SC	SC	SC*	SC	83,545	103,033	151,609
Mahar	SC	SC	SC	SC	6,760	12,221	17,706
Mahli	SC	SC	ST	ST			
Mal	SC	SC	SC*	SC	117,704	158,419	204,775
Mallah	SC	SC	SC*	SC	12,366	21,596	38,101
Mech	SC	ST	ST	ST			
Munda	SC	ST	ST	ST			
Musahar	SC	SC	SC	SC	13,058	12,426	17,628
Malpahariya	SC	SC	ST	ST			
Nagesia	SC	SC	ST	ST			
Namasudra	SC	SC	SC*	SC	729,057	980,524	1,692,233
Nat	SC		SC*	SC	899	74	3,376
Nuniya	SC	SC	SC*	SC	17,561	21,531	41,531
Oroan	SC	ST	ST	ST			
Paliya	SC	SC	SC*	SC	73,997	100,571	116,819
Pan	SC	SC	SC]	SC]	3,370]	3,690]	9,328]
Sawasi							
Pasi	SC	SC	SC	SC	13,881	20,478	21,367
Patni	SC	SC	SC*	SC	6,288	12,781	22,466
Pod	SC	SC	SC*]	SC]	875,525]	975,352]	1536,197]
Pundra							
Rabha	SC	SC	ST	ST			
Rajbanshi	SC	SC	SC*	SC	1,201,717	1,353,919	2,258,760
Rajwar	SC	SC	SC	SC	41,133	53,168	85,374
Santal	SC	ST	ST	ST			
Sarki (Nepali)			SC*	SC	5,232	5,337	11,292

(Continued on next page)

1	2	3	4	5	6	7	8
Sunri	SC	SC	SC*	SC	106,870	166,418	252,331
Tiyar	SC	SC	SC*	SC	39,633	79,786	82,108
Turi	SC	SC	SC	SC	19,048	23,190	28,446
Unclassified/ Unspecified					309,721	749,196	25,710
Total No. of caste	76(77)	58(59)	62(81) / 50*(57*)	59(79)	62	62@	59
Source					a	b	c

Source: a — Census of India, 1961, Vol. I, India, Part V-A(1), pp. 286-92.

b — Census of India, 1971, Series 1, Paper 1 of 1975, Appendix to Table C-viii A, pp. 89-92.

c — Census of India, 1981, Series 23, Part IX(i), Table SC I, pp. 8-62.

@ Bhumij notified as Scheduled Caste in the territories transferred from the Purnea district of Bihar has not been included in this figure, though the population (678) has been included in the total Scheduled Caste population.

CHANDIGARH

	Scheduled Castes in 1966 Act	Population in 1971 Census	Population in 1981 Census
1	2	3	4
Caste			
Total		29,073	63,621
Ad Dharmi	SC	723	1,341
Bangali	SC	71	49
Barar ⎤	SC ⎤	158 ⎤	200 ⎤
Burar ⎥	⎥	⎥	⎥
Berar ⎦	⎦	⎦	⎦
Batwal	SC		41
Bauria ⎤	SC ⎤	295 ⎤	791 ⎤
Bawaria ⎦	⎦	⎦	⎦
Bazigar	SC	836	1,389
Balmiki ⎤	SC ⎤	13,355 ⎤	27,547 ⎤
Chura ⎥	⎥	⎥	⎥
Bhangi ⎦	⎦	⎦	⎦
Bhanjra	SC	32	207
Chamar ⎤	SC ⎤	7,624 ⎤	20,128 ⎤
Jatia Chamar ⎥	⎥	⎥	⎥
Rehgar ⎥	⎥	⎥	⎥
Raigar ⎥	⎥	⎥	⎥
Ramdasi ⎥	⎥	⎥	⎥
Ravidasi ⎦	⎦	⎦	⎦
Chanal	SC		90
Dagi	SC		4

(Continued on next page)

1	2	3	4
Darain	SC*		23
Dhanak	SC	207	609
Dhogri	SC]	]	20]
Dhangri			
Siggi		34]	112]
Dumna	SC]		
Mahasha			
Doom			37
Gagra	SC	1]	22]
Gandhila	SC]		
Gandil Gondola		546]	2,109]
Kabirpanthi	SC]		
Julaha		643	1,170
Khatik	SC	539]	1,887]
Kori	SC]		
Koli		40]	38]
Marija	SC]		
Marecha		221	856
Mazhabi	SC	17	338
Megh	SC		21
Nat	SC		35
Od	SC	321	928
Pasi	SC	1	18
Perna	SC		12
Pherera	SC		89
Sanhai	SC		19
Sanhal	SC		

(Continued on next page)

1	2	3	4
Sansi	SC ⎤	794 ⎤	1,344 ⎤
Bhedkut	⎥	⎥	⎥
Manesh	⎦	⎦	⎦
Sansoi	SC		104
Sapela	SC		138
Sarera	SC	94	215
Sikligar	SC	119	312
Sirkiband	SC		178
Unspecified/ Unclassified		2,402	1,115
Total No. of caste	36(56)	22	36
Source		a	b

Soruce: a — Census of India, 1971, Series 1, Paper 1 of 1975, pp. 92-93.

b — Census of India, 1981, Series 26, Part IX, pp. 6-18.

DADRA AND NAGAR HAVELI

	Scheduled Castes in		Population in		
	1962 Order		1961 Census	1971 Census	1981 Census
1	2		3	4	5
Caste		Total	985	1,332	2,041
Bhangi	SC		9	32	44
Chamar	SC		384	655	903
Mahar	SC		3	-	83
Mahyavanshi	SC]		589]	645]	943]
Dhed					
Unclassified					68
Total No. of caste	4(5)		4	3	4
Source			a	b	c

Source: a — Census of India, 1961, Vol. I, Part V-A(1), p. 310.

b — Census of India, Series 1, Paper 1 of 1975, p. 94.

c — Census of India, 1981, Series 27, Part IX, p. 18.

DELHI

	Scheduled Castes in			Population in		
	1951 Order	1956 Order		1961 Census	1971 Census	1981 Census
1	2	3		4	5	6
Caste			Total	341,555	635,698	1,121,643
Adi Dharmi	SC	SC		1,242	2,072	4,882
Agria	SC	SC		682	1,145	1,139
Aheria	SC	SC		2,818	2,119	4,080
Balai	SC	SC		20,680	42,885	69,859
Banjara	SC	SC		2,518	4,344	8,357
Bawaria	SC	SC		2,175	3,935	3,953
Bazigar	SC	SC		408	269	464
Bhangi	SC	SC		21,673	24,720	21,752
Bhil	SC	SC		155	404	1,231
Chamar	SC	SC		125,997	215,747	411,316
Chanwar Chamar	SC					
Jatya Chamar	SC					
Jatav Chamar						
Mochi	SC					
Ramdasia	SC					
Ravidasi	SC					
Raidasi						
Rehgarh	SC					
Raigar						
Chohra (Sweeper)	SC	SC		3,088	2,551	3,272
Chuhra (Balmiki)	SC	SC		52,743	107,680	222,638

(Continued on next page)

1	2	3	4	5	6
Dhanak	SC	SC	8,540	15,855	36,600
Dhanuk					
Dhobi	SC	SC	14,144	26,839	59,675
Dom	SC	SC	108	553	1,367
Gharrami	SC	SC	277	467	280
Julaha (weaver)	SC	SC	17,242	26,059	43,024
Kabirpanthi	SC	SC	2,099	2,869	4,334
Kachhandha	SC	SC	70	182	429
Kanjar	SC	SC	958	2,115	4,179
Giarah					
Khatik	SC	SC	14,392	34,412	69,409
Koli	SC	SC	19,199	42,449	92,504
Lalbegi	SC	SC	28	36	134
Madari	SC	SC	12	40	257
Mallah	SC	SC	774	3,447	17,344
Mazhabi	SC	SC	107	338	858
Meghwal	SC	SC	387	668	1,481
Naribut		SC	390	783	872
Nat (Rana)	SC	SC	117	694	1,878
Pasi	SC	SC	1,985	4,746	12,455
Perna	SC	SC		117	371
Sansi	SC	SC	1,540	3,496	5,915
Bhedkut					
Sapera	SC	SC	340	454	904
Sikligar	SC	SC	1,804	4,536	8,832
Singiwala	SC	SC		246	739
Kalbelia					

(Continued on next page)

1	2	3	4	5	6
Sirkiband	SC	SC	233	311	566
Unclassified/ Unspecified			22,630	56,115	4,293
Total No. of caste	41(46)	36(49)	34	36	36
Source			a	b	c

Source: a — Census of India, 1961, Vol. I, India, Part V-A(1), SCT-II, Part A, pp. 292-98.

b — Census of India, 1971, Series 1, Paper 1 of 1975, Appendix to Table C-viii, Part A, pp. 94-95.

c — Census of India, 1981, Series 28, Part IX, Table SC I, pp. 8-20.

GOA, DAMAN AND DIU

	Scheduled Castes in 1968 Order		Population in 1971 Census	Population in 1981 Census
1	2		3	4
Caste		Total	16,514	23,432
Bhangi	SC]		890]	1,320]
Hadi				
Chambhar	SC		4,924	6,460
Mahar	SC		7,856	12,149
Mahyavanshi	SC]		1,561]	1,876]
Vankar				
Mang	SC		326	702
Unspecified/ Unclassified			957	925
Total No. of caste	5(7)		5	5
Source			a	b

Source: a — Census of India, 1971, Series 1, Paper 1 of 1975, pp. 95-96.

b — Census of India, 1981, Series 29, Part IX, p. 10.

PONDICHERRY

	Scheduled Castes in 1964 Order	Population in 1961 Census	Population in 1971 Census	Population in 1981 Census
1	2	3	4	5
Caste	Total	56,846	72,921	96,636
Adi Andhra	SC	1,412	1,543	2,148
Adi Dravida	SC	24,411	21,944	59,410
Chakkiliyan	SC	1,098	1,419	1,558
Domban		47		
Jambuvulu	SC	14	8	237
Kudumban		8		
Kuravan	SC]	386]	476]	556
Sidhanar				
Madiga	SC	181	266	39
Mala	SC]	7	1]	11]
Mala Masti		3		
Malayan		14		
Nayadi		3		
Paky	SC	22]	40	42
Moti				
Pallan	SC	812	1,359	1,766
Paraiyan		26,417]		
Parayan	SC]		39,919]	27,151]
Sambavar				
Paravan		8		
Pulayan		11]		

(Continued on next page)

1	2	3	4	5
Cheramar		⌋		
Samban	SC	320	521	16
Thoti	SC	38	420	87
Valluvan	SC	1,384	1,713	2,783
Vannan		8		
Vetan	SC	69	419	307
Vettiyan	SC	173	201	302
Unclassified / Unspecified		-	2,672	223
Total No. of caste	15(17)	23 @	15	15
Source		a	b	c

@ No order was issued by the President specifying the Scheduled Castes in Pondicherry when the 1961 Census was undertaken. The castes specified in the Presidents Order for any of the States of Andhra Pradesh, Kerala and Madras adjoining of encircling one of the four constituents of Pondicherry were adopted for census purposes in 1961.

Source: a — Census of India, 1961, Vol. I, Part V-A(i), SCT II Part A, pp. 310-16.

b — Census of India, 1971, Series 1, Paper 1 of 1975, p. 96.

c — Census of India, 1981, Series 32, Part IX, pp. 8-12.

APPENDIX I

(Orders relating to the Scheduled Castes and Scheduled Tribes)

Orders relating to the Scheduled Castes

The Government of India (Scheduled Castes) Order, 1936, pp. 1287-1296.

The Constitution (Scheduled Castes) Order, 1950, pp. 1297-1311.

The Constitution (Scheduled Castes) (Part C States) Order, 1951, pp. 1312-1317.

The Andhra State Act, 1953, pp. 1318-1319.
(relating to Andhra Pradesh, Madras and Mysore)

The Himachal Pradesh and Bilaspur (New State) Act, 1954, p. 1320.
(in relation to Himachal Pradesh)

The Scheduled Castes and Scheduled Tribes Lists (Modification) Order, 1956, pp. 1321-1348.

The Constitution (Jammu and Kashmir) Scheduled Castes Order, 1956, p. 1349.

The Bombay Reorganisation Act, 1960, pp. 1349-1353.
(relating to Maharashtra and Gujarat)

The Constitution (Dadra and Nagar Haveli) Scheduled Castes Order, 1962, p. 1353.

The Constitution (Pondicherry) Scheduled Castes Order, 1964, pp. 1353-1354.

The Punjab Reorganisation Act, 1966, pp. 1355-1357.
(relating to the States of Haryana and Himachal Pradesh and the Union Territory of Chandigarh)

The Constitution (Goa, Daman and Diu) Scheduled Castes Order, 1968, p. 1358.

The North Eastern Areas (Reorganisation) Act, 1971, pp. 1358-1365.
(in relation to the States of Manipur, Meghalaya and Tripura and the Union Territories of Arunachal Pradesh and Mizoram)

The Scheduled Castes and Scheduled Tribes Orders (Amendment) Act, 1976, pp. 1361-1386.

The Constitution (Sikkim) Scheduled Castes Order, 1978, p. 1386.

The State of Arunachal Pradesh Act, 1986, p. 1386.

The State of Mizoram Act, 1986, pp. 1386-1387.

The Goa, Daman and Diu Reorganisation Act, 1987, p. 1387.
(relating to the State of Goa and the Union Territory of Daman and Diu)

Orders relating to the Scheduled Tribes

The Constitution (Scheduled Tribes) Order, 1950, pp. 1388-1396.

The Constitution (Scheduled Tribes) (Part C States) Order, 1951, pp. 1397-1399.

The Andhra State Act, 1953, pp. 1400-1402.
(relating to Andhra Pradesh, Madras and Mysore)

The Scheduled Castes and Scheduled Tribes Lists (Modification) Order, 1956, pp. 1403-1426.

The Constitution (Andaman and Nicobar Islands) Scheduled Tribes Order, 1959, p. 1427.

The Bombay Reorganisation Act, 1960, pp. 1427-1433.
(relating to Maharashtra and Gujarat)

The Constitution (Union Territories) Scheduled Tribes Order, 1951, p. 1434.
(in relation to Lakshadweep)

The Constitution (Dadra and Nagar Haveli) Scheduled Tribes Order, 1962, p. 1434.

The Punjab Reorganisation Act, 1966, pp. 1434-1435.
(relating to Himachal Pradesh)

The Constitution (Scheduled Tribes) (Uttar Pradesh) Order, 1967, p. 1435.

The Constitution (Goa, Daman and Diu) Scheduled Tribes Order, 1968, p. 1435.

The Constitution (Nagaland) Scheduled Tribes Order, 1970, p. 1435.

The North Eastern Areas (Reorganisation) Act, 1971, pp. 1436-1440.
(relating to the States of Manipur, Meghalaya and Tripura and the Union Territories of Arunachal Pradesh and Mizoram)

The Scheduled Castes and Scheduled Tribes Orders (Amendment) Act, 1976, pp. 1441-1459.

The Constitution (Sikkim) Scheduled Tribes Order, 1978, p. 1460.

The State of Mizoram Act, 1986, pp. 1460-1461.

The State of Arunachal Pradesh Act, 1986, p. 1461.

The Goa, Daman and Diu Reorganisation Act, 1987, p. 1462.
(relating to the State of Goa and the Union Territory of Daman and Diu)

The Constitution (Scheduled Tribes) Order (Amendment) Act, 1987, p. 1462.
(in relation to the State of Meghalaya)

The Constitution (Jammu and Kashmir) Scheduled Tribes Order, 1989, p. 1462.

The Government of India (Scheduled Castes) Order, 1936.

THE SCHEDULE

PART I — MADRAS

(1) Scheduled Castes throughout the Province :—

Adi-Andhra,	Gosangi,	Paidi,
Adi-Dravida,	Haddi,	Painda,
Adi-Karnataka,	Hasla,	Paky,
Ajila,	Holeya,	Pallan,
Arunthuthiyar,	Jaggali,	Pambada,
Baira,	Jambuvulu,	Pamidi,
Bakuda,	Kalladi,	Panchama,
Bandi,	Kanakkan,	Paniyan,
Bariki,	Kodalo,	Panniandi,
Battada,	Koosa,	Paraiyan,
Bavuri,	Koraga,	Parvan,
Bellara,	Kudumban,	Pulayan,
Bygari,	Kuravan	Puthirai Vanan
Chachati,	Madari	Raneyar
Chakkiliyan,	Madiga,	Relli,
Chalvadi,	Maila,	Samagara,
Chamar,	Mala,	Samban,
Chandala,	Mala Dasu,	Sapari,
Cheruman,	Matangi,	Semman,
Dandasi,	Moger,	Thoti,
Devendrakulathan,	Muchi,	Tiruvalluvar,
Ghasi,	Mundala,	Valluvan,
Godaga,	Nalakeyava,	Valmiki,
Godari,	Nayadi,	Vettuvan.
Godda,	Paga dai.	

(2) Scheduled Castes throughout the Provinces except in any special constituency constituted under the Government of India Act, 1935, for the election of a

representative of backward areas and backward tribes to the Legislative Assembly of the Province :—

Arnadan,	Kattunayakan,	Kuruwan,
Dombo,	Kudiya,	Malasar,
Kadan,	Kudubi,	Mavilan,
Karimpalan,	Kurichchan,	Pano.

PART II—BOMBAY

Scheduled Castes :—

(1) Throughout the Province :—

Asodi,	Dhegu-Megu,	Mahar,
Bakad,	Dhor,	Mang Garudi,
Bhambi,	Garode,	Maghval, or Menghwar,
Bhangi,	Halleer,	Mini Madig,
Chakrawadya-,	Halsar, or	Mukri,
dasar,	Haslar,	Nadia,
Chalvadi,	Hulsavar,	Shenva, or Shindhava,
Chambhar, or	Holaya,	Shinghdavor Shingadya,
Mochi gar, or	Khalpa,	Sochi,
Samagar,	Kolcha, or	Timali,
Chena-Dasaru,	Kolgha,	Turi,
Chuhar, or	Koli-Dhor,	Vankar,
Chuhra,	Lingader,	Vitholia,
Dakaleru	Madig, or	
Dhed,	Mang,	

(2) Throughout the Province except in the Ahmedabad, Kaira, Broach and Panch Mahals and Surat Districts — Mochi.

(3) In the Kanara district — Kotegar.

PART III—BENGAL

Scheduled Castes throughout the Province :—

Agaria,	Bagdi,	Bhumij,
Bind,	Bahelia,	Binjhia,

Baiti,	Bauri,	Bediya,
Beldar,	Berua,	Bhatiya,
Bhuimali,	Bhuiya,	Dhoba,
Chamar,	Dhenuar,	Dosadh,
Doai,	Dom,	Ghasi,
Gonrhi,	Garo,	Halalkhor,
Hadi,	Hajang,	Hari,
Ho,	Jalia Kaibartta,	Jhalo Malo, or Malo
Kadar,	Kan,	Kaora,
Kandh,	Kandra,	Kastha,
Kapuria,	Karenga,	Khatik,
Kaur,	Khaira,	Konwar,
Koch,	Konai,	Kora,
Kotal,	Lodha,	Lohar,
Lalbegi,	Malpahariya,	Munda,
Mahili,	Mal,	Mahar,
Mallah,	Mech,	Methor,
Muchi,	Musahar,	Nagesia,
Namasudra,	Nat,	Nuniya,
Oraon,	Paliya,	Pan,
Pasi,	Patni,	Pod,
Rabha,	Rajbanshi,	Rajwar,
Santal,	Sunri,	Tiyar,
Turi.		

PART IV — UNITED PROVINCES

Scheduled Castes :—

(1) Throughout the Province :—

Agariya,	Chero,	Khatik,
Aheriya,	Dabgar,	Kol,
Badi,	Dhangar,	Korwa,
Badhik,	Dhanuk, (Bhangi)	Lalbegi,

Baheliya,
Bajaniya,
Bajgi,
Balahar,
Balmiki,
Banmanus,
Bansphor,
Barwar,
Basor,
Bawariya,
Beldar,
Bengali,
Berya,
Bhantu,
Bhuiya,
Bhuiyar,
Boriya,
Chamar,
Dharkar,
Dhobi,
Dom,
Domar,
Gharami,
Ghasiya,
Gual,
Habura,
Hari,
Hela,
Khairaha,
Kalabaz,
Kanjar,
Kapariya,
Karwal,
Kharot,
Kharwar (except Benbansi),
Majhawar,
Nat,
Pankha,
Parahiya,
Pasi,
Patari,
Rawat,
Saharya,
Sanaurhiya,
Sansiya,
Shilpkar,
Tharu,
Turaiha,

(2) Throughout the Province except in the Agra, Meerut and Rohilkand divisions — Kori.

PART V — PUNJAB

Scheduled Castes throughout the Province :—

Ad Dharmis,
Bawaria,
Chamar,
Chuhra, or
Balmiki,
Dagi and Koli,
Dhumna,
Od,
Marija, or
Marecha,
Bengali,
Barar,
Bazigar,
Bhanjra,
Chanal,
Dhanak,
Khatik,
Kori,
Nat,
Pasi,
Perna,
Sepela,
Sirkiband,
Megha,

Sansi,	Gagra,	Ramdasis.,
Sarera,	Gandhila,	

PART VI—BIHAR

Scheduled Castes :—

(1) Throughout the Province :—

Chamar,	Halalkhor,	Mochi,
Chaupal,	Hari,	Musahar,
Dhobi,	Kanjar,	Nat,
Dusadh,	Kurariar,	Pasi,
Dom,	Lalbegi.	

(2) In the Patna and Tirhut divisions and the Bhagalpur, Monghyr, Palamau and Purnea districts :—

Bauri,	Bhumij,	Rajwar,
Bhogta,	Ghasi,	Turi,
Bhauya,	Pan.	

(3) In the Dhanbad sub-division of the Manbhum district and the Central Manbhum general rural constituency, and the Purulia and Raghunathpur municipalities :—

Bauri,	Ghasi,	Rajwar,
Bhogta,	Pan,	Turi,
Bhuiya.		

PART VII — CENTRAL PROVINCES AND BERAR

Scheduled Castes	*Localities*
Basor, or Burud, ..	Throughout the Province
Chamar, ..	
Dom, ..	
Ganda, ..	
Mang, ..	

Scheduled Castes	*Localities*
Mehtar or Bhangi, ..	Throughout the Province
Mochi, ..	
Satnami, ..	
Audhelia, ..	In the Bilaspur district
Bahna, ..	In the Amraoti district.
Balahi, or Balai ..	In the Berar division and the Balaghat, Bhandara Betul, Chanda, Chhindwara, Hoshangabad, Jabbulpore, Mandla, Nagpur, Nimar, Saugor and Wardha districts.
Bedar, ..	In the Akola, Amraoti and Buldhana districts.
Chadar, ..	In the Bhandara and Saugor districts.
Chauhan, ..	In the Durg district.
Dahayat, ..	In the Damoh sub-division of the Saugor district.
Dewar ..	In the Bilaspur, Durg and Raipur districts.
Dhanuk ..	In the Saugor district, except in the Damoh sub-division thereof.
Dhimar ..	In the Bhandara district.
Dhobi ..	In the Bhandara, Bilaspur, Raipur and Saugor districts and the Hoshangabad and Seoni-Malwa tahsils of the Hoshangabad district.
Dohar ..	In the Berar division and the Balaghat, Bhandara. Chanda, Nagpur and Wardha districts.
Ghasia ..	In the Berar division and in the Balaghat, Bhandara, Bilaspur, Chanda, Durg, Nagpur, Raipur and Wardha districts.

Scheduled Castes		*Localities*
Holiya,	..	In the Balaghat and Bhandara districts.
Jangam,	..	In the Bhandara district.
Kaikari,	..	In the Berar division, and in Bhandara, Chanda, Nagpur and Wardha districts.
Katia,	..	In the Berar divison, in the Balaghat, Betul, Bhandara, Bilaspur, Chanda, Durg, Nagpur, Nimar, Raipur and Wardha districts, in the Hoshangabad and Seoni-Malwa tahsils of the Hoshangabad district, in the Chhind-wara district, except in the Sconi sub-division thereof, and in the Saugor district, except in the Damoh sub-division thereof.
Khangar,	..	In the Bhadara, Buldhana and Saugor districts and the Hoshangabad and Seoni Malwa tahsils of the Hoshangabad district.
Khatik,	..	In the Berar division, in the Balaghat, Bhandara, Chanda, Nagpur and Wardha districts, in the Hoshangabad tahsil of the Hoshangabad district, in the Chhindwara district, except in the Seoni sub-division thereof, and in the Saugor district, except in the Damoh sub-division thereof.
Koli,	..	In the Bhandara and Chanda districts.
Kori,	..	In the Amaraoti, Balaghat, Betul, Bhandara, Buldhana, Chhindwara, Jubbulpore, Mandla, Nimar, Raipur and Saugor districts, and in the Hoshangabad district, except in the Harda and Sohagpur tahsils thereof.

Scheduled Castes		*Localities*
Kumhar,	..	In the Bhandara and Saugor districts and the Hoshangabad and Seoni-Malwa tahsils of the Hoshangabad district.
Madgi,	..	In the Berar division and in the Balaghat, Bhandara, Chanda, Nagpur and Wardha districts.
Mala,	..	In the Balaghat, Betul, Chhindwara, Hoshangabad, Jubbulpore, Mandla, Nimar and Saugor districts.
Mehra or Mahar,	..	Throughout the Province, except in the Harda and Sohagpur tahsils of the Hoshangabad district.
Nagarchi,	..	In the Balaghat, Bhandara, Chhindwara, Mandla, Nagpur and Raipur districts.
Ojha,	..	In the Balaghat, Bhandara and Mandla districts and the Hoshangabad tahsil of the Hoshangabad district.
Panka,	..	In the Berar division, in the Balaghat, Bhandara, Bilaspur, Chanda, Durg, Nagpur, Raipur, Saugor and Wardha districts and in the Chhindwara district, except in the Seoni subdivision thereof.
Pardhi,	..	In the Narsinghpura sub-division of the Hoshangabad district.
Pradhan,	..	In the Berar division, in the Bhandara, Chanda, Nagpur, Nimar, Raipur and Wardha districts and in the Chhindwara district, except in the Seoni sub-division thereof.

Scheduled Castes		*Localities*
Rajjhar,	..	In the Sohagpur tahsil of the Hoshangabad district.

PART VIII — ASSAM

Scheduled Castes :—

(1) In the Assam Valley :—

Kaibartta,	Hira,	Mehtar or Bhangi,
Bania, or	Lalbegi,	Banshpor,
Brittial-Bania,	Namasudra,	

(2) In the Surma Valley :—

Mali, or Bhuimali,	Sutradhar,	Kaibartta, or Jaliya,
Dhupi, or Dhobi,	Muchi,	Lalbegi
Dugla, or Dholi,	Patni,	Mehtar, or Bhangi
Jhalo and Malo,	Namasudra,	Bansphor,
Mahara.		

PART IX — ORISSA

Scheduled Castes :—

(1) Throughout the Province :—

Adi-Andhra,	Audhelia,	Bariki,
Bansor, or	Bavuri,	Chamar,
Burud,	Chandala,	Dandasi,
Chachati,	Dhoba or	Ghusuria,
Dewar,	Dhobi,	Godra,
Godagali,	Godari,	Haddi, or Hari.
Gokha,	Ganda,	Kandra,
Irika,	Jaggali,	Kodalo,
Katia,	Kela,	Madiga,
Mala,	Madari,	Mangan,
Mahuria,	Mang	Mochi
Mehra, or	Mehtar,	or Muchi,

Mahar, or Bhangi, Paidi,
Panchama, Panka, Relli,
Painda, Pamidi, Siyal,
Sapari, Satnami,
Valmiki,

(2) Throughout the Province except in the Khondmals district, the district of Sambalpur and the areas transferred to Orissa under the provisions of the Government of India (Constitution of Orissa) Order, 1936, from the Vizagapatam and Ganjam Agencies in the Presidency of Madras :—

Pan, or Pano,

(3) Throughout the Province except in the Khondmals district and the areas so transferred to Orissa from the said Agencies :—

Dom, or Dambo,

(4) Throughout the Province except in the district of Sambalpur :

Bauro, Bhumij, Turi,
Bhuiya, Ghasi, or Ghasia,

(5) In the Nawapara sub-division of the district of Sambalpur :—

Kori, Nagarchi, Pradhan,

(i) THE CONSTITUTION (SCHEDULED CASTES) ORDER, 1950

C.O. 19 — In the exercise of the powers conferred by clause (1) of Article 341 of the Constitution of India, the President, after consultation with the Governors and Rajpramukhs of the States concerned, is pleased to make the following Order, namely :—

(1) This Order may be called the Constitution (Scheduled Castes) Order, 1950.

(2) Subject to the provisions of this Order, the castes, races or tribes, or parts of, or groups within, castes or tribes, specified in Parts I to XVI of the Schedule to this Order shall, in relation to the States to which those parts respectively relate, be deemed to be Scheduled Castes so far as regards members thereof resident in the localities specified in relation to them in those parts of that Schedule.

(3) Notwithstanding anything contained in paragraph 2, no person who professes a religion different from Hinduism shall be deemed to be a member of a Scheduled Caste :

Provided that every member of the Ramdasi, Kabirpanthi, Mazhabi or Sikligar caste resident in Punjab or the Patiala and East Punjab States Union shall, in relation to that State, be deemed to be a member of the Scheduled Castes whether he professes the Hindu or the Sikh religion.

(4) Any reference in the Schedule to this Order to a district or other territorial division of a State shall be construed as a reference to that district or other territorial division as existing on the 26th January, 1950.

THE SCHEDULE

PART I — ASSAM

Throughout the State :—

1. Bansphor
2. Bhuinmali or Mali
3. Brittial-Bania or Bania
4. Dhupi or Dhobi
5. Dugla or Dholi
6. Hira
7. Jhalo or Malo
8. Kaibartta or Jaliya
9. Lalbegi
10. Mahara
11. Mehtar or Bhangi
12. Muchi
13. Namasudra
14. Patni
15. Sutradhar

PART II — BIHAR

1. Throughout the State :—

1. Bauri
2. Bantar
3. Bhogta
4. Chamar
5. Chaupal
6. Dhobi
7. Dom
8. Dusadh, including Dhari or Dharhi
9. Ghasi
10. Halakhor
11. Hari, including Mehtar
12. Kanjar
13. Kurariar
14. Lalbegi
15. Mochi
16. Musahar
17. Nat
18. Pan
19. Pasi
20. Rajwar
21. Turi

2. In Patna and Tirhut divisions, and the districts of Monghyr, Bhagalpur, Purnea and Palamau :—

Bhumij

3. In Patna, Shahabad, Gaya and Palamau districts:—

Bhuiya

4. In Shahabad, district : —

Dabgar

PART III — BOMBAY

1. Throughout the State : —

1. Ager
2. Asodi
3. Bakad
4. Bhambi
5. Bhangi
6. Chakrawadya-Dasar
7. Chalvadi
8. Chambhar, or Mochigar, or Samagar
9. Chena-Dasaru
10. Chuhar or Chuhra
11. Dakaleru
12. Dhegu-Megu
13. Dhor
14. Garoda
15. Halleer
16. Halsar, or Haslar, or Hulsavar
17. Holaya, or Garode
18. Kolcha, or Kolgha
19. Lingader
20. Machigar
21. Madig, or Mang
22. Mahar
23. Mahyavanshi
24. Mangarudi
25. Meghval, or Menghwar
26. Mini Madig
27. Mukri
28. Nadia
29. Rohit
30. Shenva, or Shindhaya
31. Shingdav, or Shingadya
32. Sochi
33. Timali
34. Turi
35. Vankar
36. Vitholia

2. Throughout the State except in Gujrat division : —

Mochi

3. In North Kanara district : —

Kotegar

PART IV — MADHYA PRADESH

Scheduled Castes	Localities
1. Basor or Burud	Throughout the State.
2. Bahna or Bahana	
3. Balahi or Balai	
4. Chamar	
5. Dom	
6. Mang	
7. Mehtar or Bhangi	
8. Mochi	
9. Satnami	
10. Audhelia	.. In Bilaspur district.
11. Bedar	.. In Akola, Amravati and Buldana districts.
12. Chadar	.. In Bhandara and Sagar districts.
13. Dahait or Dahayat	.. In Damoh sub-division of Sagar district.
14. Dewar	.. In Bilaspur, Durg, Raipur, Bastar, Sarguja and Raigarh districts.
15. Dhanuk	.. In Sagar district *except*, in Damoh sub-division thereof.
16. Dohor	.. In Akola, Amravati, Buldana, Yeotmal, Balaghat, Bhandara, Chanda, Nagpur and Wardha districts.
17. Ghasi or Ghasia	.. In Akola, Amravati, Buldana, Yeotmal, Balaghat, Bhandara, Bilaspur, Chanda, Durg, Wardha, Nagpur, Raipur, Sarguja, Bastar and Raigarh districts.

Scheduled Castes		*Localities*
18. Holiya	..	In Balaghat and Bhandara districts.
19. Kaikadi	..	In Akola, Amravati, Buldana, Yeotmal, Bhandara, Chanda, Nagpur and Wardha districts.
20. Katia	..	In Akola, Amravati, Buldana, Yeotmal, Balaghat, Betul, Bhandara, Bilaspur, Chanda, Durg, Nagpur, Nimar, Raipur, Wardha, Bastar, Sarguja and Raigarh districts, in Hoshangabad and Seoni-Malwa tahsils of Hoshangabad district, in Chhindwara district *except* in Seoni sub-division thereof; and in Sagar district *except* in Damoh sub-division thereof.
21. Khangar	..	In Bhandara, Buldana and Sagar districts; and in Hoshangabad and Seoni-Malwa tahsils of Hoshangabad district.
22. Kori	..	In Amravati, Balaghat, Betul, Bhandara, Buldana, Chhindwara, Jabalpur, Mandla, Nimar, Raipur, Sagar, Durg, Bastar, Sarguja and Raigarh districts; and in Hoshangabad district *except* in Harda and Sohagpur tahsils thereof.
23. Madgi	..	In Akola, Amravati, Buldana, Yeotmal, Balaghat, Bhandara, Chanda, Nagpur and Wardha districts.

Scheduled Castes		*Localities*
24. Mahar or Mehra	..	Throughout the State except in Harda and Sohagpur tahsils of Hoshangabad district.
25. Rujjhar	..	In Sohagpur tahsil of Hoshangabad district.

PART V — MADRAS

Throughout the State : —

1. Adi Andhra
2. Adi Dravida
3. Adi Karnataka
4. Ajila
5. Arunthathiyar
6. Baira
7. Bakuda
8. Bandi
9. Bariki
10. Bavuri
11. Bellara
12. Byagari
13. Chachati
14. Chakkiliyan
15. Chalavadi
16. Chamar
17. Chandala
18. Cheruman
19. Dandasi
20. Devendrakulathan
21. Dom or Dombara, Paidi, Pano
22. Ghasi or Haddi, Relli Sachandi
23. Godagali
24. Godari
25. Godda
26. Gosangi
27. Hasla
28. Holeya
29. Jaggali
30. Jambuvulu
31. Kadan
32. Kalladi
33. Kanakkan
34. Karimpalan
35. Kodalo
36. Koosa
37. Koraga
38. Kudubi
39. Kudumban
40. Kuravan
41. Kurichchan
42. Madari
43. Madiga

44. Maila
45. Mala (including Agency Malas)
46. Mala Dasu
47. Malasar
48. Matangi
49. Mavilan
50. Moger
51. Muchi
52. Mundala
53. Nalakeyava
54. Nayadi
55. Pagadai
56. Painda
57. Paky
58. Pallan
59. Pambada
60. Pamidi
61. Panan
62. Panchama
63. Panniandi
64. Paraiyan
65. Paravan
66. Pulayan
67. Puthirai Vannan
68. Raneyar
69. Samagara
70. Samban
71. Sapari
72. Semman
73. Thoti
74. Tiruvalluvar
75. Valluvan
76. Valmiki
77. Vettuvan

PART VI — ORISSA

Throughout the State : —

1. Adi-Andhra
2. Amant or Amat
3. Audhelia
4. Badaik
5. Bagheti
6. Bajikar
7. Bari
8. Bariki
9. Basor or Burud
10. Bauri
11. Bauti
12. Bavuri
13. Bedia or Bejia
14. Beldar
15. Bhata
16. Bhumij
17. Chachati
18. Chamar
19. Chandala (Chandal)
20. Cherua or Chhelia
21. Dandasi
22. Desuabhumij

23. Dewar
24. Dhanwar
25. Dharua
26. Dhoba or Dhobi
27. Dom or Dombo
28. Dosadha
29. Ganda
30. Ghantarghada or Ghantra
31. Ghasi or Ghasia
32. Ghogia
33. Ghusuria
34. Godagali
35. Godari
36. Godra
37. Gokha
38. Gunju or Ganju
39. Haddi or Hadi or Hari
40. Irika
41. Jaggali
42. Kandra or Kandara
43. Karua
44. Katia
45. Kela
46. Khadala
47. Kodalo
48. Kori
49. Kumbhar
50. Kurunga
51. Laban
52. Laheri
53. Madari
54. Madiga
55. Mahuria
56. Mala or Jhala
57. Mangan
58. Mang
59. Mehra or Mahar
60. Mehtar or Bhangi
61. Mewar
62. Mochi or Muchi
63. Mundapotta
64. Nagarchi
65. Paidi
66. Painda
67. Pamidi
68. Pan or Pano
69. Panchama
70. Panika
71. Panka
72. Pantanti
73. Pap
74. Pasi
75. Patial or Patikar or Patratanti or Patua
76. Pradhan
77. Rajna
78. Relli
79. Sabakhia
80. Samasi
81. Sanei
82. Sapari
83. Satnami

84. Sidhria
85. Sinduria
86. Siyal
87. Sukuli
88. Tamadia
89. Tamudia
90. Tiar or Tior
91. Turi
92. Valamiki or Valmiki

PART VII — PUNJAB

Throughout the State : —

1. Ad Dharmi
2. Bangali
3. Barar
4. Batwal
5. Bawaria
6. Bazigar
7. Balmiki or Chura
8. Bhanjra
9. Chamar
10. Chanal
11. Dagi
12. Dhanak
13. Dumma or Mahasha
14. Gagra
15. Gandhila
16. Kabirpanthi
17. Khatik
18. Kori or Koli
19. Marija or Marecha
20. Mazhabi
21. Megh
22. Nat
23. Od
24. Pasi
25. Perna
26. Pherera
27. Ramdasi or Ravidasi
28. Sanhai
29. Sanhal
30. Sansi
31. Sapela
32. Sarera
33. Sikligar
34. Sirkiband

PART VII — UTTAR PRADESH

(1) Throughout the State : —

1. Agariya
2. Badi
3. Badhik
4. Baheliya
5. Baiga
6. Baiswar
7. Bajaniya
8. Bajgi

9. Balahar
10. Balmiki
11. Bangali
12. Banmanus
13. Bansphor
14. Barwar
15. Basor
16. Bawariya
17. Beldar
18. Beriya
19. Bhantu
20. Bhoksa
21. Bhuiya
22. Bhuyiar
23. Boria
24. Chamar
25. Chero
26. Dabgar
27. Dhangar
28. Dhanuk
29. Dharkar
30. Dhobi
31. Dhusia, or Jhusia
32. Dom
33. Domar
34. Dusadh
35. Gharami
36. Ghasiya
37. Gual
38. Habura
39. Hari
40. Hela
41. Jatava
42. Kalabaz
43. Kanjar
44. Kapariya
45. Karwal
46. Khairaha
47. Kharot
48. Kharwar (excluding Ben-bansi)
49. Kol
50. Korwa
51. Lalbegi
52. Majhwar
53. Nat
54. Pankha
55. Parahiya
56. Pasi
57. Patari
58. Rawat
59. Saharya
60. Sanaurhiya
61. Sansiya
62. Shilpkar
63. Turaiha

2. In Bundelkhand division and the portion of Mirzapur district south of Kaimur Range :—

Gond

PART IX — WEST BENGAL

Throughout the State : —

1. Bagdi
2. Bahelia
3. Baiti
4. Bauri
5. Bediya
6. Beldar
7. Bhuimali
8. Bhuiya
9. Bhumij
10. Bind
11. Chamar
12. Dhoba
13. Doai
14. Dom
15. Dosadh
16. Ghasi
17. Gonrhi
18. Hari
19. Jalia Kaibartta
20. Jhalo Malo or Malo
21. Kadar
22. Kandra
23. Kaora
24. Karenga
25. Kastha
26. Kaur
27. Khaira
28. Khatik
29. Koch
30. Konai
31. Konwar
32. Kora
33. Kotal
34. Lalbegi
35. Lodha
36. Lohar
37. Mahar
38. Mahli
39. Mal
40. Mallah
41. Malpahariya
42. Mehtor
43. Muchi
44. Musahar
45. Nagesia
46. Namasudra
47. Nuniya
48. Paliya
49. Pan
50. Pasi
51. Patni
52. Pod
53. Rabha
54. Rajbanshi
55. Rajwar
56. Sunri
57. Tiyar
58. Turi

PART X — HYDERABAD

Throughout the State : —

1. Anamuk
2. Aray (Mala)
3. Arwa Mala
4. Beda (Budga) Jangam
5. Bindla
6. Byagara
7. Chalvadi
8. Chambhar
9. Dakkal (Dokkalwar)
10. Dhor
11. Ellamalwar (Yellammalawandlu)
12. Holeya
13. Holeya Dasari
14. Kolupulvandlu
15. Madiga
16. Mahar
17. Mala
18. Mala Dasari
19. Mala Hannai
20. Malajangam
21. Mala Masti
22. Mala Sale (Netkani)
23. Mala Sanyasi
24. Mang
25. Mang Garodi
26. Manne
27. Mashti
28. Mehtar
29. Mitha Ayyalvar
30. Mochi
31. Samagara
32. Sindhollu (Chindollu)

PART XI — MADHYA BHARAT

Throughout the State : —

1. Bagri or Bagdi
2. Balai
3. Barahar or Basod
4. Bargunda
5. Bedia
6. Bhambi
7. Bhangi or Mehtar
8. Chamar
9. Chidar
10. Dhanuk
11. Kanjar
12. Khatik
13. Koli
14. Mahar
15. Mochi
16. Nat
17. Pardhi
18. Pasi
19. Sansi

PART XII — MYSORE

Throughout the State : —

1. Adidravida
2. Adikarnataka
3. Banjara or Lambani
4. Bhovi
5. Koracha
6. Korama

PART XIII — PATIALA AND EAST PUNJAB STATES UNION

Throughout the State : —

1. Ad Dharmi
2. Bangali
3. Barar
4. Batwal
5. Bawaria
6. Bazigar
7. Balmiki or Chura
8. Bhanjra
9. Chamar
10. Chanal
11. Dagi
12. Dhanak
13. Dumna or Mahasha
14. Gagra
15. Gandhila
16. Kabirpanthi
17. Khatik
18. Kori or Koli
19. Marija or Marecha
20. Mazhabi
21. Megh
22. Nat
23. Od
24. Pasi
25. Perna
26. Pherera
27. Ramdasi or Ravidasi
28. Sanhai
29. Sanhal
30. Sansi
31. Sapela
32. Sarera
33. Sikligar
34. Sirkiband

PART XIV — RAJASTHAN

Throughout the State : —

1. Adi Dharmi
2. Aheri
3. Badi
4. Bagri
5. Bajgar
6. Bansphor

7. Bargi
8. Bawaria
9. Bhand
10. Bhangi
11. Bidakia
12. Chamar
13. Chura
14. Dabgar
15. Dhankia
16. Dheda
17. Dome
18. Gandia
19. Garancha Mehtar
20. Godhi
21. Jatia
22. Kalbelia
23. Kapadia
24. Khangar
25. Khatka
26. Kooch Band
27. Koria
28. Kunjar
29. Madari (Bazigar)
30. Majhabi
31. Mehar
32. Mehtar
33. Mochi
34. Nut
35. Pasi
36. Raigar
37. Ramdasia
38. Rawal
39. Sarbhangi
40. Singiwala
41. Sansi
42. Thori
43. Tirgar
44. Valmiki

PART XV — SAURASHTRA

Throughout the State : —

1. Bawa (Dhedh)
2. Bhangi
3. Chamadia
4. Chamar
5. Dangashia
6. Garoda
7. Garmatang
8. Hadi
9. Meghwal
10. Senva
11. Shemalia
12. Thori
13. Turi
14. Turi-Barot
15. Vankar

PART XVI — TRAVANCORE-COCHIN

Throughout the State :—

1. Ayyanavar
2. Bharatar
3. Chakkiliyan
4. Domban
5. Eravalan
6. Kakkalan
7. Kanakkan
8. Kavara
9. Kootan (Koodan)
10. Kuravan
11. Mannan
12. Nayadi
13. Padannan
14. Pallan
15. Palluvan
16. Panan
17. Paravan
18. Paraya (Sambavar)
19. Pathiyan
20. Perumannan
21. Pulayan
22. Thandan
23. Ulladan
24. Uraly
25. Vallon
26. Valluvan
27. Vannan
28. Velan
29. Vetan
30. Vettuvan

(iii) THE CONSTITUTION (SCHEDULED CASTES) (PART C STATES) ORDER, 1951

C.O. 32 — In exercise of the powers conferred by clause (I) of Article 341 of the Constitution of India, as amended by the Constitution (First Amendment) Act, 1951, the President is pleased to make the following Order, namely: —

(1) This Order may be called the Constitution (Scheduled Castes) (Part C States) Order 1951.

(2) Subject to the provisions of this Order, the castes, races or tribes, or parts of, or groups within, castes or tribes, specified in Parts I to X of the Schedule to this Order shall, in relation to the States to which those Parts respectively relate, be deemed to be Scheduled Castes so far as regards members thereof resident in the localities specified in relation to them respectively in those Parts of that Schedule.

(3) Notwithstanding anything contained in Paragraph 2, no person who professes a religion different from Hinduism shall be deemed to be a member of a Scheduled Caste :

Provided that every member of the Kabirpanthi, Mazhabi, Ram Dasia, Ravidasi or Raidasi or Sikligar caste resident in the State of Delhi and Kabirpanthi or Julaha or Keer, Mazhabi, Ramdasi or Ravidasi, Ramdasia or Sikligar caste resident in the State of Himachal Pradesh shall, in relation to that State, be deemed to be a member of the Scheduled Castes whether he professes the Hindu or the Sikh religion.

(4) Any reference in the Schedule to this Order to a district or other territorial division of a State shall be construed as a reference to that district or other territorial division as existing on the 26th January 1950.

THE SCHEDULE

PART I — AJMER

Throughout the State :—

1. Aheri
2. Bagri
3. Balai
4. Bambhi
5. Bansphod
6. Baori
7. Bargi
8. Bazigar
9. Bhangi
10. Bidakia
11. Chammar
12. Dabgar
13. Dhanak
14. Dhed
15. Dhobi
16. Dholi
17. Dom
18. Garoda
19. Gancha
20. Jatava
21. Kalbelia
22. Khangar
23. Khatik
24. Koli
25. Koria
26. Kuchband
27. Mahar
28. Meghwal
29. Mochi
30. Nat
31. Pasi
32. Raigar
33. Rawal
34. Sarbhangi
35. Sargara
36. Satia
37. Thori
38. Tirgar
39. Kanjar
40. Sansi

PART II — BHOPAL

Throughout the State :—

1. Balahi
2. Basar
3. Bedia
4. Beldar
5. Chamar
6. Chitar
7. Dhanuk
8. Dome
9. Khatik
10. Koli
11. Kanjar
12. Mehtar, Bhangi

13. Mehar
14. Mang
15. Nut
16. Silawat

PART III — BILASPUR

Throughout the State :—

1. Chamar
2. Julahe
3. Dumne(Bhanjre)
4. Chuhre
5. Hesi (Turi)
6. Chhimbe (Dhobi)
7. Bangali
8. Sarehde
9. Daule

PART IV — COORG

Throughout the State :—

1. Adi Dravida
2. Adi Karnataka
3. Adiya
4. Balagai
5. Holeya
6. Madiga
7. Muchi
8. Mundala
9. Panchama
10. Paraya
11. Samagara

PART V — DELHI

Throughout the State :—

1. Adi Dharmi
2. Agria
3. Aheria
4. Balai
5. Banjara
6. Bawaria
7. Bazigar
8. Bhangi
9. Bhil
10. Chamar
11. Chanwar Chamar
12. Chohra (Sweeper)
13. Chuhra (Balmiki)
14. Dhanak or Dhanuk
15. Dhobi
16. Dom
17. Gharrami
18. Jatya or Jatav Chamar
19. Julaha (Weaver)
20. Kabirpanthi

21. Kachhandha
22. Kanjar
23. Khatik
24. Koli
25. Lalbegi
26. Madari
27. Mallah
28. Mazhabi
29. Megwal
30. Mochi
31. Nat (Rana)
32. Pasi
33. Perna
34. Ram Dasia
35. Ravidasi or Raidasi
36. Rehgarh or Raigar
37. Sansi
38. Sapera
39. Sikligar
40. Singiwala or Kalbelia
41. Sirkiband

PART VI — HIMACHAL PRADESH

Throughout the State : —

1. Ad-dharmi
2. Balmiki or Chura or Bhangi or Sweeper
3. Bangali
4. Banjara
5. Barar
6. Bawaria
7. Bazigar
8. Hesi
9. Bhanjra
10. Chamar
11. Chanal
12. Dagi
13. Daole
14. Dhaki or Toori
15. Doom or Doomna
16. Kabirpanthi or Julaha or Keer
17. Koli
18. Mazhabi
19. Mochi
20. Nat
21. Od
22. Pasi
23. Phrera
24. Ramdasi or Ravidasi
25. Ramdasia
26. Rehar
27. Sansi
28. Sapela
29. Sikligar
30. Sirkiband

PART VII — KUTCH

Throughout the State : —

1. Bhangi
2. Chamar
3. Garoda
4. Meghwal
5. Turi
6. Turi (Barot)

PART VIII — MANIPUR

Throughout the State : —

Castes, races or tribes, or parts of, or groups within, castes or tribes specified as Scheduled Castes in relation to the State of Assam.

PART IX — TRIPURA

Throughout the State : —

1. Bagdi
2. Baiti
3. Bhunar
4. Chamar
5. Dandasi
6. Dhenuar
7. Dhoba
8. Duai
9. Dum
10. Ghasi
11. Gour
12. Gunar
13. Gur
14. Gorang
15. Jalia Kaibarta
16. Kahar
17. Kalindi
18. Kan
19. Kanugh
20. Keot
21. Kharia
22. Khadit
23. Khemcha
24. Koch
25. Koir
26. Kol
27. Kora
28. Kotal
29. Mali
30. Bhuimali
31. Mehtor
32. Muchi
33. Namsudra
34. Patni
35. Sabar
36. Mahisyadas

PART X — VINDHYA PRADESH

Throughout the State :—

1. Basor (Bansphor)
2. Chamar
3. Dahait
4. Dharkar
5. Dher
6. Dom
7. Domar or Doris
8. Kuchbandhia
9. Mehtar or Bhangi or Dhanuk
10. Mochi

THE ANDHRA STATE ACT, 1953

I. —MODIFICATIONS IN THE CONSTITUTION (SCHEDULED CASTES) ORDER, 1950.

(2) In the Schedule—

(a) for the sub-heading "Part V—Madras" and for the words "Throughout the State" thereunder, substitute "Part V-Madras and Andhra" and "Throughout each of the States" respectively:

(b) for the entry under the sub-heading "Part XII-Mysore" substitute the following :—

(1) Throughout the State except in Bellary district :—

1. Adidravida
2. Adikarnataka
3. Banjara or Lambani
4. Bhovi
5. Koracha
6. Korama

(2) In Bellary district :—

1. Adi Andhra
2. Adi Darvida
3. Adikarnataka
4. Ajila
5. Arunthathiyar
6. Baira
7. Bakuda
8. Bandi
9. Bariki
10. Bavuri
11. Bellara
12. Byagari
13. Chachati
14. Chakkiliyan
15. Chalavadi
16. Chamar
17. Chandala
18. Cheruman
19. Dandasi
20. Devendrakulathan
21. Dom or Dombara, Padi, Pano
22. Ghasi or Haddi, Relli Sachandi

23. Godagali
24. Godari
25. Godda
26. Gosangi
27. Hasla
28. Holeya
29. Jaggali
30. Jambuvulu
31. Kadan
32. Kalladi
33. Kanakkan
34. Karimpalan
35. Kodalo
36. Koosa
37. Koraga
38. Kudubi
39. Kudumban
40. Kuravan
41. Kurichchan
42. Madari
43. Madiga
44. Maila
45. Mala (including Agency Malas)
46. Mala Dasu
47. Malasar
48. Matangi
49. Mavilan
50. Moger
51. Muchi
52. Mundala
53. Nalakeyava
54. Nayadi
55. Pagadai
56. Painda
57. Paky
58. Pallan
59. Pambada
60. Pamidi
61. Panan
62. Panchama
63. Panniandi
64. Paraiya
65. Paravan
66. Pulayan
67. Puthirai Vannan
68. Raneyar
69. Samagara
70. Samban
71. Sapari
72. Semman
73. Thoti
74. Tiruvalluvar
75. Valluvan
76. Valmiki
77. Vettuvan.

The Himachal Pradesh and Bilaspur (New State) Act, 1954

The following castes were inserted :

31. Julahe
32. Dumne (Bhanjre)
33. Chuhre
34. Hese (Turi)
35. Chhimbe (Dhobi)
36. Sarehde
37. Daule

THE SCHEDULED CASTES AND SCHEDULED TRIBES LISTS (MODIFICATION) ORDER, 1956

S.R.O. 2477A, dated the 29th October, 1956 — The following Order made by the President is published for general information : —

In pursuance of section 41 of the States Reorganisation Act, 1956 (37 of 1956), and section 14 of the Bihar and West Bengal (Transfer of Territories) Act, 1956 (40 of 1956), the President hereby makes the following Order, namely : —

1. This Order may be called the Scheduled Castes and Scheduled Tribes Lists (Modification) Order, 1956.

2. (1) The Constitution (Scheduled Castes) Order, 1950, is hereby modified in the manner and to the extent specified in Schedule I.

   (2) The Constitution (Scheduled Castes) (Part C States) Order, 1951, is hereby modified in the manner and to the extent specified in Schedule II.

3. (1) The Constitution (Scheduled Tribes) Order, 1950, is hereby modified in the manner and to the extent specified in Schedule III.

   (2) The Constitution (Scheduled Tribes) (Part C States) Order, 1951, is hereby modified in the manner and to the extent specified in Schedule IV.

SCHEDULE I

[See paragraph 2(1)]

Modifications to the Constitution (Scheduled Castes) Order, 1950.

1. In paragraph 2, for "Parts I to XVI", substitute "Parts I to XIII".

2. For paragraph 4, substitute :—

"4 Any reference in this Order to a State or to a District or other territorial division thereof shall be construed as reference to the State, district or other territorial division, constituted as from the 1st day of November, 1956".

3. For the Schedule, substitute : —

THE SCHEDULE

PART I — ANDHRA PRADESH

1. Throughout the State :—

1. Chalavadi
2. Chamar, Mochi or Muchi
3. Madiga
4. Mala

2. Throughout the State except Hyderabad, Mahbubnagar, Adilabad, Nizamabad, Medak, Karimnagar, Warangal, Khammam and Nalgonda districts : —

1. Adi Andhra
2. Adi Dravida
3. Arundhatiya
4. Bariki
5. Bavuri
6. Chachati
7. Chandala
8. Dandasi
9. Dom, Dombara, Paidi or Pano
10. Ghasi, Haddi or Relli Chachandi
11. Godagali
12. Godari
13. Gosangi
14. Jaggali
15. Jambuvulu
16. Madasi Kuruva or Madari Kuruva
17. Mala Dasu
18. Madiga Dasu and Mashteen
19. Matangi
20. Mundala
21. Paky or Moti
22. Pambada or Pambanda
23. Pamidi
24. Panchama or Pariah
25. Relli
26. Samban
27. Sapru
28. Thoti

3. In the districts of Hyderabad, Mahbubnagar, Adilabad, Nizamabad, Medak, Karimnagar, Warangal, Khammam and Nalgonda :—

1. Anamuk
2. Aray (Mala)
3. Arwa Mala
4. Beda (Budga) Jangam
5. Bindla
6. Byagara
7. Chambhar
8. Dakkal (Dokkalwar)
9. Dhor
10. Ellamalwar (Yellammalawandlu)
11. Holeya
12. Holeya Dasari
13. Kolupulvandlu
14. Mahar
15. Mala Dasari
16. Mala Hannai
17. Malajangam
18. Mala Masti
19. Mala Sale (Netkani)
20. Mala Sanyasi
21. Mang
22. Mang Garodi
23. Manne
24. Mashti
25. Mehtar
26. Mitha Ayyalvar
27. Samagara
28. Sindhollu (Chindollu).

PART II — ASSAM

Throughout the State :—

1. Bansphor
2. Bhuinmali or Mali
3. Brittial-Bania or Bania
4. Dhupi or Dhobi
5. Dugla or Dholi
6. Hira
7. Jalkeot
8. Jhalo, Malo or Jhalo-Malo
9. Kaibartta or Jaliya
10. Lalbegi
11. Mahara
12. Mehtar or Bhangi
13. Muchi or Rishi
14. Namasudr
15. Patni
16. Sutradhar

PART III — BIHAR

1. Throughout the State :—

1. Bantar
2. Bauri
3. Bhogta
4. Chamar or Mochi
5. Chaupal
6. Dabgar
7. Dhobi
8. Dom or Dhangad
9. Dusadh, including Dhari or Dharhi
10. Ghasi
11. Halalkhor
12. Hari, Mehtar or Bhangi
13. Kanjar
14. Kurariar
15. Lalbegi
16. Musahar
17. Nat
18. Pan or Sawasi
19. Pasi
20. Rajwar
21. Turi.

2. In Patna and Tirhut divisions, and the districts of Monghyr, Bhagalpur, Palamau and Purnea :—

Bhumij.

3. In Patna, Shahabad, Gaya and Palamau Districts: —

Bhuiya.

PART IV — BOMBAY

1. Throughout the State *except* the districts of Buldana, Akola, Amravati, Yeotmal, Wardha, Nagpur, Bhandara, Chanda, Aurangabad, Parbhani, Nanded, Bhir, Osmanabad, Halar, Madhya Saurashtra, Zalawad, Gohilwad, Sorath and Kutch :—

1. Ager
2. Bakad or Bant
3. Bhambi, Bhambhi, Asadaru, Asodi, Chamadia, Chamar, Chambhar, Chamgar, Haralayya, Harali, Khalpa, Machigar, Mochighar, Madar, Madig, Telegu Mochi, Kamati Mochi, Ranigar, Rohidas, Rohit or Samgar.
4. Bhangi, Mehtar, Olgana, Rukhi, Malkana, Halakhor, Lalbegi, Balmiki, Korar or Zadmali.
5. Chalvadi or Channayya

6. Chenna Dasar or Holaya Dasar
7. Dhor, Kakkayya or Kankayya
8. Garoda or Garo
9. Halleer
10. Halsar, Haslar, Hulasvar or Halasvar
11. Holar or Valhar
12. Holaya or Holer
13. Lingader
14. Mahar, Taral or Dhegu Megu
15. Mahyavanshi, Dhed, Vankar or Maru Vankar
16. Mang, Matang or Minimadig
17. Mang-Garudi
18. Meghval or Menghvar
19. Mukri
20. Nadia or Hadi
21. Pasi
22. Shenva, Chenva, Sedma or Ravat
23. Tirgar or Tirbanda
24. Turi

2. In the districts of Greater Bombay, West Khandesh, East Khandesh, Dangs, Nasik, Ahmednagar, Poona, Satara North, Satara South, Kolhapur, Sholapur, Thana, Kolaba and Ratnagiri :—

Mochi

3. In the districts of Buldana, Akola, Amravati, Yeotmal, Wardha, Nagpur, Bhandara and Chanda : —

1. Bahna or Bahana
2. Balahi or Balai
3. Basor, Burud, Bansor or Bansodi
4. Chamar, Chamari, Mochi, Nona, Rohidas, Ramnami, Satnami, Surjyabanshi or Surjyaramnami
5. Dom or Dum
6. Dohor
7. Ganda or Gandi
8. Ghasi or Ghasia

9. Kaikadi
10. Katia or Patharia
11. Khatik, Chikwa or Chikvi
12. Madgi
13. Mahar or Mehra
14. Mang, Dankhni-Mang, Mang Mahashi, Mang-Garudi, Madari, Garudi or Radhe-Mang
15. Mehtar or Bhangi
16. Sansi

4. In the districts of Akola, Amravati and Buldana : —

Bedar

5. In the districts of Bhandara : —

1. Chadar
2. Holiya

6. In the districts of Bhandara and Buldana : —

Khangar, Kanera or Mirdha

7. In the districts of Amravati, Bhandara and Buldana: —

Kori

8. In the districts of Aurangabad, Parbhani, Nanded, Bhir and Osmanabad : —

1. Anamuk
2. Aray (Mala)
3. Arwa Mala
4. Beda (Budga) Jangam
5. Bindla
6. Byagara
7. Chalvadi
8. Chambhar
9. Dakkal (Dokkalwar)
10. Dhor
11. Ellamalwar (Yellammalawandlu)
12. Holeya
13. Holeya Dasari
14. Kolupulvandlu
15. Madiga
16. Mahar
17. Mala
18. Mala Dasari

19. Mala Hannai
20. Malajangam
21. Mala Masti
22. Mala Sale (Netkani)
23. Mala Sanyasi
24. Mang
25. Mang Garodi
26. Manne
27. Mashti
28. Mehtar
29. Mitha Ayyalvar
30. Mochi
31. Samagara
32. Sindhollu (Chindollu)

9. In the districts of Halar, Madhya Saurashtra, Zalawad, Gohilwad and Sorath : —

1. Bawa (Dhedh) or Dedh-Sadhu
2. Bhangi or Rukhi
3. Chamadia
4. Chamar, Nalia or Rohit
5. Dangashia
6. Garoda
7. Garmatang
8. Hadi
9. Meghwal
10. Senva
11. Shemalia
12. Thori
13. Turi
14. Turi-Barot or Dhedh-Barot
15. Vankar, Dhedh or Antyaj

10. In the district of Kutch : —

1. Bhangi
2. Chamar
3. Garoda
4. Meghwal
5. Turi
6. Turi-Barot

PART V — KERALA

1. Throughout the State : —

1. Chakkiliyan
2. Kuravan, Sidhanar
3. Nayadi
4. Pallan
5. Paraiyan, Parayan (Sambavar)
6. Valluvan

2. Throughout the State *except* Kasaragod taluk of Malabar district : —

1. Kanakkan or Padanna
2. Panan

3. Throughout the State *except* Malabar district (excluding Kasaragod taluk) : —

Paravan

4. Throughout the State *except* Malabar district : —

1. Ayyanavar
2. Bharatar
3. Boyan
4. Domban
5. Kakkalan
6. Kavara
7. Kootan (Koodan)
8. Mannan
9. Padannan
10. Palluvan
11. Pathiyan
12. Perumannan
13. Pulayan or Cheramar
14. Thandan
15. Ulladan
16. Uraly
17. Vallon
18. Vannan
19. Velan
20. Vetan
21. Vettuvan

5. In Malabar district : —

1. Adi Andhra
2. Adi Dravida
3. Adi Karnataka
4. Ajila
5. Arunthathiyar
6. Baira
7. Bakuda
8. Bandi
9. Bellara
10. Chamar or Muchi
11. Chandala
12. Cheruman
13. Godagali
14. Godda
15. Gosangi
16. Holeya
17. Kadaiyan
18. Kalladi
19. Karimpalan
20. Koosa
21. Kudumban
22. Maila
23. Mavilan
24. Moger
25. Mundala
26. Nalakeyava
27. Pambada
28. Panchama
29. Puthirai Vannan
30. Raneyar
31. Samagara
32. Samban

33. Semman
34. Thoti

6. In Malabar district (excluding Kasaragod taluk) : —

1. Gavara
2. Malayan
3. Pulaya Vettuvan

7. In Kasaragod taluk of Malabar district : —

1. Bathada
2. Hasla
3. Nalkadaya

PART VI — MADHYA PRADESH

1. In the district of Bhind, Gird, Morena, Shivpuri, Goona Rajgarh, Shajapur, Ujjan, Ratlam, Mandsaur, Bhilsa, Indore, Dewas, Dhan, Jhabua and Nimar (M.B.): —

1. Bagri or Bagdi
2. Balai
3. Banchada
4. Barahar or Basod
5. Bargunda
6. Bedia
7. Bhangi or Mehtar
8. Bhanumati
9. Chamar, Bairwa, Bhambi, Jatav, Mochi or Regar
10. Chidar
11. Dhanuk
12. Dhed
13. Dom
14. Kanjar
15. Khatik
16. Koli or Kori
17. Kotwal
18. Mahar
19. Mang or Mang Garodi
20. Meghwal
21. Nat, Kalbelia or Sapera
22. Pardhi
23. Pasi
24. Sansi
25. Zamral

2. In the districts of Chhidwara, Betul, Jabalpur, Sagar, Mandla, Hoshangabad, Nimar, Balaghat, Raipur, Bilaspur, Durg, Bastar, Surguja and Raigarh : —

1. Bahna or Bahana
2. Balahi or Balai
3. Basor, Burud, Bansor or Bansodi

4. Chamar, Chamari, Mochi, Nona, Rohidas, Ramnami, Satnami, Surjyabanshi or Surjyaramnami
5. Dom or Dumar
6. Ganda or Gandi
7. Khatik, Chikwa or Chikvi
8. Mang, Dankhni-Mang, Mang Mahashi, Mang Garudi, Madari, Garudi or Radhe-Mang
9. Mehtar or Bhangi
10. Sansi

3. In Bilaspur district :—

Audhelia

4. In Sagar and Damoh districts :—

Chadar

5. In Damoh sub-division of Sagar district :—

Dahait, Dahayat or Dahat

6. In the districts of Bilaspur, Durg, Raipur, Bastar, Surguja and Raigarh :—

Dewar

7. In Sagar district except Damoh sub-division thereof :—

Dhanuk

8. In Balaghat district :—

1. Dohor
2. Holiya
3. Madgi

9. In the districts of Balaghat, Bilaspur, Durg, Raipur, Surguja, Bastar and Raigarh :—

Ghasi or Ghasia

10. In Balaghat, Betul, Bilaspur, Durg, Nimar, Raipur, Bastar, Sarguja and Raigarh districts; in Hoshangabad and Seoni-Malwa tahsils of Hoshangabad district: in Chhindwara district *except* in Seoni sub-division thereof: and in Sagar district *except* in Damoh sub-division thereof :—

Katia or Patharia

11. In Sagar and Damoh districts; and in Hoshangabad and Seoni-Malwa tahsils of Hoshangabad district : —

Khangar, Kanera or Mirdha

12. In Chindwara, Betul, Jabalpur, Narasimhapur, Sagar, Mandla, Nimar, Balaghat, Raipur, Durg, Bastar, Surguja and Raigarh districts: and in Hoshangabad district *except* Harda and Sohgpur tahsils thereof : —

Kori

13. In Chhindwara, Betul, Jabalpur, Narasimhapur, Sagar, Mandla, Nimar, Balaghat, Raipur, Bilaspur, Durg, Bastar, Surguja and Raigarh districts : and in Hoshangabad district *except* Harda and Sohagpur tehsils thereof : —

Mahar or Mehra

14. In Sohagpur tahsil of Hoshangabad district : —

Rujjhar

15. In the districts of Datia, Tikamgarh, Chhatarpur, Panna, Satna, Rewa, Sidhi and Shahdol : —

1. Basor or Bansphor
2. Beldar or Sunkar
3. Chamar, Ahirwar, Chamar Mangan, Mochi or Raidas
4. Dharkar, Balmiki or Lalbegi
5. Dher
6. Dom
7. Domar or Doris
8. Ghasia
9. Kuchbandhia
10. Kumhar
11. Mehtar, Bhangi or Dhanuk
12. Moghia
13. Muskkan
14. Pasi
15. Sansia or Bedia

16. In the district of Raisen and Sehore : —

1. Balahi
2. Bansphor or Basor
3. Basar
4. Bedia
5. Beldar
6. Chamar, Jatav or Mochi
7. Chitar
8. Dhanuk
9. Dhobi
10. Dome

11. Kanjar
12. Khatik
13. Koli or Katia
14. Mang
15. Mehar
16. Mehtar or Bhangi
17. Pasi
18. Sansia
19. Silawat

PART VII — MADRAS

1. Throughout the State :—

1. Chakkiliyan
2. Kuravan, Sidhanar
3. Nayadi
4. Pallan
5. Paraiyan, Parayan (Sambavar)
6. Valluvan

2. Throughout the State *except* Kanya Kumari district and Shencottah taluk of Tirunelveli district :—

1. Adi Andhra
2. Adi Dravida
3. Adi Karnataka
4. Ajila
5. Arunthathiyar
6. Baira
7. Bakuda
8. Bandi
9. Bellara
10. Chalavadi
11. Chamar or Muchi
12. Chandala
13. Cheruman
14. Devendrakulathan
15. Dom, Dombara, Paidi or Pano
16. Godagali
17. Godda
18. Gosangi
19. Holeya
20. Jaggali
21. Jambuvulu
22. Kadaiyan
23. Kalladi
24. Karimpalan
25. Koosa
26. Kudumban
27. Madari
28. Madiga
29. Maila
30. Mala
31. Mavilan
32. Moger
33. Mundala
34. Nalakeyava
35. Pagadai

36. Pambada
37. Panchama
38. Panniandi
39. Puthirai Vannan
40. Raneyar
41. Samagara
42. Samban
43. Sapari
44. Semman
45. Thoti
46. Tiruvalluvar

3. In the Nilgiri district : —

Kanakkan or Padanna

4. In Coimbatore and Salem districts : —

1. Pannadi
2. Vathiriyan

5. In Kanya Kumari district and Shencottah Taluk of Tirunelveli district : —

1. Ayyanavar
2. Bharatar
3. Domban
4. Kakkalan
5. Kavara
6. Kootan (Koodan)
7. Mannan
8. Padannan
9. Palluvan
10. Panan
11. Paravan
12. Pathiyan
13. Perumannan
14. Pulayan or Cheramar
15. Thandan
16. Ulladan
17. Uraly
18. Vallon
19. Vannan
20. Velan
21. Vetan
22. Vettuvan

6. In Tanjore district : —

1. Koliyan
2. Vettiyan

PART VIII — MYSORE

1. Throughout the State *except* Coorg, Belgaum, Bijapur, Dharwar, Kanara, South Kanara, Gulbarga, Raichur and Bidar districts and Kollegal taluk of Mysore district : —

1. Adi Andhra
2. Adidravida
3. Adikarnataka
4. Banjara or Lambani

5. Bhovi
6. Dakkaliga
7. Ganti Chores
8. Handi Jogis
9. Kepmaris
10. Koracha
11. Korama
12. Machala
13. Mochi
14. Sillekyathas
15. Sudugadu Siddha

2. In the districts of Belgaum, Bijapur, Dharwar and Kanara :—

1. Ager
2. Bakad or Bant
3. Bhambi, Bhambhi, Asadaru, Asodi, Chamadia, Chamar, Chambhar, Chamgar, Haralayya, Harali, Khalpa, Machigar, Mochigar, Madar, Madig, Mochi, Telegu Mochi, Kamati, Mochi, Ranigar, Rohidas, Rohit or Samgar
4. Bhangi, Mehtar, Olgana, Rukhi, Malkana, Halakhor, Lalbegi, Balmiki, Korar or Zadmali
5. Chalvadi or Channayya
6. Chenna Dasar or Holaya Dasar
7. Dhor, Kakkayya or Kankayya
8. Garoda or Garo
9. Halleer
10. Halsar, Haslar, Hulasvar or Halasvar
11. Holar or Valhar
12. Holaya or Holer
13. Lingader
14. Mahar, Taral or Dhegu Megu
15. Mahyavanshi, Dhed, Vankar or Maru Vankar
16. Mang, Matang or Minimadig
17. Mang-Garudi
18. Meghval or Menghvar
19. Mukri
20. Nadia or Hadi
21. Pasi
22. Shenva, Chenva, Sedmá or Ravat
23. Tirgar or Tirbanda
24. Turi

3. In Kanara district : —

Kotegar or Metri

4. In the districts of Gulbarga, Bidar and Raichur : —

1. Anamuk	2. Aray (Mala)
3. Arwa Mala	4. Beda (Budga) Jangam
5. Bindla	6. Byagara
7. Chalvadi	8. Chambhar
9. Dakkal (Dokkalwar)	10. Dhor
11. Ellamalwar (Yellammalawandlu)	12. Holeya
13. Holeya Dasari	14. Kolupulvandlu
15. Madiga	16. Mahar
17. Mala	18. Mala Dasari
19. Mala Hannai	20. Malajangam
21. Mala Masti	22. Mala Sale (Netkani)
23. Mala Sanyasi	24. Mang
25. Mang Garodi	26. Manne
27. Mashti	28. Mehtar
29. Mitha Ayyalvar	30. Mochi
31. Samagara	32. Sindhollu (Chindollu)

5. In South Kanara district and Kollegal taluk of Mysore district : —

1. Adi Andhra	2. Adi Dravida
3. Adi Karntaka	4. Ajila
5. Arunthathiyar	6. Baira
7. Bakuda	8. Bandi
9. Bellara	10. Chakkiliyan
11. Chalavadi	12. Chamar or Muchi
13. Chandala	14. Cheruman

15. Devendrakulathan	16. Dom, Dombara, Paidi or Pano
17. Godagali	
18. Godda	19. Gosangi
20. Holeya	21. Jaggali
22. Jambuvulu	23. Kadaiyan
24. Kalladi	25. Karimpalan
26. Koosa	27. Kudumban
28. Kuravan	29. Madari
30. Madiga	31. Maila
32. Mala	33. Mavilan
34. Moger	35. Mundala
36. Nalakeyava	37. Nayadi
38. Pagadai	39. Pallan
40. Pambada	41. Panchama
42. Panniandi	43. Paraiyan
44. Puthirai Vannan	45. Raneyar
46. Samagara	47. Samban
48. Sapari	49. Semman
50. Thoti	51. Tiruvalluvar
52. Valluvan	

6. In Kollegal Taluk of Mysore district :—

1. Pannadi	2. Vathiriyan

7. In South Kanara district :—

1. Bathada	2. Hasla
3. Nalkadaya	4. Paravan

8. In Coorg district :—

1. Adi Dravida	2. Adi Karnataka
3. Adiya	4. Balagai
5. Holeya	6. Madiga
7. Muchi	8. Mundala
9. Pale	10. Panchama
11. Paraya	12. Samagara

PART IX — ORISSA

1. Throughout the State : —

1. Adi Andhra
2. Amant or Amat
3. Audhelia
4. Badaik
5. Bagheti or Baghuti
6. Bajikar
7. Bari
8. Bariki
9. Basor or Burud
10. Bauri
11. Bauti
12. Bavuri
13. Bedia or Bejia
14. Beldar
15. Bhata
16. Bhoi
17. Chachati
18. Chakali
19. Chamar, Mochi, Muchi or Satnami
20. Chandala
21. Cherua or Chhelia
22. Chandhai Maru
23. Dandasi
24. Dewar
25. Dhanwar
26. Dhoba or Dhobi
27. Dom, Dombo or Duria Dom
28. Dosadha
29. Ganda
30. Ghantarghada or Ghantra
31. Ghasi or Ghasia
32. Ghogia
33. Ghusuria
34. Godagali
35. Godari
36. Godra
37. Gokha
38. Gorait or Korait
39. Haddi, Hadi or Hari
40. Irika
41. Jaggali
42. Kandra or Kandara
43. Karua
44. Katia
45. Kela
46. Khadala
47. Kodalo or Khodalo
48. Kori
49. Kummari
50. Kurunga
51. Laban
52. Laheri
53. Madari
54. Madiga
55. Mahuria
56. Mala, Jhala, Malo or Zala
57. Mang
58. Mangan

59. Mehra or Mahar
60. Mehtar or Bhangi
61. Mewar
62. Mundapotta
63. Musahar
64. Nagarchi
65. Namasudra
66. Paidi
67. Painda
68. Pamidi
69. Pan or Pano
70. Panchama
71. Panika
72. Panka
73. Pantanti
74. Pap
75. Pasi
76. Patial, Patikar, Patratanti or Patu
77. Rajna
78. Relli
79. Sabakhia
80. Samasi
81. Sanei
82. Sapari
83. Sauntia (Santia)
84. Sidhria
85. Sinduria
86. Siyal
87. Tamadia
88. Tamudia
89. Tanla
90. Tiar or Tior
91. Turi
92. Ujia
93. Valamiki or Valmiki

2. In Sambalpur district : —
Kuli

PART X — PUNJAB

1. Throughout the State : —

1. Ad Dharmi
2. Bangali
3. Barar, Burar or Berar
4. Batwal
5. Bauria or Bawaria
6. Bazigar
7. Balmiki, Chura or Bangi
8. Bhanjra
9. Chamar, Jatia Chamar, Rehgar, Raigar, Ramdasi or Ravidasi
10. Chanal
11. Dagi
12. Dhanak
13. Dumna, Mahasha or Doom
14. Gagra
15. Gandhila or Gandil Gondola

16. Kabirpanthi or Julaha
17. Khatik
18. Kori or Koli
19. Marija or Marecha
20. Mazhabi
21. Megh
22. Nat
23. Od
24. Pasi
25. Perna
26. Pherera
27. Sanhai
28. Sanhal
29. Sansi, Bhedkut or Manesh
30. Sapela
31. Sarera
32. Sikligar
33. Sirkiband

2. Throughout the State *except* the districts of Patiala, Bhatinda, Mohindergarh, Kapurthala and Sangrur :—

1. Darain
2. Sansoi
3. Dhogri, Dhangri or Siggi

3. In the district of Patiala, Bhatinda, Mohindergarh, Kapurthala and Sangrur :—

Deha, Dhaya or Dhea

PART XI — RAJASTHAN

1. Throughout the State *except* Ajmer district, Abu Road taluka of Sirohi district and Sunel Tappa of Jhalawar district : --

1. Adi Dharmi
2. Aheri
3. Badi
4. Bagri
5. Bairwa or Berwa
6. Bajgar
7. Balai
8. Bansphor
9. Bargi, Vargi or Birgi
10. Bawaria
11. Bedia or Beria
12. Bhand
13. Bhangi
14. Bidakia
15. Bola
16. Chamar, Bhambhi, Jatav, Jatia, Mochi, Raidass, Raigar or Ramdasia
17. Chandal
18. Chura
19. Dabgar
20. Dhankia
21. Dheda

22. Dome
23. Gandia
24. Garancha Mehtar or Gancha
25. Garo, Garura or Gurda
26. Gavaria
27. Godhi
28. Jingar
29. Kalbelia
30. Kamad or Kamadia
31. Kanjar
32. Kapadia Sansi
33. Khangar
34. Khatik
35. Koli or Kori
36. Kooch Band
37. Koria
38. Kunjar
39. Madari or Bazigar
40. Majhabi
41. Megh or Meghwal
42. Mehar
43. Mehtar
44. Nut
45. Pasi
46. Rawal
47. Salvi
48. Sansi
49. Santia
50. Sarbhangi
51. Sargara
52. Singiwala
53. Thori or Nayak
54. Tirgar
55. Valmiki

2. In Ajmer district :—

1. Aheri
2. Bagri
3. Balai
4. Bambhi
5. Bansphod
6. Baori
7. Bargi
8. Bazigar
9. Bhangi
10. Bidakia
11. Chamar, Jatava, Jatia, Mochi or Raigar
12. Dabgar
13. Dhanak
14. Dhed
15. Dhobi
16. Dholi
17. Dom
18. Garoda
19. Gancha
20. Kabirpanthi
21. Kalbelia
22. Khangar
23. Khatik

24. Koli
25. Koria
26. Kuchband
27. Mahar
28. Meghwal
29. Nat
30. Pasi
31. Rawal
32. Sarbhangi
33. Sargara
34. Satia
35. Thori
36. Tirgar
37. Kanjar
38. Sansi

3. In Abu Road taluka of Sirohi district :

1. Ager
2. Bakad or Bant
3. Bhambi, Bhambhi, Asadaru, Asodi, Chamadia, Chamar, Chambhar, Chamgar, Haralayya, Harali, Khalpa, Machigar, Mochigar, Madar, Madig, Telegu Mochi, Kamati Mochi, Ranigar, Rohidas, Rohit or Samgar
4. Bhangi, Mehtar, Olgana, Rukhi, Malkana, Halalkhor, Lalbegi, Balmiki, Korar or Zadmalli.
5. Chalvadi or Channayya
6. Chenna Dasar or Holaya Dasar
7. Dhor, Kakkayya or Kangayya
8. Garoda or Garo
9. Halleer
10. Halsar, Halsar, Hulasvar or Halasvar
11. Holar or Valhar
12. Holaya or Holer
13. Lingader
14. Mahar, Taral or Dhegu Megu
15. Mahyavanshi, Dhed, Vankar or Maru Vankar
16. Mang, Matang or Minimadig
17. Mang-Garudi
18. Meghaval or Menghvar
19. Mukri
20. Nadia or Hadi
21. Pasi

22. Shenva, Chenva, Sedma or Ravat
23. Tirgar or Tirbanda
24. Turi

4. In Sunel Tappa of Jhalawar district :—

1. Bagri or Bagdi
2. Balai
3. Banchada
4. Barahar or Basod
5. Bargunda
6. Bedia
7. Bhangi or Mehtar
8. Bhanumati
9. Chamar, Bairwa, Bhambi, Jatav, Mochi or Regar
10. Chidar
11. Dhanuk
12. Dhed
13. Dom
14. Kanjar
15. Khatik
16. Koli or Kori
17. Kotwal
18. Mahar
19. Mang or Mang Garodi
20. Meghwal
21. Nat, Kalbelia or Sapera
22. Pardhi
23. Pasi
24. Sansi
25. Zamral

PART XII — UTTAR PRADESH

1. Throughout the State :—

1. Agariya
2. Badi
3. Badhik
4. Baheliya
5. Baiga
6. Baiswar
7. Bajaniya
8. Bajgi
9. Balahar
10. Balai
11. Balmiki
12. Bangali
13. Banmanus
14. Bansphor
15. Barwar
16. Basor
17. Bawariya
18. Beldar
19. Beriya
20. Bhantu
21. Bhuiya
22. Bhuyiar

23. Boria
24. Chamar, Dhusia, Jhusia or Jatava
25. Chero
26. Dabgar
27. Dhangar
28. Dhanuk
29. Dharkar
30. Dhobi
31. Dom
32. Domar
33. Dusadh
34. Gharami
35. Ghasiya
36. Gual
37. Habura
38. Hari
39. Hela
40. Kalabaz
41. Kanjar
42. Kapariya
43. Karwal
44. Khairaha
45. Khorot
46. Kharwar excluding Benbansi
47. Khatik
48. Kol
49. Korwa
50. Lalbegi
51. Majhwar
52. Mazhabi
53. Musahar
54. Nat
55. Pankha
56. Parahiya
57. Pasi or Tarmali
58. Patari
59. Rawat
60. Saharya
61. Sanaurhiya
62. Sansiya
63. Shilpkar
64. Turaiha

2. Throughout the State excluding Agra, Meerut and Rohilkhand divisions : —

Kori

3. In Bundelkhand division and the portion of Mirzapur district south of Kaimur Range : —

Gond

PART XIII — WEST BENGAL

1. Throughout the State : —

1. Bauri

2. Chamar, Charmakar, Mochi, Muchi, Rabidas, Ruidas or Rishi
3. Dhoba or Dhobi
4. Dom or Dhangad
5. Dosadh or Dusadh including Dhari or Dharhi
6. Ghasi
7. Lalbegi
8. Musahar
9. Pan or Sawasi
10. Pasi
11. Rajwar
12. Turi

2. Throughout the State *except* in the Purulia district and the territories transferred from the Purnea district of Bihar :—

1. Bagdi or Duley	2. Bahelia
3. Baiti	4. Bediya
5. Beldar	6. Bhuimali
7. Bhuiya	8. Bind
9. Damai (Nepali)	10. Doai
11. Gonrhi	12. Hari
13. Jalia Kaibartta	14. Jhalo Malo or Malo
15. Kadar	16. Kami (Nepali)
17. Kandra	18. Kaora
19. Karenga or Koranga	20. Kaur
21. Keot or Keyot	22. Khaira
23. Khatik	24. Koch
25. Konai	26. Konwar
27. Kotal	28. Lohar
29. Mahar	30. Mallah
31. Mal	32. Mehtor
33. Namasudra	34. Nuniya
35. Paliya	36. Patni

37. Pod or Poundra
38. Rajbanshi
39. Sarki (Nepali)
40. Sunri excluding Saha
41. Tiyar

3. In the Purulia district and the territories transferred from the Purnea district or Bihar : —

1. Bantar
2. Bhogta
3. Chaupal
4. Dabgar
5. Halalkhor
6. Hari, Mehtar or Bhangi
7. Kanjar
8. Kurariar
9. Nat

4. In the territories transferred from the Purnea district or Bihar : —

Bhumij."

SCHEDULED II

[See Paragraph 2 (2)]

Modification to the Constitution (Scheduled Castes) (Part C States) Order. 1951

1. In paragraph 1, for "Part C States", substitute "Union Territories".

2. In paragraph 2, for "Parts I to IX" and "States", substitute "Parts I to IV" and "Union Territories" repectively.

3. For paragraph 4, substitute : —

"4 Any reference in this Order to a Union Territory shall be construed as a reference to the territory constituted as a Union Territory as from the 1st day of November, 1956."

4. For the Schedule, substitute : —

THE SCHEDULE

PART I — DELHI

Throughout the Union Territory : —

1. Adi Dharmi
2. Agria

3. Aheria
4. Balai
5. Banjara
6. Bawaria
7. Bazigar
8. Bhangi
9. Bhil
10. Chamar, Chanwar, Chamar, Jatya or Jatav Chamar, Mochi, Ramdasia, Ravidasi, Rehgarh or Raigar.
11. Chohra (Sweeper)
12. Chuhra (Balmiki)
13. Dhanak or Dhanuk
14. Dhobi
15. Dom
16. Gharrami
17. Julaha (Weaver)
18. Kabirpanthi
19. Kachhandha
20. Kanjar or Giarah
21. Khatik
22. Koli
23. Lalbegi
24. Madari
25. Mallah
26. Mazhabi
27. Meghwal
28. Naribut
29. Nat (Rana)
30. Pasi
31. Perna
32. Sansi or Bhedkut
33. Sapera
34. Sikligar
35. Singiwala or Kalbelia
36. Sirkiband

PART II — HIMACHAL PRADESH

Throughout the Union Territory :—

1. Ad-dharmi
2. Badhi or Nagalu
3. Bandhela
4. Balmiki, Chura or Bhangi
5. Bangali
6. Banjara
7. Bansi
8. Barad
9. Barar
10. Batwal
11. Bawaria
12. Bazigar
13. Bhanjra
14. Chamar, Mochi, Ramdasi, Ravidasi or Ramdasia
15. Chanal
16. Chhimbe (Dhobi)

17. Chuhre
18. Dagi
19. Daole
20. Darai or Daryai
21. Daule
22. Dhaki or Toori
23. Dhaogri or Dhuai
24. Doom or Doomna
25. Dumne (Bhanjre)
26. Hali
27. Hesi
28. Jogi
29. Julahe or Keer
30. Kabirpanthi, Julaha
31. Kamoh or Dagoli
32. Karoack
33. Khatik
34. Koli
35. Lohar
36. Mazhabi
37. Megh
38. Nat
39. Od
40. Pasi
41. Phrera
42. Rehar
43. Rehara
44. Sansi
45. Sapela
46. Sarde, Sarare or Siryare
47. Sarehde
48. Sikligar
49. Sipi
50. Sirkiband
51. Teli
52. Thathiar or Thathera

PART III — MANIPUR

Throughout the Union Territory :—

1. Dhupi or Dhobi
2. Lois
3. Muchi or Ravidas
4. Namasudra
5. Patni
6. Sutradhar
7. Yaithibi

PART IV — TRIPURA

Throughout the Union Territory :—

1. Bagdi
2. Baiti
3. Bhuimali
4. Bhunar
5. Chamar or Muchi
6. Dandasi
7. Dhenuar
8. Dhoba

9. Duai
10. Dum
11. Ghasi
12. Gour
13. Gunar
14. Gur
15. Gorang
16. Jalia Kaibarta
17. Kahar
18. Kalindi
19. Kan
20. Kanda
21. Kanugh
22. Keot
23. Khadit
24. Kharia
25. Khemcha
26. Koch
27. Koir
28. Kol
29. Kora
30. Kotal
31. Mahisyadas
32. Mali
33. Mehtor
34. Musahar
35. Namsudra
36. Patni
37. Sabar.

JAMMU & KASHMIR

(The Constitution (Jammu & Kashmir) Scheduled Castes Order, 1956, C.O. 52)

Scheduled Castes

1. Barwala
2. Basith
3. Batwal
4. Chamar or Ramdasia
5. Chura
6. Dhyar
7. Doom or Mahasha
8. Gardi
9. Jolaha
10. Megh or Kabirpanthi
11. Ratal
12. Saryara
13. Watal.

The Bombay Reorganisation Act, 1966

GUJARAT

(1) Throughout the State *except* the Rajkot Division and the district of Kutch :—

1. Ager
2. Bakad or Bant
3. Bhambi, Bhambhi, Asadaru, Asodi, Chamadia, Chamar, Chambhar, Chamgar, Haralayya, Harali, Khalpa, Machigar, Mochigar, Madar, Madig, Telegu Mochi, Kamati Mochi, Ranigar, Rohidas, Rohit or Samgar
4. Bhangi, Mehtar, Olgana, Rukhi, Malkana, Halalkhor, Lalbegi, Balmiki, Korar or Zadmalli
5. Chalvadi or Channayya
6. Chenna Dasar or Holaya Dasar
7. Dhor, Kakkayya or Kankayya
8. Garoda or Garo

9. Halleer
10. Halsar, Haslar, Hulasvar or Halasvar
11. Holar or Valhar
12. Holaya or Holer
13. Lingader
14. Mahar, Taral or Dhegu Megu
15. Mahyavanshi, Dhed, Vankar or Maru Vankar
16. Mang, Matang or Minimadig
17. Mang-Garudi
18. Meghval or Menghvar
19. Mukri
20. Nadia or Hadi
21. Pasi
22. Shenva, Chenva, Sedma or Rawat
23. Tirgar or Tirbanda
24. Turi

(2) In the district of Dangs and Umbergaon taluka of Surat district :—

Mochi.

(3) In the Rajkot Division :—

1. Bawa (Dedh) or Dedh-Sadhu
2. Bhangi or Rukhi
3. Chamadia
4. Chamar, Nalia or Rohit
5. Dangashia
6. Garoda
7. Garmatang
8. Hadi
9. Meghwal
10. Senva
11. Shemalia
12. Thori
13. Turi
14. Turi-Barot or Dedh-Barot
15. Vankar, Dhedh or Antyaj.

(4) In the district of Kutch :—

1. Bhangi
2. Chamar

3. Garoda
4. Meghwal
5. Turi
6. Turi-Barot.

MAHARASHTRA

1. Throughout the State *except* the districts of Buldana, Akola, Amravati, Yeotmal, Wardha, Nagpur, Bhandara, Chanda, Aurangabad, Parbhani, Nanded, Bhir, Osmanabad and Rajura:—

1. Ager
2. Baked or Bant
3. Bhambi, Bhambhi, Asadaru, Asodi, Chamadia, Chamar, Chambhar, Chamgar, Haralayya, Harali, Khalpa, Machigar, Mochigar, Madar, Madig, Mochi, Telegu Mochi, Kamati Mochi, Ranigar, Rohidas, Rohit or Samgar
4. Bhangi, Mehtar, Olgana, Rukhi, Malkana, Halalkhor, Lalbegi, Balmiki, Kerar or Zadmalli
5. Chalvadi or Channayya
6. Chenna Dasar or Holaya Dasar
7. Dhor, Kakkayya or Kankayya
8. Garoda or Garo
9. Halleer
10. Halsar, Haslar, Hulasvar or Halasvar
11. Holar or Valhar
12. Holaya or Holer
13. Lingader
14. Mahar, Taral or Dhegu Megu
15. Mahyavanshi, Dhed, Vankar or Maru Vankar
16. Mang, Matang or Minimadig
17. Mang-Garudi
18. Meghval or Menghvar
19. Mukri
20. Nadia or Hadi
21. Pasi
22. Shenva, Chenva, Sedma or Ravat

23. Tirgar or Tirbanda
24. Turi

2. In the districts of Buldana, Akola, Amravati, Yeotmal, Wardha, Nagpur, Bhandara and Chanda :—

1. Bahna or Bahana
2. Balahi or Balai
3. Basor, Burud, Bansor or Bansodi
4. Chamar, Chamari, Mochi, Nona, Rohidas, Ramnami, Satnami, Surjabanshi or Surjyaramnami
5. Dom or Dumar
6. Dohor
7. Ganda or Gandi
8. Ghasi or Ghasia
9. Kaikadi
10. Katia or Patharia
11. Khatik, Chikwa or Chikvi
12. Madgi
13. Mahar or Mehra
14. Mang, Dankhni-Mang, Mang Mahashi, Mang-Garudi, Madari, Garudi or Radhe-Mang
15. Mehtar or Bhangi
16. Sansi

3. In the districts of Akola, Amravati and Buldana :—

Bedar

4. In the district of Bhandara :—

1. Chadar 2. Holiya

5. In the districts of Bhandara and Buldana :—

Khangar, Kanera or Mirdha

6. In the districts of Amravati, Bhandara and Buldana :—

Kori

7. In the districts of Aurangabad, Parbhani, Nanded, Rajura, Bhir and Osmanabad :—

1. Anamuk
2. Aray (Mala)
3. Arwa Mala
4. Beda (Budga) Jangam
5. Bindla
6. Byagara
7. Chalvadi
8. Chambhar
9. Dakkal (Dokkalwar)
10. Dhor
11. Ellamalwar (Yellammalawandlu)
12. Holeya
13. Holeya Dasari
14. Kolupulvandlu
15. Madiga
16. Mahar
17. Mala
18. Mala Dasari
19. Mala Hannai
20. Malajangam
21. Mala Masti
22. Mala Sale (Netkani)
23. Mala Sanyasi
24. Mang
25. Mang Garodi
26. Manne
27. Mashti
28. Mehtar
29. Mitha Ayyalvar
30. Mochi
31. Samagara
32. Sindhollu (Chindollu)."

DADRA AND NAGAR HAVELI

(The Constitution (Dadra and Nagar Haveli) Scheduled Castes Order, 1962, C.O. 64.)

Scheduled Castes

1. Bhangi
2. Chamar
3. Mahar
4. Mahyavanshi, Dhed

PONDICHERRY

(The Constitution (Pondicherry) Scheduled Castes Order, 1964, C.O. 68)

Scheduled Castes

1. Adi Andhra
2. Adi Dravida
3. Chakkiliyan
4. Jambuvulu
5. Kuravan
6. Madiga

7. Mala, Mala Masti
8. Paky
9. Pallan
10. Paryan, Sambavar
11. Samban
12. Thoti
13. Valluvan
14. Vetan
15. Vettiyan.

THE PUNJAB REORGANISATION ACT, 1966

Amendment of the Constitution (Scheduled Castes) Order, 1950

(2) After Part IV, the following Part shall be inserted, namely :—

"PART IVA—HARYANA

(1) Throughout the State :—

1. Ad Dharmi
2. Bangali
3. Barar, Burar or Berar
4. Batwal
5. Bauria or Bawaria
6. Bazigar
7. Balmiki, Chura or Bhangi
8. Bhanjra
9. Chamar, jatia Chamar, Rehgar, Raigar, Ramdas or Ravidasi
10. Chanal
11. Dagi
12. Dhanak
13. Dumna, Mahasha or Doom
14. Gagra
15. Gandhila or Gandil Gondola
16. Kabirpanthi or Julaha
17. Khatik
18. Kori or Koli
19. Marija or Marecha
20. Mazhabi
21. Megh
22. Nat
23. Od
24. Pasi
25. Perna
26. Pherera
27. Sanhai
28. Sanhal
29. Sansi, Bhedkut or Manesh
30. Sapela
31. Sarera
32. Sikligar
33. Sirkiband.

(2) Throughout the State *except* in the Mahendragarh and Jind districts :—

1. Darain
2. Dhogri, Dhangri or Siggi
3. Sansoi

(3) In the Mahendragarh and Jind districts :—

Deha, Dhaya, or Dhea."

(3) In Part X omit the word "Mohindergarh" occurring in paragraphs 2 and 3 thereof.

AMENDMENT OF THE CONSTITUTION (SCHEDULED CASTES)

(UNION TERRITORIES) ORDER, 1951

HIMACHAL PRADESH

(2) In Part II of the Schedule—

(a) for the words "Throughout the Union territory", the figures, words and brackets "1. Throughout the Union territory *except* the territories specified in sub-section *(1)* of section 5 of the Punjab Reorgansiation Act, 1966" shall be substituted;

(b) the following shall be added at the end :—

"2. In the territories specified in sub-section *(1)* of section 5 of the Punjab Reorganisation Act, 1966 :—

1. Ad Dharmi
2. Bangali
3. Barar, Burar or Berar
4. Batwal
5. Bauria or Bawaria
6. Bazigar
7. Balmiki, Chura or Bhangi
8. Bhanjra
9. Chamar, Jatia Chamar, Rehgar, Raigar, Ramdasi or Ravidasi
10. Chanal
11. Dagi
12. Darain
13. Dhanak
14. Dhogri, Dhangri or Siggi
15. Dumna, Mahasha or Doom
16. Gagra
17. Gandhila or Gandil Gondola
18. Kabirpanthi or Julaha
19. Khatik
20. Kori or Koli
21. Marija or Marecha

22. Mazhabi
23. Megh
24. Nat
25. Od
26. Pasi
27. Perna
28. Pherera
29. Sanhai
30. Sanhal
31. Sansoi
32. Sansi, Bhedkut or Manesh
33. Sapela
34. Sarera
35. Sikligar
36. Sirkiband."

(3) After Part IV, the following Part shall be inserted :—

"PART V — CHANDIGARH

1. Ad Dharmi
2. Bangali
3. Barar, Burar or Berar
4. Batwal
5. Bauria or Bawaria
6. Bazigar
7. Balmiki, Chura or Bhangi
8. Bhanjra
9. Chamar, Jatia Chamar, Rehgar, Raigar, Ramdas or Ravidasi
10. Chanal
11. Dagi
12. Darain
13. Dhanak
14. Dhogri, Dhangri or Siggi
15. Dumna, Mahasha or Doom
16. Gagra
17. Gandhila or Gandil Gondola
18. Kabirpanthi or Julaha
19. Khatik
20. Kori or Koli
21. Marija or Marecha
22. Mazhabi
23. Megh
24. Nat
25. Od
26. Pasi
27. Perna
28. Pherera
29. Sanhai
30. Sanhal
31. Sansoi
32. Sansi, Bhedkut or Manesh
33. Sapela
34. Sarera
35. Sikligar
36. Sirkiband."

GOA, DAMAN AND DIU

(The Constitution (Goa, Daman & Diu) Scheduled Castes Order, 1968 C.O. 81)

Scheduled Castes

1. Bhangi, Hadi
2. Chambhar
3. Mahar
4. Mahyavanshi, Vankar
5. Mang

The North-Eastern Areas (Reorganisation) Act, 1971.

Scheduled Castes

MANIPUR

Throughout the State :—

1. Dhupi or Dhobi
2. Lois
3. Muchi or Ravidas
4. Namasudra
5. Patni
6. Sutradhar
7. Yaithibi

TRIPURA

Throughout the State :—

1. Bagdi
2. Baiti
3. Bhuimali
4. Bhunar
5. Chamar or Muchi
6. Dandasi
7. Dhenuar
8. Dhoba
9. Duai
10. Dum
11. Ghasi
12. Gour

13. Gunar
14. Gur
15. Gorang
16. Jalia Kaibartta
17. Kahar
18. Kalindi
19. Kan
20. Kanda
21. Kanugh
22. Keot
23. Khadit
24. Kharia
25. Khemcha
26. Koch
27. Koir
28. Kol
29. Kora
30. Kotal
31. Mahisyadas
32. Mali
33. Mehtor
34. Musahar
35. Namasudra
36. Patni
37. Sabar

MEGHALAYA

Throughout the State :—

1. Bansphor
2. Bhuinmali
3. Brittial Bania, Bania
4. Dhupi, Dhobi
5. Dugla, Dholi
6. Hira
7. Jalkeot
8. Jhalo, Malo, Jhalo-Malo
9. Kaibartta, Jaliya
10. Lalbegi
11. Mahara
12. Mehtar, Bhangi
13. Muchi, Rishi
14. Namasudra
15. Patni
16. Sutradhar

ARUNACHAL PRADESH

Throughout the Union Territory :—

1. Bansphor
2. Bhuinmali, Mali
3. Brittial Bania, Bania
4. Dhupi, Dhobi
5. Dugla, Dholi
6. Hira
7. Jalkeot
8. Jhalo Malo, Jhalo-Malo

9. Kaibartta, Jaliya
10. Lalbegi
11. Mahara
12. Mehtar, Bhangi
13. Muchi, Rishi
14. Namasudra
15. Patni
16. Sutradhar

MIZORAM

Throughout the Union Territory :—

1. Bansphor
2. Bhuinmali, Mali
3. Brittial Bania, Bania
4. Dhupi, Dhobi
5. Dugla, Dholi
6. Hira
7. Jalkeot
8. Jhalo, Malo, Jhalo-Malo
9. Kaibartta, Jaliya
10. Lalbegi
11. Mahara
12. Mehtar, Bhangi
13. Muchi, Rishi
14. Namasudra
15. Patni
16. Sutradhar

THE 1976 ORDER RELATING TO THE SCHEDULED CASTES

"THE SCHEDULE

PART I — ANDHRA PRADESH

1. Adi Andhra
2. Adi Dravida
3. Anamuk
4. Aray Mala
5. Arundhatiya
6. Arwa Mala
7. Bariki
8. Bavuri
9. Beda Jangam, Budga Jangam
10. Bindla
11. Byagara
12. Chachati
13. Chalavadi
14. Chamar, Mochi, Muchi
15. Chambhar
16. Chandala
17. Dakkal, Dokkalwar
18. Dandasi
19. Dhor
20. Dom, Dombara, Paidi, Pano
21. Ellamalawar, Yellammalawandlu
22. Ghasi, Haddi, Relli Chachandi
23. Godagali
24. Godari
25. Gosangi
26. Holeya
27. Holeya Dasari
28. Jaggali
29. Jambuvulu
30. Kolupulvandlu
31. Madasi Kuruva, Madari Kuruva
32. Madiga
33. Madiga Dasu, Mashteen
34. Mahar
35. Mala
36. Mala Dasari
37. Mala Dasu
38. Mala Hannai
39. Malajangam

40. Mala Masti
41. Mala Sale, Netkani
42. Mala Sanyasi
43. Mang
44. Mang Garodi
45. Manne
46. Mashti
47. Matangi
48. Mehtar
49. Mitha Ayyalvar
50. Mundala
51. Paky, Moti, Thoti
52. Pambada, Pambanda
53. Pamidi
54. Panchama, Pariah
55. Relli
56. Sámagara
57. Samban
58. Sapru
59. Sindhollu, Chindollu

PART II — ASSAM

1. Bansphor
2. Bhuinmali, Mail
3. Brittial Bania, Bania
4. Dhupi, Dhobi
5. Dugla, Dholi
6. Hira
7. Jalkeot
8. Jhalo, Malo, Jhalo-Malo
9. Kaibartta, Jailya
10. Lalbegi
11. Mahara
12. Mehtar, Bhangi
13. Muchi, Rishi
14. Namasudra
15. Patni
16. Sutradhar.

PART III — BIHAR

1. Bantar
2. Bauri
3. Bhogta
4. Bhuiya
5. Bhumij (excluding North Chotanagpur and South Chotanagpur divisions and Santal Parganas district)
6. Chamar, Mochi
7. Chaupal
8. Dabgar

9. Dhobi
10. Dom, Dhangad
11. Dusadh, Dhari, Dharhi
12. Ghasi
13. Halalkhor
14. Hari, Mehtar, Bhangi
15. Kanjar
16. Kurariar
17. Lalbegi
18. Musahar
19. Nat
20. Pan, Sawasi
21. Pasi
22. Rajwar
23. Turi

PART IV — GUJARAT

1. Ager
2. Bakad, Bant
3. Bawa-Dedh, Dedh-Sadhu
4. Bhambi, Bhambhi, Asadaru, Asodi, Chamadia, Chamar, Chambhar, Chamgar, Haralayya, Harali, Khalpa, Machigar, Mochigar, Madar, Madig, Mochi, Nalia, Telegu Mochi, Kamati Mochi, Ranigar, Rohidas, Rohit, Samgar
5. Bhangi, Mehtar, Olgana, Rukhi, Malkana, Halalkhor, Lalbegi, Balmiki, Korar, Zadmalli
6. Chalvadi, Channayya
7. Chenna Dasar, Holaya Dasar
8. Dangashia
9. Dhor, Kakkayya, Kankayya
10. Garmatang
11. Garoda, Garo
12. Halleer

13. Halsar, Haslar, Hulasvar, Halasvar
14. Holar, Valhar
15. Holaya, Holer
16. Lingader
17. Mahar, Taral, Dhegu Megu
18. Mahyavanshi, Dhed, Dhedh, Vankar, Maru Vankar, Antyaj
19. Mang, Matang, Minimadig
20. Mang-Garudi
21. Meghval, Meghwal, Menghvar
22. Mukri
23. Nadia, Hadi
24. Pasi
25. Senva, Shenva, Chenva, Sedma, Rawat
26. Shemalia
27. Thori
28. Tirgar, Tirbanda
29. Turi
30. Turi Barot, Dedh Barot.

PART V — HARYANA

1. Ad Dharmi
2. Balmiki, Chura, Bhangi
3. Bangali
4. Barar, Burar, Berar
5. Batwal
6. Bauria, Bawaria
7. Bazigar
8. Bhanjra
9. Chamar, Jatia Chamar, Rehgar, Raigar, Ramdasi, Ravidasi
10. Chanal
11. Dagi
12. Darain
13. Deha, Dhaya, Dhea
14. Dhanak
15. Dhogri, Dhangri, Siggi
16. Dumna, Mahasha, Doom
17. Gagra
18. Gandhila, Gandil Gondola
19. Kabirpanthi, Julaha

20. Khatik
21. Kori, Koli
22. Marija, Marecha
23. Mazhabi
24. Megh
25. Nat
26. Od
27. Pasi
28. Perna
29. Pherera
30. Sanhai
31. Sanhal
32. Sansi, Bhedkut, Manesh
33. Sansoi
34. Sapela
35. Sarera
36. Sikligar
37. Sirkiband.

PART VI — HIMACHAL PRADESH

1. Ad Dharmi
2. Badhi, Nagalu
3. Balmiki, Bhangi, Chuhra, Chura, Chuhre
4. Bandhela
5. Bangali
6. Banjara
7. Bansi
8. Barad
9. Barar, Burar, Berar
10. Batwal
11. Bauria, Bawaria
12. Bazigar
13. Bhanjra, Bhanjre
15. Chanal
14. Chamar, Jatia Chamar, Rehgar, Raigar, Ramdasi, Ravidasi, Ramdasia, Mochi
16. Chhimbe, Dhobi
17. Dagi
18. Darain
19. Darai, Daryai
20. Daule, Daole
21. Dhaki, Toori
22. Dhanak
23. Dhaogri, Dhuai
24. Dhogri, Dhangri, Siggi
25. Doom, Doomna, Dumna, Dumne, Mahasha
26. Gagra
27. Gandhila, Gandil Gondola
28. Hali
29. Hesi
30. Jogi
31. Julaha, Julahe, Kabirpanthi, Keer
32. Kamoh, Dagoli
33. Karoack
34. Khatik

35. Kori, Koli
36. Lohar
37. Marija, Marecha
38. Mazhabi
39. Megh
40. Nat
41. Od
42. Pasi
43. Perna
44. Phrera, Pherera
45. Rehar, Rehara
46. Sanhai
47. Sanhal
48. Sansi, Bhedkut, Manesh
49. Sansoi
50. Sapela
51. Sarde, Sarera, Sarare, Siryare, Sarehde
52. Sikligar
53. Sipi
54. Sirkiband
55. Teli
56. Thathiar, Thathera

PART VII — KARNATAKA

1. Adi Andhra
2. Adi Dravida
3. Adi Karnataka
4. Adiya (in Coorg district)
5. Ager
6. Ajila
7. Anamuk
8. Aray Mala
9. Arunthathiyar
10. Arwa Mala
11. Baira
12. Bakad
13. Bant (in Belgaum, Bijapur, Dharwar and North Kanara districts)
14. Bakuda
15. Balagai
16. Bandi

17. Banjara, Lambani
18. Bathada
19. Beda Jangam, Budga Jangam
20. Bellara
21. Bhangi, Mehtar, Olgana, Rukhi, Malkana, Halalkhor, Lalbegi, Balmiki, Korar, Zadmalli
22. Bhambi, Bhambhi, Asadaru, Asodi, Chamadia, Chamar, Chambhar, Chamgar, Haralayya, Harali, Khalpa, Machigar, Mochigar, Madar, Madig, Mochi, Muchi, Telegu Mochi, Kamati Mochi, Ranigar, Rohidas, Rohit, Samgar
23. Bhovi
24. Bindla
25. Byagara
26. Chakkiliyan
27. Chalavadi, Chalvadi, Channayya
28. Chandala
29. Chenna Dasar, Holaya Dasar
30. Dakkal, Dokkalwar
31. Dakkaliga
32. Dhor, Kakkayya, Kankayya
33. Dom, Dombara, Paidi, Pano
34. Ellamalwar, Yellammalawandlu
35. Ganti Chores
36. Garoda, Garo
37. Godda
38. Gosangi
39. Halleer
40. Halsar, Haslar, Hulasvar, Halasvar
41. Handi Jogis
42. Hasla
43. Holar, Valhar
44. Holaya, Holer, Holeya

45. Holeya Dasari
46. Jaggali
47. Jambuvulu
48. Kadaiyan
49. Kalladi
50. Kepmaris
51. Kolupulvandlu
52. Koosa
53. Koracha
54. Korama
55. Kotegar, Metri
56. Kudumban
57. Kuravan
58. Lingader
59. Machala
60. Madari
61. Madiga
62. Mahar, Taral, Dhegu Megu
63. Mahyavanshi, Dhed, Vankar or Maru Vankar
64. Maila
65. Mala
66. Mala Dasari
67. Mala Hannai
68. Mala Jangam
69. Mala Masti
70. Mala Sale, Netkani
71. Mala Sanyasi
72. Mang, Matang, Minimadig
73. Mang Garudi, Mang Garodi
74. Manne
75. Masthi
76. Mavilan

77. Meghval, Menghvar
78. Moger
79. Mukri
80. Mundala
81. Nadia, Hadi
82. Nalkadaya
83. Nalakeyava
84. Nayadi
85. Pale
86. Pallan
87. Pambada
88. Panchama
89. Panniandi
90. Paraiyan, Paraya
91. Paravan
92. Raneyar
93. Samagara
94. Samban
95. Sapari
96. Sillekyathas
97. Sindhollu, Chindollu
98. Sudugadu Sidda
99. Thoti
100. Tirgar, Tirbanda
101. Valluvan.

PART VIII — KERALA

1. Adi Andhra
2. Adi Dravida
3. Adi Karnataka
4. Ajila
5. Arunthathiyar

6. Ayyanavar
7. Baira
8. Bakuda
9. Bandi
10. Bathada
11. Bellara
12. Bharatar
13. Boyan [excluding the areas comprising the Malabar district as specified by sub-section (2) of section 5 of the States Reorganisation Act, 1956 (37 to 1956)]
14. Chakkiliyan
15. Chamar, Muchi
16. Chandala
17. Cheruman
18. Domban
19. Gavara
20. Godagali
21. Godda
22. Gosangi
23. Hasla
24. Holeya
25. Kadaiyan
26. Kakkalan
27. Kalladi
28. Kanakkan, Padanna
29. Karimpalan
30. Kavara
31. Koosa
32. Kootan, Koodan
33. Kudumban
34. Kuravan, Sidhanar
35. Maila
36. Malayan [in the areas comprising the Malabar

district as specified by sub-section (2) of section 5 of the States Reorganisation Act, 1956 (37 to 1956)]

37. Mannan
38. Mavilan
39. Moger
40. Mundala
41. Nalakeyava
42. Nalkadaya
43. Nayadi
44. Padannan
45. Pallan
46. Palluvan
47. Pambada
48. Panan
49. Panchama
50. Paraiyan, Parayan, Sambavar
51. Paravan
52. Pathiyan
53. Perumannan
54. Pulayan, Cheramar
55. Pulaya Vettuvan
56. Puthirai Vannan
57. Raneyar
58. Samagara
59. Samban
60. Semman
61. Thandan
62. Thoti
63. Vallon
64. Valluvan
65. Vannan
66. Velan
67. Vetan
68. Vettuvan.

PART IX — MADHYA PRADESH

1. Audhelia
2. Bagri, Bagdi
3. Bahna, Bahana
4. Balahi, Balai
5. Banchada
6. Barahar, Basod
7. Bargunda
8. Basor, Burud, Bansor, Bansodi, Bansphor, Basar
9. Bedia
10. Beldar, Sunkar
11. Bhangi, Mehtar, Balmiki, Lalbegi, Dharkar
12. Bhanumati
13. Chadar
14. Chamar, Chamari, Bairwa, Bhambi, Jatav, Mochi, Regar, Nona, Rohidas, Ramnami, Satnami, Surjyabanshi, Surjyaramnami, Ahirwar, Chamar Mangan, Raidas
15. Chidar
16. Chikwa, Chikvi
17. Chitar
18. Dahait, Dahayat, Dahat
19. Dewar
20. Dhanuk
21. Dhed, Dher
22. Dhobi (in Bhopal, Raisen and Sehore districts)
23. Dohor
24. Dom, Dumar, Dome, Domar, Doris
25. Ganda, Gandi
26. Ghasi, Ghasia
27. Holiya
28. Kanjar

29. Katia, Patharia
30. Khatik
31. Koli, Kori
32. Kotwal (in Bhind, Dhar, Dewas, Guna, Gwalior, Indore, Jhabua, Khargone, Mandsaur, Morena, Rajgarh, Ratlam, Shajapur, Shivpuri, Ujjan and Vidisha districts)
33. Khangar, Kanera, Mirdha
34. Kuchbandhia
35. Kumhar (in Chhatarpur, Datia, Panna, Rewa, Satna, Shahdol, Sidhi and Tikamgarh districts)
36. Mahar, Mehra, Mehar
37. Mang, Mang Garodi, Mang Garudi, Dankhni Mang, Mang Mahasi, Madari, Garudi, Radhe Mang
38. Meghwal
39. Moghia
40. Muskhan
41. Nat, Kalbelia, Sapera, Navdigar, Kubutar
42. Pardhi (in Bhind, Dhar, Dewas, Guna, Gwalior, Indore, Jhabua, Khargone, Mandsaur, Morena, Rajgarh, Ratlam, Shajapur, Shivpuri, Ujjain and Vidisha districts)
43. Pasi
44. Rujjhar
45. Sansi, Sansia
46. Silawat
47. Zamral.

PART X — MAHARASHTRA

1. Ager
2. Anamuk
3. Aray Mala
4. Arwa Mala
5. Bahna, Bahana
6. Bakad, Bant
7. Balahi, Balai

8. Basor, Burud, Bansor, Bansodi
9. Beda Jangam, Budga, Jangam
10. Bedar
11. Bhambi, Bhambhi, Asadaru, Asodi, Chamadia, Chamar, Chamari, Chambhar, Chamgar, Haralayya, Harali, Khalpa, Machigar, Mochigar, Madar, Madig, Mochi, Telegu Mochi, Kamati Mochi, Ranigar, Rohidas, Nona, Ramnami, Rohit, Samgar, Samagara, Satnami, Surjyabanshi, Surjyaramnami
12. Bhangi, Mehtar, Olgana, Rukhi, Malkana, Halalkhor, Lalbegi, Balmiki, Korar, Zadmalli
13. Bindla
14. Byagara
15. Chalvadi, Channayya
16. Chenna Dasar, Holaya Daṣar, Holeya Dasari
17. Dakkal, Dokkalwar
18. Dhor, Kakkayya, Kankayya, Dohor
19. Dom, Dumar
20. Ellamalvar, Yellammalawandlu
21. Ganda, Gandi
22. Garoda, Garo
23. Ghasi, Ghasia
24. Halleer
25. Halsar, Haslar, Hulasvar, Halasvar
26. Holar, Valhar
27. Holaya, Holer, Holeya, Holiya
28. Kaikadi (in Akola, Amravati, Bhandara, Buldana, Nagpur, Wardha and Yavatmal districts and Chandrapur district, other than Rajura tahsil)
29. Katia, Patharia
30. Khangar, Kanera, Mirdha
31. Khatik, Chikwa, Chikvi
32. Kolupulvandlu
33. Kori

34. Lingader
35. Madgi
36. Madiga
37. Mahar, Mehra, Taral, Dhegu Megu
38. Mahyavanshi, Dhed, Vankar, Maru Vankar
39. Mala
40. Mala Dasari
41. Mala Hannai
42. Mala Jangam
43. Mala Masti
44. Mala Sale, Netkani
45. Mala Sanyasi
46. Mang, Matang, Minimadig, Dankhni Mang, Mang Mahashi, Madari, Garudi, Radhe Mang
47. Mang Garodi, Mang Garudi
48. Manne
49. Mashti
50. Meghval, Menghvar
51. Mitha Ayyalvar
52. Mukri
53. Nadia, Hadi
54. Pasi
55. Sansi
56. Shenva, Chenva, Sedma, Ravat
57. Sindhollu, Chindollu
58. Tirgar, Tirbanda
59. Turi.

PART XI — MANIPUR

1. Dhupi, Dhobi
2. Lois
3. Muchi, Ravidas
4. Namasudra
5. Patni
6. Sutradhar
7. Yaithibi.

PART XII — MEGHALAYA

1. Bansphor
2. Bhuinmali, Mail
3. Brittial Bania, Bania
4. Dhupi, Dhobi
5. Dugla, Dhobi
6. Hira
7. Jalkeot
8. Jhalo, Malo, Jhalo-Malo
9. Kaibartta, Jailya
10. Lalbegi
11. Mahara
12. Mehtar, Bhangi
13. Muchi, Rishi
14. Namasudra
15. Patni
16. Sutradhar.

PART XIII — ORISSA

1. Adi Andhra
2. Amant, Amat
3. Audhelia
4. Badaik
5. Bagheti, Baghuti
6. Bajikar
7. Bari
8. Bariki
9. Basor, Burud
10. Bauri
11. Bauti
12. Bavuri
13. Bedia, Bejia
14. Beldar
15. Bhata
16. Bhoi
17. Chachati
18. Chakali
19. Chamar, Mochi, Muchi, Satnami
20. Chandala
21. Chandhai Maru
22. Cherua, Chhelia
23. Dandasi
24. Dewar
25. Dhanwar
26. Dhoba, Dhobi
27. Dom, Dombo, Duria Dom
28. Dosadha
29. Ganda
30. Ghantarghada or Ghantra
31. Ghasi, Ghasia
32. Ghogia
33. Ghusuria
34. Godagali
35. Godari
36. Godra
37. Gokha

38. Gorait, Korait
39. Haddi, Hadi, Hari
40. Irika
41. Jaggali
42. Kandra, Kandara
43. Karua
44. Katia
45. Kela
46. Khadala
47. Kodalo, Khodalo
48. Kori
49. Kummari
50. Kurunga
51. Laban
52. Laheri
53. Madari
54. Madiga
55. Mahuria
56. Mala, Jhala, Malo, Zala
57. Mang
58. Mangan
59. Mehra, Mahar
60. Mehtar, Bhangi
61. Mewar
62. Mundapotta
63. Musahar
64. Nagarchi
65. Namasudra
66. Paidi
67. Painda
68. Pamidi
69. Pan, Pano
70. Panchama
71. Panika
72. Panka
73. Pantanti
74. Pap
75. Pasi
76. Patial, Patikar, Patratanti, Patua
77. Rajna
78. Relli
79. Sabakhia
80. Samasi
81. Sanei
82. Sapari
83. Sauntia, Santia
84. Sidhria
85. Sinduria
86. Siyal
87. Tamadia
88. Tamudia
89. Tanla
90. Tiar, Tior
91. Turi
92. Ujia
93. Valamiki, Valmiki.

PART XIV — PUNJAB

1. Ad Dharmi
2. Balmiki, Chura, Bhangi
3. Bangali
4. Barar, Burar, Berar

5. Batwal
6. Bauria, Bawaria
7. Bazigar
8. Bhanjra
9. Chamar, Jatia, Chamar, Rehgar, Raigar, Ramdasi, Ravidas
10. Chanal
11. Dagi
12. Darain
13. Deha, Dhaya, Dhea
14. Dhanak
15. Dhogri, Dhangri, Siggi
16. Dumna, Mahasha, Doom
17. Gagra
18. Gandhila, Gandil Gondola
19. Kabirpanthi, Julaha
20. Khatik
21. Kori, Koli
22. Marija, Marccha
23. Mazhabi
24. Megh
25. Nat
26. Od
27. Pasi
28. Perna
29. Pherera
30. Sanhai
31. Sanhal
32. Sansi, Bhedkut, Manesh
33. Sansoi
34. Sapela
35. Sarera
36. Sikligar
37. Sirkiband.

PART XV — RAJASTHAN

1. Adi Dharmi
2. Aheri
3. Badi
4. Bagri, Bagdi
5. Bairwa, Berwa
6. Bajgar
7. Balai
8. Bansphor, Bansphod
9. Baori
10. Bargi, Vargi, Birgi
11. Bawaria

12. Bedia, Beria
13. Bhand
14. Bhangi, Chura, Mehtar, Olgana, Rukhi, Malkana, Halalkhor, Lalbegi, Balmiki, Valmiki, Korar, Zadmalli
15. Bidakia
16. Bola
17. Chamar, Bhambhi, Bambhi, Bhambi, Jatia, Jatav, Jatava, Mochi, Raidas, Rohidas, Regar, Raigar, Ramdasia, Asadaru, Asodi, Chamadia, Chambhar, Chamgar, Haralayya, Harali, Khalpa, Machigar, Mochigar, Madar, Madig, Tẹlegu Mochi, Kamati Mochi, Ranigar, Rohit, Samgar
18. Chandal
19. Dabgar
20. Dhanak, Dhanuk
21. Dhankia
22. Dhobi
23. Dholi
24. Dome, Dom
25. Gandia
26. Garancha, Gancha
27. Garo, Garura, Gurda, Garoda
28. Gavaria
29. Godhi
30. Jingar
31. Kalbelia, Sapera
32. Kamad, Kamadia
33. Kanjar, Kunjar
34. Kapadia Sansi
35. Khangar
36. Khatik
37. Koli, Kori
38. Kooch Band, Kuchband
39. Koria

40. Madari, Bazigar
41. Mahar, Taral, Dhegumegu
42. Mahyavanshi, Dhed, Dheda, Vankar, Maru Vankar
43. Majhabi
44. Mang, Matang, Minimadig
45. Mang Garodi, Mang Garudi
46. Megh, Meghval, Meghwal, Menghvar
47. Mehar
48. Nat, Nut
49. Pasi
50. Rawal
51. Salvi
52. Sansi
53. Santia, Satia
54. Sarbhangi
55. Sargara
56. Singiwala
57. Thori, Nayak
58. Tirgar, Tirbanda
59. Turi.

PART XVI — TAMIL NADU

1. Adi Andhra
2. Adi Dravida
3. Adi Karnataka
4. Ajila
5. Arunthatiyar
6. Ayyanavar (in Kanyakumari district and Shenkottah taluk of Tirunelveli district)
7. Baira
8. Bakuda
9. Bandi
10. Bellara

11. Bharatar (in Kanyakumari district and Shenkottah taluk of Tirunelveli district)
12. Chakkiliyan
13. Chalavadi
14. Chamar, Muchi
15. Chandala
16. Cheruman
17. Devendrakulathan
18. Dom, Dombara, Paidi, Pano
19. Domban
20. Godagali
21. Godda
22. Gosangi
23. Holeya
24. Jaggali
25. Jambuvulu
26. Kadaiyan
27. Kakkalan (in Kanyakumari district and Shenkottah taluk of Tirunelveli district)
28. Kalladi
29. Kanakkan, Padanna (in the Nilgiris district)
30. Karimpalan
31. Kavara (in Kanyakumari district and Shenkottah taluk of Tirunelveli district)
32. Koliyan
33. Koosa
34. Kootan, Koodan (in Kanyakumari district and Shenkottah taluk of Tirunelveli district)
35. Kudumban
36. Kuravan, Sidhanar
37. Madari
38. Madiga
39. Maila

40. Mala
41. Mannan (in Kanyakumari district and Shenkottah taluk of Tirunelveli district)
42. Mavilan
43. Moger
44. Mundala
45. Nalakeyava
46. Nayadi
47. Padannan (in Kanyakumari district and Shenkottah taluk of Tirunelveli district)
48. Pagadai
49. Pallan
50. Palluvan
51. Pambada
52. Panan (in Kanyakumari district and Shenkottah taluk of Tirunelveli district)
53. Panchama
54. Pannadi
55. Panniandi
56. Paraiyan, Parayan, Sambavar
57. Paravan (in Kanyakumari district and Shenkottah taluk of Tirunelveli district)
58. Pathiyan (in Kanyakumari district and Shenkottah taluk of Tirunelveli district)
59. Pulayan, Cheramar
60. Puthirai Vannan
61. Raneyar
62. Samagara
63. Samban
64. Sapari
65. Semman
66. Thandan (in Kanyakumari district and Shenkottah taluk of Tirunelveli district)
67. Thoti

68. Tiruvalluvar
69. Vallon
70. Valluvan
71. Vannan (in Kanyakumari district and Shenkottah taluk of Tirunelveli district)
72. Vathiriyan
73. Velan
74. Vetan (in Kanyakumari district and Shenkottah taluk of Tirunelveli district)
75. Vettiyan
76. Vettuvan (in Kanyakumari district and Shenkottah taluk of Tirunelveli district).

PART XVII—TRIPURA

1. Bagdi
2. Bhuimali
3. Bhunar
4. Chamar, Muchi
5. Dandasi
6. Dhenuar
7. Dhoba
8. Dum
9. Ghasi
10. Gour
11. Gur
12. Jalia Kaibarta
13. Kahar
14. Kalindi
15. Kan
16. Kanda
17. Kanugh
18. Keot
19. Khadit
20. Kharia
21. Koch
22. Koir
23. Kol
24. Kora
25. Kotal
26. Mahisyadas
27. Mali
28. Mehtor
29. Musahar
30. Namasudra
31. Patni
32. Sabar.

PART XVIII — UTTAR PRADESH

1. Agariya
2. Badhik

3. Badi
4. Baheliya
5. Baiga
6. Baiswar
7. Bajaniya
8. Bajgi
9. Balahar
10. Balai
11. Balmiki
12. Bangali
13. Banmanus
14. Bansphor
15. Barwar
16. Basor
17. Bawariya
18. Beldar
19. Beriya
20. Bhantu
21. Bhuiya
22. Bhuyiar
23. Boria
24. Chamar, Dhusia, Jhusia, Jatava
25. Chero
26. Dabgar
27. Dhangar
28. Dhanuk
29. Dharkar
30. Dhobi
31. Dom
32. Domar
33. Dusadh
34. Gharami
35. Ghasiya
36. Gond
37. Gual
38. Habura
39. Hari
40. Hela
41. Kalabaz
42. Kanjar
43. Kapariya
44. Karwal
45. Khairaha
46. Kharwar (excluding Benbansi)
47. Khatik
48. Khorot
49. Kol
50. Kori
51. Korwa
52. Lalbegi
53. Majhwar
54. Mazhabi
55. Musahar
56. Nat
57. Pankha
58. Parahiya
59. Pasi, Tarmali
60. Patari
61. Rawat
62. Saharya
63. Sanaurhiya
64. Sansiya

65. Shilpkar
66. Turaiha.

PART XIX — WEST BENGAL

1. Bagdi, Duley
2. Bahelia
3. Baiti
4. Bantar
5. Bauri
6. Beldar
7. Bhogta
8. Bhuimali
9. Bhuiya
10. Bind
11. Chamar, Charmaker, Mochi, Muchi, Rabidas, Ruidas, Rishi
12. Chaupal
13. Dabgar
14. Damai (Nepali)
15. Dhoba, Dhobi
16. Doai
17. Dom, Dhangad
18. Dosadh, Dusadh, Dhari, Dharhi
19. Ghasi
20. Gonrhi
21. Halalkhor
22. Hari, Mehtar, Mehtor, Bhangi
23. Jalia Kaibartta
24. Jhalo Malo, Malo
25. Kadar
26. Kami (Nepali)
27. Kandra
28. Kanjar
29. Kaora
30. Karenga, Koranga
31. Kaur
32. Keot, Keyot
33. Khaira
34. Khatik
35. Koch
36. Konai
37. Konwar
38. Kotal
39. Kurariar
40. Lalbegi
41. Lohar
42. Mahar
43. Mal
44. Mallah
45. Musahar
46. Namasudra
47. Nat
48. Nuniya
49. Paliya
50. Pan, Sawasi
51. Pasi
52. Patni
53. Pod, Poundra
54. Rajbanshi
55. Rajwar

56. Sarki (Nepali)
57. Sunri (excluding Saha)
58. Tiyar
59. Turi.

SIKKIM

(The Constitution (Sikkim) Scheduled Castes Order, 1978, C.O. 110)

Scheduled Castes

1. Damai (Nepali)
2. Kami (Nepali), Lohar (Nepali)
3. Majhi (Nepali)
4. Sarki (Nepali)

The State of Arunachal Pradesh Act, 1986

ARUNACHAL PRADESH

Scheduled Castes

1. Bansphor
2. Bhuinmali or Mali
3. Brittial-Bania or Bania
4. Dhupi or Dhobi
5. Dugla or Dholi
6. Hira
7. Jalkeot
8. Jhalo, Malo or Jhalo-Malo
9. Kaibartta or Jaliya
10. Lalbegi
11. Mahara
12. Mehtar or Bhangi
13. Muchi or Rishi
14. Namasudra
15. Patni
16. Sutradhar.

The State of Mizoram Act, 1986

MIZORAM

Scheduled Castes

1. Bansphor
2. Bhuinmali, Mali
3. Brittial Bania, Bania
4. Dhupi, Dhobi
5. Dugla, Dholi
6. Hira
7. Jalkeot
8. Jhalo, Malo, Jhalo-Malo
9. Kaibartta, Jaiiya
10. Lalbegi
11. Mahara
12. Mehtar, Bhangi
13. Muchi, Rishi

14. Namasudra
15. Patni
16. Suthradhar.

The Goa, Daman and Diu Reorganisation Act, 1987

Scheduled Castes

The State of Goa

1. Bhangi (Hadi)
2. Chambhar
3. Mahar
4. Mahyavanshi (Vankar)
5. Mang

The Union Territory of Daman and Diu

1. Bhangi (Hadi)
2. Chambhar
3. Mahar
4. Mahyavanshi (Vankar)
5. Mang

THE CONSTITUTION (SCHEDULED TRIBES) ORDER, 1950

C.O. 22.—In exercise of the powers conferred by clause (I) of Article 342 of the Constitution of India the President, after consultation with the Governors and Rajpramukhs of the States concerned, is pleased to make the following Order, namely :—

1. This Order may be called the Constitution (Scheduled Tribes) Order, 1950.

2. The tribes or tribal communities, or parts of, or groups within, tribes or tribal communities, specified in Parts I to XIV of the Schedule to this Order shall, in relation to the States to which those Parts respectively relate, be deemed to be Scheduled Tribes so far as regards members thereof resident in the localities specified in relation to them respectively in those Parts of that Schedule.

3. Any reference in the Schedule to this Order to a district or other territorial division of a State shall be construed as a reference to that district or other territorial division as existing on the 26th January, 1950.

THE SCHEDULE

PART I—ASSAM

(1) In the Autonomous Districts :—

1. Dimasa (Kachari)
2. Garo
3. Hajong
4. Khasi and Jaintia
5. Any Kuki tribes
6. Lakher
7. Any Lushai (Mizo) tribes
8. Mikir
9. Any Naga tribes
10. Synteng

(2) In the Tribal Areas other than the Autonomous Districts :—

1. Abor
2. Aka
3. Apatani
4. Dafla
5. Galong
6. Khampti
7. Mishmi
8. Any Naga tribes
9. Singpho
10. Momba
11. Sherdukpen

(3) In the State of Assam excluding the Tribal Areas :—

1. Boro-Borokachari
2. Deori
3. Hojai
4. Kachari
5. Lalung
6. Mech
7. Miri
8. Rabha

PART II — BIHAR

(1) Throughout the State :—

1. Asur
2. Baiga
3. Bathudi
4. Bedia
5. Binjhia
6. Birhor
7. Birjia
8. Chero
9. Chik Baraik
10. Gond
11. Gorait
12. Ho
13. Karmali
14. Kharia
15. Kharwar
16. Khond
17. Kisan
18. Kora
19. Korwa
20. Lohara
21. Mahli
22. Mal Paharia
23. Munda
24. Oraon
25. Parhaiya
26. Santal
27. Sauria Paharia
28. Savar

(2) In the districts of Ranchi, Singbhum, Hazaribagh, Santal Parganas and Manbhum :—

Bhumij

PART III — BOMBAY

Throughout the State :—

1. Barda
2. Bavacha
3. Bhil, including Bhagalia, Bhil Garasia, Dholi Bhil, Dungri Bhil Dungri Garasia, Mewasi Bhil, Raval Bhil and Tadvi Bhil
4. Chodhara
5. Dhanka
6. Dhodia
7. Dubla
8. Gamit or Gamta
9. Gond
10. Kathodi or Katkari
11. Konkna
12. Koli Dhor
13. Koli Mahadev
14. Mavchi
15. Naikda or Nayak
16. Pardhi, including Advichincher and Phanse Pardhi
17. Patelia
18. Pomla
19. Powara
20. Rathawa
21. Thakur
22. Valvai
23. Varli
24. Vasava

PART IV — MADHYA PRADESH

In (1) Melghat taluk of Amravati district,

(2) Baihar tahsil of Balaghat district,

(3) Bhanupratappur, Bijapur, Dantewara, Jagdalpur, Kanker, Kondagaon, Konta and Narayanpur tahsils of Bastar district,

(4) Betul and Bhainsdehi tahsils of Betul district,

(5) Katghora tahsil of Bilaspur district,

(6) Suroncha and Gharchiroli tahsils of Chanda district,

(7) Amarwara, Chhindwara and Lakhnadon tahsils of Chhindwara district,

(8) Balod (Sanjari) tahsil of Durg district,

(9) Mandla, Niwas and Ramgarh (Dindori) tahsils of Mandla district,

(10) Harsud tahsil of Nimar district,

(11) Dharamjaigarh, Ghargoda, Jashpurnagar and Kharsia tahsils of Raigarh district,

(12) Ambikapur, Baikunthpur, Bharatpur, Janakpur, Manendragarh, Pal, Samari and Sitapur tahsils of Sarguja district :—

1. Andh
2. Baiga
3. Bhaina
4. Bharia-Bhumia, or Bhuinhar-Bhumia
5. Bhattra
6. Bhil
7. Bhunjia
8. Binjhwar
9. Birhul or Birhor
10. Dhanwar
11. Gadaba or Gadba
12. Gond [including Madia (Maria) and Mudia (Muria)]
13. Halba
14. Kamar
15. Kawar or Kanwar
16. Kharia
17. Kondh or Khond or Kandh
18. Kol
19. Kolam
20. Korku
21. Korwa
22. Majhwar
23. Munda
24. Nagesia or Nagasia
25. Nihal
26. Oraon
27. Pardhan
28. Pardhi
29. Parja
30. Saonta or Saunta
31. Sawar or Sawara

PART V — MADRAS

Throughout the State :—

1. Aranadan
2. Bagata
3. Bhottadas — Bodo Bhottada, Muria Bhottada and Sano Bhottada

4. Bhumias — Bhuri Bhumia and Bodo Bhumia
5. Chenchu
6. Gadabas — Boda Gadaba, Cerllam Gadaba, Franji Gadaba, Jodia Gadaba, Olaro Gadaba, Pangi Gadaba and Pranga Gadaba.
7. Gondi — Modya Gond and Rajo Gond.
8. Goudus — Bato, Bhirithya Dudhokouria Hato, Jatako and Joria.
9. Kosalya Goudus — Bosothoriya Goudus, Chitti Goudus, Dangayath Goudus, Doddu Kamariya, Dudu Kamaro, Ladiya Goudus and Pullosoriya Goudus.
10. Magatha Goudus — Bernia Goudu, Boodo Magatha, Dongayath Goudu, Ladya Goudu, Ponna Magatha and Sana Magatha.
11. Holva
12. Jadapus
13. Jatapus
14. Kammara
15. Kattunayakan
16. Khattis—Khatti, Kommarao and Lohara
17. Kodu
18. Kommar
19. Konda Dhoras
20. Konda Kapus
21. Kondareddis
22. Kondhs — Desaya Kondhs, Dongria Kondhs, Kuttiya Kondhs, Tikiria Kondhs and Yenity Kondhs
23. Kota
24. Kotia — Bartika, Bentho Oriya, Dhulia or Dulia, Holva Paiko, Putiya, Sanrona and Sidho Paiko.
25. Koya or Goud, with its subsects — Raj or Rasha Koyas, Lingadhari Koyas (ordinary) and Kottu Koyas.
26. Kudiya
27. Kurumans

28. Manna Dhora
29. Maune
30. Mukha Dhora — Nooka Dhora
31. Muria
32. Paigarapu
33. Palasi
34. Paniyan
35. Porjas — Bodo Bonda, Daruva, Didua Jodia, Mundili, Pengu, Pydi and Saliya
36. Reddi Dhoras
37. Savaras — Kapu Savaras, Khutto Savaras and Maliya Savaras
38. Sholaga
39. Toda
40. Inhabitants of the Laccadive, Minicoy and Amindivi Islands who, and both of whose parents, were born in these Islands.

PART VI — ORISSA

Throughout the State :—

1. Bagata
2. Baiga
3. Banjara or Banjari
4. Bathudi
5. Bhuiya or Bhuyan
6. Binjhal
7. Binjhia or Binjhoa
8. Birhor
9. Bondo Poraja
10. Chenchu
11. Dal
12. Gadaba
13. Ghara
14. Gond
15. Gorait or Korait
16. Ho
17. Jatapu
18. Juang
19. Kawar
20. Kharia or Kharian
21. Kharwar
22. Khond (Kond), or Kandha, or Nanguli Kandha, or Sitha Kandha
23. Kisan

24. Kolah-Kol-Loharas
25. Kolha
26. Koli
27. Kondadora
28. Kora
29. Korua
30. Koya
31. Kulis
32. Mahali
33. Mankidi
34. Mankirdia
35. Mirdhas
36. Munda (Munda-Lohara and Munda-Mahalis)
37. Mundari
38. Oraon
39. Paroja
40. Santal
41. Saora, or Savar, or Saura, or Sahara
42. Tharua

PART VII — PUNJAB

In Spiti and Lahaul in Kangra District :—

Tibetan

PART VIII — WEST BENGAL

Throughout the State :—

1. Bhutia
2. Lepcha
3. Mech
4. Mru
5. Munda
6. Oraon
7. Santal

PART IX — HYDERABAD

Throughout the State :—

1. Andh
2. Bhil
3. Chenchu, or Chenchwar
4. Gond (including Naikpod and Rajgond)
5. Hill Reddis
6. Kolam (including Manner varlu)
7. Koya (including Bhine Koya and Rajkoya)
8. Pardhan
9. Thoti

PART X — MADHYA BHARAT

1. Throughout the State :—

1. Gond
2. Korku
3. Seharia

2. In the Revenue District of Jhabua; in the tahsils of Sendhwa, Barwani, Rajpur, Khargone Bhikangaon and Maheshwar of the Revenue District of Khargone; in the tahsil of Sailana of the Revenue District of Ratlam; in the tahsils of Sardarpur, Kukshi, Dhar and Manawar of the Revenue District of Dhar : —

Bhils and Bhilalas (inclusive of sub-tribes)

PART XI — MYSORE

Throughout the State :—

1. Hasalaru
2. Iruliga
3. Jenu Kuruba
4. Kadu-Kuruba
5. Maleru
6. Soligaru

PART XII — RAJASTHAN

Throughout the Scheduled Areas of the State :—

Bhil

PART XIII — SAURASHTRA

Throughout the State :—

1. Adodia
2. Daffer
3. Ghantia
4. Miyana
5. Sindhi
6. Wedva Waghri

PART XIV — TRAVANCORE-COCHIN

Throughout the State : —

1. Hill Pulaya
2. Kadar

9. Malayarayar
10. Mannan

3. Kanikaran
4. Kochu Velan
5. Malai Arayan
6. Malai Pandaram
7. Malai Vedan
8. Malayan
11. Muthuvan
12. Pallcyan
13. Palliyar
14. Ulladan (Hill dwellers)
15. Uraly
16. Vishavan

THE CONSTITUTION (SCHEDULED TRIBES) (PART C STATES) ORDER, 1951

C.O. 33. — In exercise of the powers conferred by clause (I) of Article 342 of the Constitution of India, as amended by the Constitution (First Amendment) Act, 1951, the President is pleased to make the following Order, namely :—

1. This Order may be called the Constitution (Scheduled Tribes) (Part C States) Order, 1951.

2. The tribes or tribal communities, or parts of, or groups within, tribes or tribal communities, specified in Parts I to VIII of the Schedule to this Order shall, in relation to the States to which those Parts respectively relate, be deemed to be Scheduled Tribes so far as regards members thereof resident in the localities specified in relation to them respectively in those Parts of that Schedule.

3. Any reference in the Schedule to this Order to a district or other territorial division of a State shall be construed as a reference to that district or other territorial division as existing on the 26th January 1950.

THE SCHEDULE

PART I — AJMER

Throughout the State :—

1. Bhil

PART II — BHOPAL

Throughout the State :—

1. Bhil
2. Gond
3. Keer
4. Karku
5. Mogia
6. Pardhi
7. Saharia, Sosia or Sor

PART III — COORG

Throughout the State :—

1. Korama
2. Kudiya
3. Kuruba
4. Maratha
5. Meda
6. Yerava

PART IV — HIMACHAL PRADESH

In Lahaul in Chamba district and in Spiti in Madasu district :—

Tibetan

PART V — KUTCH

Throughout the State :—

1. Bhil
2. Dhodia
3. Koli
4. Paradhi
5. Vaghri

PART VI — MANIPUR

Throughout the State :—

1. Any Kuki Tribe
2. Any Lushai Tribe
3. Any Naga Tribe

PART VII — TRIPURA

Throughout the State :—

1. Lushai
2. Mag
3. Kuki
4. Chakma
5. Garo
6. Chaimal
7. Halam
8. Khasia
9. Bhutia
10. Munda incluing Kaur
11. Orang
12. Lepcha
13. Santal
14. Bhil
15. Tripura
16. Jamatia
17. Noatia
18. Riang

PART VIII — VINDHYA PRADESH

Throughout the State :—

1. Agariya
2. Baiga
3. Bhumiya
4. Gond
5. Kamar
6. Khairwar
7. Majhi
8. Mawasi
9. Panika
10. Pao
11. Bhil
12. Bedia
13. Biar (Biyar)
14. Sonr

THE ANDHRA STATE ACT, 1953

MODIFICATIONS IN THE CONSTITUTION (SCHEDULED TRIBES) ORDER 1950

In the Schedule —

(a) for the sub-heading "Part V—Madras" and for the words "Throughout the State" thereunder, substitute "Part V—Madras and Andhra" and "Throughout each of the States" respectively :

(b) for the entry under the sub-heading "Part XI—Mysore" substitute the following : —

"1 Throughout the State except in Bellary district : —

1. Hasalaru
2. Iruliga
3. Jenu Kuruba
4. Kadu-Kuruba
5. Maleru
6. Soligaru

2. In Bellary district : —

1. Aranadan
2. Bagala
3. Bhottadas — Bodo Bhottada, Muria Bhottada and Sano Bhottada
4. Bhumias — Bhuri Bhumia and Bodo Bhumia
5. Chenchu
6. Gadabas — Boda Gadaba, Cerllam Gadaba, Franji Gadaba, Jodia Gadaba, Olaro Gadaba, Pangi Gadaba and Pranga Gadaba

7. Gondi — Modya Gond and Rajo Gond
8. Goudus-Bato, Bhirithya Dudhokouria, Hato, Jatako and Joria
9. Kosalya Goudus — Bosothoriya Goudus, Chitti Goudus, Dangayath Goudus, Dodd Kamariya, Dudu Kamaro, Ladiya Goudus and Pullosoriya Goudus
10. Magatha Goudus — Bernia Goudu, Boodo Magatha, Dongayath Goudu, Ladya Goudu, Ponna Magatha and Sana Magatha.
11. Holva
12. Jadapus
13. Jatapus
14. Kammara
15. Kattunayakan
16. Khattis-Khatti, Kommarao and Lohara
17. Kodu
18. Kommar
19. Konda Dhoras
20. Konda Kapus
21. Kondareddis
22. Kondhs — Desaya Kondhs, Dongira Kondhs, Kuttiya Kondhs, Tikiria Kondhs and Yenity Kondhs
23. Kota
24. Kotia — Bartika Bentho Oriya, Dhulia or Dulia, Holva Paiko, Putiya, Sanrona and Sidho Paiko
25. Koya or Goud, with its sub-sects—Raja or Rasha Koyas, Lingadhari Koyas (ordinary) and Kottu Koyas
26. Kudiya
27. Kurumans
28. Manna Dhora
29. Maune
30. Mukha Dhora — Nooka Dhora
31. Muria

32. Paigarapu
33. Palasi
34. Paniyan
35. Porjas — Podo Bonda, Daruva, Didua, Jodia, Mundili, Pengu Pydi and Saliya
36. Reddi Dhoras
37. Savaras — Kapu Savaras, Khutto Savaras and Maliya Savaras
38. Sholaga
39. Toda
40. Inhabitants of the Laccadive, Minicoy and Amindivi Islands who, and both of whose parents, were born in these Islands."

THE SCHEDULED CASTES AND SCHEDULED TRIBES LISTS (MODIFICATION) ORDER, 1956

SCHEDULE III

[*See* paragraph 3(1)]

Modification to the Constitution (Scheduled Tribes) Order, 1950

1. In paragraph 2, for "Parts I to XIV", substitute "Parts I to XII"

2. For paragraph 3, substitute :—

"3 Any reference in this Order to a State or to a district or other territorial division thereof shall be construed as a reference to the State, district or other territorial division constituted as from the 1st day of November, 1956."

3. For the Schedule substitute :—

THE SCHEDULE

PART I—ANDHRA PRADESH

1. Throughout the State :—

1. Chenchu or Chenchwar
2. Koya or Goud with its sub-sects—Rajah or Rasha Koyas, Lingadhari Koyas (ordinary), Kottu Koyas, Bhine Koya and Rajkoya.

2. Throughout the State except Hyderabad, Mahbubnagar, Adilabad, Nizamabad, Medak, Karimnagar, Warangal, Khammam and Nalgonda districts :—

1. Bagata
2. Gadabas
3. Jatapus

4. Kammara
5. Kattunayakan
6. Konda Dhoras
7. Konda Kapus
8. Kondareddis
9. Kondhs (Kodi and Kodhu), Desaya Kondhs, Dongria Kondhs, Kuttiya Kondhs, Tikiria Kondhs and Yenity Kondhs
10. Kotia-Bentho Oriya, Bartika, Dhulia or Dulia, Holva, Paiko, Putiya, Sanrona and Sidhopaiko
11. Kulia
12. Malis
13. Manna Dhora
14. Mukha Dhora or Nooka Dhora
15. Porja (Parangiperja)
16. Reddi Dhoras
17. Rona, Rena
18. Savaras-Kapu Savaras, Maliya Savaras or Khutto Savaras
19. Sugalis (Lambadis)
20. Yenadis
21. Yerukulas

3. In the districts of Hyderabad, Mahbubnagar, Adilabad, Nizamabad, Medak, Karimnagar, Warangal, Khammam and Nalgonda : —

1. Andh
2. Bhil
3. Gond (including Naikpod and Rajgond)
4. Hill Reddis
5. Kolam (including Mannervarlu)
6. Pardhan
7. Thoti

4. In the Agency tracts :—

1. Goudu (Goud)
2. Nayaks
3. Valmiki

PART II — ASSAM

1. In the Autonomous District :—

1. Chakma
2. Dimasa, (Kachari)
3. Garo
4. Hajong
5. Hmar
6. Khasi and Jaintia, (including Khasi, Synteng or Pnar, War, Bhoi or Lyngngam).
7. Any Kuki Tribes including :—

(i) Biate, Biete
(ii) Changsan
(iii) Chongloi
(iv) Doungel
(v) Gamalhou
(vi) Gangte
(vii) Guite
(viii) Hanneng
(ix) Haokip, or Haupit
(x) Haolai
(xi) Hengna
(xii) Hongsungh
(xiii) Hrangkhwal or Rangkhol
(xiv) Jongbe
(xv) Khawchung
(xvi) Khawathlang, or Khothalong
(xix) Kipgen
(xx) Kuki
(xxi) Lengthang
(xxii) Lhangum
(xxiii) Lhoujem
(xxiv) Lhouvun
(xxv) Lupheng
(xxvi) Mangjel
(xxvii) Misao
(xxviii) Riang
(xxix) Sairhem
(xxx) Selnam
(xxxi) Singson
(xxxii) Sitlhou
(xxxiii) Sukte
(xxxiv) Thado
(xxxv) Thangugeu
(xxxvi) Uibuh

(xvii) Khelma

(xviii) Kholhou

(xxxvii) Vaiphei

8. Lakher
9. Man (Tai speaking)
10. Any Mizo (Lushai) tribes
11. Mikir
12. Any Naga Tribes
13. Pawi
14. Synteng

2. In the Tribal Areas other than the Autonomous Districts :—

All Tribes of North-East Froniter Agency including :—

1. Abor
2. Aka
3. Apatani
4. Dafla
5. Galong
6. Khampti
7. Khowa
8. Mishmi
9. Momba
10. Any Naga tribes
11. Sherdukpen
12. Singpho

3. In the State of Assam excluding the Tribal Areas :—

1. Barmans in Cachar
2. Boro-Borokachari
3. Deori
4. Hojai
5. Kachari including Sonwal
6. Lalung
7. Mech
8. Miri
9. Rabha

PART III — BIHAR

(1) Throughout the State : —

1. Asur
2. Baiga
3. Banjara
4. Bathudi
5. Bedia
6. Binjhia
7. Birhor
8. Birjia
9. Chero
10. Chik Baraik

11. Gond
12. Gorait
13. Ho
14. Karmali
15. Kharia
16. Kharwar
17. Khond
18. Kisan
19. Kora
20. Korwa
21. Lohara or Lohra
22. Mahli
23. Mal Paharia
24. Munda
25. Oraon
26. Parhaiya
27. Santal
28. Sauria Paharia
29. Savar

(2) In the districts of Ranchi, Singbhum, Hazaribagh, Santal Parganas and Manbhum : —

Bhumij

PART IV — BOMBAY

1. Throughout the State *except* the districts of Buldana, Akola, Amravati, Yeotmal, Wardha, Nagpur, Bhandara, Chanda, Aurangabad, Parbhani, Nanded, Bhir, Osmanabad, Halar, Madhya Saurashtra, Zalawad, Gohilwad, Sorath and Kutch : —

1. Barda
2. Bavacha or Bamcha
3. Bhil, including Bhil Garasia, Dholi Bhil, Dungri Bhil, Dungri Garasia, Mewasi Bhil, Rawal Bhil, Tadvi Bhil, Bhagalia, Bhilala, Pawra, Vasave and Vasave
4. Chodhara
5. Dhanka, including Tadvi, Tetaria and Valvi
6. Dhodia
7. Dubla, including Talavia or Halpati
8. Gamit or Gamta or Gavit, including Mavchi, Padvi, Vasava, Vasava and Valvi
9. Gond or Rajgond
10. Kathodi or Katkari, including Dhor Kathodi or Dhor Katkari and Son Kathodi or Son Katkari

11. Kokna, Kokni, Kukna
12. Koli Dhor, Tokre Koli, Kolcha or Kolgha
13. Naikda or Nayaka, including Cholivala Nayaka, Kapadia Nayaka, Mota Nayaka and Nana Nayaka
14. Pardhi, including Advichincher and Phanse Pardhi
15. Patelia
16. Pomla
17. Rathawa
18. Varli
19. Vitolia, Kotwalia or Barodia

2. In Dangs District :—
Kunbi

3. In Surat District :—
Chaudhri

4. In Thana District :—
Koli Malhar

5. (a) In Ahmednagar District :—
Akola, Rahuri and Sangamner talukas

(b) In Kolaba District :—
Karjat, Khalapur, Alibagh, Mahad and Sudhagad talukas

(c) In Nasik District :—
Nasik, Niphad, Sinnar, Chandor, Baglan, Igatpuri, Dindori and Kalvan talukas and Surgana and Peint Mahals

(d) In Poona District :—
Ambegaon, Junnar, Khed, Mawal and Mulshi talukas and Velhe Mahal

[(b)–(d):] Koli Mahadev or Dongar Koli

(e) In Thana District : — Thana, Murbad, Bhivandi, Bassein, Wada, Shahapur, Dahanu Palghar, Umbergaon, Jawhar and Mokhada talukas	Koli Mahadev or Dongar Koli
6. (a) In Ahmednagar District : — Akola, Rahuri and Sangammer talukas (b) In Kolaba District : — Karjat, Khalapur, Pen, Panvel and Sudhagad talukas and Matheran (c) In Nasik District :— Igatpuri, Nasik and Sinner talukas (d) In Poona District :— Ambegaon, Junnar, Khed and Mawal talukas (e) In Thana District :— Thana, Kalyan, Murbad, Bhivandi, Bassein, Wada, Shahapur, Palghar, Jawhar and Mokhada talukas	Thakur or Thakar including Ka Thakar, Ka Thakur, Ma Thakur, and Ma Thakar

7. In (1) Melghat tahsil of the Amravati District,

(2) Gadchiroli and Sironcha tahsils of the Chanda District,

(3) Kelapur, Wani and Yeotmal tahsils of the Yeotmal District : —

1. Andh
2. Baiga
3. Bhaina
4. Bharia-Bhumia or Bhuinhar-Bhumia including Pando
5. Bhattra
6. Bhil

7. Bhunjia
8. Binjhwar
9. Birhul or Birhor
10. Dhanwar
11. Gadaba or Gadba
12. Gond, including :—

   Arakh or Arrakh
   Agaria
   Asur
   Badi Maria or Bada Maria
   Bhatola
   Bhimma
   Bhuta, Koilabhuta or Koilabhuti
   Bhar
   Bisonhorn Maria
   Chota Maria
   Dandami Maria
   Dhuru or Dhurwa
   Dhoba
   Dhulia
   Dorla
   Gaiki
   Gatta or Gatti
   Gaita
   Gond Gowari
   Hill Maria
   Kandra
   Kalanga
   Khatola
   Koitar
   Koya
   Khirwar or Khirwara

Kucha Maria
Kuchaki Maria
Madia (Maria)
Mana
Mannewar
Moghya or Mogia or Monghya
Mudia (Muria)
Nagarchi
Nagwanshi
Ojha
Raj
Sonjhari Jhareka
Thatia or Thotya
Wade Maria or Vade Maria

13. Halba or Halbi
14. Kamar
15. Kawar, Kanwar, Kaur, Cherwa, Rathia Tanwar or Chattri
16. Khaiwar
17. Kharia
18. Kondh or Khond or Kandh
19. Kol
20. Kolam
21. Korku, including Bopchi, Mouasi, Nihal or Nahul and Bondhi or Bondeya
22. Korwa, including Kodaku
23. Majhwar
24. Munda
25. Nagesia or Nagasia
26. Nihal
27. Oraon, including Dhanka and Dhangad
28. Pardhan, Pathari and Saroti
29. Pardhi, including Bahelia or Bahellia, Chita

Pardhi, Langoli Pardhi, Phans Pardhi, Shikari, Takankar and Takia

30. Parja

31. Saonta or Saunta

32. Sawar or Sawara

8. In the districts of Aurangabad, Parbhani, Nanded, Bhir and Osmanabad : —

1. Andh
2. Bhil
3. Gond (including Naikpod and Rajgond)
4. Kolam (including Mannervarlu)
5. Koya (including Bhine Koya and Rajkoya)
6. Pardhan
7. Thoti

9. In the districts of Halar, Madhya Saurashtra, Zalawad, Gohilwad and Sorath : —

Siddi

10. In Nesses area in the forests of Alech, Gir and Barada : —

1. Bharwad
2. Charan
3. Rabari

11. In Zalawad district : —

Padhar

12. In Kutch district : —

1. Bhil
2. Dhodia
3. Koli
4. Paradhi
5. Vaghri

PART V — KERALA

1. Throughout the State : —

1. Kadar
2. Irular or Irulan
3. Muthuvan, Mudugar or Muduvan

2. Throughout the State *except* Malabar district :—

1. Eravallan
2. Hill Pulaya
3. Kanikaran or Kanikkar
4. Kochu Velan
5. Malakkuravan
6. Malai Arayan
7. Malai Pandaram
8. Malai Vedan
9. Malayan
10. Malayarayar
11. Mannan
12. Palleyan
13. Palliyar
14. Ulladan (Hill dwellers)
15. Uraly
16. Vishavan

3. In Malabar district :—

1. Adiyan
2. Arandan
3. Kammara
4. Kattunayaken
5. Konda Kapus
6. Kondareddis
7. Koraga
8. Kota
9. Kudiya or Melakudi
10. Kurichchan
11. Kurumans
12. Maha Malasar
13. Malasar
14. Malayekandi
15. Palliyan
16. Paniyan
17. Pulayan

4. In Malabar district (excluding Kasaragod taluk) :—

Kurumbas

5. In Kasaragod taluk of Malabar district :—

Marati

PART VI — MADHYA PRADESH

1. In the districts of Bhind, Gird, Morena, Shivpuri, Goona, Rajgarh, Shajapur, Ujjain, Ratlam, Mandsaur, Bhilsa (excluding Sironj sub-division) Indore, Dewas, Dhar, Jhabua and Nimar (M.B.) :—

1. Gond
2. Korku
3. Seharia

2. In the revenue districts of Dhar and Jhabua; in the tahsils of Sendhwa, Barwani, Rajpur, Khargone, Bhikangaon and Maheshwar of the revenue district of Nimar; in the tahsil of Sailana of the revenue district of Ratlam :—

Bhils and Bhilalas including Barela, Patelia and other sub-tribes.

3. In (1) Bastar, Chhindwara, Mandla, Raigarh and Surguja districts, (2) Baihar tahsil of the Balaghat district, (3) Betul and Bhainsdehi tahsils of the Betul district, (4) Bilaspur and Katghora tahsils of the Bilaspur district, (5) Durg and Sanjari tahsils of the Durg district, (6) Murwara, Patan and Sihora tahsils of the Jabalpur district, (7) Hoshangabad, Narsimhapur and Sohagpur tahsils of the Hoshangabad district, (8) Harsud tahsil of the Nimar district, (9) Bindra-Nawagarh, Dhamtari and Mahasamund tahsils of the Raipur district :—

1. Andh
2. Baiga
3. Bhaina
4. Bharia-Bhumia or Bhuinhar-Bhumia including Pando
5. Bhattra
6. Bhil
7. Bhunjia
8. Binjhwar
9. Birhul or Birhor
10. Dhanwar
11. Gadaba or Gadba
12. Gond, including —
    Arakh or Arrakh
    Agaria
    Asur
    Badi Maria or Bada Maria
    Bhatola
    Bhimma
    Bhuta, Koilabhuta or Koilabhuti

Bhar
Bisonhorn Maria
Chota Maria
Dandami Maria
Dhuru or Dhurwa
Dhoba
Dhulia
Dorla
Gaiki
Gatta or Gatti
Gaita
Gond Gowari
Hill Maria
Kandra
Kalanga
Khatola
Koitar
Koya
Khirwar or Khirwara
Kucha Maria
Kuchaki Maria
Madia (Maria)
Mana
Mannewar
Moghya or Mogia or Monghya
Mudia (Muria)
Nagarchi
Nagwanshi
Ojha
Raj
Sonjhari Jhareka
Thatia or Thotya

Wade Maria or Vade Maria

13. Halba or Halbi
14. Kamar
15. Kawar, Kanwar, Kaur, Cherwa, Rathia, Tanwar or Chattri
16. Khairwar
17. Kharia
18. Kondh or Khond or Kandh
19. Kol
20. Kolam
21. Korku, including Bopchi, Mouasi, Nihal or Nahul and Bondhi or Bondeya
22. Korwa, including Kodaku
23. Majhwar
24. Munda
25. Nagesia or Nagasia
26. Nihal
27. Oraon, including Dhanka and Dhangad
28. Pardhan, Pathari and Saroti
29. Pardhi, including Bahelia or Bahellia, Chita Pardhi, Langoli Pardhi, Phans Pardhi, Shikari, Takankar and Takia
30. Parja
31. Saonta or Saunta
32. Sawar or Sawara

4. In the districts of Datia, Tikamgarh, Chhatarpur, Panna, Satna, Rewa, Sidhi and Shahdol :—

1. Agariya
2. Baiga
3. Bhil
4. Biar or Biyar
5. Bhumiya including Bharia and Paliha
6. Gond, including Pathari
7. Khairwar including Kondar
8. Kol (Dahait)
9. Majhi
10. Mawasi
11. Nat, Navdigar, Sapera

12. Kubutar and Panika
13. Pao
14. Sahariya
15. Saur
16. Sonr

5. In the districts of Raisen and Sehore :—

1. Bhil
2. Bhilala
3. Gond or Daroi
4. Karku
5. Keer
6. Kol
7. Mogia
8. Pardhi
9. Saharia, Sosia or Sor

6. In Sironj sub-division of Bhilsa district :—

1. Bhil
2. Bhil Mina
3. Damor, Damaria
4. Garasia (excluding Rajput Garasia)
5. Mina
6. Sehria, Sahariya

PART VII — MADRAS

1. Throughout the State :—

1. Kadar
2. Irular

2. Throughout the State *except* Kanya Kumari district and Shencottah taluk of Tirunelveli district :—

1. Adiyan
2. Aranadan
3. Kammara
4. Kattunayakan
5. Konda Kapus
6. Kondareddis
7. Koraga
8. Kota
9. Kudiya or Melakudi
10. Kurichchan
11. Kurumans
12. Maha Malasar
13. Malasar
14. Malayekandi
15. Mudugar or Muduvan
16. Palliyan
17. Paniyan
18. Pulayan
19. Sholaga
20. Toda

3. In North Arcot, Salem and Tiruchirapalli districts :—

Malayali

4. In Coimbatore district and Tirunelveli district (*except* Shencottah taluk) :—

Kaniyan or Kanyan

5. In Nilgiris district :—

Kurumbas

6. In Kanya Kumari district and Shencottah taluk of Tirunelveli district :—

1. Eravallan
2. Hill Pulaya
3. Kanikaran or Kanikkar
4. Kochu Velan
5. Malakkuravan
6. Malai Arayan
7. Malai Pandaram
8. Malai Vedan
9. Malayan
10. Malayarayar
11. Mannan
12. Muthuvan
13. Palleyan
14. Palliyar
15. Ulladan (Hill dwellers)
16. Uraly
17. Vishavan

PART VIII — MYSORE

(1) Throughout the State *except* Coorg, Belgaum, Bijapur, Dharwar, Kanara, South Kanara, Gulbarga, Raichur and Bidar districts and Kollegal taluk of Mysore district :—

1. Gowdalu
2. Hakkipikki
3. Hasalaru
4. Iruliga
5. Jenu Kuruba
6. Kadu-Kuruba
7. Malaikudi
8. Maleru
9. Soligaru

(2) In the districts of Belgaum, Bijapur, Dharwar and Kanara :—

1. Barda
2. Bavacha or Bamcha
3. Bhil, including Bhil Garasia, Dholi Bhil, Dungri Bhil, Dungri Garasia, Mewasi Bhil, Rawal Bhil,

Tadvi Bhil, Bhagalia, Bhilala, Pawra, Vasava and Vasave

4. Chodhara
5. Dhanka including Tadvi, Tetaria and Valvi
6. Dhodia
7. Dubla, including Talavia or Halpati
8. Gamit or Gamta or Gavit including Mavchi, Padvi, Vasava, Vasave and Valvi
9. Gond or Rajgond
10. Kathodi or Katkari including Dhor Kathodi or Dhor Katkari and Son Kathodi or Son Katkari
11. Kokna, Kokni, Kukna
12. Koli Dhor, Tokre Koli, Kolcha or Kolgha
13. Naikda or Nayaka, including Cholivala Nayaka, Kapadia Nayaka, Mota Nayaka and Nana Nayaka
14. Pardhi, including Advichincher and Phanse Pardhi
15. Patelia
16. Pomla
17. Rathawa
18. Varli
19. Vitolia, Kotwalia or Barodia

(3) In the districts of Gulbarga, Bidar and Raichur :—

1. Bhil
2. Chenchu or Chenchwar
3. Gond (including Naikpod and Rajgond)
4. Koya (including Bhine Koya and Rajkoya)
5. Thoti

(4) In South Kanara district and Kollegal taluk of Mysore district :—

1. Adiyan
2. Aranadan
3. Irular
4. Kadar
5. Kammara
6. Kattunayakan
7. Konda Kapus
8. Kondareddis

9. Koraga
10. Kota
11. Kudiya or Melakudi
12. Kurichchan
13. Kurumans
14. Maha Malasar
15. Malasar
16. Malayekandi
17. Mudugar or Muduvan
18. Palliyan
19. Paniyan
20. Pulayan
21. Sholaga
22. Toda

(5) In Kollegal taluk of Mysore district :—
Kaniyan or Kanyan

(6) In South Kanara district :—
Marati

(7) In Coorg district :—
1. Korama
2. Kudiya
3. Kuruba
4. Maratha
5. Meda
6. Yerava

PART IX — ORISSA

Throughout the State :—

1. Bagata
2. Baiga
3. Banjara or Banjari
4. Bathudi
5. Bhottada or Dhotada
6. Bhuiya or Bhuyan
7. Bhumia
8. Bhumij
9. Bhunjia
10. Binjhal
11. Binjhia or Binjhoa
12. Birhor
13. Bondo Poraja
14. Chenchu
15. Dal
16. Desua Bhumij
17. Dharua
18. Didayi
19. Gadaba
20. Gandia
21. Ghara
22. Gond, Gondo
23. Ho
24. Holva
25. Jatapu
26. Juang

27. Kandha Gauda
28. Kawar
29. Kharia or Kharian
30. Kharwar
31. Khond, Kond, or Kandha, including Nanguli Kandha and Sitha Kandha
32. Kisan
33. Kol
34. Kolah-Kol-Loharas
35. Kolha
36. Koli, including Malhar
37. Kondadora
38. Kora
39. Korua
40. Kotia
41. Koya
42. Kulis
43. Lodha
44. Madia
45. Mahali
46. Mankidi
47. Mankirdia
48. Matya
49. Mirdhas
50. Munda, Munda-Lohara or Munda-Mahalis
51. Mundari
52. Omanatya
53. Oraon
54. Parenga
55. Paroja
56. Pentia
57. Rajuar
58. Santal
59. Saora, Savar, Saura or Sahara
60. Shabar or Lodha
61. Sounti
62. Tharua

PART X — PUNJAB

In Spiti and Lahaul in Kangra district :—

1. Gaddi
2. Swangla
3. Bhot or Bodh

PART XI — RAJASTHAN

1. Throughout the State *except* Ajmer district, Abu Road taluka of Sirohi district and Sunel Tappa of Jhalawar district :--

1. Bhil
2. Bhil Mina
3. Damor, Damaria
4. Garasia (excluding Rajput Garasia)
5. Mina
6. Sehria, Sahariya

2. In Ajmer district :—

1. Bhil
2. Bhil Mina

3. In Abu Road taluka of Sirohi district :—

1. Barda
2. Bavacha or Bamcha
3. Bhil, including Bhil Garasia, Dholi Bhil, Dungri Bhil, Dungri Garasia, Mewasi Bhil, Rawal Bhil, Tadvi Bhil, Bhagalia, Bhilala, Pawra, Vasava and Vasave
4. Chodhara
5. Dhanka, including Tadvi, Tetaria and Valvi
6. Dhodia
7. Dubla, including Talavia or Halpati
8. Gamit or Gamta or Gavit, including Mavchi, Padvi, Vasava, Vasave and Valvi
9. Gond or Rajgond
10. Kathodi or Katkari, including Dhor Kathodi or Dhor Katkari and Son Kathodi or Son Katkari
11. Kokna, Kokni, Kukna
12. Koli Dhor, Tokre Koli, Kolcha or Kolgha
13. Naikda or Nayaka, including Cholivala Nayaka, Kapadia Nayaka, Mota Nayaka and Nana Nayaka
14. Pardhi, including Advichincher and Phanse Pardhi
15. Patelia
16. Pomla
17. Rathawa
18. Varli
19. Vitolia, Kotwalia or Barodia

4. In Sunel Tappa of Jhalawar district :—

1. Gond
2. Korku
3. Seharia

PART XII — WEST BENGAL

1. Throughout the State :—

1. Ho	2. Kora
3. Lodha, Kheria or Kharia	4. Mal Pahariya
	5. Munda
6. Oraon	7. Santal

2. Throughout the State *except* the territories transferred from the Purnea district of Bihar :—

Bhumij

3. Throughout the State *except* in the Purulia district and the territories transferred from the Purnea district of Bihar :—

1. Bhutia including Sherpa, Toto, Dukpa, Kagatay, Tibetan and Yolmo	2. Chakma
	3. Garo
	4. Hajang
	5. Lepcha
6. Magh	7. Mahali
8. Mech	9. Mru
10. Nagesia	11. Rabha

4. In the Purulia district and the territories transferred from the Purnea district in Bihar :—

1. Asur	2. Baiga
3. Banjara	4. Bathudi
5. Bedia	6. Binjhia
7. Birhor	8. Birjia
9. Chero	10. Chik Baraik
11. Gond	12. Gorait
13. Karmali	14. Kharwar
15. Khond	16. Kisan
17. Korwa	18. Lohara or Lohra
19. Mahil	20. Parhaiya
21. Sauria Paharia	22. Savar."

SCHEDULE IV

[*See* paragraph 3(2)]

Modification to the Constitution (Scheduled Tribes) (Part C States) Order, 1951

1. In paragraph 1, for "Part C States" substitute "Union Territories".

2. In paragraph 2, for "Part I to VIII" and "States", substitute "Parts I to IV" and "Union Territories" respectively.

3. For paragraph 3, substitute :—

"3 Any reference in this Order to a Union Territory shall be construed as a reference to the territory constituted as a Union Territory as from the 1st day of November, 1956."

4. For the Schedule, substitute :—

THE SCHEDULE

PART I — HIMACHAL PRADESH

Throughout the Union Territory :—

1. Gaddi
2. Gujjar
3. Jad, Lamba, Khampa and Bhot or Bodh
4. Kanaura or Kinnara
5. Lahaula
6. Pangwala

PART II — MANIPUR

Throughout the Union Territory :—

1. Aimol
2. Anal
3. Angami
4. Chiru
5. Chothe
6. Gangte
7. Hmar
8. Kabui
9. Kacha Naga
10. Koirao
11. Koireng
12. Kom
13. Lamgang
14. Any Mizo (Lushai) tribes

15. Maram
16. Maring
17. Mao
18. Monsang
19. Moyon
20. Paite
21. Purum
22. Ralte
23. Sema
24. Simte
25. Sahte
26. Tangkhul
27. Thadou
28. Vaiphui
29. Zou

PART III — TRIPURA

Throughout the Union Territory :—

1. Lushai
2. Mag
3. Kuki, including the following sub-tribes :—
   (i) Balte
   (ii) Belalhut
   (iii) Chhalya
   (iv) Fun
   (v) Hajango
   (vi) Jangtei
   (vii) Khareng
   (viii) Khephong
   (ix) Kuntei
   (x) Laifang
   (xi) Lentei
   (xii) Mizel
   (xiii) Namte
   (xiv) Paitu, Paite
   (xv) Rangchan
   (xvi) Rangkhole
   (xvii) Thangluya
4. Chakma
5. Garoo
6. Chaimal
7. Halam
8. Khasia
9. Bhutia
10. Munda including Kaur
11. Orang
12. Lepcha

13. Santal
14. Bhil
15. Tripura or Tripuri, Tippera
16. Jamatia
17. Noatia
18. Riang
19. Uchai

PART IV — THE LACCADIVE, MINICOY AND AMINDIVI ISLANDS

Throughout the Union Territory :—

Inhabitants of the Laccadive, Minicoy and Amindivi Islands who, and both of whose parents, were born in those islands."

THE CONSTITUTION (ANDAMAN AND NICOBAR ISLANDS) SCHEDULED TRIBES ORDER, 1959, C.O. 58

Scheduled Tribes

(1) In the Andaman Islands :—

1. Andamanese including Chariar or Chari, Kora, Tabo or Bo, Yere, Kede, Bea, Balawa, Bojigiyab, Juwai and Kol,
2. Jarawas
3. Onges
4. Sentinelese

(2) In the Nicobar Islands :—

1. Nicobarese
2. Shom Pens

The Bombay Reorganisation Act, 1960

AMENDMENT OF THE CONSTITUTION (SCHEDULED TRIBES) ORDER, 1960

Part IV — GUJARAT

(1) Throughout the State *except* the Rajkot Division and the district of Kutch :—

1. Barda
2. Bavacha or Bamcha
3. Bhil, including Bhil Garasia, Dholi Bhil, Dungri Bhil, Dungri, Garasia, Mewasi Bhil, Rawal Bhil, Tadvi Bhil, Bhagalia, Bhilala, Pawra, Vasava and Vasave
4. Chodhara

5. Dhanka, including Tadvi, Tetaria and Valvi
6. Dhodia
7. Dubla, including Talavia or Halpati.
8. Gamit or Gamta or Gavit, including Mavchi, Padvi, Vasava, Vasave and Valvi
9. Gond or Rajgond
10. Kathodi or Katkari, including Dhor Kathodi or Dhor Katkari and Son Kathodi or Son Katkari
11. Kokna, Kokni, Kukna
12. Koli Dhor, Tokre Koli, Kolcha or Kolgha
13. Naikda or Nayaka, including Cholivala Nayaka, Kapadia Nayaka, Mota Nayaka and Nana Nayaka
14. Pardhi, including Advichincher and Phanse Pardhi
15. Patelia
16. Pomla
17. Rathawa
18. Varli
19. Vitolia, Kotwalia or Barodia

(2) In Dangs district, Kunbi.

(3) In Surat District :—

(a) in Umbergaon taluka, Koli Malhar, Koli Mahadev or Dongar Koli;

(b) in the other talukas, Chaudhri

(4) In the Rajkot Division, Siddi.

(5) In Nesses area in the forests of Alech, Gir and Barada :--

1. Bharwad
2. Charan
3. Rabari

(6) In Surendranagar district :—

Padhar

(7) In Kutch district :—

1. Bhil
2. Dhodia
3. Koli
4. Paradhi
5. Vaghri

Part VII-A — MAHARASHTRA

(1) Throughout the State *except* the districts of Buldana, Akola, Amravati, Yeotmal, Wardha, Nagpur, Bhandara, Chanda, Aurangabad, Parbhani, Nanded, Bhir, Osmanabad and Rajura :—

1. Barda
2. Bavacha or Bamcha
3. Bhil, including Bhil Garasia, Dholi Bhil, Dungri Bhil, Dungri Garasia, Mewasi Bhil, Rawal Bhil, Tadvi Bhil, Bhagalia, Bhilala, Pawra, Vasava and Vasave
4. Chodhara
5. Dhanka, including Tadvi, Tetaria and Valvi
6. Dhodia
7. Dubla, including Talavia or Halpati
8. Gamit or Gamta or Gavit, including Mavchi, Padvi, Vasava, Vasave and Valvi
9. Gond or Rajgond
10. Kathodi or Katkari, including Dhor Kathodi or Dhor Katkari and Son Kathodi or Son Katkari
11. Kokna, Kokni, Kukna
12. Koli Dhor, Tokre Koli, Kolcha or Kolgha
13. Naikda or Nayaka, including Cholivala Nayaka, Kapadia Nayaka, Mota Nayaka and Nana Nayaka
14. Pardhi, including Advichincher and Phanse Pardhi
15. Patelia
16. Pomla
17. Rathawa
18. Varli
19. Vitolia, Kotwalia or Barodia

(2) In Thana district :—

Koli Malhar

(3)	(a) In Ahmednagar district :— Akola, Rahuri and Sangamner talukas. (b) In Kolaba district :— Karjat, Khalapur, Alibagh, Mahad and Sudhagad talukas. (c) In Nasik district :— Nasik, Niphad, Sinnar, Chandor, Baglan, Igatpuri, Dindori and Kalvan talukas and Surgana and Peint Mahals. (d) In Poona district :— Ambegaon, Junnar, Khed, Mawal and Mulshi talukas and Velhe Mahal. (e) In Thana district :— Thana, Murbad, Bhivandi, Bassein, Wada, Shahapur, Dahanu, Palghar, Jawhar and Mokhada talukas.	Koli Mahadav or Dongar Koli
(4)	(a) In Ahmednagar district :— Akola, Rahuri and Sangamner talukas. (b) In Kolaba district :— Karjat, Khalapur, Pen, Panvel and Sudhagad talukas and Matheran. (c) In Nasik district :— Igatpuri, Nasik and Sinnar talukas. (d) In Poona district :— Ambegaon, Junnar, Khed and Mawal talukas.	Thakur or Thakar including Ka Thakur, Ka Thakar, Ma Thakur and Ma Thakar

(e) In Thana district :— Thana, Kalyan, Murbad, Bhivandi, Bassein, Wada, Shahapur, Palghar, Jawhar and Mokhada talukas.	Thakur or Thakar including Ka Thakur, Ka Thakar, Ma Thakur and Ma Thakar

(5) In (1) Melghat tahsil of Amravati district, (2) Gadchiroli and Sironcha tahsils of the Chanda district, (3) Kelapur, Wani and Yeotmal tahsils of the Yeotmal district :—

1. Andh
2. Baiga
3. Bhaina
4. Bharia-Bhumia or Bhuinhar-Bhumia including Pando
5. Bhattra
6. Bhil
7. Bhunjia
8. Binjhwar
9. Birhul or Birhor
10. Dhanwar
11. Gadaba or Gadba
12. Gond, including :—

    Arakh or Arrakh
    Agaria
    Asur
    Badi Maria or Bada Maria
    Bhatola
    Bhimma
    Bhuta, Koilabhuta or Koilabhuti
    Bhar
    Bisonhorn Maria
    Chota Maria
    Dandami Maria
    Dhuru or Dhurwa

Dhoba
Dhulia
Dorla
Gaiki
Gatta or Gatti
Gaita
Gond Gowari
Hill Maria
Kandra
Kalanga
Khatola
Koitar
Koya
Khirwar or Khirwara
Kucha Maria
Kuchaki Maria
Madia (Maria)
Mana
Mannewer
Moghya or Mogia or Monghya
Mudia (Muria)
Nagarchi
Nagwanshi
Ojha
Raj
Sonjhari Jhareka
Thatia or Thotya
Wade Maria or Vade Maria

13. Halba or Halbi
14. Kamar
15. Kawar, Kanwar, Kaur, Cherwa, Rathia Tanwar or Chattri

16. Khairwar
17. Kharia
18. Kondh or Khond or Kandh
19. Kol
20. Kolam
21. Korku, including Bopchi, Mouasi, Nihal or Nahul and Bondhi or Bondeya
22. Korwa, including Kodaku
23. Majhwar
24. Munda
25. Nagesia or Nagasia
26. Nihal
27. Oraon, including Dhanka and Dhangad
28. Pardhan, Pathari and Saroti
29. Pardhi, including Bahelia or Bahellia, Chita Pardhi, Langoli Pardhi, Phans Pardhi, Shikari, Takankar and Takia
30. Parja
31. Saonta or Saunta
32. Sawar or Sawara

(6) In the districts of Aurangabad, Parbhani, Nanded, Rajura, Bhir and Osmanabad :—

1. Andh
2. Bhil
3. Gond (including Naikpod and Rajgond)
4. Kolam (including Mannervarlu)
5. Koya (including Bhine Koya and Rajkoya)
6. Pardhan
7. Thoti.

LAKSHADWEEP

[The Constitution (Union Territories) Scheduled Tribes Order, 1951, C.O. 33]

Scheduled Tribes

Inhabitants of the Laccadive, Minicoy and Amindivi Islands who, and both of whose parents were born in those islands.

DADRA AND NAGAR HAVELI

[The Constitution (Dadra and Nagar Haveli) Scheduled Tribes Order, 1962, C.O. 64]

Scheduled Tribes

1. Dhodia
2. Dubla including Halpati
3. Kathodi
4. Kokna
5. Koli Dhor including Kolgha
6. Naikda or Nayaka
7. Varli

The Punjab Reorganisation Act, 1966

Amendment of the Constitution (Scheduled Tribes) Order, 1950

Part X shall be omitted.

Amendment of the Constitution (Scheduled Tribes) (Union Territories) Order, 1951

(2) In Part I of the Schedule—(HIMACHAL PRADESH)

(a) for the words "Throughout the Union territory", the figures, words and brackets "1. Throughout the Union territory *except* the territories specified in sub-section (1) of section 5 of the Punjab Reorganisation Act, 1966" shall be substituted; and

(b) the following shall be added at the end :—

"2. In Lahaul and Spiti district :—

1. Gaddi
2. Swangla
3. Bhot or Bodh".

UTTAR PRADESH

[The Constitution (Scheduled Tribes) (Uttar Pradesh) Order, 1967, C.O. 78]

Scheduled Tribes

1. Bhotia
2. Buksa
3. Jaunsari
4. Raji
5. Tharu

GOA, DAMAN & DIU

[The Constitution (Goa, Daman & Diu) Scheduled Tribes Order, 1968 C.O. 81]

Scheduled Tribes

1. Dhodia
2. Dubla
3. Naikda, Halapati, Talavia
4. Siddi, Nayaka
5. Varli

NAGALAND

[The Constitution (Nagaland) Scheduled Tribes Order, 1970, C.O. 88]

Scheduled Tribes

1. Garo
2. Kachari
3. Kuki
4. Mikir
5. Naga

THE NORTH-EASTERN AREAS (REORGANISATION) ACT, 1971

MANIPUR

Scheduled Tribes

1. Aimol
2. Anal
3. Angami
4. Chiru
5. Chothe
6. Gangte
7. Hmar
8. Kabui
9. Kacha Naga
10. Koirao
11. Koireng
12. Kom
13. Lamgang
14. Mao
15. Maram
16. Maring
17. Any Mizo (Lushai) tribes
18. Monsang
19. Moyon
20. Paite
21. Purum
22. Ralte
23. Sema
24. Simte
25. Suhte
26. Tangkhul
27. Thadou
28. Vaiphui
29. Zou

MEGHALAYA

1. Chakma
2. Dimasa, Kachari
3. Garo
4. Hajong
5. Hmar

6. Khasi, Jaintia, Synteng, Pnar, War, Bhoi, Lyngngam

7. Any Kuki Tribes including :—

(i) Biate, Biete
(ii) Changsan
(iii) Chongloi
(iv) Doungel
(v) Gamalhou
(vi) Gangte
(vii) Guite
(viii) Hanneng
(ix) Haokip, Haupit
(x) Haolai
(xi) Hengna
(xii) Hongsungh
(xiii) Hrangkhwal, Rangkhol
(xiv) Jongbe
(xv) Khawchung
(xvi) Khawathlang, Khothalong
(xvii) Khelma
(xviii) Kholhou
(xix) Kipgen
(xx) Kuki
(xxi) Lengthang
(xxii) Lhangum
(xxiii) Lhoujem
(xxiv) Lhouvun
(xxv) Lupheng
(xxvi) Mangjel
(xxvii) Misao
(xxviii) Riang
(xxix) Sairhem
(xxx) Selnam
(xxxi) Singson
(xxxii) Sitlhou
(xxxiii) Sukte
(xxxiv) Thado
(xxxv) Thangngeu
(xxxvi) Uibuh
(xxxvii) Vaiphei

8. Lakher

9. Man (Tai speaking)

10. Any Mizo (Lushai) tribes

11. Mikir

12. Any Naga tribes

13. Pawi

14. Synteng

TRIPURA

1. Lushai
2. Mag
3. Kuki, including the following sub-tribes :—
   - (i) Balte
   - (ii) Belalhut
   - (iii) Chhalya
   - (iv) Fun
   - (v) Hajango
   - (vi) Jangtei
   - (vii) Khareng
   - (viii) Khephong
   - (ix) Kuntei
   - (x) Laifang
   - (xi) Lentei
   - (xii) Mizel
   - (xiii) Namte
   - (xiv) Paitu, Paite
   - (xv) Rangchan
   - (xvi) Rangkhole
   - (xvii) Thangluya
4. Chakma
5. Garoo
6. Chaimal
7. Halam
8. Khasia
9. Bhutia
10. Munda including Kaur
11. Orang
12. Lepcha
13. Santal
14. Bhil
15. Tripura or Tripuri, Tippera
16. Jamatia
17. Noatia
18. Riang
19. Uchai

MIZORAM

1. Chakma
2. Dimasa, Kachari
3. Garo
4. Hajong
5. Hmar
6. Khasi, Jaintia, Synteng, Pnar, War, Bhoi, Lyngngam
7. Any Kuki Tribes, including :—

(i) Biate, Biete
(ii) Changsan
(iii) Chongloi
(iv) Doungel
(v) Gamalhou
(vi) Gangte
(vii) Guite
(viii) Hanneng
(ix) Haokip, Haupit
(x) Haolai
(xi) Hengna
(xii) Hongsungh
(xiii) Hrangkhwal, Rangkhol
(xiv) Jongbe
(xv) Khawchung
(xvi) Khawathlang, Khothalong
(xvii) Khelma
(xviii) Kholhou
(xix) Kipgen
(xx) Kuki
(xxi) Lengthang
(xxii) Lhangum
(xxiii) Lhoujem
(xxiv) Lhouvun
(xxv) Lupheng
(xxvi) Mangjel
(xxvii) Misao
(xxviii) Riang
(xxix) Sairhem
(xxx) Selnam
(xxxi) Singson
(xxxii) Sitlhou
(xxxiii) Sukte
(xxxiv) Thado
(xxxv) Thangngen
(xxxvi) Uibuh
(xxxvii) Vaiphei

8. Lakher
9. Man (Tai speaking)
10. Any Mizo (Lushai) tribes

11. Mikir
12. Any Naga tribes
13. Pawi
14. Synteng

ARUNACHAL PRADESH

All tribes of the Union Territory including :—

1. Abor
2. Aka
3. Apatani
4. Dafla
5. Galong
6. Khampti
7. Khowa
8. Mishmi
9. Momba
10. Any Naga tribes
11. Sherdukpen
12. Singpho

THE 1976 ORDER RELATING TO THE SCHEDULED TRIBES

PART I — ANDHRA PRADESH

1. Andh
2. Bagata
3. Bhil
4. Chenchu, Chenchwar
5. Gadabas
6. Gond, Naikpod, Rajgond
7. Goudu (in the Agency tracts)
8. Hill Reddis
9. Jatapus
10. Kammara
11. Kattunayakan
12. Kolam, Mannervarlu
13. Konda Dhoras
14. Konda Kapus
15. Kondareddis
16. Kondhs, Kodi, Kodhu, Desaya Kondhs, Dongria Kondhs, Kuttiaya Kondhs, Tikiria Kondhs, Yenity Kondhs
17. Kotia, Bentho, Oriay, Bartika, Dhulia, Dulia, Holva, Paiko, Putiya, Sanrona, Sidhopaiko
18. Koya, Goud, Rajah, Rasha Koya, Lingadhari, Koya (ordinary), Kottu Koya, Bhine Koya, Rajkoya
19. Kulia

20. Malis (excluding Adilabad, Hyderabad, Karimnagar, Khammam, Mahbubnagar, Medak, Nalgonda, Nizamabad and Warangal districts)
21. Manna Dhora
22. Mukha Dhora, Nooka Dhora
23. Nayaks (in the Agency tracts)
24. Pardhan
25. Porja, Parangiperja
26. Reddi Dhoras
27. Rona, Rena
28. Savaras, Kapu Savaras, Maliya Savaras, Khutto Savaras
29. Sugalis, Lambadis
30. Thoti (in Adilabad, Hyderabad, Karimnagar, Khammam, Mahbubnagar, Medak, Nalgonda, Nizamabad and Warangal districts)
31. Valmiki (in the Agency tracts)
32. Yenadis
33. Yerukulas

PART II — ASSAM

(1) In the autonomous districts :—

1. Chakma
2. Dimasa, Kachari
3. Garo
4. Hajong
5. Hmar
6. Khasi, Jaintia, Synteng, Pnar, War, Bhoi, Lyngngam
7. Any Kuki Tribes, including :—

(i) Biate, Biete
(ii) Changsan
(iii) Chongloi
(iv) Doungel
(v) Gamalhou
(vi) Gangte
(vii) Guite
(viii) Hanneng
(ix) Haokip, Haupit
(x) Haolai

(xi) Hengna
(xii) Hongsungh
(xiii) Hrangkhwal, Rangkhol
(xiv) Jongbe
(xv) Khawchung
(xvi) Khawathlang, Khothalong
(xvii) Khelma
(xviii) Kholhou
(xix) Kipgen
(xx) Kuki
(xxi) Lengthang
(xxii) Lhangum
(xxiii) Lhoujem
(xxiv) Lhouvun
(xxv) Lupheng
(xxvi) Mangjel
(xxvii) Misao
(xxviii) Riang
(xxix) Sairhem
(xxx) Selnam
(xxxi) Singson
(xxxii) Sitlhou
(xxxiii) Sukte
(xxxiv) Thado
(xxxv) Thangngeu
(xxxvi) Uibuh
(xxxvii) Vaiphei

8. Lakher
9. Man (Tai speaking)
10. Any Mizo (Lushai) tribes
11. Mikir
12. Any Naga tribes
13. Pawi
14. Syntheng

(2) In the State of Assam excluding the autonomous districts :—

1. Barmans in Cachar
2. Boro, Borokachari
3. Deori
4. Hojai
5. Kachari, Sonwal
6. Lalung
7. Mech
8. Miri
9. Rabha

PART III — BIHAR

1. Asur
2. Baiga

3. Banjara
4. Bathudi
5. Bedia
6. Bhumij (in North Chotanagpur and South Chotanagpur divisions and Santal Parganas districts)
7. Binjhia
8. Birhor
9. Birjia
10. Chero
11. Chik Baraik
12. Gond
13. Gorait
14. Ho
15. Karmali
16. Kharia
17. Kharwar
18. Khond
19. Kisan
20. Kora
21. Korwa
22. Lohara, Lohra
23. Mahli
24. Mal Paharia
25. Munda
26. Oraon
27. Parhaiya
28. Santal
29. Sauria Paharia
30. Savar

PART IV — GUJARAT

1. Barda
2. Bavacha, Bamcha
3. Bharwad (in the Nesses of the forests of Alech, Barada and Gir)
4. Bhil, Bhil Garasia, Dholi Bhil, Dungri Bhil, Dungri Garasia, Mewasi Bhil, Rawal Bhil, Tadvi Bhil, Bhagalia, Bhilala, Pawra, Vasava, Vasave
5. Charan (in the Nesses of the forests of Alech, Barada and Gir)
6. Chaudhri (in Surat and Valsad districts)
7. Chodhara
8. Dhanka, Tadvi, Tetaria, Valvi
9. Dhodia
10. Dubla, Talavia, Halpati
11. Gamit, Gamta, Gavit, Mavchi, Padvi
12. Gond, Rajgond

13. Kathodi, Katkari, Dhor Kathodi, Dhor Katkari, Son Kathodi, Son Katkari
14. Kokna, Kokni, Kukna
15. Koli (in Kutch district)
16. Koli Dhor, Tokre Koli, Kolcha, Kolgha
17. Kunbi (in the Dangs district)
18. Naikda, Nayaka, Cholivala Nayaka, Kapadia Nayaka, Mota Nayaka, Nana Nayaka
19. Padhar
20. Paradhi (in Kutch district)
21. Pardhi, Advichincher, Phanse Pardhi (excluding Amreli, Bhavnagar, Jamnagar, Junagadh, Kutch, Rajkot and Surendranagar districts)
22. Patelia
23. Pomla
24. Rabari (in the Nesses of the forests of Alech, Barada and Gir)
25. Rathawa
26. Siddi (in Amreli, Bhavnagar, Jamnagar, Junagadh, Rajkot and Surendranagar districts)
27. Vaghri (in Kutch district)
28. Varli
29. Vitolia, Kotwalia, Barodia

PART V — HIMACHAL PRADESH

1. Bhot, Bodh
2. Gaddi [excluding the territories specified in sub-section (1) of section 5 of the Punjab Reorganisation Act, 1966 (31 of 1966), other than the Lahaul and Spiti district]
3. Gujjar [excluding the territories specified in sub-section (1) of section 5 of the Punjab Reorganisation Act, 1966 (31 of 1966)]
4. Jad, Lamba, Khampa
5. Kanaura, Kinnara
6. Lahaula

7. Pangwala
8. Swangla

PART VI — KARNATAKA

1. Adiyan
2. Barda
3. Bavacha, Bamcha
4. Bhil, Bhil Garasia, Dholi Bhil, Dungri Bhil, Dungri Garasia, Mewasi Bhil, Rawal Bhil, Tadvi Bhil, Bhagalia, Bhilala, Pawra, Vasava, Vasave
5. Chenchu, Chenchwar
6. Chodhara
7. Dubla, Talavia, Halpati
8. Gamit, Gamta, Gavit, Mavchi, Padvi, Valvi
9. Gond, Naikpod, Rajgond
10. Gowdalu
11. Hakkipikki
12. Hasalaru
13. Irular
14. Iruliga
15. Jenu Kuruba
16. Kadu Kuruba
17. Kammara (in South Kanara district and Kollegal taluk of Mysore district)
18. Kaniyan, Kanyan (in Kollegal taluk of Mysore district)
19. Kathodi, Katkari, Dhor Kathodi, Dhor Katkari, Son Kathodi, Son Katkari
20. Kattunayakan
21. Kokna, Kokni, Kukna
22. Koli Dhor, Tokre Koli, Kolcha, Kolgha
23. Konda Kapus
24. Koraga
25. Kota

26. Koya, Bhine Koya, Rajkoya
27. Kudiya, Melakudi
28. Kuruba (in Coorg district)
29. Kurumans
30. Maha Malasar
31. Malaikudi
32. Malasar
33. Malayekandi
34. Maleru
35. Maratha (in Coorg district)
36. Marati (in South Kanara district)
37. Meda
38. Naikda, Nayaka, Cholivala Nayaka, Kapadia Nayaka, Mota Nayaka, Nana Nayaka
39. Palliyan
40. Paniyan
41. Pardhi, Advichincher, Phanse Pardhi
42. Patelia
43. Rathawa
44. Sholaga
45. Soligaru
46. Toda
47. Varli
48. Vitolia, Kotwalia, Barodia
49. Yerava.

PART VII — KERALA

1. Adiyan
2. Arandan
3. Eravallan
4. Hill Pulaya
5. Irular, Irulan
6. Kadar

7. Kammara [in the areas comprising the Malabar district as specified by sub-section (2) of section 5 of the States Reorganisation Act, 1956 (37 of 1956)]
8. Kanikaran, Kanikkar
9. Kattunayakan
10. Kochu Velan
11. Konda Kapus
12. Kondareddis
13. Koraga
14. Kota
15. Kudiya, Melakudi
16. Kurichchan
17. Kurumans
18. Kurumbas
19. Maha Malasar
20. Malai Arayan
21. Malai Pandaram
22. Malai Vedan
23. Malakkuravan
24. Malasar
25. Malayan [excluding the areas comprising the Malabar district as specified by sub-section (2) of section 5 of the States Reorganisation Act, 1956 (37 of 1956)]
26. Malayarayar
27. Mannan
28. Marati (in Hosdrug and Kasaragod taluks of Cannanore district)
29. Muthuvan, Mudugar, Muduvan
30. Palleyan
31. Palliyan
32. Palliyar
33. Paniyan
34. Ulladan

35. Uraly.

PART VIII — MADHYA PRADESH

1. Agariya
2. Andh
3. Baiga
4. Bhaina
5. Bharia Bhumia, Bhuinhar Bhumia, Bhumiya, Bharia, Paliha, Pando
6. Bhattra
7. Bhil, Bhilala, Barela, Patelia
8. Bhil Mina
9. Bhunjia
10. Biar, Biyar
11. Binjhwar
12. Birhur, Birhor
13. Damor, Damaria
14. Dhanwar
15. Gadaba, Gadba
16. Gond; Arakh, Arrakh, Agaria, Asur, Badi Maria, Bada Maria, Bhatola, Bhimma, Bhuta, Koilabhuta, Koliabhuti, Bhar, Bisonhorn Maria, Chota Maria, Dandami Maria, Dhuru, Dhurwa, Dhoba, Dhulia, Dorla, Gaiki, Gatta, Gatti, Gaita, Gond Gowari, Hill Maria, Kandra, Kalanga, Khatola, Koitar, Koya, Khirwar, Khirwara, Kucha Maria, Kuchaki Maria, Madia, Maria, Mana, Mannewar, Moghya, Mogia, Monghya, Mudia, Muria, Nagarchi, Nagwanshi, Ojha, Raj, Sonjhari Jhareka, Thatia, Thotya, Wade Maria, Vade Maria, Daroi
17. Halba, Halbi
18. Kamar
19. Karku
20. Kawar, Kanwar, Kaur, Cherwa, Rathia, Tanwar, Chattri
21. Keer (in Bhopal, Raisen and Sehore districts)
22. Khairwar, Kondar

23. Kharia
24. Kondh, Khond, Kandh
25. Kol
26. Kolam
27. Korku, Bopchi, Mouasi, Nihal, Nahul, Bondhi, Bondeya
28. Korwa Kodaku
29. Majhi
30. Majhwar
31. Mawasi
32. Mina (in Sironj sub-division of Vidisha district)
33. Munda
34. Nagesia, Nagasia
35. Oraon, Dhanka, Dhangad
36. Panika (in Chhatarpur, Datia, Panna, Rewa, Satna, Shahdol, Sidhi and Tikamgarh districts)
37. Pao
38. Pardhan, Pathari, Saroti
39. Pardhi (in Bhopal, Raisen and Sehore districts)
40. Pardhi; Bahelia, Bahellia, Chita Pardhi, Langoli, Pardhi, Phans Pardhi, Shikari, Takankar, Takia [in (1) Bastar, Chhindwara, Mandla, Raigarh, Seoni and Surguja districts, (2) Baihar tahsil of Balaghat district, (3) Betul and Bhainsdehi tahsils of Betul district, (4) Bilaspur and Katghora tahsils of Bilaspur district, (5) Durg and Balod tahsils of Durg district, (6) Chowki, Manpur and Mohala Revenue Inspectors' Circles of Rajnandgaon district, (7) Murwara, Patan and Sihora tahsils of Jabalpur district, (8) Hoshangabad and Sohagpur tahsil of Hoshangabad district and Narsimhapur district, (9) Harsud tahsils of Khandwa district, (10) Bindra-Nawagarh, Dhamtari and Mahasamund tahsils of Raipur district]
41. Parja
42. Sahariya, Saharia, Seharia, Sehira, Sosia, Sor
43. Saonṭa, Saunta
44. Saur

45. Sawar, Sawara
46. Sonr.

PART IX — MAHARASHTRA

1. Andh
2. Baiga
3. Barda
4. Bavacha, Bamcha
5. Bhaina
6. Bharia Bhumia, Bhuinhar Bhumia, Pando
7. Bhattra
8. Bhil, Bhil Garasia, Dholi Bhil, Dungri Bhil, Dungri Gara.sia, Mewasi Bhil, Rawal Bhil, Tadvi Bhil, Bhagalia, Bhilala, Pawra, Vasava, Vasave
9. Bhunjia
10. Binjhwar
11. Birhul, Birhor
12. Chodhara (excluding Akola, Amravati, Bhandara, Buldana, Chandrapur, Nagpur, Wardha, Yavatmal, Aurangabad, Bhir, Nanded, Osmanabad and Parbhani districts)
13. Dhanka, Tadvi, Tetaria, Valvi
14. Dhanwar
15. Dhodia
16. Dubla, Talavia, Halpati
17. Gamit, Gamta, Gavit, Mavchi, Padvi
18. Gond Rajgond, Arakh, Arrakh, Agaria, Asur, Badi Maria, Bada Maria, Bhatola, Bhimma, Bhuta, Koilabhuta, Koilabhuti, Bhar, Bisonhorn Maria, Chota Maria, Dandami Maria, Dhuru, Dhurwa, Dhoba, Dhulia, Dorla, Gaiki, Gatta, Gatti, Gaita, Gond Gowari, Hill Maria, Kandra, Kalanga, Khatola, Koitar, Koya, Khirwar, Khirwara, Kucha Maria, Kuchaki Maria, Madia, Maria, Mana, Mannewar, Moghya, Mogia, Monghya, Mudia, Muria, Nagarchi, Naikpod, Nagwanshi, Ojha, Raj, Sonjhari, Jhareka, Thatia, Thotya, Wade Maria, Vade Maria

19. Halba, Halbi
20. Kamar
21. Kathodi, Katkari, Dhor Kathodi, Dhor Katkari, Son Kathodi, Son Katkari
22. Kawar, Kanwar, Kaur, Cherwa, Rathia, Tanwar, Chattri
23. Khairwar
24. Kharia
25. Kokna, Kokni, Kukna
26. Kol
27. Kolam, Mannervarlu
28. Koli Dhor, Tokre Koli, Kolcha, Kolgha
29. Koli Mahadev, Dongar Koli
30. Koli Malhar
31. Kondh, Khond, Kandh
32. Korku, Bopchi, Mouasi, Nihal, Nahul, Bondhi, Bondeya
33. Koya, Bhine Koya, Rajkoya
34. Nagesia, Nagasia
35. Naikda, Nayaka, Cholivala Nayaka, Kapadia Nayaka, Mota Nayaka, Nana Nayaka
36. Oraon, Dhangad
37. Pardhan, Pathari, Saroti
38. Pardhi; Advichincher, Phans Pardhi, Phanse Pardhi, Langoli Pardhi, Bahelia, Bahellia, Chita Pardhi, Shikari, Takankar, Takia
39. Parja
40. Patelia
41. Pomla
42. Rathawa
43. Sawar, Sawara
44. Thakur, Thakar, Ka Thakur, Ka Thakar, Ma Thakur, Ma Thakar
45. Thoti (in Aurangabad, Bhir, Nanded, Osmanabad and Parbhani districts and Rajura tahsil of Chandrapur district)

46. Varli
47. Vitolia, Kotwalia, Barodia.

PART X — MANIPUR

1. Aimol
2. Anal
3. Angami
4. Chiru
5. Chothe
6. Gangte
7. Hmar
8. Kabui
9. Kacha Naga
10. Koirao
11. Koireng
12. Kom
13. Lamgang
14. Mao
15. Maram
16. Maring
17. Any Mizo (Lushai) tribes
18. Monsang
19. Moyon
20. Paite
21. Purum
22. Ralte
23. Sema
24. Simte
25. Suhte
26. Tangkhul
27. Thadou
28. Vaiphui
29. Zou.

PART XI — MEGHALAYA

1. Chakma
2. Dimasa, Kachari
3. Garo
4. Hajong
5. Hmar
6. Khasi, Jaintia, Synteng, Pnar, War, Bhoi, Lyngngam
7. Any Kuki Tribes including :—

(i) Biate, Biete
(ii) Changsan
(iii) Chongloi
(iv) Doungel
(v) Gamalhou
(xix) Kipgen
(xx) Kuki
(xxi) Lengthang
(xxii) Lhangum
(xxiii) Lhoujem

(vi) Gangte
(vii) Guite
(viii) Hanneng
(xix) Haokip, Haupit
(x) Haolai
(xi) Hengna
(xii) Hongsungh
(xiii) Hrangkhwal, Rangkhol
(xiv) Jongbe
(xv) Khawchung
(xvi) Khawathlang, Khothalong
(xvii) Khelma
(xviii) Kholhou
(xxiv) Lhouvun
(xxv) Lupheng
(xxvi) Mangjel
(xxvii) Misao
(xxviii) Riang
(xxix) Sairhem
(xxx) Selnam
(xxxi) Singson
(xxxii) Sitlhou
(xxxiii) Sukte
(xxxiv) Thado
(xxxv) Thangngeu
(xxxvi) Uibuh
(xxxvii) Vaiphei

8. Lakher
9. Man (Tai speaking)
10. Any Mizo (Lushai) tribes
11. Mikir
12. Any Naga tribes
13. Pawi
14. Synteng

PART XII — ORISSA

1. Bagata
2. Baiga
3. Banjara, Banjari
4. Bathudi
5. Bhottada, Dhotada
6. Bhuiya, Bhuyan
7. Bhumia
8. Bhumij
9. Bhunjia
10. Binjhal
11. Binjhia, Binjhoa
12. Birhor
13. Bondo Poraja
14. Chenchu
15. Dal
16. Desua Bhumij

17. Dharua
18. Didayi
19. Gadaba
20. Gandia
21. Ghara
22. Gond, Gondo
23. Ho
24. Holva
25. Jatapu
26. Juang
27. Kandha Gauda
28. Kawar
29. Kharia, Kharian
30. Kharwar
31. Khond, Kond, Kandha, Nanguli Kandha, Sitha Kandha
32. Kisan
33. Kol
34. Kolah Loharas, Kol Loharas
35. Kolha
36. Koli, Malhar
37. Kondadora
38. Kora
39. Korua
40. Kotia
41. Koya
42. Kulis
43. Lodha
44. Madia
45. Mahali
46. Mankidi
47. Mankirdia
48. Matya
49. Mirdhas
50. Munda, Munda Lohara, Munda Mahalis
51. Mundari
52. Omanatya
53. Oraon
54. Parenga
55. Paroja
56. Pentia
57. Rajuar
58. Santal
59. Saora, Savar, Saura, Sahara
60. Shabar, Lodha
61. Sounti
62. Tharua.

PART XIII — RAJASTHAN

1. Bhil, Bhil Garasia, Dholi Bhil, Dungri Bhil, Dungri Garasia, Mewasi Bhil, Rawal Bhil, Tadvi Bhil, Bhagalia, Bhilala, Pawra, Vasava, Vasave
2. Bhil Mina
3. Damor, Damaria

4. Dhanka, Tadvi, Tetaria, Valvi
5. Garasia (excluding Rajput Garasia)
6. Kathodi, Katkari, Dhor Kathodi, Dhor Katkari, Son Kathodi, Son Katkari
7. Kokna, Kokni, Kukna
8. Koli Dhor, Tokre Koli, Kolcha, Kolgha
9. Mina
10. Naikda, Nayaka, Cholivala Nayaka, Kapadia Nayaka, Mota Nayaka, Nana Nayaka
11. Patelia
12. Seharia, Sehria, Sahariya.

PART XIV — TAMIL NADU

1. Adiyan
2. Aranadan
3. Eravallan
4. Irular
5. Kadar
6. Kammara (excluding Kanyakumari district and Shenkottah taluk of Tirunelveli district)
7. Kanikaran, Kanikkar (in Kanyakumari district and Shenkottah taluk of Tirunelveli district)
8. Kaniyan, Kanyan
9. Kattunayakan
10. Kochu Velan
11. Konda Kapus
12. Kondareddis
13. Koraga
14. Kota (excluding Kanyakumari district and Shenkottah taluk of Tirunelveli district)
15. Kudiya, Melakudi
16. Kurichchan
17. Kurumbas (in the Nilgiris district)
18. Kurumans

19. Maha Malasar
20. Malai Arayan
21. Malai Pandaram
22. Malai Vedan
23. Malakkuravan
24. Malasar
25. Malayali (in Dharmpuri, North Arcot, Pudukottai, Salem, South Arcot and Tiruchirapalli districts)
26. Malayekandi
27. Mannan
28. Mudugar, Muduvan
29. Muthuvan
30. Palleyan
31. Palliyan
32. Palliyar
33. Paniyan
34. Sholaga
35. Toda (excluding Kanyakumari district and Shenkottah taluk of Tirunelveli district)
36. Uraly.

PART XV — TRIPURA

1. Bhil
2. Bhutia
3. Chaimal
4. Chakma
5. Garoo
6. Halam
7. Jamatia
8. Khasia
9. Kuki, including the following sub-tribes :—

(i) Balte	(x) Laifang
(ii) Belalhut	(xi) Lentei

(iii) Chhalya
(iv) Fun
(v) Hajango
(vi) Jangtei
(vii) Khareng
(viii) Khephong
(ix) Kuntei
(xii) Mizel
(xiii) Namte
(xiv) Paitu, Paite
(xv) Rangchan
(xvi) Rangkhole
(xvii) Thangluya

10. Lepcha
11. Lushai
12. Mag
13. Munda, Kaur
14. Noatia
15. Orang
16. Riang
17. Santal
18. Tripura, Tripuri, Tippera
19. Uchai

PART XVI — WEST BENGAL

1. Asur
2. Baiga
3. Bedia, Bediya
4. Bhumij
5. Bhutia, Sherpa, Toto, Dukpa, Kagatay, Tibetan, Yolmo
6. Birhor
7. Birjia
8. Chakma
9. Chero
10. Chik Baraik
11. Garo
12. Gond
13. Gorait
14. Hajang
15. Ho
16. Karmali
17. Kharwar
18. Khond
19. Kisan
20. Kora
21. Korwa
22. Lepcha
23. Lodha, Kheria, Kharia
24. Lohara, Lohra
25. Magh
26. Mahali

27. Mahli
28. Mal Pahariya
29. Mech
30. Mru
31. Munda
32. Nagesia
33. Oraon
34. Parhaiya
35. Rabha
36. Santal
37. Sauria Paharia
38. Savar".

CHAPTER II

In the Constitution (Andaman and Nicobar Islands) Scheduled Tribes Order, 1959 :—

(a) in paragraph 2, for the words "resident in the localities specified in relation to them in that Schedule", the words "resident in that Union territory" shall be substituted;

(b) for the Schedule, substitute—

THE SCHEDULE

1. Andamanese, Chariar, Chari, Kora, Tabo, Bo, Yere, Kede, Bea, Balawa, Bojigiyab, Juwai, Kol
2. Jarawas
3. Nicobarese
4. Onges
5. Sentinelese
6. Shom Pens."

SIKKIM

[The Constitution (Sikkim) Scheduled Tribes Order, 1978, C.O. 110]

Scheduled Tribes

1. Bhutia (including Chumbipa, Dopthapa, Dukpa, Kagatey, Sherpa, Tibetan, Tromopa, Yolmo)
2. Lepcha.

The State of Mizoram Act, 1986

MIZORAM

Scheduled Tribes

1. Chakma
2. Dimasa, Kachari
3. Garo
4. Hajong
5. Hmar
6. Khasi, Jaintia, Synteng, Pnar, War, Bhoi, Lyngngam
7. Any Kuki Tribes, including :—

(i) Biate, Biete
(ii) Changsan
(iii) Chongloi
(iv) Doungel
(v) Gamalhou
(vi) Gangte
(vii) Guite
(viii) Hanneng
(ix) Haokip, Haupit
(x) Haolai
(xi) Hengna
(xii) Hongsungh
(xiii) Hrangkhwal, Rangkhol

(xiv) Jongbe
(xv) Khawchung
(xvi) Khawathlang, Khothalong
(xxix) Sairhem
(xxx) Selnam
(xxxi) Singson
(xxxii) Sitlhou
(xxxiii) Sukte
(xxxiv) Thado
(xxxv) Thangngen
(xxxvi) Uibuh
(xxxvii) Vaiphei
(xxvi) Mangjel
(xxvii) Misao
(xxviii) Riang
(xvii) Khelma
(xviii) Kholhou
(xix) Kipgen
(xx) Kuki
(xxi) Lengthang
(xxii) Lhangum
(xxiii) Lhoujem
(xxiv) Lhouvun
(xxv) Lupheng

8. Lakher
9. Man (Tai speaking)
10. Any Mizo (Lushai) tribes
11. Mikir
12. Any Naga tribes
13. Pawi
14. Synteng.

The State of Arunachal Pradesh Act, 1986

ARUNACHAL PRADESH

Scheduled Tribes

1. Abor
2. Aka
3. Apatani
4. Dafla
5. Galong
6. Khampti
7. Khowa
8. Mishmi
9. Momba
10. Any Naga tribes
11. Sherdukpen
12. Singpho.

The Goa, Daman and Diu Reorganisation Act, 1987

Scheduled Tribes

The State of Goa

1. Dhodia
2. Dubla (Halpati)
3. Naikda (Talavia)
4. Siddi (Nayaka)
5. Varli

The Union Territory of Daman and Diu

1. Dhodia
2. Dubla (Halpati)
3. Naikda (Talavia)
4. Siddi (Nayaka)
5. Varli

The Constitution (Scheduled Tribes) Order (Amendment) Act, 1987

Meghalaya

after sl. 14 add the following

15. Boro Kachari
16. Koch
17. Raba, Rava

The Constitution (Jammu & Kashmir) Scheduled Tribes Order, 1989

1. Balti
2. Beda
3. Bot, Boto
4. Brokpa, Drokpa, Dard, Shin
5. Changpa
6. Garra
7. Mon
8. Purigpa

APPENDIX II ***IMMEDIATE***

No. BC. 12016/37/76-SCT.V

GOVERNMENT OF INDIA/BHARAT SARKAR

MINISTRY OF HOME AFFAIRS/GRIH MANTRALAYA

New Delhi, the 5th October, 1979

To

The Secretary to the Government of Andhra Pradesh,
Social Welfare Department,
Secretariat Building,
Hyderabad

Subject : Specification of equivalent names and name of synonyms and sub-castes/tribes of the existing Scheduled Castes and Scheduled Tribes in Andhra Pradesh State.

Sir,

I am directed to refer to the correspondence resting with your letter No. 2595/F2/78-1, dated 15-12-1978 on the above subject and to say that in the light of the Supreme Court's ruling in the case of *Bhaiya Ram Munda Vs. Anirudh Palar* (A.I.R. 1971 S.C. 2533) the Government of India has, in consultation with the Registrar General of India, decided that the entries in column (3) of the table below may be treated as equivalent names or names of synonyms and sub-castes/tribes of the Scheduled Castes and Scheduled Tribes entered in column (2) of the table for the State of Andhra Pradesh :

2. The above list of equivalent names and names of synonyms or sub-castes/tribes has been prepared by taking into account the ethnographic and other facts

Sl. No. in the SC/ST Schedule	Name of the community as given in the SC/ST Schedule	Equivalent names or names of synonyms and sub-castes/tribes
1	2	3
(a)	List of Scheduled Castes	
11.	Byagara	Byagari
14.	Chamar, Mochi, Muchi	Chamar-Ravidas, Chamar-Rohidas
35.	Mala	Mala Ayawaru
(b)	List of Scheduled Tribes	
1.	Andh	Sadhu Andh
5.	Gadabas	Bodo Gadaba, Gutob Gadaba, Kallayi, Gadaba, Parangi Gadaba, Kathera Cadaba, Kapu, Cadaba
6.	Gond, Naikpod, Rajgond	Koitur
12.	Kolam, Mannervarlu	Kolawar
13.	Konda Dhoras	Kubi
16.	Kondhs, Kodi, Kodhu, Desaya-Kondhs, Dongria Kondhs, Kuttiya Kondhs, Tikiria Kondhs, Yenity Kondhs	Kuvinga
18.	Koya, Goud, Rajah, Rasha Koya, Lingadhari Koya (ordinary), Kottu Koya, Bhine Koya, Raj Koya	Doli Koya, Gutta Koya, Kammara Koya, Musara, Koya, Oddi Koya, Pattidi Koya
29.	Sugalis, Lambadis	Banjara
32.	Yenadis	Chella Yenadi, Kappala Yenadi, Manchi Yenadi, Reddi Yenadi
33.	Yerukulas	Koracha, Dabba Yerukula, Kunchapuri Yerukula, Uppu Yerukula

relating to the community referred to above and may be used only for the purpose of verification of claims of the members of the relevant community, calling themselves by the names given in column (3) of the table above, to belong to the community in column (2) of the table.

3. The above list is not intended or shall not be treated as an alteration or amendments of the Schedules to the Presidential Orders specifying Scheduled Castes and Scheduled Tribes in relation to the Andhra Pradesh State, as any alterations or amendments of the lists of Scheduled Castes and Scheduled Tribes contained in the Presidential Orders can be made only by Parliamentary legislation.

4. The Scheduled Castes and Scheduled Tribes certificates to the eligible persons will be valid only if they are issued in the relevant name of the community entered in the Presidential Order, i.e., those in column (2) of the table and not in the names given in column (3) thereof. Before issuing such certificate, it has also to be verified that they fulfil all other conditions of eligibility set out in the Presidential Orders e.g., that the person should be a resident of the locality specified in relation to the respective Scheduled Castes/Tribes from the date of notification of the Presidential Order, etc.

5. It is further clarified that as the listed synonyms/sub-castes/sub-tribes would not form part of the Presidential Order, it would be open for any affected person to contend that the particular synonyms/sub-castes/sub-tribes is not, in fact, a part of or identical with the respective Scheduled Caste/Tribe.

6. The State Government are requested to bring the contents of this letter to the notice of all concerned authorities in the State for compliance. Copy of those instructions may also be sent to this Ministry for information and record.

Yours faithfully,
P.S. KRISHNAN
Joint Secretary to the
Government of India
Tele. No 381652

No. BC. 12016/37/76-SCT.V, New Delhi, dated the 25th October, 1979.

Copy forwarded for information to:

1. The Registrar General of India, Social Studies Unit, West Block, R.K. Puram, New Delhi-110023.
2. The Commissioner for Scheduled Castes and Scheduled Tribes, West Block-1, R.K. Puram, New Delhi-110023.
3. The Commission for Scheduled Castes and Scheduled Tribes, Lok Nayak Bhavan, New Delhi-110003.
4. All Ministries of the Government of India.

P.S. KRISHNAN
Joint Secretary to the
Government of India
Tele. No. 381652

APPENDIX-III

GOVERNMENT OF WEST BENGAL
SCHEDULED CASTES & TRIBES WELFARE
DEPARTMENT WRITERS' BUILDINGS

No.269(69)-TW/EC

MR-100/93

Dated Calcutta, the 6th June, 1994.

From : V. Subramanian

Secretary to the Govt. of West Bengal.

To : (1) The District Magistrate,

....

(2) The S.D.O.,

....

Subject : Clarification regarding the term 'Methor' in West Bengal.

Sir,

I am directed to say that 'Methor' is listed as a Scheduled Caste under Serial No. 22 in the list of Scheduled Castes in West Bengal. It is also our experience that no person engaged in the clearance of night-soil and similar duties use the term 'Methor' as their surname in this State. Actually the term 'Methor' is very much related to occupation (carrying and cleaning night-soil etc.) and is not a term denoting a surname or title. Some people engaged in the work of Methor throughout West Bengal have been using Hela, Balmiki, Bansfor, Bhangi and Other surnames after their names. In Bengal all these persons using such surnames, but engaged in clearing night-soil are by profession and/or caste "Mehtor". Hence, all persons using the above surnames and traditionally occupied in the job of carrying and cleaning night-soil may be treated as 'Mehtor' mentioned in serial No. 22 of the Schedule. In view of the above clarification it is to be clearly understood that in determining as to whether a person is a 'Methor' or not it is not to be insisted upon that the person should use 'Mehtor' as a surname/title. Reliance has to be placed on his occupation and not the surname. It may be further mentioned that in determining the caste 'Methor' reliance may be laid upon the 'traditional occupation' irrespective of present occupation of the applicants concerned.

Yours faithfully,

Secretary to the Govt. of West Bengal.

APPENDIX-IV

Names of castes excluded from, or included in the Schedules, 1950-76.

Assam

1950		No change, only area restriction was withdrawn.
1956	B(i)	1 caste (Jalkeot) was included, and
	B(ii)	2 castes sub-castes (Jhalo-Malo and Rishi) were added to the existing ones.
1976		No change.

West Bengal

1950	A(i)	4 castes (Mech, Munda, Oraon and Santal) were transferred to the Scheduled Tribes list.
	A(ii)	14 castes (Agaria, Berua, Bhatiya, Binjhia, Dhenuar, Garo, Hadi, Hajang, Halalkhor, Ho, Kan, Kandh, Kapuria and Nat) were descheduled.
1956	A(i)	7 castes (Bhumij, Kora, Lodha, Mahli, Malpahariya, Nagasia and Rabha) were transferred to the Scheduled Tribes list.
	A(ii)	1 caste (Kastha) was descheduled.
	A(iii)	2 castes (Muchi and Chamar) were included in the same group.
	B(i)	13(16) castes [Bantor, Bhogta, Chau- pal, Dabgar, Damai (Nepali), Kami (Nepali), Kanjar, Kurariar, Keot or Keyot, Hari, Mehtar and

Bhangi, Halakhor, Nat and Sarki (Nepali)] were included.

B(ii) 14 castes/sub-castes [Charmakar, Mochi, Rabidas, Ruidas, Rishi, Dhobi, Dhangad, Dusadh, Dhari, Dharhi, Duley, Koranga, Paundra, and Sawasi] were added to the existing ones.

1976 A(i) 1 caste (Bediya) was transferred to the Scheduled Tribes list.

A(ii) 1 caste (Mehtor) was merged with a bigger group.

A(iii) 1 caste (Hari) became redundant due to grouping of castes.

Bihar

1950 B(i) 2 castes (Bantar and Dabgar) were included.

B(ii) 3 castes/sub-castes (Dhari, Dharhi, Mehtar) were added to the existing ones.

1956 A(i) 2 castes (Chamar and Mochi) were brought under one group.

B(i) 3 castes/sub-castes (Dhanged, Bhangi and Sawasi) were added to the existing ones.

1976 No change.

Orissa

1950 The area restriction was withdrawn.

A(i) 1 caste (Bhuiya) was transferred to the Scheduled Tribes list.

A(ii) 1 caste (Bauro) was descheduled.

B(i) 41(50) castes/sub-castes [(1) Amat, Amant, (2) Badaik, (3) Bagheti, (4) Bajikar, (5) Bari, (6) Bauti, (7) Bavuri, (8) Bedia or Bejia, (9) Beldar, (10) Bhata (11) Cherua, or Chhelia, (12) Dosadha, (13) Dhanwar, (14) Ghantarghada or Ghantra (15) Ghogia, (16) Karua, (17) Kurunga, (18) Laban, (19) Laheri, (20)

Mewar, (21) Mundapotta, (22) Panika, (23) Pantanti, (24) Pap, (25) Pasi, (26) Patial, or Patikar, or Patratanti, or Patua, (27) Rajna, (28) Sabakhia, (29) Samasi, (30) Sanei, (31) Sidhria, (32) Sinduria, (33) Tamadia, (34) Tamudia, (35) Tiar, or Tior, (36) Dasuabhumij, (37) Dharua, (38) Gunju or Ganju, (39) Kumbhar, (40) Sukuli, and (41) Khadala] were included.

B(ii) 4 castes/sub-castes (Hadi, Jhala, Kandara, Valamiki) were added to the existing ones.

1956 A(i) 3 castes (Bhumij of 1936 list and Dasuabhumij and Dharua included in 1950) were transferred to the Scheduled Tribes list.

A(ii) 4(5) castes (Pradhan of 1936 list, Ganju or Ganju, Kumbhar and Sukuli, all included in 1950) were desched- uled.

A(iii) 3(4) castes (Chamar, Mochi or Muchi, Satnami) were clubbed together in one group.

B(i) 11(13) castes/sub-castes [(1) Bhoi, (2) Chakali, (3) Chandi Maru, (4) Gorait, or Korait, (5) Kuli, (6) Kummari, (7) Musahar, (8) Namasudra, (9) Sauntia, Santia, (10) Tanla, and (11) Ujia] were included.

B(ii) 5 castes/sub-castes [Baghuti, Duria Dom, Khodalo, Malo, Zala] were added to the existing ones.

1976 A(i) 1 caste (Kuli included in 1956) was descheduled.

U.P.

1950 A(i) 4 castes (Aheriya, Khatik, Kori, Tharu) were descheduled.

B(i) 7(8) castes (Baiga, Baiswar, Bhoksa, Dhusia or Jhusia, Dusadh, Gond and Jatava) were included.

1956 A(i) 1 caste (Bhoksa, included in 1950) was descheduled.

A(ii) 3(4) castes [(1) Chamar, (2) Dhusia or Jhusia, and (3) Jatava] were merged together into a new group.

B(i) 5 castes (Khatik and Kori, descheduled in 1950, and Balai, Musahar and Mazhabi) were included.

B(ii) 1 caste (Tarmali) was added to an existing one.

1976 No change.

Punjab

1950 B(i) 7 castes (Batwal, Kabirpanthi, Mazhabi, Pherara, Sanhai, Sanhal and Sikligar) were included.

B(ii) 2 castes/sub-castes (Mahasha and Ravidasi) were added to the existing ones.

1956 A(i) 2(3) castes/sub-castes [(1) Chamar and (2) Ramdasi or Ravidasi] were merged into a group.

B(i) 4(8) castes/sub-castes [(1) Darain, (2) Deha, Dhaya, Dhea, (3) Dhogri, Dhangri, Siggi, (4) Sansoi] were included.

B(iii) 12 castes/sub-castes (Burar, Berar, Bauria, Bhangi, Jatia Chamar, Rehgar, Raigar, Doom, Gandhil Gandola, Julaha, Bhedkut, Manesh) were added to the existing ones.

1976 No change, only the area restriction was withdrawn.

Madras (Tamil Nadu)

1950 A(i) 5 castes (Arnadan, Kattanayakan, Kudiya, Kurmans, Paniyan) were transferred to the Scheduled Tribes list.

A(ii) 3 castes (Battada, Dombo, Relli) were descheduled.

A(iii) 4 castes (Ghasi and Haddi, Paidi and Pano) were merged to form two new groups.

B(i) 1 caste (Panan) was included.

B(ii) 3 castes/sub-castes (Dom, Dombara, Relli Sachandi) were added to the existing ones.

1956 A(i) 3 castes (Koraga, Kurichchan, Malashar) were transferred to the Scheduled Tribes list.

A(ii) 17(19) castes/sub-castes [(1) Bariki, (2) Bavuri, (3) Chachati, (4) Godari, (5) Byagari, (6) Dandasi, (7) Gasi, Haddi, Relli Sachandi, (8) Hasla, (9) Kadan, (10) Kodalo, (11) Kudubi, (12) Mala Dasu, (13) Matangi, (14) Painda, (15) Paky, (16) Pamidi, (17) Valmiki] were descheduled.

A(iii) 2 castes (Chamar and Muchi) were merged to form a new group.

B(i) 23(24) castes [(1) Ayyanvar, (2) Bharatar, (3) Domban, (4) Kadaiyan, (5) Kakkalan, (6) Kavara, (7) Koliyan, (8) Kootan, Koodan, (9) Mannan, (10) Padannan, (11) Palluvan, (12) Pannadi, (13) Pathiyan, (14) Thandan, (15) Vallon, (16) Perumanan, (17) Vannan, (18) Vathiriyan, (19) Velan, (20) Vetan, (21) Vettiyan, (22) Ulladan, (23) Uraly] were included.

B(ii) 5 castes/sub-castes (Parayan, Sambavar, Sidhanar, Cheramar, Padanna) were added to the existing ones.

1976 A(i) 1 caste (Uraly, included in 1956) was transferred to the Scheduled Tribes list.

A(ii) 2 castes (Perumanan, Ulladan, both included in 1956) were descheduled.

Andhra Pradesh

1953 Same list as that of Madras.

1956 A(i) 1 caste (Valmiki) was transferred to the Scheduled Tribes list.

A(ii) 46 castes (Adi Karnataka, Ajila, Arunthathiyar, Baira, Bakuda, Bandi, Bellara, Byagari, Chakkiliyan, Cheruman, Devendrakulathan,

Godda, Hasla, Kadan, Kalladi, Kanakkan, Karimpalan, Kodalo, Koosa, Koraga, Kudubi, Kudumban, Kuravan, Kurichchan, Madari, Maila, Malasar, Mavilan, Moger, Nalakeyava, Nayadi, Pagadai, Painda, Pallan, Panan, Panniandi, Paraiyan, Paravan, Pulayan, Puthirai Vannan, Raneyar, Sapari, Semman, Tiruvalluvar, Valluvan, Vettuvan) were descheduled.

A(iii) 2 castes (Chamar and Muchi) were included together to form a new group.

B(i) 31(38) castes [(1) Arundhatiya, (2) Anamuk, (3) Aray (Mala), (4) Arwa Mala, (5) Beda (Budga) Jangam, (6) Bindla, (7) Byagara, (8) Chambhar, (9) Dakkal (Dakkalwar), (10) Dhor, (11) Ellamalwar (Yellammalwandi), (12) Holeya Dasari, (13) Kolupulvandlu, (14) Madasi Kuruva or Madari Kuruva, (15) Madiga Dasu and Mashteen, (16) Mahar, (17) Mala Dasari, (18) Mala Hannai, (19) Malajangam, (20) Mala Masti, (21) Mala Sale (Netkani), (22) Mala Sanyasi, (23) Mang, (24) Mang Garodi, (25) Manne, (26) Mashti, (27) Mehtar, (28) Mitha Ayyalvar, (29) Relli, (30) Sapru, and (31) Sindhollu (Chindollu)] were included.

B(ii) 4 castes/sub-castes (Mochi, Moti, Pambanda, Pariah) were added to the existing ones.

1976 A(i) 1 caste (Thoti) was merged with a bigger group.

Madhya Pradesh

1950 A(i) 1 caste (Pardhan) was shifted to the Scheduled Tribes list.

A(ii) 14 castes (Chauhan, Dhimar, Dhobi, Ganda, Jangam, Kaikari, Khatik, Koli, Kumhar, Mala, Nagarchi, Ojha, Panka and Pardhi) were descheduled.

B(i) 1 caste (Kaikadi) was included.

B(ii) 3 castes/sub-castes (Bahana, Dahait, Ghasi) were added to the existing ones.

1956 A(i) 2 castes (Bedar and Kaikadi) were descheduled.

A(ii) 3 castes (Chamar, Mochi and Satnami) were merged to form a bigger group.

B(i) 52(89) castes/sub-castes [(1) Bagri or Bagdi, (2) Beldar, (3) Balai, (4) Balahi, (5) Banchada, (6) Barahor or Basod, (7)Bargunda, (8) Basar, (9) Basor or Bansphor, (10) Bansphor or Basor, (11) Bedia, (12) Beldar or Sunkar, (13) Bhangi or Mehtar, (14) Balmiki, Dharkar or Lalbegi, (15) Mehtor, Bhangi or Dhanuk, (16) Bhanumati, (17) Chamar, Ahirwar, Chamar Mangan, Mochi, or Raidas, (18) Chamar, Bairwa, Bhambi, Jatav, Mochi or Regar, (19) Chamar, Jatav or Mochi, (20) Chidar, (21) Chitar, (22) Dhed, (23) Dher, (24) Dhobi, (25) Dom or Dumar, (26) Dome, (27) Domar or Doris, (28) Ganda or Gandi, (29) Ghasia, (30) Kanjar, (31) Khatik, (32) Khatik, Chikwa or Chikvi, (33) Koli or Katia, (34) Kori, (35) Kotwal (36) Kuchbandhia, (37) Kumhar, (38) Mahar, (39) Mehar, (40) Mang or Mang Garodi, (41) Mang, Dankhni Mang, Mang Mahashi, Mang Garudi, Madari, Garudi, Radhe Mang, (42) Meghwal, (43) Moghia, (44) Mushkan, (45)Nat, Kalbelia, Sapera, (46) Pardhi, (47) Pasi, (48) Sansi, (49) Sansia, (50) Sansia or Bedia, (51) Silawat and (52) Zamral] were included.

B(ii) 13 castes/sub-castes (Bansor, Bansodi, Chamari, Nona, Rohidas, Ramnami, Surjabanshi or Surjyaramnami, Dahat, Patharia, Koli, Kanera or Mirdha) were added to the existing ones.

1976 A(i) 1 caste (Madgi) was descheduled.

A(ii) 19(53) castes were merged into 8(47) new groups

[a (1) Basor, Burud, Bansor, Bansodi, (2) Basar and (3) Basor or Bansphore were merged into a new group.

(b) (1) Bhangi, Mehtar and (2) Balmiki, Lalbegi and Dharkar were merged into a new group.

(c) (1) Chamar, Ahirwar, Mochi, Raidas, Chamar, Mangan, (2) Chamar, Chamari, Mochi, Nona, Rohidas, Satnami, Ramnami, Surjyabanshi, Surjyaramnami, and (3) Chamar, Bairwa, Bhambi, Jatav, Mochi, Regar were merged into a group.

(d) (1) Dhed and (2) Dher were merged into a group.

(e) (1) Dom or Dumar, (2) Dome, and (3) Domar or Doris were merged into a group.

(f) (1) Mahar or Mehra and (2) Mehar was merged into a group.

(g) (1) Mang or Mang Garodi, and (2) Mang, Mang Mahashi, Dankhni Mang, Mang Garudi, Madari, Garudi or Radhe Mang were merged into a group.

(h) (1) Sansi and (2) Sansia were merged into a group].

A(iii) 14(23) castes/sub-castes became redundant because of grouping of castes.

[(1) Beldar, (2) Balai, (3) Balahi, (4) Bansphor or Basor, (5) Mehtar, Bhangi or Dhanuk, (6) Mehtor or Bhangi, (7) Chamar, Jatav, Mochi, (8) Dom, (9) Ghasia, (10) Khatik of Khatik, Chikwa, Chikvi group, (11) Koli or Katia, (12) Kori, (13) Mahar, (14) Mang, (15) Sansia or Bedia].

B(i) 2 castes/sub-castes were added to the existing ones (Navdigar, Kubutar).

Bombay (Maharastra since 1960)

1950 A(i) 1 caste (Koli Dhor) was trasferred to the Scheduled Tribes list.

A(ii) 2 castes (Dhed and Khalpa) were descheduled.

A(iii) 4(5) castes [(1) Holaya and (2) Garode were merged into a group and (1) Halsavar and (2) Halsar or Haslar were merged into a group] were merged to form two new groups.

B(i) 5 castes (Ager, Garoda, Mahyavanshi, Machigar, Rohit) were included.

1956 A(i) 1(2) castes (Kolcha or Kolgha) were trasferred to the Scheduled Tribes list.

A(ii) 11(16) castes/sub-castes [Chakrawadya-Dasar, (2) Chena-Dasaru, (3) Chuhar or Chuhra, (4) Dakaleru, (5) Holaya or Garode, (6) Kotegar, (7) Shindheva or Shenva, (8) Shingdav or Shingadya, (9) Sochi, (10) Timali, (11) Vitholia and (12) Mang of Mang or Madig group] were descheduled.

A(iii) 9(11) castes were merged to form 3(11) groups.

[(a) (1) Asodi, (2) Bhambi, (3) Chambhar, Samgar, Mochigar, (4) Machigar and (5) Madig were merged into a group.

(b) (1) Mahar and (2) Dhegu Megu were merged into a group.

(c) (1) Vankar and (2) Mahyavanshi were merged into a group.]

B(i) 74(120) castes/sub-castes were included.

[(1) Anamuk, (2) Aray Mala, (3) Arwa Mala, (4) Bahna, Bahana, (5) Balahi, Balai, (6) Basor, Burud, Bansodi, Bansor, (7) Bawa (Dhedh), Dedh-Sadhu, (8) Beda Jangam, Budga Jangam, (9) Bedar, (10) Chamar, Chamari, Mochi, Nona, Rohidas, Ramnami,

Satnami, Surjyabanshi, Surjyaramnami, (11) Samagara, (12) Chambhar, (13) Chamar, (14) Chamadia, (15) Mehtar, (16) Mehtar or Bhangi, (17) Bhangi or Rukhi, (18) Bhangi, (19) Bindla, (20) Byagara, (21) Chalvadi, (22) Chenna Dasar or Holaya Dasar, (23) Holeya Dasari, (24) Chadar, (25) Dakkal (Dakkal- war), (26) Dangashia, (27) Dhor, (28) Dohor, (29) Dom, Dumar, (30) Ellamalvar (Yellam- malawandlu), (31) Ganda or Gandi, (32) Garoda, (33) Garmatang, (34) Ghasi or Ghasia, (35) Holeya, (36) Holiya, (37) Holar or Valhar, (38) Kaikadi, (39) Katia or Patharia, (40) Khangar, Kanera or Mirdha, (41) Khatik, Chikwa or Chikvi, (42) Kolupuvandlu, (43) Kori, (44) Madgi, (45) Madiga, (46) Mahar, (47) Mahar, Mehra, (48) Vankar, Dhedh or Antyaj (49) Mala, (50) Mala Dasari, (51) Mala Hannai, (52) Mala Jangam, (53) Mala Masti, (54) Mala Sale (Netkani), (55) Mala Sanyasi, (56) Mang, (57) Mang, Dankhni Mang, Mang Mashashi, Madari, Garudi, Mang Garudi, Radhe Mang, (58) Mang Garodi, (59) Manne, (60) Mashti, (61) Meghwal, (62) Mitha Ayyalvar, (63) Hadi, (64) Pasi, (65) Sansi, (66) Senva, (67) Shemalia, (68) Sindhollu (Chindollu), (69) Thori, (70) Turi Barot, (71) Turi Barot or Dhedh Barot, (72) Tirgar or Tirbanda, (73) Holaya or Holer, and (74) Shenva, Chenva, Sedma, or Ravat].

B (ii) 37 castes/sub-castes [(1) Bant, (2) Bhambhi, Asadaru, Chamadia, Chamar, Chamgar, Haralayya, Harali, Khalpa, Madar, Telegu Mochi, Kamati Mochi, Ranigar, Rohit, Rohidas, (3) Chamar, Nalia, (4) Mehtar, Olgana, Rukhi, Malkana,

Halalkhor, Lalbegi, Balmiki, Korar, Zadmalli, (5) Channayya, (6) Kakkayya or Kankayya, (7) Garo, (8) Halasvar, (9) Taral, (10) Dhed, Maru Vankar, (11) Hadi, (12) Mang, Matang] were added to the existing ones.

1960 The State was bifurcated when the castes/ sub-castes peculiar to Saurastra and Kuch regions, which were included in the newly created State of Gujarat, were excluded.

A(i) 17(24) castes/sub-castes [(1) Bawa (Dhedh) or Dedh Sadhu, (2) Bhangi or Rukhi, (3) Bhangi, (4) Chamadia, (5) Chamar, (6) Chamar, Nalia or Rohit, (7) Dangashia, (8) Garoda, (9) Garmatang, (10) Hadi, (11) Meghwal, (12) Senva, (13) Shemalia, (14) Thori, (15) Turi-Barot, Dhedh Barot, (16) Turi-Barot, and (17) Vankar, Dhedh or Antyaj] were descheduled.

B(i) 1 caste (Mochi) was added with the existing ones.

1976 A(i) 1 caste (Chadar) was descheduled.

A(ii) 16(59) castes/sub-castes were merged to form 7(54) group.

[(a) (1) Chamar, Chamari, Mochi, Nona, Rohidas, Ramnami, Satnami, Surjyabanshi, or Surjyaramnami, (2) Bhambi, Bhambhi, Asadaru, Asodi, Chamadia, Chamar, Chambhar, Chamgar, Haralayya, Harali, Khalpa, Machigar, Mochigar, Madar, Madig, Mochi, Telegu Mochi, Kamati Mochi, Ranigar, Rohidas, Rohit or Samgar and (3) Samgara were merged to form a group;

(b) (1) Dohor and (2) Dhor, Kakkayya, Kankayya were merged to form a new group.

(c) (1) Holeya, (2) Holiya, and (3) Holaya or Holer were merged to form a new group;

(d) (1) Mahar or Mehra and (2) Mahar, Taral, Dhegu Meghu were merged into a group;

(e) (1) Mang Garodi and (2) Mang Garudi were merged into a group;

(f) (1) Mang, Matang, Minimadig and (2) Mang, Dankhani Mang, Mang Mahashi, Madari, Garudi or Radhe Mang were merged into a group;

(g) (1) Holeya Dasari and (2) Chenna Dasari, Holaya Dasar were merged into a group].

A(iii) 8(10) castes/sub-castes [(1) Mochi, (2) Chambhar, (3) Mehtar, (4) Mehtor or Bhangi, (5) Chalvadi, (6) Dhor, (7) Mahar, (8) Mang and Mang Garudi or Mang, Dankhni Mang ... group] became redundant due to merger of groups.

Gujarat

1960 Gujarat came into being after the bifurcation of Bombay State in 1960 when fresh list for the newly created State was issued.

1976 A(i) 9 (40) castes/sub-castes were merged into 4(37) new groups.

[(a) (1) Mochi, (2) Chamar, Nalia, Rohit, and (3) Bhambi, Bhambhi, Asadaru, Asodi, Chamadia, Chamar, Chamghar, Chambhar, Haralayya, Harali, Khalpa, Machigar, Mochigar, Madar, Madig, Telegu Mochi, Kamati Mochi, Ranigar, Rohidas, Rohit or Samgar were merged into a new group;

(b) (1) Mahyavanshi, Dhed, Vankar or Maru Vankar, and (2) Vankar, Dhedh, Antyaj were merged into a new group;

(c) (1) Meghwal, and (2) Meghval or Menghvar were merged into a new group;

(d) (1) Senva and (2) Shenva, Chenva, Sedma or Rawat were merged into a group.]

A(ii) 7(8) castes/sub-castes became redundant due to grouping of castes.

[(1)Chamar, (2) Chamadia, (3) Bhangi, Rukhi, (4) Bhangi, (5) Gorada, (6) Hadi, and (7) Turi-Barot].

Mysore (Karnataka)

1953 B(i) Due to merger of a portion of Bellary district from Madras State, 75(80) castes/sub-castes were included :

[(1) Adi Andhra, (2) Ajila, (3) Arunthathiyar, (4) Baira, (5) Bakuda, (6) Bandi, (7) Bariki, (8) Bavuri, (9) Bellara, (10) Byagari, (11) Chachati, (12) Chakkiliyan, (13) Chalavadi, (14) Chamar, (15) Chandala, (16) Cheruman, (17) Dandasi, (18) Devendrakulathan, (19) Dom, or Dombara, Paidi, Pano, (20) Ghasi or Haddi, Relli Sachandi, (21) Godagali, (22) Godari, (23) Godda, (24) Gosangi, (25) Hasla, (26) Holeya, (27) Jaggali, (28) Jambuvulu, (29) Kadan, (30) Kaladi, (31) Kanakkan, (32) Karimpalan, (33) Kodalo, (34) Koosa, (35) Koraga, (36) Kudubi, (37) Kudumban, (38) Kuravan, (39) Kurichchan, (40) Madari, (41) Madiga, (42) Maila, (43) Mala (44) Mala Dasu, (45) Malasar, (46) Matangi, (47) Mavilan, (48) Moger, (49) Muchi, (50) Mundala, (51) Nalakeyava, (52) Nayadi, (53) Pagadai, (54) Painda, (55) Paky, (56) Pallan, (57) Pambada, (58) Pamidi, (59) Panan, (60) Panchama, (61) Panniandi, (62) Paraiyan, (63) Paravan, (64) Pulayan, (65) Puthirai Vannan, (66) Raneyar, (67) Samagara, (68) Samban, (69) Sapari, (70) Semman, (71) Thoti, (72) Tiruvallu- var, (73) Valluvan, (74) Valmiki, (75) Vettuvan].

1956 A(i) 24(26) castes/sub-castes [(1) Bariki, (2) Bavuri, (3) Byagari, (4) Chachati, (5)

Chamar, (6) Dandasi, (7) Ghasi, Haddi, Relli Sachandi, (8) Godari, (9) Kadan, (10) Kanakkan, (11) Kodalo, (12) Koraga, (13) Kudubi, (14) Kurichchan, (15) Mala Dasu, (16) Malasar, (17) Matangi, (18) Painda, (19) Paky, (20) Pamidi, (21) Panan, (22) Pulayan, (23) Valmiki, (24) Vettuvan] were descheduled.

B(i) 70(131) castes/sub-castes were included : [(1) Adiya, (2) Ager, (3) Anamuk, (4) Aray Mala, (5) Arwa Mala, (6) Bakad or Bant, (7) Balagai, (8) Bathada (9) Beda Jangam, Budga Jangam, (10) Bhangi, Mehtar, Olgana, Rukhi, Malkana, Halalkhor, Lalbegi, Balmiki, Korar, Zadmalli, (11) Mehtar, (12) Bhambi, Bhambhi, Asadaru, Asodi, Chamadia, Chamar, Chambhar, Chamgar, Haralayya, Harali, Khalpa, Machigar, Mochigar, Madar, Madig, Mochi, Telegu Mochi, Kamati Mochi, Ranigar, Rohidas, Rohit, Samgar, (13) Chambhar, (14) Chamar, Muchi, (15) Mochi, (16) Bindla, (17) Byagara, (18) Chalvadi, (19) Chalvadi or Channayya, (20) Chena Dasar or Holaya Dasar, (21) Dakkal (Dakkalwar), (22) Dakkaliga, (23) Dhor, (24) Dhor, Kakkayya or Kankayya (25) Ellamalwar (Yellammalwandlu), (26) Ghanti Chores, (27) Garoda or Garo, (28) Halleer, (29) Halsar, Haslar, Hulsavar, Halasvar, (30) Handi Jogis, (31) Holar or Valhar, (32) Holaya or Holer, (33) Holeya Dasari, (34) Kadaiyan, (35) Kepmaris, (36) Kolupulvandlu, (37) Kotegar or Metri, (38) Lingader, (39) Machala, (40) Mahar, (41) Mahar, Taral or Dhegu Megu, (42) Mahyavanshi, Dhed, Vankar or Maru Vankar, (43) Mala Dasari, (44) Mala Hannai, (45) Mukri, (46) Mala Jangam, (47) Mala Masti, (48) Mala Sale (Netkani), (49) Mala

Sanyasi, (50) Mang, (51) Mang, Matang, Minimadig, (52) Mang Garodi, (53) Mang Garudi, (54) Manne, (55) Masthi, (56) Meghval, or Menghvar, (57) Mitha Ayyalvar, (58) Nadia or Hadi, (59) Nalkadaya, (60) Pale, (61) Pannadi, (62) Paraya, (63) Pasi, (64) Shenva, Chenva, Sedma or Ravat, (65) Sillekyathas, (66) Sindhollu (Chindollu), (67) Sudugadu Siddha, (68) Tirgar or Tirbanda, (69) Turi, (70) Vathiriyan].

1976 A(i) 14(17) castes/sub-castes [(1) Cheruman, (2) Devendrakulathan, (3) Godagali, (4) Karimpalan, (5) Mitha Ayyalvar, (6) Pagadai, (7) Pannadi, (8) Pasi, (9) Puthirai Vannan, (10) Semman, (11) Shenva, Chenva, Sedma or Ravat, (12) Tiruvalluvar, (13) Turi, (14) Vathiriyan] were descheduled.

A(ii) 10(33) castes/sub-castes were merged into 5(33) group.

[(a) (1) Muchi and (2) Bhambi, Bhambhi, Asadaru, Asodi, Chamadia, Chamar, Chambhar, Chamgar, Haralayya, Harali, Khalpa, Machigar, Mochigar, Madar, Madig, Mochi, Kamati Mochi, Telegu Mochi, Ranigar, Rohidas, Rohit or Samgar were merged into a group.

(b) (1) Chalavadi and (2) Chalvadi or Channayya were merged into a group.

(c) Holaya or Holer, and (2) Holeya were merged into a group.

(d) (1) Mang Garudi, and (2) Mang Garodi were merged to form a new group.

(e) (1) Paraiyan and (2) Paraya were merged to form a new group.] and (1) Bakad or Bant were split up into two separate castes.

A(iii) 8(9) castes/sub-castes became redundant due to grouping of castes.

[(1) Mehtar (2) Chambhar, (3) Chamar, Muchi, (4) Mochi, (5) Chalvadi, (6) Dhor, (7) Mahar, (8) Mang].

Kerala

1956 A(i) 1 caste (Eravalan) was trasferred to the Scheduled Tribes list.

B(i) 41(42) castes/sub-castes [(1) Adi Andhra, (2) Adi Dravida, (3) Adi Karnataka, (4) Ajila, (5) Arunthathiyar, (6) Baira, (7) Bakuda, (8) Bandi, (9) Bathada, (10) Bellara, (11) Boyan, (12) Chamar or Muchi, (13) Chandala, (14) Cheruman, (15) Gavara, (16) Godagali, (17) Godda, (18) Gosangi, (19) Hasla, (20) Holeya, (21) Kadaiyan, (22) Kalladi, (23) Karimpalan, (24) Koosa, (25) Kudumban, (26) Maila, (27) Malayan, (28) Mavilan, (29) Moger, (30) Mundala, (31) Nalakeyava, (32) Nalkadaya, (33) Pambada, (34) Panchama, (35) Pulaya Samagara, (36) Puthirai Vannan, (37) Raneyar, (38) Samagara, (39) Samban, (40) Semman, (41) Thoti] were included.

B(ii) 4 castes/sub-castes (Cheramar, Padanna, Paraiyan, Sidhanar) were added to the existing ones.

1976 A(i) 2 castes [(1) Ulladan and (2) Uraly] were shifted to the Scheduled Tribes list.

Himachal Pradesh

1954 B(i) 7(10) castes/sub-castes [(1) Dumne (Bhanjra), (2) Chuhre, (3) Chhimbe (Dhobi), (4) Daule, (5) Hese (Turi), (6) Julahe, (7) Sarehde] were included.

1956 A(i) 1(3) castes/sub-castes [(1) Hese (Turi) and (2) sub-caste Sweeper] were descheduled.

A(ii) 4(5) castes were merged into 1(5) group.

[(1) Chamar, (2) Mochi, (3) Ramdasi or Ravidasi and (4) Ramdasia were merged to form a new group].

B(i) 19(26) castes/sub-castes [(1) Badhi or Nagalu, (2) Bandhela, (3) Bansi, (4) Barad, (5) Batwal, (6) Darai or Daryai, (7) Dhaogri, or Dhuai, (8) Hali, (9) Jogi, (10) Kamoh or Dagoli, (11) Karoack, (12) Khatik, (13) Lohar, (14) Megh, (15) Rehara, (16) Sarde, Sarare, or Siryare, (17) Sipi, (18) Teli, and (19) Thathiar or Thathera] were included.

In 1966 at the time of reorgansiation of the Punjab State some areas were transferred to Himachal Pradesh from the Punjab State when as many as 36(56) castes were scheduled for the ceded areas only. But some of these castes were already notified as scheduled for the State of Himachal Pradesh while some castes/sub-castes were added with the existing castes/groups of castes. Only 12(14) castes were included in the list for the first time. The net result was that the number of castes increased to 64(96).

1966 B(i) 12(14) castes/sub-castes [(1) Darain, (2) Dhanak, (3) Dhogri, Dhangri, Siggi, (4) Gagra, (5) Gandhila, (6) Marija, (7) Perna, (8) Pher-era, (9) Sanhai, (10) Sanhal, (11) Sansoi, and (12) Sarera] were included.

B(ii) 11 castes/sub-castes [(1) Burar, Berar, (2) Bauria, (3) Jatia Chamar, Raigar, Rehgar, (4) Dumna, Mahasha, (5) Kori, (6) Bhedkut, Manesh] were added to the existing ones.

1976 A(i) 15(26) castes/sub-castes were merged into 7(26) groups.

[(a) (1) Chuhre and (2) Balmiki, Bhangi, Chura were merged to form a new group;

(b) (1) Daole and (2) Daule were merged into a group;

(c) (1) Doom, Doomna, Dumna, Mahasha and (2) Dumne of Dumne (Bhanjre) group were merged into a new group;

(d) (1) Bhanjra and (2) Bhanjre of Dumne (Bhanjre) group were merged into a new group;

(e) (1) Julaha and (2) Julahe, Kabirpanthi, Keer were merged to form a new group;

(f) (1) Phrera and (2) Pherera were merged into a new group;

(g) (1) Rehar and (2) Rehara were merged into a new group;

(h) (1) Sarde, Sarare or Siryare, (2) Sarera and (3) Sarehde were merged to form a new group].

B(i) 3 castes (Chuhra, Gandhil Gandola and Marecha) were added to the existing ones.

Rajasthan

1956 A(i) 1 caste (Khatka) was descheduled.

A(ii) 5(5) castes were merged into 1(5) group.

[(1) Chamar, (2) Jatia, (3) Mochi, (4) Raigar, and (5) Ramdasia were merged to form a new group].

B(i) 75(153) castes/sub-castes [(1) Ager, (2) Bagri or Bagdi, (3) Bakad or Bant, (4) Bairwa or Berwa, (5) Balai, (6) Bansphod, (7) Baori, (8) Bargi, Vargi or Birgi, (9) Bedia, (10) Bedia or Beria, (11) Banchada, (12) Barahar or Basod, (13) Bargunda, (14) Bhanumati, (15) Bhangi or Mehtar, (16) Bhangi, Mehtar, Olgana, Rukhi, Malkana, Halalkhor, Lalbegi, Balmiki, Asadaru, Asodi, Chamadia, Chamar, Chambhar, Chamgar, Haralayya, Harali, Khalpa, Machigar, Mochigar, Madar, Madig, Telegu Mochi, Kamati Mochi, Ranigar, Rohidas, Rohit, Samgar, (19) Chamar, Bairwa, Bhambi, Jatav, Mochi, Regar, (20) Chamar, Jatava, Jatia, Mochi, Raigar, (21) Bambhi, (22) Chandal, (23) Chidar, (24) Chalvadi or Channayya, (25) Chenna Dasar or Holaya Dasar, (26) Dhanak, (27)Dhanuk, (28) Dhobi, (29) Dholi (30) Dom, (31) Dhor, Kakkayya or Kangayya, (32) Gancha, (33) Garo, Garura,

Gurda, (34) Garoda, (35) Garoda or Garo, (36) Gavaria, (37) Halleer, (38) Halsar, Haslar, Hulsavar or Halasvar, (39) Holar or Valhar, (40) Holaya or Holer, (41) Jinger, (42) Kamad or Kamadia, (43) Kanjar, (44) Khatik, (45) Koli, (46) Kabirpanthi, (47) Kotwal, (48) Lingader, (49) Bazigar, (50) Mahar, (51) Mahar, Taral, Dhegu Megu, (52) Mahyavanshi, Dhed, Vankar, Maru Vankar, (53) Dhed, (54) Mang, Matang, Minimadig, (55) Mang or Mang Garodi, (56) Mang Garudi, 957) Meghwal, (58) Megh, Meghwal, (59) Meghaval or Menghvar, (60) Mukri, (61) Nat, (62) Nat, Kalbelia or Sapera, (63) Nadia or Hadi, (64) Pardhi, (65) Salvi, (66) Santia, (67) Satia, (68) Sargara, (69) Shenva, Chenva, Sedma or Ravat, (70) Thori or Nayak, (71) Tirgar or Tirbanda, (72) Turi, (73) Zamral, (74) Kori or Koli, (75) Kuchband] were included.

B(ii) 4 castes/sub-castes (Bhambhi, Jatava, Raidas, Gancha) were added to the existing ones.

1976 A(i) 23(29) castes/sub-castes [(1) Ager, (2) Bakad or Bant. (3) Banchada, (4) Bhanumati, (5) Chidar, (6) Barahar or Basod, (7) Bargunda, (8) Chalvadi or Channayya, (9) Chenna Dasar or Holaya Dasar, (10) Dhor, Kakkayya or Kangayya, (11) Halleer, (12) Halsar, Haslar, Hulsavar or Halasvar, (13) Holar or Valhar, (14) Holaya or Holer, (15) Kotwal, (16) Garancha Mehtar or Gancha, (17) Lingader, (18) Mukri, (19) Nadia or Hadi, (20) Kabirpanthi, (21) Pardhi, (22) Shenva, Chenva, Sedma or Ravat (23) Zamral] were descheduled.

A(ii) 29(81) castes/sub-castes were merged into 13(71) groups :

[(a) (1) Bansphor and (2) Bansphod formed a new group.

(b) (1) Bhangi, Mehtar, Olgana, Rukhi, Malkana, Halakhor, Lalbegi, Balmiki, Korar, Zadmall, (2) Chura and (3) Valmiki formed a new group.

(c) (1) Bhambi, Chamar, Jatav, Jatia, Mochi, Raidass, Raigar, Ramdasia, (2) Bhambi, Bhambhi, Asadaru, Asodi, Chamadia, Chamar, Chambhar, Chamgar, Haralayya, Harali, Khalpa, Machigar, Mochigar, Madar, Madig, Telegu Mochi, Kamati Mochi, Rani gar, Rohidas, Rohit,. Samgar, (3) Chamar, Jatava, Jatia, Mochi, Raigar, (4) Chamar, Bairwa, Bhambi, Jatav, Mochi, Regar were merged into a new group.

(d) (1) Dhanak and (2) Dhanuk were merged to form a new group.

(e) (1) Dome and (2) Dom were merged into a group.

(f) (1) Garo, Garura, Gurda and (2) Garoda were merged into a group.

(g) (1) Kanjar and (2) Kunjar formed a group.

(h) (1) Kooch Band and (2) Kuchband formed a group.

(i) (1) Mahyavanshi, Dhed, Vankar, Maru Vankar, and (2) Dheda were merged to form a group.

(j) (1) Mang Garudi and (2) Mang Garodi of Mang or Mang Garodi formed a group.

(k) (1) Megh or Meghwal and (2) Meghaval or Menghvar were merged into a new group.

(l) (1) Nut and (2) Nat formed a group.

(m) (1) Santia and (2) Satia formed a group].

A(iii) 16(20) castes/sub-castes became redundant due to grouping of castes.

[(1) Bagri, (2) Bargi, (3) Bedia, (4) Bazigar (5) Bhangi, (6) Bhangi or Mehtar, (7) Mehtar,(8) Bambhi, (9) Garoda or Garo, (10) Koli, (11) Mahar, (12) Dhed, (13) Meghwal, (14) Kalbelia, (15) Thori, (16) Tirgar, and Mang of Mang, or Mang Garodi, Nat of Nat, Kalbelia or Sapera groups].

B(i) 1 sub-caste (Garancha) was added to an existing one.

APPENDIX-V

A. Tamil Nadu (Madras) has the following common Scheduled Castes with :

(I) Kerala

(1) Adi Andhra, (2) Adi Dravida, (3) Adi Karnataka, (4) Ajila, (5) Arunthathiyar, (6) Ayyanavar, (7) Baira, (8) Bakuda, (9) Bandi, (10) Bellara, (11) Bharatar, (12) Chakkiliyan, (13) Chamar, Muchi, (14) Chandala, (15) Cheruman, (16) Domban, (17) Godagali, (18) Godda, (19) Gosangi, (20) Holeya, (21) Kadaiyan, (22) Kakkalan, (23) Kalladi, (24) Kanakkan, Padanna (25) Karimpalan, (26) Kavara, (27) Koosa, (28) Kootan, Koodan, (29) Kudumban, (30) Kuravan, Sidhanar, (31) Maila, (32) Mannan, (33) Mavilan, (34) Moger, (35) Mundala, (36) Nalakeyava, (37) Nayadi, (38) Padannan, (39) Pallan, (40) Palluvan, (41) Pambada, (42) Panan, (43) Panchama, (44) Paraiyan, Parayan, Sambavar, (45) Paravan, (46) Pathiyan, (47) Pulayan, Cheramar, (48) Puthirai Vannan, (49) Raneyar, (50) Samagara, (51) Samban, (52) Semman, (53) Thandan, (54) Thoti, (55) Vallon, (56) Valluvan, (57) Vannan, (58) Velan, (59) Vetan, (60) Vettuvan.

(II) Andhra Pradesh

(1) Adi Andhra, (2) Adi Dravida, (3) Chalavadi, (4) Chamar, Muchi, (5) Chandala, (6) Dom, Dombara, Paidi, Pano, (7) Godagali, (8) Gosangi, (9) Holeya, (10) Jaggali, (11) Jambuvulu, (12) Madiga, (13) Mala, (14) Mundala, (15) Pambada, (16) Panchama, (17) Samagara, (18) Samban, (19) Thoti.

(III) Karnataka

(1) Adi Andhra, (2) Adi Dravida, (3) Adi Karnataka, (4) Ajila, (5) Arunthathiyar, (6) Baira, (7) Bakuda, (8) Bandi,

(9) Bellara, (10) Chakkiliyan (11) Chalavadi, (12) Chamar, Muchi, (13) Chandala, (14) Dom, Dombara, Paidi, Pano, (15) Godda, (16) Gosangi, (17) Holeya, (18) Jaggali, (19) Jambuvulu, (20) Kadaiyan, (21) Kalladi, (22) Koosa, (23) Kudumban, (24) Kuravan, (25) Madari, (26) Madiga, (27) Maila, (28) Mala, (29) Mavilan, (30) Moger, (31) Mundala, (32) Nalakeyava, (33) Nayadi, (34) Pallan, (35) Pambada, (36) Panchama, (37) Panniandi, (38) Paraiyan, (39) Paravan, (40) Raneyar, (41) Samagara (42) Samban, (43) Sapari, (44) Thoti, (45) Valluvan.

(IV) Pondicherry

(1) Adi Andhra, (2) Adi Dravida, (3) Chakkiliyan, (4) Jambuvulu, (5) Kuravan, (6) Madiga, (7) Mala, (8) Pallan, (9) Paryan, Sambavar, (10) Samban, (11) Thoti, (12) Valluvan, (13) Vetan, (14) Vettiyan.

B. Kerala has the following common Scheduled Castes with :

(I) Andhra Pradesh

(1) Adi Andhra, (2) Adi Dravida, (3) Chamar, Muchi, (4) Chandala, (5) Godagali, (6) Gosangi, (7) Holeya, (8) Mundala, (9) Pambada, (10) Panchama, (11) Samagara, (12) Samban, (13) Thoti.

(II) Karnataka

(1) Adi Andhra, (2) Adi Dravida, (3) Adi Karnataka, (4) Ajila, (5) Arunthathiyar, (6) Baira, (7) Bakuda, (8) Bandi, (9) Bathada, (10) Bellara, (11) Chakkiliyan, (12) Chamar, Muchi, (13) Chandala, (14) Godda, (15) Gosangi, (16) Holeya, (17) Kadaiyan, (18) Kalladi, (19) Koosa, (20) Kudumban, (21) Kuravan, (22) Mavilan, (23) Moger, (24) Mundala, (25) Nalkadaya, (26) Nalakeyava, (27) Nayadi, (28) Pallan, (29) Pambada, (30) Panchama, (31) Paraiyan, (32) Paravan, (33) Raneyar, (34) Samagar, (35) Samban, (36) Thoti, (37) Valluvan.

(III) Pondicherry

(1) Adi Andhra, (2) Adi Dravida, (3) Chakkiliyan, (4)

Kuravan, (5) Pallan, (6) Paryan, Sambavar, (7) Samban, (8) Thoti, (9) Valluvan, (10) Vetan.

C. Andhra Pradesh has the following common Scheduled Castes with :

(I) Karnataka

(1) Adi Andhra, (2) Adi Dravida, (3) Anamuk, (4) Aray Mala, (5) Arwa Mala, (6) Beda Jangam, Budga Jangam, (7) Bindla, (8) Byagara, (9) Chalavadi, (10) Chamar, Mochi, Muchi, (11) Chambhar, (12) Chandala, (13) Dakkal, Dokkalwar, (14) Dhor, (15) Dom, Dombara, Paidi, Pano, (16) Ellamalwar Yellammalawandlu, (17) Gosangi, (18) Holeya, (19) Holeya Dasari, (20) Jaggali, (21) Jambuvulu, (22) Kolupulvandlu, (23) Madiga, (24) Mahar, (25) Mala, (26) Mala Dasari, (27) Mala Hannai, (28) Mala Jangam (29) Mala Masti, (30) Mala Sale, Netkani, (31) Mala Sanyasi, (32) Mang, (33) Mang Garodi, (34) Manne, (35) Masthi, (36) Mehtar, (37) Mundala, (38) Pambada, (39) Panchama, (40) Samagara, (41) Samban, (42) Sindhollu, Chindollu, (43) Thoti.

(II) Pondicherry

(1) Adi Andhra, (2) Adi Dravida, (3) Jambuvulu, (4) Madiga, (5) Mala, Mala Masti, (6) Paky, (7) Samban.

(III) Madhya Pradesh

(1) Chamar, Mochi, (2) Dom, (3) Mahar, (4) Mang, (5) Mang Garodi, (6) Mehtar.

(IV) Maharashtra

(1) Anamuk, (2) Aray Mala, (3) Arwa Mala, (4) Beda Jangam, (5) Budga Jangam, (5) Bindla, (6) Byagara, (7) Chamar Mochi, (8) Chambhar, (9) Dakkal, Dokkalwar, (10) Dhor, (11) Dom, (12) Ellamalvar, Yellammalawandlu, (13) Ghasi, (14) Holeya, (15) Kolupulvandlu, (16) Madiga, (17) Mahar, (18) Mala, (19) Mala Dasari, (20) Mala Hannai, (21) Mala Jangam, (22) Mala Masti, (23) Mala Sale, Netkani, (24) Mala Sanyasi, (25) Mang, (26) Mang Garodi, (27) Manne, (28) Mashti, (29) Mehtar, (30) Mitha Ayyalvar, (31) Sindhollu, Chindollu.

(V) Gujarat

(1) Chamar, Mochi, (2) Chambhar, (3) Dhor, (4) Mahar, (5) Mang, (6) Mehtar.

(VI) Rajasthan

(1) Chamar, Mochi, (2) Chambhar, (3) Dom, (4) Mahar, (5) Mang, (6) Mang Garodi, (7) Mehtar.

D. Karnataka has the following common Scheduled Castes with :

(I) Pondicherry

(1) Adi Andhra, (2) Adi Dravida, (3) Chakkiliyan, (4) Jambuvulu, (5) Kuravan, (6) Madiga, (7) Mala, Mala Masti, (8) Pallan, (9) Samban, (10) Thoti, (11) Valluvan.

(II) Madhya Pradesh

(1) Bhangi, Mehtar, Lalbegi, (2) Chamar, Bhambi, Mochi, Rohidas, (3) Dhed, (4) Dom, (5) Mahar, (6) Mang, (7) Mang Garodi, Mang Garudi, (8) Madari.

(III) Maharashtra

(1) Ager, (2) Anamuk, (3) Aray Mala, (4) Arwa Mala, (5) Bant, (6) Beda Jangam, Budga Jangam, (7) Bhangi, Mehtar, Olgana, Rukhi, Malkana, Halalkhor, Lalbegi, Balmiki, Korar, Zadmalli, (8) Bhambi, Bhambhi, Asadaru, Asodi, Chamadia, Chamar, Chambhar, Chamgar, Hara-layya, Harali, Khalpa, Machigar, Mochigar, Madar, Madig, Mochi, Telegu Mochi, Kamati Mochi, Ranigar, Rohidas, Rohit, Samgar, (9) Bindla, (10) Byagara, (11) Chalvadi, Channayya, (12) Chenna Dasar, Holaya Dasar, (13) Dakkal, Dokkalwar, (14) Dhor, Kakkayya, Kankayya, (15) Dom, (16) Ellamalvar, Yellammalawandlu, (17) Garoda, Garo, (18) Halleer, (19) Halsar, Haslar, Hulasvar, Halasvar, (20) Holar, Valhar, (21) Holaya, Holeya, (22) Kolupulvandlu, (23) Lingader, (24) Madiga, (25) Mahar, Taral, Dhegu Megu, (26) Mahyavanshi, Dhed, Vankar, Maru Vankar, (27) Mala, (28) Mala Dasari, (29) Mala Hannai, (30) Mala Jangam, (31) Mala Masti, (32) Mala Sale, Netkani, (33) Mala Sanyasi

(34) Mang, Matang, Minimadig, (35) Mang Garodi, Mang Garudi, (36) Manne, (27) Mashti, (38) Meghval, Menghvar, (39) Mukri, (40) Nadia, Hadi, (41) Sindhollu, Chindollu, (42) Tirgar, Tirbanda.

(IV) Gujarat

(1) Ager, (2) Bant, (3) Bhangi, Mehtar, Olgana, Rukhi, Malkana, Halalkhor, Lalbegi, Balmiki, Korar, Zadmalli, (4) Bhambi, Bhambhi, Asadaru, Asodi, Chamadia, Chamar, Chambhar, Chamgar, Haralayya, Harali, Khalpa, Machigar, Mochigar, Madar, Madig, Mochi, Telegu Mochi, Kamati Mochi, Ranigar, Rohidas, Rohit, Samgar, (5) Chalvadi, Channayya, (6) Chenna Dasar, Holaya Dasar, (7) Dhor, Kakkayya, Kankayya, (8) Garoda, Garo, (9) Halleer, (10) Halsar, Haslar, Hulasvar, Halasvar, (11) Holar, Valhar, (12) Holaya, Holer, (13) Lingader, (14) Mahar, Taral, Dhegu Megu, (15) Mahyavanshi, Dhed, Vankar, Maru Vankar, (16) Mang, Matang, Minimadig, (17) Mang Garudi, (18) Meghwal, Menghwar, (19) Mukri, (20) Nadia, Hadi, (21) Tirgar, Tirbanda.

(V) Rajasthan

(1) Bhangi, Mehtar, Olgana, Rukhi, Malkana, Halalkhor, Lalbegi, Balmiki, Korar, Zadmalli, (2) Bhambi, Bhambhi, Asadaru, Asodi, Chamadia, Chamar, Chambhar, Chamgar, Haralayya, Harali, Khalpa, Machigar, Mochigar, Madar, Madig, Mochi, Telegu Mochi, Kamati Mochi, Ranigar, Rohidas, Rohit, Samgar, (3) Dom, (4) Garoda, Garo, (5) Madari, (6) Mahar, Taral, Dhegu Megu, (7) Mahyavanshi, Dhed, Vankar, Maru Vankar, (8) Mang, Matang, Minimadig, (9) Mang Garodi, Mang Garudi, (10) Meghval, Menghvar, (11) Tirgar, Tirbanda.

(E) Madhya Pradesh has common Scheduled Castes with :

(I) Maharashtra

(1) Bahna, Bahana, (2) Balahi, Balai, (3) Basor, Burud, Bansor, Bansodi, (4) Bhangi, Mehtar, Lalbegi, (5) Chamar, Chamari, Bhambi, Mochi, Nona, Rohidas, Ramnami, Satnami, Surjyabanshi, Surjyaramnami, (6) Chikwa, Chikvi, (7) Dhed, (8) Dohor, (9) Dom, Dumar, (10) Ganda,

Gandi, (11) Ghasi, Ghasia, (12) Holiya, (13) Katia, Patharia, (14) Khatik, (15) Kori, (16) Khangar, Kanera, Mirdha, (17) Mahar, Mehra, (18) Mang, Dankhani Mang, Mang Mahasi, Madari, Garudi, Radhe Mang, (19) Mang Garodi, Mang Garudi, (20) Pasi, (21) Sansi.

(II) Gujarat

(1) Chamar, Bhambi, Mochi, Rohidas, (2) Bhangi, Mehtar, Lalbegi, (3) Dhed, (4) Mahar, (5) Mang, (6) Mang Garudi, (7) Meghwal, (8) Pasi.

(III) Rajasthan

(1) Bagri, Bagdi, (2) Balai, (3) Bansphor, (4) Bedia, (5) Bhangi, Mehtar, Lalbegi, (6) Chamar, Bhambi, Jatav, Mochi, Regar, Rohidas, Raidas, (7) Dhanuk, (8) Dhed, (9) Dhobi, (10) Dom, Dome, (11) Kanjar, (12) Khatik, (13) Koli, Kori, (14) Khangar, (15) Mahar, (16) Mang Garodi, Mang Garudi, (17) Mang, (18) Meghwal (19) Mehar, (20) Nat, (21) Pasi, (22) Sansi.

(F) Maharastra has common Scheduled Castes with :

(1) Gujarat

(1) Ager, (2) Bakad, Bant, (3) Bhambi, Bhambhi, Asadaru, Asodi, Chamadia, Chamar, Chambhar, Chamgar, Haralayya, Harali, Khalpa, Machigar, Mochigar, Madar, Madig, Mochi, Telegu Mochi, Kamati Mochi, Ranigar, Rohidas, Rohit, Samgar, (4) Bhangi, Mehtar, Olgana, Rukhi, Malkana, Halalkhor, Lalbegi, Balmiki, Korar, Zadmalli, (5) Chalvadi, Channayya, (6) Chenna Dasar, Holaya Dasar, (7) Dhor, Kakkayya, Kankayya, (8) Garoda, Garo, (9) Halleer, (10) Halsar, Haslar, Hulasvar, Halasvar, (11) Holar, Valhar, (12) Holaya, (13) Lingader, (14) Mahar, Taral, Dhegu Megu, (15) Mahyavanshi, Dhed, Vankar, Maru Vankar, (16) Mang, Matang, Minimadig, (17) Mang Garudi, (18) Meghval, Menghvar, (19) Mukri, (20) Nadia, Hadi, (21) Pasi, (22) Shenva, Chenva, Sedma, Rawat, (23) Tirgar, Tirbanda, (24) Turi.

(II) Rajasthan

(1) Balai, (2) Bhangi, Mehtar, Olgana, Rukhi, Malkana, Halalkhor, Lalbegi, Balmiki, Korar, Zadmalli, (3) Chamar,

Bhambhi, Bhambi, Mochi, Rohidas, Asadaru, Asodi, Chamadia, Chambhar, Chamgar, Haralayya, Harali, Khalpa, Machigar, Mochigar, Madar, Telegu Mochi, Kamati Mochi, Ranigar, Rohit, Samgar, (4) Dom, (5) Garoda, Garo, (6) Khangar, (7) Khatik, (8) Kori, (9) Mahar, Taral, Dhegu Megu (10) Mahyvanshi, Dhed, Vankar, Maru Vankar, (11) Mang, Matang, Minimadig, (12) Mang Garodi, Mang Garudi, (13) Meghval, Menghvar, (14) Pasi, (15) Sansi, (16) Tirgar, Tirbanda, (17) Turi.

(G) Gujarat has common Scheduled Castes with :

(I) Rajasthan

(1) Bhangi, Mehtar, Olgana, Rukhi, Malkana, Halalkhor, Lalbegi, Balmiki, Korar, Zadmalli, (2) Bhambi, Bhambhi, Asadaru, Asodi, Chamadia, Chamar, Chambhar, Chamgar, Haralayya, Harali, Khalpa, Machigar, Mochigar, Madar, Madig, Mochi, Telegu Mochi, Kamati Mochi, Ranigar, Rohidas, Rohit, Samgar, (2) Garoda, Garo, (4) Mahar, Taral, Dhegu Megu, (5) Mahyavanshi, Dhed, Vankar, Maru Vankar, (6) Mang, Matang, Minimadig, (7) Mang Garudi, (8) Meghval, Meghwal, Menghvar, (9) Pasi, (10) Thori, (11) Tirgar, Tirbanda (12) Turi.

(H) Bihar has common Scheduled Castes with :

(I) West Bengal

(1) Bantar, (2) Bauri, (3) Bhogta, (4) Bhuiya, (5) Chamar, Mochi, (6) Chaupal, (7) Dabgar, (8) Dhobi, (9) Dom, Dhangad, (10) Dusadh, Dhari, Dharhi, (11) Ghasi, (12) Halalkhor, (13) Hari, Mehtar, Bhangi, (14) Kanjar, (15) Kurariar, (16) Lalbegi, (17) Musahar, (18) Nat, (19) Pan, Sawasi, (20) Pasi, (21) Rajwar, (22) Turi.

(II) Orissa

(1) Bauri, (2) Chamar, Mochi, (3) Dhobi, (4) Dom, (5) Ghasi, (6) Hari, (7) Mehtar, Bhangi, (8) Musahar, (9) Pan, (10) Pasi, (11) Turi.

(I) West Bengal has common Scheduled Castes with:

(I) Orissa

(1) Bauri, (2) Beldar, (3) Chamar, Mochi, Muchi, (4)

Dhoba, Dhobi, (5) Dom, (6) Ghasi, (7) Hari, (8) Kandra, (9) Malo, (10) Mahar, (11) Mehtar, Bhangi, (12) Musahar, (13) Namasudra, (14) Pan, (15) Pasi, (16) Turi.

(J) Punjab has common Scheduled Castes with :

(I) Himachal Pradesh

(1) Ad Dharmi, (2) Balmiki, Chura, Bhangi, (3) Bangali, (4) Barar, Burar, Berar, (5) Batwal, (6) Bauria, Bawaria, (7) Bazigar, (8) Bhanjra, (9) Chamar, Jatia Chamar, Rehgar, Raigar, Ramdasi, Ravidasi, (10) Chanal, (11) Dagi, (12) Darain, (13) Dhanak, (14) Dhogri, Dhangri, Siggi, (15) Dumna, Mahasha, Doom, (16) Gagra, (17) Gandhila, Gandhil Gondola, (18) Kabirpanthi, Julaha, (19) Khatik, (20) Kori, Koli, (21) Marija, Marecha, (22) Mazhabi, (23) Megh, (24) Nat, (25) Od, (26) Pasi, (27) Perna, (28) Pherera, (29) Sanhai, (30) Sanhal, (31) Sansi, Bhedkut, Manesh, (32) Sansoi, (33) Sapela, (34) Sarera, (35) Sikligar, (36) Sirkiband.

(II) Delhi

(1) Bawaria, (2) Bazigar, (3) Chamar, Rehgar, Raigar, Ravidasi, (4) Dhanak, (5) Julaha, (6) Kabirpanthi, (7) Khatik, (8) Koli, (9) Mazhabi, (10) Nat, (11) Pasi, (12) Perna, (13) Sansi, Bhedkut, (14) Sikligar, (15) Sirkiband.

(K) Himachal Pradesh has common Scheduled Castes with :

(I) Delhi

(1) Banjara, (2) Bawaria, (3) Bazigar, (4) Bhangi, (5) Chamar, Rehgar, Mochi, Ravidasi, Raigar, (6) Chuhra, (7) Dhobi, (8) Julaha, (9) Kabirpanthi, (10) Khatik, (11) Koli, (12) Mazhabi, (13) Nat, (14) Pasi, (15) Perna, (16) Sansi, Bhedkut, (17) Sikilgar, (18) Sirkiband.

Index